P9-BBN-049

# IRAN-CONTRA
## THE FINAL REPORT

## A NOTE FROM THE PUBLISHER

On January 18, 1994, after a seven-year legal investigation, the Office of Independent Counsel, under the direction of Lawrence E. Walsh, released its final report. Entitled "Final Report of the Independent Counsel for Iran/Contra Matters," it consisted of three volumes, of which only Volume One was devoted to the investigations and prosecutions, findings and conclusions reached. The other two volumes were made up of reproductions of "indictments, plea agreements, interim reports to the Congress, and administrative matters," and of "comments and materials submitted by individuals and their attorneys responding to Volume I of the final report."

This edition, published by Times Books, a division of Random House, Inc., reproduces Volume One of the Office of Independent Counsel document in its entirety. Not one word has been omitted.

ISBN: 0-8129-2456-8

Manufactured in the United States of America

# IRAN-CONTRA
## THE FINAL REPORT

### LAWRENCE E. WALSH
#### Independent Counsel

TIMES BOOKS

RANDOM HOUSE

# REPORTS OF INDEPENDENT COUNSEL

On August 5, 1993, the Office of Independent Counsel for Iran/contra Matters submitted a three-volume report to the United States Court of Appeals for the District of Columbia Circuit, Division for the Purpose of Appointing Independent Counsel:

1. Volume I: Investigations and Prosecutions
2. Volume II: Indictments, Plea Agreements, Interim Reports to the Congress, and Administrative Matters and a third classified volume that remains under seal.

On December 3, 1993, the Court ordered that the *Final Report of Independent Counsel* be released to the public subject to the completion of an appendix, containing comments and materials submitted by individuals and their attorneys responding to Volume I of the *Final Report* pursuant to 28 U.S.C. § 594, and the filing of the completed report, with the exception of any deletions required by law or further order of the Court. These comments and materials are compiled in Volume III.

The materials from Independent Counsel's investigations that are not contained in the *Final Report* have been deposited with the National Archives. Materials are also held, some under seal, in the United States District Courts for the Districts of Columbia and Maryland and the Eastern District of Virginia and in the United States Courts of Appeals for the District of Columbia and Fourth Circuits.

OFFICE OF INDEPENDENT COUNSEL
1726 M STREET, N.W.
SUITE 300
WASHINGTON, D.C. 20036

August 4, 1993

BY HAND

The Honorable David B. Sentelle
Chief Judge
Division for the Purpose of
  Appointing Independent Counsels
United States Court of Appeals for the
  District of Columbia Circuit
3rd Street & Constitution Avenue, N.W.
Washington, D.C.  20001

Dear Chief Judge Sentelle:

Pursuant to 28 U.S.C. § 595(b)(2),*/ I submit herewith the Final Report of the Independent Counsel for Iran/contra Matters.  As required by law, it attempts to set forth "fully and completely a description of the work of the independent counsel, including the disposition of all cases brought, and the reasons for not prosecuting any matter within the prosecutorial jurisdiction of such independent counsel which was not prosecuted."

It has been an honor to serve as an independent counsel. You may be sure that I am grateful for the responsibility entrusted to me by the Division.

Sincerely,

Lawrence E. Walsh
Independent Counsel

Attachments

_____

*/This section, which is published in the "Historical and Statutory Notes" following 28 U.S.C.A. § 595 (West 1992 Supp.), continues to apply to my investigation because it was pending on December 15, 1987.

# Contributors to the Final Report

One of the most difficult and important tasks of the Office of Independent Counsel has been the preparation of this Final Report. Since this Report seeks to cover the most important aspects of a lengthy and complex investigation, it is a product of all who have served in the Office of Independent Counsel in the Iran/contra matter—the lawyers, the investigators, and the support staff. To all of them, this office owes a debt of gratitude.

In addition, Independent Counsel would like to give special recognition to the following individuals who participated in the preparation of this Report:

*Editors*, Mary J. Belcher, Michael D. Vhay, and James G. Wieghart.

*Lawyers*, Thomas E. Baker, John Q. Barrett, Steven A. Ellis, Vernon L. Francis, Craig A. Gillen, Jeffrey S. Harleston, William T. Hassler, Gregory A. Mark, Christian J. Mixter, Kenneth J. Parsigian, Charles A. Rothfeld, Laurence S. Shtasel, Christina A. Spaulding, Guy Miller Struve, William M. Treanor, Michael D. Vhay, and Samuel A. Wilkins III.

*Administrator*, Carol McCreary-Maddox.

*Financial Officer*, Philip J. Rooney.

*Researchers*, Vincent T. Colosimo, Jr., Thomas F. Cusick, Michael S. Foster, Jennifer J. Gamboli, Lisa M. Mallory, Fredrich Olsen, Kristina E. Rosenthal, Megan W. Semple, and Michael D. Tang.

*Production*, Joseph Foote, Ruth Anne Witucki Miller, Peggy J. Thume and Brenda S. Carman.

*Editorial and Clerical Support Team*, Kathleen A. Betts, Kelly Hargreaves, Calvin S. Holt, Jr., Jacob D. Kortz, Josette M. Mercer, Jennifer J. Nicholson, Allen F. Stansbury, and Denise E. Washington.

# Contents

# IRAN-CONTRA
## THE FINAL REPORT

# Executive Summary

In October and November 1986, two secret U.S. Government operations were publicly exposed, potentially implicating Reagan Administration officials in illegal activities. These operations were the provision of assistance to the military activities of the Nicaraguan contra rebels during an October 1984 to October 1986 prohibition on such aid, and the sale of U.S. arms to Iran in contravention of stated U.S. policy and in possible violation of arms-export controls. In late November 1986, Reagan Administration officials announced that some of the proceeds from the sale of U.S. arms to Iran had been diverted to the contras.

As a result of the exposure of these operations, Attorney General Edwin Meese III sought the appointment of an independent counsel to investigate and, if necessary, prosecute possible crimes arising from them.

The Special Division of the United States Court of Appeals for the District of Columbia Circuit appointed Lawrence E. Walsh as Independent Counsel on December 19, 1986, and charged him with investigating:

(1) the direct or indirect sale, shipment, or transfer since in or about 1984 down to the present, of military arms, materiel, or funds to the government of Iran, officials of that government, persons, organizations or entities connected with or purporting to represent that government, or persons located in Iran;

(2) the direct or indirect sale, shipment, or transfer of military arms, materiel or funds to any government, entity, or person acting, or purporting to act as an intermediary in any transaction referred to above;

(3) the financing or funding of any direct or indirect sale, shipment or transfer referred to above;

(4) the diversion of proceeds from any transaction described above to or for any person, organization, foreign government, or any faction or body of insurgents in any foreign country, including, but not limited to Nicaragua;

(5) the provision or coordination of support for persons or entities engaged as military insurgents in armed conflict with the government of Nicaragua since 1984.

This is the final report of that investigation.

## Overall Conclusions

The investigations and prosecutions have shown that high-ranking Administration officials violated laws and executive orders in the Iran/contra matter.

Independent Counsel concluded that:

—the sales of arms to Iran contravened United States Government policy and may have violated the Arms Export Control Act[1]

---

[1] Independent Counsel is aware that the Reagan Administration Justice Department took the position, after the November 1986 revelations, that the 1985 shipments of United States weapons to Iran did not violate the law. This post hoc position does not correspond with the contemporaneous advice given the President. As detailed within this report, Secretary of Defense Caspar W. Weinberger (a lawyer with an extensive record in private practice and the former general counsel of the Bechtel Corporation) advised President Reagan in 1985 that the shipments were illegal. Moreover, Weinberger's opinion was shared by attorneys within the Department of Defense and the White House counsel's office once they became aware of the 1985 shipments. Finally, when Attorney General Meese conducted his initial inquiry into the Iran arms sales, he expressed concern that the shipments may have been illegal.

—the provision and coordination of support to the contras violated the Boland Amendment ban on aid to military activities in Nicaragua;

—the policies behind both the Iran and contra operations were fully reviewed and developed at the highest levels of the Reagan Administration;

—although there was little evidence of National Security Council level knowledge of most of the actual contra-support operations, there was no evidence that any NSC member dissented from the underlying policy—keeping the contras alive despite congressional limitations on contra support;

—the Iran operations were carried out with the knowledge of, among others, President Ronald Reagan, Vice President George Bush, Secretary of State George P. Shultz, Secretary of Defense Caspar W. Weinberger, Director of Central Intelligence William J. Casey, and national security advisers Robert C. McFarlane and John M. Poindexter; of these officials, only Weinberger and Shultz dissented from the policy decision, and Weinberger eventually acquiesced by ordering the Department of Defense to provide the necessary arms; and

—large volumes of highly relevant, contemporaneously created documents were systematically and willfully withheld from investigators by several Reagan Administration officials.

—following the revelation of these operations in October and November 1986, Reagan Administration officials deliberately deceived the Congress and the public about the level and extent of official knowledge of and support for these operations.

In addition, Independent Counsel concluded that the off-the-books nature of the Iran and contra operations gave line-level personnel the opportunity to commit money crimes.

## Prosecutions

In the course of Independent Counsel's investigation, 14 persons were charged with criminal violations. There were two broad classes of crimes charged: Operational crimes, which largely concerned the illegal use of funds generated in the course of the operations, and "cover-up" crimes, which largely concerned false statements and obstructions after the revelation of the operations. Independent Counsel did not charge violations of the Arms Export Control Act or Boland Amendment. Although apparent violations of these statutes provided the impetus for the cover-up, they are not criminal statutes and do not contain any enforcement provisions.

All of the individuals charged were convicted, except for one CIA official whose case was dismissed on national security grounds and two officials who received unprecedented pre-trial pardons by President Bush following his electoral defeat in 1992. Two of the convictions were reversed on appeal on constitutional grounds that in no way cast doubt on the factual guilt of the men convicted. The individuals charged and the disposition of their cases are:

(1) Robert C. McFarlane: pleaded guilty to four counts of withholding information from Congress;

(2) Oliver L. North: convicted of altering and destroying documents, accepting an illegal gratuity, and aiding and abetting in the obstruction of Congress; conviction reversed on appeal;

(3) John M. Poindexter: convicted of conspiracy, false statements, destruction and removal of records, and obstruction of Congress; conviction reversed on appeal;

(4) Richard V. Secord: pleaded guilty to making false statements to Congress;

(5) Albert Hakim: pleaded guilty to supplementing the salary of North;

(6) Thomas G. Clines: convicted of four counts of tax-related offenses for failing to report income from the operations;

(7) Carl R. Channell: pleaded guilty to conspiracy to defraud the United States;

(8) Richard R. Miller: pleaded guilty to conspiracy to defraud the United States;

(9) Clair E. George: convicted of false statements and perjury before Congress;

(10) Duane R. Clarridge: indicted on seven counts of perjury and false statements; pardoned before trial by President Bush;

(11) Alan D. Fiers, Jr.: pleaded guilty to withholding information from Congress;

(12) Joseph F. Fernandez: indicted on four counts of obstruction and false statements; case dismissed when Attorney General Richard L. Thornburgh refused to declassify information needed for his defense;

(13) Elliott Abrams: pleaded guilty to withholding information from Congress;

(14) Caspar W. Weinberger: charged with four counts of false statements and perjury; pardoned before trial by President Bush.

At the time President Bush pardoned Weinberger and Clarridge, he also pardoned George, Fiers, Abrams, and McFarlane.

## The Basic Facts of Iran/contra

The Iran/contra affair concerned two secret Reagan Administration policies whose operations were coordinated by National Security Council staff. The Iran operation involved efforts in 1985 and 1986 to obtain the release of Americans held hostage in the Middle East through the sale of U.S. weapons to Iran, despite an embargo on such sales. The contra operations from 1984 through most of 1986 involved the secret governmental support of contra military and paramilitary activities in Nicaragua, despite congressional prohibition of this support.

The Iran and contra operations were merged when funds generated from the sale of weapons to Iran were diverted to support the contra effort in Nicaragua. Although this "diversion" may be the most dramatic aspect of Iran/contra, it is important to emphasize that both the Iran and contra operations, separately, violated United States policy and law.[2] The ignorance of the "diversion" asserted by President Reagan and his Cabinet officers on the National Security Council in no way absolves them of responsibility for the underlying Iran and contra operations.

The secrecy concerning the Iran and contra activities was finally pierced by events that took place thousands of miles apart in the fall of 1986. The first occurred on October 5, 1986, when Nicaraguan government soldiers shot down an American cargo plane that was carrying military supplies to contra forces; the one surviving crew member, American Eugene Hasenfus, was taken into captivity and stated that he was employed by the CIA. A month after the Hasenfus shootdown, President Reagan's secret sale of U.S. arms to Iran was reported by a Lebanese publication on November 3. The joining of these two operations was made public on November 25, 1986, when Attorney General Meese announced that Justice Department officials had discovered that some of the proceeds from the Iran arms sales had been diverted to the contras.

When these operations ended, the exposure of the Iran/contra affair generated a new round of illegality. Beginning with the testimony of Elliott Abrams and others in October 1986 and continuing through the public testimony of Caspar W. Weinberger on the last day of the congressional hearings in the summer of 1987, senior Reagan Administration officials engaged in a concerted effort to deceive Congress and the public about their knowledge of and support for the operations.

Independent Counsel has concluded that the President's most senior advisers and the Cabinet members on the National Security Council participated in the strategy to make National Security staff members McFarlane, Poindexter and North the scapegoats whose sacrifice would protect the Reagan Administration in its final two years. In an important sense, this strategy succeeded. Independent Counsel discovered much of the best evidence of the cover-up in the final year of active investigation, too late for most prosecutions.

_____

[2] See n. 1 above.

## Scope of Report

This report provides an account of the Independent Counsel's investigation, the prosecutions, the basis for decisions not to prosecute, and overall observations and conclusions on the Iran/contra matters.

Part I of the report sets out the underlying facts of the Iran and contra operations. Part II describes the criminal investigation of those underlying facts. Part III provides an analysis of the central operational conspiracy. Parts IV through IX are agency-level reports of Independent Counsel's investigations and cases: the National Security staff, the private operatives who assisted the NSC staff, Central Intelligence Agency officials, Department of State officials, and White House officials and Attorney General Edwin Meese III.

Volume I of this report concludes with a chapter concerning political oversight and the rule of law, and a final chapter containing Independent Counsel's observations. Volume II of the report contains supporting documentation. Volume III is a classified appendix.

Because many will read only sections of the report, each has been written with completeness, even though this has resulted in repetition of factual statements about central activities.

## The Operational Conspiracy

The operational conspiracy was the basis for Count One of the 23-count indictment returned by the Grand Jury March 16, 1988, against Poindexter, North, Secord, and Hakim. It charged the four with conspiracy to defraud the United States by deceitfully:

(1) supporting military operations in Nicaragua in defiance of congressional controls;

(2) using the Iran arms sales to raise funds to be spent at the direction of North, rather than the U.S. Government; and

(3) endangering the Administration's hostage-release effort by overcharging Iran for the arms to generate unauthorized profits to fund the contras and for other purposes.

The charge was upheld as a matter of law by U.S. District Judge Gerhard A. Gesell even though the Justice Department, in a move that Judge Gesell called "unprecedented," filed an amicus brief supporting North's contention that the charge should be dismissed. Although Count One was ultimately dismissed because the Reagan Administration refused to declassify information necessary to North's defense, Judge Gesell's decision established that high Government officials who engage in conspiracy to subvert civil laws and the Constitution have engaged in criminal acts. Trial on Count One would have disclosed the Government-wide activities that supported North's Iran and contra operations.

Within the NSC, McFarlane pleaded guilty in March 1988 to four counts of withholding information from Congress in connection with his denials that North was providing the contras with military advice and assistance. McFarlane, in his plea agreement, promised to cooperate with Independent Counsel by providing truthful testimony in subsequent trials.

Judge Gesell ordered severance of the trials of the four charged in the conspiracy indictment because of the immunized testimony given by Poindexter, North and Hakim to Congress. North was tried and convicted by a jury in May 1989 of altering and destroying documents, accepting an illegal gratuity and aiding and abetting in the obstruction of Congress. His conviction was reversed on appeal in July 1990 and charges against North were subsequently dismissed in September 1991 on the ground that trial witnesses were tainted by North's nationally televised, immunized testimony before Congress. Poindexter in April 1990 was convicted by a jury on five felony counts of conspiracy, false statements, destruction and removal of records and obstruction of Congress. The Court of Appeals reversed his conviction in November 1991 on the immunized testimony issue.

## The Flow of Funds

The illegal activities of the private citizens involved with the North and Secord operations are discussed in detail in Part V. The off-the-books conduct of the two highly secret operations circumvented normal Administration accountability and congressional oversight associated with covert ventures and presented fertile ground for financial wrongdoing. There were several funding sources for the contras' weapons purchases from the covert-action Enterprise formed by North, Secord and Hakim:

(1) donations from foreign countries;

(2) contributions from wealthy Americans sympathetic to President Reagan's contra support policies; and

(3) the diversion of proceeds from the sale of arms to Iran.

Ultimately, all of these funds fell under the control of North, and through him, Secord and Hakim.

North used political fundraisers Carl R. Channell and Richard R. Miller to raise millions of dollars from wealthy Americans, illegally using a tax-exempt organization to do so. These funds, along with the private contributions, were run through a network of corporations and Swiss bank accounts put at North's disposal by Secord and Hakim, through which transactions were concealed and laundered. In late 1985 through 1986 the Enterprise became centrally involved in the arms sales to Iran. As a result of both the Iran and contra operations, more than $47 million flowed through Enterprise accounts.

Professional fundraisers Channell and Miller pleaded guilty in the spring of 1987 to conspiracy to defraud the Government by illegal use of a tax-exempt foundation to raise contributions for the purchase of lethal supplies for the contras. They named North as an unindicted co-conspirator.

Secord pleaded guilty in November 1989 to a felony, admitting that he falsely denied to Congress that North had personally benefited from the Enterprise. Hakim pleaded guilty to the misdemeanor count of supplementing the salary of North. Lake Resources Inc., the company controlled by Hakim to launder the Enterprise's money flow, pleaded guilty to the corporate felony of theft of Government property in diverting the proceeds from the arms sales to the contras and for other unauthorized purposes. Thomas G. Clines was convicted in September 1990 of four tax-related felonies for failing to report all of his income from the Enterprise.

## Agency Support of the Operations

Following the convictions of those who were most central to the Iran/contra operations, Independent Counsel's investigation focused on the supporting roles played by Government officials in other agencies and the supervisory roles of the NSC principals. The investigation showed that Administration officials who claimed initially that they had little knowledge about the Iran arms sales or the illegal contra-resupply operation North directed were much better informed than they professed to be. The Office of Independent Counsel obtained evidence that Secretaries Weinberger and Shultz and White House Chief of Staff Donald T. Regan, among others, held back information that would have helped Congress obtain a much clearer view of the scope of the Iran/contra matter. Contemporaneous notes of Regan and Weinberger, and those dictated by Shultz, were withheld until they were obtained by Independent Counsel in 1991 and 1992.

## The White House and Office of the Vice President

As the White House section of this report describes in detail, the investigation found no credible evidence that President Reagan violated any criminal statute. The OIC could not prove that Reagan authorized or was aware of the diversion or that he had knowledge of the extent of North's control of the contra-resupply network. Nevertheless, he set the stage for the illegal activities of others by encouraging and, in general terms, ordering support of the contras during the October 1984 to October 1986 period when funds for the contras were cut off by the Boland Amendment, and in authorizing the sale of arms to Iran, in contravention of the U.S. embargo on such sales. The President's disregard for civil laws enacted to limit presidential actions abroad—specifically the Boland Amendment, the Arms Export Control Act and congressional-notification requirements in covert-action laws—created a climate in which some of the Government officers assigned to implement his policies felt emboldened to circumvent such laws.

President Reagan's directive to McFarlane to keep the contras alive "body and soul" during the Boland cut-off period was viewed by North, who was charged by McFarlane to carry out the directive, as an invitation to break the law. Similarly, President Reagan's decision in 1985 to authorize the sale of arms to Iran from Israeli stocks, despite warnings by Weinberger and Shultz that such transfers might violate the law, opened the way for Poindexter's subsequent decision to authorize the diversion. Poindexter told Congress that while he made the decision on his own and did not tell the President, he believed the President would have approved. North testified that he believed the President authorized it.

Independent Counsel's investigation did not develop evidence that proved that Vice President Bush violated any criminal statute. Contrary to his public pronouncements, however, he was fully aware of the Iran arms sales. Bush was regularly briefed, along with the President, on the Iran arms sales, and he participated in discussions to obtain third-country support for the contras. The OIC obtained no evidence that Bush was aware of the diversion. The OIC learned in December 1992 that Bush had failed to produce a diary containing contemporaneous notes relevant to Iran/contra, despite requests made in 1987 and again in early 1992 for the production of such material. Bush refused to be interviewed for a final time in light of evidence developed in the latter stages of OIC's investigation, leaving unresolved a clear picture of his Iran/contra involvement. Bush's pardon of Weinberger on December 24, 1992 preempted a trial in which defense counsel indicated that they intended to call Bush as a witness.

The chapters on White House Chief of Staff Regan and Attorney General Edwin Meese III focus on their actions during the November 1986 period, as the President and his advisers sought to control the damage caused by the disclosure of the Iran arms sales. Regan in 1992 provided Independent Counsel with copies of notes showing that Poindexter and Meese attempted to create a false account of the 1985 arms sales from Israeli stocks, which they believed were illegal, in order to protect the President. Regan and the other senior advisers did

not speak up to correct the false version of events. No final legal determination on the matter had been made. Regan said he did not want to be the one who broke the silence among the President's senior advisers, virtually all of whom knew the account was false.

The evidence indicates that Meese's November 1986 inquiry was more of a damage-control exercise than an effort to find the facts. He had private conversations with the President, the Vice President, Poindexter, Weinberger, Casey and Regan without taking notes. Even after learning of the diversion, Meese failed to secure records in NSC staff offices or take other prudent steps to protect potential evidence. And finally, in reporting to the President and his senior advisers, Meese gave a false account of what he had been told by stating that the President did not know about the 1985 HAWK shipments, which Meese said might have been illegal. The statute of limitations had run on November 1986 activities before OIC obtained its evidence. In 1992, Meese denied recollection of the statements attributed to him by the notes of Weinberger and Regan. He was unconvincing, but the passage of time would have been expected to raise a reasonable doubt of the intentional falsity of his denials if he had been prosecuted for his 1992 false statements.

## The Role of CIA Officials

Director Casey's unswerving support of President Reagan's contra policies and of the Iran arms sales encouraged some CIA officials to go beyond legal restrictions in both operations. Casey was instrumental in pairing North with Secord as a contra-support team when the Boland Amendment in October 1984 forced the CIA to refrain from direct or indirect aid. He also supported the North-Secord combination in the Iran arms sales, despite deep reservations about Secord within the CIA hierarchy.

Casey's position on the contras prompted the chief of the CIA's Central American Task Force, Alan D. Fiers, Jr., to "dovetail" CIA activities with those of North's contra-resupply network, in violation of Boland restrictions. Casey's support for the NSC to direct the Iran arms sales and to use arms dealer Manucher Ghorbanifar and Secord in the operation, forced the CIA's Directorate of Operations to work with people it distrusted.

Following the Hasenfus shootdown in early October 1986, George and Fiers lied to Congress about U.S. Government involvement in contra resupply, to, as Fiers put it, "keep the spotlight off the White House." When the Iran arms sales became public in November 1986, three of Casey's key officers—George, Clarridge and Fiers—followed Casey's lead in misleading Congress.

Four CIA officials were charged with criminal offenses—George, the deputy director for operations and the third highest-ranking CIA official; Clarridge, chief of the European Division; Fiers; and Fernandez. George was convicted of two felony counts of false statements and perjury before Congress. Fiers pleaded guilty to two misdemeanor counts of withholding information from Congress. The four counts of obstruction and false statements against Fernandez were dismissed when the Bush Administration refused to declassify information needed for his defense. Clarridge was awaiting trial on seven counts of perjury and false statements when he, George and Fiers were pardoned by President Bush.

## State Department Officials

In 1990 and 1991, Independent Counsel received new documentary evidence in the form of handwritten notes suggesting that Secretary Shultz's congressional testimony painted a misleading and incorrect picture of his knowledge of the Iran arms sales. The subsequent investigation focused on whether Shultz or other Department officials deliberately misled or withheld information from congressional or OIC investigators.

The key notes, taken by M. Charles Hill, Shultz's executive assistant, were nearly verbatim, contemporaneous accounts of Shultz's meetings within the department and Shultz's reports to Hill on meetings the secretary attended elsewhere. The Hill notes and similarly detailed notes by Nicholas Platt, the State Department's executive secretary, provided the OIC with a detailed account of Shultz's knowledge of the Iran arms sales. The most revealing of these notes were not provided to any Iran/contra investigation until 1990 and 1991. The notes show

that—contrary to his early testimony that he was not aware of details of the 1985 arms transfers—Shultz knew that the shipments were planned and that they were delivered. Also in conflict with his congressional testimony was evidence that Shultz was aware of the 1986 shipments.

Independent Counsel concluded that Shultz's early testimony was incorrect, if not false, in significant respects, and misleading, if literally true, in others. When questioned about the discrepancies in 1992, Shultz did not dispute the accuracy of the Hill notes. He told OIC that he believed his testimony was accurate at the time and he insisted that if he had been provided with the notes earlier, he would have testified differently. Independent Counsel declined to prosecute because there was a reasonable doubt that Shultz's testimony was willfully false at the time it was delivered.

Independent Counsel concluded that Hill had willfully withheld relevant notes and prepared false testimony for Shultz in 1987. He declined to prosecute because Hill's claim of authorization to limit the production of his notes and the joint responsibility of Shultz for the resulting misleading testimony, would at trial have raised a reasonable doubt, after Independent Counsel had declined to prosecute Shultz.

Independent Counsel's initial focus on the State Department had centered on Assistant Secretary Elliott Abrams' insistence to Congress and to the OIC that he was not aware of North's direction of the extensive contra-resupply network in 1985 and 1986. As assistant secretary of state for inter-American affairs, Abrams chaired the Restricted Inter-Agency Group, or RIG, which coordinated U.S. policy in Central America. Although the OIC was skeptical about Abrams' testimony, there was insufficient evidence to proceed against him until additional documentary evidence inculpating him was discovered in 1990 and 1991, and until Fiers, who represented the CIA on the RIG, pleaded guilty in July 1991 to withholding information from Congress. Fiers provided evidence to support North's earlier testimony that Abrams was knowledgeable about North's contra-supply network. Abrams pleaded guilty in October 1991 to two counts of withholding information from Congress about secret Government efforts to support the contras, and about his solicitation of $10 million to aid the contras from the Sultan of Brunei.

## Secretary Weinberger and Defense Department Officials

Contrary to their testimony to the presidentially appointed Tower Commission and the Select Iran/contra Committees of Congress, Independent Counsel determined that Secretary Weinberger and his closest aides were consistently informed of proposed and actual arms shipments to Iran during 1985 and 1986. The key evidence was handwritten notes of Weinberger, which he deliberately withheld from Congress and the OIC until they were discovered by Independent Counsel in late 1991. The Weinberger daily diary notes and notes of significant White House and other meetings contained highly relevant, contemporaneous information that resolved many questions left unanswered in early investigations.

The notes demonstrated that Weinberger's early testimony—that he had only vague and generalized information about Iran arms sales in 1985—was false, and that he in fact had detailed information on the proposed arms sales and the actual deliveries. The notes also revealed that Gen. Colin Powell, Weinberger's senior military aide, and Richard L. Armitage, assistant secretary of defense for international security affairs, also had detailed knowledge of the 1985 shipments from Israeli stocks. Armitage and Powell had testified that they did not learn of the November 1985 HAWK missile shipment until 1986.

Weinberger's notes provided detailed accounts of high-level Administration meetings in November 1986 in which the President's senior advisers were provided with false accounts of the Iran arms sales to protect the President and themselves from the consequences of the possibly illegal 1985 shipments from Israeli stocks.

Weinberger's notes provided key evidence supporting the charges against him, including perjury and false statements in connection with his testimony regarding the arms sales, his denial of the existence of notes and his denial of knowledge of Saudi Arabia's multi-million dollar contribution to the contras. He was par-

doned less than two weeks before trial by President Bush on December 24, 1992.

There was little evidence that Powell's early testimony regarding the 1985 shipments and Weinberger's notes was willfully false. Powell cooperated with the various Iran/contra investigations and, when his recollection was refreshed by Weinberger's notes, he readily conceded their accuracy. Independent Counsel declined to prosecute Armitage because the OIC's limited resources were focused on the case against Weinberger and because the evidence against Armitage, while substantial, did not reach the threshold of proof beyond a reasonable doubt.

## The Reagan, Bush and Casey Segments

The Independent Counsel Act requires a report as to persons not indicted as well as those indicted. Because of the large number of persons investigated, those discussed in individual sections of this report are limited to those as to whom there was a possibility of indictment. In addition there are separate sections on President Reagan and President Bush because, although criminal proceedings against them were always unlikely, they were important subjects of the investigation, and their activities were important to the action taken with respect to others.

CIA Director Casey is a special case. Because Casey was hospitalized with a fatal illness before Independent Counsel was appointed, no formal investigation of Casey was ever undertaken by the OIC. Casey was never able to give his account, and he was unable to respond to allegations of wrongdoing made about him by others, most prominently North, whose veracity is subject to serious question. Equally important, fundamental questions could not be answered regarding Casey's state of mind, the impact, if any, of his fatal illness on his conduct and his intent.

Under normal circumstances, a prosecutor would hesitate to comment on the conduct of an individual whose activities and actions were not subjected to rigorous investigation, which might exculpate that individual. Nevertheless, after serious deliberation, Independent Counsel concluded that it was in the public interest that this report expose as full and complete an account of the Iran/contra matter as possible. This simply could not be done without an account of the role of Director Casey.

## Observations and Conclusions

This report concludes with Independent Counsel's observations and conclusions. He observes that the governmental problems presented by Iran/contra are not those of rogue operations, but rather those of Executive Branch efforts to evade congressional oversight. As this report documents, the competing roles of the attorney general—adviser to the President and top law-enforcement officer—come into irreconcilable conflict in the case of high-level Executive Branch wrongdoing. Independent Counsel concludes that congressional oversight alone cannot correct the deficiencies that result when an attorney general abandons the law-enforcement responsibilities of that office and undertakes, instead, to protect the President.

Independent Counsel asks the Congress to review the difficult and delicate problem posed to the investigations and prosecutions by congressional grants of immunity to principals. While recognizing the important responsibility of Congress for investigating such matters thoroughly, Congress must realize that grants of use immunity to principals in such highly exposed matters as the Iran/contra affair will virtually rule out successful prosecution.

Independent Counsel also addresses the problem of implementing the Classified Information Procedures Act (CIPA) in cases steeped in highly classified information, such as many of the Iran/contra prosecutions. Under the Act, the attorney general has unrestricted discretion to decide whether to declassify information necessary for trial, even in cases in which Independent Counsel has been appointed because of the attorney general's conflict of interest. This discretion is inconsistent with the perceived need for independent counsel, particularly in cases in which officers of the intelligence agencies that classify information are under investigation. This discretion gives the attorney general the power to block almost any potentially embarrassing prosecution that requires the declassification of information. Independent Counsel suggests that the attorney general implement standards that would permit independent review of a decision to block a prosecution of an officer within the Executive Branch and legitimate congressional oversight.

## Classified Information

In addition to the unclassified Volumes I and II of this report, a brief classified report, Volume III, has been filed with the Special Division. The classified report contains references to material gathered in the investigation of Iran/contra that could not be declassified and could not be concealed by some substitute form of discussion.

# Office of Independent Counsel for Iran/contra Matters Summary of Prosecutions

After Independent Counsel Lawrence E. Walsh's appointment in December 1986, 14 persons were charged with criminal offenses. Eleven persons were convicted, but two convictions were overturned on appeal. Two persons were pardoned before trial and one case was dismissed when the Bush Administration declined to declassify information necessary for trial. On December 24, 1992, President Bush pardoned Caspar W. Weinberger, Duane R. Clarridge, Clair E. George, Elliott Abrams, Alan D. Fiers, Jr., and Robert C. McFarlane.

## Completed Trials and Pleas

Elliott Abrams—Pleaded guilty October 7, 1991, to two misdemeanor charges of withholding information from Congress about secret government efforts to support the Nicaraguan contra rebels during a ban on such aid. U.S. District Chief Judge Aubrey E. Robinson, Jr., sentenced Abrams November 15, 1991, to two years probation and 100 hours community service. Abrams was pardoned December 24, 1992.

Carl R. Channell—Pleaded guilty April 29, 1987, to one felony count of conspiracy to defraud the United States. U.S. District Judge Stanley S. Harris sentenced Channell on July 7, 1989, to two years probation.

Thomas G. Clines—Indicted February 22, 1990, on four felony counts of underreporting his earnings to the IRS in the 1985 and 1986 tax years; and falsely stating on his 1985 and 1986 tax returns that he had no foreign financial accounts. On September 18, 1990, Clines was found guilty of all charges. U.S. District Judge Norman P. Ramsey in Baltimore, Md., on December 13, 1990, sentenced Clines to 16 months in prison and $40,000 in fines. He was ordered to pay the cost of the prosecution. The Fourth Circuit U.S. Court of Appeals in Richmond, Va., on February 27, 1992, upheld the convictions. Clines served his prison sentence.

Alan D. Fiers, Jr.—Pleaded guilty July 9, 1991, to two misdemeanor counts of withholding information from Congress about secret efforts to aid the Nicaraguan contras. U.S. District Chief Judge Aubrey E. Robinson, Jr., sentenced Fiers January 31, 1992, to one year probation and 100 hours community service. Fiers was pardoned December 24, 1992.

Clair E. George—Indicted September 6, 1991, on 10 counts of perjury, false statements and obstruction in connection with congressional and Grand Jury investigations. George's trial on nine counts ended in a mistrial on August 26, 1992. Following a second trial on seven counts, George was found guilty December 9, 1992, of two felony charges of false statements and perjury before Congress. The maximum penalty for each count was five years in prison and $250,000 in fines. U.S. District Judge Royce C. Lamberth set sentencing for February 18, 1993. George was pardoned on December 24, 1992, before sentencing occurred.

Albert Hakim—Pleaded guilty November 21, 1989, to a misdemeanor of supplementing the salary of Oliver L. North. Lake Resources Inc., in which Hakim was the principal shareholder, pleaded guilty to a corporate felony of theft of government property in diverting Iran arms sales proceeds to the Nicaraguan contras and other activities. Hakim was sentenced by U.S. District Judge Gerhard A. Gesell on February 1, 1990, to two years probation and a $5,000 fine; Lake Resources was ordered dissolved.

Robert C. McFarlane—Pleaded guilty March 11, 1988, to four misdemeanor counts of withholding information from Congress. U.S. District Chief Judge Aubrey E. Robinson, Jr., sentenced McFarlane on March 3, 1989, to two years probation, $20,000 in fines and 200 hours community service. McFarlane was pardoned December 24, 1992.

Richard R. Miller—Pleaded guilty May 6, 1987, to one felony count of conspiracy to defraud the United States. U.S. District Judge Stanley S. Harris sentenced Miller on July 6, 1989, to two years probation and 120 hours of community service.

Oliver L. North—Indicted March 16, 1988, on 16 felony counts. After standing trial on 12, North was convicted May 4, 1989 of three charges: accepting an illegal gratuity, aiding and abetting in the obstruction of a congressional inquiry, and destruction of documents. He was sentenced by U.S. District Judge Gerhard A. Gesell on July 5, 1989, to a three-year suspended prison term, two years probation, $150,000 in fines and 1,200 hours community service. A three-judge appeals panel on July 20, 1990, vacated North's conviction for further proceedings to determine whether his immunized testimony influenced witnesses in the trial. The Supreme Court declined to review the case. Judge Gesell dismissed the case September 16, 1991, after hearings on the immunity issue, on the motion of Independent Counsel.

John M. Poindexter—Indicted March 16, 1988, on seven felony charges. After standing trial on five charges, Poindexter was found guilty April 7, 1990, on all counts: conspiracy (obstruction of inquiries and proceedings, false statements, falsification, destruction and removal of documents); two counts of obstruction of Congress and two counts of false statements. U.S. District Judge Harold H. Greene sentenced Poindexter June 11, 1990, to six months in prison on each count, to be served concurrently. A three-judge appeals panel on November 15, 1991, reversed the convictions on the ground

that Poindexter's immunized testimony may have influenced the trial testimony of witnesses. The Supreme Court on December 7, 1992, declined to review the case. In 1993, the indictment was dismissed on the motion of Independent Counsel.

Richard V. Secord—Indicted March 16, 1988 on six felony charges. On May 11, 1989, a second indictment was issued charging nine counts of impeding and obstructing the Select Iran/contra Committees. Secord was scheduled to stand trial on 12 charges. He pleaded guilty November 8, 1989, to one felony count of false statements to Congress. Secord was sentenced by U.S. District Chief Judge Aubrey E. Robinson, Jr., on January 24, 1990, to two years probation.

## Pre-trial Pardons

Duane R. Clarridge—Indicted November 26, 1991, on seven counts of perjury and false statements about a secret shipment of U.S. HAWK missiles to Iran. The maximum penalty for each count was five years in prison and $250,000 in fines. U.S. District Judge Harold H. Greene set a March 15, 1993, trial date. Clarridge was pardoned December 24, 1992.

Caspar W. Weinberger—Indicted June 16, 1992, on five counts of obstruction, perjury and false statements in connection with congressional and Independent Counsel investigations of Iran/contra. On September 29, the obstruction count was dismissed. On October 30, a second indictment was issued, charging one false statement count. The second indictment was dismissed December 11, leaving four counts remaining. The maximum penalty for each count was five years in prison and $250,000 in fines. U.S. District Judge Thomas F. Hogan set a January 5, 1993, trial date. Weinberger was pardoned December 24, 1992.

## Dismissal

Joseph F. Fernandez—Indicted June 20, 1988 on five counts of conspiracy to defraud the United States, obstructing the inquiry of the Tower Commission and making false statements to government agencies. The case was dismissed in the District of Columbia for venue reasons on the motion of Independent Counsel. A four-count indictment was issued in the Eastern District of Virginia on April 24, 1989. U.S. District Judge Claude M. Hilton dismissed the four-count case November 24, 1989, after Attorney General Richard Thornburgh blocked the disclosure of classified information ruled relevant to the defense. The U.S. Court of Appeals for the Fourth Circuit in Richmond, Va., on September 6, 1990, upheld Judge Hilton's rulings under the Classified Information Procedures Act (CIPA). On October 12, 1990, the Attorney General filed a final declaration that he would not disclose the classified information.

# Part I
# Iran/contra: The Underlying Facts

## The Contras

Independent Counsel's investigation produced a vast record of U.S. Government involvement with the Nicaraguan contras during a prohibition on military aid from October 1984 to October 1986. The Office of Independent Counsel (OIC) focused its inquiry on possible criminal activity—ranging from violations of the Boland Amendment prohibition on aid to conspiracy to violate the tax laws—in Administration efforts to assist the military and paramilitary operations of the contras. The investigation also centered on what officials knew about that assistance and what they offered when questioned about it. No effort was made to create a complete historical record of U.S. activities in the region, or even of American ties to the contras.

Independent Counsel's look at the "contra" side of Iran/contra quickly focused on critical episodes for American policy in Central America. A discussion of some of these episodes is useful for understanding the prosecutions brought or declined by Independent Counsel.

## The Reagan Administration's Contra Policy

President Reagan was an early and vigorous opponent of the Sandinista regime that seized power in Nicaragua in 1979. As a presidential candidate, Reagan advocated cutting all aid to the Nicaraguan government; as President, Reagan stepped up American activities against the Sandinistas and embraced their opponents, known as the Nicaraguan Democratic Resistance or "contras."

Reagan's posture towards the Sandinista government was highly controversial. The opponents of the Administration's anti-Sandinista policies convinced a majority of the Democratic-controlled U.S. House of Representatives to view the contras with extreme skepticism. Their efforts resulted in passage in late 1982 of an amendment introduced by Representative Edward P. Boland to the Fiscal Year 1983 Defense Appropriations bill. This first of a series of "Boland Amendments" prohibited the Central Intelligence Agency (CIA), the principal conduit of covert American support to the contras, from spending any money "for the purpose of overthrowing the government of Nicaragua." [1]

Controversy over contra policy continued past enactment of the first Boland Amendment. The Reagan Administration pushed hard for more money for the contras, while House Democrats threatened to cut off such support altogether. In early December 1983, a compromise was reached: Contra funding for FY 1984 was capped at $24 million—an amount significantly lower than what the Administration had wanted—with the possibility that the Administration could approach the Congress for supplemental funds later.

The December 1983 cap on contra aid guaranteed a crisis in the Administration's contra program the following year. As early as February 1984, Reagan's national security adviser, Robert C. McFarlane, had suggested to other Administration officials that one way to fund the contras would be to encourage other countries to contribute support. CIA Director William J. Casey agreed with the idea, and recommended several countries that had been or could be approached. By May 1984, McFarlane had convinced one of these countries, Saudi

---

[1] Defense Appropriations Act for FY 1983, § 793, Pub.L. 97–377 (1982).

1

Arabia, to contribute $1 million per month to the contra cause. McFarlane instructed his trusted assistant on the National Security Council (NSC) staff, Lt. Col. Oliver L. North, to arrange for a covert bank account to move the Saudi funds into contra hands.[2]

The Saudi contributions came just as it was clear that Congress would not increase direct American support for the contras. Disclosures in April 1984 that the CIA had secretly mined Nicaraguan harbors had wrecked the Administration's chances to persuade the Congress to lift its $24 million contra-aid cap. According to McFarlane, an undaunted President Reagan instructed McFarlane—who in turn told North—that the NSC staff had to keep the contras alive "body and soul." [3]

The NSC staff's efforts to assist the contras in the wake of Congress's withdrawal of funding took many forms. Initially it meant extending its earlier initiative to increase third-country contributions to the contras. Casey and McFarlane broached the subject of such funding at a June 25, 1984, meeting of the National Security Planning Group (NSPG), consisting of the President, Vice President Bush, Casey, McFarlane, Secretary of State George Shultz, Secretary of Defense Caspar Weinberger, United Nations Ambassador Jeane Kirkpatrick, Chairman of the Joint Chiefs of Staff Gen. John Vessey, and presidential adviser Edwin Meese III. Shultz warned that any approach to a third country could be viewed as an "impeachable offense," and convinced the group that it needed a legal opinion from Attorney General William French Smith. McFarlane agreed and told the group not to approach any foreign country until the opinion was delivered. McFarlane said nothing about what he already had obtained from the Saudis.[4]

## The Funding Cut-Off

North's role in assisting the contras grew as Congress inched closer toward cutting all assistance to the contras. By early August, the House of Representatives had passed the toughest restrictions on contra aid yet, restrictions that became law in October 1984. This iteration of the Boland Amendment provided in pertinent part:

> During fiscal year 1985, no funds available to the Central Intelligence Agency, the Department of Defense, or any other agency or entity of the United States involved in intelligence activities may be obligated or expended for the purpose or which would have the effect of supporting, directly or indirectly, military or paramilitary operations in Nicaragua by any nation, group, organization, movement, or individual.

To comply with the law, both the CIA and the Defense Department withdrew large numbers of personnel from Central America—leaving a void that North was to fill.

Anticipating Boland, and hoping to mend fences with critics in the Congress, CIA Director Casey reorganized the leadership of the CIA's Operations Directorate that had been responsible for the contra war. Out was the flamboyant chief of the Latin American Division of the Operations Directorate, Duane R. "Dewey" Clarridge; in came Alan D. Fiers, Jr., who was made chief of the Central American Task Force (CATF) within the Latin American Division. It did not take Fiers long, however, to learn who had taken the reins on contra activities: North. "[W]ork with him," Clarridge reportedly told Fiers. As the CIA's deputy director for operations, Clair E. George, told Fiers in early November 1984, Casey had promised the President that he would take care of the contras. Any denial of operational activity by North would be just for show.[5]

With the bulk of their funds now coming via the NSC staff instead of the CIA, the contras increasingly turned to the NSC for advice and assistance. The point man for this assistance was North. McFarlane enjoined North from getting involved in direct fund-raising for

---

[2] A broader discussion of these events is found in the McFarlane chapter of this report.

[3] For broader discussions of these topics, see McFarlane and Reagan chapters.

[4] NSPG Minutes, 6/25/84, ALU 007863–76. The following day, Casey met with the attorney general and legal advisers from the CIA and Justice Department to press for an opinion. The attorney general expressed the view that discussions with third countries would be permissible as long as it was made clear that the countries would spend their own funds, and not later be reimbursed by the United States. (Memorandum from Sporkin to the Record, 6/26/84, ALV 035917.)

[5] Fiers, *George* Trial Testimony, 10/28/92, pp. 1254–69; George, *George* Trial Testimony, 11/16/92, pp. 50–52.

the contras, but approved of North's increasing contacts with them, warning North only to exercise "absolute stealth" in his meetings. North became familiar not only with the contra leadership, but with the CIA's assets and resources in Central America—all with the apparent approval and encouragement of CIA Director Casey. According to North, with CIA money down to a trickle by the summer of 1984, Casey was all too willing to "hand off" the CIA's contra operations to North.[6]

North also turned to Americans outside the Government to assist him with the contras. In the summer of 1984, on Casey's recommendation, North reached out to retired U.S. Air Force Maj. Gen. Richard V. Secord and asked him to help contra leader Adolfo Calero buy arms with his new Saudi money. Secord soon became an arms broker for the contras. North also convinced an employee of Gray & Company, Robert Owen, to meet regularly with Calero and other contra leaders to learn of their needs, deliver valuable intelligence to them, and supply them with money raised by North.[7]

By early 1985, North and his operatives were working several angles on behalf of the contras. North obtained tactical and other intelligence from the CIA and passed it to contra military commanders. Secord was probing the international arms markets for the contras and purchasing weapons for them. North also made it known that he was the "man to see" about money for the contras. When one congressman questioned the propriety of the CIA funding contra leaders, who in turn were lobbying Congress for increased contra aid, North proposed to Fiers and Deputy Assistant Secretary of State Craig Johnstone that he line up private funding. Fiers rejected the idea on grounds that it would cause Congress only to question the new source of funds.[8]

North was able to claim that he had private funds because he was lending a hand to various large- and small-scale efforts to raise money for the contras. Having learned from CIA Oper-

ations Director George, for example, that the South Koreans were interested in contributing funds to the contras, North arranged for contra solicitor retired Army Maj. Gen. John K. Singlaub to meet with South Korean officials in the United States. Saudi Arabia, whose contributions North earlier had arranged to transfer to the contras, doubled its monthly contribution in February 1985. Beginning in April 1985, North aided the efforts of two private fundraisers, Carl Channell and Richard R. Miller, by arranging for speakers to potential contributors, presenting his own briefings, and encouraging use of the White House as a stage prop for Channell and Miller's pitch—including arranging private chats and photo opportunities with the President.[9]

North also worked with McFarlane on efforts to use foreign aid as leverage with a number of Central American countries—particularly Honduras, the site of most of the contra encampments—to get them to support the contras more strongly. In February 1985, the President approved a McFarlane-North plan to assure the Honduran government of expedited economic, military, and intelligence support if it agreed to allow contra bases to remain in Honduras and permit weapons to be shipped to them. Vice President Bush traveled to Honduras the next month, underscoring with Honduran President Roberto Suazo the need for contra support and signaling what the United States would be willing to do in return. The Hondurans caught on to the linkage quickly. When President Reagan called Suazo in April 1985 to implore him to release a shipment of contra ammunition, Suazo reminded President Reagan that a high-level Honduran delegation shortly would be in Washington to discuss a $15 million aid package.[10]

## A Southern Front

By the spring of 1985 it became clear that Congress would not rescue the contras any time soon. The House defeated a $14 million supplemental aid package in March, leaving the contras to rely on North and his associates. Calero found himself surrounded not only with

[6] North, *North* Trial Testimony, 4/6/89, pp. 6781–82, 6826; Cannistraro, *North* Trial Testimony, 4/3/89, pp. 6405, 6409–10.

[7] North, *North* Trial Testimony, 4/6/89, pp. 6815–17. For further discussion of these events, see Flow of Funds chapter.

[8] Memorandum from Fiers to DC/LA, C/LA, SA/ODDO, and ADDO/DDO, Re: Status Report on Honduran Discussions, 2/12/85, DO 94090–95. For full treatments of North's early 1985 activities, see Flow of Funds and Fiers chapters.

[9] For further discussion of these events, see Flow of Funds and George chapters.

[10] For a full discussion of the early 1985 overtures to Honduras and other Central American nations, see McFarlane chapter.

recommended arms brokers like Secord—who by June 1985 had arranged several large arms shipments—but also willing broker/contribution solicitors like Singlaub. There also were arms merchants like Ron Martin, a Miami-based dealer who had been accused of consorting with drug-runners. While the NSC staff helped Saudi Arabian and other funds reach the contras, Calero had been deciding how most of the money would be spent. By May 1985, North realized that he and Secord were facing increasing competition for Calero's attention—and that contra arms purchases were getting out of their control.[11]

While he and Secord were grappling with disorganized contra procurement, North and other members of the Restricted Interagency Group on Central America (the RIG) had concluded that the contras had to step up pressure on the Sandinista regime. The RIG's chief strategic decision, reached in the summer of 1985, was to open a "southern front" in the Nicaraguan war. Up to then, the bulk of the contra forces—and the focus of American efforts to influence and support them—lay along Nicaragua's northern border with Honduras. The concentration of these forces made them an easy target for the Sandinistas and tested the tolerance of the Honduran government.

North, Fiers, and others in the RIG concluded by mid-1985 that one way to relieve contra forces in the north and to escalate the war would be to inspire opposition forces along Nicaragua's southern border to go on the offensive. Up to then, the anti-Sandinista groups in the south were splintered. A flamboyant but mercurial leader named Eden Pastora had attempted to rally them in 1984, but the CIA had since concluded that Pastora was not inclined to drive his forces into the heart of Nicaragua. The RIG decided by the summer of 1985 that it had to get opposition forces out of Costa Rica and into Nicaragua, where they could do some good for the contra cause.[12]

## A Full-Service Enterprise

North took bold steps in late June 1985 to solve the problems he perceived with contra weapons

procurement, while laying the foundation for a system that could supply both the northern and southern fronts. North convened a meeting on June 28, 1985, in Miami with Secord; Thomas Clines, a former CIA officer who by then was acting as Secord's overseas arms buyer; Raphael Quintero, another former CIA officer who had been acting as Secord's "man on the scene" in Honduras, El Salvador, and Costa Rica; Calero; and contra military commander Enrique Bermudez. The men met through the night, during which North announced that he would suspend his cash payments to Calero: Henceforth, Secord would arrange for all weapons purchases and deliveries. North also stressed to Calero and Bermudez, whose ties were closest to contra forces in the north, that they had to work with him and Secord—including sharing precious supplies—to build a viable southern front.[13]

Secord later described the June 1985 Miami meeting as a "watershed" event for him and his involvement with the contras. North convinced Secord to take charge of a covert air-delivery system, one that would mirror earlier CIA efforts to arm the contras. Thus, in addition to his activities as an arms purchaser and supplier, Secord began hiring airplane crews, acquiring or leasing aircraft, arranging for warehouses in Central America, and gaining landing rights in the region.[14]

While Secord proceeded with setting up a full-service "Enterprise," North continued to work within the RIG and elsewhere to implement his enhanced contra operation. These stepped-up efforts coincided with a significant reorganization of the State Department's Central American officers, which saw Elliott Abrams become assistant secretary for inter-American affairs; William Walker take over as Abrams' deputy; and the reassignments of Edwin G. Corr and Lewis A. Tambs as U.S. ambassadors to El Salvador and Costa Rica, respectively.

Both Corr and Tambs were informed of the RIG's decision to "open" the southern front, a decision that was a particularly critical one for Tambs. Costa Rican cooperation was deemed essential to the southern front, including

---

[11] For a full discussion of these topics, see CIA Subject #1 and Flow of Funds chapters.

[12] For a full discussion of this decision, see Abrams, Fiers, and Fernandez chapters.

[13] For a full discussion of this meeting, see CIA Subject #1 and Flow of Funds chapters.

[14] For a full discussion, see Flow of Funds chapter.

establishment of an airstrip in northern Costa Rica that would facilitate supply drops to contra forces. Tambs was charged with convincing the Costa Rican government to agree with the new American effort, while the chief of the CIA's station in San Jose, Joseph Fernandez, was responsible for working out many of the operational aspects of the RIG's plan. By August 1985, the Costa Ricans had approved the effort—a decision that coincided with promises of covert payments to a project headed by the Costa Rican president—and Tambs and Fernandez were working on sites for the airstrip.[15]

## The Nicaraguan Humanitarian Assistance Office (NHAO)

Barred by Boland from directly or indirectly supporting the contras' military and paramilitary activities, the CIA endeavored to do all it could in Central America in the way of non-paramilitary activities, both in direct support of the contras and in an effort to undermine the Sandinista regime. When faced with a roadblock in Congress, Casey and Fiers would turn to the designated contra trouble-shooter, North. Congress explicitly had cut funding to a specific non-paramilitary project against the Sandinistas, for example, in July 1985. Notwithstanding grudging promises to the congressional intelligence committees that they would comply with the ban, Casey and Fiers turned to North for substitute funding. They also encouraged other CIA assets to divert funds to the project, an arrangement that continued for at least nine months before being halted.[16]

Notwithstanding Congress's decision to withdraw funds from certain CIA projects, the Administration overall was slowly convincing members of Congress to resume direct aid to the contras. In August 1985, Congress approved $27 million in humanitarian aid to the contras, with the proviso that the State Department—not the CIA or the Defense Department—administer the aid. President Reagan quickly established the Nicaraguan Humanitarian Assistance Office (NHAO) within the State Depart-

ment and ordered NHAO to get supplies moving south.

Passage of NHAO aid gave the U.S. Government, acting principally through the CIA, new leverage in dealing with the contras—particularly those on the southern front. The process of gearing up NHAO's logistical and intelligence-gathering activities—a daunting task for a department that had little experience in logistics or air deliveries—would also give North the opportunity to insert people into NHAO who had been working covertly with him and Secord on contra resupply.

## "Bud McFarlane Just Perjured Himself for Me. God Bless Him."

North's efforts to assist the contras did not escape the attention of others in the Administration, or the press. By August 1985, more and more accounts had appeared in the media alleging that North had been giving military advice to the contras and had been behind logistical support for them. On August 16, Representative Michael Barnes, chairman of the House Foreign Affairs Committee's Subcommittee on Western Hemisphere Affairs, wrote to McFarlane asking whether the NSC staff had provided "tactical influence" on contra military operations, were "facilitating contacts for prospective financial donors," or were involved in "otherwise organizing and coordinating rebel efforts."[17] The chairman of the House Permanent Select Committee on Intelligence (HPSCI), Representative Lee H. Hamilton, dispatched a similar letter to McFarlane shortly after the Barnes inquiry.

Before responding to Barnes and Hamilton's letters, McFarlane ordered a search of the NSC's records for memoranda that bore on contra activities. The search, limited by NSC staff to Freedom of Information Act standards, resulted in identification of several "problem documents," memoranda written by North that suggested there was truth to the allegations of North's tactical support and fund-raising activities. McFarlane and North agreed that the documents could be so interpreted and pondered whether they should be altered. Ultimately, McFarlane decided not to bring the documents to Congress's attention, and instead decided to lie about North's activities in a series of letters

[15] For a full discussion of these events, see Corr, Fernandez, Fiers, Abrams, and Classified CIA Investigation A chapters.

[16] For a full discussion of this initiative, see Classified CIA Investigation B chapter.

[17] Letter from Barnes to McFarlane, 8/16/85, AKW 001510–11.

to Barnes and Hamilton in September-October 1985. North soon told Fiers, "Bud McFarlane just perjured himself for me—God bless him."[18]

## NHAO By Day, Private Benefactors By Night

Press allegations and questions from Congress did not hamper North in expanding resupply operations. In September 1985, on the recommendation of Col. James Steele, the commander of the U.S. Military Group in El Salvador, North wrote to Felix Rodriguez, an ex-CIA operative who had gone to El Salvador to fight communist guerrillas, and asked Rodriguez to help him win approval from the Salvadoran Air Force to use its air base at Ilopango for contra-resupply activities. Rodriguez successfully persuaded Salvadoran Air Force General Juan Rafael Bustillo to grant North and his people entry to the base—guaranteeing North a strategic position from which to launch air operations to both the north and the south.

Trouble with the Honduran government in October 1985 gave North the chance to infiltrate NHAO and, in the words of Fiers, "piggyback" the activities of his Enterprise onto the fledgling humanitarian program. As early as September 1985, North urged the director of NHAO, Ambassador Robert Duemling, to hire North's contra courier Owen as an "on the scene" Central American specialist for NHAO. Duemling ignored the advice. On October 10, however, the first air delivery to Central America by NHAO arrived in Honduras, carrying a television news crew. Attempting to hide their support for the contras, the Hondurans banned further U.S. flights—a move that, for the moment, prevented NHAO aid from reaching contra troops.

North seized on the Honduran fiasco to convince the RIG that Owen would not have let it happen. The RIG prevailed on an embarrassed

18 Fiers, FBI 302, 7/19/91, p. 17; Fiers, FBI 302, 7/30/91, p. 20; Fiers, *George* Trial Testimony, 7/28/92, p. 1133. Others in the Government in the summer of 1985—and later—avoided answering questions about North's involvement by deferring to McFarlane. See, for example, Letter from Casey to Hamilton, 8/28/85, E.R. 11618 (referring inquiries to McFarlane and telling HPSCI that Casey was not "in a position to answer in any authoritative way" questions about NSC support to the contras); Abrams chapter.

For further discussion of all of these events, see McFarlane, North, Poindexter, and Thompson chapters.

Duemling to hire Owen shortly thereafter, giving North a key operative within NHAO and providing Owen with a cover for his trips to Central America for North.

The Honduran ban created an additional problem for NHAO that worked to North's advantage: how to get aid into Honduras. In separate trips, North, Fiers, and newly appointed National Security Adviser John Poindexter traveled to Tegucigalpa to talk to the Hondurans, to no avail. It was not until late December 1985 that the Hondurans agreed to allow NHAO flights to resume, on the condition that they not come directly from the United States. North proposed to the RIG that Ilopango air base—the same airport North had envisioned as a point for private resupply—be used to "transship" NHAO supplies from the United States to El Salvador, and then on to Honduras. Government officials including North and Fiers traveled to the region in late December to gain Honduran and Salvadoran approval for the plan, with the help in El Salvador of North's man, Rodriguez.

By early 1986, large pieces of NHAO and what was known in official circles as the "private benefactors" operation were virtually indistinguishable. Owen was reporting on contra needs for both. Rodriguez was coordinating shipments at Ilopango for both entities. Butler buildings erected at Ilopango by NHAO were being used to store equipment for both entities. And both entities were using the flying services of Richard Gadd, a retired U.S. Air Force lieutenant colonel who had been working with Secord on air-delivery operations since August 1985. The stage was set for Gadd's air crews to be, in Fiers' words, "NHAO by day, private benefactors by night," marking a rare occasion that a U.S. Government program unwittingly provided cover to a private covert operation.[19]

## Leaning Forward

The new year brought hope to many in the Administration that Congress was not far from lifting the Boland restrictions altogether and allowing direct support for contra military activities to resume. Congress had allowed NHAO to consult with the CIA on setting up a secure

19 For a more extensive discussion of the merging of these operations, see the Fiers and Gregg chapters.

delivery system and had loosened Boland in late 1985 to permit the CIA to provide communications support and training to the contras. President Reagan instructed his advisers to propose an ambitious $100 million contra-aid program. Some in the Administration hoped that aid would be on its way as early as April 1986.

Confidence that official aid would soon resume encouraged Fiers and another CIA officer, James Adkins, to take steps that took each of them into dangerous territory. Fiers met with Gadd twice during February 1986 to learn more about Gadd's operations, hoping that his experience would prove helpful in re-establishing a CIA covert lethal resupply network. Adkins for his part ordered CIA pilots to ferry lethal and non-lethal supplies to contras in southern Honduras, using CIA helicopters. Though he clearly violated Boland, Adkins was encouraged by signs from Washington that Boland would not be around for long.[20]

The immediate need for funds and fund-raising did not cease with the new year. North and Abrams continued to give briefings and provide other assistance to groups of contributors gathered by Channell and Miller. President Reagan continued to drop by some of these sessions and grant private meetings and photo opportunities. Money raised by Channell and Miller fed the Enterprise, as did funds from the Saudis and diverted proceeds from covert sales of arms to Iran. They became all the more important when the House unexpectedly defeated President Reagan's $100 million contra-aid package in March 1986.[21]

## The Cover Unravels

North's use of a NHAO cover for private-benefactor lethal-resupply operations did not fool other U.S. officials for long. As early as late January 1986, Fiers began receiving intelligence from CIA personnel in Central America that Rodriguez was asserting himself in both NHAO and private-benefactor activities. Tensions between Rodriguez and CIA personnel became apparent to not only Fiers, but to State Department personnel as well. Reports that Rodriguez was involved in the crash of a private-benefactor

aircraft on a highway in El Salvador and that he was coordinating this with North over unsecured telephone lines ultimately prompted Fiers, at the insistence of CIA Operations Director George, to tell a senior CIA officer in the region to stay far away from the matter.[22]

At the same time Fiers was warning his personnel in Central America away from the private benefactors, he candidly admitted to at least one senior officer there that more flights under North's control would be coming. While Fiers did not understand in early 1986 just how complex North's network was in Central America—including its secure, National Security Agency-supplied, KL–43 communications devices linking North, Secord, Gadd, Steele, Quintero, and Fernandez—Fiers knew that it could provide lethal assistance, and that North had a key role in it. When contra forces in the north could not make a promised air drop of lethal supplies to their fellows in the south in April 1986, Fiers joined a plan secretly engineered by North and Fernandez to use the Enterprise instead. The Enterprise successfully delivered an L–100 aircraft full of materiel to the southern front on April 9, 1986, sealing a major effort by Fernandez and other CIA officers to wean pro-active, dissident commanders away from Pastora and keep them on the field of battle.[23]

## A Need for Bridge Financing

President Reagan gathered his NSPG for a meeting on the contras on May 16, 1986. While Director Casey reported encouraging developments in the contra war, many of those in attendance—including Secretaries Shultz and Weinberger, White House Chief of Staff Donald Regan, Casey, and Poindexter—voiced concern that all would be for naught if money was not found for the contras, and soon. Shultz suggested that the State Department approach third countries—something that Congress had permitted beginning December 1985. The President wondered aloud whether "Ollie's people" could step into the breach. Regan quickly changed the subject, but not in time to prevent Fiers and others who were attending the meeting—

---

[20] For a fuller discussion of Fiers and Adkins's activities in early 1986, see their respective chapters.

[21] For a fuller discussion of these activities, see the Flow of Funds chapter.

[22] For a full discussion of these topics, see Fiers, Corr, and CIA Subject #1 chapters.

[23] For a full discussion of these topics, see Fiers chapter.

including North and Abrams—from understanding where the President was heading.[24]

Ironically, between May 14–15, the Enterprise received an Iranian arms sales payment of $15 million, giving the Enterprise a total of $6 million for contra aid and other activities. Additional sources of funds for the contras were nonetheless in doubt. The Administration's success in convincing the House of Representatives to approve $100 million in contra aid in late June 1986 may have signaled past contributors that funds were no longer needed, at precisely the moment that they were.[25]

One way that North hoped to raise additional money was by liquidating the Enterprise's substantial assets. By July 1986, North was pressing CIA officials from Fiers up to buy all of the Enterprise's Central American assets, partly in hope of converting the proceeds to contra aid. North's pitch made clear to Fiers, George, Deputy Director of Central Intelligence Robert Gates, and Casey what was long apparent: that North was working hand-in-glove with the management and ownership of the private-benefactor operations in Central America.[26]

## The Trouble with Rodriguez

North's efforts to sell the Enterprise's planes and facilities did not escape the notice of one Enterprise associate, Rodriguez. For several months, Rodriguez had been both a nuisance and a key asset for the Enterprise and the RIG. As demonstrated in the February 1986 airplane mishap, and time and again since, Rodriguez was perceived as a "talker." Not only had he told people in El Salvador that he was working with North, he regularly boasted of his ties to the CIA, Vice Presidential National Security Adviser Donald P. Gregg, and through Gregg to Vice President Bush. With Rodriguez involved in activities that, had he been a Government official, would have violated the Boland Amendment, and with his bragging that all of his work—including that on behalf of the contras—was sponsored by the U.S. Govern-

ment, official Washington was repeatedly uneasy about Rodriguez. On numerous occasions, members of the RIG discussed how to silence him, with little success.[27]

At the same time, Rodriguez was essential to NHAO and the RIG's efforts in Central America. Rodriguez was friendly with the Salvadoran military, especially Bustillo, commander of the air facilities so essential to NHAO and private-benefactor flights. No one in the RIG had an alternative to Rodriguez for keeping the Salvadoran military happy. As a result, despite his liabilities, Government officials took Rodriguez seriously. As early as April 1986, Rodriguez had become disenchanted with many of the persons involved in the Enterprise—especially Secord, Clines, and Quintero, all of whom had been touched by scandal and whom Rodriguez suspected of profiteering at the contras' expense. Rodriguez threatened to move back to Miami and abandon the operation. It took persuasion by North and Corr to keep Rodriguez in place.[28]

Rodriguez's concerns about Enterprise profit-taking interfered, however, with North's plan to liquidate the Enterprise's assets. Saying that he was expressing Gen. Bustillo's views, Rodriguez accused the Enterprise of trying to sell off assets—particularly airplanes—that had been donated to the contras. In July 1986, Rodriguez posted armed guards around planes used by the Enterprise, thereby halting all resupply flights. Shortly thereafter, North accused Rodriguez of stealing a loaded Enterprise C–123 from a hanger in Miami and demanded that Gregg rein in Rodriguez. At Gregg's request, Rodriguez came to Washington on August 8, 1986, but instead of responding to North's charges, Rodriguez ran through his complaints about the Enterprise—including his suspicions about Clines, Secord, and Quintero; Enterprise profiteering; and Bustillo's concerns about the future of the "contras'" planes.[29]

Four days later, Gregg convened a meeting in his office to discuss Rodriguez. Many significant figures involved with contra operations—

[24] Memorandum from Burghardt to McDaniel Re: Minutes of the May 16, 1986 National Security Planning Group Meeting, 6/4/86, AKW 18802–13; Fiers, Grand Jury, 8/14/91, pp. 39–40. For more detail on the 1986 foreign solicitations, see Abrams chapter.

[25] Aid opponents delayed final implementation of the President's package until the new fiscal year, which began in October 1986.

[26] For a fuller discussion of North's efforts to sell the Enterprise assets to the CIA, see Fiers, Gates, and George chapters.

[27] For further discussion of Rodriguez's activities, see Gregg chapter. For further description of the CIA, State Department, and NSC discussions about Rodriguez, see Fiers and Abrams chapters.

[28] For further discussion, see Gregg chapter.

[29] For a full discussion of the circumstances surrounding this meeting, see Gregg chapter.

including Ambassador Corr, Col. Steele, Fiers, Lt. Col. Robert Earl of the NSC, and Deputy Assistant Secretary of State Walker—listened with amazement as Gregg aired Rodriguez's worries, and pressed Fiers on whether the CIA was planning to take over the private benefactors' operations at Ilopango. Again the RIG discussed whether Rodriguez could be replaced. Again the conclusion was no.[30]

## More Lies

As North was trying to bridge the gap in contra aid until official funds were resumed, his activities were the subject of a second wave of media speculation and congressional inquiry. Newspaper and television accounts of North's involvement with contra resupply coincided with the House's June 1986 debate on contra aid. Earlier, Representative Ron Coleman introduced a Resolution of Inquiry directing the President to provide information and documents to the House about NSC staff contacts with (1) private persons or foreign governments involved in contra resupply; (2) any contra, involving contra military activities; and (3) Robert Owen, Maj. Gen. Singlaub, and an American expatriate living in Costa Rica, John Hull.

Coleman's resolution prompted the chairmen of the House Intelligence and Foreign Affairs committees to request comments from the President. Poindexter replied on behalf of the President and knowingly repeated McFarlane's earlier lie that NSC staff "were in compliance with both the spirit and letter" of the Boland Amendments.

Not satisfied with Poindexter's response, members of the House Permanent Select Committee on Intelligence asked to meet with North. North met with 11 members of the Committee on August 6, 1986, assuring the group that he had not violated the spirit or the letter of the Boland Amendment. He also denied that he had raised funds for the contras, offered them military advice, or had contacts with Owen that were more than "casual." North's responses satisfied the Committee and effectively killed Coleman's resolution. After learning of North's

false and misleading remarks to the Committee, Poindexter replied to North, "Well done." [31]

## Exposure Within, Exposure Without

While he endeavored to hide his activities from the Congress in the summer of 1986, North was becoming progressively more explicit in his discussions with other U.S. officials about what he was doing for the contras. His efforts to sell "his planes" to the CIA were only the beginning. On August 28, 1986, during a breakfast with the RIG at the offices of Assistant Secretary of Defense for International Security Affairs Richard Armitage, North ran through a list of his contra activities, including his cash payments to contra leaders and organizations, provisions of food, and money for air operations. North's question for the RIG was simple: Should he continue his efforts? Fiers told North yes.[32]

The Enterprise was pushing ahead on an accelerated schedule of deliveries in August and September 1986. Crews were making more sorties into both northern and southern Nicaragua, some during daylight hours. San Jose station chief Fernandez, who was in direct contact with Quintero, ordered CIA personnel to relay drop zone and other information to contra forces on the Southern Front, as well as report news of deliveries.[33]

Events besides the imminent renewal of U.S. aid and the drawing down of the Enterprise's supplies for the contras were forcing North to wrap up his Central American operations. On September 25, 1986, a Costa Rican official disclosed the existence of the Enterprise's airstrip in northern Costa Rica and publicly linked it to contra resupply and an Enterprise shell corporation, Udall Resources, Inc. North scrambled to draft false press guidance with Abrams and Fiers, and assured Poindexter that he was doing his best to "keep USG fingerprints off this"—including dissolving Udall and covering its tracks.[34]

---

[30] For further description of this meeting, see Fiers and Gregg chapters.

[31] For further details of the summer 1986 inquiries and lies, see the North and Poindexter chapters.
[32] For a full discussion of the RIG's growing exposure to North's activities, see Abrams chapter.
[33] For further discussion, see Fernandez chapter.
[34] For further discussion, see Abrams chapter.

## The Hasenfus Shoot-Down

Unbeknownst to Enterprise crews at Ilopango, the accelerated resupply missions had alerted the Sandinistas to the private benefactors' air routes to drop sites in southern Nicaragua. Having repositioned radar and anti-aircraft units in the area, it was only a matter of time before an Enterprise plane was shot down by the Nicaraguans. Such was the case on October 5, 1986, when an Enterprise C–123K loaded with lethal supplies and carrying three Americans was brought down by Sandinista ground fire.

Of the crew, only one survived, an American named Eugene Hasenfus. The Sandinistas combed the wreckage of the flight and recovered scores of documents linking it to NHAO and numerous Americans working at Ilopango air base. While in Sandinista custody, Hasenfus said that he was working for the CIA, and that two CIA officers—including a "Max Gomez," the local alias for Rodriguez—had been in charge of food, lodging, and other services for the operation's pilots and crews. Within days, North had directed his Enterprise to clear out of Ilopango—planes and all—and had begun to destroy ledgers detailing his disbursements to the contras. The Hasenfus flight was the Enterprise's last.

## The End of Boland

The crash of the Enterprise C–123K could not have come at a worse time for the Administration. The President's $100 million contra-aid package was inching toward final approval, and opponents were quick to latch on to Hasenfus's claims that he had been part of an illegal CIA operation. Speaking to the public and Congress, Administration officials—including Fiers, George and Abrams—insisted truthfully that Hasenfus and his companions did not work for the CIA. They falsely denied knowing other facts, however: who "Max Gomez" was, who the private benefactors were, and whether any U.S. Government officials were involved.

The Administration's statements worked. Congress released the contra funds on October 17, 1986. North had kept the contras alive, "body and soul," despite the Boland cut-off, and the rest of the Administration had convinced the Congress that it had complied with the law. It took the November 1986 disclosures

of the Iran arms sales to pry the lid off North's contra activities once and for all. It took an independent counsel six years to ensure that concerted efforts to deny knowledge of North's contra activities—described in the rest of this report—met with a similar fate.

## The Iran Arms Sales

What we now know as the Iran arms sales, or the Iran initiative, was actually a series of related but distinct events that began in the summer of 1985 and continued through 1986. Israel sent U.S.-supplied weapons to Iran on three occasions in 1985. These shipments took place with U.S. approval, and, in one instance, with U.S. participation. They led to the release in September 1985 of one American held hostage in Lebanon. The United States delivered missiles and missile parts to Iran on five occasions in 1986, after President Reagan signed an intelligence "Finding" authorizing such shipments. These 1986 shipments led to the release of two more U.S. hostages, though terrorists seized two additional Americans in September 1986.

The first shipment of U.S.-made weapons from Israel to Iran took place August 20, 1985. But discussion and debate within the U.S. Government as to the desirability of arms sales to Iran had been going on for months at the time of the first Israeli shipment.

## The Policy Debate

In early May of 1985, Michael Ledeen, a part-time consultant to the NSC, obtained National Security Adviser Robert McFarlane's approval to meet in Israel with Prime Minister Shimon Peres to explore whether Israel would share information on Iran with the United States.

According to Ledeen, Peres expressed displeasure with Israel's intelligence on Iran and suggested that the United States and Israel should work together to improve their information about and policies toward Iran. He also mentioned a recent Iranian request to buy artillery shells from Israel. Israel would grant the request, Peres said, only if the United States had no objection. Ledeen agreed to relay the question of the proposed weapons sale to McFarlane.[35]

In the weeks after Ledeen's trip to Israel, the number of Americans held hostage in Lebanon grew. David Jacobsen, the director of the American University Hospital in Beirut, was kidnapped on May 28, 1985. Thomas Sutherland, the dean of agriculture at the University of Beirut, was seized on June 9, 1985. These abductions were in addition to the March 1985 kidnapping of Terry Anderson, chief Middle East correspondent for the Associated Press, and the January 1985 seizure of Father Lawrence Jenco, the senior Catholic Relief Services official in Beirut. Two other Americans kidnapped in 1984 remained in captivity as well: the Reverend Benjamin Weir and—of special interest to CIA Director Casey—CIA Beirut Station Chief William Buckley.

The hostages were not the only concern in U.S.-Iran affairs. Some U.S. Government officials feared increased Soviet influence in Iran. In a Special National Intelligence Estimate (SNIE) prepared in May 1985 at the request of Casey, the intelligence community warned of this Soviet threat and called for new approaches to improve Western relations with the government of Iran. One possible avenue, according to the SNIE, would be the elimination of restrictions on weapons sales to Iran.

Casey pushed for adoption of the SNIE as a National Security Decision Directive (NSDD), an operational paper for the national security community. In June 1985, the NSC staff prepared for McFarlane a draft NSDD responding to the ideas contained in the SNIE. The proposed presidential memorandum, entitled "U.S. Policy Toward Iran," recommended that the initial focus of any new policy should be on stimulating essential trade. According to the draft NSDD, the United States should:

> [e]ncourage Western allies and friends to help Iran meet its import requirements so as to reduce the attractiveness of Soviet assistance and trade offers, while demonstrating the value of correct relations with the West. This includes provision of

selected military equipment as determined on a case-by-case basis.[36]

McFarlane circulated the draft NSDD to Shultz, Weinberger, and Casey on June 17, 1985. Both Shultz and Weinberger wrote to McFarlane opposing the NSDD. Casey, on the other hand, wrote McFarlane on July 18, 1985, endorsing it.

On June 18, 1985, President Reagan made a public statement that would prove to be ironic in light of the arms-for-hostages shipments that were to occur over the next eighteen months:

> Let me further make it plain to the assassins in Beirut and their accomplices, wherever they may be, that America will never make concessions to terrorists—to do so would only invite more terrorism—nor will we ask nor pressure any other government to do so. Once we head down that path there would be no end to it, no end to the suffering of innocent people, no end to the bloody ransom all civilized nations must pay.[37]

## Manucher Ghorbanifar

McFarlane met at the White House on July 3, 1985, with David Kimche, director general of the Israeli Foreign Ministry. McFarlane later testified that Kimche raised the possibility of a renewed political dialogue between the United States and Iran. According to Kimche, Iranians who had been in contact with Israel would show their good faith by using their influence over radical groups in Lebanon to obtain the release of American hostages. These Iranians would expect a reciprocal show of good faith from the United States—most likely in the form of military equipment.

McFarlane mentioned Kimche's proposal to President Reagan. President Reagan expressed interest and instructed McFarlane to explore it further. On July 13, 1985, Ledeen told McFarlane that Adolf "Al" Schwimmer, an adviser to Prime Minister Peres, said that Peres wanted McFarlane to know that Israel's principal Iranian contact had told Kimche and Schwimmer that he was in touch with a group

---

[35] For a more detailed discussion of these events, see McFarlane chapter.

[36] Memorandum from McFarlane to Shultz and Weinberger, 6/17/85, AKW 001713–20.

[37] "The President's News Conference," Public Papers of the President, 6/18/85, p. 779.

of Iranians who wished to improve relations with the West and who could demonstrate good faith by arranging the release of the American hostages. In return, these Iranians needed to have 100 American-made TOW anti-tank missiles.

Schwimmer told Ledeen that the Iranian was Manucher Ghorbanifar. Ghorbanifar was an Iranian businessman who was well known to the American intelligence community as a prevaricator. The CIA had concluded, after past interaction with Ghorbanifar, that he could not be trusted to act in anyone's interest but his own. So strong were the CIA's views on Ghorbanifar that the Agency issued a "burn notice" in July 1984, effectively recommending that no U.S. agency have any dealings with him. Nevertheless, Ghorbanifar was to play a major role over the next year as the initial intermediary (the "First Channel") between Iran, the United States and Israel.

## Approving Israeli Sales

In mid-July 1985, McFarlane informed Shultz, Weinberger and Casey of the Israeli proposal, including the new demand for TOW missiles. Shultz cabled to say that the United States should make a tentative showing of interest in a dialogue with Iran. Weinberger was opposed. Casey's July 18, 1985, letter supporting the draft NSDD favored the Israeli proposal.

President Reagan entered Bethesda Naval Hospital on July 13, 1985, for cancer surgery. On approximately July 18, as President Reagan was recovering from his operation, McFarlane and White House Chief of Staff Donald Regan met with him in his hospital room. McFarlane outlined Kimche and Schwimmer's proposal—including the possibility of weapons shipments to Iran. President Reagan encouraged McFarlane to continue to explore the proposed dialogue but made no commitment to include weapons shipments.

McFarlane authorized Ledeen to meet with Ghorbanifar. Ledeen did so in late July 1985, accompanied by Kimche, Schwimmer and Yaacov Nimrodi, an Israeli arms merchant and business partner of Schwimmer. Ghorbanifar described a group of Iranians interested in improving relations with the United States. He repeated the notion of Iranian assistance in freeing Amer-

ican hostages in Lebanon, in return for American TOW missiles. After the meeting, Kimche agreed to brief McFarlane.

Kimche met with McFarlane at the White House on August 2, 1985. This time the issue of arms shipments was front and center. Would the United States itself sell weapons to Iran? If not, would the United States permit Israel to sell U.S.-manufactured weapons to the Iranians? If Israel sold the weapons, would the United States sell replacements to Israel? McFarlane promised Kimche that he would respond after consultations with President Reagan and other senior officers.

In early August 1985, McFarlane briefed President Reagan on Kimche's information. Vice President Bush, Regan, Weinberger, Casey and Shultz were also briefed. Shultz and Weinberger again expressed their opposition to arms sales. The various participants in the meeting had differing perceptions of President Reagan's reaction to McFarlane's report. McFarlane concluded that President Reagan would approve sales of U.S.-supplied weapons by Israel if the weapons went to reliable anti-Khomeini Iranians.

The precise date of President Reagan's decision is unclear. It was no later than August 23, 1985. On that day, President Reagan wrote in his diary that he had received a "secret phone" call from McFarlane, that "a man high up in the Iranian govt." believed he could deliver "all or part of the 7 kidnap victims." President Reagan further noted that he "had some decisions to make about a few points—but they were easy to make—now we must wait." [38] According to McFarlane, the President approved a commitment to replenish Israel's supply of missiles for those sent to Iran. McFarlane conveyed President Reagan's approval to Kimche. There was no notification to Congress.[39]

## The Summer 1985 Shipments

The Israelis had already prepared for the shipment and moved quickly. On August 20, 1985, after haggling over pricing and financing arrangements, the first shipment of 96 TOW mis-

---

[38] OIC Review of Reagan Diary Excerpts, 1987.
[39] For full treatments of the President's approval of Israeli arms sales, see McFarlane, State and Defense Department chapters.

siles arrived in Iran. No hostages were released. Ghorbanifar claimed that the TOWs fell into the wrong hands but expressed hope that further shipments would lead to the release of the hostages.

The Israelis tried to move things forward by convening a meeting in Paris on September 4 and 5. McFarlane sent Ledeen. As Ledeen put it, the "usual suspects" attended: Israelis Kimche, Schwimmer and Nimrodi, along with Ghorbanifar. During discussions that often were heated, Ghorbanifar explained that more TOWs would have to be sent—400 more—in order to gain the release of a single hostage.

Israel proceeded with an additional delivery of missiles. On September 14, 1985, an Israeli-chartered aircraft arrived in Iran carrying 408 TOWs.

McFarlane had told the Israelis that the United States wanted hostage William Buckley to be released if only one hostage were to be freed. On September 15, Reverend Benjamin Weir was released in Beirut. Ghorbanifar claimed that Buckley had been too sick to be moved. In fact, Buckley had been dead for at least two months.

The summer shipments marked Oliver North's first involvement with the Iran arms sales. During September, North asked the CIA to arrange for continuing intelligence reports on Ghorbanifar and Mohsen Kangarlu, Ghorbanifar's principal contact in the government of Iran. Charles Allen, the CIA's national intelligence officer for counter-terrorism, made the necessary arrangements. The intelligence reports were initially relayed only to McFarlane, North, Casey, and Vice Admiral Arthur S. Moreau, Jr., assistant to the chairman of the Joint Chiefs of Staff. Shultz and Weinberger did not get copies. Weinberger soon found out and was included in the distribution.[40]

## The November 1985 HAWK Shipment

Despite the disappointing results in September, discussions among the United States, Israel and Ghorbanifar continued. Ledeen continued to be the U.S. representative. In a late-September meeting in Paris, Ghorbanifar suggested Iran's

interest in various anti-aircraft missiles, including HAWK missiles.

Shortly after this meeting, North asked Ledeen to invite Ghorbanifar to Washington to discuss hostage issues. Ghorbanifar, Schwimmer and Nimrodi arrived on October 7, 1985. That same day, the Italian cruise ship *Achille Lauro* was hijacked by Palestinian terrorists. North was so heavily involved that he did not attend the scheduled meeting with Ghorbanifar. The meeting went ahead on October 8, 1985, without North. Ledeen, Ghorbanifar, Nimrodi and Schwimmer met in the Old Executive Office Building, with Ledeen serving as the primary spokesman for the Americans.

Ghorbanifar's basic proposal was for more trades: Israeli deliveries of U.S.-manufactured weaponry in return for the release of the Americans held in Lebanon. Ghorbanifar requested weapons that included HAWK anti-aircraft missiles, along with Sidewinder, Harpoon and advanced Phoenix missiles.

A few days afterward, Ledeen briefed McFarlane and North. Ledeen and McFarlane claim they each expressed distaste for further arms-for-hostages transactions and questioned pursuing the Israeli channel. Nevertheless, Ghorbanifar nudged the United States toward further meetings by promising to introduce Ledeen to a senior Iranian official. Ledeen obtained McFarlane's authorization to attend a meeting in Geneva in late October. On approximately October 27, 1985, Ledeen met in Geneva with the "usual suspects" and the supposed senior Iranian official, Hassan Karoubi.

Karoubi's precise rank or position within the Iranian government was uncertain. Karoubi apparently renewed with Ledeen the theme of better U.S. relations with a powerful faction of moderate Iranians, of whom Karoubi was one. But arms shipments were discussed as well. According to North's notes of Ledeen's briefing, Karoubi proposed a staggered exchange of hostages for 150 HAWK missiles, 200 Sidewinder missiles and 30–50 Phoenix missiles. Ledeen also told North that the Israelis wanted the replenishment of the TOWs that had been sent to Iran in August and September.

North and Ledeen met with McFarlane, who was highly skeptical of the existence of moderate Iranians. McFarlane, however, was willing

---

[40] For more complete discussions of the Israeli shipments in the summer of 1985, see McFarlane, State and Defense Department chapters.

to have Israel make further deliveries of weapons to Iran—as long as arms shipments were preceded by the release of "live Americans." Ledeen sensed that McFarlane was close to resigning and to shutting down the Iran initiative. To keep it moving forward, Ledeen maneuvered a meeting between Kimche and McFarlane in Washington. This meeting took place on November 8, 1985, with North and Ledeen present. Kimche pressed McFarlane not to abandon the efforts to contact moderate Iranians through Ghorbanifar and Israel.

Less than a week later, after a regular weekly meeting with senior CIA officials on November 14, McFarlane told Casey and John McMahon, the deputy director of central intelligence, that Israel planned to ship weapons to certain elements of the Iranian military who were willing and ready to overthrow the government of Iran. The following day, Israeli Defense Minister Yitzhak Rabin had breakfast with Casey and then met with McFarlane at the White House. Rabin asked McFarlane if the United States still approved of Israel selling arms to Iran. McFarlane replied that President Reagan continued to approve. Rabin described a contemplated shipment of HAWK missiles and raised the question of replenishment. McFarlane agreed to it and said he would assign North to follow through. Within a day or two, McFarlane advised President Reagan and Vice President Bush of the imminent Israeli delivery of HAWKs to Iran.

As with the late summer TOW shipments, Israel moved quickly once assured of American support. On Sunday, November 17, 1985—just two days after McFarlane's meeting with Rabin—Rabin telephoned North to say that Israel was ready to go forward with a shipment of 80 HAWKs, once replenishment issues were worked out. Rabin then spoke with McFarlane, who was in Geneva at a U.S.-Soviet summit. McFarlane called North, telling him to solve Rabin's replenishment problems. McFarlane also told North to keep the Israeli replenishment orders under $14 million per order. Larger weapons orders, he believed, would have to be reported to Congress.

Rabin's statements to McFarlane and North reflected a sale of 80 HAWKs. Subsequent conversations between North and Schwimmer indi-

cated that this 80-missile shipment was to be the first of a larger total delivery of as many as 500–600 HAWK missiles. Inventory checks at the Pentagon, however, showed that only 79 HAWKs were available for the immediate replenishment of Israel. North told Poindexter on Wednesday, November 20, that plans had changed. The Israelis planned to dispatch planes carrying 80 HAWKs. This was to be followed by the shipment of 40 additional HAWKs and other weapons, including more TOWs. North's notes of his conversation show that at least some weapons were to be delivered before any hostages were freed—contrary to McFarlane's order that "live Americans" go free before more weapons went to Iran.

On Tuesday, November 19, McFarlane asked Weinberger to check the availability of HAWKs. Weinberger referred the request to his military assistant, Gen. Colin L. Powell, who directed the Pentagon bureaucracy to prepare a negative response. The result was a memorandum that not only discussed price and availability of HAWKs, but also questioned the wisdom and legality of the proposed sale.

The proposed shipment later ran into logistical problems. The Israeli plan was to mask the origin of the delivery by flying the missiles from Israel to Europe,[41] loading them onto other aircraft, and then shipping them on to Iran. But the European country's officials were unwilling to allow this transfer to take place without word from the United States as to its purpose.

North requested Secord to travel to Europe to help arrange the necessary flight clearances. On Tuesday, November 19, North gave a letter to Secord on White House letterhead, signed by North for McFarlane. Secord arrived in Europe on Wednesday, November 20. North also discussed the situation with his friend Duane Clarridge, a senior CIA operations officer. Clarridge told North that the CIA could help gain overseas flight clearances. On the evening of November 19, North met with Clarridge and Vincent Cannistraro, a CIA operations officer temporarily assigned to the NSC, to discuss the flight clearances problem.

In Geneva, at the summit meeting between President Reagan and Soviet General Secretary

---

[41] The name of the country is classified.

Mikhail Gorbachev, McFarlane briefed President Reagan, Shultz and Regan on the details of the upcoming HAWKs shipment. President Reagan raised no objection. Shultz disapproved but did not try to stop the transaction. Weinberger telephoned McFarlane in Geneva that the transaction without notice to Congress would be illegal. McFarlane said the President had decided to make the transfer through the Israelis.

By late in the day on Thursday, November 21, Secord had been unable to get appropriate European government officials to grant landing rights for the Israeli shipment. After one of Secord's attempts failed, the European government asked the U.S. Embassy for information about the unusual situation. The uninformed Embassy responded that the activities were not authorized by the U.S. Government.

Secord reported to North that evening. North then telephoned Clarridge, who sent high-priority cables to senior CIA officers overseas directing them to go to work and await further instructions. On Friday morning, November 22, Clarridge told these officers to contact Secord (traveling under the alias "Copp") and offer assistance. Secord mistakenly said he needed no help.

The project rapidly deteriorated during Friday. An El Al 747 leased by the Israeli military took off from Tel Aviv with 80 HAWKs on board headed for Europe. Late Friday morning, clearances were denied by the European country. Secord called the senior CIA field officer with an urgent request for assistance.

North obtained State Department permission to involve the Embassy in the quest for clearances. The U.S. charge d'affaires in the European country tried to have the European foreign minister called out of a cabinet meeting to receive a call from McFarlane. The European country stated that a formal diplomatic note from the United States explaining the circumstances would be required before clearances could be approved. McFarlane did not reach the foreign minister until late Friday night. But even this proved elusive: Senior foreign ministry officials on Saturday morning said they knew nothing of McFarlane's agreement with the foreign minister, and said that a note was still required.

Lacking flight clearances, the El Al 747 was forced to return to Israel. Schwimmer canceled the charter for two other jets that were to transport additional HAWKs. With the planes Israel had reserved no longer available, North again turned to Clarridge for help. Clarridge met late Friday afternoon with an officer from the CIA's Air Branch and told him that new charters for a bulky shipment were needed as soon as possible. The Air Branch told Clarridge that a plane belonging to a CIA proprietary airline (an airline secretly owned by the CIA) might be available. Clarridge obtained the approval of Edward Juchniewicz, the CIA's associate deputy director for operations. The CIA proprietary airplane flew to Israel to load missiles.

Clarridge's office became the nerve center of the ill-fated HAWKs shipment. North joined Clarridge there on Saturday, along with Allen and the CIA Air Branch officer. Clarridge sent cables to CIA personnel at two overseas locations seeking to obtain overflight clearances and landing rights for the CIA's proprietary aircraft. After much effort, the aircraft landed in Tehran late Sunday night, November 24.[42]

## November Post-Mortem

Only 18 HAWKs were delivered to Iran, instead of the planned 80. These 18 HAWKs were not what the Iranians wanted. The Iranians had been given the impression that the "I–HAWKs" (improved HAWKs) were capable of shooting down planes at high altitudes. They were not. To make matters worse, the missiles carried Israeli "Star of David" markings, which angered the Iranians. No hostages gained their freedom.

The HAWKs shipment caused problems at the CIA as well. The CIA's extensive involvement in the logistics of the delivery, its efforts to gain foreign clearances, and the use of the proprietary aircraft for an Israeli weapons delivery were "covert actions" that required a Presidential Finding. Further operations were put on hold while a proper Finding was drafted.

After checking with McFarlane and Regan to make sure that President Reagan would sign a Finding, Casey sent a draft Finding to Poindexter on November 26, 1985. Poindexter

---

[42] For a more complete treatment of the events of November 1985, see McFarlane, Thompson, Shultz, Defense, and Clarridge chapters.

had informed President Reagan on the morning of Monday, November 25, that the HAWKs had been delivered to Iran. On November 26, President Reagan had approved the continuation of the Israeli arms-for-hostages operation. On December 5, 1985, President Reagan signed the Finding requested by the CIA that: (1) stated the CIA's activities were part of an authorized effort to secure the release of American hostages in exchange for shipments of weapons, (2) directed that Congress not be notified, and (3) retroactively sought to approve the CIA activities already completed. Just under a year later, on November 21, 1986, Poindexter secretly destroyed the signed Finding because, he said, he felt its existence—and its plain arms-for-hostages language—would embarrass President Reagan.

## The December–January Meetings

On December 4, 1985, President Reagan announced McFarlane's resignation and appointed Poindexter to replace him. Poindexter soon told Ledeen that he would no longer be used by the NSC in the initiative. North assumed primary responsibility for the project.

The debacle of the HAWKs shipment was barely a week old, yet things began moving again toward more transactions. Secord met in Paris on December 1, 1985, with Ghorbanifar, Kimche, Schwimmer and Nimrodi. Ghorbanifar registered the Iranians' anger and proposed additional exchanges of large numbers of weapons in return for the release of the American hostages. The meeting ended with an agreement that the group would meet again in London on December 6.

North sent Poindexter a computer message on December 4, 1985, outlining a broad new program of Israeli weapons sales to Iran as part of an arms-for-hostages operation—a sequential exchange of 3,300 TOWs and 50 HAWKs for the release of all U.S. hostages and one French hostage. North contemplated an exchange in five separate phases coordinated over a single 24-hour period. North expressed the view that cutting off the arms shipments so soon after angering the Iranians with the HAWKs ship-

ments risked the lives of the American hostages.[43]

Poindexter briefed Shultz by telephone on December 5, 1985. Shultz told Poindexter that he opposed the arms-for-hostages deals that had taken place and that were contemplated. At the CIA that same day, McMahon held a meeting with Juchniewicz, Deputy Director for Intelligence Robert Gates, and others to discuss American efforts to free the hostages. Notes from this meeting indicate that these CIA officials were aware that the November shipment carried to Iran by the CIA's proprietary aircraft had contained missiles.

North flew to London on December 6, 1985, to meet with Ghorbanifar, Secord, Kimche, Schwimmer and Nimrodi. The group discussed details of the proposed Israeli sale of 3,300 TOWs and 50 HAWKs to Iran in return for the release of all hostages. But the discussion was only a preliminary one. President Reagan planned to meet with his senior advisers on Saturday, December 7, 1985, to discuss whether and how to proceed with the Iran arms sales.

The December 7 meeting in the White House residence included Reagan, Regan, Shultz, Weinberger, McMahon (in Casey's absence), Poindexter and McFarlane. Shultz and Weinberger voiced their strong opposition to the Iran arms sales on both legal and policy grounds. McMahon attacked some of the basic assumptions behind the arms sales—especially the presence of "moderates" in Iran with whom the United States could deal. Poindexter favored a continuation of past efforts through the Israelis, and told those gathered that he had a proxy to express Casey's support for going ahead with the arms sales. The result of the December 7 meeting was inconclusive. President Reagan expressed no clear decision except to send McFarlane immediately to London, where North and the other negotiators were already talking. McFarlane was to inform the intermediaries that the United States was willing to pursue political rapprochement with Iran and to negotiate the release of hostages, but that these steps should precede or be independent of any further arms sales.

---

[43] On December 5, North converted the computer message into a memorandum for Poindexter. He distributed copies to those involved in the transaction, including the Israelis.

McFarlane met in London on December 8 with Secord, North, Ghorbanifar, Kimche, Schwimmer and Nimrodi. McFarlane engaged in heated exchanges with Kimche and Ghorbanifar, both of whom favored more arms-for-hostages shipments. Like two ships passing in the night, McFarlane spoke of political goals while Ghorbanifar complained about the November HAWKs shipment and called for more arms-for-hostages transactions. McFarlane came away from the meeting extremely pessimistic about breaking out of the arms-for-hostages mold, and adverse to any further interactions with Ghorbanifar.

The next day, North wrote a memorandum to McFarlane and Poindexter that took issue with McFarlane's assessment of the arms-for-hostages operations. North's basic points were that interacting with Ghorbanifar, though not optimal, had led to the release of Weir and was the best channel the United States had into the Iranian government. As North viewed it, the downside of further arms-for-hostages transactions was a small number of weapons being sent to Iran with no results. The downside of breaking off the Israeli-sponsored channel, on the other hand, was the potential for severe harm to the hostages. North concluded that it would be a mistake to walk away from Ghorbanifar at that point.

North's December 9, 1985, memorandum mentioned one additional ''option'' that had not yet been discussed. He suggested that the United States, under an appropriate covert action Finding, could sell arms directly to Iran using Secord as an intermediary who could serve as a watchdog over Ghorbanifar. A form of North's proposal eventually became the working model of the direct U.S. arms sales to Iran that took place in 1986.

McFarlane briefed President Reagan on the London meeting on December 10, 1985, in the presence of Weinberger, Casey, Regan, Poindexter and North. McFarlane warned the group that Ghorbanifar was a man of no integrity whose promises and representations could not be trusted. Ghorbanifar and the Israelis were focused primarily on arms-for-hostages transactions and were unlikely to pursue an expanded political dialogue between the United States and Iran through other means. McFarlane

recommended that the United States have no further involvement in the Iran arms sales. McFarlane did, however, mention that one option was simply to let the Israelis continue shipping weapons in the hope that the United States might get some benefit.

President Reagan did not express any conclusive decision at the December 10 meeting, but several present believed that he was unwilling to abandon an operation that might lead to the release of the American hostages. President Reagan clung to McFarlane's comment that simply letting Israel go forward without any formal U.S. commitment or involvement might help American hostage-recovery efforts. President Reagan also expressed concern, first raised by McFarlane, that abruptly breaking off the arms shipments would anger the Iranians and might lead to the death of one or more hostages.

As the December 10 meeting broke up, it was clear to Casey and other observers who knew President Reagan well that he had not yet decided to put a stop to the Israeli arms shipments to Iran. President Reagan had very powerful feelings about the hostages, and a strong sense that it was his duty to do all he could to gain their release.

## The NSC Iran Operation

Poindexter sensed President Reagan's willingness to continue with some sort of weapons sales to Iran. Poindexter discussed with North several steps that needed to be taken to lay the groundwork for future shipments. The first involved developing a better Finding that could serve as authority for future transactions. Next was a change in personnel, replacing Ledeen, Schwimmer and Nimrodi with North and Amiram Nir, an Israeli counter-terrorism expert and adviser to Prime Minister Peres.

North deviated from Poindexter's direction for a change in personnel. North instructed Ledeen to push the CIA to develop an intelligence relationship with Ghorbanifar. Ledeen met during December 1985 with Casey, Clarridge and Allen, advocating to each that Ghorbanifar be used in any future operations involving Iran. Casey had a favorable reaction, but knew of the CIA's ''burn notice'' on Ghorbanifar. In an effort to get beyond this bad history, Casey told George to reexamine

Ghorbanifar's potential as an intelligence contact.

George did as asked. CIA officers polygraphed Ghorbanifar and reported that the CIA's earlier appraisal of Ghorbanifar was correct: The man could not be trusted. Despite the debacle of the November HAWKs shipment and this negative assessment from career CIA officials, Casey still viewed Ghorbanifar as a potential link to the government of Iran and those who could influence the holders of the hostages. Casey wrote President Reagan a private letter stating that one option for pursuing the Iran arms sales was the continued use of Ghorbanifar as an intermediary.

The Israelis wasted little time. Nir came to Washington, D.C., on January 2, 1986, and met with Poindexter and North. He proposed a broad new initiative. Israel would get things rolling by sending 500 TOW missiles to Iran. Iran would then cause all American hostages in Lebanon to be released. Israel would then arrange the release of certain Hezbollah prisoners in southern Lebanon. If all went well, Israel would send 3,500 more TOWs to Iran, which would foreswear further hostage-taking and terrorism. The United States would promptly replenish the missiles delivered by Israel to Iran.

Nir's proposal was well-received by Poindexter and North. There appeared to be little risk for the United States. At worst, if no hostages were released, Israel would be out 500 TOWs with no U.S. obligation to replenish them. North immediately began the process for creating a new, more sophisticated Finding to support the operations proposed by Nir. Beginning on January 3, 1986, CIA General Counsel Stanley Sporkin and North prepared a Finding authorizing the CIA to sell arms to Iranians, which contemplated no notification of Congress and recited the broad goal of improved relations with Iran. North and Sporkin met with Casey about the Finding on January 5, 1986. Over North's objection, Casey and Sporkin added language in the draft expressing the goal of hostage recovery.

Attorney General Edwin Meese III approved the procedures described in the Finding on Monday, January 6, 1986. That same day, Poindexter informed President Reagan of the new Israeli plan. Regan, Vice President Bush,

and Poindexter's deputy Donald Fortier also were present. Poindexter gave the President the draft Finding produced by North, Sporkin and Casey. Poindexter thought the Finding needed editing, but President Reagan, not realizing that he had been given a draft, signed it.

President Reagan called a National Security Council meeting for the following day, Tuesday, January 7, to consider the Nir proposal and the new Finding. President Reagan, Vice President Bush, Shultz, Weinberger, Meese, Casey, Poindexter and Regan all took part. Only Shultz and Weinberger expressed opposition. Weinberger argued that the operation violated the Arms Export Control Act (AECA). Meese responded that the President could authorize the weapons transfers from the Defense Department to the CIA, and by the CIA to Iranians. It was very clear that President Reagan wanted to go forward.

Over the next several days, North and Noel Koch, principal deputy assistant secretary of defense for international security affairs, addressed the method by which the United States could replenish TOW missiles that Israel sold to Iran. This involved pricing discussions within the Department of Defense (DoD), and pricing negotiations with the Israelis. It became clear that any U.S. shipment of TOWs to Israel that exceeded $14 million had to be reported to Congress. Resale by Israel of weapons acquired from the United States also required prior notice to Congress and an eligible buyer. This conflicted with the Administration's decision not to notify Congress, and Iran's status as a sponsor of terrorism.

These problems led Poindexter and North back to direct sales to Iran via the Economy Act. North, Poindexter and Casey further decided that an extra layer of deniability would be provided if Secord were inserted. Several possible versions of Secord's role were considered. It was decided that the CIA would buy from DoD, and, after payment, transfer the weapons to Secord as its agent to transfer them to Iran.

On January 16, 1986, Poindexter met at the White House with Weinberger, Casey, Meese and Sporkin to discuss the structure of the proposed arms sales. Meese approved the sale under the Economy Act and the National Security Act without notice to Congress prior to completion of the transactions.

The next day, Poindexter gave President Reagan a revised Finding authorizing the use of third parties to transfer the weapons. Vice President Bush, Regan and Fortier were present. President Reagan signed the Finding under the impression that it was essentially the same as the Israeli plan he discussed on January 7.

## The February 1986 TOW Shipments

A series of organizational meetings followed the signing of the January 17 Finding. On January 20, Poindexter convened a meeting in the White House Situation Room to discuss the next steps and to introduce Secord to the senior officials of the CIA with whom he would be dealing. Poindexter, North, Secord, George, Sporkin, Deputy Chief of the CIA's Near Eastern Division Thomas Twetten and NSC Counsel Paul Thompson attended this meeting. The group discussed what the CIA's role would be under the Finding, and, to some extent, what Secord's role would entail. Poindexter designated North as the NSC's operational contact. George designated Twetten as North's counterpart at the CIA.

North traveled to London for a meeting on January 22, 1986, with Ghorbanifar, Nir and Secord to discuss the timing and structure of the transaction. The topics included weapons prices, delivery schedules, and the sequential shipments of arms for the release of American hostages. North returned to Washington and met on January 23 with Twetten, Koch, Secord and Allen to analyze the steps to prepare for the intra-governmental weapons sales from DoD to the CIA. They also discussed the logistics of transferring weapons from DoD inventories to Iran via Secord.

One day later, on January 24, 1986, North sent Poindexter a memorandum titled ''Notional Time Line for Operation Recovery.'' The document laid out in detail the anticipated sequence of events, culminating in the release of the American hostages. North sent a copy of the time line to Clair George. The next day, January 25, 1986, North met at CIA Headquarters with Gates, McMahon, George, Twetten and Allen. The group reviewed the time line and discussed

providing Iran with samples of intelligence regarding Iraq.

In the days following, Twetten and other CIA officers worked closely with the U.S. Army to plan and coordinate the details of the arms shipments. Preparations continued, but when North, Twetten, Secord and Nir traveled to London on February 6, 1986, to finalize plans for the first weapons shipment, Ghorbanifar was a no-show. No meeting took place.

Nevertheless, the first shipment of 500 TOW missiles was delivered to Iran on February 18, 1986. The logistics for the transfer followed what would become a regular pattern. Ghorbanifar deposited funds, borrowed from Saudi businessman Adnan Khashoggi, into a Swiss bank account controlled by Secord. Secord transferred the price fixed by DoD to a CIA account. The CIA purchased the TOW missiles from the U.S. Army. Secord then arranged for Southern Air Transport, a Miami-based aircraft charter company, to ferry the missiles from the United States to Israel. An Israeli charter carried the weapons on the last leg to Iran. The planes that took these first 500 TOWs into Iran returned with 17 HAWKs rejected by Iran after the November 1985 shipment. Apparently, the Iranians had test-fired one.

After the 500 TOWs were delivered, North and other U.S. officials had their first face-to-face meeting with Iranian officials. This took place in Frankfurt, West Germany, on February 25, 1986. The ostensible leader of the Iranian delegation was Kangarlu, a person described by Ghorbanifar as a senior member of Speaker of Parliament Rafsanjani's staff. Ghorbanifar, North, Nir, Twetten, Secord and Secord's business partner Albert Hakim were also present.

North pushed Kangarlu for commitments on the release of hostages. Kangarlu, on the other hand, emphasized the additional types of weapons that Iran wanted from the United States. The meeting in Frankfurt ended with no significant agreements or plans.

On the return flight to the United States, Twetten complained to North about Secord and Hakim's role. Twetten felt that an intelligence professional was needed. North responded that he trusted Secord, whom North said was working with him on his contra-resupply operations in Central America. Twetten protested that the intertwining of Secord in these two separate operations was an even stronger reason to eliminate him from the Iran transactions. Twetten reported his concerns about Secord and Hakim to George.

A few days later, on February 27, 1986, 500 additional TOWs were delivered to Iran. The delivery of 1,000 TOWs was followed by silence. No hostages were released.

## The Diversion

North's disclosure to Twetten that Secord and Hakim were helping North in his Central American activities understated the extent to which the NSC's Iran and contra operations were overlapping. In late November 1985, the North/Secord Enterprise found that it had $800,000 left over from the initial $1 million deposited by Israel with the Enterprise to facilitate the abortive November 1985 series of HAWK missile shipments. North told Secord that the Enterprise could keep the money and apply it to the Enterprise's contra-resupply operation. Although no U.S.-generated proceeds were involved, the principle of an Iran/contra "diversion" was now in place.

The NSC's Iran operations provided North with the elements essential for implementing a diversion scheme with Secord. In his January 1986 meetings with Ghorbanifar, North learned that the Iranians were willing to pay $10,000 a piece for TOW missiles. North structured what became the February 1986 TOW transactions so as to have the funds from Iran pass into an Enterprise account before payments were made to the CIA. North then succeeded in negotiating a price of $3,700 per TOW from the DoD—never disclosing the true spread between that price and the price that the Iranians would pay.

The February 1986 TOW shipments netted the Enterprise millions of dollars. North realized that the Iranian arms sales were the ideal covert fund-raiser. By April 1986, North specified this side benefit of the Iran arms sales to his superiors in a memorandum titled, "Release of the American Hostages in Beirut." A copy of this memorandum, later found in November 1986 by Department of Justice attorneys, explained the details of the transaction and explicitly described how proceeds from the Iran arms sales could be used to support the contras in Nicaragua.

## A Mission to Tehran

Casey, North, Poindexter, George and Twetten met at the CIA on February 27, 1986, to assess what had taken place in Frankfurt. George and Twetten were skeptical of further negotiations, but the others decided to press on. In deference to the CIA professionals, it was agreed to include in the operation George W. Cave, a retired CIA officer with expertise on Iran. He was to serve as an adviser and a reliable translator. Cave replaced Twetten as the CIA officer directly working on the Iran arms sales.

Cave traveled to Paris on March 7 with North and Twetten for another meeting with Kangarlu. Nir and Ghorbanifar were there as well. Once again, the two sides had significantly different agendas. Kangarlu focused on weapons and intelligence on Iraq, North on hostages and a broader political dialogue between the two countries. Ghorbanifar brought to this Paris meeting a listing of 240 HAWK missile spare parts that the Iranians desperately needed. He dangled an idea raised once before that an American delegation visit Iran. Each side agreed to work on the other's demands.

Ghorbanifar grew concerned that, having put the United States and Kangarlu in direct contact, he might be left out of the transactions. He complained to Nir, who urged the United States to involve Ghorbanifar. To assuage Ghorbanifar's concerns, he was invited to Washington, D.C., in early April 1986. There, Ghorbanifar met with Cave, Allen, Twetten and North on April 3 and 4, 1986, to discuss arrangements for a trip to Iran by a U.S. delegation. Ghorbanifar promised that the hostages would be released once the American party arrived in Tehran. Poindexter selected McFarlane as the leader of any U.S. delegation.

Several international incidents, including the U.S. bombing of Libya, delayed the mission to Tehran. A U.S. Customs sting that had resulted in Ghorbanifar's arrest also set the plans back. The sting hurt Ghorbanifar's finances, and since he had to arrange bridge financing for the arms sales, they remained in suspense as the parties waited for Ghorbanifar to raise new capital.

With no specific plans in place for a meeting in Iran, North, Cave, Nir and Ghorbanifar met on May 6 and 7 in London to work out the final details. Ghorbanifar promised that the U.S. officials would meet with the most senior officials in the Iranian government. On May 8, 1986, Cave briefed senior CIA officials, including Casey and George, and CIA personnel prepared logistical details. President Reagan was briefed on the mission on the morning of May 12, 1986.

On May 14 and 15, Ghorbanifar deposited a total of $15 million into Secord's Swiss account. On May 22, 1986, North, in a memorandum to Poindexter, described in meticulous detail the steps to take place. All Americans held hostage in Lebanon were to be freed within three days of the Americans' arrival in Tehran.

The American delegation was McFarlane, North, Cave and NSC staff officer Howard Teicher. They traveled to Iran on aircraft arranged by Secord. They delivered one pallet of HAWK spare parts. The rest were left in Israel pending the promised release of U.S. hostages.

The U.S. party arrived in Tehran on May 25, 1986, accompanied by Nir and a CIA communications specialist. They waited for over an hour for Ghorbanifar and Kangarlu. McFarlane, North, Cave, Nir and Teicher were then taken to the top floor of the former Tehran Hilton Hotel. Their plane was taken to another spot at the airfield for unloading.

They remained in Tehran for approximately three and a half days of intermittent negotiations. Little was accomplished. The Iranians were in no position to arrange for the immediate release of all American hostages. They admitted they could only hope to facilitate the release of one or two. But even that had not been arranged.

The Iranians demanded that all of the HAWK spare parts be delivered to Iran and demanded additional weapons. The Iranians urged extending the mission as they tried to encourage the release of two hostages. A plane from Israel loaded with additional spare parts departed for Iran but was ordered to return in mid-flight to Israel, because no hostages were to be freed. The American party departed on the morning of May 28, 1986. It was clear that Ghorbanifar had made inconsistent and untenable promises to both sides.

During the return trip while changing planes at Tel Aviv airport, North, to diminish the humiliation, told McFarlane that some of the arms sales proceeds were going to the contras. McFarlane thought to himself, "Oh, shit."

## The Pricing Dispute

McFarlane briefed President Reagan, Vice President Bush, Poindexter and Regan about the Tehran mission on May 29, 1986. He did not reveal the diversion. There was no decision to end the arms sales, despite the disappointing results in Tehran. While U.S. officials waited to see what would happen, things got worse. Kangarlu called Cave on approximately June 23, 1986, and informed him that the Iranians had obtained a DoD pricing list reflecting prices for HAWK spare parts. The Iranians determined that they had paid up to six times the list price for the TOWs and HAWK spare parts they had received. Cave alerted North and Allen. Cave continued conversations with Kangarlu during June and July. North blamed Ghorbanifar.

CIA officials suspected that North had been padding the weapons prices for some time. At a meeting in Twetten's office in late April of 1986 to discuss the prices of the HAWK spare parts, North had told Cave and Twetten that he would have to add in his "mark up" to DoD's prices when determining the price Iran was to pay. At that time, Cave assumed that the "mark up" was intended to cover Secord's shipping and handling costs. The news from Kangarlu left both Cave and Allen puzzled.

The pricing impasse continued into July. North refused to talk with Nir until more hostages were released. Ghorbanifar was in agony because he had paid Secord in advance for the undelivered spare parts and the Iranians would not reimburse him. Khashoggi and his associates who had loaned the purchase price to Ghorbanifar were not fully paid.

On July 24, 1986, American hostage Father Lawrence Jenco was released by his captors. Two days later, North, Nir, Cave and Ghorbanifar met in Frankfurt to discuss what would happen next. Nir and Ghorbanifar urged the United States to send Iran the undelivered HAWK spare parts. Ghorbanifar and Kangarlu said that they and an American hostage would be killed if Iran received nothing in return for the Jenco release.

On July 29, 1986, in the King David Hotel in Jerusalem, Nir briefed Vice President Bush on the status of the Iran arms sales. Vice President Bush and his chief of staff, Craig Fuller, described the briefing first as a discussion of counter-terrorism and later as a general review of the hostage-rescue proposals, without mention of an Iran/contra diversion. Vice President Bush discussed the meeting with North on his return.

That same day, North relayed Ghorbanifar's warning to Poindexter in a memorandum titled "Next Steps on the American Hostages." North sought permission to send Iran the remaining HAWK spare parts. President Reagan approved North's request the next day. Secord arranged the delivery for August 3 and 4, 1986.

## The Second Channel

At this point, U.S. officials began moving through two different channels to continue the Iran arms sales. North met in London with Nir and Ghorbanifar on August 8, 1986. Ghorbanifar presented a seven-step plan for the sequential exchange of additional TOW missiles for the remaining U.S. hostages. At about the same time, through a contact in London, Hakim learned that a nephew of Rafsanjani's was interested in establishing contacts with the United States. This led to a meeting in Brussels on approximately August 25, 1986, between Secord and "the Nephew." North continued to advocate the use of Ghorbanifar, but Poindexter decided on the Nephew and his contacts, who became known as "the Second Channel."

American Frank Reed was taken hostage in Beirut on September 9, 1986. The next day, Poindexter told North to pursue the Second Channel and avoid Ghorbanifar if possible. Two days later, on September 12, 1986, Joseph Cicippio was taken hostage in Beirut. Thus, after a full year of working with Ghorbanifar on the Iran arms sales, and after repeated shipments of TOWs, HAWKs and HAWK spare parts, the score seemed to be two hostages re-

leased (Weir and Jenco) and two new hostages taken (Reed and Cicippio).

The Nephew came to Washington on September 19 and 20, 1986. He engaged in protracted meetings with North, Cave and Secord. They developed a seven-step plan involving sequential arms deliveries and hostage releases. North sent minutes of the meetings to Poindexter and George. Four days later, Poindexter met with Casey, George, North and Cave. All agreed that the Second Channel should be pursued.

Ghorbanifar repeatedly complained about his financial losses. Nir warned North in early September that Ghorbanifar's money problems, and his anger over being cut out of future deals, jeopardized the operational security of the Iran arms sales.

By October 2, U.S. efforts were being conducted through the Second Channel. Nir had been excluded. North, Secord, Cave and Hakim met with the Second Channel in Frankfurt on October 6–8, 1986. North presented his seven-point plan, but he and Secord left the meeting after learning of the Hasenfus crash in Nicaragua. Hakim continued the negotiations and worked out a nine-point proposal that went beyond the plan advanced by North. It included interceding with Kuwait to release Da'wa terrorist prisoners, a position wholly contrary to that stated by President Reagan and Shultz.

By October, the story of the diversion to the contras of proceeds from the arms sales had leaked from North to Fiers and to George, and from Allen to Deputy Director for Intelligence Richard Kerr, Gates and Casey. Casey was told by Roy Furmark, a former business contact, that certain Canadian financiers who had lent funds to Ghorbanifar were unpaid and were threatening public disclosure—including Ghorbanifar's claim that significant funds had been diverted from arms sales proceeds to support the contras. Casey and Gates urged Poindexter to consult White House counsel. He said he preferred to discuss it with Paul Thompson, NSC counsel.

North continued to pursue the Second Channel. On October 28, 1986, 500 U.S. TOW missiles that had been sent to Israel in May were delivered to Iran. The United States sent replacement TOWs of a more recent vintage to Israel on November 7 and 8, 1986.

North, Cave, Secord and Hakim met with the Nephew in Mainz, West Germany, on October 29 and 30, 1986. Three days later, on November 2, 1986, hostage David Jacobsen was released.

## Exposure and Cover-Up

On November 3, 1986, an article describing McFarlane's trip to Tehran appeared in *Al-Shiraa*, a Lebanese publication. Rafsanjani acknowledged the McFarlane visit the following day. On approximately November 8, North, Cave, Secord and Hakim had a final meeting with the Nephew, agreeing to put things on hold in view of the growing publicity.

The arms sales became the top news story of the day. Within the Administration, officials at the NSC and the CIA scrambled to put together an account of what had taken place. The President's most senior advisers and Cabinet officers met on November 10, 1986, to develop their strategy. Those who had opposed the sales all along, particularly Shultz, saw in the exposure of the arms sales exactly what they had predicted: a policy disaster. All the President's advisers could agree on was to say nothing, or as little as possible.[44]

The White House released a press statement later that afternoon. While not confirming or denying the arms sales, the statement asserted that "no U.S. laws have been or will be violated and . . . our policy of not making concessions to terrorists remains intact." Some of the President's advisers, including White House Counsel Peter Wallison, were not as confident that laws had not been broken, particularly with respect to the 1985 arms sales. The Reagan Administration sidestepped the issue in briefings of congressional leaders two days later by denying involvement in any transfers before January 1986.

By the weekend of November 15–16, 1986, both congressional intelligence committees had called for briefings on the arms sales by Secretaries Shultz and Weinberger, CIA Director Casey, and National Security Adviser Poindexter. The efforts to prepare for these briefings exacerbated the tensions within the na-

tional security community over the arms sales. Shultz publicly stated that he was against further sales, but added that he could not speak for the Administration. Weinberger adopted a posture of continuing but silent opposition to the sales and firm support for the President. The CIA bureaucracy was scrambling to find out who had done what in the initiative, an effort that uncovered facts that proved embarrassing to the NSC and the CIA about the November 1985 HAWK shipment. North unsuccessfully tried to deny that it was he who drew the CIA into its support of the HAWK shipment.

As the congressional briefings—set for November 21, 1986—approached, Shultz and his advisers suspected that the CIA and NSC were trying to hide the facts surrounding the Government's activities in 1985, prior to the January 17, 1986, Finding which provided a legal basis for the arms sales. Shultz approached the President on November 19 and 20, 1986, in an attempt to persuade him to transfer the continuing responsibility for Iran policy back to State. Shultz pointed out mistakes in the President's public statements. President Reagan acknowledged that he had known of the November 1985 HAWKs shipment but insisted that it was not an arms-for-hostages swap.

By November 20, the Administration had agreed that Casey would brief the intelligence committees on Capitol Hill, while Poindexter would brief selected members at the White House. That afternoon, Meese and Assistant Attorney General Charles Cooper, Casey, Gates, Poindexter, Thompson and North met in Poindexter's office to discuss Casey's testimony. Legal issues involving the 1985 shipments dominated the discussion. Casey had brought a draft statement that read: "We in the CIA did not find out that our airline had hauled HAWK missiles into Iran until mid-January [1986] when we were told by the Iranians." This statement conflicted with what Casey and other CIA personnel had known in 1985 about the shipment. Nevertheless, North revised the statement to read: "No one in the USG," or U.S. Government, knew before January 1986 that weapons had been shipped.

Actions taken by State Department Legal Adviser Abraham Sofaer ultimately resulted in the

---

[44] Full discussions of these and other events in November 1986 are found in the North, Poindexter, Meese, Regan, State Department, Defense Department and CIA officials in November 1986 chapters.

deletion of this specific misstatement from Casey's prepared testimony.

Casey and Poindexter's presentations the next day were incorrect, misleading, and at times criminally false. Poindexter lied about U.S. involvement in and knowledge of the 1985 shipments. Casey meanwhile claimed that he did not learn of the cargo of the November 1985 HAWK shipment until January 1986, but he conceded that others in the CIA could have known earlier. Casey also gave misleading testimony about the flow of funds in the arms sales, the extent of presidential approval for them, and his knowledge of who in the NSC was running the Iran operation.

While Casey and Poindexter were giving their accounts of the initiative, Meese—who was aware of the conflicting statements and was having increasing concerns about the lawfulness of the 1985 activities—met with the President and told him that it was "absolutely necessary" that someone develop a coherent overview of the matter. The President agreed and directed Meese to report his findings at a meeting of senior advisers set for Monday, November 24, 1986.

Meese gathered his team around mid-day on November 21, 1986. He then called Poindexter to tell him he wanted to get all relevant documents from the NSC. Following Meese's call, Poindexter had Thompson gather the documents, including the only known signed copy of the December 1985 "retroactive" Finding that clearly stated that the HAWK shipment was an arms-for-hostages deal. With Thompson and North present, Poindexter destroyed the Finding. He said he feared that it would be a political embarrassment.

Document destruction at the NSC did not stop with Poindexter. North returned to his offices in the early evening of November 21 and shredded stacks of memoranda and messages. Meanwhile, Meese's staff had begun reviewing pertinent intelligence and interviewing witnesses. Meese himself handled the President's most senior advisers. Meeting with Meese on the morning of November 22, 1986, Shultz told him that the President had acknowledged only

two days earlier knowing about the November 1985 HAWK shipment.

While Meese was conducting interviews, two Justice attorneys were at the NSC reviewing documents. They discovered one that North had not shredded: a copy of his April 1986 memorandum that explained the diversion. Meese was told of the memorandum during lunch on November 22. His inquiry continued, culminating in the questioning of North on November 23, 1986. North lied about his knowledge of the cargo of the November 1985 HAWK shipment, claiming as he had in the November 20 meeting that he thought at the time that the cargo was oil-drilling equipment. He also denied knowing about any retroactive Finding that covered the shipment, although he suggested that "someone ought to step up and say it was authorized." Meese then confronted North with the diversion memorandum. A shaken North admitted that the diversion had occurred but attributed it to the Israelis.

On November 24, 1986, Meese privately reported the diversion to President Reagan, Vice President Bush, and Regan, and questioned McFarlane and Poindexter about it. Meese reported his findings, other than the diversion, to a meeting of President Reagan and his senior advisers, including Vice President Bush, Shultz, Weinberger, Casey, Regan and Poindexter on the afternoon of November 24. Meese reviewed the 1985 activities and asserted that the 1985 arms shipments could have been illegal. Meese reported further that, contrary to what Shultz had told him, the President did not know in November 1985 that arms were being shipped to Iran. Virtually everyone at the meeting knew better, but no one corrected the Attorney General.

On the morning of November 25, 1986, Meese disclosed the diversion to the full Cabinet and Congressional leaders. At noon, President Reagan and Meese announced at a nationally televised press conference that proceeds from the Iran arms sales had been diverted to support the contras, and that Poindexter had resigned and North had been reassigned to the U.S. Marines.

# Part II
# History of the Investigation

## The Initial Investigation, 1986–1988

The criminal investigation into the Iran/contra matters was begun on November 26, 1986, by the Federal Bureau of Investigation at the order of the attorney general. Agents assigned to the investigation, which the FBI called "Operation Front Door," secured and began analyzing thousands of documents in National Security Council offices. They conducted preliminary interviews with officials from the White House; Justice, State and Defense departments; Central Intelligence Agency and National Security Agency. The FBI investigation focused on the Iran arms sales and the Iran/contra diversion—in contrast to the broader probe subsequently undertaken by Independent Counsel, which included the investigation of aid to the Nicaraguan contra rebels.

After Independent Counsel was appointed on December 19, 1986, FBI Director William H. Webster assigned members of the bureau's investigative team to the Office of Independent Counsel (OIC).

Investigations by other bodies into Iran/contra were proceeding rapidly by December 1986. The President had appointed a special review board, known as the "Tower Commission," to study the role and procedures of the National Security Council staff.[1] The House and Senate intelligence and foreign affairs committees were conducting their own inquiries into the matter, and, by the time Independent Counsel was appointed, both houses of Congress had agreed to appoint special committees to investigate.[2]

The initial outlines of Iran/contra emerged through interviews conducted by Attorney General Edwin Meese III in his November 21–25, 1986, investigation. Lt. Col. Oliver L. North, a National Security Council staff member, confirmed to Meese that, in fact, there had been a diversion of Iran arms sales proceeds to the Nicaraguan contras. National Security Adviser John M. Poindexter admitted a general awareness of this fact.

President Reagan, Vice President Bush and Cabinet members had publicly denied any awareness of the Iran/contra diversion. These denials, however, did not address broader questions about the extent of their knowledge and approval of the other Iran and contra operations of North, Poindexter and others.

Additional elements of the secret Iran and contra operations became known through aggressive investigative reporting by the media, including the fact that North and others had destroyed reams of sensitive documents as the Attorney General conducted his initial investigation. Senior Reagan Administration officials made statements to the press and to the early congressional investigations about their own knowledge of or roles in Iran/contra, adding to a growing body of facts and, in some cases, falsehoods.

By the end of December 1986, congressional testimony had been given by McFarlane, Direc-

---

[1] The Tower Commission's members were former Senators John Tower and Edmund Muskie and former National Security Adviser Brent Scowcroft. Scowcroft became President Bush's national security adviser in 1989 and held that post throughout Bush's presidency.

[2] The Senate Select Committee on Secret Miliary Assistance to Iran and the Nicaraguan Opposition was formally established by Senate Resolution 23 on January 6, 1987, and the House Select Committee to Investigate Covert Arms Transactions with Iran was established by House Resolution 12 on January 7, 1987.

tor of Central Intelligence William J. Casey,[3] Meese, Secretary of State George P. Shultz, Secretary of Defense Caspar W. Weinberger, White House Chief of Staff Donald T. Regan and others.

Despite the seeming gusher of information from a variety of sources, by early January 1987 the most central Iran/contra operatives had refused to testify, invoking their Fifth Amendment privilege against self-incrimination. This group included Poindexter, North, North's secretary Fawn Hall, retired Air Force Maj. General Richard V. Secord and his business partner Albert Hakim. Others would follow this course as the investigation reached them.

It was clear there would be few, if any, friendly witnesses available to Independent Counsel's investigation. It also was clear that although a general outline of what happened would be quickly known, the development of solid proof, immune to impeachment, would be developed only after the analysis of thousands of documents and by the carefully structured questioning and immunization of subordinate figures.

Independent Counsel viewed his mandate as a charge to determine who had committed crimes, and how high up the true responsibility for those crimes went. In prosecuting the central operatives in the Iran/contra matter—namely North and Poindexter—Independent Counsel hoped the question of higher complicity could be resolved.

## Office Organization and Investigative Plan

In December 1986, in what proved to be a serious underestimate, Independent Counsel decided to recruit a full-time staff of 10 associate counsel, supplemented by part-time senior lawyers. Because some of the lawyers could not move to Washington, Independent Counsel organized a three-city operation: the central investigation in Washington, a legal research and analytical office in New York City, and a small office in Oklahoma City for Independent Coun-

sel's use of classified information when he was not in Washington.

The Washington office temporarily occupied two vacant chambers of the U.S. Courthouse, with additional space in the basement of the FBI building. By late February 1987, the General Services Administration had leased space at 555 Thirteenth Street, N.W., in downtown Washington, while the building was still under construction and offices could be built to comply with specifications required for the use and storage of highly classified information.

It was decided that the Office of Independent Counsel would investigate broadly. It would resist seeking a quick indictment on some fragment of the facts unless that type of prosecution could produce quickly a witness useful in exposing the criminal activities central to OIC's responsibility. The office had a reasonably optimistic expectation that it could make prosecutorial decisions on major indictments by early fall 1987.

The Justice Department in late December 1986 presented 36 pending investigative matters from around the country that arguably fell within OIC's broad jurisdiction. Independent Counsel accepted only those that held a significant possibility of misconduct by Government officers.

Following the pattern set by the initial FBI probe, OIC divided its investigative work among several teams, including: the White House/National Security Council/Justice Department team, which would question officials and review documents from those entities; the CIA/State Department team; and the flow-of-funds/Defense Department team, which was responsible for negotiating with Switzerland, Israel and other foreign countries through which the funds passed and for investigating the Pentagon.

As the investigation progressed and the prosecutable cases became more apparent, the makeup and focus of the teams changed. Also, because many Iran/contra matters overlapped across several areas of team work, investigative boundaries were not rigid.

With the expectation that Congress would grant immunity to central figures likely to be prosecuted by this office, Independent Counsel moved quickly to interview witnesses and review hundreds of thousands of documents from

---

[3] After the public exposure of the Iran/contra diversion on November 25, 1986, Casey gave testimony to several congressional committees. He was hospitalized with a fatal brain tumor in early December 1986 and died before giving further testimony or being questioned by the Office of Independent Counsel.

key agencies. In addition to the FBI agents already detailed to OIC, agents from the Customs Bureau and Internal Revenue Service were temporarily assigned to Independent Counsel with the goal of building criminal cases as quickly as possible.

On January 28, 1987, the first federal Grand Jury that would hear evidence on Iran-contra matters was convened in the District of Columbia.[4]

## Liaison With Other Agencies

Because the Iran/contra matter spanned several Executive agencies, and because other investigations were underway, it was necessary for Independent Counsel to establish liaison procedures with the White House; Congress; the departments of Justice, State and Defense; the Central Intelligence Agency; and the National Security Agency. Typically, a team of lawyers in each agency was appointed to work with Independent Counsel. The agency teams oversaw document production and requests for witness interviews and other information from OIC.

Liaison with Congress and the White House was of highest importance during the early phases of the investigation.

Weekly meetings were held with representatives of the Select Iran/contra Committees before central figures gave their immunized testimony. Although OIC's concerns over the immunity issue dominated these discussions, Independent Counsel and committee representatives had mutual fact-gathering concerns. OIC was precluded by grand jury secrecy rules from sharing certain information with the Committees, but it could sometimes provide the Committees with documents and evidence gathered outside the grand jury process.

OIC had nearly daily contact with the White House. Independent Counsel had requested all relevant documents from the offices of the President and Vice President, from the NSC,

from White House staff members, and from administrative offices. It was necessary to gain an understanding and conduct searches of White House computer systems. Finally, OIC had to make arrangements with White House officials to review President Reagan's diary and ultimately to obtain his testimony and the testimony of Vice President Bush.[5]

President Reagan in December 1986 appointed former Ambassador David M. Abshire to coordinate responses to the Iran/contra investigations of Independent Counsel, Congress and the Tower Commission. Abshire served in the post through March 1987, when his duties were assumed by White House Counsel A.B. Culvahouse.

## Early Document Production

The Office of Independent Counsel spent January and February 1987 heavily engaged in obtaining and reviewing documents. This work continued through the fall of 1987, when certain Executive agencies were still responding to OIC document requests.[6]

The Department of Justice had issued an initial request for relevant documents to each agency in late November 1986, but its focus was more narrow than the area Independent Counsel was subsequently appointed to investigate. OIC made expanded document requests based on its broad mandate.

The documents requested by the OIC included handwritten and typed notes, computer records and disks, diaries, appointment calendars and schedules, tapes and films, phone logs, correspondence, memos, messages, reports, studies, minutes, transcripts, work papers, agendas, announcements, computer notes and messages, telegrams, teletypes, bank records and other records. Independent Counsel sought all materials relevant to Iran/contra from each Executive agency; its request to the White House, which included the NSC, was the most expansive. From the White House, OIC sought the production of any materials pertaining to (1) the sale or shipment of arms to Iran, and contacts with nine listed Iranians; (2) the sale or shipment of arms to Iran, using but not limited

[4] The first Grand Jury sat for 24 months, expiring January 27, 1989. A second Grand Jury was convened in the District of Columbia on May 15, 1990 and sat until May 15, 1992. Chief Judge Aubrey E. Robinson, Jr., granted Independent Counsel's requests for the extension of both grand juries for six months beyond the normal 18-month period because of the complex nature of the evidence being presented. In addition, Iran-contra evidence was heard by grand juries sitting in the Eastern District of Virginia in Alexandria (resulting in the *Fernandez* indictment) in Baltimore, Md. (resulting in the *Clines* indictment), and later in the District of Columbia (resulting in the *Weinberger* indictment).

[5] See Reagan and Bush chapters.
[6] CIA response to the February 1987 document request continued into February 1988. Production alternated between withholding and flooding with key documents not produced until after months of delay.

to any of 26 listed intermediaries; (3) the diversion of proceeds from the Iranian arms sales to the Nicaraguan contras or insurgents elsewhere, involving but not limited to 25 listed individuals and business concerns; (4) the provision of support to the Nicaraguan contras, including possible contacts with 71 listed individuals and organizations; (5) meetings of 17 listed Administration working groups; (6) the calendars, schedules, phone logs and travel records of 34 listed White House and other officials; (7) computer messages generated or received by 35 White House staff members; and a variety of more specific items.

It was impossible for Independent Counsel to determine early in the investigation whether the agencies were complying in good faith with the document requests. As in other complex investigations, what was missing often became obvious only after a thorough review of what had been received.

Some early document production problems, however, were apparent. The CIA, for example, held back document production until late February 1987—only after Independent Counsel suggested that subpoenas might have to be issued to force compliance.[7] At the White House, certain documents deemed relevant by FBI agents were subsequently reviewed and deemed irrelevant by White House counsel; the issue took several months for OIC to finally resolve in its favor. Production from the National Security Agency was uneven.[8] Certain individuals throughout the Administration had relevant personal notes that were produced either late or in incomplete form, or both; in some cases, individuals falsely claimed not to have any notes at all.[9]

Although Independent Counsel was able to recover hundreds of thousands of relevant materials, the disturbing fact remained that some of the most important documents almost certainly were destroyed in October and November 1986, as the Iran and contra operations became publicly exposed.

## Witnesses Begin To Tell the Story

The individuals most directly involved in the Iran and contra operations—North, Poindexter, Secord and Hakim—by early 1987 had all refused to testify, invoking their Fifth Amendment protection against self-incrimination. Joseph F. Fernandez, the CIA station chief in Costa Rica who assisted North in supplying the contras, refused to talk, as did Thomas G. Clines, a former CIA officer who worked with Secord and Hakim in the "Enterprise" that supported the Iran and contra covert operations.

McFarlane was an exception. He testified before Congress and the Grand Jury voluntarily. But McFarlane was not involved in implementing the Iran/contra diversion or many of the activities in question in 1986, after he resigned as national security adviser. Also, McFarlane was misleading in many of his early interviews with Independent Counsel; it was only after he entered into plea negotiations that he offered more complete testimony.

It was clear from the beginning that Independent Counsel would have to question President Reagan and Vice President Bush at some point. Unlike other witnesses, neither person could be repeatedly called to testify, especially in the absence of incriminating evidence. Additionally, Vice President Bush had answered questions by the FBI in an early interview before Independent Counsel's appointment, and both had been questioned by the Tower Commission. Independent Counsel decided to wait until the investigation had matured before approaching President Reagan and Vice President Bush. Ultimately, the President answered written interrogatories for the Grand Jury in the fall of 1987, gave a deposition for the defense in the *Poindexter* trial early in 1990, and answered a final round of questions in an interview with Independent Counsel in the summer of 1992. Bush gave a videotaped deposition for the Grand Jury early in 1988 but arrangements for a final interview in 1992 and 1993 were brought to an impasse by his insistence that the questioning be very limited in scope.

---

[7] Independent Counsel decided to avoid initially issuing subpoenas for Executive branch documents for several reasons: (1) subpoenas enforceable by the court may require greater specificity than document requests; (2) subpoena litigation would consume time that the office could not afford as it worked quickly to outpace the congressional grants of immunity to key individuals; and (3) subpoenas could be used as a last resort, when all else failed. In the later phases of OIC's investigation, when greater specificity was possible and when the congressional hearings were concluded, subpoenas were used when necessary.

[8] See Classified Appendix.

[9] It was not until 1990 that OIC's continuing investigation began discovering the extent to which personal notes were withheld from Independent Counsel.

Senior Administration officials who continued in Government service typically testified without seeking grants of immunity from Congress or Independent Counsel. Additionally, most support staff who remained in the Government after the Iran/contra affair was exposed answered questions voluntarily.

Cabinet officers and presidential advisers generally professed little knowledge of the Iran and contra activities. Attorney General Meese, White House Chief of Staff Regan, Secretary of State Shultz and others admitted to greater or more specific knowledge only after repeated questioning by Independent Counsel and when confronted with evidence contradicting their earlier statements.

Some of the most significant witnesses were those who came in frequent contact with North and Poindexter, either as associates or subordinates, and who were potentially indictable. Most of these individuals requested immunity from prosecution in exchange for their testimony against others more central to Iran/contra matters.

A witness refusing to testify may be given immunity at the request of the prosecutor. Customarily, the witness first makes a proffer—or detailed outline—of the facts he or she will testify to in court in order to obtain immunity. Independent Counsel almost always conditioned grants of immunity on a witness's willingness to make a proffer.

One of the earliest witnesses to make a proffer was Fawn Hall, who had been North's secretary on the National Security Council staff. Like McFarlane, Hall was a difficult witness who provided information only after a series of interviews. Although Hall testified against North reluctantly, she provided valuable evidence of his destruction and alteration of official documents in November 1986, and about his extensive contacts and activities on behalf of the Nicaraguan contras. Hall testified that, with North's knowledge, she smuggled classified documents out of the White House on November 25, 1986.

Hall also told Independent Counsel that North kept detailed notebooks of his daily activities and that she had seen them in his counsel's office after the Iran-contra affair was exposed. Hall's revelation caused Independent Counsel

to launch a lengthy effort to subpoena the notebooks, whose potential evidentiary value was clear.[10]

Robert L. Earl, one of North's closest coworkers at the NSC, was granted immunity in exchange for testimony about North's destruction of documents in November 1986. Earl also described a conversation he had with North and an associate Craig Coy, on November 25, 1986. According to Earl, North told them that President Reagan had called him to express his regret at North's firing and said that the President told North that it was important that Reagan "not know." Earl inferred from this statement that North had been cast in the scapegoat's role with the President's knowledge.[11]

Dozens of NSC and White House officials were interviewed and re-interviewed. Some could provide only fragments of information about North and Poindexter's activities. Some potentially more significant witnesses, such as former NSC counsel Paul B. Thompson, made themselves available for questioning on numerous occasions but were never fully forthcoming in their answers.

One of the earliest areas of investigation to bear fruit exposed North's fund-raising activities with Carl R. "Spitz" Channell and Richard R. Miller. Under the auspices of a tax-exempt organization, the National Endowment for the Preservation of Liberty (NEPL), contributions were solicited to buy weapons for the contras. Wealthy contributors, some of whom were given immunity, testified that North had described the weapons needs of the contras in soliciting their donations, providing clear evidence that NEPL was using tax-exempt privileges for illegal purposes. This investigation resulted in Channell and Miller pleading guilty in the spring of 1987 on tax-fraud conspiracy charges, with each naming North as a co-conspirator.[12] As part of their plea agreements, Channell and Miller cooperated with Independ-

---

[10] North's notebooks could not be obtained by OIC until North took the witness stand in his trial in April 1989. The trial court ruled that North had waived his right against self-incrimination by deciding to testify in his own defense, and therefore copies of the notebooks would be produced to Independent Counsel.

[11] Earl, Grand Jury, 5/1/87, pp. 118–19. See Earl chapter.

[12] See Channell and Miller chapter. North was charged in March 1988 with conspiracy to commit tax fraud but was acquitted of the charge.

ent Counsel and provided extensive evidence against North.

Another area of early concern was North's contra-resupply operation in Central America, which was ostensibly financed and carried out by a "private benefactor" organization sympathetic to the contra cause, but which, in fact, was run by Secord under North's control. U.S. Government involvement in this operation defied the ban on military aid to the contras imposed from October 1984 to October 1986 by the Boland Amendment.

Members of the Administration's Restricted Inter-Agency Group (RIG) on Nicaragua were questioned about North's contra-support activities. The testimony of Assistant Secretary of State Elliott Abrams and CIA Central American Task Force Chief Alan D. Fiers, Jr.—neither of whom received immunity from prosecution—was proven later to be untruthful.

Robert W. Owen was immunized and gave detailed testimony about his role as North's private liaison to the Nicaraguan contras. He described carrying secret military information and large amounts of cash and traveler's checks to contra leaders on North's behalf.

Richard B. Gadd and Robert C. Dutton—the men who were employed by Secord to run the contra-resupply operation in Central America—were granted immunity and testified extensively about the organization's activities and finances.[13] Rafael Quintero, Secord's Central American representative, also was granted immunity in exchange for testimony about the weapons and other lethal assistance provided to the contras.

The contra leaders whom North assisted were questioned. Adolfo Calero, who resisted testifying until late March 1987, described North's contra-support activities in highly sympathetic terms. His testimony, however, exposed North's violations of the Boland Amendment. Many other contra figures also were interviewed, providing an increasingly explicit picture of Reagan Administration efforts to provide military support.

U.S. ambassadors to Central America were interviewed about their knowledge of the contra-resupply operation. Some, such as former Ambassador to El Salvador Edwin G. Corr,

falsely denied details of their knowledge. Others testified more forthrightly; for example, the former ambassador to Costa Rica, Lewis A. Tambs, testified candidly about his participation in opening a "southern front" of contra fighters.

Testimony about North's contra-aid activities, as well as documentary proof that he reported many of these activities to both Poindexter and McFarlane, showed that they and North had obstructed congressional inquiries about contra assistance in 1985 and 1986.

In investigative terms, much of the information on the Iran arms sale initiative in 1986 was laid out in documents. The record was less clear, however, on the 1985 shipments in which Israel was involved. Independent Counsel was effectively blocked from interviewing Israeli nationals by the government of Israel, although OIC attempted to subpoena them on visits to the United States.[14]

McFarlane provided testimony about the 1985 Iran arms shipments, but it was in doubt because of conflicting testimony given by other senior Administration officials. Michael Ledeen, a former NSC consultant who helped set up the Iran arms sales in the summer of 1985, was questioned. Duane R. "Dewey" Clarridge, the CIA officer whom North enlisted in a November 1985 shipment of U.S. HAWK missiles from Israel to Iran, testified untruthfully about the shipment.

After questioning CIA and State Department officials, it became clear that testimony delivered by Poindexter and Casey in November and December 1986 was false regarding their knowledge of the 1985 arms shipments, particularly the November 1985 HAWK shipment.

---

[13] Dutton also provided details of the final Iran arms shipments.

[14] In February 1987, the Israeli government made an agreement with the Select Iran/contra Committees to supply written historical and financial chronologies in lieu of live testimony. Independent Counsel, who was not aware of this agreement until after the fact, informed the Israelis that he was not a party to the agreement and reserved the right to issue subpoenas and to take other action as OIC saw fit.

OIC in May 1987 subpoenaed the former director general of the Israeli Foreign Ministry, David Kimche, who had proposed the Iran arms initiative to Administration officials in the summer of 1985. The subpoena was served during a visit by Kimche to the United States. At the request of the State Department and in accordance with lengthy negotiations with the Israelis, Independent Counsel eventually agreed to withdraw the subpoena and accept a commitment by the Israelis to supply OIC with chronologies, historical and financial, and with additional information.

The chronologies, although highly useful in certain respects, were not a true substitute for live witness testimony.

Evidence about the Iran/contra diversion was extremely difficult to obtain. Few witnesses admitted to knowledge of it, although some were found later to be lying. Proving that the diversion had occurred, and understanding its mechanics, required access to the secret Swiss financial records of the North-Secord-Hakim covert-operation Enterprise. These records could not be obtained until late in 1987, after lengthy negotiations with the Swiss government and litigation with Hakim and Iranian businessman Manucher Ghorbanifar.

By late April 1987, Secord decided to testify without immunity before Congress. In the same period, he received limited immunity from Independent Counsel, allowing him to be questioned with the agreement that nothing he said to OIC could be used against him as direct evidence in a criminal prosecution, unless he committed perjury. This did not preclude Independent Counsel from prosecuting him with evidence from other sources.

Secord provided valuable information about both the Iran and contra operations, as well as about the diversion. He was not truthful about the extent of his personal financial interests in the Enterprise.

The flow-of-funds investigative team, while awaiting Swiss financial records, developed extensive information about the money trail in documents from U.S. banks and from bank accounts in countries other than Switzerland. Also, Willard I. Zucker, who managed the Swiss financial accounts of the North-Secord-Hakim Enterprise, proffered testimony in exchange for immunity. Zucker could not provide the Enterprise's Swiss bank records because he was not a signatory on the accounts. Until the records were released, under the Swiss secrecy laws, he could not even be interviewed. But, through his American lawyers, he did inform OIC of Hakim's establishment of a fund for North's family, constituting an illegal gratuity to a Government official.

## The Swiss Financial Records of the Enterprise

At the heart of the covert Iran/contra Enterprise run by North, Secord and Hakim were its financial records, protected in Switzerland by strict banking-secrecy laws. Both Independent Counsel and the Select Committees were vitally interested in obtaining these records, as was the Tower Commission.

To bring a criminal indictment incorporating the diversion of Iran arms sales proceeds to the contras, and to expose other financial corruption, the Swiss records were essential.

The Department of Justice in December 1986 requested access to the Swiss records under the Treaty for Mutual Assistance in Criminal Matters between the United States and Switzerland. It would take a full year from the time of that request before Independent Counsel received the banking documents.

The Select Committees sought the assistance of Independent Counsel in acquiring the Swiss records, but they could not wait for the treaty process to play out. Over the objections of Independent Counsel, they granted immunity to Hakim to obtain financial documents.[15] The presidentially appointed Tower Commission also asked for Independent Counsel's help on the Swiss records, but its reporting deadline was too early to obtain them.

The Swiss Office for Police Matters on February 27, 1987, initially authorized the release of the records to Independent Counsel. Hakim and Ghorbanifar appealed the decision in two Swiss courts. By September 1987, both appeals were denied as frivolous.

After Independent Counsel's request worked its way through a system weighted heavily in favor of bank secrecy, the Swiss authorities on November 3, 1987, made available most of the records requested. The records contained the proof essential to a conspiracy indictment against North, Poindexter, Secord and Hakim and to charge the Iran/contra diversion as a crime.

---

[15] During the wait for the Swiss records, OIC considered immunizing Hakim, who as a signatory on the bank accounts could have authorized their release. It was decided, however, that a possible Hakim prosecution should be pursued. He was then believed to be the architect of the financial schemes to conceal the Enterprise operations, cheat the contras and bribe North. He also refused to give a proffer of his probable testimony.

It is noteworthy that the financial documents Hakim provided to Congress pursuant to his immunity grant were partially fabricated to conceal the recipients of the profits. This fact was revealed in the 1990 trial of Clines.

## Early Challenge to Independent Counsel's Constitutionality and the Parallel Appointment

On February 24, 1987, North challenged the Independent Counsel in a legal action, *North* v. *Walsh*, to test the constitutionality of the Ethics in Government Act under which Independent Counsel was appointed. In a parallel action before another judge, former presidential aide Michael Deaver brought action against Whitney North Seymour, Jr., who was the Independent Counsel prosecuting him. The District Court dismissed *North* v. *Walsh* as premature, but the Deaver motion was not dismissed.

The day after North filed his legal challenge, Walsh sought a back-up appointment as Independent Counsel from the attorney general. The attorney general made the appointment on March 5, 1987, closely paralleling the court appointment.[16] In July 1987, U.S. District Chief Judge Aubrey E. Robinson, Jr., held that the appointment was valid, allowing Independent Counsel to continue the Grand Jury investigation of Iran/contra after the Court of Appeals, in another case, had held the independent counsel statute unconstitutional.[17]

## Congressional Immunity Grants

Congress's perceived need to quickly and publicly resolve the grave political questions posed by Iran/contra nearly derailed OIC's efforts to bring high officials to justice. No adverse factor shaped or constricted Independent Counsel's criminal investigation more than the congressional immunity grants made to North, Poindexter and Hakim. The trial convictions of North and Poindexter were ultimately reversed on appeal because they prevailed in arguing that the testimony of witnesses in their trials was not proved to be unaffected by their highly publicized immunized congressional testimony.

OIC's most pressing concern from the outset of its work was that the Select Committees would grant immunity to targets of the criminal investigation, compelling them to testify before Congress while guaranteeing that nothing they said could be used against them in a criminal proceeding. The law was clear that Congress controlled the political decision of whether immunity grants were justified by the importance of the hearings even though they could destroy a criminal prosecution. With the exception of the congressional and criminal investigations of the Watergate scandal in the 1970s, the situation confronting Independent Counsel was unprecedented. In the Watergate scandal, two congressionally immunized witnesses—John Dean and Jeb Stuart Magruder—were judged guilty of crimes, but both men had pleaded guilty before their cases came to trial. Criminal charges against Gordon Strachan were dismissed because of immunity problems.[18]

President Reagan had first proposed in December 1986 that North and Poindexter be granted immunity after they refused to testify voluntarily before the Senate Select Committee on Intelligence, which was conducting a preliminary investigation into Iran/contra. He said their testimony would exculpate him. The intelligence committee resisted his proposal. Yet that, in the end, was exactly what the Select Committees did.

In early meetings between Independent Counsel and the leaders of the Select Iran/contra Committees, the leaders forthrightly stated that they were likely to grant immunity to central figures. In response, Walsh doubled the size of the OIC staff and took steps to focus the investigation on the gathering of as much evidence as possible before the grant of immunity tainted any of it.

Independent Counsel repeatedly warned the committees that such immunity grants, coupled with the high level of national exposure of the Iran/contra hearings, would pose serious if not insurmountable obstacles to prosecuting central figures. Independent Counsel also argued that key witnesses would have little incentive to testify fully and truthfully before Congress if they received immunity before impeaching or corroborating evidence had been gathered.

---

[16] In making the back-up appointment, the Attorney General referred to the President's desire to take every possible step that Independent Counsel's investigation continue. This support was intended to obviate any constitutional conflict based on the view that the appointment of Independent Counsel was an unconstitutional intrusion upon the powers of the President.

[17] Legal challenges to the constitutionality of the independent counsel statute continued into 1988, when a federal appeals court panel in January struck down the law as unconstitutional in a case brought against Independent Counsel Alexia Morrison. The Supreme Court on June 29, 1988, reversed the appeals court ruling and upheld the constitutionality of the statute.

[18] Watergate Special Prosecution Force Report, p. 52 (1977).

Independent Counsel met repeatedly with representatives of the committees to persuade them to seek alternatives to immunity grants to the central figures. But, frustrated by North and Poindexter's continuing refusal to testify voluntarily, the Select Committees decided to immunize North, Poindexter and Hakim.[19]

The Select Committees worked on tight, self-imposed deadlines. Counsel told OIC that they felt that the scandal should not be left hanging over the President. Their public hearings were to begin in early May 1987 and they planned to issue a final report by November 1987.[20]

Independent Counsel urged the Select Committees to delay granting immunity to North and Poindexter for as long as possible, to give OIC more time to gather criminal evidence that could not be tainted, by any immunized testimony. A compromise was reached between OIC and the Committees in March 1987, setting the timing for immunity grants for North and Poindexter, as well as the methods for insulating the private testimony Poindexter was to give before appearing publicly.[21]

OIC issued its First Interim Report to Congress on April 28, 1987, a week before the public Iran/contra hearings began. "The allegations in the investigation concern possible violations of public trust and possible misuse of position by high Government officials and their manipulation by former Government officials," Independent Counsel reported. "In such matters,

the public is entitled to a fair and deliberate prosecutive judgment."

The interim report informed Congress and the public that more than 800 witness interviews had been conducted, hundreds of boxes of White House and other agency documents had been reviewed, and that an ongoing Grand Jury investigation was "proving fruitful." This unusual public accounting of the criminal investigation's progress was issued to enable the Select Committees and Congress to make an informed decision in granting immunity that would gravely handicap and, possibly, frustrate these potential prosecutions.[22]

Providing concrete proof of Independent Counsel's progress were the guilty pleas in late April and early May 1987 of Carl R. "Spitz" Channell and Richard R. Miller. Both men pleaded guilty to conspiring to defraud the Government by raising money for contra weapons under the auspices of a tax-exempt organization, and both named North as a co-conspirator. These guilty pleas gave Independent Counsel the option of bringing an early tax-fraud case against North, but it was decided that the charges should be incorporated into a more comprehensive indictment against North and others.

In late May 1987, North's attorney told the Select Committees that his client would not give immunized testimony privately before his public appearance. He claimed the Committees were entitled to the testimony only once. This was a dangerous proposition for the Committees. Not only would they not be prepared for North's public appearance by questioning him privately first, they would have no prior statements with which to impeach any self-serving or exculpatory testimony he might give. Independent Counsel urged the Committees not to strike such a deal with North. Nevertheless, it was clear that the they were determined to have North's testimony. They were unwilling to await the outcome of litigation. As Senator Warren Rudman, Vice-chairman of the Senate Select Committee, put it, "I would find it inconceivable . . . that these hearings could ever

---

[19] Independent Counsel persuaded the committees not to immunize Clines, Secord and Hakim's business partner in the Iran/Contra Enterprise. Clines was later successfully prosecuted and convicted of four crimes.

[20] Some Committee members publicly expressed their frustration with the pace of Independent Counsel's criminal investigation.

[21] Under a Memorandum of Understanding dated March 24, 1987, the Committees agreed not to vote on immunizing North before June 4, not to question him privately before June 15, and not to call him for public testimony before June 23. In exchange, Independent Counsel agreed not to seek an automatic 20-day deferral of North's immunity grant, as he was entitled to under the federal use immunity statute. For Poindexter, the Committees agreed not to vote on immunity before April 20, not to question him privately before May 2 or three days before the start of public hearings, and not to call him to testify publicly before June 15. To insure against leaks of Poindexter's private testimony, the Committees agreed that only three attorneys and a court reporter would be present and that the notes of the private session would not be transcribed or removed from a Committee vault before June 15. The attorneys who questioned Poindexter privately would not disclose his answers to Committee members or others before June 15 except under "certain extraordinary circumstances"—that is, if he provided evidence of an impeachable offense. Independent Counsel agreed in return not to seek a 20-day deferral of Poindexter's immunity grant.

[22] Independent Counsel's First Interim Report is reprinted in Volume II of this report.

be complete without the testimony of Col. North.'' [23]

In May and June 1987, when it was highly unlikely that either Poindexter or North would incriminate the President, immunity was granted, and, in July, their testimony was taken and publicly exposed. The President's December 1986 proposal was thereby carried out.

## Early Indictments Weighed

To minimize the problems caused by the expected grants of congressional immunity, Independent Counsel beginning in mid-February 1987 considered indicting North and others on obstruction-of-justice charges, based chiefly on evidence of document destruction.

In March, Independent Counsel considered a list of potential targets for prosecution, subjects for further investigation and candidates for immunity. This included a tentative outline for the prosecution of North and others and included document destruction and illegal fundraising for the contras. It was decided not to try to obtain an indictment before the Select Committees granted immunity. There was no possibility that a case could be tried before North and Poindexter were called as witnesses. The confrontation with Congress and the ensuing litigation to compel the testimony could be expected not only to expand the danger of tainting the projected trial, but also to hamper and even threaten the continuation of the investigation.

While cautioning against a fragmentary indictment, Independent Counsel in March 1987 required the investigative teams to produce a summary of their possible cases, witnesses, trial documents and outlines of the applicable laws. Then, ''canning'' procedures were established so that each team could begin filing under seal with the U.S. District Court for the District of Columbia their case summaries, draft indictments, witness leads and trial exhibits. This was done to provide proof when needed that the criminal evidence OIC gathered early in its investigation could not have been ''tainted,'' or influenced, by the subsequent congressional testimony of immunized witnesses.

In early June 1987, Walsh prepared a lengthy analysis of a possible indictment based upon

information available before North and Poindexter testified before the Committees. Secord, who was also likely to be indicted, had already testified before the Committees but had done so without immunity.[24]

On June 29 and 30, 1987, there was a further consideration of an immediate indictment, a week before North's scheduled public appearance on Capitol Hill. The proposed indictment of North, Poindexter, Secord and Hakim included a conspiracy to violate the Boland Amendment's prohibition on military aid to the Nicaraguan contras, acts of obstruction and false statements to Congress. It could not include charges related to the diversion.[25] Although proof of obstruction by North and Poindexter was in hand, and although substantial evidence of Boland violations had been collected, the investigation was not complete. After lengthy discussion, Independent Counsel and a large majority of the staff favored waiting for the Swiss bank records so that charges on the Iran/contra diversion and the effort by Hakim and Secord to corrupt North could be included.

Other factors weighed heavily against an early indictment, including the legal and political confrontation that would have resulted from indicting North just before his scheduled congressional testimony. Had North been under indictment when called by Congress to testify, his probable refusal to do so would have resulted in a firestorm that OIC might not have been able to withstand. A simultaneous attack by the defendants and Congress on Independent Counsel could have resulted in a premature effort by the courts to deal with the immunity problem in the abstract and the possible destruction of the prosecution of North and Poindexter and also the ongoing investigation.[26]

---

[23] *Los Angeles Times*, ''The Iran-Contra Hearings . . .'', 6/4/87.

[24] Independent Counsel invited each of the potential defendants to make a proffer—or outline—of testimony he could give if he agreed to cooperate with the criminal investigation, to begin possible plea negotiations. Attorneys for North, Poindexter and Hakim rejected OIC's proposal.

[25] These charges required the Swiss bank records and Zucker's testimony because OIC was unwilling to rely upon Zucker's proffers through his counsel.

[26] It was always the effort of Independent Counsel to proceed to indictment and trial with immunity safeguards of his own design and to have court litigation develop as a review of the conduct trial, rather than to obtain some kind of pre-trial or pre-indictment prescription. Quite apart from the dangers of litigation, if Poindexter or North did testify, the indictment would have been subjected to a free-swinging, highly publicized attack by North, Poindexter and their congressional supporters, to which OIC could not have listened, let alone respond.

The decision was made not to indict but to take all steps necessary to keep the probable prosecution of North, Poindexter and others free of taint from their immunized congressional testimony.

## North Delivers His Immunized Testimony

Independent Counsel was fully aware of the potential problems posed by North's immunized testimony, which was finally delivered to intense public interest in early July 1987. But the Select Committees, by not insisting on privately questioning North in advance of his public appearance and by agreeing that his testimony would be limited in time, expanded the problem. Without the advantage of prior private testimony, the Committees were not able to restrict North's testimony to narrowly responsive answers. The Committees publicly and blindly examined a hostile, articulate, immunized witness without the protection and guidance of a significant prior statement.

Although OIC shielded itself from North's testimony, it quickly became clear that North had turned the tables on the Select Committees. Ollie North T-shirts and other North memorabilia were being sold on the streets of Washington. It looked as though North's charismatic qualities had enabled him to exploit his underdog role. North had bested the Congress of the United States in what was perceived to be its most ostentatious display of investigatory power since Watergate.

OIC in the spring of 1987 had doubled its staff to speed the investigation and to preserve a core of trial attorneys and paralegals who would remain unexposed to the testimony. A smaller team of attorneys and support staff became exposed, or "tainted," to serve as a buffer between the outside world and the "untainted" staff, and to investigate potential defendants not immunized by Congress. The untainted staff members could not read about or in any way monitor the immunized testimony. Inadvertent exposures—such as overheard conversations or glimpses of banner headlines—occurred and were recorded in a special file, which would later be reviewed by the court to determine whether the incidents impermissibly tainted the prosecutions. Independent Counsel asked the Iran/contra grand jurors to avoid the immunized testimony, and Grand Jury witnesses were told not to refer to it or base their testimony on it.[27]

In the two weeks following North's public testimony, Independent Counsel considered whether the investigation and prosecution could continue. Could the staff avoid becoming exposed to his testimony? What should be done with Grand Jury and potential trial witnesses who saw all or part of the immunized performance? Should OIC accept what might be inevitable—an inability to prosecute North—and try to use him as a witness?

By early August 1987, after a full review of the legal questions, OIC decided that it would continue to pursue a prosecution of North. Discussions with North's counsel left no illusion of possible cooperation. The popularity of one of the subjects of the investigation could not be permitted to deter Independent Counsel from applying the rule of law where, under less extraordinary circumstances, it would be applied. Prior court holdings on the effects of limited immunity kept OIC from simply surrendering the prosecution. The outcome would have to be resolved by the courts after OIC rigidly avoided any use of the immunized testimony.

On August 9, 1987, Independent Counsel delivered an address at the American Bar Association meeting on "Truth and the Rule of Law." He announced his decision to continue to pursue the prosecution of immunized figures. Every reasonable precaution would be taken to respect constitutional protections, but the issue of the adequacy of these precautions would be left to the courts, he said. Finally, the popularity or unpopularity of possible defendants could not affect prosecutorial decisions.

## The Swiss Records Are Obtained and an Indictment Is Written

The elements of a comprehensive indictment against North, Poindexter, Secord and Hakim fell into place as the questioning of witnesses

---

[27] Teams of OIC attorneys later became exposed to those portions of the immunized testimony that did not affect the individual trials they worked on. Independent Counsel Walsh and others who were involved in the broadest aspects of the investigation and trials remained unexposed to all the immunized congressional testimony until the completion of the *Poindexter* trial in April 1990.

and review of documents continued into the fall of 1987.

The ability to charge the Iran/contra diversion as a crime remained a pivotal concern, as OIC awaited the release of the Swiss financial records. It was the disclosure of the diversion, after all, which shocked the public and caused the appointment of Independent Counsel. In addition, it was expected that the Swiss records would show not only profiteering by Secord and Hakim, but also the possible financial corruption of North.

By October 1987, OIC was ready to evaluate the assistance to the Nicaraguan contras by North and other Government officers during the 1984–1986 period in which the Boland Amendment prohibited such aid. Although the Boland Amendment itself carried no criminal sanctions, these activities and the deceit with which they were concealed could be used as elements in a conspiracy charge. Such a charge of conspiracy would provide the necessary unity for the other counts likely to be included in an indictment.

After the Swiss records became available in November 1987,[28] a comprehensive indictment could be written. Evidence would now support the charges that would reflect the over-pricing of the missiles sold to Iran, and the subsequent diversion of the profits; the personal enrichment of Secord and Hakim; and the gratuities paid to North.

Cases were also under consideration against McFarlane and former CIA Costa Rican station chief Joseph F. Fernandez, as well as a narrower case against another CIA officer working in Central America, James L. Adkins, who had been illegally involved in resupplying the Nicaraguan contras.

It was decided that Fernandez and Adkins would not be included in the broader indictment, because the possible charges against them were limited to contra operational support. This distinguished them from the other potential defendants whose activities extended to both the Iran arms sales and the Iran/contra diversion.[29]

Unlike Fernandez, McFarlane was linked to both the Iran and contra matters. Unlike North,

Poindexter, Secord and Hakim, however, McFarlane apparently played no role in approving or implementing the Iran/contra diversion.

In January and February 1988, evidence was collected and presented to support an indictment charging a corrupt conspiracy among North, Poindexter, Secord, and Hakim, and possibly McFarlane.[30] Its elements included: (1) an unauthorized covert action to support military activities in Nicaragua in violation of the Boland Amendment ban on military aid to the contras;[31] (2) using the Iran arms sale to create a slush fund to be spent at the direction of North and Poindexter, and for self-enrichment; and (3) endangering the hostage-rescue effort by pursuing unauthorized activities. Other charges would include false statements to Congress, obstruction of official inquiries, the payment and receipt of illegal gratuities, and the destruction and alteration of official documents.

In February 1988, McFarlane entered into plea negotiations. On March 11, 1988, McFarlane pleaded guilty to four misdemeanor counts of withholding information from Congress and agreed to cooperate with Independent Counsel, allowing him to testify in a future trial of North, Poindexter, Secord and Hakim.[32]

Independent Counsel met for a final time with counsel for those who would be named in the indictment to discuss the possibility of plea negotiations. His effort was rejected. On March 16, 1988, a 23-count indictment was returned against Poindexter, North, Secord and Hakim.

## Litigation, 1988–1990

Following the March 1988 indictment of North, Poindexter, Secord and Hakim, OIC became heavily engaged in pre-trial work, responding to more than 100 defense motions and to discovery requests for hundreds of thousands of documents. Much time was devoted to trying

---

[28] Before they could be used effectively, there were weeks of translation, computerization, analysis, and lengthy interviews of Zucker and his assistants.

[29] A separate indictment was brought later against Fernandez.

[30] It is not necessary, in a conspiracy, that all defendants be party to all activities.

[31] Under the National Security Act and related Executive Orders, covert action ("special activities") by the CIA required authorization of a Finding by the President with notice to Congress either through the intelligence committees or the congressional leadership. Such activities undertaken by Government officials outside the CIA required the written authorization of the President. See The Operational Conspiracy: A Legal Analysis.

[32] McFarlane was later identified in a bill of particulars as a coconspirator of North, Poindexter, Secord and Hakim.

to resolve complications caused by the congressional grants of immunity to three of the defendants. Also, there were problems arising from the fact that the Iran/contra criminal cases were intertwined with issues of national security, requiring lengthy negotiations with the intelligence agencies to review and declassify thousands of pages of documents for possible use at trial.

Significant pre-trial and trial issues are described in detail in the individual case sections of this report. For the purposes of understanding the progression of Independent Counsel's work, however, the most important are noted briefly here.

On June 8, 1988, U.S. District Judge Gerhard A. Gesell ordered the severance of the *North, Poindexter, Secord* and *Hakim* cases, based on the fact that each of the defendants except Secord had received immunity to testify before Congress. Nothing they said in their widely publicized congressional testimony could be used against them in a criminal proceeding. Although Independent Counsel took extensive measures to shield its cases from the testimony, the defendants successfully argued that their constitutional rights would be violated if they could not use at trial possibly exculpatory immunized testimony given by their co-defendants. The severance doubled the length of time needed to try these cases. Independent Counsel decided to try North first.

A further substantial delay occurred after severance. The court was moving firmly toward a September 1988 trial of North, but North's counsel convinced the court in an *ex parte* presentation that extensive further classified information was necessary for the defense. The production could not be accomplished by the intelligence agencies in time for a September trial. To avoid the need for this additional discovery, the court proposed a trial without the conspiracy and diversion counts. Independent Counsel moved to sever but not dismiss those counts. North, however, claimed he needed a postponement to assimilate material already produced to him. Under those circumstances, the court vacated the trial date and denied Independent Counsel's motion to sever the counts as moot. The discovery schedule was extended into the fall. Hearings on the use of classified information at trial did not start until November 30.

On January 13, 1989, Judge Gesell dismissed the central conspiracy and theft charges against North because the Reagan Administration refused to declassify certain information deemed relevant to these charges. The Reagan and Bush Administrations, while yielding on some issues, continued to resist the declassification of others, requiring extensive negotiations between Independent Counsel and the intelligence agencies throughout the *North* trial.

The trial of North on 12 charges began in February 1989. On May 4, the jury convicted North on three felony counts.

Because the central conspiracy and theft charges were dropped against North, it was likely that the same charges would be dismissed in the cases of Poindexter, Secord and Hakim. As a result, Independent Counsel subsequently dismissed or narrowed the charges on his own motion. In *Secord*, Independent Counsel presented additional evidence to the Grand Jury, resulting in a second indictment of Secord on April 7, 1989, on nine additional charges of obstruction, false statements and perjury.

In April 1989, former CIA Costa Rica station chief, Fernandez, was indicted in Alexandria, Virginia, for false statements to the CIA inspector general and the Tower Commission. This indictment was similar to an earlier indictment of Fernandez—brought in 1988 in the District of Columbia and dismissed on venue grounds—but was stripped of a conspiracy charge to minimize classified information problems.

In late July 1989, as jury selection was beginning in *Fernandez*, the Department of Justice—over the objections of Independent Counsel—obtained a stay of the trial to appeal trial Judge Claude M. Hilton's rulings allowing Fernandez to introduce certain classified information in his defense. On September 29, 1989, the U.S. Court of Appeals for the Fourth Circuit ruled that the attorney general had no standing to appeal Judge Hilton's rulings in a case prosecuted by Independent Counsel. As a result of this ruling, the trial was rescheduled for November, and Independent Counsel resumed negotiations with the intelligence agencies over the classified information at issue.

Throughout the late summer and early fall of 1989, Independent Counsel attempted to persuade the intelligence agencies that the critical part of the classified information at issue in *Fernandez* was, in fact, well known to the public. In this time, Independent Counsel briefed the intelligence committees on the problems presented by the dispute. It was Independent Counsel's position that the importance of the prosecution outweighed the intelligence agencies' insistence that the information remain officially deniable.

In an effort to resolve the matter, Independent Counsel in October 1989 sought a meeting with President Bush to discuss the need to declassify the information needed to prosecute *Fernandez*. The President declined to meet with Independent Counsel, stating that the Attorney General was his representative in the matter. The Administration remained steadfast in its refusal to allow the information to be disclosed, causing the dismissal of all charges against Fernandez on November 24, 1989.

Despite the dismissal of *Fernandez*, the attorney general had indicated that he might reconsider the declassification of the information if Independent Counsel appealed Judge Hilton's rulings in the Fourth Circuit. Independent Counsel accordingly became involved in an appeals process that would take another 11 months before it was ultimately resolved, affirming Judge Hilton's rulings. In October 1990, after the appeals ruling was issued, the attorney general notified the trial court that it was his final determination that the classified information could not be disclosed, and the case was finally dismissed.

In November 1989, Secord and Hakim entered guilty pleas. Just a few days before his trial was scheduled to begin, Secord pleaded guilty to the felony charge of false statements to Congress. Hakim pleaded guilty to the misdemeanor charge of illegally supplementing the salary of a Government official (North). As part of the Hakim guilty plea, Hakim's company, Lake Resources Inc., pleaded guilty to a corporate felony of defrauding the Government in the Iran/contra diversion. Hakim entered into an agreement, which he subsequently breeched, to assist the United States in recovering Iran arms sales proceeds still on deposit in Switzerland.

In late 1989 and early 1990, *Poindexter* pretrial issues were resolved. In February 1990, U.S. District Judge Harold H. Greene ruled that former President Reagan could be called to testify in Poindexter's defense. In order to accommodate the former President, a two-day videotaped deposition was taken in Los Angeles, California, on February 16 and 17, 1990. This was shown in full as part of the defense case in Poindexter's trial.

Also in preparation for the *Poindexter* trial, Independent Counsel prevailed in obtaining North as a witness, after Judge Greene rejected North's assertion that he could not separate his testimony from Poindexter's immunized testimony before Congress.

On February 22, 1990, a Grand Jury hearing Iran/contra evidence in Baltimore, Maryland, returned an indictment of Thomas G. Clines, who had worked with Secord and Hakim in both the Iran and contra operations. The *Clines* indictment centered on his filing false tax returns in 1985 and 1986.

The *Poindexter* trial began March 5, 1990. Unlike North, Poindexter did not take the witness stand. On April 7, 1990, the jury convicted him of the five felony counts on which he was tried.

In July 1990, North's convictions were vacated because it had not been shown to the extent required by the Court of Appeals that his widely publicized immunized testimony did not affect the testimony of witnesses against him. In November 1991, Poindexter's conviction was reversed for the same reason. The Supreme Court denied certiorari in both cases.

Following the convictions of North and Poindexter, and the guilty pleas of Secord and Hakim, a second, final phase of investigative work was begun by the Office of Independent Counsel, described in detail in the following section. In addition to this final phase of investigative work and the resulting trials, the Office of Independent Counsel was engaged in 1990 and 1991 in appeals and other areas of litigation, described more fully in the individual case sections.

# The Continuing Investigation: 1990–1993

The completion of the trials of North and Poindexter in 1989 and 1990, respectively, marked the beginning of an important phase of Independent Counsel's criminal investigation: For the first time both men became available to OIC for questioning. Having convicted the individuals most operationally involved in Iran/contra, Independent Counsel focused on the supporting roles played by officials in the CIA, Defense and State departments, and the supervisory role of the principal members of the President's National Security Council.

The reactivated investigation, known as the "continuing investigation," was directed by Deputy Independent Counsel Craig A. Gillen. It focused initially on fewer than a dozen individuals who were suspected of having assisted or having falsely denied knowledge of Iran/contra activities. At the same time, the OIC reviewed whether the Executive agencies, in response to the initial phase of the criminal investigation in 1987 and 1988, had cooperated fully with Independent Counsel's document requests. There was evidence that this had not been the case.

It was Independent Counsel's hope that the continuing investigation could be completed and final prosecutorial decisions made within six months following the completion of the *Poindexter* trial in April 1990. Instead, it took three years, prolonged by the discovery of previously withheld notes and other documents by high-ranking Reagan Administration officials, and the need to re-question key figures based on new information gleaned from these documents and obtained from cooperating witnesses.

The development of the continuing investigation can be viewed in three segments:

—The first, from January 1990 to July 1991, focused on the possibly false testimony of 10 former Reagan Administration officials in the Office of the Vice President, State Department, Central Intelligence Agency and on the National Security Council staff. The testimony in question related primarily to support of the contras during the Boland prohibition on U.S. military aid from 1984 to 1986. Limited attention was given to U.S. knowledge and involvement in the November 1985 HAWK missile shipment to Iran. This phase involved the questioning of North, Poindexter and Fernandez, following the disposition of their criminal cases.

—The second, from July 1991 to November 1991, began with Independent Counsel's decision to prosecute Fiers, who had worked closely with North as the CIA's Central American task force chief. This phase was fueled by Fiers' subsequent decision to plead guilty and the investigative leads generated by his cooperation. It led to the indictments of former CIA Deputy Director for Operations Clair E. George, and former CIA official Duane R. Clarridge, and to the guilty plea of former Assistant Secretary of State Elliott Abrams.

—The third, from October 1991 to the spring of 1993, dealt with the discovery and analysis of previously withheld notes and documents that directly contradicted the testimony of some of the most senior Reagan Administration officials. This phase focused on efforts by senior officials to respond to the November 1986 public exposure of Iran/contra, their concerns over the possible impeachment of President Reagan and an attempt by some to falsely minimize his knowledge of a November 1985 shipment of U.S. HAWK missiles from Israel to Iran. This investigative phase led to the indictment of former Defense Secretary Caspar W. Weinberger.

## Phase I: Focus on Contra Support

### Questioning North and Poindexter

As of January 1990, North had not been questioned by OIC for investigative purposes, although he had been cross-examined at his trial in 1989. Most of Independent Counsel's staff had not even been exposed to his 1987 testimony before the Select Iran/contra Committees. North had testified before the committees in general terms about what Reagan Administration officials knew concerning his activities but he had not been questioned in detail about specific possible violations of law by those officials.

The Committees questioned North about a limited number of entries he had made in notebooks but he had never been systematically examined about the hundreds of pages of notes of his meetings, telephone conversations and agreements with various Administration officials reflecting Iran/contra activities. North's notebooks, from January 1984 to November 1986, contained highly detailed but sometimes cryptic information that only he could fully explain.

OIC obtained copies of North's notebooks when he took the witness stand at his trial in April 1989. After the trial, it was necessary to question him about his notebooks and to follow up, from an investigative standpoint, on his congressional testimony. Most provocative were North's generalized assertions during his 1987 congressional testimony that there was widespread knowledge among Administration officials of his activities. Many of his notebook entries seemed to corroborate those claims.

North's appearance before the Grand Jury was delayed to avoid disrupting his appearance in Poindexter's trial in the spring of 1990. In late April and early May 1990, OIC sought North's voluntary cooperation in the investigation, which would have permitted him to answer questions outside the Grand Jury in a more informal setting. Independent Counsel took the extraordinary step of submitting to North's attorneys four sets of questions describing the general parameters of a major portion of the continuing investigation. Ultimately, no agreement could be reached.

Independent Counsel then obtained a court order granting him immunity and compelling his testimony before the Grand Jury. On May 15, 1990, North moved to quash his Grand Jury subpoena, claiming that OIC was improperly using the Grand Jury to prepare its final report, that he was being harassed, and that Independent Counsel was setting up a "perjury trap". On May 24, 1990, the District Court denied North's motion.

North's Grand Jury testimony began on June 1, 1990. Independent Counsel obtained North's testimony in several areas:

—His contacts from 1984 to 1986 with the Office of the Vice President, and specifically with Donald P. Gregg, the national security adviser to Vice President Bush,

focusing on the knowledge that OVP personnel had about North's contra-related activities and about the contra support activities of former CIA operative Felix Rodriguez.

—The extent to which North discussed his contra-related activities with members of the RIG, in which representatives of several Executive Branch agencies shared information on Central American issues.

—His relationship with RIG member Alan D. Fiers, Jr., the CIA's Central American task force chief, and the extent to which Fiers participated in or was knowledgeable of North's contra-related activities during 1985 and 1986.

—His relationship with former CIA official Duane "Dewey" Clarridge in two areas: their involvement in the November 1985 HAWK missiles shipment to Iran, and in the 1984 CIA "hand off" of contra-support responsibilities to North and the NSC.

—His knowledge of whether Paul Thompson, general counsel to the NSC in 1985 and 1986, had any role in false representations to Congress made by national security advisers McFarlane and Poindexter in 1985 and 1986, respectively, about North's contra-support activities. Additionally, North was asked about Thompson's knowledge of and access to the December 5, 1985, covert-action Finding signed by President Reagan, which sought to retroactively approve the November 1985 HAWK missile shipment to Iran, and Thompson's witnessing of the destruction of the Finding by Poindexter.

In some instances, North had specific recollections of events detailed in his notes and was able to confirm their apparent meaning. In other instances, he could not recall or clarify the substance of notebook entries. North affirmed before the Grand Jury the accuracy of his prior testimony in other forums. This pattern of varying degrees of usefulness was true throughout the range of topics covered in his questioning.

North's series of appearances before the Grand Jury were halted for six months, after the U.S. Court of Appeals for the District of

Columbia Circuit on July 20, 1990, issued its opinion in his case. The appeals court vacated North's convictions on the grounds that his immunized congressional testimony had possibly tainted his trial, and it ordered further hearings in the trial court. North filed an additional motion to quash his Grand Jury subpoena, alleging that because of the possibility of a re-trial, his constitutional rights would be violated by his continued compelled appearance before the Grand Jury. North also asserted that he was entitled to transcripts of his prior Grand Jury testimony.

North's motion to quash the subpoena was denied on October 26, 1990; his motion for reconsideration was denied on November 16, 1990. On November 17, 1990, North's attorneys informed Independent Counsel that North would not comply with the court's order to compel his testimony and would be held in contempt. From November 1990 through January 1991, North litigated the Grand Jury issue. On January 29, 1991, North was held in contempt by the District Court and was denied bail, and the Court of Appeals declined to stay these judgments. Before being incarcerated, North purged himself of contempt by continuing his testimony before the Grand Jury.

Most of North's testimony was completed by March 15, 1991. He was called back for limited questioning in November 1991.

Following Poindexter's sentencing in early June 1990, Poindexter testified, under a court order granting him use immunity, five times before the Grand Jury between June 27, 1990 and March 6, 1991.

Poindexter was questioned about Thompson's involvement in responding to the 1986 congressional inquiry into North's contra-support activities. He was asked about Thompson's knowledge of the Iran arms sales Findings and about his witnessing Poindexter's destruction of the 1985 Finding. He was asked also about Thompson's role in gathering documents for Attorney General Meese's investigation of the Iran arms sales in November 1986.

Poindexter's later Grand Jury appearances in November 1991, and March 1992 focused on a broader scope of inquiry, including the knowledge and involvement of President Reagan, Vice President Bush, the Cabinet and NSC staff members regarding Iran/contra matters.

## Focus on Ilopango

During the spring and summer of 1990, the investigation focused on the contra-resupply operation runs from Ilopango airbase in El Salvador. OIC undertook to establish the extent of U.S. Government knowledge of and participation in the Ilopango operation during the Boland prohibition on U.S. military aid. It was also important to determine U.S. Government knowledge of the contra-support activities of Felix Rodriguez, a former CIA officer who used the alias "Max Gomez" and who was in Central America ostensibly to assist the Salvadoran government's fight against communist guerrilla forces.

Following the October 5, 1986, shootdown of a contra-resupply aircraft which originated at Ilopango, Reagan Administration officials denied any U.S. Government connection to the flight. They also denied knowledge of "Max Gomez," whom American Eugene Hasenfus, upon his capture by Nicaraguan soldiers, had publicly identified as a CIA agent involved in the contra-resupply operation.

The continuing investigation sought to learn what Elliott Abrams, Clair George and Alan Fiers knew about the Ilopango operation and Rodriguez prior to their October 1986 appearances before congressional committees investigating the Hasenfus shootdown. Abrams, George and Fiers had denied that they were aware of who was behind the contra-resupply flights.

It was also important to determine what information was conveyed, and at how early a date, to the Vice President's national security adviser, Gregg, about Rodriguez's activities at Ilopango on behalf of the contras.

## Steele and Corr

The initial phase of the Ilopango inquiry began with Army Col. James J. Steele, who was the military group commander at the U.S. Embassy in El Salvador during 1985 and 1986. Colonel Steele in December 1986, appearing before the Senate Select Committee on Intelligence (SSCI), testified that he tried not to actively assist the contra-resupply operation, that he had not provided such assistance, and that he did not think anyone at the U.S. Embassy had. He said that humanitarian supplies for the contras were kept in a separate place from the lethal material, which he had not seen at Ilopango.[33]

During 1990 and 1991 Steele was interviewed by OIC six times and appeared before the Grand Jury once. In the course of this questioning and after failing a lie-detector test, Steele recanted critical aspects of his earlier testimony. His truthful admissions provided the continuing investigation with a valuable basis by which to gauge the truthfulness of others testifying about the same events.

In his initial interviews with the continuing investigation, Steele denied that Gregg was aware of Rodriguez's contra-related activities before August 1986. He confirmed Gregg's own testimony.

He agreed to submit to a polygraph examination by the FBI. In the opinion of the polygraph examiner, his answers were indicative of deception on this question of Gregg's knowledge of Rodriguez's contra-related activities before July and August 1986. Following the examination, Steele remembered a meeting in approximately January 1986, when he visited Gregg's office and mentioned to Gregg Rodriguez's activities on behalf of the contras.

During his interviews, Steele was confronted with certain documents and North notebook entries indicating that he was an active participant in the resupply operation at Ilopango. Steele then admitted being involved in discussions concerning certain resupply flights and other aspects of the operation.[34] Steele admitted going on board a cargo plane at Ilopango in April 1986 prior to its dropping lethal supplies to the contras' southern fighting front. Steele believed that he told Corr about the lethal cargo on the flight.[35] Steele acknowledged informing Corr of his activities and of the lethal contra-resupply operation. He said he informed Corr of everything that wasn't "below his noise level."[36] Steele stated that both he and Corr knew that North was working very closely with the contra-resupply operation.

Following the Hasenfus shootdown, Corr and Steele discussed the Salvadoran officials' denial of a connection between the Salvadoran government and the Hasenfus flight, which originated at Ilopango airbase in El Salvador. It was clear to Steele that Corr was in a "damage control mode."[37]

Because of Steele's candor during his 1990 and 1991 interviews, he was not subjected to charges based upon his earlier misstatements. Steele acknowledged active participation by U.S. Government personnel in the contra-resupply operation at Ilopango. His information provided a much clearer picture of the activities at Ilopango.

Corr, the U.S. ambassador to El Salvador during the 1985–1986 period, was interviewed in January 1991 to follow up on Steele's statements.

Corr was questioned about an April 20, 1986, meeting at the U.S. Embassy in San Salvador, with Steele, North and Secord.[38] Corr denied meeting with both North and Secord, although he acknowledged a perfunctory meeting with Secord, which he said was not related to the resupply operation.

In April 1991, Corr was compelled to testify before the Grant Jury pursuant to a grant of use immunity. He was subpoenaed also to produce relevant documents. As the result, Corr produced in April and May 1991 notes of conversations which not previously produced to Iran/contra investigators. They reflected conversations with Abrams and others during 1986.

Many of Corr's newly produced notes were highly relevant to his knowledge and that of others within the State Department following the Hasenfus shootdown. One note reflected an October 14, 1986, telephone conversation with Abrams just a few hours before Abrams appeared before the House Permanent Select Committee on Intelligence to testify about the shootdown. The note reflects that Corr and Abrams discussed Rodriguez and his role in El Salvador.[39]

By the date of the call, Corr was fully aware of Rodriguez's role with the contra-resupply operation at Ilopango. During Abrams' testimony,

[33] Steele, SSCI Testimony, 12/18/86, pp. 10–14, 18–22, 36–37, 46–49.
[34] Steele, FBI 302, 9/18/90, p. 5.
[35] Ibid., 2/4/91, p. 7.
[36] Ibid., 9/17/90, p. 5.

[37] Steele, FBI 302, 2/5/91, p. 6.
[38] Secord became a cooperating witness following his plea agreement with OIC in November 1989.
[39] Corr Note, 10/14/86, ALW 0032906.

a few hours after his telephone conversation with Corr, Abrams did not reveal Rodriguez's role with the resupply operation at Ilopango.

## Tambs and Fernandez

OIC questioned former U.S. Ambassador to Costa Rica Lewis Tambs. Tambs had previously testified candidly about his activities in Costa Rica to help open a southern fighting front for the contras. In March 1990, Tambs gave testimony about his conversations with Abrams and other officials regarding the opening of a southern front, as well as U.S. Embassy involvement in facilitating the building of a secret contra-resupply airstrip in Costa Rica. He also testified about the extent of Reagan Administration knowledge of the activities of Fernandez, the CIA chief of station in Costa Rica. He supplied information about the knowledge that Fiers and Abrams had of Fernandez's contra-support activities.

Fernandez was ordered to testify under a grant of use immunity in October 1990, after the case against him was dismissed. He appeared six times before the Grand Jury between November 1990 and January 1991. Fernandez was asked to explain CIA cable traffic, encoded messages that were relayed on special communications devices known as KL–43s between the contras and the resupply operation, and excerpts from North's notebooks.

He was helpful in providing information about the knowledge his CIA superiors had regarding his contacts with the contra-resupply operation, and about Abrams' knowledge of the secret contra-resupply airstrip in Costa Rica.

## The Gregg Inquiry

In the summer of 1990, Donald Gregg agreed to submit to a polygraph examination. It concerned, among other things, when he first learned of Felix Rodriguez's contra-support activities and when, if ever, he relayed that information to Vice President Bush. In response to an FBI polygraph examiner's questions, Gregg reasserted his earlier statements that he was not aware of Rodriguez's involvement in contra support before August 1986 and that he had not relayed the information to the Vice President.

In the opinion of the FBI examiner, Gregg's answers to the relevant questions indicated deception. OIC intensified its inquiry as to the when and to what extent the Office of the Vice President was aware of Rodriguez's contra-support activities at Ilopango airbase.

In the late summer and fall of 1990, former members of Vice President Bush's staff were interviewed. The investigation re-analyzed the testimony of Col. Samuel Watson, Gregg's assistant, regarding Rodriguez's contra-support activities and particularly the purpose of Rodriguez's meetings with Vice President Bush in 1986.

Rodriguez testified twice before the Grand Jury in May 1991 about his contacts with the Office of the Vice President and his contra-resupply activities at Ilopango. He denied discussing activities with Gregg prior to August 1986 or ever with Bush.

## Previously Withheld Documents

One of the major difficulties confronting the continuing investigation was the passage of time since the Iran/contra events had occurred, and the corresponding lack of witness recollection of specific details. To combat this problem, OIC carefully searched for previously unproduced, contemporaneously created documents such as notes that would reflect on Iran/contra matters.

The search for previously undiscovered documents was fueled also by the fact that most significant Iran/contra witnesses were reluctant to provide truthful information unless they were confronted with difficult-to-refute documentary evidence. Much of the early phase of the continuing investigation focused on contradictions between the prior sworn testimony of Reagan Administration officials and contemporaneously created documents.

Members of the Restricted Interagency Group (RIG) on Central America, for example, generally denied knowledge of North's extensive contra-support activities. North's notebooks indicated that he had in fact exposed the RIG to a full airing of his activities as early as the summer of 1986. As a result, the investigation sought to discover the existence of notes made by other RIG members, which could either corroborate or contradict North's assertions. An extensive search was conducted in late 1990 and early 1991, but no additional relevant notes of RIG members were found at that time.

There was additional concern that some relevant documents had not been produced in 1987, because the early production of documents had been in response to document requests rather than compelled by grand jury subpoena. The investigation in 1990 and 1991 spent a great amount of time reviewing bodies of government records that potentially contained Iran/contra documents.[40] In some cases, these reviews did result in the discovery of significant evidence.

Additional witness interviews also led OIC to previously unseen Iran/contra notes. Former White House counsel Peter Wallison, interviewed concerning his dealings with Thompson during November 1986, disclosed that he kept a diary of his work experiences in the White House. Wallison's diary was significant in the investigation of the November 1986 activities of President's Reagan's closest advisers.

During the summer of 1990, the investigation began searching for State Department documents that might reflect Abrams' knowledge of North's contra-resupply activities. OIC discovered that M. Charles Hill, an executive assistant to Secretary of State George P. Shultz, had produced to criminal and congressional investigators in 1987, only those portions of his notebooks that related to the Iran arms sales—not to contra-related activities.

During the summer of 1990, OIC reviewed approximately 12,000 pages of Hill's handwritten notes, recording, in almost verbatim form, conversations between high-level State Department officials. In addition, Shultz was in the habit of giving Hill a read-out, or recounting, of important meetings he had with the President and other senior Administration officials.

The 1990 review of Hill's notes prompted the investigation to seek, but not initially find, another significant set of notes—those of former Defense Secretary Weinberger. In an August 7, 1987 note that Hill took about the Select Committee hearings, Shultz stated "Cap [Weinberger] takes notes but never referred to them so never had to cough them up."[41] Based upon the Hill note, OIC in October 1990 asked Weinberger about whether he had taken notes that had not been previously produced; he said he had not. It was not until November 1991 that Weinberger's notes at the Library of Congress were discovered, as will be described later.

After the Hill notes had been reviewed, Shultz and Hill were interviewed in December 1990 at the Hoover Institution in Stanford, California. The interviews, coupled with certain Hill notebook entries, raised concerns about prior testimony by Weinberger and other high-ranking Reagan Administration officials regarding the November 1985 HAWK missile shipment to Iran. This ultimately became a central focus of the investigation.

## Phase II: The Fiers Plea

In early 1991, the goal of the continuing investigation was to complete the questioning of relevant witnesses to determine whether to prosecute Fiers, Thompson, Clarridge, Gregg, Watson, Abrams and Corr. The Fiers investigation was the first to reach a conclusion. Independent Counsel determined that, based on the evidence, the prosecution of Fiers was necessary.

OIC negotiated with Fiers' attorneys in May and June 1991. In an effort to reach a plea agreement, Fiers proffered information that indicated his extensive knowledge of Iran/contra matters.

In his proffer, Fiers inculpated himself and others regarding their knowledge of North's contra-support activities and of the diversion of the funds from the Iran arms sales to the contras prior to it becoming public in November 1986. Because Fiers worked closely with North and Abrams on the RIG, he was able to provide valuable information on U.S. Government involvement in contra-support activities.

---

[40] In its search for previously undiscovered evidence, the continuing investigation in January 1990 sought access to the millions of documents seized by the United States following the December 1989 arrest of Gen. Manuel Noriega in Panama. OIC sought to review any Panamanian documents that might reflect upon Noriega's contacts with North, Abrams, the CIA or any U.S. Government official regarding contra-support efforts.

FBI Special Agent Michael S. Foster, who had been assigned to OIC since December 1986, along with two paralegals, traveled to Panama to review seized documents of possible relevance. On one occasion, the FBI agent observed index cards referring to document files entitled (1) Bush, (2) Irangate, (3) CIA, and (4) Contras. Because of the logistical chaos that occurred subsequent to Noriega's arrest, however, these files were not available for immediate Independent Counsel review. When these files were ultimately obtained, their contents were not helpful.

[41] Hill Note, 8/7/87, ANS 0002776.

Fiers was reluctant to implicate others unless he had a specific recollection of an event. Fiers' caution enhanced his credibility. On July 9, 1991, Fiers tendered a plea of guilty to two misdemeanor counts of withholding information from Congress and agreed to cooperate with Independent Counsel's office.

From the beginning of the continuing investigation, there was a focus on the testimony of George, Abrams and Fiers before congressional committees in October 1986 following the shootdown of the Hasenfus plane. That testimony was given days before $100 million was to be appropriated by Congress for United States funding for the contras. Fiers admitted that protection of the $100 million appropriation was a factor in the concealment of facts from Congress about the contra-resupply operation at Ilopango.

In October 1986, Congress was interested in learning what Abrams, George and Fiers knew about who was behind the contra-resupply flights, who funded them, and whether, as Hasenfus had publicly alleged, a former CIA agent named "Max Gomez" (Rodriguez's alias) was helping run the resupply operation at Ilopango airbase. Fiers acknowledged that Congress was not told what he, George and Abrams knew about North's connections to the contra-resupply operation and about Felix Rodriguez's activities at Ilopango. Fiers revealed conversations that he had with George prior to the congressional testimony, in which George stated that he "did not want to put the spotlight on Oliver North or the White House." [42]

Fiers also disclosed that North had told him in the spring and summer of 1986 that Iran arms sales proceeds were being diverted to the contras. Fiers admitted that he had conversations with George and other CIA officials about North's assertions of an Iran/contra diversion, long before its public exposure in November 1986.

Fiers supplied convincing proof of North's claim that he had exposed other members of the RIG to his contra-support activities in the summer of 1986 and sought their advice on whether they should be continued. Fiers confirmed North's assertions. He said North did this on more than one occasion, beginning as

early as July 1986. Fiers remembered a RIG meeting in Abrams' office in which North went over, item-by-item, activities being conducted on behalf of the contras and asked if they should continue. Fiers said North's recounting of the contra-support activities was followed by an awkward silence, and Fiers finally responded to North about which activities should be continued.

Corroborating North's testimonial assertions and North's notebook entry of a RIG meeting on August 28, 1986, OIC in the fall of 1991 discovered at the Department of Defense a September 2, 1986, handwritten note by Army Col. Stephen Croker, reflecting information he received from Lt. General John Moellering who had attended an August 28 RIG meeting. The Croker note corroborated North and Fiers' testimony. The note reads:

> . . . $1m [million]/month 32 people—private
> ops [operations]
> flying planes for resupply in country do we want to keep it going or choke off . . .[43]

Fiers also described a September 19, 1986, meeting of RIG members in the Pentagon. During that meeting North discussed the possibility of paying Panamanian Gen. Manuel Noriega $1 million in non-U.S. Government funds to commit acts of sabotage against the Nicaraguan government. Fiers understood that $1 million in cash would come from "Project Democracy," the contra-resupply operation being run by Secord at North's direction. Fiers' description of this RIG meeting shed new light on a Charles Hill notebook entry of September 20, 1986, in which Abrams described to Hill the Noriega proposal and how it would be funded by money from non-U.S. Government sources.[44] Fiers' testimony, corroborated by newly-discovered documents, greatly strengthened the possibility of a prosecution of Abrams for false statements to Congress.

Previously unproduced State Department notes were located in 1991 reflecting Abrams' knowledge as early as 1985 about North's role in providing lethal supplies to the contras. The

---

[42] Fiers, Grand Jury, 8/16/91, pp. 11–12.

[43] Croker Note, 9/2/86, ALZ 0034813–14.
[44] Hill Note, 9/20/86, ANS 0001617.

newly discovered notes indicated that Abrams was not truthful when he told the Select Committees in the summer of 1987 that he determined there was nothing legally questionable in North's activities.[45] Following the discovery of Hill's contra-related notebook entries, OIC discovered that another Shultz assistant, Nicholas Platt, executive secretary for the State Department, had significant notes that had not been produced to congressional and criminal investigators. One Platt note reflected the September 4, 1985, Shultz admonition to Abrams to monitor North's contra activities.

[SHULTZ]: What is happening on other support for contras for lethal aid etc.— E. ABRAMS doesn't have the answer. Stayed away let Ollie North do it. Fundraising continuing—weapons stocks are high. We have had nothing to do with private aid. Should we continue?

Hate to be in position, [Shultz] says, of not knowing what's going on. You're supposed to be managing overall Central American picture. Ollie can go on doing his thing, but you, [Abrams], should know what's happening.[46]

Platt's notes indicated that by September 1985, Abrams and Shultz knew North was involved in lethal assistance to the contras. According to Platt's notes, Shultz told Abrams that North could continue "doing his thing," but Abrams needed to be informed.

Throughout the summer and fall of 1991 the investigation focused on the possible indictments of Abrams, George and Clarridge. A case against Abrams appeared likely based on information provided by North and Fiers and newly obtained documentary evidence. As a result of the Fiers plea in July 1991 and his public acknowledgement of cooperation with the investigation, two CIA officials and one former CIA official came forward and volunteered additional information regarding the Clarridge investigation.

During July and August 1991, despite the efforts of Independent Counsel, George was unwilling to admit any criminal misconduct. The Grand Jury on September 6, 1991, returned an

indictment charging George with 10 felonies, including obstruction of Congress and the Grand Jury, false statements and perjury.

Similarly, Clarridge declined to enter into plea discussions with Independent Counsel. Clarridge in November 1991 was indicted on multiple felony counts.

Following the September 1991 indictment of George, negotiations began with Abrams' attorneys. Abrams was confronted with a multi-count felony indictment. An agreement was reached, and Abrams pleaded guilty on October 7, 1991, to two counts of withholding information from Congress.

Abrams agreed to cooperate with the continuing investigation. He provided information useful to a potential Gregg prosecution. His pleas expedited the work of the office, although they did not lead to other prosecutions.

The development of Fiers as a witness, and the continuing investigation of other CIA officials, was complicated in the summer of 1991 by President Bush's nomination of Robert Gates as CIA director. As a result of the Fiers plea— particularly his admission that he had discussed the Iran/contra diversion with other CIA officials before its public disclosure—the Senate Select Committee on Intelligence called Fiers and other CIA officials to testify about Gates's knowledge of the diversion. Fiers was subsequently immunized to provide testimony to SSCI, but the Committee declined to immunize certain individuals who were potential investigative targets.

## Phase III: NSC Principals

As of October 1991, the continuing investigation had resulted in the pleas of Fiers and Abrams and the felony indictments of George and Clarridge. At this point, the investigation began its third significant phase.

### Shultz's Congressional Testimony Contradicted by Notes

During October and November 1991, the investigation continued analyzing the notes of State Department officials Hill and Platt relating to the Iran arms sales. OIC discovered that portions of highly relevant notebook entries had not been given to Congress or to the criminal investigation before 1990. Additionally, portions of Hill and Platt's separate notes that had not

---

[45] See Abrams chapter.
[46] Platt Note, 9/4/85, ALW 0036261.

been produced closely corresponded to one another in terms of their substance and the events they reflected.

The majority of the notes that were not produced dealt with contemporaneously recorded conversations in which Shultz reports his conversations with the President, the Vice President or other Cabinet officials. These notes also contradicted Shultz's congressional testimony about his knowledge of the Iran arms sales.

Consequently, the investigation in early 1992 concentrated on collecting notes from other State Department officials that might reflect further upon the level of department knowledge of the Iran arms sales that existed in 1985 and 1986.

Additional notes of mid-level State Department employees were found. From these notes, OIC was able to reconstruct the level of contemporaneous knowledge that Shultz and other State Department officials had about the Iran arms sales in 1985 and 1986. OIC's findings indicated that Shultz's testimony concerning his knowledge about the arms sales was incorrect. The next step was to determine whether the mistakes were deliberate or inadvertent.

An investigation was conducted into how the State Department collected relevant documents for the congressional and criminal investigations and whether certain individuals in the State Department intentionally withheld relevant notes reflecting a greater level of knowledge about the Iran arms sales by Shultz and others than was acknowledged in 1986 and 1987 congressional testimony. The investigation revealed that some notes that had been produced in 1986 and 1987 to congressional and criminal investigators had been redacted to exclude material that showed greater knowledge by State Department officials about the Iran arms sales.

Shultz gave two lengthy interviews to OIC in 1992. He acknowledged the accuracy of Hill's notes, agreed that they were relevant and should have been produced, and stated that if he had reviewed them prior to his testimony before Congress, his testimony would have been very different. He admitted that portions of his congressional testimony were wrong.

OIC also interviewed Hill and Platt to find out whether there was an intentional effort to withhold relevant portions of notes from Congress.[47]

## The Weinberger Notes

In October 1990, OIC, based on a lead provided by Hill's notes, interviewed former Defense Secretary Weinberger about whether he had failed to produce relevant notes to Iran/contra investigators. Weinberger stated that after his first year in office, it was not his practice to take notes because he could not use them, in light of the many meetings he had to attend, to dictate memoranda. Despite these assertions, Independent Counsel obtained Weinberger's permission to review his papers, which had been deposited at the Library of Congress, for any Iran/contra information.

After mistakenly searching for relevant documents in the classified section of the Weinberger collection at the Library of Congress, OIC in late 1991 discovered in the unclassified section approximately 7,000 pages of handwritten notes by Weinberger, including nearly 1,700 from the 1985–1986 Iran/contra period.[48] These notes reflect conversations Weinberger had with the President and other Cabinet officials, providing a unique, contemporaneous record of many significant Iran/contra events. Weinberger's notes contradicted his prior testimony regarding the extent and timing of his knowledge and the knowledge of others within the Administration about the Iran/contra matters.

The notes contradicted Weinberger's testimony on his knowledge of and discussions within the Administration about the November 1985 HAWK missile shipment to Iran, the issue of replenishing Israeli stocks after that country in 1985 sent TOW missiles to Iran, and the issue of Saudi support for the contras. After extensive discussions with Weinberger's counsel, Weinberger was indicted on June 16, 1992, on five felony charges, including obstruction, perjury and false statements.

## The Regan Notes and the November 1986 Investigation

The discovery of other highly relevant, previously non-produced notes continued through the final phase of the continuing investigation.

---

[47] See State Department chapter.
[48] Many of these notes contain information that is highly classified.

In 1992, OIC discovered the existence of notes of former White House Chief of Staff Donald T. Regan that had not been previously produced. Independent Counsel obtained access to these notes.

The most significant of the Regan notes recorded a November 24, 1986, meeting among President Reagan and his most senior advisers, including Regan, Vice President Bush, Poindexter, CIA Director William J. Casey, Meese and Weinberger.

The Regan notes of the November 24, 1986, meeting, and Weinberger's notes, reveal that Meese, notwithstanding his contrary knowledge following a weekend investigation into the facts of the arms sales, told the group that President Reagan hadn't known about the November 1985 HAWK missile shipment to Iran. He acknowledged that it was probably illegal. The meeting notes, combined with Hill's notes of Shultz's read-out to him following the meeting, and the Wallison diary which recounted the Reagan Administration's legal concerns surrounding the arms sales, caused the continuing investigation to focus on the Meese investigation and his assertions at the November 24, 1986, meeting to determine whether there was a deliberate effort by senior officials to cover up the President's involvement in the November 1985 HAWK shipment.

Independent Counsel in 1992 attempted to re-question the participants of the November 24, 1986, meeting about it and about the November 1986 period generally. In the spring and summer of 1992, OIC reinterviewed President Reagan, Regan, Shultz and Meese. Weinberger was facing trial and was not available to be questioned. It was decided that questioning of President Bush would be deferred until after the November 1992 election; subsequent efforts to question him about this meeting were rejected by him.[49]

---

[49] President Reagan was among those who could not recall details of the key events in question. After several hours of careful interrogation in a deposition in Los Angeles in July 1992, Independent Counsel determined that the lack of recollection was genuine. Those who had worked with President Reagan had said that although the President absorbed the facts necessary to make a decision, once it was made he seemed to have the capacity for, as one witness put it, erasing the facts from his mind, like deleting data from a computer. Once the policy was set, it was said that he held his subordinates to that policy without much further reflection on how the policy developed. Furthermore, his lack of memory was reflected also in subjects not directly relevant to the inquiry.

## The Investigation is Closed and Reopened: The Bush Diary

In September 1992, Independent Counsel reported to the special D.C. Court of Appeals panel that appointed him that the investigation was complete, barring unforeseen developments at the upcoming trials of Weinberger and Clarridge. The full resources of the OIC then became trained exclusively on the trial of pending cases and on drafting a final report.

On December 11, 1992, the White House unexpectedly informed Independent Counsel that President Bush had not produced to the investigation previously requested diaries relevant to Iran/contra. The review of Bush's diary notes, and the circumstances surrounding his failure to produce them earlier, required the investigation to re-open.

On December 24, 1992, President Bush pardoned Weinberger, who was to be tried in less than two weeks, and Clarridge, scheduled for trial in March 1993, as well as four others already convicted.

During late December and January 1993 the diaries were produced. They did not justify reopening the investigation. Independent Counsel's efforts to requestion President Bush about Iran/contra matters were thwarted by Bush's insistence that the questioning be limited to the subject of his failure to produce his previously requested diaries. This limitation was unacceptable to OIC, which over the course of its continuing investigation had gathered significant new evidence about which it wanted to question Bush.

President Bush was the first President to grant a pardon on the eve of a trial. The question before Independent Counsel was, and remains, whether President Bush exercised his constitutional prerogative to pardon a former close associate to prevent further Iran/contra revelations. In the absence of evidence that the pardon was secured by corruption, Independent Counsel decided against taking the matter before the Grand Jury.

The continuing investigation resulted in the discovery of large caches of previously withheld contemporaneous notes and documents, which provided new insight into the highly secret events of Iran/contra. Had these materials been produced to congressional and criminal investigators when they were requested in 1987,

Independent Counsel's work would have proceeded more quickly and probably with additional indictments.

With the passage of time, mounting office expenses and dwindling staff resources, Independent Counsel decided not to prosecute certain individuals. Prosecutorial decisions were based primarily on the seriousness of the crimes, the certainty of the evidence, the likelihood that the targeted individual could provide valuable information to the investigation, and the centrality of the individual to the Iran/contra events.

Independent Counsel's decision to pursue the investigation beyond the *Poindexter* trial resulted in these major findings:

—that there was extensive knowledge of North's contra-support activities by high-ranking officials in the CIA, State and Defense departments;

—that false testimony was given to and highly relevant documents were withheld from the congressional and criminal Iran/contra investigations, despite representations of cooperation by the Reagan and Bush Administrations;

—that, contrary to their testimony, Bush, Shultz and Weinberger were kept informed of the details of the Iran arms sales; and

—that senior Administration officials in November 1986 were being invited to conceal President Reagan's involvement in the November 1985 HAWK missile shipment to Iran by Attorney General Meese who believed that it was possibly illegal.

# Chronology of Key Public Events

Oct. 5, 1986: Nicaraguan soldiers shoot down a contra-resupply plane; Eugene Hasenfus, an American, survives.

Nov. 3, 1986: Lebanese newspaper *Al-Shiraa* reports that the United States secretly sold arms to Iran.

Nov. 6, 1986: President Reagan denies arms were sold to Iran.

Nov. 13, 1986: President Reagan acknowledges weapons were sold to Iran but denies that the arms were sold to win the release of American hostages.

Nov. 19, 1986: President Reagan holds a news conference at which he denies U.S. involvement in shipments prior to January 1986.

Nov. 25, 1986: White House discloses contra diversion from the Iran arms sales.

Dec. 1, 1986: Tower Commission appointed by President Reagan.

Dec. 4, 1986: Meese requests appointment of Independent Counsel on Iran/contra.

Dec. 6, 1986: Swiss financial records of Enterprise requested by Department of Justice pursuant to treaty.

Dec. 19, 1986: Walsh appointed Independent Counsel.

Jan. 6, 1987: Senate creates Iran/contra committee.

Jan. 7, 1987: House creates Iran/contra committee.

Jan. 29, 1987: Senate Select Committee on Intelligence issues report on Iran/contra.

Feb. 7, 1987: Swiss Office for Police Matters approves request for financial records; Albert Hakim and Manucher Ghorbanifar appeal.

Feb. 26, 1987: Tower Commission issues Iran/contra report.

March 5, 1987: Walsh receives parallel appointment as Independent Counsel from Justice Department.

March 18, 1987: Walsh reaches agreement with House and Senate Iran/contra committees to delay voting on and obtaining immunized testimony by North and Poindexter.

April 28, 1987: Independent Counsel submits First Interim Report to Congress on potential problems caused by immunity grants.

April 29, 1987: Carl "Spitz" Channell pleads guilty to conspiracy to defraud the United States.

May 5, 1987: Congress begins public hearings on Iran/contra.

May 6, 1987: Richard R. Miller pleads guilty to conspiracy to defraud the United States.

July 7–10 and July 13–14, 1987: North testifies publicly under grant of immunity before Congress.

July 15–17 and July 20–21, 1987: Poindexter testifies publicly under grant of immunity before Congress.

Nov. 10, 1987: Swiss financial records of Enterprise received by Independent Counsel.

Nov. 18, 1987: Congress issues Iran/contra report.

Jan. 22, 1988: The U.S. Court of Appeals for the District of Columbia strikes down the Independent Counsel law as unconstitutional.

March 11, 1988: McFarlane pleads guilty to withholding information from Congress.

March 16, 1988: North, Poindexter, Secord and Hakim indicted on conspiracy to defraud the United States and other charges.

June 8, 1988: Judge Gesell orders separate trials for North, Poindexter, Secord and Hakim due to problems caused by congressional grants of immunity.

June 20, 1988: Fernandez indicted in District of Columbia for conspiracy and false statements to the CIA Inspector General and the Tower Commission.

June 29, 1988: Supreme Court upholds the constitutionality of the Independent Counsel law.

Oct. 19, 1988: Judge Robinson dismisses *Fernandez* case without prejudice on venue grounds.

Jan. 13, 1989: Central conspiracy and theft charges against North are dismissed because of classified information problems.

Jan. 31, 1989 to May 4, 1989: *North* trial, resulting in three-count conviction.

April 7, 1989: Secord is indicted on nine additional charges of obstruction, false statements and perjury.

April 21, 1989: Fernandez indicted on false statement and obstruction charges in Eastern District of Virginia.

July 24, 1989: Attorney general obtains a stay of the *Fernandez* trial to appeal Classified Information Procedures Act (CIPA) rulings.

Aug. 23, 1989: The Fourth Circuit U.S. Court of Appeals hears oral arguments in *Fernandez* on the attorney general's right to appeal under CIPA.

Sept. 19, 1989: Walsh testifies before the legislative subcommittee of the House Permanent Select Committee on Intelligence on CIPA and submits a report to the House and Senate judiciary committees and the Senate Intelligence Committee.

Sept. 29, 1989: The Fourth Circuit rules that the attorney general does not have standing under CIPA to appeal trial court rulings in cases prosecuted by Independent Counsel. It dismisses the appeal and remands the case to the district court.

Nov. 8, 1989: Secord pleads guilty to making false statements to Congress.

Nov. 21, 1989: Hakim pleads guilty to illegally supplementing the salary of a Government official; Lake Resources Inc. pleads guilty to a corporate felony of diverting Iran arms sales proceeds to the contras.

Nov. 24, 1989: *Fernandez* is dismissed after the attorney general refuses to allow the disclosure of certain classified information at trial. Independent Counsel files notice with the Fourth Circuit U.S. Court of Appeals that the Government will appeal the trial court's CIPA rulings.

Dec. 11, 1989: Independent Counsel submits Second Interim Report to Congress on CIPA.

Dec. 12, 1989: Walsh testifies on CIPA in closed session of the legislative subcommittee of the House Intelligence Committee.

Feb. 6, 1990: *North* appeal oral arguments.

Feb. 16–17 1990: Reagan gives videotaped deposition in *Poindexter*.

Feb. 22, 1990: Thomas G. Clines is indicted on tax charges.

Feb. 22, 1990: Walsh testifies on CIPA in a closed session of the Senate Intelligence Committee.

March 5, 1990 to April 7, 1990: *Poindexter* trial, resulting in five-count conviction.

July 20, 1990: U.S. Court of Appeals for the District of Columbia Circuit vacates North's convictions and orders further hearings by trial court on immunity issue.

Sept. 6, 1990: Fourth U.S. Circuit Court of Appeals upholds trial court's rulings in *Fernandez*.

Sept. 4–18, 1990: *Clines* trial, resulting in convictions on four felony charges.

Oct. 12, 1990: *Fernandez* dismissed after attorney general notifies trial court that he has made a final determination not to withdraw CIPA 6(e) affidavit to bar use of classified information.

Oct. 24–25, 1990: Walsh reports to the congressional intelligence and judiciary committees on final outcome of *Fernandez.*

May 28, 1991: Supreme Court declines review of *North* case.

July 9, 1991: Alan D. Fiers, Jr., pleads guilty to withholding information from Congress.

Sept. 6, 1991: Clair E. George is indicted on 10 counts of perjury, false statements and obstruction.

Sept. 16, 1991: Case against North is dismissed on motion of Independent Counsel after two days of hearings by the trial court.

Oct. 7, 1991: Elliott Abrams pleads guilty to withholding information from Congress.

Nov. 15, 1991: U.S. Court of Appeals for the District of Columbia Circuit reverses Poindexter's convictions.

Nov. 26, 1991: Duane R. Clarridge is indicted on seven counts of perjury and false statements.

Feb. 27, 1992: Fourth Circuit U.S. Court of Appeals affirms Clines' convictions.

May 21, 1992: Clair George is reindicted on two additional charges after three are dismissed with Independent Counsel's consent; George now faces nine felony charges.

May 25, 1992: Thomas Clines begins serving 16-month jail sentence.

June 16, 1992: Former Defense Secretary Caspar W. Weinberger is indicted on five felony charges of obstruction, perjury and false statements in congressional and Independent Counsel investigations.

June 24, 1992: Walsh issues Third Interim Report to Congress, stating that investigation is in its final phase and focusing on whether high-ranking Administration officials beginning in November 1986 tried to obstruct official investigations into the 1985 Iran arms sales.

July 13, 1992: *George* trial begins.

August 26, 1992: Mistrial declared in *George* case after jury fails to reach a verdict. Independent Counsel announces that the case will be retried.

Sept. 17, 1992: Walsh informs Chief Judge George MacKinnon, of the Independent Counsel appointing panel, and Attorney General William Barr that the investigation is complete barring unforeseen developments at the remaining trials.

Sept. 29, 1992: Judge Hogan dismisses Count 1, an obstruction of Congress charge, in the *Weinberger* case on grounds it does not conform to the *Poindexter* appeals ruling on the obstruction statute.

Oct. 19, 1992: *George* retrial on seven counts begins.

Oct. 30, 1992: Weinberger is re-indicted on a false statement charge, replacing the previously dismissed Count 1 obstruction charge.

Dec. 7, 1992: Supreme Court declines to review *Poindexter.*

Dec. 9, 1992: George is found guilty on two counts of false statements and perjury before Congress; sentencing is set for February 1993.

Dec. 11, 1992: Judge Hogan dismisses the new one-count indictment against Weinberger on statute of limitations grounds, leaving four charges remaining.

Dec. 11, 1992: White House informs Independent Counsel that President Bush has kept diaries relevant to Iran/contra, which have never been produced to investigators.

Dec. 24, 1992: President Bush pardons Weinberger, Clarridge, McFarlane, Fiers, Abrams and George. Independent Counsel denounces pardons.

Jan. 5, 1993: *Weinberger* trial was scheduled to begin.

Feb. 8, 1993: Independent Counsel issues Fourth Interim Report to Congress on the *Weinberger* case and the presidential pardons.

# Part III
# The Operational Conspiracy: A Legal Analysis

The central and perhaps the most important criminal charge developed by Independent Counsel was the conspiracy charge against Oliver L. North, John M. Poindexter, Richard V. Secord and Albert Hakim. According to that charge—set forth as Count One of the indictment returned on March 16, 1988—these four men conspired to defraud the United States by deceitfully (1) supporting a war in Nicaragua in defiance of congressional controls; (2) using the Iran arms sales to raise funds to be spent at the direction of North and Poindexter, rather than the United States Government; and (3) endangering the effort to rescue Americans held hostage in Lebanon by pursuing ends that were both unauthorized and inconsistent with the goal of releasing the hostages.[1]

The Reagan Administration was unambiguously hostile to this count. In a move that Judge Gerhard A. Gesell described as "unprecedented," the Justice Department in November 1988 filed an amicus brief supporting North's claim that the count was legally insufficient and should be dismissed.[2] Subsequently, having been informed by Independent Counsel that the conspiracy count could be tried only if a small amount of classified information were declassified, the Administration refused to release that information. Because there was no way to appeal such a refusal to declassify, Independent Counsel was forced in January 1989 to drop Count One in *North* and a related charge that

the diversion of profits from the Iran arms sales was a theft of Government funds.

Although Count One was not tried, it was established *as a matter of law* that if North, Poindexter, and the others had done what they were charged with doing, they had committed criminal acts. In rejecting the challenges of the Department of Justice and North, Judge Gesell ruled that the count "allege[d] [a] well-established offens[e]" and that the activity set forth in the count was criminal.[3] He stated: "The indictment clearly alleges a conspiracy which involved concealing the very existence of the profits of the enterprise from the start and hiding from Congress information relating to the conspirators' assistance for the Contras."[4] In addition to holding that the indictment set forth a crime, Judge Gesell also found that his review of the evidence presented to the Grand Jury indicated there was probable cause that that crime had in fact been committed.[5]

At the heart of the Iran/contra affair, then, were criminal acts of Reagan Administration officials that the Reagan Administration, by withholding non-secret classified information, ensured would never be tried. Yet Judge Gesell's decision marked an important, if incomplete, accomplishment of Independent Counsel. Judge Gesell's decision unambiguously established that high national security officials who engage in a conspiracy to subvert the laws of this country have engaged in criminal acts, even when the laws themselves provide no criminal sanctions.

---

[1] Count One charged a violation of 18 U.S.C. § 371. The bill of particulars in *North* stated that among the co-conspirators not indicted were National Security Adviser Robert C. McFarlane; CIA Station Chief Joseph F. Fernandez; Fawn Hall, North's secretary; and Robert Earl, North's assistant.

[2] *Memorandum of Law of the United States Filed by the Department of Justice as* Amicus Curiae *with Respect to the Independent Counsel's Opposition to the Defendant's Motions to Dismiss or Limit Count One* (filed November 18, 1988).

[3] *U.S.* v. *North,* 708 F. Supp. 375, 380 (1988).

[4] Ibid., p. 377.

[5] 698 F. Supp. 300, 315 ("The grand jury transcript and exhibits reflect solid proof and ample probable cause to indict on each and every count.").

A successful prosecution would have allowed Independent Counsel to present comprehensively the results of his investigation into the operational conspiracy. Much of the evidence of the conspiracy was presented at the trials of the dismembered individual charges of obstruction and false statements but the questions of intent were different, the diversion of funds from Iran to the contras was peripheral rather than central, and the absence of the conspiracy charge deprived the *North* case of its cohesiveness and completeness.

The following discussion is an attempt to present in an abbreviated fashion what would have been Independent Counsel's case at a conspiracy trial of North, Secord, Poindexter and Hakim, and an explanation of the criminal nature of their actions.

## Overview of Count One

In summary the proof would have shown three separate but intertwined activities, each specified in the indictment as an object of the conspiracy.

First, using Government resources, the conspirators conducted an unauthorized covert program in support of the contras. Because they feared that Congress would stop them if it knew of their activities and because they feared, as well, the political consequences of that exposure, they deceived Congress about the fact that they were providing this support. By so doing, the conspirators obstructed Congress's legitimate functions of regulating governmental expenditures and overseeing foreign covert actions.

Second, North and Poindexter used their Government positions to create a hidden slush fund under the exclusive control of the conspirators. This conflict of interest affected North and Poindexter's actions in numerous ways. On a mundane level, they permitted significant profits to be generated for the benefit of the private members of the conspiracy and less significant benefits to North. On a power-grabbing level, North—in order to increase the body of funds under his control for covert activities—used his position to drive down the amount that the U.S. Government received from the Iran arms sales and to inflate the amount that the Iranian purchasers paid the conspirators.

Third, by secretly pursuing their own ends, the conspirators outraged the Iranians they were attempting to persuade and thus jeopardized the success of the Iran initiative. In particular, the initiative's goals of establishing improved relations with Iran and securing the release of American hostages held by groups sympathetic to that country were jeopardized by the conspirators' private objective to overprice the weapons in order to secure additional proceeds for unauthorized purposes.

The following explanation of the charge of conspiracy to defraud brought against North, Poindexter, Secord, and Hakim begins with a brief discussion of what the crime of conspiracy to defraud the United States is. After that general explanation, each object of the conspiracy will be discussed: first, the evidence as to each object, and then why that object was criminal.

## Federal Conspiracy Law and Iran/contra

The federal conspiracy statute, 18 U.S.C. § 371, states that it is a crime to conspire to "defraud the United States, or any agency thereof in any manner or for any purpose. . . ." The attempt to carry out the three objectives described above—in other words, the attempt to interfere in a deceitful fashion with lawful governmental processes—constituted a classic conspiracy to defraud the United States. Almost a century of case law established that § 371 makes criminal deceitful schemes to obstruct the lawful functions of Government, either by defeating enforcement of legal restrictions or by using governmental authority to further illegitimate ends. Far from breaking new ground, Judge Gesell's ruling in *North* simply followed precedent. Fraud is criminal even when those who engage in the fraud are Government officials pursuing presidential policy.

The authoritative definition of the crime was set out by the Supreme Court almost 70 years ago in *Hammerschmidt* v. *United States*. In that case, Chief Justice Taft, speaking for a unanimous Court, stated:

To conspire to defraud the United States means primarily to cheat the government out of property or money, *but it also means to interfere with or obstruct one of its law-*

*ful governmental functions by deceit, craft or trickery, or at least by means that are dishonest.* It is not necessary that the Government shall be subjected to property or pecuniary loss by the fraud, but only that its legitimate official action and purpose shall be defeated by misrepresentation, chicane, or the overreaching of those charged with carrying out the governmental intention.[6]

Over the years the Supreme Court has frequently reaffirmed the validity of Chief Justice Taft's definition. For example, shortly before the Grand Jury indicted North and Poindexter, the Supreme Court in *McNally* v. *United States*[7] declared that § 371 barred deceitful interference with governmental operations. In that case, the Court declared that Congress specifically designed § 371 to protect not merely property rights, but the interests of the Government in fair administration of its functions for the benefit of the entire population.[8]

Section 371 extends beyond the traditional concept of a conspiracy as simply an agreement to commit a substantive crime. Early in this century, the Supreme Court held that a conspiracy to defraud the United States need not involve conduct that violates another independent criminal statute.[9] From the start of this century, the requisite element of fraud has been construed expansively so as to encompass not only a scheme to cheat the Government out of money, but also—in fact, especially—deceitful conduct aimed at obstructing the Government's ability to implement its programs, and to administer its affairs honestly and in accordance with the law.[10]

Similarly, in interpreting the mail and wire fraud statutes, courts repeatedly have found deceitful interference with governmental operations to be criminally fraudulent. For example, in *United States* v. *Diggs*,[11] the Court of Appeals upheld the wire fraud conviction of a congressman who had secretly used monies from his clerk-hire allowance to pay certain of his district office expenses. The Court stated that the Congressman did not have "*unfettered power to divert monies intended for one purpose to another, completely unauthorized purpose*," and concluded that by carrying out this secret diversion Diggs had "defrauded the public . . . of his faithful and honest services."[12]

Such basic principles of the law of conspiracy and the law of fraud were applied in an important case growing out of Watergate, *United States* v. *Haldeman*.[13] Three of President Nixon's closest advisers—Robert Haldeman, John Ehrlichman, and John Mitchell—were charged with conspiring to defraud the United States by, among other things, "attempting to get the CIA to interfere with the Watergate investigation being conducted by the FBI."[14] There was no hint in the case that they had been motivated by a desire to enrich themselves, and there was no criminal statute punishing Executive Branch officials for manipulating the Central Intelligence Agency for political reasons. Nonetheless, the Court of Appeals accepted that the Watergate conspirators' "misuse of the CIA" defrauded the United States because it denied the Government of its "right to have the officials of its departments and agencies transact their official business honestly and impartially, free from corruption, fraud, improper and undue influence, dishonesty and obstruction."[15]

In short, long before Iran/contra, it had been established beyond question that deceptive schemes to prevent the enforcement of civil statutes or other Government policies reflected in law—whatever form such schemes may

---

[6] 265 U.S. 182, 188 (1924) (emphasis added).

[7] 107 S. Ct. 2875 (1987).

[8] Ibid., at 2881 n.8, quoting *Curley* v. *United States*, 130 F. 1, 7 (1st Cir.), *cert. denied*, 195 U.S. 628 (1904). See also *Dennis* v. *United States*, 384 U.S. 855, 861 (1966) ("It has long been established that this statutory language is not confined to fraud as that term has been defined in the common law. It reaches 'any conspiracy for the purpose of impairing, obstructing, or defeating the lawful function of any department of government.' ") (quoting *Haas* v. *Henkel*, 216 U.S. 462, 479 (1910)); *United States* v. *Johnson*, 383 U.S. 169, 172 (1966); *Lutwak* v. *United States*, 344 U.S. 604 (1953); *Glasser* v. *United States*, 315 U.S. 60, 66 (1942).

[9] See, for example, *United States* v. *Keitel*, 211 U.S. 370, 393 (1908).

[10] See, for example, *Curley* v. *United States*, 130 F. 1, 9–10 (1st Cir.), *cert. denied*, 195 U.S. 628 (1904).

[11] 613 F.2d 988 (D.C. Cir. 1979), *cert. denied*, 446 U.S. 982 (1980).

[12] Ibid., at 995, 998 (emphasis in the original). While the Supreme Court in *McNally* rejected the theory on which cases such as *Diggs* had been prosecuted, the Court emphatically did *not* conclude that the conduct in those cases was not fraudulent; rather, its holding was based solely on the history of the mail fraud statute, which the Court determined was "limited in scope to the protection of property rights." 107 S.Ct. 2875, 2882. As pointed out above, the *McNally* Court was careful to distinguish § 371 cases brought on the same theory that was rejected as to § 1341 in *McNally*. Mail fraud cases brought under this theory thus remain persuasive authority in interpreting § 371.

[13] 559 F.2d 31 (D.C. Cir. 1976), *cert. denied*, 431 U.S. 933 (1977).

[14] Ibid. (quoting jury instructions).

[15] Ibid., at 122 & n.255 (quoting jury instruction).

take—fall squarely within the ambit of the crime of conspiracy to defraud the United States. The teaching of *Hammerschmidt* and its progeny can be reduced to the following: It constitutes fraud within the meaning of 18 U.S.C. § 371 to breach the public trust by agreeing, through deceitful or dishonest means, to prevent the Government from conducting its operations and implementing its policies honestly and faithfully, and in accordance with applicable legal constraints and guidelines.

Under *Hammerschmidt* and the cases that followed it, a conspiracy must have two elements. First, it must involve "interfere[nce] with or obstruct[ion of a] lawful governmental function[]. . . ." [16] The ways in which Poindexter, North, Secord and Hakim interfered with governmental functions are spelled out in more detail below. The secret contra war activity obstructed Congress's control of the appropriations process and its oversight of covert operations. North and Poindexter's self-dealing defeated the public's right to have Government officers pursue officially sanctioned ends, rather than inconsistent private ends.

The second element of a criminal conspiracy is that the interference with governmental operations must be accomplished by deceit. In the absence of deceit, an agreement to interfere with governmental operations is not a conspiracy to defraud the United States, although it may constitute some other crime. The conspiracy charged by Independent Counsel involved activities that were shielded by a campaign of lies and deceptions from Government officials who could have disagreed with those activities and might have sought to stop them. It was that deceit which, in Independent Counsel's opinion, made the conspiracy criminal. Over the objections of North and the Reagan Justice Department, Judge Gesell, in the only definitive judicial statement on Iran/contra and the conspiracy law, found that Independent Counsel's view was right.

There follows an abbreviated presentation of the evidence that would have supported the conspiracy charge. First, the secret support of the contras; second, the self dealing diversion; and third, the corruption of President Reagan's Iranian initiative.

---

[16] 265 U.S. 182, 188.

## First Object of the Conspiracy: The Secret War Activities

The crux of the first charged object of the conspiracy was an agreement to provide military assistance to the Nicaraguan contras and to deceive Congress about the fact that support was being provided.[17] Poindexter, North, and their co-conspirators carried out their "secret war" in a way calculated to defeat legal restrictions governing the conduct of military and covert operations and congressional control of appropriations, and they concealed their activities from legitimate congressional oversight.

Had the case been tried as indicted, the Government's proof of U.S. secret war activities would have fallen into three broad categories: (1) the organization and direction of a resupply operation to provide the contras with logistical and other support; (2) funding of the resupply operation, including exploitation of the Iran initiative; and (3) attempts to conceal from Congress the conspirators' involvement in these activities.

### The Evidence

#### Organization and Direction of the Resupply Network

During the last half of 1984 and the first half of 1985, North had developed a loose structure for contra support. Secord, responding to contra requests through North, was selling arms. Thomas G. Clines, a Secord associate, arranged for their purchase; Hakim, assisted by Swiss money manager Willard I. Zucker, set up the structure to finance the activities with funds provided to the contras through North and raised primarily by President Reagan and National Security Adviser Robert C. McFarlane.

The creation of the conspirators' more tightly organized secret resupply network dated from

---

[17] Paragraph 13(a)(1) of Count One stated that the conspirators sought to defraud the United States:

> by impeding, impairing, defeating and obstructing the lawful governmental functions of the United States, including compliance with legal restrictions governing the conduct of military and covert action activities and congressional control of appropriations and exercise of oversight for such activities, by deceitfully and without legal authorization organizing, directing and concealing a program to continue the funding of and logistical and other support for military and paramilitary operations in Nicaragua by the Contras, at a time when the prohibitions of the Boland Amendment and other legal restrictions on the execution of covert actions were in effect.

a June 28, 1985, meeting in Miami, Florida. This meeting was attended by, among others, North, Adolfo Calero (political leader of one contra faction known as the FDN), Enrique Bermudez (commander of the FDN's military forces), Secord, Clines and Rafael Quintero, an associate of Secord. At the Miami meeting, North informed Calero and Bermudez that the contras would no longer be left to decide what arms they would purchase or from whom they would buy them. In the future, North would provide the contras with materiel, and Secord would deliver it to the contras in the field. In addition, North directed that actions be taken to develop and resupply a "southern front" along the border of Costa Rica and Nicaragua.

Following the Miami meeting, North assumed a central role in the contra war effort. Using Robert W. Owen as a courier, North provided the contras with significant military advice and guidance. At the same time, with the assistance of Secord, North in the following fashion secretly brought into being the resupply operation that he had described on June 28.

*First,* North directed Owen and William Haskell, another North courier, to travel to Costa Rica and help activate a southern military front. Owen and Haskell, aided by CIA Costa Rican Station Chief Joseph F. Fernandez, undertook to build a clandestine airstrip to be used to resupply it. Haskell eventually negotiated the acquisition of property for the strip, which was funded using Swiss accounts controlled directly by Secord and Hakim, and indirectly by North. Within the United States, North attended planning sessions and personally commissioned private individuals to do preliminary site work and engineering tasks necessary for the construction of a usable airstrip.

North arranged for Haskell and Owen to be introduced to Fernandez. Fernandez minimized and concealed from his superiors at the CIA the true nature of his contacts with North and North's private representatives. Fernandez and North eventually developed a secret communications network using National Security Agency (NSA)-supplied KL–43 encryption devices, outside normal CIA communications channels. In addition, telephone records show over 100 calls from Fernandez to North during the period August 1985 until November 1986. Under the

direction of North, Fernandez and U.S. Ambassador to Costa Rica Lewis A. Tambs used their influence as representatives of the United States to obtain the support of senior Costa Rican officials for the airstrip project.

*Second,* North directed Secord to purchase aircraft capable of resupplying contra forces. From January to August 1986, private parties working on behalf of North and Secord purchased four military aircraft costing approximately $1.8 million, as well as additional equipment for operation of these aircraft. The funds for these purchases came from Hakim and Secord's secret Swiss bank accounts.

North took an active part in the purchase of the aircraft. He reviewed and approved a technical proposal for the resupply organization solicited by Secord from Richard B. Gadd, a Secord associate. North and Secord then directed Gadd in November 1985 to approach the Government of Venezuela in an unsuccessful attempt to purchase military aircraft. North used his influence as a Government official to vouch for Gadd's *bona fides* with the government of Venezuela. Similarly, North exercised final approval on major expenditures for equipment. In January 1986, North personally directed Secord to provide Gadd with over $100,000 for anticipated costs. Later in 1986, North directed Secord to purchase a package of spare parts required by the resupply operation that cost in excess of $200,000. North personally approved the purchase of a fourth military aircraft in August 1986 at a cost of $250,000. When there was a dispute between Gadd and Secord as to the ownership of the aircraft, North resolved it in favor of Secord's Enterprise.

*Third,* North secretly undertook to obtain the use of Ilopango air base in El Salvador for his resupply operation. In a letter dated September 20, 1985, North requested that Felix Rodriguez, an American citizen with close ties to the commander of the Salvadoran Air Force, solicit permission to use the base for his resupply operation. North gave Rodriguez a code name for a representative of Secord who would be assigned there.[18] In December 1985, Secord's assistant in charge of Central Amer-

---

[18] In that letter, North explicitly directed Rodriguez *not* to advise a particular CIA official of the proposed resupply project. North advised Rodriguez, "AFTER READING THIS LETTER PLEASE DESTROY IT." (Letter from North to Rodriguez, 9/20/85, AKW 022740.)

ican operations, Quintero, using that code name, obtained through Rodriguez the consent of the commanding officer.

*Fourth*, at North's instruction, Secord through Clines purchased in Europe and delivered to Central America thousands of pounds of arms from December 1985 to September 1986. The cost of purchase and transport of these arms was paid from the secret Swiss accounts.

*Fifth*, North, with the assistance of Secord, secretly directed the actual administration of the resupply project during 1986. Secord hired first Gadd and then Robert Dutton as project managers. Gadd and Dutton, through the corporation Amalgamated Commercial Enterprises (ACE), in turn hired numerous other employees. By the summer of 1986, the resupply operation had over 20 full-time employees whose combined salaries totalled over $60,000 per month. The cost of equipment and salaries for the operation was paid from the Enterprise's secret Swiss accounts.

The activities at the Ilopango air base were supervised by Quintero for Secord. Rodriguez served as liaison with the base commander, General Juan Rafael Bustillo. Additional assistance and supervision was provided by the military group detailed to the U.S. Embassy in El Salvador.

Gadd and Dutton reported directly to Secord. At the same time, they had frequent—often daily—contact with North, from whom they accepted guidance and direction. North frequently gave them orders regarding specific operations, usually in order to accelerate resupply drops to the contras.

In April 1986, for example, North commandeered an aircraft provided to the State Department's Nicaraguan Humanitarian Assistance Office (NHAO) by Southern Air Transport (SAT) for the delivery of U.S.-approved humanitarian supplies to Ilopango. SAT was also an Enterprise subcontractor for the delivery of weapons. Contrary to SAT's contract with NHAO and the legal limits on the U.S. humanitarian activities, North directed the aircraft to drop a load of weapons to the southern front of Nicaragua. North was able to accomplish this because the aircraft was being leased by Gadd, pursuant to Gadd's State Department contract (which North had helped Gadd obtain) for

delivery of humanitarian aid. North personally coordinated planning of this operation with Secord and Fernandez and Enterprise representatives at Ilopango using their network of KL-43 communication devices.

Later in April 1986, it was North and Secord who secretly met at Ilopango with Salvadoran and contra military leaders, as well as personnel of the U.S. Embassy, to resolve disputes regarding the resupply operation and its disappointing lack of success. Contra leaders criticized the quality of the aircraft being used and requested funds with which to purchase their own aircraft. North responded that the aircraft had been donated and that funds were unavailable to purchase alternative aircraft.

Under North's and Secord's direction, the resupply operation in 1986 improved and ultimately delivered to the contras in the field in Nicaragua thousands of pounds of arms previously purchased by Secord. North generally received detailed inventories of the lethal supplies provided contra forces. The resupply operation also delivered substantial quantities of nonlethal aid and engaged in projects such as training contra forces in the use of explosives. These operational activities of the Enterprise ended in early October 1986 when an Enterprise aircraft was shot down over Nicaragua, killing three crew members and leading to the capture of Eugene Hasenfus, an American who told his Nicaraguan captors that he was working for the CIA.

## Funding of the Resupply Operation

Funds for the secret war came primarily from three sources: (a) the National Endowment for the Preservation of Liberty (NEPL); (b) the Iran arms sales; and (c) foreign governments. As set forth in the "Flow of Funds" chapter of this Report, the total amount of funds deposited in Enterprise accounts in Switzerland was $47.6 million. By the time the Iran/contra affair became public, the Enterprise had given to the contras or had spent on efforts related to the contras approximately $17.6 million of these funds.

## Foreign Donations

From December 1984 through July 1985, the contras paid into Enterprise accounts approximately $11.3 million for a variety of services and goods. Most of these funds came from the Saudis, who contributed $32 million in 1984 and 1985. The Saudi funds were nearly exhausted by mid-1985.

After North held his June meeting in Miami, the contras were no longer the direct recipient of such funds. Thereafter, the conspirators directed to Enterprise bank accounts all funds from third countries that had been solicited by U.S. officials on behalf of the contras, even though some of them had been restricted for only humanitarian purposes.

In August 1985, North asked Gaston Sigur, an NSC staff officer, to arrange a meeting between North and an official of the Taiwanese government for the purpose of soliciting funds for the contras. Following this meeting, North had Sigur confirm the decision by Taiwan to provide the contras with $1 million. North then directed Robert Owen to deliver an envelope containing the number of an Enterprise account to the Taiwanese official. On September 20, 1985, $1 million was received by the Enterprise. In late 1985, North renewed his request, via Sigur, that Taiwan provide additional funds to the contras. In February 1986, a second transfer of $1 million was received in an Enterprise account.

Similarly, in June 1986, when the State Department planned to raise $10 million for the contras from the Sultan of Brunei, North undertook to divert the funds to the Enterprise by giving one of its Swiss account numbers to Assistant Secretary of State Elliott Abrams. Fawn Hall, North's secretary, apparently made a transcription error in the account number so the funds were misdirected and never received.

On November 20, 1985, the Enterprise received $1 million from the government of Israel to pay the Enterprise for transporting a number of shipments of weapons from Israel to Iran. That weapons transfer was abandoned after the first shipment. The Enterprise's expenses for that shipment were less than $200,000, but the Enterprise kept the balance.

## NEPL

Beginning in the spring of 1985, North, working primarily with Carl R. "Spitz" Channell, the president of NEPL, arranged for this tax-exempt organization to sponsor briefings and receptions designed in part to raise

funds for the contras. North gave briefings at the White House and the Old Executive Office Building (OEOB) for audiences of prospective contributors concerning the war in Nicaragua and the needs of the contras. To assist Channell in his solicitation of purportedly tax-deductible contributions, North identified specific military and other needs of the contras.

In addition to general briefings for groups of contributors, Channell, his assistant Daniel Conrad, and their business associate Richard R. Miller of International Business Communications (IBC), arranged private briefings by North to individual prospective contributors. The private briefings were given from June 1985 to late September 1986 in a variety of locations, including North's office at the OEOB. Prior to some of these briefings, Channell or Conrad advised North of the amount of money that would be solicited from a particular contributor immediately following the private meeting. North would then include in some of his briefings a discussion of the need for specific pieces of military equipment and their cost, knowing that contributors to whom this information was provided would be immediately solicited to purchase the items he had discussed.

North thanked those who gave contributions to NEPL, either in person, by telephone, or in writing on official NSC stationery. As further inducement to contribute to NEPL, North and Channell told some prospective contributors that, if they donated a specified amount to the contras, they would be given private meetings and photo opportunities with the President. North and Channell arranged several such meetings between contributors and President Reagan.

Between June 1, 1985, and November 25, 1986, North and his NEPL partners raised approximately $6.3 million for the contras, and transferred $3.3 million to Calero and to the Enterprise for contra expenses. To conceal both the source of this money and his own participation, North personally directed that approximately $1.7 million be transferred from NEPL through IBC to corporate bank accounts in the Cayman Islands, and then ultimately to Enterprise bank accounts in Switzerland.

## Exploitation of the Iran Arms Sales

The Iran arms sales were the major source of the Enterprise's funds for the secret war activities. In all, the Enterprise received slightly more than $30 million for the sale of Government arms and returned only $12.2 million to the United States. At least $3.6 million was to fund the Enterprise's resupply operation in support of the contras.

## Concealment

Soon after the June 1985 meeting in Miami, a series of congressional inquiries sought to determine exactly what the U.S. Government, and North in particular, were doing on behalf of the contras. McFarlane, Poindexter and North responded by actively deceiving committees of Congress with a series of false statements and by other efforts to ensure that Congress would never find out about the secret contra military support.

The first false statements came in McFarlane's September 5, 1985, letter to the House Permanent Select Committee on Intelligence, a letter on which McFarlane, Poindexter, and North all worked. The letter contained false denials of North's fund-raising activities and his provision of tactical advice to the contras, as well as a false assurance that no one on the NSC staff had "violate[d] the letter or spirit" of the Boland prohibition on military aid. September 12, 1985, and October 7, 1985, letters under McFarlane's signature, both jointly drafted by North and McFarlane, contained similar false statements.

McFarlane's replacement by Poindexter as national security adviser on December 4, 1985, did not alter the pattern of deceit. North continued to work to prevent dissemination of information about his activities. On June 16, 1986, North sent Fernandez a KL–43 message that stated in part:

> I do not think we ought to contemplate these operations without [Quintero] being on scene. Too many things go wrong that then directly involve you and me in what should be deniable for both of us.[19]

On May 15, 1986, Poindexter sent this computer message to North:

> I am afraid you are letting your operational role become too public. From now on I don't want you to talk to anybody else,

including Casey, except me about any of your operational roles. In fact you need to generate a cover story that I have insisted that you stop.[20]

North responded to Poindexter on the same day with a computer note that said "Done." North subsequently had Robert Dutton inform Enterprise employees in El Salvador that the resupply operation had been taken over by a new entity known as "B.C. Washington."[21]

In the summer of 1986, Congress renewed its inquiries. On July 21, 1986, responding to a House resolution of inquiry, Poindexter sent letters to two committee chairmen, stating that McFarlane's 1985 letters to Congress accurately described the activities of the NSC staff. When members of the House Intelligence Committee questioned North in person, he falsely denied his contra-support activities.

The deception continued after one of the resupply organization's planes carrying Hasenfus was shot down in October 1986. Congress was about to authorize resumption of contra support by the CIA, with an appropriation of $100 million. Administration officials denied any connection with the aircraft. In October and November 1986, North altered, destroyed, and removed documents and official records relating to the resupply operation. On November 23, 1986, he lied to the attorney general to conceal Secord's operation and his own responsibility in directing the secret resupply activities and the control of the funds used to finance them. Between November 22 and 29, 1986, Poindexter unsuccessfully tried to delete from the White House computer system all of his communications with North. Finally, on December 8, 1986, McFarlane told the House Foreign Affairs Committee that he was unaware that the government or citizens of Saudi Arabia had been involved in financing the contras.

## The Secret War Activities as a Conspiracy to Defraud the United States

The contra-support activities of the conspirators were charged as criminal because they were

---

[19] KL–43 Message from North to Fernandez, 6/16/86, AKW 004389.

[20] PROFs Note from Poindexter to North, 5/15/86, AKW 021378.
[21] Nevertheless, on June 10, 1986, Poindexter reminded North via computer: "I still want you to reduce you visibility." (PROFs Note from Poindexter to North, 6/11/86, AKW 021426–27.)

designed to deceive Congress and to obstruct and frustrate Congress's constitutional powers. The essence of the crime was not the provision of support for the contras *per se*, nor were the conspirators charged simply with conspiring to violate the Boland Amendment as such. Rather, the essence of the crime was the deceit of Congress. In the language of the indictment, North violated § 371 not simply by agreeing to "organiz[e]" and "direct[]" the program of military support for the contras, but by agreeing to organize and direct the program *"deceitfully and without legal authorization,"* and by *"concealing"* that program (emphasis added). In other words, what the conspirators did was criminal because United States Government support of the contras was a matter within congressional oversight and a matter that Congress could legitimately legislate about and because the conspirators used fraud to keep Congress from discharging these responsibilities.

In particular, the conspirators' plan to fund the contras and keep Congress from finding out about that funding interfered with governmental functions in two ways specified in the indictment: by contravening specific "legal restrictions governing the conduct of military and covert action activities" and more generally by defeating "congressional control of appropriations and exercise of oversight for such activities."

### Legal Restrictions on Covert Action

In recent years, spurred by revelations of controversial covert actions undertaken without suficient accountability, Congress and the President have erected a complex web of restrictions, rules, and notification requirements to assure that past abuses by our intelligence agencies are not repeated. Congress has also enacted specific restrictions on covert action in particular regions.[22] The most pertinent of these restrictions is, of course, the Boland Amendment, which essentially prohibited expenditure of U.S. funds in support of the contras. But the Boland Amendment must be understood in the context of the entire system of restrictions on covert action adopted since 1970.

Responding to "allegations of substantial, even massive wrong-doing within the 'national intelligence' system," the special Senate investigating committee known as the Church Committee found in 1976 that "presidents and administrations have made excessive, and at times self-defeating, use of covert action," and that these uses were in large part attributable to Congress's "fail[ure] to provide the necessary statutory guidelines to carry out their necessary missions in accord with constitutional processes."[23]

Recognizing that covert action remained necessary in "extraordinary circumstances involving grave threats to U.S. national security," and that the nature of covert action made it impossible to "assur[e] public participation in assessing each covert action," the Church Committee was insistent that "the mechanisms of executive branch review and control and of legislative intelligence oversight must serve" to prevent abuses of covert action.[24] The result of the Church Committee's 18-month investigation was a series of interlocking restrictions on covert actions that, in combination, required that significant covert actions be supported by an explicit presidential authorization and reported to the relevant congressional oversight committees.

At the time of the Iran/contra operational conspiracy, the central pillars of this structure were the Hughes-Ryan Amendment of 1974 and Executive Order 12333, as supplemented by National Security Decision Directive 159. The Hughes-Ryan Amendment, responding to the same revelations of "excessive" and "self-defeating" use of covert action that led to the creation of the Church Committee, prohibited expenditure of funds to support covert action operations by the CIA abroad

> unless and until the President finds that each such operation is important to the national security of the United States and reports, in a timely fashion, a description

---

[22] In addition to the various versions of the Boland Amendment, discussed below, see, for example, the congressional cut-off of funding for military actions in Angola (the "Clark Amendment," P.L. 94–329, Title IV, § 404, 90 Stat. 757 (1976), 22 U.S.C. § 2293 note) and Cambodia (P.L. 93–51, 87 Stat. 134 (1973)).

[23] U.S. Senate Select Committee to Study Governmental Operations With Respect to Intelligence Activities, Final Report, Book I: Foreign and Military Intelligence, S.Rep. No. 755, 94th Cong., 2d Sess. 1, 425 (1976) (hereafter, "Church Committee Report").

[24] Ibid., pp. 446–47.

and scope of such operation to the appro-priate committees of the Congress. . . .25

The remedy of the Amendment was to require (1) formal approval and certification by the President—thus preserving political and legal accountability by the President for covert ac-tion—and (2) the provision of timely informa-tion to the Congress so that it can oversee and, if necessary, take action concerning, such covert activity.

While the Hughes-Ryan Amendment initially applied only to the CIA, in 1980, Congress modified Hughes-Ryan. It left intact the limita-tion of the Finding requirement to CIA covert activities.26 But it recodified the congressional-notification requirement as part of the newly enacted 50 U.S.C. § 413. Between 1984 and 1986, § 413 required that appropriate congres-sional authorities be "informed of all intel-ligence activities which are the responsibility of, are engaged in by, or are carried out for or on behalf of, *any* department, agency, or entity of the United States," and thus imposes a reporting requirement for both CIA and non-CIA covert operations.27

In addition to these statutes, executive or-ders—most recently Executive Order 12333—have long forbidden Government agencies other than the CIA from carrying out covert actions unless there is a presidential determination that the use of some agency other than the CIA "is more likely to achieve a particular objec-tive." 28 National Security Decision Directive 159 requires that this determination be in writ-ing. Since the Executive Branch is required to keep the intelligence oversight committees of the Congress "fully and currently informed of all intelligence activities which are the respon-sibility of, are engaged in by, or are carried out for or on behalf of, *any* department, agency, or entity of the United States," 29 these execu-tive orders have given Congress an additional

means of keeping itself informed of covert ac-tivities in the Executive Branch.

Taking the Hughes-Ryan Amendment and Executive Order 12333 together, the law gov-erning accountability for covert action is clear: Personal presidential accountability and report-ing to Congress are the rule for all covert ac-tions.

In addition to this basic structure of restric-tions on covert military actions, Congress placed additional limitations on covert assist-ance to the contras in Nicaragua, principally through a series of laws known as the "Boland Amendments." They are relevant primarily as the law the conspirators were determined to evade.

There were four different versions of the Bo-land Amendment in the years 1982–1986. Only the last two applied during the period relevant to Count One. Section 8066(a) of the Depart-ment of Defense Appropriations Bill, enacted in the Further Continuing Appropriations Act of 1985,30 was in effect from October 12, 1984, to December 19, 1985. It provided:

> During fiscal year 1985, no funds available to the Central Intelligence Agency, the De-partment of Defense, or any other agency or entity of the United States involved in intelligence activities may be obligated or expended for the purpose or which would have the effect of supporting, directly or indirectly, military or paramilitary oper-ations in Nicaragua by any nation, group, organization, movement or individual.

The second relevant Boland Amendment was enacted on December 4, 1985, as part of the Intelligence Authorization Act for fiscal year 1986.31 In effect until October 18, 1986, this statute provided:

> Funds available to the Central Intelligence Agency, the Department of Defense, or any other agency or entity of the United States involved in intelligence activities may be obligated and expended during fiscal year 1986 to provide funds, materiel, or other assistance to the Nicaraguan democratic re-sistance to support military or paramilitary operations in Nicaragua only as authorized

---

25 P.L. 93–559, § 32, 88 Stat. 1804.
26 22 U.S.C. § 2422. (Repealed by 8/14/91, P.L. 102–88, Title VI, § 601, 105 Stat. 441.)
27 50 U.S.C. § 413(a)(1) (1982).
28 The version of this prohibition in effect at all times relevant to Count One is found in Part 1.8(e) of Executive Order 12333, 46 Fed. Reg. 59941, 59945 (Dec. 4, 1981). Similar restrictions have applied since President Carter promulgated Executive Order 12036, 43 Fed. Reg. 3674 (1978).
29 50 U.S.C. § 413(a)(1) (1982) (emphasis added).

30 P.L. 98–473.
31 P.L. 99–169.

in section 101 and as specified in the classified Schedule of Authorizations referred to in section 102, or pursuant to section 502 of the National Security Act of 1947, or to section 106 of the Supplemental Appropriations Act, 1985 (P.L. 99–88).

The "classified schedule" authorized a limited amount of funds for communications equipment and communication training for the contras.[32] Neither the classified schedule nor any of the statutes enumerated permitted the provision by the Government of lethal materiel for the contras' military or paramilitary efforts. The Boland Amendments were always provisions in appropriation acts. They did not provide for criminal sanctions.

While the two versions of the Boland Amendment differed slightly, they shared a common purpose: Congress clearly intended to oversee U.S. support for contra military operations, to limit the amount spent on such assistance and, indeed, during certain periods relevant to this indictment, to prohibit such assistance entirely. As Representative Boland, the principal sponsor of the Amendment, explained during the final debate for the fiscal year 1985 Boland Amendment, it did not leave open loopholes for covert U.S. support for the contras. Congressman Boland stated that the Amendment "clearly ends U.S. support for the war in Nicaragua. . . . There are no exceptions to the prohibitions." [33]

While the activities of the conspirators fell within the prohibitions of the Boland Amendment, its precise interpretation was not critical to the criminality of the conspiratorial objective charged in Count One. Rather, the indictment charged that the defendants conspired to defraud the United States "by . . . obstructing the lawful government functions of the United States, including compliance with legal restrictions governing the conduct of military and covert action activities." The crux of the crime of conspiracy to defraud the United States, as the cases cited earlier make clear, is *not* a conspiracy to *violate* some particular provision of law. The essence of the crime, rather, is to "*interfere with or obstruct* one of [the Government's] lawful governmental functions by *deceit, craft or trickery. . . .*" [34]

Even if the conspirators' actions somehow had fallen within a loophole in the Boland Amendment, the entire operation of the Enterprise to support the contras was deliberately designed to defeat the restrictions on covert action Congress had enacted to prevent its "excessive" and "self-defeating" abuse. The Enterprise, under the direction of the NSC staff, provided support for the military and paramilitary activities of the contras outside the CIA, without the presidential Finding required by Executive Order 12333 or the reporting to congressional intelligence committees required by 50 U.S.C. § 413. To the extent that CIA resources were coopted by the Enterprise for use in this venture, that too was done without a presidential Finding, as required by the Hughes-Ryan Amendment. And, of course, the entire funding operation was at best a deliberate and deceptive attempt to evade the plain intent of the Boland Amendment.

Against this extensive background of congressional investigation, legislation and Executive action to control and limit covert action in general, and covert military support for the Nicaraguan contras in particular, the system of preserving presidential accountability and congressional oversight over covert action constituted a lawful function of the United States. The Boland Amendment, moreover, shows at the very least that Congress had expressed its interest in strictly supervising covert action in Nicaragua as an exercise of that function. North was one of the NSC team making drafting suggestions to Congress to liberalize Boland. The conspirators were fully aware of Congress's efforts to exercise its oversight function, and the danger of serious retaliation, including the end of all hopes for congressional support for the contras. Accordingly, they deliberately did their utmost to defeat the system by deceitfully concealing

---

[32] In addition to the communication equipment and training, the 1986 Intelligence Authorization Act permitted United States employees to provide "advice" to the contras, including advice on the "effective delivery and distribution of materiel." (Senator Durenberger, 131 Cong. Rec. S16074 (1985).) However, the agencies could not "engage in activities . . . that actually amount to participation in the planning or execution of military or paramilitary operations in Nicaragua by the Nicaraguan democratic resistance, or to participation in logistics activities integral to such operations." (H.R. Rep. 373, 99th Cong., 1st Sess. at 16 (1985).)

[33] 130 Cong. Rec. H11980 (1984).

[34] Hammerschmidt, 265 U.S. at 188.

their operation from Congress, and acting without a formal presidential Finding.

## Congress's Appropriations and Oversight Functions

The second way in which the secret contra-support efforts interfered with governmental functions is that they denied Congress its legitimate role of regulating Government expenditures and of overseeing covert activities.

Our constitutional order emphatically reserves the powers of taxing and spending to Congress. That "the power of the purse belongs to Congress" is fundamental to our system of government.[35] The Appropriations Clause of the Constitution[36] provides that "No Money shall be drawn from the Treasury, but in Consequence of Appropriations made by Law"—thus guaranteeing that money may not be spent for purposes that have not been approved by the representatives of the people. The Boland and Hughes-Ryan Amendments are specific exercises of Congress's power to deny funds to programs disapproved by Congress.

But Congress also has a broader responsibility in foreign affairs. No less an authority than James Madison argued that Congress had plenary authority over foreign affairs.[37] The conspiracy charge was not, however, premised on such an extreme position. It was based instead on the uncontrovertible and non-controversial proposition that Congress has *some* role to play in foreign affairs.

The congressional powers to regulate foreign commerce,[38] to define offenses against international law,[39] to raise and support armies,[40] and to tax and spend "for [the] common de-

fense,"[41] make it apparent that Congress has a major role to play in defining foreign policy cooperatively with the President. Although Congress has not prohibited covert foreign operations, it has put in place requirements of reporting and accountability that enable it to exercise substantial control over particular operations when necessary.[42] The Constitution provides Congress with a key role in determining whether resources should be committed to foreign adventures, such as those engaged in by the Iran/contra conspirators.

Congress thus has a right as part of its oversight function to demand information about covert activities. It also has a right as part of its appropriations function to deny funding to covert activities. Both functions were impaired by the actions of the Iran/contra conspirators. In other words, Congress's powers are impaired not merely when Government officials deceitfully fund foreign military activities that Congress has specifically refused to fund (as was the case with the Boland Amendment); Congress's powers are also impaired when Government officials deceitfully fund and conduct foreign military activities *and* scheme to prevent their actions from coming to congressional attention by fraud, concealment, deception and disinformation.

Thus, even if it were the case that the conspirators in some way avoided violating both the Boland Amendment and the specific legal controls over covert action, the broader problem with their deceitful activities would have remained: The conspirators, aware of statutory efforts to limit and allow Congress to monitor funding for the military operations of the contras, chose to hide their activities from Congress—with the aim of ensuring that Congress would not have the opportunity to consider whether to close such a loophole. The entire point of their pattern of deceit and evasion, Count One charged, was to defraud the United States by acting unilaterally and thereby thwarting the normal processes of constitutional government.

---

[35] L. Tribe, *American Constitutional Law* 256 (1988).

[36] Article I, § 9, cl. 7.

[37] 6 J. Madison, *Writings*, 138, 147–50 (Hunt ed. 1910), cited in L. Henkin, *Foreign Affairs and the Constitution*, pp. 82–83 (1972). As Professor Henkin summarizes Madison's argument:

> Basically, . . . Congress is the principal organ of government and has all its political authority, in foreign affairs as elsewhere, except that specifically granted to the President (alone or with the Senate). The determination of foreign policy and the control of foreign relations lay with Congress under the Articles of Confederation and, with particularized exceptions, the Constitution left them there. The powers of Congress are not limited to domestic "law-making," narrowly conceived: witness, to Congress is expressly given the most important foreign affairs power, the power to declare war. . . .

(Ibid.)

[38] Art. I, § 8, cl.3.

[39] Ibid., cl. 10.

[40] Ibid., cl. 12.

[41] Ibid., cl. 1.

[42] 22 U.S.C. § 2422 (Repealed by 8/14/91, P.L. 102–88, Title VI, § 601, 105 Stat. 441); 50 U.S.C. § 413 (1982).

## The Boland Amendment was Violated

The applicability of Boland to the actions of North and others was an issue of importance when the Iran/contra affair became public. The majority and minority reports of the Select Committees reached opposing conclusions as to whether Boland had been violated.[43]

As previously noted, the conspirators were not charged with having conspired to violate the Boland Amendment. Nonetheless, it is clear that the conspirators did violate that statute. As Independent Counsel argued prior to the *North* trial,[44] Independent Counsel could as a matter of law have framed the conspiracy charge in that fashion, and its evidence at trial would have proved that the conspirators violated the Boland Amendment.

More to the point, the Boland Amendment entered into the conspirators' motivations for lying to Congress: It was certainly the critical part of the statutory framework that they were either violating or evading. It was central to the statements of both McFarlane and Poindexter to Congress that the NSC staff was in compliance with both the "spirit and the letter" of Boland.

While the Boland Amendment went through four versions, the relevant statutory language was clear and never changed. Many of the activities in which the conspirators engaged—including provision of weapons and funding for weapons, strategic and tactical advice about the conduct of military operations, and supervision of the Enterprise's resupply efforts—were unambiguously prohibited to those entities covered by the Amendment.[45] The description of its breadth of application did not change at all in the period covered by Count One. Both versions of the Boland Amendment in effect from October 12, 1984, to October 18, 1986, expressly applied to the Central Intelligence Agency, the Department of Defense, and "any other agency or entity of the United States involved in intelligence activities." [46]

The Select Committees' disagreement centered on whether the NSC was covered by the Amendment. In determining, however, whether there was a conspiracy to violate the Boland Amendment, that question need not be reached, for two reasons. First, the Boland Amendment explicitly covered the CIA, and co-conspirator Fernandez, as the station chief in Costa Rica, was a CIA employee. His activities are discussed in greater detail elsewhere in this Report, but in short, by his efforts to facilitate construction of a clandestine airstrip in Costa Rica for contra resupply, his promises to contra leaders of military supplies, and his role in carrying out those promises, Fernandez—on instructions from North—did precisely what he was barred from doing by Boland.

Second, North himself was covered, since his salary was paid by the Department of Defense, another entity specified by the Boland Amendment. The legislative history of the Boland Amendment clearly explains that its prohibitions applied to *all* Defense Department funds—including those used to pay salaries.[47]

More broadly, the NSC itself was covered. The critical question was whether the NSC was covered as an "entity of the United States involved in intelligence activities." The NSC was such an entity. The National Security Act of 1947, the statute that created the NSC,[48] charges it to "assess and appraise the objectives, commitments, and risks of the United States in relation to our actual and potential military power, in the interest of national security. . ."—virtually a definition of strategic intelligence.[49] More specifically, the Act then establishes the CIA—the archetypal "agency involved in intelligence activities"—"*under* the National Security Council," and assigns the CIA the responsibility of "coordinating the intelligence activities of the several Government departments and agencies in the interest of na-

---

[43] *Compare* Report of the Congressional Committees Investigating the Iran-Contra Affair, pp. 395–410 (majority report; Boland Amendments violated "in letter and spirit") (hereinafter cited as majority report); Ibid., pp. 489–500 (minority report; Boland Amendments not violated) herein cited as Minority Report).

[44] Government's Memorandum of Points and Authorities in Opposition to Defendant's Motions to Dismiss or Limit Count One (filed October 25, 1988), pp. 48–82.

[45] There may be doubt about the peripheral coverage of the Amendments—for example, as to whether the Amendment in effect in fiscal year 1986 barred provision of logistical advice to the contras.

[46] Section 8066 of Department of Defense Appropriations for fiscal year 1985, as enacted in P.L. 98–473; Section 106 of the Intelligence Authorization Act for Fiscal Year 1986, P.L. 99–569.

[47] For example, during the final debate on the Boland Amendment, Representative Boland stated that the Amendment "clearly prohibits any expenditure, including those from accounts for salaries and all support costs." 130 Cong. Rec. H11980 (1984).

[48] The same Act also establishes the NSC staff. 50 U.S.C. § 402(c).

[49] 50 U.S.C. § 402(b)(1) (1982).

tional security . . . *under the direction of the National Security Council.*" 50

The basic operating charter of the NSC during the years in question, Executive Order 12333, is to the same effect. President Reagan's order states that the purpose of the NSC is to

act as the highest Executive Branch entity that provides review of, guidance for and direction to the conduct of all national foreign intelligence, counterintelligence, and special activities, and attendant policies and programs.51

Accordingly, the NSC was, by its very charter, an "entity involved in intelligence activities." 52

Thus, at every stage of the debates on the fiscal year 1985 version of the Boland Amendment, both sponsors and opponents of the legislation described it as involving a total and complete cut-off of all U.S. support for the contras. This understanding of the Boland Amendment as ending all support for the war in Nicaragua would be incomprehensible if the amendment in fact were intended to eliminate only support by certain agencies. Indeed, such an intent would make little sense in any case.

Plainly, Congress did not intend to prohibit aid to the contras by only a few agencies, and permit the same type of covert assistance from others. The restriction was placed on the budgets of the CIA and the Defense Department, and made generally applicable to other

"agenc[ies] . . . involved in intelligence activities" not other "intelligence agencies." In other words, the restriction was not limited to agencies with traditional intelligence functions. If *any* Government entity undertook an intelligence activity its appropriation became unavailable for support of the contras. Only with this view could Congress believe that it had "end(ed) support for the war in Nicaragua" by passing the Boland Amendment. Otherwise, the Amendment would have become to a large extent an empty gesture, merely transferring the military assistance program for the contras from the presumably competent hands of the military and intelligence community to some branch of the Government with less relevant experience and skills. Such was obviously not the congressional intent.

There is only one specific reference to the NSC in the legislative history of the relevant Boland Amendments. By the summer of 1985, press reports of North's activities had come to the attention of Congress.53 The classified legislative history of the fiscal year 1986 version of the Boland Amendment demonstrates that the framers of the legislation—supporters and opponents of American support for the contras—specifically understood and intended the Amendment to apply to the NSC and its staff. For example:

—On May 9, 1985, during the House Permanent Select Committee on Intelligence mark-up of the Intelligence Authorization Act for fiscal year 1986, Representative Hyde, a supporter of aid for the contras, stated: "As I read (the Boland Amendment), no funds available to the CIA, the Department of Defense or any other agency or entity involved in intelligence activities—and I presume the President is (covered], because he has a National Security Council—may be obligated or expended to support directly or indirectly military or paramilitary in Nicaragua. . . ." 54

50 50 U.S.C. § 403(a), (d) (emphasis added).

51 Executive Order 12333, Part 1.2(a), 46 Federal Register 59941, 59942 (December 4, 1981), *reprinted in* 50 U.S.C.A., pp. 59–67 (1988 Supp.). The Church Committee had noted that the NSC had been an "effective means for exerting broad policy control over at least two major clandestine activities—covert action and sensitive data collection." (Church Committee Report, p. 427.) The Committee recommended that the NSC should be given broad policy-making responsibility for all of "the intelligence activities of the United States, including intelligence collection, counterintelligence, and the conduct of covert action." (Ibid., p. 429.) It is precisely this recommendation that is taken up by Executive Order 12333.

52 In a pre-trial motion challenging Count One, North contended that the statutory language "agency or entity involved in the intelligence activity" had a particular technical meaning, one excluding the NSC. The legislative history of the Amendments, however, establishes that Congress intended no such technical meaning of "agency . . . involved in intelligence activities. . . ." Rather, Congress intended the definition of intelligence agencies to be sufficiently broad to accomplish its objectives. It cannot successfully be argued that the Boland Amendment applies only to agencies that "have operational responsibility for conducting intelligence activities." The statutory language—"*involved in* intelligence activities"—is much broader, and plainly is broad enough to cover an agency or entity "involved in" intelligence activities by directing and supervising them.

53 In the 1984 debates concerning the fiscal year 1985 appropriations act, there was, of course, no special reason for Congress to focus specifically on the NSC. Congress dealt with the problem generically, and, as indicated above, intended by their broad proscription of the use of funds for military- or intelligence-related agencies in support of the contras to cut off all United States funding for their activities.

54 Transcript at 7.

—On November 7, 1985, during the House and Senate conference on the Intelligence Authorization Act for fiscal year 1986, the following colloquy occurred:

*Senator Leahy*: It is also your understanding that [the Boland Amendment] would preclude the National Security Council—I am thinking about a long discussion you and I had with Bud McFarlane about Colonel North. *This precludes the National Security Council from going out soliciting, I mean, I think that would be pretty well an agency involved in intelligence matters.* Am I correct in that?

*Representative Hamilton*: Yes.[55]

# Second Object of the Conspiracy: Self-Dealing

The second charged object of the conspiracy to defraud was to "depriv[e] the Government of the United States of the honest and faithful services of employees free from conflicts of interest, corruption and self-dealing. . . ."[56] More specifically, Count One charged that the defendants conspired to "deceitfully us[e] the influence and position of [North and Poindexter] to generate funds"—including the proceeds of the Iran arms sales—which were then held by Secord and Hakim at the disposal of Poindexter and North for the support of projects of their choice, including aid to the contras. In effect, Count One concerned the creation of a secret slush fund, in which Secord and Hakim agreed to hold funds generated by North and to apply them to purposes selected by North outside the normal channels of governmental accountability.

At its core, the self-dealing aspect of the conspiracy consisted of four elements: (1) North and Poindexter's use of their official positions to make funds available to Secord and Hakim; (2) Secord and Hakim's use of some of these funds to support projects designated by Poindexter and North; (3) Secord and Hakim's retention of some of these funds for their personal use; and (4) all of the conspirators' efforts to conceal their corrupt arrangement, which each found beneficial.

# The Evidence

In 1986, elements in Iran paid $30 million for weapons from U.S. arsenals, a price negotiated by North, the nominal representative of the U.S. Government. Of that $30 million, the United States received $12 million. The remainder went to the Enterprise, and its expenses totalled about $2 million. Its compensation, although never specifically set, would have been expected to have some reasonable relationship to its services. It was not an entity that bought for its own account with a risk as to resale. It was a service agency. About $16 million, money that should have been deposited in the U.S. Treasury, was secretly kept by the conspirators, after they had secretly generated those funds.

### The Israeli Initiative

The early history of the Iran arms sales is related in Part I of this Report. This discussion is concerned with the evidence against those charged with conspiracy.

By September 1985, after McFarlane had assured Israel of U.S. authorization to transfer U.S.-origin weapons to elements in Iran, North took an active interest. His participation in the initiative arose from his official duties regarding terrorism and hostages. On September 15, 1985, an American, Reverend Benjamin Weir, was released in Beirut by his captors. Shortly before Weir's release, on September 9, 1985, North had directed the intelligence community to take certain measures in anticipation of the possible release of an American hostage. This was the first of many directions that North was to give to the intelligence community in connection with efforts to secure the release of American hostages by means of the developing channel to Iran.

The second Israeli shipment of arms to Iran took place on November 24, 1985. At that time, Israel sent 18 HAWK missiles to Iran in what was to be the first of several deliveries, but problems with the missiles led to the cancellation of the subsequent shipments. Moreover, Is-

---

[55] Transcript at 38 (emphasis added). In connection with the Fiscal Year 1986 renewal of Boland, the Senate Intelligence Committee chairman also received a staff memorandum stating that the NSC was covered by the Boland Amendment. (See September 23, 1985 Memo from Gary Chase and Bernard McMahon to Senator Durenberger at 9: "In the absence of clear legislative history indicating that the phrase 'involved in' was meant to be read narrowly as 'conducting' it is difficult to quarrel with the proposition that the NSC is 'involved in' intelligence activities".)

[56] Count One, ¶ 13(a)(2).

rael encountered difficulties in the shipment of the HAWKs. Israeli Defense Minister Yitzhak Rabin called McFarlane, and McFarlane directed North and Poindexter to help with the shipment.

North's assistance consisted of coordinating logistical arrangements for the shipment: He confirmed the availability of CIA proprietary aircraft for use in executing the transfers, enlisted Secord to supervise and participate in the actual delivery, worked to obtain necessary flight clearances, and ensured that adequate preparations were made for the reception of any hostages whose release might ensue. The Israelis paid Secord $1 million for his assistance. When the HAWK shipments were cancelled, Secord was left with a surplus of $800,000.

This November 1985 transaction was the subject of the indictment in three respects: (1) North's direction that Israeli funds, intended to cover the transportation costs for delivery of materials to Iran, be deposited into an Enterprise bank account, (2) the Enterprise's retention and use of excess Israeli funds, and (3) Poindexter and North's attempted concealment in November 1986 of NSC participation in the November 1985 transaction. In the course of the initial Israeli arms sales, McFarlane, Poindexter, North and Secord became involved in the initiative, and the pattern of using arms sales to Iran to generate funds was established.

## The United States Initiative

In December 1985 and January 1986, despite serious disagreements within the Reagan Administration about the advisability of pursuing arms shipments to Iran, North helped move the initiative forward. He was now principally responsible for the initiative; Poindexter had replaced McFarlane as national security adviser, and NSC consultant Michael Ledeen had been told that he was no longer part of the initiative. In a December 9, 1985, memorandum to Poindexter and McFarlane, North suggested, as an alternative to the prior Israeli activities, that the Government itself commence deliveries. North suggested Secord as a conduit.

Thus, in a January 15, 1986, computer note to Poindexter, North recounted conversations with CIA Director Casey and U.S. Army Gen. Colin Powell in which he had identified Secord as "a purchasing agent" and "an agent for the CIA." At the same time, North advised Poindexter of a critical piece of information that they did not share with non-conspirators: "the Iranians have offered $10K per TOW." [57]

The effective Finding signed by President Reagan on January 17, 1986, limited the provision of arms, equipment and related material to elements in Iran to three specific purposes: "(1) establishing a more moderate government in Iran, (2) obtaining from [elements in Iran] significant intelligence not otherwise obtainable, to determine the current Iranian Government's intentions with respect to its neighbors and with respect to terrorist acts, and (3) furthering the release of the American hostages held in Beirut and preventing additional terrorist acts by these groups." While working on the Finding, North had been advised by Stanley Sporkin, the general counsel of the CIA, that a Finding must specifically enumerate each purpose to be accomplished by a particular covert action. Nonetheless, the Finding signed by the President did not authorize the generation of surplus funds to be used for the contras, or for any other unspecified covert action.

At three different points in North's memorandum for presentation to the President by Poindexter explaining the Finding, North described the intermediary who would transfer the arms to Iranians as an "agent" of the CIA, without any suggestion that Secord would operate independently of Government control and retain (subject to direction by North and Poindexter) more than 60 percent of the funds received from the Iranians. North recommended that rather than using the Israelis to deliver weapons, "the CIA, using an authorized agent as necessary, purchase[d] arms from the Department of Defense under the Economy Act and then transfer[red] them to Iran. . . ." He further stated: "Therefore it is proposed that Israel make the necessary arrangements for the sale of the 4,000 TOW weapons to Iran. Sufficient funds to cover the sale would be transferred to an agent of the CIA. The CIA would then purchase the weapons from the Department of Defense and deliver the weapons to Iran through the agent." [58] By portraying the

[57] PROFs Note from North to Poindexter, 1/15/86.

[58] Memorandum from Poindexter (prepared by North) to the President, 1/17/86, AKW 001919.

intermediary as a U.S. Government agent, North failed to reveal that the Enterprise would treat the proceeds of the arms sales as its own and did not present this aspect to President Reagan for authorization.[59]

Secord never controlled the disposition of the weapons. President Reagan, through Poindexter, retained full control over the weapons after Secord received them and up to the point of actual delivery to Iran.

President Reagan was informed and personally approved both February shipments of TOWs. During his May trip to Tehran, McFarlane, in consultation with the White House, turned back to Israel the second load of HAWK spares, even though Iranian arms dealer Manucher Ghorbanifar had paid Secord for them the full, marked up, purchase price and Secord had paid the CIA the lower price set by the Department of Defense. Only with President Reagan's personal approval was this second plane load of weapons and parts subsequently delivered.

## Generating a Surplus

In each of the 1986 Iranian transactions, North, operating with Poindexter's knowledge and approval, exercised control over the money received by Secord from the Iranians.

During its life, the Enterprise had three bank accounts at Credit Suisse in Geneva, Switzerland, through which it received funds totaling $47.6 million: the Energy Resources account ($11.3 million); the Lake Resources account ($31.5 million); and the Hyde Park Square Corporation account ($4.8 million). North directly or indirectly (through Calero) was responsible for virtually every penny that flowed into those three accounts. Accordingly, he was consulted on major expenditures. Of this $47.6 million, $28.6 million was received as a result of the sale of U.S. Government weapons to Iran.

The generation of funds for the Enterprise began almost immediately after the January 17 Finding was signed. With Secord installed as a participant in the initiative, he and North traveled to London on behalf of the United States for a meeting on January 22, 1986, with

Ghorbanifar and Amiram Nir, an Israeli official involved in the transaction. At that meeting, North set the price for the Government weapons, as he was to do in all subsequent transactions. According to a tape-recording seized from North's office by the FBI, Ghorbanifar confirmed a willingness to pay $10,000 per TOW; North accepted that offer and directed Ghorbanifar to pay $10 million for 1,000 TOWs into the Enterprise's Lake Resources account. They agreed that after the hostages were released, an additional $30 million would be deposited to an Enterprise account and an additional 3,000 TOWs delivered to Iran. Accordingly, North contemplated that within a short period of time a total of $40 million would come under the control of the Enterprise.

On January 23, 1986, North met with an official of the Defense Department and two officials of the CIA, including Charles Allen, to provide them with a detailed briefing of events in London. North advised them of anticipated steps, but he advised them that Secord would receive and pass on to the CIA *only* $6,000 per TOW, or a total of $6 million—knowing well that $10 million was the negotiated price and that Secord would not pass on to the CIA the full amount received.

North had actually told CIA officials that the quoted price of $6,000 per TOW was too high. The Defense Department later cut the price to $3,469 per TOW. The total requirement, including handling costs, was $3.7 million for 1,000 TOWs. The surplus North contemplated to be received by Secord over the amount to be paid to the Government was, at that time, more than $25 million out of a total sales price of $40 million.

On or about February 7, 1986, $10 million was deposited in an Enterprise account by the Iranians. On or about February 10–11, 1986, $3.7 million was transferred from the account to a CIA Swiss account. Between February 18 and 27, 1986, 1,000 TOWs, in two installments, were shipped to Iran. Secord's direct expenses in connection were less than $1 million. The surplus was almost $6 million.[60] Subsequently,

---

[59] In an *ex parte* statement to Judge Harold H. Greene, filed September 20, 1988, Poindexter claimed he told President Reagan that Secord was a "middleman" acting in a private capacity. This was inconsistent with contemporaneous note that he briefed the President from North's memorandum, which described Secord as an agent of the CIA.

[60] The transfer of the first 1,000 TOWs did not result in the release of the American hostages as expected and further negotiations with Ghorbanifar ensued.

in March and April 1986, the Enterprise made deliveries of weapons to Central America.

## HAWK Spare Parts

In the spring of 1986, in a meeting in Paris attended by North, Ghorbanifar, George Cave (a CIA annuitant expert in Iranian affairs) and another CIA official, Ghorbanifar raised the possibility of obtaining HAWK spare parts. After further discussions with Ghorbanifar, on April 5 or 6, 1986, North prepared a memorandum for Poindexter setting forth details of a proposed HAWK spare parts deal which referred to the allocation of $12 million from the arms sales to the contras.[61]

The price that the Iranians paid for the HAWK spare parts was $15 million. North and his assistant, Robert L. Earl, arrived at this figure by multiplying the prices obtained from the CIA by a factor of 3.7. In bringing Earl in to work on the pricing of the HAWK spare parts, North emphasized both the special secrecy of the inflated prices and of the fact that the extra money was to go to the contras.

On or about May 14–15, 1986, $15 million was deposited for the Iranians to an Enterprise account. On May 16 and 21, 1986, a total of $1.685 million was deposited by Israel into an Enterprise account to pay for the replenishment by the United States of the 50₄ TOWs shipped by Israel to Iran in August and September 1985. On May 15, 1986, $6.5 million was transferred by the Enterprise to a CIA Swiss account for the HAWK spare parts for Iran and the replenishment TOWs for Israel. On May 16, 1986, North reported to Poindexter in a computer note that "the resistance [contra] support organization now has more than $6M [million] available for immediate disbursement."[62] In May 1986, the Enterprise again shipped weapons to Central America for the contras.

On May 20–22, 1986, replenishment TOWs were shipped to Israel as well as the HAWK spare parts en route to Iran. Subsequently, one pallet of spare parts was delivered to Tehran aboard the plane carrying an American delegation led by McFarlane. When talks aborted without the release of any hostages, the remaining spare parts were left in storage in Israel. Nevertheless, the Enterprise had received full payment for all of the HAWK spare parts. None of those funds was ever returned.

Through May and June, North sought to persuade Poindexter and, through him, the President to permit the second shipment of spare parts to go forward to extricate Ghorbanifar from his embarrassment. During this period, North had Amiram Nir brief Vice President Bush during a visit to Israel. In particular, Nir undertook to convince Bush that the arms shipments should continue with the hostages being released one or two at a time rather than all at once.

On July 26, 1986, one hostage, Father Lawrence Jenco, was released. On North's recommendations, transmitted through Poindexter, the President approved the shipment to Iran of the remaining spare parts.

During the summer of 1986, fissures began to develop in North's scheme. The Iranians had obtained an accurate microfiche price list for HAWK spare parts. With the list, the Iranians realized that they had been massively overcharged—by approximately 600 percent.

As the summer of 1986 progressed, pricing complaints continued and intensified. At one point, when confronted with these complaints, North told Allen of the CIA to tell the Iranians that the price they had paid was correct and that it was higher than the microfiche because it was difficult to locate the HAWK spare parts. In another conversation, relayed to North, Ghorbanifar complained to Allen that he was being unfairly blamed for the overcharges. He explained to Allen that he paid $15 million to Secord and that he had marked up his prices by only 41 percent; not 600 percent. North's reaction to Allen's report of this conversation was to question the trustworthiness of Ghorbanifar. North also requested that the CIA generate a false microfiche price list to provide to the Iranians and extinguish the complaints. North further sought to have Cave fabricate a letter which would appear to explain and justify the spare parts prices.

## The Second Channel and the October 1986 TOW Shipment

In the late summer and fall, primarily as a result of Hakim's efforts, the conspirators began

---

[61] Memorandum from North to Poindexter, 4106, AKW 004352–59. The discovery of this memorandum by the Department of Justice in November 1986 led, in part, to the Attorney General's announcement of the Iran/contra diversion on November 25, 1986.

[62] PROFs Note from North to Poindexter, 5/16/86, AKW 021383.

working with another Iranian who came to be known as the "second channel." Though the Iranian interlocutor had changed, the conspirators continued to use the Iran initiative to generate excess funds for the Enterprise.

At a meeting with the second channel in October 1986, North learned, as he reported to Poindexter in a computer note dated October 10, 1986, that the Iranians would pay $3.6 million for 500 TOWs, or $7,200 each.[63] Six days later, he learned from Earl that the CIA would be charging the Enterprise $2.037 million for the TOWs, approximately the same price it had been charged in the February sale. Subsequently, 500 TOWs were shipped to Iran. Again North had arranged for the shipment to generate a surplus for the Enterprise.

## Concealment of the Diversion

During the summer of 1986, Charles Allen informed his supervisor, Deputy Director of Central Intelligence Robert M. Gates, and then Casey of his concerns that North and Secord had generated funds from the Iran arms sales to divert to the contras; he further warned that Ghorbanifar might go public with allegations concerning the pricing of the weapons. Private businessman, Roy Furmark, who had complained to Casey that Ghorbanifar had not repaid certain Canadian lenders, also disclosed details of the financing of the arms shipments and conveyed Ghorbanifar's suspicion that funds had been diverted to Central America. When Allen told North, North again attempted to deflect the inquiries, responding that Furmark should not be trusted. Casey related these concerns to Poindexter and suggested he consult the counsel to the President. Poindexter said he would prefer to discuss it with the NSC counsel.

In November 1986, the conspirators engaged in a cover-up. North began the shredding and destruction of documents and materials, including those relating to the diversion; North's explanation to McFarlane for the later discovery of the diversion memo was "I missed one." On November 23, 1986, in a meeting with the attorney general and other Justice Department officials at which he was confronted with that memo, North confirmed the existence of the

diversion but lied about his role in it by claiming that (1) the NSC had no involvement in the diversion; that (2) the Israelis had determined how much of the proceeds from the arms sales were diverted to the contras; and that (3) he, North, had advised contra leader Adolfo Calero to open bank accounts in Switzerland to receive the proceeds of the diversion. When asked by FBI agents about the diversion, Poindexter misleadingly minimized his knowledge and support of North's activities, saying only that he knew North "was up to something," and that he could have stopped his subordinate but did not. Between November 22 and November 29, 1986, Poindexter tried to delete from his White House computer system all the messages that he had received and sent, including those that revealed the diversion.

## Self-Dealing and Conspiracy Law

As discussed above, the self-dealing aspect of the conspiracy involved two Government officials—North and Poindexter—using their positions to create a substantial pool of funds under their control; the transmission of these funds to Secord and Hakim and their subsequent disbursement at North's direction (with the general approval of Poindexter) for a variety of purposes, including expenditures for contra arms deliveries, payments to contra leaders, radio transmitters for a foreign country, the purchase and operation of a small cargo vessel, personal payments to Secord and Hakim, and the allocation of a smaller amount to North; and the use of deception to create this pool of funds and to hide its existence and the way it was disbursed.

As a result of this scheme, the United States was deprived of the honest and faithful services of Poindexter and North because these two Government employees had undisclosed conflicts of interests. Specifically, North and Poindexter had an undisclosed interest in using their positions for the private purpose of creating and increasing the pool of funds under their personal control. For instance, when North was negotiating with the Iranians concerning the sale of arms, he had a duty as an employee of the Government to pursue single-mindedly the purposes of the Iran initiative; at the same time

---

[63] PROFs Note from North to Poindexter, 10/10/86.

he had a secret and conflicting goal of obtaining as much money as possible for the Enterprise.

This was not a technical or minor conflict of interest. North, with Poindexter's permission, in effect negotiated both the price the Iranians would pay and the considerably lower price the Government would receive. He exploited his position to exact from the Iranians a high selling price, while concealing from the Government the nature of the price spread and his control over the excess proceeds. President Reagan authorized the sale of weapons to elements in Iran for carefully specified objectives. Rather than limit their operation to the specified goals of the initiative, North and Poindexter used their control of the initiative to fund the Enterprise. In effect, the Government officials had a hidden interest in maximizing the mark-up of the ostensible middlemen, Secord and Hakim, at the expense of the United States.

The scheme charged in the self-dealing object of the indictment's conspiracy count—¶13(a)(2) of Count One—constituted a classic fraud on the Government. The thrust of the fraud was a breach of the public trust: Poindexter and North's use of their public office for execution of the Iran arms sales was driven by a concealed and wholly improper motive—a desire to generate a concealed fund for use in financing unauthorized activities designated by them. The implementation of that scheme obstructed the lawful conduct of the Government's business within the meaning of the cases outlined earlier by depriving the Government of the honest and faithful services of its employees.

An impressive series of precedents established that a public official who conspired to deprive the United States of his honest and faithful services by acting on matters in which he had a hidden conflict of interest properly violated 18 U.S.C. § 371.[64] Schemes to deprive

the Government of the honest and faithful services of its employees by creating a conflict of interest were held fraudulent in a long line of cases decided under the mail and wire fraud statutes prior to the decision in *McNally* v. *United States*.[65] One of these cases, which has already been discussed, was directly analogous to the activities of North and Poindexter. In *United States* v. *Diggs*, the Court of Appeals affirmed the conviction of a member of Congress who diverted funds authorized for staffing his Washington congressional office and applied them to the payment of, among other things, the expenses of maintaining an office in his home district.[66] The defendant argued that the use of the funds for that purpose was legitimate.[67] The Court concluded, however, that Diggs defrauded the public when he allocated public funds in accordance with his private agenda, rather than in compliance with legislative dictates.

Accordingly, a crime was committed when Poindexter and North undertook to channel funds to Secord and Hakim, retaining the concealed right to control a portion of those funds. The establishment of a privately controlled fund for Government officials, their secret arrangement to increase the fund and the diversion of those funds for unauthorized purposes deprived the United States of the honest and faithful services of its employees, in violation of 18 U.S.C. § 317.

---

[64] See, for example, *United States* v. *Lane*, 765 F.2d 1376 (9th Cir. 1985) (upholding conspiracy to defraud United States charge based on agreement of defendants, state administrators of job training program, to channel federally-funded contracts to each other); *United States* v. *Burgin*, 621 F.2d 1352, 1356–57 (5th Cir.), *cert. denied*, 449 U.S. 1015 (1980) (upholding conspiracy to defraud United States charge based on state legislator's agreement to direct federally funded state contracts to entity that, in turn, agreed to funnel part of profits to legislator); *United States* v. *Johnson*, 337 F.2d 180, 185–86 (4th Cir. 1964), *aff'd on another issue*, 383 U.S. 169 (1966) (upholding conspiracy to defraud United States charge based on Congressman's agreement to exert influence on Department of Justice to win dismissal of pending indictment in exchange for payments characterized as campaign contributions); *Harney* v. *United States*, 306 F.2d 523 (1st Cir.), *cert.*

*denied*, 371 U.S. 911 (1962) (upholding conspiracy to defraud charge based on a scheme pursuant to which state official arranged a federally-funded land condemnation at an inflated cost in exchange for seller's agreement to channel a portion of the proceeds to state official, among others); *United States* v. *Sweig*, 316 F. Supp. 1148, 1155–56 (S.D.N.Y. 1970) (upholding indictment charging that aide to House Speaker entered into scheme by which co-conspirator took fees from people with matters before federal agencies with the promise that he would use the influence of the office of the Speaker on their behalf).

[65] 107 S.Ct. 2875 (1987). Justice Stevens collected more than a dozen examples of such cases in his dissent in *McNally*. 107 S.Ct. at 2883 n.1. As previously noted, although *McNally* rejected the theory on which those cases had been prosecuted, it did so as a matter of interpretation of the mail fraud statute. The Court specifically approved § 371 cases brought on the same theory.

[66] 613 F.2d 988 (D.C. Cir. 1979), *cert. denied*, 446 U.S. 982 (1980). It was also alleged and proved that defendant had diverted some of the money to pay his personal expenses, but because the indictment had charged in the same counts both personal and congressional uses of the funds, the Court was required to consider whether the use of the funds for expenses which, though incurred for legitimate governmental purposes, were not authorized to be paid from the funds in question. (Ibid. at 994.)

[67] Ibid., p. 994.

# Third Object of the Conspiracy: The Corruption of the Iran Initiative

The final substantive object of the conspiracy—set forth in ¶ 13(a)(3) of Count One—was that the conspirators "deceitfully exploit[ed] for their own purposes and corrupt[ed] a United States Government initiative involving the sale of arms to elements in Iran" by bending their efforts toward the enrichment of the Enterprise and the pursuit of its goals, "rather than pursuing solely the specified governmental objectives of the initiative, including the release of Americans being held hostage in Lebanon." [68]

Much that has been said earlier concerning the self-dealing aspect of the conspiracy applies as well to the objective of corrupting the Iran initiative, because that corruption was in effect a specific instance—and by far the most important instance—in which the conspirators manifested the conflict of interest with which the self-dealing charge was concerned. The corruption of the effort to release the hostages by North and Poindexter to finance the Enterprise and the contras epitomized the broader conflict of interest. [69]

Paragraph 13(a)(3) is alleged as a separate objective because it set forth two additional ways in which the conspiracy impaired Government functions:

*First*, the use of the initiative as a private fund-raising device made it significantly less likely that the purposes for which the initiative was undertaken would be accomplished. As set forth in the Finding, those purposes were "(1) establishing a more moderate government in Iran, (2) obtaining from them significant intelligence . . . and (3) furthering the release of the American hostages held in Beirut and preventing additional terrorist acts. . . ." Poindexter and North promoted their private, unauthorized ends at the cost of putting at hazard the presidential objective they were supposed to be pursuing, including that of saving the lives of the Americans held hostage in Lebanon.

*Second*, more broadly, the creation and diversion of excess proceeds to the Enterprise for unspecified covert action impaired another Government function, that of presidential control of covert activity. National Security Decision Directive 159 and Executive Order 12333 give the President the power to define the scope of covert activities. The President alone can authorize covert activities; he alone can determine whether to assign such activities to agencies other than the CIA; and, by stating the activity's rationale in the Finding authorizing it, he alone can specify what the covert action is intended to achieve. By diverting the proceeds of the Iran initiative to providing support to the contras without an explicit presidential Finding, the conspirators converted a covert action authorized for particular purposes to the accomplishment of unauthorized goals. Their scheme therefore undermined presidential control of covert activities, as well as impairing the congressional power of oversight over them and its control by appropriation.

The corruption of the Iran arms sales to the private purposes of the conspirators was the logical outcome of the conspiracy's other two objects. First, the creation and diversion of excess proceeds from the Iran arms sales helped impede through concealment and deceit congressional participation in the orderly administration of foreign affairs under the Constitution. Second, the corruption of the hostage-release effort brought to fruition the conflict of interest of Government officers and the deprivation of their honest and faithful services.

---

[68] The bill of particulars specified that the deception involved in this aspect of the agreement was directed at both Congress and the Executive branch, and that the conspirators' "own purposes" toward which the Iran initiative was diverted were: (1) "providing support of military or paramilitary operations in Nicaragua by the Contras;" (2) "providing radios to an entity" in a foreign country; (3) "purchasing and operating the [ship] Erria;" and (4) "providing profits to defendants Secord and Hakim."

[69] The conduct constituting the corruption of the Iran initiative also served the conspiratorial goal charged in ¶ 13(a)(1) of Count One (the secret war objective), since the money obtained from the diversion of profits from the arms sales to Iran was used to support the conspirators' illegal Enterprise in support of the contras.

# Part IV
# Investigations and Cases:
# The National Security Council Staff

At the center of the covert Iran and contra operations were three members of President Reagan's National Security Council staff: National Security Adviser Robert C. McFarlane; McFarlane's deputy and successor, Vice Adm. John M. Poindexter; and the deputy director of political-military affairs, Lt. Col. Oliver L. North.

It is the duty of the national security adviser to brief the President daily on foreign and domestic developments of national security concern, and to integrate and keep him apprised of the views of his National Security Council. The national security adviser heads the NSC staff. The principal members of the NSC in the Iran/contra matters were the President, the Vice President, the secretaries of state and defense and the director of the CIA.

Beginning in 1984 through most of 1986, members of the NSC staff implemented President Reagan's foreign-policy directive to keep the Nicaraguan contras alive as a fighting force, despite a law—the Boland Amendment—prohibiting U.S. aid for their military activities. Largely acting through North, their contra-support activities included approaches to foreign countries and private American citizens for funding; the provision of military and tactical advice and intelligence; and working with private operatives, chiefly retired Air Force Maj. Gen. Richard V. Secord and Albert Hakim, to supply weapons.

In 1985, in what was originally a separate undertaking from the contra-support operation, McFarlane initiated contacts with Israel leading to the sale of U.S. weapons to Iran in an effort to free American hostages held by pro-Iranian terrorists in Beirut; in 1986, the NSC staff under Poindexter continued in this effort through direct U.S. arms sales to Iran. Poindexter authorized North to arrange the diversion of Iran arms sales proceeds to the contras, secretly marking up the prices for U.S. weapons and relying on the excess proceeds to help finance the contra-resupply operation, subsequently called the "Enterprise," which was run by Secord and Hakim under North's direction.

The NSC staff members in these operations could not have carried out many of their activities without the support or knowledge of officials in other agencies: most prominently the CIA, State Department and the Department of Defense. Nevertheless, after public exposure, the Reagan Administration used the most dramatic dimension of the Iran/contra affair—the Iran/contra diversion—to focus public attention and to blame the NSC staff for what went wrong.[1] On November 25, 1986, President Reagan announced the firing of North and the resignation of Poindexter. Attorney General Edwin Meese III then disclosed the Iran/contra diversion, erroneously stating that only three U.S. officials knew about it: North, Poindexter and McFarlane.

The criminal prosecutions showed that members of the NSC staff, although most directly involved in the operations, were not the only participants in Iran/contra matters. Rather, these matters often were not aberrant acts but part of a widespread pattern of covert conduct condoned at the highest levels of Government.

---

[1] On November 24, 1986, the day before the Iran/contra diversion was to be publicly announced, White House Chief of Staff Donald T. Regan recommended a damage-control strategy that put the NSC staff in the line of fire: ". . . Tough as it seems[,] blame must be put at NSC's door—rogue operation, going on without President's knowledge or sanction. When suspicions arose he took charge, ordered investigation, had meeting of top advisers to get at facts, and find out who knew what." (Memorandum from Regan, 11/24/86, ALU 0138832.)

# Chapter 1
# United States v. Robert C. McFarlane

Robert C. "Bud" McFarlane was President Reagan's national security adviser from October 1983 to December 1985. He briefed the President daily about world events and conferred regularly with Vice President Bush, Secretary of State George P. Shultz, Secretary of Defense Caspar W. Weinberger and CIA Director William J. Casey, who were the principal members of President Reagan's National Security Council.

Prior to becoming national security adviser, McFarlane had been deputy to his predecessor William Clark; counselor to Alexander M. Haig, Jr., when he was secretary of state; a member of the staff of the Senate Armed Services Committee; and military aide to Henry Kissinger when he was national security adviser to President Nixon. An Annapolis graduate, he commanded the first U.S. Marine battery to land in the Republic of South Vietnam. He completed two tours, each characterized by the heavy fighting in I-Corps just south of the demilitarized zone that separated North and South Vietnam. He received a Bronze Star for valor and other individual and unit decorations. He resigned from the U.S. Marine Corps as a lieutenant colonel.

As national security adviser, McFarlane headed the President's NSC staff, which was designed to assist the President in integrating the views of Government agencies responsible for national security matters. McFarlane regularly advised President Reagan on foreign and domestic issues of national security significance. He ordinarily based this advice on consultations with the NSC members, and on objective analyses by their agencies and the NSC staff.

Under President Reagan, the NSC staff assumed a role beyond that of an advisory or coordinating body: It at times became operational, taking on primary responsibility for the execution of the Iran and contra covert operations. McFarlane did not shrink from the operational tasks that were of high personal interest to the President. He delegated some of them to a hard-driving NSC staff member, Marine Lt. Col. Oliver L. North, McFarlane's deputy director of political-military affairs.

In 1984, President Reagan directed McFarlane to keep the financially strapped Nicaraguan contras alive as a viable fighting force, despite a ban on U.S. military assistance, McFarlane assigned the job to North. North kept McFarlane generally informed of his efforts on behalf of the contras, which McFarlane told North to undertake in utmost secrecy. When Congress in 1985 inquired about press reports of North's contra-aid efforts, McFarlane denied the allegations.

In 1985, McFarlane and Casey were the chief advocates of weapons sales to Iran in exchange for the release of American hostages held by pro-Iranian terrorists in Beirut; again, McFarlane turned to North to help implement, in utmost secrecy, the arms-for-hostages deals. Although McFarlane resigned as national security adviser in December 1985, he stayed in contact with his former deputy and successor, Navy Vice Adm. John M. Poindexter, and with North. He remained involved in the Iran weapons sales, acting as President Reagan's emissary on a mission to Tehran in May 1986. In November 1986, McFarlane helped Poindexter and North conceal details of the Iran initiative, just as they had done when the operation was underway.

Beginning in December 1986 after the public exposure of Iran/contra, McFarlane voluntarily provided information to Congress, to President Reagan's Tower Commission and to Independent Counsel. Because McFarlane was only partially truthful, it was difficult for investigators to determine on which matters he could be believed. Further complicating the matter was the fact that McFarlane's testimony was, in some crucial respects, at odds with that of other senior Reagan Administration officials. McFarlane, for example, stood alone in insisting that President Reagan had approved the earliest 1985 sales of U.S. arms to Iran by Israel and had agreed to replenish Israeli weapons stocks. It was only after contemporary notes recording the events in question were discovered late in Independent Counsel's investigation that much of what McFarlane said could be verified. His desire to keep secret certain contra-assistance activities resulted in criminal charges being brought against him.

After lengthy negotiations with Independent Counsel, McFarlane on March 11, 1988, pleaded guilty to four misdemeanor charges that he unlawfully withheld information from Congress about North's contra-support activities and about the solicitation of foreign funding for the contras. As a condition of his plea, he agreed to cooperate with the ongoing criminal investigation. On December 24, 1992, McFarlane was one of six Iran/contra defendants pardoned by President Bush.

## McFarlane's Involvement in Aiding the Contras

The contra effort was a matter of high priority to President Reagan and his Administration. The President compared the contras' struggle against Nicaragua's communist-supported Sandinista government to that of the American revolutionaries who fought and triumphed over British rule. But the contra war engendered battles on Capitol Hill, where military funding was alternately won and lost by narrow margins.

Early in 1984, President Reagan gave McFarlane responsibility for keeping the contras alive "body and soul." [1] McFarlane took this charge seriously, seeking ways to deal with the problem of rapidly depleting funds and later an all-out ban on contra aid imposed by the Boland Amendment in October 1984. McFarlane testified that the President was angry about the funding cut-off and viewed Congress's actions as a ploy not only to injure the contras but to damage him politically.[2]

On January 6, 1984, the President's National Security Planning Group (NSPG) approved "immediate efforts to obtain additional funding of $10–15 million from foreign or domestic sources to make up for the fact that the current $24 million appropriation [for the contras] will sustain operations only through June 1984." [3] McFarlane was responsible for the implementation of this plan with the assistance of North and another NSC staff member, Constantine Menges.

In late March 1984, Casey sent a memo to McFarlane urging him to explore with Israel and other countries the possibility of obtaining weapons and financial aid for the contras.[4] Subsequently, McFarlane in April 1984 dispatched NSC staff member Howard Teicher to ask the Israelis for assistance; the mission was unsuccessful.[5] Although McFarlane later characterized the Teicher approach to Israel as "perfectly legal," he was intent on keeping it secret, because such a disclosure would be "annoying to and upsetting to the Congress" and "embarrassing" to Israel.[6] When Secretary of State Shultz learned of Teicher's mission from the U.S. Embassy in Israel, McFarlane informed Shultz that Teicher had gone to Israel "on his own hook." [7]

Despite the failed approach to Israel, McFarlane continued his secret search for third-country funding for the contras. In May 1984, he met with Prince Bandar, the Saudi Arabian ambassador to the United States, and explained President Reagan's strong concern that the gap in the financial support of the contras be filled. According to McFarlane, "it became pretty obvious to the Ambassador that his country, to gain a considerable amount of favor and, frankly, they thought it was the right thing to do,

[1] McFarlane, *North* Trial Testimony, 3/10/89, p. 3946.

[2] Ibid., 3/14/89, pp. 4357–59.
[3] Memorandum from North and Menges to McFarlane, 1/13/84, AKW 038381.
[4] Memorandum from Casey to McFarlane, 3/27/84, ER 13712.
[5] Teicher, Grand Jury, 6/24/87, pp. 10–12.
[6] McFarlane, *North* Trial Testimony, 3/15/89, p. 4619.
[7] Shultz, Select Committees Testimony, 7/23/87, pp. 31–33.

they would provide the support when the Congress cut it off.'' [8]

A few days later, Prince Bandar contacted McFarlane and volunteered $1 million a month for the contras. Bandar said that the donation signified King Fahd's gratitude for past Reagan Administration support of the Saudi government.[9] McFarlane subsequently obtained from North a contra bank account number where a donation could be made, and McFarlane gave the number to Prince Bandar.

A day or two after the Saudis agreed to provide a million dollars a month to the contras, McFarlane informed President Reagan and Vice President Bush.[10] He said he also informed Shultz and Weinberger that money had been provided to the contras through the end of the year, but neither pressed him for details.[11]

The topic of third-country funding for the contras dominated a June 25, 1984, meeting of President Reagan's National Security Planning Group (NSPG). Casey advocated such a plan. Shultz quoted White House Chief of Staff James Baker (who was not in attendance) as stating that such solicitations would constitute an ''impeachable offense.'' The group, however, agreed that a legal opinion should be sought from the Justice Department. Underscoring the extreme secrecy surrounding the matter, President Reagan warned against leaks, stating, ''If such a story gets out, we'll all be hanging by our thumbs in front of the White House until we find out who did it.'' [12]

None of the participants in the NSPG meeting—which included the President, Vice President, Shultz, Weinberger, Casey, then-presidential counselor Edwin Meese III and McFarlane—apparently raised the fact that the successful Saudi solicitation had already occurred. McFarlane, who was most knowledgeable about

it, stated: ''I propose that there be no authority for anyone to seek third party support for the anti-Sandinistas [contras] until we have the information we need, and I certainly hope none of this discussion will be made public in any way.'' [13]

The day after the NSPG meeting, Casey met with Attorney General William French Smith. Smith determined that third-country funding of the contras was legally permissible as long as no U.S. funds were used for the purpose, and as long as there was not an expectation on the part of the third country that the United States would repay the aid.[14]

Over the course of the following year, Saudi Arabia gave a total of $32 million to the contras.[15] Taiwan later contributed $2 million.

## McFarlane Gives North the ''Body and Soul'' Directive

McFarlane continued to discuss the issue of contra funding with the President and his top advisers throughout the spring and summer of 1984. McFarlane said, ''He [President Reagan] let us know very clearly in that spring and summer of 1984 that we were to do all that we could to make sure that the movement, the freedom fighters [contras], survived and I think the term at the time that's come up here and there was that we were to do all we could to keep them together body and soul.'' [16]

McFarlane said he discussed the President's directive with his NSC deputy, Donald Fortier, and with North. McFarlane knew that Fortier and North ''were very resourceful people and would go out and do a number of things that they believed would achieve what the President told me and them he wanted and that is, to keep this movement going as healthy as we could so that ultimately we could win the vote in the Congress, as we did the following year.'' [17] Fortier was assigned to handle the political and legislative aspects of seeking renewed

---

[8] McFarlane, *North* Trial Testimony, 3/10/89, p. 3933.

[9] McFarlane, FBI 302, 3/10/87, p. 6. See Classified Appendix on the nature of this support.

[10] McFarlane, Select Committees Testimony, 5/11/87, pp. 38–39. McFarlane, *North* Trial Testimony, 3/13/89, pp. 4203–04, said he notified the President of the first Saudi contribution in June 1984 by putting the information on a card that he slipped into the President's daily briefing book. He said he either told the President in writing on the card or orally that ''no one else knows about this'' and the President responded, either in writing or orally, ''Good, let's just make sure it stays that way.'' When McFarlane learned from Bandar of a second donation in February 1985 and brought it to the President's attention, he said he got the same response.

[11] Ibid.

[12] NSPG Minutes, 6/25/84, ALU 007876.

[13] Ibid.

[14] Memorandum for the Record from Sporkin, 6/26/84, ALV 035917.

[15] North attempted to persuade McFarlane to seek even more Saudi funding in a March 16, 1985, memorandum, recommending an additional $25 to $30 million for the purchase of arms and munitions; McFarlane responded, ''doubtful.'' Between late February and the end of March 1985, the Saudis contributed a total of $32 million to the contras.

[16] McFarlane, *North* Trial Testimony, 3/10/89, p. 3946.

[17] Ibid., p. 3949.

contra support on Capitol Hill;[18] North was to act as a liaison with the contra forces, acting as a symbol of continued Reagan Administration support despite Congress's decision to withhold assistance.[19]

In October 1984, President Reagan signed into law the Boland Amendment, a provision added to a 1985 omnibus appropriations bill, which forbade the use of U.S. Government funds appropriated to any agency involved in intelligence activity for the support of military or paramilitary action in Nicaragua.

McFarlane testified that he believed that the NSC staff's actions were restricted by the Boland prohibition on aid to the contras, and he said he specifically gave his staff instructions not to raise money for the contras.[20] McFarlane stated he made clear to North that "no one could solicit, encourage, coerce, or broker the transmission of money . . . to the contras."[21]

After the Boland Amendment was enacted, McFarlane said that CIA Director Casey expressed concerns that North was doing more than the law permitted. "I believe that he said that he had learned that Col. North was conveying intelligence information, as I recall, to the leadership of the freedom fighters [contras] and that that seemed to him to be a questionable activity, whether it was allowed or not," McFarlane said.[22]

In response to Casey's concerns, North sent McFarlane a memo titled "Clarifying Who Said What to Whom" on November 7, 1984.[23] In it, North described contra leader Adolfo Calero's desire for intelligence reports to help the contras "take out" Soviet-made Hind helicopters obtained by Nicaragua. North reported that he got the intelligence Calero needed from Robert Vickers, a CIA national intelligence officer, and from Army Gen. Paul Gorman. North assured McFarlane that—contrary to Casey's

concerns—he had not discussed contra financial arrangements and the provision of intelligence with CIA Central American Task Force Chief Alan D. Fiers, Jr.[24]

McFarlane and other Administration officials repeatedly claimed that there was a "compartmentation" of knowledge regarding North's activities, and that only a limited number of people were made privy to the information. In many cases, Independent Counsel found that this claim was feigned, and many officials knew much more than they initially admitted. Even McFarlane found Casey's inquiry into North's activities in November 1984 as "very odd at the time" because "Bill Casey knew what Ollie was doing."[25]

## McFarlane, North and the President

North reported many of his contra-assistance efforts to McFarlane. McFarlane testified that he reported almost daily to President Reagan on changes in the military situation in Nicaragua.[26] Asked by the Select Committees whether he ever withheld information from the President to protect him, McFarlane answered no, "and I believe the President was conscious of everything I did that was close to the line."[27] Because McFarlane generally denied knowledge of North's legally questionable activities, however, it was not possible to determine whether McFarlane ever reported North's unlawful acts to the President.

In some notable instances, there is documentation that McFarlane elevated certain contra-assistance issues to the President and his Cabinet, setting into motion contacts between President Reagan and other heads of state. These contacts resulted in increased foreign aid and other favors to those countries that assisted the contras.

On February 11, 1985, McFarlane received from North and another NSC staff member, Raymond Burghardt, a draft memo for circulation to Shultz, Weinberger, Casey and Joint

18 McFarlane, FBI 302, 2/16/88, p. 7.
19 McFarlane, Grand Jury, 5/4/87, pp. 10–13.
20 McFarlane, *North* Trial Testimony, 3/10/89, p. 3975.
21 McFarlane, Grand Jury, 4/29/87, p. 21. There is documentary evidence that McFarlane was sensitive to questions of legality, even before the most extreme Boland restrictions were in place. In a September 2, 1984, memorandum to McFarlane, for example, North asked to approach a private donor to obtain a "civilian" helicopter for use on the contras' northern fighting front; McFarlane noted, "I don't think this is legal." (Memorandum from North to McFarlane, 9/2/84, ALW 019179.)
22 McFarlane, *North* Trial Testimony, 3/10/89, p. 3977.
23 Memorandum from North to McFarlane, 11/7/84, AKW 000329–30.

24 Also in the fall of 1984, Fiers attended an extraordinary meeting in which Casey asked North whether he was assisting the contras, and North assured him that he was not. Fiers said that Clair E. George, the CIA's deputy director for operations, told him after the meeting that this exchange had been a "charade", allowing meeting participants to deny knowledge of North's activities. See Fiers chapter.
25 McFarlane, *North* Trial Testimony, 3/15/89, p. 4645.
26 McFarlane, Select Committees Testimony, 5/13/87, pp. 10–12.
27 Ibid., p. 81.

Chiefs Chairman Gen. John Vessey, the principal members of the Crisis Pre-Planning Group (CPPG). The memo, reflecting the substance of a CPPG discussion several days earlier, sought "agreement in a strategy for enticing the Hondurans to greater support for the Nicaraguan resistance [contras]," specifically, release of $75 million in embargoed economic aid. It also sought CPPG concurrence on a draft letter from President Reagan to President Roberto Suazo of Honduras, signaling continued U.S. assistance to Suazo and recognizing Honduras' continued support for the contras.[28]

As a result of the North-Burghardt memo, on February 19, 1985, McFarlane sent a memo to President Reagan attaching a proposed letter to Suazo. McFarlane explained to the President, "The CPPG agreed that an emissary should again proceed to Honduras carrying the signed copy of your letter and, in a second meeting, very privately explain our criteria for the expedited economic support, security assistance deliveries, and enhanced CIA support." [29] The President approved the plan.[30]

On April 25, 1985, McFarlane enlisted President Reagan's help in unsnagging a contra weapons shipment that the Honduran military had seized.[31] McFarlane recommended that the President call Suazo. "The Honduran military this morning stopped a shipment of ammunition . . ." McFarlane informed the President:

President Suazo will need some overt and concrete sign of this commitment in order to forestall his military in taking action against the FDN [contras] . . . [I]t is essential that you call President Suazo to reassure him that we intend to continue our support for the freedom fighters [contras] and that you are examining actions for which Congressional approval is not required.[32]

In a handwritten note on McFarlane's memo recommending the phone call, President Reagan recorded the substance of his conversation with Suazo:

Expressed his respect of me & his belief we must continue to oppose Communism. Will call his mil. commander & tell him to deliver the ammunition. Pledged we must continue to support the freedom [fighters] in Nicaragua. Then he spoke of a high level group coming here next week about [illegible] mil. in aid(?) . . . [illegible] both Shultz & Weinberger will meet with them.[33]

On October 30, 1985, North sent a memo to McFarlane titled "Reconnaissance Overflights," reporting on contra military developments.[34] According to notations on the document, Poindexter briefed President Reagan on North's recommendations that two reconnaissance aircraft be deployed to collect intelligence for the contras. North stated explicitly in the memo, "You should also tell the President that we intend to air-drop this intelligence to two Resistance [contra] units deployed along the Rio Escondito, along with two Honduran provided 106 recoilless rifles which will be used to sink one or both of the arms carriers which show up in the photograph at Tab I." A handwritten note by Poindexter on the memo indicated that the "President approved." [35]

## The 1985 Congressional Inquiries and "Problem Documents"

Although McFarlane and North tried to keep their contra-support activities secret, it was impossible to conceal completely such an ambitious project involving individuals throughout Central America and in Washington. In the summer of 1985, a series of press reports raised serious, detailed allegations of North's fundraising and other contra-support activities, in apparent violation of the Boland prohibition on contra aid. These press reports prompted inquiries to McFarlane from Rep. Michael Barnes, chairman of the House Foreign Affairs Subcommittee on Western Hemisphere Affairs, and

---

28 Memorandum from North and Burghardt to McFarlane, 2/11/85, ALU 0086481–82.

29 Memorandum from McFarlane to President Reagan, 2/19/85, ALU 0101807.

30 McFarlane, *North* Trial Testimony, 3/15/89, pp. 4531–32.

31 McFarlane, Recommended Telephone Call, 4/25/85, ALU 0097413–14.

32 Ibid.

33 Ibid. The question mark in parentheses was part of President Reagan's handwritten note.

34 Memorandum from North to McFarlane, 10/30/85, ALU 0068483–86.

35 Ibid.

Rep. Lee Hamilton, chairman of the House Permanent Select Committee on Intelligence.

McFarlane and North recognized the serious problems posed by the press stories. Despite the danger, North continued his clandestine activities. In an August 10, 1985, memo to McFarlane, North described efforts to assist a southern military front for the contras from Costa Rica. North noted, referring to the press reports: ''I am sincerely sorry that this very difficult time has occurred and wish to reiterate my offer to move on if this is becoming a liability for you or the President.'' [36] McFarlane responded by approving North's obtaining a false passport and personal papers using an alias for a trip to Central America.

In testimony since the public exposure of Iran/contra in November 1986, McFarlane took general responsibility for North's activities as his superior, while professing little knowledge of his actual contra-support efforts. There is extensive documentary evidence, however, that North reported regularly to McFarlane about many of his activities.

Some of the most detailed and explicit memos that North wrote to McFarlane were identified by NSC general counsel Paul B. Thompson in August 1985, after Congress asked McFarlane to respond to press allegations about North. Thompson, whom McFarlane had asked to gather documents relevant to the congressional inquiries, pulled six aside as potentially troubling in their contents. McFarlane called these the ''problem documents.'' [37]

They were culled from the NSC's ''System IV'' document file, which is a permanent, official collection of highly classified material, carefully logged and strictly controlled. Thompson and another NSC staff member, Brenda Reger, decided not to search North's office for documents that might have been responsive to the congressional inquiries but were not logged into the official NSC system. [38] The six System IV ''problem documents'' were:

1. A North to McFarlane memo of December 4, 1984, titled ''Assistance for the Nic-

araguan Resistance.'' [39] This three-page memo first described a meeting North had with a Chinese official in Washington regarding a transfer of Chinese-made SA–7 missiles and missile launchers for the contras. The official expressed concern because the end-user certificates indicated that the missiles were bound for Guatemala, which was on unfriendly terms with China. North explained to the Chinese official that the Guatemalan end-user certificates were false and that the weapons were, in fact, destined for the Nicaraguan contras. [40]

In the memo's second part, North described efforts by retired U.S. Army Maj. Gen. John Singlaub to seek military aid for the contras in South Korea and Taiwan.

The third part of the memo recounted a meeting North had with David Walker, a British military-security expert whom North wanted to introduce to Calero to conduct sabotage against Nicaragua. North added that efforts would be made to help Calero ''defray the cost'' of employing Walker.

2. A North to McFarlane memo dated February 6, 1985, titled ''Nicaraguan Arms Shipments.'' [41] North reported that a Nicaraguan merchant ship, the *Monimbo,* would be carrying weapons from Taiwan to the Sandinistas. North proposed that the cargo be seized and delivered to the contras, and/or that the ship be sunk. North suggested seeking the assistance of the South Korean military to sink the ship. He also sought McFarlane's authorization that Calero be given intelligence on the *Monimbo.* Poindexter added in a handwritten note at the bottom of the memo, ''We need to take action to make sure ship does not arrive in Nicaragua.''

---

[36] PROFs Note from North to McFarlane, 8/10/85.
[37] McFarlane, *North* Trial Testimony, 3/13/89, pp. 4084–85, and 3/16/89, p. 4796.
[38] See Thompson chapter.

[39] Memorandum from North to McFarlane, 12/4/84, AKW 037386–88.

[40] This sale of weapons to the contras was the first executed by retired U.S. Air Force Maj. Gen. Richard Secord and Albert Hakim. Washington attorney Thomas Green and a Canadian weapons dealer, Emanuel Weigensberg, were the chief investors. See Flow of Funds section.

[41] Memorandum from North to McFarlane, 2/6/85, AKW 011528 (2 pages).

3. A North to McFarlane memo dated March 5, 1985, titled "Guatemalan Aid to the Nicaraguan Resistance." [42] North attached a memo for McFarlane to send to Shultz, Weinberger, Casey and Vessey seeking their views on increased U.S. aid to Guatemala. North told McFarlane, "The real purpose of your memo is to find a way by which we can compensate the Guatemalans for the extraordinary assistance they are providing to the Nicaraguan freedom fighters [contras]." North attached fabricated end-user certificates provided by Guatemala, to allow the contras to receive $8 million in weapons under the guise of receipt by Guatemala. Also attached was a "wish list" of military items needed by Guatemala. North added, "Once we have approval for at least some of what they have asked for, we can ensure that the right people in Guatemala understand that we are able to provide results from their cooperation on the resistance [contra] issue." McFarlane approved and signed North's proposed memo to Shultz, Weinberger, Casey and Vessey.

4. A North to McFarlane memo of March 16, 1985, titled "Fallback Plan for the Nicaraguan Resistance." [43] North reported on possible options if Congress did not approve renewed funding for the contras, informing McFarlane that money from the "current donors" (Saudi Arabia) would keep the contras supplied until October 1985. North proposed that President Reagan publicly seek donations to a tax-exempt organization; McFarlane noted "not yet" on the memo in the margin next to North's recommendation that the President announce the formation of a tax-exempt contra fund. When North recommended that the "current donors" be urged to provide an "additional $25–30M[illion] to the resistance [contras] for the purchase of arms and munitions," McFarlane noted: "doubtful." McFarlane briefed the President on this memo.[44]

5. A North to McFarlane memo dated April 11, 1985, titled "FDN Military Operations." [45] North summarized contra funding from July 1984 to April 9, 1985, and reported on growth in troop strength from 9,500 to more than 16,000. He attached a detailed list of contra weapons purchases and deliveries between July 1984 and February 1985, and stated that the contras had spent approximately $17 million of the $24.5 million available to them since U.S. funding was cut off. Although the Secord Enterprise was not mentioned, North categorized the non-Secord purchases as "Independent Acquisition." North again recommended that "the current donors [Saudi Arabia] be approached to provide $15–20M[illion] additional between now and June 1, 1985."

6. A North to McFarlane memo dated May 31, 1985, titled "The Nicaraguan Resistance's Near-Term Outlook." [46] North reported on contra operations to cut Nicaraguan supply lines and other actions on the northern front "in response to guidance . . . ." He noted that plans were underway for the CIA to take back intelligence-gathering and political operations, once certain portions of the Boland prohibitions were lifted by Congress. He reported that, "The only portion of current activity which will be sustained as it has since last June, will be the delivery of lethal supplies."

The documents were clearly responsive to a letter from Chairman Barnes dated August 16, 1985, in which he asked McFarlane to "provide Congress with all information, including memoranda and any other documents, pertaining to any contact between Lt. Col. North and Nicaraguan rebel leaders as of enactment of the Boland Amendment in October, 1984." [47] Hamilton followed with a similar request in a letter dated August 20, 1985. A short while later, the Senate Select Committee on Intelligence (SSCI) also sought information about North's alleged activities.

42 Ibid., 3/5/85, AKW 015554–65D.
43 Ibid., 3/16/85, AKW 000536–38.
44 McFarlane, *North* Trial Testimony, 3/10/89, p. 4017.

45 Memorandum from North to McFarlane, 4/11/85.
46 Ibid., 5/31/85, ALU 008429–31.
47 Letter from Barnes to McFarlane, 8/16/85, AKW 001511.

The Barnes and Hamilton inquiries arrived at the White House while McFarlane was in California with President Reagan. When McFarlane returned to Washington, he met with North to discuss the problem documents that Thompson had identified.

". . . [T]hese are the ones [the documents] that had passages in them that in my mind I thought a congressman might criticize or believe was—was not allowed by the Boland Amendment," McFarlane later explained.[48] He said he met with North several times and discussed the documents because "they were documents that at least I did not fully understand and I figured a congressman wouldn't either and so I wanted to know what the truth was so I could answer it."[49]

McFarlane gave North a list of the problem documents, which North taped to his desk.[50] McFarlane said North suggested that he re-write at least one of the memoranda—the May 31, 1985, document—"to make sure that it was clear."[51] McFarlane told OIC that North's stated intention was to make the documents more accurately reflect the facts of the situation.[52] North's changes to the document, however, were obviously intended to obscure his contra-aid efforts.[53] McFarlane asked NSC counsel Paul Thompson about the legality of altering NSC documents and was told that both the original and the altered document should be filed with an explanation of the changes. McFarlane said he threw away the altered memo.[54]

In addition to reviewing the problem documents with North, McFarlane said they discussed the press allegations that North had been fund-raising for the contras. "I asked him how he responded to the charge that he had been raising money, and he explained how he had conducted himself whenever he had been speaking in public and explained to me why this was not a violation of law, in his judgment, and we went over it in some detail."[55] McFarlane said North assured him that although he made public speeches on behalf of the contras, he always explained that he, personally, could not raise funds because he was a Government official.[56]

McFarlane testified that it was not "clear" to him that North was involved in delivering weapons to the contras, despite memos indicating that he was.[57] McFarlane admitted that North reported to him in 1985 that a secret airstrip was being constructed in Costa Rica to resupply the contras, but he claimed he did not know what North's role was in establishing a southern military front for the contras. McFarlane said:

> . . . He was reporting to me that one [a southern front] was being set up but I'd been in the military for 20 years and I knew quite well that the activities of a single officer devoted to setting up an entire front for an army is inconsequential.[58]

McFarlane and North drafted letters of response to Congress that were patently false.[59] On September 5, 1985, McFarlane wrote Hamilton:

> . . . I can state with deep personal conviction that at no time did I or any member of the National Security Council staff violate the letter or spirit of the law. . . . It is equally important to stress what we did not do. We did not solicit funds or other support for military or paramilitary activities either from Americans or third parties. We did not offer tactical advice for the conduct of their military activities or their organization.[60]

[48] McFarlane, *North* Trial Testimony, 3/13/89, p. 4077.

[49] Ibid., p. 4085.

[50] In November 1986, North retrieved from the System IV files five of the six documents on the list and attempted to alter their substance. A sixth document, the December 4, 1984, document could not be located by the System IV officer at the time of North's request. North's secretary, Fawn Hall, altered the documents that North retrieved. North's purpose was defeated, however, because both the altered and unaltered versions of the documents were found in the NSC files by investigators.

[51] McFarlane *North* Trial Testimony, 3/13/89, p. 4109.

[52] McFarlane, FBI 302, 4/15/87, p. 5.

[53] Instead of referring to the "guidance" the contras had received from the NSC staff about cutting Nicaraguan supply lines, North inserted the word "awareness;" he deleted the entire passage of the document regarding the delivery of lethal supplies.North was tried and convicted of altering and shredding official documents; his conviction was overturned on appeal.

[54] McFarlane *North* Trial Testimony, 3/13/89, pp. 4114–15.

[55] Ibid., p. 4074.

[56] Ibid., pp. 4074–75.

[57] Ibid., 3/10/89, p. 4035.

[58] Ibid., p. 4038.

[59] North was charged with obstruction of and false statements to Congress in regard to the 1985 false responses. He was not convicted of those charges.

[60] Letter from McFarlane to Hamilton, 9/5/85, AKW 001528–29.

On September 12, 1985, McFarlane sent Barnes a letter containing virtually identical false denials of contra-aid activities by North and the NSC staff.[61]

In addition to written representations, McFarlane on September 5, 1985, met with leaders of the Senate Select Committee on Intelligence and assured them no laws had been broken and no NSC staff member had aided the contras or solicited funds on their behalf. On September 10, 1985, he made similar assurances in a meeting with Hamilton and other House Intelligence Committee members; the Hamilton meeting was followed up with written questions and answers, in which McFarlane again misrepresented the facts.[62] In these responses, he stated that North had not helped facilitate the movement of supplies to the contras and that no one on the NSC staff had an official or unofficial relationship to fund-raising for the contras.

Despite McFarlane's denials, Barnes on September 30, 1985, sought from McFarlane "oral and documentary" information, including memoranda, on NSC staff involvement in contra assistance.[63] McFarlane invited Barnes to meet with him at the White House on October 17, 1985. McFarlane showed Barnes a large stack of NSC documents described as relevant to his inquiry. McFarlane told Barnes, however, that the material could not leave the White House— that members of Congress could review them there.

Barnes did not take up McFarlane's offer. On October 29, 1985, he again requested that McFarlane turn over the documents to the House Intelligence Committee, which had facilities for safeguarding classified materials.[64] McFarlane did not respond.

McFarlane later admitted that his responses to Congress were "too categorical" and they were at the least, overstated.[65] He claimed, however, that he did not lie. He explained that he understood that Congress was primarily concerned with fund-raising for the contras—not the other types of violations exposed by North's memoranda.

McFarlane said North did not tell him certain things, because, "he was probably trying to protect me."[66] McFarlane was asked whether North raised objections when they were drafting the false responses to Congress:

Q: Did Colonel North say anything to indicate that he believed that these statements were just flat-out lies?

A: No, but that's not his fault. It's mine.

Q: You say it's your fault. But you also say you didn't do anything wrong. Is that—do I understand your testimony correctly?

A: I have said over and over again I did a lot of things wrong.

Q: Did you lie to Congress, Mr. McFarlane, in connection with these statements right here?

A: At the time I didn't believe it but at the time I was wrong and I admit that.[67]

McFarlane insisted that he did not lie to Congress. Instead, he claimed, he merely told them his version of the truth:

You do not lie to the Congress, that in my experience and working nine years on the White House staff it was often the case that congressmen would not always tell us everything on their agenda and similarly the Executive branch didn't always tell everything on its agenda to the Congress. You don't lie. You put your own interpretation on what the truth is.[68]

In 1986, after McFarlane resigned as national security adviser, North continued to seek his advice on a range of contra-related matters, making it clear that he was still actively involved in contra support.[69] In the spring and summer of 1986, after a new round of press allegations of North's activities spurred a new

61 Letter from McFarlane to Barnes, 9/12/85, AKW 001512–14.
62 Letter from McFarlane to Hamilton, 10/7/85, AKW 001540–48.
63 Letter from Barnes to McFarlane, 9/30/85, AKW 001515–16.
64 Letter from Barnes to McFarlane, 10/29/85, AKW 011734–36.
65 McFarlane, FBI 302, 9/13/90, p. 13.
66 McFarlane, *North* Trial Testimony, 3/13/89, p. 4184.
67 Ibid., pp. 4168–69.
68 Ibid., pp. 4129–30.
69 On April 21, 1986, for example, North in a computer note to McFarlane expressed his frustration over a shortage of contra funds: "There is great despair that we may fail in this effort and the resistance support acct. is darned near broke. Any thoughts where we can put our hands on a quick $3–5 M?" North added, "the pot is almost empty." (PROFs Note from North to McFarlane, 4/21/86, AKW 001150–51.)

round of congressional inquiries, McFarlane raised concerns about North's vulnerability with Poindexter in a computer message dated June 11, 1986.[70] McFarlane said, "I was worried in Colonel North's behalf. It didn't have anything to do with truth or falsity, but as a human being."[71] McFarlane continued:

Q: Was Colonel North worried in his own behalf when he talked to you?

A: Some.

Q: And did he tell you why he was concerned about having to talk to the people in Congress about his activities?

A: No.

Q: Did you ask him?

A: No. It was on the telephone and I don't think I would have.

Q: Do you know what his concerns would be, so that you didn't have to ask him, I mean?

A: No. I recognized, as I had the year before, that there certainly were understandable reasons for him to be concerned because many in the Congress would certainly not agree with what he did, whatever he did.[72]

## McFarlane and the Iran Arms Sales

McFarlane, along with CIA Director Casey, was an early exponent of the view that the United States should reopen ties with Iran to influence events after the death of the Ayatollah Khomeini. Independent Counsel did not charge McFarlane with any crime stemming from the arms initiative. As one of its originators and prime movers he provided valuable testimony regarding its genesis.

By the end of June 1985, six Americans were being held hostage by pro-Iranian Shi'ite Muslim terrorists in Beirut.[73] Other acts of terrorism

were launched against Americans, including the hijacking of a TWA jet in June 1985 and the murder of one of its passengers, U.S. Navy diver Robert Stetham.

Iran had, since the taking of the U.S. Embassy in 1979, been barred from receiving U.S. weaponry, and the United States, through a policy known as "Operation Staunch," discouraged weapons sales by other countries. In January 1984 Iran was officially declared by the State Department to be a sponsor of international terrorism, making it subject to additional arms-export restrictions.

Against this troubling backdrop, McFarlane dispatched Michael Ledeen, an NSC consultant, in the spring of 1985 to sound out Israeli officials about the possibility of establishing contacts inside Iran, in hopes of building ties with more moderate factions there. During the 1985 arms shipments, Ledeen acted as a conduit for information between Israeli officials, Israeli and Iranian arms brokers, and the NSC staff.[74] By using Ledeen as a private intermediary, McFarlane pretended not to have official NSC involvement in these overtures. Ledeen said he "had an understanding with Mr. McFarlane that neither of us would keep anything in writing regarding this initiative."[75]

Ledeen said he learned in March 1985 from a Western European intelligence official that Iran's political situation was fluid and that the United States could gain valuable information from the Israelis.[76] At about this time, Ledeen said he discussed with former CIA official Theodore Shackley a meeting Shackley had in late 1984 with an Iranian (Manucher Ghorbanifar), who told him it might be possible to ransom the release of American hostage William Buckley, the CIA's station chief in Beirut. According to Ledeen, Shackley in April or May

---

[70] PROFs Note from McFarlane to Poindexter, 6/11/86, AKW 021425.

[71] McFarlane, *North* Trial Testimony, 3/13/89, pp. 4234.

[72] Ibid., pp. 4234–35.

[73] The American hostages were William Buckley, the CIA's chief of station in the Lebanese capital; Presbyterian minister Benjamin Weir; Father Lawrence Martin Jenco, a Catholic priest; Associated Press re-

porter Terry Anderson; David Jacobsen, a hospital administrator; and Thomas P. Sutherland, a university dean.

[74] Ledeen was an early subject of Independent Counsel's investigation because of allegations that he personally profited from the Iran arms sales. No evidence was found supporting these allegations, although Ledeen admitted that he asked Israeli arms brokers Adolf (Al) Schwimmer and Yaakov Nimrodi to open a bank account in October 1985 to cover Iran arms sales expenses. Ledeen said an account was opened in Switzerland, that Schwimmer and Nimrodi gave him the number, and that he subsequently gave it to North. After the Iran arms sales became public, he received a letter from Credit Suisse stating that the account was never used and no money was ever deposited in it. (Ledeen, Grand Jury, 9/18/87, pp. 125–27, and Letter from Credit Suisse to Ledeen, 4/23/87.)

[75] Ledeen, Grand Jury, 9/18/87, p. 34.

[76] Ibid., pp. 21–23.

1985 asked him to relay to the Administration a memo on the ransom plan that had already been rejected by the State Department in December 1984.[77] Ledeen said he gave the Shackley memo to North.[78]

Ledeen traveled to Israel on McFarlane's behalf in early May 1985 and met with Israeli Prime Minister Shimon Peres. According to Ledeen, Peres asked him to carry a request back to McFarlane. Peres said Iran wanted to purchase from Israel U.S.-made artillery shells or pieces, and Israel could not make the sale without U.S. approval.[79] Shortly after his return to the United States in mid-May 1985, Ledeen relayed the results of his meetings in Israel and also the Peres request. Ledeen said McFarlane checked on the request and subsequently told Ledeen "that it was okay but just that one shipment and nothing else." [80] McFarlane claimed not to have remembered any discussion with Ledeen regarding artillery parts.[81]

In Israel, meanwhile, talks were progressing among Israeli officials, including Adolf (Al) Schwimmer, an adviser to Prime Minister Peres; Israeli arms dealer Yaakov Nimrodi; and Iranian entrepreneur Manucher Ghorbanifar. Ghorbanifar had proposed that Israel sell Iran 100 U.S.-made TOW missiles; as a sign of the power of his contacts in Iran, he would obtain the release of CIA Station Chief Buckley.[82]

In early June 1985, McFarlane approved a second trip by Ledeen to Israel, but it was canceled because Secretary of State Shultz was angry when he learned after the fact of Ledeen's earlier secret mission.[83] When U.S.

Ambassador to Israel Samuel Lewis learned of Ledeen's previous visit, he complained to Shultz; when Shultz confronted McFarlane on the matter, McFarlane informed Shultz that Ledeen was there on his own, not on an NSC assignment.[84]

On June 17, 1985, McFarlane circulated a draft National Security Decision Directive (NSDD) on Iran to Shultz, Casey and Defense Secretary Weinberger, recommending the option of selling military equipment to Iran in an effort to re-open ties. Shultz and Weinberger opposed the draft NSDD; Casey endorsed it.

On July 3, 1985, David Kimche, the director general of Israel's Foreign Ministry, met with McFarlane in Washington. McFarlane's recollection of the discussion was:

> . . . In this conversation, there was no request for arms, in any respect, nor linkage made between arms and the release of the hostages although Mr. Kimche did advert to the possibility that arms might be raised in the future. He asked that I provide the U.S. Government position.
>
> Within two or three days, I conveyed this information to the President as well as to the Secretaries of State and Defense. The President reflected on the matter and gave his approval to such a political dialogue. I conveyed this information to Mr. Kimche. . . .[85]

McFarlane heard shortly after his Washington meeting with Kimche about a request from Ghorbanifar for 100 TOW missiles. On July 7, 1985, Kimche, Nimrodi, Schwimmer, Ghorbanifar and international financier Adnan Khashoggi met in Geneva, where Ghorbanifar proposed the TOW missile sale to strengthen his position in Iran. As in earlier meetings, Ghorbanifar claimed he could obtain the release of American hostages as a result.[86] On July 8, 1985, Kimche, Nimrodi, Schwimmer, Khashoggi and Ghorbanifar met with Ghorbanifar's Iranian contact in Hamburg, West Germany. The participants discussed TOW mis-

[77] Memorandum from Shackley to Walters, 11/22/84.

[78] Ledeen, Grand Jury, 9/18/87, p. 48. Despite the lack of documentation by McFarlane and Ledeen, North's notebooks suggest the timing of Ledeen's early contacts regarding Iran. North's notebooks on January 15, 1985, reflect a call to CIA counterterrorism official Duane R. Clarridge, regarding Ledeen. (North Notebook, 1/15/85, AMX 000327.) On March 21, 1985, North noted: "Mtg w/Ledeen—Wants to make trip to Israel—RCM [McFarlane] . . ." On April 28, 1985, North noted, "Call Clarridge re Ledeen [] Iranian." (North Notebook, 4/28/85, AMX 000626.)

[79] Ledeen, Grand Jury, 9/18/87, p. 30.

[80] Ibid., p. 37.

[81] McFarlane, Tower Commission Testimony, 2/19/87, p. 93.

[82] Israeli Historical Chronology, Part One, 7/29/87, p. 5, AOW 0000018, as released in Select Committees Report, pp. 164–65.

[83] Ledeen, Grand Jury, 9/18/87, pp. 40–41. North's notebooks reflect that he discussed the impending trip with Ledeen on June 3, 1985: "Call from Ledeen—Re Iran contact—so many people making approaches—confused as to intermediary—could we sit down and talk—Mullah's want to meet with a 'person we can deal with'—Ledeen leaving Friday on trip for Bud [McFarlane]—Gone for week—Ted Shackley 320–2190 (H) 522–3253 (O)." (North Notebook, 6/3/85, AMX 000732.)

[84] McFarlane, FBI 302, 3/10/87, p. 4.

[85] McFarlane, SSCI Testimony, 12/7/86, p. 9.

[86] Israeli Historical Chronology, Part One, 7/29/87, pp. 12–13, AOW 0000025–26, as released in Select Committees Report, p. 166,

siles and hostages, and the possibilities of U.S.-Israeli cooperation on the matter.[87]

On July 11, 1985, Schwimmer at Kimche's direction met with Ledeen in Washington. Schwimmer told Ledeen that Ghorbanifar thought the American hostages could be freed and that selling TOW missiles to Iran would improve U.S.-Iran relations.[88] Continuing the rapid pace of events in July 1985, Ledeen relayed to McFarlane the information Schwimmer had given him. McFarlane told Ledeen he would have to study whether the United States should sell TOW missiles to Iran.[89] Shortly after meeting with McFarlane, Ledeen left for Israel, where he met with Israeli officials and Ghorbanifar.

McFarlane informed Shultz by way of a back-channel cable on July 14, 1985, about Kimche's proposal that 100 TOWs be shipped to Iran.

McFarlane's testimony about the July-August 1985 period wavered in terms of precise dates, but it remained relatively consistent regarding the progression of events. McFarlane said he informed President Reagan of the Kimche proposal to sell arms to Iran when Reagan was recovering from cancer surgery at Bethesda Naval Hospital in July 1985.[90] According to McFarlane, the President said "that he could understand how people who were trying to overthrow a government would need weapons, but we weren't yet sure about whether they were legitimate. So he said that we, the United States, could not do it."[91]

McFarlane reported the President's response to Kimche, and Kimche requested a second meeting. On August 2, 1985, Kimche met with McFarlane at the White House and told McFarlane that the Iranian contacts the Israelis had developed were legitimate. According to McFarlane, Kimche asked, "What if Israel were to deliver the TOWs, not the United States, would that be different? Would you agree with that?"[92] Kimche asked McFarlane for the official U.S. position and McFarlane agreed to report it to the President.

McFarlane said Kimche asked whether the United States would sell replacement weapons to the Israelis if the TOW missiles came from their stocks. McFarlane said he told Kimche: "David, that's not the point. You've been buying missiles from us for a long time and you always can. You know that. The issue, and I will get you an answer, is whether it should be done at all."[93]

McFarlane said in the week following his August 2 meeting with Kimche, there were meetings at which the TOW missile sale was discussed; he repeatedly testified that Shultz, Weinberger, Vice President Bush, Poindexter and White House Chief of Staff Donald Regan were either present in those meetings or kept apprised of the discussions.[94] McFarlane said, President Reagan "decided that he would approve Israel's delivery of HAWK—excuse me—TOW missiles, and that if Israel came to us to purchase replacements they could do that."[95] McFarlane said the replenishment issue, as part of his presentation of the Kimche proposal, was discussed with Shultz and Weinberger.[96] McFarlane said shortly thereafter he notified Kimche of the President's decision.[97]

On August 20, 1985, Israel—working through Nimrodi, Schwimmer and Ghorbanifar—transferred 96 U.S.-made TOW missiles to Iran via chartered aircraft. No hostages were freed following the initial TOW missile shipment, al-

---

[87] Ibid., pp. 13–14, AOW 0000026–27, as released in Select Committees Report, p. 166.

[88] Ledeen, Grand Jury, 9/18/87, pp. 44–45. Ledeen said this was the first time he had ever heard of Ghorbanifar; he said he did not realize at the time that the memo he had received earlier from Shackley about ransoming Buckley was based on a meeting with Ghorbanifar. (Ibid., pp. 47–49.)

[89] Ibid., p. 53.

[90] McFarlane, *North* Trial Testimony, 3/16/89, p. 4761. According to "The Public Papers of the President, 1985," Appendix A, p. 1513, McFarlane on July 18, 1985, "briefed the President on the conclusion of round two of the U.S.-Soviet nuclear and space arms negotiations and also on terrorism and efforts to combat it." McFarlane's schedule also shows a meeting with the President and Secretary of State George Shultz at Bethesda Naval Hospital at 11 a.m. on Friday, July 19, 1985.

[91] Ibid.

[92] Ibid., p. 4762.

[93] Ibid.

[94] In an interview with the Tower Commission, McFarlane was perplexed by a lack of White House meeting agendas for the late July-early August 1985 time frame where all or more than two or three of the NSC principals gathered. "[I]t is those meetings where Iran was discussed," he said. " . . . I called the Executive Secretary at the NSC and I asked are there agendas for each of the following meetings, and I gave them six meetings from July 22 to August 7, and he said no, there are no agendas for meetings at which the President met with all of them on at least two occasions. I don't know." (McFarlane, Tower Commission Testimony, 2/19/87, p. 19.)

[95] McFarlane, *North* Trial Testimony, 3/16/89, p. 4764.

[96] McFarlane, FBI 302, 3/20/92, p. 5.

[97] McFarlane, *North* Trial Testimony, 3/16/89, p. 4764.

though Ghorbanifar continued to promise their release.[98]

In September 1985, Ledeen provided North with information to allow surveillance of Ghorbanifar and his contacts.[99] By this point, North had become involved in logistical aspects of arranging for the hostages to leave Lebanon. A note taken by a Shultz aide, Nicholas Platt, on September 4, 1985, reflects information that North, Ledeen and McFarlane were involved in obtaining the release of hostages, via Israel providing "equipment" to Iran.[100]

On September 14, 1985, a second shipment of 408 TOW missiles from Israel to Iran was made, finally resulting in the release of one American hostage, Reverend Benjamin Weir. Ledeen said the Weir release "confirmed the legitimacy of Ghorbanifar as a channel to powerful people in Iran."[101] But U.S. officials clearly expected more. The fact that Buckley had not been released was of special concern, because Administration officials had sought his return first.[102] Throughout September and October, Ledeen continued to act as McFarlane's private liaison with Israeli officials and Ghorbanifar in the arms-for-hostages deals.[103] Instead of further releases following Weir, however, there were increasing demands by Ghorbanifar for more weapons. In early October 1985, the terrorist group believed to be holding the hostages in Beirut reported that Buckley was dead.

In October 1985, Ledeen told McFarlane the Iranians wanted several types of missiles, including Phoenix and Harpoon missiles. McFarlane said it was "out of the question, it's nuts, just forget about it."[104]

North noted an October 30, 1985, discussion with Ledeen, in which Ledeen described a recent meeting he had with one of Ghorbanifar's Iranian contacts, Hassan Karoubi, in Geneva. The notes state: "what's Rqd. [required] to get hostages out." North then noted, 150 HAWKS, 200 Sidewinder missiles, and 30–50 Phoenix

missiles.[105] The notes also reflect the Israelis' continuing concern over replenishment of the TOW missiles they shipped to Iran in August-September 1985, the fact that Buckley had not been released, and McFarlane's apparent belief that arms sales should be stopped unless more hostages are freed.

By November, Ghorbanifar and his Iranian contacts were seeking U.S.-made Improved HAWK missiles from Israel. Israel proceeded to make plans for a shipment. On November 8, 1985, McFarlane met with Kimche in Washington.[106]

On November 9, 1985, McFarlane told Weinberger that hostage-release efforts were tied to arms sales to Iran. Noting a call from McFarlane, Weinberger wrote: "wants to start 'negot.' exploration with Iranians (+ Israelis) to give Iranians weapons for our hostages . . ."[107] On November 10, 1985, Weinberger noted a discussion with McFarlane, stating, "we might give them—thru Israelis—Hawks but no Phoenix."[108] On November 14, 1985, Shultz aide Charles Hill noted a conversation between Shultz and State Department official Michael Armacost, stating, "in last few days Bud [McFarlane] asked Cap [Weinberger] how to get 600 Hawks + 200 Phoenix to Iran. Its [sic] highly illegal. Cap won't do it I'm sure. Purpose not clear. Another sign of funny stuff on Iran issue. . ."[109]

McFarlane met with Israeli Defense Minister Yitzhak Rabin on November 15, 1985, in Washington, shortly before McFarlane left for the Geneva summit of President Reagan and Soviet leader Mikhail Gorbachev. McFarlane said, "I believe that his [Rabin's] purpose in coming was simply to reconfirm that the President's authority for the original concept was still valid. We hadn't changed our minds. And I reconfirmed that that was the case."[110] McFarlane said Rabin told him that the Israelis were about

[98] Israeli Historical Chronology, Part One, 7/29/87, p. 27, AOW 000040, as released in Select Committees Report, p. 168.

[99] Ledeen, Grand Jury, 9/18/87, pp. 103–04.

[100] Platt Note, 9/4/85, ALW 0036259.

[101] Ledeen, Grand Jury, 9/18/87, p. 105.

[102] McFarlane, FBI 302, 3/20/92, pp. 1, 12.

[103] Among these meetings, on October 7 and 8, 1985, Ledeen met in Washington with North, Schwimmer, Nimrodi and Ghorbanifar.

[104] McFarlane, Grand Jury, 5/4/87, p. 59.

[105] North Notebook, 10/30/85, AMX 001836.

[106] McFarlane Calendar, 11/8/85, MF 856–57.

[107] Weinberger Note, 11/9/85, AKW 018126.

[108] Ibid., 11/10/85, ALZ 0039775.

[109] Hill Note, 11/14/85, ANS 0001187. McFarlane said he did not believe he ever raised with Weinberger a request for 600 HAWKs and 200 Phoenix missiles for Iran, because he had rejected such a request by Ledeen in October and was strongly opposed to it. (McFarlane, FBI 302, 3/20/92, pp. 14, 15.)

[110] McFarlane, Tower Commission Testimony, 2/19/87, p. 36.

to make another arms shipment to Iran, but he did not mention HAWKs.[111]

On November 14, 1985, McFarlane and Poindexter discussed hostage-release efforts with Casey and his deputy John McMahon. McMahon memorialized this meeting for the record, noting that: ". . . McFarlane then told us about the Israeli plan to move arms to certain elements of the Iranian military who are prepared to overthrow the government.''[112]

During the Reagan-Gorbachev summit in Geneva, McFarlane informed President Reagan and White House Chief of Staff Donald T. Regan of the impending arms shipment and the anticipated hostage release. On November 19, 1985, McFarlane also informed Shultz in Geneva of the impending shipment by Israel to Iran. Hill's notes reflect a secure call between McFarlane and Shultz:

> Bud [McFarlane] talked to Kimche. 4 host[a]g[es] to be released Thursd[a]y. Isr[ael]. will fly plane w[ith] 100 Hawk to [a European city]. Transfer to another plane. If host[a]g[e]s released, plane will go to Iran. If not, Israel. Isr[ael]. will buy from us to replace & be p[ai]d by Iran. . . .[113]

Weinberger, who was in Washington, received a call from McFarlane in Geneva. He noted that McFarlane "wants us to try to get 500 Hawks for sale to Israel to pass on to Iran for release of 5 hostages Thurs[day]."[114] Although Weinberger had opposed the principle of trading arms for hostages in White House meetings with the other NSC members, he asked his chief military aide U.S. Army General Colin Powell to research the viability of McFarlane's request. Powell reported back that the large quantity of HAWKs at issue could not be shipped without congressional notification. Weinberger on November 19, 1985, called McFarlane in Geneva with the information.[115] On November 20, 1985, McFarlane informed Weinberger in a call from Geneva: ". . . President has decided to do it thru Israelis."[116]

Israeli Defense Minister Rabin called McFarlane in Geneva and told him there was a problem getting an arms shipment through a European country. McFarlane called Poindexter in Washington to help, and North undertook a series of steps in response. North told McFarlane there were two problems: the European country was not granting landing rights, and the missiles needed to be loaded onto another aircraft because they were coming from Tel Aviv in an El Al plane with Israeli markings. At North's request, McFarlane, who was in Rome, contacted officials in the European country to seek permission to land.[117]

On November 22, 1985, McFarlane, who was in Rome, contacted the foreign minister of the European country where landing rights were being sought.[118]

Ultimately, the HAWK missiles went from Israel by way of a west Asian country on November 24, 1985. When the missiles arrived in Iran, they were rejected as the wrong type of HAWK. Consequently, only one planeload bearing 18 HAWK missiles was delivered. No hostages were released.[119]

On or about November 25, 1985, Ledeen received a frantic phone call from Ghorbanifar, asking him to relay a message from the prime minister of Iran to President Reagan regarding the shipment of the wrong type of HAWKs. Ledeen said the message essentially was "we've been holding up our part of the bargain, and here you people are now cheating us and tricking us and deceiving us and you had better correct this situation right away."[120]

Ledeen relayed the message to Poindexter, and Poindexter informed Ledeen he was no longer needed for the project, that instead the Administration would use a person with more technical expertise.[121] Ledeen said North informed him in December 1985 that the arms deals "had been shut down."[122] Despite this

111 McFarlane, FBI 302, 3/20/92, p. 14.
112 Memorandum for the Record by McMahon, 11/15/85, ER 32809–10.
113 Hill Note, 11/18/85, ANS 0001200.
114 Weinberger Note, 11/19/85, ALZ 0039795.
115 Ibid., ALZ 0039797.
116 Ibid., 11/20/85, ALZ 0039799.

117 McFarlane, Grand Jury, 5/4/87, pp. 60–64.
118 PROFs Note from North to Poindexter, 11/22/85, AKW 002068.
119 The failed HAWKs shipment resulted in the illegal involvement of the CIA. North had enlisted the help of CIA official Duane "Dewey" Clarridge to unsnag the landing-rights problem in the European country and to obtain the name of a CIA proprietary airline that could transfer the missiles to Iran. Clarridge's action caused CIA officials to insist, following the weekend of the HAWK shipment, that the President sign a covert-action Finding retroactively authorizing a CIA role. See Clarridge chapter.
120 Ledeen, Grand Jury, 9/18/87, p. 133.
121 Ibid., pp. 134–35.
122 Ibid., p. 150.

information, Ledeen continued his contacts with Ghorbanifar into a new phase of the arms shipments, meeting with Duane Clarridge and Charles Allen of the CIA, in early December 1985 to "brief them on Ghorbanifar, who he was, how I had known him, what we had done with him, to lay the groundwork for possible cooperation between them and him." [123]

## McFarlane's Resignation: The Iran Initiative Continues

McFarlane resigned as national security adviser on December 4, 1985. In announcing McFarlane's departure to the press, President Reagan said: "I should warn you that I'll probably be calling on you from time to time for your wise counsel and advice." [124] In an exchange of letters regarding McFarlane's resignation, President Reagan again hinted that he would continue to use his former national security adviser in a special capacity, stating: "I trust you will still permit me to call on you from time to time." [125] The President immediately called McFarlane into service, as further arms sales to Iran were under consideration.

On December 5, Poindexter notified the NSC principals that there would be an off-the-schedule meeting on Saturday, December 7, in the White House residence to discuss whether the Iran initiative should continue.

On the morning of December 7, President Reagan met with McFarlane, Shultz, Weinberger, Regan, McMahon and Poindexter. Weinberger's notes reflect a discussion of HAWKs and TOWs that the President believed would go to "moderate elements in Army" in Iran; Weinberger objected strongly on the grounds that the U.S. embargo on arms sales to Iran would make such a sale illegal, even if it were done through Israel. Regan and Shultz agreed with his position, but the President was adamant that he should not pass up a chance to free the hostages. [126]

McFarlane said he was the principal speaker at the December 7 White House meeting, describing the progression of the Iran arms sales since August and asking the NSC principals whether the initiative should continue. [127] As a result of the meeting, McFarlane was dispatched to London to meet for the first time with Ghorbanifar. North, meanwhile, was already in London, meeting with Secord, Kimche, two other Israeli officials, and later Ghorbanifar. [128]

According to Weinberger's notes, McFarlane's mission to London was to "advise President's decision that we will not ransom our hostages—he will discuss with UK possibility of their selling some arms to negotiators." [129] Shultz was told by Poindexter:

> . . . Bud [McFarlane] is to ask them [Iran] to release hostg. [hostage]. Then, we prep[ared] to work for better rel[ations]. If rejected, he auth[orized] to go to [Great Britain which] sells arms to IR[an] anyway & see if [they] will pick up sale. I s[ai]d its [sic] still US arms. Just more complicated & we more vulnerable. P[resident] annoyed. McF[arlane] had him sold on it. [130]

On Sunday, December 8, 1985, McFarlane met at the London home of arms dealer Nimrodi, with North, Secord, Ghorbanifar, Schwimmer, Kimche and an Israeli defense official. McFarlane stated the position of the United States, that it welcomed discussions with Iran and an improvement of relations. The release of the hostages would be important evidence of a similar desire by the Iranians. Such a release would be followed by an appropriate effort to supply arms. [131] Ghorbanifar responded that he would not transmit this position for fear that the hostages would be killed. McFarlane walked away from his meeting with Ghorbanifar with a mixed impression of his political knowledge and personal character:

> . . . while he seemed to have a rather agile and creative mind for intrigue and in retrospect, a rather accurate view of the politics

[123] Ibid., p. 158.

[124] "Remarks Announcing the Resignation of Robert C. McFarlane as Assistant to the President for National Security Affairs and the Appointment of John M. Poindexter," 12/4/85, *Public Papers of the Presidents,* 1985, p. 1440.

[125] "Letter Accepting the Resignation of Robert C. McFarlane as Assistant to the President for National Security Affairs," *Public Papers of he Presidents,* 1985, p. 1443.

[26] Weinberger Note, 12/7/85, ALZ 0039831.

[127] McFarlane, FBI 302, 3/20/92, p. 20.

[128] Secord, Select Committees Testimony, 5/6/87, pp. 11–14.

[129] Weinberger Note, 12/7/85, ALZ 0039832, ALZ 0039838.

[130] Hill Note, 12/9/85, ANS 0001246.

[131] Memorandum from North to McFarlane and Poindexter, 12/9/85, AKW 02088–91.

within Iran, he was a person of intrigue and conspiracy and not a diplomat. Kind of a north end of a south bound horse. And I didn't think we should do business with the man.[132]

On December 10, 1985, McFarlane met at the White House with the President, Weinberger, Casey, Regan, and Poindexter to brief them on his meeting in London with Ghorbanifar. McFarlane told them he found him untrustworthy. According to McFarlane, he told the group that he told Ghorbanifar to tell the Iranians that, "We will talk with them [the Iranians], but no more weapons." [133] According to Weinberger's notes of the meeting, McFarlane called Ghorbanifar "corrupt, duplicitous— not to be trusted." [134] Weinberger's notes also reflect that five options for future hostage-release efforts were discussed, including "US deal with Iranians + give up Israeli cover." [135]

The December 10, 1985, meeting, in which McFarlane recommended no further dealings with Ghorbanifar, marked McFarlane's last involvement for several months in the Iran arms sales. McFarlane's pessimistic report did nothing to stop the arms deals; instead, in January 1986 President Reagan approved direct U.S. arms sales to Iran. Also, Ghorbanifar remained involved as an intermediary, although, confirming McFarlane's assessment, he failed polygraph tests administered to him by the CIA.[136]

## The Tehran Mission

Poindexter and North continued to keep McFarlane apprised of developments on the Iran arms sales in 1986. McFarlane's special relationship with the NSC staff was demonstrated by the fact that he remained in regular contact with them via a White House PROFs computer terminal in his home.[137]

On February 27, 1986, North reported in a PROFs message to McFarlane about discussions

he had just had in Frankfurt with an Iranian official, Mohsen Kangerlu, in which the Iranians sought a high-level meeting with U.S. officials. North noted that neither Poindexter nor Casey were "very enthusiastic" about such a plan, but he told McFarlane "you shd [should] be chartered" to attend such a meeting.[138] Later that same day, McFarlane in a PROFs note to North told him Poindexter had asked and he agreed to go to a meeting with Iranians the following week. McFarlane told North, "So hunker down and get some rest; let this word come to you in channels, but pack your bags to be ready to go in the next week or so." [139]

The mission would not, in fact, occur, until May 1986, following a series of meetings between North, Ghorbanifar, CIA officials, Secord, Hakim and Israeli counterterrorism official Amiram Nir, both in the United States and Europe. North regularly reported on breaking developments to McFarlane. The two men continued to enjoy close relations.[140]

Negotiations for a high-level meeting with Iranian officials continued through April. On April 21, 1986, Poindexter told McFarlane that the Iranians were insisting on a delivery of HAWK missile parts before releasing the hostages. Poindexter said the U.S.-Iran meeting should take place first, followed by the release of the hostages, and concluding with the delivery of the HAWK parts. Poindexter told McFarlane, "The President is getting quite discouraged by this effort. This will be our last attempt to make a deal with the Iranians." [141] In response, McFarlane told Poindexter: "Your firmness against the recurrent attempts to up the ante is correct. Wait them out; they will come around. I will be flexible." [142]

[132] McFarlane, SSCI Testimony, 12/7/86, p. 33.

[133] McFarlane, FBI 302, 3/20/92, p. 21.

[134] Weinberger Meeting Note, 12/10/85, ALZ 0040644B.

[135] Ibid. These options tracked with an options paper dated December 9, 1985, that North prepared for McFarlane and Poindexter; the fifth option described in the paper was for the United States to sell arms directly to Iran, acting pursuant to a Presidential covert-action finding, using Secord as an operative. (Memorandum from North to McFarlane and Poindexter, 12/9/85, AKW 002088–91.)

[136] See Casey chapter.

[137] PROFs was the name of the NSC computer program; it stood for Professional Office system.

[138] PROFs Note from North to McFarlane, 2/27/86, AKW 072209.

[139] PROFs Note from McFarlane to North, 2/27/87, AKW 072211.

[140] In a March 10, 1986, message to North, McFarlane expressed concern over renewed scrutiny by Congress over North's contra-aid activities, suggesting that North join him in the private sector at the Center for Strategic and International Studies (CSIS), a Washington think tank. He painted a simple scenario for North's future: "1. North leaves the White House in May and takes 30 days leave. 2. July 1st North is assigned as a fellow at the CSIS and (lo and behold) is assigned to McFarlane's office. 3. McFarlane/North continue to work the Iran account as well as to begin to build other clandestine capabilities so much in demand here and there. Just a knee jerk musing." (PROFs Note from McFarlane to North, 3/10/86, AKW 001141.)

[141] PROFs Note from Poindexter to McFarlane, 4/21/86, AKW 021469.

[142] PROFs Note from McFarlane to Poindexter, 4/22/86, AKW 021474.

In early May, North and CIA annuitant George Cave met in London with Ghorbanifar and Nir, where the groundwork finally was laid for a meeting between McFarlane and high-level Iranian officials, as well as financial arrangements for the arms deal. Among the officials Ghorbanifar said would meet with an American delegation were the president and prime minister of Iran and the speaker of the Iranian parliament.

Before McFarlane left for the meeting, scheduled to take place in Tehran, Poindexter briefed McFarlane on the plan: When the American party arrived in Tehran, two of the American hostages would be released to the U.S. ambassador in Beirut; then, a second aircraft carrying HAWK parts would depart from Tel Aviv, Israel, en route to Tehran, and two more American hostages would be released to the U.S. ambassador; upon confirmation that the releases had taken place, a third aircraft carrying HAWK parts would depart Tel Aviv for Tehran, and at that point the remains of Buckley would be turned over.[143]

McFarlane, North, Cave, NSC staff member Howard Teicher, and two CIA communications specialists left Washington for Iran via Frankfurt and Israel on May 23, 1986. In Israel, Secord and Nir—who had replaced Kimche as the Israeli official in the arms deals—joined the group. Only a portion of the HAWK spare parts expected by the Iranians was loaded onto the aircraft that the party was taking to Iran.

On May 25, 1986, the McFarlane party arrived in Tehran at 8:30 a.m. local time, bringing with them HAWK spare parts. The rest of the parts expected by the Iranians remained in Israel, to be flown in once the hostages were released in Lebanon. The Americans were escorted to the former Hilton Hotel. According to North's notes of a secure message transmitted to the White House, "We have been treated politely, though heavily escorted by Rev[olutionary] Guard types who are also physically and technically surveilling our rooms."[144] That evening, the McFarlane party began three days of largely fruitless talks with Iranians.

McFarlane expected the hostage releases to begin when they arrived in Tehran, and asked the deputy-level officials with whom they met the first evening why that hadn't occurred. He was also disappointed that he was not meeting with higher-level officials. Already, it was clear that the Iranians and Ghorbanifar had not agreed on the hostage-release plan that Ghorbanifar had previously laid out to the Americans.[145]

According to notes taken by Teicher, the Iranian officials with whom they met the first night:

> . . . were in a bargaining mode. They claimed the [HAWK] spares were inadequate and used, and that we couldn't keep a man on the plane. After an hour of polite exchanges, Bud got steamed. Nonetheless, things didn't seem to be too off-track; until during dinner we learned that contrary to our refusal, they had taken our man off the plane. This stimulated a flurry of angry exchanges which in the end proved unsat. [unsatisfactory]. By 11:00, after shish, caviar, ice cream things were beginning to look grim. Bud [McFarlane] threatened + started to pack. At 11:30 we broke up + called it a night.[146]

According to North's notes, McFarlane opened the meeting with a broad political discussion, telling the Iranians that President Reagan instructed him "to do what is necessary to find common ground for discussions in future." [147] McFarlane said the "very fact that I am here is proof that we have turned page of history." [148] North's notes also reflect that the Iranians were upset with the limited amount of HAWK spare parts the Americans had brought with them.

On May 26 McFarlane met again with Iranian officials. According to Teicher's notes, the "meeting w/Bud doesn't go well, deservedly. He finally walks out basically telling them to fix the problems + we can then resume a dialogue. They tell us that a special representative will soon be here to meet w/Bud." [149] In a memo of the discussion prepared by Teicher,

143 McFarlane, FBI 302, 3/13/87, pp. 10–11.
144 North Note, 5/25/86, AMX 001128.
145 McFarlane, FBI 302, 3/13/87, pp. 12–13.
146 Teicher Note, 5/25/86, AKW 005419.
147 North Note, 5/25/86, AMX 001129.
148 Ibid., AMX 001132.
149 Teicher Note, 5/26/86, AKW 005420.

the Iranian official told McFarlane that more preparations had to be made before discussions could begin with McFarlane at the "ministerial" level; McFarlane expressed disappointment and told him before a dialogue could begin with the United States, "[t]he preliminary problem in Lebanon must be overcome." [150]

That evening North, Teicher, Cave and Nir met—without McFarlane—with an Iranian foreign affairs adviser to the speaker of the Iranian Parliament. Teicher described this as "our most serious meeting," lasting several hours.[151] The next day, May 27, the Iranian adviser informed the American delegation that the hostage-holders in Beirut had been contacted and put heavy conditions on the release of hostages, including the release of Dawa terrorists imprisoned in Kuwait.

On the late afternoon of May 27, McFarlane told the Iranian foreign affairs adviser that the President had already tried in three previous weapons shipments to Iran to establish a dialogue with that country:

But his instructions to me in sending me here were that if this 4th try didn't achieve results it was pointless to pursue an ineffective dialogue. I can understand that there may have been misunderstandings + I don't point to any bad faith. But my Pres.'s instructions are firm, w/o [without] results we are to discontinue the talks. These are very firm instructions. All the items that have been paid for are loaded + poised for release the minute the hostages are in our custody. Their prompt delivery w/i [within] 10 hours is our solemn commitment . . . to the problem raised by the captors, the Dawa prisoners, it is much on our mind as it has been raised before. Our position is derived from our policy which respect's [sic] all nations judicial policies. We cannot ignore their process. I am sad to report this. I respect what you said. I will report to my Pres. But I cannot be optimistic.[152]

In the late evening of May 27, the Americans said they would give the Iranians until 4 a.m. the following morning to free all the hostages. An aircraft carrying the remainder of the HAWK spare parts would arrive in Tehran at 10 a.m.; if the hostages were not freed by 4 a.m., the aircraft would be ordered back in midflight. The Iranian foreign affairs adviser asked about the hostage-takers' demand for the Dawa prisoners, and North proposed a statement that the United States would make every effort to achieve their release and fair treatment.[153] At 11:30 p.m., after "more wrangling" between McFarlane and the Iranian foreign affairs adviser, Teicher noted:

. . . we conclude that they're just stringing us along. RCM [McFarlane] gives order to pack/depart. We discovered 15 minutes earlier that all day the plane was not refueled . . . leaving us semi-stranded.[154]

At 1:30 a.m. on May 28 Tehran time, Poindexter called McFarlane and told him that President Reagan said to launch the plane carrying HAWK parts from Tel Aviv, but if there were no word on hostage releases by 4 a.m., to leave Tehran; the Iranians asked that they be given until 6 a.m.[155]

After a series of false signals throughout the night resulting in no hostage release, the McFarlane party left Tehran at approximately 9 a.m., May 28.[156] The plane carrying the second portion of HAWK parts from Tel Aviv to Iran turned back in mid-flight.

---

[150] Memorandum of Conversation from Teicher, 5/26/86, AKW 005310–12.

[151] Teicher Note, 5/26/86, AKW 005421.

[152] Ibid., 5/27/86, AKW 005449–50.

[153] Memorandum from Teicher, 5/27/86, AKW 005327.

[154] Teicher Note, 5/27/86, AKW 005452.

[155] Ibid., 5/28/86, AKW 005452. In testimony to the Select Committees, McFarlane said that North called the second plane to leave Tel Aviv for Tehran and that he (McFarlane) learned of North's order after the fact. (McFarlane, Select Committees Testimony, 5/12/87, p. 79.) North said he gave the order for the second plane to leave Tel Aviv based on the previously established schedule. (North, Select Committees Testimony, 7/9/87, pp. 113–15.) Teicher's notes indicate that the order for the plane to leave Tel Aviv came from President Reagan early on the morning of May 28, 1986: "12:45 Bud [McFarlane] talks to John [Poindexter]. Advises us to hold pending discussion w/RR [Reagan]. 1:30 [a.m.] JMP [Poindexter] calls. RR says launch second plane. If no word on hostage release by 4:00, leave Tehran. 2:00 [a.m.] RCM [McFarlane] meets [Iranian foreign affairs adviser]. They ask for us to delay until 6. They will get answer on hostages. RCM says if they give us a time we will launch A/C [aircraft] from T.A. [Tel Aviv] so that it will land here 2 hours after hostages in U.S. custody. 2:20 conveyed to Washington. Maybe they're serious now." (Teicher Note, 5/28/86, AKW 005452.)

[156] Teicher Note, 5/28/86, AKW 005452–53.

## McFarlane Learns of the Diversion

McFarlane said he left Iran feeling that the United States had been "conned." [157] The Americans stopped in Tel Aviv where, on the airport tarmac, North attempted to cheer up McFarlane by revealing to him the fact of the Iran/contra diversion. McFarlane said North told him: "It's not a total loss, at least some of the money from this deal is going to Central America." [158] McFarlane, already troubled by the Reagan Administration's failed series of approaches to Iran, received North's statement in silence, finding that it only deepened his distress.[159]

After returning to Washington, McFarlane, accompanied by North, briefed President Reagan, Vice President Bush and Regan on the Tehran mission. McFarlane was concerned about North's revelation regarding the Iran/contra diversion, but said he shared the information with no one. He recommended to Poindexter that North be reassigned to the Marine Corps.[160]

## McFarlane's Response to the Public Exposure of Iran/contra

McFarlane was one of the first principals to speak publicly about the Iran arms sales after they were exposed in the press in early November 1986. These reports focused on the fact that McFarlane had made a secret mission to Tehran bringing spare weapons parts and a cake. Iranian Parliament Speaker Rafsanjani confirmed the reports, calling the mission a sign of U.S. "helplessness." [161] McFarlane on November 6 publicly dismissed the reports as "fanciful." [162] On November 7, 1986, McFarlane sent a computer message to Poindexter, complaining that Donald Regan was pinning the blame on him in briefings to the press. In the computer message, McFarlane recounted the early Iran arms sales, beginning with discussions with the Israelis in June 1985, mentioning the 1985 TOW shipment but not the November 1985 HAWKs, going straight to a description of his December 1985 meeting in London with Ghorbanifar.[163]

On November 8, 1986, McFarlane sent a PROFs message to North: "SUBJECT: Audit trail [—] I hope to daylights that someone has been purging the [intelligence] files on this episode." [164]

On November 15, 1986, McFarlane sent a PROFs message to Poindexter, expressing concern about the way the White House was handling the rapidly unfolding public exposure of the Iran arms sales:

> . . . I lived throught [sic] Watergate John. Well-meaning people who were in on the early planning of the communications strategy, didn't intend to lie but ultimately came around to it. I don't know how Regan will tend. He might choose two courses; either to push it off on someone outside the White House, which is fine with me, or he might go ahead with a "sell it on its merits" strategy. If the latter is the course followed, it must not be confrontational, but open and candid.
>
> The judgments made on this and other matters in the next four or five days will be crucial. . . .[165]

By the time McFarlane raised his concerns about a "communications strategy," however, Administration officials had already lied to the public and to Congress, most notably on November 12, 1986, when Poindexter falsely told congressional leaders there was no U.S. involvement in the 1985 Israeli arms sales to Iran.

On November 18, Poindexter asked McFarlane to come to the White House to review an Iran arms sales chronology that the President would use in a press conference the following evening. At about 8 p.m., McFarlane came to North's office. North showed him a CIA chronology in which North thought there were errors.[166] North told McFarlane that Administration lawyers, whom North did not name, had

---

[157] McFarlane, FBI 302, 2/17/88, p. 10.
[158] Ibid., 4/15/87, p. 11.
[159] Ibid.
[160] Ibid.
[161] Facts on File, 11/7/86.
[162] Ibid.

[163] PROFs Note from McFarlane to Poindexter, 11/7/86, AKW 002047.
[164] PROFs Note from McFarlane to North, 11/8/86, ALU 049630.
[165] PROFs Note from McFarlane to Poindexter, 11/15/86, AKW 077240.
[166] McFarlane, North Trial Testimony, 3/14/89, pp. 4262, 4267.

pinpointed legal problems with the November 1985 HAWK shipment:

Q: . . . Now, what did Colonel North say about the lawyers identifying a problem with the 1985 HAWK shipment?

A: I believe that it was a matter of whether or not the involvement of the CIA was appropriate.

Q: And by appropriate do you mean whether or not it was legal?

A: Yes. Or properly executed by decision.[167]

North told McFarlane that U.S. officials believed at the time that the cargo of the shipment was oil-drilling equipment.

McFarlane said his own recollection about the November 1985 shipment was uncertain:

Q: Did it cross your mind that he [North] may be feeding you a cover story or asking you to join with him in a cover story?

A: At the time I don't think so. Within a couple of days what I did learn led me to believe that yes, this really was a HAWK shipment and I began to recall more about it. But that evening I didn't.[168]

McFarlane told the Tower Commission that the November 18 chronology prepared by North "was not a full and completely accurate account of those events, but rather this effort to blur and leave ambiguous the President's role."[169]

McFarlane revised a version of the chronology that had made plain the fact that in November 1985 the Israelis provided HAWK missiles to Iran. He omitted reference to the HAWKs and referred instead to a shipment of equipment:

Q: Now, was that done to solve this problem that the lawyers had raised and Colonel North had told you about?

A: Well, it didn't solve that problem but it was done that way to solve a problem in my mind, that the statement in the draft that there was a HAWK shipment together with Colonel North's statement that we

hadn't learned of that until later on, I wasn't really willing to accept and so by saying equipment which I had said publicly before it seemed to me not to contradict the truth but it didn't say anything that was false or that I did not know for sure.[170]

Beside the HAWKs problem, McFarlane knew that another complication was looming: the possible disclosure of the Iran/contra diversion. In a November 18 or 19 meeting with North, Teicher, Deputy National Security Adviser Alton Keel and Poindexter, according to McFarlane,

. . . someone made the summary remark, well, we don't have a problem, and just popping off I said, well, I believe you have a problem about the use of the Iranian money and after a moment—Colonel North and Mr. Teicher had left the room, Colonel North came back and said Howard [Teicher] isn't aware of that, and I think that was it.[171]

On November 21, 1986, Ledeen asked McFarlane to come to his house because Ledeen felt that Keel had "muzzled" him, and he wanted to start speaking out.[172] According to Ledeen, McFarlane on the morning of November 21, 1986, advised him "when I described my own role in this affair that I should not get too far out in front and that I should not portray myself as having gone to Israel originally to carry out a specific mission for him at his request," which was what Ledeen, in fact, had done.[173] It was Ledeen's belief that McFarlane was trying to "protect" him, that "he would just simply try to be nice to me and leave me out of it . . ."[174]

While McFarlane was at Ledeen's house in a Maryland suburb of Washington, North arrived. According to McFarlane, North asked Ledeen, "What concerns me is not what happened but what are you going to say happened?" Ledeen said, "I've just gone through with Bud what I did as part of this and my

168 Ibid., p. 4272.
169 McFarlane, Tower Commission Testimony, 2/21/87, p. 43.
170 McFarlane, North Trial Testimony, 3/14/89, p. 4281.
171 Ibid., p. 4277.
172 McFarlane, Grand Jury, 5/4/87, pp. 170–73.
173 Ledeen, Grand Jury, 9/30/87, p. 77.
174 Ibid., p. 78.

role was nothing more than being a person who listened at meetings and reported what I heard." North then told Ledeen, "You and I can talk some more this afternoon." [175]

Besides his familiarity with the details of the 1985 HAWKs shipment, Ledeen also had potentially explosive knowledge about financial irregularities in the Iran transactions. Ghorbanifar had told him of excessive mark-ups and that investors in the deals who claimed they were owed $10 million were threatening to go public. Ledeen had approached both North and Casey about the problem in September or October 1986. [176]

As McFarlane and North left Ledeen's house, North said, according to McFarlane:

. . . he was worried that Michael may have made some personal gain in this whole thing. I said, "What do you mean?" and he said, "I think that Schwimmer" who refers to Mr. Al Schwimmer, an Israeli who was involved as one of their participants—that Mr. Schwimmer and Michael had, he thought—he, North, thought, had some kind of agreement to share some of the gain from the sales. I didn't pursue it any further and neither did he. [177]

As McFarlane and North drove toward downtown Washington, North made "statements on his part that he intended to try to protect me and the President," according to McFarlane:

Q: Did he say how he was going to protect you and the President?

A: Well, at some point in the trip, the fact of documents being shredded was

raised and that seemed to me to be an expression of perhaps trying to protect me from documents which while explainable were certainly likely to create criticism and argument. . . .

Q: And you say the documents that he was going to shred would protect you from embarrassment?

A: Well, he didn't say that exactly. He said simply that we are going to have to have a shredding party or something like that, an offhand remark, but I took it, it was my interpretation, that he said it to relieve any fears that I might have in my mind that I was going to be embarrassed by documents.

Q: And what you had in mind were the documents that you and he had reviewed back in 1985 before you sent those letters to Congress, right?

A: Those, plus probably hundreds of others that—certainly, people who don't agree with you can find a basis to criticize hundreds of things, simply because they disagree. He didn't specify. [178]

According to McFarlane, he told North: "Don't worry about me. Tell it like it is and it will be okay." [179]

## Meese Questions McFarlane

On the morning of November 21, 1986, President Reagan authorized Attorney General Edwin Meese III to conduct an inquiry into the Iran arms sales.

Specifically, Meese was confronted with the problem that Casey and Poindexter had told Congress that they had not known at the time of the November 1985 HAWKs shipment that the cargo was weapons. Shultz, meanwhile, had told other Administration officials that he was told by McFarlane at the Geneva summit in November 1985 that a HAWK transfer was going to occur. Hill, Shultz's executive assistant, had notes of the Shultz-McFarlane discussion.

---

[175] McFarlane, Grand Jury, 5/4/87, pp. 174–175. At a meeting with Ledeen in the Old Executive Office Building later that day, North became more specific about his concerns. Ledeen said North asked him, "Look, the basic question here is what will you say when you are asked or what would you say if you are asked about a shipment of HAWK missiles [to Iran] in November of 1985?" Ledeen said, "I said I would tell the truth which was that I was aware of it, that I knew that it had happened, but that I was not aware or could not recall who had made the decision to do it or when that decision had been made." North said, "Fine." (Ledeen, Grand Jury, 9/30/87, pp. 81–82.)

[176] Ledeen, Grand Jury, 9/30/87, pp. 57–63. Arms financier Adnan Khashoggi concocted the story that there was a threatened exposure in order to pressure the U.S. Government into paying him $10 million to repay his investors. See the Flow of Funds chapter.

[177] McFarlane, Grand Jury, 5/6/87, pp. 74–75. Ledeen believes North heard from Nir rumors that Ledeen was profiting from the arms sales. Ledeen denied that he profited. (Ledeen, Grand Jury, 9/30/87, pp. 16–20.) Independent Counsel found no evidence that he did. Israel never gave OIC access to financial accounts or records.

[178] McFarlane, *North* Trial Testimony, 3/14/89, pp. 4285–86.
[179] Ibid., p. 4286.

McFarlane was Meese's first interview subject. Meese, with Assistant Attorney General Charles Cooper taking notes, questioned McFarlane for two hours on the late afternoon of November 21, 1986, about the genesis of the Iran arms sales. According to Cooper's notes of the meeting, McFarlane described the Iran initiative as beginning in July and August 1985 when Kimche and other Israeli officials approached the United States. McFarlane told Meese he briefed the President and Regan about it, and while the President was interested in a dialogue he was cautious about sending weapons. McFarlane said Ledeen reported to him about Israeli contacts in Iran. McFarlane said he talked with Shultz, and that Poindexter remembered a meeting with the "Family Group" (Shultz, Weinberger and McFarlane) and the President, when the President was in pajamas, either in Bethesda Naval Hospital or during his recovery from surgery at the White House in July 1985.[180] Cooper's notes reflect that McFarlane said he learned of the 1985 shipment of TOWs from Ledeen, and McFarlane briefed the President, Weinberger, Shultz and probably Casey. McFarlane said he knew of no one in the U.S. Government who had contact with the Israelis regarding the transfer of TOWs.[181]

McFarlane told Meese he believed he first learned of the November 1985 HAWK shipment when he was preparing to go to Iran in May 1986, according to Cooper's notes. McFarlane told Meese that at the Geneva summit in November 1985 he learned that Israel had shipped oil equipment. McFarlane then described North's involvement in sorting out the logistical problems, at Rabin's request. ". . . M. [McFarlane] remembers no mention in all this of arms," according to Cooper's notes. But when Meese told McFarlane that Shultz said they discussed the HAWKs shipment in Geneva, McFarlane "doesn't remember chat w/G.S. [Shultz], but probably had one," Cooper noted.[182]

At the conclusion of his interview, McFarlane had a private conversation with Meese, out of Cooper's earshot. McFarlane testified that he told Meese at this point that the President was

"four-square behind" the arms sales from the beginning.[183] McFarlane said Meese expressed relief at this because the President's approval in advance of the sales would constitute a Finding. McFarlane said after telling Meese of the President's prior approval:

Ed said, Bud, I know that, and I can understand why. And, as a practical matter, I'm glad you told me this because his legal position is far better the earlier that he made the decision. . . . It was very clear and acknowledged by the Attorney General that the President had approved the policy providing for Israeli sale of weapons to Iran in the expectation of the U.S. sale of replacement part items.[184]

According to Meese, McFarlane "said something to the effect that I have been taking a lot of this on my shoulders in the speech I gave this last week and what I have said this last week but I want you to know—it was something to the effect he wanted me to know that the President was generally in favor of pursuing the Israelis' ideas all along." [185] Meese said he responded: "It might even be helpful to the President, not hurtful, if he generally supported this from the start." [186]

Immediately following his interview with Meese, McFarlane called North from a pay phone outside the Justice Department and told him about the interview. North's notes indicate that McFarlane said: "RR [Reagan] said—of course in July—Intent of Pres[ident] is important—RR said he wd [would] support 'mental finding.' " [187] McFarlane said:

. . . I talked to him and said that I had finished an interview with the attorney general and that the attorney general had said that he was relieved to learn that the President had approved the Iranian initiative and

---

[180] Cooper Note, 11/21/86, ALV 071808.
[181] Ibid., ALV 071808–09.
[182] Ibid, ALV 071810.

[183] McFarlane, Tower Commission Testimony, 2/21/87, p. 56.
[184] Ibid., pp. 56–58.
[185] Meese, Select Committees Testimony, 7/28/87, p. 93.
[186] Ibid. According to Cooper, Meese told him that McFarlane told him privately: "You know, I am trying and I am hopeful that I can keep the President's interests uppermost in this. I am trying to protect the President." (Cooper, Select Committees Testimony, 6/25/87, pp. 79–80.) Cooper later said, "I think he made a reference to the fact that, you know, the President was for this from the beginning or something like that," which Cooper said was inconsistent with what McFarlane had said in the interview. (Cooper, Grand Jury, 1/11/88, pp. 101–103.)
[187] North Notebook, 11/21/86, AMX 001707.

that the—he believed that because he had approved it, the President had approved it, that that justified the actions that were taken after the approval.[188]

McFarlane also called Abraham Sofaer, the State Department legal adviser, to try to obtain a copy of the Charles Hill note that reflected his conversation with Shultz in Geneva about the HAWK shipment.[189] He was not successful.

In a late night PROFs note to Poindexter on November 21, McFarlane described his interview with Meese. Among other things he wrote:

. . . The only blind spot [o]n my part concerned a shipment in November '85 which still doesn't ring a bell with me.

But it appears that the matter of not notifying about the Israeli transfers can be covered if the President made a "mental finding" before the transfers took place. Well on that score we ought to be ok because he was all for letting the Israelis do anything they wanted at the very first briefing in the hospital. Ed seemed relieved at that. . . .[190]

On November 23, 1986, McFarlane met with North and North's attorney, Thomas C. Green, at McFarlane's downtown office. According to McFarlane, North:

. . . was going over in his own mind, aloud, what he thought the problems would be in the unfolding of the investigation. And he said that he had spent a lot of time on all the facts and he believed that the only potential problem might be the use of some of the funds from Iran in Central America.

And I said, well, that was approved, wasn't it? And he said, yes. You know I wouldn't do anything that wasn't approved.

And I said, well, tell it like it is and it will be okay, Ollie.[191]

North told McFarlane the diversion was a matter of record.[192]

On November 24, 1986, Meese met with McFarlane again and told him about the weekend discovery of the Iran/contra diversion. North had, in an interview on November 23, told Meese that McFarlane was only one of three Government officials—including North and Poindexter—who knew about the diversion. Meese asked McFarlane whether this was true; McFarlane said yes.

Meese was to report the results of his weekend investigation at a meeting of the President's senior advisers—including the President, Vice President Bush, Poindexter, Casey, Weinberger and Shultz—on the afternoon of November 24, 1986. That morning, Shultz remarked to his executive assistant Hill: "They may lay all this off on Bud [McFarlane]. That won't be enough." [193]

At the meeting, Regan asked about the 1985 HAWK shipment—who knew about it, who authorized it, and whether President Reagan was told. According to notes of the meeting, Poindexter responded that McFarlane conducted the 1985 sales all alone, without documentation.

Poindexter, of course, was involved personally in the 1985 arms sales and was present in meetings at which McFarlane briefed others on the matter.

Following Poindexter's statement, Meese described the November 1985 HAWK shipment to Iran. According to two sets of notes, Meese indicated that the shipment was not legal but the President had not been aware of it.[194]

Shultz told Hill after the meeting:

. . . I s[ai]d I knew something of what he did. An Aug 85 mtg w[ith] P[resident] & me & Bud. Bud s[ai]d all deniable. I s[ai]d impossible. They rearranging the record. . . . P [President] now saying he didn't know what Bud was up to. . . .[195]

188 McFarlane, *North* Trial Testimony, 3/14/89, pp. 4293–94.
189 Ibid., p. 4297.
190 PROFs Note from McFarlane to Poindexter, 11/21/86, AKW 021677.
191 McFarlane, *North* Trial Testimony, 3/14/89, p. 4299.
192 Ibid., p. 4300. McFarlane told a closed congressional hearing late in 1986: "Thinking about what I've said today, I can recall one thing that is certainly a very, very volatile thing to say if in the public domain, and that is that I believe the President must have known about this diversion of resources. It seems to me that that ought to be a matter, and it will surely become a matter, of record with Admiral Poindexter's testimony. But that is speculation on my part. . . ." (McFarlane, SSCI Testimony, 12/7/86, NK 0001205.)
193 Hill Note, 11/24/86, ANS 0001898.
194 Regan and Weinberger Notes, 11/24/86.
195 Hill Note, 11/24/86, ALW 0059439, ALW 0059441.

On November 25, 1986, Meese publicly disclosed the Iran/contra diversion. He named McFarlane, along with North and Poindexter, as the only three U.S. Government officials who knew about it.

## McFarlane Conceals the Saudi Donations From Congress

On December 8, 1986, McFarlane testified under oath before the House Committee on Foreign Affairs. He was asked:

> There have been also press reports that the Saudis have been indirectly involved in financing the contras. Are you aware of any such activities?

McFarlane replied:

> I have seen the reports and I have heard that the Saudis have contributed. The concrete character of that is beyond my ken.[196]

In another response at the same hearing, McFarlane stated:

> I did not solicit any country at any time to make contributions to the contras . . . I have no idea of the extent of that or anything else . . . I know of no such solicitation of funds from any third country.[197]

McFarlane later explained that these questions took him by surprise because he had been called to testify regarding the Iran initiative, not the contras. He said he tried to deter further questioning with his answers.[198] He felt an obligation to preserve the confidence of Prince Bandar and attempted to give an answer that was incomplete—not false—but was unable to quite carry it off. As to the questions regarding solicitation, he repeatedly claimed that he did not solicit Prince Bandar. He said he explained to him the difficulty confronting President Reagan in light of the contra-funding cut-off, but McFarlane said he did not ask for funds. He knew, however, that Prince Bandar would be bright enough to understand that a contribution would be welcome and would invite future goodwill.[199]

---

196 McFarlane, House Foreign Affairs Committee Testimony, 12/8/86, pp. 57–58.
197 Ibid., p. 66.
198 McFarlane, FBI 302, 2/16/88, pp. 2–3.
199 Ibid., 2/17/88, p. 3.

## The Guilty Plea

On March 11, 1988, to resolve all criminal charges against McFarlane growing out of the Iran/contra affair, Independent Counsel recommended that McFarlane be permitted to enter a plea of guilty to four misdemeanors, each charging him with unlawfully withholding material information from Congress. The charges to which he pleaded guilty were:

1. In his September 5, 1985, reply to Chairman Hamilton, he unlawfully withheld material information when he stated, "From that review I can state with deep personal conviction that at no time did I or any member of the National Security Council staff violate the letter or spirit of the law. . . . We did not solicit funds or other support for military or paramilitary activities either from Americans or third parties."

2. In his September 12, 1985, reply to Chairman Barnes he stated, ". . . I want to assure you that my actions, and those of my staff, have been in compliance with both the spirit and the letter of the law. . . . Throughout, we have scrupulously abided by the spirit and the letter of the law. None of us has solicited funds, facilitated contacts for prospective potential donors, or otherwise organized or coordinated the military or paramilitary efforts of the resistance. . . . There has not been, nor will there be, any such activities by the NSC staff."

3. In his October 7, 1985, response to questions forwarded by Hamilton, he answered, "Lieutenant Colonel North did not use his influence to facilitate the movement of supplies to the resistance." He also stated, "There is no official or unofficial relationship with any member of the NSC staff regarding fund raising for the Nicaraguan democratic opposition. This includes the alleged relationship with General Singlaub." His letter also denied knowledge of the source of funds supporting the contras.

4. On December 8, 1986, he withheld material information from the House Committee on Foreign Affairs as follows:

Q: There have also been press reports that the [nationals of a third country] have been indirectly involved in financing the contras. Are you aware of any such activities?

A: I have seen the reports and I have heard that the [nationals of such third country] have contributed. The concrete character of that is beyond my ken.

As a condition of the recommendation and acceptance of the plea, McFarlane agreed to cooperate with the Office of Independent Counsel. At his request, the Court also agreed that he would be sentenced before he was required to give trial testimony against another person. On March 3, 1989, McFarlane was sentenced to two years probation, 200 hours of community service, and a $20,000 fine.

In recommending the acceptance of this plea of guilty, Independent Counsel gave up the opportunity to prosecute McFarlane as a member of the conspiracy to defraud the United States by conducting an unauthorized covert activity,[200] for making false statements to Congress, and for obstruction of a congressional investigation. The strength of such felony prosecutions would lie in the admissions of McFarlane and the documentary proof of memoranda from North to McFarlane. In addition, members of the NSC staff could have testified to North's direct access to McFarlane, notwithstanding their difference in rank.

The weaker side of a McFarlane prosecution would have been that neither Poindexter nor North was available as a witness against McFarlane. Both had refused to testify without immunity and Independent Counsel was not willing to grant it, particularly when each refused to even give a proffer of his prospective testimony. Casey, who might have been able to give some information as to McFarlane's participation, was dead. Prior admissions by McFarlane were carefully hedged: At no time did he admit deliberately misleading Congress or making a false statement. He contended that he was not adequately informed of North's activities and that even though there were memoranda from North to him, they were not carefully read for Boland

violations in view of the heavy volume of material he was required to review each day, particularly when information as to a Boland violation was slipped into the context of a larger memorandum on a broader subject.

In addition, a McFarlane prosecution posed procedural problems. The first question was whether he should be included in the indictment of Poindexter, North, Secord and Hakim or whether he should be indicted separately. Ordinarily, it would have been preferable to try all defendants at once. McFarlane, however, posed a problem of severance. First, he was not a participant in the diversion which was the central feature of the original indictment. Second, whereas he had confessed to a point, North and Poindexter had given their testimony only after receiving immunity and the Government could not have exposed it at trial. Third, there could have been an inconsistency between the confessions of McFarlane and the probable testimony of North and Poindexter—especially on the critical questions of the extent of McFarlane's knowledge of North's activities and the extent of North's authorization by McFarlane. Fourth, the indictment as then planned and as finally drawn, alleged a conspiracy beginning in late June 1985, when North and Secord took control of contra resupply, well after North's last surviving operational memorandum to McFarlane.

Tactically, there was a need on the part of the prosecution for a witness who could, to some extent, act as a narrator, linking together the complex activities that were the subject matter of the litigation contemplated in the original indictment and explaining the background against which these activities were conducted. Also, McFarlane was a witness against North as to the diversion, the center of the March 1988 indictment.

Other factors also played a role in Independent Counsel's decision to accept McFarlane's guilty plea to misdemeanor charges. In February 1987, McFarlane attempted to commit suicide. It was clear from his extensive meetings, interviews and testimony thereafter that he continued to suffer as a consequence of his role as national security adviser in Iran/contra policies. Independent Counsel also gave McFarlane credit for his willingness—unlike Poindexter and

---

[200] McFarlane, however, was an unindicted co-conspirator in Count One of the March 1988 indictment of Poindexter, North, Secord and Hakim.

North, who invoked their Fifth Amendment privilege and refused to testify without immunity—to assist the investigation at an early date, prior to his plea.

In the end, although it was recognized that McFarlane would be a very imperfect witness because of his persistent, almost ritualistic denials of knowledge of much of North's conduct, it was decided to recommend the plea and get his agreement for cooperation. This was done even though Independent Counsel realized that the prosecution of Poindexter and North would be seriously hampered by the jury's realization that McFarlane—their superior—had been permitted to plead guilty to crimes less severe than those for which his subordinates were on trial.[201]

## Conclusion

There is no question, from Independent Counsel's perspective, that President Reagan put McFarlane in a difficult position by charging him to keep the contras together, "body and soul," during the Boland cut-off of U.S. aid. It is also Independent Counsel's belief that McFarlane put his subordinates in an equally difficult position by delegating to them the

[201] Much later it also became apparent that the difficulties with classified information that arose in the *North* case would have certainly arisen in a prosecution of McFarlane.

operational tasks to carry out the President's directive, and by joining them in a criminal effort to keep their activities concealed from Congress.

There is no evidence that McFarlane or any NSC staff member raised concerns to the President that his policy directives were causing them to undertake actions that might be unlawful, although the NSC staff discussed such concerns among themselves and took steps to cover their tracks.

McFarlane's willingness to allow the NSC staff to take on operational duties—while affording the President and the CIA, State and Defense departments a degree of deniability—came at a cost to him. His efforts to keep North's activities and the Saudi donation concealed from Congress resulted in his guilty plea.

Furthermore, in testimony regarding the 1985 Iran arms sales, McFarlane contradicted other senior officials on critical points. McFarlane repeatedly testified that he kept the NSC principals briefed and was insistent that the President had approved the 1985 shipments. It was not until Independent Counsel in 1990, 1991 and 1992 obtained previously unproduced notes from Hill, Weinberger, Regan and others that the truthfulness of many of McFarlane's statements regarding the early shipments could be proven.

# Chapter 2
# United States v. Oliver L. North

Oliver L. North, a Marine lieutenant colonel assigned to the National Security Council staff beginning in 1981 until he was fired on November 25, 1986, was the White House official most directly involved in secretly aiding the contras, selling arms to Iran, and diverting Iran arms sales proceeds to the contras.

North, who was deputy director of political-military affairs, reported many of his activities to his superiors, National Security Adviser Robert C. McFarlane and later John M. Poindexter. He claimed to have taken much of his direction from Central Intelligence Agency Director William Casey.[1]

More significantly, North testified repeatedly that he believed President Reagan was aware and approving of his activities. North was unable to offer direct proof of presidential knowledge and authorization. Both McFarlane and Poindexter, who were North's channel to the President, have either claimed ignorance of certain of North's activities or said they deliberately shielded the President from such details. President Reagan in written interrogatory answers to Independent Counsel also denied knowledge of North's illegal conduct. Although the Office of Independent Counsel could not prove that President Reagan directly approved North's criminal actions, there is no doubt that he and his national security advisers allowed North to operate with unprecedented latitude in furtherance of Administration policies.

North was indicted in March 1988 on 16 Iran/contra charges, along with Poindexter, retired U.S. Air Force Maj. Gen. Richard V. Secord and Albert Hakim in a 23-count indictment. After the cases were severed and the central conspiracy charges were dropped due to classified-information problems, North stood trial beginning in February 1989 on 12 counts. On May 4, 1989, he was found guilty of three counts, including aiding and abetting obstruction of Congress, shredding and altering official documents, and accepting an illegal gratuity from Secord. North's convictions were vacated on July 20, 1990, after the appeals court found that witnesses in his trial might have been impermissibly affected by his immunized congressional testimony.

## The Decision to Prosecute

It is no exaggeration to say that the *North* case was central to the investigation into the entire Iran/contra matter. This may be difficult to understand in view of North's middle-level position on the NSC staff. It gave him no statutory power to command and control activities within the NSC, much less other areas of the vast government bureaucracy such as the departments of State and Defense and the CIA. Despite these limiting factors, it was clear from the earliest stages of OIC's investigation that North had working control of the Secord-Hakim covert-action Enterprise.

North amassed the authority to carry out his role through a combination of factors, including:

(1) President Reagan's directive to McFarlane to keep the contra forces together "body and soul," despite the Boland Amendment funding cut-off,[2] and the President's determination to pursue the release of American hostages at whatever cost.

---

[1] See Casey chapter.

[2] McFarlane, *North* Trial Testimony, 3/10/89, p. 3946.

(2) An extraordinary delegation of authority to North by McFarlane and Poindexter in executing the contra and Iran operations.

(3) The decision by President Reagan, Casey and others to run covert operations out of the NSC, where there was no institutional framework for conducting such operations and no system of accountability or oversight.

(4) The designation of North as the secret point man for contra support after CIA assistance was cut off by the Boland prohibition.

(5) The perception, promoted by North and his operational partners, that their activities were known to and authorized by the President, making others more willing to support and less eager to question them.

(6) North's powerful, can-do persona, his enthusiastic commitment to both operations, and his ruthlessness to make them succeed.

Independent Counsel viewed the prosecution or cooperation of North as the key to the secrets behind the Iran/contra affair. When North refused to enter into plea negotiations leading to a cooperation agreement, it left no alternative but to proceed with prosecution, even though it presented unusual difficulties.

The most serious obstacle to North's prosecution was the immunity grant extended him by the Select Committees that in 1987 investigated the Iran/contra matter. North's nationally televised testimony under that grant of use immunity, which guaranteed that nothing he told Congress could be used against him in a criminal proceeding, greatly complicated Independent Counsel's investigation and raised serious questions as to whether North could ever be tried. A second and equally formidable challenge was whether North would try to "graymail" his prosecution by claiming the need for classified information that could not be declassified for trial.

## Pre-Trial Proceedings

The Grand Jury on March 16, 1988, returned a 23-count indictment charging North,

Poindexter, Secord and Hakim with conspiracy to defraud the Government, theft of Government property and wire fraud. North was charged also with obstruction of congressional investigations and false statements to a congressional committee and the attorney general, shredding and altering official documents, acceptance of an illegal gratuity from Secord in the form of a home-security system, conversion of traveler's checks and tax-fraud conspiracy.

The four-defendant case, *U.S.* v. *Poindexter*, was assigned to Judge Gerhard A. Gesell of the U. S. District Court for the District of Columbia. The battle to bring the case to trial was fought on a number of fronts, with the defense filing over 100 pre-trial motions. The principal issues were the validity of the indictment itself; the application of *Kastigar* v. *United States*,[3] the ruling which set the standard for the protection of immunized witnesses from prosecution and which would govern the rules to keep the trial free of the immunized congressional testimony given by North, Poindexter and Hakim; the application of the Classified Information Procedures Act (CIPA), which governs the disclosure of classified information in trials; and immense discovery demands, which required the prosecution to turn over hundreds of thousands of documents to the defendants.

The defendants' first successful challenge to the March 1988 indictment was a motion for severance of the four cases. They successfully argued that their intention to use the immunized testimony of their co-defendants in their own defenses prevented a joint trial.[4]

The severance of the four trials on June 8, 1988, was a major setback for Independent Counsel.[5] He elected to try North first. Because North was tried alone, without his superior and co-conspirators, he was better able to present himself as a fall guy and blame others for his misdeeds. But the worst impact of severance was the delay it imposed on Independent Counsel's investigative and trial schedule. This put off for a year the completion of the Poindexter,

---

[3] 406 U.S. 441 (1972).

[4] North also contended that evidence which would be admissible against his co-defendants would not be admissible against him, a factor which weighed in favor of severance. North attempted to use the immunized testimony of Poindexter at trial, but Judge Gesell upheld the Government's objection to such use.

[5] Judge Gesell ruled from the bench to sever the trials, after hearing oral arguments on the matter.

Secord and Hakim cases and the opportunity to question them, which was essential to the investigation.

North's challenges to the indictment were virtually all rejected by the court. One count was dismissed with the Government's consent. One count was dismissed on the court's own motion to avoid confusion at trial.

The most significant ruling by Judge Gesell was his upholding as a crime Count One of the indictment, which described the Iran/contra conspiracy in detail. Count One charged a conspiracy to defraud the United States by deceitfully conducting a covert action in violation of executive orders and statutory restraints. Trial on this count, which was dismissed later because the Administration refused to declassify information material to North's defense, would have disclosed the Government-wide activities that supported the Iran and contra operations.[6]

Judge Gesell also ruled that:

—Briefings by Executive officials of congressional committees, even though informal and unsworn, may be "proceedings" under the obstruction statute.

—The federal statute prohibiting false statements covers false and deceitful statements in official correspondence from Executive Branch officials responding to congressional committees.

## Kastigar: The Problem of the Congressional Immunity Grants

Prior to severance, the immunized defendants requested a pre-trial hearing to preview the Government's case witness-by-witness to see whether it could be tried without the improper use of their immunized testimony. Independent Counsel urged that this review be deferred until after trial when the actual trial record would be available for analysis. He argued that immunity was a bar to conviction, not to trial. The District Court granted a limited pre-trial hearing. It agreed to inquire into (a) Independent Counsel's procedures for insulating his staff from immunized testimony, (b) the extent to which the Grand Jury heard evidence affected by that testimony, and (c) the independent leads to proposed witnesses and other evidence. After two

days of evidentiary hearings, Judge Gesell reviewed Independent Counsel's investigative leads, the Grand Jury proceedings, and the internal files of OIC that documented its efforts to insulate itself from immunized testimony. He permitted extensive examination of Independent Counsel in sworn testimony regarding insulation procedures adopted to protect OIC from being "tainted" by exposure to immunized testimony.

In the end the court held that (1) the Office of Independent Counsel effectively protected itself from undue exposure to immunized testimony, (2) there was no direct use of immunized testimony in the Grand Jury, (3) Independent Counsel's instructions to the grand jurors and Grand Jury witnesses to avoid using immunized testimony were effective, (4) Independent Counsel had untainted leads to each of its witnesses, and (5) immunized testimony did not enhance the focus of Independent Counsel's investigation.[7]

The three immunized defendants immediately appealed the court's ruling. They also petitioned the Court of Appeals for a writ of mandamus to compel a more extensive, pre-trial *Kastigar* hearing. Independent Counsel successfully opposed the appeal on grounds that the question could be reviewed after judgment and that interlocutory review was not warranted. The Court of Appeals ruled that Judge Gesell had "a considerable degree of discretion to fashion the procedure most conducive to resolving fully and fairly all issues regarding the use of immunized testimony at trial."[8]

Following severance, *Kastigar* requirements continued to hamper the orderly trial of the case. During 10 days of jury selection, North succeeded in having all prospective jurors who had any recollection or impression of his immunized testimony excused for cause.[9] The court

---

[6] See The Operational Conspiracy: A Legal Analysis chapter.

[7] *U.S.* v. *Poindexter*, 698 F.Supp. 300, 305–09, 314–16 (D.D.C. 1988). The court later refused to reconsider either its legal view of "use" under *Kastigar* or the preliminary decisions which shaped the factual record upon which the court based its ultimate conclusions. See Motion for Reconsideration . . . , *North*, (D.D.C. June 28, 1988); Order, *North* (July 13, 1988).

[8] See Petition of Defendants . . . for a Writ of Mandamus, *In re Poindexter*, No. 88–3097 (D.C. Cir. July 20, 1988); *U.S.* v. *Poindexter*, 859 F.2d 216, 222 (D.C. Cir. 1988).

[9] The court's careful method of excusing jurors who admitted exposure to North's immunized testimony drew fire from North both during trial and on appeal. The Court of Appeals nevertheless concluded that Judge Gesell's method of screening the jurors was proper. *See* Defendant's Motion to Stay the Proceedings . . . Pending the Selection of

rejected North's pretrial motion to suppress the testimony of prosecution witnesses on the grounds that all of them had been exposed to immunized testimony. The court also denied his requests at trial for hearings before the testimony of each prosecution witness. The court instead decided to warn each witness prior to testimony to testify only from his or her personal knowledge, and not to testify to any matter learned or derived from North's immunized appearance before Congress. During trial, Judge Gesell dismissed one prospective witness who said he was unable to comply with this instruction.

## Classified Information and Discovery Problems

In addition to *Kastigar* problems, Judge Gesell had to confront the problems posed by the likely use of classified information at trial. Using steps prescribed by CIPA, Judge Gesell began carefully sifting North's requests to disclose in his defense certain classified information; if the Government refused to allow material evidence to be disclosed, or if it failed to provide adequate substitutions, charges could be dismissed. Before and during the trial, CIPA problems dominated and very nearly overwhelmed the case.

First, Judge Gesell ordered the construction of a secure facility operated at Government expense to house the classified documents for use of the defendants. After a large, downtown office was remodeled to provide adequate security, Independent Counsel produced to the defense in pretrial discovery more than 100,000 pages of classified and almost 200,000 pages of unclassified documents. This represented only a fraction of what the defendants would ultimately receive.

North and his co-defendants demanded in discovery a search throughout the Government for any and all documents touching on Iran/contra and also on other highly sensitive activities which they claimed were analogous in some respects. Once located, all documents had to be reviewed, redacted, and annotated as to clas-

sification. At the same time, North claimed that he himself had no countervailing responsibility to indicate which classified materials were truly relevant to his defense. In the first challenge to CIPA's requirements, North raised numerous arguments, ranging from complaints that the statute unconstitutionally forced him to disclose defense strategies, to the charge that those responsible for reviewing the materials were too slow and arbitrary in their work.

On July 5, 1988, Independent Counsel presented to the court a 151-page summary of 395 documents that the Government intended to use in its case-in-chief against North. An Interagency Review Group (IRG)—made up of representatives from the departments of State, Defense and Justice, the CIA, NSC and National Security Agency, and which was responsible for protecting classified information—required numerous redactions, or omissions, in many documents.

Meanwhile, Judge Gesell, with the consent of Independent Counsel, met privately with North and heard a presentation of his defense in order to better judge the materiality of the classified documents he planned to introduce at trial. As a result of that presentation, the details of which were never disclosed to the prosecution, Judge Gesell afforded North wider discovery, set three deadlines for North to file notices of the classified information that North expected to disclose, and set trial for September 20, 1988.

It soon became clear that neither the intelligence agencies nor North could meet Judge Gesell's schedule. In July 1988 alone, the Government produced 350,000 pages of documents in response to the court's expanded discovery order. Independent Counsel reported that full production would require additional months of work. North, meanwhile, sought a continuance in order to absorb the documents already produced.

The court suggested the feasibility of avoiding the mounting discovery and CIPA problems by dropping the first three counts of the indictment. In hopes of saving these crucial counts, Independent Counsel moved that Counts One through Three be severed from the rest of the case and tried later. North followed up with an 85-page CIPA notice objecting to most of the deletions of classified information proposed by the Government for its case-in-chief documents, and he tendered an unspecific 265-page description of the classified documents he intended to disclose in his defense.

In response to North's motion for a delay necessary for his trial preparation, Judge Gesell cancelled the September trial date. He gave the Government until October 10, 1988, to comply with discovery orders. He denied the motion to sever the first three counts as moot. He struck North's CIPA notices, extended the deadline for filing new notices to November 14, 1988, and directed North to make his notices complete and specific. The Government met the discovery deadline. North's November CIPA notices again contested virtually all of the deletions in the Government's case-in-chief documents and contained a two-inch-thick list of classified documents he intended to submit for his defense, again without spelling out their relevance.[10]

Judge Gesell conducted seven days of closed hearings, beginning November 30, 1988, to hear arguments regarding the appropriateness of the redactions on the classified documents in the Government's case-in-chief.[11] To speed the proceedings and minimize confrontations over classification issues during these hearings, Independent Counsel withdrew 100 of its proposed exhibits, and North withdrew 10,000 pages of his documents.

Judge Gesell on December 12, 1988, made several critical CIPA decisions. He wrote that a "fully open, public trial [was] essential" to obtaining justice for North. In the Government's case-in-chief documents, he approved redactions designed to protect the identities of CIA personnel and cooperating foreign nationals, the locations of overseas CIA stations, and intelligence sources and methods. But he also ruled that if the Government introduced all of its proposed evidence, it would have to disclose the identities of certain countries and foreign leaders. These

subjects appeared ont the Interagency Review Group's list of items that could not be disclosed under any circumstance, even if it meant dismissal of the case—these items became known in Judge Gesell's courtroom as the "drop-dead" list. Also, Gesell held that certain intelligence reports could only be used in verbatim form, even if that disclosed an intelligence source which the intelligence agencies claimed to be secret. Although Independent Counsel would have proceeded without these reports, North claimed they were also material to his defense.

As for North's claimed need for classified information for his defense, Judge Gesell observed that North had again failed to comply with CIPA in his notices of classified information he intended to disclose. Judge Gesell stated that North's CIPA notices reflected "deliberate disregard" of the court's orders regarding specificity and materiality. In response, Judge Gesell sanctioned North by permitting him to introduce only 300 classified documents. Over North's objections, the court turned over to the intelligence agencies and to Independent Counsel North's third CIPA notice, which included a 162-page narrative of proposed testimony by North and/or other unidentified defense witnesses. Judge Gesell set the trial date at January 31, 1989.

As a result of Judge Gesell's December 12, 1988 CIPA rulings, the heads of the intelligence agencies met with President Reagan's national security adviser to determine whether to permit the disclosure of the information so the trial could proceed, or to ask Attorney General Richard Thornburgh to file a CIPA affidavit refusing to do so, thus forcing dismissal of the case. At that time, no attorney general had ever taken such a step.

The classified information at issue included the names of Latin American countries and officials referred to in certain documents, even though the country identities and the facts spelled out in the documents were publicly known. The intelligence agency heads also refused to permit the disclosure of the nature of intelligence reports circulated to Defense Secretary Caspar W. Weinberger, Casey, Deputy CIA Director Robert M. Gates and others, which exposed the U.S. arms sales and Iranian

---

[10] North attempted by these broad notices to refrain from disclosing certain classified materials that allegedly were most critical to his defense, and thus central to his claim that the CIPA process violated his constitutional rights. While allowing North to preserve his constitutional objections, the court directed North to submit a final CIPA notice *ex parte* and *in camera* by December 19, 1988, or face preclusion of the evidence.

[11] Independent Counsel's presentations on CIPA issues were directed by Associate Counsel Christian J. Mixter.

claims of being overcharged.[12] Judge Gesell ruled that the nature of the intelligence enhanced its credibility and thus would be material to the defense.

In advance of the meeting of the intelligence heads, Independent Counsel on December 20, 1988, filed a brief with Attorney General Richard Thornburgh stressing the importance of the *North* prosecution. Independent Counsel made clear that the refusal to declassify the information at issue would result in dismissal of central counts against North. Independent Counsel's brief included an extensive collection of press reports, including a book, to demonstrate that the information was not in fact secret. Independent Counsel offered to meet with the group to present his argument, but Thornburgh did not acknowledge the offer.

The meeting went forward in the White House Situation Room on December 21 without Independent Counsel. Associate Counsel to the President William Landers informed Independent Counsel that evening that the agencies would refuse to permit the use of the classified information at North's trial and that Thornburgh would file a CIPA affidavit forcing dismissal of the case if necessary to prevent the information's disclosure. That message was confirmed in subsequent letters from Assistant Attorney General Edward S.G. Dennis, Jr., and CIA Director William H. Webster.

The Reagan Administration's position made it clear that important counts against North were in jeopardy. Independent Counsel unsuccessfully moved for reconsideration of Judge Gesell's order. An appeal of Judge Gesell's rulings as to what was material to the defense was not promising. A trial judge, particularly one as diligent as Judge Gesell, is allowed wide discretion on such matters. Moreover, an appeal would have made an immediate trial impossible, even if the appeal were expedited.

More promising was an effort by Independent Counsel to reach agreement with the intelligence agencies by offering to drop two major counts of the indictment: the conspiracy and theft charges associated with the diversion.[13] These were the counts to which the intelligence

reports at issue were relevant. They were also the counts the Administration most feared.[14] In return for dismissal of Counts One and Two, Independent Counsel obtained tacit agreement from the departments of Justice and State not to block the disclosure of the identities of certain Latin American countries which, if withheld, would have forced the dismissal of many of the remaining counts.

After obtaining this assurance of support, Independent Counsel informed Thornburgh on January 4, 1989, that he would move for the dismissal of the conspiracy and theft counts. The motion was made the following day. After the attorney general filed his affidavit confirming the need to withhold the information, Counts One and Two were dismissed on January 13, 1989.

The dismissal of the conspiracy and theft counts did not end the conflict over classified information in *North*. The court conducted two more days of hearings on North's additional CIPA notices, which laid out 300 proposed defense trial documents. On January 19, 1989, the court did not rule in advance on each item. The court defined categories of classified information that could or could not be exposed. The court permitted North to use classified information in accordance with those categories relevant to seven specific purposes and for the purpose of impeaching witnesses.[15]

The intelligence agencies were outraged. Judge Gesell's order did not literally comply with the precise pre-trial procedures of CIPA by giving the Government in advance of trial the opportunity to challenge each specific intended use of classified information, one document at a time. However, as Judge Gesell pointed out, CIPA never contemplated such an extensive use of classified information, and there were limits to the court's ability to resolve all questions of materiality before the trial developed.

---

[12] See Classified Appendix.

[13] These were Counts One and Two. In late November 1988, the court had dismissed another major count, wire fraud, on the grounds that it essentially duplicated Count Two.

[14] In an earlier effort to dismiss Count One, the conspiracy count, Thornburgh had filed an amicus brief against Independent Counsel in support of defendant North.

[15] North could use the information to show that (1) the chronologies charged in the indictment were correct, (2) his answers to Attorney General Meese were true in November 1986, (3) his answers to various congressional inquiries were also true, (4) he was directed to testify falsely, (5) he did not destroy documents, (6) money donated to the contras were for legitimate, tax-deductible purposes, and (7) he lacked intent to violate the law.

As the jury was being selected, the intelligence agencies pressed Independent Counsel to get the court to agree to a system whereby the Government would be given 24-hour's advance notice from North of his intent to use classified information in his documents. Independent Counsel offered two proposals, but Judge Gesell rejected both. At the same time, OIC attorneys worked continuously with the intelligence agencies to draft acceptable substitutions for key pieces of the most sensitive classified information in the North documents.

On February 8, 1989, the day before the jury was to be sworn and opening statements were to be delivered, the attorney general attempted to intervene in the case. He filed a motion to compel literal adherence to CIPA procedures, seeking to stay the trial until the issue was litigated. Independent Counsel opposed the attorney general's motion. Judge Gesell denied the attorney general's request. In response, the attorney general, over the opposition of Independent Counsel, filed an appeal. Judge Gesell excused the jury to await action by the Court of Appeals.

The Court of Appeals denied two motions by the attorney general for a stay of North's trial, agreeing with Judge Gesell and Independent Counsel that the attorney general had no standing to appeal. Although the attorney general obtained a stay from the Supreme Court, during a weekend of negotiations Independent Counsel and the Department of Justice agreed on procedures satisfactory to Judge Gesell. The stay was lifted. Independent Counsel and the attorney general proposed to Judge Gesell a list of nine categories of information requiring prior notice to Independent Counsel by North, so that Independent Counsel could give the Government the opportunity to weigh the impact of public disclosure. The court approved most of the proposal, but stated that Independent Counsel, not the attorney general, bore sole responsibility for the prosecution and would be the Government's sole representative in court.

North was unsuccessful in graymailing the Government into dropping additional charges on grounds of classification. Only one intelligence agency persisted in abusing its classification powers during the trial by stubbornly refusing to consider declassifying even the most mundane and widely known "secrets" under its jurisdiction. But the attorney general declined to support that agency in its extreme positions.[16]

Little classified information was divulged during the trial without the Government having had an opportunity to approve its release. Hardly a day went by, however, without controversy. Evenings and weekends were spent in lengthy negotiations between Independent Counsel and the intelligence agencies in an effort to resolve disputes and head off problems. A major achievement was the negotiation of a 42-page Government admission of facts surrounding "quid pro quo" arrangements between the United States and Central American countries for the benefit of the contras, introduced in lieu of the disclosure of classified documents.

Confrontations over CIPA prompted Judge Gesell to observe later that the statute "was ill-suited to a case of this type and amendments are needed to recognize practical difficulties."[17] After trial, the only challenge North raised on appeal to Judge Gesell's CIPA rulings was his decision to allow the Independent Counsel and the intelligence agencies to review the 162-page summary of anticipated defense testimony. The Court of Appeals agreed with North that Judge Gesell "did not move straightforwardly down the procedural path" of CIPA, and that he erroneously failed to order the Government to notify North of the classified information with which the Government expected to rebut North's information. However, the appeals court refused to reverse convictions on CIPA grounds, holding that North failed to demonstrate any surprise or prejudice as a result of trial errors: "In the absence of any showing by North of actual injury, we find no constitutional violation arising out of the application of CIPA in this case."[18]

## The North Trial

Public interest in the *North* case remained high, despite months of pre-trial proceedings and three weeks of jury selection. After the jury was finally sworn in on February 21, 1989, there were long lines of spectators vying for

---

[16] See Classified Appendix.
[17] See Transcript, North (D.D.C. Apr. 6, 1989); *U.S.* v. *North*, 713 F. Supp. 1452 (D.D.C. 1989).
[18] *North*, 910 F.2d at 898–903.

the 14 or 15 public seats available in Judge
Gesell's courtroom. Outside the courthouse,
North's arrivals and departures were recorded
by waiting camera crews throughout the eight-
week trial.

With the dismissal of the central conspiracy
and theft charges against North, the prosecution
trial team [19] faced the difficult job of proving
beyond a reasonable doubt a case consisting
of 12 individual charges without the central
charges to which they had been appended. They
included obstructing a congressional investigation, shredding documents, accepting a bribe
and tax-fraud conspiracy.

In summary, the charges, renumbered, were:

*Count One:* Obstruction of Congress in
September and October 1985, when congressional committees sought information
on press reports alleging that North was
engaged in a variety of contra-support activities, in violation of the Boland prohibition on U.S. aid. The indictment charged
that North and McFarlane obstructed Congress by falsely denying in three letters
North's contra-assistance efforts. The first
letter was sent September 5, 1985, to the
House Permanent Select Committee on Intelligence (HPSCI); the second, on September 12 to a House Foreign Affairs subcommittee; and the third, on October 7 to
HPSCI, responding to additional questions.

*Counts Two, Three, and Four:* False statements to Congress, charging specific misrepresentations in the three letters described
in Count One. These included statements
that North had not solicited funds or other
support for the contras, had not provided
military advice to them, and had not used
his influence to facilitate the movement of
supplies to the contras.

*Count Five:* Obstruction of Congress in
August 1986, charging that in a presentation to HPSCI members and staff, North
falsely denied press accounts that he: (1)
had given military advice to the contras;
(2) had knowledge of specific military actions conducted by the contras; (3) had

contact with retired Maj. Gen. John K.
Singlaub within the previous 20 months;
(4) raised funds in support of the contras;
(5) advised and guided Robert W. Owen
with respect to the contras; and (6) had
frequent contact with Owen.

*Count Six:* Obstruction and aiding and
abetting in the obstruction of congressional
investigations in November 1986, charging
that North helped draft a false chronology
of the Iran arms sales and altered and destroyed documents in response to congressional inquiries into the Iran initiative.

*Count Seven:* Obstruction of a presidential
inquiry conducted by Attorney General
Edwin Meese III from November 21–23,
1986. The indictment charged that North
made false statements to Meese on November 23, including that: (1) the NSC had
no involvement in the diversion of Iran
arms sales proceeds to the contras; (2) the
Israelis determined how much of the proceeds from the arms sales were diverted
to the contras; and (3) North had advised
contra leader Adolfo Calero to open bank
accounts in Switzerland to receive the diverted funds. The indictment also charged
that North obstructed the Meese inquiry
by altering, destroying, concealing and removing relevant official documents.

*Count Eight:* False statements on November 23, 1986, charging the specific misrepresentations North made to Meese as
described in Count Seven.

*Count Nine:* Concealing, removing, muti-
lating, obliterating, falsifying and destroying official NSC documents relevant to the
Iran/contra matter from November 21–25,
1986.

*Count Ten:* Receipt of an illegal gratuity,
charging North with accepting a home-security system paid for by Secord, in exchange for official acts performed by
North.

*Count Eleven:* Conversion of traveler's
checks, charging that North from April
1985 to July 1986 personally used $4,300
in traveler's checks from approximately

---

[19] The *North* case was tried by Associate Counsel John W. Keker,
Michael R. Bromwich and David M. Zornow.

$90,000 in checks given to him by Calero for hostage-release and contra-related expenses.

*Count Twelve:* Conspiracy to defraud the United States, the Department of the Treasury and the Internal Revenue Service. The indictment charged that beginning in the spring or summer of 1985, North and others conspired to defraud the United States by illegally using a tax-exempt organization, the National Endowment for the Preservation of Liberty (NEPL), to solicit money for weapons for the contras and other unlawful purposes.[20]

Although the *North* trial was hard fought, with few exceptions the underlying facts were not truly in dispute. The principal issue was whether North acted with criminal intent. The prosecution presented more than 30 witnesses and hundreds of trial exhibits demonstrating that North did, in fact, perform the acts charged in the indictment. Instead of disproving the facts, North's defense centered on his claims that all his actions were known to and approved by his superiors, that although he knew certain of his actions were wrong, they were justifiable in light of the need for covert action in a dangerous world, and that he never believed any of his actions were unlawful.

At issue, then, was North's intent in performing these acts. The jury had to decide whether North's motives were criminal, or whether he acted out of good intentions in difficult circumstances—whether he was, as he claimed, a "pawn in a chess game being played by giants."[21]

It was clear that North's job at the NSC was to implement two of the President's most important policy goals: the sustenance of the contras despite the Boland prohibition on U.S. aid, and the release of American hostages being held by pro-Iranian terrorists in Beirut. It was also clear that North worked tirelessly in pursuit of these goals.

To prosecute North successfully, the Government was required to distinguish for the jury North's illegal actions from those that were legitimate, and it had to prove those crimes beyond a reasonable doubt.

The Government's task was complicated by the fact that most of its key witnesses were hostile to the prosecution of North. These witnesses reluctantly described their knowledge of the criminal acts of which North was accused, but at every opportunity sought to help the defendant:

—McFarlane, who testified about the false letters sent to Congress and other efforts to conceal North's contra-assistance activities, said: "I believe that I am at fault, not him." [22] After testifying on direct examination that North informed him on the weekend of November 21–23, 1986, that there would be a "shredding party," McFarlane asserted on cross-examination that he believed North intended to destroy documents only to protect McFarlane: "I took it not as an act of malice, but just a statement to me that he was going to make sure that I wasn't hurt. And I took it as a statement of a subordinate trying to be loyal . . ." [23]

—Meese, whose testimony was central to proving two of the charges against North, likened his fact-finding interview with North on November 23, 1986, to a "chat among colleagues," although he had previously testified that discovery of the diversion—the subject of his interview with North—had caused him to fear the possible impeachment of the President.

—North's secretary Fawn Hall testified extensively about helping North alter, shred and remove from the White House official NSC documents. She also testified about the blank traveler's checks North kept in his office to distribute to contra leaders. On cross-examination, she described North as a "tireless" and "inspirational" boss, who was "never lazy or self-serving." [24] Hall suggested that repeated questioning by Congress and the OIC caused her to testify that she recalled certain things more clearly

---

[20] Private fund-raisers Carl R. Channell and Richard R. Miller pleaded guilty to identical charges in 1987, naming North as a co-conspirator in the tax-fraud scheme.

[21] North, *North* Trial Testimony, 4/7/89, p. 6928.

[22] McFarlane, *North* Trial Testimony, 3/13/89, p. 4146.

[23] Ibid., 3/14/89, p. 4287.

[24] Hall, *North* Trial Testimony, 3/22/89, p. 5419.

than she actually did, including incriminating evidence she provided against North.[25]

—Calero gave detailed testimony for the prosecution about North's role in supplying weapons and other support to the contras during the Boland cut-off period. On cross-examination, he described North as a "savior," for whom the Nicaraguans should "erect a monument for . . . once we free Nicaragua."[26]

—Colorado beer magnate Joseph Coors, after testifying about his $65,000 payment to NEPL which was unlawfully solicited as a tax-deductible contribution, stepped down from the witness chair and shook hands with North in full view of the jury.

—Gen. Singlaub, who testified about his contacts with North in soliciting contributions for the contras from foreign countries, saluted North following his testimony, also in full view of the jury.

On April 6, 1989, North took the stand in his own defense. For six days, North admitted to having assisted the contras during the Boland prohibition on U.S. aid, to having shredded and removed from the White House official documents, to having converted traveler's checks for his personal use, to having participated in the creation of false chronologies of the U.S. arms sales, to having lied to Congress and to having accepted a home security-system from Secord and then fabricating letters regarding payment for the system. But, North testified, "I don't believe I ever did anything that was criminal."[27]

North described how, in 1984, he was directed by McFarlane and Casey to sustain the contras during the Boland funding cut-off of U.S. aid. "I understood it [the assignment] very clearly to be that I would be the one to replace the CIA for each of these activities," North said, referring to the efforts he was about to undertake to assist the contras.[28] North also testified that "I was told not to tell other people, not to talk about it, to keep my operational

role very, very secret, that it should not be something that others came to know about."[29]

North described how he and Secord, in order to replace the CIA in assisting the contras, in their covert-action Enterprise created a "mirror image outside the government of what the CIA had done."[30] He claimed he never made a single trip or contact "without the permission, express permission, of either Mr. McFarlane or Admiral Poindexter, and usually, when I could, with the concurrence of Director Casey . . ."[31]

North defended himself against the charges that he helped McFarlane and Poindexter obstruct and make false statements to Congress in 1985 and 1986 by characterizing these actions as part of a political dispute that had nothing to do with law-breaking. On direct examination by his attorneys, North cast himself as a victim of circumstances when he lied repeatedly about his contra-assistance efforts to HPSCI members and staff who were pursuing a resolution of inquiry into those activities at an August 6, 1986, meeting at the White House:

Q: How did you feel about being put in that position? You knew that Mr. McFarlane had denied them the information in 1985 in three letters. You knew that Mr. McFarlane had denied them the information twice on Capitol Hill in 1985. You knew that there was a letter from Admiral Poindexter referring back to these letters saying to answer the question. How did you feel about being told by your boss to go into a meeting on August 6th, 1986?

A: I felt like a pawn in a chess game being played by giants. It was a situation where I had been sent to do a lot of things, almost everything that was in that Resolution of Inquiry, by the direction of the President of the United States, I had been told by Admiral Poindexter and by Mr. McFarlane countless times; that I had given the commitment of the United States in the name of the President to the resistance [contra] leadership, to the people in those other countries, the people in foreign governments all over 18 or 19 countries, and

25 Ibid., 3/23/89, p. 5423.
26 Calero, *North* Trial Testimony, 2/23/89, pp. 2054–2055.
27 North, *North* Trial Testimony, 4/10/89, p. 7134.
28 Ibid., 4/6/89, p. 6782.

29 Ibid.
30 Ibid., p. 6817.
31 Ibid., p. 6829.

that those were things I was told could not, should not and will not be revealed, and yet there was a very strong likelihood that they would be asked, and they were; that the things I had done with the resistance itself in delivering everything from medicine for jungle leprosy to ammunition, to the bases we built for deliveries for the resistance, the arrangements I had made with foreign governments to deliver surface-to-air missiles and ammunition, all of those things I had been told to give the commitment of the United States that it wouldn't be revealed.

I had been told specifically that the Saudi aid that the President had gotten and that Mr. McFarlane had gotten will never be revealed. And by this time we were also using monies from the sale of arms to the Nicaraguan resistance—to the Iranians to help the Nicaraguan resistance, and that would never be revealed.

And I was put in this situation where having been raised to know what the Ten Commandments are, that it would be wrong to do that, but I never perceived that it would be unlawful.[32]

In November 1986, after the Iran arms sales became public, North said he went along with what appeared to be a top-level agreement not to reveal information regarding the 1985 arms sales, including the fact that the President retroactively authorized in a covert-action Finding the November 1985 shipment of HAWK missiles to Iran. "That 1985 shipment, particularly the HAWK shipment in November of 1985, had been a disaster. And we had, throughout, denied that we were involved in it, even though we were. And the reason we denied that is because the Iranians themselves were so upset about it," North said.[33]

North said on cross-examination that on November 20, 1986, during preparation of congressional testimony for Casey and Poindexter, an entire roomful of individuals knew that false assertions were being drafted when North suggested that they say no one in the U.S. Govern-

ment knew the true cargo of the November 1985 HAWK missile shipment to Iran. North said he knew it was false, Poindexter knew it was false, NSC counsel Paul Thompson knew it was false, Casey knew it was false, and North said he assumed Meese, Assistant Attorney General Charles Cooper, and Deputy CIA Director Gates knew it was false.[34]

On November 21, 22 or 24, 1986, North said he witnessed Poindexter destroy what may have been the only signed copy of a presidential covert-action Finding that sought to authorize retroactively CIA participation in the November 1985 HAWK missile shipment to Iran. North said the Finding was destroyed because its language made clear that it was a swap of arms-for-hostages, and because public revelation of the fact that the United States had been involved in the ill-fated shipment would jeopardize the lives of Americans still being held hostage in the Middle East.[35] Asked whether he felt he was part of a "den of thieves," North answered he felt he was among honorable men. He said:

We sat and tried to formulate and put the very best possible face on what was a diplomatic disaster and a political catastrophe in this country, but I did not regard it to be a criminal act. Nor did I regard the place in which I worked to be a den of thieves.[36]

North denied that he gave false information to Meese in Meese's fact-finding interview of November 23, 1986.[37] He disputed the accuracy of notes taken during the interview.[38]

North testified that he was shocked to hear Meese in a press conference on November 25, 1986, refer to the possibility of criminal action in connection with the Iran/contra diversion. North said he was also surprised to hear Meese suggest that the President did not know about the November 1985 shipment until months later. North said Meese's assertion "was not only contrary to my knowledge and my participation, it was contrary to what I had said the very day before, or on Sunday. It was contrary to

---

[32] Ibid., 4/7/89, pp. 6928–29.
[33] Ibid., 4/10/89, p. 7079.

[34] Ibid., 4/12/89, pp. 7624–7632.
[35] Ibid., pp. 7601–17.
[36] Ibid., pp. 7620–21.
[37] Ibid., 4/10/89, pp. 7091–97.
[38] Ibid., 4/13/89, p. 7684.

what I believed the President had authorized. It was contrary to what I believed all of the other people I had worked with up the chain in the Cabinet knew to be the truth.'' [39]

North blamed his decision to remove classified NSC documents from his office on November 25, 1986, on Washington, D.C., attorney Thomas C. Green. According to North, Green asked him in the wake of his public firing, ''Do you have anybody or anything to protect yourself?'' As a result, North said, ''I gathered up a number of documents that I believed would indicate or show that I had had the authority to do what I had done over the course of those two operations. I put them in my briefcase, along with my notebooks, and left the Executive Office Building with him [Green].'' [40]

After North left the White House and went with Green and Secord to a hotel in Northern Virginia, he received a call from President Reagan. North testified:

> The President came on the line and he said, I want to thank you for all your work. I am sorry that it happened the way that it did. He said, ''You are an American hero.'' He asked me to understand that it was—he just hadn't known or didn't know, words to that effect. I thanked him for the phone call and told him that I was sorry that this had created so much difficulty for him, for the country. [41]

North had difficulty on cross-examination explaining why he destroyed some NSC records, as he claimed, to protect the lives of individuals involved in the Iran and contra operations, but had taken with him from the White House more than a dozen notebooks containing 2,000 pages of names and details on operations, including some highly classified information. [42]

North also had difficulty on cross-examination explaining why he was told by Casey to keep careful track of the payments he made to contra leaders out of an ''operational fund''

in his office, and why he was subsequently told by Casey in October 1986, following the shootdown of a contra-resupply plane in Nicaragua, to destroy the ledger in which he kept track of those disbursements. [43] North testified that $4,300 in traveler's checks given to him by Calero for the operational fund, and which North spent at grocery stores, gas stations and other retail outlets, were to reimburse himself for operational expenses he paid from his own pocket. [44] He said he was not nervous about destroying the only record he kept of the operational fund disbursements because he never believed he would ever be accused of doing anything dishonest with the money. [45]

North testified that he had $15,000 in cash in a metal box bolted to a closet floor in his home, saved from pocket change and a decades-old insurance settlement. [46] This, North said, was the source of funds for a car he bought in October 1985. North could not explain why he paid for the car in two cash payments—the second after North had visited Secord. He said he could not recall the October 1985 payment. [47]

North claimed no awareness of a $200,000 investment account that Secord's business partner Albert Hakim set up for North in Switzerland, although he did admit that he sent his wife Betsy to Philadelphia in March 1986 to meet with Willard I. Zucker, the Secord-Hakim Enterprise's financial manager. North said he believed the purpose of Betsy North's trip to Philadelphia was for her to identify herself to Zucker in case North didn't return from a dangerous trip to Iran. North said he assumed that in the event of his death, something would be done ''that was proper and honorable and nothing wrong in any way,'' denying that the investment account was a bribery attempt by Hakim. [48]

North was unable to blame others for his acceptance of a home security-system from Secord, except to explain that he accepted the system in response to reported terrorist threats on his life. North admitted that after the

[39] Ibid., 4/10/89, pp. 7104–07.

[40] Ibid., pp. 7109–10. North's attorney Brendan V. Sullivan, Jr., in early December 1986 returned to NSC counsel Paul B. Thompson 168 pages of documents North took with him from the White House. Included were copies of the undated memo in which North described the diversion of Iranian arms sales proceeds to the contras.

[41] Ibid., p. 7111.

[42] Ibid., pp. 7159–60.

[43] Ibid.

[44] Ibid., pp. 7141–45.

[45] Ibid., pp. 7196–97.

[46] Ibid., pp. 7145–49.

[47] Ibid., pp. 7145–53.

[48] Ibid., pp. 7184–98. Hakim pleaded guilty in November 1989 to attempting to supplement the salary of North, based partly on the establishment of the $200,000 investment account. See Hakim chapter.

Iran/contra affair became public, he exchanged false back-dated letters with Glenn Robinette, a former CIA officer who worked for Secord in installing the system, suggesting payment arrangements. "[I]t was a fairly stupid thing to do," North said.[49]

North was insistent that many of the activities charged in the indictment were authorized and concealed to protect foreign nationals and others involved in his covert operations. North also reasserted his belief through most of 1986 that President Reagan had approved even the diversion of Iran arms sales proceeds to the contras:

Q: You understood that you had the approval of the President to use those monies to undertake operations?

A: I'm absolutely certain of the fact that I believed throughout from early February [1986] when we began the concept or putting in place the concept of using Iranian arms sale monies to aid the Nicaraguan resistance and to do those other things, that I deeply believed that I had the authority of the President to do it.[50]

North said on November 21 or 22, 1986, he showed Poindexter a copy of the diversion memo and assured him incorrectly that all copies had been destroyed. He asked Poindexter "at that point if the President knew and he told me the President did not know. . . ."[51]

## Important Evidence Emerging at Trial

A total of 49 witnesses testified during the eight-week trial: 17 for the defense (including North) and 32 for the Government.[52] Hundreds of exhibits were admitted into evidence, many of them previously classified Top Secret and beyond, dealing with secret communications and operations over a several-year period, and covering events in the Middle East, Europe, Africa, Central and South America and Asia.

## Poindexter's Destruction of the Finding

For the prosecution, which had been shielded from immunized congressional testimony, one of the most important items of new evidence to emerge from the trial was North's eyewitness description of Poindexter's destruction of the presidential covert-action Finding authorizing the November 1985 HAWK shipment. Although Poindexter had testified to that destruction in the congressional hearings, Independent Counsel had not heard his immunized testimony. In two-and-a-half years of investigation, no other witness—including NSC counsel Paul Thompson, whom North said also witnessed the event—had provided Independent Counsel with this information.[53]

North subsequently testified about the destruction of the Finding in the *Poindexter* trial. Although it was not one of the charges against Poindexter because Independent Counsel had no evidence of the destruction when the indictment was returned, it provided important corroborating evidence of his obstruction of and false statements to Congress in November 1986 about the November 1985 arms shipment. The information also caused Independent Counsel to request Thompson and to consider bringing charges against him based on this information.[54]

## The Quid Pro Quo Admission

In lieu of the disclosure of classified information deemed relevant by Judge Gesell to North's defense, the Government for trial purposes only admitted to a 42-page statement of facts describing an elaborate series of secret Reagan Administration contacts with foreign countries in efforts to assist the contras, primarily during the prohibition on U.S. aid. This document, which became known as the "Quid Pro Quo" admission, among other things described these alleged activities:

—The delivery of Israeli-seized PLO weapons to the contras; in exchange, the Department of Defense assured Israel that the United States would be flexible in its approach to Israeli military and economic needs.

[49] Ibid., pp. 7203–10.

[50] Ibid., 4/12/89, pp. 7564–65.

[51] Ibid., p. 7566.

[52] One of Independent Counsel's witnesses, Thomas Claggett, a businessman who contributed to the contras, was excused by Judge Gesell after he indicated that he could not fully comply with the judge's *Kastigar* instructions.

[53] See Thompson chapter.

[54] Ibid.

—Various forms of assistance to the contras from El Salvador, Guatemala, Honduras and other countries in Central and South America; in exchange, the United States provided increased economic and other aid.

—Approaches for funding to Saudi Arabia, Taiwan, China, South Korea and Brunei, and approaches to other countries for special weapons purchases.

—Discussions with Panamanian dictator Manuel Noriega about committing acts of sabotage against the Nicaragua Sandinista government in exchange for U.S. help in rehabilitating Noriega's public image.

—Secret contacts by President Reagan and other top-ranking officials with foreign leaders about assisting the contras, and similar approaches by U.S. ambassadors abroad.

## The "Heads of State" Documents

North entered into evidence seven documents indicating greater knowledge and involvement by President Reagan in contra-assistance efforts than had previously been made public.[55] Six of the documents described White House approaches to Honduras regarding contra aid in February and March of 1985, outlining incentives to be provided to the Hondurans for their continued support to the contras. The seventh document indicated that in October 1985, National Security Adviser McFarlane sought President Reagan's approval of U.S. reconnaissance

overflights of Nicaragua, and notations suggested that the President was informed about the illegal air-drop of recoilless rifles to the contras.

Most of these documents were obtained by Independent Counsel in 1988 in response to discovery requests by North, which resulted in the production of 15,000 pages of White House materials not previously produced to OIC despite comprehensive requests. Of the seven defense documents regarding Honduras and the recoilless rifle drop, OIC had received in response to its original White House document request only that document about the rifle drop.

Following the trial, Independent Counsel pursued the question of why documents had not been produced to the criminal investigation until North's discovery request. The House and Senate intelligence committees also sought to determine why Congress had not received the documents in 1987.[56] The reasons for non-production were not clear. Three of the original documents were found to have been segregated from NSC institutional files and kept in a special "heads of state" file, which apparently was not searched in response to earlier document requests.

Independent Counsel in June 1989 sought through the National Archives "prompt access" to all documents relevant to Iran/contra matters contained in the heads-of-state file, which had been shipped to the Reagan Presidential Library in California.[57] In December 1989, several documents were returned from California in response to Independent Counsel's request.[58] These documents did not contain significant new information.

## North's Notebooks

When North took the witness stand, Judge Gesell granted Independent Counsel's long-standing request for access to North's daily, detailed working notes, filling 2,617 pages from

---

[55] The documents were: a February 19, 1985 memo to President Reagan from McFarlane concerning a proposed letter to President Suazo of Honduras, which President Reagan approved; a February 20, 1985 memo to McFarlane from North and Raymond F. Burghardt of the NSC staff, and a notation from Poindexter; a October 30, 1985 memo to McFarlane from North with a notation by Poindexter indicating President Reagan's approval of reconnaissance overflights of Nicaragua, with attachments concerning the air-drop of recoilless rifles to the contras; a February 22, 1985 memo to McFarlane from Burghardt seeking authorization to carry a presidential letter to U.S. Ambassador John Negroponte in Honduras to be transmitted to President Suazo; a February 11, 1985 memo to McFarlane from North and Burghardt regarding a special emissary to Honduras to brief President Suazo on "conditions" for expedited assistance, with a handwritten notation from Poindexter to McFarlane regarding who the emissary should be, and attaching a memo to Secretary of State George P. Schultz, Weinberger, Casey and Joint Chiefs of Staff Chairman Gen. John W. Vessey describing an agreement for expedited aid to Honduras "as an incentive to the Hondurans for their continued support to those in jeopardy along the border;" and an April 25, 1985 memo from McFarlane recommending that President Reagan call President Suazo, bearing President Reagan's handwritten notations of the call.

[56] At least four of the seven *North* trial documents apparently had never been provided by the White House to the Select Committees in 1987. Two had been provided in a different form, without the questionable notations or without certain attachments. The status of one document's production to Congress was never clearly determined. (HPSCI report to Rep. Lee Hamilton, 6/28/89.)

[57] Letter from Christian J. Mixter to John P. Fawcett, National Archives, 6/27/89.

[58] Letter from Patricia Aronsson to Christian J. Mixter, 12/14/89.

January 1, 1984 to November 25, 1986.[59] Earlier OIC efforts to subpoena the spiral-bound notebooks, which North removed from the White House when he was fired in November 1986, failed because North successfully argued that their production would violate his Fifth Amendment protection against self-incrimination.[60]

The notebooks were not immediately made public at the *North* Trial because they contained highly classified information. They included names, phone conversations, meetings and lists of action items North recorded diligently throughout the day. Although the prosecution team quickly reviewed the notebooks in preparation for cross examining North, their cryptic contents, level of great detail and sheer volume made digesting them for use at trial nearly impossible. But they provided invaluable leads and information for further investigation.[61]

## Presidential Authorization

North's attorneys effectively employed a higher-authorization defense, repeatedly eliciting testimony and exhibiting documents showing that North executed many of his secret activities with the knowledge and approval of his superiors. Important elements of this defense were the quid-pro-quo admission of facts and the seven documents indicating presidential awareness of certain contra-assistance efforts described above. Although North testified that he believed he had his immediate superiors' and even presidential approval for all he did, he offered no hard proof of presidential awareness of any of his criminal acts.

In mounting his higher-authorization defense, North attempted to subpoena President Reagan and President Bush to testify. Judge Gesell on January 30, 1989, quashed the Bush subpoena, ruling that the defendant had "made no showing that President Bush has any specific information relevant and material to the charges of the indictment which makes it necessary or appropriate to require his appearance." At the same time, the court ordered that President Reagan would "remain subject to call" and additional consideration would be given the matter if the defense could support a claim that he "ordered, directed, required or, with advance knowledge, condoned" any of the criminal actions of which North stood accused.[62]

On March 31, 1989, Judge Gesell quashed North's subpoena of President Reagan. His memorandum and order stated:

> . . . Whether or not authorization is a defense, authorization is not established by atmosphere, surmise or inference. The written record has been exhausted in this regard. The trial record presently contains no proof that defendant North ever received any authorization from President Reagan to engage in the illegal conduct alleged, either directly or indirectly, orally or in writing. No such authorization to any obstruction or false statement count has been identified in materials submitted to the Court by the defense either in CIPA proceedings or on the public record. Additionally, the Court has examined President Reagan's responses to extensive interrogatories furnished by him under oath to the

---

[59] Independent Counsel only received copies, however; North retained the original notebooks at the secure facility that had been created for his defense facility in 1988.

[60] The Select Iran/contra Committees obtained redacted copies of the North notebooks in 1987, under the terms of North's immunity agreement. The Senate Foreign Relations Committee in April 1988 sought to subpoena unedited copies of the notebooks, finding the Select Committees' versions unusable because North's lawyers had blacked out large portions of text.

[61] In view of the enormous amount of highly classified, compartmented information in the North notebooks, Independent Counsel is at a loss to explain why attorneys general Meese and Thornburgh declined to recover the notebooks from North, who removed them from the NSC after he was fired November 25, 1986. The Government did not recover North's *original* notebooks until Independent Counsel obtained them pursuant to a Grand Jury subpoena, and after additional litigation by North in 1991.

When the Senate Foreign Relations Committee in June 1989 asked OIC for copies of the notebooks, Independent Counsel responded that he had no objection to their release but that the NSC, as the agency from which the notes originated, would have to approve their release. At that point, to assist the Senate committee, Independent Counsel attempted to return copies of the notebooks to the NSC. The NSC refused to accept them when an OIC courier tried to deliver them to the Old Executive Office Building. In October 1989, the Department of Justice informed OIC that the NSC was concerned about its "legal right to receive this material without judicial authorization and notice to the defendant. . . ." (Letter from Edward S.G. Dennis to Walsh, 10/2/89.)

Only after OIC was sued under the Freedom of Information Act by two public interest groups—the National Security Archive and Public Citizen—for access to the notebooks did the Justice Department finally accept custody of copies of North's notes. In May 1990, approximately 2,000 pages of notes were declassified and made public. Independent Counsel subsequently sent copies of the declassified notebooks to the Senate Foreign Affairs Committee and a classified, uncensored version to the Senate Select Committee on Intelligence.

[62] *North*, Order Re: Motion of the President and the President-Elect to Quash the Defendant's Subpoenas. Government's Motion to Quash Defendant's Subpoenas Duces Tecum to the President and the Custodian of Records of the Executive Office of the President, 1/30/89.

grand jury as well as references (filed herewith under seal) to portions of Mr. Reagan's personal diary developed by Independent Counsel during the investigatory stages of this matter. Nothing there even remotely supports an authorization claim.

Accordingly, the Court holds that neither defendant North nor his counsel has presented any basis which warrants the Court to exercise its discretion by enforcing the ad testificandum [for testifying] subpoena served on President Reagan. There has been no showing that President Reagan's appearance is necessary to assure Lt. Col. North a fair trial. . . .[63]

## The Jury's Verdict

The jury was sequestered and began deliberating April 22, 1989. After deliberating for 64 hours over a 12-day period, the jury on May 6, 1989, returned a verdict of guilty on three counts and not guilty on nine. North was found guilty of:

—Aiding and abetting an obstruction of congressional inquiries in November 1986 (Count Six).

—Destroying and falsifying official NSC documents (Count Nine).

—Receiving an illegal gratuity (Count Ten).

## The Sentence

Judge Gesell on July 5, 1989, sentenced North to two years probation, $150,000 in fines and 1,200 hours community service. He told North

that a jail sentence would "only harden your misconceptions" about public service and how he had tarnished it.[64] Stating that North's notoriety had caused him problems but also made him wealthy, Gesell ordered North to serve in an inner-city youth-counseling program as an administrator.[65]

The fact that North was not given a jail sentence, as Independent Counsel had recommended, gave North little incentive for cooperating with the ongoing criminal investigation. Indeed, North litigated against the Independent Counsel for months in an attempt to escape giving testimony to the Grand Jury. The court's decision not to impose jail time on North was a contributing factor also in lighter sentences imposed in subsequent Iran/contra cases.

In imposing sentence, Judge Gesell expressed his views of the case this way:

The indictment involves your participation in particular covert events. I do not think that in this area you were a leader at all, but really a low-ranking subordinate working to carry out initiatives of a few cynical superiors. You came to be the point man in a very complex power play developed by higher-ups. Whether it was because of the excitement and the challenge or because of conviction, you responded certainly willingly and sometimes even excessively to their requirements. And along the way you came to accept, it seems to me, the mistaken view that Congress couldn't be trusted and that the fate of the country was better left to a small inside group, not elected by the people, who were free to act as they chose while publicly professing to act differently. Thus you became and by a series of circumstances in fact and I believe in your mind part of a scheme that reflected a total distrust in some constitutional values.

Now, a trial is a very extraordinary thing. As you stand there now you're not the fall guy for this tragic breach of the public trust. The jury composed of everyday citi-

---

[63] *North*, Memorandum and Order, 3/31/89. Following his convictions on three charges, North appealed on several grounds, including the fact that he was unable to call President Reagan to testify. In a dissenting opinion issued July 20, 1990, (pp. 44–45), U.S. Appeals Court Judge Laurence Silberman agreed with North's argument, writing:

Presidents, even ex-Presidents, may not be called to testify capriciously or needlessly. But this is not such a case. North worked in the White House, only one step removed from the President himself, with what appears to have been enormous responsibility. He has been convicted of violating criminal statutes (never before employed as here) and his defense is that he was *lawfully* doing the President's bidding, and doing so with regard to a substantive area of national security policy, which, whatever one's view of those policies, would have been thought at the core of the Chief Executive's constitutional responsibility. His immediate superior, Admiral Poindexter, was unavailable as a defense witness. Under these circumstances, for the trial judge to have refused to compel Reagan's testimony, was to deprive North of a fair trial.

[64] Gesell, *North* Sentencing Hearing, 7/5/89, p. 36.

[65] Subsequently, it is Independent Counsel's understanding that North fulfilled his community-service requirement, but payment of the fine was suspended pending the outcome of his appeal.

zens your supporters mocked and mocked throughout the trial understood what was taking place.[66] Observing that many others involved in the events were escaping without censor or with prosecutorial promises of leniency or immunities they used their common sense. And they gave you the benefit of a reasonable doubt.

You're here now because of your own conduct when the truth was coming out. Apparently you could not face disclosure and decided to protect yourself and others. You destroyed evidence, altered and removed official documents, created false papers after the events to keep Congress and others from finding out what was happening.

Now, I believe that you knew this was morally wrong. It was against your bringing up. It was against your faith. It was against all of your training. Under the stress of the moment it was easier to choose the role of a martyr but that wasn't a heroic, patriotic act nor was it in the public interest.[67]

## The North Appeal

North appealed his convictions on all three counts on a variety of grounds. North's most serious appeals issues related to Judge Gesell's application of the *Kastigar* decision in keeping North's trial free of taint from his immunized congressional testimony and the application of the Classified Information Procedures Act during the trial.

The appeals were argued at the United States Court of Appeals for the District of Columbia

Circuit on February 6, 1990. The court ruled on July 20, 1990.

By a 2–1 vote, the Appeals Court set aside North's convictions. The divided court ruled that Judge Gesell erred in failing to hold a full hearing as required by *Kastigar* to ensure that the prosecution witnesses made no use of North's immunized congressional testimony.

The Court of Appeals disagreed sharply with the Independent Counsel and Judge Gesell's definition of "use" under the federal use-immunity statute. The Court of Appeals determined that the statute, as interpreted in *Kastigar*, prevented "evidentiary" uses of immunized testimony including "the use of immunized testimony by witnesses to refresh their memories, or otherwise to focus their thoughts, organize their testimony, or alter their prior or contemporaneous statements. . . ." The court observed that Judge Gesell never inquired into these uses of immunized testimony, and it held that warnings to witnesses not to testify to anything they did not know or recall first-hand did not insure against such uses.[68]

The Court of Appeals did not reject Judge Gesell's *Kastigar* rulings in their entirety. The court upheld his determination that Independent Counsel did not present any of North's immunized testimony to the Grand Jury or trial jury. The court also affirmed the District Court's holdings that Independent Counsel did not use the immunized testimony to guide its prosecutorial or trial decisions, and that Independent Counsel had proven untainted leads to all of its witnesses.

Nevertheless, the court remanded all three convictions to the District Court for a "witness-by-witness [and,] if necessary . . . line-by-line and item by item" inquiry into the content as well as the sources of grand jury and trial witness testimony.[69]

On September 4, 1990, Independent Counsel petitioned for rehearing by the panel and suggested a rehearing by the *en banc* (full) Court of Appeals. The panel granted the petition in part on November 27, 1990, and released a lengthy opinion, but it did not modify its judg-

66 Judge Gesell was referring to media opinion pieces and public statements by North supporters expressing the view that the jury was too ill-informed about current affairs to pass judgment on North. They argued this based on the fact that none of the jurors claimed to be knowledgeable of or interested in North or the Iran/contra matter before being sworn in. It was North's attorneys, however, who insisted on selecting a jury virtually unaware of their client's widely publicized congressional testimony.

In pre-trial hearings regarding jury selection and possible problems stemming from the publicity that had surrounded the Iran/contra matter, Judge Gesell said it was his experience in presiding over high-profile cases, including some of the Watergate cases, that ordinary citizens pay little attention to the national news events occurring around them in Washington. Because of this, he said, it was possible to pick a fair-minded jury even in the most publicized cases.

67 Gesell, *North* Sentencing Hearing, 7/5/89, pp. 35–36.

68 *North*, 910 F.2d at 856.
69 Ibid., 910 F.2d at 872.

ment. Over two dissents, the full court denied the request for rehearing *en banc*.[70]

On May 28, 1991, the Supreme Court denied Independent Counsel's petition for certiorari.[71] At that point, Independent Counsel decided to return for additional *Kastigar* hearings in Judge Gesell's court, as prescribed by the Court of Appeals. In two days of remand hearings, McFarlane testified that his trial testimony was "colored" by, and that he was deeply affected by, North's immunized congressional testimony. Independent Counsel then consented to dismiss the remaining counts of the indictment.[72]

## Conclusion

Despite the dismissal of North's convictions, the prosecution of the case showed that even individuals entrenched in national security matters can be held accountable for crimes committed in the course of their official duties. It was not classified information, after all, that caused North to prevail on appeal. It was Congress's political decision to grant immunity to North, despite the danger it posed to prosecution.

Obtaining the convictions against North put CIPA and *Kastigar* to extreme tests.

It exposed structural problems in the CIPA law when central conspiracy counts had to be dismissed because of the Reagan Administration's refusal to declassify information deemed necessary to a fair trial of the case. This raised serious questions about whether the Reagan Administration—which in the Iran/contra matter had sought the appointment of Independent Counsel to investigate and prosecute possible crimes because of an appearance of conflict of interest—in fact had the final say in determining what crimes could be tried.[73]

In *North*, the Court of Appeals extended the protections afforded to defendants who receive limited immunity. Not only must prosecutors fully shield themselves from immunized testimony—as the court determined Independent Counsel had done—but now all prosecution witnesses must essentially prove that they were not influenced in any way by the defendant's immunized testimony. As Chief Judge Patricia M. Wald in her dissenting opinion wrote: The procedural regime set forth in the majority ruling "makes a subsequent trial of any congressionally immunized witness virtually impossible."[74] This is particularly true where, as in the *North* case, many prosecution witnesses are hostile to the Government and favorable to the defense.

Not since the Watergate prosecutions of the 1970s had a case been tried against a more politically charged backdrop. Although Independent Counsel has been criticized for pursuing the prosecution of North after he had been granted immunity by Congress, the congressional hearings did nothing to hold North or others responsible for the crimes they committed. This, Congress said, was the role of Independent Counsel.

---

[70] *North*, 920 F.2d at 940.

[71] *North*, 111 S. Ct. 2235.

[72] Order, *North* (D.D.C. Sept. 16, 1991) (dismissing Counts Six, Nine, and Ten of Indictment, with prejudice).

[73] This question was posed again in Independent Counsel's case against former CIA Costa Rican Station Chief Joseph F. Fernandez, whose trial was stayed in 1989 and whose case was dismissed in 1990 after the Bush Administration refused to declassify information deemed relevant to his defense. See Fernandez chapter.

[74] *North*, 910 F.2d at 924.

# Chapter 3
# United States v. John M. Poindexter

Navy Vice Adm. John M. Poindexter was appointed as President Reagan's national security adviser on December 4, 1985, succeeding Robert C. McFarlane, whom Poindexter had served under as deputy for two years. Poindexter's White House career ended November 25, 1986, when he was forced to resign in the wake of the public disclosure of the Iran/contra diversion.

Poindexter, Lt. Col. Oliver North and McFarlane were the three individuals Attorney General Edwin Meese III identified on November 25, 1986, as knowledgeable of the diversion. Poindexter's supervision of North and his own participation in the Iran and contra operations were early focuses of Independent Counsel's investigation.

As in the case against North, criminal evidence against Poindexter had to be gathered quickly before he was compelled to testify on Capitol Hill in the summer of 1987 under a grant of limited immunity. Otherwise, the prosecution of Poindexter was likely to be challenged on the grounds that it was derived from or in some way influenced by his immunized congressional testimony.

On March 16, 1988, Poindexter was indicted on seven felony charges arising from his involvement in the Iran/contra affair, as part of a 23-count multi-defendant indictment. He was named with North, retired Air Force Maj. Gen. Richard V. Secord and Albert Hakim as a member of the conspiracy to defraud the United States Government by effecting the Iran/contra diversion and other acts.

After the cases were severed and two of the original charges dismissed, Poindexter was tried and convicted in April 1990 of five felonies, including: one count of conspiring to obstruct official inquiries and proceedings, two counts of obstructing Congress, and two counts of false statements to Congress.[1] U.S. District Judge Harold H. Greene sentenced him to a six-month prison term. In November 1991, Poindexter's convictions were overturned on appeal. In December 1992, the U.S. Supreme Court declined to review the case.

Poindexter joined the National Security Council staff in June 1981, following a distinguished naval career that included battleship command and high-ranking Pentagon posts. In October 1983 he became deputy to National Security Adviser McFarlane; among his subordinates was North. During Poindexter's one-year tenure as national security adviser, which began in December 1985, he oversaw the Iran/contra operations in which North was directly involved.

In November 1986, as the secret operations were becoming publicly exposed, Poindexter became the senior Administration official responsible for briefing the President's other top advisers about the Iran arms sales. In a series of White House meetings with other officials and members of Congress throughout the month, he repeatedly laid out a false version of the transactions that distanced President Reagan from the legally questionable 1985 arms shipments made through Israel, particularly the November 1985 HAWK-missile transaction.

Although Poindexter was the spokesman, he was not alone responsible for knowing the facts. Virtually every other senior official, including President Reagan, who heard his version of the arms sales in briefings throughout November 1986 had reason to believe it was wrong. Yet

---

[1] The *Poindexter* case was tried by Associate Counsel Dan K. Webb, Christian J. Mixter, Howard M. Pearl, and Louise R. Radin.

no one, according to contemporaneous notes of those briefings, spoke up to correct Poindexter.

Poindexter along with North and others in November 1986 attempted to shred and alter the paper trail reflecting their Iran/contra activities. Among other things, Poindexter destroyed the only existing signed presidential covert-action Finding that was intended to authorize retroactively CIA involvement in the November 1985 HAWKs shipment.

Poindexter and North were less successful in eradicating the computer-message trail of their Iran/contra activities. Poindexter and North often communicated through a special channel that Poindexter, a computer expert, had set up on the NSC computer system. This channel, known as "Private Blank Check," allowed Poindexter and North to relay messages to each other without their being routed through channels in which others on the NSC staff could screen them.

Between November 22 to 29, 1986, North deleted from his computer file 736 messages, and Poindexter deleted 5,012 messages during the same period.[2] Despite these deletions, the White House routinely saved back-up tapes containing all data in the system for two weeks to protect against inadvertent loss. When the Iran/contra affair was exposed in late November 1986, the White House Communications Agency, which manages the NSC computer system, retained the back-up tapes dating from November 15. Investigators, therefore, were able to retrieve copies of all messages that were in the Poindexter-North computer files in mid-November 1986 before most of the deletions occurred. These computer messages became important evidence in both the *Poindexter* and *North* trials.

Poindexter admitted to many of his activities before the Select Committees in July 1987 under a grant of testimonial immunity, which prevented his admissions from being used against him in any criminal proceeding. Because President Reagan did not testify in that forum, Poindexter was called to answer the question that dominated the hearings: Did the President know about and approve the diversion of the Iran arms sales proceeds to the contras? Poindexter answered no, "the buck stops here

with me."[3] He said he deliberately withheld the information from President Reagan because "I wanted the President to have some deniability so that he would be protected. . . ."[4]

Facing a criminal trial, Poindexter confronted a different dilemma: It was no longer a question of protecting the President but defending himself against five felony charges. Before Congress, Poindexter's most significant testimony corroborated President Reagan's repeated denials of awareness of the Iran/contra diversion. In the courtroom, Poindexter mounted a higher-authorization defense, attempting to convince the jury that the President had approved his actions, including those that resulted in criminal charges. Instead of taking the stand in his own defense, however, he called President Reagan to testify.

# Pre-Trial Proceedings

U.S. District Judge Gerhard A. Gesell in June 1988 ordered that the multi-defendant case against Poindexter, North, Secord and Hakim be severed.[5] Following severance, Poindexter's case was transferred to Chief Judge Aubrey E. Robinson, Jr., and then to Judge Greene, who presided over further proceedings.

All of Poindexter's substantive challenges to the validity of the indictment were dismissed before trial. The remaining important issues concerned: (1) the preservation of the conspiracy charge; (2) the resolution of classified-information disputes; (3) the resolution of issues related to Poindexter's immunized congressional testimony, under the ruling known as *Kastigar*; and (4) the defendant's successful effort to secure trial testimony from former President Reagan.

## Preserving and Narrowing the Conspiracy Charge

Problems with classified information led to the dismissal of the central conspiracy charges before the *North* trial, and similar problems were expected to arise in the case against Poindexter. On June 20, 1989, Independent Counsel moved

---

[2] Williams, *Poindexter* Trial Testimony, 3/15/90, pp. 1752–65.

[3] Poindexter, Select Committees Testimony, 7/15/87, p. 95.
[4] Ibid., p. 101.
[5] For a more detailed description of the severance of the multi-defendant case, see North chapter.

to eliminate the original broad conspiracy charges based upon the supply of the contras and the diversion and to substantially narrow the charge of conspiracy to violate other substantive criminal statutes, forbidding false statements and obstruction. After filings and oral argument, the court granted the Government's motion.

The charge was refocused on the illegal act of conspiring with North and Secord to conceal activities from Congress. Independent Counsel argued successfully that this narrowing of the conspiracy charge would minimize the classified-information problems that plagued the *North* prosecution.

## Classified Information Issues

The Classified Information Procedures Act (CIPA) allowed the trial court effectively to resolve issues involving the use of classified documents and testimony in *Poindexter*. Judge Greene's supervision of the CIPA process and fruitful negotiations between counsel for the Government and Poindexter resolved most disputes with a minimum of delay.

In contrast to *North*, there was no prolonged or significant litigation concerning the form or scope of Poindexter's CIPA notices to the court to disclose classified information at trial. Between November 27, 1989, and March 13, 1990, Poindexter served 11 such notices, including eight that listed classified documents he wanted to use at trial, two describing possible classified testimony, and one focused solely on information he wanted to elicit at the deposition of President Reagan.

Judge Greene ordered that all differences over classified information be negotiated between the parties before being brought before the court. Judge Greene held six closed CIPA hearings before the trial began and supplemented those with several shorter hearings during trial. Most of his rulings on the relevance and admissibility of classified information, and on the adequacy of substitutions proposed by the Government, were made from the bench.

Taken together, Poindexter's CIPA notices listed approximately 1,200 documents, only a small fraction of which were ultimately introduced at trial. Most classified information was covered by Government stipulations to certain

facts and other unclassified substitutions. This allowed the trial to proceed smoothly, without the conflicts that complicated *North* or the case against former CIA station chief Joseph F. Fernandez, which was dismissed due to classified-information problems.[6]

## Kastigar Proceedings

Poindexter was compelled under a grant of use immunity to testify in 1987 before the Select Committees investigating Iran/contra. As did the other Iran/contra defendants who gave immunized testimony before Congress, Poindexter moved to dismiss the indictment on the theory that it violated the standards enunciated in *Kastigar* v. *United States*,[7] arguing that his immunized testimony was used against him in the Grand Jury and at trial. This argument proved unsuccessful on the trial level but ultimately prevailed in the Court of Appeals.

Before their trials were severed, Poindexter moved jointly with North and Hakim, who also had received immunity to testify before Congress, to have the charges against them dismissed on the ground that the evidence against them was tainted by their immunized testimony. Judge Gesell denied that motion. However, in deference to defense claims that they would use one another's possibly exculpatory immunized testimony, Judge Gesell in June 1988 severed the trials.

Poindexter renewed his *Kastigar* motion before Judge Greene in August 1989. After briefing and argument,[8] the court ordered that two evidentiary hearings be held. At the first, the court heard testimony from Associate Counsel Dan K. Webb and Howard M. Pearl concerning their exposure to Poindexter's immunized testimony before joining the Office of Independent Counsel. Webb and Pearl joined the OIC staff in 1989 and had not, before their appointments, been subject to OIC's procedures to insulate itself from Poindexter's immunized testimony. Judge Greene found their exposure to Poindexter's testimony to be insignificant and allowed both attorneys to participate in the trial.

---

6 See Fernandez chapter.

7 406 U.S. 411 (1972).

8 The *Poindexter* case was tried before the Court of Appeals ruled in *North* that witness hearings were necessary to permit the trial of an immunized defendant.

The second set of court hearings concerned trial witnesses, whose testimony may have been tainted by Poindexter's immunized testimony. Judge Greene accepted Judge Gesell's earlier review of Grand Jury witnesses and declined to re-examine his findings. He also refused to dismiss the indictment on the basis of potential grand juror exposure to the immunized testimony.

Regarding trial witnesses, the court took extensive measures to ensure that Poindexter's immunized statements were not used against him. The court ordered the Government to make an *ex parte* submission (later disclosed to Poindexter) of all statements made by potential trial witnesses before Poindexter gave his immunized testimony before Congress in July 1987. The court found that all of the proposed testimony of most of the potential witnesses had been memorialized before Poindexter appeared publicly on July 15, 1987, and therefore was not tainted.

As for those witnesses whose expected trial testimony would not be limited to the evidence OIC had sealed with the court prior to Poindexter's immunized testimony, Judge Greene required additional information. He concluded that the Government had failed to establish that five of its potential witnesses were free of taint and ordered them to appear at a pre-trial hearing. Two of the three witnesses who ultimately appeared at trial credibly affirmed that their anticipated testimony would not be influenced in any way by Poindexter's immunized testimony; the third, North, refused to do so.

North stated at the pre-trial hearing that he was unable, with respect to any subject, to distinguish what he had personally done, observed or experienced from what he had learned from watching Poindexter's immunized testimony.[9] As for Poindexter's destruction of the December 1985 presidential covert-action Finding—important evidence in the obstruction of Congress—North acknowledged that he had seen Poindexter destroy a piece of paper but insisted that he did not know it was a Finding until Poindexter stated that fact in his immunized testimony before Congress.

The court rejected North's pre-trial testimony as not believable. North, the court found, "appears to have been embarked at that time [at the hearing] upon the calculated course of attempting to assist his former colleague and co-defendant . . . by prevaricating on various issues . . ."[10]

In a separate post-trial ruling, the court added that as far as the destruction of the Finding was concerned, North's testimony at his own trial about the event was inconsistent with his claim that he could not remember it independent of Poindexter's immunized testimony. The court found it "inherently incredible" that North did not remember "his participation in an event he witnessed first hand and that was as dramatic, indeed historic, as the tearing up of an extremely rare Presidential Finding."[11]

## The Reagan Subpoena

One of the most notable aspects of the *Poindexter* case was the defendant's successful attempt to call former President Reagan to testify at his trial by videotaped deposition.

Poindexter first sought presidential and vice presidential notes from OIC as part of his pre-trial discovery requests. In a pre-trial hearing on September 6, 1989, Poindexter's attorneys told the court that presidential notes would reflect that Poindexter informed the President of his denials to Congress in 1986 of NSC activity in support of the contras, and that the notes would "show what the President was told about what was being done to support the contras in Central America, and the President's consent and ratification and approval of that activity."[12] In seeking vice presidential notes, Poindexter's attorneys told the court that "anytime he [Bush] missed a meeting, Admiral Poindexter briefed him on it afterwards."[13]

The court, before making a decision on whether to compel OIC to produce these documents, on September 11, 1989, directed Poindexter to file an *ex parte* memo explaining precisely how these documents would assist his defense.[14] It required from Independent Counsel a legal memorandum concerning its responsibil-

9 North Testimony, *Poindexter* Pre-trial Hearing, 12/13/89, pp. 374–77.

10 Opinion, *Poindexter*, 3/8/90, p. 9.
11 Ibid., 5/29/90, pp. 32–40.
12 Robinson, *Poindexter* Pre-trial Hearing, 9/6/89, p. 18.
13 Ibid., p. 19.
14 Opinion, *Poindexter*, 9/11/89, p. 22.

ity to produce presidential and vice presidential documents not in OIC's possession.

Independent Counsel in a filing on September 18, 1989, told the court that the office did not have in its possession presidential notes, but rather had been granted access to notes and allowed to copy only a portion of them with special permission. As far as President Reagan's diary was concerned, Independent Counsel had been allowed to review typed extracts of portions deemed relevant by White House counsel, but the President had retained custody of his diary, which both he and the national archivist regarded as personal records, making them unaccessible under the Presidential Records Act unless their production were compelled by subpoena.[15]

Attached to Independent Counsel's filing was a declaration by John Fawcett, assistant archivist for the Office of Presidential Libraries of the National Archives and Records Administration. Fawcett stated that President Bush's vice presidential records were transferred to the archives at the end of the Reagan Administration, but, "No personal diary of former Vice President Bush has been specifically identified as being included in the Vice Presidential records. However, these Vice Presidential records have not yet been processed." [16]

On September 25, 1989, Poindexter's attorneys informed the court that "the defendant is willing to seek access to the personal diaries and notes of former President Reagan and former Vice President Bush pursuant to a . . . subpoena." [17] After reviewing Poindexter's *ex parte* submission on the materiality of presidential and vice presidential documents, the court on October 24, 1989, ruled that there was sufficient likelihood that President Reagan's documents would be material to the defense. Judge Greene differentiated between Reagan and Bush documents, however, because "the Vice President had no operational authority with respect to Poindexter," because the information

contained in vice presidential papers may be largely cumulative, and because of deference to the sitting President Bush.[18]

On November 3, 1989, Poindexter filed with the court a classified petition for leave to serve subpoenas on former President Reagan and the National Archives, seeking materials and testimony relevant to Iran/contra activities in 67 categories. On November 16, Judge Greene granted Poindexter's petition. Both President Reagan and the National Archives moved to quash the subpoena for documents.

In a pre-trial hearing December 4 the court stated that its order covered only documents, and not the President's possible trial testimony. On December 18 Poindexter sought the court's leave to subpoena President Reagan to testify at trial. In deciding whether Poindexter could subpoena President Reagan's testimony, Judge Greene asked Poindexter to submit a list of specific questions he intended to ask. Poindexter submitted a list of 183 questions, which were not made available to Independent Counsel.[19] The court ruled that the questions directly related to the charges in the indictment and to Poindexter's anticipated defense.

In his February 5, 1990, ruling upholding the testimonial subpoena of Reagan, Judge Greene described Poindexter's proposed questions as falling into 12 categories. These included: (1) the frequency and occasions on which President Reagan and Poindexter met; (2) the President's view of the Boland Amendment and how it applied to contra support; (3) whether the President authorized Poindexter to seek foreign support for the contras; (4) what instructions the President gave Poindexter regarding meetings with Central American officials, and what information Poindexter subsequently relayed back to the President; (5) presidential discussions with Central American leaders concerning contra support; (6) presidential discussions with Poindexter regarding actions to be taken if Congress did not renew contra aid; (7) presidential knowledge of North's relationship to Iran/contra figures; (8) Poindexter's

---

[15] Government's Memorandum Concerning Presidential and Vice Presidential Documents that Are Not in the Possession of Independent Counsel, 9/18/89.

[16] Ibid., Exhibit A. President Bush in December 1992 for the first time informed Independent Counsel that he had kept a diary as vice president from 1986 to 1988. See Bush chapter.

[17] Defendant's Response to Government's Memorandum Concerning Presidential and Vice President Documents That Are Not in the Possession of Independent Counsel, 9/25/89, p. 2.

[18] *U.S.* v. *Poindexter*, 725 F. Supp. 13, 28–31 (D.D.C. 1989). Judge Greene added that with respect to Bush documents, he would reevaluate the matter if Poindexter at a later date showed a more pressing need for them.

[19] In 1993, during preparation of this report, Independent Counsel obtained copies of these questions and other *ex parte* submissions from Poindexter's case.

briefings of the President regarding a congressional inquiry in 1986 into North's activities; (9) Poindexter's communications with Congress at the direction of the President; (10) whether Poindexter informed the President about Secord's status; (11) discussions Poindexter had with the President regarding a chronology of the Iran arms sales prepared in November 1986; and (12) the President's knowledge of the arms shipments to Iran.

In his opinion explaining his decision to uphold Poindexter's subpoena of President Reagan, Judge Greene concluded:

> Former President Ronald Reagan is claimed by Admiral Poindexter to have direct and important knowledge that will help to exonerate him from the criminal charges lodged against him. In view of the prior professional relationship between the two men, and defendant's showing discussed above, that claim cannot be dismissed as fanciful or frivolous. That being so, it would be inconceivable—in a Republic that subscribes neither to the ancient doctrine of the divine right of kings nor to the more modern conceit of dictators that they are not accountable to the people whom they claim to represent or to their courts of law—to exempt Mr. Reagan from the duty of every citizen to give evidence that will permit the reaching of a just outcome of this criminal prosecution. Defendant has shown that the evidence of the former President is needed to protect his right to a fair trial, and he will be given the opportunity to secure that evidence.[20]

President Reagan did not claim executive privilege once he was ordered to testify.

The seven-hour videotaped deposition of the former President was taken February 16 and 17, 1990, in the Los Angeles federal courthouse, near his residence. The public and the press were not allowed to attend the deposition. Transcripts and the opportunity to view the videotape were made available to members of the press before the trial.

As for Poindexter's subpoena for documents from the former President, Judge Greene ordered President Reagan to make diary entries

available for the court's *in camera* review. After its review, the court ordered President Reagan to produce the relevant diary entries to Poindexter in the absence of a claim of executive privilege. President Reagan, joined by the Bush Administration, claimed executive privilege as to the diary entries on February 5, 1990. On March 21, the court granted the Reagan-Bush motions to quash the subpoena for the diary entries, concluding that Poindexter's defense would be adequately served by the President's testimony.

## The Poindexter Trial

The month-long *Poindexter* trial, which resulted in a five-count conviction on April 7, 1990, centered largely on the testimony of two witnesses: Oliver North for the prosecution and former President Reagan for the defense.

Both men attempted to help the defendant in their appearances on the witness stand, but each had given prior testimony harmful to Poindexter, and they could not deviate from that under threat of perjury charges.[21] North could not abandon his earlier defense stance that he dutifully reported his activities—including those found to be crimes—to his superior, Poindexter. President Reagan was compelled at trial to state, as he had previously, that he repeatedly told his aides to obey the law and that he was unaware of their criminal acts.

Poindexter chose not to testify at his trial.

Although Poindexter and North had destroyed and altered official papers and computer messages, the prosecution offered convincing documentary evidence that Poindexter was kept apprised of North's efforts to provide military aid to the Nicaraguan contras while it was outlawed from October 1984–October 1986 by the Boland Amendment; that Poindexter adopted false statements McFarlane and North made to Congress; and that Poindexter had been fully aware of the ill-fated November 1985 HAWK missile

---

[20] *U.S.* v. *Poindexter*, 732 F. Supp. 142, 159–60 (D.D.C. 1990)

[21] Before taking the witness stand in *Poindexter*, North had testified before the Select Committees in July 1987, at his own trial in 1989, and at a *Poindexter* pre-trial hearing in 1990.

President Reagan was questioned by his Tower Commission on two occasions in early 1987. More significantly, the President in November 1987 answered 53 written interrogatories from Independent Counsel, which were submitted as sworn testimony to the federal Grand Jury investigating the Iran/contra affair.

shipment to Iran, which he subsequently tried to conceal from Congress.

## The Trial Testimony of Oliver L. North

The testimony of North, named as a co-conspirator in the case, was important to proving each of the five charges against Poindexter:

—Count One, that Poindexter conspired with North and Secord to obstruct congressional inquiries of Iran- and contra-related matters, to make false statements to Congress, and to falsify, remove and destroy official documents.

—Count Two, that Poindexter obstructed Congress in 1986 when it was investigating media allegations that North was raising funds and providing military aid to the contras. In letters to three committees, Poindexter answered questions by repeating denials McFarlane made before Congress in 1985 of North's involvement in contra-support activities, even though Poindexter knew the denials to be false. He set up a meeting with the House Intelligence Committee in August 1986 in which he knew North would have to give false testimony, and afterward congratulated North on his performance.

—Count Three, that Poindexter obstructed Congress in November 1986 by participating with North in the preparation of false chronologies of the secret U.S. arms sales to Iran and by making false statements to the House and Senate intelligence committees. Specifically, Poindexter falsely asserted that no U.S. official knew before January 1986 that HAWK missiles had been shipped to Iran in November 1985. The indictment stated that North as early as November 20, 1985, told Poindexter about the shipment in advance and advised him of it again after the fact in late 1985.

—Counts Four and Five, that Poindexter made false statements about the HAWK shipment to the House and Senate intelligence committees on November 21, 1986. As in Count Three, the false statement charges were based on North's informing Poindexter about the shipment in 1985.

In four days of trial testimony, North reluctantly recounted his central operational role in the Iran/contra affair. He described the extensive contra-resupply network he ran with Secord and Hakim,[22] his contra fund-raising efforts, and the military advice he gave the contras. He testified that he kept his bosses McFarlane and Poindexter fully informed of his activities and that he acted only with their approval.[23]

North, who was forced to testify for the prosecution under a grant of immunity, frequently claimed that he could not recall many of the incidents in question, some of which had occurred several years before. North admitted a wide range of contra-support and Iran-related actions only when confronted with prior testimony in which he had provided extensive details.

North admitted that he lied in August 1986 when he told the House Permanent Select Committee on Intelligence (HPSCI) he was not engaged in raising funds or providing military support to the Nicaraguan contras.[24] North described exchanges with Poindexter before and after the meeting that directly implicated Poindexter in a scheme to frustrate the congressional investigation.[25]

HPSCI was one of three congressional committees pursuing a House inquiry into reports of North's contra-aid activities. North testified that prior to appearing before the committee in the White House Situation Room, he told Poindexter he would be asked about "things that I had been told never to reveal."[26] In response, Poindexter told him, "You can handle it, you can take care of it," according to North.[27]

After receiving reports of North's statements to HPSCI, which Poindexter knew were false,

22 North objected to the prosecutor's use of the word "Enterprise" to describe the profit-making web of contra- and Iran-related operations he undertook with Secord and Hakim. He also objected to the use of the word "testimony" in reference to the false statements he made before the House Permanent Select Committee on Intelligence in August 1986, and the word "diversion" to describe the scheme in which he, Poindexter and others diverted Iran arms sales proceeds to the contras.
23 North, *Poindexter* Trial Testimony, 3/12/90, pp. 1275–76.
24 Ibid., 3/9/90, pp. 1042–43.
25 Ibid., 3/12/90, p. 1083.
26 Ibid., 3/9/90, p. 1033.
27 Ibid.

Poindexter by way of his computer sent North a terse congratulatory message: "Well done." [28]

Based on the statements of North and Poindexter, HPSCI Chairman Lee Hamilton informed other members of Congress that the media allegations about North could not be proven. North's false testimony, in combination with Poindexter's perpetuation of McFarlane's previous lies, successfully frustrated the congressional oversight process. It was not until Nicaraguan soldiers on October 5, 1986, shot down a contra-resupply plane carrying American Eugene Hasenfus that Congress renewed its investigation into North's activities.

North testified that he kept Poindexter apprised of his involvement in the covert sales of U.S. arms to Iran in 1985 and 1986, including the operation's most secret aspect: the Iran/contra diversion. He sent Poindexter five or six memos stating that overcharges to the Iranian buyers would generate millions of dollars for diversion to the contras.[29] North said Poindexter told him the diversion should never be revealed.[30] North said he reported the diversion plan to Poindexter because he thought that projects funded by it "ought to have the authority of the President behind them." [31]

North testified that in November 1985, he became directly involved in an Israeli shipment of U.S. HAWK missiles to Iran at McFarlane's behest.[32] North said he got permission from both McFarlane, who was then the national security adviser, and Poindexter, then deputy national security adviser, to enlist Secord's help in resolving logistical problems surrounding the shipment.[33] He also got McFarlane and Poindexter's permission to supply the Israelis with the name of a CIA-connected airline to assist.[34] North outlined the details of the planned HAWK shipment in a computer note to Poindexter on November 20, 1985.[35] By memoranda on December 4 and on December 9, 1985, North informed Poindexter that the

Iranians were unhappy with the shipment and wanted the missiles to be retrieved.[36]

When CIA officials insisted after the HAWK shipment that the President should retroactively authorize the agency's participation in the operation, CIA Director William J. Casey on November 26, 1985, gave Poindexter a covert-action Finding for President Reagan's signature.[37] North testified that he saw the signed Finding either in Poindexter's office safe or in the safe of NSC counsel Paul Thompson.[38]

After public exposure of the Iran arms sales in November 1986, North—at Poindexter's request—prepared a chronology of U.S. involvement in the Iran arms sales, which underwent a series of re-writes. North testified that McFarlane removed from the chronology North's factual account of the November 1985 HAWKs shipment and substituted a cover story: that although the CIA became involved in the November 1985 shipment after Israel encountered logistical difficulties, U.S. officials at the time believed the cargo to be oil-drilling parts and did not learn until January 1986 that the true cargo was weapons.[39]

Asked whether the McFarlane revision was part of a plan to "cover up" the existence of the November 1985 Finding, North answered: "I don't know that cover up is the right word. I listened to the President's press conferences, I listened to statements being made by people and they just didn't talk about it." [40] North said McFarlane told him the cover story should be incorporated into the chronology because the 1985 Finding authorizing the weapons shipment described too directly an arms-for-hostages swap, which, if exposed, would politically embarrass the President.[41]

The same oil-drilling-parts cover story was part of a CIA-prepared chronology that Casey and his deputy, Robert Gates, brought to a White House meeting on November 20, 1986, with Poindexter, North, Meese, Cooper and Thompson. The purpose of the meeting was

[28] PROFs Note from Poindexter to North, 8/11/86, AKW 018921.
[29] North, *Poindexter* Trial Testimony, 3/12/90, pp. 1107–11.
[30] Ibid., pp. 1103–05.
[31] Ibid., p. 1111.
[32] Ibid., pp. 1118–20.
[33] Ibid., pp. 1121–22.
[34] Ibid., pp. 1122–27.
[35] PROFs Note from North to Poindexter, 11/20/85, AKW 002066.

[36] PROFs Note from North to Poindexter, 12/4/85, AKW 002070–73; Memorandum from North to McFarlane and Poindexter, 12/9/85, AKW 002088–91.
[37] Memorandum from Casey to Poindexter, 11/26/85, AMY 000651–52.
[38] North, *Poindexter* Trial Testimony, 3/12/90, p. 1245.
[39] Ibid., pp. 1188–98.
[40] Ibid., p. 1191.
[41] Ibid., pp. 1190–91.

to prepare Casey and Poindexter for their congressional testimony the following day. North was asked at trial:

> Q: . . . did it become clear to you by the time McFarlane tells you that [the finding was too close to an arms-for-hostage swap] and by the time you see the CIA show up with this phony chronology, then at least did it appear to you that there was some effort or plan going on to cover up with U.S. involvement because of that finding?

> A: Well, there is no doubt in my mind that I came to realize that finding was a disaster, and I understood that.[42]

North testified that he altered and destroyed numerous documents in October and November 1986 that would have revealed details of the Iran and contra operations. He said he assured Poindexter that he had "taken care of" the documents that reflected his activities.[43] He said he told Poindexter all the documents describing the Iran/contra diversion were destroyed, after learning from Poindexter on November 21, 1986, that Attorney General Meese would be conducting a weekend investigation into the Iran arms sales.[44] North also testified that he altered other original NSC documents, after receiving Poindexter's permission to retrieve them from the NSC document-archiving system.[45]

More important, North reluctantly testified that he saw Poindexter destroy the only known copy of the signed presidential Finding that sought to authorize retroactively the November 1985 shipment of HAWK missiles to Iran.[46] North's eyewitness account of the destruction of the Finding provided significant proof of Poindexter's intent to conceal facts about the HAWK missile shipment from Congress in November 1986.[47]

North's wide-ranging testimony enabled the prosecution to streamline its witness list to only nine other individuals, many of whom supplemented the central details provided by North.

## The Trial Testimony of President Reagan

Before the trial of Poindexter, President Reagan had not testified publicly about Iran/contra. On February 16 and 17, 1990, he gave a seven-hour videotaped deposition as a defense witness. No classified matters were discussed and executive privilege was not invoked in response to any question. The videotaped deposition was shown in full, therefore, to the *Poindexter* jury during the trial on March 21 and 22, 1990.[48]

In direct examination, defense counsel sought to show presidential knowledge and approval of Poindexter's activities. But President Reagan frequently claimed memory lapses when questioned about specific exchanges he may have had with Poindexter and about his knowledge of individuals and details involved in the Iran and contra operations.

Although President Reagan exhibited virtually no detailed knowledge of the Iran/contra matter, he made clear to the jury that it had his imprimatur, calling it "a covert action that was taken at my behest."[49] President Reagan said North was the only person he remembered being involved in the arms initiative.[50] He could not recall being briefed by Poindexter on the May 1986 trip by McFarlane and North to Tehran, but he said he did recall signing a Bible for Iranians.[51] President Reagan testified that the amount of weapons sold to Iran totaled $12.2 million.[52]

Asked specifically about the November 1985 HAWK shipment to Iran, President Reagan said he recalled a plan in which the Israelis would turn their plane around in mid-delivery of the weapons if no hostages were released.[53] He did not recall when he became aware of the No-

---

[42] Ibid., pp. 1208–09.

[43] Ibid., p. 1218.

[44] Ibid., pp. 1120–21.

[45] Ibid., pp. 1224–27.

[46] Ibid., 1252–54.

[47] The destruction of the 1985 Finding was not charged as a separate crime in the indictment of Poindexter because Independent Counsel did not learn of it until North testified about it at his own trial in April 1989. Poindexter had told the Select Committees in 1987 that he destroyed the only signed copy of the 1985 presidential Finding. Independent Counsel did not learn of this statement at the time, however, because the OIC had taken measures to insulate itself from all immunized testimony. Even if Independent Counsel had been aware

of the Poindexter testimony, OIC could not have used it in any criminal proceeding against Poindexter under the terms of immunity grant.

[48] Immediately after each tape was shown to the jury, a copy was given to the television networks, allowing the public to see President Reagan's only courtroom testimony on the Iran/contra affair.

[49] Reagan, *Poindexter* Trial Deposition, 2/16/90, p. 9.

[50] Ibid., p. 21.

[51] Ibid., p. 24.

[52] Ibid., pp. 154–55.

[53] Ibid., pp. 24–25.

vember 1985 HAWK shipment;[54] he did not recall Poindexter telling him in November 1986 that others in the White House were having trouble remembering when they learned of it.[55]

President Reagan also claimed virtually no memory of the November 1986 period in which his top advisers were scrambling to limit public exposure of the Iran arms sales. He only generally recalled telling members of Congress about the arms sales on November 12, 1986.[56] He could not remember receiving any information from Poindexter for any of his presentations on the matter in that time.[57] The former President could not remember asking Poindexter to assemble the facts on the arms sales.[58] He could not recall that Poindexter briefed the House and Senate intelligence committees on November 21, 1986.[59]

Defense counsel's questions suggested that their client had significant exchanges with the President during the arms-sale period and its aftermath. But Reagan's lack of recollection, and lack of specificity when he did remember events or individuals, left those questions unresolved.

President Reagan provided more helpful testimony for the defense on the subject of contra-support operations. Calling the Boland prohibition on contra funding a "disaster,"[60] Reagan testified that he urged his aides to do what they could to support the contras, while staying "within the law."[61] Reagan recalled that Saudi Arabia's King Fahd pledged millions of dollars for the contras.[62] He said he told his aides not to solicit contributions for the contras directly but to tell people how they could contribute if they wanted to help.[63]

Asked whether Poindexter briefed him on the contras, President Reagan said: "Oh yes, I depended on him for that."[64] He said he had no reason to believe that Poindexter was not keeping him fully informed.

Asked to describe what he knew about North's responsibilities in the White House, President Reagan said:

> Well, he was mainly performing tasks, as I understand it, for the NSC, but he—his background and record had been one of being decorated for heroism and so forth in the Vietnamese conflict, and that he had been a very bold and brave soldier—Marine.
>
> And—so, he was—it was my impression, not from any specific reports or anything, that in through all of this that he was communicating back and forth between on the need for the support of the Contras and so forth.[65]

In addition to professing a benign view of North and his activities, President Reagan indicated general knowledge of and support for the contra-resupply operation in Central America:

> Q: Do you recall any discussions that he [Poindexter] may have had with you about the construction of an airstrip down there in Central America?
>
> A: Well, I did hear—we had learned that there was a rather primitive lane in there in the jungle near the border of Costa Rican [sic], and that was then being put into better shape as a usable airstrip.
>
> Q: Did you have any—do you recall any discussion about who was constructing the airstrip?
>
> A: Well, no. I assume it was the Costa Rican government.
>
> Q: And do you know what that airstrip was going to be used for?
>
> A: Well, I know that—I hoped that it would be used in the delivery of when once again we could supply, keep the Contras supplied, that it could be involved in the—used there, if there was need for a refueling or anything of that kind of a plane.[66]

[54] Ibid., pp. 33–36.
[55] Ibid., pp. 38–39.
[56] Ibid., pp. 37–38.
[57] Ibid., p. 30.
[58] Ibid., p. 28.
[59] Ibid., pp. 44–45.
[60] Ibid., p. 69.
[61] Ibid., pp. 53–54.
[62] Ibid., pp. 74–75.
[63] Ibid., pp. 53–54.
[64] Ibid., p. 116.

[65] Ibid., p. 131.
[66] Ibid., p. 121.

President Reagan was then asked whether he knew who would be using the Costa Rican airstrip for contra resupply. His answer reflected knowledge of the operation supposedly being funded and run by private citizens—the so-called "private benefactors"—that was in fact being run by Secord at North's direction:

Q: Do you know who it was that was going to be using the airstrip? It was going to be used for supplying the Contras, but do you know who it was that was actually going to be doing the supplying and using the airstrip?

A: No, I do not on that. I don't think— I don't think I ever considered that it would be military planes of ours. So, possibly some of those that weren't officially planes of ours that had been helping in the past in deliveries to the Contras and so forth.

Q: Earlier this morning or earlier today, I should say, you mentioned General Secord. That you knew that he was involved in the Contra supply effort.

Was it part of his operation you thought that he might be using the airstrip?

A: I can't say that I actually recall that, but it seems to me logical that he would have been involved in that.[67]

President Reagan, who winked and smiled at Poindexter from the witness stand, did not hide his contempt toward congressional inquiries into NSC staff contra-support activities. Shown misleading letters written by Poindexter in July 1986 to the committees of Congress that were investigating allegations of North's contra efforts, Reagan said: "I am in total agreement. If I had written it myself, I might have used a little profanity." [68]

In cross-examination, the prosecution was able to impeach much of President Reagan's testimony. This was possible because Reagan late in 1987 had answered, under oath, 53 written interrogatories for Independent Counsel and the Grand Jury investigating the Iran/contra matter.

The July 21, 1986, letters—in which Poindexter embraced and perpetuated the lies McFarlane had told Congress about North's contra-support activities a year earlier—were a key element in the obstruction charges against the defendant. Under cross-examination by the prosecution, President Reagan was asked whether he was aware that the Poindexter letters repeated McFarlane's previous lies. The former President equivocated:

Well, I simply—no, I did not have this information, but I have a great deal of confidence in the man who was quoted as sending these letters, McFarlane. And I have never—I have never caught him or seen him doing anything that was in any way out of line or dishonest. And so, I was perfectly willing to accept his defense.[69]

President Reagan said he did not know that McFarlane had pleaded guilty to withholding information from Congress in connection with the false letters.[70]

Asked whether he approved either the McFarlane or Poindexter letters to Congress, the former President said he had no recollection of doing so, adding that his memory could be faulty.[71] Asked directly whether he would approve of sending false information to Congress, President Reagan conceded that he would not.[72] Would he have authorized Poindexter to make false statements to Congress? President Reagan again attempted to assist his former aide: "No. And I don't think any false statements were made." [73]

President Reagan also testified that he did not approve the destruction of Iran/contra documents by Poindexter, and that he was not told about their destruction.[74] But the former President, in response to subsequent questioning, described the dilemma in which he placed his aides in November 1986 by instructing them that certain information could not be revealed because "it will bring to risk and danger to

---

[67] Ibid., p. 122.
[68] Ibid., pp. 146–47.

[69] Ibid., p. 151.
[70] Ibid., pp. 220–21.
[71] Ibid., pp. 150–51.
[72] Ibid., pp. 151–52.
[73] Ibid., p. 158.
[74] Ibid., p. 160.

people that are held and with the people that we were negotiating with.'' [75]

Asked again whether he approved the destruction of alteration of any Iran/contra records, President Reagan said: ''And this, I cannot answer. I cannot recall because it is the possibility that there were such papers that would violate the secrecy that was protecting those individuals' lives.'' [76] President Reagan had denied in response to the earlier written interrogatories that he approved the destruction and alteration of documents; when confronted with his previous testimony he stated that it was truthful.

On the issue of the contras, President Reagan said he ''never had any inkling'' that North was guiding their military strategy.[77] But Reagan muddied the issue in a later statement about North:

> I know that he [North] was very active, and that was certainly with my approval, because I yesterday made plain how seriously I felt about the Contra situation and what it meant to all of us here in the Americas. And, so, obviously, there were many things that were being done. But, again, as I say, I was convinced that they were all being done within the law.[78]

In questioning about the Iran/contra diversion, President Reagan surprisingly asserted that he had no proof that a diversion had occurred:

> And to this day, I still with all of the investigations that have been made, I still have never been given one iota of evidence as to who collected the price, who delivered the final delivery of the weapons, or what was—whether there was ever more money in that Swiss account that had been diverted someplace else. I am still waiting to find those things out and have never found them out.[79]

Asked whether he had approved a diversion, Reagan again stated:

> May I simply point out that I had no knowledge then or now that there had been

a diversion, and I never used the term. And all I knew was that there was some money that came from some place in another account, and that the appearance was that it might have been a part of the negotiated sale. And to this day, I don't have any information or knowledge that that wasn't the total amount that—or that there was a diversion.[80]

Asked again whether he would have approved a diversion, President Reagan said he would not. But, he added, ''No one has proven to me that there was a diversion.'' [81]

President Reagan said he did not recall that the Tower Commission concluded in March 1987 that, in fact, a diversion had occurred. ''I, to this day, do not recall ever hearing that there was a diversion,'' he said.[82] Shown that portion of the Tower Commission report describing the diversion, Reagan said: ''This report—this is the first time that I have ever seen a reference that actually specified there was a diversion.'' [83]

Asked whether Poindexter should have told him about an Iran/contra diversion, Reagan said: ''Yes. Unless maybe he thought he was protecting me from something.'' [84]

## The Verdict and Sentencing

After six days of deliberation, the jury on April 7, 1990, found Poindexter guilty of each of the five felony charges against him. Judge Greene on June 11, 1990, sentenced Poindexter to six months imprisonment on each of the five counts, to be served concurrently.

In imposing the sentence, Judge Greene noted complaints by Poindexter's supporters that the most he was guilty of was having become embroiled in a political quarrel between the White House and Congress. Judge Greene stated:

> Whatever may have been the nature of the original dispute, what the defendant and his associates did was emphatically not a part of the normal political process.

[75] Ibid., p. 252.
[76] Ibid., p. 255.
[77] Ibid., p. 170.
[78] Ibid., p. 189.
[79] Ibid., p. 155.

[80] Ibid., p. 156.
[81] Ibid., p. 157.
[82] Ibid., p. 240.
[83] Ibid., p. 243.
[84] Ibid., pp. 243–44.

. . . When Admiral Poindexter and his associates obstructed the Congress, what were they seeking to accomplish? In a word, it was to nullify the decision that body had made on the issue of supplies to the Contras. . . .

President Reagan did not, or for parliamentary reasons he could not, veto the bill [which contained the Boland prohibition on contra aid]. He did not attempt to assert his own constitutional powers or take the issue to the people, and at the conclusion of the political process the Boland Amendment thus became law.

No problem. What the president was unwilling or unable to do—to defeat this law—Admiral Poindexter, together with Oliver North and others, did on their own. They decided that the policy embodied in the Boland Amendment was wrong, and they went about to violate it on a large scale and for a lengthy period, and then to lie about their activities to prevent the Congress and the public from finding out. . . .

With all due respect to the distinguished military records of Admiral Poindexter, Colonel North, General Secord, and the others, they have no standing in a democratic society to invalidate the decisions made by elected officials . . . As I said several times during the trial, it is immaterial to this criminal case who was right and who was wrong about the wisdom of the Contra policy. That is not what this trial was about. The jury and this court were not competent to decide for this nation whether resistance forces in Nicaragua should or should not have been supplied with weapons.

But more importantly for present purposes, neither was Admiral Poindexter. When he and his associates took it upon themselves to make that decision anyway, to implement it on a broad scale, and to work actively to keep what they were doing from the Congress and the public, they not only violated various statutes. They were also in violation of a principle fundamental to this constitutional Republic—that those elected by and responsible to the people shall make the important policy decisions, and that their decisions may not be nullified by appointed officials who happen to be in positions that give them the ability to operate programs prohibited by law. It is unfortunate that, whatever may be his view of his own purposes and actions, the defendant still gives no evidence of recognizing that principle and the seriousness of its violation.

Given the nature of the offenses, the sentencing principle that is primarily applicable here is that of deterrence, and as a practical matter, deterrence means meaningful penalties. If the court were not to impose such a penalty here, when the defendant before it was the decision-making head of the Iran-contra operation, its action would be tantamount to a statement that a scheme to lie to and obstruct Congress is of no great moment, and that even if the perpetrators are found out, the courts will treat their criminal acts as no more than minor infractions.

A message of that kind could not help but encourage others in positions of authority and secrecy to frustrate laws that fail to accord with their notions of what is best for this country, and to carry out their own private policies in the name of the United States. . . .[85]

## The Appeal

A three-judge panel of the U.S. Court of Appeals for the District of Columbia Circuit in a 2–1 decision on November 15, 1991, reversed Poindexter's convictions on the grounds that his trial was impermissibly tainted by his immunized congressional testimony. The *Poindexter* ruling was based on the appeals court decision in the *North* case, which extended the protections of the use immunity statute to prohibit use of any witness whose testimony has been refreshed or shaped in any way by the defendant's immunized testimony. In his dissenting

---

[85] Judge Greene, *Poindexter* Transcript of Sentencing, 6/11/90, pp. 18–22

opinion, Chief Judge Abner Mikva noted that the majority ruling "tells future defendants that all they need to evade responsibility [to testify at trial] is a well timed case of amnesia."[86]

The *Poindexter* appeals panel also overturned the two obstruction convictions on the grounds that the statute was "unconstitutionally vague" in its proscription of "corruptly" endeavoring to impede a congressional inquiry. The appeals panel ruled that a defendant's lying to Congress does not constitute obstruction unless the defendant corruptly influences someone else to do so. Again, Chief Judge Mikva dissented, finding it "obvious . . . that Poindexter 'corruptly' obstructed the congressional investigation when he lied to Congress."[87]

In October 1992, Independent Counsel petitioned the U.S. Supreme Court to review the *Poindexter* case. Independent Counsel said the appeals court ruling that the obstruction statute was unconstitutional "leaves a large gap in the criminal law, while endorsing a method of analyzing constitutional vagueness challenges that could prove enormously destructive to a substantial body of federal legislation."[88] The petition noted that at least 17 other laws besides the obstruction statute at issue use the word "corruptly" to define an element of the offense.[89]

On immunized testimony, Independent Counsel in its petition to the Supreme Court said the appeals ruling in *Poindexter* would

> make almost impossible the prosecution of any case involving public immunized statements that requires testimony by persons sympathetic to the accused, such as co-conspirators or other associates. And the dangers of abuse and manipulation are magnified by the court of appeals' view, expressed in *North*, that a witness inclined to assist the defense may become disqualified from testifying at trial by the simple

expedient of soaking *himself* in the defendant's immunized statements.[90]

Independent Counsel also noted that the appeals ruling

> . . . will have its most profound impact on cases involving public immunized testimony before Congress—cases that, by definition, involve issues of the most fundamental import. If the court of appeals has erred, this Court should right that error before significant further damage is done to the legislative oversight function.[91]

The U.S. Supreme Court in December 1992 declined, without comment, to review the *Poindexter* case.

## Conclusion

Poindexter was responsible for providing President Reagan with advice on national-security matters of highest importance. What his conviction showed was that a jury of ordinary citizens can sort and weigh complex evidence and agree that obstructing and lying to Congress is a serious act worthy of felony conviction.

The *Poindexter* trial served the public interest in another sense. Poindexter's determination to call President Reagan as a witness allowed the public the rare opportunity to see him testify for seven hours about the Iran/contra matter.

The completion of the *Poindexter* trial in April 1990, two years after the original indictment was returned, necessitated the re-activation of the criminal investigation into Iran/contra. For the first time, Poindexter and North were available for questioning by Independent Counsel. Although this decision was questioned by some, Independent Counsel determined that his Iran/contra investigative mandate could not be fulfilled until the central operational figures were interrogated to find out whether other high-ranking officials helped support and cover up their activities.

---

[86] *U.S.* v. *Poindexter*, 951 F.2d 369, 390 (D.C. Cir. 1991).

[87] Ibid.

[88] *U.S.* v. *Poindexter*, Crim. No. 88–0080–01, Petition for Writ of Certiorari by United States of America, at 9 (October 1992).

[89] Ibid., p. 10.

[90] Ibid., p. 22.

[91] Ibid., p. 29.

# Chapter 4
# Paul B. Thompson

Paul B. Thompson, a Navy commander who was detailed to the National Security Council (NSC) staff in June 1983, became military assistant to National Security Adviser Robert C. McFarlane in January 1985. In June 1985, he also became NSC general counsel. When McFarlane resigned in December 1985 and was replaced by his deputy, Vice Adm. John M. Poindexter, Thompson retained his dual post.

As military assistant, Thompson provided administrative support to the national security adviser. Most paperwork passed through Thompson on its way to the national security adviser,[1] and NSC staff members would often schedule meetings or communicate with the national security adviser through Thompson.[2] Poindexter, unlike McFarlane, allowed Thompson to sit in on meetings in his office.[3] Both McFarlane and Poindexter occasionally gave documents to Thompson to store in safes in or near his office.[4]

As general counsel, Thompson provided legal advice to McFarlane and Poindexter, although he consulted on many issues with White House counsel and counsel for other agencies and departments.[5] McFarlane in particular preferred to use Thompson only as an avenue for getting legal advice from others on important or complex matters.[6]

Thompson was not involved in the operational details of either the Iran arms initiative or the contra-resupply effort. In his position as military assistant to McFarlane and Poindexter, however, Thompson did become involved in the criminal acts of others in Iran/contra.

Independent Counsel's investigation of Thompson focused on his role in Poindexter's destruction of a presidential Finding on November 21, 1986. Independent Counsel also investigated Thompson's role in McFarlane's false denials to Congress in 1985 regarding Lt. Col. Oliver L. North's contra-support efforts, and his role in Poindexter's false statements to Congress about North in 1986. In relation to these matters, OIC was concerned also with statements made by Thompson to congressional and criminal investigators that were potentially false or misleading.

Although there was strong evidence for a possible false statements and obstruction case against Thompson, Independent Counsel ultimately decided not to prosecute him. The evidence and the reasons for not prosecuting are detailed below.

---

[1] Poindexter, Grand Jury, 6/27/90, p. 12. Ronald K. Sable, FBI 302, 8/6/90, p. 2. McFarlane said his papers were routed through Thompson or secretary Wilma Hall. (McFarlane, FBI 302, 3/11/87, p. 2.) Thompson said his paperwork role expanded under Poindexter. (Thompson, Grand Jury, 5/13/87, pp. 20–22.)

[2] McFarlane, FBI 302, 9/13/90, p. 3; North, Grand Jury, 6/6/90, pp. 9–10; Sable, FBI 302, 8/6/90, p. 2. As Thompson himself put it, "I was the military assistant to the National Security Adviser and wherever he was in the world, I was the one that stayed up all night on the phone." (Thompson, Select Committees Deposition, 7/24/87, p. 74.)

[3] Poindexter, Grand Jury, 6/27/90, p. 75; McFarlane, FBI 302, 9/13/90, pp. 2, 3. According to NSC Legislative Affairs Director Ronald K. Sable, Thompson was Poindexter's "right hand." (Sable, Grand Jury, 8/10/90, p. 11; and Sable, FBI 302, 8/6/90, p. 2.)

[4] McFarlane, FBI 302, 9/13/90, p. 2; Poindexter, Select Committees Deposition, 6/17/87, p. 368; Poindexter, Select Committees Testimony, 7/15/87, pp. 45–46.

[5] Rodney B. McDaniel, Grand Jury, 4/4/90, pp. 14–17; Sable, Grand Jury, 8/10/90, p. 91.

[6] McFarlane, FBI 302s, 9/13/90, pp. 2, 10, and 3/13/87, p. 8.

## Thompson's Role in the November 1985 HAWK Shipment and the Destruction of the Finding

In November 1985, while Thompson and McFarlane were in Geneva with President Reagan, Israeli Defense Minister Yitzhak Rabin called McFarlane for assistance in making a shipment of U.S.-made HAWK missiles from Israel to Iran. Over the next several days, McFarlane was in contact with North in Washington about operational details, in an attempt to facilitate the shipment.

Thompson was frequently the point of contact between North and McFarlane, relaying messages about the planned shipment between the two. Among the messages that Thompson relayed was a request from North for McFarlane to call the prime minister of a European country to obtain landing rights for the plane carrying the HAWK missiles from Israel to Iran.[7] In addition, Thompson informed Poindexter, who was also in Washington, that McFarlane had asked North for help with an "Israeli aircraft problem." Because they were speaking on a non-secure phone line, however, Thompson was not more specific about the project and suggested that Poindexter ask North for the details.[8]

In his first congressional deposition, Thompson minimized his role in the November 1985 HAWK shipment, claiming that he did not inform McFarlane of North's reason for asking him to call the prime minister of a European country and that, at the time, he had "no idea" what the call was about.[9] Subsequently, although Thompson acknowledged that he knew that McFarlane's call involved landing rights for an aircraft and that the Israelis had an interest in the plane, Thompson continued to assert that he did not know that the plane was carrying weapons or that its destination was Iran.[10]

In passing substantive messages between North and McFarlane about the transaction, Thompson did gain some information about the shipment—so much so that when he gave McFarlane one message from North, McFarlane registered surprise at the extent of Thompson's knowledge.[11] Independent Counsel obtained no conclusive evidence, however, contradicting Thompson's assertions that he did not know the cargo or destination of the HAWKs flight.[12]

After the November 1985 HAWK shipment, the CIA sought a Presidential Finding to authorize retroactively its involvement in the shipment. On December 5, 1985, Poindexter presented the Finding to the President, and he signed it.[13] Poindexter kept the Finding in his immediate office.[14]

Poindexter later contended that he was unhappy with the language of the 1985 Finding because it justified the arms shipments to Iran as a narrow, arms-for-hostages deal rather than a broad initiative to improve relations with moderates in the Iranian government.[15] He discussed a more broadly worded draft Finding with President Reagan on January 6, 1986, and the President signed the draft. The President signed a final version of a Finding authorizing the Iran arms sales on January 17. Because of the extreme sensitivity of all three Findings—the December 1985, and January 6 and 17, 1986, Findings—copies were not distributed through regular channels to the State and Defense departments, and the CIA.[16] Poindexter retained personal custody of the January 17, 1986, original Finding in an envelope that also contained the December 1985 Finding and the

---

[7] North, Grand Jury, 6/6/90, p. 10; McFarlane, FBI 302, 9/13/90, p. 17; Thompson, Select Committees Deposition, 3/9/87, pp. 105–107; Thompson, Grand Jury, 5/20/87, pp. 63–66; Thompson, FBI 302s, 11/29/86, p. 3, 4/3/87, p. 3, 5/19/87, p. 6, and 1/3/91, pp. 3–4.

[8] Poindexter, Select Committees Deposition, 5/2/87, pp. 80–81, and 6/17/87, p. 344; Poindexter, Select Committees Testimony, 7/15/87, pp. 39–40; Poindexter, Grand Jury, 6/27/90, pp. 61–63, and 10/31/90, p. 23.

[9] Thompson, Select Committees Deposition, 3/9/87, pp. 106–107.

[10] Thompson, Grand Jury, 5/20/87, pp. 63–66; see also Thompson, FBI 302s, 11/29/86, p. 3, 4/3/87, p. 3, 5/19/87, p. 6, and 1/3/91, pp. 3–4.

[11] Thompson, FBI 302, 5/19/87, p. 6.

[12] North told the Select Committees it was "possible" that Thompson did not know the truth about the HAWK shipment. (North, Select Committee Testimony, 7/7/87, pp. 102–104.) But in his trial, North said he believed that Thompson knew that the plane was bound for Iran and had weapons on board. (North, *North* Trial Testimony, 4/12/89, pp. 7630–7632.) North later told the Grand Jury that it was "inconceivable" that Thompson "would not have known what was on that airplane in November of 1985." (North, Grand Jury, 6/15/90, p. 74.) McFarlane said although Thompson acted as a channel for information between him and North, he probably would have "cloaked" the operation from Thompson. (McFarlane, FBI 302, 9/13/90, pp. 17–18.)

[13] Poindexter, Select Committees Deposition, 5/2/87, pp. 105–106; Poindexter, Select Committees Testimony, 7/15/87, pp. 41–44.

[14] Poindexter, Select Committees Deposition, 6/17/87, pp. 367–368; Poindexter, Select Committees Testimony, 7/15/87, p. 45; Poindexter, Grand Jury, 6/27/90, pp. 66–67.

[15] Poindexter, Select Committees Testimony, 7/15/87, p. 45; Poindexter, Grand Jury, 6/27/90, pp. 71, 75–78, and 10/31/90, pp. 19–20.

[16] Poindexter, Grand Jury, 6/27/90, pp. 69, 72–73.

January 6 Finding, and permitted no other copies to be made.[17]

Thompson participated peripherally in the drafting of the January 17, 1986, Finding. On the evening of January 16, Poindexter, Attorney General Edwin Meese III, Secretary of Defense Caspar Weinberger, CIA Director William Casey, and CIA General Counsel Stanley Sporkin met in Poindexter's office.[18] During the meeting, Poindexter called in Thompson and asked him whether the executive order establishing an arms embargo of Iran was still in effect. Either Weinberger or Meese also asked Thompson whether Iran was still on the State Department's list of countries sponsoring international terrorism.[19] At about this time, Thompson had a general discussion with Sporkin about withholding congressional notification of a Finding.[20]

On either January 17 or January 20, 1986, Poindexter handed Thompson the envelope that contained the three Findings so that Thompson could show the signed version of the January 17 Finding to three CIA officials—Sporkin, Deputy Director for Operations Clair E. George, and Thomas Twetten, deputy chief of the Near East Operations Division.[21] Throughout most of 1986, Thompson kept the envelope containing the three Findings in the safe in his office.[22]

Thompson conceded that he was the knowing custodian of the January 17, 1986, Finding at "various times" throughout 1986,[23] but he flatly denied having any knowledge of the 1985 Finding.[24]

On the morning of November 21, 1986, President Reagan authorized Attorney General Meese to conduct a fact-finding inquiry into the Iran arms sales. The White House meeting at which the inquiry was authorized was attended by the President, Meese, White House Chief of Staff Donald T. Regan and Poindexter. One focus of Meese's inquiry was to resolve a conflict within the Administration about the November 1985 HAWK shipment: Secretary of State George Shultz said he knew at the time of the shipment that the cargo was HAWKs because McFarlane had briefed him, but NSC and CIA officials were stating that the Government did not know the true nature of the shipment until after the fact.

According to Poindexter, early in the afternoon of November 21, 1986:

> the Attorney General called me and said, "In following up on our discussion with the President this morning," he said, "I would like to be able to send over a couple of my people to look at the files and records that you have and could you have somebody pull them together and I'll have my people get in touch with Commander Thompson," who was my military assistant, also the General Counsel for the NSC, and the primary liaison with the Attorney General's front office.
>
> So immediately after the telephone call from the Attorney General, I called Commander Thompson on the intercom and told him about the Attorney General's request and I asked him to take responsibility for pulling the material together.
>
> After I finished talking to him, I called Colonel North, told him the same thing. I wanted him to clearly understand the directions that I had provided to Commander Thompson about pulling the material together. He said that he would do that.[25]

Later on November 21, Poindexter said Thompson:

[17] Thompson, Grand Jury, 5/20/87, pp. 79–80, 84–85.

[18] Ibid., pp. 57–58; Thompson, FBI 302s, 11/29/86, p. 2, and 4/3/87, p. 3.

[19] Thompson, Select Committees Deposition, 3/9/87, pp. 43–44; Thompson, Grand Jury, 5/20/87, pp. 57–58; Thompson, FBI 302s, 11/29/86, p. 2, 4/3/87, p. 3, and 7/22/88, p. 7.
According to Poindexter, Thompson was in and out of the meeting. (Poindexter, Select Committees Deposition, 5/2/87, p. 151; Poindexter, Grand Jury, 6/27/90, pp. 18, 74–75.) Poindexter said Thompson's sole contribution to the meeting was to retrieve a copy of the Arms Export Control Act from his office (Ibid., pp. 70–71, 74–75, 85–87; Poindexter, Grand Jury, 10/31/90, p. 21.)

[20] Thompson, Grand Jury, 5/20/87, pp. 31–33, 58–60.

[21] Ibid., pp. 25–35; Thompson, FBI 302s, 11/29/86, pp. 2–3, and 5/19/87, p. 4.

[22] Poindexter said Thompson had custody of the envelope beginning some time in 1986. (Poindexter, Grand Jury, 6/27/90, p. 102, and 10/31/90, pp. 31–32.) Thompson certainly had the Findings in his safe on October 21, 1986, when Poindexter sent him a computer note asking him to make a copy of "the very sensitive finding" on the Iran initiative for Casey. (PROFs Note from Poindexter to Thompson, 10/21/86, ALU 049972).

[23] Thompson, Select Committees Deposition, 7/24/87, p. 30; see also Thompson, Select Committees Deposition, 4/28/87, pp. 45–46; and Thompson, Grand Jury, 5/20/87, pp. 79–80.

[24] Thompson, Select Committees Deposition, 4/28/87, p. 47.

[25] Poindexter, Select Committees Deposition, 5/2/87, pp. 109–10.

brought in to my office the envelopes that I had given him earlier containing the material we had on the Iranian project in the immediate office, which was essentially the various Findings, and he pulled out this November Finding, it was actually signed in December, and my recollection is that he said something to the effect that, "They'll have a field day with this," or something to that effect.

. . . And my recollection is that the import of his comment was that up until that time in November of 1986, the President was being beaten about the head and shoulders, that this was—the whole Iranian project was just an arms-for-hostages deal.

. . . [W]hen he made his comment, I said, 'Well, let me see the Finding,' and he pulled it out and gave it to me, and I read it . . .[26]

Poindexter said the 1985 Finding gave the impression that the Iran initiative was nothing more than an arms-for-hostages deal, and

I, frankly, didn't see any need for it at the time. I thought it was politically embarrassing. And so I decided to tear it up, and I tore it up, put it in the burn basket behind my desk.[27]

North, who was in Poindexter's office at the time, witnessed the destruction of the Finding and later gave testimony regarding it.[28] According to both North and Poindexter, Thompson was present when Poindexter destroyed the 1985 finding.[29]

In Thompson's first congressional deposition, he admitted that he spoke to Poindexter on the afternoon of November 21 and that Poindexter told him that Justice Department personnel would be coming over to review the NSC's Iran arms sale files. According to Thompson, later that afternoon Assistant Attorney General Charles Cooper called him and said that two

Justice Department officials would be coming over to review North's files.[30] In this initial testimony, Thompson volunteered no information about the destruction of the 1985 Finding.

Subsequently, Thompson changed his testimony. In one OIC interview and in two Grand Jury appearances, Thompson categorically denied that he had any conversation with Poindexter on November 21 about the Justice Department's fact-gathering inquiry.[31] More importantly, in a congressional deposition in April 1987, Thompson stated that he had no knowledge at all of the 1985 Finding:

Q. The CIA has produced what they call a mini-Finding which was drafted by Stan Sporkin, General Counsel at the CIA, shortly after the November '85 shipment. Have you ever seen the document I have just described?

A. *No.*

Q. To your knowledge was it ever signed by the President?

A. Not to my knowledge.

Q. Did anybody ever tell you that it was signed by the President?

A. No.

Q. Have you seen—I've not shown it to you because I did not bring it with me, but have you ever seen the document I'm referring to?

A. *No.* There was an earlier Finding involving Iran from early January, but you're talking about yet a different Finding.

Q. Yes. I'm talking about one that would have been drafted in late November or early December of 1985.

A. *No.* That sounds like that Finding didn't go anywhere.

MR. McGRATH [Associate White House Counsel]: The Finding you are referring to is substantially different than the ones that Mr. Thompson saw in late January.

26 Poindexter, Select Committees Testimony, 7/15/87, pp. 47–49.
27 Ibid., p. 48.
28 North, *North* Trial Testimony, 4/12/89, pp. 7612–13, 7615–18; North, *Poindexter* Trial Testimony, 3/12/90, pp. 1252–55.
29 Poindexter, Select Committees Deposition, 5/2/87, p. 114; Poindexter, Select Committees Testimony, 7/15/87, pp. 48–49; North, *North* Trial Testimony, 4/12/89, pp. 7613, 7615; North, *Poindexter* Trial Testimony, 3/12/90, p. 1250, and 3/14/90, p. 1539.

30 Thompson, Select Committees Deposition, 3/9/87, p. 90.
31 Thompson, FBI 302, 4/22/87, pp. 8–9; Thompson, Grand Jury, 6/1/87, pp. 7–9.

MR. EGGLESTON [Deputy Chief Counsel, House Select Committee]: It's a Finding that relates to the November '85 shipment and it's a ratification Finding, if you will. It's a Finding which in the last paragraph, since the events had already taken place, is a Finding which states in the last paragraph or maybe the last sentence that "this Finding ratifies the prior actions by the Central Intelligence Agency."

BY MR. EGGLESTON: (Resuming)

Q. I take it that description of it doesn't bring anything to your mind, Mr. Thompson.

A. *No.*[32]

Thompson also stated in the spring of 1987 that he had no knowledge of anyone at the National Security Council or the White House, other than North, destroying or altering any documents relevant to the Iran arms sales.[33]

In May 1987, during a closed deposition before the Select Committees staff pursuant to an immunity order, Poindexter was the first witness to reveal that he destroyed the 1985 Finding, and he said Thompson was aware of that destruction. The next month, the Select Committees questioned Thompson about it.

On June 26, 1987, after being questioned by the Committees, Thompson was interviewed at his initiative by an OIC attorney and an FBI Special Agent. Thompson stated that the Senate Select Committee had asked him whether he had any information about the destruction of documents by a senior White House official from November 17–25, 1986. Thompson said he now remembered a meeting at which Poindexter asked him to retrieve Poindexter's Iran file from Thompson's safe.[34] After he retrieved the file, Thompson stated, Poindexter went through it, looked at one document, commented that this was not it, and then ripped up the document.[35] Thompson said the document that Poindexter destroyed could have been the January 6, 1986, Finding, the January 17, 1986, Finding, the December 1985 Finding, or

another Finding.[36] Thompson had told a similar story to the staff of the Senate Select Committee the same day.[37]

In July 1987, Poindexter appeared before the Select Committees. In that nationally televised appearance, Poindexter testified that Thompson removed the 1985 Finding from the safe in Thompson's office on November 21, 1986, brought it to Poindexter, told Poindexter, "They'll have a field day with this," and watched without objection as Poindexter destroyed the finding.[38] After hearing that testimony, Thompson in a congressional deposition attempted to explain the inconsistency between his prior testimony and Poindexter's. Thompson now admitted that, contrary to his earlier testimony, he *had* discussed the fact-finding inquiry with Poindexter on November 21. According to Thompson:

I met with him [Poindexter] in his office for about 30 seconds, and he told me that Meese was going to send people over, to be cooperative, and at that time he handed me this accordion file . . . with his working papers, and said basically, "Here is what I have got. Let them see what you have, and assist them in whatever else they want to do in the staff."[39]

Thompson said that he did not look through the file that Poindexter handed him immediately. Rather, according to Thompson, an hour or two later he joined a meeting in Poindexter's office that probably was attended by North, Poindexter's Deputy Alton Keel, and NSC Executive Secretary Rodney McDaniel.[40] Thompson said:

Right during the conversation while I was there, the Admiral kept saying, "There is yet another document." Or, "There is some memo that we still haven't come up with that I know has to be somewhere."

When I heard him say those words, I thought to myself, perhaps it is among the working papers that he gave me earlier,

---

[32] Thompson, Select Committees Deposition, 4/28/87, pp. 47–48 (emphasis added).

[33] Thompson, Grand Jury, 6/1/87, pp. 87–89.

[34] Thompson, FBI 302, 6/26/87, pp. 2–3.

[35] Ibid., p. 2.

[36] Ibid., pp. 2–3.

[37] Memorandum from Terry A. Smiljanich to the File, 6/26/87, pp. 3–5, AMY 000174–76.

[38] Poindexter, Select Committees Testimony, 7/15/87, pp. 47–48.

[39] Thompson, Select Committees Deposition, 7/24/87, p. 32.

[40] Ibid., p. 34.

and since I had not looked at them, perhaps it would be helpful one more time for him to look at them. So I got back up, went out and came back in carrying his accordion file. . . .

And the conversation continued. I came back in. The conversation continued on a subject I can't recall, but I assume it had to do with general posturing and strategy in dealing with the congressional requests and press requests and so forth. We had just finished briefing both the House and Senate committees, and I suspect we were trying to have a discussion as to where we stood on the issue. At any rate, as the conversation was continuing, I would open the file and quickly take out documents, look at them to see their general subject matter, and I would hand them to him.

He was sitting off to my left, and he would just kind of look at them and drop them or leave them on his lap. One document we came to he ripped up, not as a major action, but merely as he came to it. He ripped it up saying, "This is no longer necessary." Or, "This has no future." That document turns out to have been the finding of the fall of 1985.[41]

Thompson provided no explanation for recanting his earlier testimony that he had not talked to Poindexter on November 21 about the fact-finding inquiry and that he had no knowledge of document destruction (other than North's) related to the Iran initiative.

## Thompson's Role in False Denials to Congress Regarding North's Contra Activities

Independent Counsel investigated Thompson's role in McFarlane's false responses to Congress in the summer of 1985, when two committee chairmen asked about press allegations of North's contra-aid activities.

In response to the inquiries, which came while McFarlane was out of town, NSC staff member Brenda Reger informed Poindexter that she would search NSC institutional files but not North's personal files.[42] NSC Deputy Executive Secretary Robert Pearson in a computer note to Thompson reiterated this fact,[43] and Thompson informed McFarlane.[44]

The decision not to search the files in North's office was an important one. Some of the memoranda that North had written about his contra activities were not logged in on the NSC institutional file system and, therefore, were not uncovered in Reger's search. Although Reger and Pearson were apparently concerned enough about the possibility that there were "non-log" memoranda in North's office to document in writing the limits of their search, there is no evidence that Reger, Pearson or Thompson knew with certainty that North's office contained relevant non-log documents.[45]

In his first Select Committees deposition Thompson minimized his knowledge of the limits of Reger's document search in August 1985:

Q. Did you, in the course of preparing this response [to the congressional inquiries], did you search Mr. North's own office, his personal office?

A. No, I did not. I relied on a normal system search and that was performed under the auspices of our Directorate of Information Policy, Brenda Reger.

Q. Do you know whether there was a conscious decision not to search his office?

A. I am not aware of any decision not to.[46]

There is ample evidence that Thompson was aware of the decision not to search North's office. As described above, Thompson (1) received Reger's memorandum dated August 20,

---

[41] Ibid., pp. 33–36. Poindexter contradicted Thompson's account again in the Grand Jury. (Poindexter, Grand Jury, 10/31/90, pp. 42–43.) In addition, Poindexter stated that he could not recall giving Thompson any documents related to the Justice Department's fact-finding inquiry on November 21. (Ibid., p. 57.)

[42] Memorandum from Reger to Poindexter, 8/20/85, AKW 026758–59.
[43] PROFs Note from Pearson to Thompson, 8/23/85, AKW 026746.
[44] McFarlane, FBI 302, 9/13/90, pp. 4–5.
[45] Thompson may not have been involved in the initial decision not to search North's office. According to Thompson, he was on vacation in Maine at the time that the first congressional inquiry was received and was not aware at the time of the decision. (Thompson, Grand Jury, 5/13/87, pp. 58, 60–62.) Poindexter, however, noted that Thompson and Reger "normally worked very closely together on these issues." (Poindexter, Grand Jury, 6/27/90, p. 37.)
[46] Thompson, Select Committees Deposition, 3/9/87, p. 38.

1985 (a copy of which was retrieved from Thompson's personal files); (2) received Pearson's computer note dated August 23; and (3) informed McFarlane that a decision had been made not to search North's office.[47]

After completing the NSC institutional file search, Reger sent Thompson the documents that appeared to be relevant to the congressional inquiries. Thompson then reviewed the documents and noted that several raised concerns. These documents—all memoranda written by North—appeared to indicate that North had been fund-raising for and providing military assistance to the contras, in apparent violation of the Boland Amendment.[48] When McFarlane returned from California at the end of August 1985, Thompson presented him with the entire stack of documents and pointed out the existence of the "problem documents." [49]

In his first congressional deposition, Thompson did not mention his own review of the documents or that he pointed out the problem documents to McFarlane. In fact, Thompson said he could not recall the documents but was sure nothing in the documents caused him to conclude that North's contacts with the contras were "excessive." [50] In Thompson's next congressional deposition, when asked whether he reviewed the documents before he gave them to McFarlane, he replied, "I can't recall that I did." [51] When asked whether he discussed the contents of the memoranda with McFarlane, Thompson answered, "Not really." [52]

Before the Grand Jury, Thompson admitted he reviewed the documents before giving them to McFarlane, but Thompson downplayed the significance of that review, claiming it was only to determine relevance and whether the documents were covered by executive privilege. Thompson was then asked:

Q. Did you direct his [McFarlane's] attention to any documents in particular . . .?

A. Well, I think I had—as I recall we had the documents according to systems and the most sensitive documents are in system 4 which is where they should be. I think I told him that the ones in system 4 contained information that needed to be looked into.

Q. Did you explain what you meant by needed to be looked into?

A. I don't recall that I did.[53]

On the significance of his review, Thompson said:

I did not spend a lot of time then—my role at that time, I was not acting as a counsel who had been asked to do an investigation. I was forwarding these papers to the national security advisor who was tasked with responding to Congress. . . . I was helping him get ready to respond.[54]

After receiving the "problem" documents from Thompson, McFarlane reviewed them and then met with North.[55] According to Thompson, before North and McFarlane met, Thompson asked North whether he was raising funds for the contras or providing military assistance to

---

[47] Also, in early September 1985, Thompson showed the President's Intelligence Oversight Board Counsel Bretton G. Sciaroni the documents that had been gathered in the search of NSC institutional files and told him that North's office had not been searched for documents. (Sciaroni, Grand Jury, 6/1/87, pp. 14–19; Select Committees Deposition, 6/1/87, pp. 20–21; and FBI 302s, 5/22/87, p. 1, and 3/19/87, p. 2.)

[48] Thompson, Grand Jury, 5/13/87, pp. 68–71; Select Committees Deposition, 7/24/87, pp. 3–7.

[49] McFarlane, Grand Jury, 4/29/87, pp. 108–10; Select Committees Testimony, 5/11/87, p. 185, and 5/12/87, p. 69.

McFarlane retained the documents while he worked on the responses to the congressional inquiries. (McFarlane, Grand Jury, 4/29/87, pp. 109–10; Thompson, Grand Jury, 5/13/87, p. 71; Thompson, Select Committees Deposition, 4/28/87, p. 24.) At the end of each day, however, McFarlane gave the documents back to Thompson for Thompson to store in the safe in his office. (McFarlane, Grand Jury, 4/29/87, p. 110; McFarlane, Select Committees Testimony, 5/11/87, p. 190, and 5/12/87, p. 145; Thompson, FBI 302, 4/1/87, p. 7.) For more information on the problem documents, see McFarlane chapter.

[50] Thompson, Select Committees Deposition, 3/9/87, pp. 36–40.

[51] Ibid., 4/28/87, p. 23.

[52] Ibid., p. 22.

[53] Thompson, Grand Jury, 5/13/87, pp. 68–70.

[54] Ibid., p. 169.

[55] McFarlane said he asked North to alter the memoranda to reflect his activities more accurately. Subsequently, McFarlane asked Thompson whether it would be proper to alter the memoranda, and Thompson informed McFarlane that it would not be unless the originals were preserved and the changes in the memoranda marked. See McFarlane chapter.

Although Thompson's account of his exchange with McFarlane about altering documents is essentially consistent with McFarlane's, Thompson described it as a "very generic" discussion "about document creation, classification and control." (Thompson, Select Committees Deposition, 4/28/87, p. 30). Thompson called it "the typical conversation between the head of the agency and counsel of an agency, as to when a document achieves permanent status, when it can be modified, when it can be changed to reflect differences of facts or views." (Thompson, Select Committees Deposition, 7/24/87, pp. 7–8.)

them. North, according to Thompson, told him he was not.[56]

McFarlane responded to Rep. Lee Hamilton, chairman of the House Permanent Select Committee on Intelligence (HPSCI), on September 5, 1985, stating that, based on his review of relevant NSC documents, no one on the NSC staff violated the letter or spirit of the law, and they did not solicit funds for contra military or paramilitary activities.[57] One week later, McFarlane made the same assertions in a letter to Rep. Michael Barnes, chairman of the House Foreign Affairs Subcommittee on Western Hemisphere Affairs.[58]

The letters that McFarlane wrote Barnes and Hamilton were false.[59] There is little evidence, however, that Thompson played any significant role in their drafting. The evidence on the question of Thompson's knowledge of the falsity of the letters is mixed. McFarlane believed that, because Thompson reviewed almost all of the paperwork that flowed through McFarlane's office, Thompson was aware that the letters were false.[60] Neither McFarlane nor North, however, could recall specifically discussing with Thompson the true extent of North's activities on behalf of the contras in 1985.[61]

Thompson claimed that he did not know the letters were false. According to Thompson, before the NSC received the congressional inquiries, he had no knowledge of the extent of North's activities.[62] Although seeing the "problem documents" in August 1985 raised concerns in his mind about North's activities, Thompson said that he believed North when he denied raising funds for the contras or providing military assistance to them.[63]

While the NSC staff was formulating a response to the congressional inquiries, the President's Intelligence Oversight Board (PIOB) was conducting its own inquiry into North's activities. PIOB Counsel Bretton G. Sciaroni spoke to North and Thompson, who each denied that North was providing military assistance to the contras or raising funds for them.[64] In addition, Thompson showed Sciaroni a stack of NSC documents, which Sciaroni reviewed in Thompson's office.[65] According to Sciaroni, Thompson told him that he was being shown all of the relevant documents that the NSC had retrieved in its file search and that the NSC had shown the same documents to the congressional committees.[66] Several of the problem documents were not in the stack of documents that Thompson showed to Sciaroni, however.[67]

In 1986, Congress again sought White House responses to press reports of secret contra-support activities being run by North. In response to a House resolution of inquiry, Poindexter falsely denied the allegations. In letters to the chairmen of the House Permanent Select Committee on Intelligence (HPSCI), Foreign Affairs Committee and Armed Services Committee, he cited McFarlane's false letters of 1985, reasserting that the press allegations were wrong. Poindexter was convicted in 1990 for obstructing Congress in connection with these letters.[68]

The extent of Thompson's involvement in the drafting of Poindexter's false letters is unclear. Poindexter denied that Thompson had any substantive role in drafting them.[69] After Poindexter received the inquiries, however, he did speak to Thompson about McFarlane's re-

[56] Thompson, Select Committees Depositions, 3/9/87, pp. 37–38, 4/28/87, pp. 24–25, and 7/24/87, pp. 5–6; Thompson, Grand Jury, 5/13/87, pp. 72–73; Thompson, FBI 302s, 4/1/87, p. 7, 4/27/87, p. 6, and 1/3/91, p. 8. North remembers no such meeting. (North, *North* Trial Testimony, 4/11/89, pp. 7406–08). McFarlane did not recall hearing about a meeting either. (McFarlane, FBI 302, 9/13/90, p. 11.)

[57] Letter from McFarlane to Hamilton, 9/5/85, AKW 001528–29.

[58] Letter from McFarlane to Barnes, 9/12/85, AKW 001512–14.

[59] In March 1988, McFarlane admitted that he had unlawfully withheld information from Congress and pleaded guilty to four misdemeanor charges, two of which were based on these letters.

[60] McFarlane, FBI 302, 9/13/90, p. 14.

[61] North, Grand Jury, 6/6/90, pp. 14, 48; McFarlane, FBI 302, 9/13/90, pp. 7–9.

[62] Thompson, Grand Jury, 5/13/87, pp. 44–45; Thompson, Select Committees Deposition, 7/24/87, pp. 2–3.

[63] Thompson, FBI 302, 1/3/91, p. 8.

[64] Sciaroni, Select Committees Testimony, 6/8/87, pp. 4, 17–19, 26–27, 124–126; Sciaroni, Grand Jury, 6/1/87, pp. 14–18, 22–25; Sciaroni, FBI 302s, 11/4/87, pp. 1–2, and 3/19/87, p. 2.

Thompson acknowledged that he met with Sciaroni. (Thompson, Select Committees Depositions, 4/28/87, p. 13.) Thompson did not remember, however, speaking to Sciaroni specifically about North's activities in support of the contras. (Thompson, Select Committee Depositions, 4/28/87, pp. 37–38, and 7/24/87, pp. 15–16.) In the Grand Jury Thompson had no specific recollection of meeting with Sciaroni. (Thompson, Grand Jury, 5/20/87, pp. 10–11.)

[65] Sciaroni, Select Committees Testimony, 6/8/87, p. 19–20; Sciaroni, Grand Jury, 6/1/87, pp. 18–19; Sciaroni, FBI 302, 3/19/87, p. 2.

[66] Sciaroni, Select Committees Testimony, 6/8/87, pp. 4, 19–20, 43; Sciaroni, Grand Jury, 6/1/87, pp. 18–19, 55–57; Sciaroni, FBI 302, 3/19/87, p. 2. Thompson could not recall whether he showed Sciaroni the documents gathered in response to the congressional inquiries. (Thompson, Select Committees Deposition, 4/28/87, pp. 38–39; Thompson, FBI 302, 5/6/87, p. 4.)

[67] Sciaroni, Select Committees Testimony, 6/8/87, pp. 20–25, 43–44; Sciaroni, Grand Jury, 6/1/87, pp. 20–22; Sciaroni, FBI 302, 11/4/87, pp. 1–2.

[68] This conviction was overturned on appeal. See Poindexter chapter.

[69] Poindexter, Grand Jury, 6/27/90, pp. 114–19.

sponses to Congress the previous year.[70] Moreover, Thompson was the NSC point of contact with White House Counsel Peter Wallison in formulating a response: Thompson sent Wallison a draft of Poindexter's letter, received Wallison's response, made suggestions within the NSC on how best to incorporate Wallison's suggestions, and (along with Reger and Wallison) concurred when NSC Legislative Affairs Director Ronald Sable sent the final draft to Poindexter for his signature.[71]

Soon after Poindexter sent the letters to Congress, Thompson appeared before HPSCI with Sable and briefed the committee. According to Sable, the subject was North's activities on behalf of the contras, and Thompson answered most of the questions consistent with Poindexter's earlier written denials.[72] Thompson's memory of the briefing, however, was quite different. According to Thompson, the briefing:

> had nothing to do with North. It had to do with the alleged disinformation campaign that was directed against [Libya], appearing in the press at the time and Chairman Hamilton wanted to find out some background as to how the thing came about so I went up and explained it to them.[73]

OIC's attempts to obtain independent evidence from HPSCI about the subject matter of this briefing were unsuccessful.

## Independent Counsel's Decision Not to Prosecute Thompson

After Independent Counsel obtained felony convictions of both North and Poindexter, a Grand Jury in 1990 and early 1991 heard extensive evidence regarding Thompson in the areas previously described.

Independent Counsel concluded that the Grand Jury's investigation did not produce sufficient evidence to charge Thompson for involvement in the efforts of McFarlane and Poindexter to obstruct congressional inquiries into North's contra-aid activities. Although there was some evidence that Thompson helped draft letters to Congress that he knew to be false, the evidence did not appear to be sufficient to establish guilt beyond a reasonable doubt on a charge of aiding and abetting or of conspiring to make false statements to Congress. Similarly, although Thompson flagged for Poindexter the December 1985 Finding as a potential problem, there was only circumstantial evidence that Thompson acted with the intent of facilitating its destruction.[74]

The evidence that Thompson had obstructed justice, committed perjury, and made false statements before Congress and the Grand Jury was much stronger. Thompson's assertions that he had no knowledge of the December 1985 Finding and no knowledge of the destruction of documents seriously obstructed Independent Counsel's investigation. Two of the three people present when the Finding was destroyed—North and Poindexter—had valid Fifth Amendment claims against testifying before the Grand Jury in the spring of 1987. Therefore, only Thompson was available to describe the destruction of the Finding. He did not. As a result, Independent Counsel did not learn of Poindexter's destruction of the Finding until North testified about it at his own trial in April 1989.[75]

Because of the strength of the evidence and the seriousness of the likely charges, Independent Counsel considered an indictment of Thompson in late 1990. In January 1991, Thompson agreed to a voluntary interview but provided little new information.[76] In April 1991, Thompson was informed through counsel that

---

[70] Poindexter, Select Committees Deposition, 5/2/87, pp. 192–193.

[71] Memorandum from Thompson to Wallison, 7/15/86, ALU 005415–18; Memorandum from Wallison to Thompson, 7/17/86, ALU 005411–14; Note from Thompson to Sable and Reger, 7/18/86, AKW 038265–67; Memorandum from Sable to Poindexter, 7/21/86, AKW 042397–98.

Thompson testified that he was aware of the fact that the letter was being sent and that, although he could not "specifically recall" seeing the letter at the time, "I think I saw it." (Thompson, Grand Jury, 6/1/87, p. 6.) Sable initially speculated that Thompson drafted Poindexter's letter. (Sable, FBI 302, 1/8/88, p. 11.) Subsequently, Sable stated that he believed that North drafted the letter but that Thompson provided input into the response. (Sable, Grand Jury, 8/10/90, pp. 34, 38–40, 43, 45–46, 80; Sable, FBI 302, 8/6/90, pp. 3–4.)

[72] Sable, Grand Jury, 8/10/90, pp. 65–68; Sable, 302, 8/6/90, p. 5.

[73] Thompson, Select Committees Deposition, 3/9/87, p. 51. Sable had no memory of the subject of disinformation being raised during the briefing. (Sable, FBI 302, 10/9/90, p. 2.)

[74] In addition, Independent Counsel concluded that there was not sufficient evidence to prove beyond a reasonable doubt that Thompson knowingly made false statements to the President's Intelligence Oversight Board in August-September 1985.

[75] Poindexter told Congress in the summer of 1987 that he destroyed the December 1985 Finding, but the testimony was immunized and could not be used against him directly or indirectly in a criminal prosecution. See Poindexter chapter.

[76] Thompson, FBI 302, 1/3/91, p. 7.

he was a target of the Grand Jury's investigation into perjury, obstruction of justice, and
false statements; he was invited to appear before
the Grand Jury but declined.

Independent Counsel did not recommend that
the Grand Jury return an indictment of Thomp-

son. This decision was based on the long passage of time since the events in question,
Thompson's peripheral role in the Iran/contra
matter, and the simultaneous development of
strong cases against more centrally involved
Government officials.

# Chapter 5
# Fawn Hall

Fawn Hall was Lt. Col. Oliver L. North's secretary on the National Security Council staff from February 1983 until North was fired on November 25, 1986. In November 1986, Hall participated with North and other NSC staff members in obstructing official investigations and altering, destroying, and removing official Iran/contra-related documents from the White House.

At a very early point in the investigation, Independent Counsel granted Hall immunity in exchange for truthful testimony about her activities and those of North and others in connection with Iran/contra. Hall provided valuable evidence against both North and former National Security Adviser John M. Poindexter, in whose trials Hall was an important, although reluctant, Government witness.[1]

As North's secretary, Hall was generally aware of his involvement in the Iran arms sales and in supporting the contras, as well as his correspondence and contacts with numerous individuals involved in both projects.[2] Hall maintained records of North's meetings and his incoming telephone calls, and she typed memoranda and letters for him. Because of her proximity to North, Hall became aware that North was engaged in financial activities on behalf of the contras.[3] Hall did not, however, sit in on North's meetings, listen to his telephone conversations, or discuss North's activities with him, and so, according to her testimony, "I did not know many of the details relevant to the Iran and contra initiatives." [4]

Hall's first involvement in the criminal activity of North and others occurred on Friday, November 21, 1986, when North learned that the Department of Justice was conducting a fact-finding inquiry into the Iran arms sales. North retrieved a number of original documents from the NSC's institutional files indicating that he had violated the Boland Amendment by aiding the contras. North marked handwritten revisions on the original documents, changing the text so that it would appear that North had not violated the Boland Amendment. Then he asked Hall to replace the original documents with new, altered documents that contained his changes. Hall did so.[5]

Hall, however, did not complete the process of altering the documents given to her by North. She interrupted her work to help North shred documents. Some time in the early evening of November 21, Hall saw that North

> opened the five-drawer safe [in his office] and began to pull items from it and I joined him in an effort so that he would

---

[1] Because Hall testified before the Grand Jury in March and April 1987—before North and Poindexter testified to Congress under the grant of use immunity—Hall was able to testify at the trials of both North and Poindexter without serious *Kastigar* objections from the defense.

[2] For example, Hall knew and provided information about the relationship between North and every person listed in his Rolodex. (Hall, FBI 302, 2/12/87, afternoon session, pp. 1–30.)

[3] Hall, Select Committees Testimony, 6/8/87, pp. 242–44. On one or two occasions, Hall saw North writing in a financial ledger in his office, which Hall believed to be related to the contras. (Hall, Select Committees Testimony, 6/8/87, pp. 233–35; Hall, Grand Jury, 4/22/87, pp. 37–45.) In addition, on June 21, 1985, Hall asked to borrow money from North; North produced three $20 traveler's checks

that were drawn on a Central American bank, gave them to Hall, and said, according to Hall, something to the effect of " 'Make sure you return—pay back the money. It is not mine.' " (Hall, Select Committees Testimony, 6/8/87, pp. 237–40.) Moreover, some time in the summer or fall of 1986, an individual involved with the contras called to complain that a certain contra leader had not received a delivery that he was expecting; based on what was said, Hall concluded that the expected delivery was in fact a transfer of funds. (Hall, Select Committees Testimony, 6/8/87, pp. 241–44; Hall, Grand Jury, 4/22/87, pp. 28–32.)

[4] Hall, Select Committees Testimony, 6/8/87, p. 186.

[5] Hall, *North* Trial Testimony, 3/22/89, pp. 5311–16, and 3/23/89, pp. 5373–80, 5385–87; Hall, *Poindexter* Trial Testimony, 3/14/90, pp. 1598–1600.

not have to—wasting his time shredding. As he pulled documents from each drawer and placed them on top of the shredder, I inserted them into the shredder.

At the same time, I asked him if I could go ahead and shred the PROFs notes and phone logs. He acknowledged I should go ahead and do that, and I did so.[6]

Hall shredded documents in piles of 12–18 pages for between 30 minutes and one hour; she estimated that she shredded approximately one-and-a-half feet of documents.[7] Although shredding documents was part of the daily routine at the NSC, Hall had never shredded documents in such a large quantity.[8]

The following Tuesday, November 25, 1986, President Reagan publicly fired North because of his involvement in the Iran/contra diversion. NSC director of information policy, Brenda Reger, then secured suite 302 of the Old Executive Office Building—a two-floor suite that contained the offices of North, Hall, Lt. Col. Robert L. Earl, Cmdr. Craig P. Coy, and two other staff members—and refused to allow any removal of documents without her approval.

After Reger secured suite 302, Hall remembered that she had not completed the process of altering and destroying the original NSC documents North had requested on the previous Friday. In addition, Hall observed that documents related to the Iran arms sales and the contras that were similar to the documents that she and North had shredded were still in the suite.[9] Hall then began concealing these documents in her clothes to remove them from suite 302 without Reger's knowledge. She placed some documents inside her boots and others inside the back of her skirt.[10]

Hall went upstairs in the suite to Earl's office and told him what she was doing. Hall either asked Earl to take the documents out of the suite or he volunteered to do so; Earl then placed the documents in a pocket of his suit coat. A few minutes later, Hall returned to Earl's office, retrieved the documents, and concealed them under her clothes. She asked Earl whether he could see the documents, and Earl responded that he could not.[11]

Either before or after she began to hide the documents in her clothes, Hall called North who was out of the office. Because Reger and others were in the suite, Hall spoke in a whisper and tried to convey in vague terms that there was a problem with the documents and that it was important for North to return to the office.[12] North agreed to return and informed Hall that Thomas Green, who was then serving as North's attorney, would accompany him.[13]

When North and Green arrived in suite 302, North went into his private office to receive a phone call, and Hall followed him. She either stated or indicated that she had documents in the back of her skirt and asked North whether he could see them; North replied that he could not.[14] Hall then carried the concealed documents out of suite 302, accompanied by North and Green.[15]

While Hall, North, and Green were at the elevator bank on the third floor of the Old Executive Office Building, according to Hall

I indicated with a gesture or words that I wanted to give him [North] the documents, and he said—he turned to me and said, "No, just wait until we get outside," and we went down the elevator, exited the Old Executive Office Building on 17th St., and again I indicated with a word or gesture that I wanted to pass the documents,

---

[6] Hall, Select Committees Testimony, 6/8/87, p. 284.

[7] Hall, Grand Jury, 3/20/87, pp. 72–74.

[8] Hall, Select Committees Testimony, 6/8/87, p. 290.

[9] Hall, *North* Trial Testimony, 3/22/89, pp. 5354–58; Hall, *Poindexter* Trial Testimony, 3/14/90, pp. 1654–56.

[10] Hall, *North* Trial Testimony, 3/22/89, pp. 5359–60, 5362; Hall, *Poindexter* Trial Testimony, 3/14/90, p. 1657. Hall removed about 16 pages of documents from the office. (Hall, *North* Trial Testimony, 3/23/89, p. 5407.) Hall initially falsely stated to the OIC that she concealed and removed from the NSC only hard-copy print-outs of North's PROFs computer notes. (Hall, FBI 302s, 1/29/87, morning session, p. 7; 2/5/87, pp. 13–14; and 2/8/87, p. 7.) Hall subsequently acknowledged, however, that she also removed unaltered copies of the documents that she had begun altering on November 21 at North's request. (Hall, FBI 302, 2/27/87, p. 6.)

[11] Hall, Grand Jury, 3/18/87, pp. 201–2; Hall, FBI 302s, 1/29/87 (morning session), pp. 7, 9, 2/5/87, pp. 13–14, 2/8/87, p. 7.

[12] Hall, *North* Trial Testimony, 3/22/89, p. 5361; Hall, *Poindexter* Trial Testimony, 3/14/90, p. 1657.

[13] Hall, *North* Trial Testimony, 3/22/89, p. 5361.

[14] Hall, *North* Trial Testimony, 3/22/89, pp. 5364–65, and 3/23/89, pp. 5390–91; Hall, *Poindexter* Trial Testimony, 3/14/90, p. 1658. In one early OIC interview of Hall, she stated that when Green and North entered suite 302, she told both of them that she had some documents in her possession and neither Green nor North advised her that she should not remove the documents from the office. (Hall, FBI 302, 1/29/87, morning session, p. 7.)

[15] Hall, *North* Trial Testimony, 3/22/89, pp. 5363–65, and 3/23/89, p. 5391; Hall, *Poindexter* Trial Testimony, 3/14/90, pp. 1658–59.

and Tom Green said, ''No, wait until we get inside the car.''

We crossed 17th St., got in Tom Green's car on G St., took off, and I started pulling the documents from my boots, pulled them from my back, indicated to Colonel North, I believe at this time, I had not completed the process of replacing the altered documents in the files and that I had started the Xeroxing, but I had, in fact, left the originals in the office.

As we turned the corner, Tom Green was dropping us both off at the parking lot where our cars were parked. Tom Green turned to me and asked me if I was asked about shredding what would I say, and I said, ''We shred every day.'' And he said, ''Good.'' [16]

Hall's final involvement in illegal activities occurred three days later, on Friday, November 28, 1986. After Hall learned that the FBI had asked to interview her, Earl and Coy over the coming weekend, Hall and Earl spoke together about the events of the previous week. According to Hall, she and Earl agreed that neither would disclose to the FBI that Hall had removed documents from the office on November 25.[17]

By granting Hall immunity, Independent Counsel sacrificed the possibility of charging Hall with conspiracy to obstruct justice and illegally destroying, altering, and removing official NSC documents. In return, however, Independent Counsel obtained important evidence of wrongdoing by Hall's superiors, including North and Poindexter.[18]

At the trial of North, Hall was an important Government witness who provided testimony central to obtaining felony convictions for obstructing Congress in November 1986 and for illegally destroying, altering, and removing NSC documents. At Poindexter's trial, Hall provided testimony for the Government to obtain a felony conviction for conspiring to obstruct Congress.

---

[16] Hall, Select Committees Testimony, 6/8/87, p. 306. Two days later, when Hall was asked by Jay Stephens of the White House counsel's office about the reports of shredding documents in North's office, Hall said, ''I told him that we shred every day, and I led him to believe that there was nothing unusual about what had occurred.'' (Hall, Grand Jury, 3/20/87, pp. 48–9; Hall, FBI 302, 2/27/87, p. 4.)

[17] Hall, Grand Jury, 3/20/87, pp. 38–40; Hall, FBI 302, 2/8/87, pp. 1–2.

[18] Hall was an unindicted co-conspirator in Count One of the March 1988 indictment of North, Poindexter, Secord and Hakim. This count—which charged the Iran/contra diversion as a conspiracy to defraud the U.S. Government—was not tried due to classified-information problems.

# Chapter 6
# Robert L. Earl

Marine Lt. Col. Robert L. Earl served on the National Security Council staff from February to December 1986. He worked closely as a subordinate to Lt. Col. Oliver L. North on counter-terrorism activities, including the Iran arms sales. Earl was aware of North's plan to use profits from the arms sales to support the contras, and in the summer of 1986 Earl helped North calculate the marked-up prices of the arms sold to Iran. In November 1986, Earl attempted to conceal evidence regarding the arms sales to Iran and the diversion of profits to the contras. He destroyed NSC documents, assisted North in the destruction of documents, assisted North's secretary, Fawn Hall, in the illegal removal of NSC documents, conspired with Hall to make false statements to the FBI, and made false statements to the FBI.

On April 15, 1987, Independent Counsel granted Earl immunity from prosecution in exchange for his truthful testimony. He provided important evidence about the Iran arms sales and North's contra-resupply network, including the diversion of profits from the arms sales to the contras.[1]

North and Earl met many years before Earl was detailed to the NSC. The two attended the Naval Academy in Annapolis at the same time and became friends while attending an amphibious warfare training school in the early 1970s. Subsequently, their career paths in the Marine Corps crossed on a number of occasions.

In the summer of 1985, Earl was assigned to work on the Vice President's Task Force on Terrorism. In its final report, the task force recommended that the NSC add staff to address terrorism on a full-time basis. To implement this recommendation, Earl and Coast Guard Cmdr. Craig P. Coy, who had also served on the Vice President's task force, were assigned to the NSC staff in February 1986. Earl and Coy both reported to North, who supervised the NSC staff's counter-terrorism activities. In May 1986, North, Earl, Coy and Hall moved into suite 302 of the Old Executive Office Building.

In April 1986, before North traveled to Tehran with former National Security Adviser Robert C. McFarlane, North briefed Earl about the Iran arms sales.[2] At the same time, according to Earl, North informed him about one of the initiative's most secret aspects: that a portion of the proceeds from the arms sales to Iran was to be used to support the contras.[3]

Later, during the summer of 1986, North asked for Earl's help in determining the prices of the various pieces of military equipment requested by the Iranians.[4] Based on information provided to him by North regarding the pricing in prior arms sales to the Iranians, Earl determined that the average mark-up of the sales had been 370 percent. For consistency, Earl applied a 3.7 multiplier to the cost of the equipment from the Department of Defense to calculate the price that the Iranians would have to pay for each item. Earl understood that one purpose of the 370 percent mark-up was to generate funds for the contras.[5]

---

[1] In addition, because Earl testified before the Grand Jury in May and June 1987—before North testified to Congress under the grant of use immunity—Earl was able to testify at North's trial without serious objections from the defense that his testimony was tainted by North's congressional appearance.

[2] Earl, *North* Trial Testimony, 3/23/89, pp. 5531–32, 5555. Before North left for Iran, he told Earl that if he did not return, Earl should destroy the contents of the bottom drawer of his safe. (Ibid., p. 5564.)

[3] Ibid., pp. 5532–33.

[4] Ibid., pp. 5537–38.

[5] Ibid., pp. 5538–45.

On Friday, November 21, 1986, North learned that the Department of Justice was conducting a fact-finding inquiry into the Iran arms sales. North asked Earl to give him the entire contents of Earl's file on Iran and told Earl about the fact-finding inquiry. From this exchange, Earl understood that North was going to destroy the contents of his file.[6] Believing that he was following North's cue, Earl then went through his own files and destroyed his copies of documents and computer notes that related to the Iran arms sales.[7] Earl also observed North going through his own files later that same day, segregating documents to be destroyed.[8] Fawn Hall, meanwhile, was feeding a large number of documents into the shredder.[9]

Earl said North told him after returning from a White House meeting on November 21 "that it was time for North to be the scapegoat."[10] According to Earl, North said "he had asked the Attorney General if he could have—I'm not sure whether it was 24 or 48 hours—and that the Attorney General replied that he didn't know whether he could have that long, or something to that effect."[11] Independent Counsel was not able to corroborate Earl's testimony.

On Saturday, November 22, 1986, North told Earl that the shredder in suite 302 was broken. North and Earl discussed the location of other shredders in the OEOB or the White House. Later, Earl saw North leave their office suite with a pile of documents; Earl understood that North was planning to use the shredder in the Situation Room of the White House to shred the documents.[12]

On the afternoon of Tuesday, November 25, 1986, after North had been fired and NSC staff member, Brenda Reger, had sealed suite 302 so that documents could not be removed, Hall told Earl that she needed to take some documents from the suite. She either asked Earl to take the documents out of the suite or Earl volunteered to do so; Earl placed the documents in one of his suit coat pockets, but a few minutes later Hall retrieved them. After concealing the documents under her clothes, Hall asked Earl whether he could see them and Earl said no. Hall subsequently left suite 302 with the documents concealed under her clothes.[13]

On the evening of November 25 or 26, Earl testified that he had a conversation with North and Coy on the stairway adjoining the two floors of suite 302. According to Earl, it concerned a call that North had received from President Reagan on November 25, after North was fired. "Colonel North turned and confided, 'And you know what'—again I don't have the exact wording so I'm just going to relay the thrust of what he said—that the President had told him that it was important that he not know; that he was told that it was important that he not know."[14] Independent Counsel was not able to corroborate Earl's testimony regarding this conversation.

Three days later, on Friday, November 28, 1986, the FBI contacted Earl and asked to interview him during the weekend. That evening, Earl and Hall agreed that neither would disclose to the FBI that Hall had removed documents from suite 302 after Reger sealed it on November 25.[15]

On Saturday, November 29, 1986, Earl was interviewed about Iran/contra by two FBI agents. During the interview, Earl made a number of false statements. Earl falsely stated that he merely "suspected" but did not know that North was diverting the profits from the arms sales to the contras.[16] In addition, Earl falsely stated that he did not observe North or anyone else in suite 302 engaging in an unusual destruction or shredding of documents in November 1986.[17] Earl subsequently admitted that he lied to the FBI agents in this interview.[18]

In April 1987, Independent Counsel granted Earl full immunity from prosecution for his role in Iran/contra. In exchange, Independent Counsel obtained Earl's testimony about the roles

[6] Ibid., 3/28/89, pp. 5616–17.

[7] Ibid., pp. 5608, 5620–21, 5633–34, 5641.

[8] Ibid., pp. 5616, 5620.

[9] Earl, Grand Jury, 5/1/87, p. 91; Earl, Select Committees Deposition, 5/2/87, p. 72.

[10] Earl, Grand Jury, 5/1/87, p. 82.

[11] Ibid., p. 86.

[12] Earl, *North* Trial Testimony, 3/28/89, p. 5625.

[13] Earl, Grand Jury, 5/1/87, pp. 121–25; Earl, FBI 302, 4/30/87, p. 2; Hall, Grand Jury, 3/18/87, pp. 201–2; Hall, FBI 302, 1/29/87, morning session, pp. 7, 9; Hall, FBI 302s, 2/5/87, pp. 13–14, and 2/8/87, p. 7.

[14] Earl, Grand Jury, 5/1/87, pp. 118–19.

[15] Hall, Grand Jury, 3/20/87, pp. 38–40; Hall, FBI 302, 2/8/87, pp. 1–2. Earl testified that he "repressed" his memory of this conversation "almost totally" and that he could not "recall almost anything from that conversation." (Earl, Select Committees Deposition, 5/2/87, p. 94; see also Earl, FBI 302, 4/30/87, p. 2.)

[16] Earl, FBI 302, 11/29/86, p. 8.

[17] Ibid., p. 10.

[18] Earl, *North* Trial Testimony, 3/28/89, pp. 5636, 5640–41.

of North and others in Iran/contra. At North's trial, Earl's testimony confirmed the documentary evidence that showed that North knowingly and intentionally diverted some of the profits from the Iran arms sales to the contras and that North planned the diversion as early as April or May of 1986. Earl also complemented Hall's account of North's role in the illegal destruction and removal of documents from the NSC from November 21–25, 1986.

# Chapter 7
# Thomas C. Green

Thomas C. Green served briefly as attorney for Lt. Col. Oliver L. North during November 1986. In connection with this representation, there is evidence that Green assisted North and North's secretary Fawn Hall in removing official National Security Council documents from the White House after North was fired.

On the afternoon of November 25, 1986, the NSC director of information policy, Brenda Reger, had secured North and Hall's office suite 302 of the Old Executive Office Building and refused to allow any removal of documents without her approval. Subsequently, Fawn Hall decided to remove certain documents secretly and hid them inside her clothing. Hall called North back to the office, and North informed Hall that Green would accompany him.[1]

After North and Green arrived, Hall informed North—but apparently not Green—that she had documents in the back of her skirt. Hall carried the concealed documents out of suite 302, accompanied by North and Green.

While Hall, North and Green were at the elevator bank on the third floor of the Old Executive Office Building, according to Hall, she indicated to North that she had documents. She said that after they left the building, she indicated she wanted to "pass the documents, and Tom Green said, 'No, wait until we get inside the car.'" She said she took the documents out of her clothes once they were in Green's car. As Green dropped her off at her car, she said he asked her "if I was asked about shredding what would I say, and I said, 'We shred every day.' And he said, 'Good.'"[2]

Based on Hall's testimony, Green's conduct on November 25 raised questions. First, if Green told Hall not to hand the documents to North on the street but to "wait until we get inside the car," it could have been instinctive prudence, or it could have been that Green knew that Hall had in her possession documents that she had illegally removed from the NSC offices, and that he was aiding and abetting a crime. Second, Green asked Hall about what she would say if she were asked about destroying documents. By approving testimony by Hall that would mislead investigators, Green could be said to have exposed himself to a charge that he attempted to obstruct justice.[3]

Additionally, North testified that Green advised him to remove documents from his office after his firing. According to North, Green asked him whether he had "anybody or anything to protect yourself?" In response to Green's question, North said he "gathered up a number of documents that I believed would indicate or show that I had had the authority to do what I had done over the course of those two [Iran and contra] operations. I put them in my briefcase, along with my notebooks, and left the Executive Office Building with him [Green]."[4]

When Green was called before the Grand Jury in April 1987, he refused to testify, citing his Fifth Amendment right not to incriminate himself, his clients' constitutional rights to effective representation by counsel, and the attor-

---

[1] Hall, *North* Trial Testimony, 3/22/89, p. 5361.
[2] Hall, Select Committees Testimony, 6/8/87, p. 306.

[3] Two days later, when Hall was asked by Jay Stephens of the White House counsel's office about the reports of shredding documents in North's office, according to Hall, "I told him that we shred every day, and I led him to believe that there was nothing unusual about what had occurred." (Hall, Select Committees Testimony, 6/8/87, p. 309.)
[4] North, *North* Trial Testimony, 4/10/89, pp. 7104–7.

ney-client and attorney work-product privileges.[5]

North was not available as a witness until after his conviction. Independent Counsel deter-

mined that a prosecution of Green, based essentially on the testimony of the person who removed the documents, Hall, would not be useful to the investigation.

---

[5] Green, Grand Jury, 4/3/87.

# Part V
# The Flow of Funds: The Prosecution of the Private Operatives

## Overview

Amid the complexities of Iran/contra were crimes of a more common sort: those committed for personal enrichment.

Once Reagan Administration officials decided to conduct foreign policy off the books, outside of congressional funding and oversight channels, crimes of greed followed. The decision to flout Government procedures meant that private profiteers could control tens of millions of dollars without accountability, under a cover of secrecy and with the claimed cachet of the White House. The decision to employ the same profiteers in two covert but disparate operations led to the commingling of funds and to the Iran/contra diversion. In short, the privatization of Government covert operations presented fertile ground for financial wrongdoing.

The overarching money crime in the Iran/contra affair formed part of the central conspiracy charge against Lt. Col. Oliver L. North, Vice Adm. John M. Poindexter, retired Air Force Maj. Gen. Richard Secord and Albert Hakim. The four co-defendants were charged in March 1988 with conspiring to use proceeds from the sale of U.S. arms to Iran to create a slush fund that could be spent at their own discretion, although the proceeds belonged to the United States. The co-defendants were charged also with theft of Government property, by embezzling and converting to their own use the proceeds generated by the arms sales to Iran.[1]

Other money-related crimes stemmed from the Iran/contra affair, resulting in the convic-tions of those most centrally involved. These included filing false tax returns, the offer and acceptance of illegal gratuities,[2] and fraud.

CIA Director William Casey in 1984 paired North of the National Security Council staff with Secord to supply the Nicaraguan contras in anticipation of a Government funding cut-off.[3] Secord and his business partner Hakim quickly seized the opportunity to graft their business interests onto the policy goals of the Reagan Administration. Former CIA agent Thomas G. Clines became the third man in this profitable venture that came to be known as "the Enterprise."[4]

There were several funding sources for the contras' weapons purchases from the Enterprise: donations from foreign countries that had received U.S. favors, donations from wealthy Americans sympathetic to President Reagan's pro-contra policies, and later the diversion of proceeds from U.S. arms sales to Iran.

In addition to selling weapons, the Enterprise principals with the backing of North assembled a private air force of small planes, pilots and crews to supply the contras with weapons and other lethal materiel. To make deliveries in Nicaragua, they built a secret airstrip in Costa Rica and worked practically unfettered on a Salvadoran military airbase. They purchased a Dan-

---

[1] These central charges were dropped in January 1989 because the Reagan Administration refused to release classified information deemed relevant by the trial court to the defense case of North, the first of the co-defendants to be tried.

[2] North's conviction for accepting a gratuity was reversed because of immunity granted to permit his congressional testimony.

[3] North told Congress that Casey wanted to have "an overseas entity that was capable of conducting operations or activities of assistance to U.S. foreign policy goals that was . . . stand-alone . . . self-financing, independent of appropriated monies and capable of conducting activities similar to the ones that we had conducted here. . . ." (North, Select Committees Testimony, 7/10/87, pp. 314–15.) By the time North testified, Casey was dead.

[4] In interviews with OIC and congressional investigators during 1987, Secord coined the term "the Enterprise" to describe the covert operations he and others undertook on behalf of the Reagan Administration. The phrase was not used by the participants while the operations were ongoing.

ish freighter for trans-oceanic weapons shipments and for use in other covert projects. They obtained from foreign officials specious end-user certificates for weapons purchases, so that the true recipients—the contras—could not be identified and weapons laws could be evaded. They put at North's disposal a network of shell corporations and Swiss bank accounts, through which transactions were concealed and laundered.

In late 1985 and throughout 1986, the Enterprise became centrally involved in the Reagan Administration's secret arms sales to Iran. This proved a more lucrative business venture than supplying the contras. Tens of millions of dollars were funneled through Enterprise accounts, ostensibly in support of an effort to obtain the release of Americans held hostage in the Middle East, and secondarily to renew ties to Iran. But the profiteers of the Enterprise corrupted the legitimate humanitarian and political goals of the Iran operation by inflating the prices for the weapons and by putting business interests ahead of their duties as Government agents.

The links between the private operatives were long-standing. The Secord-Clines relationship dated back to the 1960s, when both had worked in secret Government operations in Southeast Asia. Secord and Hakim met in the late 1970s, while Hakim was seeking to do business with the United States in Iran and Secord was a U.S. official stationed there. By the early 1980s, Secord and Hakim were business partners specializing in weapons-related ventures, and Clines also had become an international entrepreneur.[5]

---

[5] Before Iran/contra, all three men had been subject to investigative scrutiny. Hakim was the subject of an investigation examining whether he had bribed Iranian officials on behalf of the Olin Corporation, but he was not prosecuted. Secord was investigated while a Pentagon official for his ties to Edwin Wilson, the former CIA agent serving a life sentence for smuggling arms to Libya's General Kaddaffi; Secord was not prosecuted, but he admitted receiving from Wilson the free use of a private plane. Clines, who had been Wilson's case agent at the CIA, also was the subject of a criminal investigation probing Wilson's activities. As a result of that investigation, a corporation that Clines owned, SSI, pleaded guilty to theft of government property and paid the fine of $100,000 with money from Secord.

Professional fundraisers also profited by the Reagan Administration's decision to finance its foreign-policy goals outside the congressional-appropriations process. They used the White House, the President's name and other accoutrements of official power to profit illegally. Beginning in 1985, North joined with Carl R. "Spitz" Channell and Richard R. Miller to solicit donations for the contras from wealthy Americans, and ultimately to divert these contributions to the Enterprise. Especially generous donors were rewarded with personal meetings with President Reagan and private briefings from North. Raising money for weapons and other lethal supplies was not a charitable activity under U.S. tax laws, but North, Channell and Miller illegally used a tax-exempt organization, the National Endowment for the Preservation of Liberty (NEPL), for this purpose.

To investigate these money trails, Independent Counsel obtained the Swiss financial records of the Enterprise, bank documents from other foreign countries, extensive domestic financial records, and also the immunized testimony of Enterprise and NEPL officers and employees.[6] Willard I. Zucker, the Enterprise's Swiss financial manager, was given immunity to illuminate the financial structure of the Iran and contra operations.

As detailed in the following sections, Secord and Hakim pleaded guilty to profit-related crimes. Clines was convicted after a jury trial for tax-related felonies. One of the Enterprise's principal corporations, Lake Resources Inc., pleaded guilty to the corporate felony of theft of U.S. Government property by diverting Iranian arms sales proceeds to the contras. Channell and Miller pleaded guilty to conspiracy to commit tax fraud, naming North as a co-conspirator.[7]

---

[6] All grants of immunity were preceded by proffers of testimony.
[7] North was convicted of accepting an illegal gratuity from Secord; he was charged with but not convicted of tax fraud. His conviction was set aside on appeal.

# Chapter 8
# The Enterprise and Its Finances

Secord and Hakim in 1983 founded Stanford Technology Trading Group International (STTGI).[1] Hakim was chairman of the board. Secord was president. STTGI was wholly controlled by them. In the fall of 1984, North introduced Secord to contra leader Adolfo Calero to assist Calero in the purchase of arms, using the proceeds of a contribution from Saudi Arabia.

In 1985 and 1986, weapons sales to the contras and Iran generated an increasing proportion of STTGI's income; by 1986, the business of STTGI *was* the Enterprise. Financial management of all Enterprise assets was done in Switzerland by Compagnie de Services Fiduciaire (CSF), controlled by Willard Zucker, an American tax lawyer living in Geneva.[2]

Secord and Hakim decided very early—by mid-1985 at the latest—to conceal the sources of their income through a variety of schemes. One of their purposes was to avoid the payment of income taxes. In addition to the protection afforded by Switzerland's strict bank-secrecy laws, Zucker at the direction of Secord and Hakim erected a maze of dummy corporations and bank accounts to conceal the true sources and recipients of funds.[3]

More than $47.6 million flowed from the Iran and contra operations into the Swiss Enterprise accounts. The receiving accounts were: Energy Resources International, S.A. ($11.3 million); Lake Resources Inc. ($31.5 million); and Hyde Park Square Corporation ($4.8 million). (See "Enterprise Gross Receipts" chart, next page.)

From its receipts, the Enterprise transferred to a CIA Swiss account a total of $12.2 million to be paid to the Department of Defense for U.S. weapons sold to Iran. The Enterprise also disbursed $17.6 million for weapons purchases for the contras and contra-related expenses.

Shortly after the Iran/contra matter became public in late November 1986, the Swiss government at the request of the United States froze the accounts of the Enterprise. At the time, 16 out of 21 corporate and investment accounts of the Enterprise contained a total of $7.8 million.

The direct U.S. weapons sales to Iran, which began early in 1986, generated by far the largest revenues for the Enterprise.

Unlike the contra sales transactions, the Enterprise did not buy and sell the Iran arms as brokers or for its own account. It acted as agent, a front, for the true owner of the arms, the United States. The sales were incidental to a presidential direction and a presidential objective. Sales and delivery to the ultimate purchaser were at all times subject to the control of the President, acting through Poindexter and North. As agent, the Enterprise was a service organization collecting funds for the United

---

[1] STTGI is distinct from Stanford Technology Corporation ("STC"), founded in 1974 by Hakim. Hakim and Secord subsequently formed a number of shell corporations in Switzerland with related names, including StanTech Services S.A.; Stanford Technology Corporation Services, S.A.; and Scitech, S.A.

[2] Zucker had provided Hakim with financial services since the mid-1970's, when Hakim still lived in Iran. Swiss fiduciaires combine functions that Americans associate with money managers, bankers and lawyers. The services CSF provided to the Enterprise included inter-bank and inter-account transfers, cash disbursements to individuals, expense payments, investments, currency deals, the establishment of financial accounts and shell corporations, and bookkeeping.

[3] The Enterprise's Swiss corporate accounts were: Energy Resources International, S.A.; Lake Resources Inc.; Hyde Park Square Corporation; Albon Values Corporation; Defex, S.A.; Dolmy Business, Inc.; Gulf Marketing Consultants, Ltd.; Stanford Technology Corporation Services, S.A.; Stantech Services, S.A.; Toyco, S.A.; and Udall Research Corpora-

tion. The investment accounts were: Richard V. Secord; C. Tea; Albert Hakim; Korel Assets; Scitech Trading Group, Inc.; Lake Resources Inc.; B. Button; and A.H. Sub-accounts #1, #2 and #3.

**ENTERPRISE GROSS RECEIPTS**
**NOVEMBER 1984 - NOVEMBER 1986**

FUNDS DEPOSITED TO
ENERGY RESOURCES
INTERNATIONAL, S.A.
ACCOUNT NUMBER 230774-42-1
CREDIT SUISSE
GENEVA, SWITZERLAND

<u>SOURCE:</u>

CONTRAS       $11,349,700.00

                            $11,349,700.00

FUNDS DEPOSITED TO
LAKE RESOURCES, INC.
ACCOUNT NUMBER 3864-30-22-1
CREDIT SUISSE
GENEVA, SWITZERLAND

<u>SOURCE:</u>

IRAN          $25,000,000.00

ISRAEL         2,685,000.00

TAIWAN         2,000,000.00

NEPL AND
OTHER
DONORS         <u>1,863,000.00</u>
              $31,548,000.00

FUNDS DEPOSITED TO
HYDE PARK SQUARE CORPORATION
ACCOUNT NUMBER 339825-32-1
CREDIT SUISSE
GENEVA, SWITZERLAND

<u>SOURCE:</u>

IRAN          $3,600,000.00

CIA            <u>1,200,000.00</u>

              <u>$4,800,000.00</u>

GROSS RECEIPTS

<u>$ 47,697,700.00</u>

NOTE: FIGURES ROUNDED FOR EASE OF
PRESENTATION; BANK CHARGES OF
$1,743.53 ARE NOT INCLUDED.

SOURCE: OIC ANALYSIS OF ENTERPRISE FINANCIAL RECORDS

States and delivering weapons for the United States.

In 1986 the Enterprise received $30.3 million from the sale of this U.S. Government property to Iran and for replacement TOW missiles to Israel. Only $12.2 million was returned to the United States. Direct expenses of the Enterprise were approximately $2.1 million. Thus, the amount of U.S. Government funds illegally held by the Enterprise as its own was approximately $16 million.[4]

# The Enterprise and the Contra Arms Sales

In late 1984, Secord and Hakim, at North's request, began selling weapons and other lethal supplies to the contras. They acted as brokers, buying weapons from other arms dealers and paying for them with money provided by Calero, whose funds primarily came from secret donations by Saudi Arabia.[5] Beginning in mid-1985, private and foreign-country donations to the contras were deposited directly into the accounts of the Enterprise to supply the contras, effectively eliminating Calero as a money-handler, with the exception of what remained in the contra account from the Saudi donations.

In 1985 and 1986, there were ten pro-rated profit distributions among members of the Enterprise for the contra weapons sales. The draws from these sales between April 1985 and September 1986 amounted to $4.579 million. The distributions occurred in seven numbered phases, and three that were unnumbered. (See "Contra Arms Sales, Pro-Rated Profit Distributions" chart, next page.)

## Phase I, Contra Arms Sales (November 1984–March 1985)

Secord late in 1984 arranged an initial sale of weapons to the contras through a Canadian firm, TransWorld Arms (TWA), headed by Emanuel

Weigensberg. TWA's supplier was a Portuguese weapons firm known as Defex, which arranged for the purchase of a shipload of weapons from the People's Republic of China. Due to unexpected delays, the weapons did not arrive in Central America until April 1985.

The contras paid $2.3 million for the weapons. According to Enterprise books, total profits on the "Phase I" contra weapons sale amounted to $720,400. Weigensberg at TWA received one-third of this amount ($240,133), as did Thomas Green, the Washington, D.C., lawyer who had introduced Secord to TWA. Secord and Hakim split the remaining amount equally, each receiving $120,066.

Due to delays in delivery of the Phase I shipload of weapons and in order to eliminate Weigensberg and Green from the profit shares, Secord recruited two former colleagues, Clines and Rafael Quintero, to arrange a second purchase of arms. Clines' acquaintance with the owner of Defex (Portugal) enabled Secord to work directly with that company. All profits from this and later arms sales were allocated to Secord, Hakim and Clines. Quintero was paid a monthly salary plus bonuses for successful arms deliveries.

## Phase II of the Contra Arms Sales (January–March 1985)

A second order, Phase II, was filled in two plane loads of arms purchased from Defex Portugal: one delivered in January and the second in March 1985. Secord arranged for air transport with the help of Richard Gadd, an Enterprise sub-contractor who had served under Secord in the Air Force. Gadd in turn enlisted a Miami air charter company, Southern Air Transport (SAT), which then subcontracted these flights to a second carrier.

CSF's books show that the contras paid $1.235 million for the weapons in these two shipments. Total profits were $310,840. Secord and Hakim each received 40 percent of the profits (or $124,336 each), and Clines 20 percent ($62,168).

## Phase III of the Contra Arms Sales (March–May 1985)

Secord made plans for a third shipment of arms to the contras in the spring of 1985. The weap-

---

[4] The compensation of a proprietary or private "cut-out" for the CIA is usually set in advance. This was not done for Secord. Although technically an agent for the CIA, he operated under the direction of the national security adviser. Under these circumstances, a claim for compensation would have been limited to that which was agreed to by a properly authorized Government officer and which was reasonable for the services rendered—not half the proceeds.

[5] The Saudis in mid-1984 began donating $1 million a month to the contras; in 1985, they doubled that amount. In all, the Saudis gave $32 million for the purpose of resupplying the contras during the period in which U.S. aid was prohibited by the Boland Amendment.

## CONTRA ARMS SALES, PRO-RATED PROFIT DISTRIBUTIONS

| PHASE | DATE | AMOUNT | RICHARD SECORD | ALBERT HAKIM | THOMAS CLINES | SCITECH | THOMAS GREEN | WEIGENSBERG TWA (Trans World Arms) |
|---|---|---|---|---|---|---|---|---|
| I | 04/17/85 | $720,400.10 | $120,066.68 | $120,066.68 | | | $240,133.37 | $240,133.37 |
| II | 04/11/85 | 310,840.00 | 124,336.00 | 124,336.00 | 62,168.00 | | | |
| III | 07/16/85 | 1,554,839.24 | 621,936.62 | 621,936.62 | 310,966.00 | | | |
| IV | 12/17/85 | 252,000.00 | 100,800.00 | 100,800.00 | 50,400.00 | | | |
| | 02/07/86 | 330,000.00 | 165,000.00 | 165,000.00 | | 16,000.00 | | |
| V | 04/17/86 | 161,000.00 | 50,000.00 | 50,000.00 | 45,000.00 | 8,833.00 | | |
| VI | 05/20/86 | 88,303.00 | 26,490.00 | 26,490.00 | 26,490.00 | 26,390.00 | | |
| VII | 06/02/86 | 263,891.00 | 79,167.00 | 79,167.00 | 79,167.00 | 3,728.00 | | |
| | 06/20/86 | 37,277.00 | 11,183.00 | 11,183.00 | 11,183.00 | 86,133.00 | | |
| | 08/20/86 | 861,327.00 | 258,398.00 | 258,398.00 | 258,398.00 | | | |
| Total | | $4,579,877.34 | $1,557,377.30 | $1,557,377.30 | $843,772.00 | $141,084.00 | $240,133.37 | $240,133.37 |

SOURCE: OIC Analysis of Enterprise Financial Records

ons arrived in Honduras from Portugal in June 1985 on a leased Danish freighter, the *Erria*, which the Enterprise purchased a year later. CSF's books show that the contras paid $6.407 million for the arms. Total profits were $1.5 million; Secord and Hakim got 40 percent each ($621,936 each), and Clines 20 percent ($310,966).

## Summer 1985: Calero's Purchasing Power Is Removed, the Creation of the "Defex" Account to Disguise Profits, and the Lake Account

In late June 1985, North and Secord met in Miami with Calero and contra military commander Enrique Bermudez to inform them that private contributors would begin paying the suppliers—the Enterprise—directly for weapons, rather than giving money to the contras to buy the weapons themselves. In the future, funds raised from private donors and from third countries were to be deposited into the accounts of the Enterprise, effectively allowing it to corner the contra-arms market.

Shortly after the Miami meeting, Secord and Hakim devised a new system for distribution of the profits. They had the Enterprise's Swiss fiduciaire CSF in July 1985 create a Liberian shell corporation named "Defex S.A." The new corporation was intentionally given a name similar to that of the Portuguese arms company, Defex, to enable Secord and Hakim to conceal from the contras the high mark-ups of the Enterprise, by having their financial records suggest that the marked-up prices they charged for arms were being paid to Defex, the supplier.

CSF opened the Defex S.A. bank account at Union de Banques Suisse (UBS) in Fribourg, Switzerland, on July 23, 1985. More than $3 million went through the Defex S.A. bank account between July 1985 and August 1986.

Zucker described the purpose of creating the Defex S.A. account—to hide the profits—in a memo to his assistant Roland Farina on July 8, 1985. Zucker told Farina that Defex Portugal, the Lisbon-based arms supplier from which the Enterprise (under the name Energy Resources) purchased the contra weapons, may

> . . . seek to approach Energy's customer [the contras] directly, thereby seeking to cut out Energy, and offer similar merchan-

dise at significantly lower prices, explaining to the ultimate customer that Energy has kept for itself a large commission.

> To counter this possibility, we have created a LIberian [sic] company with the name DEFEX. S.A. Energy would like us to pay to the account of this Liberian Company "DEFEX" the spread or commission earned on the transactions . . . In this manner, we can show debit advices on the Credit Suisse account of Energy for transfers made to DEFEX, and those together with all of the other disbursements made, will more or less equal the amounts received by Energy.

> . . . The objective, I repeat, is to have in hand sufficient debit advices in Energy so that if any questions are asked whether the entire amount received was expended, we can show payments approximating the amounts received to DEFEX or for expenses relating to the shipments.[6]

A further change in the financial structure of the Enterprise in the summer of 1985 helped disguise the money trail further. Payments from the contras for the first series of arms sales went into the Enterprise account named Energy Resources International. In the summer of 1985, after taking control of all contra supply, Secord and Hakim created a new receiving account, Lake Resources. In July and August 1985, they had CSF transfer all funds out of Energy and into Lake, through the Defex S.A. account and an account of a Zucker-controlled company named Audifi S.A. After Lake was formed, all Enterprise receipts were effectively commingled in that account, regardless of their origin.

## Phase IV of the Contra Arms Sales (December 1985)

Secord and Hakim arranged a fourth shipment of arms to the contras in December 1985. The weapons were purchased by Calero with funds remaining in his account; transportation and other expenses were covered by funds from Calero and other sources commingled in the Lake account.

---

6 Memorandum from Zucker to Farina, 7/8/85, AMU 005189.

The weapons were delivered to El Salvador on December 15, 1985. On December 17, CSF credited Secord's personal account, known as "Korel Assets," with $100,800 in profits. The same day, Hakim received $100,800, and Clines received $50,400 in cash.

## The February 1986 Distribution

On February 6 and 7, 1986, CSF distributed $165,000 to both Secord's Korel account and the Hakim account.[7] This distribution was distinctive for several reasons: It did not follow any arms shipment to Central America, Clines did not share in the distribution, and it was not assigned a phase number. Most importantly, the distribution was made literally hours before the Enterprise received the first payment for a $10 million U.S. weapons shipment to Iran.

Secord and Hakim drew out their Lake Resources account apparently in anticipation of the payment for the Iran shipment, which represented the start of a lucrative new venture for the Enterprise.

## Phases V–VII of the Contra Arms Sales (March–June 1986)

Between February 27 and May 23, 1986, the Enterprise paid Defex Portugal about $860,000 for contra weapons. Weapons were delivered to Central America in March, April and May in three shipments. CSF books show profit distributions between April and June, numbered Phases V through VII, totaling $550,471. In addition, there was an unnumbered distribution of $37,277 on June 20, 1986, resulting from the Phase VII shipment.

## The Undelivered Shipment and Distribution (July–September 1986)

In July 1986, the Enterprise paid Defex (Portugal) $2.6 million and $500,000 to another dealer, Monzer Al Kassar, for contra weapons. In late July, a shipment of arms left Portugal for Central America aboard the recently acquired Enterprise freighter, the *Erria*.[8] Accord-

ing to Thomas Parlow, the *Erria's* Danish shipping agent, the freighter was carrying arms picked up in Poland and Portugal.[9]

As the *Erria* was nearing Bermuda, Parlow, acting on instructions from Hakim, ordered it to slow its speed and await further instructions. Clines then directed the ship to work its way slowly back to Portugal.[10] When it arrived in Portugal it could not obtain permission to enter the port. In this mid- to late-August 1986 period, Secord ordered Clines to try to sell the cargo or dump it at sea, according to Parlow. The vessel headed for Spain, where it remained anchored for two weeks.

As the *Erria* made its circuitous journey, the CIA through a series of commercial entities arranged to buy the weapons aboard. According to CIA officials, they did not learn the identity of either the owner of the ship or its cargo until January 1987, when a newspaper article named the Secord-Hakim Enterprise as the owner of the ship and the weapons.

The CIA paid $2.1 million for the arms shipment, including shipping and handling costs.[11] According to the private arms dealer who bought the arms for the CIA, he paid $1.6 million for the weapons. Of that, the Enterprise received $1.2 million, and the remainder went to Parlow or Defex, who worked together to re-sell the weapons.

The Enterprise paid $3.1 million to arms suppliers for this shipment, but sold it to the CIA for only $1.2 million. In a conventional business, this would have represented an enormous loss. The Enterprise partners, however, split more than $861,000 in claimed profits on the transaction. Because the money originally used to purchase the weapons came from commingled funds in Enterprise accounts—including U.S. funds generated by the sale of arms to Iran and funds donated to the contras—Secord, Hakim and Clines, in effect, allocated to themselves funds that either rightfully belonged to the United States or the contras. In addition, the CIA helped cushion the blow of any loss

---

[7] The financial records provided by Hakim to Congress in 1987 inaccurately showed distributions one year apart (one in February 1985 and a second in February 1986), thus concealing the apparent 50–50 split between Secord and Hakim.

[8] Clines, Hakim and William Haskell, an associate of North, traveled to Copenhagen in April 1986 to purchase for approximately $320,000 the *Erria*, which the Enterprise had leased a year earlier for a weapons shipment to the contras. The ship was purchased by the Enterprise in the name of Dolmy Business Inc., a Panamanian shell company.

Thomas Parlow became the *Erria's* Danish shipping agent. According to Parlow, Hakim would telephone Parlow to direct movement of the ship, and Parlow would communicate those directions to the ship's captain. (Parlow, FBI 302, 3/5/87, pp. 2–3.)

[9] Ibid., p. 3.

[10] The ship apparently was ordered back to Europe because it was to be used in an impending U.S.-Israeli venture involving Iran.

[11] CIA Inspector General's Report, July 1987, p. 38.

the Enterprise might have felt by paying for the arms at a reduced price. Independent Counsel obtained no evidence that these arms ever reached the contras.

## The Finances of the Contra-Resupply Operation

In addition to selling arms to the contras, the Enterprise in the late summer of 1985 began assembling a full-service resupply operation in Central America that would air-drop weapons and other goods to contra forces in the field. In December 1985, North instructed Secord to establish an operating fund of $150,000 for Richard Gadd, whom Secord had hired to manage the resupply operation.[12] In response, the Enterprise wire-transferred $100,000 to Gadd for start-up costs.[13]

The resupply operation, known as "Project Democracy," was organized and fully running by the spring of 1986. Enterprise expenditures on this effort flowed principally to four commercial entities:

1. *Eagle Aviation Service and Technology (EAST)*. This company was run by Gadd, who was experienced in Government contracts involving covert activity. EAST received $550,007 from the Enterprise for contra-related expenses, including work on the construction of a secret airstrip in Costa Rica, payments for communications specialists, a demolitions expert and some pilots and crews.

2. *Amalgamated Commercial Enterprises, Inc. (ACE)*. This Panamanian corporation was set up by Southern Air Transport at Gadd's request to serve as a financial "cut-out"—or extra layer of concealment for the true owners of the contra-resupply operation—for billing purposes. After its creation in late 1985, ACE received and disbursed $1,540,956 in Enterprise funds for the operation. This included payments for two C–7 and one C–123 airplanes, for services provided by Corporate Air Services (see below); and for Southern Air Transport expenses not directly reimbursed by the Swiss Enterprise accounts.

3. *Southern Air Transport (SAT)*. This Miami air-charter company was used by the Enterprise in both the contra and Iran operations. In 1985 and 1986, it received $1,935,596 for contra-related services, including the purchase of a C–123 cargo plane, repair and maintenance of aircraft, sale of spare parts and the supply of cash advances to the resupply operation in Central America. In addition, the Enterprise paid SAT $200,000 for a Jetstar aircraft used by Secord and others for contra-related travel.

4. *Corporate Air Services (CAS)*. Gadd employed this Pennsylvania company owned by Edward T. de Garay as the on-site manager of the resupply operation. CAS received from the Enterprise Swiss accounts and through ACE $457,769 for salaries and other expenses.

## Summer–Fall 1986: The Enterprise Tries to Sell Its Contra-Resupply Operation to the CIA

As Congress in the summer of 1986 moved toward lifting the ban on U.S. military aid to the contras and toward final approval of a $100 million funding bill, the Enterprise envisioned another possible business opportunity: CIA assumption of its resupply operation in Central America. As a result, North, Secord and other members of the Enterprise readied the resupply network for possible sale to the CIA.

Secord in the spring of 1986 asked Robert Dutton, who had replaced Gadd as manager of the resupply operation, to prepare a description of Enterprise assets; North later asked Dutton to add a price list.[14] Dutton's memo describes how extensive the operation had grown by mid-1986.

In describing the organizational structure, Dutton stated that "Benefactor Company," or "B.C. Washington" had operational control of all assets in support of the resupply operation, or "Project Democracy." He stated that all contracts and payments went through Amalgamated Commercial Enterprises (ACE), which acted as the broker for SAT in Miami, which provided aircraft and maintenance and other support.

Dutton valued the resupply operation's assets at $4.089 million, which included, among other items, two C–123 cargo jets; two C–7 planes;

---

[12] Gadd, FBI 302, 7/14/87–7/15/87, p. 13.
[13] Ibid.

[14] Undated Dutton outline of the resupply operation; attached list of assets and expenditures dated 7/21/86, 00001–15.

a Maule aircraft;[15] a secret Santa Elena, Costa Rica, airstrip; the Santa Elena property; spare parts; and munitions and supplies.

Dutton described Project Democracy's operating locations: Washington, "the hub for all operational project information;" "Cincinnati," the code name for Ilopango air base in El Salvador, where aircraft were based and four houses maintained in the city for about 18 employees; "The Farm," the air base at Aguacate, Honduras, used as a "launch and recovery site for support missions;" "The Plantation," the secret Santa Elena, Costa Rica, airstrip for refueling and emergency landing; and "Maintenance Support Miami," where a support crew worked closely with SAT for procurement and delivery of required items. Dutton listed 25 salaried employees of the resupply operation, including managers, flight crews and others.

Dutton proposed two options for transferring the assets of the resupply operation to the CIA: (1) sale of the assets for less than the estimated value of $4 million; or (2) leasing the assets to the CIA for $311,500 per month plus add-ons. Dutton stated that the first option was preferable.

But the CIA was not eager to associate itself with the Enterprise resupply network, whose illicit operation had been concealed from Congress despite repeated inquiries. North in a computer message to Poindexter on July 15, 1986, complained about the CIA's reluctance to purchase the resupply network's assets: "It would simply be ludicrous for this to simply disappear just because CIA does not want to be 'tainted' with picking up the assets and then have them spend $8–10M of the $100M to replace it—weeks or months later."[16] In July 1986, North, at a meeting with Abrams and Fiers, described the Enterprise assets in Central America.

North asked Poindexter to speak to Casey about the matter; Poindexter agreed to talk to Casey, adding that he (Poindexter) had told CIA Deputy Director Robert M. Gates that "the private effort should be phased out."[17] According

to Alan Fiers, chief of the CIA's Central American task force in 1986, Fiers advised against CIA assumption of the operation's assets.[18]

## Dismantling the Operation

The Nicaraguan shootdown of the contra-resupply plane carrying American survivor Eugene Hasenfus on October 5, 1986, settled irrevocably the question of CIA assumption of Enterprise assets. With a $100 million contra-funding bill awaiting final approval in Congress, the agency could not associate itself in any way with the Enterprise operation. CIA officials had publicly and in closed congressional testimony disavowed any involvement with it.

General Juan Rafael Bustillo, the Salvadoran military chief at Ilopango air base, ordered the resupply crews out of the country. The planes were flown to Aguacate air base and the Hondurans later took possession of them.[19] Luis Posada, whose alias was Ramon Medina and who handled expenses for the pilots and crews, cleaned out the houses where resupply personnel had stayed, retrieved documents and delivered them to Quintero, who then gave them to Dutton.[20] Posada also terminated the operation's leases, paid the bills and disposed of radio equipment, cars and other goods.[21] The Salvadoran Air Force took possession of the operation's warehouse of parts and supplies at Ilopango.[22]

North's notebooks reflect a series of conversations with Secord and others about obtaining a lawyer for Hasenfus, who was imprisoned and facing trial in Nicaragua, as well as discussions about death benefits and funeral arrangements for the pilots killed in the crash.[23] William Haskell, North's friend who performed a variety of Enterprise-related duties on his behalf, and resupply manager Edward de Garay went to Panama to obtain a lawyer for

---

effect." (Poindexter, Select Committees Deposition, 5/2/87, pp. 208–9.)

[18] Fiers, Grand Jury, 8/14/91, p. 77.

[19] Ibid., p. 5.

[20] Dutton, who received immunity from prosecution, provided these documents to OIC.

[21] Posada, FBI 302, 2/3/92, pp.25–26.

[22] Ibid., p. 26.

[23] North's Notes, dated October 8–10, 13–15, 1986, AMX001574–93. At Secord and Hakim's request, Zucker hired a Swiss lawyer for Hasenfus. Zucker said the Swiss lawyer was unable to contact Nicaraguan officials and did not continue with the case. (Zucker, FBI 302, 5/16–18/88, pp. 4–5.)

---

[15] In 1985 and 1986, the Enterprise purchased four Maule aircraft, but apparently was offering only one as part of its resupply-operation package.

[16] PROFs Note from North to Poindexter, 7/15/86, AKW 018917.

[17] PROFs Note from Poindexter to North, 7/26/86, AKW 021732. Poindexter told Congress he believes he told Gates "that these assets are available and you ought to look at them, or something to that

Hasenfus, who was imprisoned and facing trial in Nicaragua; their mission was not a success.[24]

In December 1986, John Piowaty, an air-support manager for the resupply operation, at Dutton's request carried $6,000 in cash from Southern Air Transport in Miami to Sally Hasenfus, Eugene Hasenfus's wife.[25] This amount represented two months' salary for Hasenfus, who was released from jail and allowed to return to the United States in December 1986.

North testified that Abrams asked him to "raise the money to pay" for the retrieval of the bodies of pilots Wallace Sawyer and William Cooper from Nicaragua.[26] According to Piowaty, Dutton told him that the families of the pilots who were killed in the shootdown would each receive $60,000 in benefits. The families, however, never received such payments.[27] The Enterprise did arrange to have delivered $3,000 in cash to a Magnolia, Arkansas, funeral home for Sawyer's burial costs.[28]

The Enterprise attempted to establish a defense fund for Hasenfus from allocations intended for the contras. In early October 1986, before the shootdown, Secord and Hakim at North's request had three checks issued to pay outstanding contra grocery bills. These checks were made payable to Aquiles Marin, a contra representative, and sent to Rafael Quintero in Miami. Only one check for $75,000 went to the contras. Following the shootdown, Secord told Quintero to set aside a second $75,000 check and a third $50,000 check to establish a defense fund. Quintero endorsed the $75,000 check, forging Marin's signature, and mailed it with the unendorsed $50,000 check to the Banque Intercommerciale de Gestion in the Bahamas; Quintero instructed the bank to use the $75,000 check for a defense fund and to hold the $50,000 check for him (Quintero).[29]

---

[24] Gadd, FBI 302, 7/6/87–7/7/87, pp. 22–23; Haskell, FBI 302, 7/6/87, p. 11.

[25] Piowaty, FBI 302, 6/22/87.

[26] North, Select Committees Testimony, 7/8/87, pp. 167–68.

[27] Piowaty, FBI 302, 6/22/87, p. 4.

[28] McAlister, FBI 302, 5/4/87, pp. 1–3. Independent Counsel obtained no evidence indicating that a similar payment was made for Cooper's funeral.

[29] Quintero, FBI 302, 9/1/87.

# The Enterprise and the Sale of U.S. Arms to Iran

## The 1985 Israeli Sales

Private arms dealers in 1984 began suggesting to U.S. officials that if weapons were sold to Iran, Iranians could gain the release of Americans held hostage by terrorists in Lebanon. Manucher Ghorbanifar, an Iranian exile and former CIA informant who had been discredited by the agency as a fabricator, was a driving force behind these proposals.

By August 1985, Israel had obtained, through National Security Adviser Robert C. McFarlane, President Reagan's approval to sell U.S. arms to Iran and to replenish Israeli weapons stocks.

In 1985, there were two Israeli sales of U.S. weapons to Iran: 504 TOW missiles in August and September 1985, and 18 HAWK missiles in November 1985. The Israelis relied on international financier Adnan Khashoggi to raise "bridge financing" for the deals, because the Iranians would not pay for the weapons until they were delivered, and Israel would not ship the weapons before Iran paid for them.

Although no U.S. funds were involved in the November 1985 HAWKs transaction, the Enterprise derived a windfall. As described elsewhere in this report, the HAWK shipment encountered logistical difficulties, resulting in the direct involvement of North and Secord. North told the Israelis to transfer $1 million to the Enterprise's Lake Resources account in Geneva to pay for airlifting the missiles to Iran; they did so on November 20, 1985.[30] The Israelis thought the million-dollar request was reasonable based on an anticipated four flights to ship 80 HAWKs at $250,000 per flight.[31]

After the first 18 HAWKs were delivered to Iran, the Iranians rejected them. The rest of the shipment was cancelled. The Enterprise had spent only $127,700, on the single shipment. The difference—approximately $870,000—remained in the Lake Resources account commingled with funds from other

---

[30] Israeli Financial Chronology, 4/26/87, AOW 0000182, as released in Select Committees Report, p. 179.

[31] Ibid.

sources; it was used for aid to the contras and other purposes.[32]

## Direct U.S. Arms Sales to Iran: The Enterprise as U.S. Agent

In January 1986, the Reagan Administration decided to sell weapons directly from U.S. stocks to Iran, eliminating Israel as an intermediary and employing Secord as an agent to make the sales and transport the arms, masking official U.S. involvement. President Reagan authorized the direct sales in a January 17, 1986, covert-action Finding. Under the Finding, Secord, acting as an agent of the CIA, would sell arms to brokers representing the Iranians, who then would sell them to Iran. Secord would obtain payment in advance from the Iranians and deposit in a CIA account the amount the CIA was to pay the Department of Defense for the weapons. The CIA would purchase the weapons from the Department of Defense at cost under the Economy Act;[33] Secord would deliver them to Iran.

Ghorbanifar, as broker for Iran, borrowed funds for the weapons payments from Khashoggi, who loaned millions of dollars to Ghorbanifar in "bridge financing" for the deals. Ghorbanifar repaid Khashoggi with a 20 percent commission after being paid by the Iranians.

The Reagan Administration's 1986 decision to sell weapons directly to Iran eliminated the Israeli arms dealers from the initiative. Amiram Nir, an Israeli counter-terrorism official, became the Israeli representative in the negotiations. At North's request, he gave Ghorbanifar the number of the Lake Resources account, into which deposits for the arms purchases were to be made.[34]

## February 1986: 1,000 TOW Missiles

In January 1986, North and Secord negotiated on behalf of the United States the sale of 4,000 TOW missiles to Iran. Ghorbanifar agreed to pay $10,000 for each TOW. The terms and conditions negotiated by North and Secord required an initial sale of 1,000 TOW missiles for $10 million, and subsequent sales of an additional 3,000 TOW missiles for $30 million. North falsely informed DoD and the CIA that Secord would receive only $6,000 per TOW, or a total of $6 million. The Defense Department established its price as $3,700 per TOW missile for its sale to the CIA and the price to be paid to the CIA by Secord.

Between February 7 and February 18, 1986, Khashoggi deposited $10 million into the Enterprise's Lake Resources account.[35] On February 10–11, 1986, $3.7 million was transferred from Lake to a CIA account for the weapons. Between February 17 and 27, 1986, 1,000 TOWs were shipped to Iran. In addition, 17 HAWK missiles from the failed November 1985 shipment were returned from Iran to Israel.

The Enterprise's direct expenses in connection with the transportation of the weapons were about $716,000, leaving a surplus of $5.6 million. The plan to sell 3,000 more TOW missiles on the same terms to Iran did not materialize.[36]

Iran paid higher prices for the weapons than those already inflated by the Enterprise, because Ghorbanifar added large commissions of his own. Khashoggi said his commission was split with Ghorbanifar; Roy Furmark, who had introduced Khashoggi to Ghorbanifar; and Triad International Marketing, a Khashoggi business.[37]

Further complicating the matter, Israel had expected to pay for the replacement of TOWs it sent to Iran in 1985 from Enterprise markups on the 1,000 TOWs sold to Iran in February

---

[32] Secord testified before Congress that the Israelis did not ask for their money back. He said he discussed the matter with North in December 1986, and North told him they could use the money "for whatever purpose we wanted. We actually expended it on the Contra project." (Secord, Select Committees Testimony, 5/5/87, p. 95.) Because of the commingling of funds in the Lake Resources account, however, it is not possible to directly tie the Israeli deposit to an expenditure of funds on the contras.

[33] The Economy Act permitted sales at cost between Government agencies.

[34] Allen, Grand Jury, 1/4/88, pp. 46–47; Secord, Grand Jury, 5/14/87, p. 339.

[35] Khashoggi transferred $5 million from his own Bank of Credit and Commerce account in Monte Carlo to Lake Resources, and he raised the remaining $5 million from two investors: He borrowed $2.5 million from a wealthy woman in Monte Carlo and $2.5 million from Galliot Lines S.A., owned by Syrian banker Oussama Lababidi. (Khashoggi, FBI 302, 5/8/87, p. 8.)

[36] As originally contemplated by North and Secord, the Enterprise would have drawn off roughly $22 million after expenses, if 4,000 TOWs had been sold. This calculation is arrived at by quadrupling the surplus of $5.6 million on the 1,000 TOW deal.

[37] Ibid., p. 11. Ghorbanifar described a similar split. (Ghorbanifar, OIC Deposition, 12/9/87, p. 142.)

1986. According to the Israelis, however, North claimed the proceeds were less than anticipated and would not cover the cost of the replenishment.[38]

## May–August 1986: HAWK Parts to Iran; Israeli TOWs Replenished

In the spring of 1986, North negotiated on behalf of the United States a sale of 240 HAWK missile spare parts to Iran. He also negotiated with representatives of Israel for the purchase of 508 U.S.-made TOW missiles to replace those shipped by Israel in August and September of 1985. In combination, these transactions resulted in $16.685 million being deposited by Iranian and Israeli representatives into the Enterprise's Lake Resources account in Geneva.

The CIA charged the Enterprise $3,469 for each of the 508 TOW missiles sold for replenishment to the Israelis, plus shipping and handling costs. This cost was passed on to the Israelis. For the HAWK spare parts for Iran, the CIA charged $4.337 million, plus shipping and handling. North, however, had multiplied this true cost by a factor of 3.7 in setting the price to be paid by Ghorbanifar.

On May 14–16, 1986, a total of $15 million in bridge financing was deposited into the Lake Resources account by Khashoggi, acting on behalf of Ghorbanifar. On May 15–16, 1986, Israel deposited a total of $1.685 million in the Lake account.[39] Of the total $16.685 million deposited, only $6.5 million was paid to the United States for the Iranian and Israeli weapons purchases. The expenses involved in these shipments were about $1 million, resulting in a surplus of $9.2 million for the Enterprise.

## Khashoggi and Ghorbanifar Encounter Financial Problems; a "Second Channel" into Iran Is Pursued

In raising the $15 million bridge financing for the HAWKs spare parts, Khashoggi in April 1986 asked British entrepreneur Tiny Rowlands

to invest. After Rowlands declined, Khashoggi turned to Oussama Lababidi who, using the name "Kremdale Corporation," put up $5 million. The remaining $10 million came from Vertex International in the Cayman Islands, backed by investors Ernie Walter Miller and Donald Fraser of Canada. Khashoggi said he created a company "Trivert International," to handle the Vertex loan.[40]

In June 1986, the Iranians obtained a U.S. price list for the HAWK spare parts. After seeing the list, they refused to pay the radically inflated amount—$24 million—Ghorbanifar had charged them. As a result, Ghorbanifar paid back Khashoggi a total of only $8.1 million on the $15 million bridge-financing loan, which with the 20-percent bridge-financing commission required payment to Khashoggi of $18 million.

While these financial disputes were brewing, the Reagan Administration decided to pursue a "second channel" into the Iranian parliament, cutting out Ghorbanifar, his Iranian contact and Nir. When Poindexter told Nir about the second channel in September 1986, Nir responded that making a switch would require paying off Ghorbanifar's $10 million debt to the financiers.[41]

## October–November 1986: 500 TOWs Sold; Hakim Seeks More

In October 1986, North and Secord on behalf of the United States negotiated a sale of 500 TOW missiles to Iran. The United States charged $3,469 per TOW missile, plus shipping and handling, while the Enterprise charged the Iranians $7,200 per TOW. The Iranians, no longer acting through Ghorbanifar but through a "second channel," paid $3.6 million, deposited on October 29, 1986, into the Enterprise account known as Hyde Park Square Corporation. The Enterprise paid the CIA $2.037 million for the TOWs. Direct expenses incurred

[38] Israeli Financial Chronology, 4/26/87, p. 20, AOW 0000190, as released in Select Committees Report, p. 224.

[39] Although the Israelis expected the replenishment to be paid from mark-ups on the Iran weapons sales, they finally agreed to pay this amount after Nir was informed that sufficient funds were not being generated. (Israeli Financial Chronology, 4/26/87, pp. 26–67, AOW 0000196–97, as released in Select Committees Report, pp. 224–341.)

[40] Khashoggi, FBI 302, 5/8/87, p. 10, and 11/4/87, p. 5. According to bank records obtained by Independent Counsel, on May 14, 1986, a $10 million payment was made into Lake Resources by Trivert International by order of W.E. Miller. On May 16, 1986, Lake Resources received $5 million from Garnet Overseas at BCCI; Garnet received the funds from Khashoggi's account and Khashoggi's account received the funds from Ray Trading. Because Ghorbanifar only repaid $8 million, the investors lost $7 million of their initial investment. Ghorbanifar received from Iran only $4 million; it is unclear where he obtained the other $4 million to partially repay the investors.

[41] Allen, Grand Jury, 8/9/91, pp. 122–25.

by the Enterprise came to less than $200,000. The Enterprise cleared $1.463 million as a result.

In October 1986, Hakim in meetings with Iranian representatives took on the role of arms dealer and hostage negotiator. He proposed a nine-point plan for the phased release of the American hostages, based on further arms shipments and other conditions to be met by the United States.[42] These negotiations did not result in further arms sales.

Hakim told Independent Counsel that he had expected Iran to invest $50 million in future arms sales.[43]

## Fall 1986, the Arms Sales Unravel: Exposure and Cover-Up

In August 1986, Ghorbanifar complained to Furmark that the mark-ups charged by the Enterprise were going to the contras or Afghan rebels. Ghorbanifar told Furmark: "No sooner than we pay money, it probably is going down south."[44]

Khashoggi also was upset about being cut out of the U.S. arms sales by the establishment of the "second channel" into Iran. He said he devised a "ploy" to get CIA Director Casey to repay the $9.9 million he felt he was owed for the HAWK-parts investment. Aware of Furmark's past ties to Casey, Khashoggi said he told Furmark on October 1, 1986, that the bridge loan from the HAWKs parts deal had not been repaid and that Canadian investors (Miller and Fraser with a $10 million participation) might sue, publicly exposing the U.S. arms sales to Iran.[45]

Before Furmark approached Casey with this information, there had been other attempts to warn the Reagan Administration. Charles Allen of the CIA learned of Ghorbanifar's financial difficulties in August 1986; he knew previously

about the mark-up in arms sales prices from intelligence reports; he had suspected that the extra funds were used for an Iran/contra diversion. In August, Allen warned his superior, CIA Director of Intelligence Richard Kerr. Kerr warned Deputy Director for Central Intelligence Robert Gates.[46] By early October, Allen warned Casey.

Ghorbanifar complained to his original U.S. sponsor, Michael Ledeen, an NSC consultant. Ledeen testified that Ghorbanifar told him that Canadian investors were owed $10 million from the Iran deals and might go public; Ledeen at some time told North and Casey, but the date is unclear.[47] Nir also in mid-September warned CIA and NSC officials that Ghorbanifar needed $10 million or his creditors might expose the arms sales.[48]

North was aware that he would have to pay Ghorbanifar some amount of money to eliminate him from the deals. In a September 10, 1986, memorandum to Casey, Allen relayed that North had told him that Poindexter believed that "to cut Ghorbanifar out, Ollie will have to raise a minimum of $4 million."[49]

Furmark met with Casey in Washington on October 7, 1986, to warn of possible exposure of the Iran arms sales. Furmark said he told Casey about Khashoggi's financial problems and mentioned the Lake Resources account, which Casey said he believed was an Israeli account. Furmark did not, at this meeting, mention Ghorbanifar's belief that the money had gone to the contras.[50] Casey told Furmark that CIA officials would get in touch with him for additional information.

CIA officers Allen and George Cave then met with Furmark. On October 22, Furmark told them that Iran proceeds possibly were being diverted to the contras. In early November 1986, Furmark met with Allen and gave him Ghorbanifar's bank account number. On No-

---

[42] In these meetings, Hakim was continuing a process begun by North, who, on behalf of President Reagan, presented a seven-point plan for hostage release.

[43] Hakim, FBI 302, 2/20/91, p. 14. Hakim told Congress that had the United States renewed ties to Iran, he and Secord expected a 3 percent share of an expected $15 billion-a-year arms market. (Hakim, Select Committees Deposition, 5/23/87, pp. 256, 263–64.)

[44] Furmark, FBI 302, 2/22/88, p. 10.

[45] Khashoggi, FBI 302, 5/8/87, p. 11.

Fraser said he did not threaten to sue, and it was likely that Miller didn't either (Fraser, Select Committees Deposition, 4/29/87, pp. 58–59). Khashoggi said he sold stocks in April 1987 to repay Fraser and Miller. (Khashoggi, FBI 302, 5/8/87, p. 11.)

[46] See Gates chapter.

[47] Ledeen, FBI 302, 12/17/86, p. 13. Also, Ledeen, Grand Jury, 9/30/87, pp. 57–60, 64–65, 114–16.

[48] Allen, Grand Jury, 1/4/88, pp. 22–26. Members of the Enterprise, meanwhile, were apparently trying to shut down the Ghorbanifar-Khashoggi operation through other means. On September 2, 1986, Hakim informed Allen that Ghorbanifar and "his banker" were involved in a planned shipment of 1,250 TOWs to Iran. Allen alerted Customs and the FBI, which reported back that there was no evidence to substantiate the claim. (Ibid., p. 11.)

[49] Ibid., p. 20.

[50] Furmark, FBI 302, 2/22/88, p. 10.

vember 24, 1986, Furmark said he met again
with Casey and showed him records indicating
that Khashoggi had put up $25 million for the
arms sales, and that $10 million was owed.

## The Iran/Contra Diversion

Because of the commingling of Enterprise
funds, it was not possible to determine precisely
how much money was diverted from the Iran
arms sales proceeds to the contras. After direct
U.S. sales of arms to Iran began in February
1986, the amount of proceeds diverted to the
contras that could have been proved at trial
was $3.6 million. It probably was at least $1.1
million more.[51]

North, in his testimony, attributed to Nir and
Ghorbanifar the idea for a diversion of arms
sales funds to the contras. In the *Poindexter*
trial, although uncertain, he fixed the date in
December 1985 or January or February of
1986.[52] As early as November 14, 1985,
North's notebooks show that he discussed with
Nir a plan to obtain the release of the hostages
by payments to certain Middle Eastern factions.
The questions they discussed included: "How
to pay for; how to raise $," and a possible
solution was to set up a "joint" Israeli-U.S.
"covert op." According to the Israelis, North
apparently told Israeli defense officials in a
meeting in New York on December 6, 1985,
that he intended to divert funds from the arms
sales to the contras.[53]

Secord said North pressed him to send funds
from the Iran operation to the contra operation.[54] Secord claimed he did not view this

as a diversion, but simply as shifting funds from
one of his operations to another.

The diversion to the contras was only one
dimension of a much larger theft of Government
funds generated by the Iran and Israeli-replen-
ishment transactions. The Enterprise in 1986 illegally diverted for its own purposes $16 mil-
lion generated by the sale of U.S. property to
Iran.

Enterprise Theft of 1986 U.S. Arms Sales Proceeds

[In millions]

| | |
|---|---|
| Amount Charged for U.S. Weapons to Iran and Israel | $30.3 |
| Amount Paid to the U.S. | 12.2 |
| Enterprise Expenses | 2.1 |
| Funds Owed to U.S. | $16 |

The funds from inflated arms prices went
into the network of Swiss accounts controlled
by Hakim, Secord and North. Funds from all
sources were commingled, laundered, and disbursed to a variety of individuals and entities.
Although approximately $16 million was with-
held, only $7.8 million remained in the Enter-
prise Swiss accounts when they were frozen
in December 1986.[55]

## Enterprise Benefits to Secord and Hakim

Secord and Hakim benefited substantially as a
result of their involvement in the Iran and
contra operations. Secord in 1985 and 1986 received $2 million in direct personal benefits

[51] The $3.6 million diversion estimate does not include expenditures OIC could not provide evidence for at trial but were, in fact, contra-related, including: the purchase of a $200,000 Jetstar by the Enterprise for contra-related travel; a $500,000 weapons purchase from Monzer Al Kassar, who was not available to testify; and about $535,000 that was used to purchase, operate and insure the Danish freighter, the *Erria*, which was not used exclusively for contra operations.

Independent Counsel arrived at the diversion figure of $3.6 million by calculating the Enterprise's total contra-related expenses following the first direct U.S. shipment of arms to Iran in February 1986, less the amount of funds in Enterprise accounts specifically deposited on behalf of the contras. The Enterprise's contra-related expenses after February were conservatively estimated at $6.7 million. The amount deposited for the contras was $3.1 million. Thus, the amount that was clearly diverted from the arms sales was $3.6 million.

[52] North, *Poindexter* Trial Testimony, 3/13/90, p. 1092.

[53] Israeli Historical Chronology, 7/29/87, pp. 55–56, AOW 000068–69, as released in Select Committees Report, p. 197.

[54] Secord, FBI 302, 3/12/88, p. 4.

[55] Sixteen of 21 Swiss Enterprise accounts had funds remaining in them when they were frozen in December 1986. The total at that time was $7,814,899.24. Since then, at least $3 million in interest has accrued. The accounts and balances at the time the funds were frozen were:

| | |
|---|---|
| Albon Values Corp. | $5,494.16 |
| Defex S.A. | $88,662.50 |
| Dolmy Business Inc. | $6,508.85 |
| Gulf Marketing Consultants Inc. | $235.36 |
| Hyde Park Square Corp. | $1,136,815.47 |
| Lake Resources Inc. | $430.60 |
| Stanford Technology Corp. | $13,955.99 |
| Stantech Services S.A. | $15,806.48 |
| Toyco S.A. | $25.73 |
| B. Button | $211,990.71 |
| Hakim Albert | $259,593.46 |
| AH/Subaccount 1 | $2,129,151.51 |
| AH/Subaccount 2 | $2,051,909.30 |
| AH/Subaccount 3 | $157,146.12 |
| Korel Assets | $1,547,035.75 |
| Scitech Trading Group Inc. | $190,137.25 |
| Total | $7,814,899.24 |

The Swiss Enterprise accounts that had no funds in them in December 1986 were: Energy Resources International S.A., Udall Research Corp., C. Tea investment account, Lake Resources investment account, and Richard V. Secord investment account.

from the Enterprise, and more than $1 million in cash payments. Hakim in 1985 and 1986 received $2.06 million in direct benefits, and more than $550,000 in cash.

The benefits fell into three broad categories: pro-rated profit distributions on contra weapons sales, for which each received $1,557,377; money from Enterprise accounts that went into Secord-Hakim business ventures, amounting to $520,000 each;[56] and funds withdrawn from Enterprise accounts for personal use, including repairs to a Secord plane amounting to $5,729, payments of $20,000 each by Secord and Hakim for a business venture in the Middle East, and $3,000 each for investment in a catfish business venture.

Cash payments to Secord in 1985 and 1986 totaled approximately $1,037,000. About $14,000 could be traced to the payment of business expenses, and nearly $20,000 was cash Secord withdrew from his profit account. The remaining $1.003 million in cash payments to Secord were for unknown purposes.

Hakim in 1985 and 1986 received $550,000 in cash from the Enterprise. Hakim spent about $32,000 of this on business expenses, and about $39,000 were withdrawals from his profit account. Hakim received approximately $478,500 in cash for unknown purposes.

In addition, the Enterprise transferred at least $696,000 in 1985 and 1986 from its foreign accounts into Secord and Hakim's domestic company, STTGI. Secord and Hakim went to great lengths to conceal this income—using false loan documents and invoices—to suggest that the transfer of cash to STTGI was a loan.

Secord and Hakim took other steps to keep their profits hidden. As described earlier, in mid-1985 they created a receiving account—Defex, S.A.—with virtually the same name as a Portuguese weapons supplier to create the false impression that they were paying almost the same price for contra weapons as they were charging the contras. Also in mid-1985, Secord instructed Zucker to remove Secord's name from all Enterprise accounts and to transfer his profits into a code-named account. He closed the "Richard V. Secord" investment account and opened an investment account named "Korel Assets." In December 1986, Secord attempted to get Zucker to agree to a false story that Secord had foresworn his profits.

Finally, Secord and Hakim did succeed to some extent in disguising their benefits. Hakim provided the Select Committees in 1987 a set of financial records that did not identify payments to himself, Clines and Secord. These financial records were recorded in what was known as the "Hakim Ledger," pursuant to Hakim's instruction to Zucker in 1986 to collapse the individual profit accounts. OIC reconstructed the profit accounts with the help of a former assistant to Zucker, Roland Farina, who had coded the receipts to show the profit account to which they would have been allocable had they not been collapsed.

---

[56] Secord and Hakim apparently lost substantial sums in each of these business ventures, all of which occurred in 1986. None of the money was ever returned to the Swiss Enterprise accounts from which it came.

Secord and Hakim in 1986 shared jointly in the following investments:

| | |
|---|---|
| Tri-American Arms | $150,000 |
| Quinnault Timber | $130,000 |
| Forways | $760,000 |
| Total | $1,040,000 |

Tri-American Arms was a Colorado arms-manufacturing venture; Quinnault Timber involved the development of timberland in Washington state; and the Forways investment was in a New Jersey military parts manufacturing concern partly owned by the Enterprise's money manager, Willard Zucker.

# Chapter 9
# United States v. Richard V. Secord

Retired Air Force Maj. Gen. Richard V. Secord flew 285 combat missions while serving in Southeast Asia during the 1960s. From 1975 to 1978, he was chief of the Air Force Section of the U.S. Military Assistance Advisory Group in Iran, where he met Albert Hakim, who would later become his business partner in the Enterprise. Secord was promoted to major general in May 1980 and was the ranking Air Force officer in charge of rescue efforts for U.S. hostages held in Iran during 1980–81. After serving as deputy assistant secretary of defense for international security affairs from 1981 to 1983, he retired from the Air Force following allegations of improper dealings with former CIA agent Edwin Wilson, who was convicted of smuggling arms to Libya.

Upon leaving the Air Force, Secord went into business with Hakim, co-founding in 1983 Stanford Technology Trading Group International (STTGI). Using a complex web of secret Swiss bank accounts and shell corporations managed by Willard Zucker at Compagnie de Services Fiduciaires (CSF) in Geneva, they built a lucrative Enterprise from covert-operations business assigned to them by Lt. Col. Oliver L. North.

Secord brought important operational skills to the Iran/contra transactions supervised by North. He disclosed most of his operational exploits in testimony before Congress and to criminal investigators, but he lied when he claimed that he acted as a volunteer for the benefit of the United States and that he personally did not profit from his participation.

One of Secord's central purposes in establishing and carrying out the operations of the Enterprise was the accumulation of untaxed wealth in secret overseas accounts. Testimony and records obtained from the Enterprise's Swiss financial manager, Willard Zucker, show that Secord personally received at least $2 million from his participation in the Enterprise during 1985 and 1986, that he set up secret accounts to conceal his untaxed income, and that he later lied and encouraged others to lie to keep it concealed.

Secord was indicted in March 1988 for conspiring with North, Vice Adm. John M. Poindexter and Hakim to defraud the U.S. Government of money and services, and for theft of Government property. After the trials were severed and the main conspiracy counts dropped due to problems with classified information, the Grand Jury in April 1989 charged Secord with nine additional felonies as a result of his false testimony before Congress in 1987.

Secord pleaded guilty on November 8, 1989, to the felony charge of lying to Congress about illegal gratuities he provided to North.[1] Secord entered his plea five days before he was to be tried on 12 felony charges. As part of his plea, Secord promised to cooperate in the pending trials and ongoing investigation of Independent Counsel.

## Secord's Finances

In July 1985 Secord instructed Zucker at CSF to delete references to Secord's name from all Enterprise profit accounts. Zucker transferred funds from the "Richard V. Secord" account to one maintained under the name of a shell corporation known as "Korel Assets."[2] All

---

[1] The Secord guilty plea was obtained through the work of Associate Counsel Reid Weingarten, William Hassler and Antonia Ianniello, who would have prosecuted the case had it gone to trial.

[2] The name "Korel" has no particular significance. Secord rejected Zucker's first recommendation, a company known as "Homel General,"

subsequent profit distributions—totaling $1,457,568—for Secord were credited to Korel. On September 20, 1985, Secord signed a series of documents formalizing his control of the Korel account.[3]

Secord masked his withdrawal of funds from the Korel account. In September 1985, he received $52,500 for the purchase of a small $35,000 private airplane; the rest of the money went for other personal uses. He and Zucker used a series of specious, misleading telex messages to make it appear that Secord had purchased the airplane not for himself but for a wealthy Arab. In 1986, Secord purchased a Porsche using $31,827 withdrawn from Korel. Secord later claimed that he believed this car to be the fruit of a loan from an Arab acquaintance. In spring 1986, Secord, Thomas G. Clines and others vacationed at a German weight-reduction spa using $4,600 from Korel and Clines's profit account.

Although Secord denied ownership of the Korel account before his guilty plea, he eventually admitted ownership of the account as part of his testimony at the trial of Clines.[4]

During 1985 and 1986, Secord received $1.037 million in cash payments from the Enterprise. About $34,000 was accounted for as legitimate business expenditures or withdrawals from his profits, leaving more than $1 million in unaccounted-for cash withdrawals by Secord.

Of the unexplained withdrawals, three totaling $796,000 stand out. On May 15 and 21, 1986, Secord personally received cash payments of $225,000 and $260,000. Secord said he provided this money to Israeli official Amiram Nir, but there is no supporting documentation.[5] In July 1986, Secord withdrew $311,000 in cash, which he said he provided to the Iranian arms dealer Manucher Ghorbanifar, also without documentation.[6] Nir, who has since died, was unavailable to OIC to verify Secord's account. The Israelis denied that their government ever received these funds, whether or not Nir did. The Israelis, however, were unwilling to provide a witness to testify to these facts. Ghorbanifar also denied receiving $311,000 from Secord.[7]

Secord received two additional cash payments that could be traced as far as his home. In late September 1986, Zucker personally delivered to Secord's wife $50,000 in cash at a restaurant in New Jersey.[8] On November 17, 1986, William Haskell, a courier for North and Secord, delivered an unknown amount of cash to Secord at Secord's home.[9] Haskell received the cash from David Morabia at Republic National Bank in New York.[10]

Secord claimed to have no specific memory of what was done with the cash he received in late 1986. To the extent he received cash, however, he said he was sure he spent it on operational matters.

Despite Secord's suggestion that the money went to operational expenses, the Enterprise had effectively ceased Central American activities after a contra-resupply aircraft carrying Eugene Hasenfus was shot down over Nicaragua on October 5, 1986. None of the operatives received significant amounts of cash from Secord after that. The Enterprise generally did not deal in cash on the Iranian side. The obvious inference is that Secord retained the cash for his own use.

On January 24, 1987, the Israelis refunded to Secord $23,000 in cash remaining from an Enterprise account in Israel. Secord originally denied having received this money, but when confronted with a receipt, he admitted receiving it and claimed it was used for travel expenses in 1987 in response to investigations of the Enterprise's activities.

The calculations described above contrast with Secord's financial profile reported to the Internal Revenue Service and with Secord's testimony to the Select Committees in 1987. Secord and his wife reported adjusted gross in-

apparently because it could have suggested a reference to Secord's military rank.

[3] The documents signed by Secord included a standard Swiss Fiduciary Agreement and three Mandatory Agreements authorizing Zucker to invest funds and otherwise act on behalf of Korel. The Fiduciary Agreement defines Secord as "mandator," and begins by stating: "WHEREAS the Mandator is the principal shareholder of KOREL ASSETS INC."

Zucker, who received immunity from Independent Counsel, did not testify before Congress. Hakim, who received limited use immunity from Congress to testify, was the Select Committees' chief source for Enterprise financial information. Zucker produced these Korel documents to Independent Counsel, but they were not produced to congressional investigators by Hakim.

[4] Secord, *Clines* Trial Testimony, 9/5/90, p. 193.

[5] Secord, OIC Interview, 3/9/88, pp. 106–07.

[6] Secord, Grand Jury, 1/22/88, pp. 150–51.

[7] Ghorbanifar, OIC Deposition 12/10/87, p. 94.

[8] Zucker, FBI 302, 12/12–18/87, p. 24.

[9] Haskell, FBI 302, 7/6–7/87, p. 14.

[10] David Morabia, his father Elliot and his mother Nan assisted Zucker in laundering cash deliveries to various U.S. clients. See Other Money Matters chapter.

come of $147,000 in 1985, which consisted mainly of Secord's salary. Secord's personal return for 1985 shows none of the income he realized on arms sales to the contras or Iran.

On Schedule B of his 1985 personal return, Secord answered "no" when asked whether he had any foreign financial accounts. Secord was not charged with giving false information on his income tax form because the Swiss financial records available to Independent Counsel at the time of his indictment could not be used in a tax case, under the provisions of the treaty through which the records were obtained. But Secord's failure to give honest answers on his tax forms provides evidence of his motive in attempting to deliberately conceal his profits.

## Secord's Testimony to Congress and Independent Counsel

In December 1986, when subpoenaed by the congressional intelligence committees, Secord refused to testify, invoking his Fifth Amendment right against self-incrimination. In late April 1987, however, Secord agreed to testify voluntarily before the Select Iran/contra Committees; he also agreed to be interviewed by OIC.[11] Secord, the Committees' first witness, testified from May 5 to 8, 1987. He was recalled and deposed by Congress in June 1987.

Secord's congressional testimony can be characterized in two ways: He provided an enormous amount of largely truthful information regarding the Enterprise's operational workings; his responses to questions about its financial activities were much less candid. Secord's testimony to OIC followed the same pattern: It was generally accurate as to operational matters and blatantly false regarding his personal finances.

OIC investigators were handicapped in early interviews with Secord by a lack of access to the Swiss financial records of the Enterprise, which did not become available until November 1987. The absence of these records, together with the need to remain unexposed to records produced by Hakim to Congress under a grant of limited immunity, made it difficult to exam-

ine Secord on specific transactions. This problem was largely cured by the time Secord was deposed by Independent Counsel for two days in January 1988, after receipt of Swiss records. Secord, nevertheless, continued to lie about his personal finances.

## Secord Indicted: March 1988 and May 1989

In March 1988, Secord was indicted with North, Poindexter and Hakim on conspiracy and theft charges and on three additional charges involving illegal gratuities offered or paid to North. The trials of the four defendants were severed because of problems arising from the grants of immunity by Congress. The conspiracy and theft charges were dismissed due to classified-information problems,[12] leaving Secord to face the three remaining North-gratuities charges.

In May 1989, Secord was charged in a supplemental indictment with nine additional counts of obstruction, perjury and false statements. In November 1989, he pleaded guilty to one felony charge of false statements to Congress, admitting that he lied when he denied that North had received personal benefits from the Enterprise.

## Gratuities to North: The Basis for the Guilty Plea

Four of the criminal charges facing Secord involved illegal gratuities for North. The evidence showed that Secord and Hakim wanted to ensure that North would continue in his position as an NSC staff member so that they could continue to profit from the covert operations that North oversaw.

Specifically, the charges centered on Secord paying for a $16,000 security system for North's home in Great Falls, Virginia. In addition, Secord and Hakim established for North and his family a $200,000 Swiss investment fund. Because North was a Government official, the gifts amounted to illegal gratuities. As a result of these facts, Secord pleaded guilty to lying in the following exchange with congressional investigators in June 1987:

---

[11] In February 1987, Secord appeared before the Grand Jury investigating Iran/contra and refused to testify. In March, he appeared before U.S. District Chief Judge Aubrey E. Robinson, Jr., in response to a corporate subpoena and denied having custody of Enterprise records. Otherwise, Secord did not respond to OIC inquiries during early 1987.

[12] See North chapter.

Q: Mr. Secord, did there—are you aware of any money from the Enterprise which went to the benefit of Mr. North?

A: No.

## The North Security Fence

In the spring of 1986, Secord introduced North to Glenn A. Robinette, a former CIA agent who became involved in a variety of operations for the Enterprise. At Secord's request, Robinette purchased and installed for North a home-security system, after North was reportedly targeted for assassination by the Abu Nidal terrorist group. On May 19, 1986, Robinette paid a subcontractor $6,000 for part of the system's installation. On May 20, Robinette received from Secord $7,000 in cash.

During July and August, Robinette spent an additional $8,000 on the North security system. Following a request from Robinette to Secord, the Enterprise issued a check for $9,000 to Robinette on August 20.

After exposure of the Iran/contra affair in November 1986, Secord, Robinette and North tried to cover up the gratuity paid to North. In December 1986, North asked Robinette to send him a "bill" for the security system. Robinette sent North two back-dated bills dated July and September 1986. North in turn sent Robinette two back-dated letters in which arrangements for future "payment" of the security system were discussed. When Robinette informed Secord of the letters he had sent North, Secord said, "Fine. Glad you did." [13]

## The "B. Button" Account and Phantom Job Discussions

Secord and Hakim in 1986 provided a fund for North and his family by establishing a $200,000 Swiss investment account, the "B. Button" account. Evidence regarding this account was part of the Government's proffer to support Secord's guilty plea.

In February 1986, Secord and Hakim asked Zucker in Switzerland to find a way to transfer Enterprise money to North to help defray the costs of educating his children. First, they arranged a meeting between Zucker and North's wife, Betsy. Zucker met with Mrs. North in Philadelphia in March 1986, where he got information from her regarding the North children. As a first step, Zucker opened a new Enterprise bank account—Hyde Park Square Corporation—with a $200,000 deposit. Using a Government encryption device to relay a message, Secord in April 1986 informed North of the existence of a "200 K Insurance Fund."

In May 1986, Zucker transferred the $200,000 from the Hyde Park Square account to an account titled "B. Button." In Zucker's handwritten notes, "Mrs. Button's" phone number was the same as North's residence. Zucker called Mrs. North a few weeks after establishing the B. Button account, but Mrs. North was unavailable for another meeting. Zucker reported this to Secord. Independent Counsel could not prove that North accepted or received any of the money.

During the summer of 1986, Zucker continued to look for ways to transfer funds to the North family. In September 1986, at Hakim's urging, Zucker met with a Washington, D.C., attorney to create a phantom real-estate job for Mrs. North so that bogus commissions could be paid to her. This arrangement was never consummated.

Secord also provided cash to North. In September 1985, North purchased a vehicle for $9,500, shortly after Secord gave North $3,000 in cash, according to Secord's handwritten notes. North testified at his trial that he paid for the vehicle with money from a $15,000 cash fund kept in a metal box in his bedroom closet, in which he deposited pocket change.[14]

## Obstruction, Perjury and False Statements

In addition to the four gratuity-related charges against Secord, he faced eight charges based on false testimony to Congress about his Enterprise profits. The charges, in summary, were:

—*Obstruction of Congress.* Secord testified falsely about his economic interest in and benefits from the Enterprise, as well as about its financial structure and the manner in which accounts were manipulated to conceal individual profit interests.

[13] North was convicted in 1989 of accepting an illegal gratuity— the home-security system—from Secord. This conviction was overturned on appeal.

[14] North, *North* Trial Testimony, 4/10/89, pp. 7150–51.

—*"Korel" perjury.* Secord in May 1987 falsely testified before the congressional Select Committees that: (1) Enterprise profits had been kept for him under his name and not under a pseudonym; (2) Korel was not his company and not a repository for his profits; and (3) his interest in Korel was no different from his interest in the other companies constituting the Enterprise. In fact, profits from the Enterprise were kept for Secord in the Korel account, which was established and maintained exclusively for him. As mentioned previously, Secord subsequently admitted in the *Clines* trial that Korel was, in fact, his investment account.

—*Perjury regarding the foreswearing of profits.* Secord testified falsely to the Select Committees in May 1987 that: (1) he waived all interest in Enterprise profits in July–August 1985 and thereafter retained no personal economic interest in Enterprise companies; (2) his personal profits were returned to the Enterprise; and (3) Zucker only managed personal profits for Secord of about $400,000 for a period of months until those funds were "washed out" when he foreswore his profits.

In fact, Secord retained an economic interest in the profits of the Enterprise, continued to receive benefits from it and used Zucker on a continuous basis to manage the Korel account, which held in excess of $1 million in profits. While Secord said he was foreswearing his profits in July 1985, he was actually arranging to conceal his profit distributions in Korel, signing a fiduciary agreement with CSF in September.

Zucker was never informed that Secord had foresworn his profits until a discussion with Secord in December 1986 in Geneva, after the Iran/contra affair was publicly exposed. According to Zucker, Secord said: "you do remember that I said that I had renounced all interest in any of these accounts." [15] Zucker did not respond, knowing the assertion was false.

---

[15] Zucker, FBI 302, 11/6–10/87, pp. 4–5.

—*Perjury regarding Iranian proceeds.* Secord testified falsely before the Select Committees in May 1987 that: (1) he did not personally receive any money from the Iran arms sales beyond his $6,000 monthly salary; (2) he and Hakim agreed not to make a profit on the sales; and (3) Hakim received no profit from the sales. In fact, both Secord and Hakim did receive personal funds from the Iran arms sales, and Secord received funds beyond his monthly salary.

—*Perjury about payments to STTGI.* Secord testified falsely before the Select Committees in May 1987 that it was "his belief" that $500,000 that STTGI received from CSF was "the result of the line of credit loan that [STTGI] signed with CSF in 1985." STTGI actually received at least $700,000. According to Zucker and CSF documents, none of it constituted a loan from CSF.

—*Perjury about "Tri-American Arms."* Secord lied to the Select Committees in May 1987 about an investment in Tri-American Arms, a Colorado weapons company. First, Secord testified falsely that a $150,000 transfer to Tri-American Arms came from Hakim's profit distribution and not from other Enterprise funds. Second, he falsely denied that one of the purposes of Tri-American was to sell weapons to the contras.

In fact, it is undisputed that the $150,000 transfer to Tri-American Arms came from an Enterprise disbursement account—Albon Values—and not from Hakim's personal funds. Notes taken at a meeting of would-be investors in April 1986 showed that weapons sales to the contras were contemplated, and Secord himself told a federal law-enforcement agent in 1986 that one of the potential markets was the contras.

—*Perjury about the Defex Account.* Secord before the Select Committees in May 1987 falsely asserted that the Enterprise's "Defex" account was established to hide the source and location of Enterprise funds from arms dealers. In fact, the Defex S.A. account was opened to conceal from contra leaders and U.S. officials the profits Secord and his partners were receiving on weapons sales to the contras.

—*Perjury about foreign bank accounts.* Secord falsely denied before the Select Committees in May 1987 that he had any beneficial interest in any foreign financial accounts, with the exception of a British checking account with a small balance. In fact, Secord had substantial beneficial interests in Swiss Enterprise accounts.

# Chapter 10
# United States v. Albert Hakim

Albert Hakim, an Iranian-born American citizen, did not claim to be a patriot, acting out of unselfish interests in the Enterprise. He described himself as a businessman with a clear profit motive. But like retired Air Force Maj. Gen. Richard V. Secord, he concealed the size of his personal profits for tax purposes. He also arranged illegal gratuities to North in order to use North's Government office to serve his own money-making interests.

On November 21, 1989, Hakim pleaded guilty to an information charging a misdemeanor count of supplementing the salary of a Government officer, North. Hakim's corporation, Lake Resources Inc., pleaded guilty to a corporate felony of illegally diverting to the contras and to other unauthorized purposes U.S. funds generated by the sale of arms to Iran.[1]

Following his guilty plea, Hakim entered into a separate civil agreement with Independent Counsel. Under the agreement, Hakim agreed to accept $1.7 million of the funds on deposit in Swiss accounts and waive his claim to the remainder of the $9 million[2] in funds frozen in the Swiss Enterprise accounts in December 1986. From the amount he received, Hakim agreed to settle two other claims on the funds— $800,000 claimed by Zucker for legal expenses and $120,000 claimed by Phillippe Neyroud, Hakim's Swiss lawyer, for legal fees.[3] This was to leave the United States the only claimant of the funds. It was to have received $7.3 mil-

lion. The agreement, which had been approved by the Department of Justice, did not bar the United States from seeking civil damages from Hakim or taking tax action against him. Although Hakim agreed to take all steps necessary to facilitate the recovery of the funds by the United States, he subsequently refused to carry out his agreement.[4]

## Criminal Charges Brought

In March 1988, Albert Hakim was charged with five felonies as a co-defendant with Vice Adm. John M. Poindexter, Lt. Col. Oliver L. North and Secord. He was charged with conspiracy to defraud the United States, illegal conversion of U.S. Government property, wire fraud, conspiracy to pay illegal gratuities to North, and offering to pay an illegal gratuity to North.

The first two of these charged offenses— the conspiracy and theft charges—would have been dismissed due to classified-information problems, had the case against Hakim gone to trial; the third had previously been dismissed as duplicative.[5] The remaining counts involved Hakim and Secord's attempts to provide North with gratuities to encourage him to remain on the National Security Council staff and continue to use Secord and Hakim in pursuing his efforts with Iran.

As described earlier, in 1985 and 1986, Albert Hakim had received $2.06 million from the Enterprise. He also received $550,249 in cash; $478,508 of which went for unknown purposes. Hakim also used Enterprise funds to invest with Secord in over $1,040,000 worth of business ventures.

---

[1] The guilty pleas of Hakim and Lake Resources were obtained by Associate Counsel Stuart E. Abrams, Geoffrey S. Berman and William M. Treanor, who would have prosecuted the case had it gone to trial.

[2] As of December 31, 1986, the amount of Enterprise funds frozen in Swiss accounts at the request of the United States was $7.8 million. As of December 1989—the time of Hakim's agreement—approximately $1.2 million in interest had accrued, bringing the total to $9 million.

[3] Since this agreement was under negotiation, Secord filed a claim in the Swiss courts for the money in the Enterprise accounts.

[4] The recovery of the funds is now being pursued through litigation.

[5] See Secord chapter.

## Gratuities to North

In support of Hakim's guilty plea, Independent Counsel offered evidence to show that by early 1986, Secord and Hakim had become aware that North was having family problems because of reported threats on his life, the long hours he worked, and his financial difficulties. Because Secord and Hakim believed that North's wife was pressing him to leave the NSC, they attempted to reduce her anxiety by providing North with gratuities.

Secord took the lead. He arranged for a $16,000 security system to be installed at North's home, paid for by Enterprise funds.6 Hakim then undertook to transfer a significant sum of money from Swiss Enterprise accounts to North. Early in 1986, Hakim instructed Zucker, the money manager of the Swiss Enterprise accounts, to meet with Mrs. North to discuss the provision of financial support for North's children. Mrs. North traveled to Philadelphia to meet Zucker on March 6, 1986. She gave him the ages and school prospects of her children. After Zucker reported this meeting to Secord and Hakim, they directed him to set up a $200,000 investment account for North in Switzerland. As previously explained, this account, called the B. Button account, was calculated to produce funds for the education of North's children as they needed it.

In June 1986, Hakim asked Zucker to speak to Mrs. North a second time. Hakim told Zucker to tell Mrs. North that they had "advanced the ball," that something had been done. Zucker called Mrs. North on June 4, 1986, and asked her to meet with him in Philadelphia on June 5 or 6. She declined, saying she had other commitments. The $200,000 is among those funds still frozen in Swiss bank accounts.

After the establishment of the Button account, Hakim had several more conversations with Zucker in which he urged Zucker to find other ways to get money to North. These included the possibility of someone making a gift to the Norths, the possibility of finding Mrs. North a no-show job, the possibility of providing her with unearned real estate commissions, or the possibility of providing some commission or fee for allegedly introducing business to someone.

As he attempted to pursue these options, Zucker had several conversations with Washington attorney David Lewis. In one he asked whether someone needed a broker's license to receive a real estate commission in Washington, D.C., or Maryland. In a subsequent conversation, Zucker told Lewis that he had a client who wanted to get money to someone in the form of a commission or a job and asked Lewis whether he knew of anyone who might be of assistance.

## Possible Tax Crimes

Records obtained by Independent Counsel pursuant to the Swiss Treaty showed that Albert Hakim engaged in tax fraud with respect to his 1985 income tax returns, substantially underreporting his gross income and taxable income, and failing to file reports on his foreign financial accounts.

The treaty under which Independent Counsel obtained the Enterprise financial records from Switzerland explicitly provides that the records cannot be used in the prosecution of tax crimes. Unless the records could be obtained from some source other than pursuant to the treaty, they could not be used in a tax prosecution. Thus, though the financial records showed Hakim had violated tax laws, they could not be used in a criminal prosecution against him.

## The Lake Resources Plea

Hakim was the principal shareholder in Lake Resources, Inc., a Panamanian shell corporation established in May 1985. This corporation was the owner of the account at Credit Suisse Bank in Geneva that was the Enterprise account that received the proceeds from the Iran arms sales.

At the time Hakim entered his guilty plea on November 21, 1989, Lake Resources pleaded guilty to a corporate felony charge of illegally diverting from the U.S. Government $16.2 million in proceeds from the sale of U.S. arms to Iran.

---

6 Secord pleaded guilty to falsely denying before Congress that North had benefitted from the Enterprise. See Secord chapter.

# Chapter 11
# United States v. Thomas G. Clines, a.k.a. "C. Tea"

Thomas G. Clines, a retired CIA agent, earned nearly $883,000 helping retired Air Force Maj. Gen. Richard V. Secord and Albert Hakim carry out the secret operations of the Enterprise. Clines oversaw the logistics of purchasing weapons from private suppliers in Europe and arranging for their delivery to Central America. In early contra weapons sales in 1985, he received 20 percent of the profits; in 1986, he began receiving a third of the profits from the contra sales.

In February 1990, following the guilty pleas and promises of cooperation by Secord and Hakim, Clines was indicted and charged with concealing from the Internal Revenue Service the full amount of his Enterprise profits for the 1985 and 1986 tax years. He was charged also with denying on his 1985 and 1986 income-tax returns his foreign financial accounts, in which he hid his Enterprise profits and from which he and his surrogates transferred thousands of dollars to his U.S. bank accounts.

In September 1990, Clines was convicted of four income-tax-related felony charges, following a two-week jury trial in U.S. District Court in Baltimore, Maryland, before Judge Norman P. Ramsey.[1]

## The Charges

Clines was charged with two felony counts of falsely underreporting his gross receipts on his 1985 and 1986 tax returns. He was charged also with two felony counts of falsely denying

having foreign financial accounts on his tax returns for 1985 and 1986.

Clines on his 1985 tax return falsely reported his gross receipts as totaling $265,000—or $203,431 less than his income from his Enterprise activities proved at trial. On his 1986 tax return, Clines reported his gross receipts as $402,513—or $57,009 less than he actually received from the Enterprise. In both cases, Independent Counsel's estimates of Clines' underreported income were conservative.

Regarding his foreign financial accounts, Clines denied having such accounts on 1985 and 1986 income tax forms requiring their disclosure. In fact, Independent Counsel proved through extensive documentation and testimony that Clines had knowledge and control of large sums of money abroad in two secret Swiss accounts: the "T.C." capital account he maintained with Compagnie de Services Fiduciaires (CSF) in Geneva in 1985, and the "C. Tea" investment account he maintained with CSF in 1986.

## The Clines Trial

The central prosecution witnesses at the *Clines* trial were Secord, who was compelled to testify under a cooperation agreement with Independent Counsel, and Willard Zucker, the CSF financial manager of the secret Swiss Enterprise accounts and shell corporations, who also testified under a grant of immunity from prosecution. Thomas Cusick, a special agent with the Internal Revenue Service, testified about the complex financial structure of the Enterprise.

Clines, a 30-year veteran of the CIA, after leaving the agency in 1978, had developed significant contacts with arms dealers in Western Europe and behind the Iron Curtain. In 1985

---

[1] The prosecution's case was presented by Associate Counsel Stuart E. Abrams, Geoffrey S. Berman and William M. Treanor.

The trial was held in U.S. District Court in Baltimore because Clines' accountant was based in Bethesda, Maryland, and filed Clines' tax forms there.

and 1986, after becoming involved in the Enterprise, Clines was responsible for locating and
purchasing weapons abroad and shipping them
to Central America. He worked primarily with
the arms company Defex Portugal, maintaining
a small office at the company in Lisbon. When
the Enterprise became involved in secret U.S.
weapons shipments to Iran late in 1985, Clines
also became active in this aspect of its activities.[2]

In 1985, Clines began receiving 20 percent
of the profits from each arms shipment, plus
expenses. He received his first share in April
1985, when $310,840 was distributed among
Secord and Hakim, who each received
$124,366, and Clines, who got $62,168. A capital account was maintained by CSF for Clines.
He had some of this money wired from this
account to the United States, withdrew some
of it in cash, and transferred some amounts
to a third party for his benefit. In 1985, a total
of $155,000 was wired from Clines' capital ac-
count to his account at First American Bank
in Virginia. Clines also made cash withdrawals
from the TC capital account totaling $217,820.
At trial the evidence showed that Clines' gross
receipts in 1985 were at least $468,431. This
figure represented $423,431 from the Enterprise
and $45,000 from non-Enterprise sources. The
estimate was conservative.

In 1986, as the Enterprise continued selling
arms to the contras, its involvement in the secret
U.S. sale of arms to Iran generated a new
source of funds for Clines, Secord, and Hakim.
Clines' share of the distributions increased to
30 percent, like Secord and Hakim. (The final
10 percent of the distribution went to Scitech,
a company jointly owned by Secord and
Hakim.) As a result of these pro-rated distributions, Clines received $420,238 in 1986. In ad-
dition, Clines received four small distributions
from the Enterprise in 1986. On February 18,
1986, CSF transferred $7,000 to the bank ac-
count of a friend of Clines in South Carolina
for Clines' personal benefit. On May 2, 1986,
CSF wired $1,137 and on July 7, 1986, CSF

wired $1,147 to the Klinik Buchinger to pay
for Clines' attendance at that weight-reduction
clinic. On November 10, 1986, CSF transferred
$30,000 into an investment account that Clines
maintained with CSF. Thus, Clines' total receipts from the Enterprise in 1986 were at least
$459,522.[3]

When Clines opened an Enterprise account
in late spring or early summer 1986, he decided
to use an assumed name. Zucker suggested ''C.
Tea,'' and Clines agreed. Clines signed the
agreement using his assumed name, C. Tea;
his real name does not appear on that document.
Clines earned income of $17,135.10 on the de-
posits in the C. Tea account during 1986.

Enterprise activities were effectively curtailed
in November 1986 with the exposure of the
Iran arms sales. Clines expressed concern about
his inability to obtain his funds. Hakim, at
Clines' request, persuaded Zucker[4] to release
Clines' funds.

When Zucker began to liquidate Clines' investment account on December 4, 1986, Clines
instructed Zucker that he wanted the funds
transferred to a numbered Swiss bank account
that Zucker recognized as Defex Portugal.
Clines gave Zucker a letter specifying that the
money was to be transferred for ''services rendered.'' On December 19, 1986, CSF transferred $311,600 as directed. Thereafter, Clines
told Secord in December 1986 that he had received his money from Zucker.

At trial, Clines acknowledged that he had
the C. Tea funds transferred to a Defex Portugal
account so it could be handled for Clines' by
Defex head Jose Garnel. According to Clines,
only $266,000 had been transferred to Defex

---

[2] Clines accompanied Secord in late November 1985 to Europe to
facilitate a snagged shipment of U.S. HAWK missiles from Israel to
Iran. In the summer of 1986, Clines became involved in an unsuccessful
Ross Perot-funded hostage-rescue operation in which the Enterprise's
Danish freighter, the *Erria*, waited off the coast of Cyprus where
a $1 million exchange was to be made for a hostage release. This
operation did not result in a release.

[3] Clines also received $70,000 in other payments from the Enterprise
in 1986. But since the underlying documents did not clearly establish
the nature of these additional funds, they were not included in the
estimate of Clines' underreporting. In addition, in 1986 Clines' bank
accounts in the United States received wire transfers of $160,000 from
unknown foreign sources. This money was not included in calculating
Clines' true gross receipts.

[4] The Government proffered at trial that, if permitted to testify about
his conversation with Hakim, Zucker would testify that ''Mr. Hakim
alerted Mr. Zucker to the fact that Mr. Clines was a former CIA
field operative and was potentially violent, and [Mr. Hakim] suggested
that Mr. Zucker should give him his money back.'' (Zucker, *Clines*
Trial Testimony, 9/7/90, p. 551.) The Government contended that this
testimony was admissible as to Zucker's state of mind, since, on the
cross-examination of Secord, defense counsel had elicited testimony
that Zucker was a ''basket case'' in early December 1986. (Secord,
*Clines* Trial Testimony, 9/5/90, p. 214). The Court ruled the substance
of the Hakim-Zucker conversation inadmissible. (Zucker, *Clines* Trial
Testimony, 9/7/90, pp. 552–53.)

from the C. Tea account. In fact, $311,600 had actually been transferred. Clines testified that he only learned this after being indicted. Clines described a complicated series of personal "loans" between him and Garnel. He said he believed Garnel deliberately concealed the true amount and stole the difference from him.

The Garnel-Clines "loans" were among a series of Clines' financial maneuvers to conceal income. In addition, Clines stored large amounts of cash in Swiss safety deposit boxes, withdrawing and carrying funds to banks and individuals, who would subsequently wire the amounts to his U.S. bank accounts. He also signed over real estate holdings to friends and family, while continuing to pay for them and claiming the payments as income-tax deductions.

In his 1985 and 1986 tax returns, Clines followed a consistent practice: He reported what he believed the Government knew and could prove against him, and nothing more. Beginning in 1982, Clines used as his accountant Melvyn Leshinsky, in Bethesda, Maryland. As previously discussed, Clines' gross receipts in 1985 were at least $468,431. The figure he actually reported was $265,000, a shortfall of $203,431. The basis for the $265,000 figure was Clines' January 10, 1986, letter to Leshinsky listing his gross income for 1985 "as reflected on my bank statements"—exactly the amount that he brought into the United States that was traceable to him. The money that Clines left abroad was not reported.

In answering "no" to the question whether Clines had an interest in or authority over a foreign account, Leshinsky specifically asked Clines whether he had an account in any foreign country; Clines said he did not. In 1983, Clines and various of his corporate entities had been the subject of a criminal investigation. Leshinsky in the context of that investigation, found that Clines controlled a bank account in Bermuda in 1981 and had not reported it. Leshinsky had to have Clines file a corrected form. Given this prior record, it was clear that Clines was familiar with the reporting requirement for foreign accounts.[5]

Leshinsky also prepared Clines' 1986 income tax return. Initially, Clines represented to Leshinsky that his gross receipts were $297,673. Later, he informed Leshinsky his gross receipts were $342,673. On the income tax returns as filed, his gross receipts were listed as $402,513, or $57,009 less than his proven gross receipts.

The 1986 income tax return also contained a false denial that Clines had a foreign account. Again, Leshinsky had asked Clines whether he had a foreign account, and Clines answered no. None of the $17,135 Clines earned in income from his C. Tea account was reported.

At trial, Clines claimed that the underreporting on tax returns arose from his inability to understand the difference between net and gross income. He referred to his 1985 capital account as his "profit account," but said he did not believe it was reportable. He nonetheless acknowledged control over the funds. He admitted that the answer on his income tax returns stating that he did not have a foreign account was "incorrect."[6]

Secord attempted to confuse the jury by suggesting that Government evidence against Clines was based on inaccurate financial records fabricated, or "cooked," by Hakim.[7] In fact, some financial records *were* reconfigured by Zucker at Hakim's request. In late 1986, Hakim instructed CSF to collapse separate profit accounts into one ledger so that payments to Clines, Secord and himself could not be identified. This document, according to Zucker, was known as the "Hakim ledger." The "Hakim ledger," however, was not what the Government used to prove its case. As described previously, Independent Counsel reconstructed the profit accounts, going piece by piece through thousands of pages of foreign and domestic bank records that illuminated in detail the true financial

---

[5] In March 1987, after Clines had been subpoenaed by the Office of Independent Counsel, Leshinsky, Clines, and Clines' then-lawyer John Stein met to review Clines' finances. Clines stated in essence that when his 1985 income tax returns were filed, he had not grasped the difference between net and gross and that the figure on his income

tax returns for gross receipts was actually his net receipts. The three agreed that Clines should file an amended return. The amended return was eventually filed on November 2, 1987. On that return, a gross receipts figure of $486,490 was reported. The cost-of-goods-sold figure of $152,640 was $68,850 short of offsetting the increase in the gross receipts from the original return. The cost-of-goods-sold figure was unsubstantiated: Clines did not provide Leshinsky with any support for that figure. Clines did not tell Leshinsky of reimbursements that he had received from the Enterprise for expenses.

[6] Clines, *Clines* Trial Testimony, 9/14/90, p. 1305.

[7] Secord, *Clines* Trial Testimony, 9/5/90, p. 219.

machinations of the Enterprise and Clines' personal profits.[8]

---

[8] The key to understanding the collapsed profit accounts was provided by Roland Farina, an assistant to Zucker, who retained codes on the Hakim ledger that corresponded to the receipts.

## Verdict and Sentence

The jury found Clines guilty on all four counts in the indictment on September 18, 1990. On December 13, 1990, Judge Ramsey sentenced Clines to 16 months in prison and a $40,000 fine. On appeal, the convictions were affirmed by the U.S. Court of Appeals for the Fourth Circuit. The Supreme Court denied certiorari.

# Chapter 12
# U.S. Efforts To Recover the Enterprise Funds

In December 1986, before Independent Counsel was appointed, the Swiss government at the request of the Department of Justice froze the Enterprise accounts maintained in Switzerland. Sixteen accounts contained funds totaling $7.8 million. While the initial U.S. request for assistance included a request for return of the funds, Independent Counsel's efforts to recover the funds for the United States began in earnest in early 1989, after the bank account records of the Enterprise had been obtained under the Swiss-American Treaty on Mutual Assistance in Criminal Matters and after the indictments of Lt. Col. Oliver L. North, Vice Adm. John M. Poindexter, retired Air Force Maj. Gen. Richard V. Secord and Albert Hakim were secured.

In Switzerland, the request for the return of the funds was before the Federal Office for Police Matters. The Office of Independent Counsel made its request through the Justice Department's Office of International Affairs.

Under the mutual assistance treaty, the U.S. request for the return of the funds had to be based on crimes recognized by Swiss law. In the Iran/contra request, the crimes were conspiracy to defraud and embezzlement, which corresponded to Counts One and Two of the indictment brought in March 1988 against North, Poindexter, Secord and Hakim. These counts were eventually dropped because the Reagan Administration refused to declassify certain information the court deemed relevant to the defense of North.[1] It was Independent Counsel's position, however, that the evidence it had provided to the Swiss authorities was sufficient to prove that a fraud on the U.S. Government had occurred.[2]

Challenging the U.S. request for return of the funds were claims in Switzerland reportedly made by Secord, Hakim, Willard Zucker, and Hakim attorney Phillippe Neyroud. Although Hakim, after his criminal plea in November 1989, agreed to settle his claim for $1.7 million of the funds and to settle the claims of others within that amount, he later reneged on the agreement.

In February 1992, the Federal Office for Police Matters advised the Office of Independent Counsel that it would not return the funds to the United States because the conspiracy and embezzlement charges had been dismissed. Independent Counsel's appeal of the ruling was rejected by the Swiss Federal Tribunal on grounds that the United States had no standing to appeal.[3]

Independent Counsel had received the assistance of Richard Owen in the Criminal Division of the Department of Justice. In 1992 OIC requested, pursuant to the Independent Counsel Act, that the Department of Justice's Civil Division take over the matter in the Swiss civil courts.[4] It at first declined. It then assigned a liaison attorney. With the change of Administration, it has now aggressively undertaken efforts to recover the stolen funds. That litigation is pending. At the time of this report to the court, the Enterprise funds, plus several million dollars in interest that has accrued since December 1986, remain frozen in Switzerland.

---

[1] Although as part of the Hakim plea agreement, Lake Resources Inc. in November 1989 pleaded guilty to a corporate felony of defrauding the U.S. Government in the Iran/contra diversion, Swiss law does not recognize corporate criminality. The Lake Resources guilty plea, therefore, could not support Independent Counsel's request for return of the funds.

[2] The standard of proof in the Swiss courts in this matter was "reasonable suspicion." The indictment and Judge Gerhard A. Gesell's upholding of Count One as a crime met the standard of proof.

[3] Decision, Proceeding Nos. 1A.125/1992 and 1A.233/1992 (Swiss Federal Tribunal Mar. 29, 1993).

[4] 28 U.S.C. § 596(b)(2), (1987) P.L. 101–191, 101 Stat. 1305.

# Chapter 13
## Private Fundraising: The Guilty Pleas of Channell and Miller

As funding prospects for the contras grew increasingly dim in the spring of 1984, one source of funds for the contras was wealthy American citizens sympathetic to President Reagan's contra policy and willing to donate large sums to send weapons and other military supplies to the contras. Lt. Col. Oliver L. North of the National Security Council staff worked principally with two private fundraisers—Carl R. "Spitz" Channell and Richard R. Miller—to solicit donations through a tax-exempt foundation, the National Endowment for the Preservation of Liberty (NEPL).

NEPL in 1985 and 1986 received $6,323,020 for the contras. Because of overhead costs, commissions and salaries taken by the fundraisers, it disbursed to the contras at North's direction only $3,306,882.

In the spring of 1987 Channell and Miller each pleaded guilty to a felony: conspiracy to defraud the United States. Together they provided extensive information about their fundraising activities. The pleas were based on Channell and Miller's illegal use of a tax-exempt organization to raise funds for non-charitable items, including weapons and other lethal supplies for the contras.[1]

On April 29, 1987, Channell pleaded guilty to a felony charge of conspiracy to defraud the United States. At the time of his plea, Channell entered into an agreement with Independent Counsel requiring him to cooperate with the investigation and to provide truthful testimony in future court proceedings.

On May 6, 1987, Miller entered a plea of guilty to the felony charge of conspiring to defraud the United States. At the time of his plea, Miller agreed to cooperate with Independent Counsel's investigation and to provide truthful testimony in subsequent court proceedings.

Supplementing the information provided by Channell and Miller, a number of their subordinates and associates entered into cooperation agreements with Independent Counsel in exchange for immunity from prosecution. They included: Channell employees Daniel L. Conrad, F. Clifton Smith, Krishna S. Littledale and Jane McLaughlin; Miller associate Francis Gomez; and Channell-Miller consultant David Fischer.

Both Channell and Miller in the allocutions preceding their guilty pleas identified North as an unindicted co-conspirator. Both men testified at the trial of North, who was acquitted of the charge of conspiracy to commit tax fraud and making false statements to Congress regarding his fundraising activities.[2]

## National Endowment for the Preservation of Liberty (NEPL)

Channell formed NEPL in 1984. He obtained Internal Revenue Service approval to operate it as a tax-exempt organization based on his representations that its activities were not for profit and focused on the study, analysis and evaluation of the American socioeconomic and political systems. NEPL was exempted from taxes under Section 501(c)(3) of the Internal Revenue Code, which covers groups organized exclusively for "religious, charitable, scientific, testing for public safety, literary or educational"

---

[1] The Channell and Miller guilty pleas were obtained principally through the work of Associate Counsel Michael R. Bromwich and David M. Zornow.

[2] The private fundraising in which North engaged with Channell and Miller also formed part of the central diversion-conspiracy charge against North, which was dismissed due to classified-information problems before the case came to trial.

purposes. Channell was NEPL's president and Daniel L. Conrad its executive director.

Channell had years of experience in raising funds for conservative political causes. As a result, he was asked by White House officials early in 1985 to help organize a "Nicaraguan Refugee Fund Dinner" to raise money for the contra cause. Channell became disenchanted with the way the dinner-planning had been conducted, and in April 1985 he approached White House political director Edward Rollins to offer his assistance in promoting President Reagan's contra policies.

He was referred to White House political aide John Roberts, who in turn directed him to Miller, a private public relations consultant who ran a firm known as International Business Communications (IBC).[3] According to Channell, Roberts told him that Miller and his partner Frank Gomez "are the White House—outside the White House."[4]

By the late spring of 1985, Channell and Miller had begun raising money for direct aid to the contras through NEPL.[5] Channell had developed a fundraising technique in which a comparatively small number of wealthy potential contributors were invited to briefings with Administration officials in Washington and then solicited for donations.

## The North Briefings

The success of the Channell-Miller operation was dependent on donors recognizing its close

ties to the White House. Miller introduced Channell to North, who in June 1985 began giving personal and group briefings for NEPL contributors on the war in Nicaragua and the needs of the contras. North's dramatic presentation style prompted many wealthy donors to give tens of thousands of dollars immediately following these briefings.

North testified that he received permission from his immediate superior Donald Fortier and from National Security Adviser Robert C. McFarlane in 1985 to engage in fundraising with Channell and Miller.[6] North said he was told, however, that he could not solicit donations directly for the contras under the Boland prohibition. As a result, North said, he would provide information about contras needs and then leave it to Channell and others to follow with a solicitation. North's participation in these fundraising events gave a clear White House endorsement to the Channell-Miller operation, and although North may not have specifically asked for money, he was a party to a joint effort to solicit it. He had no other purpose in briefing wealthy donors.

Following the first NEPL briefing at the White House in June 1985, Channell presented contra leader Adolfo Calero with a $50,000 check. But shortly after this direct payment, Channell expressed concerns to North that the donations might be unwisely used if they were given directly to contra leaders.[7] North told Channell to direct funds to Miller at IBC. Miller, in turn, transferred the bulk of these funds to a Cayman Islands bank account, I.C. Inc., that he had established in coordination with North.[8] At North's direction, Miller transferred $1.7 million to the Enterprise's Swiss accounts. (See "Flow of Funds from Contributors through NEPL to Lake" chart, next page.)

---

[3] In 1984, Miller and his partner Gomez began providing public relations advice to contra leader Adolfo Calero. Calero's Nicaraguan Development Council between September 1984 and May 1985 paid $55,000 in retainer fees to IBC. (Miller, FBI 302, 7/8/87, p. 4.)

[4] Channell, Select Committees Deposition, 9/1/87, p. 53.

[5] Shortly before Miller and Channell joined forces, Miller and North in March 1985 began pursuing a promised contra donation from a man named Mousalreza Ebrahim Zadeh, also known as Al-Masoudi, who fraudulently represented himself as a member of the Saudi royal family. Miller and North referred to him as "the prince."

In various efforts to assist Zadeh throughout 1985 and to obtain from him a promised $14 million donation to the contras, Miller estimated that he disbursed more than $270,000 in IBC funds, which had been earmarked for the contras and raised by Channell's NEPL organization. (Miller Grand Jury, 6/17/87, p. 104.) According to Miller, North was aware of these expenditures and said that the needs of the contras were so great that money spent on Zadeh from funds intended for the contras were justified.

By the fall of 1985, the FBI had begun investigating Zadeh for bank fraud. The FBI informed Miller that Zadeh was not a Saudi prince but an Iranian national and con-man. Despite this warning, Miller remained in contact with Zadeh to obtain information about American hostages in the Middle East and continued to pay some of his expenses. In 1986 Zadeh pleaded guilty to bank fraud charges. (Miller, FBI 302, 7/8/87.)

[6] North, *North* trial testimony, 4/10/89, p. 7217.

Fortier died in August 1986. McFarlane denied authorizing fund solicitation, but he pleaded guilty in March 1988 to misleading Congress based in part on false representations he made about NSC staff fundraising activities in letters in 1985 to the House Permanent Select Committee on Intelligence and the House Foreign Affairs Subcommittee on Western Hemisphere Affairs. See McFarlane chapter.

[7] In June 1985, North and Secord informed contra leaders that they would no longer receive money directly for weapons purchases, but that funding would go to the Enterprise, which would purchase weapons for them.

[8] The name of I.C., Inc., was later changed to Intel Co-operation, Inc.

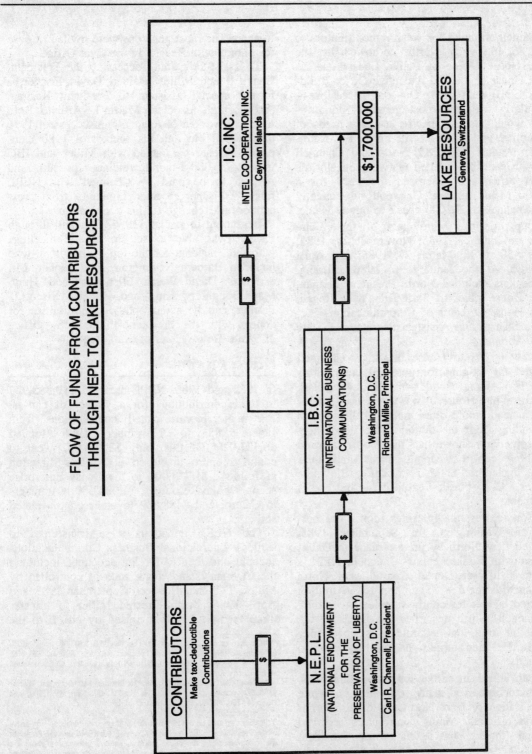

FLOW OF FUNDS FROM CONTRIBUTORS
THROUGH NEPL TO LAKE RESOURCES

Channell arranged for wealthy contributors to attend briefings by North, co-hosted by the White House Office of Public Liaison, at the White House or the Old Executive Office Building (OEOB) next door. On some occasions—particularly with the most generous donors—North would discuss specific military needs of the contras, and their specific costs. For example, on August 23, 1985, North and Channell met with contributor Ellen Garwood in North's OEOB office and discussed the need for a $75,000 Maule aircraft; Garwood subsequently gave Channell a $75,000 check to buy a Maule.

Group briefings were held at the White House on June 27, 1985; November 21, 1985; January 30, 1986; March 27, 1986; and April 16, 1986. At the January 30, 1986, briefing, the speakers included North, President Reagan, White House Chief of Staff Donald T. Regan, White House Director of Communications Patrick Buchanan, and Assistant Secretary of State Elliott Abrams.

Following White House briefings, Channell arranged for lodging for potential contributors at the Hay-Adams Hotel, across Lafayette Park from the White House. It was at the Hay-Adams that Channell would often make his direct pitch for funding from the donors. Potential donors were sometimes shown lists that North prepared describing contra weapons needs and their prices, including SAM–7 missiles, Blowpipe missiles, C–4 plastic explosives and other equipment.

In some cases, the briefings took place outside of Washington. In September 1985, Channell flew North by private plane to Dallas to meet with Bunker Hunt.[9] Channell, NEPL's executive director Daniel Conrad, and North brought with them a $5 million to $6 million projected budget for contra supplies. According to Channell, North described the needs of the contras but told Hunt he couldn't ask for money himself. He then turned the meeting over to Channell.

As an added incentive for future donations, contributors received thank-you letters on White House stationery from North and other Administration officials. Major contributors received personal thanks in letters from President Reagan. The most generous were invited to pose for photos with Reagan in the Oval Office.

To assist in gaining access to the President, Channell and Miller retained David Fischer, a former special assistant to President Reagan, and Fischer's associate, Martin L. Artiano. Both men had worked in Reagan's unsuccessful 1976 presidential bid and his successful 1980 campaign. Fischer contracted with Miller and IBC for a $20,000-a-month retainer for him and Artiano to be paid by Channell with NEPL funds.[10] Fischer received immunity from prosecution in exchange for his cooperation.

Beginning in January 1986, Channell through Fischer was able to set up private meetings with the President for the top contributors, who included Barbara Newington, Fred Sacher, Mr. and Mrs. David Warm, Ellen Garwood, Hunt, May Dougherty King and Robert Driscoll.[11] Fischer said he set up photo opportunities for donors with the President through the Office of White House Chief of Staff Regan.[12]

## NEPL Income

In 1985 and 1986, NEPL received $10,385,929 in total contributions for a variety of causes. The major contra-related contributions from June 1985 to November 1986 totaled $6,323,020. Of this, only $3,306,882 went to contra support, disbursed at North's direction as follows: $1,738,000 to the Swiss Enterprise account Lake Resources; $1,080,000 in transfers to Calero; and $488,882 to other contra-related activities.

The NEPL donations were transferred to Miller's International Business Communications account and then to foreign accounts, including the Cayman Islands bank account controlled by Miller, I.C. Inc. Between September 1985 and April 1986, North directed Miller to transfer more than $1.7 million raised by NEPL to the

---

[9] Channell, *North* Trial Testimony, 3/8/89, pp. 3414–15.

[10] Fischer denied allegations that he received $50,000 from NEPL for each meeting he set up with President Reagan. (Fischer, FBI 302, 5/5/87, p. 4; Grand Jury 12/2/87, p. 69.) Independent Counsel found no evidence supporting these allegations.

[11] Newington contributed $1,148,471; Sacher $400,000; the Warms $355,232; Garwood $2,546,598; Hunt $475,000; King $921,500; and Driscoll $106,000. These were the top donors.

[12] Fischer, FBI 302, 3/18/87, p. 3.

Fischer said that he described to Regan these individuals as supporters of the President and the Republican party. Fischer said that the President was told, preceding the photo sessions, general information about the people, including the fact that they supported his contra policy. (Fischer, Grand Jury, 12/2/87, pp. 49–53.)

Enterprise's Lake Resources account in Switzerland, including:

| | | |
|---|---|---|
| 9/20/85: | $130,000 | from the I.C. Inc. account |
| 9/26/85: | $100,000 | from the I.C. Inc. account |
| 11/1/85: | $150,000 | from the I.C. Inc. account |
| 11/18/85: | $48,000 | from the I.C. Inc. account |
| 12/16/85: | $300,000 | from the IBC account |
| 1/21/86: | $360,000 | from the I.C. Inc. account |
| 4/11/86: | $650,000 | from the I.C. Inc. account |
| Total: | $1,738,000 | |

North also directed Miller to transfer NEPL funds to other projects. These disbursements included $200,000 for a purported Arab ''prince'' who promised to make a sizable donation to the contras;[13] and $75,000 to the Institute for Terrorism & Subnational Conflict, to pay the salary of Robert W. Owen, North's personal courier to the contras. About $450,000 went to a Cayman Islands entity, World Affairs Counselors Inc., through which Miller and Gomez paid themselves for their fundraising services.

On two occasions, Roy Godson of the Heritage Foundation helped solicit funds from private donors.[14] In the fall of 1985, Godson, at North's direction, informed Miller that an anonymous donor wanted to make a large contribution to the Catholic church in Nicaragua. Based on a plan agreed to by Godson and Miller, the donor contributed $100,000 to the Heritage Foundation, which then forwarded the money to a Miller-Gomez entity known as the Institute for North-South Issues (INSI). Miller and Gomez took a $20,000 commission and forwarded $80,000 to their I.C. Inc. account in the Cayman Islands.

In November 1985, North spoke with another private donor about the needs of the contras and the Nicaraguan Catholic church.[15] North informed Miller that Godson had located the donor, who would be making a $60,000 contribution.[16] The money was deposited directly into the INSI account and then transferred to the Lake Resources Account in Switzerland. Miller and Gomez took no commission on this donation.

After business expenses, Channell and Miller earned substantial sums for their work. Channell was paid $345,000 during the two-year period; his associate Conrad was paid $270,000. Including ''commissions'' totaling $442,000, Richard Miller and Frank Gomez and their firm, IBC, received approximately $1.7 million. Public relations contractors David Fischer and Martin Artiano received $662,000.

---

[13] Miller, FBI 302, 6/11/87, p. 2. See n. 5.
[14] Miller, FBI 302, 7/8/87, pp. 10–11.

[15] Richard MacAleer, FBI 302, 9/30/87, p. 2.
[16] Miller, FBI 302, 7/8/87, p. 10.

# Chapter 14
# Other Money Matters: Traveler's Checks and Cash Transactions

Nearly $6 million dollars in cash and traveler's checks changed hands in the course of the Iran and contra operations of Lt. Col. Oliver L. North and the Enterprise.[1] The full extent of the cash transactions will never be known because of a purposeful lack of documentation. Traveler's checks were purchased by contra leader Adolfo Calero and used as a convenient form of currency. They were largely traceable as far as who cashed them, but the task was complicated by their volume—25,637 checks—and the illegibility of many of the recipients' signatures.

The largest cash transfers originated with the Enterprise primarily in connection with: (1) cash deliveries in the United States from foreign Enterprise accounts to Albert Hakim, Richard V. Secord and Thomas G. Clines; and, (2) the transportation of cash from Southern Air Transport (SAT) in Miami to the Enterprise's contra-resupply operation in Central America. Independent Counsel traced the movement of a total $2.7 million in 97 separate cash transactions through records supplied by the Swiss Government and Enterprise financial manager Willard Zucker. In addition, more than $450,000 in cash deliveries from SAT and from other Enterprise sources to the resupply operation were analyzed based on SAT and Swiss financial records, and on interviews with SAT financial officers and couriers who took the cash to Central America.

A separate but related area of investigation was the "operational fund" that North admitted keeping in his office. He estimated that $150,000 to $200,000 in cash from Secord and $100,000 in blank traveler's checks from contra leader Adolfo Calero passed through this fund. From the fund, which North said he established at CIA Director William Casey's direction, North made payments to contra leaders and paid other expenses. North testified that he kept track of the payments in a ledger, which he said he destroyed in October or November 1986 to protect the identities of those involved in the unraveling operation.[2]

Finally, large sums of cash were traced in connection with a North-directed hostage-rescue operation using two Drug Enforcement Agency agents detailed to him. This operation, which did not come to fruition, was to have included bribes and hostage-ransom payments, funded largely by a contribution from H. Ross Perot. North continued to use these DEA agents in other operations involving large amounts of cash, making them subject to investigative scrutiny, but no prosecution resulted.

## The Traveler's Checks

North was charged in March 1988 with converting to his personal use $4,300 worth of traveler's checks, provided to him by Calero in support of the contras and hostage-rescue efforts. The Government at trial showed that North used these checks at supermarkets, gas stations and other stores. North, did not dispute the expenditures, but said he used the traveler's checks to reimburse himself for operational expenses

---

[1] This estimate includes approximately $2.7 million in cash transactions between February 1985 and November 1986 reflected in the Swiss records of the Enterprise, and $2.7 million in traveler's checks cashed in 1985 and 1986, which could be identified and traced by the Office of Independent Counsel. In addition, more than $450,000 in cash was delivered from Southern Air Transport and other sources to the Enterprise's contra-resupply operation in Central America.

[2] North, *North* Trial Testimony, 4/10/89, pp. 7134–45. North's daily notebooks, which were obtained by Independent Counsel when North took the stand in his trial, reflect various payments to contra leaders, but these notebooks apparently were separate from the ledger North claims to have kept.

he had paid out of his pocket.[3] The jury acquitted North of the traveler's-check-conversion charge.

North estimated that he received from Calero about $100,000 in blank traveler's checks, which went into an operational fund he kept in his office. He said the checks were used to make payments to about 40 contra leaders and to reimburse himself for expenses.[4] North said he discussed the operational fund with Casey and national security advisers Robert C. McFarlane and John M. Poindexter.[5] Asked why he kept such a fund, North said he believed it allowed him to operate outside the Boland Amendment prohibition on the expenditure of appropriated funds.[6] Calero said it was necessary for North to make the payments to contra leaders because of politically sensitive relationships between Calero and rival faction heads.[7]

Calero said his lawyer, Carlos Morales, purchased the blank traveler's checks for him from BAC International Bank in Miami, using funds transferred from the contras' Cayman Island bank accounts.[8] Calero sent some of the blank traveler's checks to Honduras for expenses there, others were used to pay the travel expenses of contra leaders, and on occasion they were spent on contra supplies in the United States. In addition, payments were made to the families of contras living in the United States.[9]

In February or March 1985, North asked Calero for $15,000 to $25,000 in traveler's checks for a hostage-rescue operation, shortly after the contras' Cayman Islands bank account had received $15 million from Saudi Arabia.[10]

Calero on several occasions sent some of the checks to North via Robert W. Owen, North's personal courier to the contras.[11] Owen estimated that he gave out more than $30,000 in traveler's checks to contra leaders at North's behest.[12] According to OIC's analysis, Owen cashed 426 checks totaling $45,880. In October 1985, North gave Owen $1,000 in traveler's checks as a wedding gift.[13]

Both Owen and North's secretary, Fawn Hall, were aware of the checks North kept in his operational fund.[14] According to North and Owen, at least one other White House official, Johnathan Miller, a State Department employee detailed to the National Security Council staff, helped North distribute the traveler's checks from the fund to contra leaders.[15] In an interview with OIC, however, Miller claimed little awareness of North's contra efforts and divulged nothing about his knowledge of North's cash fund. Miller said his contacts with North were limited to policy issues and education efforts relating to the contras.[16] When Miller subsequently appeared before the Grand Jury, he refused to testify.[17]

There are no known documents explaining the traveler's check expenditures, which totaled $2,691,950. Calero said he initially kept a journal of the traveler's checks disbursements but discontinued the practice; he said the journal was no longer available.[18] He said he wrote no memoranda describing the check expenditures because the contras were involved in a covert operation.[19] As a result, OIC obtained no record of what the payments were intended for—only who endorsed the blank traveler's checks. Even then, on about a fifth of the traveler's checks—4,982 checks totaling $479,010—the signatories' names were illegible.

## The Cash Drops

In order to transfer money from the Swiss Enterprise accounts into the United States while avoiding financial reporting requirements, Zucker employed a New York bank officer, Nan Morabia, her husband Elliot, and their son David to make cash drops to Hakim, Secord and others on their behalf. Beginning in early 1985, Zucker would contact Nan Morabia and

[3] North, *North* Trial Testimony, 4/6/89, p. 6849.

[4] Ibid., pp. 6841–6851. According to OIC's analysis of the traveler's checks signatories, North cashed in his true name 49 checks totaling $4,940. In addition, he cashed 37 checks totaling $2,420 using his alias, William P. Good.

[5] Ibid., 4/10/89, p. 7135.

[6] Ibid., p. 7173.

[7] Calero, *North* Trial Testimony, 2/23/89, p. 2081.

[8] Calero, FBI 302, 9/22/87, p. 1.

[9] Ibid., pp. 1–10.

[10] Ibid., p. 4.

[11] Ibid., p. 6.

[12] Owen, *North* Trial Testimony, 2/27/89, p. 2427.

[13] Ibid., p. 2272. Clear evidence of abuse was difficult to establish because no records of the purpose of the expenditures were kept or at least produced to Independent Counsel.

[14] Fawn Hall testified that North gave her $60 in traveler's checks from the fund for a beach trip; she repaid the loan. (Hall, Select Committees testimony, 6/8/87, p. 458.)

[15] North, *North* Trial Testimony, 4/6/89, p. 6851; and Owen, *North* Trial Testimony, 2/27/89, p. 2427.

[16] Johnathan Miller, FBI 302, 5/1/87, p. 5.

[17] Johnathan Miller, Grand Jury, 5/27/87.

[18] Calero, FBI 302, 9/22/87, p. 2.

[19] Ibid., p. 3.

inform her that Hakim or Secord needed a certain amount of cash; Nan Morabia would communicate this to her husband Elliot, who provided and delivered the cash or had their son David deliver it.[20] Zucker wired from Enterprise accounts an equal amount to an account named "Codelis" at the Trade Development Bank in Geneva. This account was controlled by two brothers, Edgar and Elie Mizrahi, who were family friends of the Morabias.[21]

According to Nan Morabia, she arranged at Zucker's request six cash drops, ranging in amount from $5,000 to $60,000.[22] David Morabia said he became involved at his father's request in drops to Hakim and to a man carrying Secord's business card, who was later identified as William Haskell, a North courier.[23] David Morabia said he did not know the amounts of cash involved.

David Morabia delivered to Hakim in May 1986 $100,000 at the New York Hilton Hotel. He delivered to Haskell in November 1986 at the Summit Hotel in New York an uncertain amount, possibly totaling $100,000. Elliot Morabia delivered $100,000 in cash to Hakim in New York, on uncertain dates, possibly in June and August 1986; he delivered $50,000 more to Hakim in late October 1986. Nan Morabia delivered $7,000 in cash to Robert W. Owen at Republic National Bank in New York in August 1985, and she delivered to Zucker in New York in late September 1986 cash totaling $50,000.[24]

The Morabias' drops do not reflect the full extent of the cash deliveries to Hakim and others. Zucker sometimes made the deliveries himself or had other individuals make them.[25]

Mrs. Morabia said she understood the purpose of the secret cash deliveries was to avoid Currency Transaction Reports, requiring that cash transactions involving $10,000 or more be reported to the Federal Government.[26] The drops were made surreptitiously—code names and phrases were used when the parties met in person, so that each could determine the other's good faith. David Morabia said he sometimes would carry with him a half of a dollar bill; the recipient of the cash would have to present the missing half in order for the drop to be made.[27]

Nan and David Morabia were given immunity from prosecution in exchange for their testimony. Elliot Morabia died in March 1987 before he could be questioned.

## SAT's Cash Deliveries to the Resupply Operation

Once the contra-resupply network was operational in Central America in 1986, cash was transported to the region from Southern Air Transport's petty-cash funds at the request of the operation's managers Richard Gadd and later Robert Dutton. According to OIC's analysis of SAT financial records, the Miami company disbursed approximately $467,000 in cash in connection with the contra-resupply operation.

The cash was carried in amounts ranging from several thousand dollars up to $50,000 by resupply pilots and other employees traveling from Miami to Ilopango airbase in El Salvador, where it was used for fuel purchases.[28] The Enterprise reimbursed these cash advances with wire transfers to SAT accounts.[29] In addition to the SAT cash transactions, Gadd's company, Eagle Aviation Service and Technology (EAST), issued a total of $43,000 in cash on four occasions for transfer to the fuel fund in Central America.[30]

Once the cash was delivered to Ilopango airbase in El Salvador, fuel fund deposits were made by Enterprise employees Luis Posada

20 Nan Morabia was an officer of the Republic National Bank in New York, which handled many of the Enterprise's wire transfers, but she said the cash-delivery operation was conducted by her outside bank channels. (Nan Morabia, FBI 302, 11/16/87, p. 4.)

21 Ibid., 2/17/88, p. 2.

22 Ibid., p. 2.

23 David Morabia, FBI 302, 2/19/88, p. 3.

24 In addition to cash payments to Enterprise figures, Nan Morabia said that on November 26, 1986, she delivered $150,000 in cash to Adnan Khashoggi, an Iran arms sales financier, in New York. She said this cash delivery was an authorized payment from the account of Samir Trabigulsi, who has not been identified as an Iran/contra figure. Khashoggi, who had already been questioned in Paris by the time Nan Morabia informed Independent Counsel of this cash drop, was not asked about it. (Nan Morabia, FBI 302, 2/17/88, p. 9.)

25 Zucker, FBI 302, 11/6–10/87, p. 9.

26 Nan Morabia, FBI 302, 11/16/87, p. 2. In addition to Currency Transaction Reports, these cash drops also circumvented Currency and Monetary Reports, which are required for cash being transported in or out of the United States.

27 David Morabia, FBI 302, 2/8/88, pp. 1–2.

28 William Langton, FBI 302, 4/30/87, p. 2.

29 Ibid., p. 1. Also, Robert H. Mason, Grand Jury, 6/19/87, pp. 11–12.

30 Cynthia Dondlinger, FBI 302s, 3/19/87, 4/6/87, 4/12/87.

(alias Ramon Medina) and Felix Rodriguez, and recorded by William Cooper.[31]

Rafael Quintero, Secord's representative in Central America, personally carried to Central America at least $30,000 in cash from SAT in Miami. He said he also received cash several times from Secord's office in northern Virginia for delivery to Central America.[32]

On at least one occasion, cash was carried from SAT in Miami to North in Washington. In August 1986, Shirley Napier, Secord's secretary, flew to Miami to pick up a package containing $16,000 in cash.[33] Napier delivered the cash to Fawn Hall, North's secretary.[34] Hall gave the cash to North. On the same day, he gave $10,800 in cash to one of the DEA agents involved with him in hostage-rescue efforts.

North testified that it was "reasonable" to conclude that the purpose of using cash in the Enterprise operations was that it was untraceable.[35] Independent Counsel was able to identify 21 transactions involving approximately $357,000 in cash in which North participated.

In conducting its contra and Iran operations, the Enterprise employed couriers whom North personally trusted to deliver traveler's checks and cash, as well as to relay secret information. Rob Owen, in addition to handling traveler's checks for contra leaders, picked up and delivered $16,500 in cash. William Haskell, a tax accountant whom North sent on a variety of missions, received an estimated $143,905 in cash and dispersed $116,600 that could be traced. Both Owen and Haskell received immunity from prosecution in exchange for their testimony about their roles as North's couriers.

## The Cash: The DEA Hostage-Rescue Operation

The largest lump sum of cash North is known to have handled was $200,000 provided to him in May 1985 for a hostage-rescue effort. Ross Perot provided the money for the operation, which North conducted with two Drug Enforce-

ment Agents temporarily detailed to the NSC staff.

In all, Perot made available $1.3 million for this operation. In addition to the previously mentioned $200,000 which was paid to a DEA informant, Perot provided another $100,000 through the FBI, and $1 million for a hostage-ransom payment that was never made. The $1 million in ransom money was returned to Perot. Other funding for the operation came from the CIA, which spent $50,000 for payments to informants; and the DEA, which spent $49,098 for travel expenses and informant payments. Finally, North generated approximately $150,900 in traveler's checks and currency from Calero, Hakim and Richard R. Miller, a private fundraiser.

Independent Counsel investigated possible conversions of any of the large sums of cash and traveler's checks for personal purposes by the DEA agents. Possible misuse of small amounts was found in the case of one of the DEA agents, whose names are protected. It did not merit prosecution.

## Third-Country Funding and the Missing Brunei Funds

From 1984 through 1986, Administration officials approached more than a dozen foreign countries for various forms of assistance for the contras.[36] Most of them responded positively, providing weapons, weapons end-user certificates, training, equipment and other aid for the contras. Three countries—Saudi Arabia, Taiwan and Brunei—made or attempted to make substantial cash contributions. The Saudis donated $32 million between July 1984 and March 1985. Taiwan contributed a total of $2 million in September 1985 and February 1986.

In the summer of 1986, Secretary of State George P. Shultz and Assistant Secretary Elliott Abrams decided to solicit $10 million from the Sultan of Brunei. Although Shultz originally was to have made the approach, he failed to do it. Abrams instead solicited the contribution from a Bruneian official at a meeting in London.[37]

---

[31] Dutton, Grand Jury, 5/11/87, p. 39.

[32] Quintero, FBI 302, 12/28/87, pp. 8–9.

[33] Napier, FBI 302, 4/2/87, p. 5. Napier was involved in another cash transaction in March 1986, when she picked up $15,000 in cash from two branches of First American Bank and delivered it to Hakim at STTGI offices in Northern Virginia.

[34] Ibid., p. 5.

[35] North, *North* Trial Testimony, 4/10/89, p. 7163.

[36] These included Saudi Arabia, Israel, China, Taiwan, South Korea, Chile, Singapore, Venezuela, England, South Africa, Brunei, Panama, Honduras, Salvador, Guatemala and Costa Rica.

[37] Abrams, FBI 302, 11/5/87, p. 5. See Abrams chapter.

Abrams provided the Bruneian official with a bank account number into which the deposit should be made. Abrams had obtained it from North. But the number—which was to have been for the Enterprise's Lake Resources account in the Credit Suisse bank Geneva—had two numbers transposed, and the subsequent $10 million deposit went into the wrong account.[38]

After the United States submitted to Switzerland its initial request for assistance in investigating possible Iran/contra crimes in December 1987, Swiss authorities noted the similarity of the two account numbers. The individual who controlled account number 368.430.22.1 had not been identified by the United States as among a list of individuals involved in Iran/contra. Therefore, the magistrate executing the request concluded that this individual was not involved in activities subject to the request. The magistrate stated that this individual benefitted from the transfer of funds solely because of the transposition of figures in the account number.

Independent Counsel late in 1989 obtained new information indicating that the $10 million Brunei contribution passed through an account or accounts controlled by or on behalf of Bruce Rappaport, a Swiss businessman with ties to certain individuals involved in the Iran/contra affair.[39] In August 1989, Rappaport's lawyers received from Credit Suisse bank a letter disclaiming Rappaport as the recipient of the Brunei funds. It stated: "Credit Suisse knows the identity of the person in whose account the Sultan of Brunei's $10 million was placed. Neither Bruce Rappaport, nor any entity directly or indirectly controlled by Bruce Rappaport was the recipient of the Sultan of Brunei's $10 million."[40] Despite Credit Suisse's denial, Independent Counsel sought further information regarding the deposit through the State Department, but these efforts did not resolve the question.

In October 1990, Independent Counsel questioned Rappaport, under an immunity agreement, about his knowledge of the Brunei funds.[41] Rappaport said the account that received the Brunei deposit was not his, and that it did not belong to any of his family members or to any companies in which he had an interest. He said the Brunei money was not transferred from one of his accounts into any other account, and the money was not converted into some other form, such as certificates of deposit owned or controlled by him. Rappaport said he did not know whose account received the Brunei deposit.

Independent Counsel was unable to determine the recipient of the $10 million Brunei deposit. Although Swiss authorities continued to refuse to identify the recipient, they did report that the money was returned to Brunei.[42]

---

[38] Instead of Lake Resources account number 386.430.22.1, the number North provided to Abrams, on a card typed by North's secretary Fawn Hall, was 368.430.22.1.

[39] Rappaport had participated from 1984 through early 1986 in a plan to build an oil pipeline from Iraq through Jordan to the Gulf of Aqaba. Rappaport and his representatives met repeatedly with individuals at the National Security Council to secure financing for a "political risk" insurance package to protect Rappaport's projected investment in the pipeline. Among the individuals with whom he met were McFarlane and CIA Director William Casey, a long-time friend.

The Aqaba pipeline was never built. However, during the precise time that Israel, individuals from the NSC staff and Rappaport were discussing U.S. Government financing and the division of profits from the pipeline, many of the same individuals from the NSC staff were participating (along with Israel) in the arms sales to Iran in November 1985 and February 1986.

Allegations of improper use of influence by Attorney General Edwin Meese III on behalf of Rappaport were investigated in 1987 by Independent Counsel James McKay.

[40] Rappaport, FBI 302, 10/2/90, pp. 1–2.

[41] Ibid.

[42] Rappaport also said he did not know North or Abrams. He said he had met on June 24, 1985, with McFarlane. Rappaport said either McFarlane or E. Bob Wallach, a long-time friend of Attorney General Meese, told Rappaport in that time frame that the NSC had a "piggy bank account" with many millions of dollars in it which could be used for emergency purposes. Rappaport said he thought he was told about the money because it might have been available for the Aqaba pipeline project. Rappaport said he believed McFarlane controlled the fund. McFarlane said Meese in mid-1985 recommended that he meet with Rappaport concerning the Aqaba pipeline. (Rappaport, FBI 302, 10/2/90, p. 4.)

According to McFarlane, Rappaport asked if Israel assured him it would support the project, would he help get funding for it. McFarlane said he thought such a project, with Israel's endorsement, would promote goodwill in the region. McFarlane recalled that he talked to the Export-Import Bank and possibly representatives of Overseas Private Investments Corporation (OPIC) regarding the project. (McFarlane, FBI 302, 9/27/90, pp. 9–10.)

# Part VI
# Investigations and Cases:
# Officers of the Central Intelligence Agency

The Central Intelligence Agency's role in the Iran/contra affair was in large measure a manifestation of Director William J. Casey and President Reagan's shared goal of rolling back Soviet-supported communist regimes around the world. Casey and Reagan mutually supported the cause of the Nicaraguan contras. This support inspired Lt. Col. Oliver L. North's efforts to supply the contras in defiance of the Boland Amendment's prohibition on U.S. military aid. Casey also respected Reagan's concern for the Americans held hostage in Lebanon. Casey was an early and vigorous advocate of the Iran arms sales and was strongly against telling Congress about them until all of the hostages were released—a position consistent with his general attitude as director of central intelligence that Congress be told as little as possible.

Casey's support of the contras and his backing of the Iran arms sales had direct consequences for the officers under his direction. Casey's position on the contras gave his chief of the Central American Task Force, Alan D. Fiers, Jr., a green light to "dovetail" the CIA's Central American activities with those of North's contra-resupply operation. With Casey's encouragement, Fiers also used North to replace CIA funding of a classified project banned by Congress in the summer of 1985.

As for the Iran arms sales, Casey was largely responsible for forcing the CIA's Directorate of Operations, the U.S. Government's covert-action arm, to rely on operatives whom they distrusted, whom they could not monitor, and who ultimately laid the groundwork for the infamous diversion of Iran arms profits to the contras. Casey supported the decision to have the national security adviser direct the operations of the Iran arms sales. He also overrode strong opposition from seasoned CIA professionals to using Manucher Ghorbanifar, retired Air Force Maj. Gen. Richard V. Secord, and Albert Hakim in the effort. Ghorbanifar was "a liar and has a record of deceit," warned Casey's deputy, John McMahon. "[W]e would be aiding and abetting the wrong people." [1] Thomas Twetten, a senior agency official, returned from meetings in Europe shocked to learn that Secord and Hakim, whom North told Twetten were assisting him in Central American operations, were principals in the Iran initiative. Casey, who had originally paired Secord and North in contra resupply, overrode these concerns.

When the Iran/contra affair became public in late 1986, at least three of Casey's subordinates—Fiers, Clair E. George, and Duane R. Clarridge—responded to Congress in keeping with the tone set by Casey throughout his tenure at the CIA: Tell Congress as little as possible and keep the spotlight off the White House. Independent Counsel found that key Agency officials were better informed and more directly involved in the contra-resupply effort and in the Iran arms sales than they previously admitted.

It would be wrong, however, to blame all of the improper conduct of CIA officers on Casey. Some CIA officers had their own motives for violating the law during the course of the affair, or for denying knowledge of it once it came into public view. For example, James L. Adkins, chief of a CIA facility in Central America, acted out of what he claimed were "humanitarian" motives in supplying the contras in violation of the Boland cut-off of contra aid, without any demonstrable tie to

---

[1] DIRECTOR 705574, 1/25/86, ER 24834–35.

Casey or other CIA officials. Joseph F. Fernandez, a CIA station chief in Costa Rica, disregarded explicit warnings from his superiors: He deliberately violated the Boland restraints, and subsequently lied to federal investigators out of friendship for North and to protect himself. The claims of faulty memories by ''CIA Subject #1,'' a counterpart of Fernandez's in Central America, and Robert M. Gates, deputy director of the CIA, were self-protective.

The accounts that follow in this section are based on an exhaustive review of CIA cables and documents, and from extensive interviews with former and present Agency employees.

Independent Counsel's investigation resulted in a comprehensive analysis of CIA activities in the Iran arms sales and in contra resupply during the mid-1980s. Despite this investigation, the last word about the CIA in Iran/contra cannot be written. Casey suffered a seizure in his office on December 15, 1986, and died on May 6, 1987. Independent Counsel never questioned him, and the investigation recovered only a few contemporaneous notes written by him.[2] A potentially significant area of inquiry was thus closed to Independent Counsel.

Casey's death also provided an opportunity for many—most importantly, North and Fiers—to attribute activities and decisions to the late director, without rebuttal from him. That Casey was close to both North and Fiers cannot be disputed. As the head of an agency that had no supervisory authority over North, Casey had an impressive number of individual contacts with the National Security Council staffmember. Casey also interceded with the White House in May 1984 to keep North on the staff of the National Security Council, characterizing North's impending transfer back to the Marine Corps as a ''critical problem'' for the Administration's Central American program.[3] As for Fiers, Casey personally put Fiers in charge of the contra program as the ''full Boland'' restrictions went into effect, and both men regularly sidestepped the CIA's chain of command to work exclusively on the program. Nevertheless, important charges about Casey's conduct were made only after his death, making verification in many instances impossible.

The OIC charged four CIA officials with criminal offenses: George, the deputy director for operations and the third highest-ranking CIA official; Clarridge, chief of the Agency's Latin American Division and, later, its European Division; Fiers; and Fernandez. George was convicted by a jury of two felony counts of false statements and perjury before Congress. Clarridge was charged with seven counts of perjury and false statements. Fiers pleaded guilty to two misdemeanor counts of withholding information from Congress. The case against Fernandez, who was charged with four counts of false statements and obstruction, was dismissed after the CIA, backed by Attorney General Richard Thornburgh, refused to declassify information sought by the defense.

President Bush pardoned George, Clarridge and Fiers on December 24, 1992, before Clarridge could be tried.

---

[2] Independent Counsel learned in November 1987 that after Casey had resigned as DCI in January 1987, the CIA removed safes, telephones and other Agency equipment and materials from Casey's three homes. The CIA later returned to Casey's widow, Sophia, 25 boxes of unclassified papers, documents and other materials. (Murphy, FBI 302, 11/5/87, pp. 1–2.) A subpoena directing Mrs. Casey to produce to the Grand Jury ''any and all'' documents, diaries, notes, calendars and other materials maintained by Casey in his capacity as director of the CIA had little result. Mrs. Casey reported that the boxes had been sent to the Hoover Institution at Stanford University. Family members who reviewed the boxes said that no CIA material or documents or notes relevant to Iran/contra were included. (Sophia Casey, Grand Jury, 3/7/88, pp. 7–18.)

Renewed interest in possible Casey documents and relevant Iran/contra materials was spurred in 1992 with the opening of the Casey Library and statements by Casey's biographer, Joseph Persico, that Mrs. Casey had made available to him all of Casey's personal papers. Despite extensive effort, no significant materials were recovered.

[3] Meese Notes, 5/15/84, 55301467; Kelley, *North* Trial Testimony, 4/3/89, pp. 6272–74.

# Chapter 15
# William J. Casey

William J. Casey served as director of central intelligence from January 1981 until he resigned on January 29, 1987, incapacitated by a brain tumor. Casey had been director of President Reagan's successful 1980 campaign, but his appointment as CIA director was not seen as a political reward. During World War II, Casey had a distinguished record in the Office of Strategic Services, the forerunner of the CIA, serving as intelligence chief for Europe. He also was an experienced Washington hand, having served as head of the Securities and Exchange Commission and as under secretary of state for economic affairs in the Nixon Administration. As CIA director, Casey and President Reagan shared similar world views, at the center of which was their determination to roll back communism and bring about the collapse of the Soviet Union.

The Iran/contra investigations and prosecutions could not have been pursued without developing evidence on Casey's role, particularly guidance or authorization he may have provided in the commission of illegal acts. Because Casey did not have the opportunity to answer questions arising from the evidence, however, Independent Counsel did not conduct his investigation with an eye toward establishing Casey's guilt or innocence.[1]

There is evidence that Casey played a role as a Cabinet-level advocate both in setting up the covert network to resupply the contras during the Boland funding cut-off, and in promoting the secret arms sales to Iran in 1985 and 1986. In both instances, Casey was acting in furtherance of broad policies established by President Reagan.

There is evidence that Casey, working with two national security advisers to President Reagan during the period 1984 through 1986— Robert C. McFarlane and Vice Admiral John M. Poindexter—approved having these operations conducted out of the National Security Council staff with Lt. Col. Oliver L. North as the action officer, assisted by retired Air Force Maj. Gen. Richard V. Secord. And although Casey tried to insulate himself and the CIA from any illegal activities relating to the two secret operations, using there is evidence that he was involved in at least some of those activities and may have attempted to keep them concealed from Congress.

## Casey, North and the Contras

There is abundant evidence that President Reagan was determined that the contras be sustained as a viable military force during the period of the Boland cut-off, from October 1984 to October 1986.[2] When President Reagan was asked in written interrogatories from Independent Counsel whether he authorized Casey, among others, to take action with respect to the contras during the Boland cut-off period, Reagan said the question was too broad to answer specifically. He conceded that Administra-

---

[1] For example, North, at his trial, testified to conversations with Casey. By that time in his investigation, as indicated below, Independent Counsel did not use his resources just to check the truth of some of North's statements.

[2] The Boland Amendment was signed into law by President Reagan as part of Public Law 98–473. It expressly prohibited the use of appropriated funds from being obligated or expended in support of military or paramilitary operations in Nicaragua, stating in relevant part:

> During fiscal year 1985, no funds available to the Central Intelligence Agency, the Department of Defense, or any other agency or entity of the United States involved in intelligence activities may be obligated or expended for the purpose or which would have the effect of supporting, directly or indirectly, military or paramilitary operations in Nicaragua by any nation, group, organization, movement, or individual.

tion policy was to support the contras: "Thus, Administration officials were generally authorized to implement that policy."[3]

But the President also stated that he never authorized the transfer of CIA contra duties to the NSC and did not recall discussing such a transfer with anyone. The President also stated that he did not authorize anyone to violate the Boland Amendment or other laws in implementing his policy to support the contras.[4]

There is evidence that Casey welcomed North's taking over some of the activities done by the CIA prior to enactment of the Boland Amendment. North testified that in the spring of 1984, as CIA funds appropriated by Congress to assist the contras began to run out, he was directed by McFarlane to set up a secret account for the contras to accept Saudi Arabia's $1-million-per-month contribution. McFarlane directed North to contact Casey to find out which of the contra leaders should receive the contributions and get foreign accounts for the money transfers.[5]

Casey and McFarlane in the spring of 1984 were aware that contra funds were running out and discussed alternative means of financing.[6] In a March 27, 1984, memo to McFarlane, Casey endorsed McFarlane's plan to seek funding from third countries, including Israel. Casey stated that the CIA was exploring possible contributions from the Israelis and another country.[7]

At a June 25, 1984, meeting of the National Security Planning Group (NSPG), Casey debated with Secretary of State George P. Shultz the legality of obtaining contra funding from third countries in the face of the Boland restrictions. Shultz declared that White House Chief of Staff James Baker, who was not at that meet-

ing, had said that soliciting aid from third countries might be "an impeachable offense." Casey insisted that "[w]e need the legal opinion which makes clear that the U.S. has the authority to facilitate third country funding for the anti-Sandinistas. . . ."[8] The following day, Casey and CIA General Counsel Stanley Sporkin met with Attorney General William French Smith and legal advisers from the Justice Department to press for such an opinion, framing the issue in terms of aid from "other nations in the region." Smith expressed the view that discussions with third countries for such assistance would be permissible as long as it was made clear that the countries must spend their own funds and would not be reimbursed by the United States.[9]

While the CIA was, in May 1984, still able to supply, direct, and advise the contras, it was already apparent to the Administration that Congress was going to pass very restrictive legislation, perhaps even an outright ban on contra assistance in the coming fiscal year. North testified that in the spring and summer of 1984, he was instructed on the CIA's contra operation, introduced to the CIA officials with whom he would be dealing and brought together with contra leaders.[10] North said Casey also gave him the names of CIA assets in Central America with whom to work. North said Casey "told me to work with them because they were totally reliable people, that they had worked with the CIA before, that they were people who we could trust in Central America."[11]

North testified that at Casey's direction in late summer 1984, he recruited Secord, a retired

---

[3] Answers of the President of the United States to Interrogatories, *In re Grand Jury Investigation*, Answer to Question 9 (hereafter, "Reagan, Grand Jury Interrogatories"). President Reagan stated: "As I have stated in these Interrogatory answers, it was the consistent policy of my Administration to advocate the support of the Freedom Fighters by the Congress, the American people, and our friends and allies abroad. Thus, Administration officials were generally authorized to implement that policy."

[4] Ibid., Answers to Questions 14–17.

[5] North, *North* Trial Testimony, 4/6/89, pp. 6778–79.

[6] In a June 11, 1984, memo, CIA General Counsel Stanley Sporkin advised Casey that the $24 million FY 1984 appropriation for CIA assistance to the contras had virtually run out, and told Casey further that under the Anti-Deficiency Act, 31 U.S.C. §§ 1341–1519, sanctions could be imposed directly on CIA officers if spending beyond the $24 million cap occurred. (Memorandum from Sporkin to Casey, 6/11/84, ER 46099.)

[7] Memorandum from Casey to McFarlane, 3/27/84, ER 13712.

[8] Minutes of NSPG meeting, 6/25/84, ALU 007863–76.

[9] Memorandum from Sporkin to the Record, 6/26/84, ALV 035917.

[10] North, *North* Trial Testimony, 4/6/89, p. 6781–6782:

Through the summer, as a consequence of my having been sent down and meeting with resistance [contra] leadership, having given Mr. McFarlane the accounts to set up funding for them, slowly but surely more and more of that CIA responsibility had been, I suppose, passed on to me. I don't recall that there was any specific break point up until late in the summer where I was finally told, Okay, you have got it all, but it did occur just before the bill [the Boland Amendment] passed into law, having been fought bitterly by the Administration and by some supporters up in Congress. There was finally a point in time where Director Casey set up a number of meetings with me and the resistance, some of them down south in Central America, some in Miami, some in Washington, through he and his people. And basically, what we would call a hand off, just like in basketball, I suppose, you got the ball, go on with it. And certainly that was fully in force by October when the bill was passed.

[11] Ibid., p. 6826. Independent Counsel was unable to corroborate North's story.

Air Force major general skilled at clandestine operations, to set up his contra-supply network.[12] According to North, Secord's operation was modeled on prior CIA operations, using a series of organizations to obtain weapons and deliver them to the contras.

In late July 1984, Casey took North to a meeting in a Central American location of all of the CIA's senior field officers in the region. "Director Casey told me he wanted me to see them eyeball-to-eyeball and them to see me, so we would know each other in the event, his words were, something went wrong," North said.[13] North testified that Casey advised him to set up a secret account to accept foreign contributions to the contras so that arms and other purchases would be controlled by him rather than the contra leaders.[14] North testified that at the end of 1984, he also set up an operational account in his office to provide funds for the contra and later the hostage-release operations.[15] North said Casey gave him a ledger to keep an accurate account of the cash and traveler's checks disbursements from the fund. North said he destroyed the ledger in October or November 1986 at Casey's direction when it appeared that the secret contra-supply effort would be publicly exposed following the downing over Nicaragua of one of the operation's aircraft and the capture of crew-member Eugene Hasenfus.[16]

Casey demonstrated his high regard for North as a Central American player by asking Presidential counselor Edwin Meese III in the spring of 1984 to intercede when North was scheduled to be detailed back to the Marines. A Meese notebook entry on May 15, 1984, shows a call from Casey: "Critical problem re Central America: Keep Ollie North from being trf'd back to USMC. Will F [follow up] + call GEN

Kelley [P. X. Kelley, Commandant of the Marine Corps]." Although he had misgivings about extending North's tour at the NSC, Kelley agreed to do so.[17]

The only testimony linking the President to Casey's purported decision to install North as the action officer for the contras was the hearsay testimony of CIA official Vincent Cannistraro at the *North* trial. Testifying as a defense witness, Cannistraro described a series of meetings in the spring and summer of 1984 in which he said the "hand off" to North was effected. Cannistraro said in June 1984 in a meeting in Casey's office attended by Duane R. (Dewey) Clarridge, then head of the CIA's Latin American Operations Division; Joseph F. Fernandez, then an officer in the CIA's Central American Task Force; and contra leader Adolfo Calero, Casey had told Calero that

> speaking on behalf of the President of the United States, [Casey] wanted to assure the freedom fighters [the contras] that the United States government would find a way to continue its support to the freedom fighters after the 30th of September, 1984, if the Boland Amendment became part of the operational restrictions against the involvement of the CIA.[18]

Cannistraro said that Casey explained that North, "as a member of the National Security Council, would not be subject to those restrictions and that North would be a principal point of reference." [19] Casey said that "he had discussed this with the President of the United States and that it was agreed with the President that this was how it should be handled." [20]

Aside from North's testimony, the most important evidence of Casey's role in handing off to North the CIA's contra-support operations is testimony from Alan D. Fiers, Jr., chief of the CIA's Central American Task Force.[21] Fiers

[12] Ibid., p. 6815. According to a North computer message, Casey also later approved Secord's involvement in the covert arms sales to Iran, designating him as a CIA agent to serve as an intermediary in 1986. (PROFs Note from North to Poindexter, 1/15/86, 012.) Under the January 17, 1986, Presidential Finding, which Casey and CIA General Counsel Stanley Sporkin helped North put together, the U.S. Army sold the TOW missiles to the CIA, who in turn passed them on to Secord, the unnamed "third party" in the Finding, who then delivered them to Iranian agents.

[13] North, *North* Trial Testimony, 4/6/89, p. 6841.

[14] Ibid., 4/10/89, pp. 7267–68, 7273–84.

[15] Ibid., 4/6/89, pp. 6841–49.

[16] Ibid., 4/10/89, pp. 7138–39. Independent Counsel was unable to corroborate North's testimony concerning the ledger or Casey's instruction to destroy it.

[17] Meese Notes, 5/15/84, 55301467 (emphasis in original); Kelley, *North* Trial Testimony, 4/3/89, pp. 6272–74.

[18] Cannistraro, *North* Trial Testimony, 4/3/89, pp. 6404–5.

[19] Ibid., p. 6405. Casey and President Reagan took the position that the President and the NSC were not covered by the Boland restrictions, an interpretation not shared by Congress or Independent Counsel.

[20] Ibid., pp. 6409–10. Independent Counsel was unable to corroborate Cannistraro's testimony.

[21] Fiers pleaded guilty on July 7, 1991, to two charges of withholding information from Congress, including facts about secret Government efforts to support the contras during Boland. He was a key Government

was appointed to that position by Casey in late August 1984, about a month before the Boland cut-off became effective. Fiers, following his guilty plea, testified that shortly after he assumed his new position in approximately mid-September 1984, he was called at his home by Clarridge, and was asked to come in to the office. Once there, Fiers was introduced to North by Clarridge. "He [Clarridge] said, 'He's [North] someone you need to get to know. He's got responsibilities at the NSC for Central America and you'll be working with him.'"[22] In early November 1984 Fiers said he was again called into Clarridge's office and told: "Alan . . . you've got to cooperate with Ollie [North]. Ollie has got special responsibilities here for— for things in Central America and I want you to work with him."[23] Fiers said he was concerned that Clarridge's directive "would draw me into a collaboration with Ollie North that took me beyond the bounds of that [the Boland cut-off] restriction."[24]

Shortly after Fiers reported his concerns about North to Clarridge's successor as chief of the Latin American Division and to Clair E. George, CIA deputy director for operations, Fiers was summoned to a meeting with Casey, George, the new chief of the Latin American Division, and North. Fiers gave this account of the meeting:

> . . . the director sort of leaned back in his chair and said, "Ollie, Alan says you're operating in Central America" or words to that effect. "Are you operating in Central America?" And then the director said to me, "Alan, tell Ollie what you told—what you said." And I was sort of taken aback and kind of rounded the edges off—softened—the conversation that had taken place between Dewey [Clarridge] and myself . . . Well, the director then said, "Now Ollie, I don't want you operating in Central America. You understand that?"

And Ollie said, "Yes, sir. I understand it."[25]

After the meeting, George told Fiers that he had just witnessed a charade: "Alan, you've got to understand what happened in there. What we saw was for our consumption. Sometime in the dark of night Bill Casey has told the President: I'll take care of Central America, Mr. President; don't worry about it. And what you saw was essentially for our consumption." Fiers said he replied to George, "Wow, if that's true and if it blows it will be worse than Watergate."[26]

To Fiers, the message from George, the third highest ranking officer in the CIA, was clear: North, with Casey's support and direction, was taking on the CIA's role of supplying and advising the contras during the period of the Boland prohibitions.

This message was underscored to Fiers shortly after the "charade" meeting by two separate incidents. The first involved a request from North for CIA-produced intelligence on Nicaraguan air defenses, which would have been valuable to the contras but which Fiers could not produce under the Boland restrictions. When Fiers declined to produce it, within 24 hours he was summoned to bring the requested intelligence to George's office. Describing the incident, Fiers said: "I took it upstairs and gave it to him [George] and said, 'What are you going to do with it?' And he said, 'Never mind, just give it to me.'"[27]

The second example cited by Fiers involved a policy paper he was asked to write by Casey on what the United States ought to do to advance its goals in Central America. While his task force was in the final process of completing the paper, Fiers said, North called and asked for a copy. After Fiers refused to provide it to North, Fiers got a call from Casey asking him to bring the policy paper to the director's office in the Old Executive Office Building adjacent to the White House. After working into the night to complete the paper, Fiers gave this account of delivering it to Casey the following morning:

---

witness in the trial of Clair E. George, the former deputy director for operations at the CIA. George was convicted on December 9, 1992, of two felony charges of perjury and false statements before Congress. Both George and Fiers were pardoned by President Bush on December 24, 1992.

22 Fiers, *George* Trial Testimony, 10/28/92, pp. 1254–57.
23 Ibid., pp. 1257–58.
24 Ibid., p. 1261.

25 Ibid., pp. 1263–64.
26 Ibid., p. 1264.
27 Ibid., p. 1269.

I went down with it and he [Casey] looked at it and he said, "Now, take it down and give it to Ollie North." And I thought to myself, wow, I just got rolled big time. I took it down and gave it to Oliver North. And I came away with two conclusions: that Ollie North had the ability to work down in my chain of command and to cause to override me if and when I didn't do something.[28]

Casey was aware that North was raising money for the contras. He referred a potential contributor, beer magnate Joseph Coors, to North, explaining to Coors that he, Casey, could not be involved in assisting the contras because of the Boland restrictions.[29]

Casey, like other Administration witnesses when asked by congressional committees how the contras were managing to prosper during the Boland cut-off period, professed ignorance.[30]

In September 1986, in response to allegations that the CIA had provided $50 million to the contras over the past two years, Casey replied to the Senate Intelligence Committee: "The CIA has not provided any assistance whatsoever to support military or paramilitary operations in Nicaragua beyond that which was specifically authorized by Congress in the FY86 Intelligence Authorization Act. This Agency has scrupulously adhered to congressional restrictions in the past and will continue to do so in the future."[31]

In August 1984 CIA General Counsel Stanley Sporkin determined that a draft version of the Boland prohibition and the subsequent congressional floor debate "make it clear that this restriction is intended by its sponsors to halt CIA activities supporting the Contras."[32] While strict Agency guidelines were issued to appraise CIA field personnel of this reading, Casey's increased contacts with North show that he did not regard himself as cut off from the contras.[33]

By the late summer of 1986, Congress was prepared to lift the Boland restrictions, put the CIA back fully in play in Central America and appropriate $100 million in contra assistance. As the CIA prepared to move back into contra support and the North/Secord Enterprise was preparing to phase out, North attempted to sell the Enterprise's resupply assets to the CIA. North prevailed on George, Deputy CIA Director Robert M. Gates and Casey to intercede on behalf of the Enterprise. Fiers fought North off. "All three times I told each one the same thing, that they were not the right airplanes, they were heavy on maintenance, I didn't want to contaminate the old program with the new program," Fiers said. "They all understood the points . . . there was no argument, they all nodded their head [sic]. And this time Ollie didn't roll me in other words."[34]

## Casey and the Iran Arms Sales

Casey was an early advocate of finding an opening to Iran. He worked closely with McFarlane, who shared his view that the policy that existed at the end of 1984 was not adequate. The Iran policy then in effect essentially called for direct U.S. response with force if Iran should undertake terrorist attacks against the United States and a U.S.-led international embargo on all arms sales to Iran. The policy was based on a State Department study completed in October 1984, which concluded that the death of Ayatollah Khomeini was a precondition for any improvement in the Iran-U.S. relationship.

In the spring of 1985, reports began filtering back to the CIA that hostage William Buckley, a former CIA station chief in Lebanon, was being tortured. According to former Attorney

---

28 Ibid., p. 1271.

29 North, *North* Trial Testimony, 4/10/89, pp. 7220–21.

30 See, for example, Letter from Casey to Hamilton, 8/28/85, ER 11618 (explaining that Casey was not "in a position to answer in any authoritative way" inquiries whether the NSC was providing support to the contras).

31 Letter from Casey to Durenberger, 9/25/86, DDO TS8366–86.

32 Memorandum to Sporkin, 8/10/84, DO 182616–13.

33 Disregarding unrecorded Casey-North meetings and telephone calls, the number of recorded contacts between them is impressive. In 1984, nine meetings with North are noted on Casey's schedule; in 1985, there were six meetings; in 1986, nine meetings are recorded. These do not include group meetings at the NSC or elsewhere where both were present. North and Casey were also in frequent telephone contact. There were numerous phone calls between Casey and North in the fall of 1984, after Boland went into effect. Between October 12 and October 31 they spoke on the phone 12 times and met twice, according to Casey's schedules. Another spurt of contacts occurred in April 1985, when 13 calls with North are recorded on Casey's schedules. According to Casey's official schedules, Casey spoke with North 67 times on the phone in 1984, 54 times in 1985, and 44 times in 1986. Independent Counsel did not attempt to ascertain the substance of these contacts on a meeting-by-meeting or phone-call-by-phone-call basis.

34 Fiers, *George* Trial Testimony, 10/28/92, pp. 1333–34.

General Edwin Meese III, Buckley's fate was of special concern to Casey.[35]

In early spring 1985, Casey directed CIA National Intelligence Officer Graham Fuller to draft a paper suggesting a new Iran policy. Fuller, in a May 17, 1985, memorandum to Casey, suggested that the Iranian arms embargo might work against U.S. interests by moving the Iranians, who were desperately seeking arms on the world market to carry on their war with Iraq, toward a closer relationship with the Soviet Union. The Fuller memorandum to Casey, which was circulated as a Special National Intelligence Estimate (SNIE) to the NSC, State and Defense, contained several themes that were later picked up by McFarlane and Casey in support of the arms-for-hostages proposal. The first was that Iran was losing the war with Iraq; second was the notion that encouraging U.S. allies to resume arms sales to Iran would stop an Iranian drift toward the Soviet Union; third was the concept that the "arms door" was an opening which "might encourage the emergence of Iran's moderates into a greater policy role." [36]

On May 30, 1985, Casey asked in a meeting with Poindexter about the status of a new National Security Decision Directive (NSDD) on Iran. Poindexter replied that the NSC was pulling together a policy paper on Iran.[37] Two weeks later in a memorandum to Chief of CIA's Near East Division titled, "Release of Hostages," Casey described a conversation with his personal friend, John Shaheen, about an offer from indicted Iranian arms trader Cyrus Hashemi to set up contact with "leading figures in the Iranian Government." Shaheen had been told the Iranians were interested in obtaining TOW missiles.[38]

In mid-June 1985, the NSC produced a draft NSDD entitled "U.S. Policy Toward Iran," proposing, among other things, a resumption of limited arms sales to Iran as a means of seeking an opening. It adopted much of Fuller's memorandum to Casey. Casey supported the draft NSDD in a July 18 memorandum to McFarlane, stating: "I strongly endorse the thrust of the draft NSDD on *U.S. Policy Toward Iran*, particularly its emphasis on the need to take concrete and timely steps to enhance U.S. leverage in order to ensure that the USSR is not the primary beneficiary of change and turmoil in this critical country." Casey did not mention Fuller's "arms door" concept.[39] Both Shultz and Defense Secretary Caspar Weinberger strongly opposed the draft NSDD. The opposition of Shultz and Weinberger effectively blocked any formal change in U.S. policy and the draft NSDD was abandoned.

While the discussion over whether to use the "arms door" to Iran was taking place, McFarlane was acting. He authorized Michael A. Ledeen, a part-time NSC consultant on anti-terrorism, to ask Israeli Prime Minister Shimon Peres to check on a report that the Israelis had access to good sources on Iran. By early August 1985, Ledeen's talks had led to a direct approach by Israeli officials to McFarlane, to obtain President Reagan's approval to ship U.S.-supplied TOW missiles to Iran in exchange for the release of American hostages in Beirut. McFarlane said he briefed the President, Regan, Shultz, Weinberger, Casey and perhaps the Vice President about the proposal in July and August 1985.[40] McFarlane said that Casey recommended that Congress not be informed of the arms sales.[41]

In testimony to the House Permanent Select Committee on Intelligence (HPSCI) on November 21, 1986, Casey said he was first informed about contacts with Iran by McFarlane in the early fall of 1985, after the Israeli shipment of 504 TOWs in August and September.[42]

Charles Allen, the CIA national intelligence officer for counterterrorism, was asked by North in early September 1985 to arrange for collection of intelligence about arms broker Manucher

[35] Meese, Grand Jury, 11/20/87, p. 83.

[36] Memorandum from Fuller to Casey and McMahon, 5/17/85, ER 15478–83.

[37] Memorandum from McMahon to the Record, 5/31/85, ER 25830–31.

[38] Memorandum from Casey to Chief, Near East Division, DO, 6/17/85, ER 15126–27. In the memo, Casey noted Hashemi's claim that Vice President Bush's brother, Prescott, had approached the Iranians. Casey's schedules indicate that Casey received calls from Prescott Bush on March 1, 1985, and May 15, 1985. They are the only calls from Prescott Bush noted in the Casey schedules from 1984 to 1987.

[39] Memorandum from Casey to McFarlane, 7/18/85, AKW 00075–79.

[40] See McFarlane, Shultz, and Defense Department chapters.

[41] McFarlane, Select Committees Testimony, 7/14/87, pp. 243–45 ("It seems to me that at the July and August meetings in 1985 with the President and his Cabinet officers that Mr. Casey expressed the view that Congress should not be advised [of the arms initiative], and the President agreed with him, that—I don't recall any dissent from that position at the time.").

[42] Casey, HPSCI Testimony, 11/21/86, p. 5.

Ghorbanifar, his Iranian contact Mohsen Kangarlu, and their contacts in Lebanon. North said the request was related to a possible release of hostage Buckley.[43]

On September 13, 1985, Allen informed Casey of North's request when he called Casey in New York to tell him that the intelligence reports ordered by North indicated a possible hostage release[44] and arms transaction. Allen testified that North had directed him to restrict the intelligence reports to McFarlane, North, Casey and his deputy John McMahon, the secretary of defense and his senior military adviser, but to exclude Shultz and the State Department.[45]

The year-long intelligence effort initiated by North provided a steady stream of information. It included information as to bank accounts and weapons shipments and, beginning in the summer of 1986, references to a price spread between what the Iranians were paying for the equipment and what was being charged by the Department of Defense. Although Casey was among the listed recipients of this intelligence, it is not known how closely he followed the reports. A note from Defense Secretary Weinberger's diary of September 20, 1985, written after Weinberger learned of "strange" reports about an arms-for-hostages swap, indicated that Casey followed at least the early reports: "Called Bill Casey - he too is surprised by [intelligence reports] + suspects Bud [McFarlane] is not telling us all he knows or has promised."[46] The reports at that time contained information about the Israeli TOW shipments to Iran and the release of hostage Benjamin Weir.

Casey and McMahon met with McFarlane and Poindexter on November 14, 1985. According to McMahon's Memorandum for the Record:

> McFarlane then briefed on Ollie North's visit to London [Classified Information Withheld] ** [McFarlane then told us about the Israeli plan to move arms to certain elements of the Iranian military

who are prepared to overthrow the government].[47]

The following morning, Casey had breakfast with Israeli Defense Minister Yitzak Rabin, who was in Washington to learn whether the President still approved the Israeli arms sales to Iran. Later that day, McFarlane assured Rabin of the President's continuing approval.[48]

Casey was on a trip to Asia when the delivery of 18 HAWK missiles from Israeli stocks was finally made on November 24, 1985. The proposed shipment of 80 HAWK missiles ran into trouble when the El Al 747 cargo aircraft that the Israelis had commissioned for the task could not obtain landing rights in a European city. Neither Casey nor his deputy McMahon were available the weekend of November 21, 1985, so Clarridge undertook a series of operations largely on his own—including granting an NSC request to use an Agency proprietary airline.[49] When McMahon, on Monday, November 25, learned that a CIA proprietary was involved, he decided a presidential Finding authorizing the covert action was required. He called Sporkin, who agreed that a Finding was necessary.[50] A Finding drafted by Sporkin the next day described the Iran initiative as a straight arms-for-hostages arrangement.[51]

Casey agreed with the necessity of the Finding and forwarded it to Poindexter the same

---

[47] Memorandum from McMahon to the Record, 11/15/85, ER 32809–10 (second set of brackets and asterisks in original).
[48] McFarlane, Grand Jury, 5/6/87, pp. 34–35.
[49] See Clarridge chapter.
[50] McMahon, Grand Jury, 9/18/91, pp. 8–12.
[51] Draft Finding, ALV 014320. Sporkin's draft Finding for the President provided:

I have been briefed on the efforts being made by private parties to obtain the release of Americans held hostage in the Middle East, and hereby find that the following operations in foreign countries (including all support necessary to such operations) are important to the security of the United States. Because of the extreme sensitivity of these operations, in the exercise of the President's constitutional authorities, I direct the Director of Central Intelligence not to brief the Congress of the United States, as provided for in Section 501 of the National Security Act of 1947, as amended, until such time as I may direct otherwise.

DESCRIPTION

The provision of assistance by the Central Intelligence Agency to private parties in their attempt to obtain the release of Americans held hostage in the Middle East. Such assistance is to include the provision of transportation, communications, and other necessary support. As part of these efforts certain foreign material and munitions may be provided to the Government of Iran which is taking steps to facilitate the release of American hostages.

All prior actions taken by U.S. Government officials in furtherance of this effort are hereby ratified.

---

[43] Allen, Grand Jury, 12/18/87, pp. 19–21.
[44] Hostage Benjamin Weir was released two days later.
[45] Allen, Grand Jury, 12/18/87, pp. 22–25, 128–29.
[46] Weinberger Note, 9/20/85, ALZ 0039671.

day, November 26, 1985.[52] Poindexter testified
that the President signed the Finding on December 5, 1985.[54] Poindexter also testified that he
destroyed the Finding on November 21, 1986,
after the Iran arms sales had been publicly revealed and Congress was initiating inquiries on
the matter.[55] President Reagan did not recall
signing the Finding[53] and no copy of the signed
Finding was ever located by the OIC.

The Administration in December 1985 and
January 1986 continued to weigh alternatives
on how to pursue the Iran arms sales.
McFarlane, who resigned as national security
adviser on December 4, 1985, had soured on
the arms-for-hostages deals and had become
skeptical that arms broker Manucher
Ghorbanifar and his Iranian contacts were interested in anything except buying additional arms
from the United States. This left Casey and
Poindexter, who succeeded McFarlane as national security adviser, as the two main protago-
nists for going forward with the arms deals.
Weinberger and Shultz remained opposed. But
the President, ever sensitive to the plight of
the hostages, seemed willing to be convinced.
It was against that backdrop that a second phase
of the Iran arms sales began, this time under
direct U.S. auspices and control.

Poindexter scheduled a meeting of the President's top national security officials for December 7, 1985, to discuss the future of the Iran
arms sales. Casey could not attend. His deputy,
John McMahon, described the Agency's negative views of Ghorbanifar's reliability and questioned the existence of a moderate faction in
Iran. Poindexter claimed to have Casey's personal proxy in support of the proposal. A fol-

low-up meeting was set for December 10, 1985,
to hear McFarlane's report on an upcoming
meeting with Ghorbanifar in London.

On December 10, 1985, McFarlane recommended that the Administration have no further dealings with Ghorbanifar. Casey's memorandum of the meeting indicated that McFarlane
suggested other options. There was general support for a dialogue with other Iranian
intermediaries on a "purely intelligence basis
being alert to any action that might influence
events in Iran." But Casey indicated that another McFarlane option—simply letting the Israelis continue the arms deals on their own—
was generally opposed because it would be a
"little disingenuous and still bear the onus of
having traded with the captors and provide an
incentive for them to do some more kidnapping.
. . ." While the President stated no conclusion
at the meeting, Casey came away with probably
the clearest reading of the President's mind,
observing in his memorandum to McMahon:

> As the meeting broke up, I had the idea
> that the President had not entirely given
> up on encouraging the Israelis to carry on
> with the Iranians. I suspect he would be
> willing to run the risk and take the heat
> in the future if this will lead to springing
> the hostages. It appears that Bud
> [McFarlane] has the action.[56]

Despite Casey's report that McFarlane "has
the action," the record indicates that some of
the "action" as far as continuing the Iran arms
sales stayed with Casey. There were two troubling aspects of continuing the Iran arms sales
through the Israelis and Ghorbanifar: (1)
Ghorbanifar's unreliability and (2) legal problems stemming from selling weapons from Israeli stocks, on account of congressional reporting requirements under the Arms Export Control
Act. Casey took steps to defuse these problems.
On December 18, Casey was called by North,
according to Casey's schedule. It was their first
documented telephone conversation since early
October 1985. While there is no direct proof
of the substance of the conversation, the following day, Casey met with Ledeen and asked
Ledeen to talk to Ghorbanifar about taking a

---

[52] Memorandum from Casey to Poindexter, 11/26/85, AMY 000651–
52. Casey directed that it "should go to the President for his signature
and should not be passed around in any hands below our level."
The CIA never received a copy of the signed Finding. But in a December 7, 1985, Memorandum for the Record, McMahon noted, "After
repeated calls to NSC personnel on 27 November and during the week
of 2 December continuously receiving assurances of the President's
intent to sign the Finding, we were notified on 5 December that indeed
the Finding was signed." (Memorandum from McMahon to the Record,
12/7/85, ER 32388–89.)

[53] Reagan, *Poindexter* Trial Deposition, 2/17/90, pp. 230–33. When
presented with his response to interrogatories posed by Independent
Counsel in which he did not deny signing the Finding, Reagan responded that he still did not deny signing the Finding, but simply
did not recall it.

[54] Poindexter, Select Committees Deposition, 5/2/87, pp. 105–07.

[55] Poindexter, Select Committees Testimony, 7/15/87, pp. 46–48.
North said he was present at the time Poindexter destroyed the Finding.
(North, *North* Trial Testimony, 4/12/89, pp. 7616–18.)

[56] Memorandum from Casey to McMahon, 12/10/85, ER 10409.

lie-detector test at the CIA.[57] Later that day, Casey met at the White House with Poindexter and McMahon. On the next day, December 20, Casey met with Secord to discuss both the Iran arms sales and the contra-resupply operation.[58] Before taking his Christmas holiday, Casey met on December 23 with Clair George, the chief of the CIA's Near East Division, and the chief of the CIA's Iran Branch, to be briefed on the branch chief's meeting with Ghorbanifar in Washington the previous day.[59]

On the more complex question of how to avoid the legal problems created by arms sales to Iran from Israeli stocks, North and CIA General Counsel Sporkin began drafting "an expanded Finding" on January 2, 1986.[60] Casey, who was in Florida, sanctioned the collaboration by phone, but instructed Sporkin to keep him advised.[61] North and Sporkin opted for sales from Defense Department stocks to the CIA under the Economy Act. This gave control of the sales and pricing to the United States.

The proposal to resume arms sales to Iran was formally discussed at a White House meeting on January 7, 1986, attended by the President, Vice President Bush, Regan, Poindexter, Weinberger, Shultz, Meese and Casey. Weinberger memorialized the meeting in his diary notes for January 7 in succinct terms:

> Met with President, Shultz, Poindexter, Bill Casey, Ed Meese, in Oval Office—President decided to go with Israeli-Iranian offer to release our 5 hostages in return for sale of 4000 TOWs to Iran by Israel—George Shultz + I opposed - Bill Casey, Ed Meese + VP favored—as did Poindexter.[62]

Despite being informed of Ghorbanifar's failing a polygraph test on January 11, Casey noted that Ghorbanifar nevertheless appeared to have information on terrorist threats. He directed Charles Allen to meet with Ghorbanifar and learn more about him.

Casey was involved in planning how the new Iran arms sale operation would be conducted. In a memorandum dated January 13, 1986, Casey outlined two options for proceeding with TOW sales to Iran from U.S. stocks. Option 1 would have the Israelis buy improved TOWs from the United States and have the Israeli's ship older, basic TOWs in their arsenal to Iran. Casey pointed out that the Iranians had already placed $22 million for the transaction into a Swiss account, which was sufficient to pay for the basic TOWs but was not enough for the improved TOWs, which would cost about $44 million. Casey noted that Sporkin "feels that the most defensible way to do it from a legal standing" was through a CIA purchase of the weapons from the Defense Department. But he added: "We prefer keeping the CIA out of the execution even though a Presidential Finding would authorize the way Defense would have to handle the transactions."[63]

On January 15, North reported to Poindexter that Casey said that Weinberger would continue to be a roadblock in the Iran arms sales unless Weinberger was informed that the President had ordered it to go forward. North also reported that Casey saw no problem with having Secord deal directly with the Department of Defense in the missile purchases as an "agent of the CIA."[64] On January 16, Casey met with Poindexter, Weinberger, Attorney General Meese and Sporkin at the White House to discuss the Iran arms sales.[65]

President Reagan signed the third and final Iran arms sales Finding on January 17, 1986. The President, Vice President, Chief of Staff Regan and Poindexter's deputy, Donald Fortier, were briefed by Poindexter from a cover memo which stated that the CIA would purchase 4,000 TOWs from the Department of Defense and deliver them to Iran through "an agent of the CIA."[66] Casey informed Clair George that the President had signed the new Finding and directed George to attend a meeting at the White House Situation Room on January 20 to discuss its implementation. George, Sporkin and Thom-

[57] Ledeen, Grand Jury, 9/18/87, pp. 170–73.

[58] Secord, OIC Deposition, 4/30/87, pp. 1–5; Secord, Select Committees Testimony, 5/5/87, pp. 192–97.

[59] Iran Branch Chief, FBI 302, 12/4/86, pp. 2–3. The CIA administered a polygraph examination to Ghorbanifar on January 11, 1986. The results indicated that Ghorbanifar showed deception on 13 of 15 questions. The only two questions for which no deception was noted were his name and place of birth.

[60] Sporkin, Select Committees Testimony, 6/24/87, pp. 37–38.

[61] Ibid., pp. 49–50.

[62] Weinberger Note, 1/7/86, ALZ 0039883.

[63] DCI Talking Points, 1/13/86, ER 10410–11. Leaving the execution of the initiative to North and Secord paved the way for profiteering and the diversion.

[64] PROFs Note from North to Poindexter, 1/15/86, 012.

[65] Sporkin, Grand Jury, 3/2/88, pp. 61–64.

[66] Memorandum from Poindexter to Reagan, 1/17/86, AKW 001918–20.

as Twetten, deputy chief of the CIA's Near East Division, attended the meeting, which was presided over by Poindexter. To the surprise of the CIA contingent, Secord also attended. The meeting concluded with the understanding that the CIA should make the financial and logistical arrangements necessary for the TOW missiles to be transported to Iran.[67] Thus, despite protests by virtually all of the Agency's top officials, Secord and Ghorbanifar were to play key roles in the Iran arms sales.

There is evidence that Casey followed the meetings and subsequent arms transfers connected with the Iran initiative throughout 1986. On January 25, while Casey was overseas, McMahon cabled Casey to inform him that as a result of a meeting between North and Ghorbanifar in London, North had agreed that the CIA would furnish highly sophisticated intelligence to the Iranians, including "a map depicting the order of battle on the Iran/Iraq border showing units, troops, tanks, electronic installations. . . ." McMahon noted that "[e]veryone here at headquarters advises against this operation not only because we feel the principal involved [Ghorbanifar] is a liar and has a record of deceit, but, secondly, we would be aiding and abetting the wrong people." Notwithstanding McMahon's strong objections, Casey did not change his mind. As a result, Allen passed the intelligence to Ghorbanifar in London on January 25.[68]

On January 27, Casey met at various times with McMahon, Gates, George, and Clarridge. He spoke on the phone with Twetten three times and with Poindexter and the President, but Independent Counsel was unable to learn the subject of these meetings. The following day, Casey met with Gates, George and Allen to discuss Allen's meetings with Ghorbanifar in London.[69]

In early February, Casey participated in meetings with Allen, George and Twetten to discuss the Iran arms sales. He also talked to North before North, Secord and Nir were to meet in London on February 5. On February 18, the day after the first direct U.S. shipment of 500 TOWs was delivered in Tehran, Casey met with North. After the February 25 meeting of North, Secord, Hakim, Twetten and Nir with Ghorbanifar and Iranian representatives in Frankfurt, Casey was briefed by North and Twetten. Casey also met with North, Poindexter, George and Twetten at the White House. The same day, Casey met privately with the President. Talking points prepared for Casey by McMahon indicate that he suggested to the President that the Israelis and Ghorbanifar should not be included in the initial meetings with Iranian leaders in Iran. Casey suggested that the American party consist of McFarlane, North, Twetten, a staffer for McFarlane, and CIA annuitant George Cave. He also suggested that Secord fly to Tehran to set up a secure communications facility.[70]

Casey spent the first two weeks of March abroad. Immediately upon his return on March 15, he met on hostage-related matters with McMahon, Gates, George, Clarridge and Twetten. During the remainder of the spring and summer, Casey was kept informed on progress and problems with the Iran initiative by North and CIA officers involved with the project, particularly Cave, Allen and Twetten.

Casey was out of the country from July 4 to 15, 1986. The day after his return, Casey met with his Near East experts—including Clarridge—then followed up with a private session with North at the Old Executive Office Building. Independent Counsel could not prove the substance of these meetings.

The release of American hostage Father Lawrence Jenco on July 26, 1986, was attributed to the Iranians, in a July 28 Casey memorandum to Poindexter. The memorandum advised that the United States maintain the Ghorbanifar-Kangarlu contact in order to facilitate the release of the rest of the hostages and provide an opening to factions in Iran that could be dealt with in the future.[71]

In late July and throughout August, Ghorbanifar complained repeatedly about the price of the HAWK spare parts that had been sold to the Iranians. The overcharging complaints of the Iranians were presented in the

[67] Twetten, Grand Jury, 1/22/88, pp. 27–34; Twetten, *George* Trial Testimony, 8/6/92, pp. 2315–23; Sporkin, Grand Jury, 3/2/88, pp. 69–74.

[68] DIRECTOR 705774, 1/25/86, ER 24834–35; Allen, SSCI Testimony, 12/5/86, pp. 14–15.

[69] Allen, Select Committees Deposition, 4/24/87, pp. 360–62.

[70] DCI Talking Points, 2/27/86, ER 1997–98.

[71] Memorandum from Casey to Poindexter, 7/28/86, ER 31324–26.

intelligence reports which were delivered to the executive suites of the CIA. On September 8, 1986, Casey was briefed by Allen and Cave. Since early July, Cave had been involved in negotiations with Iranians who eventually became "the second channel" into Iran. On September 9, North informed Allen that Poindexter had approved use of the second channel. Allen expressed his concern that an unhappy Ghorbanifar might pose a security threat and North conceded he might have to take money out of "the reserve" to solve this problem. In a memo on this exchange sent to Casey the next day, Allen stated that "[t]o cut Ghorbanifar out, Ollie will have to raise a minimum of $4 million." [72] Allen called Casey early that same afternoon.

On September 17, Casey met with Allen, Cave, and CIA lawyer Bernard Makowka to discuss gathering intelligence during a visit by a nephew of Iranian Majlis Speaker Rafsanjani. Casey talked to both North and Poindexter about the arrangements. Casey was asked to ensure that the nephew was cleared to come into the United States.[73] Following the meetings with the nephew on September 19 and 20, George Cave briefed Casey and Clair George on September 22. According to a computer note from North to Poindexter that same day, Casey reportedly was concerned about "bringing the Sec State [Shultz] up to speed on results. I told him this was your call. Casey is urging a [meeting] on Wed[nesday] among you, Casey, Cave and me to discuss situation prior to discussion w/ Shultz." [74] The following day, Casey met with Poindexter, Cave, North and Twetten at the White House "re George Cave discussion." [75]

On October 2, Casey was called by North. A North memorandum to Poindexter on the same day proposed a trip to Frankfurt by North, Secord and Cave to meet with the nephew. The memorandum asked Poindexter to tell Casey to prepare "an appropriate intelligence package"

for the Frankfurt meeting.[76] On October 9, Casey and Gates had lunch with North in Casey's office at Langley to discuss the Frankfurt talks with Rafsanjani's nephew.[77]

## Casey and the Diversion

In 1986, the CIA arranged for the sale of 2,008 TOW missiles and a variety of HAWK spare parts to Iran in three separate transfers on February 13, May 23 and November 3. Agents acting for Iran deposited $28.6 million in the Swiss accounts controlled by Secord; approximately $1.7 million more was deposited by Israel for replenishment weapons.[78] Only $12,237,000 was deposited in CIA accounts. This enormous price differential—approximately $18 million—paved the way for the Iran/contra "diversion."

North testified that the idea of using "residuals" from the Iran arms sales to assist the contras was first suggested to him by Israeli official Amiram Nir or Ghorbanifar in late 1985 or January 1986.[79] North said both Casey and Poindexter endorsed the idea.

Independent Counsel obtained no documentary evidence showing Casey knew about or approved the diversion. The only direct testimony linking Casey to early knowledge of the diversion came from North. When asked by the Select Committees when Casey learned of the diversion, North replied:

Actually, my recollection is Director Casey learned about it before the fact. Since I am confessing to things, I may have raised it with him before I raised it with Admiral Poindexter, probably when I returned from the February—from the January discussions.

Q. You are referring now to the trip during which you had the discussion with Mr. Ghorbanifar in the bathroom?

A. Yes, I don't recall raising the bathroom specifically with the Director, but I do recall talking with the Director and I don't

[72] Memorandum from Allen to Casey, 9/10/86, ER 19179. It is not known whether Casey saw the memo.

[73] PROFs Note from North to Poindexter, 9/17/86, AKW 021694. See also PROFs Note from Poindexter to North, 9/17/86, AKW 2021696.

[74] PROFs Note from North to Poindexter, 9/22/86, AKW 021708.

[75] Casey Schedules, 9/23/86, ER 411–12.

[76] Memorandum from North to Poindexter, 10/2/86, AKW 007234–50. The memorandum does not indicate whether Poindexter approved North's recommendation.

[77] Gates, Grand Jury, 6/26/87, pp. 7–11.

[78] See Flow of Funds chapter.

[79] North, *Poindexter* Trial Testimony, 3/12/90, p. 1092.

remember whether it was before or after I talked to Admiral Poindexter about it.

I was not the only one who was enthusiastic about this idea and I—Director Casey used several words to describe how he felt about it, all of which were effusive. He referred to it as the ultimate irony, the ultimate covert operation kind of thing and was very enthusiastic about it.[80]

North indicated that Casey not only saw the profits from arms sales as a source of aid to the contras, but also as a means of financing other similar unauthorized covert operations:

At various times, he [Casey] and I talked about the fact that it might be necessary at some point in the future to have something, as he would put it, to pull off the shelf and to help support other activities like that. And none of those aside from the ones we talked about in terms of co-operation with Israel, the ones I referred to in my notes as TA–1, 2, and 3, or TH–1, 2, and 3, I don't recall exactly which—aside from those operations, he was looking forward to the possibility of needing to support other activities beyond that, and that is why I am not exactly certain as to what perhaps was intended beyond the use of those moneys for support of the Nicaraguan Resistance and the other purposes that I described to you earlier, in that I had, I think, communicated that to General Secord and he did prepare a layout which showed how other of those commercial entities could be used to support activities in other places besides Central America and besides U.S.-Israeli operations, besides the hostage recovery operations.[81]

The credibility of North's testimony is weakened by the fact that he never made such assertions while Casey was alive. In fact, when questioned by Attorney General Meese on November 23, 1986, about the diversion, North said the only persons in Government who knew about the diversion were McFarlane, Poindexter and himself. However, North did tell one of

his NSC staff associates, Lt. Col. Robert L. Earl, that he had told Casey about the diversion. In testimony at North's trial, Earl said that North told him in May or June 1986 that he had informed Casey of the use of profits from the Iran arms sales to assist the contras. Referring to North, Earl said:

He said that he had talked to Director Casey about the provision of certain parts of the money paid by the Iranians to— in support of the contras and that Director Casey had—had been impressed by the manipulation of the situation to the disadvantage of the Ayatollah, that we were taking some of the Ayatollah's money and applying it to a cause that the Ayatollah did not support.[82]

Another person who was told of the diversion by North was Fiers, but North did not tell Fiers about Casey's knowledge.[83]

Casey denied knowledge of the diversion. While he did not seem surprised on November 24, 1986, when Regan informed him that Meese had learned about the diversion, Regan reported that Casey did not admit prior knowledge. He denied knowing about the diversion in his congressional testimony following the public disclosure by Meese on November 25, 1986. He also denied knowing about the diversion to Clair George and CIA General Counsel David Doherty during a meeting on November 20, 1986.[84]

Regardless of his knowledge, Casey was at least instrumental in setting up a situation which made the diversion possible. North testified that Casey directed him in mid-1985 to take control of the funds going to the contras from third-country solicitations and contributions from private citizens. Casey approved North's suggestions in December 1985 and January 1986 for restructuring the Iran initiative, resulting in North and Secord's effective control of the

---

[80] North, Select Committees Testimony, 7/8/87, p. 124.
[81] Ibid., pp. 126–27.

[82] Earl, *North* Trial Testimony, 3/28/89, p. 5601.
[83] Fiers, *George* Trial Testimony, 10/28/92, p. 1338. Fiers said after North mentioned the diversion a second time, in late summer 1986, Fiers told his superior and Clair George. Fiers said George's response was, "Well, Alan, now you're one of a handful of people that know that, and keep it under your hat or keep it to yourself." (Ibid., p. 1340.) Fiers said he believed George's response was in reference to the fact of the Iran arms sales, not the diversion.
[84] Doherty, FBI 302, 11/13/87, p. 6.

funding for the arms purchases from Defense stocks and the payments from the Iranians.

Casey's meetings with North were also frequent during the crucial period leading up to and following the creation of the so-called "diversion memo" prepared by North in early April 1986 for approval by Poindexter and President Reagan. The month before, George Cave wrote a memo for the record reporting Ghorbanifar's proposal "that we use profits from these deals and others to fund support to the rebels in Afghanistan. We could do the same with Nicaragua." [85] Casey's schedule shows a private meeting on April 7, 1986, with the President, after a Casey meeting with Clarridge and Allen. Independent Counsel could not obtain direct evidence of the purposes for these meetings. That same day, North wrote a computer note to McFarlane which stated, "Per request of JMP [Poindexter] have prepared a paper for our boss which lays out arrangements." [86] On April 9, Casey met privately with North at the OEOB after having met with President Reagan in the morning. Again, Independent Counsel could not obtain direct proof of the purpose of this meeting.

In October and November 1986 Casey was confronted with growing evidence from a variety of sources of a diversion. His inactivity in responding to this evidence has yet to be explained. On October 1, Allen informed Gates of his mounting concerns regarding a diversion from the arms sales. After hearing his concerns, Gates advised him to speak with Casey as soon as possible. [87] Allen and Gates did not meet with Casey until October 7, when Allen briefed Casey on the reliability of the "second channel" into Iran. Allen told Casey of his concerns over a possible diversion of Iran arms sales funds to the contras, explaining that he had only a series of indicators, but no hard evidence. Allen said Casey seemed disturbed and called it a dangerous situation. Gates stated that if reports of the diversion were true, North had gone too far. Casey agreed. [88]

Casey then disclosed that Roy Furmark, a New York businessman and former client, had told him earlier that day that Adnan Khashoggi was a financial backer of Ghorbanifar and that Khashoggi and his Canadian investors were owed money by Ghorbanifar. [89] In describing his initial conversation with Furmark to the House Appropriations Committee, Casey later said that Furmark was informed by Khashoggi that the Canadians were threatening a lawsuit, which could publicize the Iran initiative. Following his meetings with Furmark and Allen, Casey called Poindexter that same afternoon. [90] In a memo dated October 8, Casey also informed the chief of the CIA's Near East Division, Tom Twetten, of his conversation with Furmark. [91]

On October 9, Casey and Gates met for lunch with North to receive a report on the Iran arms sales "second channel" into Iran. According to Gates, the discussions also focused on security problems posed by a dissatisfied Ghorbanifar and unhappy Canadian investors and the claim by Eugene Hasenfus, who had been shot down over Nicaragua and captured that week, that he was working for the CIA. North told Gates the CIA was "absolutely clean" in the Hasenfus matter. North also made a passing reference to Swiss bank accounts and the contras, according to Gates. After the meeting, Gates said he asked Casey about the meaning of North's mention of the Swiss bank accounts:

I mentioned the comment about the Swiss bank accounts, and because it was new information to me, or something that I hadn't been exposed to—I asked him if he understood what North was talking about—whether there was anything we should be concerned about in all of that. His reaction was that it gave me the impression that he hadn't even heard or had not picked up on what North had to say.

[85] Memorandum from Cave, 3/7/86, DO 25936–37 (dated by Cave on December 11, 1986). Cave wrote a second memo in April referring to Ghorbanifar's "scheme to use the profits to support the Afghan rebels." This memo did not refer to the contras. There is no evidence that Casey ever saw either of the Cave memos.

[86] PROFs Note from North to McFarlane, 4/7/86, AKW 01145.

[87] Allen, FBI 302, 6/24/87, pp. 4–5.

[88] Ibid., p. 5. Gates disputed this account. See Gates chapter.

[89] Ibid.

[90] Casey, House Appropriations Committee Testimony, 12/8/86, pp. .19–20.

[91] Memorandum from Casey to Twetten, 10/8/86, DO 84625. In the memo, Casey said Furmark believed the Canadian investors had been talking to Senators Leahy, Cranston and Moynihan, claiming that on the latest arms shipment they came up $10 million short.

Basically, in effect, said there was nothing to be concerned about then.[92]

On October 14, Allen sent identical memoranda to Casey and Gates outlining "problems that I see with our initiative towards Iran." Allen described the threat posed by Canadian investors and expressed concern that Ghorbanifar's allegations would include the claim that "the Government of the United States, along with the Government of Israel, acquired a substantial profit from these transactions, some of which profit was redistributed to other projects of the U.S. and of Israel."[93] Late in the day, Casey phoned Poindexter, then met with North, Twetten, and Cave at CIA headquarters.[94]

Gates said he was so disturbed by the Allen memorandum that the following day he obtained permission from Casey to give the information to CIA General Counsel Doherty. Doherty recommended that the Allen memorandum be provided to Poindexter.[95] Later in the afternoon of October 15, Gates and Casey met with Poindexter in the Old Executive Office Building where Casey showed Poindexter the Allen memorandum and asked him to read it immediately. According to Gates, Casey then expressed concern that the project was out of control and urged that the whole Iran affair be made public.[96] On October 16, Casey directed Allen to meet with Furmark, who was in Washington at that time. Allen interviewed Furmark at the OEOB. Casey had three telephone conversations with Furmark that day and Furmark returned to New York on a flight with Casey and Casey's wife. The day after his meeting with Furmark, Allen wrote to Casey that his conversation with Furmark "only served to underscore the serious concerns that I outlined to you in my memorandum of 14 October."[97]

On October 20, Casey met with President Reagan and Poindexter at the White House. Two days later Casey met early in the day with Allen. Allen and Cave then flew to New York to meet again with Furmark. Among other things, Furmark told Allen and Cave that Ghorbanifar believed that millions of dollars from the arms sales were earmarked for Central America. The following day, Casey was briefed on the meeting with Furmark. Casey directed Cave to write a memorandum for Casey's signature for forwarding to Poindexter. In the memorandum, which apparently was not sent, Cave repeated Furmark's claim that Ghorbanifar believed the bulk of $15 million in profits was earmarked for Central America.[98]

On November 6, 1986, three days after the Iran arms sales were publicly exposed, Casey met with Gates and Poindexter at the White House, where Casey recommended that Poindexter have White House Counsel Peter J. Wallison review the Iran affair. Poindexter said he did not trust Wallison to keep his mouth shut and that NSC Counsel Paul B. Thompson would conduct the review.[99] The next day, Allen wrote still another memorandum to Casey on his continuing debriefing of Furmark. Among other things, Allen wrote:

> The Canadians intend to expose fully the US Government's role in the backchannel arms transactions with Iran. They believe Lakeside [probably referring to Lake Resources, an Enterprise shell company] to be a proprietary of the US Government; they know that former Major General Richard Seccord [sic] is heavily involved in managing the arms transactions to Iran for Oliver L. North, and that Secord is also involved in assisting North in the support the [sic] Contras in Nicaragua.[100]

On November 10, Casey attended a meeting with the President, Vice President, Poindexter, Poindexter's deputy Alton G. Keel, Shultz, Weinberger, Meese and Regan. It was at this meeting that Poindexter, at Reagan's request, gave an account of the Iran arms sales. Poindexter falsely stated that they began in

[92] Gates, Grand Jury, 6/26/87, pp. 7–11.

[93] Memorandum from Allen to McMahon, 10/14/86, ER 127–34.

[94] Independent Counsel was unable to establish direct evidence of the purpose of this meeting.

[95] Gates, Grand Jury, 6/26/87, pp. 19–20.

[96] Ibid., pp. 20–21.

[97] Memorandum from Allen to Casey and Gates, 10/17/86, ER 46446–48.

[98] Memorandum from Casey to Poindexter, ER 19051–53. On November 25, after Meese learned of the diversion, Casey appeared to be upset to learn that the memorandum had not been sent. But, according to Allen, he said, "Well, it doesn't matter, I briefed Admiral Poindexter on the substance of this." (Allen, Grand Jury, 1/4/88, pp. 107–8.)

[99] Gates, Grand Jury, 6/26/87, pp. 23–25.

[100] Memorandum from Allen to Casey and Gates, 11/7/86, ER 46449–52.

1986 with the signing of the January 17, 1986, Finding, leaving out the 1985 Israeli shipments. There was no mention of a diversion.

On November 12, Poindexter repeated his performance for the same group but with congressional leaders present. Senator Robert Byrd asked if "anything happened" in 1985, and Poindexter answered that there were "contacts," but no materials were shipped.[101]

On November 16, Casey departed on a three-day trip to Central America. Before he left, he directed Gates to take charge of preparing testimony on the Iran arms sales for Senate and House intelligence committee hearings set for November 21. While Casey was in Central America, Shultz emerged as the sole dissenter to a cover story that the President did not have prior knowledge of the 1985 HAWK shipment and did not authorize it.

Casey returned from his Central American trip on the evening of November 19. En route, he rewrote the proposed testimony which had been prepared under Gates's direction and had been flown down to Casey by Norman Gardner, a special assistant to Clair George. At a meeting held November 20 to help prepare Casey's testimony, North suggested that Casey state that "no one in the U.S. Government" knew the nature of the cargo in the November 1985 HAWKs flight "until January 1986." Casey, who had been prepared to state that no one in the CIA knew the nature of the cargo until January 1986, marked North's suggested change into his documents.[102]

The proposed statement brought Casey into direct conflict with Shultz, who contended that he was briefed in Geneva by McFarlane prior to the shipment in November 1985 and told that the cargo would be missiles. It also was at odds with Sporkin's recollection that he learned soon after the November 1985 flight that the cargo was missiles. Conflicts such as these led to a very thin description of the CIA's

1985 activities in Casey's November 21 testimony.[103]

Casey was so angry at Shultz's public airing of his opposition to the Iran arms sales that in a letter to the President on November 23, 1986, he urged that Shultz be fired.

On Friday I spent over five hours discussing and answering questions for the House and Senate Intelligence Committees on our effort to develop a relationship with important elements in Iran. I was able to deal with all of their questions with no problem while, at all times, insisting on the value and need for this. A full house of each of the Committees was present throughout and, except for the expected partisan posing by Bobby Byrd and Jim Wright, when they went out to speak to the cameras, the members took it well.

As to the manner in which Shultz had conducted himself regarding the Iran disclosures, Casey said:

The public pouting of George Shultz and the failure of the State Department to support what we did inflated the uproar on this matter. If we all stand together and speak out I believe we can put this behind us quickly. Under Secretary of State Armacost sat through my briefing like a bump on a log, opening his mouth only to deny any involvement or knowledge. . . . Rich Armitage, who accompanied me for Defense, was helpful in explaining the rules on arms transfer and was forthcoming and supportive whenever he had the opportunity. . . . You need a new pitcher! A leader instead of a bureaucrat. I urge you to bring in someone like Jeane Kirkpatrick or Paul Laxalt, who you may recall, I recommended for State in 1980.[104]

In response to conflicting accounts over the 1985 Israeli arms shipments to Iran, President Reagan on November 21, 1986, directed Meese to conduct an inquiry to develop a "coherent" account of the Iran initiative.[105] During the weekend of the Meese inquiry, Casey had con-

---

[101] Weinberger Meeting Notes, 11/12/86.

[102] North, *North* Trial Testimony, 4/12/89, pp. 7628–33. Casey's executive assistant later testified that Casey returned to CIA Headquarters with this draft and promptly misplaced it. Casey's Executive Assistant Statement to SSCI, as set forth in Nomination of Robert M. Gates to be Director of Central Intelligence, Sen. Exec. Rpt. 102–19, 102d Cong., 1st Sess., pp. 65–66 (Oct. 24, 1991). Evidence uncovered by Independent Counsel supports this officer's testimony. See Conduct of CIA Officers in November 1986 chapter.

[103] See ibid.

[104] Letter from Casey to Reagan, 11/23/86, AKW 020592.

[105] Meese, Grand Jury, 2/17/88, pp. 47, 122.

tact with all of the principals involved in the initiative except McFarlane. There are no notes on these contacts. Testimony that exists about these contacts is often illogical, or not believable, in the context of the weekend's dramatic developments. Casey's schedules and witness testimony show:

Friday, November 21:

4:25 p.m. Call to Poindexter
5:20 p.m. Call to Regan
Evening Meese called Casey about inquiry

Saturday, November 22:

9:55 a.m. Call to Meese
10:05 a.m. Meeting with Gates
10:05 a.m. Call from Sporkin
10:10 a.m. Call to Meese
10:10 a.m.
Meeting with Gates, George, Twetten, Clarridge, Kerr, Layton, Allen, Cave, Gries, and Kinsinger
10:15 a.m. Call to Poindexter
12:25 p.m. Call from Sporkin
12:35 p.m. Call to Poindexter
12:50 p.m. Call to Cave
12:52 p.m. Call to Allen
12:55 p.m. Meeting with Cave
1:15 p.m. Lunch with Poindexter and North
3:46 p.m. Call to Meese
Evening meeting at residence with Meese

Sunday, November 23:

10:20 a.m. Call to Meese
10:25 a.m. Call to Allen
10:30 a.m. Meeting with Allen and Doherty
10:37 a.m.
Meeting with Cooper, Allen, Doherty, Jameson
10:55 a.m. Call to Allen
11:05 a.m. Call from Michael Deaver
11:07 a.m. Call to Deaver
11:12 a.m. Call from Sporkin
11:17 a.m.
Meeting with Doherty (joined by Allen at 12:10 p.m.)

12:30 p.m. Meeting with Doherty and Jameson
1:20 p.m. Call to President Reagan
3:30 p.m. Meeting with Deaver

Monday, November 24:

10:25 a.m.
Meeting with Twetten and Casey Executive Assistant
10:30 a.m. Meeting with Allen and Cave
10:35 a.m.
NSPG pre-brief with George, Kerr, Twetten
12:45 p.m. Meeting with Allen and Cave
2:00 p.m. NSPG meeting, White House
5:10 p.m. Meeting with Furmark
5:20 p.m. Call to North
5:25 p.m. Call to Twetten
6:00 p.m. Call from George
6:15 p.m. Meeting with Cave
6:35 p.m. Meeting with Regan
7:05 p.m. Call to Poindexter

Tuesday, November 25:

6:30 a.m. Call to Meese, who subsequently dropped by Casey's home
7:20 a.m. Meeting with Allen
7:25 a.m. Call to Richard Allen
8:00 a.m. Meeting with George
8:25 a.m. Call to Meese
8:30 a.m. Call to Twetten
8:45 a.m. Call to Doherty
8:46 a.m. Call to George
8:50 a.m. Meeting with Twetten
8:55 a.m. Call from Gates
9:00 a.m. Meeting with Doherty
9:15 a.m. Call to Weinberger
10:15 a.m. NSPG meeting, White House
11:00 a.m.
Meeting with Congressional Leaders at White House
11:58 a.m. Call from Allen
12:02 p.m. Call to Poindexter
3:00 p.m. NSPG meeting on interim restraint
5:10 p.m. Call from Clarridge
5:12 p.m. Call to Regan
5:25 p.m. Meeting with Allen and Cave
5:40 p.m. Call from Twetten

6:10 p.m. Call from Fred Ikle

Some of the more significant contacts were:

—The evening of Friday, November 21, when Meese said he told Casey he was launching an inquiry into the Iran initiative at the President's request. Meese said he did not schedule an interview with Casey because he already had Casey's prepared remarks from the November 21 hearings before the Senate and House intelligence committees. Meese told Casey he wanted to speak with Sporkin and McMahon.[106]

—November 22, when Meese said he received calls from Casey at 9:55 a.m. and 3:46 p.m. and visited Casey that evening. Meese told the Grand Jury that the reason Casey called in the afternoon was that he wanted to provide information. Meese said he went to Casey's home that evening but did not take notes of their conversation. Meese said Casey disclosed to him the information given him by Furmark about the disgruntled Canadian investors. Meese did not recall Casey mentioning the contras or the diversion. Meese said he did not tell Casey about the diversion memo his staff had uncovered that afternoon at the White House because he was not certain where it would lead.[107] Meese said Casey told him he had spoken to Poindexter about the funds and that Poindexter had assured him that nothing wrong had occurred. Meese still did not discuss the diversion with Casey. Meese said Casey "may have" discussed the December 1985 Finding with him at that time, but he wasn't sure. The December 1985 Finding "wasn't particularly important at this stage because it really didn't alter anything that had happened," Meese said. He said Casey did not tell him about his two-hour meeting with Poindexter earlier that day.[108]

—November 22, when Casey had lunch with Poindexter and North, Poindexter said that the topic of discussion was Casey's testimony from the day before. Poindexter said there was no discussion of the diversion. Poindexter said he did not tell Casey about his destruction the day before of the December 1985 Finding.[109]

—November 24, when Casey called Assistant Attorney General Charles Cooper. Cooper said Casey, who had never called him before, asked whether Cooper had come across the name "Lakeside Resources" in the course of the Meese inquiry. This was apparently a reference to the Enterprise's Lake Resources account, which was misidentified by Furmark to Allen, who subsequently used the name "Lakeside" in a memo to Casey on October 7, 1986. Cooper said the name had some familiarity, but he could not place it.[110]

—November 24, when at 6:35 p.m. Regan met with Casey at the CIA and told him what Meese had discovered about the diversion. Regan said Casey did not act surprised, but his reaction was one of concern for the impact on the contras. Casey also expressed concern that public disclosure would close down contacts with Iran. Regan said that Casey reminded him that he had mentioned Furmark and unhappy Canadian investors. Regan could not recall when Casey first mentioned Furmark to him. He has given various estimates of when this occurred, from late October 1986 to November 20, 1986.[111]

—November 25, when Casey called Meese at home and asked him to drop by on his way to work. Meese told Casey about the diversion, and Casey told Meese he would send him a copy of a memo about Furmark's allegations. Meese said that while he was at Casey's home, Regan placed a call to Meese to tell him he would be asking for Poindexter's resignation that morning.[112]

—Early on November 25, when Casey asked Allen to gather the Furmark memo-

[106] Meese, Grand Jury, 12/21/87, pp. 101–4.
[107] Ibid., pp. 143–44.
[108] Ibid., pp. 138–39, 141–52.

[109] Poindexter, Select Committees Testimony, 7/21/87, pp. 71–75.
[110] Cooper, Select Committees Testimony, 6/25/87, pp. 147–49.
[111] Regan, FBI 302, 7/14/87, pp. 19–27, 92–94.
[112] Meese, Select Committees Testimony, 7/28/87, pp. 157–59.

randa so that he could send them to Meese immediately. Allen said that Casey told him some very serious developments were about to happen. Casey was frantically trying to find a copy of the memorandum of October 24, 1986, which outlined Furmark's diversion allegations and which Casey said he thought had been sent to Poindexter but apparently had not.[113]

## Casey's Testimony to Congress

Casey's virtually identical opening statements on November 21, 1986, to both the House and Senate intelligence committees[114] were incorrect or incomplete in several respects:

1. Casey concealed the U.S. role in the 1985 TOW and HAWK shipments. He limited the CIA's involvement to providing an Agency proprietary to transport "cargo" from Israel to Iran. Casey failed to mention the September 1985 stepped-up intelligence on Iran and Lebanon and individuals involved in the Iran initiative.

2. In the responses Casey omitted the December 5, 1985, retroactive Finding:

—Regarding the CIA's involvement in November 1985 Casey said that McMahon directed that no further flights take place without a Presidential Finding. But Casey did not mention that McMahon demanded a Finding to cover the November 1985 shipment, nor did he mention that he had sent a draft Finding to Poindexter with directions that the President sign it.

—Casey stated there had been "only two findings" in the past 10 years on Iran, which did not count the after-the-fact December 5, 1985, Finding.[115]

—Again failing to mention the December 1985, Finding, Casey stated that the January 17, 1986 Finding was only the second time notice of a Finding was withheld from Congress by Presidential directive, the first time being President Carter's brief withholding of notification of a Finding regarding the aborted 1980 Iranian hostage-rescue effort.

3. Casey testified that the Agency's proprietary flight crew was told the cargo contained oil-drilling equipment. While Casey's testimony was technically correct—the flight crew initially was told the cargo was oil-drilling equipment— CIA field personnel quickly learned and communicated back that the cargo was missiles.[116]

4. Casey's description of the Iran arms sales focused almost exclusively on the geopolitical rationale for seeking an opening to Iran. He mentioned the hostage issue only in passing, even though the initiative was an arms-for-hostages operation.

5. Casey's description of the money flow in the 1986 weapons shipments was inaccurate and incomplete. He did not mention the roles of Secord and the Enterprise in the arms deals. Casey testified that the Iranian funds were deposited in an Israeli account, then transferred to a sterile CIA account, when in fact the funds were deposited by the Iranians into the Enterprise's Swiss accounts controlled by Secord, operating as an "agent for the CIA." Whether or not Casey knew the precise details of the money flow, he laid it out to the committees as if he did. He was accompanied by others who did know the flow but did not correct him, as they did on other occasions when he misspoke. Casey withheld from the committees a central aspect of the arms transfer—the role of Secord as the CIA's "agent."

Nor did Casey disclose his information of a substantial diversion. In fact, he assured the committees:

I would like to reiterate that the funds for the material I have enumerated as well as all associated costs were provided by the Iranians, funding for Iran was transferred to CIA for deposit in a covert funding mechanism. . . . This action provided secure means for controlled payment and ac-

[113] Allen, Grand Jury, 1/4/88, pp. 74–75.

[114] Casey appeared before HPSCI and SSCI with these CIA officers: George, Doherty, Comptroller Daniel Childs; Allen; a special assistant to George (called CIA Subject #2 in Conduct of CIA Officials in November 1986 chapter); David Gries; and another member of Gries staff. George's special assistant Norman Gardner was at the afternoon HPSCI hearing; W. George Jameson was at the SSCI session. Also present before both panels were Under Secretary of State Michael H. Armacost and his executive assistant; Assistant Secretary of State Richard W. Murphy; State Department Legal Adviser Abraham D. Sofaer (morning session of HPSCI only); two deputy assistant secretaries of state; Assistant Secretary of Defense Richard Armitage; and a Department of Defense legal adviser. John Bolton of the Department of Justice attended the SSCI session only.

[115] There is, however, no direct proof Casey knew the December 5, 1985, Finding had been signed.

[116] See Clarridge chapter.

countability of all the funds associated with this program. The Iranian funds, a total of $12,237,000 were deposited in a special account in a Swiss bank.[117]

While the House committee did not focus on the contents of the November 1985 shipment, they questioned Casey as to whether the President authorized the shipment. Casey alluded to a shipment made by the Israelis that "violated our law." Later, Casey, without mentioning the HAWK shipment but apparently referring to it, said it was sent without the President's knowledge and "we ultimately required the Israelis to reverse," meaning get the materials back. This led Representative Dwyer to ask:

Mr. Dwyer: One more point I would like to have cleared up in my mind, the Israelis transferred some equipment to the Iranians. We apparently were chagrined because they transferred that equipment and the Israelis got the equipment back. Is that what I heard?

CIA Subject #2: That is correct.

Mr. Allen: That is right.

Mr. Dwyer: There must be an excellent relationship between the Israelis and the Iranians to deliver the equipment and say, hey, look, we made a mistake; you got to give us the equipment back. Is that really what happened?

Mr. Casey: I don't know if they actually got the equipment back.

CIA Subject #2: We got it back.

Mr. Allen: The Israelis obtained back the equipment, 17 of them.

Mr. Casey: There is a good relationship between the Iranians and Israelis.

Mr. Dwyer: But how was it that—how did they get it back? Does anybody know? I mean who went and got it?

Mr. Casey: They probably shipped it back. I don't know.

Mr. Allen: I think it was brought back in the February–March time frame by one of the flights that went in with TOW missiles. So that they were retrieved.[118]

When questioned about why the CIA played a support role in the Iran arms sales while the NSC supervised it, Casey conceded that the NSC's principal role is to advise the President, not to conduct operations. Asked by Representative McCurdy, "Who headed the team? Who called the shots? Was it Poindexter or Casey?," Casey replied: "I think it was the President." Asked by McCurdy if the NSC had managed similar operations, Casey replied, "I am trying to think. Apart from the Central American thing which has NSC people involved in it, I don't know of any." [119] Pressed later by Representative Brown about how the NSC got involved in running the Iran initiative, Casey conceded, "I don't think that is a good idea. It happened. It happened first because the Administration wanted to pursue something that the Congress that created the CIA and Defense Department should not do and that is this Central American business." [120]

Questioning of Casey by the SSCI focused more sharply on how the CIA could fail to know that the cargo in the November 1985 shipment consisted of HAWK missiles. Casey originally stated that the people "running the airplane were told that they were oil field parts." [121]

Casey incorrectly testified that McFarlane briefed him about the Israeli initiative before he left for a trip overseas "without getting into the arms aspect of it." [122] This conflicts with McMahon's memo for the record on the McFarlane briefing which indicated that McFarlane made it clear that the initiative involved the shipment of arms.

Casey also incorrectly testified about North's active participation in drafting the January 17, 1986, Presidential Finding. Asked who in the NSC participated in the drafting, Casey, who worked closely with North and Sporkin on the Finding, said: "I really can't tell you all who

[117] Casey, HPSCI Testimony, 11/21/86, pp. 17–18.

[118] Ibid., pp. 101–2.
[119] Ibid., pp. 42–43.
[120] Ibid., p. 64.
[121] Casey, SSCI Testimony, 11/21/86, p. 32.
[122] Ibid., p. 62.

might have been in. I would just be guessing.''[123]

On December 8, 1986, Casey testified before the House Defense Appropriations Subcommittee. Casey denied all knowledge of a diversion. He stated that while he had heard reports of a diversion to Central America from Furmark in early and mid-October, he had no firm proof until told of Meese's discovery by Regan on November 24, 1986.

Casey continued to withhold information about Secord's role as an agent of the CIA in the initiative and to misstate the money flow for the 1986 TOW and spare HAWK missile parts. He withheld his knowledge of North's central role in the contra-resupply effort, attributing the flow of funds to the contras to unnamed "private benefactors."

When he appeared before the House Foreign Affairs Committee on December 10, 1986, Casey's testimony on the diversion was similar to his account two days earlier to the House Defense Appropriations Subcommittee, except he did add that "[i]t's barely conceivable" that North and Poindexter initiated the diversion on their own.[124] On contra support, Casey testified that the CIA learned in the spring of 1986 of "private benefactor supply activity being conducted out of Ilopango" air base in El Salvador and said the Agency did not permit its people to become involved.[125] As to who the "private benefactors" were, Casey said "I have heard speculation over a period of time, various rich people, other countries, but it was all rumor." Asked if the Saudis ever contributed to the contras, he said, "I have seen press reports to that effect," but he said he never inquired about those reports.[126]

Casey's most difficult testimony came on December 11, 1986, before the House Permanent Select Committee on Intelligence, before whom he had previously testified on November 21, 1986.

Casey said he did not inform the committee of a possible diversion at his previous appearance because "I had to protect the ongoing operation which the NSC and the President and everybody else hoped would bring additional hostages out."[127] Asked if he had informed Reagan about the rumors of a diversion, Casey said, "No, I didn't tell the President. I didn't think it reached that order. . . . I don't bother the President about little details like that."[128]

Casey faced tough questions over the December 5, 1985, Finding. The committee asked whether there were "any other covert activities or findings that this committee has not been informed of." Casey said "No," explaining that a November 26, 1985, draft Finding was "sent up and it didn't get completed until January 17th."[129] After being confronted with a copy of the November 26 draft Finding and asked whether it was sent to the President for signing, Casey replied:

It wasn't this. It was the one he signed as far as I remember. I guess we just passed it around for discussion. There was an objection to this all prior action clause, I think on the part of the NSC and it was taken out before it was finally signed.

Casey said he did not think it was sent to the President: "It didn't get accepted. It was not accepted. It was redrafted."[130] Casey was shown a memo for the record from McMahon dated December 7, 1985, in which McMahon stated that the Finding was cleared by Casey, who "called McFarlane and Don Regan to ascertain that indeed [the shipment] had Presidential approval and to get assurances that a Finding would be so signed." The memo went on to say that the CIA was notified on December 5, 1985, that the Finding had been signed by the President. Casey's final word on the subject was: "Maybe that finding was signed but it was certainly signed on January 17th, the ultimate Finding. I don't think one was signed in between. . . . Maybe it was possible that it was signed and it was replaced by another Finding."[131]

## Conclusion

Casey's conduct in October and November 1986 certainly can be questioned. His actions when

---

123 Ibid., p. 76.
124 Casey, HFAC Testimony, 12/10/86, p. 53.
125 Ibid., pp. 20–21.
126 Ibid., pp. 154–55.

127 Casey, HPSCI Testimony, 12/11/86, p. 6.
128 Ibid., pp. 119, 184.
129 Ibid., pp. 80, 89.
130 Ibid., pp. 92–94.
131 Ibid., pp. 155–56.

confronted with mounting evidence of a diversion were more consistent with the behavior of a person aware of the diversion and concerned with keeping it concealed, than with the behavior of a responsible official learning for the first time that one of the President's top covert foreign policy initiatives had been illegally subverted.

When Allen and Gates met with Casey in early October 1986 to share Allen's concerns about a possible diversion, Casey, who had independently received similar reports from his friend Furmark, did not request an immediate investigation. He did not call the President or the Attorney General. Instead, he directed Allen to write another memorandum. And Casey called Poindexter, the man in charge of the operation presumably gone bad. The next day, Casey and Gates had lunch with North, the man who was running the operation. Again, Casey did not confront North or demand to know what was going on. Instead, he talked about operational details, warned North about dissatisfied Canadian investors, and obtained from North a disingenuous clean bill of health for the CIA on any involvement in the illegal contra-supply operation.

In separate appearances before the House and Senate intelligence committees on November 21, Casey made no mention of his suspicions of a diversion. There is no evidence that he told the Attorney General even after he learned that Meese, at the President's direction, was conducting an inquiry to get a coherent picture of the Iran arms sales. It was not until after Meese publicly announced the diversion on November 25 that Casey made available to Meese the final Allen memorandum outlining a possible diversion.

The objectivity, professionalism, and integrity of the Central Intelligence Agency were compromised by Casey's attitude and behavior in connection with the Iran venture. To a large degree, the CIA's top professionals were dragged against their better judgment into supporting a questionable venture conducted by NSC staff who lacked competence and expertise in covert operations. At Casey's insistence, two persons—Ghorbanifar and Secord—were placed in key roles, although Agency leaders considered them to be unreliable and unfit for such important and sensitive assignments. As a result, key Agency officials felt obliged to adopt a cynical see-no-evil, hear-no-evil, report-no-evil posture.

# Chapter 16
# Robert M. Gates

Robert M. Gates was the Central Intelligence Agency's deputy director for intelligence (DDI) from 1982 to 1986. He was confirmed as the CIA's deputy director of central intelligence (DDCI) in April of 1986 and became acting director of central intelligence in December of that same year. Owing to his senior status in the CIA, Gates was close to many figures who played significant roles in the Iran/contra affair and was in a position to have known of their activities. The evidence developed by Independent Counsel did not warrant indictment of Gates for his Iran/contra activities or his responses to official inquiries.

## The Investigation

Gates was an early subject of Independent Counsel's investigation, but the investigation of Gates intensified in the spring of 1991 as part of a larger inquiry into the Iran/contra activities of CIA officials. This investigation received an additional impetus in May 1991, when President Bush nominated Gates to be director of central intelligence (DCI). The chairman and vice chairman of the Senate Select Committee on Intelligence (SSCI) requested in a letter to the Independent Counsel on May 15, 1991, any information that would "significantly bear on the fitness" of Gates for the CIA post.

Grand Jury secrecy rules hampered Independent Counsel's response. Nevertheless, in order to answer questions about Gates' prior testimony, Independent Counsel accelerated his investigation of Gates in the summer of 1991. This investigation was substantially completed by September 3, 1991, at which time Independent Counsel determined that Gates' Iran/contra activities and testimony did not warrant prosecution.[1]

## Gates and the Diversion

Gates consistently testified that he first heard on October 1, 1986, from the national intelligence officer who was closest to the Iran initiative, Charles E. Allen, that proceeds from the Iran arms sales may have been diverted to support the contras.[2] Other evidence proves, however, that Gates received a report on the diversion during the summer of 1986 from DDI Richard Kerr. The issue was whether Independent Counsel could prove beyond a reasonable doubt that Gates was deliberately not telling the truth when he later claimed not to have remembered any reference to the diversion before meeting with Allen in October.

Allen did not personally convey to Gates his concerns about the diversion until October 1, 1986.[3] Allen testified, however, that he became worried during the summer of 1986 that the

---

[1] Independent Counsel made this decision subject to developments that could have warranted reopening his inquiry, including testimony by Clair E. George, the CIA's former deputy director for operations. At the time Independent Counsel reached this decision, the possibility remained that George could have provided information warranting reconsideration of Gates's status in the investigation. George refused to cooperate with Independent Counsel and was indicted on September 19, 1991. George subpoenaed Gates to testify as a defense witness at George's first trial in the summer of 1992, but Gates was never called.

[2] See, for example, Gates, Grand Jury, 5/1/91, p. 135 ("Q. Do you recall that in this time frame also you became initially—well, let me not characterize it—you became aware of what is now referred to as the diversion.[sic] A. Yes. I had a meeting with the NIO, the national intelligence officer, Charlie Allen, on the 1st of October."); Gates, SSCI Confirmation Hearing, 2/17–18/87, p. 13 (response to written interrogatory about his knowledge of the diversion).

[3] Allen believed, however, that he sent a memorandum to Gates discussing, among other things, how much money North needed to pay Manucher Ghorbanifar from the Iran initiative. (Memorandum from Allen to the DCI, Subject: American Hostages, 11/10/86, ER 19739; Allen, Grand Jury, 1/4/88, pp. 19–21.) Independent Counsel was unable to corroborate Allen's testimony.

Iran initiative would be derailed by a pricing impasse that developed after former National Security Adviser Robert C. McFarlane failed in his attempt to secure release of the hostages during his trip to Tehran in May 1986. Lt. Col. Oliver L. North of the NSC staff had inflated the price to the Iranians for HAWK missile spare parts that were to be delivered at the Tehran meeting by a multiple of 3.7. Manucher Ghorbanifar, who brokered the parts sale, added a 41% markup to North's price of $15 million. With another increase added by Ghorbanifar during the Tehran meeting, the Iranians were charged a total of $24.5 million for HAWK spare parts priced by the Defense Department at $3.6 million.[4]

In late June 1986, Mohsen Kangarlu, Ghorbanifar's channel to the Iranian government, informed the CIA through Agency annuitant George Cave that the Iranians had evidence that they were being drastically overcharged for HAWK missile spare parts. Kangarlu asked the Americans to lower the price. Led by North, the Americans first attempted to blame Ghorbanifar for the overcharges. When blaming Ghorbanifar failed to break the impasse in U.S.-Iran talks, North sought to convince the Iranians that the pricing was fair, and attempted to provide the Iranians with falsified pricing documents.[5]

A frightened and angry Ghorbanifar finally called Allen in late August 1986 to complain that the situation had become unbearable. He told Allen that he had borrowed $15 million to finance the HAWK parts transactions, and that he was now being pursued by his creditors for repayment. Ghorbanifar insisted that it was not his markup, but the U.S. Government's, that was responsible for the pricing impasse. Ghorbanifar then pleaded with Allen to do something to resolve the issue. Allen told Ghorbanifar that he would bring the matter to North's attention.[6]

By this time, Allen had concluded that something was deeply wrong with the Iran initiative.[7]

Allen related his concerns to Cave, Duane R. Clarridge, a senior officer in the CIA's Directorate of Operations, and North. North told Allen not to believe Ghorbanifar because he was a liar. Instead, North insisted that Allen stick to the story that gathering the HAWK spares was expensive and to not break ranks with other U.S. officials on the pricing cover story.[8]

Having received no satisfaction from North or Clarridge, Allen brought his concerns to Richard Kerr, who was DDI and Allen's immediate superior. Kerr's deputy, John Helgerson, joined their meeting. Allen testified:

> I went through what was occurring. I brought Mr. Kerr up to date on the initiative. I met with him occasionally to brief him orally on the White House effort and the Agency support. He had asked to be kept informed when I had something useful to say, so I worked my way through the current problem—the fact that after the failure of the McFarlane trip to Tehran, there had been a hiatus and efforts had been made to move this process along; but the Iranians had begun to complain very strongly about the price being charged.
>
> Then I went through the rationale of why I believed that the United States was charging excessive costs to the Iranian government for the arms and that profits from

---

[4] Allen, Grand Jury, 8/9/91, pp. 100–02.
[5] Cave, Grand Jury, 8/30/91, pp. 94–99; Allen, Select Committees Deposition, 6/29/87, pp. 534–40.
[6] Allen, Grand Jury, 8/9/91, pp. 110–13.
[7] Ibid., pp. 113–15:

I had begun to think along those lines, after the 15th of August 1986, when it was clear that with White House support, Major General Secord and Mr. Hakim had established a new link or a new channel into the government of Iran. It was clear that they were dealing with Hashem Rafsanjani, Ali Hashem Rafsanjani, who was a nephew, I believe, of the current President Rafsanjani.

It was clear to me that Mr. Hakim and Major General Secord were moving to take over the control of the operation; that they were moving to exclude Mr. Ghorbanifar—that was very clear. I was very much aware that Mr. Hakim by that time and Mr. Secord were involved in other matters, relating to the contras in Central America.

It appeared to me that Mr. Ghorbanifar's call was sort of the final indicator that something was deeply awry—that the problem was not Mr. Ghorbanifar; the problem was the operation being directed by U.S. officials. And I then came to the analytic judgement—based on all these indications that money was being diverted from the profits from the sale of arms to Iran to the contras in Central America.

I did not have hard proof of this. In fact, I had no direct evidence in writing from anyone. It was simply aggregating a series of indicators into a conclusion. And at that point it was at that time or shortly thereafter, I recall walking out from the building to my car late in the evening and thinking very deeply about this—thinking of the fact that two operations were probably being combined—that the lives of the hostages were being actually endangered by such a reckless venture; [a]nd I raised the point with Mr. Cave at the office.

[8] Ibid., p. 115.

the sale of the arms were being diverted to Central America.

I made it clear I did not have direct evidence, but that when you put the indicators together, it sounded as if two separate problems or projects were being mixed together. And I pointed out to him that it made no sense to me and in fact could endanger the hostages in Lebanon.

Allen believed he also told Kerr and Helgerson that retired U.S. Air Force Major General Richard V. Secord and Albert Hakim were involved in both the Iran arms sales and the NSC's contra project. Allen related the markups alleged by Ghorbanifar, and described intelligence reports that indicated that the Iranians were upset by the high prices.[9]

Allen testified that this information made Kerr visibly upset. Kerr told Allen to "stay on top of the issue" and to "keep him advised of any new developments." According to Allen, Kerr pulled him aside later that same day and expressed "deep concern." Kerr believed that if Allen's story were true, the arms sales ultimately would be exposed.[10]

In various interviews, Kerr admitted Allen told him of his suspicions. Kerr also corroborated Allen that Helgerson was present at the meeting. Kerr's account of his reaction to Allen's information, however, differed from Allen's. Kerr said that, as a general matter, he did not find Allen credible—that Allen was "a person who started and put out his own fires"—and therefore he did not take his allegations as seriously as Allen said he did. Kerr had Helgerson there, he stated, to calm Allen down.[11]

Still, Kerr admitted that he took Allen's concerns seriously enough to bring them to Gates, who was Kerr's immediate superior. Kerr acknowledged this meeting in two interviews with the CIA's inspector general, and in an interview with the Select Committees. Kerr stated that he did not remember when this meeting took place, dating it some time between May and

September 1986.[12] In an interview with the inspector general on December 4, 1986, Kerr stated that Gates's response was, "God only knows what Ollie is up to." A memorandum for the record written by a CIA attorney reporting Kerr's interview with the Select Committees recites that Kerr testified that when he informed Gates of Allen's concerns, "Gates responded that he was aware that rumors were circulating that profits were being made on the sales of arms to Iran and that money from the arms sales was being made available to the Contras."[13]

Kerr told Independent Counsel that he did not recall Gates referring to other rumors of a diversion at this meeting.[14] The Select Committees' report of the interview did not contain the statement that Gates was aware of "rumors" of a diversion, but it did state that Gates told Kerr to "keep him informed." Accordingly, the evidence was clear that Gates's statements concerning his initial awareness of the diversion were wrong: Kerr brought him the information from Allen over a month earlier than Gates admitted. This would have been material because it suggested that the CIA continued to support North's activities without informing North's superiors or investigating. By October, when Gates claimed he first remembered hearing of the diversion, Casey ordered an inquiry and later made a report to Poindexter; but, by then, the Hasenfus aircraft had been shot down and Casey and Gates were beginning to cover.

Gates's defense was that he did not recall the Kerr meeting.[15] To say the least, this was

---

[9] Ibid., pp. 117–18.

[10] Ibid., pp. 118–19.

[11] Kerr, FBI 302, 7/31/91, pp. 4–5; see also Helgerson, FBI 302, 9/5/91, pp. 4–5.

[12] Gates's calendar shows frequent meetings with Kerr in late August 1986, but this is inconclusive evidence of when the meeting occurred. Dating the meeting is made even harder by the close working and personal relationship between Kerr and Gates. According to Diane Edwards, Gates's secretary, Kerr was in regular contact with Gates and was among a handful of people who could see Gates without an appointment. (Edwards, FBI 302, 8/23/91, pp. 1–2.)

[13] Working Notes, Kerr, CIA IG Interview, 12/4/86; Memorandum from Pearline to the Record, Subject: Interview of Dick Kerr, 9/10/87, OCA 87–3899. Pearline stood by his notes of Kerr's Select Committees' interview. (Pearline, FBI 302, 9/12/91, p. 5.) Helgerson told the OIC that Kerr informed him shortly after speaking with Gates of their conversation. (Helgerson, FBI 302, 9/5/91, p. 5.)

[14] Kerr, FBI 302, 7/31/91, p. 5. Kerr admitted that he and Gates had reviewed the incident several times since. (Ibid.)

[15] In testimony he gave before the Select Committees' report was issued, Gates made no reference to a meeting with Kerr. In two later Grand Jury appearances, however, Gates acknowledged the conflict between his recollection of events and Kerr's, but he insisted that he

disquieting. He had been told by a very senior officer that two of President Reagan's personal priorities were in danger—not something an ambitious deputy director of central intelligence would likely forget. Allen was acting as a whistle-blower in a difficult situation. His concern was for the safety of the hostages and the success of the efforts of the President. His information suggested serious malfeasance by Government officials involved in a clandestine and highly sensitive operation. Even though Gates may have believed Allen to be excessively concerned, could such an expression of concern be forgotten, particularly after it had been corroborated within a few weeks? Logically, Gates could ignore or forget the Allen report only if he already knew of the diversion and he knew that Casey and Poindexter knew of the diversion. Gates also was on the distribution list for highly reliable intelligence that should have informed him of the pricing dispute among Kangarlu, Ghorbanifar, and the U.S. Government, although it did not refer specifically to any diversion of funds. Gates claimed that he rarely reviewed the intelligence.[16] North testified that he did not discuss the diversion with Gates or in Gates's presence. Gates also never met with Richard Secord, whom Gates was aware of only as a "private benefactor" (the CIA's term for non-Government donors to the contras) by July 1986.[17]

Notwithstanding Independent Counsel's disbelief of Gates, Independent Counsel was not confident that Kerr's testimony, without the support of another witness to his conversation with Gates, would be enough to charge Gates with perjury or false statements for his testimony concerning the timing of his knowledge of the diversion.

## Gates and North's Contra Activities

Gates maintained consistently that he was unaware that North had an operational role in supporting the contras. He testified that he believed that North's activities were limited to putting contra leaders in contact with wealthy American donors, and to giving the contras political advice.[18] While sufficient circumstantial evidence exists to question the accuracy of these statements, it did not adequately establish that Gates knowingly was untruthful about his knowledge of North's activities.

Gates first met North at meetings of the Crisis Pre-Planning Group (CPPG) beginning in 1982, when Gates was deputy director of intelligence. Gates claimed that his contacts as DDI with North were almost exclusively in the CPPG context, apart from meetings on intelligence assignments. Other than these meetings, Gates said that he had little to do with North. He was nonetheless aware of allegations that North was involved on some level with contra support.[19]

Notwithstanding his claims, Gates was aware of information that caused others to question the legality of North's activities. The most obvious source of concern should have been Allen's allegations, discussed above, about North's corruption of the Iran arms sales to support the contras. But other evidence—available before October 1, 1986—should have alerted Gates to North's contra support role.

did not recall the meeting. (Gates, Grand Jury, 2/19/88, pp. 22–23; Gates, Grand Jury, 5/1/91, p. 140.)

[16] Gates, Grand Jury, 2/19/88, pp. 13–14 (found intelligence "confusing," so he stopped reading it); Gates, Grand Jury, 5/1/91, p. 138 (intelligence showed "a couple of Iranian arms dealers . . . lying to each other," so he stopped reading it).

[17] North, *North* Trial Testimony, 4/12/89, pp. 7552–55; Gates, Grand Jury, 5/1/91, pp. 71–72, 87–88. Gates admitted that he and others were concerned about Secord's involvement in the Iran initiative because of Secord's prior contacts with unsavory individuals, but he did not link these concerns with the diversion. (Gates, SSCI Testimony, 12/4/86, pp. 80–85; Gates, Select Committees Deposition, 7/31/87, p. 13.)

[18] Gates, Grand Jury, 5/1/91, pp. 59–60; Gates, Grand Jury, 2/10/88, pp. 74–75; Gates, Select Committees Deposition, 7/31/87, p. 30; Gates, Grand Jury, 6/26/87, p. 36.

[19] Gates, SSCI Testimony, 12/4/86, pp. 69–71; Gates, FBI 302, 5/15/87, p. 1. One disturbing evolution in Gates's description of his knowledge is the degree to which he relied on McFarlane's false assurances to Congress in 1985 that North was not involved in contra resupply. Before the Select Committees, Gates claimed that the CIA, as a whole, was aware of McFarlane's statements, and that the Agency relied on them:

> I might add, you know, there's been a great deal of attention drawn to the letter that McFarlane sent to Mr. Hamilton avowing that whatever North was doing was legal and proper. The House Intelligence Committee were not the only ones who read that letter and were not the only ones who believed it. So there was a predisposition that while we didn't know or certainly from my standpoint, I think from the standpoint of others as well, that while we didn't know entirely what North was up to, the presumption was that it was proper because of that letter.

But when the Select Committees asked if he specifically was aware of McFarlane's representations at the time McFarlane made them, Gates was quick to deny that he was. (Gates, Select Committees Deposition, 7/31/87, pp. 32–33.) In his 1991 Grand Jury testimony, Gates reversed his position. (Gates, Grand Jury, 5/1/91, p. 82.)

Gates became deputy director of central intelligence on April 18, 1986. As DDCI, Gates had at least two sources of information about North's activities: CIA personnel—particularly Alan D. Fiers Jr.—who had duties relating to Central America, and his regular contacts with National Security Adviser John M. Poindexter and others at the NSC.

## The Cannistraro Question

In the spring and summer of 1986, Gates became involved in a debate over what role Vincent Cannistraro, a CIA officer detailed to the NSC, should play in the $100 million contra program that was expected to take effect in October 1986. There was concern that if Cannistraro replaced North, the CIA would be drawn into North's contra supply activities. Gates discussed Cannistraro's assignment with a number of CIA and NSC personnel, including Fiers, Clair E. George, and Poindexter. Gates met with Cannistraro himself in an attempt to resolve the situation. OIC's inquiry focused on whether Gates, in the course of these discussions, learned about North's role in contra operations.

By the time Gates became DDCI, Fiers was chief of the CIA's Central American Task Force (CATF). Fiers ran the CIA's support for the Nicaraguan contras and planned for the day when the CIA would again be allowed to provide lethal support to the insurgents. Fiers did not readily share information about his unit's operations in Nicaragua. This had led to complaints with the CIA's intelligence analysis directorate. [20]

According to both Fiers and Gates, Gates's role in the contra program increased significantly once he became DDCI. Fiers testified

Gates became "intricately involved" in developing policy and coordinating interagency work on the contras. Fiers dealt with Gates on requests from the NSC and on structural discussions with other Executive Branch agencies about the contra program. Fiers kept Gates informed "generally, on our state of planning and the nature of our operations." Fiers met with Gates regularly and weekly. [21]

Fiers testified that he did not lay out to Gates his extensive knowledge about North's activities. [22] From two events, however, Fiers concluded that Gates too was aware of North's operational role with the contras. The first incident involved Cannistraro, who had been Fiers's predecessor as chief of CATF.

Cannistraro, then detailed to the NSC, was nominally in charge of monitoring all U.S. covert-action programs. By June 1986, North's operational activities caused Cannistraro concern. [23] In mid-1986, media reports repeated earlier assertions that North was linked to contra military aid. As an important House vote on renewed contra aid approached, on June 24, 1986, a resolution of inquiry was introduced in the House to inquire about North's activities. On June 25, after the House approved a $100 million military and humanitarian aid package, Representatives Lee Hamilton and Dante Fascell wrote the President for comment on the resolution of inquiry; that night, CBS News ran a program that expressly linked North to the private contra-aid network.

On June 26, Cannistraro suggested in a computer note to Poindexter that the new contra-aid program should be a "regularized C[overt] A[ction] program which would normally fall under my responsibility." Poindexter agreed in a computer note sent to NSC Executive Secretary Rodney McDaniel that same day:

> Yes, I would like to regularize it. The Vince-Ollie relationship would be the same as between Vince and Howard [Teicher, another NSC staffer] on Afghanistan. Ollie will have mixed reactions. He has wanted CIA to get back on the management of

[20] One of the protesters was Robert Vickers, the CIA's national intelligence officer for Latin America from July 1984 to November 1987. Vickers told Gates that Fiers was not keeping him informed about the contras. (Vickers, FBI 302, 4/28/87, p. 4; Kerr, FBI 302, 7/31/91, p. 6.) Vickers did not remember this meeting with Gates in his most recent interview. (Vickers, FBI 302, 5/15/91, p. 5.) Vickers also complained to Cannistraro about being cut out of the new interagency group on Nicaragua, and asked Cannistraro to assist him in getting into the group. Cannistraro brought up Vickers's concern with Gates in a meeting at Gates's office. Cannistraro told Gates that Vickers "was very knowledgeable and was a real student of Central America," and he recommended that Vickers be included in meetings of the new interagency group. (Cannistraro, FBI 302, 7/24/91, p. 9.) A PROFs note from Cannistraro to Rodney McDaniel, Executive Secretary of the NSC, corroborates Cannistraro's efforts to get Vickers involved and Cannistraro's meeting with Gates. (PROFs Note from Cannistraro to McDaniel, 7/21/86, AKW 022235.)

[21] Fiers, Grand Jury, 8/14/91, pp. 44–45; Gates, Grand Jury, 5/1/91, pp. 12–14.

[22] Fiers's knowledge of North's contra-resupply activities is discussed more fully in the Fiers chapter.

[23] Cannistraro, FBI 302, 9/18/90, p. 2; Cannistraro, FBI 302, 7/24/91, p. 9.

the problem and we need to lower Ollie's visibility on the issue. Talk to him about it and I will follow up when I get back.[24]

Fiers recalled Cannistraro's move to take the contra program away from North, as well as Poindexter's concerns about North's program. The question of who would run the anticipated contra-aid program was important to Fiers and the CIA. Fiers had been planning the CIA's program "in earnest." According to Fiers, Gates was intimately involved in structuring the new program, both within the CIA and the Executive Branch as a whole. Gates admitted he was aware that Poindexter had been contemplating changes in who oversaw contra issues at the NSC.[25]

In the midst of the struggle over who would run the contra-aid program, Cannistraro visited Gates at his office. Cannistraro told Independent Counsel that he came to express his desire to return to the CIA's Directorate of Operations (DO).[26] Gates promised to urge the directorate to take Cannistraro back. But soon Cannistraro's future became an item on the agenda for one of Gates' weekly meetings with Poindexter. On July 10, 1986, Paul Kinsinger, an aide to Gates, sent Gates a memorandum that stated:

> Vince Cannistraro called to say that Poindexter wanted to discuss how we are going to coordinate the Nicaragua program. Attached is a short memo to you from the Director, you may recall, that lays out the Director's views.
>
> Vince also said that Poindexter would want to know whether Ollie North should be involved. Peggy [Donnelly, a CIA officer assigned to the DCI-DDCI executive offices] checked with the DO and they say yes.[27]

The DO officer mentioned in Kinsinger's memo was Fiers. Fiers recalled that he specifi-

cally talked about Cannistraro's duties with Gates. Fiers was concerned that having Cannistraro in the management of the new program would bring a CIA officer "into the proximity of operations that I knew to go on, that were someplace we didn't want CIA officers to be." Fiers recalled voicing this concern not only to Gates, but to George and Casey as well.[28]

Fiers made it clear in several meetings in Gates's office that he wanted North to stay involved in contra aid—and have Cannistraro kept out. Fiers recalled telling Gates:

> I just think I said, if Vince were to take over the Central American account, he can't be doing the same thing that Ollie is doing with the private sector people in lining up support for the resistance. That crosses over the Boland Amendment, and it's just someplace that we don't want to be. We've got to keep Vince away from that. And, I think those probably were my exact words, or very similar to that.

Fiers testified that Gates "understood me. We all understood that to be the case, and we were going to have to keep Vince away from that." [29]

On July 10, 1986, Gates raised the Cannistraro issue with Poindexter. Gates wrote after their meeting:

> I followed up on Vince Cannistraro's assignment. Poindexter clearly wants to keep Vince indefinitely and while I told him that Clair did not have to have a final answer before the end of August, his reaction strongly suggested to me that he will keep Vince there. I also repeated our concern that *should Vince take over the Central American account, that he should have nothing to do as a CIA employee with the private sector people Ollie North had been dealing with in support of the Contras.*

Cannistraro remained at the NSC,[30] and was not transferred.

[24] Cannistraro, FBI 302, 9/18/90, p. 3; PROFs Note from Cannistraro to McDaniel, 6/26/86, AKW 019032; PROFs Note from Poindexter to McDaniel, 6/26/86, AKW 021436.

[25] Fiers, Grand Jury, 8/14/91, pp. 53–57; Gates, FBI 302, 5/15/87, pp. 4–5; Gates, Grand Jury, 5/1/91, pp. 103–04.

[26] Cannistraro claimed that he had long-standing differences with DO chief Clair George, which is why Cannistraro went to Gates. (Cannistraro, FBI 302, 7/24/91, p. 6; see also Gates, FBI 302, 5/15/87, p. 4; Gates, Grand Jury, 5/1/91, pp. 83–84.)

[27] Note for ADCI, Subject: Late Item for Poindexter Meeting, 7/10/86, ER 27199–206.

[28] Fiers, Grand Jury, 8/14/91, pp. 58–59.

[29] Ibid., pp. 59–60.

[30] Memorandum from Gates to the Record, Subject: Meeting with Adm. Poindexter, 7/11/86, ER 27195–97 (emphasis added); Gates, FBI 302, 5/15/87, pp. 4–5. See also Poindexter, Select Committees Deposi-

Gates's explanation of these events was that he wanted to keep Cannistraro from becoming entangled with the contras for political reasons—and not because he was concerned about North. Gates was concerned, he said, about Congress finding a CIA employee anywhere close to the situation. Gates claimed he had not considered the legality or nature of what North was doing on behalf of the contras: "I had no concerns—I had no reason to have concerns based on what was available to me about North's contacts with the private sector people, but I didn't think a CIA person should do it." [31]

Gates acknowledged that he might have raised the Cannistraro issue with Fiers, but he did not recall it. He did not recall any conversations with Fiers and he claimed not to recall any recommendation from Fiers one way or the other.[32]

Given the accusations swirling about North's support of the contra rebels, and the prospect of a formal Congressional inquiry into North's actions, Gates must have been concerned about the nature of his activities as a threat to the planned resumption of support to the CIA. It was, however, also politically wise to keep Cannistraro away from any activities that resembled North's. Independent Counsel did not believe that provable evidence of Gates's awareness of North's operational activities would sustain a prosecution for his denials to the Select Committees or to OIC.

## Sale of Enterprise Assets

North attempted to sell aircraft and a vessel, the *Erria*, that were owned by the Enterprise to the CIA. The proposed sales were discussed in Gates's presence at meetings with Poindexter. Gates also spoke about the aircraft with Fiers,

who discouraged their purchase. These discussions must have provided some additional knowledge about North's role in contra resupply.

The *Erria* had carried munitions to Central America for the contras.[33] Poindexter, Gates and Casey discussed the *Erria* at one of their weekly meetings in May 1986. Memoranda prepared for that meeting associated North with the *Erria*. Cannistraro recalled that discussion of the ship at a Poindexter-Gates meeting suggested Gates knew the *Erria* was used in support of North's contra operation.[34]

At a later meeting, Gates and Poindexter discussed North's proposal that the CIA buy the Enterprise's aircraft. In a computer note to Poindexter dated July 24, 1986, North complained that the CIA was unwilling to purchase the Enterprise assets and urged Poindexter to ask Casey to reconsider. Poindexter responded that he *did* "tell Gates that the private effort should be phased out. Please tell Casey about this. I agree with you." Poindexter later elaborated that he had told Gates that the Enterprise's assets were available for purchase, and that Gates said he would check on the matter.[35]

North's calendar and pocket cards show that North scheduled a meeting with Gates for July 29, 1986, three days later. Gates's calendar also shows a meeting with North on July 29.[36] About this time, Gates approached Fiers and asked why the Central American Task Force would not purchase North's, or "the private

---

tion, 5/2/87, pp. 200–02 (giving his reasons for easing North out of the contra effort, and North's reluctance to leave).

[31] Gates, Grand Jury, 5/1/91, pp. 79–83, 85. The information that Gates claimed to have about North consisted of "rumors" from various Government officials that North had put contra leaders in touch with Secord and retired U.S. Army Major General John K. Singlaub. Gates testified that at the time he did not know that North had "hands-on" involvement with contra resupply. (Ibid., pp. 86–89.)

[32] Ibid., pp. 110–11. Fiers said that a "note-taker" usually attended his meetings with Gates. This note-taker was Kinsinger. Fiers remembers telling Kinsinger—whom Fiers did not remember by name—occasionally not to write down things such as disparaging comments or other matters because of their sensitivity. Fiers also would ask Kinsinger to leave the room for matters that he wanted to discuss privately with Gates. (Fiers, Grand Jury, 8/14/91, pp. 45–46.) Kinsinger kept none of his notes for the period that he served as Gates's aide. (Kinsinger, FBI 302, 7/25/91, p. 8.)

[33] North, *North* Trial Testimony, 4/7/89, pp. 6883–84. North approached several CIA officers with his proposal. North asked Cannistraro to convince the CIA to purchase the ship as a floating broadcast platform. Cannistraro found out that CIA officers had considered the matter and had declined North's offer because of the ship's association with Thomas Clines. (Cannistraro, Grand Jury, 6/15/87, pp. 53–65; see also Twetten, Select Committees Deposition, 4/22/87, pp. 181–82; Haskell, FBI 302, 7/6–7/7/87, p. 10.)

[34] Memorandum from Cannistraro to Poindexter, Subject: Agenda for Your Weekly Meeting . . . , 5/14/86, AKW 045227–28; Memorandum, Item . . . Poindexter May Raise With The DCI at their 8 May Meeting, 5/8/86, ER 143–5 91–0041; Gates 1986 Appointment Book, 5/15/86; DCI Schedule, 5/15/86, ER 598; Kinsinger, FBI 302, 7/25/91, p. 9; Cannistraro, FBI 302, 7/24/91, p. 10. See also Poindexter, Select Committees Deposition, 5/2/87, pp. 221–22 (recounting discussions with the CIA about its purchasing the *Erria*).

[35] See PROFs Note from North to Poindexter, 7/24/86, AKW 021735; PROFs Note from Poindexter to North, 7/26/86, AKW 021732; Poindexter, Select Committees Testimony, 5/2/87, pp. 187–88, 228.

[36] North Schedule Card, 7/29/86, AKW 002640; Gates 1986 Appointment Book (Doc. No. 258). When asked about this meeting by SSCI in his second confirmation hearings, Gates could not recall the meeting. (SSCI Confirmation Nomination of Robert M. Gates to be Director of Central Intelligence, Sen. Exec. Rpt. No. 102–19, 102d Cong., 1st Sess., p. 80 (Oct. 24, 1991). 10/19/91, p. 85.)

benefactor's,'' aircraft. According to Fiers, Gates accepted Fiers' explanation that the aircraft were in poor condition and unduly risky for the CIA. Fiers also ''vaguely'' recalled discussing ''phasing out the private Contra aid effort'' with Gates in July 1986. Both men agreed that the private effort was a political liability for the Agency. From their discussions, Fiers—like Cannistraro—concluded that Gates was aware that ''North was running a private supply operation.'' [37]

Gates denied discussing phasing out the private resupply effort with Poindexter. Asked about Poindexter's message to North, Gates testified that he examined his records upon reading the message and could find no evidence that such a meeting with Poindexter occurred. Gates claimed, ''If Poindexter made a comment to me like that, it would have been in the context of once the authorized program is approved there would be no point in having any of these private benefactors any longer.'' Neither did Gates recall meeting with North about the *Erria* during this time.[38]

The evidence established that Gates was exposed to information about North's connections to the private resupply operation that would have raised concern in the minds of most reasonable persons about the propriety of a Government officer having such an operational role. Fiers and Cannistraro believed that Gates was aware of North's operational role. The question was whether there was proof beyond a reasonable doubt that Gates deliberately lied in denying knowledge of North's operational activities. A case would have depended on the testimony of Poindexter. Fiers would not testify that he supplied Gates with the details of North's activities. In the end, Independent Counsel concluded that the question was too close to justify the commitment of resources. There were stronger, equally important cases to be tried.

## Obstruction of the Hasenfus Inquiries

There was conclusive evidence that in October 1986, following the Hasenfus shootdown, Clair George and Alan Fiers obstructed two congressional inquiries.[39] Gates attended meetings where the CIA's response to these inquiries was discussed. None of the evidence, however, links Gates to any specific act of obstruction.

The background for Congress's inquiries into the Hasenfus shootdown is discussed in the Fiers and George chapters. By October 9, 1986, the Senate Committee on Foreign Relations (SCFR) had set a hearing on the shootdown for October 10, 1986, and the House of Representatives Permanent Select Committee on Intelligence (HPSCI) had set a hearing for October 14, 1986. Gates's main concern during this period was convincing Congress that the CIA had sponsored no resupply flights. He appeared before SSCI on October 8, 1986, and gave the committee brief biographies of the pilots on the downed plane. He responded to Senator Cohen when asked whether the plane was owned by a CIA proprietary:

No, sir. We didn't have anything to do with that. And while we know what is going in—going on with the Contras, obviously as you indicate, by virtue of what we come up here and brief, I will tell you that I know from personal experience we have, I think, conscientiously tried to avoid knowing what is going on in terms of any of this private funding, and tried to stay away from it. Somebody will say something about Singlaub or something like, we will say I don't want to hear anything about it.[40]

To the extent that Gates spoke for others in the CIA, this was wrong. It was true that the Hasenfus plane was not owned by a CIA proprietary. But as set forth in the Fiers, George, and Fernandez chapters, several individual CIA officers had not stayed away from ''private-benefactor'' activities. There was no evidence, however, that Gates knew this as early as October 8, 1986, although he did know by then of the concern that North and Secord were diverting funds from the Iran arms sales to the contras.[41]

---

[37] Fiers, Grand Jury, 8/14/91, pp. 68–69; Fiers, FBI 302, 8/1/91, pp. 14, 16. See also Sen. Exec. Rpt. No. 102–19, p. 80.
[38] Gates, Grand Jury, 2/10/88, pp. 76–77.

[39] See George and Fiers chapters.
[40] Gates, SSCI Testimony, 10/8/86, p. 9.
[41] Gates was informed by Allen about the diversion, North, and Secord on October 1, 1986, and met with Allen and Casey about them on October 7.

The day after his SSCI testimony Gates double-checked his statements with a number of people. He met with Fiers and George at 10:10 a.m. on October 9 and was told "that there had been no contact between—that the Agency wasn't involved in the Hasenfus matter at all." Gates then had lunch with Casey and North. North had just returned from negotiations in Frankfurt with the "Second Channel" to the Iranian government. North briefed Gates and Casey on the progress of the negotiations. The discussion then turned to the contras. North testified at trial and before the Grand Jury that during this luncheon, Casey told him that North's Iran and contra operations were unraveling, and that he should begin to clean up both of them. North specifically recalled being told by Casey about allegations by Roy Furmark of a diversion; he did not recall telling Gates about the diversion or going into detail about the nature of his operations. North also did not recall whether Gates was there when Casey told North to clean up his operation.[42]

In his testimony about the lunch, Gates stressed his attempt to get North to confirm that the CIA was not involved with the Hasenfus crash. Gates claimed that he was not invited to the lunch, and that he "crashed the lunch" because he wanted to speak with North. Gates said that Casey discussed the Furmark allegations with North and told him that the situation had to be straightened out. Gates remembered no instruction from Casey to North to start cleaning up operations, but did recall asking North directly whether any CIA personnel had been involved in the resupply network. Gates said that North told him that the CIA was "absolutely clean." North made a "cryptic comment" about Swiss bank accounts, which Gates claimed not to have understood. Gates stated that he then left Casey's office for ten minutes, and returned to ask Casey alone about North's comment about Swiss accounts. Casey

seemed not to have picked up on the comment, and Gates dropped it.[43]

Gates changed his story in only one significant way between his early testimony and his final Grand Jury appearance: He expressly added that he left Casey and North alone together during lunch.

Gates wrote an exculpatory memo the next day. Gates wrote:

> North confirmed to the DCI and to me that, based on his knowledge of the private funding efforts for the Contras, CIA is completely clean on the question of any contacts with those organizing the funding and the operations. He affirmed that a clear separation had been maintained between the private efforts and CIA assets and individuals, including proprietaries.

Gates recorded North's purportedly exculpatory statement uncritically, even though he was by then clearly aware of the possible diversion of U.S. funds through the "private benefactors." Although, in testimony before SSCI, Gates admitted that his concerns about Allen's allegations were behind the questioning of North, he did not ask North whether a diversion had occurred. He was interested only in eliciting statements protective of his Agency.[44]

After his lunch with North and his post-lunch discussion with Casey, Gates met again with Casey and George at 1:45 p.m. on "Directorate Reporting." Casey then briefed congressional leaders about the downed aircraft. Casey and Gates then met with George, Fiers and the CIA's congressional affairs chief, David Gries. Gates, George and Gries stated that they did not recall what occurred at this meeting. Fiers recalled that the meeting concerned whether it would be Gates or George who testified on October 10 before SCFR. Fiers testified that he, Casey and George had decided earlier on October 9 that George was to testify. As Fiers recalled it, the later meeting was to give Gries the opportunity to argue in favor of Gates testifying. The content of the next day's briefing,

[42] DDCI Appointments—Thursday, 10/9/86, AKY 006296; Gates, Grand Jury, 5/1/91, pp. 176–77; Fiers, Grand Jury, 8/16/91, pp. 6–7; North, *North* Trial Testimony, 4/12/89, pp. 7552–57; North, Grand Jury, 3/8/91, pp. 30–32. Casey testified in December 1986 that the October 1986 luncheon included questions concerning a possible diversion. (Casey, HPSCI Testimony, 12/11/86, pp. 120–21; Casey, House Appropriations Subcommittee Testimony, 12/8/86, p. 102.)

[43] Gates, Grand Jury, 5/1/91, pp. 177–79; Gates, Grand Jury, 6/26/87, pp. 8–11; Gates, Select Committees Deposition, 7/31/87, pp. 23–29, 33–35; Gates, Grand Jury, 2/19/88, pp. 46–47; Gates, FBI 302, 5/15/87, p. 5. When confronted with Gates's account of the meeting, Casey did not dispute it. (Casey, HPSCI Testimony, 12/11/86, pp. 180–81.)

[44] Memorandum from Gates to the Record, Subject: Lunch with Ollie North, 10/10/86, ER 24605; Gates, SSCI Testimony, 12/4/86, p. 20.

except for the categorical denial made in the CIA's opening statement, was not discussed.[45]

The early evening meeting of Casey, Gates, George, Fiers, and Gries ended Gates's involvement with the preparation of the CIA's testimony concerning the Hasenfus crash. The only other evidence relating to Gates during this period was a meeting that took place in Casey's office around the time of George and Fiers's briefing of HPSCI on October 14, 1986. During this meeting, Fiers told George and Casey that the Hasenfus inquiries would not end until someone took responsibility for the private resupply flights. Fiers recommended that Secord take responsibility. George turned to Casey and said, "Bill, you know Secord has other problems," and the conversation ended soon after. Fiers had a vague recollection of Gates being present for part of the conversation, and then leaving the room. Fiers was uncertain if Gates heard his remarks about Secord.[46]

At most, the evidence showed that Gates was in and around meetings where the content of George and Fiers's testimony was discussed, and that he participated in two briefings that helped lull congressional investigators into believing that the CIA was not involved in facilitating private resupply flights. The evidence shows further that Gates was aware of at least general information suggesting involvement by North and Secord with the contras, and that Gates did not disclose this information—or argue that it should be disclosed. For Gates, the CIA's task in October 1986 was to distance the CIA from the private operation, in part by locking North into statements that cleared the CIA of wrongdoing.[47]

In the end, although Gates's actions suggested an officer who was more interested in shielding his institution from criticism and in shifting the blame to the NSC than in finding out the truth, there was insufficient evidence to charge Gates with a criminal endeavor to obstruct congressional investigations into the Hasenfus shootdown.

## Gates and Casey's November 1986 Testimony

The events leading up to the preparation of false testimony by Director Casey in November 1986—preparations that Gates nominally oversaw—are set forth in a separate chapter of this Report. There was insufficient evidence that Gates committed a crime as he participated in the preparation of Casey's testimony, or that he was aware of critical facts indicating that some of the statements by Casey and others were false.

## Conclusion

Independent Counsel found insufficient evidence to warrant charging Robert Gates with a crime for his role in the Iran/contra affair. Like those of many other Iran/contra figures, the statements of Gates often seemed scripted and less than candid. Nevertheless, given the complex nature of the activities and Gates's apparent lack of direct participation, a jury could find the evidence left a reasonable doubt that Gates either obstructed official inquiries or that his two demonstrably incorrect statements were deliberate lies.

---

[45] George, Grand Jury, 4/5/91, pp. 72–73; Gates, Grand Jury, 5/1/91, pp. 197–98; Gries, FBI 302, 4/9/91, pp. 4–5; Fiers, Grand Jury, 8/16/91, pp. 19–20.

[46] Ibid., pp. 40–43.

[47] Indeed, according to Allen, when Allen first discussed rumors of a diversion with Gates on October 1, 1986, Gates told Allen he

---

"didn't want to hear about Central America" and "I've supported Ollie in other activities . . . but he's gone too far." (Allen, Grand Jury, 1/4/88, pp. 31–33.) See also Gates, SSCI Testimony, 12/4/86, pp. 18–19 (confirming that he told Allen that he "didn't want to hear anything about funding for the Contras").

# Chapter 17
# United States v. Clair E. George

Clair E. George served as deputy director for operations (DDO) of the CIA from July 1984 through December 1987, after a long and distinguished career in the CIA's Directorate of Operations (DO) that began in 1955. During his tenure at the CIA, he completed numerous overseas assignments, often in dangerous locations. His primary activity was the recruitment of foreign agents to work clandestinely for the United States. Interspersed with these tours of duty abroad were assignments at CIA headquarters in Langley, Virginia, during which George coordinated the CIA's activities in various parts of the world. He rose through the ranks at CIA during this progression of assignments.

As director of the Agency's clandestine operations, George was the CIA's third-in-command and highest ranking of the four CIA officers prosecuted by Independent Counsel. During his term as DDO, George was responsible for the CIA's covert actions and espionage activities worldwide. The only individuals senior to George in the Agency were CIA Director William J. Casey, Deputy Director of Central Intelligence John N. McMahon, and McMahon's successor, Robert M. Gates.[1] George was the highest ranking CIA official convicted after trial since the Agency was formed under the National Security Act of 1947.[2]

The very fact that Independent Counsel was able to bring the *George* case to trial was a significant achievement. The prosecution of any CIA officer is inherently difficult because of the issues of secrecy involving national security information of the highest classification. These problems are magnified when the defendant is the director of the CIA's global spy network and the criminal charges against him relate to his conduct in carrying out his official responsibilities. Thus, Independent Counsel had to ensure that the case against George could survive the stringent requirements of the Classified Information Procedures Act (CIPA), which is designed to prevent the disclosure of national security information while at the same time not inhibiting a defendant's right to a fair trial. The CIPA procedures were a major hurdle in the *George* case as the defense sought to block trial by claiming that huge quantities of the nation's top secrets needed to be exposed to put on George's defense.[3]

The *George* case was also important in Iran/contra because Clair George was one of a small group of high officials who was unavoidably a supervisor having oversight of both ventures and had, therefore, substantial knowledge of both the secret arms sales to Iran and the secret contra-resupply operation. This meant that George was one of the few officials who could have provided Congress with specific and crucial information on the Iran arms sales and the illicit contra-resupply network when both

---

[1] McMahon served as DDCI from 1982 until March 26, 1986, when he retired. Gates was deputy director for intelligence from 1982 until he was appointed to replace McMahon in April 1986. Gates became acting director of the CIA when Casey became ill in December 1986.

[2] After he had left the Agency, former CIA Director Richard M. Helms pleaded nolo contendere in 1977 to a misdemeanor charge of withholding information from Congress during testimony about CIA activities in Chile in connection with the overthrow and murder of Marxist President Salvador Allende in 1970.

[3] Much of the pre-trial litigation in the *George* case revolved around classification problems in discovery and in working through the CIPA process. There were more than 10 pretrial motions relating to CIPA and over 80 hours devoted to hearings regarding classification issues. Although the classified information problems in the *George* case were formidable, the pre-trial obstacles were surmounted largely through excellent cooperation and diligence on the part of the Inter-Agency Review Group, a group made up of representatives from the intelligence community, and thoughtful application of the CIPA procedures by U.S. District Judge Royce C. Lamberth.

operations began unraveling publicly in October and November of 1986.

George was not only privy to many of the details concerning the Iran/contra affair, he was also aware that other senior Government officials were aware of the same information. Moreover, George knew that many of these officials were withholding information or lying about what they knew.

During the investigation of the CIA's role in Iran/contra, Independent Counsel uncovered evidence indicating that George was a well-informed supervisor of the CIA's support of the NSC effort to supply military aid to the contras and to sell weapons to Iran. The evidence indicated that George was aware of information he later denied knowing. The relevant evidentiary documents were, for the most part, either created, reviewed or received by George. The witness testimony came primarily from individuals who had worked closely with George, or who had provided information to his most senior, trusted assistants.

Independent Counsel's case against George centered on testimony he gave before the Senate Foreign Relations Committee on October 10, 1986, the House Permanent Select Committee on Intelligence on October 14, 1986, and a federal Grand Jury investigating Iran/contra in 1991. The charges against him involved statements he made in the wake of the October 5, 1986, shootdown in Nicaragua of the contra-resupply plane carrying American Eugene Hasenfus. George was charged with falsely denying before Congress knowledge of who was behind the contra-resupply operation and the true identity of Max Gomez, a former CIA operative whose real name was Felix Rodriguez and whom Hasenfus had publicly identified as part of the resupply operation. According to the charges, George also falsely denied contacts with retired U.S. Air Force Major General Richard V. Secord, who was involved in both the Iran and contra operations.

George was tried in the summer of 1992 on nine counts of false statements, perjury and obstruction in connection with congressional and Grand Jury investigations. This trial ended in a mistrial after the jury was unable to reach a verdict on any count. George was retried in the fall of 1992 on seven counts, resulting in

convictions on two charges of false statements and perjury before Congress. Before George was sentenced, President Bush pardoned him on December 24, 1992.

## George and Contra Support

Beginning in early 1985, George was aware that North was the key player in the Reagan Administration's secret contra-resupply operations. For example, CIA officers in South Korea informed CIA headquarters on January 28, 1985, that retired U.S. Army Major General John K. Singlaub had asked the governing political party to contribute $2 million to the contras. The Koreans told CIA personnel that some signal from the U.S. Government endorsing the Singlaub request would be necessary.[4] George called North to inform him of the developments. North's notes from February 4, 1985, describe a call from "Clair" which relayed the information provided by CIA personnel in South Korea. According to North's notes, George said that the South Koreans were "increasingly inclined to contribute $2M" but that they "[n]eed W[hite] H[ouse] indication."[5] George also called North on February 2 and 5, 1985, to discuss the potential South Korean contribution to the contras.[6]

In a February 6, 1985, memorandum from North to McFarlane, North discussed Singlaub's solicitation of the South Koreans as a possible means of obtaining short-term financing for the contras:

> Regarding [the Contras' short-term financing needs], as a consequence of GEN Singlaub's recent trip, both the Taiwanese and the South Koreans have indicated [to CIA field personnel] that they want to help in a "big way." *Clair George (CIA) has withheld the dissemination of these offers and contacted me privately to assure that they will not become common knowledge.*[7]

Documents indicate that George was aware of the identity of others who were secretly arranging for arms shipments to the contras. In

---

[4] CIA Cable, 1/28/85, ER 29941, *George GX 5*.
[5] North Notebook, 2/4/85, AMX 000427, *George GX 8*.
[6] North Notebook, 2/2/85, AMX 000421 & 2/5/85, AMX 00043, *George GX 7 & GX 9*.
[7] Memorandum from North to McFarlane, 2/6/85, ALU 130089–90, *George GX 10* (emphasis added).

the first half of March 1985, George sent a memorandum to national security adviser Robert C. McFarlane regarding reports that a Canadian arms dealer was purchasing weapons in China on behalf of Secord for shipment to Guatemala.[8] Alan D. Fiers, Jr., chief of the CIA's Central American Task Force from 1984 to 1986 testified that there was no doubt within the CIA that the arms purchased by Secord were headed to the contras.[9]

In the latter part of 1985, Congress authorized the sending of humanitarian aid to the contras. To oversee this aid, the Reagan Administration created an entity within the State Department known as the Nicaraguan Humanitarian Assistance Office, or "NHAO." During late 1985 and early 1986, NHAO humanitarian-supply flights began being routed through Ilopango air base in El Salvador. At the same time, Felix Rodriguez was based at Ilopango and was coordinating North's secret weapons shipments to the contras.[10] As the early months of 1986 passed, the two operations became indistinguishable, both using the same equipment and pilots, and both being coordinated by Rodriguez.

CIA personnel in Central America had been instructed to abide by the Boland Amendment's restrictions on aiding the contras. But as the NHAO and "private benefactor" operations at Ilopango grew, and as Rodriguez's role expanded, a senior CIA official in Central America grew more uncomfortable remaining on the sidelines. Guidance from headquarters was slow in coming, and finally, on February 7, 1986, the officer, known in the *George* trials as "Officer #1," wrote a frustrated, sarcastic cable to headquarters. The cable described a recent incident in which a NHAO plane had crash-landed in El Salvador. Officer #1 had been unaware of the event until later, because Rodriguez was "coordinating" all of his actions with North and leaving everyone else in the dark. The cable, titled "End the Silence," ended with the question, "What is going on back there?"[11]

The cable raised eyebrows at CIA headquarters. Fiers discussed it with George, whose reaction was unambiguous. George ordered Fiers to go to El Salvador and instruct Officer #1 to keep his nose out of the activities at Ilopango. Those activities, George told Fiers, were being run by "Ollie North" and the White House.[12]

In April 1986, CIA headquarters received cable traffic from Europe regarding Thomas Clines, a former CIA employee whose association with convicted arms trafficker Edwin Wilson had given him a bad reputation within the CIA.[13] According to one cable, Clines was planning a large shipment of arms from Europe to Honduras and ultimately to the contras. Fiers discussed this and similar cables with George. Both men were concerned about Clines's involvement with contra resupply, but, according to Fiers, George told him not to get involved in what was a sensitive operation.[14]

Additional documentary evidence regarding the private benefactors shows that key details were reported to George's office on October 9, 1986, on the eve of his Senate Foreign Relations Committee testimony. After Eugene Hasenfus, a captured resupply operation employee, had accused the CIA of being involved in contra-resupply operations, the CIA received a cable from Central America plainly stating that "Max Gomez," whom Hasenfus had named as a resupply manager, was a local alias used by Rodriguez.[15] The cable also explicitly discussed Rodriguez's involvement with the private benefactors:

[At a lunch with a senior CIA officer in Central America,] Rodriguez stated that he was [in El Salvador] in a dual capacity. One of his duties was to advise the Salvadoran Air Force in counter-insurgency tactics. The other was to participate in private benefactors' (unnamed) efforts to assist the FDN.[16]

This cable arrived at the CIA at 8:50 p.m. on October 9, 1986 and three copies were sent

---

[8] Memorandum from George to McFarlane, 3/6/85, ER AKW 031346–47, *George* GX 12.

[9] Fiers, Grand Jury, 8/12/91, pp. 49–50. Fiers further testified that he vaguely recalled discussing the memorandum on Secord's arms purchases in China with George.

[10] North's secret network of personnel that supplied weapons to the contras became known later in 1986 as the "private benefactors."

[11] CIA Cable, 2/7/86, DO 10959, *George* GX 32.

[12] Fiers, Grand Jury, 8/12/91, pp. 150–53.

[13] CIA Cable, 4/28/86, *George* GX 37.

[14] Fiers, Grand Jury, 8/14/91, pp. 30–33. At his trials, George acknowledged that he read cables regarding Clines and the contras.

[15] CIA Cable, 10/9/86, *George* GX 45.

[16] Ibid., ¶ 2.

to George's office. This information subsequently appeared in the briefing book and other papers prepared for George's use during congressional testimony over the next several days.[17] Copies of this briefing book and the Rodriguez papers were retrieved from one of George's CIA office files, or "soft files," suggesting that he received and retained them.[18]

George denied having been involved in the drafting of the opening statement he gave to the Senate Foreign Relations Committee on October 10 and HPSCI on October 14. Drafts of that opening statement, however, show that George played an active role in the preparation of the opening statement, directing subordinates to remove significant information from it. One draft had contained language regarding the NHAO operations conducted at Ilopango. The language was crossed out, with the notation "deleted by DDO" written in the margin.[19] On another copy of the same draft, one recovered from George's "soft" files, the same sentence is crossed out. FBI experts identified George's fingerprints on the page where the NHAO information was deleted.[20]

Besides the documents discussed above, numerous statements by a variety of witnesses, including subsequent statements made by George himself, showed that George's knowledge of the contra-resupply operation was extensive.[21]

Alan D. Fiers, Jr., who served as chief of the Central American Task Force within the Directorate of Operations, had day-to-day responsibility for CIA operations in Central America. From 1984 through 1986, Fiers's duties brought him in close contact with North and resupply operatives, including Rodriguez. In turn, Fiers reported significant information regarding the contra-resupply operation to George and others.

In the latter part of 1984, George was aware of North's activities in Central America. North during this time called Fiers asking for sensitive information on Nicaraguan air defenses. Fiers refused. He believed the information was too "operational," and "could only be used in conjunction with some support of air drops or contra activity." [22] Within a day, George called Fiers and asked for exactly the same information. Fiers brought it to George's office and asked if George intended to give the data to North. George responded that Fiers did not have to worry about what George would do with the information.[23]

Fiers testified that George was also aware of Rodriguez's presence in El Salvador by early 1985. Rodriguez had been recommended by individuals within the office of Vice President Bush to work with the Salvadoran military on counterinsurgency operations. Because of Rodriguez's ties to the White House, George and other CIA officials knew that any dealings with Rodriguez could have broader political implications.[24] Thus, Rodriguez's identity and whereabouts were a topic of discussion within the CIA by early 1985.

Fiers put many of the documents discussed above in context. Fiers recalled discussing Singlaub's solicitation of the Koreans with George. The upshot of this conversation was that North should be called so that he could take care of the situation.[25] Fiers also recalled discussing with George Secord's 1985 weapons purchases in China on behalf of the contras. There was no doubt within CIA where the arms were headed.[26] Further, Fiers discussed with George the April 1986 cables from Europe that indicated that Clines was purchasing arms on behalf of the contras. When Fiers pressed for more information, George told him not to get involved.[27]

When Fiers received the "End the Silence" cable from Officer #1 in February 1986, George responded decisively.[28] He instructed Fiers to tell Officer #1 that the activities at Ilopango were not something the CIA should be involved in. George said that those activities were being handled by North and the White House. If Offi-

---

17 Briefing Book, Tab H, DO 44536–44535, *George* GX 119.

18 "Soft file" is another term for a personal or working file. George retained certain documents of extreme sensitivity in soft files in his safe. (George, *George* Trial Testimony, 8/14/92, p. 3545.)

19 Draft, "Subject: DDO's Opening Statement," ANT 1771–73, *George* GX 48.

20 Draft, "Subject: DDO's Opening Statement," DO 44828–26, *George* GX 105.

21 A detailed recounting of these statements would be too lengthy for this report. What follows are highlights of the key points made by various witnesses.

22 Fiers, Grand Jury, 8/12/91, pp. 24–26.

23 Ibid., pp. 25–26.

24 Ibid., pp. 30–32.

25 Ibid., pp. 33–34.

26 Ibid., pp. 49–50.

27 Fiers, Grand Jury, 8/14/91, pp. 30–32.

28 Fiers, Grand Jury, 8/12/91, pp. 151–52.

cer #1 could not keep out of it, George threatened to replace him.[29]

During the summer of 1986, Congress appeared ready to approve $100 million of unrestricted aid for the contras to be administered by the CIA—in particular, by Fiers and the Central American Task Force. North hoped that the CIA would buy the airplanes that the resupply operation had been using to deliver secret weapons shipments to the contras.[30] Fiers was not interested. The planes were old, needed maintenance, and were not fuel-efficient. Fiers also wanted the new CIA program to be free from the taint of the equipment used by North's secret network.[31] Fiers told North this. Shortly thereafter, George pressed Fiers on his reasons.[32] Fiers's position ultimately prevailed, and the CIA did not buy the planes. George's efforts to change Fiers's mind nevertheless indicated that George was hearing from North about the operation.

Finally, Fiers provided important information about the preparation of the opening statement George gave to the congressional committees in October 1986. George ordered him to remove from the draft opening statement a section discussing the way the NHAO humanitarian aid flights out of Ilopango had become intertwined with private-benefactor lethal resupply flights out of the same facility.[33] George told Fiers that this information would turn a spotlight on the White House and the Reagan Administration's links to the lethal resupply operation. George did not want to be the first person to expose that link.[34]

Louis Dupart, Fiers's compliance officer, corroborated portions of Fiers's testimony. Dupart testified that he prepared the initial draft of the statement on the evening of October 9, 1986, and left it on Fiers's desk at approximately 2:30 a.m. or 3:00 a.m. on October 10.[35] When Dupart came to work later that morning, Fiers was upstairs with George, going over the proposed opening statement.[36] When Fiers came back downstairs to the Task Force, he had a copy of the opening statement with some changes in it.[37] Dupart later wrote on one version of the draft opening statement the words "Deleted by DDO."[38]

George also told Fiers, who was to testify alongside him on Capitol Hill, that the CIA was not going to inform the committees that Gomez was an alias for Rodriguez. Fiers objected, telling George that he, Fiers, knew for a fact that Gomez was Rodriguez. But George instructed Fiers to answer any questions about Gomez by saying that the CIA was still checking into Gomez's identity.[39]

Fiers also explained that George aided an effort to conceal headquarters knowledge of the activities of CIA Costa Rican station chief Joseph F. Fernandez. Despite the Boland Amendment's ban on most forms of CIA support for the contras, Fernandez continued to have direct contacts with the resupply operation and North. In October 1986, Fernandez informed Fiers that there were phone records in Costa Rica that would show numerous calls between Fernandez and the resupply operation's quarters at Ilopango. Fiers told his immediate superior, and the division chief, in turn, informed George.[40]

Despite learning in October of Fernandez's misconduct, Fiers, the division chief and George took no steps to correct George's inaccurate testimony to two congressional committees that the CIA had no involvement with the contra-resupply operation. Louis Dupart threatened to inform the CIA general counsel if the record was not corrected. On November 25, 1986—the date of the public exposure of the diversion, Poindexter's resignation and North's dismissal—the three men simply agreed to say they had met on the Fernandez matter on November 10, even though this was pure fiction.[41] The division chief wrote a memorandum on Novem-

[29] Ibid., pp. 151, 153.

[30] Fiers, Grand Jury, 8/14/91, p. 68.

[31] Ibid., pp. 68–69.

[32] Ibid., p. 69. Others besides George pressed Fiers on the same point, including CIA Director Casey and CIA Deputy Director Gates.

[33] Fiers, Grand Jury, 8/16/91, pp. 10–12.

[34] Ibid., pp. 11–12.

[35] Dupart, Grand Jury, 3/15/91, p. 27.

[36] Ibid., pp. 28–29.

[37] Ibid., p. 29.

[38] Draft, "Subject: DDO's Opening Statement," ANT 1771–73. See also Draft, "Subject: DDO's Opening Statement," DO 44828–26.

[39] Fiers, Grand Jury, 8/16/91, p. 21.

[40] Fiers, Grand Jury, 8/16/91, p. 57. When asked by SSCI on December 3, 1986, if he had "any knowledge of any activities by any official of CIA in conjunction with or in cooperation with North to raise private funds or otherwise assist in providing private assistance to the contras," George replied, "I do not." (George, SSCI Testimony, 12/3/86, p. 57.)

[41] Fiers, Grand Jury, 8/16/91, pp. 62–63.

ber 26, 1986 that and referred to this non-exist-
ent meeting in the first sentence.[42]

Another witness who called the truthfulness
of George's testimony into question was a CIA
officer who testified at George's second trial
as "CIA Officer #7." In October 1986, Officer
#7 was employed in the Air Branch of George's
Directorate of Operations. But from February
through June of 1986, before joining the CIA,
Officer #7 had worked as a pilot flying contra-
resupply flights out of Ilopango airbase. He also
helped set up the air operation at Ilopango, and
trained other pilots—including Wallace Sawyer,
one of the Americans killed when Hasenfus's
plane was shot down over Nicaragua. Officer
#7 had extensive knowledge of the secret
contra-resupply network operating out of
Ilopango. He also was working in George's directorate at the time George told the congressional committees in October 1986 that he did
not know the identities of the persons behind
the resupply flights.[43]

Shortly after the Hasenfus shootdown, Norman N. Gardner, Jr. one of George's two special assistants, sought out Officer #7 while he
was attending an antique auto show in Hershey,
Pennsylvania. Gardner asked him to return to
CIA headquarters. The two men met in
Gardner's office, which was located in George's
suite of offices, prior to George's HPSCI testimony on October 14, 1986. Officer #7 told
Gardner the full story of his contra-resupply
activities.[44] Gardner then accompanied George
to the HPSCI hearing. When Independent Counsel asked Gardner whether he informed George
of Officer #7's information prior to the HPSCI
hearing, Gardner claimed his rights under the
Fifth Amendment and refused to testify.[45]

When Fiers learned of Officer #7's story, he
spoke with both Gardner and George about how
to handle the situation.[46] Fiers urged interviewing Officer #7 immediately and addressing
head-on any problems caused by his recent em-
ployment. But George wanted to "slow-roll"
any action taken with respect to Officer #7 and
the information he had provided about the

contra-resupply operations. Officer #7's information was never used to correct George's testimony.[47]

## George and the Iran Arms Sales

Fiers recounted to Independent Counsel that
around the time of George's HPSCI testimony,
Fiers and George met in Director Casey's office. Fiers suggested to Casey and George that
congressional interest in the Hasenfus crash and
the secret resupply flights would not abate until
someone stood up and took responsibility for
the flights.[48] Casey asked Fiers who that should
be, and Fiers suggested Secord. According to
Fiers, George then "looked at the Director and
said, 'Bill, you know Secord has other problems.' "[49]

George knew where Secord's "other problems" lay: in the Iran arms sales.[50] Fiers testified that North had told him in late summer
1986 that profits from the arms sales were being
used to support the contras. Fiers said he reported North's statements to George, who told
Fiers that only a handful of people in the U.S.
Government knew of this. Fiers interpreted this
to mean the arms sales, not the diversion.[51]

In his 1986 congressional testimony, George
deflected questions about Secord by stating that
he did not know him.[52] Documents show that
George knew what Secord's role was in the
Iran arms sales. White House gate logs from
January 20, 1986, show that George attended
a meeting on that day with Secord and others
in the White House Situation Room to discuss
the operation.[53] According to Secord, he was
introduced to George at this meeting, and the

[42] Memorandum from Division Chief to the DDO, 10/26/86, DO
166541–39, *George* GX 131.

[43] CIA Officer #7, FBI 302, 6/21/91, pp. 1–2.

[44] Ibid., p. 3.

[45] Gardner, Grand Jury, 8/7/91, p. 8.

[46] Fiers, Grand Jury, 8/16/91, pp. 54–55.

[47] Ibid., p. 55.

[48] Fiers, Grand Jury, 8/14/91, p. 41.

[49] Ibid.

[50] George told the Senate Select Committee on Intelligence on December 3, 1986, that he had not learned of the diversion until Attorney
General Meese's announcement of it on November 25, 1986. To a
follow-up question inquiring whether George had any indication that
anyone else at CIA knew of the diversion prior to Meese's statements,
George replied, "None whatsoever." (George, SSCI Testimony,
12/3/86, pp. 29–30.)

[51] Fiers, Grand Jury, 8/14/91, pp. 104–05. Fiers was not alone in
recalling telling George about the diversion in advance of Meese's
announcement. George Cave testified to SSCI that he had informed
George in late October or early November of 1986 of allegations
by Roy Furmark that arms sales proceeds had been diverted to the
contras. (Cave, SSCI Testimony, 12/2/86, pp. 89–90.)

[52] George denied knowing Secord in his testimony to SSCI on December 3, 1986. Before SFRC on October 10, 1986, George denied
ever having had contact with Secord.

[53] White House Gate Log 1/20/96, ALU 49624–27, *George* GX 52.

group discussed the role Secord was to play in the Iran arms sales.[54]

Shortly after this meeting, on January 24, 1986, North prepared what he termed a "notional" time line for "Operation Recovery," North's code name for the arms-for-hostages deal with Iran.[55] The document described in detail the logistics of the Iran arms sales, particularly Secord's role. The only copy of the document at CIA was kept in George's safe, and George discussed the document with his senior subordinates before January 27, 1986.[56] Although the document referred to Secord by his code name "Copp," a colleague of George at the CIA who reviewed the Notional Time Line with him, Thomas Twetten, testified that George knew "Copp" was Secord.[57]

In late February 1986, George approved the issuance of false or "alias" passports for Secord and for Albert Hakim, Secord's business partner.[58] George knew that these passports were needed in order to facilitate Secord and Hakim's roles in the Iran arms sales.[59]

As the Iran arms sales progressed, George was briefed on important details by Twetten and George Cave, the CIA operative closest to the day-to-day events of the Iran arms sales.[60] CIA records indicate that after meetings in London in early May 1986, Cave briefed George and other CIA officials about Secord including his role as financial intermediary.[61] According to Cave, George expressed concern about Secord's involvement.[62] Records indicate that at a subsequent meeting on May 9, 1986, George and other CIA and NSC officials discussed Secord's role again.[63] As discussed in more detail below, CIA officers testified that

George was present at yet another meeting in mid-May 1986 prior to McFarlane's mission to Tehran at which Secord's role was discussed in detail.

As an Iranian "Second Channel," [64] or Iranian contact, was being cultivated in the late summer of 1986, George was kept informed of the developments. After the Second Channel came to Washington in mid-September 1986 for in-depth meetings with North, Cave and Secord, North prepared and sent to Poindexter transcribed minutes of the meetings.[65] This document stated on its front page that Secord had been one of the three U.S. participants in the talks. North's cover memorandum to Poindexter recited that "[t]he only other copy of this memorandum of conversation has been given (by hand) to the DDO of CIA." [66]

North's memorandum contained information that would have been of great interest to George. The Second Channel reported that the Iranians possessed a 400-page transcript of the torture/debriefing of William Buckley, the former CIA station chief in Beirut who had been taken hostage and killed by terrorists in Lebanon.[67] George had been "extremely emotionally involved" in the Buckley matter.[68]

On November 18, 1986, two weeks after details of the Iran arms sales began to appear in the press, George gave a briefing to congressional staffers on the CIA's role in the initiative. A memorandum of that briefing written by the chief counsel of Senate intelligence committee recited that George told the staffers that the CIA received money directly from Iran, and made no mention of Secord's role as a financial intermediary.[69] A contemporaneous internal CIA document retrieved from George's working files contained a handwritten notation next to a similar assertion that Iranian funds went directly to the CIA. The notation is "Gorba > Secord > CIA Account > DOD." [70] A CIA

---

54 Secord, OIC Interview, 5/14/87, p. 318.

55 George, *George* Trial Testimony, 8/13/92, p. 3307.

56 Twetten, Grand Jury, 8/21/91, pp. 33–34, 36.

57 Ibid., p. 33.

58 Twetten, Grand Jury, 1/22/88, p. 85. Twetten had recommended that George *not* approve the issuance of the passports. George took the matter to Director Casey, who instructed him to issue the passports.

59 George, *George* Trial Testimony, 8/13/92, p. 3324. The passports were introduced into evidence at George's trials. See Alias Passport for Richard V. Secord (Richard J. Adams), DO 69903, *George* GX 57; Release for Alias Passport for Secord, DO 69904, *George* GX 58; Alias Passport for Albert Hakim (Ibrahim Ibrahamian), DO 69870, *George* GX 59; Release for Alias Passport for Albert Hakim, DO 69871, *George* GX 60.

60 Cave, Grand Jury, 8/30/91, p. 26.

61 Casey Schedule, 5/8/86, ER 609, *George* GX 61; Cave, Grand Jury, 8/30/91, pp. 78–79.

62 Ibid., pp. 80–81.

63 Memorandum for the Record by Robert Earl, 5/9/86, AKW 8904–06, *George* GX 72.

64 The "Second Channel" referred to a group of Iranians, including a nephew of Rafsanjani, who were viewed as more promising intermediaries for releasing the hostages.

65 Memorandum from North to Poindexter, 9/25/86, AKW 7291–7308, *George* GX 98.

66 Ibid., AKW 7291.

67 Ibid., AKW 7293–94.

68 George, Select Committees Deposition, 4/24/87, p. 131.

69 Memorandum to the Record by Daniel Finn, 11/19/86, SSCI Covert Action Document 86–3964, *George* GX 77.

70 Subject: CIA Involvement in NSC Iran Program, DO 44620–17, *George* GX 68.

witness identified the writing as George's.[71] The document indicates that George clearly understood the path of the Iran arms money and Secord's role in the Iran arms sales.

Following the November 18, 1986, briefing, George's two special assistants, Norman Gardner and an officer referred to in this report as "CIA Subject #2," met with North. A one-page document containing North's notes of that meeting was retrieved by FBI agents from the "burn bag" in North's office one week later.[72] North recorded the points made by George at the briefing. North then wrote "Not reveal Dick Secord."

Significant witnesses added to the documentary record of George's knowledge of Secord's role in the Iran arms sales. Thomas Twetten, who later became deputy director for operations, testified that during his return from a meeting in Europe relating to the Iran arms sales, North told him that Secord and Hakim were working with North in Central America.[73] Twetten was concerned that Secord and Hakim were involved in both operations. He reported North's comments to George, including the information about Secord and Hakim's conflicting roles.[74]

Twetten also discussed with George North's Notional Time Line, which frequently referred to actions to be taken by "Copp."[75] Twetten testified that George knew that Copp was an alias for Secord,[76] and that George was aware of the flow of funds associated with the Iran arms sales—including Secord's role.[77]

After Twetten's meeting in Europe, George assigned Cave, an experienced CIA operative who spoke fluent Farsi, to work with North as an interpreter. Cave briefed George throughout 1986 on important issues relating to the arms sales.[78] After a meeting in London in early May 1986, he explained to George and others at the CIA the financial arrangements, including Secord's role in the flow of funds.[79] Cave recalled George expressing concern over Secord's

involvement in the Iran arms sales.[80] And prior to traveling with McFarlane to Tehran in late May 1986, Cave informed George and other CIA officials about the role Secord was playing with respect to the Tehran mission: arranging for aircraft and supervising other logistical details.[81]

In August through October 1986, Cave kept George informed also of Secord's involvement in the development of the Second Channel.[82] Then in October 1986, Cave informed George of Roy Furmark's allegations of a diversion of funds from the Iran arms sales to the contras.[83]

In an April 24, 1987 deposition taken by the staff of the Senate Select Committee, George himself made significant admissions that contradicted his 1986 congressional testimony. First, regarding Secord, he admitted that he had a clear memory of Secord's presence at the Situation Room meeting on January 20, 1986. In conflict with his October 10, 1986, denial to the Senate Foreign Relations Committee of ever having had contact with General Secord, and his December 3, 1986 denial to SSCI that he had ever had any meetings with Secord, George testified:

Q: When did you know that Secord and North were associated together in their efforts on behalf of the Contras?

A: Well, my mind is so riveted on the day when I saw them both standing there together that I might have to say, if there was ever any question, that was the day, in the White House situation room.[84]

## George's False Testimony

### George's Congressional Testimony

George testified on several occasions before various congressional committees and other investigative bodies. The charges brought against him arose out of this testimony. On two occasions, George essentially denied the CIA's knowledge of and involvement in the contra-resupply network: On October 10, 1986, before the Senate Committee on Foreign Relations

71 George subsequently acknowledged at trial that the writing was his. George, *George* Trial Testimony, 8/13/92, p. 3461.
72 North Note, AKW 32705.
73 Twetten, Grand Jury, 8/21/91, pp. 36–38.
74 Ibid., pp. 41, 44–45.
75 Ibid., p. 26.
76 Ibid., pp. 33–34.
77 Ibid., p. 35.
78 Cave, Grand Jury, 8/30/91, p. 26.
79 Ibid., pp. 78–79.

80 Ibid., pp. 80–81.
81 Ibid., pp. 48–49, 85.
82 Ibid., p. 115.
83 Cave, SSCI Testimony, 12/2/86, pp. 44, 89–90.
84 George, Select Committees Deposition, 4/24/87, p. 44.

(SFRC) and on October 14, 1986, before the House of Representatives Permanent Select Committee on Intelligence (HPSCI). On December 3, 1986, George testified before the Senate Select Committee on Intelligence (SSCI) regarding the CIA's role in the Iran arms sales.

During his testimony before SFRC, the focus of the committee's inquiry was the recent downing of a contra resupply plane within Nicaragua. Two Americans died in the crash. The sole survivor, an American named Eugene Hasenfus, claimed that he was working for the CIA and had flown numerous missions delivering lethal supplies to contra forces inside Nicaragua. In light of these statements, the committee wanted to know (1) whether Hasenfus's assertions about CIA involvement were true, and (2) if not, what knowledge the CIA had regarding the persons coordinating the contra resupply effort of which the downed flight was a part. On October 10, 1986, George told the Senate Foreign Relations Committee:

[MR. GEORGE]: . . . We learned that support flights had American citizens involved.

[SENATOR KERRY]: When was this?

[MR. GEORGE]: Oh, I would say probably around March of this year, Senator. *However, we were not aware of their identities.*

*           *           *

However, to reiterate my opening remarks, we did not directly or indirectly assist them. We provided a great deal of intelligence about supplies into Nicaragua, and I believe that those of you who followed the ''National Intelligence Daily'' over the last two or three months will have noted that we have provided several articles about the growing amount of supplies being provided over land and by air to the Contras inside Nicaragua. I would only conclude in saying that at no time did we attempt to investigate those Americans. That is not our responsibility. On those occasions in the past, where we have come across Americans who we have determined were violating law, we have made that information available to the Department of Justice. *We do not know the individuals*

*involved in this affair which led to the downing of the airplane,* and we do not know the details of supply routes which they used. Thank you, Mr. Chairman.[85]

During the same SFRC testimony, George made the following statements regarding Secord:

[SENATOR KERRY]: . . . How about General Secor[d]? Do you have any contact with General Secor[d]?

[MR. ABRAMS]: I never met him. I read in today's paper that he is alleged to be behind all of this. But I have never met him.

[SENATOR KERRY]: You have never had any contact with him at all?

[MR. ABRAMS]: None whatsoever.

[SENATOR KERRY]: What about you?

[MR. GEORGE]: *No.* I know his name well and I have known his name for years. *But I do not know the man.*[86]

Four days later, George testified before HPSCI about the same subjects. Like SFRC, HPSCI was interested in learning what George knew about the Hasenfus allegations and the individuals behind the secret contra-resupply flights. Once again, George made statements indicating he had little information on these topics. He denied knowing the identities of the individuals who were behind the secret contra-resupply flights of which the downed flight was a part:

[MR. CHAIRMAN]: There are a number of airplanes that take off there to supply the Contras regularly. You don't know who they are?

[MR. FIERS]: We know the airplanes by type. We knew, for example, there were two C–123s and two C–7 cargoes. We knew that they were flying out of Ilopango and we knew they were flying both from [another location in Central America] and

---

[85] George, SFRC Testimony, 10/10/86, pp. 29–31. In this and other quoted passages of George's testimony, the specific statements later charged in the indictment are underscored.

[86] Ibid., pp. 74–75.

from [another location in Central America] into Nicaragua. We knew in some cases much less frequently that they were flying down the Pacific air corridors into southern Nicaragua for the purposes of resupply, but as to who was flying the flights and who was behind them, we do not know.

[MR. CHAIRMAN]: And you still don't?

[MR. FIERS]: No.

[MR. GEORGE]: *No, sir.*

[MR. FIERS]: We know from the newspapers that a company called Corporate Air Services is the company that appears to have some involvement with them, but——

[MR. GEORGE]: *What we know at this point is* as [Alan] says, *is from the press.*[87]

Second, George denied to HPSCI knowing whether "Max Gomez" was actually involved in providing supplies to the contras. Hasenfus had stated at an October 9, 1986, press conference in Managua, Nicaragua, that he and numerous other crew members had been flying contra resupply missions out of Ilopango air base. Hasenfus had claimed that Max Gomez and Ramon Medina, two Cubans who purportedly worked for the CIA, were overseeing the operation. Congress wanted to know whether this was true.

Before the SFRC, George stated that he had some tentative information that the name Max Gomez was an alias for a former CIA employee. But George said his information was not firm and needed further checking.

Between George's October 10 testimony and his HPSCI appearance on October 14, several major newspapers reported that Max Gomez was an alias for Felix Rodriguez. According to these reports, Rodriguez had close contacts inside the office of Vice President George Bush. So by the time of George's HPSCI testimony, Max Gomez's true identity—Felix Rodriguez—had become common knowledge. For this reason, George agreed that the CIA could no longer fail to acknowledge that Gomez was Rodriguez.[88] But Rodriguez's specific activities on behalf of the contras were still not fully

understood, and HPSCI was looking for detailed information.

This led to the following interchange between George and Representative Matthew McHugh:

[MR. McHUGH]: . . . Do any of you gentlemen know Ramone [sic] Medina? His name has been mentioned.

[MR. GEORGE]: That was the other name mentioned by Mr. Hasenfus. He mentioned two. We have identified the first as Felix Rodriguez, and correct me, Alan or Elliott, we don't know what that second name means.

[MR. FIERS]: We still are trying to find out who Ramone Medina is.

[MR. McHUGH]: I'd like to be clear in my own mind as to whether you or anybody in the Government knows as a matter of fact whether Mr. Gomez or Rodriguez was involved in providing supplies to the Contras.

[MR. GEORGE]: *I do not know that per se. I do not. Or any record I have ever read.*[89]

On November 28, 1986, the Senate Select Committee on Intelligence began a formal investigation into the circumstances surrounding the Iran arms sales and the use of funds generated by these sales for contra resupply operations. On December 3, 1986, George testified under oath as part of SSCI's investigation.

By then, Secord's name had been publicly linked to both the Iran arms sales and the secret contra resupply network. This produced the following dialogue between George and Keith Hall, the Committee's deputy staff director:

[MR. HALL]: Was it your understanding that Colonel North or anybody else in the National Security Council or any private parties would have some responsibilities and roles in the financial transactions?

[MR. GEORGE]: I'm told that an individual that had—I'm told after the fact that an individual who did have a role in the financial affairs of this enterprise was Richard Secord.

---

[87] George, HPSCI Testimony, 10/14/86, pp. 20–21.
[88] Fiers, Grand Jury, 8/16/91, pp. 43–44.

[89] George, HPSCI Testimony, 10/14/86, p. 40.

[MR. HALL]: Were you aware of any role that Colonel North played?

[MR. GEORGE]: I have no information on Colonel North and funds.

[MR. HALL]: Can you tell us what role Secord did play?

[MR. GEORGE]: *I cannot.* Please.

\*       \*       \*

[MR. HALL]: Are there any other details associated with this project that you have not already discussed with us that you are aware of?

[MR. GEORGE]: *No. . . .* I am sure [the people I put into the initiative] told me many, many things that I, sitting here before you, can't recall off the top of my head, and I have again, as I said, gone out of my way not to sit down with Mr. Cave and Mr. Twetten and everyone else and say now let's all remind each other what happened here, because I understand that's the way it should be. But I at no time felt uncomfortable that the law was broken or that we knew money was being siphoned off or——

[MR. HALL]: Did you have—

[MR. GEORGE]: I was a little disturbed about some of the players in the affair. I think I was worried about—I was worried about, you know, who was Hakim and where is his role in this, and *the good General Secord whom I had never laid eyes on* but whose name I was familiar with.

\*       \*       \*

[MR. HALL]: Did you ever ha[ve] any meetings with General Secord?

[MR. GEORGE]: [The witness nodded in the negative.] [90]

## George's Grand Jury Testimony

In early 1991, Independent Counsel was investigating the testimony given by George and others before Congress in October 1986. In late June 1990, Independent Counsel received drafts of the opening statement showing that important information about the origins of the secret contra-resupply effort had been deleted. The preparation of the opening statement became an area of investigative concern for Independent Counsel.

On April 5, 1991, George appeared before a federal Grand Jury in the District of Columbia. He was asked for information regarding the preparation of his opening statement:

Q: . . . During our meeting in our office, the Office of Independent Counsel, you indicated that you did not edit anything out of these drafts?

A: *I do not recall editing these drafts at all.*

Q: Okay.

A: *I was finally handed Draft Number whatever it was, and that was it.*

\*       \*       \*

Q: On page two of Draft 3, at the bottom of that I will read the following sentence and it has three lines through it. It says, "Subsequent to the 1984 cutoff, Ilopango airfield in San Salvador was used to support the democratic resistance as a transit point for congressionally authorized humanitarian assistance." And then by the third line through that sentence, it says, "Deleted by DDO."

First of all, is that your handwriting?

A: It's not my handwriting.

Q: Did you direct that portion of the draft be excised?

A: *I cannot believe I did.*

Q: Do you know who did?

A: *I do not.* Uh, as we said previously, "deleted by DDO" could be by DO, the Director of Operations and they were confusing terminologies. *I do not recall getting to this kind of detail in preparing this statement.*[91]

---

[90] George, SSCI Testimony, 12/3/86, pp. 19, 30–31.

[91] George, Grand Jury, 4/5/91, pp. 70–80, 82–83.

## The George Prosecution

On September 6, 1991, a federal Grand Jury in the District of Columbia returned a 10-count felony indictment against George, charging him with perjury, false statements and obstruction of congressional and Grand Jury investigations.

Based on the narrow interpretation of the obstruction statute expressed in *United States* v. *Poindexter*,[92] which was decided after the *George* indictment was returned, Judge Royce C. Lamberth dismissed three obstruction counts in *George* on May 18, 1992. In light of the *Poindexter* decision, the Government did not object. On May 21, 1992, a federal Grand Jury in the District of Columbia returned a supplemental two-count indictment charging violations in conformity with the holding in *Poindexter*. George's efforts to dismiss the new counts were unsuccessful. The case proceeded to trial on nine counts.[93]

On August 26, 1992, the Court declared a mistrial in light of the jury's inability, despite protracted deliberations, to reach a unanimous verdict on any count. The Court scheduled a second trial to begin on October 19, 1992.

Independent Counsel took steps to simplify the *George* case at retrial based on the experi-

ence at the first trial.[94] First, he moved to dismiss the two obstruction counts. Second, he chose to delete certain specific charged statements in other counts, where more than one statement was charged as false.[95] The retrial began as scheduled on October 19, 1992.

The case went to the jury on November 19, 1992. After eleven days of deliberation, the jury returned on December 9 with a verdict of guilty on Counts 4 and 5 and acquittal on the other five counts. Count 4 charged that George made false statements before HPSCI on October 14, 1986, in denying knowledge about Rodriguez's role in the contra-resupply operation. Count 5 charged that George committed perjury before SSCI on December 3, 1986, in denying knowledge about North and Secord's role in the Iran initiative.

The Court set sentencing of George for February 18, 1993. Before sentencing could take place, President Bush granted a full and unconditional pardon to George and five other Iran/contra defendants on December 24, 1992. Three of the five had, like George, been convicted of crimes prior to receiving their pardons. In view of the pardon granted to George, the Court dismissed the indictment with prejudice on January 15, 1993.

## Conclusion

The documentary and testimonial evidence presented against George in the two trials refuted the view that the secret Iran/contra operations

---

[92] 951 F.2d 369 (D.C. Cir. 1991).

[93] The charges faced by George in the first trial under the consolidated indictment included:

—Count 1: False statement to the SFRC on October 10, 1986, about knowledge of individuals involved in contra-resupply, including Rodriguez, North and Secord.

—Count 2: False statements to SFRC on October 10, 1986, about knowledge of Secord and his involvement in both the Iran arms sales and contra-resupply.

—Count 3: Obstruction of Congress stemming from his actions on October 9–10, 1986, by directing Fiers to delete portions of George's SFRC testimony regarding the use of Ilopango air base for contra-resupply and by telling Fiers not to reveal that Max Gomez was an alias for Rodriguez.

—Count 4: Obstruction of Congress stemming from his actions on October 9–14, 1986, by instructing Fiers not to convey certain facts regarding the use of Ilopango air base for contra-resupply.

—Count 5: False statements to HPSCI on October 14, 1986, about his knowledge of individuals involved in contra-resupply, including North, Secord and Rodriguez.

—Count 6: False statements to HPSCI on October 14, 1986, about his knowledge of Rodriguez's involvement in contra-resupply.

—Count 7: Perjury before SSCI on December 3, 1986, about Secord's role in the Iran initiative and about his contact with Secord.

—Count 8: Obstruction of a federal Grand Jury on April 5, 1991, regarding the preparation of testimony before the SFRC on October 10, 1986.

—Count 9: Perjury before a federal Grand Jury on April 5, 1991, regarding his role in preparing testimony given the SFRC on October 10, 1986.

[94] Both trials were conducted by Deputy Independent Counsel Craig A. Gillen, assisted by Associate Counsel Jeffrey S. Harleston, Michael D. Vhay, and Samuel A. Wilkins III.

[95] The charges faced by George in the second trial were simplified. They included:

—Count 1: False statements before SFRC on October 10, 1986, about the identity of individuals involved in contra-resupply, including Rodriguez, North and Secord.

—Count 2: False statements before SFRC on October 10, 1986, about his contact with Secord and Secord's involvement in the Iran initiative.

—Count 3: False statements before HPSCI on October 14, 1986, regarding his knowledge of the identity of individuals involved in contra-resupply, including North, Rodriguez and Secord.

—Count 4: False statements before HPSCI on October 14, 1986, about his knowledge of Rodriguez's involvement in contra-resupply.

—Count 5: Perjury before SSCI on December 3, 1986, about Secord's role in the Iran initiative.

—Count 6: Obstruction of a federal Grand Jury on April 5, 1991, regarding his role in the preparation of testimony to SFRC on October 10, 1986.

—Count 7: Perjury before a federal Grand Jury on April 5, 1991, regarding his denial of editing his opening statement to SFRC on October 10, 1986.

were essentially run out of the NSC and that high Administration officials at the various departments of Government, including the CIA, Defense and State, were unaware of the details or not involved in the activities. George was in a position to provide this crucial information to Congress when various congressional committees, in attempting to fulfill their constitutional oversight responsibility, began official inquiries into the Iran/contra affair. But instead George chose to evade, mislead and lie.

# Chapter 18
# United States v. Duane R. Clarridge

Duane R. "Dewey" Clarridge was a career CIA officer whose major posts included chief of the Latin American Division, chief of the European Division, and chief of the Counterterrorism Center. He retired from the CIA in 1987 after being formally reprimanded for his role in the Iran/contra affair.

As chief of the Latin American Division from 1981 to 1984, Clarridge directed CIA efforts to support the Nicaraguan contras. One of the people helping Clarridge during this period was Lt. Col. Oliver L. North of the National Security Council staff. When Congress passed the Boland Amendment and cut off all aid to the contras in October 1984, Clarridge allegedly passed off responsibility for supporting the contras to North.

The investigation of Clarridge focused on his knowledge of and role in both parts of the Iran/contra affair—the arms-for-hostages trades with Iran and the effort to secure covert foreign funding for the contras after Congress cut off U.S. aid. In November 1985, when North became involved in an Israeli effort to ship U.S.-made HAWK missiles to Iran to secure the release of U.S. hostages being held in Lebanon, he turned to Clarridge, then chief of the CIA's European Division, for assistance. Clarridge testified extensively about his role in the operation, but steadfastly denied contemporaneous knowledge that the shipment contained weapons. Clarridge also testified at length about his efforts to support the contras, but denied soliciting support from third countries or even knowing about discussions of such efforts. In both instances, there was strong evidence that Clarridge's testimony was false.

On November 26, 1991, a federal Grand Jury indicted Clarridge on seven counts of perjury and false statements to congressional investigators and to the President's Special Review Board (the Tower Commission) stemming from his testimony about his role in the November 1985 arms shipment to Iran.[1] The OIC decided not to seek an indictment against Clarridge for false testimony about CIA efforts to solicit third-country funding for the contras, primarily because the solicitation effort in which Clarridge was involved was called off at the last minute by his superiors.

Counts One through Three of the Indictment charged Clarridge with perjury (18 U.S.C. § 1621) before the Senate Select Committee on Intelligence on December 2, 1986. Count One was based on the following exchange:

> Mr. Newsom: At what point did you . . . have knowledge that the cargo of the plane was actually weapons?
>
> Mr. Clarridge: Well, as I say, the trouble is that when I really got a fix on it was in January when Charlie [Allen] debriefed a—the Iranian go-between in all this.[2]

---

[1] On December 10, 1992, Judge Harold H. Greene ruled that Counts One and Two and Counts Six and Seven were multiplicitous, and ordered the OIC to choose between Counts One and Two and between Counts Six and Seven. Count One charged Clarridge with lying to the Senate Select Committee on Intelligence about when he learned, *from any source,* that the cargo of the November 1985 shipment was weapons. Count Two charged Clarridge with lying to the same Committee when asked specifically when *North* told him the plane contained weapons. The court ruled those statements were essentially the same lie, and ordered the OIC to choose between them. At the time Clarridge was pardoned, the OIC's motion to reconsider that ruling was pending.

Counts Six and Seven did charge essentially the same lies, but the statements were made to different entities. The false statements charged in Count Six were made to the staffs of the Select Committees while the false statements charged in Count Seven were made to the Committee members themselves. At the time of the pardon, the OIC had not yet chosen between Counts Six and Seven.

[2] Clarridge, SSCI Testimony, 12/2/86, p. 20.

In Count Two, in response to a question about whether North had ever told him the cargo of the flight from Israel to Iran was military equipment, Clarridge answered: "No, and I can't say that he [North] knew. I can't say for sure that he knew." [3]

In Count Three, Clarridge was asked whether he had any concern about using the CIA proprietary airline for a mission like this. He responded that "it seemed to be a straight commercial deal. In other words, private people apparently hiring our proprietary." [4] Senator Thomas Eagleton then asked: "Didn't you have a second thought or question, 'Here's a hotshot from the NSC who's on this interagency group coming to my personal office, one on one. Maybe this might be a shade more than a commercial endeavor.'" Clarridge responded: "I'm sorry, I didn't see it any more than what he was telling me." [5]

Count Four charged Clarridge with perjury for testifying before the House Permanent Select Committee on Intelligence on December 11, 1986, that a November 25, 1985, CIA cable from an Asian country stating that the pilot of the proprietary had said that the cargo was military equipment was "the first indication that we had that maybe that something other than oil drilling equipment was on the plane." [6]

Count Five charged Clarridge with making false statements for testifying before the Tower Commission on December 18, 1986, as follows:

[T]he question was asked when did I feel that that shipment in November, the 25th, had had weapons on board. By the 26th or 27th—and I can't give you a precise date—Charlie Allen was showing me [intelligence reports] . . . that indicated that that flight had had munitions or something on board. [7]

Count Six charged Clarridge with perjury before the Select Iran/contra Committees for the following exchanges:

Mr. Eggleston: As of this early time [November 22, 1985], your initial conversations with Colonel North, did you know

or had you been informed by Colonel North what was on the plane?

Mr. Clarridge: No, I was not.

\*          \*          \*

Mr. Eggleston: . . . it is your understanding as of that time [November 22] that the cargo onboard is oil drilling equipment . . . ?

Mr. Clarridge: Yes.

\*          \*          \*

Mr. Eggleston: The person who gave you the problem knew [the cargo was weapons]. The person you gave the problem to solve [a senior CIA field officer in a European country] knew. The person who was helping, [the chargé d'affaires to the European country], knew. The [European] government knew. But you did not know?

Mr. Clarridge: That is the way it was.

\*          \*          \*

Mr. Eggleston: You had not heard . . . other than this cable . . . that reflected what the pilots had said . . . that it [the cargo] was anything other than oil-drilling equipment?

Mr. Clarridge: I had not. [8]

Finally, Count Seven charged Clarridge with making false statements in a deposition before the staffs of the Select Committees, when he stated that he had no knowledge that the cargo was weapons as of November 21 or 23; that North never told him in November 1985 that the cargo was military equipment; and that as of November 25, 1985, he believed the cargo was oil parts.

The Clarridge trial, which would have been the final Iran/contra prosecution, was scheduled to begin March 15, 1993. [9] Trial was precluded by President Bush's December 24, 1992, pardon of six Iran/contra defendants, including Clarridge.

3 Ibid., p. 73.
4 Ibid., p. 14.
5 Ibid., pp. 56–57.
6 Clarridge, HPSCI Testimony, 12/11/86, p. 69.
7 Clarridge, Tower Commission Testimony, 12/18/86, p. 14.

8 Clarridge, Select Committees Deposition, 8/4/87, pp. 8, 21, 32, 42.
9 Had the *Clarridge* case gone to trial, it would have been conducted by Associate Counsel Paul J. Ware, Kenneth J. Parsigian, and David J. Apfel.

## Clarridge's Role in the November 1985 HAWK Shipment

In the summer of 1985, President Reagan approved an Israeli plan to ship weapons to Iran in exchange for the Iranians' pledge to use their influence to persuade Lebanese kidnappers to release American hostages. With U.S. acquiescence, Israel shipped 504 U.S.-made TOW missiles to Iran in August and September of 1985, and U.S. hostage Benjamin Weir was released as a result.

Israel was planning another shipment, this time of HAWK missiles, in November 1985, when it ran into difficulty obtaining requisite flight clearances.[10] Israeli Defense Minister Yitzhak Rabin sought assistance from National Security Adviser Robert C. McFarlane, who directed North to help the Israelis in obtaining the flight clearances.[11] The plan called for an Israeli El Al 747 to fly 80 HAWK missiles into a European country, transfer them to other planes, and then fly the missiles, one plane at a time, into Iran.[12] The first delivery was supposed to trigger the release of two hostages, followed by another delivery, another release, and a third delivery and a third release.[13]

North enlisted retired Air Force Maj. Gen. Richard Secord to go to the European country to obtain the necessary clearances to land the El Al flight.[14] North also brought Clarridge into the mission to get a senior CIA field officer in the European country to assist Secord.[15] Late on November 21, 1985, Clarridge sent cables to the senior officer and his deputy instructing them to report to the office and stand by for

messages.[16] The cables were sent "flash" priority, which is the second highest priority for CIA cables and requires immediate attention.[17] The senior field officer and his deputy went to their office where they received another flash cable from Clarridge instructing them to contact Secord, who was using the code name "Copp," and offer him assistance.[18] The cable indicated that Secord was on assignment for the National Security Council and that the mission was so sensitive that the senior field officer should not discuss it with the U.S. ambassador to the European country.[19] The senior field officer contacted Secord, who indicated he did not require assistance at that time; the senior field officer cabled that information back to Clarridge and awaited developments.[20]

At that time, Secord was confident that his contacts at a private company in the European country would get him access to the foreign minister, who would grant the necessary clearances.[21] Unfortunately for Secord, the private company's contacts were not helpful and an attempt by the company's president to bribe a European country official to secure the necessary clearances not only failed but angered the European government.[22] Thus, by 12:50 p.m European country time on November 22, 1985, the entire operation was in jeopardy and Secord telephoned the senior CIA field officer with an urgent request for assistance.[23] The senior

10 North, Select Committees Testimony, 7/7/87, pp. 133–134, 156–157.

11 Ibid.

12 North Notebook, 11/17/85, AMX 001865; Ibid., 11/18/85, AMX 001866–71. There is some evidence that the initial plan called for as many as 500–600 HAWKs to be shipped. There was also some talk of 120 HAWKs. The number actually on the El Al plane, however, was only 80. Transferring the HAWKs from the El Al plane to the other planes was necessary because poor relations between Israel and Iran made it untenable to fly an Israeli plane into Iran.

13 Ibid., 11/20/85, AMX 001878–81.

14 North, Select Committees Testimony, 7/7/87, pp. 135–36, 157; Letter from McFarlane to Secord, 11/19/85, AKW 000001.

15 North, Grand Jury, 2/1/91, pp. 20–21. Precisely when Clarridge became involved in the mission would have been a key issue at trial. Clarridge testified that he first learned of the mission on November 21, 1985, when North called seeking his assistance. (Clarridge, Select Committees Deposition, 8/4/87, p. 6.) The OIC would have established at trial, however, that Clarridge was involved and knew the flight would be carrying weapons at least by November 19.

16 DIRECTOR 624839, 11/22/85, DO 21379; DIRECTOR 624939, 11/22/85, DO 21378. (The cables are dated November 22, 1985 because CIA cables use "Zulu," or Greenwich mean time).

17 The only precedence higher than "flash" is "critic," which is rarely used and is only for events like an attack on an embassy or a coup. (CIA Field Communications Officer, Select Committees Deposition, 7/13/87, pp. 18–19.) When a "flash" message is sent, the intended recipient will be contacted at home, if necessary, and must open the message within thirty minutes. (Ibid., p. 18.)

18 Senior CIA Field Officer, Select Committees Deposition, 4/13/87, pp. 4–5. The actual cable is missing. The senior field officer referenced that cable, DIRECTOR 625103, however, in his cable back to Clarridge in which he indicated that he had spoken with Copp and offered "all assistance" but that Copp did not require assistance at that time. (CIA Cable, 11/22/85, DO 21380.)

19 Senior CIA Field Officer, Select Committees Deposition, 4/13/87, p. 5.

20 Ibid., pp. 5–6; CIA Cable, 11/22/85, DO 21380.

21 Secord, FBI 302, 3/11/92, p. 4. Indeed, Secord apparently believed, and informed the senior CIA field officer in the European country, that the foreign minister of the European country had orally approved the clearances before November 22, 1985, but had failed to sign the papers. (CIA Cable, 11/22/85, DO 21381.) The OIC was not able to verify that oral approval.

22 CIA Cable, 11/23/85, DO 21397–96.

23 Ibid.

CIA field officer immediately made inquiries [24] and suggested to Clarridge that a more formal diplomatic approach should be made by the second-ranking person in the U.S. Embassy, who was the chargé d'affaires. The senior CIA field officer indicated that Secord approved of involving the chargé and was seeking approval from Washington.[25] Clarridge cabled back that the NSC wanted the senior CIA field officer to bring the chargé into the operation and to "pull out all the stops" because the El Al plane was only one hour from aborting.[26]

The cables between Clarridge and the senior CIA field officer over the next day show extensive knowledge and involvement by both men in trying to salvage an operation that North later described as "a bit of a horror story." [27] First, it was discovered that when the president of the private concern used by Secord had been in contact with European country authorities on November 20, 1985, he claimed to be working with a retired U.S. general. The authorities had checked with the U.S. Embassy and were told the Embassy knew nothing of such an operation and that the United States remained opposed to arms sales to Iran.[28] Thus the senior CIA field officer had to explain to European country officials that while the Embassy's position had been correct on November 20, circumstances had changed by November 22.[29]

The next problem was that the foreign minister of the European country was the only person who could approve the clearances, and he was in a cabinet meeting. The senior CIA field officer asked a lower-level ministry official to pull the foreign minister out of the meeting and was told that would require a formal statement from the U.S. Embassy.[30] Secord told the senior CIA field officer he had called the White House and recommended authorizing the chargé to pull the foreign minister out of the cabinet meeting. Secord noted that McFarlane was being pulled out of a meeting with the Pope in order to telephone the foreign minister. Clarridge then telephoned the senior CIA field officer and instructed him to have the chargé formally request that the foreign minister be pulled out of the cabinet meeting.[31]

While waiting for the foreign minister, the El Al plane had to abort and return to Israel.[32] The NSC was still hoping that McFarlane could reach the foreign minister and revive the operation for the next day, November 23.[33] With that hope in mind, Clarridge cabled CIA officers in an Asian country requesting advice and assistance in obtaining clearances for three planes to fly through that country's airspace en route from a European country to Iran and back on November 23 or 24.[34] Clarridge explained that this was a "National Security Council initiative" that had "the highest level of USG [U.S. Government] interest." [35] He described the mission as "humanitarian in nature" and in "response to terrorist acts," and told the senior CIA official in the Asian country not to inform the Ambassador.[36]

When the European cabinet meeting ended, the foreign minister still would not approve the flights. Instead, his aide informed the chargé that the U.S. Embassy would have to send a diplomatic note stating the type of aircraft, the routes to and from the European country, and the cargo.[37] Late at night on November 22 (European country time), McFarlane finally reached the foreign minister by telephone and persuaded him to approve the flights without a diplomatic note.[38] It was not until mid-morning the next day, however, that the chargé was able to contact anyone in the Ministry of Foreign Affairs.[39] When the chargé did reach the secretary general of the Foreign Ministry and then the chief of the Cabinet of the Foreign Minister, they knew nothing of McFarlane's deal with the foreign

[24] See Classified Appendix.

[25] CIA Cable, 11/23/85, DO 23197–96. The Ambassador was out of the country.

[26] DIRECTOR 625908, 11/22/85, DO 21383. Clarridge also telephoned the senior CIA field officer with approval for bringing the chargé into the operation. (Senior CIA Field Officer, Select Committees Deposition, 4/13/87, p. 13.)

[27] North, Select Committees Testimony, 7/7/87, p. 137.

[28] Chargé d'Affaires, Select Committees Deposition, 5/27/87, pp. 8, 14; CIA Cable, 11/22/85, ALW 0034616–17; CIA Cable, 11/22/85, DO 21384.

[29] CIA Cable, 11/22/85, DO 21384; Senior CIA Field Officer, Select Committees Deposition, 4/13/87 p. 12.

[30] CIA Cable, 11/22/85, DO 21384; Senior CIA Field Officer, Select Committees Deposition, 4/13/87, p. 13.

[31] Ibid.

[32] CIA Cable, 11/22/85, DO 21386.

[33] DIRECTOR 626226, 11/22/85, DO 21388.

[34] Ibid., DO 21389.

[35] Ibid.

[36] Ibid.

[37] CIA Cable, 11/23/85, DO 21391; Senior CIA Field Officer, Select Committees Deposition, 4/13/87, p. 16.

[38] DIRECTOR 626552, 11/22/85, DO 21390; Chargé d'Affaires, Select Committees Deposition, 5/27/87, p. 9.

[39] Ibid., pp. 9–10.

minister and insisted that a diplomatic note was required.[40]

On Saturday, November 23, North telephoned CIA intelligence officer Charles Allen at home and asked him to go to his office and show Clarridge a collection of intelligence reports concerning Mohsen Kangarlu, Iran's director of security, and Manucher Ghorbanifar, the Iranian expatriate arms dealer who was serving as an intermediary between Israel and the Iranians.[41] At about the same time, North was beginning to seek alternate routes for delivering the missiles and asked Clarridge if the CIA could recommend a reliable charter.[42] Clarridge began checking into charters, and North headed in to the CIA to meet with Clarridge.[43]

Allen arrived at the CIA before North and showed the packet of intelligence reports to Clarridge per North's instructions. Allen explained to Clarridge that North wanted him to understand that this was "a very serious initiative under way by the White House."[44] Allen told Clarridge that the reports had been very tightly held and they discussed the highly sensitive nature of the operation.[45] Clarridge leafed through the intelligence reports and told Allen that he understood this was a serious initiative; Allen left the reports with Clarridge who said he would read them.[46]

While waiting for North, Clarridge called the CIA Air Branch seeking the name of a reliable charter. The Air Branch recommended that North use a CIA proprietary airline.[47] Clarridge then called his superior, acting Deputy Director for Operations Edward Juchniewicz, to inform him that North wanted to use a CIA proprietary.

According to Clarridge, Juchniewicz approved North's using a CIA proprietary.[48]

About an hour after Allen left Clarridge's office, North arrived.[49] The mission was now proceeding on two separate fronts. While the senior CIA field officer and the chargé were still trying to obtain clearances from the European country, North was attempting to set up a series of flights using the CIA proprietary and flying through a different city, perhaps in a second European country.[50] Clarridge, who was monitoring efforts in the first European country, was simultaneously attempting to arrange clearances for a CIA proprietary to fly from Israel through an Asian country's airspace with a possible stopover in the second European country "for deception purposes," that is, to satisfy the Asian country's concerns about being involved with a direct flight from Israel to Iran.[51] Clarridge informed senior field personnel in both the second European country and the Asian country that the mission was essential to the release of the U.S. hostages.[52] By this time, a CIA Air Branch officer was in Clarridge's office to discuss staffing the proprietary flights and arranging an "appropriate cover . . . so it would look like a normal charter activity."[53] Allen had also returned to Clarridge's office along with another CIA intelligence official, Dr. Joseph Markowitz; thus, Clarridge, North, Allen, the CIA Air Branch

40 Ibid.; CIA Cable, 11/23/85, DO 21397–96; Senior CIA Field Officer, Select Committees Deposition, 4/13/87, pp. 17–18. The chargé ultimately confirmed that the phone call between the foreign minister and McFarlane occurred, but the foreign minister thought he agreed only to approve the clearances if he received the necessary background information—i.e., a diplomatic note about the cargo and the purpose of the mission. (Chargé d'Affaires, Select Committees Deposition, 5/27/87, p. 20.)

41 Allen, Grand Jury, 12/18/87, pp. 52–55. Ghorbanifar's codename was "Ashgari." As a result, these intelligence reports have come to be known as the A–K, or Ashgari-Kangarlu, Reports.

42 Clarridge, SSCI Testimony, 12/2/86, pp. 5–6.

43 Allen, Select Committees Deposition, 4/21/87, p. 160.

44 Ibid., p. 157.

45 Ibid., 7/2/87, p. 669; Allen, Grand Jury, 12/18/87, p. 54.

46 Allen, Select Committees Deposition, 4/21/87, p. 157; Ibid., 7/2/87, p. 669; Allen, FBI 302, 1/10/91, p. 2.

47 Clarridge, SSCI Testimony, 12/2/86, pp. 5–6.

48 Ibid. Juchniewicz, who placed the call from Clarridge on November 22, has told somewhat conflicting stories about this event. He testified that Clarridge told him only that North was searching for a reliable charter, not that he had specifically requested assistance. (Juchniewicz, SSCI Testimony, 12/4/86, p. 4.) Later, he testified, North called him at home and inquired about using a CIA proprietary. Juchniewicz testified that he told North the proprietary was a "strictly commercial venture" that anyone could hire. (Ibid., p. 5.) When he was interviewed by the OIC in 1991, however, Juchniewicz told a version of the events that more closely parallels Clarridge's testimony. He said that Clarridge had come to his office and said that North needed a plane to ship some oil-drilling equipment. He asked if it would be a problem for North to use the CIA proprietary and Juchniewicz said he did not see it as a problem. (Juchniewicz, FBI 302, 10/8/91, p. 2.) At that time, Juchniewicz did not recall a phone call from North. (Ibid., p. 3.)

49 Allen, Select Committees Deposition, 7/2/87, p. 670.

50 For a brief period, there was some thought that the flights by the CIA proprietary might still be able to fly through the first European country. (CIA Cable, 11/23/85, DO 21397; Senior CIA Field Officer, Select Committees Deposition, 4/13/87, p. 18; Clarridge, Select Committees Deposition, 4/27/87, pp. 45–47.)

51 DIRECTOR 627461, 11/23/85, DO 21402 (to Asian country personnel); DIRECTOR 627576, 11/23/85, DO 21404 (to second European country personnel).

52 Ibid.

53 Allen, Select Committees Deposition, 4/21/87, pp. 162–63.

officer, and Markowitz were all in Clarridge's office working on the operation.[54]

The situation in the first European country finally collapsed on the afternoon of November 23, 1985. Despite his telephone conversation with McFarlane, the foreign minister was still insisting on a diplomatic note that said the purpose of the mission was to secure the release of the U.S. hostages. McFarlane and his deputy, Vice Admiral John M. Poindexter, determined that the United States would not send a formal note mentioning the hostages, but could tell the European country that the mission was "humanitarian" in nature.[55] Finally, McFarlane and Poindexter decided to terminate efforts to run the planes through the European country. Clarridge cabled a message from Poindexter to the chargé to send the following note to the European government: "We regret that your government was unable to fulfill the USG [U.S. Government] request for this humanitarian mission."[56]

Meanwhile, negotiations with the Asian country were continuing. It agreed to permit one flight, not three as requested, with the possibility of more the next day; the Asian government also insisted on information about the cargo the plane would be carrying.[57] According to Clarridge, that was the first time he asked North what the cargo was and North told him it was spare parts for the oil industry.[58] Clarridge cabled that information to a senior CIA field officer to relay to the Asian country authorities.[59] After another day of negotiations and cables between Clarridge and CIA field personnel, the Asian country permitted one plane to traverse its airspace. The plane, which left Israel late on November 24 and arrived in Iran early on November 25, carried 18 HAWK missiles from Israel to Iran with a stop in an intermediate country.[60]

At that time, four additional flights were planned, and Clarridge continued his efforts to arrange necessary clearances. The Asian country authorities were upset about the stop in the intermediate country, so Clarridge arranged for the remaining four flights to stop in the second European country.[61] A senior CIA field officer cabled Clarridge on November 25 that the Asian country authorities were also upset about confusing accounts about the cargo of the completed flight. According to Asian country authorities, the proprietary's ground personnel had said the cargo was medical supplies; CIA field officers, at Clarridge's direction, had told them it was spare parts for the oil industry; and the pilot had told Asian country ground controllers it was military equipment.[62] In response to that cable, Clarridge checked with North, who confirmed that the cargo was spare parts for the oil industry.[63] Clarridge cabled that information back to the field.[64]

Clarridge continued working on arrangements for the remaining four flights until mid-December, when they were finally called off.[65]

## The Case Against Clarridge

When the arms sales to Iran first became public in November 1986, the Reagan Administration was concerned about the legality of the 1985 shipments.[66] The November 1985 HAWK shipment was particularly troubling because a CIA

[54] Ibid., 7/2/87, pp. 670–72.

[55] Chargé d'Affaires, Select Committees Deposition, 5/27/87, pp. 10–11; Clarridge, SSCI Testimony, 12/2/86, pp. 4, 10–11; CIA Cable, 11/23/85, DO 21405; CIA Cable, 11/23/85, DO 21406; DIRECTOR 627621, 11/23/85, DO 21407; DIRECTOR 627627, 11/23/85, DO 21410.

[56] Chargé d'Affaires, Select Committees Deposition, 5/27/87, pp. 11–12; DIRECTOR 627621, 11/23/85, DO 21407; DIRECTOR 627627, 11/23/85, DO 21410.

[57] CIA Cable, 11/23/85, DO 21412.

[58] Clarridge, Tower Commission Testimony, 12/18/86, p. 7.

[59] DIRECTOR 627797, 11/24/85, DO 21416.

[60] Clarridge, SSCI Testimony, 12/2/86, pp. 15–16; CIA Cable, 11/25/85, DO 21428.

[61] Clarridge, SSCI Testimony, 12/2/86, p. 16.

[62] CIA Cable, 11/25/85, 21428.

[63] Clarridge, Tower Commission Testimony, 12/18/86, p. 9. Clarridge later determined that the pilot probably did not tell the ground controllers anything about the cargo and that the Asian country authorities were "on a fishing expedition" trying to find out what the cargo was. (Ibid.)

[64] DIRECTOR 628289, 11/25/85, DO 31394–95.

[65] Clarridge, SSCI Testimony, 12/2/86, p. 25. On Monday, November 25, Deputy Director of Central Intelligence John McMahon told Clarridge that no more flights should take place without a Presidential Finding authorizing such flights. (McMahon, Select Committees Deposition, 6/1/87, p. 105; Clarridge, SSCI Testimony, 12/2/86, pp. 18–19.) Apparently, Clarridge did not understand McMahon's instruction to preclude *planning* for further flights. (Clarridge, Select Committees Deposition, 8/4/87, pp. 47–48.) McMahon was surprised that such planning took place and considered it a violation of his instructions. (McMahon, Select Committees Deposition, 6/1/87, p. 105.)

[66] The 1986 shipments were made pursuant to a written Presidential Finding under the National Security Act. Under that act, the President was required to give Congress "timely" notice of the covert action of shipping weapons to Iran. In the Administration's view, the President could withhold notification from Congress for a reasonable period to protect the lives of the hostages. Because neither the statute nor the case law defined "timely" notice, Administration officials were not nearly as concerned about the legality of the 1986 shipments as they were about the 1985 shipments, which were not made pursuant to a Finding.

proprietary airline had transported the weapons, and the CIA had been heavily involved in attempting to influence foreign governments to obtain clearances for the flight without a written finding authorizing such action under the National Security Act.

On November 20, 1986, CIA Director William J. Casey, Attorney General Edwin Meese III, Poindexter, North and others met to prepare Casey's testimony to Congress on the arms shipments. The group agreed that Casey would testify that no one in the U.S. Government was aware that weapons were on the November 1985 flight by the CIA proprietary. The story was that the CIA believed the cargo was oil-drilling equipment and that the true nature of the cargo did not become clear until January 1986.

Later that day, Abraham D. Sofaer, State Department legal adviser, protested to the Department of Justice that Casey's planned testimony was wrong because Secretary of State George P. Shultz had been informed in advance of the November 1985 HAWK shipment by McFarlane. That revelation sparked an inquiry by Meese that focused on who in the U.S. Government had contemporaneous knowledge that the November 1985 shipment contained HAWK missiles.[67]

When Meese falsely stated at a November 25, 1986, press conference that the President was not aware of the November 1985 HAWK shipment until February 1986, but that others in the Government "probably" knew,[68] attention focused on who in the Government had known of the HAWK shipment but had failed to inform the President (or had failed to report to their superiors, who in turn might have informed the President). Because he had directed the CIA's efforts in the November 1985 HAWK shipment, Clarridge, along with North, was one of the lower-level officials suspected of being involved in a "rogue" operation without Presidential approval. As a result, everyone investigating Iran/contra—the Tower Commission, the CIA's inspector general, Congress, and Independent Counsel—questioned Clarridge at length about his role in the November 1985

HAWK shipment, as well as his efforts on behalf of the contras.

The critical questions about Clarridge's testimony regarding the November 1985 shipment are not what he did, but what he knew about the mission and when he knew it. Although Clarridge testified in detail before the Tower Commission and congressional investigators about his role in facilitating the shipment, he steadfastly maintained that he did not know until after the mission was completed that the shipment contained weapons.

All of the charges against Clarridge were based on evidence that he knew prior to November 24, 1985, that the shipment contained weapons. Six of the seven counts charged Clarridge with a variety of false statements about his knowledge of the cargo of the November 1985 shipment, while the other count charged him with falsely stating that he believed the use of the CIA proprietary was a "straight commercial deal." At trial, Independent Counsel would have proven in three ways that Clarridge learned before November 24, 1985, that the November 1985 shipment contained weapons: (1) from discussions with North, (2) from a cable sent to Clarridge by the senior CIA field officer in the first European country, describing the mission as an arms-for-hostages exchange—a cable that has never been found—and (3) from the intelligence reports given to Clarridge by Allen to brief Clarridge on the mission.

## Discussions With North

The most direct evidence that North told Clarridge prior to November 24, 1985, that the shipment contained weapons is the testimony of CIA official Vincent Cannistraro. In November 1985, Cannistraro was a career CIA officer who had been detailed to the NSC where he served as director of intelligence programs. On November 19, 1985, Cannistraro received a call from North, who said he needed to meet with Cannistraro and Clarridge that evening at a McLean, Virginia restaurant called Charley's Place.[69] Cannistraro had plans that evening, but

[67] See Meese chapter.
[68] Transcript of Meese press conference, 11/25/86, ALV 014375.

[69] Cannistraro, Grand Jury, 8/2/91, pp. 10–11. Cannistraro was unable to precisely date the meeting other than to state that it occurred before the November 24, 1985 shipment. (Ibid., pp. 14, 57; Cannistraro, FBI 302, 7/24/91, pp. 3–4.) North's calendar for November 19, 1985 lists

North insisted that the meeting was important and Cannistraro relented.[70]

Cannistraro arrived at Charley's first, followed by Clarridge; North arrived later.[71] Cannistraro and Clarridge were having drinks and talking while waiting for North when Cannistraro told Clarridge that North was shipping weapons to Iran in an attempt to free the U.S. hostages; Clarridge indicated that he already knew.[72] When North arrived, he told Clarridge and Cannistraro that he needed Clarridge's help getting clearances to fly a shipment of military equipment to Iran from the first European country.[73] North said he needed authorization from Poindexter to bring Clarridge into the operation, and he called Poindexter from Charley's seeking such authorization.[74] North then reported to Clarridge and Cannistraro that Poindexter had approved using Clarridge to obtain the clearances.[75] Several days after the Charley's meeting, Cannistraro asked Clarridge what had happened and Clarridge responded that he had made some arrangements for the flight.[76]

Cannistraro's testimony establishes that Clarridge knew by November 19, 1985—two days before Clarridge testified he first learned of the operation—that North was trying to ship arms to Iran, through the European country, to secure the release of U.S. hostages. North's notebook provides further evidence that Clarridge knew of the operation by November 19, 1985.[77]

North gave conflicting testimony about when he told Clarridge the shipment contained arms. During the *Poindexter* trial, North testified that he "made sure" the CIA knew that weapons were going to be on the CIA proprietary flight.[78] In his July 7, 1987, Select Committees testimony, however, North stated several times that he could not say whether he informed Clarridge that the shipment contained arms before or after the flight.[79] He did not remember the Charley's Meeting, but conceded "it could well have happened."[80]

There is documentary evidence that North and Clarridge discussed the operation in great detail before December 4, 1985. North wrote Poindexter a long computer message about the operation on December 4, 1985. In it, he discussed both the November HAWK shipment, which the Iranians had rejected as having the wrong type of missile, and the plans for further shipments.[81] The plan called for the Israelis to provide 50 HAWKs and 3,300 TOWs in five staggered shipments beginning on December 12; one or two of the five American hostages and one French hostage would be released after each shipment.[82] After describing the plan, North wrote:

> Dewey is the only other person fully witting of this entire plan. Copp is not briefed on [another classified aspect of the plan]—though he suspects. The Israelis are in the same position. Dewey and I have been through the whole concept twice looking for holes and can find little that can be done to improve it given the "trust factor" with the Iranians.[83]

While the computer note does not establish that North told Clarridge the cargo was weapons before November 24, it does contradict Clarridge's testimony that he did not get "a fix on" the cargo until "January [1986] when Charlie Allen debriefed . . . the Iranian go-between in all this."[84] It also contradicts Clarridge's testimony that his only involvement

---

a 7:00 p.m. meeting at "Charlie's [sic] Place Vince + Dewey [Clarridge's nickname]." Clarridge's calendar for that evening has only an illegible erasure. (North Calendar, 11/19/85, AKW 003910.)

[70] Cannistraro, Grand Jury, 8/2/91, pp. 10–11, 50–51. Cannistraro recalls North urging him to attend the meeting "because Americans are dying face down in the mud." (Ibid., pp. 50–51.)

[71] Ibid., p. 12.

[72] Ibid., p. 13. Cannistraro's memory of the conversation is vivid because he thought the news that North was shipping weapons to Iran would be "a real shocker to Mr. Clarridge." He was surprised to learn that Clarridge already knew. (Ibid., p. 50.)

[73] Ibid., pp. 15–16; Cannistraro, FBI 302, 7/24/91, p. 4. Cannistraro could not recall the precise language North used to describe the cargo, but was positive North identified the cargo as military equipment:

> . . . I can't recall whether he specifically said HAWK missile parts or TOWs or what; but he indicated there was military equipment on board. . . . I'm not positive he said missiles. He said military equipment. My impression is that he said missiles, but I can't be 100 percent certain of it.

(Cannistraro, Grand Jury, 8/2/91, p. 15.)

[74] Ibid., pp. 16–17.

[75] Ibid., p. 16.

[76] Cannistraro, FBI 302, 7/24/91, p. 5.

[77] See Classified Appendix.

[78] North, *Poindexter* Trial Testimony, 3/12/90, pp. 1197–98.

[79] North, Select Committees Deposition, 7/7/87, pp. 165, 184.

[80] North, Grand Jury, 11/15/91, p. 104.

[81] PROFs Note from North to Poindexter, 12/4/85, AKW 002070–73.

[82] Ibid.

[83] Ibid., AKW 002073.

[84] Clarridge, SSCI Testimony, 12/2/86, p. 20.

with the planning for shipments in December 1985 was "getting the aircraft clearances." [85] Clarridge disputed the story told in the December 4, 1985 computer note, claiming not to remember any conversations during early December 1985 with North about the operation, and specifically denying that he and North had gone over the "whole concept twice." [86] Indeed, Clarridge testified that as late as the middle of December 1985, when he pointed out to North that reliable intelligence reports were "beginning to . . . suggest" that the cargo had been weapons, that North still maintained it was oil-drilling equipment. [87]

Finally, the relationship between North and Clarridge makes more compelling the evidence that North told Clarridge that the cargo of the November 1985 shipment was weapons. North and Clarridge had a close working relationship, dating back to Clarridge's work in support of the contras when he was chief of the Latin American Division. According to former Deputy Director of Central Intelligence John McMahon, "North thought that Duane Clarridge was the best guy in CIA . . . [b]ecause he was . . . an action-oriented guy who would get things done." [88] He described North and Clarridge as "professionally close" and "peas in a pod." [89] The husband of a CIA employee who had worked for Clarridge recalled a CIA Christmas party he attended at which Clarridge was wearing an "Ollie North is an American Hero" T-shirt. [90]

Given North's admiration for Clarridge, it makes little sense for him to have kept Clarridge in the dark about the cargo when virtually everyone else involved in the mission—North, Allen, Poindexter, numerous CIA field personnel in the European country, Secord, the chargé, and even officials of the European country—knew that weapons were being shipped. [91] Clarridge has testified that he was not informed about the cargo because of "compartmentation"; that is, he did not have a "need to know." [92] But excluding Clarridge from information about the cargo was inexplicable when persons with much smaller roles in the operation were aware that the cargo was weapons. [93] Moreover, North testified that there would not have been any reason for him not to have told Clarridge that the cargo was weapons. [94]

In fact, not informing Clarridge that the cargo was weapons would have been inconsistent with North's disclosures when he brought others in to help with the mission. When Secord was having trouble obtaining the clearances and asked North to get the U.S. Embassy involved, North called Ambassador Robert Oakley, who was then director of the State Department's counter-terrorism unit. According to Oakley, North said he needed to get a plane into the first European country in order to ship arms to Iran, and wanted Oakley to authorize involving the chargé there. [95] Oakley agreed and called Clarridge to tell him that the State Department was aware of the operation and that Clarridge should contact the foreign minister of the first European country for assistance. [96] Although Oakley cannot recall the details of his conversation with Clarridge, he had no doubt that Clarridge knew the cargo was weapons. [97] North was "completely up front" about the cargo with Oakley, and there was no suggestion of compartmentation. [98]

## The "Missing" Cable

North was not the only person who contemporaneously informed Clarridge that the cargo of

[85] Ibid., p. 25.
[86] Clarridge, Select Committees Deposition, 4/27/87, pp. 102–03.
[87] Clarridge, SSCI Testimony, 12/2/86, pp. 75–76.
[88] McMahon, Grand Jury, 9/18/91, pp. 60–61.
[89] McMahon, FBI 302, 7/22/87, p. 4; FBI 302, 3/26/87, p. 2.
[90] [Classified Identity Withheld], FBI 302, 9/16/91, p. 2.
[91] In a hearing before the Select Committees, Clarridge was involved in the following exchange regarding the anomaly of his not knowing that the shipment contained weapons while nearly everyone else involved with operation did know:

    Mr. Eggleston: The person who gave you the problem [North] knew. The person you gave the problem to solve [the senior CIA field officer in the European country] knew. The person who was helping, [the chargé], knew. The [European] government knew. But you did not know?

    Mr. Clarridge: That is the way it was.

(Clarridge, Select Committees Deposition, 8/4/87, p. 32.)

    With respect to the chargé's knowledge and the knowledge of the European government, see Chargé d'Affaires, Select Committees Deposition, 5/27/87, pp. 20–22. Allen's knowledge has been discussed previously in this section.

[92] Clarridge, Select Committees Deposition, 4/27/87, p. 49.
[93] For example, a CIA secretary in the European country on November 23, 1985, was aware that the cargo was weapons, as was a CIA communications officer in that country. (CIA Field Secretary, FBI 302, 9/23/92, p. 2; CIA Field Communications Officer, Select Committees Deposition, 7/13/87, p. 67.)
[94] North, Grand Jury, 2/1/91, p. 128.
[95] Oakley, FBI 302, 11/14/91, p. 1.
[96] Ibid., pp. 1–2.
[97] Ibid., p. 1.
[98] Ibid. (quotation is from FBI 302, which paraphrases Oakley).

the November 1985 shipment was weapons. On November 23, 1985, the senior CIA field officer in the first European country sent Clarridge a cable explaining that the cargo was HAWK missiles. Although Clarridge has steadfastly maintained that he never received any such cable, there is overwhelming evidence that the cable was sent. CIA communications experts would have testified that, under the circumstances, there is no reason that the cable would not have been received in Washington.[99]

On Saturday, November 23, 1985, the senior CIA field officer, the chargé and Secord were still trying to recycle the mission through the first European country, using three planes instead of the original El Al plane that had aborted its flight and returned to Israel when clearances were not obtained. At about 11:30 a.m. European country time, Secord called the senior CIA field officer to seek assistance in arranging for the planes that would fly to Iran.[100] During that conversation, Secord asked if the officer had been briefed on the operation. When the officer replied that he had not, Secord suggested they meet.[101]

The senior CIA field officer and Secord met at Secord's hotel shortly thereafter. They sat in the officer's car and discussed the operation for approximately ten minutes.[102] Secord told the officer that HAWK missiles were being shipped to Iran in exchange for the release of U.S. hostages.[103] The officer promptly returned to his office and wrote two cables: (1) a round-up report on the morning's events in which he mentioned the meeting with Secord, and (2) a detailed report on his meeting with Secord in which he reported that the cargo being shipped to Iran was HAWK missiles.[104] The officer sent the first cable to Clarridge at 2:13 p.m. European country time, and the second

cable, in which he mentioned the HAWK missiles, shortly thereafter.[105]

The senior CIA field officer's testimony is supported by four persons who were in his office that day: a CIA field communications officer, who sent the cable; the chargé; a CIA operations officer; and a CIA administrative officer. Furthermore, the CIA cable call-numbering system indicates that a cable was sent from the European country at the appropriate time. This was the only cable missing from the file Clarridge kept of cables he received from the European country during the November 1985 operation.[106]

The CIA field communications officer was on duty at the senior CIA field officer's office on Saturday, November 23, 1985, when the senior officer claims to have sent the critical cable.[107] The communications officer testified that he regularly reads the cables he transmits and that he distinctly remembers transmitting a cable on November 23, 1985, that a shipment of HAWK missiles was being sent from Israel to Iran. He remembered the cable so clearly because it angered him that Israel was shipping weapons to its "arch-enemy" and that the United States was trying to help; the communications officer personally felt Iran was "the enemy" because he had a good friend who had been held hostage by Iran for 444 days in 1980.[108] Finally, the communications officer noted that he "had nothing to gain" by supporting the senior officer's story because he and the senior officer disliked each other. He simply felt he had a professional obligation to tell what he remembered.[109]

---

[99] The CIA inspector general conducted an exhaustive search for the "missing cable," electronically checking the files and systems of the CIA field officers involved in the November 1985 shipment and those at CIA headquarters. The inspector general also interviewed relevant CIA personnel. Independent Counsel then conducted his own search, interviewing additional witnesses and searching files from various CIA field locations by hand.

[100] Senior CIA Field Officer, Select Committees Deposition, 4/13/87, p. 18.

[101] Ibid., pp. 18–19.

[102] Ibid.

[103] Ibid.

[104] Ibid., pp. 25, 32–33; Senior CIA Field Officer, Deposition in lieu of Grand Jury testimony, 4/8/87, pp. 33–35.

[105] CIA Cable 63397, 11/23/85, DO 21397–96; Senior CIA Field Officer, Deposition in lieu of Grand Jury testimony, 4/8/87, pp. 33–35 (senior CIA field officer recalls sending the first cable at approximately 12:30, but the cable, DO 21397–97, indicates the transmission time as 1413, or 2:13 p.m., Zulu (Greenwich) time which was the same as European country time). The senior officer was clear that he sent the more detailed cable about 30 minutes after the round-up cable. (Senior CIA Field Officer, Select Committees Deposition, 4/13/87, pp. 25–26.)

[106] One cable Clarridge sent to the European country, DIRECTOR 625103, is also missing. (Memorandum from CIA Iran/contra Task Force to Scopeletis, 7/8/87, ¶ 2.)

[107] CIA Field Communications Officer, Select Committees Deposition, 7/13/87, pp. 11, 66–67.

[108] Ibid., p. 67; CIA Field Communications Officer, IG Interview, 7/13/87, p. 1.

[109] CIA Field Communications Officer, Select Committees Deposition, 7/13/87, pp. 68–69; CIA Field Communications Officer, IG Interview, 7/13/87, p. 1; FBI 302, 5/8/92, p. 2. In his interview with the CIA inspector general, the communications officer was quite graphic in describing his relationship with the senior officer, stating that the senior

The chargé also recalls the "missing" cable. He was in the senior CIA field officer's office when the officer returned from his meeting with Secord. According to the chargé, the senior CIA officer returned "around midday" and briefed him on the meeting with Secord.[110] Later, the senior officer showed the chargé a cable to CIA headquarters in which he discussed the meeting with Secord. The chargé did not recall whether he read the cable or the senior officer read it to him, but the chargé was certain the cable indicated that the cargo of the shipment going from Israel to Iran was HAWK missiles.[111] The senior CIA officer told him he was sending the cable to CIA headquarters, and the chargé "has no doubt" that the cable was sent.[112]

Another CIA operations officer in the European country also saw the cable informing CIA headquarters, that is, Clarridge, about the details of the Secord briefing.[113] On November 23, 1985, the senior CIA officer asked the operations officer to become involved in obtaining flight clearances for the Israeli aircraft.[114] The operations officer later learned that Secord had informed the European country authorities that he was seeking clearances for a plane carrying HAWK missiles from Israel en route to Iran.[115] Secord reportedly had told the officials that the missiles would be flown on one plane then transferred to another plane and flown into Iran.[116] Secord reportedly suggested that, as a cover story, the European country could say that a transfer had occurred at an airport in their country but that the cargo was oil-drilling equipment.[117]

When the CIA operations officer returned to the senior field officer's office, he told the senior officer what he had learned about Secord's overtures. The senior CIA officer said he had heard essentially the same story from Secord.[118] The senior CIA officer said he was pleased that the operations officer's information matched Secord's.[119] The senior officer told the operations officer to prepare a cable for CIA headquarters with his report, which the operations officer did, specifically mentioning that the cargo was HAWK missiles and that oil-drilling equipment was a cover story.[120] Meanwhile, the senior officer was preparing his own cable on the Secord meeting.[121] The two officers compared their cables and found them to be "[b]asically, the same thing."[122] The operations officer was not sure whether the senior officer sent both cables or simply combined the two into a single cable.[123] In either event, the operations officer did see a final draft of a cable to "C[hief]/EUR," reporting the details he had learned and what the senior officer had learned from Secord, between 1:00 p.m. and 2:00 p.m. on November 23, 1985.[124] The senior officer showed the operations officer the draft before taking it up to the communications center to send out.[125]

The operations officer received a "come-back copy" of the cable the following Monday.[126] A "come-back copy" is a copy generated by the CIA communications system for each cable sent. It indicates the time and date the cable was transmitted.[127] The operations officer reviewed the "come-back copy" and found that

---

officer regarded communicators as "creatures that 'crawled out from under the rocks, the lowest form of life.'" Carla Scopeletis, who interviewed the senior officer for the CIA, observed that "[i]t was hard not to be convinced that [the communications officer] believes he saw such a cable. Moreover, his true feelings about [the senior officer] were very apparent as well. I don't think this is a man lying or speculating to save his boss." (CIA Field Communications Officer, IG Interview, 7/13/87, p. 1.)

[110] Chargé d'Affaires, FBI 302, 3/11/92, p. 3; Chargé d'Affaires, Select Committees Deposition, 5/27/87, pp. 34–36. The Chargé's recollection that the briefing occurred "around midday" is consistent with the cable traffic and the senior CIA field officer's testimony that he met with Secord at approximately 11:30 a.m. (CIA cable, 11/23/85, DO 21397–96; Senior CIA field officer, Select Committees Deposition, 4/13/87, p. 19.)

[111] Chargé d'Affaires, FBI 302, 3/11/92, pp. 3–4; Chargé d'Affaires, Select Committees Deposition, 5/27/87, pp. 34–36.

[112] Chargé d'Affaires, Select Committees Deposition, 5/27/87, p. 36; Chargé d'Affaires, FBI 302, 3/11/92, p. 5.

[113] CIA Operations Officer, Grand Jury, 9/13/91, pp. 5–6.

[114] Ibid., pp. 9–10; CIA Operations Officer, FBI 302, 9/12/91, pp. 2–3. See also Classified Appendix.

[115] CIA Operations Officer, FBI 302, 9/12/91, pp. 2–3.

[116] Ibid.

[117] Ibid.

[118] Ibid., p. 3.

[119] Ibid., p. 4.

[120] Ibid., p. 3; CIA Operations Officer, Grand Jury, 9/13/91, pp. 18–20.

[121] Ibid., pp. 18, 21.

[122] Ibid., p. 21.

[123] Ibid., pp. 38–39.

[124] CIA Operations Officer, FBI 302, 9/12/91, p. 3; CIA Operations Officer, Grand Jury, 9/13/91, pp. 21–23.

[125] CIA Operations Officer, FBI 302, 9/12/91, pp. 3–4. The round-up cable, which immediately preceded the "missing" cable, was sent from the European country at 1413 or 2:13 p.m.

[126] Ibid., p. 4; CIA Operations Officer, Grand Jury, 9/13/91, pp. 24–26.

[127] Ibid.

it contained the same information as his original draft cable.[128]

Finally, a CIA administrative officer in the European country also saw a copy of the "missing" cable, which reported on the senior officer's briefing by Secord. The administrative officer was taking all of the cables up to the communications center for the senior officer on Saturday, November 23, 1985, and recalls a cable that described the Secord briefing in detail, including that the cargo Secord was trying to ship to Iran was HAWK missiles. The administrative officer remembered being upset that trading "HAWKs for Hostages" would encourage terrorists to "grab us and get missiles." [129]

Assuming the "missing cable" was sent, the next question is, was it received at CIA headquarters in Langley, Virginia? The cables between Langley and the European country that weekend were sent in Clarridge's "privacy channel"—a special channel for "background exchanges on sensitive issues between Chiefs of Division and [senior field officers]. . . ." [130] Privacy channel cables may be retained only "temporarily"; they must be destroyed once the "issue in question is transferred to the command channel or when the temporary circumstances end." [131] Although the senior CIA officer in the European country destroyed all of his copies of the cables, Clarridge instructed his secretary to retain copies in an unofficial, "shadow" file.[132] Clarridge's secretary maintained carbon copies of the cables in a file "in a corner of her desk," while the originals went to CIA field chronological files and were routinely purged in accordance with normal practice.[133] Clarridge's secretary kept the file even after Clarridge left to become chief of the Counterterrorism Center because she "never got around to throwing the material away." [134] When the Iran/contra affair became public in November 1986, Clarridge called his former

secretary to see if she still had the file, and she sent the entire file to him.[135] It turned out that Clarridge had retained the CIA's only file of the November 1985 cables.

The CIA cable system automatically assigns a number, in sequential order, to each cable transmitted from a particular location.[136] Thus, Country X Cable 63397 would be followed by Country X Cable 63398, and so on.[137] When the CIA inspector general conducted an investigation of the "missing cable," he recovered copies (either from Clarridge's file or from CIA electronic searches) of every cable sent out of the European country on November 22 and 23, 1985 except one.[138] The cable immediately preceding the missing cable is unrelated to the arms shipment.[139] The cable before that is the round-up cable the senior field officer sent in which he referenced his meeting with Secord but did not provide details. That cable was transmitted at 2:13 p.m. European country time on November 23, 1985. The cable after the missing cable, which is also about the arms shipment, was transmitted at 2:53 p.m. European country time on November 23, 1985. Thus, the missing cable was transmitted between 2:13 and 2:53 p.m. European country time on November 23, 1985. That corresponds with the senior CIA field officer's testimony that he sent the cable in which he identified the cargo as HAWK missiles approximately 30 minutes after he sent the round-up cable, and with the CIA operations officer's testimony that he saw a final draft of such a cable between 1:00 p.m. and 2:00 p.m. on November 23, 1985.

At trial, CIA cable communications experts would have explained how once a cable is given a number and transmitted, there is virtually no way for that cable to disappear from the system.[140] If a number is skipped on the receiving

[128] CIA Operations Officer, FBI 302, 9/12/91, p. 4. The operations officer vividly recalls the "come-back copy" because he used it later that week as a reference in drafting another cable. (See Classified Appendix.)

[129] CIA Administrative Officer, FBI 302, 10/31/91, p. 4.

[130] Memorandum from McMahon re: Privacy Channel Correspondence, 4/14/80.

[131] Ibid.

[132] CIA Secretary, IG Interview, 4/10/87; Clarridge, IG Interview, 4/10/87, p. 1.

[133] CIA Secretary, IG Interview, 4/10/87.

[134] Ibid.

[135] Ibid. Clarridge recalls that he asked his new secretary to contact his former secretary. (Clarridge, IG Interview, 4/10/87, p. 1.)

[136] CIA Communications Expert, FBI 302, 11/21/91, p. 2.

[137] The numbers are assigned based on when each cable is sent, not when it is printed at the receiving end. When numerous cables are sent, they often queue up at the printer on the receiving end. Higher-priority cables will jump the queue and be printed before lower priority cables that were sent earlier. (DDO Duty Officer, FBI 302, 7/16/92, p. 2.)

[138] Memorandum from CIA Iran/contra Task Force to Scopeletis, 7/8/87, p. 3, ¶8.

[139] Ibid.

[140] CIA Communications Expert, FBI 302, 11/21/91, pp. 2–3. When asked if he knew of any explanation for the missing cable, former Deputy Director for Operations Clair E. George testified, "I suppose

end, the supervisor on the receiving end automatically inquires about the missed number, usually each hour.[141] Thus, if the missing cable had not been received in Langley, inquiries would have been made.[142] There is no record of any such inquiry, no record of any power outage, and no record of a mechanical problem with the system in the European country during the relevant period.[143] In addition, if the missing cable had been sent by flash precedence, as it surely would have been, the message center in Langley would have been required to acknowledge its receipt, and such acknowledgment would have been automatically generated by the system within a minute of transmission.[144]

Thus, all the evidence confirms that the "missing cable" was sent. The only evidence suggesting the cable was not received is the testimony of Clarridge and former Deputy Director for Operations Clair E. George that they do not recall such a cable. Because the missing cable, like all the cables between Clarridge and senior CIA field officers that weekend, was sent in the privacy channel, only Clarridge and George would have received copies.[145] Clarridge could have destroyed his copy of the cable at any time, even after he retrieved the working file from his secretary in 1986.[146] George has testified that on Monday, November 25, 1985, he instructed both his secretary and Clarridge to collect the relevant cables and bring them to him.[147] Whether Clarridge or George's secretary was the last to see the package of cables delivered to George is unclear. In addition, a CIA cable duty officer who was on duty on November 23, 1985 in Langley has testified that if the named recipient of a privacy channel cable had requested that he be given *all* the copies of the cable—including the copy slated for the Directorate of Operations—the duty officer probably would have complied.[148]

## The A–K Reports

The third way Clarridge learned that the cargo of the November 1985 shipment was weapons was from the A–K Intelligence Reports Allen showed him on November 23, 1985. The A–K Reports concerned negotiations between Iranian expatriate arms dealer Manucher Ghorbanifar (code named "Ashgari," the "A" of A–K) and Iran's Chief of Security Mohsen Kangarlu (the "K" of A–K). Distribution of the reports was extremely limited.[149]

On Saturday, November 23, 1985, North asked Allen to show the A–K Reports to Clarridge to brief him on the mission. Allen gave the reports to Clarridge to read, telling him that this was

> an extremely sensitive NSC initiative, that . . . had been held with a small number of people in Washington at the White House and Defense and within the Central Intelligence Agency, that the Department of State was not part of this process, and that through this process we had obtained the release of Reverend Weir [a U.S. hostage in Lebanon released in September 1985]. . . .[150]

Allen left the reports with Clarridge for approximately half an hour.[151]

Clarridge admitted that he saw the A–K Reports and that they were given to him to brief him on the mission.[152] He read the reports with at least sufficient scrutiny to glean that the purpose of the mission was to secure the release of the U.S. hostages being held in Lebanon.[153] According to Clarridge, however, there was

---

three times in the last 20 years I have seen a cable eaten alive by the relay station. . . . The odds are so high, I am afraid we would be foolish to think that happened." (George, Select Committees Deposition, 8/5/87, p. 296.)

[141] CIA Communications Expert, FBI 302, 11/21/91, pp. 2–3.

[142] Ibid. See also Iran/contra Telecommunications Review of Late November 1985, 6/19/87, ¶14 (prepared by CIA) ("Missing check numbers are serviced back to the field within hours, at most.").

[143] Ibid., ¶13; CIA Field Communications Officer, Select Committees Deposition, 7/13/87, p. 21.

[144] Ibid. pp. 36–38; CIA Communications Expert, FBI 302, 11/21/91, p. 3.

[145] CIA Cable Duty Officer, FBI 302, 7/10/92, p. 3.

[146] The secretary who maintained the file did not read the cables. CIA Secretary, IG Interview, 4/10/87.

[147] George, Select Committees Testimony, 8/5/87, p. 293.

[148] DDO Duty Officer, FBI 302, 7/16/92, p. 3. The duty officer also testified that the copy of a privacy channel cable slated for the Directorate of Operations ("DO") would normally print out automatically at the DO Registry. If, however, the named recipient of the cable was coming in to pick it up, the cable duty officer could print it out on his own printer. This would be especially likely when the Registry was closed. Ibid., p. 2.

[149] Allen, Grand Jury, 1/11/91, pp. 61–62.

[150] Ibid., p. 47.

[151] Ibid.

[152] Clarridge, Select Committees Deposition, 4/27/87, pp. 36–38.

[153] Clarridge, Select Committees Testimony, 8/4/87, pp. 13–14.

nothing in the reports about weapons, at least not that he could recall.[154]

In fact, the reports are replete with references to an arms-for-hostages swap, including specific references to HAWK, TOW, Phoenix, Harpoon, and Sidewinder missiles.[155] As Allen put it, the "the principal content of the intelligence [reports] reflected negotiations relating to military equipment."[156] After reading the reports, Allen said, he had "no doubts" the cargo of the November 1985 shipment was military equipment and that it was "clear" to him that North's assertion that the cargo was oil-drilling equipment was "a cover story."[157] North similarly agreed that the packet of reports Allen showed Clarridge made it "very obvious" that the cargo was missiles.[158] Finally, there is no reference in any of the reports to oil-drilling equipment.[159]

---

[154] Ibid.

[155] Allen, Grand Jury, 1/11/91; A–K Reports, 9/15/85–11/22/85, AMW 0001918–91.

[156] Allen, Grand Jury, 1/11/91, pp. 66, 68 (the file of reports Allen showed Clarridge "refers directly on a consistent basis to military equipment").

[157] Allen, FBI 302, 1/10/91, p. 3. In his testimony before congressional investigators, Allen was never quite so forthcoming. When questioned about North's assertion that the cargo was oil-drilling equipment, Allen testified that he "had doubts . . . as to whether Colonel North was being totally candid. . . ." (Allen, Select Committees Deposition, 4/21/87, p. 165.) At other times he referred to a "suspicion" he had that the cargo was weapons. (Ibid., 7/2/87, pp. 674–78; ibid., 6/29/87, pp. 625–26.) He never admitted to congressional investigators, however, that he *knew* the cargo was weapons. (See Allen, Select Committees Deposition, 7/2/87, p. 678, denying certainty about cargo but admitting "suspicion.")

Whether from the A–K Reports or otherwise, however, Allen was quite certain that the cargo was weapons. On Monday, November 18, 1985, Allen told intelligence officials responsible for the reports that a "planeload of arms" was going into Iran, "probably" on Wednesday, November 20, 1985. (Classified Communications Log, November 18, 1985.) On November 22, 1985, Allen told these officials that a "planeload of arms is now over the Med[iterranean] en route to Iran." (Classified Communications Log, 11/22/85, AMW 0000548.)

The Classified Communications Logs raised serious questions about Allen's evasive congressional testimony about his knowledge of the cargo. Independent Counsel decided not to pursue possible perjury and false statements charges against Allen because he admitted his knowledge of the cargo in interviews with Independent Counsel and in testimony before the Grand Jury, and assisted the investigation with truthful testimony about the knowledge of others.

[158] North, Grand Jury, 2/1/91, pp. 113–15. North was shown a packet of the A–K Reports dating from September 1985 to November 22, 1985. (Ibid., p. 114.) Allen testified that he showed Clarridge all the A–K Reports he had for that period. (Allen, Grand Jury, 1/11/91, p. 15.)

[159] Ibid., p. 66. There are a very few references to using the proceeds from oil sales to pay for military equipment, but no references to oil-drilling equipment. (Ibid.)

## Admission Evidence

In December 1986, Clarridge attended a CIA Christmas party wearing an "Ollie North is an American Hero" T-shirt.[160] At the party, Clarridge had a heated argument with the husband of a CIA employee who worked for Clarridge, about congressional oversight of the CIA.[161] Clarridge was generally opposed to congressional oversight, while the husband was defending it.[162] According to the husband, Clarridge "had no real use for Congress."[163]

The CIA employee who worked for Clarridge also recalled that Clarridge said at the party that he "had slipped something by Congress" or "really slipped by Congress."[164] The CIA employee said Clarridge moved his hand forward in a sliding motion while making the statement.[165]

## Count Three—"Straight Commercial Deal"—Evidence

In Count Three, Clarridge was charged with perjury for testifying that he believed the November 1985 flight by the CIA proprietary airline from Israel to Iran was a "straight commercial deal." While the evidence set forth above that Clarridge knew the cargo of the flight was weapons would have been sufficient to disprove Clarridge's stated belief that it was a "straight commercial deal," there is additional evidence material only to that count.

---

[160] [Classified Identity Withheld], FBI 302, 9/16/91, p. 2. A CIA employee who worked for Clarridge remembered Clarridge's wearing an Ollie North button rather than a T-shirt. ([Classified Identity Withheld], FBI 302, 9/9/91, p. 4.)

[161] [Classified Identity Withheld], FBI 302, 9/9/91, pp. 3–4; [Classified Identity Withheld], FBI 302, 9/16/91, pp. 1–2.

[162] Ibid.

[163] [Classified Identity Withheld], FBI 302, 9/16/91, p. 2. Clarridge had a reputation for being less than forthcoming with Congress. Juchniewicz, Clarridge's superior, said that Clarridge "never told anyone a full story." (Juchniewicz, FBI 302, 3/20/91, p. 14.) Clarridge, he said, would "dance around a question" and would not tell Congress anything unless specifically asked. (Ibid.) Senator Thomas Eagleton, who questioned Clarridge extensively, was asked at the trial of Clair George whether he assumed everyone testifying on behalf of the CIA would lie to Congress. He responded, "I didn't trust Dewey Clarridge. We knew he was lying." (Eagleton, *George* Trial Testimony, 11/5/92, p. 2317.)

[164] [Classified Identity Withheld], FBI 302, 9/9/91, p. 3. Later in the interview, the employee said she was not certain Clarridge had made the comment at the Christmas party, but that he had said it a day or two after his congressional testimony. (Ibid., p. 4.) Clarridge testified before the congressional committees investigating Iran/contra on December 2, 1986 and December 11, 1986 and before the Tower Commission on December 18, 1986.

[165] [Classified Identity Withheld], FBI 302, 9/9/91, p. 3.

The text of the false statements charged in Count 3 is emphasized in the following exchange from Clarridge's December 2, 1986, testimony under oath before the Senate Select Committee on Intelligence:

Mr. Newsom: At that time, did you have any concern about the [sic] whether necessary or sufficient authority existed to use a U.S. proprietary aircraft under the control of the CIA for this kind of mission?

Mr. Clarridge: For oil spare parts?

Mr. Newsom: For using the CIA proprietary to fly a mission destined for Iran.

Mr. Clarridge: Well, the way I talked to Juchniewicz about it was that this would, although the NSC was interested in it, *it seemed to be a straight commercial deal. In other words, private people apparently hiring our proprietary.* That was the reason that he felt he [Juchniewicz] didn't have to go any higher apparently on the approval process.[166]

       \*      \*      \*

Sen. Eagleton: . . . You thought this was a commercial undertaking, right, this flight? We're going back to this flight.

Mr. Clarridge: *Right.*[167]

       \*      \*      \*

Sen. Eagleton: Didn't you have a second thought or question, "Here's a hotshot from the NSC [North] who's on this interagency group coming to my personal office, one on one. Maybe this might be a shade more than a commercial endeavor."

Mr. Clarridge: *I'm sorry, I didn't see it any more than what he was telling me.*[168]

While the charged quotes do not state it expressly, the underlying premise of Clarridge's professed belief that the operation was a "straight commercial deal" was that the cargo was normal commercial cargo—oil-drilling equipment. The committee's concern about the use of the CIA proprietary airline paralleled its concern about Iran/contra generally: that unsupervised operatives like North and Clarridge were running the affair with minimal authorization from those in charge. Clarridge's response, "For oil spare parts?" implies that authorization for using the proprietary was not a major problem because the cargo was oil spare parts which are commercial. In response to Eagleton's follow-up questioning to the passage quoted above, Clarridge makes the point more clearly:

Sen. Eagleton: The second time the guy from the NSC [North] comes back.

At that second time, did that cause you to say, "Well, gee, I wonder if this is completely commercial"?

Mr. Clarridge: You know, you have to believe in people once in awhile. A fellow says it's, you know, this flight has got all spare parts on it.[169]

Conversely, if Clarridge knew the cargo was military equipment, he did not believe that the operation was a "strictly commercial deal."[170]

---

[166] Clarridge, SSCI Testimony, 12/2/86, pp. 13–14.
[167] Ibid., p. 54.
[168] Ibid., pp. 56–57.

[169] Ibid., p. 60.
[170] Clarridge was formally reprimanded and reduced in rank for "provid[ing] assistance to the NSC staff in connection with [shipping arms to Iran] . . . without appropriate authorizations." (Letter from Webster to Clarridge, 12/16/87.) In a memorandum for the record of his meeting with Clarridge to discuss the reprimand, Webster wrote that he told Clarridge that he was "culpable in respect to his testimony before Congress" and for "fail[ing] to keep his senior officials properly apprised and to obtain appropriate authorizations" in connection with the use of the CIA proprietary in November 1985. (Memorandum from Webster to the Record, 12/16/87.) In other words, Clarridge was reprimanded for failing to tell Juchniewicz the truth about the operation when he sought approval for using the proprietary. According to Juchniewicz, even if Clarridge thought the cargo was "commercial," he had an obligation to inform Juchniewicz that the purpose of the mission was to secure the release of the hostages and that the flight was going into Iran. (Juchniewicz, FBI 302, 3/20/91, p. 13.) If he knew the cargo was weapons, it would have been even more critical that he inform his superiors. (Ibid.) Thus, once Clarridge lied to Juchniewicz, he had to lie to Congress to conceal the first lie. If he was reprimanded merely for not informing Juchniewicz that the mission was about the hostages and that the flight was going into Iran, Clarridge might well have been fired for failing to inform Juchniewicz that the cargo was weapons.

Clarridge testified that he thought Juchniewicz had been reviewing the flash cables between headquarters and the European country and thus knew all about the mission. (Clarridge, Tower Commission Testimony, 12/18/86, p. 5.) Flash priority cables in a division chief's privacy channel are screened, with only the most important of them being forwarded to Juchniewicz's level. (Hohing, FBI 302, 7/10/92, pp. 1–2; Juchniewicz, FBI 302, 3/20/91, pp. 11–12.) According to Chimera Hohing, who was reviewing the cables in November 1985, she would pass on only 75–150 of the roughly 1000 cables she screened per day. (Hohing, 7/10/92, p. 2.) She would decide which cables were

Clarridge seemed to distinguish a commercial deal that the "NSC was interested in," from an NSC operation. Everything Clarridge knew and said about the operation at the time, however, belies that purported belief.

First, Clarridge repeatedly testified that he knew the purpose of the operation was to secure the release of the hostages—hardly a "strictly commercial" deal.[171] Second, the cables Clarridge sent to the first European country identify the "Subject" as "NSC Mission." [172] Third, when Allen gave Clarridge the reliable intelligence reports he told him this was

> an extremely sensitive NSC initiative, that . . . had been held with a small number of people in Washington at the White House and Defense and within the Central Intelligence Agency, that the Department

of State was not part of this process, and that through this process we had obtained the release of Reverend Weir.[173]

Finally, in a cable Clarridge sent to the senior CIA officer in the second European country on November 25, 1985, he wrote: "One of the key elements for [the Asian country] is the requirement that they have at least a good approximation when the aircraft is going to enter their airspace eastbound. . . . *If this were a normal commercial flight,* it probably wouldn't make much difference to them but under the circumstances it does." [174]

## Soliciting Third-Country Support for the Contras

Independent Counsel also investigated Clarridge's role in soliciting funding from a third country for the contras. Clarridge testified that he did not solicit funds from the country and that he was unaware of discussions within the CIA about soliciting third-country funding for the contras. Although CIA cables about a spring 1984 trip that Clarridge took to the country belie Clarridge's testimony, Independent Counsel decided not to pursue false statement and perjury charges against Clarridge. The reasons for Independent Counsel's decision are set forth in the Classified Appendix.

---

important based on content, not precedence (flash, immediate, etc.). She did not think it likely that she would have forwarded cables about flight clearances and weapons being shipped to Iran. (Hohing, FBI 302, 7/13/92, p. 3.)

The testimony of John McMahon, former Deputy Director of Central Intelligence, was that Clarridge would withhold information from his superiors if he thought the superior would impede an operation he believed in. (McMahon, FBI 302, 2/15/91, p. 9.) Juchniewicz agreed, stating that Clarridge "never told anyone a full story," and that Clair George and McMahon never felt that Clarridge "squared with them." (Juchniewicz, FBI 302, 3/20/91, p. 14) (quotations are from the report, which paraphrases Juchniewicz). McMahon believed that using oil-drilling equipment as a cover story within the CIA would have been a good way to get the operation "through the CIA hierarchy without setting off alarms. . . ." (McMahon, FBI 302, 2/15/91, p. 9) (quotations are from the report, which paraphrases McMahon).

[171] *See, e.g.,* Clarridge, SSCI Testimony, 12/2/86, pp. 10–11; Clarridge, Select Committees Deposition, 12/11/86, p. 63; Clarridge, Tower Commission Testimony, 12/18/86, pp. 3–4.

[172] The cables Clarridge sent to the second European country also identify the "Subject" as "NSC Mission," while the cables Clarridge sent to the Asian country identify the "Subject" as "NSC Request."

[173] Allen, Grand Jury, 1/11/91, p. 47.
[174] DIRECTOR 628959, 11/25/85, DO 21443 (emphasis added).

# Chapter 19
# United States v. Alan D. Fiers, Jr.

Alan D. Fiers, Jr., was the chief of the Central Intelligence Agency's Central American Task Force (CATF) from October 1984 until his retirement in 1988. An extraordinary career officer—with accolades that included the CIA's Distinguished Officer Rank, the CIA's highest award—Fiers was the CIA headquarters official most heavily involved with efforts to support the contras. After 1984, Fiers was perhaps second only to CIA Director William J. Casey in the extent of his contact with Lt. Col. Oliver L. North's efforts to keep the contras supplied, notwithstanding the limits of Boland Amendments upon contra aid.

On July 9, 1991, Fiers pleaded guilty to two counts of withholding information from Congress. Fiers entered the plea as part of an agreement to cooperate with Independent Counsel's investigation. On January 31, 1992, Chief Judge Aubrey E. Robinson, Jr., sentenced Fiers to one hundred hours of community service to be performed within one year of his sentence. Fiers was pardoned by President Bush on December 24, 1992.

Fiers's cooperation with Independent Counsel was extensive and exemplary. No other Iran/contra defendant assisted OIC with the degree of professionalism exhibited by Fiers. Many pieces of the Iran/contra puzzle fell into place solely because of the information provided by Fiers. Fiers also was the principal witness for the Government in the two trials of Clair E. George.

What follows is a discussion of Fiers's involvement in the Iran/contra affair.[1] Independent Counsel's analysis relies primarily on evidence other than that provided by Fiers pursuant to his cooperation agreement with Independent Counsel. This analysis caused Independent Counsel to conclude that Fiers had made false statements and committed the perjury that led to his prosecution. These include:

—Denying knowledge of the true identity of "Max Gomez," an alias for Felix Rodriguez, and knowledge of to whom he was reporting.

—Denying CIA contacts with the contra-resupply operation at Ilopango air base in El Salvador.

—Denying knowing the identities of any of the "private benefactors."

—Denying that North discussed his contra-resupply activities, and denying knowledge of North's fund raising, supply-providing, and intelligence-passing activities, as well as North's connection with arranging flights into the Ilopango air base.

—Denying that any American citizen was providing aid to the contras outside of the law.

—Denying North's account of an August 1986 RIG meeting where North claimed he revealed all of his Central American activities in support of the contras.

## Fiers' Knowledge of Contra Resupply

Fiers became chief of the CATF on October 9, 1984, shortly before the "full" Boland restrictions on contra aid took effect. By all indi-

---

[1] Because the Department of Justice specially referred two aspects of Fiers's Iran/contra activities to Independent Counsel, these matters are treated in other sections of this report. See Classified CIA Investigations A and B.

cations, Fiers was fully in control of task force operations and ran them with a firm hand.[2]

Fiers learned by late 1985 of a private network that was supporting the contras. He knew that North was a manager in this effort, and that Felix Rodriguez and Richard Gadd were involved in its day-to-day operations. Fiers approved specific activities that facilitated the network's operations. On one occasion, Fiers encouraged the network to drop supplies to contra units operating in northern Costa Rica and southern Nicaragua (the so-called contra "southern front").

During 1986, Fiers also learned that an airstrip had been built at Santa Elena, Costa Rica, by the "private benefactors" involved in contra resupply to facilitate aerial resupply. He became aware in April or May of 1986 that the Chief of the CIA's station in San Jose, Costa Rica, Joseph Fernandez, was passing CIA intelligence directly to the operation to facilitate resupply missions to the southern front. Fiers helped develop a plan to terminate Fernandez's direct involvement with the network, but it was scrapped after other task force officers criticized it as being too risky, both legally and politically. Although Fernandez continued to facilitate resupply drops after August 1986 without informing headquarters of his actions, Fiers knew from Fernandez's activities prior to August 1986 that he was in direct contact with the resupply network, and was facilitating its operations, at the time Fiers was first questioned about the resupply effort in October 1986.

Fiers dated the beginning of his knowledge of the "private benefactors" resupply operation and their involvement with U.S. officials around a meeting held on November 9, 1984, in Director Casey's office.[3] Fiers' own experience arose from events that occurred the following year, beginning with Fiers' realization that North was raising funds on behalf of the contras.

In a February 1985 memorandum written by Fiers to his superiors at the CIA, Fiers reported that North could line up funding for contra lead-

ers Arturo Cruz, Sr., and Edgar Chamorro, who to that point had been receiving money from the CIA. By using private funding, Fiers believed these contra representatives could continue to lobby Congress without it appearing that Government funds were supporting the contras to influence legislation.[4]

## Secord

In early March 1985, the CIA received reports that retired Air Force Maj. Gen. Richard V. Secord was seeking to buy weapons from the Peoples' Republic of China, for delivery to Guatemala. Fiers passed this information to North. This was the first document to link them. North noted on March 7, 1985:

Mtg w Fiers
[CIA] Source—businessman in Boston
"knows": Canadian Arms Broker Working
    w/ Secord
Went to China
Secord working w/ USG
China refused Guat EUC's [End User Certificates]
Moroccan EUC's used
1st Shipment Feb
offshore bank Cayman/Bahamas

## Rodriguez

In the fall of 1985, North recruited a former CIA officer named Felix Rodriguez, who was working in El Salvador, to join the "private benefactors." Rodriguez's work led to a significant confrontation between Fiers and Rodriguez in February 1986, as well as a meeting in Washington in August of that year where Rodriguez's role in contra resupply was fully aired. Together these events showed Fiers just what Rodriguez was doing for the resupply operation.

On December 30, 1985, a delegation from the Restricted Interagency Group on Central America (the RIG) arrived at Ilopango air base

---

[2] See, for example, Deputy Chief of CATF (DC/CATF), FBI 302, 2/28/91, p. 2 ("All of CATF was a support mechanism for Fiers, who ran it all."); Chief #2, Latin America Division (C/LA #2), Grand Jury, 5/8/91, p. 25 ("Alan was Mr. Central America. I mean he went to every congressional hearing, he went to every place, and when you really wanted to know what [the] policy was, Alan was the guy to talk to."); Deputy C/LA, FBI 302, 5/2/91, pp. 5, 11.

[3] See description of the meeting in the George chapter.

[4] Memorandum from Fiers, re: Status Report on Honduran Discussions, 2/12/85, DO 94090–94; Fiers, Select Committee Deposition, 5/1/87, pp. 22–24. North professed not remembering any specific conversation about funding with Fiers, but had "absolutely no doubt that it occurred." (North, Grand Jury, 1/18/91, p. 36.) Fiers subsequently acknowledged to the Independent Counsel that he knew more than he had previously disclosed about North's fund-raising activities in 1985, particularly an incident where Fiers helped refer intelligence to North concerning South Korean interest in contributing to the Contras. (See Fiers, Grand Jury, 8/12/91, pp. 40–45 and George chapter.)

to discuss using the air base as a transshipment point for U.S. Government humanitarian assistance provided by the Government's Nicaraguan Humanitarian Assistance Office (NHAO). The delegation consisted of Fiers, North, Deputy Assistant Secretary of State William G. Walker, and Cresencio Arcos, the deputy director of NHAO.[5] Numerous meetings took place during this visit, including one among North, Salvadoran Air Force Gen. Juan Bustillo, U.S. Military Group commander Col. James J. Steele, and Rodriguez.[6] The meetings resulted in agreements on use of Ilopango air base as a transshipment point for NHAO assistance to the contras. A consensus also was reached that Rodriguez and Steele would pass information about NHAO flights to CIA field personnel.[7]

Fiers provided general guidance to CIA field personnel on tracking NHAO shipments out of Ilopango in a cable dated January 4, 1986. CIA personnel were to monitor the arrival of all equipment brought in by NHAO, and to report in detail on shipments from Ilopango—including the contents of each load, the destination of the flight and type of aircraft used. Personnel were also instructed "to confirm that none of the supplies are diverted to [Eden Pastora's] organization." [8]

NHAO supplies began landing at Ilopango in January 1986. With large amounts of supplies arriving and no contra logistics team in place,

coordination problems arose. North noted that U.S. Ambassador to El Salvador Edwin G. Corr and Steele were becoming concerned about what CIA Officer #1 was reporting about these problems to Washington, and that Bustillo wanted to deal with Rodriguez, not the CIA:

> Amb & Steele concerned
> [CIA Officer #1] msg to Wash re mtg he had w/Bustillo re movement of matl [material] through El Salv.
> [CIA Officer #1] advised Bustillo that he [CIA Officer #1] had a reporting reqmt Bustillo told this is overt program—reported back to D.C.
> Bustillo very concerned that [CIA Officer #1] involved
> Does not want to deal w/ CIA wants no reports is going to shut down OP
> Bustillo wants CIA out or he will shut this off will work only w/Steele and Maximo

Ambassador Corr's notes indicate that he attempted to persuade Fiers to limit distribution of Officer #1's reports.[9]

In late January 1986, CIA field personnel—including CIA Officer #1—began to complain that Rodriguez was attempting to take over coordination of NHAO flights. Personnel in one location reported to Headquarters:

> [Personnel believe] additional confusion being introduced into San Salvador scenario by Felix ((Rodriguez)), who has somehow become involved in the San Salvador end of the NHAO system. He repeatedly was the person who receipted for the NHAO shipment to Ilopango, and he has become involved in conflict with both [the contra air force commander and the contra logistics coordinator at Ilopango] by insisting that all matters relating to the Ilopango logistics system be channelled through him.

[5] CIA Officer #1, Grand Jury, 3/16/90, pp. 31, 40–42, 51; CIA Officer #1, FBI 302, 4/19/91, p. 3; CIA Officer #1, Grand Jury, 5/22/91, pp. 8–13, 16–19. Fiers later told the Independent Counsel that shortly before this trip, he talked with North about a weapons resupply flight that was on its way from Europe. (Fiers, FBI 302, 7/17/91 AM, p. 13; Fiers, FBI 302, 7/17/91 PM, p. 11; Fiers, FBI 302, 7/23/91, p. 4.) Also during this period, Fiers learned from North that Rodriguez was using the alias "Max Gomez." (Fiers, FBI 302, 7/17/91 PM, p. 7.) By the end of December 1985, Fiers had concluded that Rodriguez was "North's man" at Ilopango and was "greasing the skids" for Contra resupply activities there. (Fiers, FBI 302, 7/23/91, p. 3.)

[6] CIA Officer #1's stand-in during the RIG's December 1985 visit placed Fiers in these "closed door" sessions. ([Classified Identity Withheld], FBI 302, 11/20/90, p. 5; [Classified Identity Withheld], CIA IG Interview, 2/12/87, p. 2.) Fiers insisted that he was not in these meetings. (Fiers, FBI 302, 7/17/91 PM, p. 13.) Notes prepared by Ambassador Corr in February 1986 confirm Fiers's account. (Corr Notes, 2/9/86, ALV 1399–1400.)

[7] DIRECTOR 672514, 12/30/85, DO 39663; DIRECTOR 672517, 12/30/85, DO 58061; Corr Notes, 2/9/86, ALV 1399–1400; Corr, Grand Jury, 4/26/91, pp. 86–90; [Classified Identity Withheld], Grand Jury, 5/31/91, pp. 47, 67–82.

[8] DIRECTOR 677959, 1/4/86, DO 84690; CIA Officer #1, Grand Jury, 5/22/91, pp. 13–15. The cable also noted that CIA field personnel would assist Contra forces in Honduras in placing an FDN communicator at Ilopango. (Ibid.) On the significance of the ban on providing assistance to Eden Pastora, see section below.

[9] North Notebook, 1/22/86, AMX 00927 (emphasis in original); CIA Cable, 1/16/86, DO 10458; Corr Notes, ALV 1396. CIA Officer #1 felt during this period that Corr was cutting him out of the machinations at Ilopango. (CIA Officer #1, FBI 302, 4/19/91, p. 4.) Fiers later disclosed to Independent Counsel that he was aware by October 1985 that someone was complaining to North about CIA Officer #1. (Fiers, FBI 302, 7/17/91 PM, p. 8.) Fiers also did not dispute the implication of North's notes. (Fiers, Grand Jury, 8/12/91, pp. 128–29.)

CIA Officer #1 agreed and further informed CATF headquarters:

> [We are] standing by for final decision on who will do what at Ilopango. Until this determined, our preference is to stay away from all other players. . .at moment there does not seem to be convenient way to be partially involved; it's either us or the other group (i.e., Rodriguez and Col. Steele).[10]

CIA Officer #1 pressed again for guidance in a special message addressed to Fiers on February 6, 1986.

Meanwhile, Ambassador Corr, who was in Washington, had spent the last two days meeting with North, Fiers, Assistant Secretary of State Elliott Abrams, and Abrams's deputy Walker about the situation at Ilopango—particularly Officer #1's performance. Corr's notes from one of these meetings state in part:

> Re-hash of earlier mtgs w/ North & Fiers. I said I'd prefer early promotion & transfer of [CIA Officer #1], emphasizing that he'd done a superb job of pulling USG intel effort together. Said that perhaps same qualities that enabled him to do this were detrimental on the Contra question.

Corr later wrote that another topic during this meeting was "coordination among Front Office, [CIA Officer #1], Steele, *Felix*, and UNO/FDR." [11]

On February 6, 1986, a private-benefactor C–7 aircraft crashed on a highway in El Salvador, its crew frantically unloading cargo on the way down. In frustration, CIA Officer #1 sent a cable to Fiers with a subject line that read "END THE SILENCE":

> 1. [My last cable asked Fiers] for update on the Salvadoran aspects of Washing-

ton negotiations on NHAO/UNO-FDN/Ilopango et al, to be available by OOB [opening of business] this morning, 7 February. Nothing arrived. Given that two weeks have passed since that awful mix-up on this subject at HQS, with sloppy repercussions here,[12] do not feel our request for a timely response was unreasonable.

> 2. Minutes ago Charge [David] Passage came to [me] with story that presumed NHAO-chartered Caribou aircraft on ill-fated supply run to Ilopango via Mexico made emergency landing yesterday, 6 February, on road in Southwest El Salvador. Charge says his source was Felix Rodrigues [sic] who apparently has been "coordinating" all of this with Ollie North (one supposes on open phone). [I] had to say, honestly, that [I] knew nothing of this Caribou and indeed had not heard anything from [Fiers] on this subject for two weeks.

> 3. Rodrigues has just called Charge to advise that UPI [United Press International] is on the downed Caribou and wants a story. Charge's position is that he has no knowledge re this A/C. God knows what Felix Rodrigues is saying.

> 4. What is going on back there? [13]

Fiers cabled CIA Officer #1 four hours later and told him that CIA Deputy Director for Operations Clair George had instructed Fiers to meet Officer #1 at Ilopango to discuss NHAO operations in San Salvador. Fiers came to Ilopango from Honduras, where he had reached agreement with the Honduran government over the size of aircraft and other rules that would govern flights of NHAO aircraft from Ilopango to contra bases in Honduras. Fiers met Officer #1. He and another CIA field officer took Fiers past a Southern Air Transport C–130, on which supplies were being loaded. It exceeded the size of aircraft acceptable to Honduras. Fiers asked the loaders where the plane was headed, and

[10] CIA Cable, 1/25/86, DO 39674–73; CIA Cable, 1/27/86, DO 39675; CIA Officer #1, FBI 302, 4/19/91, p. 7; CIA Officer #1, Grand Jury, 5/22/91, pp. 21–32. Officer #1 testified that during this period, his personnel had to compete with Rodriguez and Steele for NHAO flight manifests. Cables state that Rodriguez personally arranged for at least one humanitarian resupply flight from Guatemala to Ilopango without informing CIA personnel. (CIA Officer #1, Grand Jury, 3/16/90, pp. 42–43; CIA Cable, 1/27/86, DO 39676.)

[11] Corr Notes, 2/5/86, ALW 33715–16; Corr, Grand Jury, 5/29/91, pp. 96–106; ALV 1399–1400 (emphasis added). UNO/FDR was an acronym for the principal contra organization that operated out of Honduras.

[12] CIA Officer #1 testified that his reference here was to the cables discussed above. (CIA Officer #1, Grand Jury, 5/22/91, pp. 35–36.)

[13] CIA Cable, 2/6/86, DO 84797; CIA Cable, 2/7/86, DO 58911; CIA Officer #1, FBI 302, 4/19/91, pp. 8–10; CIA Officer #1, Grand Jury, 5/22/91, pp. 32–37, 42–43.

was told that it was going to Honduras—on Felix Rodriguez's authority.[14]

Fiers and Officer #1 drove to Rodriguez's quarters at the air base, where Fiers told Rodriguez that he could not send the plane to Honduras. Rodriguez said that he had North's permission. Fiers told Rodriguez to call North. Rodriguez dialed North's number, spoke briefly with North, then handed the phone to Fiers. Fiers convinced North that the plane could not fly over Honduran airspace, and North said, "Okay, give me Felix." North cancelled the flight.[15]

Fiers had to admit that by this time, that he knew that North had involved Rodriguez in coordinating NHAO shipments at Ilopango. Fiers also knew that C–7 Caribous, like the one that crashed on the highway in El Salvador were linked to Rodriguez and were controlled by private benefactor Richard Gadd [16]—and that these planes carried arms when they were not carrying NHAO goods. He knew as well that Rodriguez had arranged to bring the C–7s into Ilopango.[17]

CIA Officer #1 told Independent Counsel that even before the confrontation with Rodriguez, he and Fiers took a drive to talk about NHAO operations at Ilopango. Fiers disclosed that there would be "more flights" similar to the ones Officer #1 was now seeing, flights that Fiers "would not handle." Fiers told Officer #1 that these new flights would be managed by North, and that they would be lethal resupply missions. Officer #1 pressed Fiers to "get a handle on this;" Fiers told Officer #1 not to worry—that he would "take care of Ollie North." [18] Subse-

quent to his meeting Fiers at Ilopango, CIA Officer #1's was "promoted" to another post.[19]

Fiers's "trouble with Felix" arose on at least three other occasions.[20] Rodriguez was a topic of discussion at a meeting of senior CIA field officers in May 1986, when Fiers, his new superior and the field officers attempted to fix once and for all problems associated with the private benefactors.[21] Fiers's concern regarding Rodriguez was also reflected in a secure phone conversation with a senior CIA field officer in August 1986. Fiers said:

[A]pparently, Felix Rodriguez is. . .getting himself out of control and about to get himself and General Bustillo into . . . trouble. . . . [I]t appears that . . . Bustillo and Felix Rodriguez took off from Miami . . . in a C–123K that did not belong to them. . . . [W]e have checked . . . with everybody in Washington, including the Vice President's office, and . . . there is no writ anywhere for Felix Rodriguez in any way to be involved with anything to do with Nicaragua, the Nicaraguan Resistance or . . . C–123s or C–7s or anything else operating out of Ilopango. . . . [W]e checked and we've got to try to get [Rodriguez] out of the Nicaraguan pot because he is really . . . muddying the waters and is going to cause us big problems just at a time when we don't need them. . . .[22]

Rodriguez also was the center of an August 12, 1986, meeting in Donald P. Gregg's office. Fiers testified that the meeting focused on Rodriguez's frictions with the private benefactors and on whether the CIA would purchase the resupply operation's planes.[23] The partici-

---

[14] DIRECTOR 726822, 2/7/86, DO 84799; CIA Officer #1, FBI 302, 4/19/91, pp. 9–10; CIA Officer #1, Grand Jury, 5/22/91, pp. 43–50; Fiers, Grand Jury, 4/17/87, pp. 107–13; Fiers, Select Committees Deposition, 5/1/87, pp. 102–05.

[15] Ibid., pp. 104–05; [Classified Identity Withheld], FBI 302, 4/18/90, p. 10; CIA Officer #1, Grand Jury, 3/16/90, pp. 52–54; CIA Officer #1, FBI 302, 4/19/91, pp. 9–10; CIA Officer #1, Grand Jury, 5/22/91, pp. 49–53; Rodriguez, Grand Jury, 5/3/91, pp. 86–88, 157, 199–210; Chief #1, Latin American Division (C/LA #1), Grand Jury, 8/28/91, pp. 48–50, 75–77. North did not recall the incident. (North, Grand Jury, 2/8/91, pp. 13–14.)
Despite North's orders, Rodriguez made one last effort to get his C–130 to Honduras. See CIA Subject #1 chapter.

[16] Fiers' knowledge of Gadd is discussed in more detail below.

[17] Fiers, Select Committees Deposition, 5/1/87, pp. 72–73, 99–100; Fiers, Select Committees Testimony, 8/5/87, p. 13.

[18] CIA Officer #1, FBI 302, 4/19/91, p. 10; CIA Officer #1, Grand Jury, 5/22/91, pp. 46–49, 53–56. North's notebook suggests that Fiers discussed the incident with North upon Fiers's return from Ilopango. A February 11, 1986 entry reads: "Fiers—Why clearing out Ilopango". (North Note, 2/11/86, AMX 955.)

[19] CIA Officer #1, FBI 302, 4/19/91, p. 10. For an example of a sanitized reference to Rodriguez, see CIA Cable, 2/14/86, DO 101121. Fiers admitted to Independent Counsel that he "probably" ordered CIA Officer #1 not to mention Rodriguez in cables. (Fiers, FBI 302, 7/19/91, pp. 3–4.)

[20] After pleading guilty, Fiers disclosed that he discussed security concerns about Rodriguez with North on several occasions in 1986. (Fiers, FBI 302, 7/18/91 AM, p. 2.) Fiers also revealed that the RIG discussed Rodriguez, his whereabouts, and his plans to return to El Salvador on October 8, 1986, in the wake of the Hasenfus crash. (Fiers, FBI 302, 7/23/91, p. 9.)

[21] C/LA #2, Grand Jury, 5/8/91, pp. 30–45. This meeting is discussed in greater detail below.

[22] PRT–250 Conversation, 8/6/86.

[23] Fiers later explained that he turned down North's offers of the planes because they were old, poorly maintained and heavy users of

pants uncomfortably agreed that they would try to work with Rodriguez, and Fiers so informed his field personnel.[24]

## Gadd

Richard Gadd was the first manager of the North/Secord contra-resupply network. He also supervised contracts for deliveries of NHAO aid to Central America. Fiers admitted he met with Gadd around February 7 or 8, 1986—the same week a private benefactor C–7 aircraft crashed in El Salvador, and the same time that Fiers had confronted Rodriguez at Ilopango. Fiers testified that his meeting with Gadd made him uncomfortable, and that he never met Gadd again.[25]

According to Gadd, some time in January or February 1986 he received a message from Secord, who relayed a request from North that Gadd brief a CIA official on air operations at Ilopango. Gadd received a phone number of an individual named "Cliff," whom Gadd knew to be Fiers.[26]

At Fiers' suggestion, Gadd and one of his employees met Fiers and a CIA annuitant who was in charge of air logistics for the Central American Task Force. The annuitant was also the task force's airlift liaison to NHAO. They met at Charley's Place, a restaurant near CIA headquarters. The meeting lasted two to three hours. Fiers said little, remaining aloof and allowing the annuitant to do most of the questioning. Gadd testified that he told both men about his efforts to airlift guns and ammunition from Europe to Central America, and on into Nicaragua, using C–123 aircraft.[27]

Fiers later added two details to the Gadd story, first that he had met Gadd alone the day before, and second, that North had encouraged him to meet with Gadd, whom North called "Colonel East." North told Fiers that Gadd could be helpful to Fiers in "running this stuff"—meaning contra resupply—once official aid to the contras resumed.[28]

## The Airstrip

Joseph F. Fernandez was the CIA's chief of station in San Jose, Costa Rica from 1984 to 1987. His involvement in the construction and planning of a "private benefactor" airstrip near Santa Elena, Costa Rica, and the effort by the CIA to induce Costa Rican President Luis Monge to permit construction of the airstrip, are discussed elsewhere in this report.[29] The focus of this section is Fiers's knowledge of what was occurring at Santa Elena.

The first information available to Fiers of private benefactor efforts to build the airstrip appeared on August 13, 1985, in a cable from Fernandez. Fernandez informed Fiers that President Monge had agreed to allow construction of an airstrip, and Fernandez asked Fiers for guidance on facilitating it. Fiers responded that Monge's interest in supporting the contras was "gratifying," but he told Fernandez that the CIA could not be involved in pushing the airstrip.[30]

At the conclusion of a Senior Interagency Group meeting on February 12, 1986, North showed photographs of the airstrip, then under construction, to everyone in attendance. North did not say that he was building the airfield, but Fiers inferred that he was behind it. Fiers

---

fuel. Fiers also did not want to "contaminate" the $100 million program with planes that could be traced back to North's program. (Fiers, *George* Trial Testimony, 10/28/92, pp. 1333–34.)

[24] Fiers, Select Committees Deposition, 5/1/87, pp. 120–31.

[25] Ibid., pp. 82–84.

[26] Gadd, Grand Jury, 10/16/87, pp. 63–64; Gadd, FBI 302, 2/19/91, p. 4; Gadd, Grand Jury, 6/19/91, pp. 5–7. North did not remember setting up the briefing, but did recall that Fiers and others were concerned at this time about NHAO money paying for lethal supplies. (North, Grand Jury, 2/8/91, pp. 109–12.)

[27] Gadd, Grand Jury, 10/16/87, pp. 65–69; Gadd, Grand Jury, 6/19/91, pp. 7–11, 13–15. Gadd said in 1991 he was not sure whether Fiers was aware of the NSC's involvement with his operation. (Gadd, FBI 302, 2/19/91, p. 4) In his first Grand Jury appearance, however, Gadd testified that it was "clear" from the circumstances surrounding the meeting that "Fiers was aware of North's involvement in all of this." (Gadd, Grand Jury, 10/16/87, pp. 69–70.) Gadd said, however, that Fiers never mentioned North's name. (Ibid., p. 70.) The annuitant, for his part, gave interviews to Independent Counsel in 1987 and 1988, and never admitted to meeting with Gadd and Fiers. (CIA Annuitant, FBI 302, 6/12/87; CIA Annuitant, FBI 302, 2/9/88.) He included

Fiers in a meeting with Gadd only when pressed, in May 1991. The annuitant acknowledged learning that Gadd was involved with lethal Contra resupply efforts, but denied that he learned it during the February Charley's Place meeting. (CIA Annuitant, FBI 302, 5/1/91, p. 7.) Gadd's associate, John Cupp, could not recall if lethal contra-resupply efforts were discussed during the meeting. (Cupp, FBI 302, 3/26/91, p. 4.)

[28] Fiers, FBI 302, 7/18/91 AM, p. 5; Fiers, FBI 302, 7/18/91 PM, p. 2; Fiers, Grand Jury, 8/12/91, pp. 168–70.

[29] See Fernandez and Classified CIA Investigation A chapters.

[30] SAN JOSE Cable, 8/13/85, DO 189740–38; SAN JOSE Cable, 8/14/85, DO 189743–41; WASHINGTON 497837, 8/17/85, HC 10; Fiers, Select Committees Testimony, 8/4/87, pp. 264–65. Fiers later admitted to Independent Counsel that he remembered these cables clearly, but denied that they contained any hidden instructions to Fernandez. Fiers assumed that the private benefactors, perhaps with North's help, would find a way to get the airstrip built. Fiers also described discussions during September 1985 with North and Abrams about these cables. (Fiers, FBI 302, 7/30/91, p. 14, and Classified CIA Investigation A chapter.)

thought that North was reckless to show the pictures at such a meeting, and he told North, "You ought to keep your mouth shut." [31]

In early September 1986, the new President of Costa Rica, Oscar Arias, threatened to expose the airstrip and its connection to the "private benefactors." Fiers consulted with an extremely upset North. At Abrams' request, Fiers called Fernandez. Fernandez claimed that the situation had been handled through a CIA asset. The situation, however, was merely delayed. On September 25, 1986, a Costa Rican official revealed the airstrip in a press conference. According to a memo to National Security Adviser John M. Poindexter from North, Fiers, Abrams, and North prepared the false press guidance to cover it. [32]

## Clines

By February 1986, Fiers knew that Rodriguez, North, and Gadd were engaged in lethal resupply of the contras. By April he could add another name to his list: Thomas Clines.

Clines was a former CIA officer who had begun working with the Enterprise in 1985 as an arms purchaser. On April 28, 1986, CIA personnel in Europe cabled headquarters about business discussions between Clines and a CIA source concerning a possible shipment of arms from Portugal, and possibly Poland, along the lines of earlier shipments to the contras. The cable reported that the shipment in question was "directly dependent for time being on successful passage of bill in U.S. Congress providing funding support for Nicaraguan 'contras.'" [33]

Fiers called North on May 2, 1986. North's notes state:

—Lisbon—reporting on Clines
—Poland -> Honduras
—Direct contact w/
—People are reporting

North remembered that CIA stations worldwide were reporting on arms purchases on behalf of the contras. North testified that Fiers probably called him to brief him on one report, and to suggest improvements in the operational security of his program. [34]

Fiers testified that he spoke to North about Clines, essentially to warn North and his contacts away from him. [35]

## Advice and Information

Alan Fiers not only learned about private benefactor activities—he assisted them. North's notebook reveals, for example, a discussion on April 2, 1986, with Fiers concerning Blowpipe missiles, in which Fiers apparently gave North a source for the missiles and a price. North remembered discussing Blowpipes generally with "a lot of different people," possibly including Fiers. North testified that information about his search for Blowpipes was "not the kind of information I held back from Alan Fiers or any of the other people that I had to deal with." [36]

Fiers assisted the private benefactors by providing them information, such as flight vectors and clearances, that assisted their air deliveries. [37] Much of this assistance was done indirectly, and therefore legally. In one instance, however, Fiers encouraged and perhaps directed

[31] Fiers, Select Committees Deposition, 5/1/87, pp. 60–61; Fiers, Select Committees Testimony, 8/4/87, pp. 270–72; Croker, Grand Jury, 9/13/91, pp. 54–57. Fiers later told Independent Counsel that the evening of the meeting, he questioned Gadd about the airstrip and its use. (Fiers, FBI 302, 7/30/91, p. 19.)

[32] Fiers, Select Committees Deposition, 5/1/87, pp. 63–64; Memorandum from North to Poindexter, Subject: Press Guidance re Costa Rican Airstrip, 9/30/86, AKW 002131–39. Fiers later admitted that this further proved to him that North was closely tied to the private benefactors. Fiers also feared that press inquiries about the airstrip would lead to revelation of North's operation. (Fiers, FBI 302, 8/1/91, p. 6.)

[33] CIA Cable, 4/28/86, DO 187161–60.

[34] North Notebook, 5/2/86, AMX 1093; North, Grand Jury, 2/8/91, pp. 114–18. North recalled receiving calls about the operational security of the resupply operation from others at the CIA, including Director Casey, deputy directors of central intelligence John McMahon and Robert Gates, and Clair George. North recalled that eventually, by agreement with Casey and George, the reports were "restricted so that there would not be a widespread dissemination of the fact that arms were being purchased in foreign countries by specific individuals or by the resistance. . . ." (Ibid., p. 115.) North also said that he "undoubtedly" communicated to Secord that there was a security leak, and may have done so without Fiers's knowledge or consent. (Ibid., p. 119.) Someone undoubtedly reported the leak to Clines. CIA personnel in Europe reported in June 1986 that the source who had reported the April discussions had received an "angry phone call" from Clines warning him to "stop talking 'to those other people'" about a ship Clines had recently purchased. Clines also reportedly told the source that these "other individuals" were not involved and had no need to know what he was doing, and that he would no longer do business with the source "if he could not keep his mouth shut." (CIA Cable, 6/19/86, DO 13000–12999.)

[35] Fiers, Select Committees Deposition, 5/1/87, p. 35; Fiers, Select Committees Testimony, 8/5/87, p. 65.

[36] North, Grand Jury, 2/15/91, pp. 38–39, 76. Fiers later admitted these conversations. (Fiers, Grand Jury, 8/14/91, pp. 21–22.)

[37] Fiers would later reveal to Independent Counsel that on Clair George's instructions, he provided intelligence to North in February 1985 that North intended to pass to the Contras illegally. See George chapter.

a lethal "private benefactor" mission to forces that had been promised lethal aid by the CIA.

## The CIA and the Southern Front

Prior to 1985, the bulk of U.S. Government effort and resources earmarked for the contras benefited those elements arrayed against the Sandinista regime along Nicaragua's border with Honduras, on Nicaragua's northern frontier. By August 1985, officials in the CIA and other federal agencies had decided that they could press the Sandinistas harder if there were a politically and militarily viable contra force along Nicaragua's southern border with Costa Rica—a "southern front."

Prior to August 1985, contra forces along Nicaragua's southern border were commanded by Eden Pastora, a charismatic ex-Sandinista who enjoyed significant political support in the U.S. Congress. The CIA viewed Pastora as a militarily ineffective personality who would not take his forces out of Costa Rica. This produced diplomatic friction between the American and Costa Rican governments. Further, as evidence mounted that Sandinista spies and drug smugglers had penetrated Pastora's inner circle, the CIA believed that Pastora had become a security and public relations risk. The CIA saw Pastora as a difficult and opportunistic leader who also did not share United States objectives for the region.[38]

The task of shaping a Pastora-free, viable Southern Front fell primarily to Fernandez. As chief of the CIA station in Costa Rica, Fernandez carefully helped neutralize Pastora's influence among contras who were operating in Costa Rica and persuaded his military commanders to join the United Nicaraguan Opposition (UNO).[39] Fernandez pursued these actions under Fiers' supervision, and kept CIA headquarters informed of his progress.

Fiers and Fernandez began planning to separate Pastora's commanders from their leader in the spring of 1985. Both viewed the effort as a critical objective for the CIA in the contra

war.[40] Their plans crystallized in early August 1985. North noted on August 6, 1985, a call from Fiers during which they discussed Fiers' plans:

—Alfonso [Robelo] alone is not enough in South

\*      \*      \*

—Told Robelo to get in touch w/3 Pastora [commandantes]
Gonzalez
Lionel
Omar

—Fold 3 commandantes, into [UNO][41]

The next day, Fiers cabled Fernandez with a "Strategy for the Southern Front." Fiers wrote that "a cohesive and viable southern front has not evolved" and that the CIA was "left with the problem of trying to develop an alternative organization which could be folded into our overall objectives." CIA headquarters had reached this conclusion in light of "consensus having developed that neither we nor [UNO] could work with any confidence with [Pastora]." The cable suggested that an effective and complementary course of action would be to "have [Arturo Cruz, Jr.] seek out Southern Commanders who we understand to have a positive record (such as 'Ganso,' 'Lionel' and 'Omar') and begin a dialogue with them on behalf of [UNO] with the objective of bringing them into the overall effort."[42]

Fernandez, who eventually was given responsibility for persuading Pastora's commanders to abandon him, responded by cable on August 8, 1985. Fernandez suggested bringing Pastora's military commanders under Fernando ("El Negro" or "Blackie") Chamorro, who for much of 1986 served as military commander for the southern front. Fernandez also concurred in efforts to wean Pastora's commanders away from him, suggesting that these commanders and other sympathetic individuals would "unite

[38] Fiers, Select Committees Deposition, 5/1/87, pp. 37–40; Fernandez, Grand Jury, 11/19/90, pp. 59–67; CIA Officer #1, Grand Jury, 5/22/91, pp. 15–16.

[39] UNO was a contra organization under the leadership of Alfonso Robelo, Adolfo Calero, and Arturo Cruz, Sr. UNO was created in 1985 under the auspices of the CIA and the State Department to unify the various elements of the resistance.

[40] Fiers, Select Committees Deposition, 5/1/87, pp. 40–41; Fernandez, Grand Jury, 11/19/90, pp. 69–70.

[41] North Notebook, 8/6/85, AMX 001305. North did not recall the specifics of this conversation, but he admitted that he discussed these kinds of matters regularly with Fiers. (North, Grand Jury, 1/18/91, p. 40.)

[42] DIRECTOR 482618, 8/7/85, DO 186312–11.

with [UNO] once its programs are funded and under way.''[43]

Fiers denied authorizing such activities until after Congress amended its restrictions on aid to the contras in December 1985, and allowed for expanded political activities in support of the contras. On December 31, 1985, Fernandez reported to Fiers that four commanders within Pastora's organization, known as the ARDE, were ''planning to abandon Pastora and ally themselves with UNO/FDN'' and Fernando Chamorro. Fiers responded by asking Fernandez for a plan to contact the dissidents, whom CIA officers would later dub the ''Newly Aligned Commanders'' or ''NACs.''[44]

## Supporting the NACs

The success of the CIA's effort to enlist dissident Pastora commandantes in the UNO/FDN cause depended in large part on the acquisition and delivery of lethal and non-lethal support to them. The CIA provided communications equipment and training for the NACs as permitted by law. This alone, however, would not have drawn the NACs into the field. As plans were made in early February 1986 to move these forces into southern Nicaragua, it became a priority for the CIA to get supplies to them. The NACs and Fernando Chamorro were promised support, both lethal and non-lethal, to enter southern Nicaragua.[45]

Two CIA paramilitary officers testified that Fernandez authorized CIA officers to promise support to the NACs to induce them to join UNO.[46] Rafael Quintero, a former CIA opera-

tive who helped coordinate ''private benefactor'' activities in Central America, also testified that Fernandez made such promises to the NACs.[47] Other evidence—most notably from North and Robert Owen[48]—indicates that North and others promised lethal support to the NACs during this period.

Confirmation of CIA offers of lethal support also came from Fernando Chamorro. In February 1986, Chamorro, on instructions from Fernandez, traveled to Washington, D.C. He met with a ''Mr. Cliff.'' (Fiers's cover name was Cliff Grubbs.) ''Mr. Cliff'' congratulated Chamorro on the unification of the southern troops with UNO and reaffirmed promises of increased assistance. Chamorro was told that in terms of arms, whatever Chamorro thought was necessary, ''he would receive.''[49]

Fiers admitted that he encouraged CIA officers and others to lead the NACs to believe that Fiers would do whatever was possible under the law to support them if they left Pastora. The NACs were to be offered communications equipment, humanitarian aid, and an equal share of U.S. weapons once Congress had resumed aid to the contras. Fiers also testified that he twisted Adolfo Calero's arm to get the FDN to release weapons from FDN stocks for the NACs, and that he spoke with North about the Southern Front's need for arms—knowing that North might be able to influence Calero.[50]

CIA cables and other evidence from early 1986 establish that, to seal the NACs' allegiance to UNO, the Central American Task Force actively promoted non-lethal airdrops, and later, lethal missions to them. Soon after the NACs' defection, Fiers informed the San Jose station that the task force wanted to ensure that the NACs received ''some demonstrable material benefit as a result of their decision,'' and noted that NHAO had authorized money and other aid to the NAC forces. Fiers pushed for a NHAO drop to the southern forces that was accomplished on March 6, 1986.[51]

[43] Fernandez, Grand Jury, 11/19/90, pp. 71–72; SAN JOSE Cable, 8/8/85, DO 181545–41.

[44] Fiers, Select Committees Deposition, 5/1/87, p. 41; SAN JOSE Cable, 12/31/85, DO 100930–29; DIRECTOR 676529, 1/3/86, DO 10336.

[45] Fernandez, Grand Jury, 11/19/90, p. 73; SAN JOSE Cable, 2/4/86, DO 100961.

[46] [Classified Identity Withheld], Grand Jury, 6/5/87, pp. 21–22; [Classified Identity Withheld], Grand Jury, 4/13/88, p. 14. These officers and a third paramilitary officer also testified that Fernandez ordered them to provide training (permitted by law) in map reading and drop site selection for the southern forces. The third paramilitary officer, who arrived in San Jose in August 1986, essentially chose drop sites for Enterprise resupply drops with Fernandez's knowledge. The third officer knew that private sources were supplying the arms, but he assumed the activities were authorized by CIA headquarters. ([Classified Identity Withheld], Grand Jury, 1/20/88, pp. 34–36; [Classified Identity Withheld], Grand Jury, 4/13/88, p. 20; [Classified Identity Withheld], Grand Jury, 6/5/87, pp. 26–27.) Fernandez admitted only to authorizing training. (Fernandez, Grand Jury, 12/19/90, pp. 6–9.) He also denied authorizing his subordinates to promise aid to the NACs. (Fernandez, Grand Jury, 11/19/90, pp. 82–83.)

[47] Quintero, Grand Jury, 1/6/88, pp. 105–6.

[48] North, Grand Jury, 2/8/91, p. 46; Memorandum from TC [Owen] to BG [North], 2/10/86, p. 1 (''Once [Chamorro's] column reaches its destination, they will request a large amount of goods and they have been promised they will get what they need'').

[49] Chamorro, FBI 302, 11/17/87, p. 4.

[50] Fiers, Select Committees Deposition, 5/1/87, pp. 42–49.

[51] DIRECTOR 684429, 1/9/86, DO 10392; Fernandez, Grand Jury, 11/19/90, p. 94. According to Fernandez, these drops had to be in

Despite having received humanitarian aid, Fernando Chamorro complained that the U.S. Government had abandoned its commitments to the NACs, who by that time had been in southern Nicaragua for a month without having received fresh ammunition or other lethal supplies. Chamorro had attempted to arrange for an airdrop sponsored by the FDN, the contra organization in Honduras, to the southern forces on March 7 or 8, 1986, only to have the mission scrubbed by the FDN, Fernandez, and U.S. Ambassador to Costa Rica Lewis Tambs.

On March 11, 1986, Fernandez informed Fiers that Chamorro's forces had established a secure drop zone in southern Nicaragua. Fernandez also reported that the NACs had made an "urgent request" for ammunition. Headquarters replied, suggesting that a "list of items needed be obtained and sent through UNO secure commo net and drop of ammunition be arranged through UNO/FDN."[52]

On March 15, 1986, Fiers directed Fernandez and other CIA personnel in Central America to assist a drop of lethal supplies by UNO/FDN to the NACs. By this time, according to CIA field reports, Chamorro and the NAC forces had received the March 6 NHAO drop and were dividing it among themselves. Fernandez related that the UNO/South leadership had given priority to a lethal drop, noting that the NACs were ready to receive supplies at their secure drop zone. Fiers responded:

1. Note [your cable] planning to expedite ammunition resupply for [Southern] forces. Hqs views this as positive step to expand NAC forces. If the ammunition drop can be made with the UNO/FDN aircraft it will go a long way toward promoting UNO/FDN/FARN unity.

2. Suggest this drop be expedited by the FDN to speed up the development of NAC

forces and [CIA field personnel] assist as appropriate.

By this cable, Fiers instructed Fernandez and other CIA personnel in Central America not only to encourage an FDN drop to the NACs, but to make sure that it happened.[53]

Handwritten notes by Fiers on cables received by CIA headquarters during late March-early April 1986 urged headquarters personnel to move ahead with plans for a drop of supplies.[54]

## A Lethal Mission for the Southern Front

Three events prompted North and Secord to stage its first aerial delivery of supplies to the southern front on the night of April 11, 1986, after the CIA was blocked from a lawful means of delivery.

The first development came in Congress. On March 20, 1986, the House of Representatives rejected the Reagan Administration's request for 100 million dollars for contra aid.

The second event was the imminent collapse of the newly formed NAC alliance, a collapse fueled in part by private American donors. Pastora vied with the CIA and UNO for the NAC commanders' allegiance throughout January-May 1986. In early March 1986, Pastora traveled to Washington and was received by the State Department. He returned to Costa Rica insisting that he would be receiving supplies from the U.S. Government. The Central American Task Force assured a worried Fernandez that, although the State Department had met with Pastora, "no commitments were made to support him or his troops." In a separate communication, the task force "strongly" suggested that a

message be sent to Newly Aligned Commanders . . . alerting them to rumors being circulated by [Pastora], and setting the record straight. They should be made aware that as soon as some basic operational problems are resolved they will be

Nicaragua because the CIA "felt that if [the NACs got] their supplies inside Costa Rica, they might never go back into Nicaragua. So we put the carrot out there and let them go." (Ibid., p. 95.) Fiers explained his rationale by cable: [W]e do not view [Pastora] in vicious or malicious terms, but rather see him as a tragic figure, who for multiple reasons. . .is incapable of a positive contribution. It is also important to point out that supplies will be made available to FRS [contra] units in the field via NHAO, if they (the unit commandantes) so request. (FYIO [For Your Information Only]: specific plans to this end are being made.) DIRECTOR 677959, 1/4/86, DO 84690.

[52] SAN JOSE Cable, 3/11/86, DO 11405; Fernandez, Grand Jury, 11/19/90, pp. 127–28; DIRECTOR 776030, 3/13/86, DO 11467.

[53] SAN JOSE Cable, 3/13/86, DO 100977; DIRECTOR 780844, 3/15/86, DO 11534; Fiers, Select Committees Testimony, 8/5/87, p. 18.

[54] SAN JOSE Cable, 4/1/86, DO 101154–53.

receiving further supplies from UNO, rpt [repeat] UNO.[55]

Soon after Pastora's trip, retired Army Maj. Gen. John K. Singlaub traveled to Costa Rica. During his visit Singlaub met with Pastora and attempted to negotiate an agreement with him, purportedly on behalf of the United States. Word of a Singlaub-Pastora agreement stoked the already tense competition for the NACs and momentarily gave the advantage to Pastora. Shortly after hearing about the agreement, Fiers cabled Fernandez and other CIA personnel in Central America that Singlaub's actions did not reflect a new posture toward Pastora, and that the NACs should be reminded that any and all U.S. support would come through UNO. Fiers also wrote that in view of Singlaub's ''agreement,''

it is more crucial than ever that we maintain our commitment to the NAC's and that the required drop be made at the absolutely first possible opportunity. Recognizing aircraft problems, request [CIA personnel in Central America] ensure that [the FDN] understands urgency and assigns proper priority to this mission.[56]

Despite Fiers' efforts, news of the Singlaub-Pastora accord spread quickly through the NAC coalition. UNO/FARN commander Ramon and NACs Lionel and Oscar threatened to march back towards the Costa Rican border if they did not receive the arms they were promised as soon as possible. Moreover, Franklin and Navigante—the NAC commanders most loyal to Pastora and most skeptical of their UNO/FDN brethren in the north—informed other NACs that they remained allied with Pastora's ARDE. In short, in the days immediately preceding North's lethal resupply mission, the nascent southern front was teetering.[57]

The third event that forced a private benefactor drop to the NACs was UNO/FDN's inability to stage its own mission. CIA personnel in Central America reported on April 1, 1986, ten days before North's mission, that the FDN had scheduled a drop to the NACs on April 3, using an FDN-owned DC–3 aircraft. The proposed route would have taken the FDN aircraft twice over Costa Rican air space. It also called for landing at the San Jose international airport if the mission had to abort.[58]

Fernandez objected that any flight that crossed Costa Rican air space would violate American assurances to President-elect Arias. Fernandez also argued that the route would make the flight vulnerable to detection by Sandinista radar and anti-aircraft fire. Fernandez suggested an alternative route.[59]

CIA headquarters agreed and directed other CIA personnel in Central America to change the route. In response, CIA field personnel reported that the FDN's airplane was having mechanical problems, and that the FDN flight crew was too inexperienced to fly the prescribed route. Angry and concerned, Fernandez cabled headquarters and his Central American colleagues:

UNO/South is currently making arrangements *with sources other than FDN* for a smaller resupply drop utilizing a C–123 aircraft which will be able to fly the preferred route mentioned previous traffic. That drop is tentatively scheduled for the week of 6 April. In the event that [Calero] cannot assist and if San Jose cannot be assured that DC–6 will follow flight plan recommended believe that [FDN] drop should be held in abeyance until further notice.

The FDN mission was scrapped and the FDN's pre-packed load of lethal materiel designated for the NACs remained in Honduras.[60]

The North-Secord Enterprise resupplied the NACs by air within a week by commandeering an aircraft in Ilopango under NHAO contract. A Southern Air Transport L–100 under contract to the private benefactors—which had delivered NHAO supplies to Ilopango from the United States—dropped a mixed load of arms and non-

[55] DIRECTOR 772442, 3/11/86, DO 11375; DIRECTOR 773931, 3/11/86, DO 100976.

[56] AMEMB SAN JOSE 0144, 3/27/86, ALV 5011–12; DIRECTOR 799822, 3/28/86, DO 10799. Fernandez testified that the drop to which Fiers referred was the lethal drop contemplated by the FDN. (Fernandez, Grand Jury, 12/19/90, p. 48.)

[57] Fernandez, Grand Jury, 12/19/90, p. 55; SAN JOSE Cable, 4/1/86, DO 101154–53.

[58] CIA Cable, 4/1/86, DO 11714.

[59] SAN JOSE Cable, 4/2/86, DO 11741.

[60] DIRECTOR 809755, 4/3/86, DO 101156; CIA Cable, 4/4/86, DO 11782; SAN JOSE Cable, 4/5/86, DO 101158 (emphasis added); CIA Cable, 4/7/86, DO 101159; Fernandez, Grand Jury, 12/19/90, p. 52.

lethal supplies to the NACs on the night of April 11, 1986.

Fernandez, North, and Secord were the moving forces behind the L–100 mission. The most direct evidence of Fiers' involvement in the drop was a KL–43 message, one written a few days before April 9, 1986. In this message North informed Secord that he had briefed Fiers on the L–100 flight and secured Fiers's approval for the mission. The message states:

The unit to which we wanted to drop in the southern quadrant of Nicaragua is in desperate need of ordnance resupply. We had planned to do a material drop from the supplies we are bringing into Ilo Pango [sic] but the units—headed by [NACs] Ramon, Lionel and Navigante cannot wait. Have therefore developed an alternative plan which Cliff [Fiers] has been briefed on and in which he concurs. The L–100 which flies from MSY [Miami] to Aguacate' on Wednesday should terminate it's [sic] NHAO mission on arrival at Aguacate. At that point it should load the supplies at Ilo Pango which—theoretically [CIA Subject #1] is assembling today at Aguacate—and take them to Ilo Pango. These items should then be transloaded to the C–123 after being properly rigged. On any night between Wednesday, Apr 9, and Friday, Apr 11 these supplies should be dropped by the C–123 in the vicinity of 11 22 15N and 84 18 00W—SSE of Nueva Guinea. The A/C shd penetrate Nicaragua across the Atlantic Coast shouth [sic] of Monkey Point. Call signs freqs and zone marking light diagram to be provided to Ralph [Quintero] at Ilo Pango by the new UNO Sur operator we are taking care of. Hope we can make this happen the right way this time. If we are ever going to take the pressure off the northern front we have got to get this drop in—quickly. Please make sure that this is retransmitted via this channel to Joe [Fernandez], Ralph, Sat [Southern Air Transport] and [the US military group commander in El Salvador, Colonel James] Steele. [Robert] Owen already briefed and prepared to go w/ the L–100 out of MSY if this will help. Please advise soonest.

North, Fiers, and Abrams' calendars show that the three of them met at 3:00 p.m. on April 4, 1986, and at 4:30 p.m. on April 10, 1986. North's calendar and schedule cards show that he met with Fiers alone on April 8, 1986, at 4:30 p.m., and that he met with Fiers alone at the CIA at 9:00 a.m. on April 11, 1986—the morning after a first failed attempt to drop lethal supplies to the NACs. The meeting also was on the heels of a request by Secord that North learn whether there was intelligence indicating that the Sandinistas knew of the attempted drop.[61]

By April 13, 1986, the CIA had published news of the L–100 drop to other U.S. government agencies. Fernandez cabled CIA headquarters with word of the drop's success on April 12, and sent an elated KL–43 message to North at midnight that same day. The drop had the desired effect on the NACs. Shortly after the drop, Fernando Chamorro met with NAC leaders and convinced them to resume negotiations with UNO. By the end of May, the NACs publicly announced an agreement to align themselves with UNO under Chamorro. Meanwhile, Pastora had turned himself in to Costa Rican authorities and had applied for political asylum—thereby ending his military influence.[62]

## Fiers's Effort to Insulate Fernandez

Continuing from April to October 1986, Fernandez passed intelligence directly to Rafael Quintero, Secord's Central American representative. To remove himself from direct contact with the resupply operation, Fernandez began working to place a UNO/South representative at Ilopango air base as a liaison between the resupply operation and UNO/South. Although this plan was ultimately rejected by Fiers—and although Fernandez continued to pass information directly to Quintero without informing headquarters—Fiers learned enough between April and July 1986 to know that Fernandez

61 KL–43 Message from Secord to North, 4/11/86, AKW 4413; Fiers, Select Committees Deposition, 5/1/87, pp. 91–92; Fiers, Select Committees Testimony, 8/4/87, pp. 271–72. North claimed not to remember either briefing Fiers on the mission or writing the KL–43 message. North did not dispute the message, however. (North, Grand Jury, 2/8/91, p. 94.)

62 CIA Intelligence Cable, 4/12/86, DO 101167; SAN JOSE Cable, 4/16/86, DO 12126; CIA Intelligence Cable, 4/29/86, DO 100997; CIA Intelligence Cable, 5/7/86, DO 101012; SAN JOSE Cable, 3/15/86, DO 12637.

was in direct contact with the private resupply network in 1986.

Fernandez first announced his plan to place a UNO/South communicator at Ilopango on April 8, 1986. Ultimately, it was decided that the UNO/South communicator would be housed and would use radio equipment provided by the "private benefactors." [63]

At least one senior CIA official learned that Fernandez was involved in passing information directly to the benefactors in April 1986. C/LA #2, who was to become Chief of the CIA's Latin American Division and Fiers' direct superior on May 1, 1986, visited San Jose in April. Fernandez and C/LA #2 were friends. Shortly after C/LA #2 arrived, Fernandez told him this about his contacts with the resupply operation:

—he was passing intelligence to the private benefactors to facilitate the delivery of supplies, including guns and ammunition, to the southern front;

—he had not previously told headquarters about these activities;

—North had introduced him to the private benefactors;

—he communicated with the private benefactors by "communications gear" used in conjunction with the telephone and manufactured by TRW;

—he had received this gear [a KL–43 device] from the private benefactors; and

—at the request of Ambassador Tambs, he was monitoring the construction of an airfield that was being paid for and would be used by the private benefactors.[64]

C/LA #2 expressed concern and promised to look into the situation when he returned to Washington and to provide guidance. C/LA #2 remembered more than one meeting after his return in which he discussed Fernandez's predicament with Fiers. He did not tell Fiers about the mysterious "communications gear" ob-

tained by Fernandez, but he told Fiers everything else.[65]

C/LA #2 and Fiers agreed that Fernandez's direct contacts with the private benefactors were contrary to CIA policy. They believed that the solution was to place a UNO/South communicator at Ilopango, and to inform Fernandez of this decision personally at a regional conference of senior CIA officers later in May 1986. C/LA #2 and Fiers presented their proposal to Fernandez as planned, provoking a wider discussion among the senior CIA field officers in attendance about Fernandez's contacts with the private benefactors. C/LA #2 and Fiers directed the officers to help place the UNO/South communicator at Ilopango.[66]

By July 10, 1986, the arrangements were complete and were reported to the CATF. It was only then that Louis Dupart, the task force compliance officer and a lawyer, decided that the plan took the CIA too close to the line drawn by the Boland Amendment restrictions on contra aid. Dupart persuaded Fiers that the move was politically and legally risky, and that the CIA could not be involved in any effort to place a contra liaison to the private benefactors at Ilopango. Dupart and Fiers informed the field of their decision on July 12, 1986. Fiers assured C/LA #2 that the contras would place the communicator on their own.[67]

Fiers knew as early as May 1986 that Fernandez had passed information directly to the "private benefactors." No one at the CIA—including Fiers—disclosed this information to any congressional committee in October 1986,

[63] SAN JOSE Cable, 4/8/86, DO 11890; SAN JOSE Cable, 7/10/86, ANT 3729–30.

[64] C/LA #2, Grand Jury, 4/29/88, pp. 15–31; C/LA #2, Grand Jury, 5/8/91, pp. 15–24.

[65] Ibid., pp. 25–31; C/LA #2, Grand Jury, 4/29/88, pp. 24, 36–42; Fernandez, Grand Jury, 11/19/90, pp. 131–32. C/LA #2's calendar shows meetings with Fiers on May 2, 5, 6, 7, 8, 9, 12 and 13, 1986. Fiers denied C/LA #2's account. (Fiers, FBI 302, 7/19/91, p. 14.)

[66] C/LA #2, Grand Jury, 4/29/88, pp. 45–52; C/LA #2, Grand Jury, 5/8/91, pp. 31–46; [Classified Identity Withheld], FBI 302, 3/24/87, p. 2; DIRECTOR 830033, 4/16/86, DO 12111; Fernandez, Grand Jury, 12/19/90, pp. 70–76. Only one officer who attended the May 1986 meeting, CIA Subject #1, failed to recall the discussion of Fernandez's contacts with the private resupply operation. (CIA Subject #1, Grand Jury, 6/5/87, pp. 65–66.) Fernandez recalled that Quintero's name came up during the meetings, as the officers joked about Quintero's arranging a delivery of pizza to the private benefactors at Aguacate. (Fernandez, Grand Jury, 12/19/90, p. 106.) For his part, Fiers testified before cooperating with the Government that C/LA #2 did not speak with him upon C/LA #2's return from his April 1986 trip, and that the first he heard of Fernandez's situation was at the May 1986 meeting. (Fiers, Select Committees Deposition, 5/1/87, p. 114; Fiers, Grand Jury, 4/17/87, pp. 116–19, 126.)

[67] Dupart, Grand Jury, 4/27/88, pp. 66–71; DIRECTOR 959273, 7/12/86, DO 169558; C/LA #2, Grand Jury, 4/29/88, pp. 61–63; C/LA #2, Grand Jury, 5/8/91, p. 63.

when questioned about CIA contacts with the private resupply network.

## Fiers's Request for North's Financial Assistance

Fiers joined one last attempt in July 1986 to use North's private resupply operation after the House of Representatives approved an Administration-backed effort to provide the contras with $100 million in assistance. By May 1986 it was clear to some that "bridge financing," until the contras would eventually receive aid from the U.S. Government, would be necessary. A computer message from North to Poindexter indicates that Fiers and Abrams turned to North for some of this aid.

> All seriously believe that immediately after the Senate vote the [contras] will be subjected to a major Sandinista effort to break them before the U.S. aid can become effective. PRODEM [Project Democracy] currently has the only assets available to support the [contras] and the CIA's most ambitious estimate is 30 days after a bill is signed before their own assets will be available. This will be a disaster for the [contras] if they have to wait that long. *Given our lack of movement on other funding options, and Elliot/Allen's plea for PRODEM to get food to the resistance ASAP, PRODEM will have to borrow at least $2M to pay for the food. . . .* The only way that the $2M in food money can be repaid is if CIA purchases the $4.5M worth of PRODEM equipment for about $2.25M when the law passes.[68]

North tried to enlist the CIA in extricating himself from "private benefactor" operations; he sought the Restricted Interagency Group's (RIG's) advice as well. In at least one RIG meeting prior to October 1986—meetings that Fiers attended—North exposed his role in pri-

vate assistance to the contras, with such detail that Fiers had a comprehensive understanding of his activities.[69]

## Exposure

### The Hasenfus Crash

Fiers' control of Central American issues for the CIA extended beyond management of regional operations. Fiers also had a unique command of the CIA's relationship with Congress on Central American affairs throughout 1985 and 1986. The Task Force was not subject to the same control by the CIA's Office of Congressional Affairs (OCA) as other Agency units, but despite (or perhaps because of) this autonomy, relations with the Hill were positive. Members of Congress admired Fiers and his ability to give them details of Central American operations. Fiers was the one to whom Congress turned when it wanted answers about the specifics of the Nicaragua program. As a result, Fiers spent hours speaking with people from the Hill. It was a task that he enjoyed.[70]

Fiers was more than a knowledgeable mouthpiece on Central America. He was politically astute, something which earned him credit at Agency headquarters but which sometimes frustrated those in the field. Fiers's chief political interest beginning in late 1985 was persuading the Congress to let the CIA back into the "resistance game"—that is, appropriate funds to the CIA so that the Agency could support and better influence the contras.[71]

Fiers worked hard to persuade Congress to support President Reagan's 1986 proposal to appropriate $100 million in contra aid. His chief contribution to this effort was demonstrating that the Agency was abiding by the law. Fiers underestimated the delays. Both Fiers and CIA

---

[68] PROFs Note from North to Poindexter, 7/24/86, AKW 021735 (emphasis added). Fiers later admitted to Independent Counsel that he and Abrams had sought aid from "Project Democracy." (Fiers, Grand Jury, 8/14/91, pp. 72–76.) Fiers said that North had approached him about this time with an offer to sell the private benefactors' planes to the CIA, (Fiers, FBI 302, 7/19/91, p. 18); and that Fiers had pleaded with several senior CIA officials in July 1986 to keep a CIA detailee to the NSC, Vincent Cannistraro, away from the "private sector people" with whom North was dealing. (Fiers, Grand Jury, 8/14/91, p. 59.)

[69] Fiers later corroborated North's general account of these discussions. (Fiers, FBI 302, 7/22/91, p. 14; Fiers, FBI 302, 8/2/91, pp. 9–10.) For further discussion of these meetings, see Abrams Chapter.

[70] Fiers, Tower Commission Testimony, 1/8/87, pp. 18–19, 22; C/LA #2, Grand Jury, 4/29/88, pp. 72–73; Memorandum for DCI & DDCI, Subject: Meeting with VADM Poindexter, 13 November, 1700 Hours, 11/12/86, ER 27230; Pearline, FBI 302, 3/4/91 302; Memorandum re: HPSCI Request for a Briefing on Downed Cargo Plane, 10/9/86, DO 112485; Fiers, Select Committees Testimony, 8/5/87, p. 60; Gries, FBI 302, 4/9/91, p. 2.

[71] Fernandez, Grand Jury, 12/21/90, p. 89; Fiers, Tower Commission Testimony, 1/8/87, pp. 21, 27, 60; Fiers, Grand Jury, 4/17/87, pp. 79–85; Fiers, Select Committees Testimony, 8/5/87, pp. 171–72; Dupart, Grand Jury, 4/27/88, pp. 20–21; Fiers, Select Committees Deposition, 5/1/87, pp. 16–17.

field officers promised supplies to the contras in anticipation of renewed aid, but they could not deliver. Efforts to demonstrate compliance were thus redoubled.[72]

Eventually the House approved the $100 million aid package on June 25, 1986, but the final steps toward enacting the package came slowly. The October 5, 1986, crash of the Hasenfus C–123 could not have occurred at a more inopportune time.

The Hasenfus crash unleashed chaos in the Central American Task Force. The Task Force spent the Monday following the crash, and most of the rest of the week, scrambling for information. Matters were made worse on Tuesday, October 7, when Nicaragua announced that the plane had CIA backing.[73] That same day a staff member of the House Permanent Select Committee on Intelligence (HPSCI) called the CIA to seek the identities of the private benefactors. Fiers equivocated about the cargo of the Hasenfus plane—despite having received specific cables on the subject—and denied knowing who sponsored the flight: "I can assure you that we won't touch any of that stuff, we have come too far to commit political suicide." Later, to another HPSCI staffer, Fiers stressed that he was trying "to be as up front as possible and we don't want to hide any information from anybody."[74]

The controversy continued. Director Casey and Deputy Director Gates briefed ranking members of HPSCI and the Senate Select Committee on Intelligence (SSCI) on October 9, only to have one member say he was "shaken" by the disclosures. HPSCI met on the morning of October 9 to hear House Speaker Tip O'Neill report that the Hasenfus crash was "mysterious still." The Chairman of HPSCI, Rep. Lee Hamilton, decided that he would call the CIA for a briefing. Likewise, the Senate Committee on Foreign Relations told the CIA that it wanted a hearing the next day about the crash, the history of the Central America covert-action program, and CIA compliance with the law.[75]

CATF was told that it would be responsible for putting a statement together for Deputy Director Gates. The deputy chief of CATF cabled all Central American personnel for information about their contacts with the Hasenfus crew and Hasenfus's press statements about CIA contacts. Another CATF officer contacted a senior CIA officer in Central America by secure phone to learn his knowledge of Felix Rodriguez.[76]

Fiers ordered Dupart, who was on leave, back to the office. Fiers told him, "[T]his is it. This is what you were hired for," and instructed him to prepare testimony and a briefing book. Fiers later left to join Casey, Clair George (who had replaced Gates as the lead witness for the Agency), and David Gries from the Office of Congressional Affairs about the next day's testimony.[77]

Dupart worked into the night. In his draft, the CIA categorically denied direct or indirect CIA involvement in "private benefactor" operations. The statement acknowledged only that the Agency had passed intelligence legally to the contras, who may have passed the information to private groups that aided deliveries of supplies.[78]

The rest of the story of Dupart's draft testimony is treated elsewhere.[79] After drafting the testimony, Fiers and George joined Abrams to appear before the Senate Foreign Relations Committee at 10:11 am on October 10, 1986. George read from his opening statement that

---

[72] Fiers, Select Committees Testimony, 8/5/87, pp. 192–93; Dupart, Grand Jury, 3/15/91, pp. 11–13.

[73] Dupart, FBI 302, 2/19/91, p. 2; Strother, FBI 302, 3/8/91, pp. 4, 6–7.

[74] Ibid.; Memorandum to Fiers, Subject: Request from HPSCI Staffer Giza, 10/7/86, DO 166462; Memorandum for the Record by Strother, Subject: Request from Dick Giza, 10/7/86, DO 166472–71; Memorandum for the Record by Strother, Subject: Telephone Call from Steve Berry, 10/7/86, DO 166474–73; CIA Cable, 10/6/86, DO 101228; SAN JOSE Cable, 10/6/86, DO 101254–52; DDO Duty Officer, FBI 302, 4/30/91. Fiers later told Independent Counsel that he read DO 101228 late on the afternoon of October 6, 1986. He also admitted talking with North, who said that the Hasenfus plane was one of his and that he was dismantling his operation. (Fiers, FBI 302, 7/22/91, pp. 10–11.) Fiers admitted that his aim during this period was to protect North and not disclose his knowledge of North's operation. (Fiers, FBI 302, 7/30/91, pp. 5, 8.)

[75] Lugar, SCFR Hearing, 10/10/86, p. 44; Durenberger, SSCI Hearing, 12/9/86, pp. 22–23; HPSCI Session, 10/9/86, pp. 3–5, 23; Memorandum for EPS/LG by Randolph, Subject: HPSCI Request for a Briefing on Downed Cargo Plane, 10/9/86, DO 112485; Memorandum for the Record by Rice, Subject: SFRC Briefing—Airplane Crash in Nicaragua, 10/9/86, DO 169160.

[76] Ibid.; CIA Cable, 10/9/86, DO 177158. The Task Force officer who spoke with the senior officer, who was identified as CIA Officer #2 in U.S. v. George, did not recall telling Fiers about his conversation or the cable summarizing it, which arrived around 6:00 p.m. (CATF Officer, FBI 302, 6/6/91, pp. 11–12.)

[77] Dupart, FBI 302, 2/1/88, pp. 8–9; Dupart, Grand Jury, 4/27/88, pp. 39–40; Dupart, FBI 302, 2/19/91, pp. 3–4; Casey Schedule, 10/9/86, ER 379; George, FBI 302, 3/11/91, p. 5.

[78] Dupart, FBI 302, 2/1/88, pp. 8–9; Dupart, Grand Jury, 4/27/88, p. 43; Dupart, FBI 302, 2/19/91, pp. 6–7; DDO's Opening Statement, ANT 1779–82.

[79] See George chapter.

the CIA "has not been involved directly or indirectly in arranging, directing, or facilitating resupply missions conducted by private individuals in support of the Nicaraguan Democratic Resistance." "Not only do we wish to share what we know with all the members of the Senate," said George, "but this is very critical testimony for us because there is some question as to our legal behavior. We want to share with you the frank, open facts, because it is not anything that we want to have hanging over our head at any moment, that we broke the law in our performance in Nicaragua or Central America." [80]

Fiers remained silent throughout George's opening statement. The Committee chairman asked Fiers at the end of George's statement whether Fiers had "anything additional, or are you in support of Mr. George's testimony?" Fiers replied: "That's it. Yes." [81]

Fiers and George repeated their false testimony and disavowals on October 14, 1986, this time before HPSCI. The next day, Fiers briefed Sen. John Kerry, two Senate foreign relations staff members, and later Sen. Edward Kennedy on the contras—again denying CIA complicity in resupply activity. Fiers' aim in these briefings, like the ones before them, was to head off an effort by Sen. Tom Harkin to stop the $100 million aid package. [82]

## Fernandez

Fiers' efforts to persuade Congress that the CIA had no involvement with the private benefactors succeeded. On October 17, 1986, Congress released the $100 million contra-aid package. In the wake of this vote, Fiers traveled with an interagency group to Central America, where he learned that Fernandez had been in telephone contact with the private benefactors since the regional meeting in May 1986. Returning to

Washington on October 23, Fiers informed C/LA #2 of the news, but not Dupart. [83]

Fernandez returned to Washington for consultations on Saturday, October 25. The following Monday, Fernandez met with C/LA #2 about the private benefactors. C/LA #2 learned for the first time in this meeting that the "communications gear" that Fernandez told him about in April was a KL–43 encryption device. Fernandez described the device as National Security Agency issue, and said that he got it from North. Fiers may have joined this meeting late; in any event, C/LA #2 understood that Fiers would talk to George and continue discussions with Fernandez. Fernandez returned to San Jose two days later. [84]

Unaware that the Fernandez situation was about to compromise his work as the CATF's compliance officer, Dupart penned a memorandum on November 4, 1986, in which he boasted of the task force's responses to Congress in the wake of the Hasenfus crash. Two days later Dupart traveled to San Jose to explain the new contra-aid rules, only to learn from Fernandez that he had been in contact with the private benefactors since early 1986. "Shocked" by this information, Dupart instructed Fernandez to report the matter to headquarters by special cable. [85]

Dupart returned to Washington on November 10. Dupart advised Fiers privately of what he had learned from Fernandez. He warned Fiers that the CIA had to correct its October testimony before Congress. Fiers was surprised by Dupart's reaction, and claimed he never "perjured" himself. Dupart told Fiers that perjury was not the issue, but rather, frank disclosure. [86]

Despite Dupart's warning, Fiers did not take any steps to correct the testimony until November 26, the day after North was fired and after

[80] George, Senate Foreign Relations Committee Testimony, 10/10/86, pp. 16, 29–31, 51–52.

[81] Fiers, Select Committees Testimony, 8/5/87, pp. 90–91; Fiers, Senate Foreign Relations Committee Testimony, 10/10/86, p. 31.

[82] Memorandum for the Record by Dorn, Subject: Briefing for Senator Kerry, 10/16/86, DO 166519–18; Dupart Notes, ANT 01783–89; Dupart, Grand Jury, 4/27/88, pp. 45–48, 110–11; Dupart, Grand Jury, 3/15/91, pp. 56–73; Memorandum by Buckman, Subject: Briefing for Senator Kennedy, 10/15/86, ER 28571.

[83] 132 Cong.Rec., No. 144, at H 11068, S 16638; Dupart, Grand Jury, 4/27/88, pp. 48–49; C/LA #2, Grand Jury, 4/29/88, pp. 73–77; C/LA #2, Grand Jury, 5/8/91, pp. 61–63.

[84] Ibid., pp. 69–71, 79–84; Dupart, FBI 302, 2/1/88, pp. 4–5; C/LA #2, Grand Jury, 4/29/88, pp. 77–93; Fernandez, Grand Jury, 1/4/91, pp. 39–40; SAN JOSE Cable, 10/30/86, DO 22949.

[85] Dupart, FBI 302, 2/19/91, pp. 7–8; Memorandum for General Counsel by Dupart, Subject: The Compliance Process and the Crash of the Private Benefactors C–123 Transport Aircraft, 11/4/86, DO 169157–58; Dupart, FBI 302, 4/3/87, pp. 4–5; Dupart, FBI 302, 2/1/88, pp. 5; Dupart, Grand Jury, 4/27/88, pp. 51–58; Dupart Notes, ANT 1790; Fernandez, Grand Jury, 1/4/91, pp. 42–44.

[86] Dupart, Grand Jury, 4/27/88, pp. 62–63; Dupart, FBI 302, 2/1/88, p. 6; Dupart, FBI 302, 2/19/91, pp. 7–8; Dupart Notes, ANT 1790.

Attorney General Edwin Meese III announced the diversion to the contras of profits from the Iran arms sales. On November 26, Fiers, C/LA #2, and George met to discuss what to do about the Fernandez matter. After the meeting, C/LA #2 wrote a memorandum to George about his involvement with the Fernandez/private benefactor issue, and recommended review by the CIA's inspector general.[87]

On December 4, NBC broadcast the connection between the pilots of the Hasenfus flight and "Tomas Castillo," Fernandez's alias. The next day HPSCI asked the CIA to respond to NBC's allegations—triggering the CIA's first admission to HPSCI that the October 1986 testimony had been incorrect.[88] On December 9, 1986, Fiers told SSCI that Fernandez had been in contact with private benefactor Quintero. Fiers stated that he discovered the matter in a conversation with Fernandez in late October. Sen. David Durenberger asked Fiers: "Are there any other incidents like that that you want to leave with us today?" Fiers replied: "No, no, no. That's the one." [89]

## Official Inquiries

During 1987, Fiers began admitting that he knew more about North's involvement in contra resupply than he had disclosed previously. For example, Fiers admitted that he knew that North and Fernandez talked often about the contras. Fiers acknowledged that he had a general sense in 1985–86 that North had a relationship with Secord, and that Secord was involved in contra weapons purchases. He also admitted that North tried to sell the CIA Enterprise assets.[90]

Fiers had a tougher time explaining his efforts with respect to the southern front and his knowledge of Felix Rodriguez. About the former, Fiers gradually gave a more complete account of the May 1986 regional meeting, where he "really developed an understanding of this whole private benefactor program. . . ."

In answer to the question, "Did you ever during this period of '85 and '86 have reason to believe that the private benefactors or individuals within the private benefactors had received information generated by the CIA," Fiers said, "I had no hard reason to believe it but I also wouldn't have doubted it." Fiers also admitted to a hazy memory about the Costa Rican airstrip, North's showing pictures of the airstrip, and North and Fernandez's role in the "flap" over the airstrip's exposure.[91]

Fiers denied, however, that he had promised southern front commanders lethal aid, or that he authorized subordinates to do so. He did acknowledge discussing the southern front and its problems with North, "within the context of legislation" and in deciding whether to deal with Eden Pastora. Fiers denied asking North to try to find a way to supply the front, as well as prior knowledge of or briefings on the April 1986 L–100 flight. Fiers did describe in May 1987, however, how the CIA passed flight vectors via Fernandez to what he believed was UNO/South, attributing these activities to being "a little too far forward leaning" in anticipation of renewed U.S. funding.[92]

Fiers could not square his previous testimony about North with what he knew about Rodriguez. Fiers admitted that he first became aware of Rodriguez's relationship with North and Ilopango in December 1985. Fiers also admitted to his confrontation with Rodriguez at Ilopango in early 1986, and eventually divulged the phone call to North. From this Fiers admitted that he had concluded that Rodriguez was keeping North informed of the private benefactor operation at Ilopango and that North was influencing it through Rodriguez. Fiers also admitted to attending the August 1986 meeting in Donald P. Gregg's office concerning Rodriguez.[93]

When it came time to appear before the Iran/contra Committees, Fiers was clearly prepared to answer questions about his and

[87] Memorandum for the DDO by C/LA #2, Subject: Possible Impropriety in San Jose, 11/26/86, DO 62341–39; C/LA #2, Grand Jury, 4/29/88, pp. 100–01; C/LA #2, Grand Jury, 5/8/91, pp. 89–91. Fiers later disclosed that George directed that C/LA #2's memorandum fabricate an account of a meeting on November 10, 1986, that never happened. See George chapter.
[88] Dupart, FBI 302, 4/3/87, p. 4; Dupart, FBI 302, 2/1/88, p. 10.
[89] Fiers, SSCI Testimony, 12/9/86, pp. 30–32.
[90] Fiers, Grand Jury, 4/10/87, pp. 30–31, 39–40, 45–46; Ibid., 4/17/87, pp. 175–78.

[91] Fiers, Grand Jury, 4/10/87, pp. 38–45; Ibid., 4/17/87, pp. 118–130, 156–71, 179–80; Fiers, Select Committees Deposition, 5/1/87, pp. 56–57.
[92] Fiers, Select Committees Deposition, 5/1/87, pp. 43, 47, 49, 108–13; Ibid., 5/11/87, pp. 12–17; Fiers, Select Committees Testimony, 8/5/87, p. 21.
[93] Fiers, Select Committees Deposition, 5/1/87, pp. 71–72, 100–06; Fiers, Grand Jury, 4/17/87, pp. 107–16, 120–27.

George's testimony of October 14, 1986.[94] Fiers acknowledged that he intentionally remained silent before HPSCI on that day, but denied that it was because he knew of Fernandez's problems. Fiers was less prepared, however, to talk about other false testimony such as his responses to Sen. David Boren in December 1986 to a question of his knowledge of any involvement by persons associated with the U.S. Government in resupply activities. Fiers could say only that he had been "exposed" and "nervous" during his testimony. As for questions about North, Fiers said that he had been "cutting some very tight corners" and was "technically correct, specifically evasive" in October 1986.[95]

## The Fiers Plea and Cooperation

Count One of the criminal information to which Fiers pleaded guilty charged Fiers with withholding information concerning his knowledge of the diversion of funds from the Iran arms sales to the contras during a November 25, 1986, briefing of SSCI. Fiers had claimed that the first time that he had heard of the diversion was from a Cable News Network broadcast of Meese's November 25, 1986, news conference, and that he was aware of no official above him in the CIA hierarchy who was aware of this information.[96]

As he admitted in 1991, Fiers knew that these statements withheld material information from Congress because North had given him information about the diversion on two occasions in 1986, and because Fiers communicated this information to his superiors. Fiers reported these contacts to his superiors, and purposely avoided telling SSCI about them during his November 25, 1986 briefing.

In Count Two of the information, Fiers was charged with concealing his knowledge of North's resupply operation from HPSCI, during this exchange:

[MR. CHAIRMAN]: You don't know whose airplane that was?

[MR. George]: I have no idea. I read—except what I read in the paper.

[MR. CHAIRMAN]: I understand, but you don't know?

[MR. FIERS]: No, we do not know.

[MR. CHAIRMAN]: There are a number of planes that take off there to supply the Contras regularly. You don't know who they are?

[MR. FIERS]: We know what the planes are by type, we knew, for example, there were two C–123s and two C–7 cargoes. . . . We knew in some cases much less frequently that they were flying down the Pacific air corridors into southern Nicaragua for the purposes of resupply, but as to who was flying the flights and *who was behind them we do not know.*

[MR CHAIRMAN]: And you still don't?

[MR. FIERS]: No.

These statements withheld Fiers's actual knowledge about the operations and sponsorship of the resupply flights. Fiers was aware generally from November 1984 through November 25, 1986, that North was actively involved in coordinating lethal assistance for the contras. Fiers coordinated CATF activities with North to facilitate North's efforts. As a result, Fiers became aware by February 1986 that North was involved specifically in coordinating flights carrying lethal supplies to the contras from Ilopango air base in El Salvador. This knowledge was reinforced throughout 1986 in a variety of meetings and conversations, some solely between Fiers and North, others attended by other Government officials.

After pleading guilty, Fiers spent over 100 hours reviewing documents and notes, recounting events to FBI agents and the Grand Jury, and preparing himself for trials. Information obtained from Fiers contributed significantly to Independent Counsel's investigation of Iran/contra, particularly his investigation of the activities of the CIA, the Department of State, and the RIG on Central America. Fiers gave

---

[94] Fiers had earlier defended this testimony in a Select Committees deposition, arguing that his answer about ownership of private benefactor planes was literally true. Fiers, Select Committees Deposition, 5/11/87, pp. 42–44.

[95] Fiers, Select Committees Testimony, 8/5/87, pp. 59–63, 80, 121–22, 116–17.

[96] Information, *United States* v. *Fiers*, Crim. No. 91–0396 (D.D.C. July 8, 1991). Fiers' guilty plea was obtained by Deputy Independent Counsel Craig A. Gillen and Associate Counsel Vernon L. Francis and Michael D. Vhay.

critical evidence against Clair George, and would have been a major witness against Elliott Abrams had Abrams not pleaded guilty. At the cost of alienating those with whom he worked, Fiers broke the conspiracy of silence within the Reagan Administration that concealed the widespread high-level support for North's illegal contra resupply activities.

# Chapter 20
# United States v. Joseph F. Fernandez

The beginning and end of the case against Joseph F. Fernandez were unprecedented. The indictment of Fernandez represented the first time that a CIA chief of station had been charged with crimes committed in the course of his duties as a CIA officer. The dismissal of *Fernandez* derived from the first and only invocation by the attorney general of his power to prohibit the introduction of classified information at trial. As a result, Independent Counsel was deprived of the opportunity to demonstrate at trial the crucial role Fernandez played in the contra resupply operation run by Lt. Col. Oliver L. North and retired U.S. Air Force Major General Richard V. Secord, as well as the extent to which Fernandez tried to obstruct the inquiries of official investigative bodies attempting to learn the facts of the Iran/contra matter.

## The Fernandez Indictments

Fernandez was originally charged in a five-count indictment returned on June 20, 1988, by a federal Grand Jury sitting in the District of Columbia. Fernandez was accused of conspiring with North, Secord and others to defraud the United States, obstructing an investigation by the Tower Commission, and making false statements. The indictment alleged that the conspirators deprived Congress of its ability to oversee the operation of covert actions pertaining to Nicaragua by establishing and running a military support enterprise which was unaccountable to the CIA and, in turn, to Congress. By operating outside of prescribed channels, Fernandez prevented those with oversight authority from monitoring activities that were at the heart of congressional concern regarding Central American policy.[1]

The activities undertaken by Fernandez—most at a time when the CIA was forbidden from "participation in the planning or execution of military operations" or "participat[ion] in logistics activities integral to such operations"—included: (1) participation in the planning and construction of an airstrip in Costa Rica to serve the contra resupply operation; (2) mobilization of a contra fighting force on the southern front through inducements of lethal resupply; and (3) coordination of the southern front resupply effort. When questioned about these activities in early 1987 by investigators working separately for the Tower Commission and the CIA's inspector general, Fernandez made false statements regarding his relationship with North and Secord, the origin of the Costa Rican airstrip, and his involvement in and knowledge of the resupply operation.

The indictment alleged that the conspiracy took place within the District of Columbia and elsewhere, and that the obstruction and false statements occurred in the Eastern District of Virginia where Fernandez had been questioned. Independent Counsel properly presented the combined charges to a Grand Jury sitting in the District of Columbia, and following return of the indictment, Fernandez spent several months making various motions to dismiss it. It was only after litigating for three months that Fernandez moved to dismiss four of the counts on grounds of improper venue. In response, Independent Counsel moved to dismiss the entire indictment without prejudice, in order to avoid separate indictments in two separate districts for crimes that were entirely connected.

---

[1] Indictment, *U.S.* v. *Fernandez*, No. 88–0236 (D.D.C. June 20, 1988).

Independent Counsel's motion was granted on October 19, 1988.

On April 24, 1989, as the *North* trial was ending, Fernandez was indicted by a Grand Jury sitting in the Eastern District of Virginia.[2] In an effort to avoid the issues under the Classified Information Procedures Act that had plagued *North,* Independent Counsel did not seek the return of the conspiracy charge contained in the District of Columbia indictment. This was consistent with Independent Counsel's decision on January 13, 1989, to dismiss similar conspiracy charges in *North.*

The four-count Virginia indictment charged that during a three-week period in January 1987, Fernandez made false and misleading statements to two official investigative bodies—the CIA's Office of Inspector General and the Tower Commission—that were examining the facts surrounding the Iran/contra affair. These statements created a distorted picture of Fernandez's activities in support of the contras during the time of the Boland Amendment prohibitions on U.S. aid. More specifically, the indictment alleged that Fernandez made these false statements:

1. That the airstrip was a Costa Rican initiative, rather than an initiative of Fernandez, North, Secord and others;

2. That the airstrip was designed to help defend Costa Rica from a Nicaraguan invasion, rather than to support the resupply of the contras;

3. That Fernandez's contacts with Rafael Quintero, a member of the North-Secord "private benefactor" network, were limited to the occasions of the resupply flights, rather than including their work together on the airstrip and other projects;

4. That Fernandez did not know that North was involved in the resupply operation, when in fact the two worked closely together on this project; and

5. That Fernandez did not know that the supplies he had assisted in delivering to the contras in September 1986 contained

---

[2] Pre-trial and trial proceedings in *Fernandez* were supervised by Associate Counsel Laurence S. Shtasel, Geoffrey S. Stewart, and Geoffrey S. Berman.

weapons and ammunition, when in fact Fernandez knew that they were.[3]

Independent Counsel further sought to prove that Fernandez endeavored to obstruct these investigations by making these and 25 other misleading statements (13 to the Inspector General and 12 to the Tower Commission) pertaining to:

1. His involvement with the airstrip;

2. His dealings with the resupply operation;

3. His relationship with North; and

4. His contacts with Felix Rodriguez, a representative of North and Secord in El Salvador.

## Summary of the Evidence

From mid-1985 through October 1986, while the Boland Amendment prohibited the CIA from supporting military and paramilitary operations in Nicaragua by the contras, Fernandez played a crucial role in an effort spearheaded by North and Secord to provide lethal support to the contras. Fernandez's activities for the North-Secord operation centered largely on two interconnected activities. Both of these projects focused on developing a contra "southern front" along the Costa Rica/Nicaragua border that would complement contra forces arrayed to the north along the Honduras/Nicaragua border.[4]

First, beginning in August 1985, Fernandez assisted North, Secord and others in building a refueling airstrip at Santa Elena in remote

---

[3] Indictment, *U.S.* v. *Fernandez,* No. CR89–0150–A (E.D.Va. Apr. 24, 1988).

[4] Fernandez admitted to the Tower Commission that opening a southern front was his "one mission" received from the newly appointed U.S. ambassador to Costa Rica, Lewis Tambs, in July 1985. (Fernandez, Tower Commission Testimony, 1/28/87, pp. 8–12.) Tambs was knowledgeable of many of Fernandez's activities set forth in this chapter, especially those concerning the airstrip at Santa Elena, discussed later in this section. (See also Classified Investigation A, set forth in the Classified Appendix to this Report, which describes Tambs' involvement in a possibly illegal quid pro quo to Costa Rican President Luis Monge to induce the Costa Ricans to permit construction of the airstrip.) Independent Counsel concluded in November 1987 to go forward with a case against Fernandez in hopes of eventually using Fernandez as a witness. The demise of Boland conspiracy charges in *North* in January 1989 and Independent Counsel's subsequent decision not to seek conspiracy charges in the second indictment of Fernandez ended Independent Counsel's plans to prosecute other conspirators. Tambs later voluntarily testified in Independent Counsel's investigation. See History of Investigation chapter.

northwest Costa Rica that was designed to facilitate aerial resupply of the contras. Second, throughout the first nine months of 1986, Fernandez worked closely with Rafael Quintero, North and Secord's representative in Central America, both in building the airstrip and in coordinating the actual resupply flights that delivered weapons, ammunition and supplies to contra troops along the Southern Front.

Both of these efforts were designed to encourage the contras in northern Costa Rica to move back inside Nicaragua and resume fighting the Sandinistas. Fernandez urged contra leaders, directly and through CIA field personnel, to take up this struggle and induced them by promising lethal and non-lethal supplies. In the words of one CIA paramilitary officer, Fernandez authorized provision to the contras of everything from "beans to bullets" if they would re-infiltrate Nicaragua and provide a military counterpoint to the contras to the north.[5] Having made these assurances, Fernandez worked closely with Quintero and North to follow through with their plans to construct an airstrip and resupply contra forces in the south.

## The Airstrip

In August 1985, Fernandez began assisting efforts to construct an airstrip to be used as an emergency landing strip and refueling point for contra-supply aircraft making the long round trip from Ilopango, El Salvador, to the southern front. Because the aircraft could not fly over Nicaragua, they flew off-shore along the Pacific coast to the Costa Rican border, then along the border to drop sites just inside Nicaragua.[6]

Fernandez sent two CIA paramilitary officers to northwest Costa Rica to locate an appropriate site for the strip. The officers surveyed a potential location at Santa Elena and reported to Fernandez that it was a feasible site.[7] During the fall of 1985, Fernandez also consulted with Robert Owen, a representative of North, both

to design an overall strategy for the southern front and to obtain permission from Coast Rican officials to construct the airstrip.[8]

Also during the fall of 1985, Fernandez worked with William Haskell, an associate of North and Secord, who ultimately purchased land for the airstrip on behalf of Udall Corporation, a company established by Secord. Fernandez traveled to the airstrip site with Haskell and provided assistance to Haskell's efforts.[9] In January 1986, Haskell introduced Fernandez to Quintero, who took over the coordination of the airstrip project at Secord's request.[10]

In January 1986, Quintero and Fernandez traveled to inspect the site for the airstrip; after this trip, Fernandez modified the layout of the airstrip to accommodate the swampy terrain.[11] During the next three months, Quintero made numerous trips to Costa Rica to oversee construction of the airstrip. Fernandez explained to Quintero that Congress was expected to reverse its prior prohibition on CIA military support for the contras and the airstrip was, therefore, being built in anticipation of renewed funding for CIA contra-support efforts. Fernandez stated that the object was to have the airstrip ready by the time Congress changed its course.[12] Some months later, in the spring of 1986, Quintero learned that Congress had rejected renewed funding for the contras. When Quintero raised this issue, Fernandez announced that the airstrip project and the contra-resupply operation would continue nonetheless.[13]

The airstrip was completed, although it proved to be less significant in the resupply

---

[5] [Classified Identity Withheld], Grand Jury, 6/5/87, pp. 21–25. See also [Classified Identity Withheld], OIC Deposition, 5/28/87, pp. 41–46, 49–51; [Classified Identity Withheld], Grand Jury, 4/13/88, pp. 14–18.

[6] Fernandez, Tower Commission Testimony, 1/28/87, pp. 9, 12–14; SAN JOSE Cable, 8/8/85, DO 181545–41; SAN JOSE Cable, 8/13/85, DO 189740–38; SAN JOSE Cable, 8/14/85, DO 101720–19.

[7] [Classified Identity Withheld], OIC Deposition, 5/28/87, pp. 25–26, 52–54; [Classified Identity Withheld], FBI 302, 10/13/87, p. 3.

[8] Fernandez, Tower Commission Testimony, 1/28/87, pp. 14–15; Owen, Grand Jury, 11/13/87, pp. 52–58; Owen, North Trial Testimony, 2/27/89, pp. 2446–47 and 3/1/89, pp. 2705–07; Memorandum from TC [Owen] to BG [North], 8/25/85; [Classified Identity Withheld], OIC Deposition, 5/28/87, pp. 23–24, 29.

[9] Fernandez, Tower Commission Testimony, 1/28/87, pp. 16–17; Quintero, FBI 302, 11/13/87, p. 10; [Classified Identity Withheld], OIC Deposition, 5/28/87, pp. 24–25; Haskell, FBI 302, 7/6–7/87, pp. 4–6.

[10] Fernandez, Tower Commission Testimony, 1/28/87, pp. 16–17; Quintero, FBI 302, 11/13/87, p. 10; Quintero, FBI 302, 11/23/87, p. 4; Quintero, North Trial Testimony, 3/2/89, pp. 2916–17.

[11] Ibid.

[12] Quintero, Grand Jury, 1/6/88, p. 95. In his November 1987 interviews, Quintero attributed this explanation for the airstrip to Secord. (Quintero, FBI 302, 11/13/87, pp. 10–11; Quintero, FBI 302, 11/23/87, p. 4.)

[13] Quintero, Grand Jury, 1/6/88, p. 96. See also KL–43 Message from Secord to North, 6/6/86, ALU 003835 (asking North to "light a fire" under Fernandez to get increased guard protection for the airstrip).

operation than was originally expected. The landing strip would get muddy after a rain, and on one occasion a plane got stuck there.[14] While Fernandez would later assert that the purpose of the airstrip was to provide defensive support to Costa Rica in the event of an invasion by Nicaragua, this purported objective was a cover story. An airstrip built for these reasons would have been redundant, since the U.S. Army's Southern Command maintained its own airport, with a paved airstrip, only one hour's drive from Santa Elena. In fact, Fernandez told U.S. Army Lt. Col. John Taylor, head of the U.S. Military Group in Costa Rica and a man who had unwittingly discovered the airstrip, that it was Fernandez's project.[15]

## The Resupply Operation

During the first nine months of 1986, Fernandez spent considerable time coordinating the resupply of weapons and ammunition to the contras along the southern front. Through the use of a KL–43—a National Security Agency communication device supplied to Fernandez by North—Fernandez was able to send encoded messages over the telephone to Quintero and North about the supply needs of the contras, flight path information, coordinates for specific air drops, and the overall plan for the enhancement of the southern front.[16]

From January through September 1986, Fernandez communicated with those overseeing the North-Secord operation. Telephone records reveal hundreds of calls between Fernandez and North and Quintero. During calls with Quintero, Fernandez would provide material requirements of the contras (including weapons lists) and would dictate locations for air drops. On a number of occasions, Fernandez postponed or cancelled scheduled drops.[17]

To improve the efficiency of the resupply operation, Fernandez used CIA field personnel. Beginning in August 1986, Fernandez relied on a CIA paramilitary officer to "get the job done."[18] Fernandez would tell the officer to determine coordinates for a drop on a designated date. The officer would then evaluate the best site for the drop, then give the drop coordinates, call signals and bonfire configurations to Fernandez, who would pass this information to Quintero.[19]

Despite Fernandez's later statements that he was a mere conduit for information,[20] Fernandez clearly played an important role in shaping the strategy for the southern front. Fernandez's principal goal was to link the southern front forces with contra troops to the north. Fernandez indicated that he wanted to use systematic placement of air drops to create northward movement of the southern front units.[21] Following the first successful lethal air drop in April 1986, Fernandez sent a KL–43 message to North that stated in part:

> Our plans during next 2–3 weeks includes [sic] air drop at sea for UNO/KISAN [contra] indigenous force area Monkey Point, maritime deliveries NHAO [humanitarian] supplies to same, NHAO air drop to UNO South, but w/ certified air worthy aircraft, lethal drop to UNO South, Negro [Chamorro] visit to UNO South Force with

---

14 Quintero, FBI 302, 11/13/87, pp. 12–13; Quintero, FBI 302, 11/23/87, pp. 15–16; Fernandez, Tower Commission Testimony, 1/28/87, pp. 25–26.

15 Taylor, FBI 302, 1/30/89, p. 5. See also KL–43 Message from Secord to Dutton, 7/29/86, 0360–61 (proposing that Dutton negotiate with Fernandez "re future use" for airstrip); Galvin, FBI 302, 6/13/87, pp. 3–4 (Southern Command unaware of purpose for airstrip).

16 Fernandez, Tower Commission Testimony, 1/28/87, pp. 52–56; Quintero, FBI 302, 11/13/87, p. 14; Quintero, FBI 302, 11/23/87, pp. 5–6; KL–43 Message from Fernandez to North, 3/3/86, AKW 004421; KL–43 Message from Secord to North, 4/9/86, AKW 004416; KL–43 Message from Fernandez to North, 4/12/86, AKW 004410; KL–43 Message from North to Fernandez, 4/15/86, AKW 004409. See also messages cited in n.16 below.

17 Fernandez, Tower Commission Testimony, 1/28/87, pp. 33–34; Quintero, FBI 302, 11/13/87, pp. 13–14. See also these KL–43 messages, all of which involve Fernandez or which report on conversations with Fernandez: Secord to North, 3/24/86, AKW 004419 & 004424; Secord to North, 4/9/86, ALU 003840; Secord to North, 4/16/86, AKW 004408; Secord to North, 4/23/86, AKW 004403; Quintero to Secord, 4/23/86; Secord to North, 5/2/86, AKW 004401; Secord to North, 5/12/86, ALU 003834; Secord to North, 6/2/86, AKW 004393; Secord to North, 7/11/86, 00371; Quintero to Secord, 7/16/86, 00367; Steele to Earl, 8/18/86, 00342; Fernandez to Quintero, 9/2/86, 00308–09; Dutton to Quintero, 9/9/86, 00413; Quintero to Dutton, 9/10/86, 00410; Fernandez to Quintero, 9/10/86, 00414; Dutton to North, 9/17/86, 00423; Fernandez to Quintero, 9/17/86.

18 [Classified Identity Withheld], Grand Jury, 1/20/88, pp. 27–28, 40–41.

19 Ibid., pp. 29–40; SAN JOSE Cable, 12/7/86, DO 166532. On one occasion, Fernandez had the paramilitary officer bring a map bearing drop site coordinates to his home to show to Quintero. ([Classified Identity Withheld], Grand Jury, 1/20/88, pp. 48–50, 58; Quintero, FBI 302, 11/13/87, p. 15.)

20 See, for example, SAN JOSE Cable, 12/7/86, DO 166532; Inspector General Notes, 1/11/87, ER 8820; "Ex-CIA Agent is Bitter Over Iran Affair," The New York Times, 11/27/89, p. A31.

21 [Classified Identity Withheld], Grand Jury, 4/13/88, pp. 8–19.

photogs, UNO newspapers, caps and shirts, and transfer of 80 UNO/FARN recruits now in Costa Rica carrying all remaining cached lethal materiel to join UNO South Force. My objective is creation of 2,500 man force which can strike northwest and link-up with quiche to form solid southern force. Likewise, envisage formidable opposition on Atlantic Coast resupplied at or by sea. Realize this may be overly ambitious planning but with your help, believe we can pull it off.[22]

The need for secrecy regarding Fernandez and North's roles in the resupply operation was emphasized in a KL–43 message from North to Fernandez in June 1986:

We are committed to commencing drops to FDN [contras] by C–7 tomorrow night but can delay for one night to do your drop if we can get the necessary info for the pilots. To facilitate, have asked Ralph [Quintero] to proceed immediately to your location. I do not think we ought to contemplate these operations without him being on scene. Too many things go wrong that then directly involve you and me in what should be deniable for both of us.[23]

As a result of Fernandez's efforts, resupply operations had improved greatly by September 1986. During that month alone, six successful lethal air drops were made along the southern front.[24] The resupply operation came to an abrupt halt in early October 1986, however, when a private benefactor plane carrying, among others, Eugene Hasenfus, was shot down over Nicaragua.

## Investigation and Obstruction

In the aftermath of the downing of the Hasenfus aircraft, Fernandez took steps to erase records of his relationship with North and Quintero. In the Fall of 1986, Fernandez approached Eva Groening, a State Department employee working at the U.S. Embassy in San Jose, and instructed her to remove from the general files all records of his telephone calls. Groening iso-

lated Fernandez's telephone records—which documented the hundreds of calls to North and Quintero—and placed them in a personal safe. When Groening completed her tour in Costa Rica, she did not take these records with her.[25]

Some months after Fernandez arranged to have his telephone records removed from their proper place of storage, Independent Counsel requested these records from the Embassy. They could not be located. The Costa Rican telephone company provided the records to Independent Counsel in August 1988. At trial, these records would have demonstrated that there was frequent contact between Fernandez and North, and Fernandez and Quintero—particularly at the times of attempted resupply flights.

The downing of the Hasenfus airplane and the exposure of secret sales of arms to Iran sparked two official investigations, both of which sought in part to examine the role of the CIA in these operations. One investigation was made by the CIA's inspector general; the other was by the President's Special Review Board, the Tower Commission.

In January and February 1987, Fernandez was interviewed on several occasions by both of these bodies.[26] During these interviews, Fernandez gave false and misleading answers on matters at the core of the investigations. Fernandez provided inaccurate information about his involvement with the airstrip, insisting that it was a Costa Rican initiative to help defend against a Nicaraguan invasion. Fernandez stated that he dealt with Quintero only on the occasions of resupply flights, failing to mention his numerous contacts with Quintero in connection with the construction of the airstrip. Fernandez claimed that he did not know that North had been involved in the resupply network, despite the fact that he had worked with North closely on this very project for nine months. Fernandez also asserted that he did not know that the supplies that he had assisted in delivering to the contras in September 1986 were lethal. Fernandez further denied having ever communicated with Secord—even though he had met with Secord, Quintero and Costa

---

[22] KL–43 Message from Fernandez to North, 4/12/86, AKW 004410.
[23] KL–43 Message from North to Fernandez, 6/16/86, AKW 004389.
[24] SAN JOSE Cable, 9/10/86, DO 72985; SAN JOSE Cable, 9/15/86, DO 73134; SAN JOSE Cable, 9/30/86, DO 77565.

[25] Groening, FBI 302, 1/6/89, pp. 1–3.
[26] Fernandez was interviewed by Tower Commission staff on January 21, 1987. Fernandez testified to the Commission on January 28, 1987. Fernandez was interviewed by the CIA's Office of Inspector General on January 11, January 24, and February 2, 1987.

Rican Security Minister Benjamin Piza in March 1986 to discuss the airstrip—or Felix Rodriguez, even though Fernandez had several conversations with him about the resupply operation.[27]

At the time Fernandez was initially questioned by CIA and Tower Commission investigators, neither Fernandez nor the investigators knew that on some occasions, messages transmitted by the KL–43 machine were printed and retained. Fernandez thus believed that no permanent record of his extensive, ongoing relationship with North and Quintero existed that would disprove his denials of involvement with either the airstrip or the resupply operation. When some of the KL–43 messages were discovered by Tower Commission investigators, Fernandez was forced to concede that he had been untruthful in his responses. On January 28, 1987, Fernandez admitted to the Tower Commission that he had been "less than candid or even misleading" in his answers.[28] Fernandez told the Commission he was "stunned" when he was shown written copies of his KL–43 messages.[29] That led to this exchange:

General Scowcroft: That stunned you in what way? That they existed?

Mr. Fernandez: Yes, that they existed— not in the sense that I was—in the way that the communications between Colonel North and I and Mr. Quintero and I, who was Colonel North's I guess representative, although never defined in that way, were things that were written on this machine. It was all in digital. There were no hard copies—see hard copies—of things. It was sort of startling because, up until that time, I had been recalling everything I had said from memory.[30]

## Pretrial Proceedings

In both the District of Columbia and Virginia proceedings, Fernandez made a number of motions to dismiss the indictments. All of the motions that Fernandez directed at the legal sufficiency of the charges that were adjudicated were denied.

As in *North*, the most significant legal issues raised by Fernandez concerned immunity granted him by Congress in return for his testimony and the protective requirements of *Kastigar* v. *United States*, 406 U.S. 441, 458 (1972), and his demands for classified information. While the court had little difficulty disposing of Fernandez's *Kastigar* challenge, Fernandez's CIPA claims ultimately resulted in dismissal of the case.

## Kastigar

Fernandez argued from the start that his prosecution was barred by *Kastigar* because he had provided testimony to Congress under a grant of immunity. Judge Claude M. Hilton of the Eastern District of Virginia adopted procedures proposed originally by the District of Columbia court and ordered the Government to submit *in camera* and *ex parte* an explanation of Independent Counsel's measures to insulate the *Fernandez* case from Fernandez's immunized congressional testimony.[31] After reviewing the Government's papers, Judge Hilton concluded that there had been no violation of *Kastigar*.[32]

## Classified Information (CIPA)

### Relevancy Hearing

Fernandez filed notices under the Classified Information Procedures Act (CIPA) on May 24, June 23, July 3, and July 7, 1989, that identified the classified information he proposed to disclose at trial. The district court conducted hearings on the notices on July 10, 13, and 14, 1989. On the first day of hearings, over the Government's objection, the district court ruled orally and without written opinion that two broad categories of classified information were material to Fernandez's defense: the operational details of three highly sensitive projects in

[27] Inspector General Notes, 1/11/87, ER 8820–25; Inspector General Notes, 1/24/86, ER 8826–36; Inspector General Notes, 2/2/86, ER 8792–98; Black, Grand Jury, 5/13/88, pp. 9–11, 13–24; Fernandez, Tower Interview, 1/21/87, ALU 3818–20.

[28] Fernandez, Tower Commission Testimony, 1/28/87, p. 5.

[29] Ibid., pp. 3–4. See also Fernandez, Tower Interview, 1/21/87, ALU 3821–26; Bruh, FBI 302, 10/2/87, p. 2 (Fernandez admitted, "You have me and my career is ruined!").

[30] Fernandez, Tower Commission Testimony, 1/28/87, p. 4.

[31] Ibid., pp. 22–23; Memorandum Opinion and Order, *Fernandez*, slip. op. at 4–5 (E.D. Va. June 15, 1989).

[32] Order, *Fernandez* (E.D. Va. June 15, 1989); Memorandum Opinion and Order, *Fernandez* (E.D. Va. July 10, 1989). Unlike North and Poindexter, Fernandez did not give his immunized congressional testimony in open, nationally televised hearings, but in executive session. Thus, dissemination of his immunized testimony was much more limited and therefore posed less of a problem for the trial judge. (Ibid., pp. 5–6.)

Costa Rica, none of which was described or implicated by the indictment or was in any way a part of the Government's case-in-chief; and the identity of three CIA stations or facilities in Central America.

Fernandez argued that he had to introduce documents showing highly classified operational details of the three projects in order to demonstrate the fear of the Costa Rican government of the military threat posed by Nicaragua.[33] Fernandez contended that Costa Rica's concern about Nicaragua, in turn, supported the truth of his statement to the CIA's inspector general that the Santa Elena airstrip—an entirely separate project—too was a Costa Rican initiative to protect itself. The court ruled that evidence establishing the origin, purpose, development and magnitude of these programs was admissible.[34]

The second category of classified information deemed relevant to Fernandez's defense involved the identity of three specific CIA facilities and stations, all of which remain classified. Fernandez argued it was critical that he show the understanding of CIA headquarters and high-ranking CIA officials of the activities of the North-Secord contra-resupply operation. Fernandez argued that the knowledge of CIA officials about these activities made it less probable that he would have lied intentionally about these subjects. The district court determined that Fernandez could identify these stations and facilities.[35]

## Rejection of Substitutions

On July 12, 1989, Independent Counsel moved under CIPA for substitutions for the classified information deemed relevant to Fernandez's defense by the trial court. Along with its motion, Independent Counsel filed affidavits by Assistant Attorney General Edward S.G. Dennis, Jr., and two intelligence officials, which stated that the three projects could not be disclosed without serious injury to national security. They similarly stated that official acknowledgement of the existence of the three disputed CIA facilities would adversely affect national security.[36]

The Government's first proposed substitutions addressed Fernandez's evidence of the three projects in Costa Rica. The court rejected the Government's initial proposal on July 13, 1989—the day after it was offered. The court acknowledged that "[w]e are not talking about details. We are not talking about trying these programs." Nevertheless, the court insisted that Fernandez could "introduce into evidence the fact that they did have other serious ongoing programs." [37] In the court's view, "hard core programs that really shows [sic] that America is doing something other than talking" went directly to Fernandez's defense that the Costa Ricans wanted American involvement with the airstrip. The court suggested that an adequate substitution would show "that there were three or four other specific, substantial programs going on at the same time" as the airstrip.[38]

The Government broadened its proposal on July 14, 1989. The text of the Government's revised substitution is set forth in the Classified Appendix to this Report. The revised substitution conceded, that "Fernandez, as well as other United States Government officials, provided support for these specific projects," and that "[a] substantial amount of Fernandez's time during his tenure as Chief of Station" was spent working on them. The Government was also prepared to concede that the projects

> were all fully discussed in cables and in face to face meetings between . . . Fernandez and CIA Headquarters. Once it was determined that . . . Fernandez, as well as other CIA personnel, would participate in these projects, there was ongoing communication between the Costa Rica Station and Headquarters regarding the implementation, functioning and success of these projects. During the period 1984 through 1986, over forty cables—providing background, operational details, mutual concerns and the results of these important projects—were exchanged between

---

[33] Defendant's Second Notice Pursuant to Section 5 of CIPA, *Fernandez* (E.D. Va. July 3, 1989).

[34] Transcript, Closed CIPA Hearing, Fernandez, 7/10/89, pp. 48–50.

[35] Ibid., pp. 34–40.

[36] Affidavit of Assistant Attorney General Edward S.G. Dennis, Jr., *Fernandez* (E.D. Va. July 12, 1989); Declaration of Deputy Director

for Operations of the Central Intelligence Agency, *Fernandez* (E.D. Va. July 12, 1989); Declaration of [Classified Identity of Agency Director Withheld], *Fernandez* (E.D. Va. July 12, 1989).

[37] Transcript, Closed CIPA Hearing, *Fernandez*, 7/13/89 p. 74.

[38] Ibid., p. 76.

Fernandez and senior CIA officers at Langley, Virginia.

\*       \*       \*

During the period late-1984 through 1986, CIA Headquarters at all times was informed of, and approved, Fernandez's role in these projects. Fernandez's immediate superior was consulted extensively about his work, and senior officers were also familiar with Fernandez's work on these projects.

The day that the Government offered the revised substitution, the district court rejected it. The court ruled that it did not adequately disclose the instigation and magnitude of the programs; that, having been charged with lying about the airstrip operation, Fernandez would be permitted to show "there were three operations that were set up which . . . were set up in the same kind of way, that shows how they were done, the purpose for doing them, who instigated them, and for what purposes. And also the magnitude of them." To do this, Fernandez would be permitted to prove "any and all circumstances of these operations, subject only to my rulings on relevancy of how much detail he needs to go into." [39] In the court's view, Fernandez could "get on the stand and testify to whatever he knows about these three operations, subject only to the relevancy of the amount of detail that I will let him put in. . . . I am ruling that it is all relevant. It is all relevant evidence." [40] Accordingly, the court did not review individual documents, adding:

I suppose every prosecutor would like the proposition of being able to put on their live witnesses and then have a defendant get on the stand and tell his story and only be able to corroborate it with a brief stipulation. . . . I don't believe that the prosecutors should be permitted to do that. I think the defendant ought to have leeway, in order to have a fair trial, to put on that evidence which is relevant to corroborate his defense, and would so rule. [41]

On July 24, 1989, the district court rejected the Government's offer to narrow the indictment to eliminate the charges relating to the airstrip. Judge Hilton stated:

While we did discuss at the previous hearing, reference was made as an example concerning the statement about the airstrip, it really goes broader than that in terms of some allegations as to other meetings and the fact that there may have been or at least the defendant alleges that these programs were overlapping or intertwined.

So, your proposal I don't believe is really any different than before. If it is, that would not be acceptable. [42]

On the separate issue of CIA stations, on July 12, 1989, the Government was prepared to concede this about the stations and facilities in Central America:

1. The CIA maintains a presence in various foreign countries in furtherance of its intelligence collection activities and certain covert operations. The offices the CIA maintains in foreign countries generally are referred to as "stations." In addition, the CIA has other facilities abroad from which it collects intelligence or manages covert operations. These other facilities sometimes are referred to as "facilities" or "bases."

2. In 1984 through 1986, the CIA had stations and facilities in various countries in Latin America.

3. Throughout the period from 1984 to 1986, the CIA had officers and employees working in the countries of [Classified Country Names Withheld]. [43] Certain of these officers and employees worked on matters involving the contras. CIA officers and employees also collected intelligence concerning (a) the activities of the Sandinista regime in Nicaragua, (b) Nicaraguan military activities, (c) the activities of the political leadership of the contras, (d) the contras' military activities, (e) the contras'

---

[39] Transcript, Closed CIPA Hearings, *Fernandez*, 7/14/89, pp. 5–6.
[40] Ibid., pp. 7–8.
[41] Ibid., pp. 9–10, 14.

[42] Trial Transcript, *Fernandez*, 7/24/89, p. 8.
[43] While the names of these countries have been withheld here, the Government would have admitted them at trial had the trial court approved the Government's July 12, 1989, submission.

logistical requirements, (f) the contras' receipt of arms, food, clothing and other materiel, and (g) certain activities of private benefactors who were supplying the contras with lethal and non-lethal aid.

The Government also agreed that Fernandez could refer to "a CIA employee located in [Country Name Withheld]" [44] or "a CIA employee located in [Country Name Withheld]," [45] and that these employees could be described as being familiar with matters such as the operations at [Location Withheld] [46] or the operations of the contras in [Country Name Withheld]. [47] The Government also agreed that a chief of station could be identified as "a senior CIA officer."

On July 13, 1989, the district court rejected the Government's proposed substitution concerning CIA facilities and personnel in Central America. The court insisted that Fernandez was entitled to "divulge the identity of those . . . particular two stations." [48] It held that the substitution would be acceptable, however, if it identified only two CIA stations in Central America. [49]

On July 24, 1989, the Government offered a new proposal on CIA facilities. It agreed that Fernandez could identify the two Central American stations and the CIA facility by means of a key card given to each juror. Witnesses would refer to the stations and the facility by number, but the jurors would know the real location. [50] In this way, while the Government would avoid publicly acknowledging the facilities, the jury would be able to follow in complete detail Fernandez's evidence about them. The district court rejected this proposal without explanation, except to say that it regarded it as a "repeat of what I ruled on better than a week ago." [51]

## The Attorney General's Intervention & Affidavit

After the district court rejected the Government's proposals to eliminate CIPA problems

from *Fernandez,* the Department of Justice moved over the objection of Independent Counsel to intervene, stay the proceedings, and appeal the district court's rulings. The district court summarily rejected the Department's move. [52] The Department then obtained a stay from the U.S. Court of Appeals for the Fourth Circuit, pending appeal. After full briefing and argument, the Fourth Circuit dismissed the Department's appeal on grounds of lack of jurisdiction and lifted its stay. [53] The case was returned to the district court. On November 22, 1989, for the first time in history, Attorney General Richard Thornburgh filed an affidavit under CIPA § 6(e) that barred disclosure at trial of information pertaining either to the three programs or the CIA's disputed stations and facilities. [54]

Facing the prospect of dismissal of the case, Independent Counsel proposed to the district court less severe responses to the Attorney General's affidavit, including a narrowing of the charges to avoid the need for testimony regarding the three CIA programs, and certain findings of fact against the Government. On November 24, 1989, the district court rejected these proposals and entered a dismissal order. The court repeated its view that narrowing the charges would not satisfy the court's ruling that the evidence in question was "essential to this defendant to enable him to defend himself against the charges in this case . . ." [55] The court described the Government's proposals for alternative sanctions as a request "essentially for a rehearing of the rulings previously made in regard to the admissibility and the necessity of the defendant to divulge this information." [56]

## Fourth Circuit Appeal

On September 6, 1990, the Fourth Circuit affirmed Judge Hilton's CIPA rulings and his de-

---

[44] See note 43 above.
[45] See note 43 above.
[46] See note 43 above.
[47] See note 43 above.
[48] Transcript, Closed CIPA Hearing, *Fernandez,* 7/13/89, p. 65.
[49] Ibid., p. 66.
[50] Trial Transcript, *Fernandez,* 7/24/89, p. 5.
[51] Ibid., p. 8.
[52] Ibid., p. 13.
[53] *U.S.* v. *Fernandez,* 887 F.2d 465 (4th Cir. 1989).
[54] Although the existence of the disputed facilities had from time to time been publicly reported, the intelligence agencies and the Attorney General concluded that it would be detrimental to national security if the U.S. Government acknowledged their presence through Government documents or Government witnesses. Independent Counsel attempted to persuade the Attorney General to release the information because of its prior exposure. Independent Counsel was unsuccessful. The Attorney General's decision in *Fernandez* to preclude, pursuant to CIPA § 6(e), the introduction of classified information at trial was not subject to judicial review.
[55] Hearing on Motions, *Fernandez* Transcript, 11/24/89, p. 10.
[56] Ibid.

cision to dismiss with prejudice the indictment against Fernandez. The three-judge appeals panel ruled that Judge Hilton did not abuse his discretion in holding that Fernandez needed to disclose classified information to demonstrate that CIA headquarters was provided "with detailed information about the resupply program, and that CIA headquarters urged . . . encouragement and assistance to the lethal aid resupply network." [57] The court observed:

> All of the charges against Joseph Fernandez concern what he was doing as the CIA station chief in Costa Rica in the mid-1980's, including the nature of his assignments, the persons with whom he worked, and the context in which he carried out certain acts. Because his trial was essentially going to be about the truth of his version of these activities, he must be allowed to tell the jury exactly what he was doing as the CIA's station chief in Costa Rica. The nature of the charges against him demand that he be able to place his job before the jury in a concrete, palpable context, and that he be able to explain his understanding of the world in which he worked. Only against such a background could the jury realistically and fairly evaluate his allegedly false statements.[58]

Following the Fourth Circuit's decision, Independent Counsel invited the Attorney General to reconsider his decision. The Attorney General declined, informing Judge Hilton that there would be "potentially serious damage to national security" from disclosure of the two categories of classified information deemed relevant to Fernandez's defense.[59]

### The Public Nature of the Classified Information

Independent Counsel did not challenge the need to protect the three CIA programs. He was willing to drop the charges to which the programs had been held to pertain. The critical information that would have permitted trial of the other charges was the location of two well-

known CIA stations. Each had been identified in *North*. They were regularly mentioned in the press—even in the obituary of a former station chief. The intelligence agencies' submissions to the Attorney General were not specific enough to rebut this fact. They were general reiterations of the need to preserve "deniability" of well-known facts.

## Conclusion

The Attorney General's actions in *Fernandez* were an unprecedented and unwarranted intrusion into the prosecution of a case conducted by an Independent Counsel. It is clear that the Attorney General's refusal to hear Independent Counsel on the need for continued secrecy, and his decision not to release limited classified information, stemmed solely from his uninformed assessment of the merits of the prosecution, and not from an informed balance of competing policy interests. In a report to Congress dated October 24, 1990, a representative of the Attorney General explained that the Attorney General blocked disclosure of classified information in *Fernandez* because

> those who are familiar with the case assess it as a relatively weak one which would not have been brought had Fernandez been willing to cooperate with the investigation. While a criminal conviction might assist the Independent Counsel in gaining Fernandez's cooperation, other mechanisms are available in the Federal criminal justice system to elicit that cooperation.[60]

In *Fernandez* or any other case prosecuted by an Independent Counsel, it is not up to the Attorney General to assess its merits or its investigative purpose. In fact, although Fernandez's testimony to Congress was immunized and could not have been used against him, the Attorney General must have known that Fernandez admitted to the Select Committees that he had lied to both the Tower Commission and the CIA's Inspector General. Further, in a newspaper interview following Judge Hilton's dismissal of the case, Fernandez stated that he would have incriminated higher-ups in

---

[57] *U.S.* v. *Fernandez*, Top Secret Opinion, p. 29 (4th Cir. 1990).
[58] Ibid., pp. 42–43.
[59] *Fernandez* Notice of Lodging (E.D. Va. Oct. 12, 1990) (filing Letter from James S. Reynolds to Hon. Claude M. Hilton, 10/12/90).

[60] Letter from W. Lee Rawls to Anthony C. Beilenson, 10/24/90, p. 5.

the CIA and other Administration officials had the case gone to trial.[61] It should have been Independent Counsel's decision—not the Attorney General's—whether this evidentiary information should have been developed at trial or by some other means.

---

[61] "Ex-Agent is Bitter Over Iran Affair," *The New York Times*, 11/27/89, p. A31.

# Chapter 21
# CIA Subject #1

CIA Subject #1 was a senior CIA field officer in Central America from 1984 through 1987. His identity as a CIA officer is classified. Independent Counsel learned in early 1987 that CIA personnel under Subject #1's supervision had illegally resupplied the contras. While Independent Counsel determined that Subject #1 was unaware of this activity,[1] other evidence raised questions about his contacts with persons working on behalf of the contra-resupply operation run by Lt. Col. Oliver L. North and retired U.S. Air Force Maj. Gen. Richard V. Secord, and Subject #1's knowledge of these activities.

Subject #1's responses to this evidence were unconvincing. Nevertheless, for the reasons set forth below, Independent Counsel chose in the summer of 1991 not to prosecute Subject #1. This unclassified chapter describes some of the highlights of Subject #1's contacts with the North-Secord Enterprise, his false statements to congressional investigators and Independent Counsel, and Independent Counsel's reasons why he declined to seek an indictment. A more complete version of this chapter is found in the Classified Appendix.

## Subject #1 and the North/Secord Enterprise

### The Honduran Arms Competition

The genesis of the North-Secord effort to help the contras purchase weapons is described elsewhere in this report.[2] The halt to U.S. aid to the contras opened the door to a host of arms dealers.[3] These dealers realized that, since the bulk of the contra forces was in Honduras, an essential element to providing them with weapons was good relations with the government of Honduras. One way the North/Secord Enterprise hoped to obtain Honduran government approval for its services to the contras was through CIA Subject #1.

Secord and his associate Thomas G. Clines, a former CIA agent, knew Subject #1 from their service together in Southeast Asia during the Vietnam War. Clines knew Subject #1 particularly well, as Subject #1 had been Clines's deputy for four years. Clines and Subject #1 remained in contact. They met socially as late as December 1984, when Clines and another former CIA operative, Rafael Quintero, were on a business trip in Mexico City. Subject #1's contacts with Secord and Clines "from the old . . . days" were well known to North, who talked to Secord frequently about Subject #1.[4]

Subject #1 was aware of the post-Boland competition among international arms dealers. Chief among these competitors was Ron Martin, a Miami-based arms dealer who had been the focus of investigation by the Bureau of Alcohol, Tobacco and Firearms for many years, and who at one time had been charged with providing arms illegally to narcotics traffickers. Martin had been approached about selling arms to the

---

[1] See Adkins chapter and Adkins Classified Appendix. Subject #1 may have conveniently forgotten witnessing, however, a confrontation between James L. Adkins and another CIA officer, during which Adkins admitted that he had authorized CIA pilots to ship lethal materials to the Contras. Subject #1 admitted witnessing part of the argument, but never testified that Adkins confessed his wrongdoing.

[2] See Secord and North chapters.

[3] See the Flow of Funds section.

[4] Secord, Grand Jury, 1/25/91, pp. 3–4; Clines, Grand Jury, 4/19/91, p. 26; Secord, OIC Interview, 5/13/87, pp. 105, 113. According to Quintero, the Mexico City meeting occurred because he and Clines had bumped into Subject #1's wife. The men met later with Subject #1. (Quintero, FBI 302, 4/9/91, p. 10; Quintero, Grand Jury, 1/6/88, p. 55.) Subject #1 did not tell Independent Counsel about the Mexico City meeting until well after Quintero first disclosed it. Subject #1 never mentioned that Quintero was with Clines. (CIA Subject #1, FBI 302, 6/24/88, p. 2.)

contras in late 1984 by a former U.S. military attache to Nicaragua, Col. James McCoy. McCoy assured Martin that such sales would have U.S. Government approval.[5]

Over time McCoy and a Honduran-based U.S. national who was working for McCoy, Mario Dellamico,[6] convinced Martin to get into the contra arms market. Martin and McCoy developed a plan to ship a storehouse of weapons into Honduras, where the Honduran government would take possession of them. The contras then could purchase weapons from this supply as they needed. Martin obtained financing for this proposal from Enrique DeValle, the brother of a former Panamanian president. Martin was responsible for purchasing and shipping the weapons; Dellamico's job was to intercede with the Honduran government (that is, the Honduran military) and contra military commander Enrique Bermudez.

Subject #1 became aware of Martin's "Arms Supermarket" by mid-February 1985. CIA officers learned from Calero and others that the Honduran government had agreed to permit an "international arms supplier to establish a stock of ammunition and weapons parts in Honduras upon which the FDN [contras] could draw as needed [on] a cash-and-carry basis." CIA officers further reported that the Honduran government had issued end-user certificates for weapons transactions to the supplier.[7]

## A Meeting in Honduras

By May 1985 the supermarket was worrying the North-Secord Enterprise. A large shipment of arms purchased by the Enterprise in Europe was on board the Danish freighter *Erria* and on its way to Honduras in May 1985 when North noted during a meeting with Secord: "'Martin' setting up munitions 'supermarket' in Tegu[cigalpa]." Intelligence reports a week later stated that the contras were entertaining an offer by "an international arms dealer" to

store a stock of munitions in Honduras, from which contras could make purchases as required. North noted that he had to raise the matter with the contra leadership when they next spoke.[8]

North and Calero met on May 13, 1985. North starred as "to do" items "Check w/ Ron Martin 'Supermarket' being set-up by Aplicano" (a colonel in the Honduran army) and "Secord/Aplicano meeting." [9] North spoke with Secord four days later, noting:

Ron Martin & Mario del Amico (Cuban American) wanted in Guatemala for criminal activity Dealing w/ AUTOMEX in Lisbon & CRADDOCK in U.K.

\*            \*            \*

—Promised to sell weapons thru "supermarket"
—Probably levered by HOAF personnel
—DEFEX people [Secord's suppliers] will not work w/
—MARTIN letter of credit floating all over Lisbon
—Prices from Secord based on adequate lead time.

North further noted this report from Secord, whose "on scene" man in Honduras was Quintero:

View from on scene:

—Mario more & more in picture

\*            \*            \*

—serious logistics problems
—Possible Martin interference w/ Puerto Cortez delivery
—Ship arrives 1 June 85—Danish vessel [10]

After talking with Secord, North phoned Calero. Calero said that a representative of the arms supermarket had quoted him prices on AK–47 and M–16 ammunition. The Honduran military was said to guarantee that the arms supermarket would not "run short." [11] On May

---

[5] Martin, FBI 302, 4/13/92, p. 2. Martin told Independent Counsel that he learned later from Calero and a Honduran military officer that the U.S. Government sanctioned private weapons sales to the contras. Calero told Martin, however, that some U.S. officials disliked Martin. (Ibid., p. 8.)

[6] According to Dellamico, but contrary to many of the transcripts and documents cited in this chapter, this is the correct spelling of his name.

[7] Field Intelligence Report, 2/11/85, DO 94825. This report was disseminated throughout the intelligence community, including the NSC, by Classified Intelligence Report, 2/19/85, DO 181966–64.

[8] North Note, 5/1/85, AMX 000638; Classified Intelligence Report, 5/8/85, DO 175558; North Notebook, 5/9/85, AMX 000658.

[9] Ibid., 5/13/85, AMX 000668.

[10] North Note, 5/17/85, AMX 000679–80.

[11] Ibid.

20, 1985, North noted Calero's assessment that "Supermarket is proceeding." [12]

As Secord and North had discussed, the *Erria* was due at the Honduran port of Puerto Cortes in early June. Clines and Quintero departed for Honduras on May 31, 1985, to meet the vessel. Clines and Quintero were not the only ones, however, who were interested in what was arriving. Ron Martin had heard of the *Erria* from his own sources in Portugal, who said that the Enterprise was selling the contras old equipment at outrageous prices. Sensing an opportunity to shame his rivals, Martin ordered Dellamico to arrange with Col. Aplicano to secure as much paperwork as possible about the *Erria's* cargo. [13]

With the help of the Honduran military, Dellamico boarded the *Erria* shortly after it arrived in Puerto Cortes. Dellamico convinced the *Erria's* captain that he was a representative of the purchasers and obtained a cargo manifest. Dellamico received the papers shortly before Clines and Quintero reached the ship. Clines confronted the captain, who explained that he thought Dellamico worked for Clines. Clines angrily threw Dellamico off the ship. [14]

That same day—witnesses are not sure if it was before or after the fight with Dellamico—Clines and Quintero met with CIA Subject #1. Accounts of the meeting, which Subject #1 denies, differ.

—Quintero testified that as he and Clines were awaiting the arrival of the *Erria*, they heard rumors that a ship carrying weapons had been sunk in the Caribbean. Clines tried to telephone Subject #1 to confirm the story. [15] The *Erria* arrived safely, and

afterwards Subject #1 picked up Quintero and Clines at the Maya Hotel in Tegucigalpa. Subject #1 took them to his residence for lunch. Quintero and Clines asked Subject #1 how they could contact the leaders of the anti-Sandinista Miskito Indians. Subject #1 reportedly advised them not to go to a Miskito encampment at Rus-Rus, but instead contact the leadership in Tegucigalpa. [16] They then discussed the *Erria* shipment, particularly Clines, Quintero, and North's role in it. [17] Quintero recalled asking Subject #1 if the CIA had been reporting on Quintero's many trips to Honduras. Subject #1 replied no, to which Quintero responded, "Fine, that's great, because Oliver North is going to be very happy about knowing that I'm coming here and there are no reports going around that I am doing any work here." Quintero asked Subject #1 for his telephone numbers, which Quintero wrote down in his address book. [18] They then discussed Martin, Dellamico, and Dellamico's relationship with Col. Aplicano. [19]

—Clines corroborated only a few aspects of Quintero's story. According to Clines, Quintero said that he had been advised previously that they should contact Subject #1. Quintero already had Subject #1's phone number. [20] Clines agreed that the three met with Subject #1 at his residence for forty minutes, around noon. Subject #1 acted as if he had met Quintero before. According to Clines, however, the only topic of discussion was where he and Quintero could meet the leadership of the

---

[12] Ibid., 5/20/85, AMX 000687.

[13] Quintero Passport; Martin, FBI 302, 4/13/92, p. 11.

[14] Martin, FBI 302, 4/13/92, p. 11; Clines, Grand Jury, 4/19/91, pp. 27–28; Quintero, FBI 302, 11/13/87, p. 7. Quintero told Independent Counsel that he had first met Dellamico in late April 1985, somewhere near the Guatemalan/Honduran border. Quintero was in Guatemala supervising the first Secord arms shipment to the contras. According to Quintero, Dellamico arrived at the border with a Honduran military officer, who was to take possession of the arms shipment prior to its delivery to the contras. (Quintero, FBI 302, 11/13/87, p. 5.) Dellamico has denied ever meeting Clines or Quintero. (Dellamico, FBI 302, 2/4/92, p. 7.) Martin claims, however, to have learned all that he knows about the *Erria* incident from Dellamico. Martin told Independent Counsel that he used the manifest and other documents that Dellamico took from the *Erria* to try to convince Calero that Secord was "ripping off" the contras. (Martin, FBI 302, 4/13/92, p. 11.)

[15] In the Grand Jury, Quintero testified that Clines's call to Subject #1 came after their lunch meeting with Subject #1, and that Clines actually spoke with him. (Quintero, Grand Jury, 1/6/88, p. 61.)

[16] According to Quintero, he and Clines contacted the Tegucigalpa office, only to learn that Indian leader Wycliffe Diego was in Miami. (Ibid., pp. 62–63.)

[17] In a 1991 interview with Independent Counsel, however, Quintero said that he and Clines did not discuss contra resupply with Subject #1, although Quintero "assumed" Subject #1 knew about it. (Quintero, FBI 302, 4/9/91, p. 9.)

[18] In 1991, however, Quintero said that Clines gave him Subject #1's telephone number. (Ibid., p. 11.)

[19] Quintero, FBI 302, 11/13/87, pp. 6–7; Ibid., 12/28/87, pp. 4–5; Ibid., 4/9/91, pp. 9–10; Quintero, Grand Jury, 1/6/88, pp. 54–63; Quintero, North Trial Testimony, 3/2/89, pp. 2982–86.

[20] Quintero's telephone records reveal several calls to Subject #1. Quintero could not recall why he made the telephone calls, or if he reached Subject #1. (Quintero, FBI 302, 12/28/87, p. 5.)

Miskito Indians.[21] Clines testified that they did not discuss contra resupply with Subject #1, as Clines wanted to "keep [Subject #1] out of trouble" with the Boland Amendment.[22]

On June 5, 1985, CIA field officers reported that the Honduran military backed the arms supermarket. This report, which was placed into an intelligence memorandum sent to North the next day, valued the arms destined for the supermarket at $17 million. CIA field officers said that a Honduran military official had discussed the proposal with Calero, and that Calero had provided a list of weapons that the Supermarket should carry. CIA field officers concluded that the arrangement "should help solve the problem [the contras] are now having with the time lag between the ordering and subsequent delivery of munitions."[23]

## A Meeting in Virginia

The North-Secord Enterprise's frustration with how the contras spent their money prompted North to call a meeting of Secord, Clines, Quintero, Calero and Enrique Bermudez in Miami in late June 1985. During the meeting, North noted:

—Supermarket

   —Honduran E.U.C.'s
   —L & M Equipment
   —del Amico
   —Martin [24]

After the meeting, which Secord described as a "watershed" for him, North asked Secord to set up his own private airlift operation to benefit the contras. Starting this operation occupied Secord throughout the summer and early fall of 1985.[25]

In setting up his private airlift service for the contras, Secord met with CIA Subject #1.

On July 11, 1985, North was told by Alan D. Fiers, Jr., Subject #1's superior as chief of the CIA's Central American Task Force (CATF), that Subject #1 was in town and that he would call North that evening. New intelligence reports revealed that a shipment of 1,300 tons of arms from Poland had arrived in Honduras for the supermarket. These reports indicated that another shipment was due in August, and that while contra commander Enrique Bermudez was "dubious" about the supermarket concept, the supermarket's terms and prices sounded to Bermudez "almost too good to be true."[26]

As Fiers promised, Subject #1 called North on the evening of July 11. North wrote down Subject #1's local telephone number, then noted:

—passed # to Dick

Subject #1 met with Secord, Clines, and Quintero at Secord's home the next day. While Secord is unsure whether Clines or North told him that Subject #1 was in town, Secord was certain that North set up the meeting.[27]

The witnesses to the July 12, 1985, meeting at Secord's home gave different accounts of what was discussed.

   —Clines described the meeting as very brief, lasting no more than a few minutes. Clines said he was not privy to the entire conversation and did not recall hearing about the contras. Clines could not recall even if Quintero was there.[28]

---

[21] According to Clines, Subject #1 said that the Miskito leaders were not in Honduras, but rather were in Miami. Compare with n.16 above.
[22] Clines, Grand Jury, 4/19/91, pp. 28–33.
[23] CIA Cable, 6/5/85, DO 94828–26; Memorandum from George, 6/6/85, AKW 22961–64. CIA officers further noted that the Honduran military was expecting a cut of the supermarket's profits or "a good deal" on its own munitions purchases in return for granting Martin his "franchise. . . ." (CIA Cable, 6/5/85, DO 94828–26.)
[24] North Note, 6/28/85, AMX 000820.
[25] Secord, OIC Interview, 4/29/87, pp. 31–38; Secord, Select Committees Testimony, 5/5/87, pp. 164–69; Secord, Grand Jury, 1/16/91, pp. 7–9; Quintero, Grand Jury, 1/6/88, pp. 66–75.

[26] Secord, OIC Interview, 4/29/87, pp. 37–38; Secord, Select Committees Testimony, 5/5/87, pp. 168–69; Secord, Grand Jury, 1/16/91, p. 9; Quintero, Grand Jury, 1/6/88, pp. 73–75; CIA Subject #1 Travel Records; CIA Cable, 7/9/85, DO 178759; CIA Cable, 7/9/85, DO 107993, DO 108034; CIA Field Intelligence Report, 7/10/85, DO 181999–98; CIA Information Report, Subject: Scheduled Arrival in Honduras of Arms Shipment from Poland for the Nicaraguan Democratic Force, 7/22/85, DO 175398–96; CIA Field Intelligence Report, 7/10/85, DO 107991–90. CIA headquarters directed its officers in Central America to find out more about the Supermarket shipments. (DIRECTOR 447814, 7/11/85, DO 178758; DIRECTOR 448583, 7/11/85, DO 178757.)
[27] North Note, 7/11/85, AMX 001222; CIA Subject #1, FBI 302, 5/16/91, p. 5; Secord, FBI 302, 2/26/88, pp. 2–3; Secord, Grand Jury, 1/25/91, pp. 8–11. Quintero says that Secord told him at the time that North had set up the meeting. (Quintero, Grand Jury, 1/6/88, pp. 83–87; Quintero, North Trial Testimony, 3/2/89, pp. 2986–87.) North's secretary wrote "Secord [CIA Subject #1]" in the 7:00 am to 10:00 am slot on North's appointment calendar for July 12, 1985. (North Calendar, 7/12/85, AKW 003872.)
[28] Clines, Grand Jury, 4/19/91, pp. 34–35.

—Secord recalled the meeting more vividly, saying he told Subject #1 that he "wanted to get a handle" on what was happening in Honduras. They discussed the general tactical situation of the contra war, the extent of Honduran government support for the contras, and how best to ensure effective private deliveries to the contras ("a common theme," according to Secord, since the June 1985 Miami meeting).[29]

—Quintero corroborated Secord. Quintero said that Secord had called him in Miami and told him to come to Washington. Quintero and Clines went with Secord to meet with Subject #1. The meeting was short but friendly, revolving around the contras and events in Honduras. One topic was how Martin and Dellamico were working with the Honduran government to block Secord from selling and airlifting weapons to the contras.[30] Subject #1 said that he had spoken with North about Martin and the Honduran problem, but that he did not want to assist Secord in solving it.[31]

Secord reported the meeting to North later the same day. North's notes corroborate Secord and Quintero's version of the meeting:

—mtg. tonight w/Dick/Rafael/Tom w/ Romero FDN Log Chief

—[CIA Subject #1] discussions re Supermarket
   —HO Army plans to seize all mat'l when supermarket comes to a bad end
   —$14M to finance came from drugs

—[Subject #1] expects HOAF to seize the supermarket's assets when the supermarket folds.
—[Subject #1] likes light A/C [aircraft] ASAP
   Doesn't like goons [slang term for C–47]
   Should get CASA 212's [32]

## Watching the Arms Supermarket

Subject #1's actions subsequent to the July 12, 1985 meeting are consistent with Quintero's characterization of him as an intelligence officer who was unwilling to side either with the Enterprise or the Supermarket in their rivalry. Subject #1 returned to Central America and secretly recounted to Fiers later that he would begin collecting more intelligence about the supermarket. Subject #1 further passed on his understanding that the contras were about to make their first purchases from Martin:

My concern is the source of the funds for the Supermarket (10 to 14 million USD). We cannot conceive that the backers of this program are doing it for patriotic or altruistic reasons and we hope UNO/FDN leader[s]hip will exercise prudence and conduct an in-de[p]th check of sources of the financial backing before becoming involved.[33]

Subject #1's subsequent reports reflected the CIA's concerns that Martin and McCoy had an "unsavory past," but Subject #1 did not attempt to exploit this anxiety to the Enterprise's advantage.[34]

Cables from the Fall of 1985 support the view that Subject #1 was honestly monitoring, rather than choosing sides in, the supermarket/Enterprise competition. Fiers cabled Subject #1 on September 17, 1985, that Calero urgently needed to know more about the supermarket, as Calero was "under increasingly in-

---

[29] Secord, FBI 302, 2/26/88, pp. 2–3; Secord, Grand Jury, 1/25/91, pp. 8–10.

[30] Secord told Independent Counsel that at this time, Calero had been saying that Martin was pressuring him to buy arms from the supermarket. "I believe that starting about August of '85 a number of desperate groups started focusing on me and my men as great threats, one was Ron Martin and his group. They saw me and my group as a threat to their business which we weren't even aware of." Mario Dellamico "was seen by all of us—that means Clines, Secord, Quintero—as hostile to our interests. . . ." (Secord, OIC Interview, 4/29/87, pp. 55–56; Secord, Grand Jury, 1/16/91, pp. 40, 54–56, 70; Secord, Grand Jury, 1/25/91, pp. 52–53.)

[31] Quintero, FBI 302, 12/28/87, p. 6; Quintero, FBI 302, 4/9/91, pp. 9–10; Quintero, Grand Jury, 1/6/88, pp. 83–87; Quintero, *North Trial Testimony*, 3/2/89, pp. 2986–87. Quintero provided other details that are presented in the Classified Appendix.

[32] North Note, 7/12/85, AMX 001225.

[33] CIA Cable, 8/29/85, DO 94841. By late August 1985, North's interest in Martin and McCoy had flared once again. He may have prompted CATF to run traces on the men. (North Note, 8/28/85, AMX 001341; DIRECTOR 511129, 8/28/85, DO 94835; CIA Cable, 8/29/85, DO 94837.) On August 30, 1985, North noted information similar to what had been reported by DO 94837. (North Note, 8/30/85, AMX 001343.) See also CIA Cable, 8/30/85, DO 94843 (confirming DO 94837 and reporting on ATF investigation of Martin's operations).

[34] All of the examples of this conduct are classified and are thus set forth in the Classified Appendix.

tense pressure'' from Bermudez and others ''to avail himself of . . . the warehouse.'' Subject #1 suggested that Calero question the supermarket's backers himself. Calero did just that, prompting Martin and McCoy to offer to fly a CIA representative to Panama City to meet ''the banker financing the supermarket transaction and to examine the paperwork.''[35]

Calero reported his discussions with Martin and McCoy to Subject #1 on September 27, 1985. Subject #1 relayed Calero's information via special channels to Fiers. Subject #1 argued against accepting Martin's invitation to examine the supermarket's records: ''There is no advantage for [CIA] to get involved in anything like this nor do we wish to be seen as the approval mechanism on whether or not [Calero] buys from Martin.'' Subject #1 recognized, however, that Calero wanted to buy from Martin. Subject #1 wrote that Martin's

> prices are good, the credit terms excellent and the material newer and in better condition than that UNO/FDN [contras] has received from other sources. [Calero] wants to be told if [U.S. Government] has any information that would make his involvement with the Supermarket an unwise decision. [Calero] will hold back on purchases until he hears . . . but he has to make some move soon.

The CIA ended up making no recommendation to Calero about the supermarket, and Calero purchased weapons from it.[36]

## Subject #1 and 1986 Resupply Activities

Subject #1's agnosticism towards the arms supermarket and the North-Secord Enterprise

manifested itself in an incident that occurred in February 1986—an episode that made Subject #1 aware of a link between the two resupply operations in the persons of Dellamico and Felix Rodriguez. Subject #1 had met Rodriguez in the early 1980s. Subject #1 later claimed that he and Rodriguez had a falling-out in 1984, shortly before Rodriguez headed to El Salvador, and never spoke again. Evidence from as early as January 1985 suggests, however, that Subject #1 kept aware of Rodriguez's activities.[37]

## Subject #1 and NHAO #4 Transshipment

In September 1985, Subject #1 and other CIA field personnel began assisting a new U.S. Government humanitarian assistance program for the contra rebels. Sponsored by the State Department's Nicaraguan Humanitarian Assistance Office (NHAO), the new aid was to travel from the United States directly to Honduras, to be shipped overland to contra bases. Unfortunately, excessive press coverage of the first NHAO mission to Honduras soured the Honduran Government on the program and resulted in a temporary ban on NHAO flights into Honduras.[38]

The halt to NHAO flights began in mid-October 1985. After a series of official visits from persons including North, National Security Adviser John M. Poindexter, U.S. Ambassador to Honduras John Ferch, and Subject #1,[39] the Honduran government eventually agreed to allow NHAO-sponsored flights to resume over

---

[35] DIRECTOR 534371, 9/17/85, DO 94859; CIA Cable, 9/18/85, DO 94860; CIA Cable, 9/27/85, DO 94864. Calero called North a few days after meeting Martin with a full report. North noted:
—Martin said that Calero has created probs w/ weaps
—''Damned ship is not mine''
—preoccupied—believes that [Calero] has screwed up the supermarket.
—says he has someone who has invested heavily + bank support.
—Says he wants to see [CIA Subject #1]. Take him to Panama to show him paperwork.
—Says he has a valid contract w/ Honduran Govt.
(North Note, 9/24/85, AMX 001773.)
[36] CIA Cable, 9/27/85, DO 94864; Calero, FBI 302, 6/10/91, pp. 5–6. Subject #1 shared his views about the Supermarket with U.S. Government personnel in Honduras. (See, for example, Comee, FBI 302, 5/17/91, pp. 10–12.)

[37] CIA Subject #1, FBI 302, 5/16/91, pp. 1–2. North noted, for example, during a trip to Honduras in late January 1985 (emphasis in original):
*Discussion w/ [Subject #1]*
La Quinta, Las Vegas,
—FDN Air Arm
—Felix too involved w/ Alvarez
—Not enough money to do what's needed
—Parachutes.
(North Note, 1/30/85, AMX 000409.)
[38] CIA Cable, 10/10/85, DO 22975; CIA Cable, 10/16/85; CIA Cable, 10/16/85, ER 33056–57; DIRECTOR 584237, 10/23/85; CIA Cable; CIA Cable, 10/24/85, DO 22976; CIA Cable, 10/25/85, DO 2298; CIA Subject #1, FBI 302, 5/16/91, pp. 4–5.
[39] CIA Subject #1 Travel cables; CIA Subject #1, Select Committees Deposition, 4/25/87, pp. 94–105; CIA Subject #1, FBI 302, 5/16/91, p. 11; CIA Cable, 11/9/85; CIA Cable, 11/11/85, DO 22983; CIA Cable, 11/13/85, DO 7409; CIA Cable, 11/15/85; CIA Cable, 11/16/85; CIA Cable, 11/18/85, DO 22984; CIA Cable, 11/20/85, DO 7443; CIA Cable, 11/21/85, DO 7451; CIA Cable, 11/27/85, DO 7475; CIA Cable, 12/2/85; DIRECTOR 637248, 12/2/85, DO 7488; North Notebook, 12/13/85, AMX 001933–34; CIA Cable, 12/13/85, DO 8527; CIA Cable, 12/17/85, DO 8544; CIA Cable, 12/17/85, DO 8545.

Honduran airspace—provided that the flights originated from El Salvador.[40]

NHAO worked to mount the first in the new series of flights—embarking from the United States to Ilopango air base in El Salvador, and then crossing to contra bases in Honduras—in January 1986. CIA officers in Central America were charged with obtaining clearances for these flights from the Honduran military. As a result, CIA officers in Central America began learning about the contractors who were making NHAO's deliveries—some of whom were delivering lethal supplies for the North-Secord operation. In seeking clearances for the first drop, proposed for the contra base at Yamales, field officers reported their concern that a "possible conflict in aircraft use" could jeopardize it. Officers said that another Honduran project was using "an L–100 . . . , operated by Dick ((Gadd)), who in turn gets his aircraft from Southern Air in Miami." Gadd, an associate of Secord, was known by CIA field personnel to be a NHAO contractor. CIA field personnel feared that if Gadd used the NHAO mission as a way to lessen his expenses on the other project, the Hondurans would get angry. The drop to Yamales was eventually cancelled, at the Hondurans' insistence.[41]

## Rodriguez and Dellamico

By late January 1986 CIA personnel in Central America, including those closest to Subject #1, recognized a second American citizen, Felix Rodriguez, in NHAO and private lethal resupply efforts. CIA field personnel had been asked in late January to facilitate the movement of contra logistics officers to Ilopango air base and to set up a contra communications network linking Honduras and El Salvador. CIA headquarters complained that CIA officers closest to Subject #1 were responding slowly. CIA officers closest to Subject #1 tried to put the blame elsewhere:

[Officers] believe additional confusion being introduced into San Salvador scenario by Felix ((Rodriguez)), who has somehow become involved in the San Salvador end of the NHAO system. He reportedly was the person who receipted for the NHAO shipment to Ilopango, and he has become involved in conflict with both UNO/FDN [contra] air force commander Col Juan ((Gomez)) and UNO/FDN San Salvador logistics chief Lopez by insisting that all matters relating to the Ilopango logistics system be channelled through him. According to Col Gomez, Rodriguez implied that he was employed by [CIA] without actually saying so. . . .

Other field personnel warned that, in fact, logistics officer Lopez was being "dominated" by Rodriguez and the Chief of the U.S. Military Group in El Salvador, U.S. Army Col. James Steele.[42]

Ten days later, CIA officers closest to Subject #1 reported that the Hondurans finally had granted permission for resumption of contra resupply flights. CIA officers expected the flights would begin promptly, and were stumped when they learned that Lopez had been told to stop work on the first load. CIA officers closest to Subject #1 suspected Rodriguez. Fiers soon announced that he would travel to Honduras and

40 CIA Cable, 12/20/85, DO 8556; AMEMB TEGUCIGALPA 17411, 12/20/85, ALW 30596–602; DIRECTOR 665928, 12/21/85, DO 8572; DIRECTOR 667352, 12/24/85. Subject #1 grudgingly provided testimony on this subject to Congress in 1987. (CIA Subject #1, Select Committees Deposition, 4/25/87, pp. 32–36.)

41 CIA Subject #1, FBI 302, 4/9/87; DIRECTOR 683461, 1/9/86; DIRECTOR 685439, 1/10/86; CIA Cable, 1/10/86; CIA Cable, 1/10/86, DO 84692; DIRECTOR 687081, 1/10/86; CIA Cable, 1/13/86, DO 20034. See also DIRECTOR 691558, 1/15/86, DO 39668 (advising that Gadd will move supplies for NHAO from cancelled Yamales drop, and has arranged for construction of Butler buildings at Ilopango).

Subject #1 denied knowing the background of the cables discussing Gadd when questioned about them in 1987. (CIA Subject #1, OIC Interview, 8/28/87, pp. 102–3.) Other cables suggest that personnel other than Subject #1 may have been close to the situation. (See, for example, CIA Cable, 1/15/86, DO 83565; CIA Cable, 1/18/86, DO 83567–66.) Subject #1's deputy believed he may have been the first senior official in the region to learn of Gadd's activities, although the deputy told Independent Counsel that DIRECTOR 687081 should have been sufficiently important to CIA Subject #1 for him to know what Gadd was doing in Honduras. (Field Deputy, FBI 302, 6/7/91, pp. 7–8.)

For other cables about Gadd's activities in Honduras, see DIRECTOR 760645, 3/3/86; and CIA Cable, 3/3/86, DO 103566 (proposal to use Gadd to erect warehouses at Aguacate); CIA Cable, 3/10/86; CIA Cable, 3/11/86, DO 103566; CIA Cable, 3/12/86, DO 85474; DIRECTOR 778444, 3/14/86, DO 177472 (squabble among CIA field personnel over the unannounced appearance of "NHAO communications specialist" described as a Gadd employee); DIRECTOR 780844, 3/15/86, DO 11534; CIA Cable, 3/17/86; DIRECTOR 803080, 3/29/86; CIA Cable, 4/1/86, DO 85492; DIRECTOR 807942, 4/2/86, DO 85493; CIA Cable, 4/3/86, DO 85494 (CIA field activities in arranging contra-sponsored drops of lethal and non-lethal supplies to contra forces on

the Nicaraguan "Southern Front;" Gadd mentioned as NHAO and private benefactor contractor).

42 CIA Cable, 1/18/86, DO 83567–66; CIA Cable, 1/23/86, DO 84696; CIA Cable, 1/24/86, DO 10534; CIA Cable, 1/24/86, DO 10545; DIRECTOR 706924, 1/25/86, DO 10548; CIA Cable, 1/25/86, DO 39672; CIA Cable, 1/27/86, DO 39675. See also CIA Cable, 1/27/86, DO 39676 (reporting from Col. James Steele that a January 26 NHAO flight was arranged by a contact of Rodriguez).

El Salvador to consult with officers about NHAO transshipment operations.[43]

Fiers went first to Honduras to cement an agreement on obtaining clearances of NHAO flights. He then traveled to Ilopango air base, where he witnessed the loading of a Southern Air Transport C–130 with supplies for the contras. Concerned that the flight would upset the new American-Honduran rapprochement, Fiers went to Rodriguez's quarters at Ilopango and persuaded North to have him cancel the flight.[44]

Or so Fiers thought. Two days later, CIA officers closest to Subject #1 reported that Rodriguez attempted to make a second end-run around the official clearance system—this time, with the help of Mario Dellamico:

> It appears that the private citizen in San Salvador [45] who was sowing confusion on the question of a C–130 flight to Honduras did not give up easily. While we have not established the time of day of the request, during the day on 9 Feb he did contact his counterpart in Tegucigalpa, [Mario Dellamico], and requested that clearance for the L–100 be obtained. [Dellamico] met with Honduran Army Commander Col Thumann morning of 10 Feb, without having discussed the subject with any other interested party in Honduras, and subsequently appeared at UNO/FDN Directorate house saying he had obtained clearance for the aircraft and needed to travel to San Salvador immediately to coordinate the flight from that end. Per Col Thumann's office, no such approval was granted, and Hondurans had merely agreed to consider the subject, somewhat reluctantly and based on appeals by [Dellamico] that were

not necessarily true. This situation has been corrected.[46]

By February 14, 1986, contra shipments from Ilopango to Aguacate had resumed. CIA personnel reported to the Central American Task Force that "[t]he role of the now infamous local 'private American citizen' has been reduced to that of an 'on-looker' at the NHAO/UNO/FDN warehouse at Ilopango." [47]

CIA Subject #1 denied hearing anything about Rodriguez's private resupply activities until October 1986. In a May 1991 interview, Subject #1 explained his ignorance of repeated mentions of Rodriguez in field cable traffic by insisting that other field personnel wrote the cables and were more knowledgeable of the resupply operation.[48] Subject #1's excuse is unconvincing. First, as is clear from the events of 1985, Subject #1 was the CIA officer in the area most knowledgeable of Dellamico's activities in Honduras.[49] Subject #1 also knew that Dellamico had high contacts in the Honduran military—specifically, with Col. Thumann—and that he was a friend of Rodriguez.[50] Second, Subject #1 was heavily involved in trying to persuade the Honduran government to allow resumption of NHAO resupply operations—a critical U.S. objective in early 1986.

The most telling evidence of Subject #1's contemporaneous knowledge of the Rodriguez/Dellamico clearance incident is, however, a contemporaneous KL–43 message from North to Secord. The message states in part:

> Regarding the El Salvador problem, we may have created one of our own with Maximo [Felix Rodriguez's alias]. While our L–100 was on the ground in El Sal he apparently called to Mario Del Amico . . . and asked Del Amico to go to the general staff to get flight clearance from Ilopango to Aguacate. Thumann, the Hon-

---

43 CIA Cable, 2/7/86, DO 84703; CIA Cable, 2/8/86, DO 178737.

44 For a more complete account of Fiers's confrontation with Rodriguez, see Fiers chapter.

45 According to Fiers, he instructed CIA personnel in Central America during his February 1986 trip to keep Rodriguez's name out of CIA cables. (See Fiers chapter.) CIA field personnel thus began using phrases like "private citizen in San Salvador" as euphemisms for Rodriguez. For an example of an exchange among CIA field personnel (not including Subject #1, who was in Miami) that reflects an understanding of the meaning of this euphemism, see CIA Cable, 2/28/86, DO 85445; CIA Cable, 3/1/86, DO 85451; CIA Cable, 3/2/86, DO 103559.

46 CIA Cable, 2/11/86, DO 10987. This cable raised Fiers' temperature. (See DIRECTOR 731090, 2/11/86 (report "disturbing").) See also CIA Cable, 2/15/86, DO 11038; CIA Cable, 2/15/86 (reporting angry reaction of a contra leader).

47 CIA Cable, 2/14/86, DO 101121.

48 Some CIA cables do suggest that Subject #1's deputy was heavily involved in discussions with the Honduran government about clearances. (See, for example, CIA Cable, 2/19/86, DO 11062; CIA Cable, 2/27/86, DO 85443–42.)

49 See Classified Appendix.

50 CIA Subject #1, FBI 302, 5/16/91, p. 6.

duran Chief of Staff—who had just cleared the FDN C–47 flight clearances[—]told Del Amico that he would quote consider the request unquote. Thumann then called [CIA Subject #1] and asked him what the hell was going on since he—Thumann—was reluctant to give any clearances at all but that [Subject #1] had brought enough pressure to bear with [Subject #1] that he—Thumann—had no choice and now Del Amico was asking for more before the first flight of the C–47 had even taken place. [Subject #1] told Thumann—without checking with Fiers—to stand down on the Del Amico request and that Del Amico might well be a close friend of Calero but he was no friend of ours. . . . The bottom line is that Felix has once again exceeded his mandate and has dissembled with us—or at least allowed himself to hear from Del Amico that the L–100 was cleared. I have no reason to disbelieve [Subject #1] and find the story about Amico to be plausible.[51]

North's account of the Dellamico/Rodriguez "end run," which describes Subject #1 as a knowledgeable witness, is corroborated by the former U.S. military adviser to Honduras, Col. William C. Comee. Colonel Comee told Independent Counsel in May 1991 that he was in frequent contact with Subject #1 during February 1986. According to Comee, Subject #1 was very upset by the "end run" around the CIA's clearance system—not because a private resupply flight was involved, but rather because it ruffled the delicate Honduran relationship.[52]

---

[51] Secord, OIC Interview, 5/13/87, pp. 118–19; KL–43 Message from North to Secord, AQT 000002. The KL–43 message refers to upcoming talks between Fiers and Gadd. Independent Counsel's evidence is that these meetings occurred on February 12, 1986. See Fiers chapter.

[52] Comee, FBI 302, 5/17/91, pp. 2–3. See also CIA Cable, 4/24/86, DO 177531, DO 83790; CIA Cable, 4/26/86, DO 3792 (attributing resupply confusion to "local contractors" identified as Rodriguez and Quintero).

Independent Counsel was unable to prove another Boland violation attributed to Subject #1 in a later North KL–43 message. In early April 1986, the North-Secord Enterprise arranged for another L–100 cargo plane to drop lethal supplies to contra forces operating on the Nicaraguan "southern front." Preparations for this drop were at their peak on April 10–12, 1986. Prior to the drop, North sent a KL–43 message to Secord that stated that Subject #1 would be assembling supplies at the contra base at Aguacate and moving them to Ilopango Air Base in time for the L–100's mission. (KL–43 Message, from North to Secord, 4/86.) To the best of Secord's knowledge, however, Subject #1 played no part in the L–100 mission and did not assemble materials at Aguacate. Subject #1's travel records confirm that he was

## Subject #1's False Statements

### Meetings With Quintero, Secord, and Clines

Subject #1 first testified that he had no contact with Quintero, Secord and Clines between 1984 and 1987. The FBI Form 302 of an interview Subject #1 gave on April 9, 1987, to agents assigned to Independent Counsel states: "[CIA Subject #1] advised that during his assignment in [Central America] he had no contact with the following people: Richard Secord . . . and Thomas Clines." Subject #1 did indicate that one source of supplies for the contras was the supermarket managed by Martin. Subject #1 stated that he never met Martin, however, "and the CIA was told to stay away from him." [53] But on April 25, 1987, in a deposition for the Select Committees, Subject #1 admitted that he had met Secord and Clines:

Q: Richard Secord. What knowledge do you have of this individual?

A: Oh, I knew Richard Secord for a number of years.

Q: Let's say after 1984, the beginning of 1984. Have you seen Secord?

A: Yes.

*             *             *

Q: What was the nature of that contact?

A: *Well, I ran into him. I'm not sure how it occurred.* But he invited me to stop by his place for a cup of coffee. I'm not sure if it was '84 or '85. And I did.

Q: That was his home?

A: Yes.

*             *             *

---

out of Central America at the time. Secord admitted, however, that Subject #1's subordinates occasionally interceded with contra leaders in the north to free up supplies for the Southern Front—an apt description of what the Enterprise accomplished with its April L–100 flight. (Secord, Grand Jury, 1/25/91, pp. 17–18; Secord, Select Committees Testimony, 5/6/87, p. 147; CIA Subject #1, OIC Interview, 8/28/87, pp. 107–11; CIA Subject #1 Travel Cables.)

[53] CIA Subject #1, FBI 302, 4/9/87, pp. 1–2. The special agents' handwritten notes are consistent with the Form 302 prepared following their interview with Subject #1. One agent noted specifically: "Tom Clines—never in Hond [Honduras]."

Q: Did he have any specific reason to see you at that time?

A: *It was more just shooting the breeze, as I recall.*

Q: Did he make any statements, to your recollection, that would indicate that he was involved in private support to the contras?

A: *No.*

Q: Did he give you any reason to believe that he sought something or sought some assistance from you with respect to that?

A: *No. No, sir.*

\*     \*     \*

Q: When is the last time you saw Mr. Clines?

A: It was at Secord's house.

Q: At that same function?

A: Yes.

Q: Did Secord or Clines explain why they were together at that time?

A: No, they did not.

Q: Was this a family function?

A: It was just in the morning.

Q: Just the three of you?

A: *And Secord's wife.*

Q: Did Clines give you any reasons to believe that he was involved in Central American-related things?

A: *No.*

\*     \*     \*

Q: Do you recall the nature of the discussion you did have at that time?

A: *No, I don't. It was just a general how are you doing type of thing. Have a cup of coffee.*

Q: How long did that last?

A: Forty-five minutes, an hour at the most.

Subject #1 continued to deny having met Quintero.[54]

Subject #1 was called before a federal Grand Jury on June 5, 1987. Subject #1 once again denied knowing Quintero. He acknowledged meeting Secord and Clines once in 1985, but he claimed not to recall how the meeting came about.

Q: What went on at the meeting, do you know?

A: He just asked how I was doing, how things were going—basically that's it— what's the situation we're fighting in Nicaragua? Nothing memorable, actually.

Q: Were they asking you or you asking them?

A: They're asking me. It was more just a chat—how ya' been? Haven't seen you in a long time.

Q: When did you first become aware, if ever, that [C]lines had a business relationship with Secord.

A: *I didn't know he had a business relationship with Secord.* I just thought they were personal friends from back in those days in the late sixties.

Q: Did you ever become aware that they had a relationship?

A: *Not until this most recent stuff that's come out.*

Q: What about General Secord. When did you become aware that he had an involvement in Central America and supplying the Contras?

A: *I don't know. I guess when it came out in the press, frankly.*

Q: In other words, in '87?

A: *Whenever that was, yes.*

\*     \*     \*

---

[54] CIA Subject #1, Select Committees Deposition, 4/25/87, pp. 76–79, 81 (emphasis added). Subject #1 was questioned by counsel for the minority of the Senate Select Committee. Statements by counsel during the deposition indicate that Subject #1 had advance notice of some of the questions.

Q: Did you know of the relationship, or did Colonel North ever advise you of the relationship between North and Secord?

A: *Negative.*

\*          \*          \*

Q: Did you have any knowledge of Oliver North's involvement in fund raising or in providing materials [for the contras]?

A: *No, I did not.*

\*          \*          \*

Q: When Secord had you over to his house . . . was he having you over because you are old friends, or was he having you over to, essentially, probe for information?

A: *I assumed he was having me over because we are old friends. Or I knew him from the old days.* That may have not been the case, of course, now. That's what I assumed.[55]

Independent Counsel interviewed Subject #1 again in June 1988 about his contacts with the North-Secord Enterprise. During that interview, Subject #1 admitted for the first time that he and his wife had met Clines (but not Quintero) in Mexico City sometime in 1984. As for the July 1985 meeting, Subject #1 said that either Secord had telephoned him or they had run into each other. Subject #1 admitted that he was close to North, but denied ever giving Clines or Quintero his telephone numbers. The FBI agent who attended the interview noted:

[CIA Subject #1] did not recall discussing Contra resupply in Honduras with Secord, Clines, or North. He did not recall meeting with Secord or Clines to discuss setting up a Contra resupply operation or obtaining Honduran flight clearances for such an effort. . . . As far as [Subject #1] knew, Clines was not involved in purchasing weapons for the Contras.[56]

Subject #1 was interviewed one last time by Independent Counsel in May 1991. Subject #1

continued to deny (1) knowing as early as 1985 that Clines was involved in weapons shipments to the contras, (2) ever meeting Quintero, or meeting Quintero and Clines in Honduras (although he confirmed that the Miskito Indians had an office in Tegucigalpa), or (3) ever giving Quintero, Clines, or Secord his telephone number. He asserted that his first memories of the meeting at Secord's house may not have been good because the primary purpose for his extended leave in Washington in the summer of 1985 was to resolve certain upsetting family matters. He did not recall discussing the arms supermarket with North, but he admitted that such a discussion would not have been unusual. Subject #1 denied discussing the supermarket with Secord during their meeting.

## Knowledge of Rodriguez and Other Private Benefactors

CIA Subject #1 claimed not to know much about the NHAO transhipment operation when questioned about it less than eighteen months after it began:[57]

Q: So you don't recall a specific period in which humanitarian assistance was coming only from Ilopango and not from the United States directly?

A: *No, but it could very well have happened.*

Q: So at some point, at any rate, supplies were coming in, humanitarian supplies were being received at Aguacate and they could have come from one of two sources, either from the mainland United States directly or from El Salvador, from Ilopango?

A: Yes.

Q: What was the role of [CIA field personnel] with respect to making arrangements to assist NHAO in providing the assistance in this matter?

A: Well, we were requested, I believe after the flights resumed, to obtain flight clearances from the Hondurans to allow those aircraft to come.

---

55 CIA Subject #1, Grand Jury, 6/5/87, pp. 65, 58–62, 72, 86–87 (emphasis added). In a deposition taken in August 1987, CIA Subject #1 repeated many of these points. (CIA Subject #1, OIC Interview, 8/28/87, pp. 106–9.)

56 CIA Subject #1, FBI 302, 6/24/88, pp. 3, 5.

57 The classified text of this exchange makes Subject #1's denials more unbelievable than they are rendered here.

Q: Did [field personnel] obtain clearances for flights from Ilopango?

A: *I don't know.* I had the feeling flights from Ilopango were sort of—the FDN may have done those themselves and it was sort of catch as catch can when a bird was coming. And there was traffic that went back and forth, but my recollection would have been from the States.

Q: So you can confirm that [field personnel were] making flight clearance arrangements for deliveries from the United States?

A: I have been told that and read that, but I did not remember that.

Q: But you cannot recall, at any rate, [ ] assistance in making similar arrangements for the flights from Ilopango?

A: *I can't recall that, no.*

Subject #1 was more categorical in denying knowing about Rodriguez:

Q: When did you become aware that Max Gomez or Felix Rodriguez was located at Ilopango?

A: Oh, I had heard Max Gomez was going to Salvador and Ilopango when I was still in [Classified Location], so that must have been '83 or early '84.

Q: Did you at some point link Gomez with the humanitarian assistance program?

A: *No.*

Q: When did you become aware that Gomez was performing some function with respect to deliveries to the FDN at Aguacate from Ilopango?

A: *I don't recall. Perhaps the newspapers.*

Q: Did you become aware at some point that private air crews had been retained by someone to shuttle supplies between Ilopango and Aguacate?

A: What time period are we talking about—during the NHAO period?

Q: Yes. Let's say in the period of November of '85 to March of '86.

A: *No, I did not.*

Q: So it's your belief that the private air crews did not appear on the scene prior to the winding down of the NHAO program?

A: *As far as I know.*

*     *     *

Q: At the point that the humanitarian program was winding down were you generally aware that the contras were the beneficiaries of a private supply network that was operating out of Ilopango?

A: I'd say yes.

Q: Did you associate that network with Max Gomez' presence at Ilopango?

A: *No.*

Q: So it was your understanding that Gomez was at Ilopango solely to assist the Salvadoran government's counter-insurgency effort?

A: I may have heard that he was involved in, you know, some of these other things, but Max Gomez was involved in that for quite some time. That was his reason for being there, the insurgency effort, whatever he did with the insurgents or counter-insurgency, yes.[58]

Subject #1's testimony on these subjects was slightly more straightforward in his August 1987 deposition for Independent Counsel. He admitted that officers under his command—most likely those closest to James Adkins—were responsible for clearing NHAO flights into Honduras. He denied learning, however, of a link between NHAO and the private benefactors:

Q: Were you involved in [clearances for NHAO flights]?

A: We would also get the cable; sure.

Q: You personally though?

A: The cable would go to both locations.

---

[58] CIA Subject #1, Select Committees Deposition, 4/25/87, pp. 35–36, 37–38, 46–47 (emphasis added).

Q: Would the air ops officer under Adkins command check with you before he talked to the Honduran government to get the clearance?

A: Probably with someone [close to Subject #1] or [Adkins] would talk to him probably, yes.

Q: Do you remember someone talking to you about some of the clearances, any clearances?

A: No, not really. Since I first discussed these I had forgotten that we did the clearances to tell you the truth.

\*          \*          \*

Q: Did you ever make a connection between the NHAO flights and the private lethal flights?

A: The private lethal flights?

Q: Yes.

A: You mean the two?

Q: Yes.

A: *No.*[59]

## The Decision Not to Prosecute

Independent Counsel uncovered very little evidence that CIA Subject #1 participated in or facilitated the affairs of the North-Secord Enterprise. Subject #1 also appears not to have knowingly violated any of the statutory restrictions on assistance to the contras that were in effect from 1984 to 1986—particularly the Boland Amendment. This left the possibility of charging Subject #1 with false statements, obstruction, or perjury. Independent Counsel's decision whether to prosecute Subject #1 rested on (1) the strength of the case against him, (2) the significance of his obstruction of the Iran/contra investigations, and (3) the prospects for furthering Independent Counsel's investigation.

The strongest evidence against Subject #1 concerned his meetings with Secord, Clines, and Quintero in 1985. Independent Counsel believed that the circumstantial and direct evidence about these meetings was overwhelming. Nevertheless, the three principal witnesses to the 1985 meetings were carrying significant baggage by 1991. Secord had pleaded guilty to providing false testimony; Clines had been convicted of tax evasion; and Quintero had testified only under immunity. Moreover, while the witnesses agreed that the meetings had occurred, they disagreed as to what had been discussed. Could their testimony convince a jury that Subject #1's motive for covering up the 1985 meetings was to distance himself from the Enterprise when Quintero, Secord, and Clines could not agree whether Subject #1 had been told about it?[60]

The evidence of Subject #1's contemporaneous knowledge of Rodriguez and the NHAO transshipment operation was likewise powerful. Much of the Rodriguez/NHAO case relied on CIA cables, many of which were written or released by Subject #1. Nevertheless, in many significant instances, proving Subject #1 released a cable would have been impossible, as the original cables had been destroyed by the CIA in the ordinary course of its business.

The strengths of a Subject #1 case were overshadowed by the relative insignificance of his false statements, the slim prospects for obtaining important information from him, and the resources that would have been required to obtain a conviction. Subject #1 sought only to distance *himself* from the Enterprise. No evidence suggested that he was covering for anyone else, or that he had particularly valuable information concerning the matters about which he lied. There was no evidence of a special relationship between Subject #1 and North; he did not appear to be a confidant of Alan D. Fiers, Jr., or other senior officials at CIA; and Independent Counsel had scant evidence that Subject #1 was involved in situations that could have incriminated other senior CIA officials.

---

[59] CIA Subject #1, OIC Interview, 8/28/87, pp. 97–98, 102 (emphasis added).

[60] With respect to the meeting at Secord's house, Independent Counsel also would have had to overcome an emotional preoccupation defense.

# Chapter 22
# James L. Adkins

James L. Adkins was the chief of a CIA facility in Central America from January 1986 until May 1987.[1] Independent Counsel found that from January 1986 until October 1986, when lethal U.S. Government aid to the contras was prohibited, Adkins knew and approved of contra-resupply missions by CIA pilots, in violation of the Boland Amendment. Independent Counsel also found that Adkins approved of the provision of thousands of dollars of aviation fuel to the contras—fuel that was mischarged to CIA accounts—and lied to investigators from the CIA's Office of Inspector General about his activities.[2] Despite the evidence, Independent Counsel concluded in November 1987 that he would not bring criminal charges against Adkins, principally because prosecution would not have advanced Independent Counsel's investigation into the Iran/contra affair.

Much of the information gathered during Independent Counsel's investigation of Adkins is classified and came from classified sources. A complete account of the investigation is set forth in the Classified Appendix to this report.

---

[1] In May 1987, the CIA placed Adkins on administrative leave. The Agency later forced Adkins to resign.

[2] Inspector's Notes, Adkins Interview, 3/26/87, ANT 003312–14; Inspector's Notes, Adkins Interview, 5/7/87. Independent Counsel found additional evidence that Adkins authorized activities that violated the Mrazek Amendment, Title II of the Military Construction Appropriations Act of 1987, Pub. L. 99–500, but concluded that the legal guidance that was provided to Adkins about the Amendment was insufficient to prove beyond a reasonable doubt that Adkins knew his conduct was illegal.

# Chapter 23
# Conduct of CIA Officials in November 1986

Independent Counsel investigated the concerted conduct of senior CIA officials in response to early congressional inquiries into the Iran/contra affair in November 1986. This investigation was substantially complete as of November 17, 1991, by the end of the statutory limitations period for the conduct under investigation. Upon completion of this investigation, Independent Counsel decided not to seek additional indictments.[1] The chief reason was the unavailability of three key witnesses—former CIA Deputy Director for Operations Clair E. George, his former special assistant, Norman H. Gardner, Jr., and most importantly, former CIA Director William J. Casey.[2]

## Congressional Inquiries Into the Iran Initiative

After the secret U.S. arms sales to Iran became exposed in the first week of November 1986, they quickly caught the attention of the Congress. They contained at least three troublesome aspects: (1) The sale of arms to a "terrorist state" was contrary to express policy, and in violation of export restrictions; (2) The link between the arms sales and the release of American hostages also contradicted the stated Reagan Administration position of not dealing with kidnappers; (3) The Administration had failed to inform Congress of the initiative.[3]

The Reagan Administration first responded to these reports with a series of public denials. When this strategy failed, President Reagan decided to address the nation on November 13, 1986. In anticipation of this address, four congressional leaders received a briefing on November 12, 1986, about the arms sales.[4] President Reagan opened the briefing by assuring the leaders that the sales were legal and that arms had not been exchanged for hostages. National Security Adviser John M. Poindexter described the Iran initiative without disclosing—and sometimes affirmatively disclaiming—activities in support of the arms sales prior to a Presidential covert-action Finding dated January 17, 1986. Casey was among those present.[5]

## CIA Briefing

On November 13, shortly before the President's speech, Poindexter and Casey briefed five senators and three congressmen on the speech and the January 17 Finding. Once again Poindexter denied any U.S. Government activity before the January 17 Finding "except talk," while Casey remained largely silent. By the next day, however, it was clear to Casey that the Administration's briefings and the President's speech had not satisfied the intelligence oversight commit-

---

[1] At the time Independent Counsel reached this decision, one former CIA official, Clair E. George, was under indictment for perjury committed in December 1986. George's December 1986 statements were consistent with false statements he made during November 1986. For reasons that will be described below, Independent Counsel declined to bring charges for George's November 1986 statements.

[2] By all accounts, despite showing some signs of the illness that eventually took his life, Casey was a commanding figure at the Agency during most of November 1986. He also knew, or was in a position to know, about aspects of the Iran initiative that others in the CIA professed to have never learned. In short, Casey was a man whose potential knowledge of the Iran initiative and control of the CIA was such that putative defendant could have cast doubt on a Government case concerning CIA conduct in November 1986 by attributing responsibility to the deceased Casey.

[3] 50 U.S.C. § 501 (1982). On congressional reaction to news of the Iran initiative, see Hamilton, *Poindexter* Trial Testimony, 3/19/90, pp. 2177–78; "Hill Probes of NSC Planned," *The Washington Post*, 11/10/86, A1; "Congress Members Predict Move to Curb President's Secret Diplomacy," *Los Angeles Times*, 11/15/86, Pt. I, 9.

[4] By this time, the House Permanent Select Committee on Intelligence (HPSCI) had called for briefings on the Iran initiative by Poindexter, Shultz, Secretary of Defense Weinberger, and Casey. (Letter from Hamilton to Poindexter, 11/10/86, *North* Trial, GX 119.)

[5] For a more complete discussion of this briefing, see Reagan and Meese chapters.

tees.[6] Casey contacted Deputy National Security Adviser Alton G. Keel for guidance on what to tell the House and Senate intelligence committees in scheduled appearances the following week. Keel passed along Casey's request to Poindexter, who in turn directed the National Security Council's operating officer on the Iran project, Lt. Col. Oliver L. North, to respond to the director's queries.[7]

On Saturday, November 15, 1986, Casey spoke with Senators Durenberger and Leahy of the Senate Select Committee on Intelligence (SSCI). Casey and Durenberger agreed that committee staffers would meet with CIA personnel on Tuesday, November 18, 1986, to receive a preliminary briefing on the initiative and to advise the CIA of SSCI's concerns. This briefing would be the first expansive CIA presentation to Congress by persons closely associated with the Iran operation.[8]

The CIA briefed committee staffers on the morning of November 18 at CIA headquarters. CIA Deputy Director for Operations Clair E. George was the principal speaker, supported by the deputy chief of the CIA's Near East Division;[9] the Director of the Office of Congressional Affairs, David Gries; CIA comptroller, Daniel Childs; an executive assistant to Casey (EA/DCI);[10] two special assistants to George, Norman H. Gardner, Jr., and CIA Subject #2;[11] counsel to the Operations Directorate (DO), W. George Jameson; and the head of a DO congressional liaison unit, George W. Gerner. The NSC's director of legislative affairs, Ronald K. Sable, also attended.

While the briefing was not transcribed, Gerner took notes. These notes indicate that from the outset of the briefing, Clair George attempted to limit himself to describing his directorate's support to what he called "the White House initiative to Tehran," and tried to avoid discussing the legal or political wisdom of the project. George nevertheless stated this about the CIA's involvement:

—In prepared remarks, George implied that Iranians deposited funds for American arms directly into a CIA account. In fact, Iranian payments passed through several hands (including those of retired Maj. Gen. Richard V. Secord) before reaching CIA accounts.

—In response to a staffer's question, George stated that, "to the best of his knowledge," a CIA proprietary was used on only *one* occasion in the course of the initiative. Later George stated that there was no CIA support to the initiative prior to 1986. In fact, a CIA proprietary was also used to ship Israeli HAWK missiles to Iran in November 1985.

—In response to press reports of arms shipments before the January 17 Finding, George responded that this "could be true, but it wasn't us." CIA Director of Congressional Affairs David Gries echoed George's remarks. Again, these statements ignored the November 1985 HAWK shipment carried by a CIA proprietary.[12]

## The Director Testifies

The next congressional briefings by the CIA came on Friday, November 21, 1986, in Casey's appearances before HPSCI and SSCI.[13] Casey came before each committee with a prepared statement and a retinue of advisers, along with representatives from the State and Defense departments.[14] In both appearances, Casey was

[6] November 14 was also the day that the CIA formally notified the intelligence committees of the January 17 Finding.

[7] PROFs Note from Pearson to Poindexter, 11/14/86, AKW 021641; North Notebook, AMX 001684; DCI Phone Log, 11/14/86, ER 320.

[8] George, Select Committees Deposition, 4/24/87, pp. 126–27. By November 18, the briefing had been expanded to include staff from HPSCI.

[9] The deputy's identity is classified.

[10] The identity of Casey's assistant is classified. In *United States v. George,* the assistant was called CIA Officer #8.

[11] The identity of this officer is classified. It is disclosed in the Classified Appendix to this chapter.

[12] Gerner, Memorandum for the Record, 11/18/86, ER 29688–95. Notes taken by two SSCI staffers, Edward Levine and Daniel Finn, corroborate Gerner's account of the briefing. (Finn, Memorandum for the Record, Subject: Iranian Arms Deal, 11/19/86, SSCI 86–3964; Levine, Memorandum for the Record, Subject: CIA Briefing on support to the Iran Arms Program, 11/18/86, SSCI 86–3958.)

[13] Both of these appearances came on the heels of two separate briefings of the members of the intelligence committees by Poindexter. Gardner attended these briefings and remained silent as Poindexter lied about prior presidential approval for the November 1985 HAWK shipment. Gardner later denied that he went to these briefings to insure that Casey and Poindexter were saying the same thing. (Gardner, *Poindexter* Trial Testimony, 3/23/90, pp. 2676–79, 2689–91.)

[14] Casey appeared before HPSCI and SSCI with these CIA officers: George; CIA General Counsel David Doherty; Comptroller Childs; National Intelligence Officer Charles Allen; CIA Subject #2; Gries; and another member of Gries's staff. Gardner joined Casey for his afternoon HPSCI session; George Jameson joined Casey for his SSCI appearance. Also present with Casey before HPSCI and SSCI were Under Secretary of State Michael H. Armacost and his executive assistant; Assistant Secretary of State Richard W. Murphy; State Department Legal Adviser Abraham D. Sofaer (HPSCI morning session only); two deputy assistant

the primary spokesman. In his opening remarks to HPSCI, Casey volunteered that "[t]he CIA's involvement [with the Iran initiative] began in late November of 1985" when the CIA was asked to recommend an airline to transport "bulky cargo to an unspecified location in the Middle East." Casey suggested that the CIA's associate deputy director for operations, Edward Juchniewicz, and the deputy director of central intelligence at the time, John McMahon, had approved the flight, although McMahon "directed that we would not provide any future flights into Iran in the absence of a Finding." [15]

Casey went on to describe briefly the financial mechanics of the arms sales:

> First, the Iranian intermediary would deposit funds in an Israeli account, the funds would then be transferred to a sterile US-controlled account in an overseas bank. Using these funds the CIA would work with the Army Logistics Command to obtain any material and the material would then be transported to Israel for future shipment to Iran.

Casey fielded questions from HPSCI members, House Majority Leader James Wright and House Minority Leader Robert Michel. The questioning of Casey went past the allotted time, forcing HPSCI to ask Casey to return that afternoon. [16]

Casey's intervening appearance before SSCI was marked by much sharper exchanges than those that had occurred before HPSCI. After Casey repeated his HPSCI opening statement, Senate Minority Leader Robert Byrd raised the possibility of placing all of the witnesses under oath. Chairman Durenberger denied the request and the questioning of Casey began with Sen. Leahy. Leahy had attended a briefing by Poindexter that morning and had learned that there had been activities in 1985—prior to the signing of a Presidential Finding authorizing such activity. Leahy quickly inquired about the November 1985 HAWK shipment and the

CIA's contemporaneous knowledge of its contents. Casey explained that the CIA did not know of the contents until some time in January 1986, but pleaded that he was uncertain whether the air crew had learned earlier than that. Leahy pressed the issue, because he could not square the CIA's attributing the flight to the NSC with what Poindexter had told him: that the NSC had just learned about the flight. [17]

Casey returned to HPSCI for further questioning at 1:50 p.m. Chairman Hamilton sought a summary of "all the arms transfers that reached Iran pursuant to this initiative, both direct transfers from the United States, which may have gone through Israel, but nonetheless were basically direct, and transfers by the Israeli government to Iran in which the President approved." At Clair George's suggestion, CIA Subject #2 recited a list of shipments. This list included the September 1985 Israeli shipment of TOW missiles to Iran, the February, May, and November 1986 TOW shipments, and the May 1986 U.S. shipment of HAWK spare parts to Iran. CIA Subject #2 did not include, however, the November 1985 U.S.-assisted shipment of 18 HAWK missiles to Iran. CIA Subject #2 also did not disclose the shipment upon closer questioning:

> The Chairman. Now, what about the amount of arms sent from Israel to Iran?
>
> Mr. Childs. We don't have that.
>
> Mr. George. We don't have that, Mr. Chairman.
>
> The Chairman. Other than these?
>
> CIA Subject #2. Other than the September 1985 shipment of TOWs we don't know.

The members of HPSCI also questioned the CIA on the extent of presidential approval for Israeli actions in the initiative, including the November 1985 HAWK shipment:

> The Chairman. Well, look, there have been reports in the press that I have seen, $40, $60 million has been sent in by Israel. Under the law Israel could not ship those without the approval of the President. Am I right about that?

secretaries of state; Assistant Secretary of Defense Richard Armitage; and a Department of Defense legislative affairs representative. John Bolton of the Justice Department attended the SSCI session only.

[15] Casey, HPSCI Testimony, 11/21/86, pp. 5–6. In early December 1986, Casey corrected this testimony to say that DDCI McMahon had not approved the flight. (Casey, Defense Appropriations Subcommittee Testimony, 12/8/86, p. 10.)

[16] Casey, HPSCI Testimony, 11/21/86, pp. 11, 51.

[17] Casey, SSCI Testimony, 11/21/86, pp. 7–26, 31–36.

Mr. [Richard] Armitage [Assistant Secretary of Defense]. That is right.

The Chairman. How many times did the President give his approval for Israel to ship arms into Iran?

Mr. Allen. None to our knowledge, sir.

The Chairman. The President did not approve any arms shipments by Israel directly into Iran?

Mr. Allen. We don't know.

Mr. George. We don't know.

Mr. Allen. We don't know that and—

Mr. George [sic]. What do you mean we don't know it?

Mr. Allen. We don't know.

The Chairman. You mean the President hasn't told you?

Mr. Allen. We have no knowledge of that as part of this project whatsoever.

Mr. George. We received the missiles, we transported them to Israel and away they go. We don't know whether or what transpires. We bring them to Kelly Air Force Base I should say.[18]

Casey returned to CIA headquarters, angry that his Directorate of Operations had not served him well in preparing his testimony. Gardner reported to Poindexter later that afternoon that ''nothing that we did up there today has done anything to answer their concerns about the whole Iran activity.'' [19]

## The CIA's Incorrect Statements

At least seven of the statements described above were incorrect:

(1) George's statement to intelligence committee staff on November 18, 1986, that the Iranians deposited funds directly into a CIA account for the purchase of arms;

(2) George's twin denials that same day of any CIA support for the Iran initiative prior to the January 17 Finding;

(3) David Gries's denial that there had been CIA support for the Iran arms sales prior to the January 17 finding;

(4) The prepared remarks of Casey on November 21, 1986, that CIA involvement with the arms sales began in November 1985;

(5) Additional prepared remarks by Casey, echoing George's statement about the flow of funds;

(6) CIA Subject #2's failure to include the November 1985 HAWK shipment in the list that he recited to HPSCI on November 21, 1986, of all of the arms shipments by the Israelis and the Americans in support of the initiative; and

(7) Allen and George's denials before HPSCI of knowing whether the President had approved Israeli arms shipments prior to the January 17 Finding.

As in most other investigations involving illegal false statements, the key questions in assessing the liability of senior CIA officials for these statements were, first, whether each official knew at the time he spoke that his statement was false, and second, whether that official deliberately made that statement. The answers to some of these questions are found upon close examination of what happened at the CIA prior to Casey's appearances before the intelligence committees on November 21, 1986.

## Disclosure and Alarm

According to Charles Allen, the National Intelligence Officer for Counter-Terrorism and the CIA analyst who worked most closely with the Iran initiative, the CIA's first response to the public disclosures of the initiative in early November 1986 was no response. Allen departed on a trip to Israel, during which he met with the Israeli representative in the 1986 arms sales, Amiram Nir. Nir quizzed Allen on how the United States would respond to the disclosures,

[18] George, HPSCI, 11/21/86, pp. 75–79.
[19] Doherty, FBI 302, 10/30/91, p. 19; Gardner, *Poindexter* Trial Testimony, 3/23/90, pp. 2695–96.

and Allen was chagrined to admit that the United States apparently intended to do nothing.[20]

Unbeknownst to Allen, some in the U.S. Government, even in the CIA, were preparing to respond to the growing firestorm. Poindexter asked North on November 5, 1986, to prepare a chronology of involvement in the initiative. The next day, after a morning staff meeting, the chief of the CIA's Iran Branch (C/Iran) [21]—who was the CIA's day-to-day operational contact with the NSC in the late stages of the initiative—decided on his own that he would prepare a chronology of CIA involvement. C/Iran's chronology contained generally accurate statements about CIA involvement in the Iran arms sales, including a note that CIA activities began in September 1985. On the advice of his immediate superior, Chief of the CIA's Near East Division Thomas Twetten, C/Iran personally delivered a copy of his chronology to North on November 6. Upon reading the section concerning the CIA's 1985 activities, North expressed amazement that C/Iran wrote about it, since "you were not involved." [22]

For their part, Casey and Deputy CIA Director Robert Gates' stated concerns about the arms sales focused on their legality. Casey and Gates met with Poindexter on the morning of November 6, 1986, to discuss what to do about allegations that profits from Iranian arms sales had been diverted to other covert projects. According to Gates, Casey proposed that Poindexter raise these allegations with White House Counsel Peter Wallison. Poindexter said he would take up the matter with NSC Counsel Paul B. Thompson instead. After the meeting, Gates returned to CIA headquarters and ordered

CIA General Counsel David Doherty to take his first look at the January 17, 1986 Finding.[23]

The day after C/Iran wrote his chronology, he revised and sent it to Associate Deputy Director for Operations Bertram Dunn and Casey.[24] What Dunn and Casey did with the chronology is not known. Dunn later denied having seen the chronology or having had any role in preparing CIA responses to inquiries about the Iran initiative. CIA Subject #2, who worked as closely with Dunn as he did with Clair George, stated that he did not recall seeing the chronology—with its explicit references to CIA activities in 1985—at the time he was drafting testimony for George in November 1986.[25]

## Preparing for Clair George's Briefing

During the week of November 9, 1986, it became clear to Casey that the controversy surrounding the Iran initiative would not abate. Organized efforts thus began to write the story of the Agency's involvement with the arms sales.[26] After a senior staff meeting on Novem-

[20] Allen, FBI 302, 11/6/91, p. 3. On the day before leaving on this trip, Allen met at the Key Bridge Marriott for the third time with Roy Furmark, an associate of arms-sales financier Adnan Khashoggi. Furmark earlier had given Allen evidence that profits from the Iran arms sales may have been diverted to other projects, including the contras. Furmark told Allen that investors in the initiative who had not been paid were threatening to expose it. (Memorandum from Allen to Casey, 11/7/86, ER 46449–52.)

[21] The identity of this officer is classified. He testified as C/Iran Branch #2 in the second *George* trial.

[22] Subject: Background and Chronology of Special Project, 11/6/86, ER 24517–20; Earl Note, 11/5/86 & 11/6/86; Earl, FBI 302, 4/21/87, p. 2; Earl, Select Committees Deposition, 5/30/87, pp. 53–55; Earl, *North* Trial Testimony, 3/23/89, pp. 5546–47; C/Iran, FBI 302, 10/29/91, pp. 6–7; WAVE Records, ALU 049209–17; 11/6/86, ER 18195–98; AKW 10038–45; North, *Poindexter* Trial Testimony, 3/13/90, pp. 1443–47; Earl Note, 11/10/86; Earl, Select Committees Deposition, 5/30/87, pp. 76–77.

[23] Gates 1986 Appointment Book; DCI Schedule for 11/6/86; Gates SSCI Testimony, 12/4/86, pp. 23–24, 51, 53–59; Gates, Grand Jury, 6/26/87, pp. 23–25; Gates, SSCI Deposition, 7/31/87, pp. 36–39; Doherty Notes, 11/6/86, ER 46562; Doherty, FBI 302, 10/30/91, pp. 2–3; Doherty, FBI 302, 11/13/87, pp. 3–4; Doherty, SSCI Testimony, 12/8/86, p. 55. Gates asked the NSC for the Finding during the now famous North-Casey-Gates luncheon of October 9, 1986. See Gates chapter. Inexplicably, it took the NSC several weeks to get the Finding to Gates. (Gates, SSCI Testimony, 12/4/86; Gates, Grand Jury, 6/26/87, pp. 9–10; Gates, SSCI Deposition, 7/31/87, p. 26; EA/DCI, FBI 302, 9/12/91, pp. 6–7.)

[24] DO 44631–35 and DO 83915–18. These papers are identical. Independent Counsel obtained the first from a "DDO Iran Soft File" recovered from Clair George's safe. The second of these papers was found in a working file labeled "DO Iran/Contra Investigation," along with other papers of Gardner. Both papers bear C/Iran's handwritten note that his November 7 chronology was passed to Dunn and Casey on 11/7/86. C/Iran could not recall who asked him to send his chronology to these men. (C/Iran, FBI 302, 10/29/91, p. 71.)

[25] Dunn, FBI 302, 9/25/91, p. 17; CIA Subject #2, FBI 302, 9/17/91, p. 4.

[26] Casey also consulted with other senior Administration officials on the text of President Reagan's first public statements on the initiative and sat in on the President's first briefing of congressional leaders on the sales. See Regan chapter for a fuller discussion of the preparation of the President's statement; Letter, Casey to Poindexter, 11/10/86, ER 24035 (transmitting draft of statement); DCI Schedule, 11/10/86, ER 326–27; Letter, Casey to Poindexter, 11/10/86, ER 24032–34 (transmitting revised two-page draft statement); AKW 20674–77 (same, recovered from NSC); DCI Schedule, 11/12/86, ER 323–24; Presidential log, 11/12/86, ALU 027752.

By November 12, Casey and Gates had concluded that they could not respond to Congress unless the President lifted his order in the January 17 Finding that prohibited congressional notification of it. Poindexter agreed to end the ban. (Draft letter from Casey to Poindexter, 11/12/86, ER 27233; Gates, Grand Jury, 6/26/87, p. 25; Gates, SSCI Deposition, 7/31/87, p. 39; Gates, Grand Jury, 5/1/91, pp. 200–01.)

ber 12, Gates asked Doherty to join George, Twetten, and him for a brief meeting. Doherty and Gates listened while George and Twetten summarized the CIA's involvement in the Iran initiative—activities that Doherty believed were consistent with the Finding he had read the previous week.[27]

Charles Allen returned from Israel on November 12 to find that the Agency had gone from nonchalance to panic. His colleague on the Iran initiative, George Cave, had returned from meetings with the Iranians in Geneva, and was now in daily contact with the White House in the preparation of the President's November 13 address. Clair George for his part instructed CIA Subject #2 on November 13 to prepare a chronology and an opening statement of the Directorate of Operations's involvement in the initiative, in anticipation of a request for CIA testimony.[28]

CIA Subject #2 claimed not to have known much about the Iran arms sales at the time George directed him to start drafting. Subject #2 thus sought out Twetten, who had been involved with the initiative since January 1986. Twetten was scheduled to leave the country on November 15, and so he turned over much of the work to C/Iran.[29]

Over the next few days (approximately November 13 through November 15) Twetten had C/Iran draft and revise several documents concerning CIA involvement in the arms sales. For some reason, all of these documents focused solely on CIA activities following the January 17, 1986 Finding.[30] This decision or under-

standing was in effect at least through Clair George's briefing of intelligence committee staff on November 18. These documents also were the source for George and Casey's later misstatements that the Iranians had deposited payments for arms directly into a CIA bank account—omitting Secord. This omission caused George Cave, who read the statements prior to November 18, to note in the margins of his copies of these documents: "Not True."[31]

Clair George reviewed C/Iran's papers prior to his briefing of intelligence committee staff on November 18.[32] George's handwritten notes on these documents are telling. George was familiar enough with the flow of funds from the Iranians to write "Gorba -> Secord -> CIA Account -> DOD" next to one of C/Iran's descriptions of the flow, and he replaced the words "Iranians deposit" in two other descriptions with the words "Channel deposit" and "System deposit." George knew or was informed of the minutiae of the initiative well enough to insert, for example, the number of communications officers and false passports provided to McFarlane's mission to Tehran in May 1986.[33]

## Did George Know the Truth?

Clair George knew during his briefing of intelligence staffers on November 18, 1986, and in his reviews that week of Casey's testimony, that there was something more to the CIA's obtaining money from the Iranians than having the Iranians make a deposit into a CIA bank account.[34] According to Cave, he informed one of George's special assistants, Gardner—most likely before George's briefing—that the de-

[27] Gates 1986 Appointment Book; Doherty, SSCI Testimony, 12/8/86, p. 55–56; Doherty, FBI 302, 11/13/87, p. 3; Doherty, FBI 302, 10/30/91, pp. 3–4. While Doherty could not recall why he was asked to this meeting, he believed that it prompted him to ask others within the CIA's Office of General Counsel (OGC) to begin drafting their own chronologies. It may have been at this point that an OGC lawyer, Bernard Makowka, told Doherty about pre-1986 activities and his involvement in the preparation of a retroactive finding that covered them. (Makowka, FBI 302, 10/11/91, p. 2.)

[28] Allen, FBI 302, 11/6/91, pp. 3–4; WAVE records, 9/28/87; Cave, Grand Jury, 1/15/88, pp. 171–172; Cave, Select Committees Deposition, 4/17/87, pp. 170–71; CIA Subject #2, FBI 302s, 3/4/88, p. 2 & 9/17/91, p. 4.

[29] CIA Subject #2, FBI 302, 9/17/91, p. 4; C/Iran, FBI 302, 10/29/91, p. 7; CIA Chronology, 2/27/87.

[30] In his October 1991 interview with Independent Counsel, C/Iran vaguely recalled instructions from Twetten that he should limit his chronology to those events occurring after the CIA's Near East Division, the Division for which both C/Iran and Twetten worked, began supporting the Iran initiative. (C/Iran, FBI 302, 10/29/91, p. 8.) CIA Subject #2 alleged that the congressional committees had limited their request for information to 1986 activities. (CIA Subject #2, FBI 302, 9/17/91, p. 15.) Independent Counsel found no evidence to support CIA Subject

#2's claim. At the 1990 trial of Poindexter, Gardner claimed that the omission of 1985 references in these documents was not part of an effort to sell a "cover story" to the Congress. (Gardner, *Poindexter* Trial Testimony, 3/23/90, pp. 2647–51.)

[31] Draft chronologies DO 44631, ER 29709, ER 18203, ER 18200, ER 18199 & ER 18202; Cave, Grand Jury, 11/22/91, pp. 13–14.

[32] The evidence includes C/Iran's comments on the draft statement ER 18203, which indicate that a draft had been passed to the DDO's office sometime during the weekend of November 15–16; statements made on documents prepared on November 17 that reflect George's comments on C/Iran's drafts; and George's near-verbatim recitation of the contents of one C/Iran document during the staff briefing. See DO 44620-17, which were retrieved from a "DDO Iran Soft File" and bear George's handwriting. In his second trial, George admitted that he used the C/Iran documents.

[33] DO 44620-17.

[34] For a fuller discussion of the evidence that supports this conclusion, see George chapter.

scription of the money flow found in George's briefing papers was inaccurate.[35]

George knew that his statement was false. George had been absent from CIA headquarters over the weekend of the November 1985 HAWK missile shipment, but he was involved in numerous events that followed in its wake. According to Juchniewicz and McMahon, George knew the "full story" about the flight within three days. McMahon also recalled repeatedly telling George to find out from the NSC—particularly Poindexter—whether the President had signed the retroactive Finding covering the shipment.[36] Further, Gardner had been at CIA headquarters when the NSC made its request for assistance for the HAWK shipment. Both he and CIA Subject #2 later conceded that they would have reviewed closely held CIA cable traffic that discussed the flight.[37] Both men denied that they remembered the flight in November 1986 until some time *after* George's erroneous briefing of committee staff on November 18.[38]

In order to charge George's misstatements concerning the November 1985 HAWK shipment, Independent Counsel would have had to prove either that George recalled the flight independently of Gardner and CIA Subject #2, or else that Gardner and CIA Subject #2 had lied themselves.[39] Independent Counsel found no direct evidence that George independently recalled the November 1985 flight in November 1986.

There was evidence that information about the flight was developed for Gardner and CIA Subject #2 prior to George's briefing, but this evidence was not sufficient to prove beyond a reasonable doubt that Gardner and CIA Subject #2 were lying. On the evening of Wednesday, November 12, 1986, a lawyer who was assigned to the CIA's Air Branch, Cynthia Erskine, had dinner with a pilot for the CIA proprietary that had ferried the HAWK missiles to Iran in November 1985. During their dinner, the pilot boasted to Erskine about flying Israeli "Gabriel" anti-aircraft missiles to Iran in November 1985, an effort that the pilot linked to the arms-for-hostages deals. Erskine repeated the pilot's story to CIA General Counsel Doherty the next morning. Later that day or the following Monday, Erskine spoke to the CIA's contact with the pilot's proprietary. That officer gave Erskine the flight records of the November 1985 shipment, which the officer was carrying.[40] Erskine used the flight records in editing a chronology prepared by the Air Branch of its involvement with the Iran arms sales, which she finished by the end of November 17. Erskine had to correct the Air Branch's chronology to reflect that missiles had been shipped in November 1985, instead of oil-drilling equipment. She attached the flight records to the chronology, which she understood was intended for George.[41]

---

[35] Cave, *George* Trial Testimony, 8/11/92, pp. 2849–51; Cave, Grand Jury, 11/22/91, pp. 27–28. It appears that George was prepared largely by his special assistants, Gardner and CIA Subject #2. Independent Counsel found no evidence that CIA Subject #2 was aware of the financial aspects of what all witnesses said was a closely held program. Two CIA officers apart from Cave who knew about the finances of the initiative, C/Iran and his predecessor, claimed that they did not speak with George about this subject close to the time of the briefing. Twetten was in the Mideast in the days leading up to the briefing, and there is no record of communications between him and George during this time.

[36] Juchniewicz, FBI 302, 10/8/91, p. 4; McMahon, SSCI Deposition, 6/1/87, pp. 95–101, 108; McMahon, Grand Jury, 10/15/91, pp. 9–10; McMahon, Grand Jury, 9/18/91, pp. 9–20. North's notebooks for November 25 and 26, 1985, support the view that George was upset about the shipment on November 25, that he spoke with Poindexter about it, and that he was aware of General Counsel Stanley Sporkin's advice to get a Finding. Independent Counsel also discovered that shortly after the shipment, George visited a European location that was involved in the November 1985 shipment. Officers who met with George during the trip, however, deny that they discussed anything with George about the shipment, other than commenting about the flurry of cable traffic. ([Classified Identity Withheld], FBI 302, 11/5/91, p. 8; [Classified Identity Withheld], FBI 302, 11/7/91, p. 5.) George testified to trying to gather facts in November 1985, but he denied that he was aware of a 1985 hostages finding. (George, Select Committees Testimony, pp. 200–01, 290–93; George, Select Committees Testimony, 8/6/87, p. 5; George, Select Committees Deposition, 4/24/87, pp. 85–86.)

[37] Gardner, Grand Jury, 4/19/91, pp. 97–100; CIA Subject #2, SSCI Testimony, 12/9/86, pp. 4–5. CIA Subject #2 testified that he did not connect the November 1985 incident to the Iran initiative until November 1986. (Ibid., p. 4.)

[38] Their stories are not consistent. Gardner claimed to have recalled the flight "vaguely" during a conversation that he and CIA Subject #2 had with North in North's office during the afternoon following George's briefing. (See text and citations at notes below.) Subject #2 recalled some aspects of Gardner's story, but linked his and Gardner's recognition of the flight to a phone call from someone in the CIA's

Air Branch, after Gardner and Subject #2 returned from North's office. (CIA Subject #2, FBI 302, 9/17/91, pp. 3–4.)

[39] Proving that CIA Subject #2 or Gardner remembered the flight prior to George's briefing could have been enough to place knowledge in George's mind, as Subject #2 said he brought the flight to George's attention immediately after learning about it in November 1986. (CIA Subject #2, FBI 302s, 3/4/88, p. 2 & 9/17/91, pp. 3–4.)

[40] Independent Counsel was unable to ask this CIA officer why he had these records. By the time Independent Counsel had interviewed Erskine, the officer was dead.

[41] Erskine, Memorandum for the Record, Subject: [Proprietary] Flight to Tehran, 11/13/86, ER 91–00487–88; Erskine, FBI 302s, 9/27/91, pp. 3–4 & 11/21/91, p. 3. Erskine became firmer in her recollection of these dates in her second interview. She was initially unable to

Erskine's story of November 13 had puzzled Doherty, as it did not square with the briefing that he had received from George and Twetten the previous day. Doherty asked the legal adviser to the Operations Directorate, attorney W. George Jameson, to question directorate personnel about the flight. Jameson initially reported on November 13 or 14 that Gardner and CIA Subject #2 were unaware of November 1985 activity. By early the next week, sometime prior to November 19, 1986, Jameson called back and said that the Operations Directorate now was acknowledging a November 1985 flight involving HAWK missiles.[42]

Charles Allen also believed that CIA Subject #2 and Gardner had been confronted prior to George's November 18 briefing of congressional staffers with memories of the November 1985 HAWK shipment. Allen testified that Gates called a meeting on November 17, 1986, to assign responsibilities for Casey's upcoming testimony. Allen recalled that many senior CIA officials attended. Allen claimed further that, after Gates had concluded his business and left the room, Allen presented details of the HAWK shipment and witnessed a debate between former Associate Deputy Director for Operations Juchniewicz and Duane R. Clarridge, the CIA officer who had coordinated the CIA's activities in support of the shipment. Allen recalled that George listened passively, while CIA Subject #2 took notes.[43]

Allen's description of this meeting could not be corroborated. Gates's calendar shows a brief meeting late in the afternoon of November 17. No one placed Allen at this meeting. Juchniewicz claimed that, while he recalled a large gathering of senior CIA officials and vaguely remembered discussions about the flight, he and Casey's calendars date this meeting as December 1, 1986. Juchniewicz did not recall speaking with anyone at the CIA prior to Casey's November 21 testimony.[44]

Questions remain unexplained about two documents generated during this period, documents which indicate recognition of the November 1985 flight at some point earlier than CIA Subject #2 and Gardner admitted:

—Gardner's handwritten notes appear on a copy of a statement drafted by C/Iran prior to George's briefing. Gardner listed on the front of the statement the dates of release of hostages Benjamin Weir, Lawrence Jenco, and David Jacobsen. On the back of the last page of the statement is a handwritten list of items that parallels the topics of concern raised by intelligence committee staffers during George's briefing, which Gardner attended. On the same page, however, are the words "'85 Trip"—an indication that, at least during George's briefing, an additional 1985 event struck Gardner as important.[45]

—CIA Subject #2 testified that, on the afternoon of November 18, he wrote a one-

---

date her completion of the Air Branch's chronology. Further, at some point after she spoke with Doherty but before she saw the CIA's contact with the proprietary, Erskine says she met an Air Branch supervisor who denied that the proprietary's flight records existed. Neither the Air Branch supervisor nor another CIA officer who was involved in the Air Branch chronology could say when he received his first instructions about it.

The finished chronologies are dated November 25, 1986, although there are undated draft chronologies that point to earlier Air Branch contacts with George's office. For his part, CIA Subject #2 recalled that the first information that reached George's office on November 18 about the November 1985 flight came from the Air Branch, and not the other way around. (CIA Subject #2, FBI 302s, 3/4/88, p. 2 & 9/17/91, pp. 3–4.)

[42] Doherty, FBI 302, 10/30/91, pp. 4–7. Doherty also may have received confirmation of the November 1985 flight on November 17, 1986, during a meeting with former CIA general counsel Stanley Sporkin. See text accompanying notes below. Jameson and Erskine's efforts could have prompted CIA Subject #2 or Gardner to contact Air Branch personnel earlier than CIA Subject #2 or Gardner has claimed. Air Branch officers could not recall when they first spoke to the DDO's office about the November 1985 flight. (See Air Branch Supervisor, Grand Jury, 11/8/91, p. 32; [Classified Identity Withheld], Grand Jury, 11/8/91, pp. 27–33.)

[43] Allen, FBI 302, 11/6/91, pp. 3–4.

[44] Gates 1986 Appointment Book; CIA Subject #2, FBI 302, 9/17/91, p. 10; EA/DCI, FBI 302, 9/12/91, p. 11; Gates, Grand Jury, 6/26/87, pp. 27–28; Gates, Select Committees Deposition, 7/31/87, p. 47; Gates, Grand Jury, 2/19/88, p. 58; Gates, Grand Jury, 5/1/91, pp. 202–03; Juchniewicz, Phone Interview, 11/8/91; DCI Calendar, 12/1/86, ER 290; Jameson, Meeting With DCI, 12/1/86, AKY 006443–48. Allen insisted that this meeting occurred on a Monday before "Casey's testimony" because he had to postpone a meeting of a public committee that met Monday evenings. (Allen, FBI 302, 11/6/91, p. 4.) December 1 was also a Monday evening, however, and it came before a series of congressional appearances by Casey in December 1986 on the Iran/contra matter. Allen also wanted to place Doherty at the meeting. (Ibid.) Doherty's conduct on November 19, see text accompanying notes 63–65 below, suggests that he was not present for any discussion with Juchniewicz about the flight prior to that date.

[45] Draft Statement, DO 84292–86. For corroboration of the timing of the draft, see draft DO 83905–11; draft DO 84074–80; Gardner, FBI 302, 6/17/87 302; draft ER 18359–65; C/Iran, FBI 302, 10/29/91; DIRECTOR 161904, 11/18/91; DO 83899–904; CIA Subject #2, FBI 302, 9/17/91. The notes of Gerner and the SSCI staffers who attended George's November 18 briefing make no mention of any 1985 trips. They do refer, however, to NSC "contacts" with Iranian representatives in Western Europe in 1985. (See sources cited in n. 12 above.)

page paper that presents the first detailed description of the November 1985 shipment. Gardner and Subject #2 visited North around 2:00 p.m., to report on George's briefing.[46] Subject #2 and Gardner then returned to Langley, where Subject #2 claimed they received a report from the Air Branch indicating that there had been a November 1985 flight in support of the initiative. Subject #2 and Gardner immediately reported the flight to George, who instructed the men to get all of the facts together. According to Subject #2, the facts of the flight were sketchy, and not easily gathered. Nevertheless, Subject #2 claimed to have written the document—a rather detailed account of the November 1985 shipment—that same afternoon, in time for Gardner to take a copy of it to Casey in Central America early the next morning.[47]

Subject #2's recollection of the timing of these events and his writing the first CIA chronology acknowledging the November 1985 flight is unconvincing. The completeness of the chronology and Gardner's briefing notes indicate that Clair George's assistants knew that George was falsely denying to congressional staffers CIA activities prior to 1986.

## Preparing Casey's Testimony

Casey's preparations for his intelligence committee testimony were handicapped by his taking a twice-postponed trip to Central America between November 16 and November 20. Before leaving, Casey instructed George to gather facts for his testimony. Casey also met with Allen on the afternoon of Saturday, November 15, to discuss the extent to which the CIA should protect in its briefings the identities of sensitive Iranian contacts. Casey and Allen agreed that the Agency would withhold six names at all costs.[48] The next day Casey spoke with Poindexter, White House Chief of Staff Donald T. Regan, and North. Casey then prepared a list of items he wished to have done before he returned, and departed for Central America.[49]

Documents that C/Iran had drafted as informational papers for George's briefing were transformed into formal, more elaborate statements about the Iran initiative. The persons principally responsible for this transformation appear to have been Jameson, C/Iran and Subject #2, although documents indicate that George exercised considerable editorial responsibilities as well.[50]

Casey instructed Gates: "It is understood that this Finding existed. Someone ought to get Stan Sporkin's recollection of the advice he gave the NSC with respect to the Finding." [51] On November 17, 1986, Doherty met with Sporkin, who had been CIA general counsel at the time of the HAWK shipment and had drafted the retroactive Finding that sought to authorize CIA involvement in it. Doherty took with him three CIA lawyers, Bernard Makowka, Edward Dietel and George Clarke, who had worked with Sporkin on this Finding. Sporkin discussed the period between the HAWK shipment and the ultimate January 17, 1986, Finding:

—Sporkin and Makowka both recalled that Sporkin talked about the November 1985 flight and his learning that there were weapons on the plane. Sporkin also mentioned "prior documents" and the drafting of a retroactive Finding. Sporkin directed Makowka to look for these drafts.[52]

—Doherty's recollection of the meeting was not that crisp. Doherty recalled

---

[46] Interestingly, North's crumpled notes of his debriefing from Gardner and Subject #2, recovered from a "burn bag" at NSC, contain the point: "Not reveal Dick Secord." (11/18/86, AKW 32705.) North did not recall these notes or the debriefing. (North, Grand Jury, 11/15/91, pp. 31–33.)

[47] Subject: CIA Airline Involvement, ER 24219; North Calendar, 11/18/86, AMX 5517–21; WAVE Records, 9/28/87; AKW 32705; CIA Subject #2, FBI 302, 9/17/91, pp. 3–4. CIA Subject #2 claimed that November 18 was further complicated with a return visit to North's office that evening to compare chronologies. (Ibid; CIA Subject #2, FBI 302, 3/4/88, pp. 3–4.) No one corroborated this visit, nor does Subject #2's name appear on White House gate logs on November 18 after his afternoon talk with North.

[48] DCI Schedule, 11/15/86, ER 317; Allen, FBI 302, 11/6/91, p. 5. Allen recalled that because of these instructions, he withheld the names of the Iranian contacts from Justice Department officials the following weekend, during Attorney General Meese's investigation into the Iran matter.

[49] DCI Schedule and Phone Logs, 11/16/86, ER 316; Memorandum, Casey to Gates, 11/16/86, ER 24305, DO 84041, ER 24256–57.

[50] Draft Statement, DO 44642–36; Draft Statement, 11/17/86, ER 7834–37; Jameson Notes, 11/17/86, ER 13980; Jameson, FBI 302, 9/20/91, pp. 7–8; Draft Statement, DO 83919–26; Draft Statement, 11/17/86, ER 7838–46; CIA Subject #2, FBI 302, 3/4/88; CIA Subject #2, FBI 302, 9/17/91.

[51] Memorandum, Casey to Gates, 11/16/86, ER 24256–57.

[52] Sporkin, *North* Trial Testimony, 4/3/89, pp. 6369–75; Makowka, FBI 302, 10/11/91, pp. 2–3; Makowka, Gates Interrog., 7/12/91, p. 3.

Sporkin, perhaps at this meeting, saying that "there was something else" drafted prior to the January 17 Finding. Three days later, Doherty sent Makowka back to Sporkin to confirm Doherty's "vague recollection" that Sporkin knew shortly after the shipment that arms were involved.[53]

—Dietel and Clark could not remember the meeting.[54]

Makowka put together soon thereafter a rough chronology of the office's involvement with the initiative, a chronology that referred to the November 1985 flight and the drafting of the retroactive Finding. Makowka also told Doherty that he remembered North saying on Christmas Eve of 1985 that the President had signed "the document" concerning the initiative and that it was in North's safe.[55]

## Doherty's Concerns

The day after the Sporkin interview, November 18, 1986, White House Counsel Wallison convened a meeting of general counsel from the State and Defense departments, NSC and CIA. Those who attended left with sharply contrasting impressions.[56] Doherty was struck most by the tone of the NSC's presentation. NSC Counsel Paul Thompson seemed to imply by what little information he provided to the group that the arms sales were a CIA operation, and that the CIA had more facts about it than the NSC. Doherty left the meeting concerned that the

NSC would shift the blame for the initiative's failures onto the CIA.[57]

Doherty learned from Jameson that the Directorate of Operations was acknowledging a November 1985 flight. This news, coupled with Thompson's remarks, caused Doherty to fear that the CIA would find itself unfairly attacked for its role in the arms sales and lacking the facts with which to fight back. Doherty requested that DDCI Gates gather the testimony team for a meeting on Wednesday, November 19. Doherty intended to use the meeting to point out the weaknesses in the Operations Directorate's facts, and to have Gates get the directorate to do better work.[58]

Gates testified that the task of preparing a statement for Casey overwhelmed him, and others have criticized Gates for not providing sufficient leadership to the project.[59] Casey cabled that he was dissatisfied with an early draft of a proposed statement, and on the morning of November 19 Gardner was dispatched to Casey in Central America. Gardner took with him many of the papers Casey had requested, but he did not take a draft of testimony that addressed Casey's criticisms.[60] Gates agreed readily to Doherty's request for a meeting of the Casey testimony team.

Prior to the meeting, Doherty spoke with two congressional staff members, State and Defense department counsel, and Assistant Attorney General Charles Cooper. What he heard only heightened his anxiety. Abraham Sofaer of the State Department complained to Doherty that he was unable to get facts from the NSC, which

---

[53] Doherty, FBI 302, 10/30/91, pp. 8, 13. In view of what Doherty called his "concerns" about the November 1985 flight—concerns he had once he had heard Erskine's story the previous week—it is puzzling that any mention by Sporkin of a November 1985 arms shipment, or even a November 1985 flight, did not prompt Doherty to react immediately. Doherty was unable to account for his lack of response to Sporkin's statements, except to suggest that perhaps he had spoken with Sporkin sometime prior to the November 17 meeting—a suggestion that, if true, would call Doherty's recollection of Jameson's first report about the November 1985 flight into question. (Ibid.)

[54] Dietel, FBI 302, 10/28/91, p. 5; Clarke, FBI 302, 9/24/91, pp. 2–3.

[55] Memorandum from Doherty to DCI, Subject: Discussion with Stanley Sporkin about the Iranian Finding, 11/18/86, ER 32384–85; Makowka, FBI 302, 10/11/91, pp. 2–3; Doherty, FBI 302, 10/30/91, p. 8; ER 32377–78 (rudimentary OGC chronology dated 11/20/86). Doherty's November 18 memorandum of the Sporkin meeting does not discuss missiles, but it does refer to a "shipment of equipment" to Iran that had prompted calls for a finding. (ER 32384–85.)

[56] See Meese and Regan chapters for a fuller account of the Wallison general counsels' meeting.

[57] Doherty Notes, 11/18/86, ER 46616; Doherty, FBI 302, 10/30/91, p. 9; Doherty Notes, prepared after 11/18/86 meeting, ER 46524; see also ER 46603; Doherty, FBI 302, 11/13/87, p. 4.

[58] Doherty, FBI 302, 10/30/91, p. 11.

[59] Gates was taking many of his directions from Casey. (Casey-Gates PRT–250 Conversation, 11/17/86.) Nevertheless, early in the evening of November 18, the growing problems with Congress's calls for briefings prompted Poindexter to call Casey directly in Central America. (Poindexter Phone log, 11/18/86, AKW 45588; Casey-Poindexter PRT–250 Conversation, 11/18/86, ER 50206–08.)

[60] CIA Chronology, 2/27/87; Gardner, North Trial Testimony, 4/4/89, pp. 6613–16; CIA Subject #2, FBI 302, 9/17/91. Subject #2 finished a draft of testimony that reflected Casey's comments some time on the morning of November 19, after Gardner had departed for Central America. (Draft Testimony, DO 44589–97.) This was the first full statement on the arms sales that included the November 1985 shipment. The statement implies that the NSC told the CIA about the cargo at the time the NSC requested the name of the proprietary. Jameson's comments on this draft suggest adding the phrase "to assist the Israelis in shipping HAWK missiles to Iran." (Draft Statement, ER 7764–72.) In his September 1991 interview with Independent Counsel, Jameson professed that he could not recall where or when he got his information. (Jameson, FBI 302, 9/20/91, p. 9.)

Sofaer perceived to be in chaos. Sofaer's concerns, as well as his appeal for a draft of Casey's testimony, made Doherty fear that Under Secretary of State Michael H. Armacost, who was scheduled to accompany Casey, would make a "bad wit[ness] for Admin[istration]." [61]

Before going to the meeting, Doherty prepared a list of imperative points to discuss with George and CIA Subject #2, in front of Gates:

—What was the extent of Casey's knowledge?

—What about Sporkin and Makowka's memories of a second finding?

—What was Charles Allen's involvement in the initiative?

—How did the CIA use proprietaries and private companies in the initiative, and who were they? [62]

Doherty testified that he raised all of these concerns in the Gates meeting, which took place at 2:30 p.m. on November 19. Just as Doherty was leaving for the meeting, Makowka handed him physical proof that Sporkin had prepared a Finding other than the January 17, 1986, Finding. Makowka had recovered from Sporkin's secretary a draft of a retroactive Finding, a "mini-Finding," that had been stored on a magnetic computer card. The draft contained an explicit arms-for-hostages equation not found in the later Finding and was intended to provide, retroactively, legal protection for the CIA's support of the November 1985 shipment. Doherty took the draft Finding to Gates's office, although he could not recall showing it to anyone other than Gates. [63]

Attending the November 19th meeting in Gates's office were Gates, George, CIA Subject

#2, two persons from the CIA's Office of Congressional Affairs, and Casey's executive assistant. Doherty took notes of the meeting. According to Doherty, his concerns forced George and his staff to "volunteer" to:

—Talk to Allen about his recollection of the mini-Finding and his activities in the initiative;

—Get all of the facts of the November 1985 flight, including interview Juchniewicz and former DDCI John McMahon about whether they had authorized it; and

—Obtain a signed copy of the mini-Finding from North. [64]

Three observations must be made about the Gates meeting. First, it should have been clear to everyone that at least Doherty was upset with the state of the Directorate of Operations' story, with less than two days to go before Casey was to brief Congress. [65] Second, as of November 19, 1986, no one in the Directorate of Operations had spoken to McMahon or Juchniewicz about the November 1985 flight— or at least no one was willing to admit he had. [66] The drafts of testimony that Subject #2 prepared both before and after the meeting avoided specifying whether Juchniewicz or McMahon had authorized the November 1985 flight. [67]

---

[61] Doherty, FBI 302, 10/30/91, p. 10; Doherty Notes, telephone conversations with Daniel Finn (SSCI) and Michael O'Neill (HPSCI), 11/19/86, ER 46620–21; Doherty Notes, telephone conversations with Abraham Sofaer (State) and Larry Garrett (Defense), 11/19/86, ER 46523.

[62] Doherty Notes, ER 46518; Doherty, FBI 302, 10/30/91, pp. 9–10. Doherty also prepared a report on what he had learned from Sofaer and the intelligence committees that morning. (Doherty Notes, 11/19/86, ER 46519.)

[63] Draft Finding, DO 44568–69; Makowka, FBI 302, 10/11/91, p. 4; Makowka, Gates Interrog., 7/12/91, pp. 3–4; Doherty, FBI 302, 11/13/87, p. 4; Doherty, FBI 302, 10/30/91, p. 11. The only copy produced to Independent Counsel of the draft finding that was uncovered by Makowka, and marked by Doherty, came from Clair George's files.

[64] Doherty Notes, 11/19/86, ER 46520; Gates 1986 Appointment Book; Doherty, FBI 302, 10/30/91, p. 11; EA/DCI, FBI 302, 9/12–9/16/91, pp. 13–14; CIA Subject #2, FBI 302, 9/17/91, p. 10; Doherty Notes, 11/19/86, ER 46519. The only thing that Gates remembered about this meeting were Doherty's concerns that the facts in the proposed testimony were "shaky." (Gates, Select Committees Deposition, 7/31/87, pp. 48–49; Gates, Grand Jury, 5/1/91 pp. 206–07.) According to Doherty's notes, Gates approved Doherty's plan to brief Cooper and the State and Defense departments on Casey's upcoming testimony. (Doherty Notes, 11/19/86, ER 46521, 46600.)

[65] Doherty told Independent Counsel that in the car on the way back from Casey's November 21 briefings, Casey complained that the Operations Directorate had done a "lousy job" of gathering the facts. (Doherty, FBI 302, 10/30/91, p. 19.)

[66] Subject #2 claimed later that he had spoken with Juchniewicz before Casey's testimony. Juchniewicz recalled only that someone attempted to reach him that week, but he did not return the call. (CIA Subject #2, FBI 302, 9/17/91, p. 11; Juchniewicz, FBI 302, 11/8/91, p. 6.)

[67] Express references in Casey's final testimony to Juchniewicz and McMahon crept into the text beginning with a draft that Casey himself (perhaps with Gardner's help) composed during Casey's return flight from Central America. (Compare Draft Testimony, 11/19/86, DO 44653–62 (Subject #2 draft); Draft Testimony, 11/19/86, DO 84277–85 (Subject #2 draft); and Draft Testimony, 11/20/86, DO 84042–52 (Subject #2 draft) with Draft Testimony, 11/20/86, DO 44671–

The third and most striking consequence of the November 19 meeting was that afterwards the team had to know that a mini-Finding had been drafted, and that the answer to whether it had been signed by President Reagan lay with the NSC. The meeting also makes the testimonies of North, Gardner and CIA Subject #2 inconsistent about the state of the CIA's knowledge of the mini-Finding prior to Casey's briefing on November 21.

—Both North and Gardner claimed that, at a meeting on November 18 among North, Gardner, and Subject #2, North told Gardner that if the CIA insisted on talking about the November 1985 HAWK shipment, then "they ought to know" that the President signed a Finding authorizing it.[68]

—In a March 1988 interview with Independent Counsel, Subject #2 recalled portions of his and Gardner's discussion with North, but he did not remember any discussion of a prior Finding.[69] If North had mentioned a prior Finding, however, it is strange that Subject #2 did not tell this to the Casey testimony team on November 19.

## "Shut Up, There is No Mini-Finding"

Allen believed that he raised questions about the existence of a prior Finding early in the week of November 17–21, 1986, or perhaps late the previous week, with Makowka, as both Allen and Makowka had been in North's office on Christmas Eve 1985 when North spoke about the "signed document." Allen believed he then called North and asked him if there had been a prior Finding. North denied it.[70] Later, Makowka called North back, asked again about

the Finding, and received another denial. Allen said that around midday on November 20, Allen raised the topic at a meeting with Casey, George, George Cave, and perhaps Gates. Allen claims that George sharply told him that he was "causing trouble" about the mini-Finding, that "it didn't exist" and that Allen should "shut up" about it.[71]

The exchange recounted by Allen explains why he told HPSCI on November 21, 1986, that he did not know whether the President had authorized Israeli shipments to Iran prior to the January 17, 1986, Finding. Despite his suspicion that there was a document reflecting approval, a superior officer, George, had told him that no such thing existed.[72] For George, the exchange with Allen raises the likelihood that George (1) spoke with North (note his "causing trouble" comment to Allen), (2) received confirmation that a Finding existed but that it could not be disclosed, (3) tried to silence Allen, and (4) lied about Presidential approval for 1985 activities when asked on November 21, 1986.

On November 19, George and CIA Subject #2 told Gates that the Directorate of Operations would find out whether the Finding had been signed. George admitted phoning North at least once during the week. George, Subject #2, and Gates also went to the White House shortly after the Casey testimony team meeting of November 19 to see Poindexter, North, Thompson, and Cave. Subject #2 stayed after the White House meeting to work with North on coordinating the NSC and CIA chronologies.[73] Despite these opportunities, however, no witness (including North) recalled that George and

---

80 (Casey/Gardner draft). See also EA/DCI, FBI 302, 9/16/91; CIA Subject #2, FBI 302, 9/17/91; Gardner, *North* Trial Testimony, 4/4/89, pp. 6620–28; Gardner, *Poindexter* Trial Testimony, 3/23/90, pp. 2654–60.) Independent Counsel found no evidence that Casey or Gardner was aware of Doherty's concern that nothing be said about authorization until someone had spoken with Juchniewicz and McMahon.

68 North, *North* Trial Testimony, 4/7/89, pp. 7044–45; North, Grand Jury, 11/15/91, p. 36. At North's trial, Gardner explained further that he told North that the CIA was only a "mechanic" in the November 1985 shipment, referring to the CIA's limited role in providing the name of a proprietary to the NSC. (Gardner, *North* Trial Testimony, 4/4/89, pp. 6610–11; see also Gardner, *Poindexter* Trial Testimony, 3/23/90, pp. 2649–50.)

69 CIA Subject #2, FBI 302, 3/4/88, p. 4.

70 Makowka corroborated Allen's story of his inquiry to North and North's denial. (Makowka, Gates Interrog., 7/12/91, p. 2.)

71 DCI Schedule, 11/20/86, ER 310; Allen, Grand Jury, 8/9/91, pp. 160–61; Allen, FBI 302, 11/6/91, p. 6. Gates and Cave did not recall George and Allen's exchange on November 20. North did not recall denying the mini-Finding's existence to Allen. (North, Grand Jury, 11/15/91, p. 36.) Indeed, at his trial North said he told Allen the opposite. (North, *North* Trial Testimony, 4/7/89, p. 7045.)

72 Allen, FBI 302, 11/6/91, p. 6.

73 North Note, 11/19/86, AMX 5522–26; Thompson, FBI 302, 4/22/87, p. 5; Gates 1986 Appointment Book; Cave, Select Committees Deposition, 4/17/87, p. 172. Those attending the meeting recall different aspects of the meeting. A CIA 2/27/87 Chronology states that the purpose of the meeting was to describe George's briefing of 11/18/86. George recalled conflict over the November 1985 flight (George, Select Committees Deposition, 4/24/87, pp. 123–26), while Subject #2 stated in his 9/17/91 FBI 302, p. 13, that the meeting was a relaxed affair. Gates had no specific recollection of the meeting.

North talked with each other about the mini-Finding.[74]

## Finishing Touches

By November 19, 1986, CIA Subject #2 was aware of the November 1985 HAWK shipment. Subject #2 had composed chronologies and drafted testimony that referred to the flight and its contents. Although parts of the story may have been in dispute—the extent of the CIA's contemporaneous knowledge of the flight's contents, or the level of authorization for the NSC's use of the proprietary airline—it was clear to Subject #2 by November 19 that a flight had taken place and that it had carried arms.[75]

The November 1985 flight was a major source of friction between the NSC and the CIA by the time Casey testified. Subject #2 admitted that he was aware of a conflict by the time he sat down with North on November 19 to coordinate chronologies. Casey and Gates, for their part, went to the White House on the afternoon of November 20 to try to settle the dispute over the flight. This dispute contributed to the ultimate decision—made around the time of a large meeting at the CIA on the evening of November 20, which Subject #2 attended—to present an extremely unspecific and thin description of the flight in Casey's prepared remarks.[76]

Subject #2 went home immediately after the large CIA gathering on November 20. Casey's executive assistant and his secretary, Deborah Geer, stayed to produce a draft of testimony that incorporated the changes discussed at the meeting. The assistant dated this draft "November 20, 2000." Doherty later reported to Casey that Sporkin was certain that he knew that weapons were on the November 1985 flight "within days" of its occurrence. Doherty thus sought and obtained Casey's permission to delete a reference from Casey's "1200" version of testimony—the version which Doherty then assumed was everyone's working copy—that stated that no one in the CIA knew about the contents of the flight until mid-January 1986. Doherty phoned Casey's assistant. On the *2000* draft, Casey's assistant deleted a single sentence that read: "Neither the airline nor the CIA knew the cargo consisted of 18 HAWK missiles." This was the *only* reference in the 2000 text to HAWK missiles.[77]

The next morning, Subject #2 got a copy of the 2000 version of Casey's testimony and took it with him to Casey's appearances on the Hill. Subject #2 made notes on the draft while Casey spoke, for he was surprised that his draft was not what Casey was reading to the committees. Subject #2 jotted in the upper right hand corner of the first page a list of the 1986 TOW missile shipments, which corresponds with the list that Subject #2 recited of all of the arms shipments to Iran.[78]

## Independent Counsel's Decision Not to Prosecute

The evidence suggests a concerted effort by CIA officials to withhold information from or lie to Congress about the November 1985 shipment of HAWK missiles to Iran. The available evidence could not, however, prove beyond a reasonable doubt that concerted action by CIA officials violated federal laws in responding to congressional inquiries about the November

---

[74] North affirmed in the Grand Jury, however, that after November 12, 1986, it was his belief that the Administration had decided that Congress was not to be told of the mini-Finding or the November 1985 HAWK shipment—a position that culminated in Poindexter's destruction of the mini-Finding on November 21, 1986. (North, Grand Jury, 11/15/91, pp. 33–35.)

[75] See also Earl Notebook, 11/20/86, AMT 733 (entry: "[CIA Subject #2]/proprietary flight-bad problems/OLN himself ask for/McMann [sic]-Casey argument-help OK this one time but thereafter need a Finding./Seacord [sic]-hired CIA proprietary for flt from T.A. [Tel Aviv] to Europe to T. [Tabriz, Iran]").

[76] DCI Schedule, 11/20/86, ER 310; Gates 1986 Appointment Book; Gates, Grand Jury, 2/19/88, pp. 62–63; Gardner, *North* Trial Testimony, 4/4/89, pp. 6629–33; Gardner, *Poindexter* Trial Testimony, 3/23/90, pp. 2660–63; Jameson, FBI 302, 9/18/91, pp. 6–7; Doherty, FBI 302, 11/13/87, pp. 4–5; Doherty 8/5/91 Gates Interrog. at 3–4. The description of the November 1985 flight in Casey's prepared statement was at its fullest on November 19. It steadily waned thereafter, particularly between noon and 8:00 p.m. on November 20. Part of the reason for this appears to have been the conflict with the NSC; another reason appears to have been disputes within the CIA over how the flight was authorized and when the CIA learned that missiles were being or had been shipped. (See drafts discussed in note 67 above; see also Doherty, FBI 302, 11/13/87, p. 15; Makowka, FBI 302, 10/11/91, pp. 6–7; Draft Testimony, 11/20/86, DO 83967–76; CIA Subject #2, FBI 302, 3/4/88, pp. 8–9; EA/DCI, FBI 302, 9/16/91, p. 6; Draft Testimony, 11/20/86, DO 83977–87; Draft Testimony, 11/20/86 [unnumbered Doherty 4:15 p.m. version]; Gries, FBI 302, 9/9/91 Interview.) Doherty found the situation so disturbing that he called Casey sometime on November 20 and implored him to postpone his congressional appearances. (DCI Phone Log, 11/20/86, ER 311; Doherty, FBI 302, 11/13/87.)

[77] Draft Testimony, 11/20/86, DO 83988–98; CIA Subject #2, FBI 302s, 3/4/88, pp. 5–6 & 9/17/91, p. 15; EA/DCI, FBI 302, 9/16/91, p. 6; Doherty, SSCI Testimony, 12/8/86, p. 10. The final Casey draft is DO 83999–84009, which Casey had typed on the morning of November 21.

[78] CIA Subject #2, FBI 302, 9/17/91, p. 16.

1985 shipment. The primary reason was that crucial witnesses to the events surrounding the Agency's responses in November 1986 were unavailable in 1991: Clair George was under indictment for false statements and perjury; Gardner had invoked his Fifth Amendment privilege against self-incrimination and had refused to give Independent Counsel a proffer; and Casey was dead.

There was evidence of individual crimes. Independent Counsel had proof beyond a reasonable doubt that Clair George knew on November 18, 1986, more about the flow of funds from the Iranians to the CIA than he told to intelligence committee staffers. By the time this proof was fully developed, however, Independent Counsel had charged essentially the same category of false statement—in a more formal setting, before SSCI—in the *George* case. As for George's denial in the November 18 briefing of CIA activity prior to 1986, the evidence did not establish beyond a reasonable doubt that George at that time remembered that a CIA proprietary had shipped weapons in 1985. George would have had two witnesses, Gardner and CIA Subject #2, who could have testified that as they helped George prepare for his briefing, they themselves had been unaware of the flight.

# Part VII
# Chapter 24
# The Investigation of State Department Officials: Shultz, Hill and Platt

From the Reagan Administration's first suggestion in June 1985 that the United States should transfer arms to Iran through the final decision in December 1986 that arms shipments would cease, Department of State officials opposed these dealings for reasons of policy and status. Department officials argued that trading arms for hostages would only increase the value and therefore the number of hostages. They also believed that the Department, not the National Security Council staff or the Central Intelligence Agency, should establish counterterrorism policy, including dealings with Iran and efforts to free hostages in Lebanon.

During 1985 and 1986, senior State Department officials monitored the U.S. contacts with Iranians quite closely, with increasing consternation. At several points, department officials attempted to stop the arms-for-hostages initiative. At least twice, they attempted to circumvent it by opening other channels to Iran. After the arms-for-hostages story broke in November 1986, the department and Secretary of State George P. Shultz eventually used the revelations to regain control over counterterrorism policy. Following a strenuous bureaucratic struggle, Shultz persuaded President Reagan to prohibit further arms transfers to Iran and to announce that the Department of State would take the lead on such counterterrorism and diplomatic matters in the future.

During the congressional investigations in December 1986 and throughout 1987, Shultz testified—to great effect—about State Department efforts to oppose arms shipments to Iran and State's limited contemporaneous knowledge of the activities in this regard of the NSC staff. In contrast to other agencies, State Department officials appeared open and cooperative; they

were the emerging heroes of the Iran/contra story and seemed to have nothing to hide.

In 1990 and 1991, however, Independent Counsel received new evidence, in the form of handwritten notes that had not been provided in response to previous document requests, suggesting for the first time that central aspects of Shultz's testimony were incorrect. Based on the notes, it appeared that Shultz and other senior Department of State officials had known significantly more about arms shipments to Iran than Shultz's testimony reflected. As a result of this new evidence, Independent Counsel conducted an investigation into whether Shultz or other department officials deliberately misled or withheld information from Iran/contra investigators.

Independent Counsel concluded that Shultz's testimony was incorrect, if not false, in significant respects and misleading, if literally true, in others, and that information had been withheld from investigators by Shultz's executive assistant, M. Charles Hill. Nevertheless, for reasons explained in this chapter, the investigation did not result in criminal charges.

## Department of State Organization and Arms Shipments to Iran

During 1985 and 1986, Shultz was the secretary of state, John C. Whitehead was deputy secretary of state and Michael H. Armacost was under secretary of state for political affairs. These senior ranking officials met daily to keep each other informed of the department's activities and relevant domestic and international events.[1]

Shultz and Whitehead were political appointees. Armacost was a career foreign service officer. During 1985 and 1986, two other senior foreign service officers occupied posts of importance in the department: Executive Secretary Nicholas Platt, and Shultz's executive assistant, M. Charles Hill.

Formally, the executive secretary was responsible for making sure that the secretary of state was adequately supported by the department bureaucracy: that matters were appropriately staffed, that deadlines were met and that appropriate guidance was given up and down the bureaucratic chain of command.[2] To fulfill that role, Platt attended and made a detailed handwritten record during most of Shultz's meetings within the department.[3] One of Platt's two deputies accompanied Shultz on all trips outside Washington, D.C., and reported back to Platt, who made notes of those reports. In addition, Platt had a close working relationship with Hill, who regularly reported to Platt what had occurred in Shultz's meetings outside the department; Platt also made notes of these reports. Platt also took notes in other meetings he attended and of significant information he acquired throughout the day. Platt created over 4,500 pages of daily handwritten notes from January 2, 1985, through February 12, 1987.[4]

Hill had served as the department's executive secretary prior to Platt. Thereafter, as Shultz's executive assistant from summer 1984 until the end of the Reagan Administration in January 1989, Hill's formal role was to write speeches and keep a record of Shultz's activities. In practice, Hill was one of Shultz's closest advisers and his principal gatekeeper. Hill regularly traveled with Shultz and, with few exceptions, attended and kept a handwritten record of Shultz's meetings in the department. In addition, Shultz regularly reported to Hill significant information he received and meetings he attended outside of Hill's presence, both to get Hill's reaction to the information and to permit Hill

to record it in his notebooks.[5] Shultz, who characterized Hill's notes as a "remorselessly precise record and a vivid picture" after using them to write his recent memoirs,[6] consistently stated that Hill's notes were accurate.[7] During the period January 1984 through December 1987, Hill filled more than 50 stenographer's notebooks with detailed, often verbatim, daily notes of Shultz's meetings, statements and activities.

The two State Department components with primary responsibility for the Middle East and counterterrorism were the Bureau of Near Eastern and Asian Affairs (NEA) and the Office of Counterterrorism and Emergency Planning (S/CT). Throughout 1985 and 1986, Assistant Secretary of State Richard W. Murphy headed NEA and Arnold L. Raphel served as his principal deputy. Ambassador Robert B. Oakley headed the counterterrorism office during 1985 through September 1986; his principal deputy was Parker Borg.

These nine senior officials—Shultz, Whitehead, Armacost, Platt, Hill, Murphy, Raphel, Oakley and Borg—together with a very few assistants, appear to have been the only State Department officials with significant contemporaneous knowledge of U.S. and Israeli contacts with Iranians and arms shipments to Iran during 1985 and 1986. Among that group, Armacost, Raphel and Oakley constituted what one participant called a "floating directorate" that monitored this activity, principally through contacts outside the department, and reported any significant developments to Shultz, often through Platt and Hill.[8]

## Department of State Evidence of Iran Arms Shipments: The Notes

The best evidence of Department of State knowledge of U.S. dealings with Iran comes from Hill and Platt's notes. It was their job to bring important information to the attention of Shultz and to communicate to others his guidance and questions. Both Hill and Platt took minute-by-minute notes that document this ex-

[1] Armacost, Grand Jury, 3/13/92, p. 6.

[2] Ibid.; Platt, Senate Foreign Relations Committee Testimony, 7/24/87, p. 35 (hearing on nomination to be United States Ambassador to the Philippines); Platt, FBI 302, 4/5/91, pp. 1–2.

[3] E.g. Platt, FBI 302, 7/14/87, p. 1; Ibid., 4/5/91, p. 2; Shultz, OIC Interview, 2/12/92, p. 65.

[4] Platt Notes, 1/2/85–2/12/87, ALW 0034815–9618.

[5] Shultz, OIC Interview, 2/12/92, pp. 4–5, 142–45.

[6] George P. Shultz, *Turmoil and Triumph* (Chas. Scribers Sons 1993), p. xiii.

[7] E.g., Shultz, OIC Interview, 12/11/90, p. 6 (describing Hill's notebooks as "a useful managerial tool" to Shultz as Secretary of State).

[8] Ross, FBI 302, 3/11/92, p. 4.

change of information in remarkably detailed fashion.

Notes taken by three other department officials supplement Platt and Hill's notes. Platt's deputy Kenneth M. Quinn took detailed notes of information he received from or passed on to Platt. Christopher W.S. Ross, the principal deputy to Armacost, took detailed notes of information he received from or passed to Armacost. Arnold Raphel took less detailed, but still valuable, notes of significant information he received.

The notes of these five officials—Hill, Platt, Quinn, Ross and Raphel—were particularly important to Independent Counsel's investigation because State Department officials committed so little about the Iran arms transfers to formal documents.[9] With the exception of a few cables and memoranda, almost everything significant that Independent Counsel was able to learn about the Department of State's role in the Iran initiative came from these handwritten notes.

## The Department of State's Production of Evidence During 1986 and 1987

On November 28, 1986, Attorney General Edwin Meese III wrote a letter to Shultz requesting that department information "be segregated and held for review by and transmission to the Federal Bureau of Investigation (FBI) upon its request."[10] Meese's request applied to

[a]ny and all material of any kind, type, or description, including, but not limited to, all memoranda, briefing materials, minutes, handwritten notes, diaries, telephone logs, . . . files and other documents of the . . . State Department, . . . from 1 January 1985 to the present, concerning the following:

1. All arms activities involving Iran;

2. All hostage negotiations or similar communications involving arms as an inducement;

3. All financial aid activities involving the Nicaraguan resistance movement which are related to Iran or Israel; [and]

4. All activities of Robert C. McFarlane, . . . Lt. Col. Oliver L. North, Vice Admiral John M. Poindexter . . . relating to 1–3 above.[11]

In response to the Meese request, the Department of State's Legal Adviser Abraham D. Sofaer, and the Assistant Secretary of State for Administration Donald J. Bouchard sent a memorandum the next day to the senior official in each department component that potentially would possess relevant information, including Hill and Platt.[12] The Sofaer/Bouchard memorandum, which the Department of Justice had reviewed and approved before it was issued at State,[13] distributed a copy of Meese's letter to each of these persons, reported that the President had ordered the Department of Justice investigation and stated that "[t]he Secretary has pledged full Department cooperation. . . ." The memorandum stated that, with regard to the phrase "All arms activities involving Iran" in the Meese letter, the department was interpreting this request,

[b]ased upon consultation with the FBI, . . . to encompass any materials concerning allegations or evidence of U.S. or U.S.-authorized arms shipments to Iran, requests by Iran for arms or alleged offers by the U.S., Israel, or other parties allegedly acting on behalf of the U.S. to supply arms.[14]

The memorandum also instructed that, with regard to named individuals such as McFarlane, North and Poindexter, "[y]ou should . . . provide information of *any* alleged activities [by

9 Although Ross was a prolific notetaker and produced a typed transcript of his relevant handwritten notes to Iran/contra investigators during 1987, he was unable to locate notes dated earlier than November 18, 1985. (Ross, FBI 302, 3/11/92, p. 1; DAMASCUS 02366, 3/30/92, ALW 0054999.) During 1992, the OIC reviewed Ross's collection of handwritten notes and confirmed the completeness of his December 1986 production of transcribed relevant entries.

10 Letter from Meese to Shultz, 11/28/86, ALV 004590–91.

11 Ibid.

12 Memorandum from Sofaer and Bouchard to Platt (S/S), Grossman (D), Ross (P), Boyce (T), Abrams (ARA), Murphy (NEA), Holmes (PM), Abramowitz (INR), Bremer (S/CT) and Lamb (DS), cc: Hill (S), Subject: Search for Documents, 11/29/86, ALV 004587–89.

13 Sofaer, OIC Interview, 4/6/92, pp. 4, 16–17.

14 Memorandum from Sofaer and Bouchard to Platt (S/S), et al., Subject: Search for Documents, 11/29/86, ALV 004587.

them]. . . .'' [15] The memorandum, which stated twice that the Meese request covered handwritten notes,[16] directed those addressed to transmit copies of responsive documents to the department's information coordinator by December 3, 1986, and to hold the original documents in their offices pending the conclusion of the investigation.[17]

On December 3, Shultz took note of the document request in a letter to Meese:

Dear Ed:

Your letter of November 28 requested that this Department segregate and hold for review by and transmission to the FBI various documents of potential relevance to your ongoing investigation. I wish to assure you personally of this Department's full cooperation as you pursue this highly important task.

In response to your request, we immediately ordered production of all documents requested. . . . Our goal is to have the requested materials in the hands of the FBI by the end of this week.

The Legal Adviser and his staff have been in close touch with the FBI investigators and will continue to pro/ide them full cooperation and assistance as the investigation proceeds.

Sincerely yours,

/s/ George [18]

Hill—who had reviewed his notebooks after the revelations of early November 1986 and located numerous notes regarding Iran, hostages, McFarlane, North and possible arms shipments [19]—began to review his notebooks again after receiving the Meese request and the Sofaer/Bouchard memorandum.[20] On December 2, 1986, Hill noted, in red pen, that "CH [Charles Hill] wkg [working] full-time on notebooks for FBI re Polecat,'' [21] a term used by Hill to describe arms-for-hostages deals with Iran.[22] Hill also received a report that afternoon from Sofaer, who had met with the FBI to discuss the sensitivity of Hill's notes and how their production could be avoided:

R/O [Readout] Abe [Sofaer] = [meeting with] CH [Charles Hill] . . . Abe mtg w [meeting with] FBI.

*          *          *

On Polecat notes, I [Sofaer] sd [said] parts sensitive, + probl [problem] of coherence in context. (S) [Shultz] wd [would] prefer to meet w [with] Dir. Webs [FBI Director William Webster] + go thru story w him orally. They accepted that + will let us know tomorrow what Dir. [Director Webster] says.[23]

---

[15] Ibid., ALV 004588 (emphasis added).

[16] Ibid. ("Please note that the request defines documents which are subject to production most broadly to include handwritten notes, diaries, and telephone logs of Department officials. . . . It is not necessary to retrieve documents that were directed to the central information system. . . . However, any . . . personal notes . . . must be produced'').

[17] Ibid., ALV 004588–89. The memorandum also directed that, "[i]f you have any question as to whether a particular document is responsive, you should forward it. L [Office of the Legal Adviser] will make the final determination of responsiveness.'' (Ibid., ALV 004589.)

[18] Letter from Shultz to Meese, 12/3/86, ALV 011058.

[19] E.g. Hill, OIC Interview, 2/21/92, pp. 18–19, 21; accord Hill Note, 11/8/86, ANS 0001743–44 ("CH bfs (S) [Charles Hill briefs Shultz] on all details of Polecat. . . . Arf [Raphel] knows more than this

chronology[.] CH—. . . does chronology of what we told since May '85") (emphasis in original); Hill Note, 11/9/86, ANS0001748. ("(S) = CH [Shultz meeting with Charles Hill] 0915 at [Shultz's] house (upstairs study)[.] CH—(hands over 3 papers—Chron [Chronology] of what we knew since May '85, . . .") (emphasis in original); Hill Note, 11/10/86, ANS 0001756 ("from CH [Charles Hill] notebooks'').

[20] On December 1, 1986, Hill made a note, and told Shultz, that the topic of Brunei's $10 million contribution to the contras was "not w/I [within] the purview of what they asked for in this investigation.'' (Hill Note, 12/1/86, ANS 0001941, emphasis in original). Hill made another note to the same effect the next day, and again passed the information to Shultz. (Hill Note, 12/2/86, ANS 001946.) Hill's notes suggest that he read the Sofaer/Bouchard memorandum closely.

[21] Hill Note, 12/2/86, ANS 0001946.

[22] Both Platt and Hill were evasive about the origin and meaning of the term "Polecat,'' which appears throughout their notes as a reference to arms-for-hostages proposals and developments. (See Hill, Grand Jury, 7/10/92 pp. 39–41, "That is what Platt and I began to call this whole thing because we associated it with Oliver North. I believe Platt made this name up. North equaled Pole . . . and Polecat was something that kind of smelled. . . . It was whatever Oliver North and McFarlane were up to.''); cf. Shultz, OIC Interview, 2/12/92, p. 46 ("That [Polecat] was Charlie Hill's characterization, I think.''). Platt's principal deputies from 1985 each confirmed that "Polecat'' was a derogatory term for Oliver North personally (North—North Pole—Polecat) and referred to the arms-for-hostages aspects of North's counterterrorism activities. (Quinn, FBI 302, 12/4/91, pp. 2–3; Brunson McKinley, FBI 302, 12/13/91, p. 3.) For a time in late 1985, Hill replaced "Polecat'' in his notes with the less pejorative term "Night Owl.''

[23] Hill Note, 12/2/86, ANS 001946. Hill's note indicates that he passed this information to Shultz. Ibid. (symbol of arrow pointing to the right with a star at the end of the arrow and a vertical line through the shaft of the arrow); accord Hill, OIC Interview, 7/9/92, pp. 8–9 (explaining meaning of the symbol).

Later that afternoon, Hill wrote, underlined and circled: "CH [Charles Hill] Reemerges from Notebook research on Polecat." [24]

Hill continued his notebook review the next day. At the top of his first page of December 3 notes, Hill wrote and circled, "CH [Charles Hill] works on Notebook Research." [25] Hill also received Sofaer's report that the FBI had determined that one agent would need to see Hill's notes:

CH Notes

$$\frac{Abe = CH}{1220}$$

Dir Webst [FBI Director Webster] doesnt want to get personally involved. One guy wd [would] go over docs [documents] w CH [Charles Hill]. Tell you what he needs + leave the rest. [26]

Hill immediately reported this proposed arrangement to Shultz, who replied, "ok, good." [27]

On Thursday, December 4, 1986, Hill provided the notes he had selected from his review to three FBI special agents who met at State with him and Michael G. Kozak, the principal deputy legal adviser. [28] Hill told the agents that he had searched his handwritten notes and other records that were available to him in the secretary's office and located a set of documents pertinent to the Iran/contra arms controversy. [29] Hill provided the agents a chronological set of 65 photocopied pages. [30] The documents Hill provided consisted of excerpted entries (some of which also were partially redacted) from 32 pages of his own notebooks; three excerpted notes by Platt dated November 19, 1985; and cables and other Department of State documents. [31] Hill did not state to the FBI agents that he had more relevant material, that he had not had time to review all of his notebooks, or that this production was the result of a partial review of the notebooks. FBI Special Agent Danny O. Coulson understood that Hill was pro-

viding everything he had that was relevant to Iran/contra within the parameters of Attorney General Meese's November 28, 1986, letter to Shultz. [32]

Pursuant to Sofaer's discussion with FBI Director William H. Webster, Hill also met privately on December 4, 1986, with Coulson, who was the senior FBI agent assigned to the Iran/contra investigation. [33] During this interview, Hill said that he possessed notes he had taken of his conversations with Shultz regarding arms sales to Iran. Hill stressed that these notes, which represented confidential conversations between Cabinet officers and the President, were extremely sensitive and asked Coulson to disseminate the notes only to individuals with an absolute "need to know." Hill then disclosed that these notes related in part to the December 7, 1985, meeting of President Reagan, Defense Secretary Caspar W. Weinberger, Shultz, White House Chief of Staff Donald T. Regan, former National Security Adviser Robert C. McFarlane, National Security Adviser John M. Poindexter and CIA Deputy Director John N. McMahon regarding selling arms to Iran. [34] After walking Coulson through the documents, which contained explosive statements attributed to President Reagan, [35] Hill provided copies of five photocopied pages to the FBI: one page of typed talking points that had been prepared for Shultz's use at the December 7, 1985, meeting; excerpted entries from three pages of Hill's December 7 notes; and one page with two excerpted notes by Platt dated December 7. [36] In his own notes, Hill subsequently made this account of the interview:

---

[24] Hill Note, 12/2/86, ANS 0001947.

[25] Ibid., 12/3/86, ANS 0001953.

[26] Ibid., ANS 0001955.

[27] Ibid.

[28] Hill, FBI 302 (Special Agent Beane), 12/4/86.

[29] Ibid., p. 1.

[30] See Ibid. (attached photocopies). Hill wrote the date of each incompletely dated or undated document on the upper right-hand corner of each photocopied page.

[31] Ibid., pp. 1–5 (itemizing the documents produced).

[32] Memorandum from FBI Special Agent Michael S. Foster re: Coulson/OIC Meeting, 3/5/92, pp. 1–2, 027774.

[33] Hill, FBI 302 (Special Agent Coulson), 12/4/86.

[34] Ibid., p. 1.

[35] Coulson's interview report states that,

[a]t the December 7, 1985 meeting, Secretary of Defense Weinberger, Secretary of State Shultz and Donald Regan opposed sale of arms to Iran as being illegal. . . . During this meeting President Reagan indicated that the American people would not understand if four hostages died because "I wouldn't break the law."

\*              \*              \*

During the course of this meeting the President indicated that "they can impeach me if they want, visiting days are Wednesday." Weinberger indicated "you will not be alone."

(Ibid., pp. 1–2.)

[36] Ibid. (attachments); ALW 0059585–88 ("original" photocopied handwritten Hill and Platt notes provided by Hill to FBI on December 4, 1986; each page is dated by Hill in red pen in upper right hand corner).

CH [Charles Hill] = [meeting with] FBI
1030–1300         Reads Polecat Record
—Parts on P [Presidential] conversations
(Dec 6, 7, 1985) read to sr. [senior]
agent only, who will discuss w the
Director.
—Asked for nothing to take away.
—astounded at the detail of fact. Much
that was new to them.
—said, personally, "if only the WH
[White House] had taken the (S)
[Secretary's] advice." [37]

Later on the afternoon of December 4, 1986, Sofaer told Hill that the FBI wanted to take possession of his original notes regarding the Brunei solicitation,[38] but added that Kozak would try to make alternative arrangements:

—Webster wants orig [original] notes +
wd [would] lock up for indep. counsel.
Kozak will work for giving copies + CH
[Charles Hill] showing originals on request.[39]

Hill also wrote some reflections that day on the process of reviewing his notebooks in re-

sponse to the Meese request and the Sofaer/Bouchard memorandum:

—Polecat
Reviewing the notebooks for the 4th time Like rereading Paradise Lost; each time something new seems to appear—not new evidence, but new interpretations impress themselves on you. The impression now shining through is that the key figures were . . . [Michael Ledeen and North].
So 2 activists—one policy driven, one operationally driven [—] play on the flaws of 2 leaders:—McF's [McFarlane's] megalomania—P's [President Reagan's] humanitarian spirit [40]

In April 1987, the OIC transmitted its omnibus document request to the Department of State. This request, which covered the period January 1, 1983, to the present, specifically called for the production of all "notes" prepared or maintained by Hill and Platt on subjects including the sale, shipment or transfer of military arms to Iran.[41] On May 28, 1987, the Office of the Legal Adviser produced various photocopied documents in response to the OIC request. One set of documents, which includes a number of excerpted Hill notebook entries, was a slightly expanded version of the chronological set of document copies that Hill had provided to the FBI special agents on December 4, 1986: It included copies of excerpts from 34 pages of his own notebooks and five excerpted notes by Platt.[42] A second set of documents consists of excerpted Platt notes, including 18 photocopied pages of excerpted notes regarding Iran that Platt had provided to Sofaer's office in December 1986.[43]

In early 1988, the Department of State also provided to the OIC a copy of the set of Hill's November and December 1986 "post-revelation" notes, which had been provided to the Senate Select Iran/contra Committee in 1987.[44]

---

[37] Hill Note, 12/4/86, ANS 0001966.
Hill later received a report of the reactions that the FBI agents had expressed to Kozak after their meeting with Hill:
y [you] impressed the hell out of them . . . one FBI sd [said] to Kozak[:] "I deal w [with] murderers, rapists, terrorists + the scum of the earth and I'm a pretty thick skinned guy—but when I hear what those guys in the WH [White House] did to the Sec of State—as a citizen—I'm furious."
(Ibid., 12/4/86, ANS 0001968.)
Two weeks later, the senior FBI agent met again with Hill to discuss these documents. Hill clarified that his notes resulting from the December 7, 1985, White House meeting were based on a general conversation and then a more detailed meeting with Shultz; Hill identified Platt as the author of the other notes Hill had produced on December 4; and Hill stated that Platt's note marked "from Rich" reflects information that Weinberger gave to Assistant Secretary of Defense Richard Armitage, who in turn reported Weinberger's comments to Platt. (Hill, FBI 302, 12/18/86; accord, Hill Note, 12/18/87, ANS 0002073: "1415—Colson [sic] = [meeting with] CH [Charles Hill] (Just to ask CH to explain relationship betw [between] the various R/O's [read outs] of the Dec 7 '85 mtg + the tp [talking points] prepared for it.[)]".)
[38] At this time, there was substantial concern among Department of State officials such as Abrams, Sofaer and Hill (who knew that Brunei had contributed $10 million to the contras but that North had claimed it never arrived) that North had absconded with the Brunei money.
[39] Hill Note, 12/4/86, ANS 0001968. Hill later told Shultz that "Webster wants orig [original] pages of notebooks.—but that wd [would] destroy 'best evidence' on other issues (2 sided pages) in order to get 'best evidence' for this [Brunei] issue." (Hill Note, 12/4/86, ANS 001970, emphasis in original.) Hill, who graduated from law school but never practiced, recalled the "best evidence rule" from "a case in [his law school] Evidence course." (Ibid.)

[40] Hill Note, 12/4/86, ANS 0001970–71.
[41] Letter from Geoffrey S. Stewart to Michael Kozak, Deputy Legal Adviser, 4/23/87.
[42] ALV 001577–1680.
[43] ALV 002710–40.
[44] Hill Notes, 11/3/86–12/31/86, ALW 021109–430 (set of photocopied, redacted pages selected from Hill's notebooks that was provided to the Senate Select Committee by the Department of State in 1987; produced by State to the OIC on January 20, 1988).

## OIC Acquires Additional Department of State Evidence During 1990 and 1991

In 1990, the OIC requested and received Hill's permission to review his original notebooks covering the period 1983 through the end of the Reagan Administration in January 1989, and to photocopy all entries relevant to the continuing Iran/contra investigation.[45] At the time, Independent Counsel's investigation was focused on support for the Nicaraguan contras and the activities and statements of sub-Cabinet officials such as Elliott Abrams, Duane R. Clarridge, Alan D. Fiers, Jr. and Donald P. Gregg. Neither Shultz nor Hill was a subject of the OIC's investigation.

The 1990 review of Hill's notebooks resulted in the OIC keeping copies of a much greater volume of relevant notes than the Department of State had produced in response to OIC and congressional requests in 1986 and 1987.[46] The OIC continued to assume the accuracy of Shultz's well-known testimony regarding his exclusion from information regarding arms shipments to Iran and his (and Hill's) seeming cooperation with each Iran/contra investigation. When Shultz and Hill were reinterviewed at the end of 1990, the OIC remained focused upon the subjects of its investigation at that time: Abrams, Clarridge and Gregg.

On April 5, 1991, the OIC also interviewed Nicholas Platt as part of its continuing investigations of Clarridge, Abrams and Gregg.[47] Platt described his notetaking practices as executive secretary and said that, although he already had reviewed his notes for any relevant Iran/contra material and turned the relevant notes over to both Congress and the OIC, his complete notes were in a safe deposit box at a local bank, and the OIC was welcome to review them and duplicate them as necessary.[48] The following Monday, an FBI special agent took custody of Platt's original notes for the period January 1985 through February 1987.[49] In May 1991, after a brief review of Platt's original handwritten notes revealed that they were highly relevant to the continuing Iran/contra investigation, the OIC requested and obtained Platt's permission to copy his entire collection of notes.[50] The OIC returned Platt's original notes later in 1991.[51]

It was not until the summer and fall of 1991, in connection with the accelerating investigations of Abrams and several CIA officials, that the OIC realized that Hill's notes were inconsistent with Shultz's testimony. Further investigation revealed that Hill had not produced these notes in 1986 or 1987, and that Platt had not produced corresponding notes of many of the same events. The OIC later obtained notes from other Department of State officials that also had not been produced to Iran/contra investigators.[52]

## Shultz's "Three Phases" of Department of State Knowledge Regarding Arms Shipments to Iran

Starting with his earliest closed-session testimony before Congress on December 16, 1986, Shultz characterized his knowledge of the Iran arms shipments in three phases: from June to

---

[45] Hill made his notebooks available to the OIC for its review off-site, first during June 1990 in a secure facility at the Hoover Institution library in Stanford, California, and then during July and August 1990 in a secure section of the National Archives and Records Administration in Washington, D.C. The OIC reviewed these documents anew, identifying and copying *all* relevant items. It was not until much later that the OIC compared its selection to Hill's original production of relevant notes.

[46] Most of the "new" Hill notes that the OIC identified and photocopied in 1990 fell into two categories. Some notes address the plethora of specific topics concerning the Nicaraguan contras (including strategy for obtaining contra aid from Congress, regional diplomatic activity and contra financial analyses) that the OIC had agreed to exclude from its request for relevant Hill notes in 1987. Other notes were created during the period April 24, 1987, through January 20, 1989, which was outside the scope of the OIC's previous requests for relevant Hill notes. The OIC accordingly was not troubled to find these notes when it reviewed Hill's notebooks in July 1990.

[47] Platt, FBI 302, 4/5/91, pp. 4–9. This interview, which the OIC had requested months earlier, had been deferred until Platt, who was serving as United States ambassador to the Philippines at the time, was in Washington for regular consultations.

[48] Ibid., pp. 2–3.

[49] Ibid., 4/8/91, p. 1.

[50] Letter from John Q. Barrett to Ambassador Platt, 5/28/91, 016491; Letter from Ambassador Platt to Barrett, 6/5/91, 016596.

[51] Platt, FBI 302, 9/24/91, p. 1.

[52] For example, in 1991 and 1992, the OIC located for the first time handwritten meeting and reminder notes that had been created contemporaneously by three junior foreign service officers (Glyn Davies, Keith Eddins and Debi Graze) who served as special assistants to Shultz during 1986–87. Although these notes were largely cumulative, repeating much information that Hill, Platt, Ross, Quinn and/or Raphel had recorded in their notes, they occasionally contained substantive information that was not recorded in any other document. These notes were not produced earlier because the Department of State failed to advise the special assistants that they had been requested. (Eddins, FBI 302, 1/28/91, p. 6; Graze, FBI 302, 8/27/92, p. 3.) When contacted directly by the OIC in 1991–92, each special assistant promptly and voluntarily provided the requested material.

November 1985, when he said he knew arms sales were debated but was not informed that any took place; from December 1985 to May 1986, when he said he knew the United States was attempting to open a dialogue with Iran but was unwilling to sell arms; and from May 4 to November 3, 1986, when he received no information of arms transfers. In essence, Shultz's testimony centered more on what he did not know than on what he did; it laid the groundwork for the widely held misperception that he and other Department of State officials were largely ignorant of the Iran arms shipments. Shultz's testimony—which was prepared by Hill and Sofaer, and reviewed by Platt—specifically characterized the development of the Iran initiative, and his knowledge of the initiative, as follows:

> The following chronology would fail to give the full picture as I saw it if I did not note at the outset that this year-and-a-half-long episode involving contacts with Iran seems to me in retrospect to have taken place in three phases: an initial period from June until November 1985 when arms transfers were periodically debated as part of an effort to improve relations with Iran and secure the release of our hostages—*during this period I learned of two proposed arms transfers, but was not informed that either was consummated*; a middle period, from December '85 to May '86, *during which I had strong evidence that we were trying to open a dialogue with Iran but were unwilling to sell arms*; and a third phase, from May 4, 1986, when I heard of a discussion in London about arms transfers and protested to the White House, until the revelations in the media beginning November 3, 1986—*during this period I received no information indicating that an arms transfer to Iran had occurred.*[53]

---

[53] Shultz, SSCI Testimony, 12/16/86, pp. 6–7 (emphasis added); accord, Shultz, House Foreign Affairs Committee (HFAC) Testimony, 1/21/87, pp. 13–14; Shultz, Tower Commission Testimony, 1/22/87, pp. 8–9. In 1992, Shultz explained that it had been his thinking that the "three phases" construct

just made the account more understandable and easier to describe. The phases were characterized, I believe, by if a phase came to an end and I concluded for one reason or another that the effort to sell arms to Iran had stopped, so that ended the phase.

The evidence contained in contemporaneous notes supports the thesis that Shultz and others in the department opposed the initiative. But it does not support the commonly accepted corollary: that they were prevented from monitoring the initiative. In fact, Shultz and his senior officials did monitor the initiative. As a result, Shultz and other top department officials had a far better understanding of the initiative than their testimony suggests. Moreover, significant aspects of Shultz's testimony were incorrect: Shultz learned in "phase one" that arms had been shipped; Shultz repeatedly complained during "phase two" that arms were still on the table; and there is strong evidence that, during "phase three," Shultz learned in both late May and late July that arms had been shipped to Iran in exchange for the release of hostages. The evidence shows that Shultz's characterization of each of the three phases set out in his testimony was incorrect: Shultz and others in the department were substantially better informed during each of the three phases than he stated.

## Phase One: "from June until November 1985 . . . I learned of two proposed arms transfers, but was not informed that either was consummated"

As Shultz told Congress, he learned during 1985 of two proposed transfers of U.S. arms to Iran: the Israeli TOW missile shipments planned for August and September, and the Israeli HAWK missile shipment planned for November. He did not admit knowledge that either was consummated.

Contemporaneous notes taken by both Platt and Hill show that Shultz and other senior Department officials received information indicating that the transfers had taken place. These notes corroborate McFarlane's contention that

---

(Shultz, OIC Interview, 2/12/92, p. 37.) Although Shultz had abandoned the "three phases" organizational scheme by the time he gave public testimony before the Select Committees in July 1987, the substance of his testimony was largely unchanged and he did, on one occasion, resurrect "three time periods" in response to a specific question. (Shultz, Select Committees Testimony, 7/24/87, pp. 87–93.) He also told the Select Committees at the beginning of his testimony that he would make no opening statement because Congress had his prior Iran/contra testimony and what he had to say was "basically the same testimony. So I don't choose to read it out again." (Ibid., 7/23/87, p. 2.)

he had kept Shultz and others informed about the Iran initiative.

Hill's notes reflect that McFarlane informed Shultz (who was traveling in Australia) by a "back channel" cable transmitted on July 14, 1985, that he (McFarlane) had been advised by an Israeli emissary of contacts with Iranians who

> were confident that they cld [could] achieve the release of the 7 hostg [hostages]. They sought some gain in return: 100 TOWS from Israel—but the larger purpose wld [would] be the opening of the private dialogue w [with] a high level American official and a sustained discussion of US-Iranian relations[.] [54]

Shultz directed Hill to "do a cautiously positive reply to say ok." [55] Shultz, by cable transmitted later that day, told McFarlane that he (Shultz) agreed

> that we should make a tentative show of interest without commitment. . . .
>
> That being said, I further agree with you that this situation is loaded with "imponderables" that call for great caution on our part. . . . I would only underscore a couple of them: the fraud that seems to accompany so many deals involving arms and Iran. . . .
>
> I suggest . . . that we give the emissary a positive but passive reply. That is tell him that he may convey to his Iranian contacts that the U.S. has been informed of the Iranian proposal and is receptive to the idea of a private dialogue involving a sustained discussion of U.S.-Iranian relations. In other words, we are willing to listen and seriously consider any statement on this topic they may wish to initiate. . . .[56]

Shultz followed up after he returned to Washington on July 19, 1985.[57] Hill made a note

that Shultz should "check w[ith] Bud" McFarlane about

> * "Emissary" from Israel re Israel-Iran contact to help w[ith] A. 7 hostages B. moderates in post-Khomeini Iran (Gorbanefar) [sic] [58]

On August 6, Hill took detailed notes of Shultz's "read out," or recounting, of his conversation with McFarlane regarding the "Israel-Iran link:"

> 3 mtgs [meetings] betw [between] Israelis + 2 or 3 from Iran (Hamburg + Tel Aviv) Bud's contact is [Israeli official David] Kimche. Was in DC on weekend. Irans [Iranians] sees IR [Iran] in shambles. See new govt as inevitable. Mil [military] + people still pro-American. Want a dialogue w [with] Amers [Americans]. Want arms from us. Want 100 TOWS from Israel. All totally deniable. Say they can produce 4 or more of hostg [hostages]. Want a meeting somewhere. So Bud is pursuing it. Shamir told Kimche he wanted to know explicitly whether I informed. Kimche sd [said] Murf [Murphy] mtg [with Syria] scares them.[59]

Hill also noted his own response to Shultz's report, and Shultz's ultimate response to McFarlane:

> CH [Charles Hill] to (S) [Shultz]
> We are being had. Isr [Israel] desperate for a big arms trade rel [relationship] w [with] Iran that US permits. They have finally hit on the way to do it.
> (S): its a mistake. I sd [said] it had to be stopped [60]

On September 4, 1985, Platt noted information—which he labeled as a matter that had

[54] Hill Note, 7/14/85, ANS 0001109 (emphasis deleted); Back Channel Cable from McFarlane to Shultz (unnumbered), 7/14/85, ALV 005092–95.

[55] Hill Note, 7/14/85, ANS 0001109. This note was not produced to the FBI, Independent Counsel, the Tower Commission or the Select Committees during 1986 or 1987.

[56] SECTO 13108, 7/14/85, ALW 001132–34.

[57] Shultz Record of Schedule, 7/19/85, ALW 0048791.

[58] Hill Note, 7/23/85, ANS 0001140. Shultz also discussed this topic at a "wrap up" meeting with his senior aides late the next day. (Hill Note, 7/24/85, ANS 0001141.) Hill made another note two days later that Shultz should "check out" this matter with McFarlane. (Hill Note, 7/26/85, ANS 0001143.) On August 5, 1985, Hill made a note indicating that he told Shultz to ask McFarlane "tonight at 6 pm" about "Peres + Isr [Israel]/Iran intel [intelligence] link[.]" (Hill Note, 8/5/85, ANS 0001152.) None of these notes was produced to the FBI, Independent Counsel, the Tower Commission or the Select Committees during 1986 or 1987.

[59] Hill Note, 8/6/85, ANS 0001154.

[60] Ibid.

lots of "juice" [61]—about Shultz-McFarlane discussions and "equipment" shipments to Iran in exchange for hostages:

—Juice—O    [Oliver    North]—Bud [McFarlane]—Ledeen—Back channels Israel-Iran—would produce 7 hostages[.] Kimche. ~~Israel~~ Israelis ~~produce~~ said they could produce—Because Iranians wanted equipment.
Past 2 days—sidebar conversations w Bud + S [Shultz]—How to move them—numbers, etc. . . .
—This AM Bud said to S—Deal is— They'll move seven hostages to beach . . .
—Ollie North will go out + arrange. He needs a fake passport ~~will get~~ We have one.[62]

On September 11, 1985, Hill noted his awareness that these exchanges would leave the United States with an obligation to replenish "arms" to Israel:

Bud [McFarlane] wkg [working] on 7 hstgs [hostages]. Don't stir it up. Its independent from Syrian effort. Iran-Israel. Shd [Should] be worked thru by end of week. (Scam on us) They [Iran] giving us what wld [would] anyway [hostages] (for Atlit [prisoners in Israel]) + then give us a bill for arms for IR [Iran] from Israel.[63]

On the evening of September 14, 1985, the balance of the Israeli TOW shipment went to Iran and Reverend Benjamin Weir was released. The next day, Platt made a note, based on a call from Oakley (who had just spoken with North) that "Polecat [is] beginning to Pay off— Weir has been released. . . . Other things could happen." [64] On September 16, Hill's first note of the day recorded his understanding of events:

Weir released + taken to CIA [facility] in Va. Secret because op. [operation] still going on. Oakley working w Ollie [North].

McF [McFarlane] + Ollie are getting us into deal where we will have to pay off Isr [Israel], IR [Iran] and Syr [Syria] for what we wd [would] get from Syria for nothing following Atlit release.[65]

On September 17, 1985, Weir's release became public and both Platt and Hill's notes reflect numerous discussions about the release. They both noted an early morning telephone call between Hill and Reginald Bartholomew, the U.S. ambassador to Lebanon.[66] Bartholomew, who had not been informed of any of the arms-for-hostages proposals leading up to Weir's release,[67] told Hill that "all signs are we didn't get Weir from Syria. As for others (IR [Iran], Isr [Israel] etc) I have no info." [68] Bartholomew, from his position outside the circle of knowledge in Washington, said it was his feeling that "Weir was let out to ~~put~~ bring letters + put pressure on us to release the Dawa prisoners [in Kuwait]." [69] Since then, Shultz has used Bartholomew's uninformed speculation that Weir was released to deliver a message regarding the Dawa prisoners as proof that it was the reason for Weir's release and that Shultz, himself, was unaware of the arms transfers that preceded Weir's release.[70] Contrary to Shultz's pretenses, Hill's notes from later in the day on September 17, 1985, show that Shultz did receive indications that arms were involved.

On the day that Weir's release was announced, NBC News had a story about an airplane that had run into trouble on its flight

---

[61] Platt Note, 9/4/85, ALW 0036258. Platt's deputy said Platt used the term "juice" to refer to anything that was "especially interesting." (Quinn, FBI 302, 12/4/91, p. 3.)
[62] Platt Note, 9/4/85, ALW 0036258–59.
[63] Hill Note, 9/11/85, ANS 0001117. This note was not produced to the FBI, Independent Counsel, the Tower Commission or the Select Committees during 1986 or 1987.
[64] Platt Note, 9/15/85, ALW 0036343.
[65] Hill Note, 9/16/85, ANS 0001123. This note was not produced to the FBI, Independent Counsel, the Tower Commission or the Select Committees.
[66] Hill Note, 9/17/85, ANS 0001125; Platt Note, 9/17/85, ALW 0036354.
[67] Bartholomew, FBI 302, 1/2/92, pp. 3–6; Hill Note, 9/17/85, ANS 0001125 ("I [Bartholomew] know precious little about origins of this or who is involved. Bud [McFarlane] has told me nothing of who else [is] involved.").
[68] Hill Note, 9/17/85, ANS 0001125.
[69] Platt Note, 9/17/85, ALW 0036354. The Dawa prisoners held in Kuwait reportedly included a close relative of a key member of the Hezbollah faction that was holding the hostages in Lebanon. (See generally Shultz, OIC Interview, 2/12/92, pp. 72, 93, 95, 159; Shultz, OIC Interview, 2/13/92, pp. 300–1.)
[70] E.g. Shultz, OIC Interview, 2/12/92, pp. 60–61, 70–73, 77, 79, 90, 113, 115, 172–73. The suggested explanations are not mutually exclusive: The terrorists could have decided to free Weir after Iran received TOW missiles from the West, and they could have told Weir that the remaining hostages would suffer unless he communicated the terrorists' demand that Kuwait free the Dawa prisoners.

back to Israel after delivering arms to Iran. Hill noted on September 17, 1985:

> NBC—Isr. [Israeli] arms to ~~arms~~ Iran.
> DC–8 flew from Iran to Isr [Israel]. Isr sd yes, but elec. + commo [electrical and communications] failure. Story is Iran Jews on board. Plane picking up spare parts. Kimche met in London in last month w [with] NSC official. + arrangements made. US interested in leverage w Iran mil. (ingratiating) over what comes after Khomeini.
> (false) Kashoggi [sic] + Nimrodi.[71]

Hill noted Shultz's reply: "Well, sometimes you have to try things." Hill's note indicates that he told Shultz *The Washington Post* had a story that Weir had been released. Hill observed that reporters "[h]ave not yet put the two [stories] together." In the margin of his notebook, he wrote: "Bud's folly is out." [72]

On September 20, 1985, after it was clear that no additional hostages would be freed, Shultz stated that he was "uncomfortable with polecat operations." [73] The next day, Shultz, Armacost and Whitehead discussed their concern for the U.S. Government position—bargaining for hostage release while publicly denying a deal. Hill recorded their discussion in his notebook:

> <u>Weir + 6 Hostg</u> [Hostages]
>
> Arma [Armacost]: I have anxiety about strange bargaining going on. Iran plane in Israel.
>
> (S): I'm not comfortable, don't know what to do about it.
>
> When Weir released, lot of people wanted to take credit for it. But looks like they let him go just to propagandize their cause.
>
> Arma—They are being cute w [with] me. Pdx [Poindexter] just says its v [very] confused.
> I wd be concerned about bargaining w Iran while we say we not doing a deal.
>
> (S): WH [White House] has taken control. When they want us to do something they will tell us.
>
> JW [Whitehead]: do you tk [think] they tell the P [President]?
>
> (S): Yes, But he doesn't appreciate the problems w [with] arms sales to Iran.[74]

In 1993, Armacost acknowledged that during the period surrounding Weir's release, arrangements involving "giving something for hostages" were "going on," and Armacost understood that one major component was arms going to Iran.[75] Armacost, although not recalling specific discussions, testified that the connection between Israel's dealings with Iran and Weir's release "surely" was something that he and Shultz discussed.[76] Oakley, who was informed by North that an arms shipment produced Weir's release,[77] generally kept Shultz informed by briefing Armacost and Platt.[78] Oakley believed that Shultz knew everything that he knew

---

[71] Hill Note, 9/17/85, ANS 0001126. Hill marked this note with stars and the symbol "H)," which indicated that he regarded the information as "interesting." This note was not produced to the FBI, Independent Counsel, the Tower Commission or the Select Committees during 1986 or 1987.

The Department of State apparently learned of NBC's information through a telephone call from NBC reporter Chris Wallace to Raphel on September 17, 1985. (See Raphel Note, 9/17/85, ALW 0062116–17; same information as Hill's 9/17/85 note; Raphel Chronology, 1987, p. 1, ALW 0056726.) A series of State Department cables during this period also referred to the reports of the plane returning to Israel running into trouble over Turkey after delivering weapons to Iran. (See Department of State cable to Beirut, Damascus and London, 9/17/85, ALW 025278–79; MANAMA 02805, 9/19/85, ALW 025287; Department of State cable to all Near East diplomatic posts, Ankara, Paris, London, Rome and Nicosia, 9/19/85, ALW 025282–83; *see also* "Rara avis," *The Economist*, 9/21/85, p. 42, ALW 025280; *cf.* RIYADH 08507, 9/23/85, ALW 025281, reporting front page *Al Riyadh* story of previous day claiming President Reagan sent U.S. official to Tehran to discuss release of hostages in Lebanon.)

[72] That same day, Platt made notes of McFarlane's report that the effort to obtain hostages other than Weir "appears not going anywhere" and wrote that this activity had turned into a "[r]ace between Syria to round up hostages so [Classified Country Name Withheld] can pay or Israelis can pay iranians with weapons sales." (Platt Note, 9/17/85, ALW 0036360.)

[73] Platt Note, 9/20/85, ALW 0036387. This note was not produced to the FBI, Independent Counsel, the Tower Commission or the Select Committees during 1986 or 1987.

[74] Hill Note, 9/21/85, ANS 0001132–33 (original emphasis). This note was not produced to the FBI, Independent Counsel, the Tower Commission or the Select Committees during 1986 or 1987.

[75] Armacost, Grand Jury, 3/13/92, p. 30.

[76] Ibid., p. 43.

[77] Oakley, FBI 302, 8/19/87, p. 2; Ibid., 11/13/91, pp. 3, 5; Ibid., 11/14/91, p. 2; accord, Oakley, Tower Commission Interview Notes, 12/17/86, p. 2, ALS 002391.

[78] E.g. Ibid.

about the Weir release because he had reported his information.[79] McFarlane and Poindexter also testified that they informed Shultz about the Israeli shipments preceding the release.[80]

Notes from November and December 1985 corroborate this testimony and reflect the working understanding within the Department of State that the Weir release had, in fact, involved arms transfers to Iran. A note taken by Raphel during a meeting with Armacost, Oakley, Borg and Ross on November 12, 1985, states that "Iranian/Israeli connection got Weir released." [81]

An early morning Hill note from November 18 reflects the same understanding. It indicates that Hill and Shultz discussed:

> McF [McFarlane] + Isr/IR [Israel/Iran] hostg [hostages]. That was attempt to see (S) [Shultz] last night. He thinks something's coming down in next week or so (not for the first time)
> —Nothing cld [could] be more
> (S): its          appropriate than a meeting
> a bad         betw [between] [a non-Iranian
> deal           intermediary] + Ollie North.
>                    Looney Tunes.[82]

The next day, Hill made another note regarding "Ollie North's hostg [hostage] caper. Ollie telling story (skewed) to Parker Borg. Using [non-Iranian intermediary] (witting) as cover." [83] Hill later received a secure telephone call from Platt in Washington, D.C. Platt reported that North told Borg he (North) had stumbled on the Israelis sending arms to Iran as a result of his contra activities. North claimed he "went to Isr [Israel] + sd [said] we know yr [you're] doing this + we want something for it—use yr [your] channel to IR [Iran] to get hstg [hostages] out. They thot [thought] all wd [would] come out w [with] Weir. Didn't.

Now will try again." [84] Hill responded to this account of North's story by stating, "I think Ollie is lying to try to make the arrangement sound more acceptable. We (he) didn't just stumble on this." [85]

A memorandum from Oakley sent electronically to Shultz in Geneva on November 18, 1985, states that,

> [t]hrough other sources and connections, those used for the release of Reverend Weir, there is an expectation of a possible break through on the hostages on November 20 or 21. [Non-Iranian intermediary] was informed of the possibility and urged to be present so he could take credit.[86]

As Shultz has testified, McFarlane informed him in Geneva the next day (November 19, 1985) that the remaining hostages were about to be released following a shipment of 120 HAWKs from Israel to Iran. Oakley's memo and McFarlane's report together told Shultz that the Weir release had involved the same kind of arms-for-hostages deal. Oakley's memorandum stated the "sources and connections" who were developing the November 1985 activity were those used for the release of the Reverend Weir. McFarlane's report disclosed these "sources and connections" included the Israelis and their arms dealers. The inference from Oakley's memorandum and McFarlane's report, then, is that the Israelis were following the same pattern in November 1985 to obtain the release of the remaining hostages, as they had in obtaining the release of Weir.

Notes from discussions leading up to the December 7, 1985, White House meeting of the President with his national security advisers confirm Shultz's and other senior department officials' awareness of the Israeli arms transfers prior to the Weir release. Shultz spoke with Poindexter on December 5, 1985, first by unsecured telephone, then on secure. Shultz reported to Hill that during the first call he (Shultz) told Poindexter,

---

79 Oakley, FBI 302, 11/14/91, p. 4.

80 E.g. McFarlane, FBI 302, 3/20/92; Poindexter, Select Committees Testimony, 7/15/87, pp. 180–81.

81 Raphel Note, 11/12/85, ALW 0062333. Raphel, who died in 1988, was not interviewed regarding this note.

82 Hill Note, 11/18/85, ANS 0001194. This note was not produced to the FBI, Independent Counsel, the Tower Commission or the Select Committees during 1986 or 1987.

83 Hill Note, 11/19/85, ANS 0001198. This note was not produced to the FBI, Independent Counsel, the Tower Commission or the Select Committees during 1986 or 1987.

84 Hill Note, 11/19/85, ALW 0058650 (misdated as 11/18/85). This note was not produced to the FBI, Independent Counsel, the Tower Commission or the Select Committees during 1986 or 1987.

85 Ibid.

86 Memorandum from Oakley to Shultz, 11/18/85, ALW 0047963–65.

I think we shd [should] say stop[.] Syria has indicated to Murf [Assistant Secretary Richard W. Murphy] that Iran [is] playing a big role + they can't influence it much. We are signalling to Iran that they can kidnap people for profit.[87]

Later, during the secure call, Shultz said, "This is paying for hostgs [hostages]—so we have broken our principles."[88] The only hostage who had been paid for at that point was Weir, and the only currency that had been discussed was arms.

Hill's notes of Shultz's report of the December 7, 1985, meeting state:

They [McFarlane and Poindexter] say Isr [Israel] sent 60 I-hawks [missiles] for release of Weir. Maybe thats why he released + maybe not. [Non-Iranian intermediary] sent back to Beirut so he can get credit for it.[89]

Hill's note shows that Shultz was informed that arms transfers in fact had been consummated in connection with the release of Weir. Thus, although Shultz stated as recently as February 1992 that he still believed that Weir was released to bring pressure on Kuwait to release the Dawa prisoners, and not because of the Israeli arms shipments, he could not maintain that he was never informed that Israel made arms shipments at or before the time of the Weir release.

Before the Select Committees in 1987, Shultz testified that McFarlane had informed Shultz and President Reagan on August 6, 1985, of an Israeli proposal to sell 100 U.S.-supplied TOWs to Iran in return for the release of four Americans held hostage in Beirut.[90] Shultz testified that he objected and heard nothing indicating that the transfer had taken place.[91]

Regarding the November 1985 HAWK shipment, numerous notes reflect that Shultz and other senior department officials were informed contemporaneously of many of its details, in-cluding discussions prior to the Geneva summit of President Reagan and Soviet Leader Mikhail Gorbachev, the flight plan, the need for over-flight clearances, the delay in the shipment and the reasons the Iranians eventually returned the missiles.

With regard to the November 1985 shipment of HAWKs, Shultz testified to Congress that he knew the shipment was planned, but that he believed that it was never consummated. At first, he believed no arms were actually sent. Later, he understood the shipment had been un-satisfactory and therefore returned. He said:

I learned about the—I learned about the proposed shipment in connection with the hostages, as I described it, in the telephone call in Geneva. But since no hostages were released, I assumed that no arms were sent. I later learned, as I testified, that a ship-ment went from Israel to Iran but was re-jected by Iran and presumably sent back; so as of that time, as far as I knew, no arms had been shipped.[92]

The shipment was not in fact sent back to Israel until February 1986. No contemporaneous State Department records indicate a belief that the shipment was immediately "sent back."[93]

## Phase Two: "from December '85 to May '86, during which I had strong evidence that we were trying to open a dialogue with Iran but were unwilling to sell arms"

Shultz's position on phase two was that during this period he "had strong evidence that we were trying to open a dialogue with Iran but were unwilling to sell arms."[94] The notes of

---

87 Hill Note, 12/5/85, ANS 0001227 (emphasis in original).

88 Ibid., ANS 0001229.

89 Hill Note, 12/7/85, ANS 0001242; accord generally Shultz, OIC Interview, 2/12/92, p. 45 ("I'm not a military person so I always have trouble with TOWs and HAWKs and things like that.").

90 Shultz, Select Committees Testimony, 7/23/87, pp. 67–68. Hill's notes do not reflect such a meeting with McFarlane and the President on August 6, 1985.

91 Ibid.

92 Shultz, HFAC Testimony, 1/21/87, p. 64.

93 Congress never asked Shultz whether he was informed that the President had approved the shipment, and he never volunteered that information. Hill's notes reflect that McFarlane told Shultz, before the shipment, that the President had approved what Shultz called at the time "A 30M [$30 million] wpns [weapons] payoff." (Hill Note, 11/22/85, ALW 0058654.)

94 Shultz, SSCI Testimony, 12/16/86, p. 6. In 1992, Shultz stated that his December 1986 testimony had incorrectly drawn the line be-tween phases two and three in early May 1986. Shultz said that he should have started phase three some time in or after early June 1986, after McFarlane's trip to Tehran with a planeload of HAWK missile battery parts. Shultz said that he had meant to draw the line between phases two and three at the point that Poindexter and Casey told him "that the whole operation was going to stand down or some phrase like that." (Shultz, OIC Interview, 2/12/92, p. 229.)

Hill, Platt and others, however, reflect Shultz's awareness of ongoing arms-for-hostages negotiations during nearly this entire period.

Both Platt and Hill took notes of a meeting between Shultz and Armacost on January 4, 1986, in which they discussed the Iran initiative. Shultz told Armacost that Israeli counterterrorism adviser Amiram Nir had met with Poindexter "to revive hostg [hostage] idea." The new deal would involve trading "3300 TOWS for hostg [hostages]." Shultz reported that he told Poindexter that the new proposal raised "all [the] same probls [problems] as before. A payment. Blows our policy." Shultz complained to Armacost, "[s]o its not dead. [Israeli Prime Minister Shimon] Peres comes to me on some things + to the NSC [staff] on others." [95]

Following a January 7, 1986, meeting at the White House, Shultz made a brief report to Hill. Hill's note of the report, under the caption "Iran Polecat," states: "P [President Reagan] decided to go ahead. Only Cap [Weinberger] + I opposed. I won't debf [debrief] anybody about it. (TOWS for hostages)." [96] Then, on January 14, Hill noted that Armacost reported to Shultz that "Hostg [hostage] dealing still going on." Shultz's response was "WH [White House] is running this. No comment[.]" [97]

Three days later, on January 17, 1986, there was another meeting at the White House to discuss the initiative. Platt noted Shultz's report of that meeting as follows: "[l]ong discussion of Polecat at lunch. He [Shultz] half shut his eyes—Want it to be recorded as[:] A[.] unwise [and] B[.] illegal." [98]

News of the new arms transactions circulated through Shultz's inner circle. Armacost's deputy Ross on January 23 noted that Quinn reported that Raphel had heard that the arms-for-hostages effort had been reactivated, that this might indicate the Iranians had come back to us, that a reported hostage-relief initiative involving New York Cardinal John O'Connor might sim-

ply be a cover,[99] and that Shultz had said the department should stay out of the activity but attempt to keep itself informed:

1/23 <u>1100 KQ</u> [Quinn]

      *        *        *

(2) AR [Raphel] info of Sat meeting
           reactivating Arms for hostages.
    Iranians came back?
GPS [Shultz]: let's stay out, just keep
    informed. No control or
    involvement.[100]

On January 24, 1986, Platt noted: "Polecat lives." [101]

On February 6, the U.S. Embassy in Paris sent a "No Distribution" (NODIS) cable to Shultz reporting that the "Embassy has been approached by a French, Swiss-based arms dealer . . . with a written prospectus alleging ongoing negotiations between the government of Iran and U.S. middlemen toward exchange of 10,000 TOW missiles for release of six U.S. hostages in Lebanon." [102] Hill noted the cable in his notebook as follows: "Polecat? NODIS from Paris. Its spreading around[.]" [103]

[99] In January 1986, Department of State officials learned of a complicated initiative to free Shi'ite detainees held by Israel in South Lebanon as a means of obtaining the freedom of the hostages in Lebanon. This supposed initiative involved such religious figures O'Connor, Terry Waite, Pope John Paul II and the Greek Orthodox Patriarch in Damascus, Syria, along with General Antoine Lahad in South Lebanon. See, e.g., Memorandum from P—Christopher Ross to the Files, Subject: Transcription of Personal Notes in Response to Request for Search for Documents, Ref: L [Sofaer] and A [Bouchard] Memorandum Dated November 29, 1986, 12/8/86, p. 5, ALV 002745–46 (Ross' translation and narrative explanation of his 1/14/86 handwritten note).

[100] Ross Note, 1/23/86 ALW 0047076; accord Memorandum from P—Christopher Ross to the Files, Subject: Transcription of Personal Notes in Response to Request for Search for Documents, Ref: L [Sofaer] and A [Bouchard] Memorandum Dated November 29, 1986, 12/8/86, p. 6, ALV 002746 (Ross' translation and narrative explanation of his 1/23/86 handwritten note).

[101] Platt Note, 1/24/86, ALW 0037163. This note was not produced to the FBI, Independent Counsel, the Tower Commission or the Select Committees during 1986 or 1987.

[102] PARIS 05480, 2/6/86, ALV 004154–60.

[103] Hill Note, 2/7/86, ANS 0001317. This note was not produced to the FBI, Independent Counsel, the Tower Commission or the Select Committees during 1986 or 1987. The Department of State replied, in a cable drafted by Oakley, to the Paris cable on February 23: "As Embassy [Paris] has surmised, the proposal described Reftel [in the Paris cable] is a scam. There is no rpt [repeat] no USG [U.S. Government] official involvement in or knowledge of the purported arrangement to transfer TOW missiles to Iran, nor is there any evidence of which USG is aware that such a transfer would produce the release of American citizens held hostage in Lebanon." (STATE 054752, 2/22/86, ALV 004161–64.) The reply appears to have been literally true, because the proposal described in the Paris cable was not the proposal the White House had approved. But, as Hill's note reflects, the cable was a foretaste of leaks to come.

[95] Hill Note, 1/4/86, ANS 0001255. This note was not produced to the FBI, Independent Counsel, the Tower Commission or the Select Committees during 1986 or 1987.

[96] Ibid., 1/7/86, ANS 0001264 (emphasis deleted). This note was not produced to the FBI, Independent Counsel, the Tower Commission or the Select Committees during 1986 or 1987.

[97] Ibid., 1/14/86, ANS 0001270. This note was not produced to the FBI, Independent Counsel, the Tower Commission or the Select Committees during 1986 or 1987.

[98] Platt Note, 1/17/86, ALW 0037151.

On February 11, Shultz attended a "family group" lunch with Poindexter, Weinberger and Casey.[104] Weinberger took extensive notes of the discussion, which revolved around the arms-for-hostages arrangements.[105] Weinberger's notes record a timeline for the anticipated hostage release that included 1,000 TOW missiles being transferred from Kelly Air Force Base in Texas to Israel on February 15.[106] According to the timeline, 500 of the TOW missiles were to be delivered to Bandar Abbas in Iran on February 16, and the second 500 TOWs would be delivered on February 19, with the U.S. hostages to be released on February 23.[107] Appearing after the timeline in Weinberger's notes is a statement attributed to Shultz: "Try to find pattern of various connections between a number of countries—ours with Iran, French with Iraq, South Africa, etc. etc."[108] The latter note indicates that Shultz was present for the entire lunch, including the recitation of the timeline.

The next family group lunch took place February 21, 1986. Afterward, Shultz reported to Hill and Platt that the "hostg [hostage] deal getting screwed up. [syndicated columnist] Jack Anderson is on to it." Shultz also reported that the hostage "[t]urnover supposed to be this weekend [as would be expected based on the timeline laid out at the February 11 Family Group lunch]. I pleaded w [with] Pdx [Poindexter] that if not pls [please] shut it down. Fr [French] got stung. Spaniards too." Shultz added, "I think we have already turned over some wpns [weapons]"—again, as would be expected based on the timeline. In fact, 1,000 TOW missiles had been delivered to Iran between February 15 and 17, 1986. Shultz concluded by stating that "at F4 [family group]

we agreed no comment on any Qs [questions]. But we will get crucified."[109]

The next development came in March, when Department officials learned that one of the Iranian negotiators was going to come to Washington, D.C., in April. Raphel reported to Quinn that a DoD component wanted to tap the Iranian's phone while he was in Washington and that the visit indicated that the initiative "was back on."[110]

Iranian arms broker Manucher Ghorbanifar did visit Washington in April 1986. On April 3, Shultz reported to Hill and Platt that he had talked to Poindexter about the visit, and about a possible meeting between McFarlane and high-level Iranians. Hill's notes state:

> Polecat VI[[111]] Money man in town w [with] $ [money] to pay for TOWS. If he pays, They'll set the McF [McFarlane] mtg [meeting]. During that mtg our hostg [hostages] supposed to be released. I [Shultz] sd [said] this all has me horrified. Region petrified that Iran will win + we are helping them. He [Poindexter] said TOWS are defensive wpns [weapons]. I sd [said] "so's yr [your] old man."[112]

Platt's notes are to the same effect.

104 Shultz Record of Schedule, 2/11/86, ALW 0049130. Shultz explained that he arranged for these periodic, principals-only gatherings, which began during McFarlane's tenure as national security adviser and continued during Poindexter's, "to create more amity among the people who tended to be fighting with each other a lot." (Shultz, OIC Interview, 2/12/92, p. 89.) These lunches, which would not occur unless all four "family" members could be in attendance, typically occurred in the White House Family Dining Room. (Ibid., pp. 89, 203.)

105 Weinberger Meeting Note, 2/11/86, ALZ 0040652A–52E.

106 Ibid., ALZ 0040652D.

107 Ibid.

108 Ibid., ALZ 0040652E.

109 Hill Note, 2/21/86, ANS 0001321. This note was not produced to the FBI, Independent Counsel, the Tower Commission or the Select Committees during 1986 or 1987.

Platt's corresponding notes are similar:
  Hostage deal. Have not wanted to know much. Getting fac screwed up to a fare the [sic] well
  —Israelis have screwed up
  —Jack Anderson has wind
  —turnover to take place this weekend
  —French have paid penalty—have not gotten people out. Spaniards got a deal.
  —Asked PDX [Poindexter] to shut it down if it doesn't work.
  —Agreed that in respect to Qs [questions] CT [State's Office of Counterterrorism] et al stonewall, but we will get crucifice crucified.

(Platt Note, 2/21/86, ALW 0037404–05.) This note was not produced to the FBI, Independent Counsel, the Tower Commission or the Select Committees during 1986 or 1987.

Platt reported this conversation to Quinn, who noted "[t]urnover of people this weekend. If it doesn't work—please shut it off. Some weapons already Exchanged." (Quinn Note, 2/21/86, ALV 002336.)

110 Quinn Note, 3/31/86, ALV 002337.

111 Hill sarcastically began to add numerals to some of his Polecat notes during 1986.

112 Hill Note, 4/3/86, ANS 0001399. This note was not produced to the FBI, Independent Counsel, the Tower Commission or the Select Committees during 1986 or 1987.

Hill's notes from April 15 indicate he told Shultz that the "plans are for Bud [McFarlane] to go to Tehran 4/25 w [with] Ollie [North] to work on hostages for arms. To see Rafsanjani[.]"[113] On April 21, Armacost reported to Shultz, as reflected in Hill's notes, that "Bud [McFarlane] may show up in Tehran on Wednesday [April 23, 1986]." The danger in this planned mission was apparent: Hill asked, "How much will we pay to get McF [McFarlane] back?" and called it "all disastrous."[114] The next day, Shultz told Hill (who labeled his note "Polecat 15") that "Ir [Iran] keeps haggling. P [President Reagan] ~~says~~ has said here's the deal + that's it, Pdx [Poindexter] says. —McF [McFarlane] [is] in town today, so wont be in Tehran tomorrow."[115]

Later that day, April 22, Armacost and Shultz discussed a Customs Department sting operation in Bermuda that had resulted in the arrest of six Israelis, charged with selling arms to Iran in violation of U.S. law. According to Hill's notes (which, in a pun on "Polecat," he labeled "Poledog"), Armacost worried aloud to Shultz that, "[i]f it breaks, Isr [Israel] may blow whistle on Polecat."[116] On April 24, Hill noted that, as a result of the "Isr [Israel] + arms to Iran sting," Poindexter had "put Bud's [McFarlane's] trip [to Iran] on ice."[117]

It was in May 1986 that McFarlane's trip to Tehran finally took place. State Department notes reflect discussions about the trip in advance, knowledge that weapons parts were transferred to Iran during the trip, and, subsequently, the mission's failure to obtain the release of the hostages.

The month of May began with a leak similar to that reported in the February 1986 Paris cable, but this time word of U.S. arms sales to Iran surfaced in London. U.S. Ambassador

Charles Price called home and demanded to know what was going on. Price's call prompted Shultz, who was at a presidential economic summit in Tokyo, to confront White House Chief of Staff Regan and Poindexter and demand that the operation be stopped.

Shultz later testified that, following this confrontation, Poindexter assured him in late May that the initiative was over.[118] No contemporaneous notes record such assurances. Platt and Hill's notes suggest that, in early May at least, Poindexter gave Shultz a more equivocal response. Hill's May 4 notes state that Shultz said,

> Pdx [Poindexter] sd [said] he told Price [that there was] no more than smidgn [smidgeon] of reality to it. I [Shultz] went thru my feelings. He [Poindexter] doesnt share it. Says we not dealing w these people. He has great decision-making equanimity. But I sd to him he has the P [President] very exposed.[119]

Platt's subsequent note regarding a Shultz-Poindexter exchange reads as follows:

> S [Shultz] made strong personal effort to turn off Polecat tues [Tuesday] AM [May 6, 1986]. Saw Regan + Pdx [Poindexter]. unloaded. D R [Regan] said he'd raise it w Pres [President Reagan]. PDX then muddied waters. . . . S did it again. ~~θ~~ No insulation between this operation + Pres. This is wrong + illegal + Pres is way overexposed. Nothing will happen CH [Hill] thinks.[120]

On May 13, Weinberger called Shultz about a specific intelligence report he had just received. The report described an "arrangement to pay for items being provided to Iran by U.S."[121] That afternoon, Weinberger brought the report to a White House meeting and showed it to Shultz. Weinberger's notes state that Shultz was "appalled" at the report that, among other things, a U.S. delegation was going to Iran and that "240 types of spare parts" Iran wanted "would be available when the dele-

[113] Ibid., 4/15/86, ANS 0001412. This note was not produced to the FBI, Independent Counsel, the Tower Commission or the Select Committees during 1986 or 1987.

[114] Ibid., 4/21/86, ALW 0053811. This note was not produced to the FBI, Independent Counsel, the Tower Commission or the Select Committees during 1986 or 1987.

[115] Ibid., 4/22/86, ANS 0001426. This note was not produced to the FBI, Independent Counsel, the Tower Commission or the Select Committees during 1986 or 1987.

[116] Ibid., ANS 0001427. This note was not produced to the FBI, Independent Counsel, the Tower Commission or the Select Committees during 1986 or 1987.

[117] Ibid., 4/24/86, ANS 0001432. This note was not produced to the FBI, Independent Counsel, the Tower Commission or the Select Committees during 1986 or 1987.

[118] E.g. Shultz, Select Committees Testimony, 7/23/87, pp. 26–28.

[119] Hill Note, 5/4/86, ANS 0001439.

[120] Platt Note, 5/8/86, ALW 0037956.

[121] AMW 0002161–62 (intelligence report).

gation arrives.'' [122] A Hill note of May 19 appears to refer to this discussion between Shultz and Weinberger. The note indicates that Hill discussed the following information with Shultz:

> Iran at F4 [family group] last Friday [May 16, 1986]? Wbgr [Weinberger] told S [Shultz] about [intelligence report] that Bud [McFarlane] wd [would] get arms there + then they see about hostg [hostages]. More + more elusive. Parts for [HAWK] anti-missile system. But we believe sys [system—Iran's HAWK missile batteries] wont work.[123]

On May 22, Hill reported to Shultz that North was bringing a non-Iranian intermediary to Cyprus, and that Catholic Relief Services was donating $10 million to poor Shias in Lebanon. Shultz responded, ''This is to be [the] cover story for our shipment of TOWs to Iranians.'' [124] Two days later, May 24, Raphel recorded in his notes that Quinn had told him about a ''transfer today—arms to Iran today.'' [125] Hill's notes from May 27 indicate that he told Shultz that Poindexter had told Weinberger ''[d]eliveries are being made of our mil [military] equip [equipment]—may see action today on release.'' Hill also told Shultz

that ''[the non-Iranian intermediary] is in Beirut with 10m [$10 million]. We have commo [communications] to him from ships (the cover).'' [126]

As Hill understood at the time, of course, this information corresponded to real, ongoing activities. On May 28, 1986, Hill accurately reported to Shultz and Platt the unsuccessful conclusion of McFarlane's trip to Iran with a cargo of HAWK missile battery parts:

> Polecat died. M.O. [McFarlane[127]] to Tehran. Talks broke down + on way back. [Non-Iranian intermediary] has left Lebanon.[128]

## Phase Three: "from May 4, 1986, . . . until the revelations in the media beginning November 3, 1986—during this period I received no information indicating that an arms transfer to Iran had occurred"

Shultz's testimony that ''during this period I received no information indicating that an arms transfer to Iran had taken place'' is most clearly incorrect with respect to the information about arms transfers he received in May. Shultz was warned by Armacost, Oakley and Raphel that the arms-for-hostages initiative had *not* been abandoned after McFarlane's failed trip to Tehran. There also is strong evidence that Shultz received information indicating arms transfers had taken place in connection with the release of Father Lawrence Jenco in July 1986.

On or about May 28, British counterterrorism counterparts confronted Oakley with the accusation that the United States was violating its ''no concessions [to terrorists] policy.'' [129] Following this confrontation, Oakley wrote to Platt what appears to be the first official State Department document complaining about the ongoing Iran initiative. Oakley's June 2, 1986, memorandum, which followed up on

[122] Weinberger Diary, 5/13/86, ALZ 0040148; AMW 0002161 (intelligence report).

[123] Hill Note, 5/19/86, ANS 0001453. This note was not produced to the FBI, Independent Counsel, the Tower Commission or the Select Committees during 1986 or 1987.

The question of Department of State access to these intelligence reports became an issue during the Select Committees investigation. Shultz consistently testified that he was denied access to the intelligence reports. (E.g. Shultz, Select Committees Testimony, 7/23/87, pp. 75–77.) Although there is no evidence that Shultz generally saw the intelligence reports that were distributed to Executive branch officials, Shultz was at least intermittently given the gist of significant developments contained in them. He had several sources of this information. The director of the Defense Department component that produced these reports, Armacost and his deputy Ross all stated, and Hill's notes reflect, that the defense official regularly called Armacost to report significant developments from the intelligence reports. (Armacost, FBI 302, 1/22/87; Armacost, Grand Jury, 3/13/92, p. 95; Ross, FBI 302, 3/11/92, pp. 3–4.) In addition, Assistant Secretary of Defense Richard Armitage, who was shown some of these reports by Weinberger and Powell, testified that he spoke to Raphel on a daily basis and informed him of significant developments from the intelligence reports; Raphel's handwritten notes reflect these discussions. (Armitage, Grand Jury, 4/29/92, p. 42.) Finally, as Weinberger's diary and meeting notes reflect, Shultz had opportunities during 1985 and 1986 to learn about the intelligence from the people who were receiving hard copies, including Weinberger, Casey, McFarlane and Poindexter.

In the May 13, 1986, instance discussed in the text, Weinberger called Shultz and told him about an intelligence report.

[124] Hill Note, 5/22/86, ANS 0001459 (note headed ''Polecat''). This note was not produced to the FBI, Independent Counsel, the Tower Commission or the Select Committees during 1986 or 1987.

[125] Raphel Note, 5/24/86, ALW 0062905.

[126] Hill Note, 5/22/86, ANS 0001462 (emphasis in original).

[127] Platt, who devised numerous nicknames for people and operations during his tenure as executive secretary, began to refer privately to McFarlane as ''the morose one'' and, for that reason, Platt and Hill each occasionally used the abbreviation ''M.O.'' in their notes to connote McFarlane.

[128] Hill Note, 5/28/86, ANS 0001463. This note was not produced to the FBI, Independent Counsel, the Tower Commission or the Select Committees during 1986 or 1987.

[129] Quinn Note, 5/28/86, ALV 002338; accord, Oakley, ''Agenda'' Calendar, 5/28/86, ALW 0043138.

Armacost's May 30 report to Shultz,[130] states that "there is no doubt as to what was going on during the last ten days in May" and complains that it "was in direct blatant violation of basic hostage policy approved, reapproved, stated and restated by the President and the Secretary of State." Oakley warned that the negotiations were continuing, they would eventually leak, the Administration would be damaged and he, therefore, urged the department had to stop the initiative.[131] Oakley expected that Platt, a good friend, would deliver the memorandum to Shultz,[132] but no contemporaneous record confirms that this occurred.[133] Oakley recalled that he received no feedback regarding his memorandum and said that, in sending it, he effectively resigned from the Department of State.[134]

Raphel next warned Shultz. On June 12, he asked Quinn to report up the chain to Shultz three significant new pieces of information: First, Armitage told Raphel about an intelligence report showing that the negotiations were continuing; second, Poindexter had just told Weinberger to "implement the tilt (toward Iran)," which would mean even more weapons sales would follow; third, Assistant Secretary Richard W. Murphy had been given a cryptic message via his counterpart in a third country from Rafsanjani, the speaker of the Iranian parliament, that indicated that the initiative was continuing. Raphel was convinced that the oper-

ation would become public and embarrass the President. Quinn's notes state that Raphel requested his views be passed on. He said: "Put [it] all together. Secretary of State must go back to President." [135] Quinn passed Raphel's report to Platt.[136] Hill's notes show that Platt reported it to Hill, who reported it to Shultz.[137]

Armacost formally warned Shultz about the continuing arms-for-hostages negotiations in an "eyes only" memorandum dated July 2, 1986. Armacost's memorandum, transmitted through Platt, told Shultz that the National Security Council was engaged in "sub rosa provision of arms" to Iran, that "a usually detached (and heretofore skeptical[)] source" was "upbeat" about the prospects for a hostage release in Lebanon the next day, and that word of this deal was getting out, through Israeli official Amiram Nir, to arms dealers who were involved as middlemen, to officials of another government and to newspaper columnist Jack Anderson.[138] Like Oakley and Raphel, Armacost warned Shultz about both the wrongness of the policy and the inevitability of public disclosure.

Clearly, as of early July 1986, Shultz was on notice that the initiative was not over, regardless of what Poindexter may have told him, and that future arms transfers to Iran were likely. Hill's notes of July 2, 1986—the same day as Armacost's memorandum—show that Hill and Shultz discussed a report of an impending hostage release:

> Polecat moves again?
> 1800 EDT delivery of hostg [hostage] in
> Beirut set for Thursday
> (119th such prediction) [139]

Shultz later told Hill that the

> Iran business [is] very uncomfortable. No
> one mentions it to me—my own fault. I

---

[130] Hill's notes of Shultz's "Welcome Home" meeting with Whitehead and Armacost include the following exchange:

> Arma [Armacost]—Polecat petered out. No Deal. But it won't go away.
> (S) [Shultz]—What does it take to get this to stop? Pdx [Poindexter] sd [said] Bud [McFarlane] was out there.

Hill Note, 5/30/86, ALW 0053818. This note was not produced to the FBI, Independent Counsel, the Tower Commission or the Select Committees during 1986 or 1987.

[131] Memorandum from Oakley to Platt, 6/2/86, ALV 004620–21.

[132] Oakley, FBI 302, 1/6/92, p. 2.

[133] The Department of State was not able to locate any record indicating Platt's distribution of Oakley's memorandum. (Letter from James E. Baker to John Q. Barrett, 2/11/92, p. 2 (018147), "The document appears to have been handled 'outside the system' in accord with the designation 'eyes only.' Such memoranda are typically not recorded or tracked. They are kept or destroyed at the recipient's discretion and do not become part of the official files of the Department unless the recipient specifically brings them 'within the system.'".) During early June 1986, the only substantive Hill and Platt notes regarding Oakley concern the possibility of nominating him to serve as United States Ambassador in Honduras. (Hill Note, 6/3/86, ANS0001478; Platt Note, 6/2/86, ALW 0038142.) Hill made an unexplained note regarding "Iran—arms sales," however, on the same day that Oakley sent his memorandum to Platt. (Hill Note, 6/2/86, ANS 0001472.)

[134] Oakley, FBI 302, 1/6/92, p. 3.

[135] Quinn Note, 6/12/86, ALV 002339.

[136] Platt Note, 6/12/86, ALW 0038225.

[137] Hill Note, 6/13/86, ANS 0001494. This note was not produced to the FBI, Independent Counsel, the Tower Commission or the Select Committees during 1986 or 1987.

[138] Memorandum from Armacost to Shultz, 7/2/86, ALV 005024.

[139] Hill Note, 7/2/86, ANS 0001524. This note was not produced to the FBI, Independent Counsel, the Tower Commission or the Select Committees during 1986 or 1987.

sd [said] if I didnt need to know dont tell me. Casey said it was dead. Its not.[140]

Shortly after Shultz received these warnings, Jenco was released on July 25. Notes from Hill, Platt, Raphel, Quinn and Ross all reflect an understanding that the release was part of an arms deal. The notes show that North told Oakley as much, and that the director of a Defense Department intelligence component called Armacost and told him about intelligence reports that indicated Jenco was released in return for arms. On July 26, the day they received this news, Platt and Armacost each had several conversations with Shultz, some by secure phone.[141] And Platt reported the news to Hill on Monday, July 28, 1986.[142]

Yet no Department of State official would say that he told Shultz about the arms deal for Jenco's release. Platt and Armacost testified in 1992 that, although it is certainly likely that they told Shultz, neither could recall whether in fact they had done so. Hill, on the other hand, stated that he did not tell Shultz because he did not believe that the reports were true.[143] Hill's notes indicate that Hill regarded the reports as an interesting item; they do not in any way indicate that Hill doubted their accuracy.[144] But Hill's notes are replete with rumors that he reported to Shultz. Armacost, Platt, Quinn and Oakley each testified that any rumor or other indication that Jenco was released in return for arms would have been, and in fact was, very significant at the time, particularly given the warnings these officials had given Shultz in June and early July. On the eve of Shultz's congressional testimony in December 1986, they discussed Jenco as one the "[a]reas of greatest vulnerability."[145] Yet, Platt and Hill

did not provide their notes concerning the Jenco release to the Department's legal adviser or investigators.

## The Aftermath: State Responds to the November 1986 Exposure of Arms Sales to Iran

Shortly after the news of the Iran initiative broke in early November 1986, senior State Department officials began a two-part response. The first, led by Shultz and Hill, was a reexamination of what the department had known and done about the arms sales. The second, led by Shultz and L. Paul Bremer, the new ambassador-at-large for counterterrorism, was an effort to stop any further sales to Iran and to take control of counterterrorism policy from the NSC staff.

According to Hill, Shultz and others at the State Department were surprised to learn in November 1986 that the White House intended to continue its arms-for-hostages efforts even after the 1985 and 1986 sales had been reported in the press.[146] Shultz was determined to try to persuade President Reagan to order an end to further sales.[147]

But from early November onward, it became clear that few if any other senior Administration officials shared Shultz's views on how to respond to the growing criticism of the Iran arms sales. While Shultz called for a full public disclosure of the facts, Weinberger and Poindexter advocated saying as little as possible.[148]

At a meeting on November 10, 1986, attended by Reagan, Bush, Shultz, Weinberger, Attorney General Edwin Meese III, Regan, Poindexter, Casey and Poindexter's deputy Alton Keel, the rift between Shultz and the others widened. Shultz pressed for assurances that no more arms would be sent to Iran; Reagan in response insisted that all present support his Iran policy and refrain from making public statements.[149] Shultz replied that he sup-

[140] Ibid., circa 7/3/86, ANS 0001528. This note was not produced to the FBI, Independent Counsel, the Tower Commission or the Select Committees during 1986 or 1987.

[141] Platt Note, 7/26/86, ALW 0038556–58, ALW 0038560; Armacost, Grand Jury, 3/13/92, pp. 117–20. This note was not produced to the FBI, Independent Counsel, the Tower Commission or the Select Committees during 1986 or 1987.

[142] Hill Note, 7/28/86, ANS 0001568. This note was not produced to the FBI, Independent Counsel, the Tower Commission or the Select Committees during 1986 or 1987.

[143] E.g. Hill, OIC Interview, 2/24/92, p. 414.

[144] Hill Note, 7/28/86, ANS 0001568. This note was not produced to the FBI, Independent Counsel, the Tower Commission or the Select Committees during 1986 or 1987.

[145] Platt Note, 12/15/86, ALW 0039344. This note was not produced to the FBI, Independent Counsel, the Tower Commission or the Select Committees during 1986 or 1987.

[146] Hill, OIC Interview, 2/21/92, p. 22.

[147] Ibid.

[148] Weinberger Diary, 11/5/86, ALZ 0040517 ("Called John Poindexter—Shultz has suggested 'telling all' on attempts to deal with Iran to get their help—strongly objected[.] I sd [said] we should simply say nothing—John agrees.").

[149] Regan Meeting Notes, 11/10/86, ALU 024685; Keel Meeting Notes, 11/10/86, AKW 047253–55; Hill Note, 11/10/86, ANS 0001764–65.

ported the President, but could not support the policy.[150] In light of Shultz's position, a press release issued by the White House that day described only "unanimous support for the President."[151]

Shultz's opposition to additional arms sales continued throughout November 1986. Hill prepared a set of talking points for Shultz to use in an attempt to persuade President Reagan to discontinue the sales.[152] Though Shultz could not remember precisely when he used these talking points with President Reagan, he remembers that talking points of this sort were his "preoccupation" in his efforts to convince Reagan that the shipments were a bad idea.[153]

Shultz appeared on CBS-TV's "Face the Nation" on Sunday, November 16, 1986. When questioned about the Iran arms sales, Shultz voiced his opposition to any further transactions. Asked whether he could speak for the entire Administration on this point, Shultz replied that he could not.[154]

On November 20, 1986, Shultz met with President Reagan to go over a list of erroneous assertions Reagan had made during a nationally televised press conference the previous evening. With Regan present, Shultz tried to convince the President that the public saw the Iran arms sales as arms-for-hostages exchanges. Shultz specifically mentioned the November 1985 HAWK shipment, which McFarlane had described to Shultz as arms-for-hostages at the time the shipment took place. Reagan replied that he knew about the November 1985 transaction, but that it was not an arms-for-hostages deal.[155]

That same day, Sofaer took action to remove what he believed to be a false statement regarding the November 1985 HAWK shipment from the testimony that Casey was to give to the intelligence committees on Friday, November 21, 1986. By late afternoon on November 20, the draft testimony stated that no one in the U.S. Government knew until early 1986 that the November 1985 flight carried missiles instead of oil-drilling equipment.[156] Sofaer knew this was false based on Hill's note of McFarlane's November 19, 1985, call to Shultz in Geneva, during which McFarlane outlined the upcoming shipment of HAWK missiles.[157] Through a series of phone calls to senior Justice Department officials, Sofaer alerted the attorney general to Hill's November 19, 1985, note, which was written proof that Casey's draft testimony contained a false statement about the November 1985 HAWK shipment.[158] Late in the evening on November 20, 1986, Sofaer received confirmation from Assistant Attorney General Charles Cooper that the false statement in Casey's testimony regarding November 1985 had been corrected.[159]

On Friday, November 21, 1986, the day of Casey's testimony, President Reagan asked Meese to conduct an inquiry into the Iran arms sales and to report his findings at a senior advisers' meeting scheduled for Monday, November 24, 1986.[160] As part of this inquiry, Meese and Cooper interviewed Shultz on Saturday morning, November 22, with Hill present. Hill and Cooper took extensive notes of the interview.[161] The November 1985 shipment was high on the list of items discussed. Shultz told Meese that President Reagan had recently acknowledged to Shultz that he (Reagan) knew about the November 1985 shipment.[162] Meese asserted later in the same interview that President Reagan had not known about the November 1985 HAWKs shipment, and that if Reagan

150 Keel Note, 11/10/86, AKW 047255; Hill Note, 11/10/86, ANS 0001768.

151 "Statement by Principal Deputy Press Secretary Speakes on the American Hostages in Lebanon," 11/10/86, *Public Papers of President Reagan*, Vol. II (1986), p. 1539.

152 Talking Points, ALW 50420–25.

153 Shultz, OIC Interview, 2/13/92, p. 318. Shultz met twice weekly with President Reagan, on Wednesdays and Fridays. (Ibid., pp. 327–28.) Shultz could not remember whether he went over these talking points with Reagan on Wednesday, November 12, 1986, or at another of these regular meetings. (Ibid., pp. 317, 326–27.)

154 Shultz, *Face the Nation* Transcript, 11/16/86, p. 12, ALW 0050352.

155 E.g. Hill Note, 11/22/86, ANS 0001881. Hill's notes also indicate that Shultz and President Reagan discussed this same subject the previous day, at their regular Wednesday meeting: "Bud [McFarlane] once told me [Shultz] about a plane of arms that wd [would] go if hostg [hostages] released—not if not. P [President Reagan] knew of this—but it didn't come off." (Hill Note, 11/19/86, ANS 0001852.)

156 Sofaer, Select Committees Deposition, 6/18/87, p. 43.

157 Hill Note, 11/19/85, ANS 001200. Hill mistakenly wrote "Tuesday, November 18" on the preceding page of notes. Earlier notebook pages confirm, however, that Hill made the notes on pages ANS 001199–1200 on Tuesday, November 19, 1985.

158 Sofaer, Select Committees Deposition, 6/18/87, pp. 38–50.

159 Ibid., pp. 49–50.

160 Meese, Select Committees Testimony, 7/28/87, pp. 224–25.

161 Cooper Notes, 11/22/86, ALV 71839–42; Hill Notes, 11/22/86, ANS 001882–89.

162 Hill Note, 11/22/86, ANS 001883.

*had* known and had not told Congress, it would be a violation of law.[163]

Shultz's effort to get control of the Iran initiative seemingly failed in a senior advisers' meeting on November 24, attended by President Reagan, Vice President Bush, Regan, Shultz, Weinberger, Casey, Poindexter and Meese. At this meeting, Meese denied Reagan's knowledge of the 1985 HAWK shipment. According to Weinberger's notes of the meeting, Meese advised the group that the November 1985 HAWK shipment was "[n]ot legal because no finding," but "President not informed." [164]

Events and revelations overtook the internal Administration debate on continuing the arms sales. On Tuesday, November 25, 1986, Meese announced during a nationally televised press conference that proceeds from the Iran arms sales had been siphoned off to supply weapons for the contras. The furor over this diversion of funds became the focus of congressional investigators. In the aftermath of the disclosure of the diversion, President Reagan handed over to Shultz and the State Department the responsibility for future dealings with Iran.[165]

Other matters required Shultz's attention during this period. He learned on December 6, 1986, that U.S. Ambassador to Lebanon John Kelly had circumvented the State Department chain of authority by having multiple unreported contacts with McFarlane and North during the second half of 1986. In August 1986, Kelly had met with McFarlane, who briefed him on the Iran arms sales. Then, between October 30 and November 4, 1986, Kelly had numerous conversations with North and retired Air Force Maj. Gen. Richard V. Secord on hostage-related arrangements with Iran. During the same period, Kelly sent and received several "back channel" messages to and from Poindexter at the White House. After discussing the matter with President Reagan, Shultz summoned Kelly back to Washington and ordered him to follow the chain of authority at all times in the future.[166]

Despite the public uproar over secret U.S. dealings with Iran, contacts with representatives of Iran continued on December 13, 1986, with Shultz's knowledge. CIA operative, George Cave, accompanied by Charles Dunbar of the State Department, met with Iranian representatives in Frankfurt, West Germany. Shultz allowed the meeting to proceed with the understanding that the Iranians would be told that American hostages must be released unconditionally and that no more weapons could be sold until it negotiated an end to its war with Iraq and stopped supporting terrorism.[167]

Dunbar called Shultz after the meeting, however, to report that the Iranians—with Cave's apparent agreement—were insisting on adhering to a formal but unsigned nine-point plan worked out earlier by North, Secord and Albert Hakim.[168] In return for the eventual release of all American hostages in Lebanon, the plan envisioned more arms shipments to Iran, as well as U.S. efforts to cause the release of the Dawa prisoners held by Kuwait.[169] Shultz alerted President Reagan to the still-extant nine-point plan. Reagan authorized Shultz to ignore "any unauthorized understandings that may have been reached," and to proceed according to Shultz's understanding outlined in the preceding paragraph.[170]

## How Shultz's Incorrect Testimony Was Prepared

The admirable role that Shultz and others in the department (particularly Bremer and Sofaer) played in November 1986, both in stopping the initiative and in urging disclosure of the events of 1985 and 1986, makes the misstatements in Shultz's testimony difficult to understand. Unlike the false testimony of Poindexter, Casey and Weinberger, the misstatements in Shultz's testimony do not fit neatly into the framework of protecting the President. To the contrary, on perhaps the most significant subject on which the others gave false testimony to protect the President—the November 1985 HAWK ship-

163 Hill Note, 11/22/86, ANS 001888.

164 Weinberger Meeting Notes, 11/24/86, ALZ 0040669MM (emphasis in original).

165 E.g. Shultz, SSCI Testimony, 12/16/86, p. 31.

166 Ibid., pp. 29–31.

167 Ibid., p. 31.

168 Ibid., pp. 31–32.

169 Ibid., pp. 32–33.

170 Ibid., p. 33. On the morning of his December 16, 1986, SSCI testimony, Shultz learned that Cave had an additional meeting with one of the Iranians after Dunbar left Frankfurt. Shultz was angry, and told SSCI he would work to remove Cave and the CIA from further contacts with Iran. (Ibid., pp. 35–36.) Cave portrayed the additional meeting as Iranian-initiated, brief and inconsequential—and stated that he relayed to State the information he received at the second meeting. (Cave, Select Committees Deposition, 9/29/87, pp. 181–82.)

ment—Shultz openly admitted being informed in advance and suffered the wrath of Administration loyalists as a result.

## Shultz's December 1986 Testimony

Shultz gave his first comprehensive testimony about his role in the Iran initiative to the Senate Select Committee on Intelligence in closed session on December 16, 1986. Hill prepared the first draft of an opening statement to be used in the testimony, based on a chronology binder he had assembled. Hill then gave the draft statement and the binder to Sofaer for review. Shultz read the prepared statement.[171]

Shortly before this testimony by Shultz, Hill had given a copy of the documents in the binder to the FBI. Both Sofaer and the FBI agent who received the copy understood that the binder included *all* of the entries in Hill's notebooks that related to the Iran initiative.

They were wrong. In putting the chronological binder together, Hill omitted more Iran-related notes than he included. Among the omitted notes are nearly every one of his notes referred to in this chapter, as itemized above. Hill's omissions were consistent with Shultz's incorrect testimony in December 1986 and thereafter.

There is strong evidence that Hill intended to mislead. First, Sofaer and the senior FBI agent independently understood that the documents they received from Hill included all of his notebook entries regarding the Iran initiative.[172]

Second, the FBI agent who interviewed Hill and received his documents, pursuant to the attorney general's request on December 4, 1986, was, by arrangement of the director of the FBI, the senior agent on the Iran/contra investigation. The agent was working on a criminal investigation of the highest levels of Government that potentially implicated the survival of the Reagan presidency. The agent met with Hill to receive his documents, because Hill insisted on dealing with the senior FBI agent involved. Hill made no statement suggesting that he had more relevant material than he was producing, or that for any reason his production was incomplete. If Hill had indicated in any way that he had not produced all of his relevant material, the agent would have demanded compliance and, if necessary, deployed assisting agents to review Hill's notes in their entirety.[173]

Third, Sofaer and other State Department attorneys spent a significant amount of time preparing Shultz to testify to Congress in 1986 and again in 1987. Frequently they worked with Shultz in Hill's presence. If they had received any indication that there might be additional relevant notes in Hill notebooks, they would have done whatever work it took to find them.

Fourth, the Department of State attorneys who worked most closely with Shultz, Sofaer and Hill in preparing Shultz to testify stated that, throughout their preparation process, they all—including Hill—treated the binder as "the Bible" of Shultz's knowledge about the Iran initiative.[174] Thus, Hill well knew and perpetuated their misperception that the binder was comprehensive.

Fifth, when Shultz was first interviewed in February 1992 after being advised of his status as a "subject" of the OIC investigation, and before he was confronted with the evidence that his testimony was wrong, Shultz defended that testimony by asserting that he was confident that it was correct because Hill had gone over and over the notebooks, pulled out everything about the Iran initiative, and given it to Sofaer and the FBI.[175]

Finally, there is significant evidence, discussed separately below, that Platt and Hill colluded to withhold information from inves-

---

[171] In his initial Iran/contra testimony, which occurred in public session, Shultz told the House Committee on Foreign Affairs that he was ready to tell "everything I knew at the time about our sales of arms to Iran" but would only be able to provide the "classified" details of my knowledge and activities . . . based on documents that I have, cable traffic and notes that were taken at the time," in a closed session of the Committee. (Shultz, HFAC Testimony, 12/8/86, pp. 58–59, 66.) Although Shultz's testimony in the December 8 public session concentrated "on looking forward," (Ibid., p. 59), he provided a brief summary concerning his knowledge of arms transfers to Iran during 1985 and 1986, (Ibid., pp. 66–67.) Shultz also told the committee that he had "already made all the information at my disposal available to the FBI." (Ibid., p. 58.)

[172] Sofaer was not present when Hill gave the agent the documents on December 4, 1986, and the agent and Sofaer never discussed the documents or Hill's statements about the documents. It is unlikely that the agent and Sofaer would independently make such a significant mistake, unless Hill gave them the wrong impression that the notes were complete.

[173] See generally, Memorandum from FBI Special Agent Michael S. Foster re: Coulson/OIC Meeting, 3/5/92, 027774.

[174] Sofaer, OIC Interview, 4/6/92, p. 42; Kozak, FBI 302, 3/4/92, pp. 5, 7.

[175] Shultz, OIC Interview, 2/12/92, pp. 6–13; cf. Hill Note, 12/15/86, ANS 0002046 ("(S) [Shultz]—. . . CH [Charles Hill] [was] Quick off the mark to go over the papers for hours.").

tigators and Sofaer. This evidence indicates a deceptive intent by Hill in his dealings with the FBI and Sofaer.

Both Hill and Shultz attempted to blame Sofaer and the Office of the Legal Adviser for Shultz's erroneous testimony. This attempt to lay the blame elsewhere is unworthy. Shultz and Hill, not Sofaer, had reason to know what Hill's notes would contain. They formulated the "three phases" characterization of Shultz's arms sales knowledge in the chronology that became his prepared statement.[176] On December 7, 1986, it was Hill who objected that Sofaer had, upon reviewing Hill's draft of the opening statement that Shultz was to make the next day before the House Committee on Foreign Affairs, "expanded your [Shultz's] record to include [what Sofaer believed to be] virtually all the facts." Hill's own notes document his argument with Sofaer that Shultz's testimony should contain "characterizations and statements on behalf of Shultz:"

> (CH—Abe [Sofaer] is depriving (S) [Shultz] of the ability to make a stmt [statement] saying how he saw the scene that in any way defends his own interest.
> i.e[.] Abe—and (S)—both saying that anythg [anything] explanatory is exculpatory + so shdnt [shouldn't] be used.
> —Abe is playing to (S)'s weakness like ON [Oliver North] played to ~~Reag~~ P [President Reagan's] weakness and Ledeen played to McF's [McFarlane's]
> —So (S) can be induced to make no stmt [statement] in his own behalf.
>
>       \*       \*       \*
>
>     CH [Charles Hill] yells—gets
>         characterizations +
>         stmts in ~~behaf~~
>         behalf of ~~self~~ (S) [177]

## Shultz's July 1987 Testimony to the Select Committees

Sofaer and his staff prepared Shultz's July 1987 testimony before the Select Committees with an eye toward the "whole picture" of Iran/contra—not to a more narrow view such as Shultz's role or what Shultz knew.[178] An attorney on Sofaer's staff, Elizabeth Keefer, collected and organized documents from other agencies relating to both the Iran arms sales and the contras.[179] Keefer created back-up briefing books containing chronologies relating to both the arms sales and the contras.[180]

Keefer was certain she spoke with Hill about these chronologies, which she recalled were cleared by Shultz's office prior to being released.[181] Keefer viewed the chronologies as important: They were a list of events that were stipulated to by Congress and the State Department, and were designed both to facilitate and limit the questioning of Shultz by committee members.[182]

Keefer and others met with Shultz on several occasions to go over his upcoming testimony. These meetings were attended by Shultz, Hill, Sofaer, Kozak and Keefer. Hill's notes were relied upon as Shultz's memory of events.[183] They were "the Bible." [184]

Sofaer confirmed Keefer's recollection that the preparation of Shultz's July 1987 testimony was intended to be thorough and definitive. Sofaer stated:

> [T]he most comprehensive collection of information that we engaged in was the last one for the joint committee. . . . That was the last and I think most authoritative. . . . [I]n those answers there would be reflected every bit of information that was brought to our attention.[185]

Sofaer's staff took a team approach to preparing sample answers for Shultz:

> It wouldn't be just one person. Everybody—this was like institutional testimony.

---

[176] E.g. Hill Note, 12/7/86, ANS 0001992 ("(S) [Shultz]—One method of summary is 3 periods."); ibid., ANS 0001993–94 ("(S)—. . . . I need a structure in the testimony that enables me to handle Q [questions]. —First phase. . . —2 Phase starts w [with] Jan [January 7, 1986] mtg [meeting]. . . .—Then 3d period up to Jacobsen release where my record essentially blank.") (emphasis in original).

[177] Ibid., 12/7/86, ANS 0001995 (emphasis in original).

[178] Keefer, FBI 302, 3/10/92, p. 2.
[179] Ibid.
[180] Ibid.
[181] Ibid., p. 3.
[182] Ibid.
[183] Ibid.
[184] Kozak, FBI 302, 3/4/92, pp. 5, 7.
[185] Sofaer, OIC Interview, 2/20/92, p. 74.

[Keefer] worked on it, [Kozak] worked on it, everybody went over every answer and compared it to the documents so that the answer would be accurate.[186]

Sofaer confirmed Hill's significant participation.[187]

## Possible Collusion by Platt and Hill

Several of the most obviously significant notebook entries that Hill did not produce correspond directly to particular entries Platt also failed to include in the set of relevant notes he compiled in early December 1986 at the request of the legal adviser's office. It is unlikely that Platt and Hill each, acting independently, would have omitted notes containing the same significant information.

The parallel omissions of Hill and Platt are the best evidence that the two acted together. Foremost among the joint omissions are Platt and Hill's July 1986 notes stating that the Jenco release "was [a] result of Polecat." [188]

First, on the same page of notes about Jenco that Platt did provide to the legal adviser, he redacted (that is, photocopied his full note and then cut off before recopying) the following passage: "release of Hostages Jenco. Result of Polecat negotiations." [189] He did not provide any part of the next page in his notes, which contains the following statement:

—Price: ITOW, side winders, 155 mm ammo. Weir was earnest money. . . .

—Armacost calls [Head of Defense Department component]—real negotiation had been whether it was 1 or 2. 24 million— 4 mil [million] laundered through Israel— rest is equipment, for which, he implied, they are paying.[190]

Second, by the time Hill on November 8, 1986, began reviewing his 1985 and 1986 notebooks for information, he was aware of press

reports alleging that Jenco had been released as part of a U.S. arms deal with Iran.[191]

Third, on a notebook page dated November 10, 1986, Hill referred back to his July 1986 note about Jenco's release:

from CH [Charles Hill] notebooks

7/28 Jenco release (July) was Polecat $24 m[illion] in wpns [weapons] next will be [Terry] Anderson

8/11 Jack Anderson on it.

9/16 Ledeen = CH [Charles Hill]—wants to tell (S) [Shultz] what's going on at Casey's request

9/17 Casey = (S) Nephew of Rafsj [Rafsanjani] will be brought in. Has infor [information] on Iran. Only P [President Reagan] knows [192]

Hill, after the public revelations had begun, located the note he had made several months earlier, and then withheld the note and the summary.[193] The note showed that he had been

---

[191] On November 6, 1986, Hill, who was in Europe with Shultz, made a notebook entry regarding that morning's *Washington Post* story:

Nov 6 Wash Post Pincus: 3 American Hostages Released During 14 Months of Negos [Negotiations] + shipments to Iran.
  —channel opened at Israeli initiative

The Story—McF [McFarlane] met in London w [with] Kimche
  is
H) out —McF then met Iranians in Eur [Europe] + Iran
  —1st US/Israeli shipment of arms was Sept 85—
    + Weir Released
  —2d was July 86 + Jenco released
  —3d was this month, + Jacobsen released.

(Hill Note, 11/6/86, ALW 0056323, emphasis in original.) The next day, on a flight from Paris to Vienna, Charles Redman, the assistant secretary of state for public affairs, told Shultz, Hill and others that "most [media] stories say 3 shipments, each related to 1 hostg [hostage]. And in meantime 3 more hostg taken." Shultz replied that, if these stories were true, "Iran has made chimps out of us." (Hill Note, 11/7/86, ANS 0001732.)

[192] Ibid., 11/10/86, ANS 0001756.

[193] Hill's November 10 note also refers back to three other entries relating to arms shipments to Iran that Hill had located in his earlier notebooks: his August 11, 1986, note (labeled "Polecat") quoting Jack Anderson's column in that morning's *Washington Post*, (Hill Note, 8/11/86, ANS 0001591); Hill's September 16, 1986, notes of a telephone call from Michael Ledeen, an NSC consultant who said he wanted to brief Shultz at Casey's request about what the United States and Israel "have been doing" with Iran, (Hill note, 9/16/86, ANS 0001610); and Hill's September 17, 1986, note of Shultz's secure telephone call to Casey, who told Shultz that United States representatives would be meeting with Rafsanjani's nephew, (Hill Note, 9/17/86, ANS 0001613.) Of these three notes, only the top half of Hill's September 16, 1986, note regarding Ledeen was produced to the FBI, Independent Counsel, the Tower Commission or the Select Committees during 1986 or 1987; the second half of Hill's Ledeen note, which he did not produce, states:

---

[186] Ibid., p. 92.
[187] Sofaer, OIC Interview, 4/6/92, pp. 65–66.
[188] Hill Note, 7/28/86, ANS 0001568; Platt Note, 7/26/86, ALW 0038555.
[189] Ibid.
[190] Ibid., ALW 0038556.

told at the time of the Jenco release in July 1986 that it had been part of a large weapons deal, and that he regarded this entry as particularly noteworthy. Hill's November 10 note suggests that he made an affirmative decision not to include the July 28, 1986, Jenco note in the chronological binder of relevant documents that he was compiling.

There is more to this Hill note. In 1987, Iran/contra investigators asked the department for a complete set of Hill's November–December 1986 "post-revelation" notes. Hill supposedly complied with this request by giving the Office of the Legal Adviser a set of photocopies that Hill described as his complete notes for November 3–December 31, 1986, and the legal adviser provided the copies to Independent Counsel and the Select Committees. Although this set of Hill's unnumbered notebook pages included 24 pages of notes that he had created on November 10, 1986, the set did not include the above-quoted single page, which referred back to Hill's July 28, 1986, note regarding an arms-for-Jenco deal. In other words, Hill failed to produce the page that might have revealed that his chronology binder was not the comprehensive set of notes that the FBI and the legal adviser believed it to be.

On December 15, 1986, the eve of Shultz's testimony before the Senate Select Committee on Intelligence, there is a Platt note that shows that he and Hill discussed their concerns about the Jenco issue.[194] By then, Platt and Hill had gone back through their notes to identify relevant material. The note shows that they discussed the July 1986 Jenco release as one of the "[a]reas of greatest vulnerability."[195] They knew Shultz was going to—and did—testify that, from May to November 1986, he had no indications that any arms were shipped to Iran,

yet both Platt and Hill's notes showed that they and Armacost, who spoke with Shultz on a daily basis, had been told about a weapons deal that produced the Jenco release.

The Platt notebook entry appears at the end of the day on December 15, 1986. Hill's notebook shows that, at 7:00 p.m. that evening, he and Platt were discussing Iran/contra events.[196] Both sets of notes show that they discussed Congress's request for testimony from Kelly, the ambassador to Lebanon.[197] Platt's notes then continue as follows:

> Areas of greatest vulnerability.
> —Jenco—released well before Jacobsen.
> How did he think that had occurred.
> What did you think.
> —Why did you avert your gaze.[198]

The notes appear to reflect concerns about possible questions Shultz might confront in the next day's testimony before SSCI. But Hill and Platt each professed not to remember this conversation when they were shown Platt's contemporaneous note.[199] Neither attempted to offer an innocent explanation. Hill, who was the first to be confronted about the conversation and had never seen the Platt note, was visibly shaken. Platt, who had spoken to Hill and reviewed the note privately before he was questioned about it by the OIC,[200] simply stated, "I have no explanation for this."[201]

Platt and Hill made other significant parallel omissions in their note productions to investigators. Contrary to Shultz's repeated testimony that he was not told about a proposed trade of HAWK missiles for hostages until McFarlane told him in Geneva on November 18 or 19, 1985, when it was too late to stop it,[202] Platt and Hill's notes show that Shultz was informed

---

—Involved at outset with the Israeli (Kimche) approach on getting us into rel. [relationship] w[ith] Iran.—for intel [intelligence], then for hostg [hostages]. McF [McFarlane] picked up on it.

—(S) [Shultz] opposed Polecat op [operation] + told P [President Reagan]—so didnt want to be part of it or informed about it. This all at the very start.

The awareness of Anderson's column, the full substance of Ledeen's call to Hill and Casey's report to Shultz regarding the so-called second channel also were not addressed by Shultz in his December 16, 1986, testimony before the Senate Select Committee on Intelligence, or in the "Iran Chronology I" that he presented to the Select Committees in July 1987.

194 Platt Note, 12/15/86, ALW 0039344.
195 Ibid.

196 Hill Note, 12/15/86, ANS 0002048.
197 Ibid. ("Kelly + Congress. Standing invitation for him to go up. We ~~are~~ (NP [Platt]) are saying he can't go until issue resolved. They say ok, but don't let him go back w/o [without] seeing us. This will blow up. —leak that P [President Reagan] says admonish, but (S) [Shultz] wants to fire. —Evans + Novak will do a column. —WH [White House] will realize JK [Kelly] a hostage to release/clnc [clearance] of the instructions.") (original emphasis); Platt Note, 12/15/86, ALW 0039344 ("—Kelly + the Congress—").
198 Ibid.
199 Hill, OIC Interview, 2/24/92, pp. 386–88; Platt, Grand Jury, 3/27/92, pp. 138–40.
200 Platt, Grand Jury, 3/27/92, pp. 23–24.
201 Ibid., p. 130.
202 E.g. Shultz, SSCI Testimony, 12/16/86, p. 17; accord, generally, Shultz, HFAC Testimony, 12/8/86, p. 66.

on November 14, 1985, before he left from Washington. Platt's note recorded the basic information:

> —Small mtg [meeting]—P [Armacost],
>    D [Whitehead], CH [Hill], S [Shultz]
> —600 hawks 200 phoenix missiles for
> Iran—Bud [McFarlane] asks Cap
>    [Weinberger].203

Hill's note, which he marked with a star and his symbol for "interesting" information, recorded:

> after
>    Arma [Armacost] = [meeting with] (S)
>    [Shultz] in last few days Bud
>    [McFarlane] asked Cap [Weinberger]
>    how to get 600 Hawks + 200 Phoenix
>    to Iran. Its highly illegal. Cap wont do
>    it Im sure. Purpose not clear. Another
>    sign of funny stuff on Iran issue. PDX
>    [Poindexter] not levelling w [with] me.
>    Framed in term of long-term rel. [relations] w mod. [moderate] els [elements]
>    in Iran.204

Second, Platt and Hill also failed to produce their respective notes of January 4, 1986, which show that Poindexter briefed Shultz on a January 2, 1986, meeting with Israeli counterterrorism adviser Amiram Nir and the latest proposal to trade arms for hostages. Platt's note reads:

> Mtg [Meeting] II w [with] S [Shultz] 1140. Another issue. Israeli—Iranians—issue not dead. Peres has 2 track approach—comes to me on some issues—goes to NSC for others.205

Hill's note recorded the detailed discussion that occurred:

> (S) [Shultz] = Arma [Armacost] POLECAT
>    Pdx [Poindexter] sd [said] NiR came to
> see him to revive hostg [hostage] idea. Wd
> [Would] id [identify] Hizbollah prisoners
> held by Lahad who not bloody + offer
> to release—and 3000 TOWS for hostg
> [hostages].

I sd [said] all same probls [problems] as before. A payment. Blows our policy. Isr [Israel] has an interest in leaking such a deal.

So its not dead. Peres [Shimon Peres, Israeli Prime Minister] comes to me on some things + to NSC on others.

~~Neww~~ Newsweek had the McF [McFarlane]-Kimche meetings but didnt run it. Kimche seems to have leaked it deliberately.

I think Pdx [Poindexter] was negative twd [toward] Nir.206

Platt and Hill also did not produce their respective notes of February 21, 1986, which show Shultz's knowledge of an impending arms-for-hostages trade and his belief that weapons had previously been delivered to Iran. Each set of notes is lengthy and detailed. Platt wrote the following:

> Hostage deal. Have not wanted to know much. Getting ~~fue~~ screwed up to a fare the [sic] well
> —Israelis have screwed up
> —Jack Anderson has wind
> —turnover to take place this weekend
> —French have paid penalty—have not gotten people out. Spaniards got a deal.
> —Asked PDX [Poindexter] to shut it down if it doesn't work.
> —Agreed that in respect to Qs [questions] CT [State's Office of Counterterrorism] et al stonewall, but we will get ~~crucifiee~~ crucified.207

Hill's notes, which correspond exactly, identify Shultz as the speaker and document his belief that weapons had been delivered by February 1986 in an effort to free the hostages in Lebanon:

> (S) [Shultz] = CH [Hill], NP [Platt]
> (S)—hostage deal getting screwed up. Jack Anderson is on to it. Turnover supposed to be this weekend. I pleaded w [with] Pdx [Poindexter] that if not pls [please] shut it down. Fr [France] got stung. Spaniards too. I think we have already turned over some wpns [weapons].

203 Platt Note, 11/14/85, ALW 0036734.
204 Hill Note, 11/14/85, ANS 0001187.
205 Platt Note, 1/4/86, ALW 0037024.
206 Hill Note, 1/4/86, ANS 0001255–56.
207 Platt Note, 2/21/86, ALW 0037404–05.

At F4 [the family group lunch] we agreed no comment on any Qs [questions]. But we will get crucified.[208]

Platt and Hill also did not produce their respective notes of April 3, 1986, which show that Poindexter told Shultz that an Iranian intermediary (Ghorbanifar) was in the United States at that time to buy TOW missiles, and of the expectation that the hostages would be released during McFarlane's trip to Iran. Platt recorded much of the detail until his notetaking stopped in mid-sentence:

—Asked PDX [Poindexter] about Iranian caper—man he dealing with is in town today—supposed to have money up front for tows—if they get the money—will next go McF [McFarlane] mtg [meeting] w [with] inside Iranians—+ hostages will be released during mtg.
S [Shultz] Said horrified—said he horrified—everyone petrified of Iran. If it leaks out that we helping—there'l [sic] [209]

Hill's note, which appears at the top of a notebook page, is consistent:

Polecat VI        Money man in town w [with] $ [money] to pay for TOWS. If he pays, They'll set the McF [McFarlane] mtg [meeting]. During that mtg our hostg [hostages] supposed to be released. I [Shultz] sd [said] this all has me horrified. Region petrified that Iran will win + we are helping them. He [Poindexter] said TOWS are defensive wpns [weapons]. I sd [said] "so's yr [your] old man." [210]

Unlike Hill, Platt's position was that he meant to provide all relevant notes to the legal adviser. Platt explained the omissions as the result of innocent oversight. Hill, on the other hand, explained that he never made a comprehensive review of his notes and that he cannot understand why so many people—Shultz, Sofaer, other Department of State lawyers, the

senior FBI agent and Iran/contra investigators—had such a wrong idea. He only went through his notes, he explained, to find the notes that documented the things that Shultz independently remembered in early November 1986. He did not go through the notes, he said, to find things that Shultz did not remember.

# Confronting Shultz, Hill and Platt With the Evidence

## Questioning Shultz

In his December 16, 1986, appearance before SSCI, Shultz described his knowledge of events relating to arms shipments to Iran. Just six weeks after public exposure, this testimony was Shultz's first opportunity to testify in a closed classified setting regarding those events. Shultz testified, under oath, that his opening statement

represents an effort on my part . . . to research out what I knew about all this.
. . .

I propose to proceed chronologically. My purpose here is to pass on the information in my possession. I strongly agree with the President that the sooner all available information is made available to Congress through appropriate investigating bodies and to the public, the sooner we will put all this behind us. . . .

I rely heavily in this review on documentary materials. My recollection of these events is far from perfect, especially because . . . my information and participation was sporadic and fragmentary. Nor have I consulted with any other participant in these events, so as to avoid any appearance of impropriety.

As the evidence unfolds in public, my recollection of certain events has from time to time been refreshed. This will certainly continue to happen. So I cannot claim to be presenting a totally complete and accurate recitation. On the other hand, I can and do promise as full and accurate a recitation as my present recollection permits. Moreover, by sticking to the written materials that reflect what information was available to me when the relevant events occurred, I feel reasonably confident that

---

[208] Hill Note, 2/21/86, ANS 0001321.

[209] Platt note, 4/3/86, ALW 0037725. This note was not produced to the FBI, Independent Counsel, the Tower Commission or the Select Committees during 1986 or 1987.

[210] Hill Note, 4/3/86, ANS 0001399. This note was not produced to the FBI, Independent Counsel, the Tower Commission or the Select Committees during 1986 or 1987.

the facts you receive from me are accurately reported.[211]

Chairman Durenberger interrupted to ask Shultz "to just share with us your habit of keeping notes and how you have refreshed your recollection on this."[212] Shultz identified Hill as his notetaker and testified that "we have researched through these [notes] very painstakingly to see what we can find on this subject."[213]

In 1991, the OIC determined, after reviewing a full set of Hill's notes regarding Iran that they were inconsistent with Shultz's testimony about his own lack of knowledge, that many of these notes had not been produced in response to earlier document requests, and that Platt had not produced corresponding notes of many of the same events.

Shultz voluntarily came to Washington in February 1992 for an interview with the OIC, lasting over a day and a half.[214] These sessions focused on the contrast between Shultz's testimony asserting his lack of knowledge of arms shipments during the so-called "three phases" and the contemporaneous notes.[215] Over the course of the interviews, Shultz's attitude evolved from combative to contrite. In the end, after confronting the evidence contained in contemporaneous notes created by his closest aides, he repeatedly admitted that significant parts of his testimony to Congress had been completely

wrong. He denied that these errors had been deliberate, stating that he always had testified to the best of his recollection. He also initially denied that relevant notes were deliberately withheld from Independent Counsel or the Select Committees and he defended Hill's integrity.

At the start of the 1992 interview, before he had reviewed significant Department of State notes or been informed that many of them had not been produced to investigators in a timely fashion, Shultz vigorously defended the completeness of Hill's document production to Iran/contra investigators[216] and, consequently, the accuracy of Shultz's own testimony. He said he had "very painstakingly" researched the notes and provided "the information in [his] possession" regarding "what [he] knew." Shultz stated that, although he had not participated personally in the document-review process during late 1986,[217] he recalled that Hill "spent several hours on a couple of days going through" his notebooks.[218] Shultz said that, "[i]n terms of time allocation, busy as we were, that was a big amount of time to allocate."[219] He minimized the nature of his directive that Hill review his notebooks and extract relevant notes in preparation for the December 1986 testimony.[220] Shultz also suggested at times that the responsibility to make relevant information available was that of Sofaer and the Office of the Legal Adviser, not Shultz (or, implicitly, Hill).[221]

Shultz primarily blamed the investigators for not reviewing Hill's complete notebooks, which Shultz claimed were readily available to anyone

---

[211] Shultz, SSCI Testimony, 12/16/86, pp. 4–5.

[212] Ibid., p. 18.

[213] Ibid., p. 19. Later, in response to a question from Senator Cohen, Shultz stated his reluctance to produce copies of his notes, but he assured the Committee that "the notes have been turned over to the FBI for investigative purposes." (Ibid., p. 102.)

[214] At the time it requested the interviews, the OIC advised Shultz that, based upon information that had not been provided during 1986 and 1987, his status had changed from prospective witness to a subject of the investigation. Shultz subsequently retained counsel, who worked with him and with Hill prior to the interviews. Shultz's counsel was provided access to all of Shultz's prior statements and it was agreed that the interview would be limited to questioning about Shultz's December 16, 1986, testimony in closed session before SSCI.

[215] Because the Department of State notes that were obtained for the first time by Independent Counsel in 1990 and 1991 were not used as trial evidence or otherwise publicized, they are largely unknown publicly. As recently as May of 1993, for example, Arthur L. Liman, who served as chief counsel to the Senate Select Committee in 1987, testified that Congress "had the full story from Secretary Shultz." (Liman, Senate Governmental Affairs Committee Testimony, 5/14/93, NEXIS Transcript, p. 22; accord Prepared Testimony of Arthur L. Liman to the Committee of Governmental Affairs of the United States Senate, 5/14/93, pp. 12–13, "the House and Senate Committees . . . served demands . . . for any notes or diaries . . . relating to Iran-Contra. . . . [Shultz] made available to us the relevant excerpts of his diaries.") This view is, by Shultz's own admission, mistaken.

[216] Shultz stated that, because it had not occurred to him in 1986 that Platt's notes could contain information independent of Hill's notebooks, he was not referring to Platt's notes when he testified that he had turned over all of his records in December 1986. (Shultz, OIC Interview, 2/12/92, p. 14.)

[217] Shultz, OIC Interview, 2/12/92, p. 8.

[218] Ibid., p. 7.

[219] Ibid., pp. 7–8. Beginning with this statement, Shultz repeatedly tried to excuse Hill's omissions by stating that Hill was too busy with his regular job responsibilities to identify the entries in his notebooks that were relevant to Iran/contra. (See, e.g., ibid., p. 13, "the process of gathering information . . . wasn't something that Mr. Hill could do", pp. 14–15 "in the time he had available", p. 19 "Bear in mind we were struggling hard with our operational duties", pp. 24–25 "Mr. Hill . . . did his best in the time he had available.")

[220] E.g. Shultz, OIC Interview, 2/12/92, p. 10. ("There wasn't any necessity to try and pin down something in a highly specific way.")

[221] E.g. ibid., p. 11 ("this was basically something that I turned over to the legal adviser, Judge Sofaer, and his associates"), pp. 12–13, 31.

who was interested.222 Yet, Hill's notebooks themselves demonstrate that Shultz always was reluctant to permit outsiders to review this comprehensive and "remorselessly precise record" of Shultz's private comments and personal reflections and communications with the President and others, including remarks regarding Vice President Bush 223 and Weinberger.224

A few examples drawn from Hill's notebooks illustrate Shultz and Hill's consistently restrictive attitude regarding dissemination of Hill's notes:

—In November 1986, it was Sofaer, acting on his own initiative, who told the Department of Justice about Hill's note establishing contemporaneous U.S. Government knowledge of the plan to ship HAWK missiles to Iran one year earlier in exchange for hostages.225 Hill was reluctant to provide a copy of that single note to the Justice Department.226

—In early December 1986, after Meese and Sofaer had ordered the gathering of all relevant notes, Hill insisted on providing meager excerpts only to the senior FBI agent.

—On December 8, 1986, during his public testimony, Shultz informed the House Committee on Foreign Affairs that he had prepared a classified statement "based on documents that I have, cable traffic and notes that were taken at the time," and would testify about their contents in closed session.227 When counsel to President Reagan and Vice President Bush subsequently requested a copy of this classified statement, Hill said that "drag feet is the way" and told Platt to "[t]ell Sofaer to do nothing[.]" 228

---

222 E.g. Ibid., pp. 14–15 ("The effort of Mr. Hill in the time he had available was to find everything in his notes that had to do with this subject. His notebooks were there. All the investigating authorities knew they were there. There was never any effort to prevent people from looking at them themselves if they wished to do so. . . . I think your phraseology . . . carries an implication that . . . they had been withheld before that [the summer of 1990], which they weren't. They were available."), pp. 16–17.

223 E.g. Hill Note, 11/9/86, ANS 0001748 ("(S) [Shultz]: Nick Brady called me last night about whether I wd [would] resign. I sd [said] what concerns me is Bush on TV saying it ridiculous to even consider selling arms to Iran. VP was part of it. In that mtg [meeting]. Getting drawn into web of lies. Blows his integrity. He's finished then. Shd [Should] be v. [very] careful how he plays the loyal lieutenant role now."); Hill Note, 11/10/86, ANS 0001771 (Shultz: "They are trying by this [press] guidance to get me to lie. What are they trying to pull on me[?] Taking the P [President] down the drain. VP, Sec Def. Sec State shd [should] on such occasions prevail on P. They aren't— So I'm alone."); Hill Note, 12/2/86, ANS 0001948 ("The VP has had a thing about wanting to be a hero about hostgs [hostages]. He wanted in ME [Middle East] trip to go to Syria. Wanted to have a hostg come back on his plane[.] There's a superficiality there."); Hill Note, 12/2/86, ANS 0001949 ("(S) [Shultz] has just read [intelligence report] summary—can't believe VP in it—if so he's finished. Up to his neck in it. A lot in here. . . . (S): To extent there is truth to this, my warning to VP was ludicrous. Washed him out of politics. Cd. [Could] cause him to have to resign. It really is getting like Watergate."); Hill Note, 12/3/86, ANS 0001953 (Shultz: "Big event today is VP speech I guess.—[Intelligence reports] show he in collaborative pattern w [with] ON [Oliver North]. An action officer[.]—If not careful he'll dissemble + it will come out that he was deceiving people."); Hill Note, 12/28/86, ANS 0002108 ("Bush has lost his chance. The [intelligence report] material. Full of VP references. He always tempted to lurch to Right. Contra + Iran tempted him. So he will cont. [continue] to aspire to Presidency w [with] money + name recognition—but whose star is fading. Dems [Democrats] maybe love to have him nominated."); Hill Note, 1/3/87, ANS 0002116 (Shultz: "The whole thing crushes Bush. I'll stop saying that to people. His only hope wd [would] be if P [President] ceases to be P. I don't think he can get elected now on his own."); Hill Note, 1/4/87, ANS 0002125, ANS 0002130 (Shultz: "And it includes Bush. He is up to his ears in Iran. His name [is] sprinkled all thru it. . . . Thats why I shut out of it. . . . VP is deeply into Iran thing + has big problem").

224 E.g. Hill Note, 6/27/84, ANS 0000705 ("(S) [Shultz]—I sd [said] [to President Reagan] I upset w [with] quality of disc [discussion] [at June 25, 1984, NSPG meeting regarding Nicaragua]. Cap [Weinberger] close to unacceptable as interlocutor (in contrast to Kirkp [Kirkpatrick]). Misstates facts. Many battles since I been here"); Hill Note, 7/16/86, ANS 0001552–53 (Shultz: "Its tiresome. Wbgr [Weinberger] dishonest. Says these outrageous things. Says ABM ty [treaty] prohibits deployment. I sd [said] it doesnt—req [requires] 6 mos [months] notice. But Pdx [Poindexter] showing no signs like Bud [McFarlane] did of getting frustrated w [with] Cap. He's strong + in the center of things. You don't have to sit in these meetings + listen to Cap. He's either stupid or dishonest, one or the other."); Hill Note, 12/28/86, ANS 0002110 ("Probl [Problem] is y [you] can't engage Wbgr [Weinberger] in discussion. He makes up mind + that's that."); but, cf., e.g., Hill Note, 12/19/86, ANS 0002078 ("Cap is an ally in some ways. A real guy. Bill Clark has no substance. An influence peddler. McF [McFarlane] + Pdx [Poindexter] [have] substance but no stature apart from job they hold. Carlucci will have it.").

225 E.g. Hill Note, 11/24/86, ANS 0001909 (Hill's "Historical Notes" at end of the day include "Key point—Sofaer blurted out CH [Charles Hill's note] of 11/18/85 [sic] to DOJ Cooper, who got Meese alarmed."); Hill Note, 11/25/86, ANS 0001916 ("The trigger of the turning point[:] It was (S) [Shultz] pounding on P [President Reagan] last Thursday about NSC not giving all the facts. It made some impression—so he asked/agreed to Meese investigation, gen'l [general] attitude, triggered by Abe [Sofaer] blurting out CH notebook facts that contradicted ON [Oliver North] statement[.] And that turned up ON wrongdoing."). Hill was upset because Sofaer's disclosure to DoJ could "be read as GPS [Shultz] fingering McF [McFarlane] on something that cd [could] get him prison." (Hill Note, 11/21/86, ANS 0001879.)

226 Hill Note, 11/21/86, ANS 0001878 (Platt secure telephone call to Hill in Ottawa, Canada; Platt reports that "Abe [Sofaer] sd [said] DOJ has asked for all records—specifically the Nov 18, 1985 [sic] conversation. P [President Reagan] auth [authorized] the investigation[.] And they want our records." Hill's response: "CH [Charles Hill] Raises hell. Stop Abe for shits sake!"); cf. (Hill Note, 11/21/86, ANS 0001879) (Sofaer subsequently calls Hill in Ottawa to reassure him regarding DOJ's request for Hill's "notebooks—wd [would] not have to be taken out of your [Hill's] possession.").

227 Shultz, HFAC Testimony, 12/8/86, p. 66.

228 Hill Note, 12/10/86, ANS 0002008. Platt's corresponding notes state that "CH [Charles Hill] does not want to hand over his testimony[.] Does not believe lawyers will hold confidentially.—Didn't

—Hill also opposed a proposal by State Department lawyers that would have urged the Senate to seek Iran/contra documents directly from State, not from Department of Justice investigators:

> —SSCI [Senate Select Committee on Intelligence] wants all docs [documents] A/G [Attorney General Meese] had gathered during first weekend of Iran investigation. L [Office of the Legal Adviser] proposes SSCI deal directly w [with] State. . . . This is dumb. Q [Question] is not docs, or evid [evidence], but docs gathered by A/G. [Therefore] SSCI shd [should] get copies of 1. (S) [Shultz] reply to draft NSDD [National Security Decision Directive] [and] 2. CH [Charles Hill] note of 11/18/86 McF = (S) sectelcon [secure telephone conversation]—and nothing else. To deal directly w [with] SSCI wd [would] open up possibility of requests for all kinds of other docs.[229]

—At the end of December 1986, Platt told Hill, who noted the information with pleasure, that SSCI's initial Iran/contra report, which had been sent to the State Department for declassification, contained "no ref [reference] to notes in any way. . . ."[230]

—In 1987, Hill's "relevant" note excerpts were provided to the Select Committees' counsel under extraordinary restrictions. Hill's notes of a July 21, 1987, meeting of the Department of State legal team that was preparing Shultz for his testimony before the Select Committees document these restrictions and Shultz's attitude regarding Hill's notes:

> 0915   (S) [Shultz] = [meeting with] MK [Michael Kozak], LK [Libby Keefer], Abe [Sofaer]

MK—Cmte [Committee] will have 7 books of docs [documents] for (S)
{3 vols [volumes] of CH [Charles Hill] notes
{2 exhibit books (IR [Iran] + Contra)
{1 classified docs books (NSPG [National Security Planning Group] notes)
None of which we have been given yet
Abe—They will only refer to books a few times
(S)—CH notes surfaced. He spent large amt [amount] of time mining them. Not public yet. Devastating if they become ~~knowed~~ known. And totally ag. [against] the agmt [agreement] by which we provided them.

> *       *       *

Abe—we have to keep notes out of the room or they will be tempted to make them part of the record.
(S)—when do we get the notes back?
LK—As soon as yr [your] test [testimony] [is] over. Belnick[231] will collect.

> *       *       *

(S)—. . . CH notes on post-revelation [period]. If published as a book, worth 5m [$5 million] at least. A fascinating tale. But terrible to have them be made public. All kinds of speculation in there.[232]

—When members and staff attorneys from the Select Committees interviewed Shultz at length on July 18, 1987, in preparation for his public testimony the next week, many of their questions were explicitly based on the excerpts from Hill's notebooks that had been made available to

---

—What would FBI think about handing over?—What would Congress think about sharing?—Do nothing for now —[.]" (Platt Note, 12/10/86, ALW 0039314.)

[229] Hill Note, 12/12/86, ANS 0002021. Later Hill notes indicate Senate Select Committee on Intelligence staff members requested a copy of Shultz's "calendar" before his testimony in December 1986. (Hill Note, 12/14/86, ANS 0002032.)

[230] Hill Note, 12/31/86, ANS 0002113.

[231] Mark A. Belnick, Esq., Executive Assistant to Arthur L. Liman, Esq., the chief counsel of the Senate Select Committee.

[232] Hill Note, 7/21/87, ANS 0002699–700. Shortly before Shultz testified publicly before the Select Committees, a congressional staff attorney asked to see Hill's original notes. Hill, who was advised by a State Department attorney that the requester was questionable, personally denied the request for access. (Ibid., 7/16/87, ANS 0002658.)

them.[233] After the interview, Shultz told Sofaer and Hill that

> [t]hese guys . . . have a glimpse of my life + activities as w [with] no one else they have called [to testify]— bec. [because] of CH [Charles Hill] notes. They poring over them.[234]

The next day, during a private meeting with Hill at Shultz's home, Shultz voiced additional concerns about outsiders reviewing Hill's notebooks:

> (S): I've read yr [your] notes on post-revelation [period]. Astonishing story; Our behavior strong. But to have it up their on [Capitol] Hill for staff + lawyers to read—devastating for WH [White House]. If [Hill's notes] were to be published . . . Nothing like it in history of the Republic.[235]

—With the cooperation of the Select Committees members and staff, almost none of Hill's notes were used as exhibits or mentioned during Shultz's public testimony before the Select Committees. When Representative Fascell referred during Shultz's testimony to a single Hill note, the occurrence was unusual enough that Hill recorded it in his notebook.[236]

—On August 7, 1987, after Shultz had completed his testimony and received Hill's note excerpts back from the Select Committees, he made his position abundantly clear:

> CH [Charles Hill] notes. They personal. We have retrieved them from the Cmte [Committee]. Not giving them out anymore.[237]

In his February 1992 interview with the OIC, Shultz indignantly denied that any information was withheld deliberately.[238] He stated that he had always cooperated fully and directed his subordinates to cooperate fully with investigators.[239] He said,

> as far as I know, but you may have some other things, all of the fundamental and important information was placed in front of people and it turned out to be very important.[240]

The OIC then confronted Shultz with handwritten notes and other documents reflecting information brought to his attention and private statements he made during the period he had labeled "phase one" of the Iran initiative (June through November 1985). He had described this in his December 1986 testimony as a period when he "learned of two proposed arms transfers, but was not informed that either was consummated." [241] Shultz was combative throughout this segment of the interview and did not acknowledge that his testimony regarding "phase one" had been incorrect.

Despite the notes suggesting otherwise, Shultz adhered to his previous statements that he had not known of Israel's August and September 1985 TOW missile shipments to Iran, which produced the freedom of hostage Weir. He repeated his belief that Weir was released to deliver a message from the Hezbollah terrorists who had held him hostage in Lebanon, demanding the release of the Dawa prisoners in Kuwait.[242] Shultz said he had "accept[ed] Weir's statement and the rationale that it contained at face value" [243] and that, consequently, any broader deal involving an arms shipment "did not come off." [244]

Shultz dismissed various handwritten notes that appeared inconsistent with his testimony. Shultz said that Hill's September 11, 1985, note

---

[233] Ibid., 7/18/87, ANS 0002667–81.

[234] Ibid., ANS 0002688.

[235] Ibid., 7/19/87, ANS 0002691 (ellipses in original).

[236] Ibid., 7/24/87, ANS 0002724 ("Fascell passes (S) [Shultz] a page of CH [Charles Hill] notes Nov 24, 1986").

[237] Ibid., 8/7/87, ANS 002776. The next line of Hill's notes suggests that Shultz contrasted his behavior with Weinberger's: "Cap takes notes but never referred to them so never had to cough them up." (Ibid.)

[238] When asked if he and Hill in the past four weeks had discussed whether relevant Iran notes had not been turned over to investigators in December 1986, Shultz called the question "outrageous" and asked, "Do I have to answer a question about whether I stopped beating my wife?" (Shultz, OIC Interview, 2/12/92, p. 26.)

[239] Ibid., pp. 34–35, 39, 56–57.

[240] Ibid., p. 25.

[241] Shultz, SSCI Testimony, 12/16/86, p. 6.

[242] E.g. Shultz, OIC Interview, 2/12/92, pp. 60–61, 70–73, 77, 79, 90, 113, 115, 172–73.

[243] Ibid., p. 71.

[244] Ibid., p. 73; accord, ibid., pp. 81–82 ("There was something that apparently was supposed to happen [in September 1985] that didn't and so it was an effort that didn't work."), p. 92 ("other things that I was aware of . . . didn't come to pass").

anticipating hostage releases and "a bill for arms for IR [Iran] from Israel" was speculation by Hill.[245] Hill's September 16 note—"McF [McFarlane] + Ollie [North] are getting us into deal where we will have to pay off Isr [Israel], IR [Iran] + Syr [Syria] for what we wd [would] get from Syria for nothing following Atlit release"—which Hill made after Weir had been released but while "op [operation] still going on," also was dismissed by Shultz as "Charlie's speculation. . . ."[246]

Shultz was hard-pressed to explain other notes. He claimed, incredibly, that Hill's September 17, 1985, note reporting the NBC story regarding a plane flying arms from Israel to Iran, *The Washington Post* story regarding Weir's release and Hill's observation that reporters "[h]ave not yet put the two together" did not necessarily indicate that Hill, himself, had "put the two things together."—even though Hill noted that in the margin.[247] Shultz speculated that his telling answer to Whitehead's question on September 21— Whitehead: "Do you think they tell the President?" Shultz: "Yes, but he doesn't appreciate the problems with arms sales to Iran."—referred not to an actual arms sale that had just occurred, but the Israeli proposal a month earlier.[248] According to Shultz, Raphel's November 12, 1985, note of his meeting with Armacost, Oakley, Borg and Ross—"Iranian/Israeli connection—got Weir released"—was the speculation of that senior group, not something he in 1992 agreed with in fact.[249] Shultz explained that, while he could not recall in 1992 what he thought at particular points during fall 1985,[250] "I testified what I thought in December [1986] when I testified before the Senate."[251]

Shultz also tried to square his knowledge of Israel's shipment of HAWK missiles to Iran in late November 1985 with his testimony that

he "was not informed" during the first "phase" that an arms transfer to Iran "was consummated." Although Shultz admitted that he had known of the HAWK missile shipment by December 6, 1985,[252] Shultz claimed that his knowledge of a HAWK missile delivery to Iran did not mean that he knew that a delivery had been "consummated":

Q: When you said not consummated, an arms transfer in fact did take place.

A: That's right.

Q: Why the use of the term consummated since you were aware that an arms transfer had taken place in November of '85?

A: Well, it had not taken place in the sense that the arms were not accepted by Iran and they were rejected so it hadn't taken place. That's what I said.

Q: They were ultimately returned but you were aware that they went there and that it was some period of time when they were returned. Is that correct?

A: Basically that's what I testified before the Senate.[253]

After learning that Hill had not produced numerous Iran/contra notes, Shultz repeatedly and emphatically declared that he and the legal adviser's office had directed Department of State personnel to produce all relevant information to investigators and denied that there had been any process of selecting which relevant notes were to be produced.[254] Shultz said that, because Hill is a person of great integrity, intellect and competence,[255] his failure to produce certain notes must be attributed to honest mistakes

---

245 Ibid., pp. 54–55.

246 Ibid., p. 66.

247 Ibid., p. 101.

248 Ibid., pp. 113–14, 117–18.

249 Ibid., p. 132. Oakley's November 18 memorandum—which was electronically transmitted to Shultz at the Geneva summit and reported that "[t]hrough other sources and connections, those used for the release of Reverend Weir, there is an expectation of a possible breakthrough on the hostages on November 20 or 21"—similarly was dismissed as a "phrase . . . which I may or may not have focused on." (Ibid., p. 163.)

250 E.g. Ibid., pp. 69, 105.

251 Ibid., p. 152.

252 Ibid., pp. 165–66; accord, Shultz, SSCI Testimony, 12/16/86, p. 20.

253 Ibid., pp. 166–67.

254 E.g. ibid., pp. 8–9. Shultz also said that the relevance of a Platt note—which recommended that Shultz talk to McFarlane in October 1985 about the "Iranian connection," based on intelligence connecting the White House to a "$100 million for spare parts for Iran," and which was not produced in 1986 or 1987—is determined not by the content of the note, but by "whether or not [the information] is available elsewhere"; to determine relevance, "you have to be Nick Platt and say where did this come from and is that something I should provide." (Ibid., p. 122.) Shultz seemed to be suggesting that notetakers did not have to produce any notes that they regarded as cumulative of available information or containing information from an unreliable source.

255 E.g. ibid., pp. 84, 142–45.

he made during the limited time he had to review his notebooks.[256]

As to his statements regarding "phase two" (December 1985 through April 1986),[257] Shultz initially explained that his testimony that the United States had been "unwilling" to sell arms to Iran during this period was a description, in hindsight, of his knowledge at the end of the phase.[258] He said he had testified to his understanding of what actually had happened.[259] Shultz attributed particular inconsistencies with contemporaneous documents to his own oversights, his failures of recollection and his aides' failures to bring specific notes to his attention before he testified in December 1986. Thus, although Hill's December 7, 1985, note indicates that Shultz was told at the White House meeting that morning that "Isr [Israel] sent 60 I-hawks," Shultz said he "must have overlooked that in some manner." [260]

Shultz said his understanding that the United States was unwilling to sell arms during this period was based on two factors: First, he claimed to be unaware of a presidential Finding legally authorizing arms shipments to Iran and, because he believed that such shipments would be illegal without a Finding, the lack of a Finding meant the United States was unwilling to ship arms to Iran;[261] second, Poindexter showed Shultz talking points on February 28, 1986, for a meeting that McFarlane was to have with Iranians that would result in the release of the hostages, and the talking points did not mention arms.[262]

Shultz was then shown several notes—none of which had been produced to Congress or Independent Counsel in 1986 or 1987—that documented his knowledge of U.S. willingness to sell arms to Iran during phase two, December 1985 through April 1986.

Shultz had no explanation to offer when he saw Weinberger's notes of the February 11, 1986, family group lunch, which contain a detailed timeline for transferring TOW missiles from the United States through Israel to Iran within the next seven days:

A: Well, I'm surprised by this because I don't recall that being set out.

Q: Can you think of any explanation why these notes would indicate such an elaborate description of the delivery of the TOWs in light of your testimony on December the 16th[, 1986]?

A: Well, the only explanation I can think of is that this represented some sort of side conversation between Weinberger and Casey as frequently happened in these meetings but I'm not remembering this.

\*      \*      \*

Q: Any other remarks about that [note] before we move on?

A: No. I don't know quite what to say about it. I am surprised by it and I don't remember it.

\*      \*      \*

[Shultz:] What does this ["French dropped some demand"] refer to at the top [of Weinberger's note] then?

Q: I don't mean to be flip but I wasn't at the meeting.

A: I feel as though I wasn't either.[263]

Shultz saw that Hill's February 21, 1986, note of Shultz's report on that day's family group lunch included his statement that "I think

[256] E.g. Ibid., p. 57 ("Well, you found something [in his September 11, 1985, notes] that Charlie probably missed. That's about the way I could express it."), p. 84 ("again I think what Mr. Hill did was make a good faith effort to find everything in his notes he could find and that doesn't necessarily mean that he found everything that was there"), p. 136 ("all I can think about is that this [November 14, 1985, note] is something that Charlie Hill missed").

[257] Ibid., pp. 166–68.

[258] Shultz, SSCI Testimony, 12/16/86, p. 6.

[259] See Shultz, OIC Interview, 2/12/92, pp. 182–83 ("My summary statement is covering the period and reflects what I knew about what happened."), p. 186 ("[A]s with all these things, you don't know what a person is ready to do until you actually do it and that's what you have to judge. You have to judge by what happens."), p. 188 ("that statement [that the U.S. was unwilling to sell arms during phase two] was intended as a summary of the behavior that I observed during the period that I identified").

[260] Ibid., p. 173; accord, ibid., p. 174 ("This does say that there was an actual shipment by Israel so somehow I missed that").

[261] Ibid., pp. 181, 199.

[262] Ibid., pp. 196–97 ("I put these things together, I think quite understandably, as meaning that when people came right up to it, they were approaching this issue of creating a better relationship with Iran on a basis to which I had no objection and which is characterized

properly by the phraseology that I used [in my December 1986 testimony].").

Although Hill's February 28, 1986, notes regarding this episode do not mention arms, Independent Counsel located no copy of the McFarlane "terms of reference" in NSC records that does not mention arms.

[263] Shultz, OIC Interview, 2/12/92, pp. 204–07.

we have already turned over some wpns [weapons].'' He was asked what his statement had meant:

> A: It must have been just a supposition, an instinct.
>
> Q: During this period of time in your testimony you were stating that you had strong evidence of a dialogue but [we] were unwilling to sell arms and this [note] indicates that your thoughts were at the time that ''we have already turned over weapons.''
>
> A: Just that I was—it must be that having had this described, I was uneasy that that might already have happened, but I don't know any more than what this says.
>
> Mr. Cutler: May we have a recess?
>
> Mr. Gillen: Just one more point before we take off.
>
> Do you feel that this note would have been helpful to investigators in '86 and '87 if it had been turned over?
>
> A: Well, it sure would have been helpful to me in preparing my testimony.[264]

After taking a break, Shultz began with a statement before questioning resumed:

> I'd like to say there[,] if there were shipments and I had known about them in my mind at the time I testified, I certainly would have testified to that effect. There was no reason for me not to set out what I knew, no reason not to, so I'm puzzled by this.[265]

Shultz agreed that Hill and Platt's April 3, 1986, notes—''Money man in town w [with] $ to pay for TOWs. . . . This all has me horrified. Region [is] petrified that Iran will win + we are helping them.'' [266]—would have helped him prepare his testimony in December 1986 because it is ''further evidence of arms being traded.'' [267] He said, ''I think if I had

this note I would have not testified the same way.'' [268]

During the examination regarding phase two, Shultz offered an explanation for his apparent failure in December 1986 to recall events that apparently had been quite striking at the times they occurred less than a year earlier:

> Q: Would the impact of a man coming to the United States ''in town to pay for TOW missiles,'' is that something that irrespective of any notes, is that something that you could have forgotten about, having that kind of knowledge in the spring of 1986 when you testified in December of '86?
>
> A: Well, I think in December '86 in trying to construct this testimony I basically relied on the information that we got up and felt that the notes and the documents were the best evidence that I had at the time and I went ahead on that. . . . Basically I relied on the notes that we had.[269]

In contrast to the examination regarding phase one, Shultz offered no opinions during the phase-two examination regarding Hill's integrity, his efforts to produce relevant notes or reasons why relevant notes may not have been produced to Independent Counsel or the Select Committees.

Shultz was then confronted with handwritten notes and other documents reflecting information brought to his attention and statements that he made during ''phase three'' (May 1986 until the revelations of early November 1986), which he had described in his December 1986 testimony as a period when ''I received no informa-

---

[264] Ibid., pp. 208–9.

[265] Ibid., p. 209.

[266] Hill Note, 4/3/86, ANS 0001399.

[267] Shultz, OIC Interview, 2/12/92, pp. 211–12.

[268] Ibid., p. 215; accord, ibid., p. 230 (''I said some things today that are—earlier today—that are inconsistent, and I said some things in my testimony that are inconsistent with things you have shown me. So I'm perfectly glad to see—I'm not glad to see but I would look at things that are written on the record and regard that as more convincing than what I remember and what I told you earlier.''), p. 236 (''if I had [a recollection of conversations from February through May 1986 regarding TOW missile shipments or sales to Iran], I would not have testified the way I did''), p. 244 (''I can't imagine I knew these things when I testified or I wouldn't have testified the way I did'').

[269] Ibid., p. 213; accord, ibid., p. 244 (''I think I had convinced myself way back when I was involved in the testimony and so on that my best approach was to take the materials, the notes, the documents and so forth, and use them as a basis for my testimony because that's what I felt I knew'').

tion indicating that an arms transfer to Iran had occurred."[270]

After reviewing notes showing his awareness in May 1986 that McFarlane had delivered HAWK spare parts to Iran, Shultz first explained that his December 1986 testimony had incorrectly drawn the date line between phases two and three in early May 1986, when he should have started phase three some time in or after early June 1986. Shultz reiterated that Poindexter and Casey had told him "that the whole operation was going to stand down or some phrase like that."[271] Shultz said that he had meant to draw the line between phases two and three at the point he received that information:

I'm just trying to . . . get a dating for the third phase; namely, when I was told that the operation was standing down. It was the period of time from then until the release of Jacobson [sic] and that I didn't have any information. That's what I testified to. That's the dating that I had in mind.[272]

Shultz then acknowledged that his information that McFarlane had delivered weapons parts to Iran was not consistent with his testimony that the United States was not willing to sell arms to Iran during phase two.[273] Shultz said that

[t]he only reason that I can think is that I was not aware in my mind at the time that I testified that that was so; this is, my purpose was to be as informative as I could be and I had no reason or incentive to hold anything back.[274]

After an overnight recess, Shultz reflected on the previous day's session. He did not contest the accuracy of the documents he had reviewed.[275] He said that the notes had surprised him because they were not consistent with, and

did not refresh, his present recollection of events.[276] Shultz stated that he also had not remembered these events at the time of his testimony in December 1986 and stated categorically that, if he had recalled or if he had had these notes before him at that time, his testimony would have been different:

At the time that I testified . . . I was not aware, I didn't remember and my memory hadn't been refreshed by written material, some materials that you showed to me, and I'm certain that if I had that material in front of me, my testimony would have been different and it would have reflected that.

I also recognize that there were times when apparently from the things that you showed me, which I'm not doubting, I knew about some planned events and I didn't renew my protest to the President. I don't know why that is. . . .[277]

Shultz then discussed his understanding of the July 1986 release of hostage Jenco, which occurred during "phase three." Shultz initially stated that he had no present recollection regarding Jenco's release.[278] After reviewing the contemporaneous documents showing that most of his senior aides (Hill, Platt, Armacost, Ross and Raphel) had been informed at the time that the release of Jenco in July 1986 was a result of a $24 million arms deal with Iran, Shultz said flatly that he was not similarly informed.[279] He admitted, however, that he would not have expected Armacost, Platt and Hill to keep such information from him.[280] Shultz also did not recall reading a series of talking points that Hill had prepared for him to use with President Reagan on or about November 12, 1986, which includes Hill's handwritten note, "July 1986:

[270] Shultz, SSCI Testimony, 12/16/86, pp. 6–7.

[271] Shultz, OIC Interview, 2/12/92, p. 229. Although Shultz asserted that there is no note on this point, (ibid., p. 229) in fact Hill's July 2, 1986, note quotes Shultz as saying, "Casey said it was dead." Hill's note also includes Shultz's rejoinder, however: "It's not." (Hill Note, 7/2/86, ANS 0001528.)

[272] Shultz, OIC Interview, 2/12/92, p. 231

[273] Ibid., pp. 231–32.

[274] Ibid., p. 232.

[275] E.g. Shultz, OIC Interview, 2/13/92, p. 252.

[276] Ibid., pp. 248, 272. Shultz added, "I don't have pinned down in my own mind even after our discussion yesterday my specific knowledge of an actual delivery of arms. . . . I am not able to pin down in my own mind right now what I must have known or not known about an actual delivery." (Ibid., pp. 254–55.)

[277] Ibid., p. 252; accord, ibid., p. 256 ("Well, I have trouble in light of the things that you brought out in explaining to myself why I didn't go back at the President, but I didn't.").

[278] Ibid., p. 286.

[279] Ibid., p. 287.

[280] Ibid., p. 290.

Jenco released, then arms shipped to Iran ($20 million U.S. $4 million Israeli)."[281]

Shultz said that, although he did not recall discussing Jenco's release with Hill in July 1986 or later during the preparation of testimony,[282] he did not believe that Hill would have withheld the Jenco information.[283] If Shultz had recalled that information, he added, his testimony would have been different:

Q: . . . When you were preparing with Mr. Hill based upon his review of his records, did he remind you of the Jenco release as a result of the Polecat $24 million in weapons?

A: I think if I knew this to be a fact when I testified, I would have testified to it.

Q: What you did testify was that "I received no information [during phase three] indicating that an arms transfer to Iran had occurred." This [November 10, 1986, Hill] note indicates that on the summary review of Mr. Hill that "the Jenco release was Polecat, $24 millon in weapons."

A: Well, as I said, if I knew that to be a fact I wouldn't have testified the way I did.[284]

## Questioning Hill

Shortly after the OIC interviewed Shultz on February 12–13, 1992, it conducted a two-day interview of Hill on February 21 and February 24, 1992. The questioning focused on his hand-written notes and their nonproduction.

Prior to interviewing Hill, the OIC had already obtained some information about Hill's actions in the weeks after the November 1986 exposure of the Iran arms sales. The State Department in 1988 had produced copies of most of his notes from November and December 1986. He had been interviewed on several occa-

sions by the FBI and the OIC.[285] He had answered written questions from OIC on January 22, 1992.[286]

The OIC had also obtained from the State Department in February 1992 a handwritten chronology prepared by Hill on November 8, 1986,[287] which appeared to record information that Shultz had received regarding the arms sales. The chronology is incomplete in subtle but important ways. For example, a May 22, 1986, entry in the chronology discusses (1) North going to Cyprus with a non-Iranian intermediary, (2) a $10 million donation by Catholic Relief Services to poor Shia Moslems in Lebanon, and the release of all hostages within a week.[288] But Hill's actual notes from May 22, 1986—which were not produced to the FBI or to Congress in 1986 or 1987—go on to quote Shultz as stating that "[t]his is to be cover story for our shipment of TOWs to Iranians."[289] The omitted quote reveals Shultz's awareness of an arms-for-hostages exchange in May 1986 that is inconsistent with Shultz's disclaimers of Iran arms sales knowledge in his testimony.

Finally, the OIC knew that Hill had limited the excerpts from his notes provided to State Department lawyers and to the FBI prior to Shultz's December 16, 1986, testimony,[290] to those consistent with the "three-phase" description given by Shultz in his testimony.

At the outset of his February 1992 OIC interview, Hill acknowledged that he had spoken with Shultz and his lawyers about the questions the OIC had asked Shultz just ten days earlier.[291] Throughout the interview, Hill denied having intentionally withheld any notes from investigators. Hill offered a multi-layered explanation for his failure to include certain relevant notes among the excerpts he gathered in preparation for Shultz's December 1986 testimony. Hill repeatedly downplayed the significance or

---

[281] Ibid., p. 321 (referring to Hill's Talking Points, circa 11/12/86, ALW 0050420).

[282] Ibid., p. 297.

[283] Ibid., p. 324.

[284] Ibid., pp. 310–11. Shultz accordingly did not agree with Platt's December 15, 1986, note calling Jenco an "[a]rea[] of greatest vulnerability." Shultz said: "My attitude was, is now and was then[,] that that's not the way to look at it. The way to look at it is that we should say, or I should say as carefully and completely as I can what I knew contemporaneously with the flow of events to the intelligence committee." (Ibid., p. 330.)

[285] Hill, FBI 302s, 12/4/86 (two interviews), 5/7/87, 7/13/87, 12/18/87, 7/23/88, 12/10/90 and 12/12/90.

[286] Letter from Craig A. Gillen to Charles Hill, 1/7/92, 017948; Letter from Charles Hill to Lawrence E. Walsh, 1/22/92, 018034.

[287] Hill Chronology, 11/8/86, ALW 50552–58. Hill had referred to this chronology in the written answers he provided to Independent Counsel on January 22, 1992.

[288] Ibid., ALW 50558.

[289] Hill Note, 5/22/86, ANS 001459.

[290] Hill, FBI 302 (Special Agent Beane), 12/4/86, p. 1; Sofaer, OIC Interview, 2/20/92, p. 23.

[291] Hill, OIC Interview, 2/21/92, pp. 5–9.

credibility of the information in notes he had omitted from these excerpts. Hill said that he had played only a minor role in preparing Shultz for his December 1986 testimony.[292]

Hill's basic position during the interview was that he was never asked to review all of his notes for all entries relevant to the Iran arms sales, and that he never undertook a review of his notes for this purpose. In early November 1986, as the Iran arms sales were first becoming public, Shultz and Hill traveled to Vienna, Austria.[293] During their travel, Shultz and Hill discussed the history of the arms sales but were unable to recall many of the details of what had occurred.[294] Upon their return to the United States, Hill spent a dozen or more hours on Saturday, November 8, 1986, reviewing his notes. This review provided the basis for his November 8, 1986, chronology.[295]

According to Hill, however, Shultz rejected the chronology the very next day, because it contained some information he had learned only after the public revelation of the arms sales. Shultz believed that the chronology did not accurately reflect what *Shultz* had known at specific points during the course of the arms sales.[296] Hill told the OIC that he then became preoccupied with assisting Shultz's efforts to quash the ongoing efforts to engage Iran in arms-for-hostages transactions.[297] Accordingly, he did not conduct any further review of his notebooks until late November or early December 1986, when he searched for information that would aid in the preparation of Shultz's upcoming congressional testimony.[298]

As Hill explained it, even this review had only a limited purpose. Hill was not searching for all notations relevant to the Iran arms sales. Rather, he was attempting "to go and get what in [Shultz's] view were the key—as best we could recall it then—what were the key elements in his effort to stop [the Iran arms sales] in the past."[299] In other words, Hill reviewed his notes *not* to refresh Shultz's memory by

identifying all relevant notes, but to provide support for those events that Shultz actually remembered.[300]

Even with this qualification, Hill was at a loss to explain why certain notes were not provided. Hill admitted that he should have included specific notes in his excerpts and had made a mistake by not doing so. These included:

—A November 14, 1985, note of Armacost telling Shultz that McFarlane had recently asked Weinberger how to get HAWK and Phoenix missiles to Iran— Hill said, "This one simply escaped me." [301]

—An April 3, 1986, note of a "horrified" Shultz telling Hill there is a "money man" in town to pay for TOW missiles, and that the McFarlane Tehran meeting—during which the hostages will be released—will be set once payment is made—Hill said, "if I had seen this and focused on it, it would have been relevant and I would have brought it to his [Shultz's] attention in that [December 1986] period. I did not do so and I fault myself for that." [302]

—An April 15, 1986, note indicating that Hill and Shultz discussed a report that North and McFarlane were going to Tehran in late April to work on "hostages for arms"—Hill said, "I don't know why I didn't catch it. I didn't catch it." [303]

—A July 16, 1986, note about Shultz and Hill discussing the possibility of using an official of another country to pursue contacts with Iran and serve as a "[w]ay out of Polecat"—Hill said he "entirely missed it in the review," called that "a lapse on my part" and said "as part of the great blank of whiteness out there, it was just not there." [304]

[292] Hill's story is inconsistent in several key respects with the recollection of Sofaer.

[293] Hill, OIC Interview, 2/21/92, pp. 18–19.

[294] Ibid., p. 20.

[295] Ibid., pp. 19, 21.

[296] Ibid., pp. 21–22.

[297] Ibid., pp. 22–23.

[298] Ibid., p. 19.

[299] Ibid., pp. 23–24.

[300] Ibid., pp. 25–27.

[301] Ibid., p. 111. Hill was asked if he checked his notes to verify Shultz's testimony that he was unable to protest the November 1985 HAWK shipment because he had no advance notice of the shipment. Hill's November 14 note shows that Shultz and the Department of State *did* have advance notice. Hill said he did not check his notes on this point: "Looking back at it, that's an error on my part." (Ibid., p. 115.)

[302] Ibid., pp. 164–69.

[303] Ibid., pp. 174–75.

[304] Ibid., pp. 223–24.

—A July 28, 1986, note reporting that Jenco was released as a result of Polecat—specifically, a $24 million weapons deal between the U.S. and Iran—Hill said this was "a major error on my part of misjudgment;" "[m]y analytical and judgmental abilities simply weren't functioning." [305]

Hill claimed that in omitting the July 28, 1986, note regarding the Jenco release, he "simply missed this period in terms of significance. It was a great gap which I now see but I did not see at that time." [306] But a note Hill wrote on November 10, 1986, plainly shows that Hill did *not* miss this note. He summarized it during his November 1986 review of his notes:

> from <u>CH</u> [Charles Hill] notebooks
>
> 7/28 <u>Jenco</u> release (July) was Polecat $24 m [$24 million] in wpns [weapons.] next will be [Terry] Anderson [307]

Hill also referred to the Jenco information when preparing materials for Shultz to use during a November 12, 1986, meeting with President Reagan.[308] In addition to written talking points,[309] Hill made several handwritten notations on a page that contained a copy of a November 12, 1986, *Washington Post* compilation of "Administration Statements on Iran." This page was stapled to the typed talking points when the OIC found these documents at the State Department in 1992. Hill's fifth handwritten notation on this page reads:

> <u>July 1986</u>: <u>Jenco</u> released, then
>                   arms shipped to Iran ($20
>                   million U.S., $4 million
>                   Israeli).[310]

Hill claimed that in 1987 he turned over all of his notes from the "after the revelation" period.[311] But the November 10 note, which summarized the July 28 Jenco note, was not among the package he produced in 1987. Hill produced 24 pages of notes he had taken on November 10, 1986, including the pages immediately *before* and immediately *after* the original page that referred to the July 28, 1986, Jenco note, but not that page itself.

He also reformulated his basic explanation of the limited purpose for which he reviewed his notes prior to Shultz's December 1986 testimony. He said he did not review his notes to buttress *all* of the points that Shultz remembered, but only to identify a narrow category of information:

> I went to my notebooks and went to the time periods that we had thought in Vienna were the key periods in Shultz's reconstruction of this at which he felt that he had enough direct information and the ability to deal with the principals of this [], that is Poindexter or whomever, and to throw himself into it and to try and he thought make a fundamental shift in the way things were going.[312]

Later, Hill offered another narrow formulation of the purpose of his search:

> What [Shultz] wanted to do was to talk about or to convey to the Senate what on key events when he was unmistakably confronted with a situation, what action he took in general outline, again given the objective that he set for himself with regard to the December testimony.[313]

Hill claimed that he was looking for only those notes that reflected times when Shultz was "unmistakably confronted" with "direct evidence" under circumstances where he could "deal with the principals" in order to cause a "fundamental shift" in U.S. policy toward Iran. With these quoted phrases, Hill exposed the selective nature

[305] Ibid., p. 226.
[306] Ibid., p. 231.
[307] Hill Note, 11/10/86, ANS 001756.
[308] Shultz's calendar for November 12, 1986, reflects a meeting with President Reagan from 1:30 p.m. to 2:00 p.m. (Shultz, Record of Schedule, 11/12/86, ALW 49611.) Shultz identified the typed talking points for his meeting with President Reagan and explained that his goal during this meeting was to prevent any further arms sales from taking place. (Shultz, OIC Interview, 2/13/92, pp. 316–18.)
[309] Hill, Talking Points, circa 11/12/86, ALW 50420–25.
[310] Ibid., ALW 50420.
[311] Hill, OIC Interview, 2/21/92, p. 245.

[312] Ibid., pp. 24–25.
[313] Ibid., p. 110. Hill later offered another version:
What [Shultz] wanted to do was simply go through the basics as he understood it in his own mind of what he had done and those related to occasions when he was in his mind presented with evidence that arms for hostages—an operation that was underway, without any doubt was taking place or on the verge of taking place, not rumor, not talked about in terms of someone is heading someplace else, or someone says somebody is in town, but actually was underway because he had to harbor the occasions at which he could take on the others.
(Ibid., pp. 178–79.)

of Shultz's testimony, as well as Hill's document production.

Asked about specific relevant notes that he did not include in the excerpts he provided to Sofaer's office and to the FBI, Hill observed variously, that the actual events differed from certain notes that anticipated them,[314] did not directly involve Shultz,[315] that Shultz and he had not really understood the information at the time they received it,[316] that the information passed on to Shultz was not sufficiently reliable,[317] that he (Hill) did not believe the information he recorded in his notes.[318]

The events recorded in some of the withheld notes were of such significance that it is difficult to believe that Hill overlooked these notes in the production process. For example, Hill noted on September 17, 1985, separate press reports that (1) Israeli arms had been sent to Iran, and (2) Weir had been released. Hill noted that "Bud's folly is out," and Shultz's reaction: "Well, sometimes you have to try things."[319] Hill recalled "virtually running into [Shultz's] office to tell him . . . [that] we've caught the guy," that is, that McFarlane's arms-for-hostages "folly" is now exposed. Shultz was "totally surprised and in a sense disbelieving," and responded that "sometimes you've got to try things." Shultz felt "resigned" and "defeated" to learn of these arms shipments.[320] Hill's explanation for not producing the notes: the events later appeared not to have happened exactly as described in the note. Nonetheless, Hill and Shultz discussed it prior to Shultz's testimony.[321]

Hill also did not include in his excerpts a May 22, 1986, note describing (1) Ollie North and a non-Iranian intermediary traveling to Cyprus, (2) a $10 million Catholic Relief Services donation to poor Shia Muslims in Lebanon, and (3) the concomitant release of all hostages.[322] Immediately after listing these three events, the note quotes Shultz as saying, "This is to be cover story for our shipment of TOWs to Iranians."[323] Though plainly relevant to what Shultz knew about the Iran arms sales, Hill did not provide this note to investigators. He explained:

[T]his is in the category of things that do not happen, stories that prove to be false, false starts, rumors, assertions that are not borne out, claims that something is going on that seems not to be going on, and therefore it is not in the realm of something where he [Shultz] has taken action.[324]

Actually, the note refers to a cover story for the expected release of hostages after McFarlane's mission to Tehran. The failure of the mission does not negate Shultz's knowledge of it.[325]

Hill explained his failure to include certain notes from September 1985 by stating that the events described were not ones in which Shultz participated in a meaningful way.[326] As Hill phrased it:

[T]he outcome of this September event to us . . . was that this was a zero and if there was an outcome it was that our suspicions are heightened but it was not part of what the Secretary—it did not make the cutoff in terms of the Secretary wanting to say what his specific role was to be.

---

314 E.g. Ibid., pp. 85–101, 205–7.

315 E.g. Ibid., pp. 107–8.

316 E.g. Ibid., pp. 198–203.

317 E.g. Ibid., pp. 214–15.

318 E.g. Ibid., pp. 135–36, 181.

319 Hill Note, 9/17/85, ANS 001126.

320 Hill, OIC Interview, 2/21/92, p. 99.

321 Ibid., p. 101. At a later point, Hill was asked if he had discussed the substance of this Weir note during Meese's interview of Shultz on November 22, 1986. Hill replied, "No, I'm quite sure I didn't go into that kind of detail at this kind of meeting." (Ibid., p. 281.) Hill was then confronted with notes that Assistant Attorney General Cooper had taken during the November 22, 1986 Shultz interview. Cooper's notes indicate that Hill *had* recited the details from his September 17, 1985 note. (Cooper Note, 11/22/86, ALV 071843.) Hill then reversed his prior answer and acknowledged that he did discuss the details. (Hill, OIC Interview, 2/21/92, p. 281.)

322 Hill Note, 5/22/86, ANS 001459. Hill recorded this note just three days after describing in a note Weinberger telling Shultz of intelligence reports that McFarlane was taking arms to Tehran as part of the arms-for-hostages operation. (Hill Note, 5/19/86, ANS 0001453.)

323 Hill Note, 5/22/86, ANS 001459.

324 Hill, OIC Interview, 2/21/92, p. 211. The nonproduction of this note is even harder to understand in light of Hill's recollection that Shultz was in "agony" after hearing of this arms-for-hostages episode. (Ibid., p. 207.) Hill continues: ". . . I think [Shultz] believes this for whatever it is, a few hours, and we leave him to his agony, and then shortly thereafter, once again the indications are that this has been a false alarm." (Ibid., p. 211.)

325 Hill claimed as late as February 1992 that he did not know that McFarlane had gone to Tehran. (Ibid., p. 211.) Hill admitted, however, that he was aware of public statements in November 1986 that such a trip had occurred and stated that, in retrospect, he should have produced to investigators notes about McFarlane's mission. (Ibid., p. 212.)

326 Hill Note, 9/11/85, ANS 001117; Hill Note, 9/16/85, ANS 001123; Hill Note, 9/17/85, ANS 001125–26; Hill Note, 9/21/85, ANS 001131–33.

My impression before the testimony was that *he wanted to confine himself to what he had actually done, taken steps to do when he was confronted with the opportunity to make an impact.*[327]

Hill claimed he omitted notes about McFarlane's trip to Tehran because Shultz and he did not fully understand the information. On Monday, May 19, 1986, five days before the trip, Hill asked Shultz if the Iran arms sales were discussed at a lunch with Casey, Weinberger and Poindexter. According to Hill's note, Weinberger told Shultz about an intelligence report that McFarlane "wd [would] get arms there [to Iran]" and "then they would see about hostg [hostages]." The note identifies the arms as anti-missile system parts.[328]

The note plainly refers to McFarlane's mission. Yet Hill claimed that he did not include this note because he did not understand it:

> Again, I don't understand this note. I didn't understand it then and because it's not in verbatim language, I can only speculate of [sic] what it might be and I hesitate to do that because I don't find enough in this, I didn't find enough in this to make anything even close to a stab in the dark about it.[329]

Hill claimed that he omitted notes as not sufficiently reliable—just "a story we hear"[330]—even when the sources were Poindexter and Weinberger. On May 22, 1986, Hill wrote: "Pdx = Wbger. [Poindexter-Weinberger]" and then "Deliveries <u>are being made</u> of our mil [military] equip [equipment]—may see action today on release."[331] Hill admitted that Shultz should be informed at the time, because "it's the principals, that is Poindexter and Weinberger, talking. . . ."[332] But he omitted the note from his excerpts:

I don't think that I would have [brought this note to the attention of those who were preparing Shultz for his testimony], given what I was looking for because, again, this was—it fits with the one we just discussed, a story we hear. It's not direct, the Secretary cannot credit it although I think that he feels that there is something going on here and he has to freeze and very shortly it doesn't happen, there is no immediate release of all the hostages.[333]

Hill failed to produce some notes, even though given to Shultz before his testimony. For example, a note taken on January 14, 1986:

> Arma [Armacost] = [meeting with] S [Shultz]. <u>Hostg [Hostage]</u> dealing still going on. Ollie [North] under pressure to produce before St [State] of Union speech. . . . (S): WH [White House] is running this. No comment[334]

Hill said he omitted it because the information was just another unreliable story about North's actions. "This document to me was part of the—I don't mean to be impertinent at all but on the laughable cavorting of North."[335] Yet, he nonetheless included this document in the chronology he initially tendered to Shultz on November 8, 1986, because he "was not making judgments of significance" about the material he included in the chronology.[336]

Lastly, there are instances where Hill downplayed the significance of information relayed to him by Shultz, claiming that Hill did not believe the information. After a January 7, 1986, meeting with the President, Shultz reported the following information to Hill, who recorded it in his notes:

> <u>Iran Polecat</u>. P [President Reagan] decided <u>go ahead</u>. Only Cap [Weinberger] & I opposed. I won't debf [debrief] anybody about it. (TOWS for hostages)[337]

[327] Hill, OIC Interview, 2/21/92, pp. 107–8 (emphasis added).

[328] Hill Note, 5/19/86, ANS 001453.

[329] Hill, OIC Interview, 2/21/92, pp. 199–200. Hill admitted that the note deals with Weinberger informing Shultz of intelligence reports that McFarlane would get arms to Iran. (Ibid., pp. 200–1.) But Hill would not acknowledge that this shipment of arms related to the hostage situation, despite the phrasing, "Bud w[oul]d get arms there and <u>then</u> they see about host[age]s." (Ibid., p. 201.)

[330] Ibid., p. 215.

[331] Hill Note, 5/22/86, ANS 001462.

[332] Hill, OIC Interview, 2/21/92, p. 215.

[333] Ibid., p. 215.

[334] Hill Note, 1/14/86, ANS 001270.

[335] Hill, OIC Interview, 2/21/92, p. 150.

[336] Ibid. Hill also found humorous the information contained in an April 21, 1986, note quoting Armacost telling Shultz that "Bud [McFarlane] may show up in Tehran on Wednesday." (Hill Note, 4/21/86, ANS 001423.) This note was not included because "I treated this with levity and I didn't believe it." (Hill, OIC Interview, 2/21/92, p. 181.)

[337] Hill Note, 1/7/86, ANS 001263.

Hill testified that even though Shultz had told him that President Reagan had decided to go forward on "Polecat," Hill did not believe that Reagan had decided any such thing:

> I didn't read it that way. . . . The national security adviser [Poindexter] would never allow the President to make a decision at an NSC or NSPG meeting. The President would give his views . . . and then go away and make a decision at some later point. . . . I said [to Shultz], "It's awful," but I wasn't reading this as an official decision.[338]

Hill also asserted that even though this note depicts Shultz's knowledge of important events relating to the Iran arms sales, this was not the precise type of information Hill was seeking during his notes review:

> [I]t's because with the Secretary's view of what the important points were, they were points at which he felt that there would be clear knowledge that an operation was taking place and that he could do something about it. That would be his recounting of what were his actions, not his recounting of what were other people's actions.[339]

The note reflects a meeting with the President at which Shultz argued against the Iran initiative and lost. Hill said it did not reflect *Shultz's* actions, but "other people's actions."

Hill struggled to explain why he included this information in the chronology he prepared for Shultz on November 8, 1986, but excluded the information from the excerpts he later turned over to Sofaer's office and to outside investigators.

> Clearly it is a matter of some significance. I feel that what we were—when the testimony was going forward, what he [Shultz] was looking for was something that he felt he knew in terms of an operation as in the case of McFarlane's call to him [in] Geneva that he could actually take action upon.

> I am now saying my own interpretation of this note at the time and it was something where he wasn't going to talk about it, therefore we did not discuss it, which was that the President at this time—and this is my own recollection of my own thoughts—had given an indication at this meeting that he was willing to consider anything to get the hostages out and that we could expect people to be running around, probably Ollie North and McFarlane, trying to cook up some kind of an operation, some kind of an arrangement—again I'm speaking for myself—that would come back, that they would take back to the President to say okay or not.

> That's the kind of event that the Secretary felt—when those events came forward, that's when he could do something himself where he was involved and not simply a listener and not simply letting someone else do something.[340]

Hill also claimed that the "TOWS for hostages" language was not a note of what Shultz said, but rather was Hill's guess as to what was going to happen.[341] But Hill could not explain where he learned what type of weapons were involved, if not from Shultz.[342]

Whatever the credibility of Hill's various explanations, the excuses all share a fundamental problem: Hill received a memorandum from Sofaer and Bouchard on November 29, 1986, calling for the production of *all* documents—including personal notes—relevant to the Iran arms sales.

The plain terms of this memorandum from the chief legal and administrative officials at State required Hill to produce all of his notes that contain information relevant to the Iran arms sales. Hill had a simple explanation why he did not turn over all relevant notes. According to Hill, Sofaer orally told him that he did not have to comply with the terms of the November 29, 1986, memorandum. As Hill explained it, he had a conversation with Sofaer before the memorandum came out:

---

338 Hill, OIC Interview, 2/21/92, pp. 135–36.
339 Ibid., p. 139.
340 Ibid., pp. 143–44.
341 Ibid., pp. 136–37.
342 Ibid., p. 137.

[Sofaer] had told me that I would have to obtain the [notes], have them in a secure place, have them close at hand, be ready to produce them as requested, and that because it already had been gathered together, they should be retained right where they were which was a few yards from his office and I should just hold myself ready which is the situation that I agreed to.[343]

Because of this understanding, Hill asserted in 1992 that "[n]o one ever asked me to produce any note," the November 29, 1986, memorandum notwithstanding.[344] Phrasing things slightly differently, Hill elsewhere stated that by following Sofaer's instructions about keeping his notes ready and available, "constructively [his notes] were turned over to the legal adviser's office although they remained in the safe where they were held." [345] Hill claimed he assumed that Sofaer and others in the legal adviser's office informed investigators that Hill's excerpts did not contain all relevant passages from his notes.[346]

Hill went so far as to assert that holding on to his notes, instead of turning them over to Department of State legal counsel and to the FBI, affirmatively helped the investigation into the Iran arms sales:

Q: Mr. Hill, how many documents do you think law enforcement officials would have received if everyone constructively produced [their] notes such as you did?

A: Well, everyone shouldn't do that. That would be a terrible mistake. They should produce their documents. I fully agree with that.

I felt that what was being done here would be more effective and a superior way to serve the investigation, which I certainly wanted to serve. . . .[347]

Sofaer directly and sharply contradicted Hill's explanation. Sofaer acknowledged that Hill was

supposed to retain his original notebooks, but that is where Hill and Sofaer's recollections diverged. According to Sofaer:

It was also true that [Hill] was required by [the November 29, 1986] memorandum, and I never excused this in any way, shape, or form, to review those notes and to provide me, among others, with information in those notes that was responsive to these demands.

You know, there are things you might forget after all the years, but that is not one of them.[348]

During this same interview, Sofaer restated the point even more forcefully:

Every single person had a total duty, an absolute duty, to supply everything called for by [the November 29, 1986] memo and thereafter to supply everything relevant to Shultz's testimony so the Secretary wouldn't make a mistake in his testimony.[349]

Sofaer explained that the reason he allowed Hill to retain possession of his notes "was because he [Hill] would be trusted to give us all the relevant information." [350] Sofaer "fully assumed that a thorough review had been made." [351] Hill never informed Sofaer that he was forwarding only those notes that matched Shultz's recollection.[352] In fact, Sofaer stated that

the thing that enabled me to authorize Shultz to testify [only] to what he knew was that everything he didn't know that we had within our power and control we were going to give to the FBI, to the Tower Board, whatever we had then, to the Iran-contra committee on the Hill, to the Independent Counsel.[353]

Thus, Hill's claim that he and the legal adviser had an understanding about the limited scope

---

[343] Hill, OIC Interview, 2/21/92, pp. 41–42. Hill repeated this description of Sofaer's oral instructions regarding Hill's notes numerous times during the interview. E.g. ibid., pp. 44, 50–51, 62–63.
[344] Ibid., p. 43.
[345] Ibid., p. 50; accord, ibid., p. 60 (where Hill described his "constructive compliance" with Sofaer and Bouchard's November 29, 1986, memorandum).
[346] Ibid., pp. 66–67, 70.
[347] Ibid., pp. 63–64.

[348] Sofaer, OIC Interview, 4/6/92, pp. 8–9.
[349] Ibid., p. 28.
[350] Ibid., p. 39.
[351] Ibid., p. 41.
[352] Ibid., pp. 9–10.
[353] Ibid., pp. 43–44.

of Hill's notebook review [354] was flatly contradicted by Sofaer.

One point of conflict between Hill and Sofaer—Hill's participation in the preparation of Shultz's testimony—was resolved. Hill at first claimed he never compared his notes with Shultz's testimony, did not review Shultz's testimony before Shultz delivered it, never read Shultz's testimony, and did not know what that testimony was. [355] Sofaer had a different recollection of the preparation of Shultz's summer 1987 testimony:

> [Hill] would sit in on the meetings and watch things, read the drafts, comment on them. He played a substantial role. . . . He would comment on what the evidence showed about what the Secretary knew, how we ought to express it, how he understood it as a result. He was a full participant in preparing the Secretary for his testimony on each occasion that the Secretary testified. [356]

When confronted with his December 7, 1986, note on Shultz's December 8, 1986, testimony, stating "ok, I /s/ [sign] off" on Shultz's December 8, 1986 testimony, [357] Hill acknowledged that his earlier recollection was incorrect. [358]

Testimony from two State Department lawyers involved in the Department's response to congressional and criminal investigators corroborates Sofaer's recollection. Neither Elizabeth Keefer nor Michael Kozak, who were on the staff of the legal adviser's office, understood that Hill reviewed his notes for the limited purpose of supporting Shultz's memory of events. Both believed that Hill conducted a complete review of all of his notes in advance of Shultz's December 1986 testimony for the purpose of identifying all information relevant to the Iran arms sales. [359] Both understood that Hill was fully obligated to comply with the terms of Sofaer's November 29, 1986, memorandum calling for the production of all relevant documents. Neither Keefer nor Kozak had excused

Hill from complying with its production instructions; and, so far as they knew, neither had anyone. [360] Each was under the impression that Hill had fully complied. [361]

Keefer described Hill's role in preparing Shultz for his congressional testimony as substantive. [362] Kozak recalled that State Department legal counsel relied on Hill for the substance of the testimony. [363]

In the meetings where Shultz's testimony was being prepared, Hill's notes were considered Shultz's recollection—even though Shultz took part in the meetings. [364] Kozak recalled that the binder of notes that Hill had identified as relevant to Iran/contra was referred to as "the Bible." [365] Everyone viewed this binder of notes as the primary source of information concerning Shultz's knowledge of the Iran/contra matter, and used it to cross-check the factual accuracy of the testimony. Even Hill referred to this binder of notes as "the Bible." [366]

Overall, Hill's explanations as to why specific relevant notes were not turned over either to Sofaer's office or to the FBI were a combination of admitted errors and strained, inconsistent rationalizations. None of his stated excuses can be squared with Sofaer, Keefer and Kozak's clear memories that Hill, like everyone else, was required by Sofaer's November 29, 1986, memorandum to produce all notes in his possession that were relevant to the Iran arms sales. Hill alone asserted that he was called upon to identify only those notes that supported selected events recalled by Shultz, and that he was exempted from the production requirements of Sofaer's memorandum.

For the most part, Hill's state of mind and intentions in November and December of 1986 must be inferred from the notes that he did not produce and his various excuses for not producing them. But a more telling source exists in Hill's own notes. On November 21, 1986, Hill and Platt had a secure conversation in

---

354 Hill, OIC Interview, 2/21/92, pp. 71–72.

355 Ibid., pp. 102–4.

356 Sofaer, OIC Interview, 4/6/92, pp. 65–66.

357 Hill Note, 12/7/86, ANS 001995.

358 Hill, OIC Interview, 2/24/92, pp. 337–38.

359 Keefer, FBI 302, 3/10/92, pp. 6, 10; Kozak, FBI 302, 3/4/92, pp. 3, 7, 11.

360 Keefer, FBI 302, 3/10/92, pp. 14–15; Kozak, FBI 302, 3/4/92, p. 6.

361 Keefer, FBI 302, 3/10/92, p. 14; Kozak, FBI 302, 3/4/92, p. 6.

362 Keefer, FBI 302, 3/10/92, p. 13.

363 Kozak, FBI 302, 3/4/92, p. 5.

364 Keefer, FBI 302, 3/10/92, p. 3.

365 E.g. Kozak, FBI 302, 3/4/92, p. 7.

366 Ibid., p. 5.

which Platt told Hill about a conversation Sofaer had with McFarlane:

MO [McFarlane] called Abe [Sofaer] + sd [said] he understood there are records in Dept [the Department of State] that cover the period & that they had been sent to Justice. Abe sd no records sent to DOJ [Justice], but he had been told some "alleged facts" from records & he had told DOJ in order to protect P [President Reagan]. Abe sd MO [McFarlane] shd [should] keep all his records. Abe sd DOJ has asked for all records—specifically the Nov [November] 18, 1985 conversation. P auth [authorized] the investigation and they want our records.

CH [Charles Hill] raises hell.
Stop Abe for shit's sake! [367]

Hill claimed that his "intemperate outburst" meant only that "[i]t sounded like Sofaer was doing the wrong thing and so I was saying slow Sofaer down." [368] Hill denied being concerned about turning over all of his records, claiming instead that "I was concerned about things being said that were not well documented and . . . that Sofaer might conceivably be going off and giving 'alleged facts.' " [369]

## Questioning Platt

Nicholas Platt appeared before the Grand Jury on March 27, 1992.[370] He had first been interviewed by Shultz's lawyers. The OIC asked Platt general questions about his actions in 1985 and 1986, and then reviewed specific notes he took during that period. Unlike Hill but like Shultz, Platt claimed that he had virtually no independent memory of the events of 1985 and 1986. Platt stated that his notes were his memory.[371]

Despite this disclaimer, Platt did recall a few relevant points. First, Platt said he passed on "virtually everything" he heard about the Iran arms sales to Shultz.[372] This did not always mean speaking with Shultz directly. Platt would most often communicate the information to

Hill.[373] Platt believed that "passing information to Charles Hill was the equivalent of passing it to the Secretary." [374]

Platt had limited involvement in the preparation of Shultz's December 1986 congressional testimony. He "did sit in on meetings that [Shultz] had about his testimony with other advisors who were charged with preparing it." [375] According to Platt, Hill was one of those charged with preparing Shultz's testimony, working in conjunction with Sofaer and others.[376]

Platt recalled receiving Sofaer's November 29, 1986, memorandum directing him and others to turn over all relevant documents, including notes.[377] Beyond this basic recollection, Platt's memory of the document-production process was, by his own admission, "flawed." [378] He did not remember what guidance he received on how to handle his personal notes.[379] He recalled reviewing his notes and marking relevant passages with paper clips.[380] But Platt could not remember when he provided copies of these relevant notes to Sofaer's office.[381] Platt made no claim that Sofaer or anyone else had exempted him from the production required by the November 29, 1986, memorandum.

Platt claimed to recall that he produced a limited number of notes on a specific subject on December 3 or 4, 1986,[382] but he acknowledged that a recent telephone conversation with Hill had "refreshed" Platt's memory of this production.[383] Platt could not recall the purpose of this limited production or the subject matter.[384] Independent of Hill's reminder, Platt could not recall producing any notes.[385]

---

367 Hill Note, 11/21/86, ANS 001878.
368 Hill, OIC Interview, 2/21/92, p. 271.
369 Ibid.
370 Prior to Platt's appearance before the Grand Jury, he was interviewed voluntarily at the OIC. (Platt, FBI 302, 3/26/92.)
371 Platt, Grand Jury, 3/27/92, pp. 17–18.
372 Ibid., p. 12.

373 Ibid., p. 8.
374 Ibid., pp. 10–11.
375 Ibid., p. 18.
376 Ibid., pp. 18–19. Platt's memory (like Sofaer's, Shultz's, Keefer's and Kozak's) conflicts with Hill's memory on this point. Hill claimed that he had little involvement in the preparation of Shultz's testimony. (Compare Hill, OIC Interview, 2/21/92, pp. 102–4, with Sofaer, OIC Interview, 4/6/92, pp. 65–66; Shultz, OIC Interview, 2/12/92, p. 151; Keefer, FBI 302, 3/10/92, p. 13; Kozak, FBI 302, 3/4/92, p. 5.)
377 Platt, Grand Jury, 3/27/92, p. 22.
378 Ibid., p. 32.
379 Ibid., pp. 27, 33. Platt remembered that there were discussions of how notes were to be treated, but could not recall the substance of those discussions. (Ibid.)
380 Ibid., p. 34.
381 Ibid., pp. 39–42.
382 Ibid., p. 23.
383 Ibid., pp. 23–24.
384 Ibid., pp. 27–28.
385 Ibid., p. 29.

Platt acknowledged that he and Hill had discussed the areas of concern that had arisen in Hill's February 1992 OIC interview.[386] Hill also reminded Platt of the various "phases" of the State Department's awareness of the Iran arms sales.[387] Hill told Platt that, as a result of Hill's interview with the OIC, Hill felt that Shultz's testimony "in one place . . . [s]hould have been worded differently."[388]

Platt was questioned about several specific notes of his that were not produced to any investigators prior to the spring of 1991. Platt admitted in almost every instance that (1) the note appeared to be relevant, (2) he did not know why it was not produced, and (3) he may have overlooked the information under the pressure of the burgeoning crisis that ensued after the arms sales were publicly disclosed.

For example, Platt was asked about a note he took on September 16, 1985, regarding the Weir release.[389] The note discusses conversations among Oakley, McFarlane and North regarding the mechanics of the hostage release and potential problems. Platt did not deny the relevance of the note, and could not explain why it was not produced:

Q: Why did you not produce this note, pursuant to the November the 29th, '86 memorandum?

A: I can't—I cannot explain, other than to say that it related to—this is a note that relates to the fact of Weir's having been released. It doesn't refer to arms for hostages, although it does mention Bud and Ollie. Anyway, I made it available later [in 1991]. I don't know why it wasn't released then. It was overlooked.

\*    \*    \*

Q: You believe now it should have been produced?

A: Yes, I would think so.[390]

Platt did not defend the omission of an October 4, 1985 note, which quotes Shultz as saying that he intends to speak with McFarlane about intelligence that points "toward 100 mil. [$100 million] deal for spare parts for Iran to be delivered in Spain."[391] Platt acknowledged that this was a significant note relating to the Iran arms sales:

I can only conjecture or speculate that it was—that I overlooked it. I have no recollection of having decided not to send it. All I can say is that I was motivated by a desire to comply with the desires of the law enforcement agencies and did the best that I could at the time.[392]

Likewise, Platt could not explain the non-production of a June 1, 1985, note that discusses NSC consultant Michael Ledeen's presence in Israel seeking "Israeli cooperation on Iran intelligence":[393]

I can't recall why it wasn't produced. I can only speculate from the context and the appearance that the reference was hidden and there isn't a specific link between Iran and arms. There's no mention of arms here.

But I can't recall why it's not there. It may just have been overlooked.[394]

As to some specific notes, including the two just discussed, Platt suggested that the information was hidden or obscure.[395] As to others, Platt asserted that the hectic circumstances of November and December 1986 made it impossible for him to do the kind of careful review done by the OIC after it acquired a complete set of Platt's notes in 1991:

---

[386] Ibid., p. 24.

[387] Ibid., pp. 24–25.

[388] Ibid., pp. 26–27.

[389] Platt Note, 9/16/85, ALW 0036349.

[390] Platt, Grand Jury, 3/27/92, pp. 70–71.

[391] Platt Note, 10/4/85, ALW 0036463.

[392] Platt, Grand Jury, 3/27/92, p. 80. Platt admitted that this note contradicted statements made by Shultz during his testimony that the State Department did not have access to intelligence reports regarding the Iran arms sales: "[the note] does indicate that the Secretary knew that [the intelligence reports] existed." (Ibid., p. 81.)

[393] Platt Note, 6/1/85, ALW 0035751.

[394] Platt, Grand Jury, 3/27/92, p. 49; accord, ibid., p. 51 (regarding the 6/4/85 Note, ALW 0035767), p. 60 (regarding the 9/13/85 Note, ALW 0036332); p. 85 (regarding the 11/14/85 Note, ALW 0036734), pp. 91–92 (regarding the 11/26/85 Note, ALW 0036809); pp. 100–1 (regarding the 1/4/86 Note, ALW 0037024), pp. 101–2 (regarding the 1/14/86 Note, ALW 0037124); pp. 102–4 (regarding the 2/21/86 Note, ALW 0037404), pp. 112–13 (regarding the 4/3/86 Note, ALW 0037725).

[395] Ibid., pp. 70, 49; accord, ibid., p. 91 (regarding a November 26, 1985 note (ALW 0036809): "let me say that from the context of it, it's pretty well hidden"), p. 92 (regarding another November 26 note (ALW 0036813): "I believe it's hidden, and I missed it.").

The milieu we were living in was one of
very high pressure, a lot of events, a lot
of activity, and review of notes—it was
very difficult for any of us to get the time
off to do the kind of careful review of
notes that this investigation suggests that
we should have been able to do.[396]

Elsewhere, Platt stated:

Well, I can only say that there were a
lot of things going on. There was a huge
amount of material to screen. . . . All I'm
saying is, when I was going through the
review process, I was preoccupied with a
lot of other things.[397]

But Platt acknowledged that some notes he
omitted were obviously significant and should
not have been overlooked.

Platt, no less than Hill, had his greatest difficulty explaining the omission of passages of
notes containing critical information about the
release of Jenco in July of 1986. The Department of State in 1987 produced a Platt note
segment from July 26, 1986, that discussed
some basic aspects of the Jenco release:

> July 26, 1986 Informal working
> group set up
> —Jencko out. Now with Amb / 10:50
> plane arrives in Syria will      1330
> Frankfurt leave via US Aircraft for
> Wiesbaden tomorrow 27th 9:00 AM.
>      ALDAC [All Diplomatic and Con-
> sular Posts] Sec [Shultz] approved
> Press Statement release this AM.
> Condolence message.—
>                          ALDAC [398]

The photocopy that the Department produced
was cropped to remove the remainder of this
page of Platt's notes, obliterating the following
additional information:

—Release of Hostage Jenco—result of
Polecat negotiations.

—Presidential statement thanking Syrians
arranged.

—next one will be Anderson.

—Dick [Murphy] calling Don Gregg. VP
[Bush] may delay departure [399]

The note continues on the top of the following
page which was not produced at all:

from Frankfurt so he can.

—Price. ITOW, side winders, 155 mm
ammo. [ammunition] via the Israelis.

—Weir was earnest money.

Charley Allen & Dewey Clarridge at the
mtg

—Armacost calls [Head of Defense Department component]—real negotiation had
been whether it was 1 or 2. 24 million—
4 mil laundered thru Israel—rest in
equipment, for which, he implied, they
are paying.

Ollie flying out tonight [400]

When shown the information that had been
cut off from the first page of his July 26, 1986,
notes, Platt was nonplussed:

Q: Can you please tell us, Ambassador,
why you chose to make a determination
that that should be redacted?

A: I have no recollection of why it was
redacted. I can only speculate that when
the page—I mean, the subject changed, and
I didn't carefully read on to the rest of
the page. There is absolutely no reason,
I don't think, why—I mean, on the face
of it, one would—would want to cut this
out.

Q: "Result of Polecat negotiations." It
shows us that Jenco was released because
of Oliver North, does it not, Ambassador?

396 Ibid., p. 109.
397 Ibid., p. 85.
398 Platt Note, 7/26/86, ALV 002739. The bottom portion of this
note that Platt produced in response to Iran/contra investigators in
1986 and 1987, which mentions a "Condolence message," apparently
does not relate to Iran/contra. W. Averell Harriman, the former diplomat, Assistant Secretary of State and Governor of New York, died
on July 26, 1986, and the Department of State released a condolence
statement from Shultz later that day. (The New York Times, 7/27/86.)

399 Platt Note, 7/26/86, ALW 0038555. Platt's July 26 notes discuss
an unrelated matter in between the Iran arms sales information Platt
produced from this page and these redacted points.
400 Platt Note, 7/26/86, ALW 0038556.

A: I have no idea why I would want to hide that. Why would I want to hide that? [401]

Platt later acknowledged: "It came to me as a surprise that it was cut off where it was—looked to me as if it looked like I had something to hide." [402]

He was confronted with the note taken on December 15, 1986, the day before Shultz's testimony before the SSCI, discussing "Jenco" as an area of "greatest vulnerability," apparently for Shultz, which then asks, "Why did you avert your gaze." [403]

Asked to explain, he testified:

Q: To whom are these questions [in the note] directed?

A: I don't know. I can't remember. I can't tell from the context of the note. It's obviously something that was discussed, and I don't know who was saying what to who here. I'm hearing it.

Q: Well, let us look at it from another angle. You were not going to testify the next day, were you?

A: No.

Q: Charlie Hill was not going to testify the next day, was he?

A: No.

Q: Secretary Shultz was going to testify the next day. Right?

A: Yes.

Q: So, when questions concerning, "What did you think? Why did you avert your gaze?"—are you referring to anyone other than Secretary Shultz?

A: It's a question that's asked by somebody in the meeting, but I don't know who.

Q: I see. And so, why are people concerned on the eve of Secretary Shultz's testimony that Jenco is one of the areas of greatest vulnerability?

A: I can't tell. I don't recall. [404]

An obvious interpretation of the December 15, 1986, note is that Shultz was indeed told in July 1986 about the arms-for-hostages basis for Jenco's release. His advisers, in a meeting on the eve of Shultz's December 16, 1986, SSCI testimony, threw out hypothetical questions that Shultz might be asked about his reaction to Jenco's release: How did you think the Jenco release occurred? Why did you avert your gaze? Production of the note to investigators would invite additional questions.

Platt did not subscribe to this interpretation. He testified that (1) he had no idea why he would want to hide the Jenco information in the July 26th note, (2) he did not know why this information was redacted or omitted, and (3) he did not recall the meaning of the December 15th note. [405]

Platt acknowledged that he had recently discussed the Jenco issue with Hill. [406] Hill told him that he had found the July 1986 information about Jenco "hard to believe" at the time he heard it. [407] Hill told him that he had overlooked his note on the real reasons behind the Jenco release. [408]

When asked whether he had recently discussed the Jenco matter with anyone other than Hill, Platt invoked the attorney/client privilege. [409] Asserting a joint defense with Shultz, Platt asserted this privilege with respect to conversations with persons *other than* his own attorney, including Shultz's counsel. [410]

Independent Counsel decided that contesting Platt's assertion of a joint privilege was not

---

[401] Platt, Grand Jury, 3/27/92, p. 129.

[402] Ibid., p. 141.

[403] Platt Note, 12/15/86, ALW 039344. Earlier in the testimony, Platt said he could not recall whether he told Shultz during a July 26, 1986, telephone call about the information Platt had learned concerning the true reason for Jenco's release. (Platt, Grand Jury, 3/27/92, p. 134.)

[404] Ibid., pp. 139–40.

[405] Ibid., pp. 129, 139–40.

[406] Ibid., p. 135.

[407] Ibid., pp. 136–37.

[408] Ibid., p. 137.

[409] Ibid., p. 135.

[410] Ibid. Subsequent correspondence revealed that Platt had an oral joint defense agreement with Shultz as to Iran/contra matters. (Letter from Platt's counsel, R. Kenly Webster, to Craig A. Gillen, 4/2/92, 018655.) Platt refused to waive the joint privilege. (Letter from R. Kenly Webster to Craig A. Gillen, 4/16/92, 018754.) Following Platt's refusal, Shultz's attorney stated that he could not waive the joint privilege unilaterally. As a result of this assertion of privilege, Platt never disclosed anything about the conversations he had in 1992 with Shultz or Shultz's counsel on the Jenco issue.

an efficient use of limited resources. Platt's testimony showed signs of rehearsal.[411] Even a successful attack upon the claim of privilege was unlikely to produce new information.

## Conclusion

### Shultz's Testimony Was Incorrect, But It Could Not Be Proven That It Was Willfully False

Independent Counsel's investigation established that central and important aspects of Shultz's testimony to congressional committees in late 1986 and 1987 regarding his knowledge of arms shipments to Iran were incorrect.

Shultz's carefully prepared testimony stated that he received no information regarding arms transfers to Iran during 1985 and 1986. It conveyed the impression that, because of his steadfast opposition to proposals to transfer arms to Iran, National Security Advisers McFarlane and Poindexter and the NSC staff had successfully concealed information from Shultz and the Department of State regarding actual arms transfers to Iran.

The contemporaneous handwritten notes of Hill and Platt demonstrate the inaccuracy of Shultz's assertions and the popular impression regarding his knowledge. Shultz was aware of Israel's TOW and HAWK missile transfers to Iran during 1985. He was aware of direct arms transfers from the United States to Iran during 1986. The notes also demonstrate that, to the extent Shultz did not have complete information

regarding the arms transfers, his situation was caused as much by his desire not to know more as it was by efforts at the NSC staff to conceal information from him.[412]

In his 1992 interviews with the OIC, Shultz did not contest the accuracy of these notes and ultimately acknowledged that his testimony had been incorrect.

Notwithstanding the gravity of Shultz's errors while testifying before Congress in 1986 and 1987, Independent Counsel declined to prosecute because the evidence did not establish beyond a reasonable doubt that his testimony was willfully false. Contemporaneous notes exposed the inaccuracy of Shultz's assertions. However difficult it may be to believe that Shultz could forget events that troubled him so deeply, it was significant that none of the contemporaneous notes created in November and December 1986 suggest that Shultz in fact remembered more or different information than that to which he testified.

### Hill Deliberately Withheld Key Notes and Prepared Inaccurate Testimony Regarding Shultz's Knowledge of Arms Transfers to Iran

Although Hill claimed a variety of explanations for his failure to produce relevant notes to Iran/contra investigators, the evidence indicates that Hill withheld these notes deliberately, in conjunction with his preparation of testimony portraying Shultz as uninformed of arms shipments to Iran and victimized by the NSC staff.

Hill withheld his notes deliberately. He was clearly instructed in 1986 to locate and produce relevant entries in his notebooks, and he was not exempted from this obligation by the legal adviser.

The direct correlation between notes not produced by Hill and Shultz's disclaimers of knowledge in official testimony also is too powerful to be an accident. Although Hill claimed that Shultz had directed him to locate only those notes that corroborated Shultz's recollections,

---

[411] For example, near the start of his Grand Jury appearance in March 1992, Platt testified that it had been his practice during 1985 and 1986 to pass along to Shultz "virtually everything" he (Platt) heard on the subject of arms shipments to Iran. (Platt, Grand Jury, 3/27/92, p. 12.) Platt acknowledged that he did not attempt to evaluate the reliability or credibility of a piece of information on this subject before passing it along. But he then attempted to volunteer a distinction lessening the likelihood that he would report "wild rumors:"

> As I recall—as I recall, that would be—that would be correct. I mean, I—there might be wild rumors that would come out; I would—normally, I would share those at least with Mr. Hill—unless he already knew them or was telling them to me.
> Q: Give us an example of what you had determined to be a "wild rumor."
> A: Well, we had a report, as I remember, that a hostage had been released and that someone paid $24 million for the release of this one guy. I mean, it was a rumor. That's an example.

(Ibid., p. 13.) Platt, himself, had not yet been asked about "the Jenco "[a]rea[] of greatest vulnerability" note. Platt attempted to reduce to a "wild rumor" his July 1986 note stating that Jenco had been released as part of a $24 million arms deal, even though his December 1986 note on the eve of Shultz's testimony characterized Jenco one of the "[a]reas of greatest vulnerability."

[412] E.g. Hill Note, 12/9/85, ANS 0001246 ("NIGHTOWL . . . —P [President Reagan] annoyed. McF [McFarlane] had him sold on it. Saw hostg [hostages] out + new stratg [strategic] rels [relationship]. So he annoyed w [with] me [Shultz] + Cap [Weinberger]. —I will let them post me. I will not pursue or ask. But will take it over when it gets messy."); cf. Hill Note, 11/19/86, ALW 0056348 "(S) [Shultz]—We knew they [the NSC staff] [were] doing somethg [something]. Not totally innocent.").

the record suggests otherwise. Shultz instructed Hill, as he instructed all Department of State employees, to locate and produce all relevant information to investigators. Sofaer, Kozak and Keefer each corroborated Shultz's recollection on this point.

Hill's notes are also too legible, and his relevant notes too easy to locate, to support his explanation for their non-production. Shultz voiced the best criticism of Hill's failure to produce obviously relevant notes:

> Well, I think I'd have to put it into the context but when you have the word Polecat underlined, I should think that's the kind of thing that would attract your attention.[413]

Although the evidence demonstrated beyond a reasonable doubt that Hill withheld relevant notes and helped prepare inaccurate testimony, Independent Counsel concluded it would not be appropriate to prosecute Hill, a subordinate to Shultz who had delivered that testimony and who was not the subject of a prosecution himself. Additionally, Hill's assertion that he was given an oral waiver from full document production by Sofaer could raise an issue of fact regarding events several years old that might create a reasonable doubt in the minds of jurors. Finally, the passage of time itself weighed against the prosecution of Hill, who promised little in the way of further investigative developments beyond what was contained in his extensive notes.

## The Evidence That Platt Deliberately Withheld Relevant Notes Is Inconclusive

Independent Counsel's investigation in 1991 and 1992 also determined that Platt failed to produce a significant quantity of relevant handwritten notes to Iran/contra investigators. Platt's omissions are not as blatant as Hill's. His notes are more fragmentary and more difficult to review. Platt did review his notes repeatedly and

made supplemental production to the legal adviser's office throughout the first few months of 1987.[414] Most importantly, in the spring of 1987, Platt left his position as executive secretary and was preparing to become United States ambassador to the Philippines. He was not involved in the continuing process of preparing Shultz's testimony and so, unlike Hill, he was not as aware of the degree to which the notes that had been produced in December 1986 became "the Bible" that defined Shultz's, and the entire Department of State's, information and knowledge regarding arms transfers to Iran.

Still, the non-production of Platt's highly relevant notes is troubling. In 1987, the Department produced an innocuous Platt note reflecting Jenco's release. The redacted portion, not discovered by investigators until 1991, reveals information linking Jenco's release to the NSC Iran initiative, weapons and ammunition. Platt had no explanation for this redaction. Whether it was done by Platt or someone else in the State Department document-production process is unsettled.

Finally, there is the question whether Platt and Hill colluded to withhold corresponding portions of their notes. Coincidence is unlikely. Platt's notes were produced to the FBI in December 1986 through Hill. Given Hill's more central role in the preparation of Shultz's testimony, even at that early date, it is possible that Platt's proposed note production in December 1986 was reviewed by Hill. Given the passage of time, the absence of direct evidence of collusion, and Platt's minimal role in the preparation of Shultz's testimony, it was determined not to seek criminal charges against him.

---

413 Shultz, OIC Interview, 2/12/92, pp. 58–59.

414 Memorandum from Platt to Executive Secretary Levitsky, 4/23/87, ALV 002717 ("I attach personal notes I have found which relate to the NDR [contras]. All the notes fall into the period Jan 1–July 1, 1985, . . . My personal notes on the contra issue for the period July 1985–November 1986 are already in Mike Kozak's possession, part of the collection made in connection with the Iran-hostages arms investigation."); Memorandum from Platt to Levitsky, 5/7/87, ALV 002712 (producing additional Platt notes regarding the contras); Memorandum from Quinn to Kozak, 5/11/87, ALV 002711 ("transmit[ting] additional notes from Ambassador Nicholas Platt in response to your request for documents relating to the Iran/Contra investigation").

# Chapter 25
# United States v. Elliott Abrams

Elliott Abrams in January 1981 joined the Reagan Administration as an assistant secretary of state for international organization affairs and later became assistant secretary for human rights. On April 19, 1985, Secretary of State George P. Shultz offered Abrams the position of assistant secretary of state for inter-American affairs (ARA), overseeing South and Central American and Caribbean issues. Shultz explained that it would be a difficult job, but Abrams quickly accepted. Shultz promised to "manage the emergence of E[lliott] A[brams] as King of L[atin] A[merica]."[1]

Abrams assumed his position at ARA in July 1985. Under Shultz, he was responsible for Central American issues and became the Reagan Administration's chief advocate on Capitol Hill for U.S. aid to the contra rebels in Nicaragua, which had been cut off in October 1984 by the Boland Amendment. During Abrams' tenure at ARA, humanitarian aid for the contras and later lethal aid were lawfully resumed.

Abrams worked closely with Lt. Col. Oliver L. North of the National Security Council Staff and Alan D. Fiers, Jr., the chief of the CIA's Central American Task Force. Together they comprised the principal members of a Restricted Interagency Group (RIG), which worked on Central American issues for the Reagan Administration.

In the course of his work, Abrams became aware of North's efforts to assist the contras militarily, despite the Boland prohibition on U.S. aid.[2] Abrams also was directly involved in secretly seeking third-country contributions to the contras.

On October 7, 1991, Abrams pleaded guilty to two misdemeanor charges of withholding information from Congress. Abrams admitted that he withheld from the Senate Foreign Relations Committee and the House Permanent Select Committee on Intelligence (HPSCI) in October 1986 his knowledge of North's contra-assistance activities. In support of his guilty plea, Abrams admitted that it was his belief "that disclosure of Lt. Col. North's activities in the resupply of the Contras would jeopardize final enactment" of a $100 million appropriation pending in Congress at the time of his testimony.[3] He also admitted that he withheld from HPSCI information that he had solicited $10 million in aid for the contras from the Sultan of Brunei.

## Abrams' Knowledge of North's Activities

After Abrams assumed the position of assistant secretary of state for ARA, he began to orient himself to his new responsibilities. On September 4, 1985, Abrams met with Shultz to discuss Central American issues. Also present were M. Charles Hill, Shultz's executive assistant, and Nicholas Platt, the executive secretary. They discussed North's contra-support activities. Abrams' notes of that meeting reflect Shultz's instruction to him to "monitor Ollie."[4]

During his testimony before the Select Iran/contra Committees in the summer of 1987,

---

[1] Hill Note, 4/19/85, ANS 0001039.
[2] It was Abrams' "working assumption" that the Boland Amendment applied to the NSC staff. Abrams, Select Committees Testimony, 6/2/87, p. 8.

[3] Government's Statement of the Factual Basis for the Guilty Plea, 10/7/91, p. 4. Abrams' guilty plea was obtained by Deputy Independent Counsel Craig A. Gillen and Associate Counsel Thomas E. Baker and John Q. Barrett.
[4] Abrams Note, 9/4/85, ALW 0041285.

Abrams explained his "monitor Ollie" notebook entry as follows:

> ". . . All these accusations about Colonel North, you want me to try to find out whether they are true and what he is up to, or do you want me to sort of leave?"

And [Shultz] said, "No, you have got to know." [5]

In later congressional testimony, Abrams explained that he believed that he carried out Shultz's directive by obtaining North's assurances that he was not soliciting funds for the contras and by McFarlane's similar assurances to Congress. Abrams said because he and North worked together in RIG meetings, he believed that he had a good understanding of what North was doing. [6]

Hill's contemporaneous notes of the September 4, 1985, meeting are more detailed:

> [ABRAMS]:—fundraising continues, arms shipments going up. I have not asked Ollie for any info[rmation] about fundraising for lethal aid.
>
> [Shultz]: We don't want to be in the dark. You suppose to be mgr [manager] of overall C.A. [Central America] picture. Contras are integral part of it. So y[ou] need to know how they getting arms. So don't just say go see the WH [White House]. It's very risky for WH. [7]

Platt's notes of the September 4th meeting are even more detailed and instructive on the extent of Abrams' knowledge of North's involvement on behalf of the contras:

> [Shultz]: What is happening on other support for Contras for lethal aid etc.—E. Abrams doesn't have the answer. Stayed away let Ollie North do it. Fundraising continuing—weapons stocks are high. We have had nothing to do with private aid. Should we continue?

Hate to be in position, [Shultz] says, of not knowing what's going on. You are supposed to be managing overall Central American picture. Ollie can go on doing his thing, but you, [Abrams], should know what's happening. [8]

Platt's notes reflect that, by September 4, 1985, Abrams knew North was involved in lethal assistance to the contras and that he informed Shultz.

As assistant secretary of state for ARA, Abrams assumed the chairmanship of the RIG, which was a senior-level working group that focused on policy in Central America. It was comprised of Abrams and his assistants, and representatives of the CIA, the Joint Chiefs of Staff, Department of Defense and the NSC staff. At the time of Abrams' swearing-in, the RIG member with the most seniority was North of the NSC staff.

Abrams' senior management team included James H. Michel as his principal deputy assistant secretary of state, and William G. Walker as his deputy assistant secretary of state for Central American affairs. On occasion, both Michel and Walker accompanied Abrams to RIG meetings.

## Abrams, North and NHAO

After Abrams took control of ARA, North continued to raise funds and assist in coordinating the provision of weapons to the contras. In September 1985, North induced former CIA officer Felix Rodriguez to assist the contra-resupply effort by setting up the servicing of aircraft at Ilopango air base in El Salvador. [9] Rodriguez had been working out of Ilopango air base, assisting the Salvadoran Air Force in counterinsurgency actions. Donald P. Gregg, Vice President Bush's national security adviser, had been instrumental in placing Rodriguez in El Salvador. While at the air base, Rodriguez used the alias "Maximo (Max) Gomez." He established an excellent relationship with General

[5] Abrams, Select Committees Testimony, 6/2/87, p. 34. By September 1985, Abrams was aware of the public allegations that North was involved in soliciting funds for the contras and assisting in providing lethal aid. (Ibid., pp. 82–83.)

[6] Ibid., p. 84; Abrams, Select Committees Testimony, 6/3/87, pp. 30–33.

[7] Hill Note, 9/4/85, ANS 0001130.

[8] Platt Note, 9/4/85, ALW 0036260. Platt's note was not produced until 1991. It raised more doubts about the veracity of Abrams' 1987 testimony that he did not believe the allegations about North's Contra activities.

[9] Letter from North to Rodriguez, 9/20/85, AKW 022740–43.

Juan Rafael Bustillo, the Salvadoran commander of the base.

In August 1985, one month after Abrams' swearing-in as assistant secretary of state for ARA, Congress modified the Boland Amendment by appropriating $27 million for humanitarian assistance to the contras. On August 29, 1985, President Reagan created the Nicaraguan Humanitarian Assistance Office (NHAO) in the State Department for the purpose of administering the appropriated $27 million.

Ambassador Robert W. Duemling set up NHAO within the State Department to administer the humanitarian assistance. A NHAO organizational meeting was held October 1, 1985, attended by Abrams' two senior aides, Walker and Michel. Duemling's notes reflect that North volunteered the services of Rodriguez to assist in the humanitarian resupply.[10]

North intruded in the NHAO operations in at least two other ways: (1) He insisted that Richard B. Gadd, who was assisting retired Air Force Maj. Gen. Richard V. Secord and North in lethal resupply, be the contractor to transport NHAO flights; (2) With Abrams, he persuaded Duemling to add to the NHAO staff North's Central American courier, Robert W. Owen.

Initially, it was planned that the humanitarian supplies would be flown from the United States into Honduras, off-loaded there and delivered in private resupply planes to the contra forces. On October 10, 1985, a NHAO aircraft flying directly from the United States to Honduras arrived with a television crew documenting the effort. This angered the Honduran government, and it rescinded its permission for NHAO planes to fly directly there from the United States. During RIG meetings on this topic, North suggested that the Ilopango air base in San Salvador be used as a transshipment point: NHAO planes would fly from the United States to Ilopango air base, unload, and the supplies would be flown into Honduras in smaller aircraft.[11]

On December 30, 1985, a meeting was held at Ilopango air base in El Salvador to discuss coordination of the NHAO flights there. Walker, North, Fiers, U.S. Ambassador to El Salvador Edwin G. Corr and U.S. Army Col. James J.

Steele, among others, represented the United States in meeting with Salvadoran General Bustillo. Rodriguez was also present.[12]

In early 1986, the NHAO resupply operation at Ilopango became merged with the North-Secord operation there supplying weapons to the contras. The same flight crews that delivered the NHAO humanitarian aid also flew the lethal resupply flights. The same aircraft were used, and the U.S. Government-sponsored humanitarian supplies were stored in the same warehouse as the weapons at the Ilopango airport. Rodriguez was the manager of the resupply effort at Ilopango. He coordinated the arrival and departure of both the lethal and humanitarian resupply flights, controlled the resupply material in the warehouse and arranged for housing for the flight crews.[13]

As the NHAO flights began arriving at Ilopango in late January and early February 1986, concern was expressed within the CIA and Department of State about North and Rodriguez's coordination of these flights. On February 7, 1986, a senior CIA officer in Central America cabled Washington, stating:

Minutes ago [Embassy] Charge [David] Passage came to [me] with story that presumed NHAO-chartered Caribou aircraft on ill-fated supply run to Ilopango via Mexico made emergency landing yesterday, 6 February, on road in southwest El Salvador. Charge said his source was Felix Rodrigues [sic] who apparently has been "coordinating" all of this with Ollie North (one supposes on open phone). [I] had to say, honestly, that [I] knew nothing of this Caribou and indeed had not heard anything from [Fiers] on the subject for two weeks.

Rodrigues [sic] has just called Charge to advise that UPI is on the downed Caribou and wants a story. Charge's position is that he has no knowledge re this A/C [aircraft]. God knows what Felix Rodrigues [sic] is saying.[14]

---

10 Duemling Notes, 10/1/85, GP 0025171.
11 Fiers, *George* Trial Testimony, 7/28/92, pp. 1141–42.
12 Corr Notes, 2/9/86, ALV 001400. Although Corr's notes indicate the meeting was held on December 28, 1986, the meeting was held on December 30, 1985. (*See* North Notebook, 12/30/85, AMX 001948.)
13 CIA Officer #7, *George* Trial Testimony, 10/30/92, pp. 1637–39; Rodriguez, *George* Trial Testimony, 8/4/92, p. 1915.
14 CIA Cable, 2/7/86, DO 58911.

Ambassador Corr's notes reflect that on the following day, February 8, 1986, Corr and Walker discussed the same concerns:

Bill [Walker] said:

COM [Chief of Mission, Ambassador John A. Ferch] in Hond[uras] knows about flight. This part of effort to restab[lish] Hond[uras] connection seems to be falling apart because Max [Gomez, an alias for Felix Rodriguez] has intervened and trying to check everything w/Ollie or others. Ollie and Max are to have nothing to do w/humanitarian assistance deliveries, etc.

I asked if I should have DCM [deputy chief of mission Passage] tell Max to release items to UNO [contra] rep[resentative].

Walker said yes.

*Note*

DCM passed "word" to Max, and he said he would comply.[15]

Another Corr note dated February 8, 1986, attributes the following statement to Walker:

Bill [Walker] said I should impress on Fiers[16] that we cannot proceed in this "fouled up manner." This is the 3d recent screw up & Washington being surprised by unknown & uncoordinated activities.[17]

## Abrams, North and the RIG

As the Reagan Administration's principal advocate of support for the contras, Abrams in 1986 continued to request that the U.S. Congress appropriate $100 million for the contras, including military aid. In March 1986 this request was narrowly defeated in the House of Representatives. Abrams, North, Fiers and other RIG members traveled to Central America on March 21, 1986, to assure the Central American governments that the Reagan Administration was still intent on pursuing funding for contra assistance.

On occasion, Abrams, North and Fiers met either before RIG meetings or immediately after

to discuss sensitive contra matters that they did not want discussed with the other RIG members. An April 25, 1986 North notebook entry reflects the topics (North, Fiers and Abrams discussed with each other:[18]

Meeting w/Elliott:

.

.

.

—Support for S [Southern]. Front.[19]
—Air base open in C.R. [Costa Rica][20]
—A/C for Arias[21]
—[Classified] operation.
—100 BP's [Blowpipes] fm. Chile[22]

On May 16, 1986, Abrams attended a National Security Planning Group meeting on Central America at the White House. The principals attending the meeting were President Reagan, Vice President Bush, Shultz, Treasury Secretary James A. Baker, Defense Secretary Caspar W. Weinberger, CIA Director William J. Casey and White House Chief of Staff Donald T. Regan. In addition, Fiers, North and supporting personnel from the various agencies attended the meeting. NSC staff member Raymond F. Burghardt's minutes of the meeting reflect that North reminded the group that the fiscal 1986 Intelligence Authorization Bill permitted the State Department to approach other governments for non-military aid for the contras. A brief discussion ensued concerning the solicitation of other countries for contra assistance. Burghardt's minutes reflect that Reagan posed the following questions:

What about the private groups who pay for ads for the contras? Have they been contacted? Can they do more than ads?[23]

---

15 Corr Note, 2/8/86, ALV 001398.

16 Fiers traveled to Ilopango on February 8th in response to the CIA cable regarding Rodriguez/North.

17 Corr Note, 2/8/86. Walker said he does not remember these conversations or whether he imparted this information to Abrams. Indeed, Walker testified that he was not aware of the name Felix Rodriguez until an August 12, 1986 meeting with Gregg. (Walker, Grand Jury, 7/31/91, pp. 69–71.)

18 Fiers, Grand Jury, 8/14/91, pp. 25–27; North Notebook, 4/25/86, AMX 1084–85. Although North does not have a specific recollection of meeting with Abrams on April 25, 1986, these issues are generally topics which he discussed with Abrams. (North, Grand Jury, 2/22/91, pp. 4–5.)

19 This note was 14 days following the first successful lethal drop to the southern front.

20 This entry reflects the progress of the opening of the airstrip at Santa Elena in Costa Rica.

21 This entry is a reference to an unsuccessful attempt to get an aircraft for the brother of newly elected Costa Rican President Oscar Arias Sanchez.

22 North Notebook, 4/25/86, AMX 001084–85. This entry references North's attempts to obtain 100 blowpipe missiles from Chile for the contras.

23 Memorandum from Burghardt to McDaniel re: May 16, 1986, NSPG Meeting, 6/4/86, AKW 018812.

Fiers' recollection of this meeting differed from the Burghardt minutes. Fiers vividly recalled Reagan asking about "Ollie's people" and inquiring whether they could help. Fiers remembers a nervous tension and then a quick response to the effect of "that's being worked on."[24]

Prior to this NSPG meeting, North had been circumspect within the RIG in describing the specific activities he was undertaking on behalf of the contras. Following the meeting, he was more outspoken.

During RIG meetings in the summer of 1986, North went over, "item by item," actions that he was directing or coordinating on behalf of the contra resupply effort.[25] North referred to the supply effort being run by him and Secord as "Project Democracy." Fiers remembered a July 1986 RIG meeting, chaired by Abrams at the State Department, wherein North listed the many activities—including aircraft descriptions and salaries being paid—that he was causing to be conducted on behalf of the contras. North inquired whether these activities should continue or be terminated. North made it very clear that he could cause Project Democracy to respond as he directed.[26] There was an awkward silence. No one responded. Finally Fiers answered either in the affirmative or negative as to each of the items listed by North.[27]

Abrams was aware that North could obtain funds for the contras from Project Democracy. By July 1986, the $27 million appropriated for humanitarian assistance had been spent and it appeared there would be a considerable gap in funding before the $100 million would be appropriated by for the contras. Abrams and Fiers requested that North cause Project Democracy to contribute $2 million for food to keep the contra resistance forces intact.[28] A July 24, 1986 computer note from North to Poindexter reflected the request: "Given our lack of movement on other funding options, and Elliott/Allen's [sic] plea for PRODEM [Project Democracy] to get food to the resistance ASAP, PRODEM will have to borrow at least $2M

to pay for the food."[29] During the RIG meeting, North informed Abrams and Fiers that he could arrange for the requested money.[30]

North testified before the Select Iran/contra Committees in 1987 that the members of the RIG were aware of what he was doing on behalf of the contras. North stated the RIG members were knowledgeable that a covert operation was being conducted by the U.S. Government to support the Nicaraguan resistance.[31] North remembered a meeting in the Pentagon with RIG members where he went down, item by item, a checklist of the activities he was directing each month or each quarter to support the contras and he asked the RIG members "point blank" whether this activity should continue.[32] North's notes of an August 28, 1986, meeting at the Pentagon reflect such a list of activities:

—UNO [contras] 60K/QTR

—UNO U.S. travel 30K/mo
—Cruz 10K
—Robello 10K
—Calero [FDN] food 500K/mo.
—[Classified Project] 20K
—Hospital
—Air Ops
     2 C–7's
     2 C–123's = 132K/mo
     3 Maules[33]

Present at the August 28, 1986, meeting were Assistant Secretary of Defense Richard L. Armitage, Lt. Gen. John Moellering, Fiers, Abrams aide Michel and Nestor Sanchez, a DoD officer assigned to the NSC staff. Abrams did not attend.

Armitage gave deposition testimony to the staff of the Select Committees on July 22, 1987. The staff followed up on North's assertion that he had informed the RIG members of his activities and requested whether they should or should not continue. Armitage was asked "do you recall, regardless of what dates, regardless of where it was, regardless of whether it had exactly the players he said—because he could have gotten all that wrong—do you recall any

---

24 Fiers, Grand Jury, 8/14/91, p. 39.
25 North, Grand Jury, 3/8/91, pp. 71–73.
26 Fiers, Grand Jury, 8/14/91, p. 75.
27 Ibid., pp. 72–76.
28 Ibid., p. 73.

29 PROFs Note from North to Poindexter, 7/24/86, AKW 018917.
30 Ibid.; Fiers, Grand Jury, 8/14/91 p. 75.
31 North, Select Committees Testimony, 7/7/87, pp. 231–32.
32 Ibid., p. 231.
33 North Notebook, 8/28/86, AMX 001442.

meeting at which he did anything close to what his testimony suggests?" His answer was: "I do not."[34]

Moellering, during a November 13, 1990, interview with the Office of Independent Counsel, reviewed North's notebook entry of August 28, 1986, and stated he did not recall any meeting when North made disclosures concerning the contra-resupply operation or the Iran initiative. Moellering stated he never knew about North's personal involvement with the resupply operation before it was reported by the press in November 1986.[35]

Michel denied the North allegations in a written memorandum, stating that he had no recollection of North indicating that he was the source of contra funding or was in control of such funding. Michel added, "[h]ad he done so, I would have considered it an amazing revelation requiring immediate attention."[36]

During the congressional investigation, no member of the RIG corroborated North's testimony that he openly discussed his contra-resupply activities with the "private benefactors" during RIG meetings. It was not until the Fiers' plea in July 1991 that a RIG member affirmed North's 1987 testimony by acknowledging that North, in RIG meetings in July, August and September 1986, discussed item-by-item the activities being conducted on behalf of the contras and requested whether the activity should continue. The testimony of North and Fiers about widespread interdepartmental knowledge of North's activities on behalf of the contras during the summer of 1986 was significantly reinforced by the belated discovery of a handwritten note of a debriefing of Moellering by Colonel Stephen Croker shortly after the August 28th meeting. In pertinent part, the note reads:

$1 M/month 32 people—private ops.

flying planes for resupply in country
do we want to keep it going or choke off[37]

During what was perceived as a transitional phase in later summer 1986 from private support to official U.S. Government support for the contras, North continued to seek guidance from the RIG about the continuation of private resupply efforts. Another meeting occurred in Armitage's office on September 19, 1986. Abrams, North and Fiers were among those in attendance. Again, North went over the items being conducted on behalf of the contras and asked whether they should continue.[38] Then, North raised a new, dramatic proposition. Manuel Noriega, dictator of Panama, had offered to have sabotage conducted inside Nicaragua for $1 million in cash; the funds would not be from the U.S. Government. Fiers understood that the funds would be from Project Democracy.[39]

On September 20, 1986, Abrams met with Platt and Hill and discussed North's proposal. Hill's notes reflect Abrams' explanation:

> Noriega offers to do some sabotage (electric pylons) that we training contras to do but which they can't do for 18 mos. Wd [would] get us on the map fast—by Oct.
>
> Do it via mercenaries who may not know who employers are. Brits.
>
> Wd do it for cash (not from USG [U.S. Government]). Wants our go-ahead. Ollie will meet him w/approval of Pdx. [Poindexter][40]

Ultimately, the decision was made not to have North cause the $1 million to be paid to Noriega.

## Abrams' Knowledge of the Costa Rican Airstrip and the Southern Front

Before Lewis A. Tambs became U.S. ambassador to Costa Rica in the summer of 1985, North instructed Tambs to assist in opening a "southern front" for contra forces in Nicaragua. Tambs believed that his instructions to open a southern front came from the Restricted Interagency Group chaired by Abrams.

[34] Armitage, Select Committees Deposition, 7/22/87, p. 242.
[35] Moellering, FBI 302, 11/13/90, p. 10.
[36] Memorandum from Michel to Shultz, 7/20/87, ALW 0032400.
[37] Croker Notes, 9/2/86, ALZ 0034813–14. Croker, who was Moellering's aide on the Joint Chiefs staff, told the Grand Jury that these notes referred to the cost of running the private benefactors operation and whether the RIG should "do something." Having not attended the meeting recounted by Moellering, Croker did not wish to speculate about what was under consideration. (Croker, Grand Jury, 9/13/91, pp. 29–43, 46–54.)

[38] Fiers, Grand Jury, 8/14/91, pp. 116–18.
[39] Ibid., pp. 118–19.
[40] Hill Note, 9/20/86, ANS 0001617.

When Tambs arrived in Costa Rica, he met with his Deputy Chief of Mission James Tull, and Joseph F. Fernandez, the CIA chief of station, to discuss ideas for opening a southern front in Nicaragua for the contras.[41] A small group of contras were located in northern Costa Rica, and both Tambs and the Costa Rican government wanted them out. But it was necessary to ensure that they would receive supplies once inside Nicaragua.[42] At the suggestion of Fernandez, Tambs approached Costa Rican President Monge to discuss the development of an airstrip in northern Costa Rica by "private benefactors" (the North-Secord Enterprise), which could be used to resupply[43] contra rebels inside Nicaragua.[44]

Tambs met with Monge on August 12, 1985. On August 13, Fernandez sent Fiers a cable stating that Monge told Tambs an airfield and resupply depot could be established as long as they were located well inside Costa Rica and away from the border area.[45]

Within days after Shultz directed Abrams to "monitor Ollie," Abrams, North and Fiers met in Abrams' office. Fiers briefed Abrams on the recent developments concerning the secret Costa Rican airfield.[46] During the discussion, Abrams asked "Why is Monge doing this?," referring to the airstrip. Fiers explained Tambs' discussion with Monge.[47]

With knowledge of the Embassy's involvement in the negotiations on the secret airstrip, Abrams attended a Chiefs of Mission meeting in Panama to discuss policy with U.S. ambassadors in his region.[48] Tambs and Abrams briefly discussed the airstrip in the hallway outside of the meeting.[49] They discussed the agreement regarding the airstrip and its purpose to supply the southern front.[50]

Another person at the Panama meeting was Corr, ambassador to El Salvador. Corr assumed his post in the summer of 1985. Corr had a habit of organizing his thoughts for important meetings by preparing written notes. His note prior to the Chiefs of Mission conference reads as follows:

To discuss w/Elliott [Abrams] and Bill [Walker]

> *         *         *

*Other Subjects*

> *         *         *

(3) Contras—3 contacts; FDN talk w/Steele (No)
(4) Rodriguez.
(5) Ollie North conversation—S[outhern] Front[51]

On his note, Corr bracketed these three topics together and placed check marks next to each one, indicating it was discussed. Although Corr said he does not have a specific recollection of discussing these topics at a meeting, he acknowledged that all three were contra-related.[52]

Ultimately, the secret airstrip was constructed at Santa Elena, Costa Rica, by one of Secord's companies, Udall Corporation, and was known as "Point West." It became a matter of public focus in September 1986. When Monge's successor, Oscar Arias, became president of Costa Rica in the spring of 1986, he was briefed about the airstrip. He was outraged and directed that it not be used for contra resupply. On September 6, 1986, in a series of late night telephone calls, Fernandez informed North and Fiers that the Costa Rican security minister planned to hold a press conference the follow-

41 Tambs, Grand Jury, 3/23/90, pp. 27–28.

42 Ibid., p. 30.

43 The flights from Ilopango to Southern Nicaragua usually were routed over the Pacific Ocean for safety. The landing strip was intended for refueling empty aircraft for the return trip and for emergency landing.

44 Tambs, Grand Jury, 3/23/90, p. 31.

45 San Jose Cable, 8/13/85, DO 189740–38. Other details of Monge's discussion with Tambs—details that Fiers later conveyed to Abrams—are set forth in the Classified Appendix to this chapter.

46 Ibid.

47 Ibid. During Abrams' testimony before the Select Committees in the summer of 1987, he testified that although he learned of the existence of the airstrip in August or September 1985, he was unaware of Tambs' involvement with the Costa Rican government regarding the airstrip until Tambs' public testimony before the Committees in the summer of 1987. (Abrams, Select Committees Testimony, 6/2/87, p. 51.) When asked whether he learned that the U.S. Government or any U.S. officials were involved in the airstrip project, Abrams responded: "Well, it was pretty clear from the way it was told to me that no U. S. Government officials were involved in the project. That would have been illegal." (Ibid., p. 52.)

48 During the meeting, the topic of the agreement reached with the Costa Ricans regarding the secret airstrip was not discussed openly. (Tambs, Grand Jury, 3/23/90, p. 37.)

49 Ibid.

50 Ibid., p. 39. Tambs claims he did not participate further in the negotiations for the purchase of the property or other arrangements with the Costa Rican government for the construction of the airstrip, which was built at Santa Elena, Costa Rica. (Ibid., p. 35.)

51 Corr Note, ALW 0033600.

52 Corr, Grand Jury, 5/29/91, p. 31.

ing day and make public the Udall Corporation's role with the Point West airstrip, alleging violations of Costa Rican laws by Udall, North, Secord, and others.[53] North discussed this impending crisis in conference calls with Abrams, Tambs and Fiers. They discussed whether to tell Arias that he would never set foot in the White House and that he would never get five cents of the $80 million promised to him by the U.S. Agency for International Development if the airstrip were revealed.[54]

After Tambs interceded with the Arias administration, the Costa Rican press conference was cancelled. Fiers acknowledged that he, Abrams and North were concerned that public revelation of the airstrip would expose the linkage of North and the White House to the contra-resupply operation.[55] Two weeks later, in spite of Tambs's intervention, on September 24, 1986, the Costa Rican public security minister held a press conference and announced the discovery of a secret airstrip in Costa Rica, which had been built and used by Udall for support to the contras.[56] False guidance for the press regarding the Costa Rican airstrip was prepared by North and coordinated with Fiers and Abrams. The press guidance was consistent with a previously concocted cover story regarding the airstrip. The press guidance was intentionally misleading, denying U.S. Government knowledge of the origins and purpose of the airstrip. It was clear to Fiers that Abrams was aware of North's connection to the airstrip.[57] Following the Costa Rican announcement of the airstrip, Abrams drafted a harshly worded cable to be sent to the Costa Rican government. A cable containing Abrams' message was stopped by Shultz aide Hill before it was sent.[58]

## The Hasenfus Shootdown

On October 5, 1986, less than two weeks after the exposure of the airstrip, a C–123 aircraft carrying weapons and supplies to the contras was shot down in Nicaragua. Two American pilots, William H. Cooper and Wallace B. Sawyer, Jr., and one Latin crew member were killed. A third American crew member, Eugene Hasenfus, parachuted out but was captured by the Nicaraguans. Over the course of the next few days, Abrams was the senior U.S. spokesman responding to the incident. He coordinated his statements with Ambassador Corr in El Salvador, talked with North and chaired a RIG meeting concerning the incident.

Corr's notes reflect a telephone conversation with Abrams in the early morning of October 8, 1986, regarding the downed plane in Nicaragua.

> . . . Nica[ragua] said [Hasenfus said] that he got instr[uction] & support from Gen. Bustillo. He said 5 airplanes—gave tail numbers. Cooper had ID card plus something from humanitarian office (NHAO)
>
> Appears that Hazenful [sic] was an mbr [member] of something called: Grupo USA-para mil grp.
>
> Ollie out of country. Back this afternoon & Elliott will get info from him.[59]

Corr's notes of the conversation with Abrams continue, relating how the U.S. Government planned to proceed and whether an upcoming presidential summit in Iceland would cause news focus to shift from the downed airplane to other events. Corr's notes also indicate that Salvadoran General Bustillo, who ran Ilopango air base where the Hasenfus flight originated, would "deny all" connection to the flight and that Salvadoran President Duarte would not comment on it.

Corr's notes focus on what should be said about the Salvadoran role:

> ACTION: Must say something about Salv role when we are asked
>
> I told him [Abrams] of my 10/7 conversation w/Vides & Bustillo [60] Elliott replied

53 North Notebook, 9/6/86, AMX 001458.
54 Ibid.
55 Fiers, FBI 302, 8/1/91, p. 6. Abrams testified that the consternation over the public revelation of the airstrip only had to do with the embarrassment of the previous Costa Rican administration. (Abrams, Select Committees Testimony, 6/2/87, p. 65.)
56 PROFs Note from North to Poindexter, 9/25/86, AKW 018884.
57 Fiers, FBI 302, 8/1/91, p. 9.
58 Hill, FBI 302, 12/10/90, p. 17.

59 Corr Note, 10/8/86, ALV 001402.
60 Before calling Abrams, Corr met with General Vides, the Salvadoran minister of defense. They agreed to say as little as possible but not to lie, because they could not be certain what Hasenfus might eventually say. Nor could they be certain about what might come out in the United States. Bustillo joined the meeting and advocated saying nothing, and if it was necessary to say something, to deny everything. Vides then agreed with Bustillo. (Corr Note, 10/7/86, ALV 001432.)

might be better if Salv brazenly deny all. Agreed w/Bustillo thesis. Simpler if Salv Mil[itary] puts out statement denying all, & [Salvadoran President] Duarte says he accepts FFAA [Salvadoran military] statement

Only alt[ernative] is if D[uarte] comes out of closet & ready to support openly a support role against Sandinistas.[61]

The Corr note continues concerning the inevitability of leaks:

There will be leaks. Cannot keep Salvadoran link wholly SECRET. Would be done as tactic. But eventually someone in USG will finally acknowledge some "winking." Salv role now more public. This would be a tactic. All will know they (GOES) [Government of El Salvador] lying, but perhaps soon forget & get on w/things

I said the key on this would be D[uarte], who has view of himself as never lying. I said I'd talk w/Salv & get back.[62]

Later, on October 8, Abrams chaired a RIG meeting concerning the downed aircraft. North did not attend. Issues such as demand for access to Hasenfus, Salvadoran denial of contra support, press guidance, and legal counsel for Hasenfus were discussed. It was agreed that Abrams would follow up with North to request that UNO (the contra umbrella organization) assume responsibility for the flight.[63]

Additionally, Fiers said it was reported at the RIG meeting that the contra-resupply planes had been moved from Ilopango to Aguacate, Honduras.[64] There was discussion about news reports linking the downed plane to Southern Air Transport (SAT), a Miami-based airline that had, in fact, contracted to service the resupply network's airplanes and to perform other duties. Fiers was concerned because SAT had been used for the NHAO delivery of humanitarian assistance to the contras.[65]

Felix Rodriguez also was discussed. It was said that Rodriguez was lying low in Miami and the press couldn't find him. There was discussion about the possibility of supporting Rodriguez financially.[66]

Abrams acknowledged phoning North regarding the Hasenfus shootdown. Abrams asked about retrieval of the bodies of Cooper and Sawyer, and North informed Abrams that the employers of Hasenfus would continue to pay the families.[67] Abrams did not explicitly ask North if he was connected with the downed aircraft. North later explained "he didn't have to ask me."[68]

On October 9, 1986, Hasenfus, then in Nicaraguan custody, publicly stated he had made 10 trips to supply the contras—six out of Ilopango airfield in El Salvador—and had worked with "Max Gomez" and "Ramon Medina," whom he alleged were CIA employees. Hasenfus stated that Gomez and Medina oversaw the housing for the crews, transportation, refueling and flight plans.[69] On the same day, Nicaraguan officials claimed that one of the crew members of the aircraft carried cards issued by the Salvadoran Air Force, identifying them as U.S. advisers. They said that one of the crew members had carried a business card of a NHAO official.

On October 10, 1986, *The San Francisco Examiner* reported that Vice President Bush, not the CIA, was the U.S. Government link to the Hasenfus flight. The newspaper said Max Gomez, whose real name was Felix Rodriguez, was assigned to Ilopango by Gregg, the national security adviser to Bush.

Later, Abrams assured Congress that the resupply operation was conducted without any coordination from the U.S. Government; that there was no direct or indirect U.S. Government involvement in contra resupply; and that no one in the U.S. Government knew who organized and paid for the Hasenfus flight.

Between October 10 and October 15, 1986, Abrams appeared three times before congressional committees as the Reagan Administration spokesman concerning the downed aircraft.

61 Corr Note, 10/8/86, ALV 001403.
62 Ibid.
63 PROFs Note from Cannistraro to Poindexter, 10/8/86, AKW 021747; Fiers, FBI 302, 7/22/91, pp. 18–19.
64 Ibid.
65 Fiers, FBI 302, 7/23/91, p. 5.

66 Ibid., p. 9.
67 Abrams, Select Committees, 6/2/87, pp. 169–170; Abrams, FBI 302, 9/28/91, pp. 33–34.
68 North, Select Committees Testimony, 7/8/87, p. 233.
69 Managua 06587, 10/9/86, ALW 0026774.

Abrams was confronted with a number of questions: Who was behind the aircraft? Who was financing the resupply operation? Was the U.S. Government involved, either directly or indirectly, in contra resupply? Who was Max Gomez? What was Max Gomez's role in contra resupply? What was Gomez's relationship to the Office of the Vice President? Were foreign governments assisting the contras?

On October 10, 1986, Abrams appeared in closed session before the Senate Committee on Foreign Relations. The chairman, Sen. Richard Lugar, said Congress was intent on learning whether there was any Government involvement with the downed aircraft: ''[V]ery clearly, members are going to want to know if not CIA, if not State Department, then who.'' [70] Lugar sought additional information regarding a *Los Angeles Times* story on October 9, which reported an elaborate system supplying the contras, and that the downed cargo plane was only one of 19 aircraft flying in support of the guerrilla war, apparently out of El Salvador.[71] Abrams responded to Lugar's inquiry in his opening statement:

> It seems to me, on the question of the ''L.A. Times'' article on there being an elaborate supply system, it seems that there clearly is an elaborate supply system.
>
> In the last two years, since Congress cut off support to the resistance [contras], this supply system has kept them alive.
>
> It is not our supply system. It is one that grew up after we were forbidden from supplying the resistance, and *we have been kind of careful not to get closely involved with it and to stay away from it.*
>
> I think that people who are supplying the Contras believe that we generally approve of what they are doing—and they are right. We do generally approve of what they are doing, because they are keeping the Contras alive while Congress takes [sic] its decision, which each House has separately, though obviously final legislation is not yet ready.

So, the notion that we are generally in favor of people helping the Contras is correct.

> *We do not encourage people to do this.* We don't round up people, we don't write letters, *we don't have conversations, we don't tell them to do this, we don't ask them to do it.* But I think it is quite clear, from the attitude of the administration, the attitude of the administration is that these people are doing a very good thing, and if they think they are doing something that we like, then, in a general sense, they are right. But *that is without any encouragement and coordination from us,* other than a public speech by the President, that kind of thing, on the public record.[72]

Four days later, on October 14, 1986, before a closed session of the House Permanent Select Committee on Intelligence (HPSCI), Abrams continued to assure Congress that the U.S. Government was not involved in the supply of contras:

> CHAIRMAN HAMILTON: Can anybody assure us that the United States Government was not involved, indirectly or directly, in any way in supply of the contras?
>
> MR. ABRAMS: I believe we have already done that, that is, I think, the President has done it, the Secretary has done it, and I have done it.
>
> CHAIRMAN HAMILTON: So the answer is the United States Government was not involved in any way.
>
> MR. ABRAMS: *In the supply.* Now again, this normal intelligence monitoring is there, but *the answer to your question is yes.*[73]

Later in the hearing, the chairman revisited the issue of U.S. Government assistance:

> CHAIRMAN HAMILTON: We will begin another round.
>
> Just to be clear, the United States Government has not done anything to facilitate the activities of these private groups, is

---

[70] Abrams, Senate Foreign Relations Committee Transcript, 10/10/86, p. 3.
[71] Ibid., p. 4.
[72] Ibid., pp. 10–11. (Emphasis added.)
[73] Abrams, HPSCI Testimony, 10/14/86, p. 17. (Emphasis added.)

that a fair statement? We have not furnished any money. We have not furnished
any arms. We have not furnished any advice. We have not furnished logistics.

MR. GEORGE: Mr. Chairman, I cannot
speak for the entire United States Government.

CHAIRMAN HAMILTON: Can you, Mr.
Abrams?

MR. ABRAMS: *Yes, to the extent of my
knowledge that I feel to be complete, other
than the general public encouragement that
we like this kind of activity.*[74]

The following day, in a public hearing before
the House Foreign Affairs Subcommittee on
Western Hemisphere Affairs, Abrams reaffirmed
his prior statements that there was no U.S. Government involvement with the downed aircraft.[75] Abrams added that no one in the U.S.
Government knew who organized and paid for
the Hasenfus flight or other flights like it:

MR. ABRAMS: I do not know the answer
to the question who organized and paid
for this flight. I don't mean to suggest
that the U.S. Government as a whole
knows absolutely nothing about the fact
that there is material getting in. For 2 years
the Contras have been kept alive by this
material, so it is clear it is getting in, but
I still don't know——

MR. BARNES: Who organized this and
who paid for it?

MR. ABRAMS: That is correct.

MR. KOSTMAYER: You have not been
told by our Government, if indeed our
Government knows, who organized and
who paid for this particular flight?

MR. ABRAMS: I wouldn't separate myself
from the Government. *We don't know.*

MR. KOSTMAYER: Do you think there
is anyone in the Government who does
know?

MR. ABRAMS: *No, because we don't
track this kind of activity.*[76]

Abrams was not truthful with the congressional committees. He was aware that North
was encouraging, coordinating and directing the
activities of the contra-resupply operation and
that North was in contact with the private citizens who were behind the lethal resupply flights.
Additionally, Abrams did not inform Congress
of his knowledge of the activities of the U.S.
Embassy in Costa Rica to help construct a secret contra-resupply airstrip in Costa Rica.

## Max Gomez/Felix Rodriguez Inquiry

Because of Hasenfus's public statements on October 9 identifying "Max Gomez" as a resupply manager, and because of press reports linking Gomez to the Office of the Vice President,
Members of Congress were especially interested
in information about Gomez. When Abrams appeared before the Senate Committee on Foreign
Relations on October 10, 1986, the committee
was interested in knowing the extent of U.S.
Government knowledge about the Hasenfus allegations concerning Max Gomez. Clair George
stated that the CIA was running the names
Gomez and Medina through their information
system and would respond accordingly.[77]

Senator John Kerry pressed the inquiry about
the alleged connection between Gomez and the
Office of the Vice President:

SENATOR KERRY: . . . Mr. Gomez,
Max Gomez, do you know whether or not
he reports to or was hired by the Vice
President of the United States?

MR. FIERS: Max Gomez is the individual—he is not in our records—I think it
is an alias for an individual who was previously employed with us. But I don't
know. If that, in fact, is the case, I don't
know who he is reporting to.

This is one of the two names.

---

[74] Ibid., p. 48. (Emphasis added.)
[75] Abrams, House Foreign Affairs Subcommittee Testimony,
10/15/86, p. 31.

[76] Ibid., p. 33. (Emphasis added.)
[77] George, Senate Foreign Relations Committee Testimony, 10/10/86,
pp. 55–56.

SENATOR KERRY: You don't know whether or not he reports to the Vice President of the United States?

MR. GEORGE: The Vice President? I don't know.

SENATOR KERRY: You don't know anything about that?

MR. ABRAMS: I have never heard any suggestion of that.

SENATOR KERRY: The suggestion comes from the Hearst newspapers in a story that started last night. A copy of the article I will have in about half an hour from now. It apparently says that Max Gomez was placed in this position by the Vice President of the United States and reports directly to him. That is the story.

MR. ABRAMS: What position?

SENATOR KERRY: I don't know. That is the story.

MR. GEORGE: That is one of the two names that Mr. Hasenfus said were the two CIA men who were running this whole thing.

MR. ABRAMS: *It really stretches credulity.*

SENATOR KERRY: Now, I don't know. I am just asking. I got a piece of paper that said this is out there and I know nothing about it, any more than you do. I just asked the question.[78]

On October 11, 1986, *The Washington Post* quoted Abrams as stating "What's kept the resistance alive has been private help. Some Members of Congress accuse us of approving of this with a wink and a nod. A wink and a nod, hell. We think it's been fine."[79]

On October 11, 12 and 13, 1986, media reports identified Gomez as Felix Rodriguez, a Cuban-American who fought in the CIA's failed invasion of Cuba at the Bay of Pigs in 1961.[80] Vice President Bush publicly acknowledged that

he had met Rodriguez two or three times, but refused to state what their relationship was. Unidentified sources were cited, stating that Rodriguez reported his activities to Vice President Bush and Bush approved of them. On October 14, 1986, *The Washington Post* quoted Vice President Bush stating three days earlier in Charleston, South Carolina, as stating that Rodriguez was a U.S. counter-insurgency adviser working directly with the Salvadoran government. The article stated that Salvadoran officials denied this.[81]

During Abrams' appearance before HPSCI on October 14, 1986, he was asked about the press allegations relating to Vice President Bush and Felix Rodriguez:

MR. STOKES: . . . Secretary Abrams, going back to your statement to the Chairman with reference to the fact that there was no involvement on the part of the U.S. Government, taking into account the allegations with reference to Vice President Bush, you are familiar with those.

MR. ABRAMS: Yes.

MR. STOKES: Does that statement also categorically include him when you say there was no involvement on the part of our Government?

MR. ABRAMS: Yes. I am going to just expand on that.

MR. STOKES: Sure. Go ahead, please.

MR. ABRAMS: My understanding of it—and it comes from the Vice President's staff—is that, as I think he has said publicly, Mr. Gregg knew Mr. Rodriguez and introduced him to the Salvadorans, in I think 1984, for work with the Salvadoran armed forces, particularly the Salvadoran air force.

What he was supposed to be a specialist in was air-ground helicopter operations, and he did work with the Salvadoran air force on that, and apparently very well, and he was a great help to them.

[78] Ibid., pp. 125–26 (Emphasis added).

[79] "Bush Is Linked to Head of Contra Aid Network," *The Washington Post,* 10/11/86, p. 2.

[80] Ibid., "Singlaub Played Double Role in Aid to Contras," *The Los Angeles Times,* 10/13/86, p. 2.

[81] "Salvadoran General Disputes Bush on Role of U.S. Advisor," *The Washington Post,* 10/13/86, p. 1.

And that is what the Vice President was aware of his doing and the Vice President has said that. *But there was no knowledge that he was, or at what point he had moved off into doing some other things which apparently he has done with the resistance.* But that was the initial involvement there.

MR. STOKES: That was the extent of it to your knowledge?

MR. ABRAMS: *That was the extent of it to my knowledge, that is right.*[82]

When Abrams became assistant secretary of state for ARA in July 1985, Rodriguez was already situated at Ilopango air base, having been placed there with the assistance of Gregg. The first indication of Abrams' knowledge of Rodriguez in El Salvador appears from a Corr note to himself made in preparation for the State Department chiefs of mission meeting in Panama in September 1985. Corr's note reflects topics he planned to address with Abrams. Rodriguez was one of three contra-related issues Corr wished to discuss with Abrams.[83]

Following the Honduran refusal to permit direct NHAO flights from the United States to Honduras, it was agreed within the RIG to use Ilopango as a transshipment point for off-loading supplies onto smaller aircraft. During December 1985, Rodriguez was openly discussed within the RIG as an individual who could be of assistance to the NHAO flights into Ilopango because of his personal relationship with Bustillo, who controlled the Ilopango air base. The fact that Rodriguez was using the alias Maximo (Max) Gomez while in El Salvador was also openly discussed within the RIG.[84]

During January and February 1986, Rodriguez's involvement in coordinating NHAO flights into Ilopango with North became of concern to the State Department and the CIA. CIA personnel in Central America cabled concern to Fiers in Washington about Rodriguez and North supposedly having coordinated a Caribou

aircraft carrying NHAO supplies that crashed in Salvador, causing press inquiries about the flight. The next day, Corr and Walker discussed the same incident by phone and expressed concern about Gomez's (Rodriguez's) intervention with NHAO flights and his coordination with North.[85]

In the summer of 1986, after the Administration's request for $100 million in contra aid passed both Houses of Congress, there was concern about what should be done with the Secord operation's assets, principally the airplanes, after the anticipated funding was approved. North advocated to the RIG that the CIA should purchase the airplanes from the operation. Rodriguez and Bustillo believed that the airplanes belonged to the contras, not to the Secord operation.

Rodriguez's concern that the Secord operation was selling shoddy goods at high prices to contras resulted in his traveling to Washington, D.C., in August 1986 to air his complaints to Gregg. After meeting with Rodriguez, Gregg organized a meeting with other Administration officials to discuss Rodriguez's complaints. Abrams' assistant Walker, Corr, Fiers and North's assistant Lt. Col. Robert L. Earl, among others, met with Gregg in his office on August 12, 1986.[86] Abrams did not attend.

Rodriguez's role in the resupply effort at Ilopango, his relationship with Bustillo and his claims of working for the CIA with the blessing of the Vice President were among the topics discussed. Earl noted this during the meeting:

12 Aug

Corr
Concerned on transition
Busti[ll]o concerned FDN [contras] getting screwed
    (re A/C).
Equip being taken?
Urgent need for resupply of [the] southern front.
—123 Miami →
Felix Rodriguez—compadres w/ Busti[ll]o.

.

.

.

[82] Abrams, HPSCI Testimony, 10/14/86, pp. 23–24 (emphasis added). Two months later, appearing before the House of Representatives Committee on Foreign Affairs, Abrams stated that ". . . prior to all of this [the Iran/Contra revelations] I don't think I ever heard of Felix Rodriguez, . . ." (Abrams, House Foreign Affairs Committee Testimony, 12/17/86, p. 79.)

[83] Corr Note, ALW 0033600. Corr does not remember if he had such a meeting with Abrams.

[84] Fiers, FBI 302, 8/2/91, p. 5.

[85] Corr Note, 2/8/86, ALV 001398.

[86] For a more complete discussion of this meeting, see Gregg Chapter.

bottom line = sell A/C & money to FDN.
Corr recommends this.
Or, ON [North] to explain who owns A/C
to
        Busti[ll]o—
Corr doesn't think this will work.
Felix needs to be eased out w/ honor.
Corr doesn't mind either way, but Corr thinks
he's been instrumental—3 months
Ilopango = [Classified—continuation
                Information Withheld]
                not 1st choice
Felix claims working w/VP blessing for CIA.

.

.

.

Corr sees no legal alternative to Felix ([CIA]
& Steele can't ~~tough~~ touch it)
Corr can't see any way to operate
Mario Delameco, Miami = Felix contact
(Cuban
    → cut this link.
Calero—Martin link = a problem too.
. . .[87]

After the shootdown on October 5, 1986,
Felix Rodriguez became a major concern. He
was discussed in the RIG meeting on October
8, chaired by Abrams, and the next day
Hasenfus named him, using his alias Gomez,
as a supervisor of the resupply operation at
Ilopango.

On October 10, 1986, during the hearing before the Senate Committee on Foreign Relations, Abrams, George and Fiers were pressed
concerning their knowledge about "Gomez"
and his reputed relationship to Vice President
Bush.[88] Later that afternoon, Abrams was interviewed by Rowland Evans and Robert Novak.
The videotape of that interview was aired on
October 11 and 12, 1986. Abrams was asked
about Max Gomez:

MR. NOVAK: All right, now, just on Friday the San Francisco Examiner reported
that, no, quoting intelligence sources, said
there was no CIA connection, but there
was connection, of all places, from Vice
President Bush's office. That Vice Presi-

dent Bush's security aid, Mr. Don Gregg,
had hired this Max Gomez, who Mr.
Hasenfus described as a CIA agent. Do
you know anything about that?

MR. ABRAMS: Not a lot. I first heard
about it on Friday morning as well. I can
say first of all *there's no Max Gomez.*
Whoever that gentleman is, he certainly
isn't named Max Gomez. So we need, first
of all, to find out who he is. Secondly,
I know nothing about any connection to
the Vice President's office whatsoever.
And thirdly, in his capacity down there
in Central America helping whoever he is,
he is not on the U.S. government payroll
in any way.

MR. NOVAK: Now, when you say gave
categorical assurance, we're not playing
word games that are so common in Washington. You're not talking about the NCS
[sic], or something else?

MR. ABRAMS: I am not playing games.

MR. NOVAK: National Security Council?

MR. ABRAMS: No government agencies,
none.[89]

Questions about Rodriguez's role in contra
resupply persisted. Hours before his appearance
before HPSCI on October 14, 1986, Abrams
called Corr to discuss the role of Rodriguez
in El Salvador. Corr's note of that telephone
conversation reads:

Elliott Abrams TELCON—10/14/86

Elliott has

    House Intel. Cmte in a couple hours.
Role of Salv, Felix [Emphasis added]
    Why are Salv saying nothing coming[90]

Corr was fully aware of Rodriguez's role in
the resupply operation located at the Ilopango

[87] Earl Note, 8/12/86 (emphasis in original).
[88] Senate Foreign Relations Committee Transcript, 10/10/86, pp. 125–
26. (Emphasis added.)

[89] Transcript of Evans & Novak Interview, 10/10/86, AKW 000964–
65. During his Select Committees testimony on June 3, 1987, Abrams
admitted that he knew by the time of his Evans and Novak interview
that Gomez was an assumed name. (Abrams, Select Committees Testimony, 6/3/87, pp. 21–22.)
[90] Corr Note, 10/14/86, ALW 0032906. Corr withheld this note from
Independent Counsel until he received immunity in 1991. See Corr
chapter.

airport. Corr does not remember discussing Rodriguez with Abrams on October 14, 1986.[91] However, Corr testified that if Abrams ever asked about Rodriguez, he would have given a full and candid explanation of what he knew about Rodriguez's activities.[92]

Abrams did not inform HPSCI of Rodriguez's role at Ilopango.[93] Two days after his HPSCI appearance on October 16, 1986, Abrams discussed Rodriguez with Shultz while they were flying to El Salvador. Hill's notes of Abrams' statement to Shultz read as follows:

> Felix Rodrigues [sic]—Bush did know him from CIA days. FR [Rodriguez] is ex-CIA. In El Salv[ador] he goes around to bars saying he is buddy of Bush. A y[ea]r ago Pdx [Poindexter] & Ollie [North] told VP staff stop protecting FR as a friend—we want to get rid of him from his involvnt [sic] w[ith] private ops. Nothing was done so he still is there shooting his mouth off.[94]

## The Brunei Solicitation

Following a May 16, 1986, National Security Planning Group meeting, in which the need for further assistance to the contras was discussed, Abrams raised with Shultz the issue of soliciting third countries for funding. Shultz instructed Abrams that he did not want a country solicited that was a large recipient of U.S. aid, fearing that a contra donation would look like a kickback from U.S. foreign aid. Additionally, Shultz did not want any right-wing dictatorships, such as Taiwan and South Korea, to be solicited because it would create an unfortunate link between those dictatorships and the contras.[95]

Abrams suggested to Shultz that the Sultan of Brunei, an oil-rich Southeast Asian country, be approached during Shultz's upcoming visit to Brunei in late June 1986. Abrams discussed with North where money should be sent in the event a solicitation was successful. North told

Abrams to "do nothing, to send no papers and to talk to no one further about this until he [North] talks to [Poindexter]."[96] North informed Poindexter that he had "the accounts and the means by which this thing [transfer of solicited funds] needs to be accomplished."[97]

On June 11, 1986, Abrams had lunch with Poindexter and they discussed Brunei as a possible donor for the contras.[98] They discussed possible methods of transferring the funds.

In June 1986, Abrams obtained bank account information from North on a card typed by his secretary, Fawn Hall. Two account numbers were transposed, ultimately resulting in the transfer of the funds into the wrong account. During his trip to Asia on June 23 and 24, 1986, Shultz took with him this index card but on the advice of U.S. Ambassador Barrington King, Shultz did not ask the Sultan of Brunei for assistance to the contras.

During July 1986, Abrams discussed the solicitation of a foreign country with Fiers. He asked Fiers for an off-shore bank account number for the transfer of funds. Abrams and Hill discussed which account to use for the Brunei solicitation and settled on the account provided by North. North told Abrams that the use of the account North provided would permit more control by the U.S. Government.[99]

A meeting was arranged for Abrams with General Ibnu, the Bruneian defense minister, in London on August 9, 1986, to discuss a $10 million contribution to the contras. Ibnu was informed that the U.S. emissary would call him using the name "Kenilworth."[100] Abrams, using this name, called Ibnu and met with him in London on August 9th, solicited funds for the contras and gave Ibnu the account information provided by North. On August 19, 1986, the Sultan of Brunei ordered the transfer of $10 million from his Citibank account via Citibank Zurich branch to Credit Suisse, Eaux Vives Branch, Geneva, account 368430–22–1, attention: Jacob Steger. On September 15, 1986, Ambassador King cabled State Department with the message: "This is to confirm that General

91 Corr, Grand Jury, 6/14/91, pp. 82–83.
92 Ibid., p. 25.
93 Abrams was accompanied by Walker during his appearance before the Senate Foreign Affairs Committee and HPSCI. Walker had attended the August 12, 1986, meeting in Gregg's office where Rodriguez's role in the private resupply effort at Ilopango was extensively discussed. He did not attempt to correct the testimony of any of the witnesses.
94 Hill Note, 10/16/86, ANS 001661.
95 Abrams, House Foreign Affairs Committee Testimony, 12/17/86, pp. 5–6.
96 PROFs Note from North to Poindexter, 6/10/86, AKW 021427.
97 Ibid.
98 Abrams, Grand Jury, 2/26/88, pp. 26–28.
99 Hill Note, 8/6/86, ANS 0001587.
100 State 244548 re: Brunei Project, 8/5/86, ALV 000394.

Ibnu assures me arrangements have been consummated.'' [101] The same date, September 15, 1986, North's notebook entry reads:

> Gaston Amb says
>
> Elliott talked w/
> —$ was deposited
> —1 wk ago.
> —Mtg w/Sultan tomorrow [102]

On September 16, 1986, Washington cabled King stating that ''[t]hose on the receiving end here cannot confirm consummation of arrangements. But they tell us that this is not unusual in view of the process involved. If you are asked on this point, we suggest that simply say that the material is apparently still in the pipe-line.'' [103]

On September 19th, Washington cabled King and requested that Brunei have the bank trace the funds.[104] Four days later, King replied that Ibnu was surprised at the non-receipt because he understood the procedures and the recipient bank. Ibnu indicated that he would run tracers on the funds.[105] On September 26, 1986, Ibnu informed King that the Sultan of Brunei had personally handled the transfer and that the recipient was quite clear. The Sultan of Brunei added that ''because of the procedures that had been used we might have to wait for a short while more before the transaction is completed.'' [106]

Congress was concerned as to the extent of the U.S. Government knowledge about foreign government assistance to the contras. At the time of Abrams' testimony in October 1986, he had personally solicited $10 million from Brunei for the contras. Although the $10 million had not arrived in the Swiss bank account recommended by North because of Hall's typing error, the State Department had been assured that the money was sent and that the transaction had been handled personally by the Sultan of Brunei.

On October 10, 1986, a *Washington Post* article stated that Saudi Arabia might be funding the contra resupply through Secord. During Abrams's appearance before the Senate Foreign Relations Committee on October 10, Senator Kerry inquired whether Abrams or the CIA representatives with him (including Clair George and Fiers) were aware of Saudi Arabia or any other foreign government supplying weapons or providing assistance to the contras.

SENATOR KERRY: Are you aware, any of you, of any deal by which, as part of the AWACS transaction or subsequent to the AWACS transaction, Saudi Arabia is supplying weapons or assistance to the Contras on our behalf?

MR. ABRAMS: No.

MR. GEORGE: No.

MR. FIERS: No, sir.

MR. ABRAMS: I think I can say that while I have been Assistant Secretary, which is about 15 months, we have not received a dime from a foreign government, not a dime, from any foreign government.

SENATOR KERRY: ''We'' being who?

MR. ABRAMS: The United States.

SENATOR KERRY: How about the Contras?

MR. ABRAMS: *I don't know. But not that I am aware of and not through us.*

The thing is I think I would know about it because if they went to a foreign government, a foreign government would want credit for helping the contras and they would come to us to say you want us to do this, do you, and I would know about that.

SENATOR EVANS: Elliott, when you said ''not a dime,'' I did not hear the rest of what you said.

MR. ABRAMS: From any foreign government to the Contras. It would not be to us, it would be to the Contras.

101 Bandar 01158 re: Brunei Project, 9/15/86, ALV 000383–84.
102 North Notebook, 9/15/86, AMX 001471 (emphasis in original).
103 State 289965 re: Brunei Project, 9/16/86, ALV 000382.
104 State 296219 re: Brunei Project, 9/19/86, ALV 000379.
105 Bandar 01195 re: Brunei Project, 9/23/86, ALV 000378.
106 Bandar 01212 re: Brunei Project, 9/26/86, ALV 000376–77.

I suspect that we would know about it, though.[107]

Four days later, on October 14th, the issue of foreign government assistance to the contras arose again during Abrams' appearance before HPSCI:

THE CHAIRMAN: Do you know if any foreign government is helping to supply the contras? There is a report in the LA paper, for example, that the Saudis are.

MR. GEORGE: No, sir, we have no intelligence of that.

MR. ABRAMS: I can only speak on that question for the last fifteen months when I have been in this job, and that story about the Saudis to my knowledge is false. I personally cannot tell you about pre-1985, but in 1985–1986, when I have been around, no.

THE CHAIRMAN: Is it also false with respect to other governments as well?

MR. ABRAMS: *Yes, it is also false.*[108]

Following public disclosure of the Iran/contra diversion on November 25, 1986, Abrams appeared along with Fiers before SSCI for a briefing on Nicaragua. Abrams was questioned about his knowledge of the mechanics of how money was diverted from arms sales to the contras. He replied as follows:

MR. ABRAMS: Well, we—after the Hasenfus shootdown we were asked about, you know, what did you know about the funding of Hasenfus and his operation. And the answer here is the same answer. That is, that we knew there were private contributions coming in, because they sure weren't surviving on the money that we were giving them, which at one time was nothing and then the 27 million came along. So there was money coming in. *But there was no reason to think it was coming from foreign governments,* and I certainly

did not inquire as to which individuals it was coming from.[109]

The questioning persisted on the issue of fundraising:

SENATOR BRADLEY: So let me ask it again. Did either one of you ever discuss the problems of fundraising by the contras with members of the NSC staff?

MR. ABRAMS: *No, I can't remember.*

SENATOR BRADLEY: Well, you would say gee, they got a lot of problems, they don't have any money. Then you would just sit there and say, what are we going to do? They don't have any money. You never said, you know, maybe we could get the money this way?

MR. ABRAMS: *No.* Other than the conversation I have—other than the Middle Eastern thing which I recounted to you. We're not—you know, *we're not in the fundraising business.*[110]

Later, Abrams assured the Committee, that until the Meese press conference, he was "fairly confident that there was no foreign government contributing [to the contras]." [111]

Later, on December 8, 1986, after consultation with senior State Department officials, Abrams corrected his testimony. However, he did not alter his October statements regarding third-country contra funding to the Senate Foreign Relations Committee. These statements were the basis for Count Two of the information to which he pleaded guilty.

Later, when confronted about his failure to tell Congress about the Brunei solicitation during his October testimony, Abrams claimed that he was acting under instructions not to divulge the Brunei solicitation at all. To the contrary, during his testimony on October 10, 1986, before the Senate Committee on Foreign Relations, Abrams informed the Committee: "I can only tell you that my injunction from the Secretary of State is never to lie." [112]

---

[107] Abrams, Senate Foreign Relations Committee Testimony, 10/10/86, pp. 75–76. (Emphasis added.)
[108] Abrams, HPSCI Testimony, 10/14/86, p. 21. (Emphasis added.)
[109] Abrams, SSCI Testimony, 11/25/86, pp. 8–9. (Emphasis added.)
[110] Ibid., pp. 14–15. (Emphasis added.)
[111] Ibid., p. 18.
[112] Abrams, Senate Foreign Relations Committee Testimony, 10/10/86, p. 49.

## Abrams Pleads Guilty

Independent Counsel's investigation focused on the veracity of Abrams' October 1986 statements to Congress concerning his knowledge of U.S. Government involvement in the contra-resupply operation, his knowledge of the role of Felix Rodriguez in contra resupply and his failure to inform Congress of the Brunei solicitation when he was asked about foreign government assistance to the contras.

The facts concerning the Brunei solicitation had been publicly exposed during the congressional hearings in the summer of 1987. The extent of Abrams' knowledge of North and Rodriguez's role in contra resupply was greatly amplified as the OIC investigation progressed. North had publicly testified in the summer of 1987 that Abrams was aware of his "full service operation" to the contras and that he discussed many of his contra-related activities within the RIG, but it was not until 1990 and 1991 that independent evidence was produced that corroborated North's assertions. In 1990 and early 1991 North was compelled to testify in greater detail about his communications with Abrams and to explain contemporaneously made notebook entries that related to Abrams. In 1990 and 1991, notes of Hill, Platt, Walker and Corr, were produced for the first time. These notes recorded conversations within the State Department regarding Abrams' knowledge of North's activities.

The "Croker note," produced by the Defense Department in 1991, corroborated North's assertion that in 1986 he had listed within the RIG, item-by-item, the activities that he was causing to happen on behalf of the contras through the private network. The 1991 production of Corr's previously withheld notes supplied details of telephone conversations between Corr and Abrams about the Hasenfus shootdown and conversations about Rodriguez's role in Salvador.

Fiers, after his plea in July 1991, supplied additional facts about the extent of Abrams' knowledge of North's involvement in the resupply effort and Abrams' knowledge about the Embassy involvement in the Costa Rican airstrip.

Independent Counsel was prepared to present a multi-count felony indictment against Abrams to the Grand Jury for its consideration in early October 1991. Abrams, through his counsel, was invited to consider a plea of guilty. Before an indictment was presented, Abrams entered into a plea agreement on October 7, 1991, and pleaded guilty to two counts of withholding information from Congress. He pleaded guilty to unlawfully withholding material information concerning North's contact with and encouragement of the people supplying the contras from the Senate Foreign Relations Committee on October 10, 1986. Additionally, he pleaded guilty to unlawfully withholding material information from HPSCI on October 14, 1986, concerning his participation in the Brunei solicitation and his expectation, as of October 14, that the $10 million from the Sultan of Brunei was on its way to the Swiss bank account he had provided.

# Chapter 26
# Edwin G. Corr

Independent Counsel began his investigation of former U.S. Ambassador to El Salvador Edwin G. Corr in the fall of 1990, based on new information obtained from U.S. Army Col. James J. Steele that raised questions about the truthfulness of some of Corr's prior testimony. Corr gave voluntary interviews to Independent Counsel in January 1991 before ending his cooperation and invoking his Fifth Amendment privilege against self-incrimination. Independent Counsel subsequently obtained a judicial order compelling Corr's testimony in April 1991 and forcing him to produce documents, under grants of immunity. The Grand Jury's subpoena resulted in production in May 1991 of hundreds of pages of relevant documents previously withheld from Independent Counsel.[1] The grant of

immunity did not, however, lead Corr to change his prior false testimony.

Because of Corr's continuing and unbelievable assertions in the Grand Jury, after his final Grand Jury appearance in June 1991, Independent Counsel focused more intensely on Corr's false statements in the Grand Jury about an April 20, 1986, meeting that he had with retired Air Force Maj. Gen. Richard V. Secord and Lt. Col. Oliver L. North of the National Security Council staff at the U.S. Embassy in San Salvador. Independent Counsel's investigation of Corr concluded in January 1992 with a decision not to indict.

This chapter discusses the evidence collected during Independent Counsel's investigation of Corr, his false statements in the Grand Jury, and Independent Counsel's reasons for not prosecuting the ambassador.

## Corr and the Private Contra Resupply Effort

Edwin G. Corr joined the U.S. foreign service in 1961. His long career included ambassadorships in Peru and Bolivia, before becoming U.S. ambassador to El Salvador in August 1985. Corr's arrival in El Salvador coincided with a significant change in the nature of covert U.S. Government support to the Nicaraguan contra rebels. That summer, North had asked Secord to set up a private airlift operation that would carry privately purchased materials, including arms, to the contras. Through the fall of 1985, Secord endeavored to set up this operation, choosing the Ilopango air base just outside of San Salvador to be the locus of his operation's transshipment and local warehousing efforts. Secord and North also worked to establish fa-

---

[1] An April 1987 request from Independent Counsel to the State Department called for Corr to produce "[a]ll correspondence, memoranda, working papers, telexes, telegrams, cables, telecopies, messages and other documents," however made, which were prepared by, received by, routed through or maintained by Corr on "the provision or coordination of support for persons or entities engaged as military insurgents in armed conflict with the Government of Nicaragua since 1984." Independent Counsel also requested all of Corr's "individual appointment calendars and schedules, card files, diaries, telephone logs, records or evidence of incoming and outgoing telephone calls, indices of correspondence, itineraries and activity reports. . . ." (Letter from Stewart to Kozak, 4/24/87; Letter from Stewart to Kozak, 4/23/87, specifically including handwritten materials in its definition of "documents"). Corr told Independent Counsel in 1991 that he and his secretary were responsible for reviewing his documents for materials demanded by the State Department on behalf of Iran/contra investigators. (Corr, FBI 302, 1/9/91, pp. 1–2.)

When compelled to produce materials in April 1991, Corr delivered 175 pages of new documents to the Grand Jury. Corr first explained that these materials, plus others previously produced to the Select Committees, constituted his relevant Iran/contra documents for July 1985 through July 1987, but he later admitted that he had omitted items demanded by the Grand Jury. (Corr, Grand Jury, 4/26/91, pp. 8–18; ALW 32449–623.) Two weeks later, after Independent Counsel had consulted with Corr's attorney, Corr produced an additional 1,480 pages of new notes and documents to the Grand Jury. (ALW 32671–34196.) Independent Counsel's review of these materials required Corr to appear three more times before the Grand Jury in late May and mid-June 1991.

cilities that would assist in the resupply of contra forces on a resurgent "southern front" on the Costa Rican border with Nicaragua.

Early in his new post, Corr became aware of allegations that North was tied to contra operations. Corr noted in a meeting with four State Department officials prior to leaving for San Salvador that North "is the NSC man for Central America. Allegedly 'man who has run the "contras." ' " [2] North's tie to the contras was reinforced in Corr's mind by events that occurred around the time of a September 1985 State Department chiefs of mission conference held in Panama—a conference that both North and Corr attended. Before going to the conference, Corr's deputy chief of mission (DCM), David Passage, wrote Corr that he had to alert Elliott Abrams, the assistant secretary of state for inter-American affairs, to three recent approaches by contra officials to Embassy officers and to Col. Steele, the commander of the U.S. Military Group in El Salvador. Passage requested guidance on these contacts, so the Embassy could maintain "squeaky-clean" operations. [3]

After receiving Passage's memorandum, Corr made a list of items that he intended to discuss in Panama with Abrams and his deputy, William Walker. The third item on Corr's list spoke directly of Passage's concerns. The fourth and fifth items, checked off by Corr and bracketed with Passage's item, also addressed the contras:

(3) Contras—3 contacts; FDN [contra] talk w/ Steele (NO)

(4) Rodriguez.

(5) Ollie North conversation—S.[Southern] Front [4]

On September 20, 1985, North had requested Felix Rodriguez, a U.S. citizen who was assisting the Salvadoran government's counter-insurgency efforts, to intercede with Salvadoran Air Force General Juan Bustillo to allow Enterprise planes to be based at Ilopango air base in El Salvador, as part of an operation to resupply contra forces. [5] Rodriguez worked in the coming months with Steele and Rafael Quintero, an associate of Secord's, to ensure that North-Secord contra-resupply operations did not run afoul of the Salvadoran military at Ilopango. [6]

Smooth relations at Ilopango became critical in late 1985. In October 1985, the Honduran government decided to limit sharply official and unofficial U.S. efforts from that country to provide supplies by air to the contras. After two months of negotiations, the Hondurans agreed to admit planes carrying U.S. Government-provided non-lethal supplies into the country, on the condition that the planes enter from El Salvador. In late December 1985, Corr met a delegation from Washington that included North, Walker, and the chief of the CIA's Central American Task Force, Alan D. Fiers, Jr., that had flown to Central America to complete work on the new non-lethal contra-supply arrangements, being administered through the State Department's Nicaraguan Humanitarian Assistance Office (NHAO). Corr learned that Bustillo gave his approval for U.S. Government-sponsored transshipment operations at Ilopango, allowing large planes to unload their cargo there for transfer onto smaller aircraft making supply drops to the contras. [7] The NHAO humanitarian-resupply operations at Ilopango gave a major boost to North's own private lethal-resupply efforts in Central America. [8]

The combination of official and unofficial contra aid efforts at Ilopango became too great a strain on base resources and the tolerance of Salvadoran officials. By January 23, 1986, Corr had learned that Bustillo had become alarmed about the visibility of the expanded operations at Ilopango. [9] During a swing through Washington in early February 1986, Corr attempted to get North and Fiers and his superiors

---

[2] Corr Notes, 8/19/85, ALW 0033531 (emphasis in original).

[3] Memorandum from DP to AMB, 9/7/85, ALV 001407 (bearing Corr's handwritten notes); Passage, FBI 302, 3/7/91, pp. 3–4.

[4] Corr Notes, ALW 0033600. Corr testified under immunity that he normally checked off items either when he had done them or when he had gone over them with someone else. (Corr, Grand Jury, 5/29/91, pp. 52–53; Corr, Grand Jury, 6/12/91, p. 149.)

[5] Letter from North to Rodriguez, 9/20/85, AKW 22740–41. Corr had heard of Rodriguez as early as July 1985 from Corr's predecessor in San Salvador, Thomas G. Pickering. Corr was also aware of Rodriguez's work with the Salvadoran military. (Corr, Select Committees Deposition, 4/30/87, pp. 4–6.)

[6] See Underlying Facts, Gregg and Fiers chapters; Secord, Grand Jury, 1/16/91, pp. 38–39.

[7] Corr Notes, 2/9/86, ALV 001399–401 (describing December 1985 meeting); Corr, FBI 302, 1/10/91, p. 5 (adopting notes as accurate record of December meeting).

[8] For a fuller description of the mingling of official and unofficial contra aid operations at Ilopango, see Fiers chapter.

[9] Corr Notes, 1/23/86, ALV 001396 (note of telephone conversation with Walker).

at the State Department to agree to reduce CIA contact with the contra-resupply efforts. Corr wanted to, in his words, "in effect become 'desk officer'" on the "contra question," [10] referring to NHAO activity. Corr returned to San Salvador only to learn that Rodriguez was interfering in humanitarian-aid efforts, with North's help. Rodriguez's actions prompted Deputy Assistant Secretary of State Walker to phone Corr and tell him that "Ollie and Max [Rodriguez's alias] are to have nothing to do [with] humanitarian assistance deliveries . . ." [11] Walker also instructed Corr to meet with Fiers in El Salvador and "impress on Fiers that we cannot proceed in this []fouled-up manner." [12] Corr did as he was told, reminding Fiers in a meeting at Corr's residence that Corr was to be "the coordinator & director of everything on this matter" until Washington determined otherwise. [13]

North and Secord's covert-action business, known as the Enterprise, was having difficulties of its own at Ilopango. Deliveries were behind schedule and over budget. Corr was apprised of some of these problems through Steele. On April 10, 1986, Quintero reported to Secord that "Col. Steele briefed U.S. Ambassador on all ongoing operations. Ambassador is on [sic] total support of our position regarding L–100, 707 and Lopez FDN [contra] attitude." [14] Nevertheless, by early April 1986, Secord had concluded that a "summit meeting" of the principals at Ilopango—including the Salvadoran military, the contras, and the Enterprise's operatives—was needed to speed up deliveries and achieve Enterprise resupply objectives. [15]

## The April 20, 1986, Meetings

On April 20, 1986, North and Secord flew with Enterprise air operations chief Richard Gadd and others by private jet from Washington, D.C., to Ilopango air base. After important meetings in Salvador—including one with Corr in his office—the passengers flew back to Washington, their mission complete. [16]

Evidence of these meetings came from a number of sources, many of which were not supplied when the Department of State first directed Corr to provide information to Iran/contra investigators in late 1986. Corr insisted that when he met with Secord in April 1986, North was not present and contra issues were not discussed. Only when key witnesses—including North, Secord and Steele—testified did the real story emerge. Backed by circumstantial eyewitness accounts and contemporaneous documents—some of which were withheld by Corr himself—these witnesses told a different tale about Corr's April 20, 1986, meeting with the principals of the Enterprise in Central America.

### Secord

Secord spoke frankly about his April 1986 trip to El Salvador. He revealed his meeting there with Corr in his earliest testimony. [17] Before Congress in 1987, Secord stated that Corr was one of the U.S. Government officials from whom he had received "moral support, certainly" on the contra-resupply project. [18] When asked to specify this support, Secord testified:

> I can't say that we had anything other than moral support from him. I did speak with him personally during my brief trip to El Salvador in April of '86. I know that he was sympathetic with our operation, and I know that he kept track of it. [19]

10 Corr Notes, 2/5/86, ALW 0033716. While he could not recall meeting with Corr on this trip, Fiers did recall that Corr wanted to coordinate resupply activities at Ilopango and keep both Steele and CIA officers in the area under his control. (Fiers, FBI 302 morning session, 7/18/91, p. 10.)

11 Corr Notes, 2/8/86, ALV 001398 (notes of telephone conversation with Walker).

12 Corr Notes, 2/8/86, ALV 001397; Corr, FBI 302, 1/10/91, p. 7 (recalling incident).

13 Corr Notes, 2/9/86, ALV 001399; Fiers, FBI 302 morning session, 7/18/91, pp. 12–13 (recalling meeting). For additional background on Fiers' visit to El Salvador, see Fiers chapter.

14 KL–43 Message from Quintero to Secord, 4/10/86; Steele, Grand Jury, 2/6/91, pp. 59–60, 77 (Steele kept Corr informed of important contra details); Ibid., pp. 92–94 (Corr briefed on L–100 flight in April 1986).

15 Secord, Grand Jury, 1/16/91, pp. 90–91, 93–95; KL–43 Message from Secord to North, 4/8/86, AKW 004417.

16 On the way back, the Jetstar made an intermediate stop in Miami, where it dropped off some passengers, refueled and cleared United States Customs. (Private Aircraft Inspection Report, 4/23/86, AOT 0000004, Customs form filled out by Jetstar crew, including passenger manifest).

17 See, for example, Secord, OIC Deposition, 4/29/87, p. 65; see also Secord, OIC Deposition, 5/14/87, pp. 371–72 (recounting contra air commander Juan Gomez's criticisms of private benefactor Caribou aircraft at the Ilopango meeting that preceded Secord's meeting with Corr).

18 Secord, Select Committees Testimony, 5/5/87, p. 191.

19 Secord, Select Committees Testimony, 5/6/87, p. 147. The next day's Washington Post, after quoting this testimony, reported that "[a] senior embassy official in El Salvador said yesterday that Corr has

Secord did not, however, mention North's presence on this trip or in Secord's meeting with Corr. Indeed, at one point Secord gave the impression that no Government officials accompanied him to El Salvador:

> Mr. Sarbanes: The help you were getting from the CIA people in Central America or the ambassadors in Central America, do you explain that simply that you came along as a private person doing, wanting to do this project and they were ready to help you, or they perceived that you were carrying out a policy supported by the Administration?
>
> Mr. Secord: The answer is both. We were in touch with them and they perceived that they were carrying out the policy of this Administration.
>
> Mr. Sarbanes: Which is what you perceived?
>
> Mr. Secord: Indeed.[20]

A more complete account of Secord's trip to El Salvador emerged in his appearance before the Grand Jury in January 1991. According to Secord, after he and North arrived at Ilopango, they met on the base with Salvadoran Air Force General Bustillo; two contra commanders, Enrique Bermudez and Juan Gomez; Steele; Quintero; and Rodriguez.[21] The topic of this meeting was improving private contra-resupply operations in El Salvador—or, in Secord's words, a summit meeting, "operationally speaking."[22] After lunch, Secord, North and Steele

were flown in a helicopter piloted (poorly) by Rodriguez to a landing zone near the U.S. Embassy in San Salvador.[23] While Rodriguez remained with the helicopter, Secord, North and Steele then had a meeting, which had been scheduled in advance, with Corr in his Embassy office. Secord recalled that Corr had to come in especially for the meeting, which suggested to Secord that the day was a Sunday. Secord testified that Corr "was very interested in how it went with Bustillo because Bustillo was truly vital to our operations as well as the operations in El Salvador."[24] According to Secord, Steele gave a "resumé of the [Bustillo] meeting, and I spoke giving my view of the meeting. North spoke . . . more than any of us."[25] Corr "was very interested, asked detailed questions, was very supportive."[26]

After Corr's first compelled Grand Jury appearance, where he adhered to his prior testimony that his meeting with Secord did not involve North or contra-resupply, Independent Counsel reinterviewed Secord. Secord repeated his sworn testimony without equivocation. He also added new detail about the day in El Salvador:

> —Bustillo provided the helicopter for the flight from Ilopango into San Salvador, and thus knew they were going to meet with Corr;
>
> —the helicopter had no doors, which made it too noisy to talk during the flight into San Salvador;

---

previously stated that 'he would not be doing his job if he did not know about' the operation, but the official added that Corr did not play any active role." ("Contra Corruption Said to Worry North," *The Washington Post,* 5/7/87, p. A30.) Corr told Independent Counsel that he "didn't watch" Secord's testimony about his meeting with Corr. (Corr, FBI 302, 1/9/91, p. 6.)

[20] Secord, Select Committees Testimony, 5/8/87, p. 82. Secord gave his brief account of his trip at a time when it was uncertain whether North would receive immunity and testify before Congress.

[21] Gadd left the group to meet with Enterprise pilots and was not present in any of the meetings that followed involving North and Secord. (Gadd, FBI 302, 7/6–7/87, pp. 19–21; Rodriguez, Grand Jury, 5/10/91, pp. 14–15; Posada, FBI 302, 2/3/92, p. 10.)

[22] Secord and Wurts, *Honored and Betrayed,* p. 273 (John Wiley & Sons, Inc. 1992) (hereafter, "*Honored*"). See also Bustillo, Grand Jury, 5/15/91, pp. 16–18, 34–36, 77–83 (confirming meeting and all attendees except Quintero; topics included problems with maintenance of contra-owned planes and provision of end-user certificates for Chilean Blowpipe missiles; Bustillo authorized Rodriguez to fly the party by a Salvadoran helicopter to downtown San Salvador); Rodriguez, Grand Jury, 5/10/91, pp. 13–15, 20–34 (Rodriguez arranged for Bermudez and Gomez to join

Bustillo at the meeting; Rodriguez and Quintero met the Jetstar when it arrived; topics included Blowpipes, unhappiness with contras' airplanes, and training of contra pilots).

[23] Secord, Grand Jury, 1/16/91, pp. 95–98; Secord and Wurts, *Honored,* p. 273. See also Quintero, FBI 302, 4/9/91, p. 12 (Rodriguez piloted North, Secord, and Steele to San Salvador for a meeting with Corr; Rodriguez reported on meeting in scant detail to Quintero afterwards); Rodriguez, Grand Jury, 5/10/91, pp. 34–38 (same).

[24] Secord, Grand Jury, 1/16/91, pp. 102–04; Secord and Wurts, *Honored,* p. 273. The significance of the Bustillo meeting may have been reinforced further in Corr's mind a few days later, when Rodriguez announced to him that he was leaving El Salvador for good. Rodriguez believed he may have told Corr at that time that the participation in contra-resupply operations of Secord and others whom Rodriguez associated with convicted arms trafficker Edwin Wilson gave Rodriguez "a sixth feeling, . . . a hunch" that he should abandon the operation. (Rodriguez, Grand Jury, 5/10/91, pp. 42–55.)

[25] Secord, Grand Jury, 1/16/91, p. 104.

[26] Ibid., p. 108. See also Secord, Grand Jury, 1/25/91, p. 81 ("Corr knew who to expect when I met him. He knew who I was.").

—the helicopter was met by an Embassy car, which Steele had arranged, that took North, Secord and Steele to the Embassy;

—the car was driven by an American, and during the ride Steele used a walkie-talkie to tell the Embassy that they were coming;

—during the meeting in Corr's office (which Secord diagrammed), Corr wore slacks and a short-sleeved shirt;

—Corr, North, Secord and Steele were present for the entire meeting;

—Secord spoke less than the others, and Corr did the most talking; "it was his meeting;" [27] and,

—during the meeting, they reviewed the situation in Nicaragua and the importance of the airlift operation; they also talked of the just-concluded Ilopango meeting concerning ways to improve the operation, Secord's plan to put more money into the operation, the need for weather reports and Sandinista order-of-battle information, the military needs of the southern front, the need for the FDN contra faction to share supplies with the southern front, and the Costa Rican airstrip.[28]

## North

Although North did not testify about any aspect of his April 1986 trip to El Salvador until he was compelled to appear before the Grand Jury in 1990, his notes suggested that he met with Corr on or about April 20, 1986. North's notebook contains no entries for the weekend of April 19–20, 1986, but he wrote this on April 21:

Mtg w/ Ed C

—Debt Relief.[29]

North initially called this "a very thrifty note" that "[c]ould well have been" taken the day after a late night trip.[30] North stated that the "Ed C" in the note "[c]ould be [Corr], I guess. Debt relief is certainly an issue that

the Salvadorans were very concerned about. . . . I just don't remember the conversation." [31] Although never confronted with North's note, Corr testified under immunity that debt relief for the Salvadoran government was one of the major issues he dealt with as ambassador,[32] and Corr's notes from this period—including a list of topics he made for an April 21, 1986, "Core Country Team Meeting"—refer to debt relief immediately after mentioning his role as "action officer" on contra issues.[33]

North's testimony about the meeting with Corr was evasive and imprecise. Although he remembered traveling on the private jet, North claimed to have great difficulty differentiating that trip from other trips to Central America. Regarding the meeting with Corr, he testified initially as follows:

I think that I may have had a meeting on this trip or it may be another one that I'm confused with with Colonel Steele, and perhaps even the ambassador although I just can't associate which trip was which.

\*          \*          \*

If I'm remembering the right trip and the right set of meetings associated with the trip, this dealt with aid to the southern front and the military operations along the southern part of Nicaragua, I think.

\*          \*          \*

Somehow I recall—whether it was this trip or another one—General Secord and I going to the embassy itself for a brief meeting with the ambassador, just saying hi. I don't recall whether it was this trip or not.

\*          \*          \*

I have this recollection of walking through the embassy because it was a very secure compound that had been attacked a number of times by the guerillas and just commenting—I think it was General Secord—it

27 As mentioned previously, Secord had testified that North was the principal speaker.

28 Secord, FBI 302, 5/9/91, pp. 3–7.

29 North Notes, 4/21/86, AMX 001074.

30 North, Grand Jury, 7/11/90, p. 102.

31 Ibid. North later testified, however, that he "would be inclined to think that's not the same Ed Corr . . . I would be inclined to think that since this [note] is the 21st, that's not it." (Ibid., 1/30/91, p. 20.)

32 Corr, Grand Jury, 5/29/91, p. 125.

33 See Corr Notes, 4/21/86, ALW 0032813, and text below.

might have been Colonel Gadd—about that kind of thing.[34]

In his next appearance, North testified that he had:

> a general recollection of bringing General Secord to the embassy, although not a specific meeting with Ambassador Corr that day other than to introduce General Secord. I remember generally doing that.

> I don't recall with anybody saying this is Dick Secord and here's all the things we're doing together . . . other than to say that these are people that have the sanction of what I thought was the President of the United States to do these kinds of activities.

> I don't recall a meeting with Ambassador Corr, or even Jim Steele, to say here's the long list of things that General Secord and I are doing together.

> *         *         *

> Q: Tell me how it [the President's approval] came up, what context it was that you communicated it to someone like Ambassador Corr.

> A: It would come up in the context of, "This is Dick Secord. He's supporting the Nicaraguan resistance operation. He's not one of these other groups that we're now familiar with that were operating in and out of the Central American region. He has our endorsement," our meaning the U.S. government endorsement, "for what he's doing. There are going to be airplanes flying in and out of here supporting the resistance." [35]

North gave this testimony when his criminal case was still pending in the court of appeals. In his Grand Jury appearances after his criminal convictions had been vacated, North testified that he had no specific recollection of meeting with Corr in the Embassy.[36]

## Steele

In Steele's earliest testimony, which contained numerous false and misleading statements concerning his own activities,[37] he revealed the Corr-Secord meeting:

> I met Secord one time in Salvador. . . . It was early '86 is the best I can say. I am not sure what month it was.

> *         *         *

> He didn't discuss the purpose of his trip with me. I know that he came in and he was on—he was there, it appeared, just for a very short period of time. I know he made a courtesy call on the ambassador and he left.

> *         *         *

> I am not aware of anybody [else with whom Secord met]. But again, I wasn't with him the whole time he was there. . . .

> The only thing that I can remember saying to Secord when he was there was it was a pretty snazzy airplane that he landed in, an executive aircraft.

> *         *         *

> But I know he went into the city and then he had a meeting—I am told he had a meeting there with the ambassador.[38]

Steele did not mention, however: North's presence; the meeting with Bustillo, Bermudez and others at Ilopango immediately preceding the Corr meeting; the helicopter ride into San Salvador; or his own involvement in setting up and attending Corr's meeting with Secord.

In his April 1987 Select Committees deposition, Steele suggested the possibility of North's presence during Corr's meeting with Secord, but he disclosed nothing about the substance of the meeting:

> [Secord] came through there on a quick trip. He was only on the ground, I would guess, for a very short time. And he met with the Ambassador, kind of a courtesy

34 North, Grand Jury, 7/11/90, pp. 88–96, 100–01.
35 Ibid., 7/13/90, pp. 14–15, 17.
36 Ibid., 1/30/91, p. 21; Ibid., 2/15/91, pp. 85–86.

37 See History of the Investigation section.
38 Steele, SSCI Testimony, 12/18/86, pp. 26–27.

call thing. I can't remember if North was with him or not. I think he was though. That's my recollection that North was with him and that he met with the Ambassador very short and he was gone.

*  *  *

No [I never learned that Secord was involved with the private resupply organization]. I had the sense that he was, but I never—I never pinned—he certainly didn't say he was, as I recall. And, you know, that was the only time that he came to El Salvador.[39]

The next day, in his first interview with Independent Counsel, Steele was more definite, at least about the meeting with Corr. Steele said that Secord came to El Salvador once in early 1986 with North, that the party flew in on a private jet, and that they met with Corr for about one hour before departing.[40]

Over time, and after many interviews with Independent Counsel, Steele's testimony coalesced on these points:

—North and Secord came into Ilopango on a private jet;

—Rodriguez told Steele that one of the things that Secord wanted to do in El Salvador was meet with Corr;

—contra leaders did come to Ilopango for a meeting, but Steele is not sure whether it was at the same time that North and Secord came there together, and Steele does not recall whether they were in the meeting with the contras;

—Rodriguez flew North, Secord and Steele by helicopter into San Salvador, and Secord criticized Rodriguez's flying abilities;

—Steele, Secord and North met with Corr in his Embassy office; and

—Steele could not recall anything about the substance of that meeting.[41]

## Corr

Apart from a few admissions made in the years following his initial false statements about his meeting with Secord, Corr made two relevant statements after the Iran/contra revelations of late 1986. The first showed Corr's early effort to deny; the second reflected Corr's concern. First, in December 1986, Sen. Christopher Dodd traveled to El Salvador and privately met with Corr at his residence. Dodd told Independent Counsel that in response to questions about contra-resupply activity at Ilopango, Corr basically denied knowing about it and answered "no" to all of Dodd's questions. Corr said he had met with North in El Salvador but said nothing about them working together. Dodd also did not recall Corr saying that he had met in the Embassy with Secord.[42]

In January 1987, Jon Wiant, then director of coordination in the Department of State's Bureau of Intelligence & Research, traveled to El Salvador as part of a "flying RIG." In two interviews, Wiant described to Independent Counsel a conversation with Corr in the Ambassador's residence. According to Wiant, Corr was "shaky, scared" and asked to speak privately to Wiant as a larger meeting was breaking up and the visitors were about to go to the airport. Wiant recalled the conversation specifically. He reported that Corr said:

> Am I in trouble? This stuff has ended up on my door step, they . . . Oliver North and someone else—have been down here to the Embassy and have done things at Ilopango, I've called and they said its okay—they meaning either Elliott Abrams or Bill Walker . . .[43]

[39] Steele, Select Committees Deposition, 4/21/87, pp. 109–10. See also Ibid., pp. 120–21 (misdirecting a question about a North-Secord-Corr meeting at Ilopango to a December 30, 1985, meeting at Ilopango that Secord did not attend).

[40] Steele, FBI 302, 4/22/87, p. 2.

[41] Steele, Grand Jury, 2/6/91, pp. 94–103.

[42] Dodd, FBI 302, 2/19/91, p. 2. See also Memorandum from FitzGerald to Abrams, undated, ALW 030446 (reporting Dodd's visit); San Salvador 15919, 12/20/86, ALW 030459–68 (same); Dlouhy, FBI 302, 5/23/91, p. 7 (recalling that Corr had a "heated meeting" with Dodd, after which Corr was very upset and said that Dodd had asked a lot of questions about contra resupply). Dodd believed, however, that he did not ask Corr directly about his meetings with persons involved in private resupply efforts. (Dodd, FBI 302, 2/19/91, p. 2.)

[43] Wiant, FBI 302, 12/9/91, pp. 6–7. See also Wiant, FBI 302, 9/19/91, pp. 6–7. In the September 1991 interview, the FBI agent's report states that Wiant "remembered being called aside by Corr and discussing a meeting that Corr had had with Richard Secord and Oliver North in April of 1986. Wiant said that Corr was upset because he

In response to the Grand Jury's subpoena, Corr produced one contemporaneous document that related to the April 20, 1986, meeting. Corr's handwritten list of items to discuss at a meeting of top Embassy officials on Monday, April 21, 1986, included this item, which Corr had checked off:

> [ck] (2) FDR—help w/in guidelines; monitor—Repeat my enjoinder that I am "action officer" on this! [44]

Corr's former deputy, David B. Dlouhy, identified the acronym "FDR" as referring to the Salvadoran Democratic Revolutionary Front, the civilian wing of the Salvadoran guerrillas,[45] "FDR" also was an acronym for the contras—one that Corr used often.[46]

## The Dlouhy Allegations

Independent Counsel obtained what appeared at first to be extremely damaging evidence against Corr in late 1991 from Corr's former deputy chief of mission (DCM) in El Salvador, Dlouhy. From 1985 to mid-1986, Dlouhy was deputy director of the Office of Central American Affairs within the State Department's Bureau of Inter-American Affairs. Dlouhy departed for El Salvador to become DCM in July 1986. During the course of his tour there, Dlouhy developed a close relationship with Corr, one that continued long after Dlouhy's assignment ended.[47]

Dlouhy's first interviews with Independent Counsel occurred in May 1991. In the first interview, which was conducted by phone because Dlouhy was overseas, Dlouhy said that he had taken a trip to El Salvador in March or April 1986 and had met with Corr and another Embassy officer. Dlouhy said that no one discussed the contras with him on this trip,

which concerned American-Salvadoran cooperation on police matters, but that at some point later he heard that Corr had met with North out at Ilopango when North had stopped briefly there. Dlouhy stated that Corr never told him that Corr had met Secord.[48] During a second telephone interview with OIC, Dlouhy reported that it became clear to him after early October 1986, from conversations with Corr or Steele, that North had come to Ilopango—but not San Salvador—and had visited Bustillo and Rodriguez but not Corr.[49]

During a second round of questioning of Dlouhy in the fall of 1991, subsequent to receiving Corr's notes, Dlouhy recalled a second trip he had made to El Salvador in April 1986. Dlouhy believed that he arrived in El Salvador some time during the week of April 14, 1986, and stayed through Sunday, April 20, 1986—the date of the Corr-Secord-North meeting. Dlouhy told Independent Counsel he recalled that:

> —Steele had said that Rodriguez had flown North and Secord to downtown San Salvador, almost hitting a flagpole with his helicopter and killing everyone aboard the aircraft. Dlouhy said that he thought Steele had told him this story shortly after the incident occurred, when Dlouhy was not yet deputy chief of the mission. Dlouhy may have learned of it while talking with Steele and Corr on the terrace of Corr's residence in San Salvador.

> —Dlouhy believed that the purpose of the trip was for the people in the helicopter to go to the Embassy and visit Corr, and that before the flagpole incident, the visitors had met at Ilopango with Bustillo and the contras.

> —Steele told Dlouhy that he, North, and Secord had met in Corr's office, but did not say what was discussed. Dlouhy assumed that the purpose of the meeting was a briefing on what had transpired at Ilopango that day.[50]

didn't like the fact that North and Secord as private benefactors, were coming into the Embassy." (Ibid., pp. 6–7.) After reading this report in December 1991, Wiant stated that the only thing he was not "positively sure about" was his statement regarding Secord being at the Embassy with North. (Wiant, FBI 302, 12/9/91, p. 7.)

[44] Corr Notes, 4/21/86, ALW 032813 (emphasis in original). Despite Corr's checking off this item, no witness recalled Corr discussing the issue in the April 21, 1986, team meeting.

[45] See, for example, Dlouhy, Grand Jury, 11/1/91, pp. 98, 102.

[46] Ibid., p. 99. See, for example, Corr Notes, 2/9/86, ALV 001399 ("3. We also discussed coordination among Front Office, . . . Steele, Felix & UNO/FDR"). Corr confirmed this under immunity. (Corr, Grand Jury, 5/29/91, p. 124.)

[47] Dlouhy, FBI 302, 5/23/91, p. 9. Dlouhy called Corr after his first telephone interview with the Independent Counsel. Dlouhy was posted to Luxembourg at the time.

[48] Dlouhy, FBI 302, 5/22/91, p. 6. See also Transcript of 5/22/91 Interview, pp. 8–9, 19–20.

[49] Dlouhy, FBI 302, 5/23/91, pp. 3–4; Transcript of 5/23/91 Interview, pp. 37–38.

[50] Dlouhy, FBI 302, 10/31/91, pp. 14–20.

Dlouhy repeated this story before the Grand Jury on November 1, 1991.[51]

Independent Counsel re-interviewed Steele on November 12, 1991, in an attempt to corroborate Dlouhy's story. Steele did not recall Dlouhy being present the weekend of April 19–20, 1986, or discussing any subject with Dlouhy at that time.[52] Almost two months later, Dlouhy provided Independent Counsel with a photocopy of his expired passport for the 1982–87 period. The passport indicated that Dlouhy arrived in San Salvador on April 16, 1986, and departed on April 20, 1986.[53] Independent Counsel also obtained Dlouhy's travel vouchers for the trip, which were ambiguous.[54] Nevertheless, Dlouhy declared in a letter to the Independent Counsel that he wished to "restrict[]" the record of his direct knowledge of events in San Salvador to the period April 16–19, 1986, stating that he may have learned about the events on April 20, 1986, from other sources, or may have confused the event with later ones.[55]

## Corr's False Testimony

Corr consistently took the position, first in response to inquiries from the Department of State and subsequently in sworn testimony, that his only contact with the party that traveled to El Salvador was a brief meeting of no substance with Secord, at which North was not present. On December 3, 1986, in conjunction with an official request from Attorney General Edwin Meese III, the Department of State directed various diplomatic posts, including San Salvador, to search for relevant "materials."[56] On December 13, 1986, San Salvador responded with an artfully worded cable.[57] In it Corr reported to the Department, and through it to the FBI, that

> LtCol. Oliver North . . . transited briefly San Salvador enroute to Honduras on December 30, 1985 with an [sic] NHAO official[58] in connection with humanitarian assistance to the Nicaraguan resistance, as well as brief stopovers on one or two other occasions. There was no activity by LtCol. North of which I or anyone else at this Post are aware of *in connection with financial aid activities related to* Iran or Israel or *the Nicaraguan resistance movement.* Retired General Richard V. Secord was in San Salvador at least once and made *a very brief courtesy call* on me on a Saturday [sic] morning *at which nothing of substance was discussed.* I do not have the dates of LtCol. North's other brief stopovers *nor of Secord's courtesy call* because my calendars were lost in the October 10, 1986 San Salvador earthquake.[59]

Corr's cabled response revealed that he had met Secord but explicitly denied that the meeting concerned anything of substance. Corr also suggested implicitly, by separating his mentions of Secord and North, that North was not present when Corr met with Secord. Finally, by limiting his statement on lack of awareness of North's contra activity to "financial aid activities," Corr's cable avoided revealing what he knew of North's involvement in the contra-resupply operation based in El Salvador.[60] At the time

---

[51] Dlouhy, Grand Jury, 11/1/91, pp. 43–96, 100. Dlouhy added a few details during this appearance. He testified that he arrived in El Salvador on April 16, 1986, (Ibid., pp. 43–44); he placed the terrace conversation after Corr had gone to church and had worked, (Ibid., p. 84); while certain that North met with Corr, he was less certain that Steele and Secord were present, (Ibid., p. 93–94); the party discussed with Corr a recent drop of lethal supplies by an Enterprise-leased L-100 aircraft, (Ibid., p. 94); and that the last incident he recalled from the trip was the terrace conversation, (Ibid., p. 100).

[52] Steele, FBI 302, 11/12/91, pp. 9–10.

[53] Dlouhy Passport, 3/15/82, ALW 048735.

[54] Dlouhy's description of his itinerary stated that he left San Salvador at 9:00 am on April 20, 1986. His travel authorization indicated, however, that Dlouhy planned to return on or about April 21, 1986, and Dlouhy attached an airline receipt indicating that Dlouhy was ticketed on a TACA Airlines flight that left at 9:00 am on April 21, 1986. (Travel Reimbursement Voucher, 4/11/86, ALW 47505-10.) Independent Counsel attempted to confirm Dlouhy's re-entry into the United States through the U.S. Customs Service, but was informed that customs declarations forms filed in the Miami District—Dlouhy's stated point of re-entry—had been destroyed. (Letter from Schmitz to SA Buckley, 1/15/92, 018022.)

[55] Letter from Dlouhy to Barrett, 1/6/92, 017949.

[56] State 374730, 12/12/86, ALV 004986–87.

[57] Corr would later testify that, while "every cable that leaves the embassy has the ambassador's name on it," he "probably wrote [this cable]" himself. (Corr, Grand Jury, 5/29/91, pp. 144–45.)

[58] This official was Cresencio Arcos, the deputy director of the State Department's Nicaraguan Humanitarian Assistance Office, NHAO.

[59] San Salvador 15584, 12/13/86, ALV 004119–20 (emphasis added). Corr's reference to the loss of his calendars was inexact. Corr himself produced appointment calendars kept by his secretary for him to the State Department in 1987.

[60] Almost five months after the December 1986 cable, when explaining his ignorance of the financial arrangements underlying contra-support activities in El Salvador, Corr volunteered that the questions in the "initial" exchange of cables had focused upon financing:

> [At] least from where I sat, things that came, or may have gone through Ilopango, it was something that had been consummated and transacted elsewhere. And at the Ilopango or at the Salvador end, you are really down to materiel . . . In Salvador it was materiel.

Corr wrote his cable, North and Secord had invoked the Fifth Amendment before congressional committees, and their refusals to testify had been widely reported by the media.

Corr's first recorded contact with Iran/contra investigators occurred on April 1, 1987, when he was interviewed by the FBI at Homestead Air Force Base in Florida.[61] The agents' report of this interview states that Corr said that North came to El Salvador two to four times, twice after Congress approved humanitarian aid to the contras in 1985, each time for a stop of one to four hours.[62] Corr did not mention Secord or any visit by him to El Salvador. Corr was not asked about documents.[63]

On April 30, 1987, Corr gave a sworn deposition to staff members of the Select Committees. In response to a series of questions about trips to El Salvador by North, by Secord, and by them together, Corr made a number of false statements:

Q: First of all, tell me if you can how many times to your recollection Oliver North actually travelled to El Salvador during the time you have been Ambassador to El Salvador, that you know of.

A: I told you last time, I don't know whether it was three or four. I know it

was two. Every time he came, it was with a group of people. . . . I just can't tell you exactly.

Q: What about any times that Oliver North came down where he wasn't a part of a contingent, an official contingency, but was either by himself or with a group of private individuals? Do you know anything about that?

A: *No, I don't think so.*

\*             \*             \*

Q: I'm asking for your best recollection. That's all I can get from you.

A: Well, that's the best I can give you. I don't recall it. *I certainly don't remember him travelling with private people.*

\*             \*             \*

Q: I asked you last time about General Richard Secord, and you described one time in which General Secord came by I believe your residence.

A: No.

Q: The Embassy? The Embassy. And I believe you described about a half-hour meeting, and you could not recall it.

A: It was a very innocuous meeting. He had either gotten in touch with Jim Steele, but anyway Jim Steele called and said that this guy was in town, did I want to meet with him. If they've got two heads, I meet with them. I said sure, you know, come on in.

And I remember him coming into the office. I remember it being very much a non-meeting, what I call a "non-meeting." We chatted a little bit about his having been the Deputy Assistant Secretary in ISA, and how are you, and how are you, and that was kind of as I recall the meeting.

Q: Do you know what he was doing in El Salvador?

A: *No.*

Q: Did he ask you to do anything for him?

---

I remember concentrating on that very much in the initial questions that came down for us to answer in writing, the stress in the language and the cables was on funding, on funding. For El Salvador, it was boots.

(Corr, Select Committees Deposition, 4/30/87, pp. 83–84.) Indeed, Meese's original request for materials focused on the activities of North and Secord only to the extent that they related to, among other things, "all financial aid activities involving the Nicaraguan resistance movement *which are related to Iran or Israel.*" (State 374730, 12/12/86, ALV 004987 (emphasis added).) On the other hand, Corr was not disposed in late 1986 to be too helpful to Iran/contra investigators. (See Corr Notes, 11/28/86, ALW 0033747, telling Steele prior to his appearing before a congressional committee in December 1986 "we have nothing to hide, but we are not anxious to speak. If insists we should do.").

[61] At some point prior to April 30, 1987, Corr was interviewed in San Salvador by Senate Select Committee staff, (See Corr, Select Committees Deposition, 4/30/87, p. 44.) He may have had a second meeting with one staffer prior to his April 30 deposition. (Ibid., pp. 91, 93, 94, 109.) During the deposition, a questioner said that an earlier meeting between them included discussion of Secord's visit to the Embassy. (Ibid., p. 96.) Independent Counsel did not obtain records of these interviews.

Corr also referred occasionally to his responses to Tower Commission inquiries. (See, for example, Corr, FBI 302, 4/1/87, p. 1; Corr, Grand Jury, 5/29/91, p. 151.) Independent Counsel's search of the Commission's records uncovered no trace of these responses.

[62] Corr, FBI 302, 4/1/87, p. 3.

[63] The FBI Form 302 of the interview suggests that the agents were unaware of Corr's cables regarding Iran/contra, including the December 13, 1986, cable quoted above.

A: He did not.

Q: Did he describe in any way his involvement in assisting the contras?

A: *No.* I think there was—[Corr interrupted by counsel, who then confers with Corr]—[o]ne thing that I think that it's important to note is that he was there as a retired military officer, as far as I was concerned, on private business. I don't think I'm capable of saying that I did not think that it might have something to do with contras, *but we certainly didn't discuss it.*

\* \* \*

Q: Were you aware when you met with General Secord that he had any type of relationship with Oliver North?

A: *I don't think so. . . .*

\* \* \*

Q: Were you ever aware of a trip to El Salvador by Colonel North in which General Secord accompanied him?

A: *I don't think so, no.*

\* \* \*

Q: Did any of your meetings. . .with North, or at any time you came in touch with North in Washington, ever deal with private resupply to the contras?

A: I'm sure we talked about private resupply to the contras. I mean, there was private resupply going through Ilopango. There was this general kind of thing that Ollie repeated a lot, you know, that we're going to get through this period; there are very admira[b]l[e] Americans and foreigners who are providing funds, you know, the world will long note what these people have done. *But in terms of any details, no.*[64]

In subsequent interviews, Corr amplified slightly his description of his meeting with Secord in El Salvador. On June 18, 1987, Corr told Independent Counsel "they may have had some general discussions about maintaining pressure on the Sandinistas. The discussion did not last long and Corr could not really remember their conversation."[65] On February 15, 1988, Corr stated that Col. Steele also was present for the meeting with Secord; that "they just talked about how bad communists were;" that Corr was "anxious to get Secord in and out because he had things to do;" and that Corr was "pretty certain he knew Secord met Bustillo."[66] On January 9, 1991, Corr said that he and Secord "talked about how there was no support for the Contras in the U.S. Congress."[67] In these interviews, however, Corr never modified or wavered from his original deposition testimony that North did not accompany Secord to El Salvador.

On April 26, 1991—after he had claimed the privilege under the Fifth Amendment—Corr was compelled to give immunized testimony before the Grand Jury. On this occasion, and again during a second Grand Jury appearance on May 29, 1991, Corr repeated his earlier false statements, insisting that only he and Secord (and, briefly, Steele) met in April 1986.[68]

## The Decision Not to Prosecute

By the fall of 1991, Independent Counsel had determined that he could prove beyond a reasonable doubt that Corr's testimony about the April 20, 1986, meeting was false. Although each of the central witnesses (North, Secord and Steele) had an imperfect recollection of the meeting and was subject to impeachment on the basis of his own false statements in prior Iran/contra proceedings, the weight of the evidence compensated for these deficiencies. Independent Counsel also determined that the evidence showed beyond a reasonable doubt that Corr recalled meeting with North and discussing contra-resupply issues on April 20, 1986. Corr's motive for not admitting the meeting with North and Secord was, as he indicated to Wiant, his obvious concern that it showed knowledge of a clear violation of the Boland Amendment, with North on the NSC staff and Secord—the operating head of contra resupply—discussing

---

64 Corr, Select Committees Deposition, 4/30/87, pp. 94, 95, 96–97, 100, 101, 109–10 (emphasis added).

65 Corr, FBI 302, 6/18/87, p. 2. See also Tylicki, Grand Jury, 12/7/87, p. 12 (interviewing agent, reiterating Corr's remarks).

66 Corr, FBI 302, 2/15/88, p. 5.

67 Corr, FBI 302, 1/9/91, p. 6.

68 Corr, Grand Jury, 4/26/91, pp. 201–05, 209–11, 213; Ibid., 5/29/91, pp. 6–7, 129, 142–43, 145–46, 153–54.

their activities with a State Department officer. Having lied in 1987, he was constrained not to change his testimony.

In November 1991, Dlouhy's Grand Jury testimony provided additional evidence that Corr's testimony about the April 20 meeting was false. Accordingly, after analyzing the proposed evidence, Independent Counsel decided to propose an indictment of Corr to the Grand Jury.

Shortly thereafter, events caused reconsideration of that decision. First, Independent Counsel located Dlouhy's passport and travel vouchers for his April 1986 trip to El Salvador, which raised doubts that he could have been in San Salvador for the April 20, 1986, conversation with Corr and Steele, to which Dlouhy had testified about in the Grand Jury. With this problematic evidence, Dlouhy recanted his Grand Jury testimony.

In light of these developments, Independent Counsel re-evaluated the other evidence against Corr. North's equivocation and a recent interview with Steele, who did not remember Dlouhy's presence, posed additional uncertainty.

At that time, both Clair George and Duane Clarridge had been indicted and were proceeding toward trial. There was no prospect that Corr would provide evidence that would assist Independent Counsel's investigation significantly. Elliott Abrams, against whom Corr would have been a witness for the Government, had resolved his situation by pleading guilty.

Finally, at this time, Independent Counsel recently had acquired former Defense Secretary Caspar Weinberger's voluminous handwritten notes and highly relevant Department of State notes. Independent Counsel believed that both the Weinberger and State Department investigations presented a more worthwhile use of his resources than a prosecution of Corr.

# Part VIII

# Officers of the Department of Defense (*U.S. v. Caspar W. Weinberger* and Related Investigations)

Defense Secretary Caspar W. Weinberger lied to investigators to conceal his knowledge of the Iran arms sales. Contrary to Weinberger's assertions, a small group of senior civilian officials and military officers in the Department of Defense (DoD), comprised of Secretary of Defense Caspar W. Weinberger and his closest aides, was consistently informed of the arms shipments to Iran in 1985 and 1986.

The OIC uncovered documents and notes and obtained testimony, which had been withheld from the Tower Commission and the Select Committees. The most important new evidence was Weinberger's own detailed daily diary notes and his notes of significant White House and other meetings regarding arms shipments to Iran. These notes, along with withheld notes of other Administration officials and additional documents that were obtained from DoD, revealed that Weinberger and other high-level Administration officials were much more knowledgeable about details of the Iran arms sales than they had indicated in their early testimony and statements.

This evidence formed the basis for the 1992 indictment of Weinberger. It also provided Independent Counsel with valuable, contemporaneous information concerning high-level participation in Iran/contra activities.

Senior officials outside the DoD, including National Security Advisers Robert C. McFarlane and his successor John M. Poindexter, kept Weinberger informed of proposals and developments. Weinberger also participated in meetings on this topic with President Reagan and other members of the National Security Council. In addition, beginning in September 1985, Weinberger, along with McFarlane and Director of Central Intelligence William J. Casey, regularly received highly classified intelligence reports containing detailed information on the negotiations and activities of Iranian government officials, private Iranian intermediaries, representatives of Israel, and the terrorists who were holding American citizens hostage. Weinberger's aides gave him additional information, which they acquired by reading the intelligence reports, from meetings and primarily from informed counterparts at the CIA, the Department of State and the NSC staff.

Throughout 1986, Weinberger continued to receive intelligence reports regarding arms-for-hostages negotiations and arms deliveries, and he continued to discuss these activities with other senior officials.[1]

## Origins of the Arms Shipments

On June 17, 1985, McFarlane sent a draft memorandum—a proposed National Security Decision Directive (NSDD) by President Reagan titled "U.S. Policy Toward Iran"—for review and comment to Secretary of State George P. Shultz and to Weinberger.[2] Among other things, the proposed presidential memorandum stated that the first component of new U.S. policy would be to

[e]ncourage Western allies and friends to help Iran meet its import requirements so as to reduce the attractiveness of Soviet assistance and trade offers, while demonstrating the value of correct relations

---

[1] After the revelation of the Iran intiative, Weinberger stated that he had "seriously contemplated resignation" in January 1986 but decided against it. (Weinberger, *Fighting for Peace: Seven Critical Years in the Pentagon* (Warner Books, 1990), pp. 383–84 (hereafter, "Weinberger, *Fighting for Peace*"). No contemporaneous document corroborates this claim.

[2] Memorandum from McFarlane to Shultz and Weinberger, "Subject: U.S. Policy Toward Iran," 6/17/85, AKW 001713–20.

with the West. This includes [the] provision of selected military equipment as determined on a case-by-case basis.[3]

After reading the memorandum, Weinberger scrawled a covering note to his senior military assistant, U.S. Army Major General Colin L. Powell:

> This is almost too absurd to comment on— By all means pass it on to Rich[ [4]]—but the assumption here is 1) that Iran is about to fall; + 2) we can deal with them on a rational basis—It's like asking Quadhaffi to Washington for a cozy chat [5]

Assistant Secretary of Defense for International Security Affairs Richard L. Armitage subsequently drafted a response with input from Fred Ikle, the under secretary of defense for policy.[6] On July 16, 1985, Weinberger sent McFarlane a memorandum that opposed issuing the draft NSDD and stated that "[u]nder no circumstances . . . should we now ease our restriction on arms sales to Iran." [7]

During July 1985, Weinberger learned from McFarlane of Israeli intelligence information regarding Iranians who were interested in opening a dialogue with the west. On July 13, 1985— the day of President Reagan's surgery at Bethesda Naval Hospital—he informed Shultz and Weinberger. McFarlane sent an "eyes only" back-channel cable to Shultz that he had met with an Israeli emissary, who had identified the Iranian contacts as Ayatollah Karoubi and an adviser to the Prime Minister named Manucher Ghorbanifar. The Israeli emissary reported that the Iranians were confident that they could achieve quickly the release of seven U.S. citizens held hostage in Lebanon. They wanted delivery of 100 TOW missiles from Israel so that they (the Iranians) could show some gain from their dealings with the west.[8] McFarlane gave the same report to Weinberger, who was at his home in Washington.[9]

In late July and August 1985, Weinberger attended meetings of senior Reagan Administration officials where this opening to Iran, through Israel, was discussed in detail. General John W. Vessey, Jr., the Chairman of the Joint Chiefs of Staff (JCS), recalled that Weinberger told him incredulously, after attending a White House meeting in the summer of 1985, that someone had proposed contacts with Iran.[10] Weinberger himself testified that he recalled attending a White House meeting in August 1985 regarding the proposed NSDD on a new policy toward Iran.[11]

According to McFarlane, President Reagan, after meeting with his senior advisers in July and August 1985 and hearing the objections raised by Weinberger and Shultz, gave McFarlane oral authorization for Israel to trans-

---

[3] Ibid., AKW 001719.

[4] Richard L. Armitage, Assistant Secretary of Defense for International Security Affairs.

[5] Weinberger Note, circa 6/18/85, ALZ 0049658. Powell also delivered a copy of the draft NSDD, with a typed version of Weinberger's note, to Deputy Secretary of Defense William Howard Taft IV, who reviewed it on June 20, 1985. (ALZ 004401 ("DEP SEC HAS SEEN").)

[6] Memorandum from Armitage to Ikle, 7/13/85, ALZ 0071353–62 (transmitting alternative draft memoranda for Weinberger's consideration in responding to McFarlane); Memorandum from Armitage to Weinberger, 7/16/85, ALZ 004400.

[7] Memorandum from Weinberger to McFarlane, 7/16/85, AKW 001710. Shultz had sent McFarlane a similar response to the draft NSDD. (Memorandum from Shultz to McFarlane, 6/29/85, AKW 005357 ("I . . . disagree with the suggestion that our efforts to reduce arms flows to Iran should be ended.").)

[8] Cable from McFarlane to Shultz, 7/13/85, ALV 005092–95 (Shultz file copy).

[9] In his 1990 book, Weinberger noted McFarlane's testimony regarding his July 13 briefings of Shultz and Weinberger, but dismissed it sarcastically:

> His "recollection" . . . exceeds mine on this, as it did on many other points. I recall no such meeting. July 13 was the Saturday the President was operated on for abdominal cancer; and I was going over office papers in the garden at our home in McLean, Virginia, and not being briefed by McFarlane.

(Weinberger, *Fighting for Peace*, p. 366.) In fact, Weinberger's diary entries for July 13, 1985—which are part of the voluminous Weinberger note collection that the OIC first located in 1991—memorialize *five* separate conversations, apparently by telephone, with McFarlane, plus Weinberger's conversation with General Powell, regarding a conversation Powell had had with McFarlane. (Weinberger Diary, 7/13/85, ALZ 0039537H–37J.)

Although none of these diary entries record substantive information regarding hostages, Israel or Iran, that omission could reflect Weinberger's apparent decision to make no detailed notes during July and early August 1985 regarding this activity. (See, e.g., Weinberger Diary, 8/6/85, ALZ 0039585–87 (no notes of a White House meeting on Iran, which Weinberger later testified he attended on this date)). On Monday, July 15, 1985, Weinberger did make a cryptic diary entry—"Saw Colin Powell—re proposed Iran"—that is consistent with McFarlane's testimony about his disclosures to Weinberger two days earlier. (Weinberger Diary, 7/15/85, ALZ 0039539.)

[10] Vessey, Select Committees Deposition, 4/17/87, pp. 30–31. In a subsequent interview, Vessey elaborated, explaining that Weinberger had first offered Vessey a ride to the White House meeting and then, after checking, had to tell Vessey that he was not invited. The next day, Weinberger told Vessey that he " 'wouldn't believe what was being proposed,' namely, negotiation with the Iranians." (Vessey, FBI 302, 6/11/92, p. 1.)

[11] Weinberger, Select Committees Testimony, 7/31/87, pp. 88–89; cf. Weinberger, Tower Commission Testimony, 1/14/87, p. 5 ("I do not have memory of an August [1985] meeting as such, but I gather that there was an August [1985] meeting, and there was certainly a meeting with the President upstairs in the residence after he got out of the hospital.").

fer U.S.-made arms to Iran, which the United States would replenish, to get the hostages released.[12] McFarlane recalled communicating the President's decisions to Weinberger.[13]

## Israel's Initial TOW Missile Shipments and the September 1985 Release of the Reverend Weir

In late August 1985, after McFarlane learned that Israel and Iran had agreed on a shipment of 100 TOW missiles,[14] he met with Weinberger at the Pentagon.[15] Powell, who attended the meeting,[16] recalled that McFarlane gave Weinberger "a sort of history of how we got where we were on that particular day"[17] and reported that there "was to be a transfer of some limited amount of materiel."[18] Weinberger's diary shows that, in a subsequent conversation with McFarlane, Weinberger advocated an agreement with the Iranians that would release all U.S. citizens being held hostage in Lebanon.[19] Weinberger's diary also shows that he and his senior aides devoted significant time during late August and September of 1985 to

planning for the release of hostages,[20] and that he approved a plan for a senior military officer[21] to represent the DoD at a meeting with Iranian representatives in Europe during that period.[22]

After the Reverend Benjamin Weir was released on September 15, 1985, Weinberger's diary refers to "a delivery I have for our prisoners."[23] Weinberger's notes show that on September 17, 1985, at a "Family Group" lunch at the White House with McFarlane, Shultz and Casey, he discussed David Kimche, director general of Israel's Foreign Ministry, who was acting as the "go between" in contacts with Iranians.[24]

---

12 McFarlane, FBI 302, 3/20/92, p. 2. In President Reagan's August 23, 1985, diary entry, which he made available for review to Independent Counsel, in excerpted form, he wrote that he had "received 'secret phone' call from Bud McFarlane—seems a man high-up in the Iranian govt. believes he can deliver all or part of the 7 kidnap victims—I had some decisions to make about a few points—but they were easy to make—now we must wait."

13 McFarlane, FBI 302, 3/20/92, pp. 3, 5, 6, 7, 9.

14 Ibid., p. 3.

15 Weinberger Diary, 8/22/85, ALZ 0039605 ("Bud McFarlane fm [from] AF1 [Air Force One]—wants to meet with me tonight—"); Powell, Select Committees Deposition, 6/19/87, pp. 5–8, 52.

16 Powell, FBI 302, 12/5/86, p. 1; Powell, Select Committees Interview Memorandum, 4/17/87, p. 2, AMY 000561. Although Powell could not supply a precise date for this meeting (Powell, Select Committees Deposition, 6/19/87, p. 39, placing this meeting "in the summer" of 1985), Weinberger's diary indicates that the meeting occurred in his office on August 22, 1985, and was attended by Weinberger, McFarlane, Powell and General Charles Gabriel, the Acting Chairman of the Joint Chiefs of Staff (Weinberger Diary, 8/22/85, ALZ 0039606–07). Weinberger's typed calendar, which corroborates the attendees and the location, indicates that the meeting lasted from approximately 7:30 until 8:10 p.m. (Weinberger Calendar, 8/22/85, LC–007474.)

17 Powell, Select Committees Deposition, 6/19/87, p. 5.

18 Powell, FBI Interview Transcript, 12/5/86, ALZ 0047719–20; accord Powell, Select Committees Deposition, 6/19/87, p. 5; see also Weinberger Diary, 8/22/85, ALZ 0039606–07 ("Bud McFarlane, Charles Gabriel, CP [Powell] in office. Peres sent Israeli Envoy to tell us 2 Iranians offered to return some of our kidnappees—want us to have better attitude toward Iran after Khomeni—I argued that we tell them we wanted all hostages back") (emphasis in original).

19 Ibid., 8/23/85, ALZ 0039608 ("Conference call—with Bud McFarlane + General Gabriel—on Iranian proposal to let us have our Kidnappees—agreed we should deal directly with Iranians + not thru Israelis + that we should get guarantees that we'll get them all—+ take them off w helos fm Tripoli Beach").

20 See, e.g., ibid., 8/24/85, ALZ 0039611A; bid., 8/26/85, ALZ 0039613; ibid., 8/29/85, ALZ 0039621–22; ibid., 9/3/85, ALZ 0039627, ALZ 0039630; ibid., 9/11/85, ALZ 0039647–48.

21 The DoD determined in 1993 that the senior military officer's name and all details relating to this subject continue to be classified. See Classified Appendix to this chapter.

22 Weinberger Diary, 8/29/85, ALZ 0039621–22. The senior military officer said that he was not aware that he had ever been considered for a meeting with Iranians and, notwithstanding Weinberger's diary notes, he stated emphatically that he had no knowledge of any dealings with Iranians. (Senior Military Officer, FBI 302, 1/28/92, p. 3.) The senior military officer also said that he never dealt with Oliver North and never heard his name mentioned in connection with the hostage Benjamin Weir's release; he described North as "simply a staff officer on the periphery. . . ." (Ibid., pp. 2–3.)

The senior military officer's account conflicts with the contemporaneous evidence. Weinberger's diary relates that the officer embarked on a mission involving travel to Vienna, Austria—at McFarlane's request and with the approval of Weinberger and General Vessey—in early September 1985 "to see if Iranians will release our hostages. . . ." (Weinberger Diary, 9/6/85, ALZ 0039637; accord Ibid., 8/29/85, ALZ 0039621–22; ibid., 9/3/85, ALZ 0039627, ALZ 0039630; ibid., 9/4/85, ALZ 0039632.) North's notebook quotes Adm. Moreau, who supervised the officer in the JCS chain of command (Senior Military Officer, FBI 302, 1/28/92, p. 2), as reporting on Wednesday, August 28, 1985, that "[senior military officer]" had been "briefed Monday." (North Note, 8/28/85, AMX 001340.) On September 4, 1985, he applied for and received a ten-year passport in a false name. (Department of State Passport Application, 9/4/85, ALW 015697 (signed by "[alias]" and bearing the Senior Military Officer's photograph); accord ALW 015698 (identification page of passport).) Contemporaneous notes show that North sought a false passport for himself and a second false passport for the Senior Military Officer; that North invoked Moreau's name while making this request; that North was going to Europe with the military officer; that they would be using the aliases; and that their reservations were in the latter alias. (Quinn Note, 8/30/85, ALV 002319 ("Secure call—Ollie North—. . . Asked for false passport for trip to Europe—"); Ibid., 9/4/85, ALV 002320 ("OLLIE—One more passport—DoD—"); Raphel Note, 9/10/85, ALW 0045285 (North/[Senior Military Officer]—to Europe); Platt Note, 9/10/85, ALW 0036312 ("Ollie North, [Senior Military Officer]—Goode, [false name]"); North Note, 9/4/85, AMX 001723 ("TICKETS & HOTEL: [false name]"); see also Platt Note, 9/10/85, ALW 0036317 ("Armacost heard from Pdx [Poindexter] . . .—That Ollie + friend going nowhere"); see generally Memorandum for the Record from Martel, "Subject: Request for Passport Retrieval," 11/25/86, ALW 015668 (passport believed issued for Senior Military Officer at the request of Ambassador Robert B. Oakley); Memorandum from Coburn to George, 10/16/87, ALW 015667; Coburn, FBI 302, 10/30/87, p. 3.)

23 Weinberger Diary, 9/15/85, ALZ 0039653F.

24 Ibid., 9/17/85, ALZ 0039659.

Weinberger, along with McFarlane and Casey, began to receive intelligence reports that provided further detailed information about dealings with Iran in exchange for hostages. Before September 17, 1985, the Pentagon copies of the first six intelligence reports on this activity were delivered to Adm. Arthur Moreau, assistant to the chairman of the JCS, rather than to Weinberger;[25] Moreau brought his copies to Weinberger's office, however, where they were read by Weinberger and Powell.[26] On September 17, Weinberger, through Powell, complained to the originating intelligence agency about not receiving direct delivery of its intelligence reports on this topic.[27] Thereafter, and continuing through the end of 1986, these reports, which were issued frequently and on a current basis, were delivered directly to Weinberger. Later in September 1985, these reports disclosed that arms were the currency of United States dealings with Iran.[28] In early October 1985, Weinberger noted that the dealings with Iran involved "arms transfers."[29] Weinberger also knew by early October 1985 that NSC staff member Lt. Col. Oliver L. North was involved in these negotiations with Iranians.[30]

## Israel's November 1985 HAWK Missile Shipment

In November 1985, McFarlane informed Weinberger that negotiations involving Israelis, Iranians and Americans for proposed weapons transfers in return for hostage releases had resumed.[31] Although Weinberger objected, the activity continued. McFarlane specifically in-

formed Weinberger that HAWK missiles were the proposed currency.[32]

In late November 1985, when McFarlane was in Geneva with President Reagan for a summit meeting with Soviet leader Mikhail Gorbachev, he gave Weinberger reports regarding this proposed transaction. On November 19, McFarlane asked Weinberger to get 500 HAWK missiles for sale from the United States to Israel, which would transfer them to Iran in exchange for the release of five hostages on November 21, 1985.[33] Weinberger passed this request to Powell,[34] who discussed it with Noel C. Koch, the acting assistant secretary of defense for International Security Affairs.[35] Powell and Koch directed Henry H. Gaffney, the acting director of the DoD's Defense Security Assistance Agency (DSAA),[36] to gather information about the availability of HAWK missiles and the legal restrictions that would apply to the proposed transfer from Israel to Iran.[37] Gaffney gave Powell a negative oral report on the proposed shipment,[38] and Powell passed this information to Weinberger later that same day. Weinberger's diary entry reads:

> Colin Powell in office re data on Hawks— can't be given to Israel or Iran w/o Cong. notification,—breaking them up into several packages of 28 Hawks to keep each package under $14 million is a clear violation[39]

Weinberger promptly passed this information to McFarlane in Geneva. McFarlane's response was non-committal.[40]

The next day, McFarlane told Weinberger that, notwithstanding the legal problems raised

---

[25] AMW 0001918–40. The apparent reason for delivering the Pentagon copy of these intelligence reports to Adm. Moreau during the first weeks of September 1985 was the fact that the senior military officer who was to meet with Iranian representatives during that period reported to the Joint Staff. (Senior Military Officer, FBI 302, 1/28/92, p. 2.) The intelligence reports, in short, were initially delivered to the senior military officer's commanding officers, Moreau and Gen. Vessey, who in turn reported with him to Weinberger. (Ibid., p. 3.) Independent Counsel was not able to obtain additional information regarding Moreau's handling of the initial intelligence reports because he died shortly before Independent Counsel was appointed in December 1986.

[26] Powell, FBI 302, 2/24/92, p. 5.

[27] Weinberger Diary, 9/17/85, ALZ 0039659.

[28] Ibid., 9/20/85, ALZ 0039671; *accord* Intelligence Report, AMW 0001937.

[29] Weinberger Diary, 10/3/85, ALZ 0039703.

[30] Ibid., 10/4/85, ALZ 0039704.

[31] Ibid., 11/9/85, ALZ 0039774.

[32] Ibid., 11/10/85, ALZ 0039775; ibid., 11/19/85, ALZ 0039795.

[33] Ibid., 11/19/85, ALZ 0039795.

[34] Powell, Grand Jury, 4/22/92, pp. 57–58.

[35] Koch, FBI 302, 3/23/92, p. 9. Koch was acting assistant secretary of defense because Armitage was traveling from November 15 to November 23, 1985. After Armitage returned to the United States in late November, Powell informed him of the activity that had occurred during his foreign trip. (Ibid., pp. 10–11.)

[36] Gaffney, who was DSAA's director of plans at the time, was acting director of DSAA during the week of November 18, 1985, because the director, Lt. Gen. Philip Gast, was traveling with the Armitage delegation, and the deputy director, Glenn A. Rudd, was out of town. (Gaffney, FBI 302, 4/9/92, p. 2; Gaffney, Select Committees Interview Memorandum, 4/10/87, pp. 3, 5–6, AMY 000542, AMY 000545–46.)

[37] Gaffney, Select Committees Deposition, 6/16/87, pp. 62–63, 73.

[38] Ibid., p. 81; Gaffney, Select Committees Interview Memorandum, 4/10/87, p. 8.

[39] Weinberger Diary, 11/19/85, ALZ 0039797.

[40] Ibid.

by Weinberger, President Reagan had decided to send HAWK missiles to Iran through Israel.[41] McFarlane later advised Weinberger that only 120 HAWK missiles would be sent, that they would be "older models," and that the hostage release would occur on Friday, November 22, 1985.[42]

Weinberger continued to discuss this planned HAWK shipment with Powell.[43] Powell provided him a succinct "point paper" written by Gaffney concerning the practical, legal and political difficulties with the proposed shipment.[44] Weinberger's diary shows that he and Powell watched for a hostage release, which did not occur, on November 22, 1985.[45] Early the next week, Weinberger received an intelligence report confirming that weapons had been shipped to Iran on November 24, 1985.[46] Subsequent reports made clear that these weapons had been HAWK missiles.[47]

## December 1985 Meetings Regarding Proposals to Transfer Additional Weapons to Iran

During the first week of December 1985, senior DoD officials addressed a proposal to ship additional missiles to Iran in exchange for hostages. On December 2, Assistant Secretary Richard L. Armitage discussed this topic with Menachem Meron, the director general of Israel's Ministry of Defense, who was visiting the United States.[48] The next day, Armitage discussed these proposals with North.[49] On December 5, Armitage met with retired U.S. Air Force Major General Richard V. Secord, who had just returned from Israel and had been deeply involved in the HAWK missile shipment of late November 1985.[50] North prepared a detailed paper for Poindexter that same day which discussed Israel's September 1985 TOW missile shipment to Iran and urged additional Israeli arms shipments to Iran with replenishment by the United States.[51]

On or about December 5–6, Armitage obtained an information paper from DSAA regarding the proposed shipment outlined in North's

---

41 Ibid., 11/20/85, ALZ 0039799. There is no record that Weinberger attempted to contact the President to voice his opposition or to seek reconsideration of this decision.

42 Ibid., 11/20/85, ALZ 0039801.

43 Ibid.; ibid., 11/21/85, ALZ 0039802.

44 "Point Paper: Hawk Missiles for Iran," ALZ 000353–54. A second copy of Gaffney's point paper, which is labeled "REVISED" in his handwriting but in fact contains only one less word, apparently was located in Weinberger's office complex during an April 1987 search for Iran/contra documents. On April 17, 1987, Col. James F. Lemon, the executive secretary in the Office of the Secretary of Defense, transmitted this version of Gaffney's point paper to the DoD general counsel and the assistant general counsel who were collecting Iran/contra documents, with a cover memorandum explaining that the point paper had been located during a search, conducted at the general counsel's instruction in response to document requests from the Select Committees, of "the Immediate Office of the Secretary of Defense, the Office of the Deputy Secretary of Defense, and the Office of the Executive Secretariat." (Memorandum from Lemon to Garrett and Shapiro, with attached "Point Paper: Hawk Missiles for Iran," 4/17/87, ALZ 0058446–48.)

Although the revised Gaffney point paper and Lemon's cover memorandum were responsive to Independent Counsel's 1987 omnibus requests for DoD documents, they were not made available to the OIC until 1992. There also is no record that the DoD Office of General Counsel ever provided this version of Gaffney's point paper or the information regarding its location in Weinberger's office to the Select Committees. When the Select Committees questioned Weinberger using Gaffney's file copy of the point paper, Weinberger said he did not recall seeing the document contemporaneously. (Weinberger, Select Committees Testimony, 6/17/87, pp. 22, 41.)

45 Weinberger Diary, 11/23/85, ALZ 0039806A ("Colin Powell— . . . no hostage release last night").

46 Intelligence report, 11/25/85, AMW 0002001–03 ("Subj: Lebanese Kidnappings: . . . Delivery Made on 24 November 1985").

47 Intelligence reports, AMW 0002010–12 (12/11/85), AMW 002016–17 (12/12/85).

48 Armitage, Meeting Log, 12/2/85, ALZ 016436. Two days after Meron's meeting with Armitage, the Director of DSAA's Israel desk, Diana Blundell, sent an information paper on Israel's HAWK missile systems through DSAA Deputy Director Rudd to Lt. Gen. Gast, the director of DSAA. (Information Paper SUBJECT: Israel—HAWK Missile System, circa 12/4/85, ALZ 0044276.) Blundell's paper contains detailed information on the status and schedule for improving Israel's HAWK missile batteries, the anticipated schedule for delivering modified missiles to Israel that would be compatible with the improved batteries, and the numbers of basic and improved HAWK missiles that Israel had received from the U.S. in the past. Blundell's cover note transmitting the information paper to Rudd and Gast says that they had requested a paper "on I–HAWK deliveries to Israel." (Memorandum from Blundell through Rudd to Gast, 12/4/85, ALZ 0044275.) Rudd's schedule indicates that, after he, Gast and Blundell had received a farewell "courtesy call" from Gen. Meron on December 2, 1985; Rudd, Gast, Blundell and others met the next afternoon "re: I–HAWK. . . ." (Rudd Schedule, 12/2/85, ALZ 0044110; ibid., 12/3/85, ALZ 0044110.) This meeting preceded Blundell's paper on I–HAWK deliveries to Israel.

Blundell's information paper and the related Rudd schedule documents are consistent with a response to an Israeli request during the first week of December 1985 for prompt replenishment of the 18 HAWK missiles that Israel had transferred to Iran the previous week. Armitage, one possible source of such a request, did not recall possessing knowledge in early December 1985 of Israel's HAWK shipment. Because the Blundell and Rudd documents were not produced by DoD to the OIC until 1992 (and apparently never were produced to the Select Committees), the OIC did not pursue the matter after Blundell stated in 1992 that she had no recollection whatsoever of the events that prompted her 1985 information paper. (Blundell, FBI 302, 5/29/92, pp. 4–5.)

49 Armitage Meeting Log, 12/3/85, ALZ 016437 ("1230–1345 Ollie North—Lunch in office").

50 Ibid., 12/5/85, ALZ 016439 ("1300—Gen Secord").

51 See Armitage section below.

paper. This paper, a one-page analysis titled "Prospects for Immediate Shipment of I–HAWK and I–TOW Missiles," was drafted by DSAA Deputy Director Glenn A. Rudd and Gaffney.[52] The paper reported that up to 75 I–HAWK missiles were available in the United States for foreign shipment and quoted a "total package price" of $22.5 million "for [shipping] 50. . . ." It reported that "3,300 I–TOWs" could be shipped from U.S. Army stocks "immediately. . . ."[53] Armitage, in collaboration with State Department official Arnold L. Raphel,[54] also created a second information paper, using a draft by Rudd and Gaffney, titled "Possibility for Leaks." The "Leaks" paper addresses the legal implications of transferring "I–HAWKs in the quantity contemplated" and "the I–TOW quantities" and says that "[t]here is no good way to keep this project from ultimately being made public."[55]

By Thursday, December 5, 1985, Weinberger had learned that President Reagan would be meeting with his senior advisers on Saturday, December 7 to discuss this proposal.[56] Weinberger and Powell, who had been out of the country from December 2 to 6, 1985,[57] met with Armitage early that Saturday morning to discuss the information papers Armitage had assembled in preparation for Weinberger's meeting with the President.[58]

At the White House meeting, Weinberger—supported by Shultz and White House Chief of Staff Donald T. Regan—argued against any more arms shipments to Iran.[59] Weinberger specifically told President Reagan that he could not violate the United States embargo on arms shipments to Iran, and that "washing" an arms transfer through Israel would not make it

legal.[60] The President rejected these legal arguments,[61] but he announced no decision by the end of the meeting. Later that day, McFarlane advised Weinberger that the President had decided not to trade more arms for hostages, but instead was sending McFarlane to London to meet with the Iranians and to discuss the possibility of Great Britain selling arms to them.[62]

Early the next week, after McFarlane had returned from London, Weinberger attended another White House meeting with the President and senior officials to discuss proposed arms shipments to Iran. Weinberger took detailed notes during this December 10, 1985, meeting. McFarlane told the group that the United States had an outstanding commitment to supply 500 replacement TOW missiles to Israel.[63] The meeting ended with an apparent decision by President Reagan not to send additional arms to Iran at that time but to pursue diplomatic contacts in an attempt to free the hostages.[64]

## January 1986 Meetings and President Reagan's Decision To Proceed With Direct Weapons Transfers From the United States to Iran

In January 1986, Israel proposed additional weapons shipments to Iran. On January 6, Poindexter briefed Weinberger regarding Israel's proposal to transfer 4,000 TOW missiles from Israel to Iran, with a commitment from the United States to replenish Israel's TOW-missile stocks.[65] The next day, Weinberger attended a

---

[52] Gaffney, Select Committees Deposition, 6/22/87, p. 24 (joint deposition with Rudd).

[53] Prospects for Immediate Shipment of I–HAWK and I–TOW Missiles, ALZ 0058747.

[54] Raphel served as the principal deputy assistant secretary of state in the Bureau of Near Eastern and Asian Affairs (NEA) during 1985 and 1986.

[55] Possibility for Leaks, ALZ 004343.

[56] Weinberger Diary, 12/5/85, ALZ 0039827 ("Colin Powell in room—re meeting Saturday with President on Iran hostages + TOW's").

[57] Ibid., 12/2/85, ALZ 0039818 (departure for Europe); ibid., 12/6/85, ALZ 0039829 (return to U.S.).

[58] Ibid., 12/7/85, ALZ 0039830 ("Met with Colin Powell + Rich Armitage—re NSC Plan to let Israelis give Iranians 50 Hawks + 3300 TOWs in return for 5 hostages—NSC will present it as a means of helping group that wants to overthrow gov't—But no assu assurance that any of this goes—weapons will go to Iranian Army.").

[59] Ibid., 12/7/85, ALZ 0039831.

[60] Ibid. ("I argued strongly that we have an embargo that makes arms sales to Iran illegal + President couldn't violate it— + that 'washing' transaction thru Israel wouldn't make it legal. Shultz, Don Regan agreed.").

[61] Ibid. ("President sd. he could answer charges of illegality but he couldn't answer charge that 'big strong President Reagan passed up a chance to free hostages'.").

[62] Ibid., ALZ 0039832, ALZ 0039838 ("Called McFarlane in Washington—he is going to London to advise President's decision that we will not ransom our hostages—he will discuss with UK Possibility of their selling some arms to negotiators.") (emphasis in original).

[63] Weinberger Meeting Notes, 12/10/85, ALZ 0040645 ("We still must replace 500 TOWs to Israel").

[64] Weinberger Diary, 12/10/85, ALZ 0039840 ("President still wants to try to get hostage released—But forcible storming would mean many deaths—decided to send Dick Walters to Damascus [with classified message].").

[65] Weinberger Meeting Note, 1/6/86, ALZ 0042650-51 ("Nir proposed selling 4000 TOWs (unimp. [unimproved])—No launchers—+ Israelis would deliver 500 via Israeli plane—if all 5 US hostages released—then Israelis want 4000 TOW replacements, + If they are caught they would want us to acknowledge that we knew of it + did not object.") (emphasis in original). Weinberger Diary, 1/6/86, ALZ 0039880 ("John Poindexter in office. Another Israeli-Iranian

White House meeting with President Reagan and other senior officials. Weinberger voiced his continuing objections to this proposal.[66] The next week, Weinberger received a briefing from Koch, the principal deputy assistant secretary of defense for International Security Affairs, who had been negotiating details relating to these shipments with an Israeli arms procurement official.[67] After hearing Koch's progress report, Weinberger commented that somebody was going to go to jail.[68]

President Reagan ultimately decided that the United States would deal with Iran directly, rather than through Israel. On January 16, 1986, Weinberger attended a White House meeting with Casey, Attorney General Edwin Meese III and CIA General Counsel Stanley Sporkin regarding a proposed presidential Finding that would authorize covert arms shipments from the CIA to Iran.[69] Although Weinberger continued to offer legal objections,[70] President Reagan signed the Finding the next day. Weinberger, through General Powell, then directed the DoD bureaucracy to make missiles available to the CIA.[71] Weinberger explicitly directed subordinates that DoD was not to be involved in shipping arms to Iran beyond selling the missiles to CIA.[72]

## DoD Knowledge of Weapons Transfers to Iran During 1986

Throughout 1986, Weinberger received periodic but detailed reports, which he recorded in his handwritten notes, concerning arms shipments to Iran to recover the hostages. In February 1986, at a "Family Group" lunch with Casey, Shultz and Poindexter, Weinberger was briefed on the schedule for sequential TOW missile shipments and hostage releases.[73] In March 1986, Weinberger learned of a proposal to send McFarlane to meet with the Iranians.[74] In April 1986, Weinberger learned that, in addition to the TOW missiles that had already been sent, HAWK missile parts would now be transferred to Iran, and that McFarlane and North would be traveling to Iran.[75] In May 1986, Weinberger discussed with Shultz intelligence reports demonstrating that McFarlane would be bringing military equipment to Iran without a commitment that all U.S. hostages would be released.[76] Near the end of May 1986, Weinberger learned that McFarlane's trip to Iran had ended in failure.[77] In July 1986, Weinberger received a briefing from Michael Ledeen, the former NSC and DoD consultant who had participated in the 1985 negotiations with Israelis and Iranians before his dismissal by Poindexter.[78] In late July 1986, Weinberger was informed that hostage Father Lawrence Martin Jenco had been released in Lebanon due to Iran's intervention and in an effort to obtain "more US weapons." [79] In October 1986, Poindexter informed

scheme offering freedom to hostages in return for TOW missiles—Told him I opposed it.'').

[66] Weinberger Meeting Note, 1/7/86, ALZ 0042655; Weinberger Diary, 1/7/86, ALZ 0039883 ("Met with President, Shultz, Poindexter, Bill Casey, Ed Meese, in Oval Office—President decided to go with Israeli-Iranian offer to release our 5 hostages in return for sale of 4000 TOWs to Iran by Israel—George Shultz + I opposed—Bill Casey, Ed Meese + VP favored—as did Poindexter.'').

[67] Ibid., 1/14/86, ALZ 0039901 ("Colin Powell + Noel Cook [sic—Koch] in office—re changes in Iran offer on hostages—'').

[68] Koch, Select Committees Testimony, 6/23/87, pp. 76, 187–88 ("I said to him—and I did not say it in a very serious way—it may not sound in context as an opportunity for levity, but I said, do we have a legal problem with this, is somebody going to go to jail, and his response was in the affirmative. But I didn't take that seriously. . . . I hadn't intended it seriously when I asked the question. We had the shared background of Watergate to bounce some of these perceptions off of, so there was that. Chiefly I assumed if there was any prospect of it being illegal, that he would have stopped it. . . . [S]ince he didn't leave, I assumed it was legal.'').

[69] Weinberger Diary, 1/16/86, ALZ 0039906A ("Met with John Poindexter, McLaughlin—re ways to increase aid + financing for Lebanon—Bill Casey—Ed Meese—Stanley Sorkin [sic—Sporkin]''); Sporkin, Select Committees Testimony, 6/24/87, pp. 126–28.

[70] Weinberger Diary, 1/17/86, ALZ 0039906D ("Saw Colin Powell—re acts prohibiting sales to Iran[;] Colin Powell (2) to Car—citation to statute above[;] Lunch with Shultz, Bill Casey, John Poindexter in W.H. [White House] Family Dining Room, re attempts to get hostages back from Hizballah—Told him of Statutes forbidding sales to Iran.'').

[71] Powell, FBI 302, 7/6/87 & 7/9/87, p. 1.

[72] Weinberger Diary, 1/24/86, ALZ 0039919 ("Noel Koch—in office—with Colin Powell—re Iranian-Hizbollah hostage release—we are not to be involved in this beyond selling to CIA'').

[73] Weinberger Meeting Note, 2/11/86, ALZ 0040652D–52E.

[74] Weinberger Diary, 3/4/86, ALZ 0040006B ("Attended lunch with John Poindexter—in his WH [White House] office—re Iran hostages. (About delays and demands—McFarlane will go as rep. to meeting if they agree.)'').

[75] Ibid., 4/10/86, ALZ 0040065 ("Saw Don Jones—re cables fm [from] Will Taft—on addl [additional] attempts to buy our kidnappees' release—with sp Hawk equipment—''); Weinberger Diary, 4/13/86, ALZ 0040072 ("[Saw] Will Taft—. . . also re sam Iran hostages—McFarlane, North going to Iran—idiocy—'').

[76] Ibid., 5/13/86, ALZ 0040147–48.

[77] Ibid., 5/29/86, ALZ 0040165.

[78] Ibid., 7/24/86, ALZ 0040303.

[79] Ibid., 7/30/86, ALZ 0040312.

Weinberger of a new channel to Iran through Rafsanjani's nephew.[80]

Weinberger complied with President Reagan's decision by selling weapons and weapons parts from DoD to CIA for onward shipment to Iran on three occasions. In February 1986, TOW missiles were sold to CIA and ultimately transferred to Iran. In May 1986, HAWK missile parts were sold by DoD to CIA and ultimately, in a partial shipment with McFarlane that month and in a second shipment in early August, transferred to Iran. In October 1986, additional TOW missiles were sold by DoD to CIA and ultimately transferred to Israel, which retained some as replenishment for earlier shipments and transferred others to Iran, producing the release of hostage David Jacobsen. Weinberger's senior military assistant informed him at the time each of these transfers to the CIA took place.[81] Weinberger also continued to receive intelligence reports on this activity throughout 1986, which provided detailed information on dealings with Iran and arms shipments in exchange for hostages.[82]

# Independent Counsel's Investigation

## Investigation of the DoD, 1986–1990

Before the discovery of Weinberger's notes in 1991, Independent Counsel's investigation had focused primarily on DoD's sale of missiles and missile parts to the CIA in 1986, and on the involvement of military officials in contra resupply activity. The inquiry into the 1986 Iran arms sales was intended primarily to obtain a thorough understanding of the mechanics of the transactions, the pricing of the TOW missiles, and whether DoD officials involved in the pricing or transfer had knowledge of the diversion of profits from the arms sales. No prosecutions resulted from this aspect of the investigation.

Weinberger was interviewed twice as a witness.[83]

## Discovery of Weinberger's Notes

Beginning in 1987, congressional investigators and the OIC repeatedly requested notes, calendars, telephone logs, diaries and other materials relevant to the Iran/contra matter from Weinberger and other high Administration officials. Weinberger produced a typewritten memorandum of one meeting, a few documents containing his handwritten marginalia, and official calendars and activity logs that were maintained by his staff. It was not until the late summer of 1990 that OIC obtained a document suggesting that he had withheld relevant handwritten notes.

An August 7, 1987, note by Secretary of State Shultz's executive assistant, M. Charles Hill, led investigators to reexamine earlier Weinberger statements regarding notes.[84] In one OIC interview, Weinberger had referred to "a habit of making notes on any piece of paper he could get his hands on." [85]

In late August 1990, Weinberger was subpoenaed to produce relevant documents, including any handwritten notes, to the Grand Jury. On September 13, 1990, his attorney assured the OIC that Weinberger had previously turned over his notes to the congressional committees investigating the Iran/contra matter or to the Library of Congress. Subsequently, Weinberger agreed to be interviewed. On September 28, 1990, in arranging the interview, Weinberger's attorney was told that two sources of information— Weinberger's previous interview with the OIC and a newly discovered document [86]—indicated that Weinberger had not turned over relevant notes to Congress.

On October 10, 1990, Weinberger, accompanied by his counsel, was interviewed by OIC attorneys in the presence of an FBI Special Agent.[87] At that time, his counsel asked to see a record of the April 7, 1988, interview. After reviewing it, Weinberger said that he disagreed with that portion of the report that stated: "he had a habit of making notes on any piece of paper he could get his hands on." Weinberger

80 Ibid., 10/3/86; ALZ 0040458.

81 Jones, FBI 302, 3/24/92, pp. 2, 6.

82 Weinberger Diary, 5/13/86, ALZ 0040146-48; ibid., 10/30/86, ALZ 0040506.

83 Weinberger, FBI 302, 12/1/86; Weinberger, FBI 302, 4/7/88.

84 Shultz told Hill that "Cap takes notes but never referred to them so never had to cough them up." (Hill Note, 8/7/87, ALW 0056370.)

85 Weinberger, FBI 302, 4/7/88, p. 2.

86 The August 7, 1987, Charles Hill note.

87 The following account of the OIC's October 10, 1990, interview of Weinberger is based upon the FBI Record of Interview, also referred to as a "302."

characterized the statement as "misleading" because it implied that it was his habit to make notes throughout his seven years as secretary of defense, which he said was not the case. Weinberger stated that during his first year as secretary of defense he had taken notes on the backs of pages in his briefing books. He said his personal secretaries initially had saved these notes for him so that he could dictate memoranda. He said he discontinued that practice after about a year, when it became apparent that he would not have time to dictate memoranda.[88] Weinberger stated that, after his first year in office, he did not regularly take notes at meetings or make a record of meetings when he returned to his office; he did not take notes of his phone calls; and he had not deliberately withheld anything from Iran/contra investigators. During the interview, Weinberger was told that a document, contemporaneously written by someone Weinberger would consider credible, said that Weinberger had withheld some of his relevant Iran/contra notes.[89] Weinberger denied the allegation and stated he was distrustful of the author and his motivations.

Weinberger and his counsel were permitted to review the FBI agent's October 10, 1990, interview report when they returned to the Office of Independent Counsel for another interview on December 3, 1990.[90] Both Weinberger and his counsel complimented the report's accuracy and thoroughness and contrasted it favorably with the report of the 1988 interview, which had suggested he was an avid notetaker.

Between the October and December 1990 interviews, the OIC obtained Weinberger's permission to review his papers at the Library of Congress. Assuming that any documents relating to Iran/contra were classified[91] and relying on Weinberger's statements that the few notes he took were scribbled on the backs and margins of documents in his briefing books, OIC investigators asked both DoD and Library of Congress personnel where such materials would be located. The investigators were directed to the classified subject list in the Library's index to the Weinberger collection.[92] Investigators found no collection of notes among the materials they examined.

When OIC investigators returned to the Library of Congress in November 1991, they reviewed the entire index and found thousands of pages of diary and meeting notes that Weinberger had created as secretary of defense. These notes, which contained highly classified information, had been stored in the *unclassified* section of the Weinberger collection.[93]

Weinberger's notes proved to be an invaluable contemporaneous record of the views and activities of the highest officials regarding those sales.[94] They revealed, among other things, that contrary to his sworn testimony, Weinberger knew in advance that U.S. arms were to be shipped to Iran through Israel in November 1985 without congressional notification, in an effort to obtain the release of U.S. hostages, and that Israel expected the United States to replenish the weapons Israel shipped to Iran. Weinberger's notes also disclosed that, contrary to his sworn testimony, he knew that Saudi Arabia was secretly providing $25 million in assistance to the contras during a ban on U.S. aid.

---

[88] At the beginning of the October 10, 1990, interview, Weinberger produced an October 1, 1990, memorandum by Kay D. Leisz, his executive assistant at that time and throughout his tenure at the DoD, regarding the OIC's request for Weinberger's notes. Leisz's memo echoed Weinberger's assertion that, other than notes he took in his briefing books during his first year as Secretary of Defense, no notes were retained. (Memorandum for the Record by Leisz, 10/1/90, ALZ 0051360.)

[89] The August 7, 1987, Hill note.

[90] Weinberger's counsel had asked to review the FBI report of the October 10, 1990, interview because of Weinberger's criticisms of the earlier FBI report.

[91] Almost all high-level documents regarding the Iran arms sales and the Reagan Administration's efforts to obtain foreign support for the contras are highly classified.

[92] In what may have been a misunderstanding, the OIC investigators did not believe they were at liberty to examine other parts of the index and therefore did not see the references to diary and meeting notes in the description of unclassified material.

[93] The OIC immediately informed the Library of Congress and the Department of Defense of the security breach. After reviewing Weinberger's notes, the DoD determined that "classified information [had] inadvertently been included in the unclassified portion of the Weinberger collection at the Library of Congress" and recalled Weinberger's diary notes and activity logs to the Pentagon pending a formal security review. (Letter from Sterlacci to Stansbury, 6/12/92, 019316.)

[94] During his interview with the Tower Commission, Weinberger lamented the fact that there were not "accurate minutes taken of all [NSC and NSPG] meetings." (Weinberger, Tower Commission Interview, 1/14/87, pp. 43–44.) He conceded that someone might have taken notes of the relevant meetings but said, "I don't know of any." (Ibid., p. 46.) Weinberger recommended strongly that accurate records be kept of such meetings in the future to show "who said what to whom and when." (Ibid., pp. 44, 46.)

## Investigation, Indictment and Pretrial Proceedings in *United States* v. *Weinberger*

By late January 1992, Weinberger's conduct had become a focus of the OIC's investigation.[95]

On March 30, 1992, the OIC notified Weinberger that he was a target of a federal Grand Jury investigation of possible crimes, including obstruction, false statements and perjury. Independent Counsel invited Weinberger's voluntary testimony before the Grand Jury. Although Weinberger ultimately declined to appear before the Grand Jury or make any statements before an FBI Agent, he did, at his request, make his own presentation to Independent Counsel and other OIC attorneys on May 12, 1992. In addition, in extended efforts to resolve the matter, OIC attorneys met frequently and at length over a 10-week period with Weinberger's counsel.[96]

In the course of these discussions, Independent Counsel asked Weinberger to provide complete and truthful information on a range of topics, including positions that Reagan Administration officials took before Congress and the public in November 1986. Weinberger and his counsel insisted, however, that Weinberger had no information to provide that went beyond his previous statements. Weinberger and his counsel claimed that Weinberger had never associated his diary notes with Iran/contra document requests because his note-taking was as habitual and unconscious as brushing his teeth. They also claimed that none of Weinberger's aides had asked him to produce his notes. Weinberger denied present knowledge of the information

recorded in his handwritten diary and meeting notes and would not acknowledge the inconsistencies between his notes and his testimony. In an effort to demonstrate that Weinberger lacked criminal intent, his attorneys also submitted to the OIC a report of a private polygraph examination of Weinberger and a psychologist's report regarding Weinberger's memory. Both concluded that Weinberger had not intentionally concealed his notes from Congress or the OIC.[97]

The OIC found Weinberger's presentations unconvincing. Independent Counsel thereafter presented an indictment to the Grand Jury, which was returned on June 16, 1992.

The indictment contained five felony counts charging Weinberger with:

—Count One, obstruction of a congressional investigation by concealing and withholding relevant notes;

—Count Two, making false statements to Congress regarding his knowledge of Saudi Arabia's funding of the contras;

—Count Three, perjury before Congress about his knowledge of the planned shipment of HAWK missiles to Iran in November 1985;

—Count Four, perjury before Congress about his knowledge of the issue of replenishing missiles that Israel had shipped to Iran; and

---

[95] In the course of the Weinberger investigation, the OIC requested and reviewed numerous DoD documents relating to the Iran arms sales and DoD's document-production efforts, and questioned more than 25 witnesses in interviews and in the Grand Jury. The central witnesses included Weinberger's personal secretaries at DoD, Kay D. Leisz and Thelma Stubbs Smith; former DoD General Counsel H. Lawrence Garrett III; former DoD Assistant General Counsel Edward J. Shapiro; former DoD officials Richard L. Armitage and William H. Taft IV; General Colin L. Powell; and Library of Congress personnel.

[96] Independent Counsel recognized that Weinberger had a distinguished public career and that he had strongly opposed the Iran arms sales. OIC representatives met with Weinberger's attorneys on at least 12 separate occasions between April 1 and May 13, 1992. After Weinberger's counsel requested additional time to work with their client, Independent Counsel agreed not to present a proposed indictment to the special Iran/contra Grand Jury whose two-year term expired on May 15, 1992. Independent Counsel met with Weinberger's attorneys on June 2, 1992, to permit a final presentation by them. Subsequently an indictment was presented to and returned by a different Grand Jury.

[97] The polygraph report concluded that no deception was indicated when Weinberger denied having intentionally misled or lied to Iran/contra investigators about his diary notes, denied having deliberately withheld his diary notes, and denied misleading investigators about his knowledge of arms transfers to Iran from August through November 1985. (Polygraph Examination Report, 5/5/92, ALZ 0046855–56.) The psychologist's report concluded that Weinberger's note-taking was so "routine, compulsive and habitual" that it was not "stored in memory for easy retrieval" and that the questioning of Weinberger "lacked sufficient specificity" to trigger a recollection of his notes. (Letter from Fishburne to Bennett, 6/1/92, pp. 3–4, ALZ 0047613–14.) Although Fishburne apparently reviewed Weinberger's congressional deposition, in which Weinberger was questioned about his note-taking (Ibid., p. 1), he did not review other evidence the Government would have used at trial to show Weinberger's consciousness of his notes.

The district court later ruled that neither the polygraph examination result nor expert testimony on memory could be admitted at trial. (Memorandum Opinion and Pretrial Order No. 15, *United States* v. *Weinberger*, Crim. No. 92–0235–TFH (D.D.C. Dec. 21, 1992).)

—Count Five, false statements to the Office of Independent Counsel and the FBI regarding his note-taking.[98]

Weinberger was arraigned on June 19, 1992, and pleaded not guilty to all charges. The case was ultimately set for trial on January 5, 1993. Hearings to resolve classified information issues under the Classified Information Procedures Act (CIPA) were scheduled for December 7, 1992, with a November 2 deadline for the Government to produce the documents it intended to use in its case-in-chief.

On September 29, 1992, the district court granted Weinberger's motion to dismiss Count One.[99] The court held that Count One, in effect, charged Weinberger with lying to Congress, which did not constitute obstruction under the decision in *United States* v. *Poindexter*.[100] Rather than appeal the district court's decision, Independent Counsel sought a new indictment charging Weinberger under 18 U.S.C. § 1001 with the same false statements to Congress that had been alleged in the original Count One. The new indictment was returned on October 30, 1992.[101] On December 11, 1992, the district court granted Weinberger's motion to dismiss

the new indictment on statute-of-limitation grounds.[102] On December 24, 1992, President Bush pardoned Weinberger. At the time of President Bush's pardon, Independent Counsel had not yet decided whether to appeal the district court's ruling.

## The Government's Case Against Weinberger

The Government's trial evidence would have demonstrated that, contrary to the impression created by his false testimony before Congress, Weinberger was a knowing participant in the initiative to send arms to Iran in return for the release of Americans held hostage in Lebanon. In the summer of 1985, Weinberger knew of President Reagan's decision to authorize Israel to send missiles to Iran and his commitment to replenish Israel's missile stocks. Beginning in late September 1985 and continuing through the end of 1986, Weinberger also received a sizeable quantity of highly classified intelligence reports regarding the Iran initiative.[103] These intelligence reports provided detailed information regarding the pricing and delivery of missiles sold to Iran and the release of American hostages in Lebanon. In particular, in very late November and early December 1985, the reports revealed that HAWK missiles

---

[98] Indictment, *United States* v. *Caspar W. Weinberger*, Criminal No. 92–0235–TFH (D.D.C. June 16, 1992).

[99] Memorandum Opinion and Pretrial Order No. 6, *United States* v. *Weinberger*, Crim. No. 92–0235–TFH, pp. 4–5 (D.D.C. Sept. 29, 1992).

[100] 951 F.2d 369 (D.C. Cir. 1991), *cert. denied*, 113 S. Ct. 656 (1992). The obstruction statute outlaws, among other things, "corruptly" "obstruct[ing]" or "imped[ing]" a congressional inquiry. (18 U.S.C. § 1505.) The Court of Appeals held in *Poindexter* that the term "corruptly" implies that a defendant must cause another knowingly to violate a legal duty and found that the term was therefore unconstitutionally vague as applied to a defendant charged with lying to Congress himself rather than causing another to do so. (951 F.2d at 379, 385–86.)

The OIC had argued that *Poindexter* did not preclude the obstruction charge against Weinberger because the indictment alleged that Weinberger had obstructed Congress not merely by lying but also by withholding and concealing his relevant notes. The *Poindexter* decision left open the possibility that concealing or destroying documents could be considered analogous to causing a witness to lie or withhold testimony and therefore would satisfy the court's interpretation of the term "corruptly." (Ibid. at 384, citing *United States* v. *Walasek*, 527 F.2d 676, 679 & n.11 (3d Cir. 1975); cf. *United States* v. *Rasheed*, 663 F.2d 843, 852 (9th Cir. 1981), *cert. denied*, 454 U.S. 1157 (1982).)

[101] Indictment, *United States* v. *Caspar W. Weinberger*, Criminal No. 92–0416–TFH (D.D.C. Oct. 30, 1992). Weinberger had moved on August 3, 1992, to disqualify Deputy Independent Counsel Craig A. Gillen from trying the case on the ground that Gillen was a witness to Weinberger's October 10, 1990, interview. Gillen withdrew voluntarily from the case on October 9, 1992, following the District Court's preliminary ruling on this issue. Substitute trial counsel James J. Brosnahan was appointed on October 15, 1992. Brosnahan would have tried the case with Associate Counsel John Q. Barrett, George C. Harris, and Christina A. Spaulding.

[102] Memorandum Opinion and Pretrial Order No. 12, *United States* v. *Weinberger*, Crim. No. 92–0235–TFH (D.D.C. Dec. 11, 1992). Although the charged statement was beyond the five-year statute of limitations, 18 U.S.C. § 3288 provides that when a count is dismissed for "any reason" after the statute of limitations has run, the prosecution may bring a new indictment based upon the same facts within six months of the dismissal. To be proper under section 3288, the new indictment must be based on "essentially the same facts as those alleged in the old indictment" so that the defendant is on notice, within the statute of limitations, of the basis for the new charges. (Pretrial Order No. 12, at 4 quoting *United States* v. *George*, 1992 U.S. Dist. LEXIS 9618 (D.D.C. July 8, 1992).)

The District Court acknowledged that, under this standard, Weinberger "clearly had notice of the factual basis for the charges" in the new indictment. (Ibid.) The court expressed "concern" that the specific statements alleged to be false had not been underlined in the first indictment but did not find this point dispositive. (Ibid., pp. 4, 6.) Rather, the court went on to hold that even though the new indictment was premised on the same *facts* as the first indictment, it impermissibly broadened the original charges because the obstruction *statute*, as construed in *Poindexter*, does not include false statements. (Ibid., pp. 5–6.)

[103] In his testimony before congressional committees, Weinberger falsely claimed that he had been cut off "to a large extent" from this intelligence until shortly before December 7, 1985, when he first received one of these reports. (Weinberger, SSCI Testimony, 12/17/86, pp. 6–9, 51; Weinberger, HPSCI Testimony, 12/18/86, pp. 39–41; Weinberger, Select Committees Testimony, 7/31/87, pp. 92–94.)

were shipped to Iran from Israel in connection with hostage-recovery efforts.

The Government's evidence also would have shown that Weinberger deliberately concealed from Iran/contra investigators his diary and meeting notes, which would have demonstrated the falsity of his testimony.

For simplicity of discussing the evidence supporting the individual counts, this Report begins with the evidence proving the falsity of Weinberger's denial of the existence of his notes, which was charged in the original Count One and Count Five. Because Count One was dismissed, this discussion begins with Count Five.

## Count Five: Weinberger's Denial of the Existence of His Notes

Count Five charged Weinberger with making false statements in the October 10, 1990, interview with members of Independent Counsel's staff and a special agent of the FBI. Weinberger's attorney had been advised beforehand that the purpose of the interview was to discuss Weinberger's notes, and Weinberger brought to the interview a memorandum from his personal secretary that addressed this very issue. During the interview, Weinberger was asked repeatedly, in several different ways, about his note-taking practices. He insisted that he rarely took notes; that, as a rule, he did not take any notes when he met with the President or other Cabinet members; and that he specifically did not take any notes during meetings concerning the Iran arms sales. Weinberger also stated that he did not make a record of his meetings when he returned to the Pentagon and did not take notes of telephone conversations. He stated that he had always followed President Reagan's instructions to turn everything over to Iran/contra investigators and said that he was not aware of any relevant notes that had not been turned over. He insisted he had not deliberately withheld anything from Iran/contra investigators.[104]

To establish the deliberate falsity of Weinberger's statements, the Government would have proved at trial that (1) Weinberger maintained voluminous notes of meetings and phone calls, many of which were relevant to Iran/contra; (2) Weinberger knew in 1987 of congressional requests for his notes and diaries but produced none of them, and went so far as to lie under oath to conceal their existence from congressional investigators;[105] and (3) on his retirement as secretary of defense, Weinberger privately deposited his notes in the Library of Congress where no one could see them without his permission.

### Weinberger's Note-Taking Practices

Throughout his career, Weinberger regularly took detailed notes, primarily in pencil, of his daily activities, including summaries of his meetings and telephone conversations. While secretary of defense, Weinberger took more than 7,000 pages of these daily "diary notes" on 5" x 7" government-issue note pads.[106] He took nearly 1,700 pages of such notes in 1985 and 1986 alone. During the same period, Weinberger compiled hundreds of pages of notes taken during White House and Cabinet meetings. More than 150 pages of these diary and meeting notes contain information relevant to Iran/contra, including information that contradicts Weinberger's sworn testimony concerning his knowledge of the Iran arms sales and of Saudi Arabian contributions to the contras.

According to General Powell, who served as Weinberger's senior military assistant from July 1983 to March 1986, Weinberger kept the 5" x 7" note pads on his desk and jotted down entries throughout the day. Weinberger stored completed note pads in his desk drawer and transferred them to the bedroom attached to his

---

[104] Weinberger, FBI 302, 10/10/90. Weinberger later claimed that he believed the OIC was inquiring only about notes he took *during* meetings and therefore did not understand the questions to include his diary notes. (Weinberger Interview, ABC "This Week with David Brinkley," 12/27/92, NEXIS Tr. at 12). This explanation is disingenuous, because Weinberger stated in his October 10, 1990, interview that he very rarely took notes during meetings—which was, in itself, false—and *also* denied that he made any other record of meetings when he returned to his office or that he took notes of telephone

conversations. In fact, Weinberger's diary notes consist primarily of notes of telephone conversations and of meetings, made after the fact.

[105] Weinberger filed a motion *in limine* on December 14, 1992, seeking to prevent the Government from introducing at trial any evidence regarding the Select Committees' requests for Weinberger's notes and diaries. The Government opposed this motion on the ground that evidence that Weinberger had deliberately concealed his notes from Congress was admissible as intrinsic evidence of the falsity of his statements to the OIC and as extrinsic evidence under Federal Rule of Evidence 404(b) to show Weinberger's motive to lie to the OIC. The district court had not yet ruled on the motion at the time of the pardon.

[106] The term "diary notes" was adopted by the Library of Congress archivists to describe Weinberger's daily notes. Although Weinberger apparently referred to these documents as his "telephone logs," (Leisz, Grand Jury, 3/6/92, pp. 34–35), this report uses the Library of Congress terminology.

office when the drawer was full.[107] Powell's successor, Admiral Donald S. Jones, said there were "better than one or two linear feet" of papers, bound together with rubber bands, on the shelf in Weinberger's bedroom at DoD.[108] Several witnesses stated that Weinberger intended to use his diary notes to write his memoirs.[109] In 1988, while working on his book *Fighting for Peace,* Weinberger and his research assistant John C. Duncan reviewed some of the Weinberger diary notes that had been deposited at the Library of Congress.[110] Duncan recalled that they joked about the illegibility of Weinberger's handwriting. They decided that Weinberger's handwritten notes would be too difficult to use as a source for *Fighting for Peace* but agreed that the notes would be useful when Weinberger wrote a more comprehensive memoir that tracked his daily experiences.[111]

Weinberger also regularly took notes of meetings on White House note pads, on the backs of documents, and on other stray pieces of paper. In addition to his own meeting notes, many of which are identified by typed or handwritten notations made by Weinberger's secretaries, Weinberger saved notes and doodles passed to him by others, which he labeled and dated himself. Some of Weinberger's meeting notes were kept in a "Handwritten Notes" file maintained by his secretaries.[112] The remainder, which include most of Weinberger's meeting notes relevant to Iran/contra, were maintained by Weinberger himself in the same manner as his diary notes.

At trial, the Government would have shown that the sheer volume of Weinberger's notes, and the care he took in maintaining them for posterity, belied his contention that his notetaking was so habitual that he never thought of his notes.[113] The Government also would have demonstrated that Weinberger could not have forgotten his notes, having recorded *in* his diary the very meetings in which he was asked by Iran/contra investigators about his notes or diaries.

## Weinberger's Knowledge of Congressional Requests for His Notes and Diaries

Weinberger's notes and other contemporaneous documents show that he knew of the Select Committees' requests for handwritten notes and diaries. Despite his direction to others to cooperate fully with the congressional investigation, Weinberger deliberately withheld his own notes from Congress and falsely denied to congressional investigators that he had contemporaneous notes of meetings and phone calls.[114]

107 General Powell described Weinberger's note-taking in detail in an affidavit obtained by Weinberger's attorneys before the indictment. (Powell, Affidavit, 4/21/92, ¶¶ 3–4, ALZ 0045089.) Powell also stated that he regarded these notes as Weinberger's personal diaries and expressed the opinion that "it is entirely possible that it would not have occurred to [Weinberger] to associate or link these private notes on the 5 x 7 pads with a governmental request for 'notes' in the context of the Iran-Contra matter." (Ibid., ¶ 3.) On two separate occasions in 1987, however, Powell told congressional Iran/contra investigators that he had no knowledge of Weinberger maintaining a "diary." (Powell, Select Committees Interview Memorandum, 4/20/87, p. 9, AMY 000568; Powell, Select Committees Deposition, 6/19/87, pp. 54–55.) The inconsistencies in Powell's testimony are discussed below.

108 Jones, FBI 302, 12/22/92, p. 4. On one occasion, Jones noticed that Weinberger was taking notes of their conversation as they were talking. (Ibid.)

109 Smith, Affidavit, 4/29/92, ¶ 5, ALZ 0045122; Leisz, Grand Jury, 3/6/92, p. 35; Duncan, Grand Jury, 3/6/92, pp. 25–26; Taft, FBI 302, 4/8/92, p. 2; accord Weinberger, *Fighting for Peace,* p. 17 (expressing hope to write later book covering on a "day-to-day basis" his seven years as secretary of defense).

Weinberger's 1981 diary notes contain repeated references to discussions with the British scholar and biographer Janet Morgan regarding his "biography + diaries." (Weinberger Diary, 3/16/81, ALZ 0060966; ibid., 3/17/81, ALZ 0060969; ibid., 3/27/81, ALZ 0060995; ibid., 3/30/81, ALZ 0061001; ibid., 4/4/81, ALZ 0061022; ibid., 4/9/81, ALZ 0061033; ibid., 10/24/81, ALZ 0061542.) Pentagon spokesperson Henry E. Catto, Jr. publicly identified Morgan in February 1982 as a prospective biographer of Weinberger. (DoD News Briefing, 2/2/82, pp. 1–2, ALZ 0070079–80.) Morgan denied in October 1992 that she had ever seen Weinberger's diary notes or discussed the notes with him as a possible basis for a biography or autobiography. (Morgan, FBI 302, 10/12/92, pp. 11–13; Morgan FBI 302, 10/14/92, pp. 2, 8.)

110 Weinberger signed the Manuscript Reading Room register on July 20, 1988. (AOZ 0000036.) Library call slips show that on the same day Duncan checked out boxes 580–85, which contain Weinberger's diary notes from his tenure as secretary of defense. (ALZ 0042861 (7–20–88, call slip); Memorandum from Teichroew to Wigdor, 12/22/92, AOZ 0000183–84 (explaining that 1980–87 diary notes were located in boxes 579–85 in 1988).)

111 Duncan, Grand Jury, 3/6/92, pp. 25–26, 34–35. *Fighting for Peace* nevertheless contains some references to Weinberger's notes. (See, for example, Weinberger, *Fighting for Peace,* pp. 96, 381.)

112 See, for example, Smith, Affidavit, 4/29/92, ¶ 7, ALZ 0045122–23.

113 Following the summary of a meeting in his diary notes, Weinberger would sometimes cross-reference his meeting notes by indicating parenthetically "see separate memo." (Weinberger Diary, 9/28/84, ALZ 0063118; ibid., 6/24/85, ALZ 0039500; ibid., 10/27/86, ALZ 0040497; ibid., 11/10/86, ALZ 0040525; ibid., 11/12/86, ALZ 0040531; ibid., 11/25/86, ALZ 0040562; ibid., 9/15/87, ALZ 0046894.) These references further demonstrate Weinberger's consciousness of his notes.

114 Both the House and Senate Select Committees considered contemporaneous notes to be particularly important to their investigation of Iran/contra. In a statement appended to the Select Committees' report on the Iran/contra investigation, Senators Inouye and Rudman—the Chairman and Vice Chairman, respectively, of the Senate Select Committee—praised President Reagan for making excerpts of his personal diaries available to the Select Committees and for instructing other executive branch officials similarly to make all of their relevant records

During Weinberger's March 11, 1987, interview with the staff of the Senate Select Committee, Chief Counsel Arthur L. Liman told him that President Reagan's diary excerpts had been very useful to the Select Committees' investigation and remarked that he hoped to use these diary excerpts at the hearings.[115] Weinberger stated that his own record-keeping habits were poor and said that he regretted he did not keep copious records of meetings as Henry Kissinger had done.[116] As staff counsel noted in a memorandum of the interview, Weinberger left the clear impression that he did not keep diaries or dictate his thoughts about a day's events.[117] When the interview was over, Weinberger made the following entry in his daily diary notes: "2 Senate staff of Special Iran Committee in office—with Larry Garrett—re my recollections of Iran events." [118]

The Senate and House Select Committees made formal written requests on April 4 and April 13, 1987, respectively, for Weinberger's notes and diaries.[119] The DoD General Counsel's office relayed these requests to DoD officials in a series of internal memoranda. At least one of these—an April 14 memorandum regarding the Senate Select Committee's document request—reached Weinberger's desk and was stamped "SEC DEF HAS SEEN APR 20 1987." [120]

A singularly incriminating document is an April 17, 1987, "Action Memorandum" from DoD General Counsel H. Lawrence Garrett III to Weinberger that described the Senate and House requests for notes and diaries.[121] Garrett advised Weinberger:

> I know you understand the nature of the obligations placed upon us by this request. I understand that these materials, if any such exist, are highly personal and sensitive. Accordingly, I would of course insist that any provision of these materials to the Committees be conducted in as discreet and limited a manner as you wish.

The memorandum further advised Weinberger that Garrett would determine what "the arrangements currently are for the review of any similar records of other top-ranking officials." It concluded by stating that Garrett would "await further information/instructions from" Weinberger. Weinberger underlined the reference to other officials and wrote a note below: "Larry—let's have a meeting after you hear what others are doing." [122]

The Garrett memorandum discredits any claim that Weinberger's subordinates simply failed to ask him for his notes. In fact, Garrett told Weinberger, specifically and in writing, that Congress had requested his handwritten notes and diaries.[123] The memorandum also belies Weinberger's claim that he had no reason to believe that the congressional document requests encompassed personal documents such as his diary notes.[124] Not only did Garrett tell him

available. Rudman and Inouye noted that administration officials had been asked to disclose *personal* documents and remarked that "[t]hose of us who keep diaries appreciate the intensely personal and private nature of the entries we make in such books, confiding our innermost concerns, aspirations and thoughts." (Majority Report, p. 637.)

[115] Weinberger, Select Committees Interview Memorandum, 3/11/87, p. 2, AMY 00205.

[116] Ibid., pp. 4–5, AMY 00207–8. Weinberger repeated his Kissinger analogy when asked again about notes during his June 17, 1987, congressional deposition. (Weinberger, Select Committees Deposition, 6/17/87, p. 79.)

[117] Weinberger, Select Committees Interview Memorandum, 3/11/87, p. 5, AMY 00208.

[118] Weinberger Diary, 3/11/87, ALZ 0042242.

[119] Letter from Belnick to Shapiro, 4/4/87, ALZ 0041455–64; Letter from Naughton to Shapiro, 4/13/87, ALT 0001378–79.

[120] Memorandum from Garrett to Under Secretary of Defense (Policy) [Ikle], Assistant Secretary of Defense (ISA) [Armitage], Assistant General Counsels (OSD), Assistants to the Secretary of Defense, et al., 4/14/87, p. 1, ALZ 0047336–51. Documents were stamped "SEC DEF HAS SEEN," with the date, after Weinberger's secretary removed them from the out box on his desk. (Leisz, Grand Jury, 3/6/92, p. 8.)

[121] Action Memorandum from Garrett to Weinberger Re: Document Request from Congressional Select Committee on Iran, 4/17/87, ALZ 0064947–48.

[122] Ibid. The Garrett memorandum was stamped "SEC DEF HAS SEEN" on June 17, 1987, indicating that Weinberger placed the document in his out box on the same day that he stated falsely in his congressional deposition that he rarely took notes.

[123] Garrett's April 17, 1987, memorandum contradicts his 1992 affidavit, which asserted that he did not discuss with Weinberger "the specific details" of any Iran/contra document request and did not ask Weinberger "about the existence of personal notes or diaries." (Garrett, Affidavit, 4/28/92, ¶¶ 7, 11, ALZ 0045034–36.) Similarly, although Weinberger's senior military assistant at that time, Gen. Gordon Fornell, asserted in an affidavit that he was "unaware of anyone ever asking Secretary Weinberger to produce his informal jottings to any body investigating the Iran-contra affair," Fornell later identified his handwritten initial "F" in the margin of Garrett's April 17, 1987, memorandum to Weinberger, next to the paragraph noting that the House Select Committee "has requested all . . . diaries . . . and handwritten notes kept by you" relating to various topics, including Iran. (Compare Fornell, Affidavit, 4/24/92, ¶ 6, ALZ 0045025–26, with Fornell, Grand Jury, 10/28/92, p. 31.)

[124] Weinberger, CNN Interview, 12/28/92, NEXIS Transcript p. 6; Weinberger, Fox Morning News Interview, 12/29/92, NEXIS Transcript p. 2.

Weinberger's secretary, Kay Leisz, said she had a general recollection that in connection with the Iran/contra document production "someone" told Weinberger that there was a distinction between "personal" and that the requests included "highly personal and sensitive" papers, but Weinberger focused specifically on that part of the memorandum in asking Garrett to find out what other officials "are doing." [125]

Weinberger's diary notes indicate that Garrett raised this subject with him again in a meeting on April 21, 1987, after which Weinberger wrote: "Larry Garrett in office—re demands by Sen—House Committees for briefings on black programs— + their demand for my diary[.]" [126]

There is also circumstantial evidence that Garrett raised the issue with Weinberger a third time, on April 30, 1987, and may have advised him of the arrangements that had been made for Iran/contra investigators to review President Reagan's diaries. On April 29, 1987, Garrett and Assistant General Counsel Edward J. Shapiro attended a White House meeting of the general counsels' group that coordinated Administration responses to the congressional and OIC Iran/contra investigations. The attorneys discussed the terms on which the Select Committees and the OIC were permitted to review excerpts of President Reagan's personal diaries.[127] The same day, Garrett sent an "Information Memorandum" to Deputy Secretary of

Defense William H. Taft IV regarding "Congressional Request for Excerpts of Relevant Portions of the Diaries of the SecDef." The memorandum advised Taft that "[w]e have been asked again by the senior legal staff of the Senate Select Committee on Iran whether the SecDef keeps diaries. . . ." The memorandum then related to Taft that White House counsel had made transcribed excerpts of President Reagan's diaries available to the Select Committees and the OIC, subject to certain restrictions. The memorandum concluded: "I do not know whether the Secretary keeps a diary, but it is obviously necessary to pursue this." [128]

Taft recalled that he had told Garrett during the Iran/contra investigation that Weinberger had regularly kept notes during the Nixon Administration, and Taft had advised Garrett to go to Leisz and Weinberger to be sure that, if Weinberger still kept such notes, everything was produced to Iran/contra investigators.[129] Although Taft could not fix the date of this conversation, Garrett's April 29 memorandum to Taft was stamped "DEP SEC HAS SEEN" on April 30, 1987. On the same day, Weinberger made the following entry in his daily diary notes: "Larry Garrett in office re preparation for Senate House staff interview on Iran hgs—also re papers to be turned over." [130]

The day after Garrett's conversation with Weinberger, on May 1, 1987, Mark A. Belnick, executive assistant to the chief counsel of the Senate Select Committee, spoke to Shapiro and recorded in a file memorandum that Shapiro "had been informed *by Secretary Weinberger's office*" that Weinberger had "no entries in his diaries responsive to [the Senate] requests," and that Weinberger had some "but not many" notes responsive to the requests.[131]

---

"official" documents, and it was her "feeling" that personal documents did not have to be produced. (Leisz, OIC Interview, 6/15/92, pp. 26–28.) Neither Weinberger nor his attorneys ever claimed that he had been advised that personal documents did not have to be produced to Iran/contra investigators. Garrett's memorandum reached the opposite conclusion, and he testified that he specifically advised Smith, in Leisz's presence, that the document requests included "personal notes." (Garrett, Grand Jury, 4/22/92, pp. 18–19.) Garrett did not recall giving Weinberger advice to the contrary. (Garrett, Grand Jury, 10/28/92, p. 32.)

[125] President Reagan's agreement to allow congressional investigators limited access to his personal diaries was also widely publicized. It also was widely known, at least by the time the congressional hearings were underway, that other Administration officials, including Shultz's executive assistant Charles Hill, had produced some of their relevant, personal notes to congressional investigators.

[126] Weinberger Diary, 4/21/87, ALZ 0042343. Weinberger's attorneys claimed that this note actually reads "demand for my *choices*" and refers not to Iran/contra but to some unspecified matter regarding "black programs" that may have been pending before the Senate and House intelligence committees in April 1987. They submitted a report from a private handwriting expert who concluded that it was "highly probable" that the disputed word was "choices." (Document Examination Report, 5/27/92, ALZ 0047624.) The OIC would have established at trial, based on comparisons to other samples of Weinberger's handwriting, that the disputed word is "diary." The "black programs" mentioned in Weinberger's note refers to an April 1, 1987, request from the staff of the Senate Select Committee for briefings on limited access ("black") programs. (Letter from Saxon to Shapiro, 4/1/87, ALZ 0054812.)

[127] General Counsels' Coordinating Group Meeting Minutes, 4/29/87, ALU 140159–64.

[128] Memorandum from Garrett to Taft Re: Congressional Request for Excerpts of Relevant Portions of the Diaries of the SecDef, 4/29/87, ALZ 0058007.

[129] Taft, FBI 302, 4/8/92, p. 2; Taft, Grand Jury, 10/28/92, pp. 27–29. Taft said he also advised Garrett that Smith and Leisz would know if Weinberger kept notes. (Taft, FBI 302, 4/8/92, p. 2.) Garrett recalled a conversation in which he told Smith and Leisz that the document requests included personal notes and he was told that Weinberger had no notes. (Garrett, Grand Jury, 4/22/92, pp. 18–19.) Garrett purported not to recall such a conversation with Taft, however.

[130] Weinberger Diary, 4/30/87, ALZ 0042366.

[131] Memorandum from Belnick to the File, 5/1/87, AMY 000361 (emphasis added). The House Select Committee continued separately to pursue Weinberger's notes and diaries. On May 22, 1987, Joseph H. Saba, staff counsel to the House Select Committee, wrote to Garrett, noting that the House Committee had received few documents from

In his June 17, 1987, congressional deposition Weinberger testified falsely that he rarely made notes of meetings—either contemporaneously or after the fact—and had no records that could supplement his memory regarding Iran/contra events.[132] As he made these statements under oath in his office, Weinberger was sitting only four feet from the desk drawer that contained his diary notes. After the deposition, Weinberger made the following entry in his daily diary notes: "Gave deposition to Senate + House staff members on Joint Iran investigation.—10:35 AM—1:10 PM Larry Garrett & Mr. Shapiro there."[133] That same day, Weinberger also placed Garrett's April 17, 1987, memorandum regarding the congressional document requests into his out box.[134]

---

Weinberger and asking for Weinberger's "diaries, appointment books, records of meetings, and handwritten notes. . . ." The letter further advised that the request "is inclusive of [Weinberger's] personal diary entries made from October 1984 through 1987, pertaining to the Boland Amendment, Iran, Nicaragua, and the Contras." (Letter from Saba to Garrett, 5/22/87, ALZ 0054598–600.)

On June 10, 1987, Saba wrote again to Shapiro, reiterating the House Committee's request for access to Weinberger's calendars and diaries, "and all other schedule-type records of the occurrence of meetings, events, and telephone conversations for the period July 1, 1985, through December 31, 1986." (Letter from Saba to Shapiro, 6/10/87, ALZ 0058754.) According to Weinberger's own diary notes, Gen. Fornell consulted him on June 15, 1987, two days before Weinberger's deposition, about "data on my calendar to be turned over to Jt. Iran Committee[.]" (Weinberger Diary, 6/15/87, ALZ 0042472.) The next day, Weinberger's official calendars and activity logs, but none of his diary or meeting notes, were produced to the House Select Committee. (Letter from Shapiro to Saxon, 6/18/87, ALZ 0055135–36 (enclosing documents produced to House Select Committee on 6/16/87 and memorandum describing documents)).

[132] Weinberger, Select Committees Deposition, 6/17/87, pp. 79–80. Ironically, given Weinberger's subsequent contention that he did not understand his "jottings" to be within the scope of congressional requests for "notes," (Weinberger, CNN Interview, 12/28/92, NEXIS Transcript p. 6), the following exchange occurred during Weinberger's congressional deposition:

Q: Do you ever take notes that are not dictated or make *jottings* when you get back [from meetings]?

A: Yes, occasionally, but comparatively rarely. I don't know that we kept those in any formal way. I don't think they have been filed or labeled. . . .

Q: If there is any chance there are——

A: I think we made this examination and whatever there is is in our so-called C&D, correspondence and directives. They have been asked to paw through everything.

Weinberger, Select Committees Deposition, 6/17/87, pp. 79–80. (emphasis added).) As discussed further below, the Government would have shown at trial that Weinberger was well aware that hundreds of pages of his diary notes and scores of pages of his meeting notes were stored in his desk and office bedroom and were not in the C&D files.

[133] Weinberger Diary, 6/17/87, ALZ 0042476.

[134] Memorandum from Garrett to Weinberger Re: Document Request from congressional Select Committee on Iran, 4/17/87, ALZ 0064947 (stamped "SEC DEF HAS SEEN JUN 17, 1987").

## Weinberger's Deposit of His Notes at the Library of Congress

Weinberger personally packed his diary notes as he was preparing to leave office in November 1987. On that day, Roger Sandler, a freelance photographer, was present to take photos for a magazine profile of Weinberger. These photos show Weinberger handling large stacks of his diary notes, neatly bundled together with binder clips and rubber bands. As Weinberger was taping boxes, he commented on his daily diary notes, and he and Sandler briefly discussed the fact that they both kept diaries.[135] Weinberger's diary notes subsequently were transferred to the Library of Congress without being submitted for classification review.[136]

Weinberger's meeting notes were transferred from the Pentagon to the Library of Congress in two sets. The "set A" notes arrived at the Library in April 1988 along with Weinberger's 1980–87 diary notes. The set A notes consist of *original* meeting notes by Weinberger and notes and doodles from others that were labeled and dated by Weinberger.[137] These notes, which include most of Weinberger's meeting notes relevant to Iran/contra, were kept by Weinberger himself and were not submitted for classification review before being transferred to the Library.[138]

The "set B" notes, which arrived at the Library in August 1988, consist of *copies* of

---

[135] Sandler, FBI 302, 7/28/92, p. 3.

[136] Receipt for 99 Unclassified Boxes of Secretary Weinberger's Personal Papers, 4/5/88, attaching Index of 14 Miscellaneous Boxes, including "Telephone Logs 1980; 1981–87," (Grand Jury Exhibit No. 326, 5/8/92.)

[137] The index of 14 miscellaneous boxes included in the April 1988 accession also listed one box of "Blank Note Pads; Notes from Meetings." (Ibid.)

[138] The following evidence indicates that Weinberger maintained the set A notes himself, separately from his secretaries' handwritten notes file: (1) none of the notes is stamped "SecDef Has Seen," indicating that they were never placed in his out box; (2) according to the Library of Congress archivist, these notes were bundled together under handwritten cover notes by Weinberger (ALZ 0040718–19) identifying them as miscellaneous notes of Cabinet and NSC meetings (Teichroew, OIC Deposition, 4/21/92, p. 37); and (3) the notes were not labeled or dated by anyone other than Weinberger. (Compare description of set B notes below.) Like the diary notes, the set A meeting notes are all originals and have no classification markings, even though they contain classified information.

The set A notes contain Weinberger's notes of the most significant Iran/contra meetings, including the December 10, 1985, White House meeting at which arms sales to Iran were discussed, the January 6 and 7, 1986, meetings on the Iran arms sales, a February 11, 1986, "Family Group" lunch meeting at which a schedule of arms transfers and hostage releases was outlined and the November 24, 1986, NSPG meeting regarding the Administration's response to public disclosure of the arms sales.

Weinberger's notes of other meetings.[139] Many of the set B notes are identified by typed or handwritten notations made by Weinberger's secretaries at the top of the first page. Unlike the set A notes, the set B notes were individually indexed and reviewed for classified information before they left DoD for the Library of Congress. The index is titled "SECRETARY Weinberger's HANDWRITTEN NOTES" and identifies the source of the notes as "VAULT." [140] Thelma Stubbs Smith, Weinberger's second personal secretary, described how the handwritten notes file maintained by Weinberger's secretaries (set B) was transferred to the vault in his inner office and that she packed these notes at the end of Weinberger's term, leaving the boxes with Defense Department C&D personnel to transfer to the Library of Congress.[141] Boxes containing meeting notes were subsequently sent to the Executive Secretariat where they were copied, sorted and indexed for transmittal to the Library.[142] Thus, contrary to Weinberger's suggestion during his congressional deposition, it appears that *none* of his meeting notes were stored in Defense Department C&D's files.[143]

Rather, both the set A and set B meeting notes were maintained outside DoD's recordkeeping system until Weinberger left office.

All of Weinberger's diary and meeting notes were deposited with the Manuscript Division of the Library of Congress as Weinberger's private property, under an agreement that provided expressly that no one could have access to Weinberger's papers without his permission.[144] Weinberger's repeated public assertions that his notes were deposited in "the most public depository in the United States" [145] are therefore grossly misleading. In fact, Weinberger refused in February 1990 to allow even the General Accounting Office access to the papers when it was attempting to monitor former agency heads' compliance with laws governing the removal of Government records.[146]

In summary regarding Count Five of the Indictment, the Government would have proven at trial that Weinberger had, since 1987, deliberately concealed his notes from Iran/contra investigators and that his false statements to the OIC in October 1990 were simply a continuation of those efforts. The Government also would have shown that Weinberger's motive for concealing his notes was simple: The notes disclosed that, contrary to his sworn testimony, Weinberger had contemporaneous knowledge of the Reagan Administration's involvement in arms sales to Iran in 1985, which Weinberger himself had argued at the time was illegal, and that he had greater knowledge of the Iran arms sales in 1986 than he had disclosed in his testimony.

Weinberger's notes also reflect frank and potentially embarrassing exchanges between President Reagan and his advisers, including President Reagan's sweeping rejection of concerns about illegality at the December 7, 1985, meeting. They also record the Administration's efforts in November 1986 to insulate President

---

[139] There is no overlap between the set A and set B meeting notes.

[140] ALZ 0040721 (3 pages) (index to 1985 set B meeting notes); ALZ 0040722 (3 pages) (index to 1986 set B meeting notes); ALZ 0040723 (3 pages) (1985 index showing classified items removed); ALZ 0040766 (1986 index showing classified items removed). The August 1988 Library of Congress accession included the "SecDef's Personal Library Vaulted Files (1981–87) and Complete Index." (ALZ 0042825 (8/9/88) (receipt for classified material).)

[141] Smith, Affidavit, 4/29/92, ¶¶ 7, 8, 10, ALZ 0045122–24. Smith suggested that the meeting notes listed on the index of 14 miscellaneous boxes included in the April 1988 Library of Congress accession (which contained the set A notes) were from the handwritten notes file in the office vault. (Ibid., ¶ 8.) The circumstantial evidence demonstrates, however, that the set B notes, rather than the set A notes, correspond to the handwritten notes file that Smith recalls packing: (1) only the set B notes were labeled by the secretaries; (2) only the set B notes contain documents stamped "SEC DEF HAS SEEN," indicating that Smith or Leisz had originally retrieved them from Weinberger's out box; and (3) the set B notes include a cover note by Leisz, attaching a set of notes on the TWA hijacking (ALZ 0060091) and a cover note by Powell to Leisz, attaching another set of notes "for your file" (ALZ 0060174).

[142] Lt. Col. Andrew Krepinevich, who worked in the Executive Secretariat in 1987–88, recalled receiving one or more boxes of material from Weinberger's vault, including a significant number of his handwritten meeting notes, to be processed for transfer to the Library. (Krepinevich, FBI 302, 3/16/92, pp. 2–3.) Krepinevich's description of these notes dovetails with Smith's description of the notes she packed, and the indices that accompanied the set B notes are identical to other indices generated by the Executive Secretariat. Although the OIC was not able to confirm the location of the original notes, Krepinevich said they would have been sent to storage at the National Archives and Records Administration's Washington National Records Center in Suitland, Maryland. (Ibid., p. 3.)

[143] Weinberger, Select Committees Deposition, 6/17/87, p. 80. The indices prepared by DoD list individual documents with their C&D-

assigned number, which has an X prefix; documents that do not have a C&D number have a blank space next to the X prefix. (See, e.g., DoD 1985 Subject Index A–I, ALZ 0043111–233.) *None* of the 1985 and 1986 set B meeting notes has a C&D number. ALZ 0040721 (3 pages) (index to 1985 set B meeting notes); ALZ 0040722 (3 pages) (index to 1986 set B meeting notes).

[144] Agreement of Deposit, 8/7/87, ALZ 0040904–6.

[145] Weinberger, Press Conference, 12/24/92, NEXIS Transcript, p. 39.

[146] General Accounting Office, Federal Records—Document Removal by Agency Heads Needs Independent Oversight, August 1991, pp. 23–25.

Reagan from knowledge of the 1985 arms sales to Iran.[147]

## Count Two: Weinberger's Denial of His Knowledge of Saudi Arabia's Financial Support for the Contras

Count Two of the Indictment charged Weinberger with making false statements to the Select Committees denying his knowledge that Saudi Arabia had contributed to the support of the Nicaraguan contras at a time when Congress had forbidden the use of appropriated funds for this purpose. One of the chief concerns of the congressional Iran/contra investigations was third-country assistance to the Nicaraguan contras.[148] Weinberger's daily diary notes and other contemporaneous documents reveal that he knew in the spring of 1984 that foreign countries including Saudi Arabia were being solicited to provide funds for the contras, and that he knew in the spring of 1985 that Saudi Arabia was providing $25 million in assistance to the contras. Yet on June 17, 1987, when he appeared as a witness before the staff of the Select Committees, Weinberger made the following statement under oath:

> Q: Do you recall learning at some point that the Saudis or some people connected with the Saudis provided funds for the contras?
>
> A: No. I don't have any memory of any contra funding or of anything connected with [the Saudis] that I can remember now.[149]

### The Importance to Weinberger of U.S. Relations With Saudi Arabia and the Survival of the Contras

Weinberger's daily diary notes during his nearly seven years as secretary of defense demonstrate that Saudi Arabia and Nicaragua were foreign policy matters of great concern to him.

During the period 1984–1987, Weinberger's daily diary notes record at least 64 separate contacts with Prince Bandar bin Sultan, the Saudi Ambassador to the United States. These

include 16 meetings, mostly private, in Weinberger's office;[150] telephone conversations on 18 separate days;[151] and 10 social events at which both men were present.[152] The subjects of Weinberger's dealings with Bandar, as recorded in Weinberger's daily diary, range from the birth of one of Bandar's children[153] to political strategy for handling the revelation of the Iran arms sales,[154] and include discussions of helping Saudi Arabia acquire United States weapon systems.[155]

Weinberger's daily diary similarly records his concern for the Nicaraguan contras and events in Central America. On hundreds of separate occasions during 1985 and 1986, he made daily diary entries about formal meetings within the Administration, telephone calls or private meetings at the Pentagon concerning such things as the latest military and political developments in the region, the prospects for obtaining funding from Congress for the contras, recent trips

---

[147] See, e.g. Weinberger NSPG Meeting Notes, 11/24/86, ALZ 0040669 (20 pages).

[148] See, e.g., Majority Report, pp. 15–16, 38–39, 44–47, 63, 69–71, 120–21.

[149] Weinberger, Select Committees Deposition, 6/17/87, p. 74.

[150] Weinberger Diary, 1/6/84, ALZ 0062780; ibid., 5/21/84, ALZ 0062949; ibid., 6/27/84, ALZ 0063000; ibid., 8/17/84, ALZ 0063062; ibid., 10/9/84, ALZ 0063133; ibid., 11/2/84, ALZ 0063161; ibid., 1/10/85, ALZ 0039233; ibid., 5/1/85, ALZ 0039404; ibid., 6/18/85, ALZ 0039488; ibid., 9/11/85, ALZ 0039648; ibid., 6/2/86, ALZ 0040174; ibid., 10/31/86, ALZ 0040508; ibid., 11/23/86, ALZ 0040556; ibid., 2/9/87, ALZ 0042167; ibid., 6/30/87, ALZ 0042496.

[151] Ibid., 2/6/84, ALZ 0062819; ibid., 2/9/84, ALZ 0062826; ibid., 5/20/84, ALZ 0062948; ibid., 6/5/84, ALZ 0062969; ibid., 10/8/84, ALZ 0063131; ibid., 11/5/84, ALZ 0063166; ibid., 7/29/85, ALZ 0039565; ibid., 10/9/85, ALZ 0039713A; ibid., 1/8/86, ALZ 0039887; ibid., 5/15/86, ALZ 0040157; ibid., 6/23/86, ALZ 0040228; ibid., 6/27/86, ALZ 0040243; ibid., 1/6/87, ALZ 0042084; ibid., 5/20/87, ALZ 0042416; ibid., 6/11/87, ALZ 0042462; ibid., 7/23/87, ALZ 0042551; ibid., 7/24/87, ALZ 0042555; ibid., 8/2/87, ALZ 0042574.

[152] Ibid., 1/31/84, ALZ 0062811; ibid., 5/6/84, ALZ 0062935; ibid., 9/24/84, ALZ 0063111; ibid., 1/20/85, ALZ 0039248; ibid., 2/13/85, ALZ 0039276; ibid., 12/10/85, ALZ 0039842; ibid., 2/5/86, ALZ 0039948; ibid., 3/4/86, ALZ 0040006D; ibid., 7/1/86, ALZ 0040254; ibid., 4/3/87, ALZ 0042295; ibid., 7/26/87, ALZ 0042559.

[153] Ibid., 7/11/87, ALZ 0042520.

[154] For example, as the Iran/contra scandal was breaking publicly, Weinberger's diary contains these notes regarding his private meeting with Prince Bandar on Sunday, November 23, 1986:

> Prince Bandar in office—Nancy Reagan—
> in a 1½ hr. talk Friday with him—he invited President to dinner at his Embassy—sd [said] she thinks Shultz should go—that he has been disloyal to the President—he sd he recommended to her that I be named Secretary of State; that I could negotiate an agreement with Soviets because no one could say I was soft on them—She feels that very few are being loyal to President + that Shultz should not have gone to Canada Friday + should support President—She would like Baker to go in as Secretary of Defense!

(Ibid., 11/23/86, ALZ 0040556.)

[155] E.g., 5/25/84, ALZ 0062956–57; ibid., 1/8/86, ALZ 0039887; ibid., 5/15/86, ALZ 0040157; ibid., 6/2/86, ALZ 0040174; ibid., 2/9/87, ALZ 0042167; ibid., 6/30/87, ALZ 0042496; ibid., 9/2/87, ALZ 0046865; ibid., 9/26/87, ALZ 0046921.

to Central America by other officials and his own dealings with contra leaders.[156]

Weinberger's congressional testimony and statements regarding Saudi funding for the contras consistently protected the false position taken by the Saudi Arabian Government: total denial of such support. On October 21, 1986, Prince Bandar issued the following press release from the Royal Embassy of Saudi Arabia in Washington, D.C.:

### Saudi Ambassador Denies Nicaraguan Involvement

The Ambassador of Saudi Arabia to the United States today issued the following statement in response to press inquiries.

"Saudi Arabia is not and has not been involved either directly or indirectly in any military or other support activity of any kind for or in connection with any group or groups concerned with Nicaragua." [157]

## Weinberger's Knowledge of Saudi Arabia's Support for the Contras

Weinberger's notes and other contemporaneous documents reveal his direct knowledge that Saudi Arabia had agreed to give financial support to the Nicaraguan contras during the period when U.S. funds for the contras were virtually exhausted and Congress had refused to appropriate additional funds.[158]

In May 1984, Prince Bandar informed National Security Adviser Robert C. McFarlane that Bandar would provide $1 million per month to the contras.[159] Weinberger's diary notes show

that, on Sunday, May 20, 1984, Prince Bandar asked Weinberger for an appointment.[160] Weinberger's very next diary note states that he

Called Bud McFarlane—re ~~agreed~~ f above—he wants to be sure there's no gap. . . .[161]

Although Weinberger's diary entry regarding his meeting with Prince Bandar shows discussion of topics other than the contras, Weinberger's diary the next day shows that he and McFarlane spoke about U.S. officials soliciting foreign countries to aid "Central America:"

Called Bud McFarlane—rhc [returned his call]—he doesn't want [Under Secretary of Defense for Policy Fred] Ikle working to get any Israeli, etc. aid for Cent Am

Called Colin Powell—re above [162]

On June 20, 1984, during a "Contra Money" meeting at the Department of State that was attended by senior Reagan Administration officials,[163] Weinberger stated his views on ensuring the survival of the contras:

Don't give up on the Congr chance, altho slim. But plan for other sources for $. Keep US fingerprints off.

\*              \*              \*

even if Congr turns us down, we must not let collapse happen [164]

Weinberger's diary notes also show his knowledge of Saudi Arabia's continuing, and expanded, support for the contras during 1985. On March 13, 1985, Weinberger made the fol-

---

[156] Weinberger's diary does not indicate, however, that he had any awareness of the contra resupply network in Central America or its connection to Oliver North during 1985 and 1986.

[157] Press Release from Bandar, 10/21/86, ALW 0063258. In 1987, Prince Bandar refused Independent Counsel's request for a personal interview and declined to provide answers to Independent Counsel's interrogatories regarding financial support for the contras. (Letter from Bandar to Shultz, 5/1/87, ALW 0063255–57.) In his letter to Secretary of State Shultz communicating this refusal to cooperate, Prince Bandar said that Saudi Arabia's "confidences and commitments, like our friendship, are given for not just the moment but the long run." (Ibid.) Prince Bandar also attached a copy of his October 21, 1986, public statement regarding the contras and asserted that "it would not be appropriate or constructive in a diplomatic or other sense to elaborate further on that clear position." (Ibid.) To Independent Counsel's knowledge, no official representative of the Saudi Kingdom ever admitted publicly that it provided money to the contras during 1984 and 1985.

[158] For a more complete discussion of third-country funding for the contras, see McFarlane chapter.

[159] E.g. McFarlane, FBI 302, 4/15/87 (morning session), p. 3 (placing Bandar's announcement in "June 1984"); McFarlane, Select Committees Testimony, 5/11/87, pp. 34–36.

[160] Weinberger Diary, 5/20/84, ALZ 0062948.

[161] Ibid.

[162] Ibid., 5/22/84, ALZ 0062950.

[163] Charles Hill, the executive assistant to Secretary of State Shultz, took detailed notes during this meeting. Hill's notes indicate that the meeting was attended by Shultz, Weinberger, Iklé, Kirkpatrick, Casey, McMahon, McFarlane, Poindexter and North, among others, and that Shultz, Weinberger, Kirkpatrick and McFarlane had a private meeting after the larger meeting had ended. (Hill Notes, 6/20/84, ANS 0000679–81.)

[164] Ibid., 6/20/84, ANS 0000680 (emphasis in original). Weinberger's corresponding diary entry is the following: "Attended meeting w/ Shultz, Jeane Kirkpatrick—Bill Casey, Bud McFarlane[,] Ikle—at State—re funding for Nicaragua—urged that we tell the Senate to stand fast on their vote despite Speaker's refusal to go along with George's requests for less. + then try to get the best we can in conference." (Weinberger Diary, 6/20/84, ALZ 0062989.)

lowing entries in his daily notes after a private meeting with General John W. Vessey, Jr., Chairman of the Joint Chiefs of Staff:

Jack Vessey in office alone—after meeting [with others]—Bandar is giving $25 million to Contras—so all we need is non-lethal aid

Called Bud McFarlane—out; l.w. [left word]

*          *          *

Called Bud McFarlane—passed on to him Jack Vessey's report that Bandar is giving $25 million to Contras— + suggested that if so—we go for covert non-lethal aid of $14 mil.[165]

Weinberger's daily notes indicate that he spoke with McFarlane again the following day about Saudi aid to the contras:

Called Bud McFarlane—No further news on Saudis gifts to Contras [166]

The following morning, March 15, 1985, Weinberger and Deputy Secretary of Defense William Howard Taft IV had their regular Friday breakfast with CIA Director Casey and Deputy Director John N. McMahon. McMahon's memorandum for the record, created that same day, documents the following discussion of the contras, including Saudi support:

Question of the support to the Contras came up. The Director [Casey] noted that we should have another meeting on it but following last week's meeting of the LSG [Legislative Strategy Group] we tended to be leaning towards non-lethal aid. I [McMahon] described the assignment given to [Assistant Secretary of State] Motley to develop different options which could be packaged and then played against Senators Lugar and Durenberger to see what combination of options in a single package might be acceptable to Congress. But I noted at the meeting that there was no agreement that we would be limited to non-lethal aid. The Director [Casey] said

that McFarlane was to meet with Lugar and Durenberger today. In closing the Secretary [Weinberger] stated that he had heard that Bandar, Ambassador of Saudi Arabia, had earmarked $25 million for the contras in $5 million increments.[167]

Credible witnesses corroborated Weinberger's knowledge of Saudi Arabia's support for the contras. General Vessey, who served as Chairman of the Joint Chiefs of Staff until he retired in September 1985, recalled that Bandar informed him on two occasions that the Saudis were funding the contras.[168] On each occasion, Vessey immediately reported Bandar's statements to Weinberger, who responded that he did not want this issue to become public.[169] Vessey recalls that he or Weinberger, during a White House conversation they had with McFarlane, urged McFarlane to support a proposed arms sale to Saudi Arabia because the Saudis were funding the contras.[170] McMahon confirmed two meetings in which Weinberger reported to McMahon and Casey that the Saudis were funding the contras.[171] McFarlane recalled a number of discussions with Weinberger regarding the Saudi contributions to the contras during 1984 and 1985. McFarlane testified that in May 1984, he told Weinberger and Shultz that an unnamed foreign country had agreed

---

[165] Ibid., 3/13/85, ALZ 0039320B–C.
[166] Ibid., 3/14/85, ALZ 0039323.

[167] Memorandum for the Record from McMahon, 3/15/85, ER 26,187–88 & ER 92–00116–17.
[168] Vessey, FBI 302, 6/11/92, pp. 6–7; accord Vessey, Select Committees Deposition, 4/17/87, pp. 5–8 (testimony regarding one occasion when Bandar told Vessey, who then reported to Weinberger, of a contribution to the contras).
[169] Vessey, FBI 302, 6/11/92, p. 7; Vessey, FBI 302, 2/11/87, p. 1.
[170] Vessey, FBI 302, 6/11/92, p. 7; cf. Vessey, Select Committees Deposition, 4/17/87, pp. 8–9 (". . . . I have wracked my mind trying to think of a conversation with McFarlane. And it seems to me that at one time we came out of a National Security Council or National Security Planning Group meeting in the NSC wing of the White House, and that some conversation with McFarlane took place about the Saudis, about them helping the contras. But I don't recall the substance of it or anything other than it being sort of a casual thing as we went out."). Although General Vessey stated in 1992 that this incident at the White House had occurred after Prince Bandar had informed him for the second time that the Saudis were funding the contras, Vessey also recalled that the subject of his and Weinberger's meeting with McFarlane was a specific classified proposal involving arms sales to the Saudis. (Vessey, FBI 302, 6/11/92, p. 7; see also Classified Appendix.) Based upon Vessey's recollection of the subject matter, contemporaneous records indicate that this conversation occurred on the morning of May 25, 1984, when Vessey accompanied Weinberger to a White House meeting on this subject. (Weinberger Diary, 5/25/84, ALZ 0062956 ("Jack Vessey in office—wants to go to meeting with President—also re [Classified Arms Sale Proposal] . . . Attended Meeting in Oval Office—with President, Bud McFarlane, ~~Shultz~~, Vice President, Shultz, Ed Meese, Baker—[specific classified weapons systems] OK for Saudi—").)
[171] McMahon, FBI 302, 5/23/88, p. 4.

to "provide for" the contras through the end of the year.[172] McFarlane also recalled Weinberger telling him in spring 1985 that Weinberger had received information that Prince Bandar had given $25 million to the contras.[173]

Throughout the 1987 period when Weinberger was testifying that he had no recollection that the Saudis had supported the contras, specific events continued to give Weinberger vivid reminders on that very subject. On January 14, 1987, for example, a reporter drew an angry response when he publicly confronted Weinberger, who denied knowing about Saudi aid to the contras.[174] Similarly, Vessey told Weinberger on February 11, 1987, that he had just told an FBI Agent of his conversations with Bandar and Weinberger about Saudi aid to the contras. Weinberger replied that he had forgotten about the conversations but agreed with Vessey's recollection.[175] Weinberger recorded this meeting in his daily diary as follows:

> Jack Vessey in office—he remembers telling McFarlane about Saudi claim they had sent funds to contras—also he has been asked to do a mission to Hanoi on POW's by Frank [Carlucci]—OK
> Discussed Secretary of Navy vacancy [176]

---

[172] McFarlane, Select Committees Testimony, 5/11/87, pp. 38–39; accord generally McFarlane, FBI 302, 4/15/87 (morning session), pp. 3–5; McFarlane, Select Committees Testimony, 5/12/87, p. 133. This probably occurred on May 24, 1984. Weinberger's diary notes indicate that he, McFarlane and Shultz discussed a classified arms sale proposal to Saudi Arabia that was pending at that time. (Weinberger Diary, 5/24/84, ALZ 0062955 ("Breakfast with Bud McFarlane, Shultz, Rich Armitage—etc—at State—re [Classified Arms Sale Proposal] for Saudi"); see also Classified Appendix.) Other evidence indicates that Prince Bandar made his decision to support the contras in the second half of May 1984.

[173] McFarlane, FBI 302, 3/10/87, p. 10; McFarlane, FBI 302, 4/15/87 (morning session), p. 5; accord Weinberger Diary, 3/13/85, ALZ 0039320C.

[174] Ibid., 1/14/87, ALZ 0042107.

[175] Vessey, FBI 302, 6/11/92, p. 8.

[176] Weinberger Diary, 2/11/87, ALZ 0042173. Less than three weeks after this meeting with Vessey and their discussion of the information they had received in 1985 regarding Saudi assistance to the contras, Weinberger made a curious diary entry:

> Jack Vessey—re reference to Tower Report to Saudis helping contras—neither of us know anything about that

(Ibid., 2/27/87, ALZ 0042210.) Weinberger's note appears to refer to McFarlane's written statement, which is quoted in the Tower Commission Report issued the previous day, that he "was separately informed by the Secretary of Defense and General Vessey that the total amount of the contribution [by a "foreign official" (Prince Bandar) to the contras] during 1985 was 25 million." (Report of the President's Special Review Board, 2/26/87, p. C–5.)

When Vessey was confronted with Weinberger's note in 1992, he said that he had no idea what it referred to and denied that he and Weinberger ever agreed to cover up their knowledge of the Saudi

## Weinberger's Previous False Testimony Regarding the Saudi Contribution

As early as the summer of 1986 Weinberger concealed from Congress his knowledge of Saudi Arabian support for the contras. On September 4, 1986, in response to a letter of inquiry from Representative Dante B. Fascell, Chairman of the House Committee on Foreign Affairs, Weinberger wrote that he "regarded [a press] allegation of Saudi funding of U.S. assistance to anti-government forces in Nicaragua as so outlandish as to be unworthy of comment from the Department [of Defense]." [177]

Later in 1986, Weinberger continued to conceal his knowledge from Congress. On December 17, 1986, during sworn testimony in closed session before the Senate Select Committee on Intelligence, Weinberger gave the following answers to Sen. Bill Bradley's detailed and persistent questions:

> Q: Have you been in any meeting since December—well, in the last 2 years—that discussed the funding for the contras outside of a direct congressional act?
>
> A: No. I did spend a lot of time trying to persuade various Members of the Senate and House that the $100 million was required, and——
>
> Q: But outside of——
>
> A: Not outside; no, sir. No.
>
> Q: You've had no discussions with any third party about provision of equipment or money to the contras?
>
> A: No, sir.
>
> Q: You've been in no meeting where it was discussed?
>
> A: To get—from outside assistance?
>
> Q: Uh-huh.

---

contribution. (Vessey, FBI 302, 6/11/92, p. 9.) Vessey also pointed out that he would not have told Weinberger on February 27, 1987, that he (Vessey) had no knowledge of the Saudi contribution because he had told the FBI, and then Weinberger, exactly the opposite only a few weeks earlier. (Ibid.)

[177] Letter from Weinberger to Fascell, 9/4/86, ALZ 012492. The press report that prompted Fascell's letter alleged that a slush fund, built into the Airborne Warning and Control Systems (AWACS) sale to Saudi Arabia, provided funds for the contras. (Ibid.)

A: No, I don't have any recollection of that. I know that there were a lot of attempts to get aid to the contras, but my efforts were concentrated entirely on trying to get the $100 million bill passed.

Q: But prior to that, in 1985 or early 1986 you had no discussions with anyone about providing funds or equipment to the contras?

A: I have no recollection of anything of that kind at all, Senator; no. I concentrated, as I said, entirely on the trying to get the Congress to approve the $100 million appropriation, which I thought then and think now was very necessary.

Q: You were in no meeting in which this was discussed?

A: I don't have any recollection of it, Senator, I really don't; no.[178]

By the time that Independent Counsel had discovered Weinberger's notes and the falsity of his testimony, the five-year statute of limitations had run on this testimony, so it was not, in itself, a basis for prosecution.[179]

In Weinberger's public testimony before the Select Committees on July 31, 1987, his denial of knowledge of Saudi support to the contras was categorical:

Q: . . . Mr. McFarlane testified that in the spring of 1985 there was a large contribution from [Saudi Arabia]. You were asked in your deposition whether you were aware at or about that time of the contribution. Do you recall being aware?

A: No. I was not aware.

Q: Let me just ask you, . . . if you would turn to . . . a memorandum for the record by John McMahon. It is dated March 15, 1985, and on the second page in paragraph 7 it refers to a meeting that you had with Director Casey at or about that time. It indicates, "Question of the support the contras came up." This is reporting on a

meeting that had taken place between yourself and Director Casey. The very last line reads, "In closing, the Sec—"—meaning the Secretary of Defense—"—stated that he had heard that—"—I will tell you what is under [the black redaction mark] there is an official [Prince Bandar]—"—had earmarked 25 million for the contras in $5 million increments." Do you have any recollection of seeing——

A: Well, I don't really. These were regular breakfast meetings that I had every week with the Director of CIA and they were very free-form discussions and meetings. The Director [Casey] and his Deputy [McMahon] and Mr. Taft and I went to these breakfasts every week and there was a lot of discussion back and forth and reports passed on and this statement that I had heard that, I don't remember saying it, but I did frequently joke with Mr. Casey to the effect that I frequently picked up things from his rival intelligence agency, which was one of the morning radio stations, and I may very well, simply been passing on that kind of report. I don't have any specific memory of it, but John McMahon is a good reporter so he probably heard this statement made.

Q: John McMahon was Deputy Director of the CIA at the time?

A: He was indeed.

Q: But you don't have any recollection of being advised by Mr. McFarlane or——

A: No.

Q:——the President or anyone else that there had been such a large contribution from [Saudi Arabia]?

A: No. The reason I am quite sure about it is that we were all making major efforts at that time to get funding for the contras from the Congress and I think probably many of the gentlemen here remember that I made lots of calls in support of various bills and particularly trying to get the $100

---

[178] Weinberger, SSCI Testimony, 12/17/86, pp. 67–68.

[179] At Weinberger's trial, evidence of this false testimony would have been admissible under Federal Rule of Evidence 404(b) and on other bases to show the motive and intent for his later lies on the same topic.

million appropriation which ultimately was voted.[180]

This testimony in July 1987 simply repeated Weinberger's false testimony from the June 17, 1987, deposition. To avoid unnecessary proliferation it was not included in the indictment as a separate charge.

## Count Three: Weinberger's Denial of His Knowledge of the Planned HAWK Missile Shipment in November 1985

Count Three of the Indictment charged Weinberger with perjury for stating falsely under oath that he had no knowledge that the November 1985 HAWK missile shipment to Iran was to take place. Weinberger repeatedly denied to congressional investigators and to the OIC that he had contemporaneous knowledge of the planning for the November 1985 HAWK missile shipment. Yet his daily diary notes demonstrate his detailed and contemporaneous knowledge. Although Weinberger opposed the shipment and warned that it would be illegal under the Arms Export Control Act, his notes indicate that, in furtherance of President Reagan's decision to proceed, Weinberger took steps to identify adequate U.S. HAWK missile inventories to replenish the Israelis.

As the Indictment states, Weinberger was asked directly about the HAWK shipment while testifying under oath before the Select Committees on July 31, 1987:

> Mr. Eggleston: The Committee has also received testimony that on that weekend of November 23 and November 24, [1985,] there was a shipment of 18 HAWK missiles from Israel to Iran. This [exhibit] was a paper that was written immediately prior to that time. Let me just ask you: Did you have any knowledge that that transfer was to take place?

Secretary Weinberger: No, I did not.

But his contemporaneous notes reveal that Weinberger was notified on November 9, 1985, by McFarlane of a new phase in the arms-for-hostages plan. After their conversation, Weinberger made the following note in his diary:

> Bud McFarlane . . . wants to start "negot." exploration with Iranians (+ Israelis) to give Iranians weapons for our hostages—I objected—we'll talk later on secure.[181]

The next day, after speaking again with McFarlane, Weinberger made this diary note:

> Bud McFarlane . . .—negotiations are with 3 Iranian dissidents who say they want to overthrow government. We'll demand release of all hostages. Then we might give them—thru Israelis—Hawks but no Phoenix.[182]

One week later—when McFarlane was in Geneva with President Reagan for a summit meeting with Gorbachev, and Weinberger was in Washington—McFarlane again telephoned Weinberger. Weinberger made a diary note of McFarlane's specific request for 500 HAWK missiles from DoD stocks:

> Bud McFarlane fm [from] Geneva—update on [summit] meetings—all OK so far— Also wants us to try to get 500 Hawks for sale to Israel to pass on to Iran for release of 5 hostages Thurs.[183]

Weinberger informed Powell of McFarlane's request.[184] Powell promptly obtained the requested information and reported back to Weinberger, who made the following diary note:

> Colin Powell in office re data on Hawks— can't be given to Israel or Iran w/o Cong. notification,—breaking them up into several packages of 28 Hawks to keep each

---

[180] Weinberger, Select Committees Testimony, 7/31/87, pp. 133–35. Although Weinberger's attorneys later claimed that this testimony showed that Weinberger did not deny making the statement recorded in McMahon's contemporaneous memorandum, the full transcript demonstrates Weinberger's calculated denial that he knew anything about Saudi assistance to the contras. The core of the testimony was Weinberger's statement that he was "quite sure" that no one had advised him of the Saudi contribution to the contras. The OIC verified the exact phrasing of the questions and Weinberger's answers throughout his testimony from videotape recordings of the Select Committee proceedings.

[181] Weinberger Diary, 11/9/85, ALZ 0039774.
[182] Ibid., 11/10/85, ALZ 0039775.
[183] Ibid., 11/19/85, ALZ 0039795.
[184] Powell, FBI 302, 2/24/92, pp. 7–8.

package under $14 million is a clear violation [185]

Weinberger, in turn, relayed Powell's information to McFarlane in Geneva. Weinberger made the following diary entry regarding McFarlane's non-committal response:

Called McFarlane in Geneva—re above—he "thanks me for call"—[186]

The next day, McFarlane informed Weinberger that, notwithstanding the legal restrictions that Weinberger had identified, President Reagan had decided to approve the proposed HAWK missile shipment to Iran. Weinberger recorded the President's decision in his diary as follows:

Bud McFarlane rmc. [returned my call] fm [from] Geneva (2)—he hasn't heard of request for logistical support for hostages—return—Told him we shouldn't pay Iranians anything—he sd [said] President has decided to do it thru Israelis.[187]

Later that day, McFarlane called to give Weinberger the latest details on the planned HAWK missile shipment, which Weinberger again recorded in his diary:

Bud McFarlane fm [from] Geneva—working on broad agreement language—Israelis will sell 120 Hawks, older models to Iranians—Friday [hostage] release

Called Colin Powell—re above [188]

On Thursday, November 21, 1985, Weinberger made additional diary entries regarding this arms-for-hostages initiative:

In office 720 Am—105 Pm

Saw Colin Powell—full statements of Geneva meetings, agreements,—etc—OK—also re Hawks for Israel-Iran

\*    \*    \*

Admiral Crowe in office—re President's decisions at Geneva—hostage rescue attempts—[189]

On Saturday, November 23, Weinberger made a diary note of his call from his home to General Powell:

Colin Powell—. . . no hostage release last night [190]

On Monday, November 25, 1985, Weinberger's diary contains a final note regarding this phase of the Iran arms sales:

Admiral Crowe in office—. . . also re Iranian ~~host~~ held hostages [191]

Because Count Three focused on Weinberger's denial of knowledge that the November 1985 HAWK missile shipment to Iran "was to take place," it was not essential to prove his knowledge of the actual shipment. Nevertheless, Weinberger did receive intelligence reports shortly after the shipment confirming that weapons had been shipped to Iran on November 24, 1985. Subsequent intelligence reports, which also were delivered to Weinberger, specified that these weapons had been HAWK missiles.[192]

---

[185] Weinberger Diary, 11/19/85, ALZ 0039797.

[186] Ibid. Powell later explained, after reviewing this note by Weinberger, that

[t]his is Mr. Weinberger's way of expressing his frustration in dealing with Mr. McFarlane. Mr. McFarlane had a habit of concluding conversations with the statement, "Thanks for the call." It was also a way of dismissing any concerns that might have been expressed in the call.

So whereas Mr. Weinberger was calling back to Mr. McFarlane to tell him this is illegal, it's a bad idea, you shouldn't be doing this, he was getting back from Mr. McFarlane something along the lines, "Thanks for the call," rather than "I agree" or "I don't agree." It was just "Thanks for the call."

So Mr. Weinberger is expressing his anxiety and frustration here that he has given information that should kill this idea right in its crib and instead of getting agreement, he's getting once again a "Thanks for the call" answer.

I am confident that this way of entering it in his personal notes was a way of expressing his annoyance and frustration that he did not succeed in killing this or he didn't know if he succeeded in killing this.

(Powell, Grand Jury, 4/22/92, p. 62.)

[187] Weinberger Diary, 11/20/85, ALZ 0039799.

[188] Ibid., 11/20/85, ALZ 0039801.

[189] Ibid., 11/21/85, ALZ 0039802–03.

[190] Ibid., 11/23/85, ALZ 0039806A. This diary note and the subsequent November 25, 1985, diary note showing that Weinberger was watching for a hostage release at the time contradict his assertion, offered for the first time after he was pardoned, that he did not believe McFarlane's statements to him and thus did not "know" that a shipment of HAWK missiles was to take place.

[191] Ibid., 11/25/85, ALZ 0039808.

[192] In his statements to various Iran/contra investigators, Weinberger adamantly denied receiving actual copies of these intelligence reports regarding arms-for-hostages transactions with Iran during 1985–86. (E.g. Weinberger, FBI 302, 12/3/90, p. 3.) Weinberger's statements were contradicted by numerous witnesses, including Powell and Armitage. Independent Counsel was unable to prosecute Weinberger for these false statements because the Executive Branch would not have declas-

## Count Four: Weinberger's Denial of Knowledge of the Replenishment Issue

Count Four charged Weinberger with perjury for stating falsely under oath that he had no knowledge of the "replenishment issue" that was created by Israel's arms shipments to Iran in 1985. The crux of that issue was that Israel wanted the United States to replenish its weapons stocks for missiles it had sent to Iran. On July 31, 1987, in sworn testimony before the Select Committees, Weinberger gave the following false answer:

Q. And in addition there are various documents which are in evidence before the Committee which refer to the Israeli desire and need for replenishment of weapons that the Israelis were sending. Did you know that replenishment was an issue?

A. No, I have no memory of that.[193]

This testimony conformed to Weinberger's previous false statements to Iran/contra investigators regarding Israel's role in arms shipments to Iran.[194]

Weinberger knew of the replenishment issue throughout 1985 and into 1986. According to McFarlane, he informed Weinberger in July and August 1985 first of Israel's proposal to send arms to Iran to achieve the release of Americans held hostage in Lebanon,[195] and then of President Reagan's decision to approve that proposal, including his agreement to replenish Israel's

weapons stocks after shipments to Iran.[196] McFarlane also reminded Weinberger in December 1985 that Israel had shipped TOW missiles to Iran in August and September 1985, and that the United States had to replenish Israel's stocks.[197] From September 1985 through the end of 1986, Weinberger received intelligence reports concerning past and proposed arms shipments to Iran in return for the release of American hostages, including the initial TOW missile shipments and a delivery of HAWKs on November 24, 1985. As discussed above, Weinberger's own notes show that, in November 1985, McFarlane advised Weinberger of President Reagan's decision to provide HAWK missiles to Iran through Israel, and that McFarlane asked Weinberger "to try to get 500 Hawks for sale to Israel to pass on to Iran for release of 5 hostages . . . ."[198]

On Saturday, December 7, 1985, Weinberger attended a meeting at the White House of President Reagan and his senior national security advisers. According to McFarlane, he reviewed the development of the Iran arms sales to that point, including Israel's August–September 1985 TOW missile shipments and the November 1985 HAWK missile shipment.[199]

On Tuesday, December 10, 1985, Weinberger attended another meeting at the White House with the President and senior advisers. On the back of his DoD daily press clippings, Weinberger took two full pages of handwritten notes during the meeting, including the following statements by McFarlane:

Bud

Sales of arms only in connection with establishment of better gov't—
Hostages only ~~infren~~ indirectly linked

———————

Separate hostage issue—
We tried that + they rejected it

---

sified even Weinberger's statements for inclusion in a proposed indictment, much less the underlying documentary evidence and testimony that would have been necessary to prove the case.

[193] Weinberger, Select Committees Testimony, 7/31/87, p. 99. As published by the Select Committees, the transcript of Weinberger's testimony erroneously reports the question quoted in the text above as, "Do you know that replenishment was an issue?"

[194] For example, during his December 17, 1986, testimony in closed session before the Senate Select Committee on Intelligence, Weinberger gave the following answer to a question from Senator Cohen:

Q: So to the best of your recollection there was no discussion about the Israelis transferring arms and us possibly resupplying them?

A: Not in my presence; no. I heard about that only much later after these things started to come out and as I say I heard—only heard that statements were being made, not that that had actually happened.

(Weinberger, SSCI Testimony, 12/17/86, p. 58.) This answer was not the subject of prosecution because the statute of limitations had run before the OIC obtained Weinberger's notes.

[195] McFarlane, FBI 302, 3/20/92, pp. 5–7; ibid., 12/3/86, pp. 2–3.

[196] Ibid., 3/20/92, pp. 3, 5–6, 9; ibid., 3/13/87, p. 4; ibid., 12/3/86, pp. 2–3.

[197] Ibid., 3/20/92, pp. 19–22; ibid., 3/31/92, pp. 2–3, 5.

[198] Weinberger Diary, 11/19/85, ALZ 0039795.

[199] E.g. McFarlane, FBI 302, 3/20/92, pp. 19–22; McFarlane, FBI 302, 3/31/92, p. 3. Shultz, who also attended, told his aides after the meeting that McFarlane and Poindexter had reported that "Isr [Israel] sent 60 I-hawks for [the] release of Weir" in September 1985. (Hill Note, 12/7/85, ANS 0001242.)

We may lose a hostage this weekend

       \*       \*       \*

Options

I accept original plan might lead to disclosure + more hostages

II—US Raid to release hostages [ ] in Beirut—some casualties inevitable

III—Continue to stand away fm it—Israeli's will go on delivering weapons + they might get hostages back

IV—Do nothing

(V—US deal with Iranians + give up Israeli cover)

covert operation to get arms to overthrow elements

       \*       \*       \*

Bud

[Classified proposed message for Syria]

-------

We still must replace 500 TOWs to Israel

-------

President—worried about hostages—let Israelis go ahead with arms sales—we'll get hostages back—

-------- 200

Weinberger's note—"We still must replace 500 TOWs to Israel"—shows that he knew of the replenishment issue that had been created by Israel's 1985 TOW missile shipments to Iran.[201]

In January 1986, after President Reagan had decided to cut out Israel by shipping arms directly from United States stocks to Iran, Weinberger received additional information about the replenishment issue. Koch reported to Weinberger on January 14, 1986, that an Israeli arms procurement official had agreed to postpone, until the hostages had been released,

the needed replenishment of the TOW missiles Israel had sent to Iran in 1985.[202] At a later point, the CIA asked Powell to increase its order for the purchase of TOWs from DoD stocks by an increment of approximately 500 missiles.[203] Powell understood that the added increment was to replenish an earlier Israeli shipment of TOW missiles to Iran, and he discussed replenishment with Weinberger at that time.[204]

## Independent Counsel's Investigations of DoD Personnel Not Prosecuted

### General Colin L. Powell

As Weinberger's senior military assistant from 1983 until March 1986, General Powell was one of the handful of senior DoD officials who were privy to detailed information regarding arms shipments to Iran during 1985 and 1986. When the arms shipments were publicly revealed in late 1986, investigators quickly learned that Powell was a knowledgeable party and interviewed him repeatedly regarding these events.

In 1992, after the OIC discovered Weinberger's voluminous notes and other withheld information, Powell was reinterviewed and gave additional testimony as part of Independent Counsel's investigation of Weinberger. During his February 1992 interview with the OIC, Powell read Weinberger's relevant diary and meeting notes for the first time.[205] Powell agreed that Weinberger's notes were accurate and found that they assisted his own recollection and understanding of events.[206]

Although Independent Counsel conducted no formal investigation at any time of General

---

200 Weinberger Meeting Notes, 12/10/85, ALZ 0040644B–45B.

201 Other phrases—the prediction that, if the United States stood away from Iran, the Israelis would "go on" delivering weapons, and the statement that dealing with Iran directly would require the United States to "give up" Israeli cover—also show Weinberger was informed of past missile shipments from Israel to Iran.

202 Koch, FBI 302, 4/2/92, pp. 9–10.

203 E.g. Powell, Select Committees Deposition, 6/19/87, pp. 80–81.

204 Powell, Grand Jury, 4/22/92, pp. 93–97; accord generally Powell, FBI Interview Transcript, 12/5/86, ALZ 0047715 ("every step along the way I kept the Secretary [Weinberger] informed as to the progress of this activity"); Powell, OIC Interview Transcript, 11/5/92, pp. 13, 24–25, ALZ 0075329–30 ("I'm sure I discussed it [replenishment] with him [Weinberger]. . . . The only thing I have a recollection of is at some point the issue of replenishment came up and I'm quite confident I had [a] fairly good memory of having made him aware of it. . . . I'm sure that we discussed the fact at that time that there was a replenishment issue or replenishment problem associated with this deal and it had to be dealt with.").

205 Powell, FBI 302, 2/24/92, p. 2.

206 E.g. Ibid., pp. 11–12.

Powell's conduct or his testimony and regarded him as merely a prospective witness,[207] the OIC did thoroughly reevaluate the conduct and prior statements of Powell and other senior DoD officials as part of its investigation of Weinberger and its preparation for his trial. On the basis of this evaluation, Independent Counsel determined that most of Powell's early statements regarding the Iran initiative were forthright and consistent. But some were questionable and seem generally designed to protect Weinberger.[208] Because Independent Counsel had no direct evidence that Powell intentionally made false statements, however, these matters were not pursued.

## Richard L. Armitage

Armitage served as assistant secretary of defense for International Security Affairs (ISA) from May 1983 until January 1989. As the head of ISA, which frequently is described as the "little Department of State" within DoD, Armitage had responsibility for all DoD programs and political and military relationships outside of NATO Europe.[209] During his tenure at the DoD, Armitage became a "major player" within the Pentagon and one of Weinberger's most trusted assistants.[210] Armitage also was an active figure throughout the executive branch who maintained extensive, daily contacts with key officials at the Department of State, the CIA and the NSC staff.[211]

From his extensive sources and contacts throughout the Government, Armitage acquired information regarding Israeli and U.S. arms sales to Iran during 1985 and 1986. During the ensuing Iran/contra investigations, Armitage was questioned in detail on numerous occasions.[212]

## Armitage's Statements Regarding Israel's 1985 Missile Shipments

In his early testimony, Armitage claimed ignorance of Israel's shipments of TOW missiles to Iran in August and September 1985, and its shipment of HAWK missiles to Iran in November 1985. He testified that he first knew that Israel had transferred missiles to Iran in 1985 when he heard CIA Director Casey testify on November 21, 1986, that the United States had replenished Israel's TOW missile stocks.[213] Regarding the November 1985 Israeli HAWK shipment, Armitage testified that although there were rumors and possibly intelligence reports "of some HAWK missiles to Israel [sic]," [214] the testimony of Casey on November 21, 1986, "was the first that I really knew of a shipment to Iran." [215]

The Tower Commission and Congress asked Armitage about meetings that he had with various principals in the Iran arms shipments. During the first week in December 1985, Armitage met separately with Israeli General Menachem (Mendi) Meron, the director general of Israel's Ministry of Defense, with Lt. Col. Oliver L. North of the NSC staff, and with retired U.S. Air Force Major General Richard V. Secord.

Armitage's records show three separate contacts with Meron in the first week of December 1985.[216] Armitage's account of these contacts was that they imparted no hard information to

[207] On December 9, 1986, prior to Independent Counsel's appointment, the FBI advised the White House, in response to its request for information, that Powell had been interviewed as a witness and was not considered a subject of investigation. (Letter from Clarke to Wallison, 12/9/86 ALU 010963; cf. Weinberger Diary, 12/10/86, ALZ 0040584 ("Saw Frank Carlucci—. . . Also Frank wants me to call Peter Wallison WH Counsel—to tell them Colin had no connection with Iran arms sales—except to carry out President's order. . . . Called Peter Wallison—Told him Colin Powell had only minimum involvement on Iran").)

[208] Powell's statements to congressional investigators in 1987 regarding Weinberger's notes and diary are addressed below in a separate section.

[209] Armitage, Grand Jury, 4/29/92, p. 7. In May 1986, Armitage also assumed responsibility for counterterrorism policy, including security assistance, counterintelligence and special forces operations. (Ibid., p. 7.)

[210] Armitage typically would see Weinberger every day, and sometimes as often as three to four times a day. (Ibid., p. 9.)

[211] Armitage readily admitted that he was "a terrible gossip" and trader of information throughout the Government regarding political, bureaucratic and policy developments. (Ibid., p. 22; accord Armitage, Select Committees Deposition, 7/22/87, p. 145).

[212] This section of the report focuses only on Armitage's knowledge and testimony regarding the Iran arms sales. Armitage also acquired direct knowledge of North's contra-support activities. See Abrams chapter.

[213] Armitage, SSCI Testimony, 12/11/86, pp. 58, 70; Armitage, Tower Commission Interview, 12/18/86, pp. 14–15, 33; Armitage, DAIG Interview, 12/24/86, p. 8.

[214] Armitage, SSCI Testimony, 12/11/86, p. 43. Armitage subsequently recalled hearing the rumor that the HAWK missiles that went from Israel to Iran were rejected "because they had the Star of David on them." (Armitage, Tower Commission Interview, 12/18/86, p. 32.) He also stated that this information may have been contained in an intelligence report. (Armitage, FBI 302, 1/31/91, pp. 1, 6.)

[215] Armitage, SSCI Testimony, 12/11/86, p. 43.

[216] On Monday, December 2, they met at 3 p.m. in Armitage's office. (Armitage Meeting Log, 12/2/85, ALZ 016436.) The next day, after Armitage had lunch with North to discuss his activities relating to Iran, Meron returned to Armitage's office for a late afternoon meeting. (Armitage Meeting Log, 12/3/85, ALZ 016437.) On December 5, Meron called Armitage on the phone. (Armitage Telephone Log, 12/5/85, ALZ 015341.)

him regarding the 1985 Israeli shipments or any information on a pending proposal for Israel to sell additional missiles to Iran. When the Tower Commission asked Armitage about his conversations with Israelis, he stated that

[w]hen Mandy Marone [sic—Mendi Meron] was around as the Director General of the Defense Ministry, I once said to him, I don't know what's going on, but I know you guys are involved, and I hear Iranians are real sleazebags and you shouldn't be involved in this kind of thing, Mandy [sic]. And he, well, other people make decisions. That was it. That's the only discussion I remember having, until after this broke.[217]

In deposition testimony to staff members of the Select Committees in 1987, Armitage denied discussing U.S. replenishment of Israeli TOW missiles with Meron.[218]

North and Armitage met in Armitage's office for lunch on December 3, 1985.[219] Armitage volunteered in his earliest statement to the FBI that his meeting with North was triggered by his review of intelligence reports in late November 1985 that Iranians were speaking with someone in the White House.[220] Armitage said that based upon the intelligence reports and after discussing his suspicions with Weinberger, Powell and Arnold Raphel of the State Department, he confronted North and asked whether he was part of discussions with Iranians.[221] According to Armitage, North responded that he had met with Iranians in Europe and, although North did not mention it, Armitage said he supposed that the meetings dealt with the hos-

tages.[222] Armitage said he also told North that because Weinberger knew nothing about this, "[y]our ass is way out," and Armitage said he urged North to inform all of the principal national security officials.[223] Armitage said that his reaction seemed to shock North, and that President Reagan called a White House meeting on this topic and invited Weinberger to attend shortly after Armitage's lunch with North.[224]

Armitage's meeting logs indicate that he met with Secord on December 5 and again on December 27, 1985,[225] but Armitage professed in a variety of inconsistent ways to recall nothing about these meetings. During his first FBI interview in December 1986, Armitage said he had last seen Secord "over one year ago" and did not know of any role Secord had played in the Iranian arms initiative.[226] Just eight days after the FBI interview, Armitage told a different story to the Tower Commission: "I found out midway, I would say roughly midway in '86 that Secord in some fashion was working with Ollie [North] on the Iranian side of this." [227] During his May 1987 congressional deposition, Armitage testified that, although he did not actually recall, "it had to be after—sometime after February of 1986" when he learned, perhaps from North or from some unidentified "Israelis," that Secord was involved in arms shipments to Iran.[228]

Armitage's statements regarding his lack of knowledge about the Israeli 1985 TOW and HAWK missile shipments to Iran and the issue of U.S. replenishment of those Israeli missile stocks—and his claimed failure to recall discussing these topics during his conversations with Meron, North and Secord during the first week of December 1985—were significant in two respects. First, they removed Armitage from

---

[217] Armitage, Tower Commission Interview, 12/18/86, p. 29.

[218] Armitage, Select Committees Deposition, 5/26/87, pp. 32–33, 118–19. Armitage agreed that he thought he would remember if he had discussed the replenishment issue with Meron. (Ibid., p. 33.)

[219] Armitage Meeting Log, 12/3/85, ALZ 016437 ("1230–1345 Ollie North—Lunch in office"). North's meeting immediately prior to the Armitage lunch was a meeting with Secord at 11:30 a.m. in North's office. (North Appointment Calendar, 12/3/85, AKW 003914.)

[220] Armitage, FBI 302, 12/10/86, p. 4.

[221] Ibid., p. 4. In his congressional testimony the next day, Armitage stated that *Weinberger*, after reading intelligence reports suggesting that Iranians were contacting U.S. officials through the White House switchboard, had assigned him to find out which officials were talking to the Iranians. (Armitage, SSCI Testimony, 12/11/86, pp. 5, 40.) The next week in his Tower Commission interview, Armitage gave a more active description of Weinberger's role: "the Secretary [Weinberger] had shown me [intelligence] that indicated somebody in the White House, quote, unquote, was meeting with Iranians." (Armitage, Tower Commission Interview, 12/18/86, p. 4.)

[222] Armitage, FBI 302, 12/10/86, p. 4; accord Armitage, SSCI Testimony, 12/11/86, pp. 5, 12–13, 41; Armitage, Tower Commission Interview, 12/18/86, pp. 4–5.

[223] Armitage, FBI 302, 12/10/86, p. 4; accord Armitage, SSCI Testimony, 12/11/86, pp. 5–7; Armitage, Tower Commission Interview, 12/18/86, pp. 4–5 ("I said to him [North], I don't think my boss knows anything about this. I doubt that Secretary of State Shultz knows anything about [this]. I think your ass is way out on a limb and you best get all the elephants together to discuss this issue.")

[224] Ibid., p. 5.

[225] Armitage Meeting Log, 12/5/85, ALZ 016439 ("1300—Gen Secord"); ibid., 12/27/85, ALZ 016457 (2:50 p.m.).

[226] Armitage, FBI 302, 12/10/86, p. 4; accord Armitage, Tower Commission Interview, 12/18/86, p. 27.

[227] Armitage, Tower Commission Interview, 12/18/86, p. 26.

[228] Armitage, Select Committees Deposition, 5/26/87, pp. 65–67; accord ibid., pp. 83–84.

a list of people who could have provided investigators with important information on the origins of the Iran arms sales and who, among the President's top national security advisers, was witting and involved. Second, by asserting personal ignorance and failure to recall the 1985 shipments, Armitage's testimony neatly dovetailed with and made more credible Weinberger's false statements regarding his own purported ignorance of the Israeli arms shipments.

## Armitage's Knowledge of Israel's 1985 Missile Shipments

Armitage claimed that he first learned that Israel had shipped missiles to Iran in 1985 when he heard Casey testify on November 21, 1986, that the United States had replenished Israel's TOW missile stocks. Significant evidence from a variety of sources shows that Armitage's knowledge predated Casey's testimony. For instance, a North notebook entry of November 18, 1986, documents a discussion with Armitage about Israel's 1985 arms shipments to Iran— three days before Armitage supposedly learned for the first time that such shipments had occurred:

> 1800
> [] Call from Armitage—Lawyers
> Israeli shipments in 1985
> —Did we know about it?
> —~~D~~ When did we promise to
>    replenish the Israelis? [229]

Armitage's knowledge about the 1985 Israeli missile shipments went back a year earlier, to his contacts with North, Meron and Secord in the first week of December 1985. During that week, the Reagan Administration and the Israelis were trying to decide whether to proceed with the Iran arms sales in the wake of the botched shipment of 18 HAWK missiles in late November 1985. The Israelis were concerned about obtaining replenishment for the HAWK missiles and 504 TOW missiles sent to Iran in August and September 1985. Another arms transfer was being contemplated.[230] Among other things, Armitage's task was to prepare briefing materials for Weinberger in advance

of a December 7, 1985, White House meeting where the future of the Iran initiative was to be debated.

## The December 2, 1985, Armitage-Meron Meeting

Classified evidence obtained from the Government of Israel, which is set forth in the Classified Appendix to this chapter, and evidence from North and Secord show that during the period Meron met with Armitage, Meron was discussing arms shipments to Iran and Israel's need for replenishment. Secord and North, on separate occasions, directed Meron to discuss these issues with Armitage. According to Secord, when Meron told him during their meeting in Israel in late November 1985 about the previous TOW missile shipments to Iran and the need for replenishment, Secord told him to talk to Armitage and to Lt. Gen. Philip Gast, director of the Defense Security Assistance Agency (DSAA), about getting the missiles replenished.[231] Secord's recollection is consistent with North's contemporaneous note of a telephone call he received from Secord on November 26, 1985:

> 1230—Call from Dick [Secord]
> —Can we supply later serial #s for Hawks?
> —How difficult is it to procure these items.
> —Met w/ D.K. [Kimche] & Mindy [sic] [Meron]
> —Mindy coming to meet w/ Rich [Armitage] & Phil [Gast] [232]

North, Secord and Meron met on the evening of December 2.[233] The next night (December 3), North sent Poindexter a lengthy PROFs computer note outlining a program for sending arms to Iran. It mentioned "discussions with Mendy Meron here in Washington which are continuing" and the problem of "replenishing Israeli stocks. . . ."[234]

[229] North Note, 11/18/86, AMX 001696.
[230] Memorandum by North, "Special Project Re Iran," 12/5/85, ALZ 0041745–52.
[231] Secord, FBI 302, 3/11/92, p. 8.
[232] North Note, 11/26/85, AMX 001911. Secord recalled reporting this information to North. (Secord, FBI 302, 3/11/92, p. 8.)
[233] North Note, 12/2/85, AMX 001920 ("Mtg [Meeting] w/ Moron [sic]") (final entry of the day).
[234] PROFs Note from North to Poindexter, 12/4/85, AKW 002070–73.

## The December 3, 1985, Armitage-North Lunch

On December 3, 1985, North had lunch with Armitage at Armitage's Pentagon office. Armitage's claim that the meeting was triggered by Weinberger's request to check an intelligence report that someone at the White House was meeting with Iranians is simply not true. The one report containing a White House telephone number—was delivered to Weinberger on October 2 or 3, 1985.[235] By December 3, 1985, North's involvement in dealings with Iran was no mystery to Weinberger. His diary demonstrates that by October 4, 1985, he knew that North was involved in negotiations with Iranians.[236]

There is strong circumstantial evidence that the discussion topics at the luncheon were past Israeli arms shipments to Iran, proposals for future shipments and the issue of replenishing Israeli missile stocks. Secord had just completed meetings in Israel with Meron and Kimche regarding replenishment and had mentioned Armitage as the DoD contact on that issue. Meron had discussed the Israeli missile shipments and the need for replenishment with Armitage the previous day. At their meeting the night before, North, Meron and Secord had also discussed replenishment.[237]

Independent Counsel was unable to obtain a dispositive account of the Armitage-North luncheon. Arnold Raphel, the deputy assistant secretary of state with whom Armitage regularly discussed the Iran initiative, took notes of a telephone call he received from Armitage immediately following the lunch with North.[238] But

Raphel died in 1988. Powell, who spoke to Armitage by telephone from Brussels, Belgium, during or immediately following Armitage's lunch with North,[239] recalled nothing more than Armitage's account of the lunch.[240]

## The December 5, 1985, Armitage-Secord Meeting

Armitage said he had no recollection of a meeting with Secord in December 1985 although his own meeting log indicated they met twice in that month. Raphel's notes, which do not identify the source of the information, contain a contemporaneous report on Armitage's meeting with Secord:

—Secord involved

Mtg. w/ Pres.—1000 Sat—w/ Pres. + arms if:—

    1—no more terrorism

    2—moderate govt in Tehan Tehran

    3—Iran wins war

    4—hostages released [241]

In the preceding weeks, Secord had been operationally involved in the shipment of 18 HAWK missiles from Israel to Iran. He had returned to the United States shortly before his meeting with Armitage.[242] Secord called Armitage at 11:15 a.m. on December 5.[243]

In contrast to Armitage's failure to recall the December 5 meeting, Secord never equivocated regarding its substance.[244] Secord consistently stated that he went to see Armitage with

---

[235] Intelligence Report, 10/2/85, AMW 0001955–57; accord Weinberger Diary, 10/3/85, ALZ 0039703.

[236] Weinberger Diary, 10/4/85, ALZ 0039704 ("Breakfast with Bill Casey + John McMahon + Will Taft—re Israeli bombing of Tunis—+ UN resolution; Ollie North's negot. with Iranians—Told them no US arms to be sold or given to Iran.").

[237] State of Israel, The Iranian Transactions—A Historical Chronology, Part One, 7/29/87, p. 54, AOW 0000067, as released in Majority Report, pp. 194, 210 n. 11.

[238] Armitage Telephone Log, 12/3/85, ALZ 015337 (Armitage called and spoke to Raphel at 2:05 p.m.). Raphel's handwritten notes contain the following:
    —Ollie
    —Scapegoat if it goes wrong
    —Iranians are sleazeballs
    —Ollie—we've lost little
    —Bud should get them all together + brief—
(Raphel Note, 12/3/85, ALW 0062382.) Ralphel's 1987 typed narration of his notes identified Armitage as the source of Raphel's information:
December 3—Assistant Secretary Armitage told me that Col. North had said that he would be made the scapegoat if the operation

goes wrong, but that we have lost little by trying. Reportedly, Col. North added that the Iranians involved are disreputable. Mr. Armitage said he suggested to Col. North that Mr. McFarlane should get all the principals together to brief on the operation. (Raphel Chronology, 1987, p. 2, ALW 0056727.)

[239] Armitage Telephone Log, 12/3/85, ALZ 015337 (Armitage takes incoming call from Powell at 12:45 p.m.).

[240] Powell, Grand Jury, 4/22/92, pp. 84–85.

[241] Raphel Note, 12/5/85, ALW 0062388. Although Raphel spoke to Armitage on a daily basis, he was not questioned about this note because Independent Counsel did not acquire it until after Raphel's death in 1988.

[242] North Appointment Calendars, 12/2/85 & 12/3/85, AKW 003914; Memorandum for the Record by Secord, "Meeting with O. North in OEB, 4 Dec @ 1930," AQT 0000050.

[243] Armitage Telephone Log, 12/5/85, ALZ 015341.

[244] See, for example, Secord, OIC Deposition, 3/9/88, p. 99 ("I didn't have any contact with the Defense Department save one meeting with Rich Armitage early on and then another one quite by accident with Noel Koch").

North's permission[245] after hearing North's report that Weinberger was opposing the arms shipments to Iran.[246] Secord thought that he might be able to convince Armitage, with whom he had worked closely in the past, of the need for such an initiative,[247] and that Armitage in turn might be able to convince Weinberger.[248] Secord recalled that he was unsuccessful: Armitage remained opposed to the Iran arms sales.[249]

Secord was uncertain about the date of his discussion with Armitage. After reviewing Armitage's meeting log, Secord said that while it was "quite possible" that he talked to Armitage in December 1985, his logic still suggested the meeting occurred "later, such as in January or February, 1986. . . ."[250]

It is reasonably clear that North, having heard Armitage's account of Weinberger's opposition to the Iran arms sales during his December 3, 1985, luncheon with Armitage, produced Secord, who was trusted by Armitage, as a means of vouching for the operation.[251]

## Armitage's Receipt of North's December 5, 1985, "Special Project re Iran" Paper

There is strong circumstantial evidence that Armitage on December 5 or 6, 1985, received a paper prepared by North containing significant information regarding the 1985 Iran arms sales and proposals for future sales.[252] The paper states explicitly that Israel, after receiving a U.S. commitment to sell replacement missiles, shipped 500 [sic] TOW missiles to Iran on September 14, 1985, two days before Reverend Benjamin Weir was released by terrorists in Lebanon. The paper describes a proposal to deliver 3,300 TOW missiles and 50 Improved

HAWK missiles from Israel to Iran in exchange for the release of five remaining U.S. citizen hostages plus one French citizen hostage and a cessation of terrorism against U.S. property or personnel. The paper declares, without using Secord's name, that "a U.S. businessman acting privately on behalf of the USG [U.S. Government]" has been negotiating this deal with the Iranians and Israelis. It states that such shipments would "significantly degrade Israeli stockpiles and require very prompt replenishment" by the United States. In an emotional summation, North's paper declares that the U.S. "must make one last try or we will risk condemning some or all of the hostages to death and undergoing a renewed wave of Islamic Jihad terrorism." For this reason alone, North's paper immediately became widely known throughout the Executive Branch.[253]

If Armitage reviewed North's paper on or about December 5–6, 1985, this would establish the falsity of Armitage's statements that he was unaware until November 1986 of Israel's 1985 arms shipments to Iran and the U.S. commitment to replenish Israel's stocks. If the North paper was used by Armitage as a basis of briefing Weinberger for the December 7, 1985, White House meeting this would have been powerful evidence that Weinberger's professed lack of early knowledge of the 1985 Israeli shipments was false.

There is no question that Armitage and Weinberger received North's December 5, 1985,

245 Secord, FBI 302, 3/11/92, p. 14.

246 Secord, Grand Jury, 1/25/91, p. 94.

247 Ibid.

248 Secord, FBI 302, 3/11/92, pp. 10, 13.

249 Secord, Grand Jury, 1/25/91, pp. 94–95.

250 Secord, FBI 302, 3/11/92, p. 11.

251 Armitage recalled that North invoked Secord's name as part of North's defense for the Iran operation. (Armitage, Tower Commission Interview, 12/18/86, pp. 26–27: "And Ollie told me[,] roughly, when I said ['] this is a bad deal [']—it was my usual talking point with Ollie when we were alone—and he said ['] and Secord's in it['].  . . . His response to me was ['] Dick Secord is really doing the Lord's work and that he's going to get the Medal of Freedom from the President, and he deserves it.[']''.)

252 Special Project Re Iran, 12/5/85, ALZ 0041745–52. This paper refines a PROFs message that North sent Poindexter on December 4, 1986. (PROFs Note from North to Poindexter, 12/4/85, AKW002070–73.

253 E.g. Platt Note, 12/5/85, ALW 0036859 ("Message from North to Iran via Israelis[:] Our arms deliveries predicated on following: 1. no more terrorism[;] 2. moderate gov[;] 3. Iran must not lose the war w Iraq.[;] 4. Release of hostages."); Ross Note, 12/5/85, ALW 0047062 (noting Raphel's report on "ON [Oliver North] message to Iran;" same four points as Platt note); Hill Note, 12/6/85, ANS 0001236 ("how they will argue [—] NP [Platt]: Ollie [North]: we shd [should] go ahead for long term stratg [strategic] int. [interest] w Iran + if we reneg [sic], there will be 4 dead hostg [hostages] + we may have to mount rescue"); Platt Note, 12/6/85, ALW 0036863 ("Arms for Hostages—Israel has been trading arms for Jews for years. Ship arms. Get 40 Iranian Jews. . . . Meron runs it[.] This specific deal—Israeli sends Hawks—Phoenix—replaced by 3300 I TOWs. Ollie has done memo to Pres [President Reagan] for 10 o clock.—should go ahead because of longer term strategic benefit—if we renege will have 4 dead hostages in 10 days—will have to move"); Hill Note, 12/6/85, ANS 0001238 ("Arma [Armacost]—Ollie told Iranians that as part of Night Owl deal—They shd give up t'ism [terrorism] [;]—install moderate govt[;]—win war w IQ [Iraq] } (!) ha ha Ollie is laughable.").

North's paper apparently was the basis of a detailed briefing that Poindexter gave Shultz over secure telephone the afternoon of December 5, 1985. (Hill Note, 12/5/85, ANS 0001228–29 ("3300 TOW. 60 Hawks Emph [Emphasis] is on rel [relations] w post-Kh. [Khomeini] Iran more than on hostages. . . .").) Independent Counsel was not able to determine whether a copy was provided to President Reagan, as Platt's note reports.

paper at some point. Armitage placed a copy of the paper in Weinberger's briefing book before the November 10, 1986, meeting of President Reagan and his senior advisers to discuss the Iran arms sales.[254] OIC obtained no testimonial evidence as to who delivered the North paper to Armitage or when it was delivered, but circumstantial evidence indicates that Armitage received North's paper on December 5 or 6, 1985: [255]

—the North paper was closely related to the series of meetings and conversations regarding arms shipments that Armitage had during that week with Meron, North and Secord;

—because Weinberger and Powell were in Europe until the night of December 6, 1985, Armitage was the senior DoD official at the Pentagon who was familiar with the Iran arms sales; he was the logical person to be informed of the North paper. By his own description, Armitage was the person who was gathering information as part of the effort to prepare Weinberger for the December. 7, 1985, White House meeting; [256]

—Poindexter briefed Shultz by secure telephone on the substance of North's paper before their December 7, 1985, White House meeting.[257] It is unlikely that the NSC staff would brief the Department of State of the proposal but not brief the DoD, which had the missiles.

—Raphel took these notes during a telephone call from Armitage at 10:05 on December 6, 1985,[258] shortly after North's visit to Armitage's office, regarding the substance of North's paper:

—arms for Jews
—David Kimche
—Mendy [Meron]/Ben Josef—procurement
—replace ~~300~~ 3300 I–TOWs in IDF [Israeli Defense Forces] [259]

—an information paper that Armitage commissioned from DSAA officials Rudd and Gaffney prior to the December 7 meeting refers to a proposal to transfer 50 Improved HAWKs and 3,300 TOWs to Iran [260]—the exact numbers specified in North's paper; and

—North brought a copy of his paper when he met with Israelis in New York City on December 6, 1985, just before North travelled to London to meet with the Iranians and Israelis in connection with the initiative.[261] It is implausible that North shared the paper with the Israelis but withheld it from Armitage.[262]

Armitage made misleading statements regarding his preparation of Weinberger for the December 7, 1985, White House meeting. Armitage told the Tower Commission that he prepared Weinberger for the meeting "orally without any paper trail." [263] In June 1987, however, the DoD belatedly produced to the Select Committees and to Independent Counsel two December 1985 briefing papers prepared by Rudd and Gaffney regarding missile shipments to Iran. Armitage ultimately stated that he probably provided these papers to Weinberger, or at least gave him an oral briefing from the

[254] During the November 10, 1986, meeting, Weinberger made extensive notes on the backs of the pages of North's December 1985 paper. After the meeting, the briefing book apparently was returned to ISA, "broken down" and refiled. Although Armitage obviously returned this document to the files, it was not produced to Congress or Independent Counsel in 1987. The OIC first located the copy of North's paper with Weinberger's notes when it reviewed a segregated collection of Iran/contra material at ISA in 1992.

[255] Armitage's logs show that North placed a telephone call to Armitage's office at 6:50 p.m. on December 5, 1985, but they apparently did not speak. The next morning, North called again and spoke to Armitage at 8:30 a.m. North arrived at Armitage's office at 9:00 a.m., and he called and spoke to Armitage by telephone at 10:05 a.m. (Armitage Telephone Log, 12/5/85, ALZ 015341; ibid., 12/6/85, ALZ 015342; Armitage Meeting Log, 12/6/85, ALZ 016441.) Although no witness explained this series of contacts, the sequence of events suggests that North called Armitage to tell him of the paper, then dropped off a copy at Armitage's office, and then called back an hour later to get Armitage's views after he had read the document.

[256] Armitage, FBI 302, 1/30/92, p. 5.

[257] Hill Notes, 12/5/85, ANS 0001228–29.

[258] Armitage, Telephone Log, 12/6/85, ALZ 015342.

[259] Raphel Note, 12/6/85, ALW 0062391; Raphel Chronology, 1987, p. 2, ALW 0056727.

[260] Prospects for Immediate Shipment of I-HAWK and I-TOW Missiles, ALZ 0058747.

[261] State of Israel, The Iranian Transactions—A Historical Chronology, Part One, 7/29/87, p. 55, AOW 0000068, as released in Majority Report, p. 197.

[262] See Classified Appendix.

[263] Armitage, Tower Commission Interview, 12/18/86, p. 5.

papers, in preparation for the December 7 White House meeting.[264]

These papers clearly related to the North proposal. The first of the Rudd-Gaffney papers, a two-page analysis titled "Possibility for Leaks," was created in response to Armitage's request for information on "the legal ramifications of the possible sale of Hawk and TOW missiles, either directly to Iran or as replacement for an Israeli shipment to Iran."[265] Although the "Leaks" paper mentions neither Israel nor Iran by name and does not itemize quantities of missiles or say that missile shipments are planned, it transparently refers to Israel as "the country involved," refers to another "country we do not sell to ourselves" (Iran), speaks of "I–HAWKS in the quantity contemplated" and "the I–TOW quantities," and reports, in its very first line, that "[t]here is no good way to keep this project from ultimately being made public."[266] Rudd specifically recalled providing this paper to Armitage on December 6, 1985.[267] Rudd also recalled that Armitage instructed him to retain no copies of the paper, and that he (Rudd) complied.[268]

The second paper, a one-page analysis titled "Prospects for Immediate Shipment of I–HAWK and I–TOW Missiles," also was created by Rudd, with Gaffney providing some of the information as a follow-on to his November 1985 point paper regarding HAWK missiles.[269] The "Prospects for Immediate Shipment" paper reported that up to 75 I–HAWK missiles, although intended for shipment to the United Arab Emirates, were still being tested in the U.S. and could be shipped elsewhere without impact and quotes a "total package price" of $22.5 million "for [shipping] 50. . . ."[270] This paper also reported that "the impact on Army of shipping 3,300 I–TOWs immediately would

be serious but not intolerable."[271] 50 HAWKs and 3,300 TOWs were the quantities and types of missiles in the proposed shipment outlined in North's December 5, 1985, "Special Project Re Iran" paper.

Armitage's false statement to the Tower Commission that he prepared Weinberger for the December 7, 1985, meeting "orally without any paper trail," suggests that the DoD's initial failure to produce the Rudd-Gaffney papers was no accident. Notwithstanding numerous requests from investigators in late 1986 and early 1987, these two papers were not produced to the Select Committees until the weekend of June 20–21, 1987—after the Tower Commission had completed its work and after the Select Committees had obtained initial testimony from numerous DoD witnesses, including Weinberger and Armitage.

On June 16, 1987, Gaffney reminded Rudd that they had created a paper for Armitage regarding TOW missiles in early December 1985,[272] and that Rudd had promptly delivered this paper to Armitage, who instructed Gaffney to destroy all copies and drafts.[273] During a deposition on the afternoon of June 16, 1987, Select Committee staff members informed Rudd that a 1986 handwritten note by Koch indicated that this "TOW paper [was] locked in RLA [Armitage's] safe, wouldn't let Rudd keep copy."[274] The next day, Rudd discussed the matter with Armitage.[275] In Rudd's presence, Armitage pulled a copy of the "Leaks" paper out of his office safe.[276] Then DoD provided both the "Leaks" paper and the "Prospects for Immediate Shipment" paper to the Select Committees.[277]

Armitage claimed that he had at the outset of the Iran/contra investigations directed his aide, Lincoln P. Bloomfield, Jr., to review Armitage's files and produce all requested, rel-

[264] Armitage, FBI 302, 3/3/92, p. 1; Armitage, Grand Jury, 4/29/92, p. 86.

[265] Rudd, Select Committees Deposition, 6/22/87, p. 3 (joint deposition with Gaffney).

[266] Possibility for Leaks, ALZ 004343–44.

[267] Rudd, Select Committees Deposition, 6/22/87, pp. 3, 18 (joint deposition with Gaffney).

[268] Ibid., pp. 18–19.

[269] Gaffney, Select Committees Deposition, 6/22/87, p. 24 (joint deposition with Rudd). Rudd accepted the logic of Gaffney's account but could not specifically recall the "Prospects for Immediate Shipment" paper. (Ibid., pp. 24–25.)

[270] Prospects for Immediate Shipment of I–HAWK and I–TOW Missiles, ALZ 0058747.

[271] Ibid.

[272] Rudd, Select Committees Deposition, 6/16/87, pp. 25, 36, 40, 45, 48–49.

[273] Gaffney, Select Committees Deposition, 6/16/87, pp. 125, 128–32.

[274] Rudd, Select Committees Deposition, 6/16/87, p. 26; Koch Note, AOX 000812.

[275] Rudd, Select Committees Deposition, 6/16/87, p. 45 ("I have no idea where it [the TOW paper] is" and have not made any inquiry to Armitage about its existence).

[276] Rudd, Select Committee Deposition, 6/22/87, pp. 19–20, 26–28 (joint deposition with Gaffney).

[277] Gaffney & Rudd, Select Committees Deposition, 6/22/87, Exhibits 1–2.

evant documents.[278] Bloomfield corroborated Armitage's account.[279] There was no evidence that Armitage and Bloomfield collaborated with anyone else to withhold documents. Independent Counsel could not prove beyond a reasonable doubt that the initial non-production and Armitage's false testimony were deliberate.

## Individuals Knowledgeable of or Involved in the Production of Weinberger's Notes

Of the chief witnesses interviewed by the OIC about the withholding of Weinberger's notes, four merit separate discussion: (1) H. Lawrence Garrett, III, DoD general counsel during the congressional Iran/contra investigation, (2) General Colin L. Powell, Weinberger's former senior military assistant, (3) Kay D. Leisz, Weinberger's confidential assistant at DoD and in his subsequent legal practice, and (4) Thelma Stubbs Smith, secretary to Weinberger at the DoD.

### H. Lawrence Garrett III

Garrett testified in the Grand Jury that he told Weinberger's secretaries, Thelma Stubbs Smith and Kay Leisz, that the Iran/contra document requests included personal notes and that Smith told him Weinberger had no notes.[280] Garrett had not personally observed Weinberger taking notes, other than scribbling marginalia on documents during meetings,[281] and had not seen Weinberger's diary notes until he was shown them by OIC investigators in March 1992.[282] When specific Weinberger notes were described to Garrett, he stated that he would have considered them relevant to Iran/contra and said, "[h]ad I known of them at the time, I would have so advised the Secretary."[283]

Garrett also implied that the failure to produce Weinberger's notes had been because of Garrett's own lack of vigilance. He asserted on several occasions that he had never asked Weinberger directly whether he had notes or diaries[284] and stated in his affidavit that he was "confident that if [he] or members of [his] staff had asked [Weinberger] specifically whether he kept diary notes, [Weinberger] would have provided them so that any relevant portions" could be produced.[285]

Garrett's April 17, 1987, memorandum to Weinberger and his April 29, 1987, memorandum to Taft—both of which DoD produced *after* the indictment, despite having been asked for such documents much earlier—indicate that, contrary to the impression conveyed by his affidavit, Garrett was diligent in attempting to obtain Weinberger's notes and diaries. When Garrett was questioned about these documents, he nevertheless insisted he had no recollection of discussing the production of notes and diaries with either Weinberger or Taft.[286]

Although Garrett's purported inability to recall anything about his efforts to obtain Weinberger's notes was sufficiently implausible to undermine Garrett's credibility, it would have been difficult to prove beyond a reasonable doubt that Garrett had intentionally perjured himself five years after writing his April 1987 memorandum. The evidence indicated that Garrett was not a witting accomplice in withholding Weinberger's notes from Congress.

### Colin L. Powell

Although Powell generally was a cooperative witness, his 1992 statements describing Weinberger's notes in detail and characterizing them as a "personal diary"[287] necessarily raise

[278] Armitage, FBI 302, 1/30/92, p. 3.

[279] Bloomfield, Grand Jury, 5/1/92, pp. 62–63.

[280] Garrett, Grand Jury, 4/22/92, p. 19 (Garrett indicated to Thelma Stubbs Smith, in the presence of Kay Leisz, "that [the requests] would include personal notes and her [Smith's] response to me was 'I don't believe there are any notes.'"); accord Garrett, Affidavit, 4/28/92, ¶11, ALZ 00400536.

[281] Garrett, Affidavit, 4/28/92, ¶11, ALZ 0045036; Garrett, Grand Jury, 4/22/92, p. 59 (Weinberger's deposition responses "would have been consistent with [Garrett's] belief from the outset, and, as I said, I did not observe the Secretary to be a copious notetaker at all of the meetings that I attended with him so it didn't trouble me. . . .")

[282] Garrett, FBI 302, 4/8/92, p. 6; Garrett, Grand Jury, 4/22/92, p. 17; accord ibid., pp. 67–68 (Garrett was not aware that at the time of Weinberger's congressional deposition, Weinberger had "several hundred pages possibly" of notes in his desk).

[283] Ibid., pp. 74–75.

[284] Garrett, Affidavit, 4/28/92, ¶11, ALZ 0045036 (Garrett "did not personally question Secretary Weinberger about the existence of personal notes or diaries."); accord Garrett, Grand Jury, 4/22/92, pp. 58, 66, 77 (Garrett did not follow up on the inquiries about notes and records raised in Weinberger's congressional deposition.).

[285] Garrett, Affidavit, 4/28/92, ¶¶11–13, ALZ 0045036–37.

[286] Garrett, Grand Jury, 10/28/92, pp. 20–21, 22, 24, 35 (Weinberger); ibid., pp. 10–11 (Taft).

[287] In an affidavit submitted by Weinberger's attorneys, Powell stated that he regarded Weinberger's daily notes as a "personal diary" and thought it "entirely possible" that Weinberger would not have understood these personal notes to be within the scope of congressional or OIC document requests. (Powell, Affidavit, 4/21/92, ¶3, ALZ 0045089.) Powell's detailed 1992 account of Weinberger's note-taking, while quite helpful to the OIC, was also consistent with a defense strategy to demonstrate that Weinberger was not secretive about his notes. Indeed, Powell, who cooperated extensively with Weinberger's counsel, provided increasingly vivid descriptions of Weinberger's notes

questions about Powell's 1987 statements to congressional investigators. Powell told the staff of the Senate Select Committee on April 17, 1987, that he did not know whether Weinberger kept a diary.[288] During Powell's June 19, 1987 deposition, the following exchange took place:

Q: Maybe I should know this, but did the Secretary keep a diary?

A: The Secretary, to my knowledge, did not keep a diary. Whatever notes he kept, I don't know how he uses them or what he does with them.

Q: Did he—

A: He does not have a diary of this ilk, no.

Q: —did he dictate memos, as some people do, so that if they ever get around to writing their—a book on the era, they have some aids; they have memoirs?

A: No, the Secretary did not dictate his daily activities, to the best of my knowledge. I've never seen it. He didn't do it and I was with him every day.

Whatever notes he took in the course of a day, I don't know what he did with them.[289]

In light of his statements in 1992, Powell's 1987 deposition testimony was at least misleading. Although Powell qualified his denial that Weinberger kept a "diary" by distinguishing that kind of record from "whatever notes [Weinberger] kept," this oblique reference to Weinberger's notes hardly constituted full disclosure.[290] Powell apparently understood that

congressional investigators wanted to know whether Weinberger kept contemporaneous records of his daily activities but failed to disclose that Weinberger's notes were a running, daily log of telephone calls and meetings. He also claimed that he did not know what Weinberger did with his notes.[291]

Nevertheless, it would have been difficult to prove that his deposition testimony was intentionally false.[292] Similarly, there was no direct evidence that Powell and Weinberger colluded to conceal Weinberger's notes from congressional investigators. Thus, while Powell's prior inconsistent statements could have been used to impeach his credibility, they did not warrant prosecution.

### Kay D. Leisz

Leisz was interviewed by the OIC on February 3, 1992, and appeared before the Grand Jury on March 6 and April 24, 1992. On the latter occasion, Leisz, who had been advised that she was a subject of the Grand Jury's investigation and had retained counsel, invoked the Fifth Amendment. On June 15, 1992, in return for an immunity agreement, Leisz gave a deposition in lieu of a Grand Jury appearance but added little to her prior testimony.

Leisz asserted in an October 1, 1990, memorandum that she had stopped maintaining Weinberger's handwritten meeting notes after his first year as secretary of defense.[293] Leisz later elaborated that she simply left Weinberger's loose meeting notes in his briefing books, which were forwarded to the Correspondence & Directives (C&D) section to be broken down and filed.[294]

Leisz adhered to this story, which Weinberger had echoed in his October 10, 1990, interview,

---

as the investigation progressed. (Compare Powell, FBI 302, 2/24/92, p. 2 with Powell, Affidavit, 4/21/92, ¶¶ 3–4, ALZ 0045089 and Powell, Grand Jury, 4/22/92, pp. 19–20, 23.)

[288] Powell, Select Committees Interview Memorandum, 4/20/87, p. 9, AMY 000568.

[289] Powell, Select Committees Deposition, 6/19/87, p. 54–55. Powell's reference to "a diary of this ilk" may refer to the notebook that Powell began to maintain when he became deputy national security adviser in January 1987. (Powell, Grand Jury, 4/22/92, pp. 14–15.)

[290] As one example of Powell's contemporaneous familiarity with Weinberger's diary notes, Powell actually helped to create Weinberger's daily diary entries for October 10, 1985, the day that U.S. military forces captured the hijackers of the *Achille Lauro* cruise ship in the Mediterranean. Weinberger, who had been flying from Canada to Maine and made an unscheduled return to Washington as the military action unfolded, apparently was too busy to create his typical log of calls and activities and asked Powell to create a chronology of the day's events for him. Later that day, Powell gave Weinberger a cover note

("Sec Def, Chronologies. Does not include all your calls. VR [very respectfully], CP") and two handwritten pages on which Powell had noted Weinberger's afternoon and evening activities. Weinberger subsequently annotated Powell's entries and filed all three pages with his daily diary notes. Weinberger's accompanying diary entry says "See attached slips for calls from + to plane." (Weinberger Diary, 10/10/85, ALZ 0039713c-13g.)

[291] In a trial preparation interview with the OIC in late 1992, by contrast, Powell stated that Weinberger, "[m]ore often than not," made notes on his 5" x 7" pad while working at his "stand up desk," and that Weinberger "put them in his desk on the right side. . . ." (Powell, OIC Interview Transcript, 11/5/92, p. 3, ALZ 0075308.)

[292] Powell's vague references to Weinberger's "notes," as opposed to his "diary," may have been calculated to avoid giving overtly false testimony while providing as little information as possible.

[293] Memorandum from Leisz for the Record, 10/1/90, ALZ 0051360.

[294] Leisz, Grand Jury, 3/6/92, p. 16.

despite overwhelming evidence that it was false.[295] For example, Weinberger's other secretary, Thelma Stubbs Smith, stated that she and Leisz had maintained a handwritten-notes file throughout Weinberger's tenure at DoD and that these notes were later transferred from Leisz's safe to the vault in Weinberger's office.[296] In addition, Leisz identified her handwritten notations on some of Weinberger's meeting notes from 1985–86.[297] Leisz had also referred to "your hand-written notes file" in a 1987 note to Weinberger;[298] another cover note by Leisz identified a collection of Weinberger's notes taken during the TWA hijacking in June 1985;[299] and a 1985 cover note from Powell to Leisz attached a set of Weinberger's meeting notes "For your File."[300] Even when confronted with this evidence, Leisz insisted that she could not recall having maintained a file of Weinberger's handwritten notes after his first year at DoD.[301]

Leisz also insisted that she was unaware of Weinberger's diary notes while at DoD and that she had not heard Weinberger refer to them as his "telephone logs" until she went with him to review the notes at the Library of Congress in December 1991.[302] Most other Weinberger aides who had similar daily contact with Weinberger eventually said they had been aware of his diary notes.[303]

Leisz's testimony, particularly about the meeting notes, was flagrantly incredible. Although the immunity agreement did not preclude prosecuting Leisz for giving subsequent false testimony in her June 15, 1992, deposition, the OIC determined that pursuing such collateral charges was not an effective use of resources.

## Thelma Stubbs Smith

In her first interview on March 5, 1992, Smith was shown examples of Weinberger's diary notes and stated that she had never seen them before. Smith also stated that she had seen Weinberger's meeting notes only when Weinberger used them to dictate memoranda, which he did infrequently, and she had thrown the corresponding notes away when a memorandum was completed. Smith further stated that she had no knowledge where any notes Weinberger may have made would have been kept. Smith said she had talked to Leisz before the interview, and Leisz had told her of the OIC's interest in the notes discovered at the Library of Congress.[304]

In Smith's second interview, on April 28, 1992, she was again shown examples of Weinberger's diary notes. This time, she said she had occasionally seen such notes on Weinberger's desk and assumed he intended to use them to write a book. Smith also disclosed, in contradiction to her earlier statement, that she and Leisz maintained a file of Weinberger's handwritten notes in a safe by Leisz's desk.[305]

In an affidavit executed the next day for Weinberger's counsel, Smith provided even more detailed information about Weinberger's notes. Smith stated that she had been "aware that Secretary Weinberger kept a pad on his desk on which he scribbled notes reflecting the date, time and other references to telephone

[295] Leisz, FBI 302, 2/3/92, p. 2; Leisz, Grand Jury, 3/6/92, pp. 17–18; Leisz, OIC Interview, 6/15/92, p. 14.

[296] Smith, Affidavit, 4/29/92, ¶7, ALZ 0045122–23. Also, as discussed above, none of Weinberger's meeting notes has a C&D file number.

[297] Leisz, OIC Interview, 6/15/92, p. 22.

[298] Leisz's typed, undated note was attached to Weinberger's notes of the November 10, 1986, White House meeting. Although the context for Leisz's note remains a mystery, she typed "I looked through your hand-written notes file and the only file I keep on dictated notes from meetings. Attached is all we have." (ALZ 0058999.) Leisz's handwritten note at the bottom says "P.S. There are no copies." (Ibid.)

[299] Leisz Note, ALZ 0060091 (covering Weinberger notes of 6/15/85, 6/16/85 and 6/24/85).

[300] Note from Powell to Leisz, 9/24/85, ALZ 0060174.

[301] Leisz, Grand Jury, 3/6/92, pp. 42–43, 44 (note to Weinberger); ibid., pp. 47–48, 49 (notes on TWA hijacking); Leisz, OIC Interview, 6/15/92, pp. 20–21 (note from Powell); ibid., p. 22 (Leisz handwriting on meeting notes).

[302] Leisz, Grand Jury, 3/6/92, pp. 25–26. Weinberger's former senior military assistant, Admiral Donald S. Jones, recalled, however, that one of Weinberger's secretaries (he could not remember if it was Smith or Leisz) had identified papers on the shelf in the bedroom adjacent to Weinberger's office as "Weinberger's notes." (Jones, FBI 302, 12/22/92, p. 4.)

[303] The latter admissions were consistent with the apparent defense strategy to emphasize that Weinberger had made no effort to hide his notes from those around him.

Leisz also testified that when she and Weinberger went to the Library in December 1991 to review the notes the OIC had found there, both

she and Weinberger were surprised to find that his diary and meeting notes were at the Library. (Leisz, Grand Jury, 3/6/92, pp. 31, 34–35.) Leisz said Weinberger had remarked about his diary notes, "these are my telephone logs; I didn't know where they were." (Ibid., p. 35.)

Weinberger's comments are odd given that he and Duncan had looked at the diary notes in the Library in July 1988 and that Weinberger had packed his diary notes and at least some of his meeting notes himself for transfer to the Library. Weinberger's attorneys, who claimed that Weinberger was well aware his diary notes were at the Library when he gave the OIC permission to review his papers there, tried to minimize this episode in a pre-indictment meeting with the OIC, explaining that Weinberger was simply suprised at the way his notes had been neatly archived in individual plastic sleeves.

[304] Smith, FBI 302, 3/5/92, pp. 2, 3.

[305] Smith, FBI 302, 3/23/92, p. 3.

calls and meetings.'' Smith also expanded her description of the handwritten notes file but said she did not believe Weinberger was aware that she and Leisz kept such a file. Smith said she did not recall being asked by anyone to gather ''documents'' relevant to Iran/contra and said that, even if she had been asked, she ''would not have thought of the handwritten notes'' because she did not consider them to be ''documents.''[306]

When questioned later before the Grand Jury about the inconsistency in her statements about the diary notes, Smith insisted that she simply had not remembered them when they were shown to her in the first interview.[307]

Smith's statements conflict with Garrett's Grand Jury testimony. Garrett said he told Smith and Leisz specifically that the document requests included ''personal notes.''[308] If Smith told Garrett in 1987 that Weinberger had no notes, her statement was deliberately false. Because of Garrett's own credibility problems, and the lack of direct proof that Smith had colluded with Weinberger and/or Leisz, the OIC did not charge Smith with complicity in withholding Weinberger's notes.

## The DoD's Lack of Cooperation With the OIC's Investigation of Weinberger

The OIC's experience with the DoD during the Weinberger investigation illustrates the unique problems Independent Counsel encountered in-vestigating possible wrongdoing by high-level officials. DoD withheld documents even in 1992. DoD employees gave defense counsel confidential communications between DoD and OIC—the Government's counsel. DoD employees improperly allowed defense counsel to review evidence being held for the OIC.

In April and May of 1992, the OIC asked the DoD to produce documents from the Office of General Counsel (OGC) and Office of the Secretary of Defense (OSD) regarding DoD's responses to Iran/contra document requests. The OGC files containing most of the information relating to DoD's Iran/contra document production, including Garrett's 1987 memoranda to Weinberger and Taft, were *not* produced to the OIC until *after* the indictment.[309] In response to additional, specific requests and subpoenas, DoD produced from OSD files another copy, and the original, of Garrett's memorandum to Weinberger, bearing the ''SEC DEF HAS SEEN'' stamp and a handwritten note by Weinberger—neither of which had been produced in response to previous document requests.[310]

Although the OIC found no conclusive proof that a DoD official had deliberately withheld these documents, the OIC received an anonymous telephone call on May 21, 1992, suggesting that investigators look in the office of Deputy General Counsel Michael A. Sterlacci for information regarding Weinberger. Several of the files produced belatedly by DoD had been stored in Sterlacci's office.[311]

---

[306] Smith Affidavit, 4/29/92, ¶¶ 5, 7, 11, ALZ 0045122–24.

[307] Smith, Grand Jury, 5/8/92, p. 31. Following Smith's Grand Jury appearance, her attorney wrote an indignant letter to the OIC objecting to the suggestion that his client had shaded her initial statements to the OIC after talking to Leisz. (Letter from Banoun to Baker, 5/8/92, 018977.) Later, Weinberger's counsel attached to a court pleading an affidavit from Smith's husband, alleging that the OIC had deliberately falsified the record of the first interview. (Affidavit of Edwin E. Smith, 12/14/92, ¶ 5, attached to Defendant's Memorandum in Opposition to OIC's Motion *In Limine* to Exclude Extraneous Evidence Concerning the OIC, 12/16/92, 024526.) The FBI agents who conducted the interview each unequivocally denied Mr. Smith's allegations. (Government's Motion to Strike Affidavit of Edwin E. Smith from Defendant's Pleadings, 12/17/92, 024558.)

[308] Garrett, Grand Jury, 4/22/92, p. 19. In the affidavit that Weinberger's counsel procured and submitted to the OIC after Garrett's Grand Jury testimony, his account of his conversation with Smith and Leisz is phrased more narrowly: ''I do recall that early on in the process I told [Weinberger's] secretaries that a document request had been received and asked them whether Secretary Weinberger had any notes *regarding the Iran-Contra affair*. They said he did not have any *such* notes.'' (Garrett, Affidavit, 4/28/92, ¶ 11, ALZ 0045036, emphasis added.) In a subsequent interview, however, Garrett again characterized Smith's statement to him as a categorical assertion that ''there weren't any notes.'' (Garrett, OIC Interview, 5/13/92, pp. 10–11, 24–25.)

[309] The OIC had determined that there was sufficient evidence from Weinberger's own diary notes, his false statements to congressional investigators and the few documents produced by DoD to prove beyond a reasonable doubt that Weinberger had intentionally withheld his notes from Congress. The new documents, however, strengthened the evidence of Weinberger's intent.

[310] Garrett's chronological files and a number of relevant subject files from his tenure as DoD general counsel similarly were not produced until October 1992, in response to a Grand Jury subpoena, despite a specific request for such files in May 1992. These files contained additional copies of Garrett's memoranda to Weinberger and Taft. Garrett had previously told the OIC that he had no chronological files. (Garrett, FBI 302, 4/8/92, p. 10.) DoD Deputy General Counsel Michael A. Sterlacci testified, however, that the files had been obtained from Garrett's former office (Garrett had recently resigned as Secretary of the Navy). (Sterlacci, Grand Jury, 10/28/92, p. 7.) Sterlacci also conceded that, although the OGC had forwarded the earlier OIC document request to Garrett, the OGC had made no effort to follow up on the matter when Garrett failed to respond. (Ibid., pp. 11–13.)

[311] According to one OGC attorney, the files had been scattered among three different offices, including Sterlacci's, before mid-1992. The attorney said that the missing files had been located when old

During the investigation, the OIC discovered that DoD officials had faxed to Weinberger's counsel copies of at least one OIC document request to DoD, which the OIC regarded as confidential. DoD's Acting General Counsel later conceded that it was not consistent with DoD policy to disclose such documents relating to an ongoing criminal investigation without at least consulting the prosecutor beforehand.[312]

OIC discovered after Weinberger's indictment that DoD personnel had given Weinberger's defense counsel apparently unsupervised access to documents the OIC had identified as evidence and left, by agreement with DoD, temporarily in DoD custody.[313] This jeopardized the integrity of original evidence in a pending criminal case and also allowed Weinberger's counsel to circumvent ordinary discovery procedures. DoD's general counsel later conceded that this conduct was not consistent with DoD policy, which provides that the Department of Justice, (in this case, the OIC) should be consulted before DoD discloses official information to a criminal defendant or other litigant.[314]

Independent Counsel decided in 1992 not to commit resources to an investigation into ongoing obstruction by the Department of Defense.

---

files were being reviewed to be sent to storage, not in response to the OIC's document requests. (White, FBI 302, 9/4/92, p. 1.)

[312] Letter from Chester Paul Beach, Jr., DoD Acting General Counsel, to Gillen, 8/8/92 (020209).

[313] This discovery was accidental. An OIC attorney arrived at the Pentagon to take custody of the documents and found that one of Weinberger's attorneys was photocopying the documents in the OGC's offices without any visible supervision by DoD personnel.

[314] DoD Directive 5405.2, 7/23/85.

# Part IX
# Investigations of the White House

The Iran/contra affair flowed from decisions made and actions taken in the White House by President Reagan and his closest advisers.

The operational aspects of Iran/contra were carried out by the national security adviser to the President and the National Security Council staff, who were aided by private operatives they recruited. Their criminal activities are related in earlier sections of this report.

This part of the report covers the actions and decisions relative to Iran/contra of President Reagan; White House Chief of Staff Donald T. Regan; Attorney General Edwin Meese III, in so far as Meese acted in his capacity as friend and adviser to the President; Vice President George Bush; Bush's national security adviser Donald P. Gregg; and Gregg's deputy, Col. Samuel J. Watson III.

The criminal investigation established that President Reagan, with the support of Vice President Bush, promulgated the two policies that drove Iran/contra:

—that the contras would be kept viable as an insurgent force during the Boland cut-off period from October 1984 to October 1986, and

—that arms would be sold to Iran, first from Israeli stocks and later directly from the United States, in exchange for the release of Americans held hostage in the Middle East.

The investigation also established that the President, Vice President and Regan were briefed regularly and in considerable detail as to the operations being conducted to carry out those policies. Independent Counsel found no credible evidence that the President authorized or was aware of the diversion of profits from the Iran arms sales to assist the contras, or that Regan, Bush, or Meese was aware of the diversion.

Similarly, Independent Counsel found no convincing evidence that Reagan formally or specifically authorized the National Security Council staff in general or Lt. Col. Oliver L. North in particular to establish a U.S. Government-coordinated covert, full-scale contra-resupply organization to replace the CIA during the Boland cut-off period. President Reagan and Vice President Bush did receive regular reports on the strengths and problems of the contras and knew that North was the Government official charged in the first instance with trying to find solutions to their problems.

The OIC found considerable evidence that the President and the Vice President knew about and, in some instances, directly participated in contra-funding efforts during this period—including third-country donations, quid-pro-quo arrangements to encourage third-country support, and contributions from private citizens. In addition, there was evidence that Bush's aides Gregg and Watson had information on North's direction of the contra-resupply effort through Gregg's close relationship with Felix Rodriguez, a former CIA operative whom North enlisted as a part of his contra-supply organization. Gregg claimed that, notwithstanding the Administration's interest in the success of the contras, he never mentioned any information regarding contra resupply to Vice President Bush, the person he was advising on national security matters.

A principal focus of this section centers on the activities of the President, the Vice President, Regan and Meese during November 1986 when the public disclosure of the Iran arms sales created a political furor, generating demands for a congressional investigation and the appointment of an independent counsel. Of particular interest to congressional leaders was whether the Iran arms sales, in the face of a U.S.-supported embargo on such sales, were in violation of any statutes, and whether the failure of the Administration to disclose the Iran arms sales to Congress was in violation of the Arms Export Control Act, the National Security Act or any other statute.

Independent Counsel concluded that President Reagan, Vice President Bush, Regan, Meese and other senior Administration officials in November 1986 undertook to "rearrange the record," as Secretary of State George P. Shultz put it in a conversation with his senior advisers, in an effort to protect the President and themselves from accusations of possible violations of law. A particular concern was that the 1985 Iran arms sales from Israeli stocks violated the congressional notification requirement of the Arms Export Control Act. Evidence to support this conclusion was obtained by Independent Counsel in 1991 and 1992 from notes, diaries and documents previously withheld from the Tower Commission, the congressional Select Committees and the OIC. The withheld evidence demonstrated that:

—President Reagan authorized the 1985 sale of TOW and HAWK missiles from Israeli stocks in an effort to free Americans held hostage even though he was warned such sales were in violation of the Arms Export Control Act.

—The President's senior national security advisers—Vice President Bush, Shultz, Secretary of Defense Caspar W. Weinberger, CIA Director William J. Casey, and Regan—were informed in 1985 of presidential approval of the transactions.

One year later, in November 1986, when Congress tried to learn the facts about the Iran arms sales, the Administration first tried to withhold information about the 1985 sales from Israeli stocks. Thereafter, Poindexter and Meese stated that the President was unaware of and had not authorized the November 1985 shipment of 18 HAWK missiles from Israel to Iran—that the initiative had been handled by former National Security Adviser Robert C. McFarlane without presidential authorization. The evidence demonstrates that Poindexter and Meese, as well as the President and his other senior advisers, knew that to be false, but they at least tentatively accommodated that position.

Independent Counsel concluded that no criminal charges should be brought against President Reagan, Vice President Bush, Meese or Regan because the belated production of notes and other documents delayed the investigation beyond the point where it could be effective.

# Chapter 27
# President Reagan

The President is the only individual granted power and responsibility by the Constitution. In other delegations of power and authority, the Constitution deals with entities—the Congress, the courts, the states. In cases of conduct involving political objectives rather than venal objectives, the procedure of impeachment, which brings into play the political judgment of both houses of Congress, would ordinarily be preferred over criminal charges and a trial by jury.

Further, the President's awesome responsibility for policy decisions necessary to our national safety was not intended to be belittled by requiring him to deal personally with the thicket of statutes, regulations, and orders that regulate Government activity. He ordinarily would be entitled to rely on his staff and Cabinet to see that his decisions are carried out in a legal manner.

But because a President, and certainly a past President, is subject to prosecution in appropriate cases, the conduct of President Reagan in the Iran/contra matter was reviewed by Independent Counsel against the applicable statutes. It was concluded that President Reagan's conduct fell well short of criminality which could be successfully prosecuted. Fundamentally, it could not be proved beyond a reasonable doubt that President Reagan knew of the underlying facts of Iran/contra that were criminal or that he made criminal misrepresentations regarding them.

President Reagan created the conditions which made possible the crimes committed by others by his secret deviations from announced national policy as to Iran and hostages and by his open determination to keep the contras to-gether "body and soul" despite a statutory ban on contra aid.[1]

In the Iran initiative, President Reagan chose to proceed in the utmost secrecy, disregarding the Administration's public policy prohibiting arms sales to nations supporting terrorism. He also chose to forgo congressional notification under the National Security Act and the Arms Export Control Act.[2] Having bypassed accountability to Congress, the President failed either to establish an effective system of accountability within the Administration or to monitor the series of activities he authorized.[3] Working in a climate of extreme secrecy and operating without accountability, National Security Adviser John M. Poindexter, Lt. Col. Oliver L. North of the National Security Council staff and others associated with the initiative invited criminal acts including profiteering on the Iranian arms sales, the diversion of some of those proceeds to aid the contras, destroying documents, and lying to Congress to cover up their criminal activities.

When the Iran initiative was exposed on November 3, 1986, the President convened a series of meetings with his top national security advisers and permitted the creation of a false account of the Iran arms sales to be disseminated to members of Congress and the American peo-

---

[1] McFarlane, *North* Trial Testimony, 3/10/89, p. 3946.

[2] See discussion on "The Iran Hostage Initiative, 1985–1986" later in this chapter.

[3] In his written answers to interrogatories requested by Independent Counsel and the Grand Jury, Reagan stated that he did not monitor the details of the Iran arms sales and had no specific knowledge of such key matters as North's role or Secord's role. The President said he did not authorize any profits from the sale of arms to Iran and that he was unaware that there were excess proceeds and that some of them were diverted to aid the contras.

ple.[4] These false accounts denied the President's knowledge and authorization of the initial sales from Israeli stocks of U.S.-made TOW and HAWK missiles to Iran in August, September and November of 1985. Attorney General Edwin Meese III and others were concerned that those sales violated the Arms Export Control Act and the National Security Act of 1947.[5] Previously withheld notes by participants in the November 12 and November 24, 1986, meetings constituted evidence of an effort to cover up the true facts of the President's authorization of the 1985 Iran arms sales. But the discovery of the notes by Independent Counsel came too late to investigate effectively and to prosecute the false statements involved.[6] The passage of time, claims of dimmed recollections and the running of the statute of limitations protected the underlying acts.

No direct evidence was developed that the President authorized or was informed of the profiteering on the Iran arms sales or of the diversion of proceeds to aid the contras.[7] Yet, it was doubtful that President Reagan would tolerate the successive Iranian affronts during 1986 unless he knew that the arms sales continued to supply funds to the contras to bridge the gap before the anticipated congressional appropriations became effective. Only Poindexter could supply direct evidence, and he denied passing on this information. The wide destruction of records by North eliminated any possible documentary proof.

As with the Iran initiative, President Reagan was apparently unconcerned as to the details of how his policy objectives for contra support were being carried out by subordinates who were operating virtually free from oversight or accountability. President Reagan made it clear to his national security advisers Robert C. McFarlane and Poindexter that he wanted to keep the contra resistance alive "body and soul." He said he told them to stay within the law, including the Boland Amendment restrictions on U.S. aid to the contras. In doing so, he confronted his staff with two virtually incompatible objectives.

This determination to surmount Boland was seized on by North and others as a justification for violating Boland and later lying to Congress about such violations. Independent Counsel found no prosecutable evidence that the President expressly authorized or was informed of the illegal features of North's operational participation in the covert contra-resupply operation and his financing of the operation. President Reagan was aware of and even encouraged some aspects of external funding for the contras, such as solicitation of aid from third countries and contributions from private benefactors. He also was aware that North was the NSC's action officer on the contras, and he was regularly briefed on the growth of the contra movement during the period when funds to assist the contras were cut off by Boland.[8]

President Reagan supplied information regarding his knowledge of these activities in sworn answers to written interrogatories posed by Independent Counsel and the Grand Jury, his testimony during the *Poindexter* trial, and a deposition by Independent Counsel in July 1992. In addition, North, Poindexter and other central figures testified during the investigation and in various trials. Documents were also produced after the Select Iran/contra Committees had completed their investigation in 1987.

President Reagan's activities were analyzed in four broad aspects: (1) the military and paramilitary support of the contras from 1984 to 1986; (2) the Iran arms sales in 1985 and 1986; (3) the October–November 1986 cover-up of these activities from mounting congressional inquiries; and (4) the President's responses and

---

[4] Two of the key meetings were on November 10 and November 12, where the principal account of the Iran initiative, given by Poindexter, left out the 1985 arms sales from Israeli stocks. At a meeting on November 24, Attorney General Meese said that the November 1985 HAWK shipment was possibly illegal but, he said, the President "didn't know."

[5] Later, the Department of Justice Office of Legal Counsel developed a purported defense for these sales. The participants in the November 24, 1986, meeting were concerned, however, with the question of legality, rightly or wrongly.

[6] Former Defense Secretary Caspar W. Weinberger was indicted by a federal Grand Jury on June 16, 1992, on five counts of obstruction, perjury and false statements. He was to be tried on January 5, 1993. Weinberger was pardoned by President Bush on December 24, 1992.

[7] Two of the key persons involved in the operations said they believed the President either had approved of their actions or would have approved of them had he been asked. Poindexter, who testified that he did not inform the President of the diversion, said he nevertheless believed the President would have approved it had it been presented to him. (Poindexter, Select Committees Deposition, 5/2/87, pp. 70–72.) North testified that he believed that the President had authorized the diversion. (North, Select Committees Testimony, 7/7/87, pp. 23–25.)

[8] Answers of the President of the United States to Interrogatories, Answer to Question 10, *In Re Grand Jury Investigation* (hereafter, "Reagan, Grand Jury Interrogatories").

testimony to the Tower Commission and to Independent Counsel.

## Military and Paramilitary Support to the Contras, October 1984 to October 1986

### Financial Support

From the congressional cut off of contra military aid until October 1986, when Congress again appropriated funds for contra assistance, there were three sources of funding developed by NSC officials to carry out President Reagan's generalized admonition to keep the contras together "body and soul": third-country grants; donations from so-called "private benefactors"; and proceeds diverted from the Iran arms sales. Of the three, third-country funding, particularly from the Saudis, was by far the biggest source, amounting to $32 million. The Taiwanese government contributed $2 million. Other governments, at the request of the Administration, made available weapons, documentation to disguise the origin of weapon shipments, and facilities to accommodate contra camps and provide logistical support. Some $1.7 million in private contributions flowed through the tax-exempt National Endowment for the Preservation of Liberty (NEPL) to accounts controlled by North, and approximately $4 million from the Iran arms proceeds diversion, also controlled by North.[9]

The Administration was advised by the attorney general that, absent a quid-pro-quo arrangement, soliciting third-country contributions which would be paid directly to the contras would not violate Boland restrictions.[10] It would obviously be difficult to proceed criminally against a President who operated on the basis of what he considered sound legal advice. The President held a similar view that he and his subordinates could publicly encourage private citizens to contribute directly to the contras without running afoul of Boland.[11]

The President denied unequivocally that he was aware of the diversion of funds from the proceeds of the Iran arms sales, or that he authorized it.[12] Independent Counsel could not prove the contrary. Poindexter testified that he did not inform the President of the diversion, and Meese and White House Chief of Staff Donald T. Regan testified that the President was "shocked" when he learned about it on November 24, 1986.[13]

Domestic fundraising for the contras presented a more complicated picture. There is no doubt that, at least beginning with his appearance at a dinner for the Nicaraguan Refugee Fund in April 1985 and continuing through mid-1986, President Reagan, like North, was a frequent and enthusiastic fundraiser for contra-related causes. The President's appeals seem to have been confined to non-lethal, "humanitarian" aid. North, in contrast, participated in direct appeals, mainly through the tax-exempt NEPL, for funds to buy weapons, a fact that Poindexter did not recall telling the President.[14] President Reagan was unquestionably aware of NEPL. He held meetings and exchanged commendatory correspondence with its officials and big contributors, often at North's request. President Reagan stated that he did not know that North wound up with actual control of the funds raised through NEPL and passed them through

---

[9] See Flow of Funds chapter.

[10] See Minutes from National Security Planning Group Meeting, 6/25/84, ALU 007863–76. Although Vice President Bush and CIA Director William J. Casey felt third-country assistance would be legal absent any quid-pro-quo arrangement, Secretary of State George P. Shultz felt that a legal opinion should be obtained; and Casey agreed. The day after the NSPG meeting, Casey and CIA General Counsel Stanley Sporkin met with Attorney General William French Smith and two of his assistants and were told by the attorney general that

> he saw no legal concern if the United States Government discussed this matter with other nations so long as it was made clear that they would be using their own funds to support the contras and no U.S. appropriated funds would be used for this purpose. The Attorney General also said that any nation agreeing to supply aid could not look to the United States to repay that commitment in the future.

An assistant to the attorney general, Mary Lawton, suggested that

> a specific written statement might be developed to make clear to cooperating nations that any decision to provide further assist-

ance to the resistance in Nicaragua would be made without any monetary promises or inducements from the United States Government which would expect them to take steps to assure that no U.S. appropriated funds would be involved in the program.

(Memorandum from Sporkin to the Record, 6/26/84, ER 21615.)

[11] Reagan, Grand Jury Interrogatories, Answers to Questions 1–4.

[12] The President denied knowledge of the diversion to the Tower Commission, in his sworn answers to Grand Jury Interrogatories, in his testimony in *Poindexter*, and in numerous public statements following the disclosure of the diversion by Attorney General Meese on November 25, 1986. (See, e.g. Reagan, Remarks at a Meeting with the President's Special Review Board, 12/1/86, *Public Papers of the Presidents*, 1986 Vol. II, 1986, p. 1591; Reagan, Address to Nation on Iran Arms and Contra Aid Controversy, 3/4/87, *Ibid.*, p. 208–11; Reagan, Interview with White House Newspaper Correspondents, 4/28/87, *Ibid.*, pp. 424–29; Reagan, Address to Nation, 8/12/87, Ibid., p. 942–45.)

[13] Meese, Grand Jury, 2/17/88, pp. 51–56; Regan, Grand Jury, 2/3/88, pp. 43–47.

[14] Poindexter, Grand Jury, 11/28/90, p. 115.

to the secret Swiss accounts managed by retired Air Force Maj. Gen. Richard V. Secord and Albert Hakim.[15] Independent Counsel could not prove that the President was aware of the misused tax-exempt status of NEPL, or that he was aware that contributions to it were used to purchase lethal materials for the contras.

In describing his understanding of NEPL, the President said in his Grand Jury Interrogatory Answer 19:

I understand that NEPL was engaged in building grass-roots support for legislation to provide military support to the NFF [contras] including the funding of a public awareness campaign.

My understanding came from briefing papers provided to me by my staff and by correspondence I received from NEPL . . . Moreover, NEPL engaged in similar public information programs for other national security issues, e.g., the Strategic Defense Initiative. I thought of their effort on behalf of the NFF as identical to these other information programs.

North stated in a May 1986 computer note to Poindexter that "the President obviously knows why he has been meeting with several select people to thank them for their 'support for Democracy' in CentAm."[16] Independent Counsel could not prove, however, that the President had more than the generalized awareness of private U.S. support for the contras reflected in his Answer to Grand Jury Interrogatories 14–17:

I was generally aware that some assistance was flowing from the private sources to the NFF and that some of this assistance would have included military support. This information was public knowledge as early as 1985 and was even mentioned in Congressional debate about a request for funding in August 1985. Until the plane carrying Mr. Hasenfus was shot down in October 1986, I do not recall knowing of specific individuals or groups engaged in this activity and was unaware of any connection with the U.S. Government. I believed such activity to be similar to the efforts by Americans in other conflicts. Even after Mr. Hasenfus was shot down, I was told that he was not participating in a U.S. sponsored operation, and I was not informed of any particulars of that operation beyond what was in the news media. It was not until after November 25, 1986, when the full details of these operations became public, that I learned the nature and extent of the private support network and the role of certain U.S. officials in it.

Although I did not seek or directly encourage private citizens to provide military support, I did encourage William Simon and others to provide humanitarian assistance through the Nicaraguan Freedom Fund (Tab 14A). I also knew, as had been previously reported in the press, that Mrs. Garwood had contributed money to refurbish a Medevac helicopter. I understood her contributions to be of a humanitarian nature, and when I met Mrs. Garwood, this subject was not discussed.

The President's knowledge was much more complete regarding the obtaining of funds for the contras from foreign governments. But Independent Counsel found no evidence that he knew that, after North had set up his secret contra-resupply operation, control over most of those contributions also passed to North. Both McFarlane and CIA Director William J. Casey sought aid from foreign governments for the contras during the first six months of 1984.[17] There is no doubt that the President was informed of the first successful effort to secure third-country funding. In May or June 1984, McFarlane advised the President that the Saudi Arabian ambassador, Prince Bandar, volunteered

---

[15] Reagan, Grand Jury Interrogatories, Answer to Question 18. Alan D. Fiers, Jr., former head of the CIA's Central American Task Force, had a vivid memory of the NSPG meeting on May 16, 1986. According to Fiers, during a discussion of the need for funds to keep contras in the field until an expected congressional appropriation became available, President Reagan said: "Can't some of Ollie's people help out?" Regan quickly changed the subject. (Fiers, Grand Jury, 8/14/91, p. 39.) The official NSPG minutes record Reagan's remarks as: "What about the private groups who pay for ads for the contras. Have they been contacted? Could they do more than ads?" (Minutes of the May 16, 1986, NSPG Meeting, 6/4/86, AKW 018802–13.)

[16] PROFs Note from North to *Poindexter*, 5/16/86, Poindexter GX 66.

[17] See McFarlane and Casey chapters; see also Reagan, Grand Jury Interrogatories, Answers to Questions 11–13.

to deliver $1 million-per-month to a contra bank account. According to McFarlane, the President responded to this information with the words "Good news" or "That's fine." [18]

On June 25, 1984, third-country solicitation was discussed at a meeting of the National Security Planning Group (NSPG). CIA Director Casey reported that the CIA was down to $250,000 remaining from the Fiscal 1984 appropriation for the contras, and that the contras had arms and ammunition to last only until August. Casey brought up the subject of third-country funding, prompting a debate between Secretary of State George P. Shultz and Casey over whether or not White House Chief of Staff James Baker, who was not at the meeting, believed that solicitation of third-country funding for the contras would be an "impeachable offense." It was decided that Attorney General William French Smith would be consulted to resolve that issue. Those who were aware of the Saudi $1 million-per-month commitment did not mention it. According to the minutes, the meeting concluded with the following exchange:

*Vice President Bush:* How can anyone object to the U.S. encouraging third parties to provide help to the anti-Sandinistas under the finding? The only problem that might come up is if the United States were to promise to give these third parties something in return so that some people could interpret this as some kind of exchange.

*Mr. Casey:* Jim Baker changed his mind as soon as he saw the finding and saw the language.

*Mr. McFarlane:* I propose that there be no authority for anyone to seek third party support for the anti-Sandinistas until we have the information we need, and I certainly hope none of this discussion will be made public in any way.

*President Reagan:* If such a story gets out, we'll all be hanging by our thumbs in front of the White House until we find out who did it.[19]

McFarlane interpreted the President's final comment as a command that Congress not be notified of third-country contributions, but not a direction to lie to Congress if asked.[20]

The President himself received promise of the next major foreign contribution to the contras, which also came from Saudi Arabia. During a February 1985 visit to Washington by King Fahd, the king volunteered to double the Saudis' contribution to the contras to $2 million per month. Reagan later informed McFarlane and, according to McFarlane, directed that the information not be shared with others.[21]

The NSC staff aided efforts to obtain both financial and other support for the contras from other third countries as well. The Republic of Korea was solicited through retired Army Maj. Gen. John K. Singlaub; no contribution resulted. Taiwan was solicited through a number of intermediaries; two donations of $1 million each were eventually received. Poindexter suspected that the President was informed of Taiwan's contribution.[22]

Finally, with regard to the contras' never-ending search for anti-aircraft missiles, the President was at least generally familiar with North's efforts to obtain foreign approvals necessary for the contras to obtain British-made Blowpipe missiles.[23] Poindexter recalled, albeit vaguely, discussing with the President efforts to get Blowpipes or Chinese-made SA–7s for the contras.[24]

During 1985 and early 1986, the President and other Administration officials were called upon to send frequent messages to Central American countries to bolster their support for the contras and to remind them of the importance of their security and aid relationships with the United States. The President personally participated in flurries of this type of activity involving Honduras in February 1985, April 1985, May 1985, and March 1986. The most graphic example was an April 25, 1985, call from Reagan to President Roberto Suazo Cordova of

---

[18] McFarlane, Grand Jury, 4/29/87, pp. 36–37.
[19] Minutes from National Security Planning Group Meeting, 6/25/84, ALU 007863–76.

[20] McFarlane, *North* Trial Testimony, 3/10/89, pp. 3941–30; Ibid., 3/15/89, pp. 4626–29.
[21] Ibid., 3/13/89, pp. 4201–6.
[22] Poindexter, Select Committees Deposition, 6/17/87, pp. 268–69. For discussion of McFarlane and North involvement in solicitation of third-country funds for the contras, see McFarlane chapter.
[23] Ibid., pp. 76–79.
[24] Poindexter, Grand Jury, 3/6/91, pp. 52–54.

Honduras, in which Reagan aksed on Suazo
to persuade the Honduran military to release
a contra weapons shipment which had been
seized by the Honduran army.[25] A briefing
memo for Reagan's use in a subsequent May
meeting with President Suazo states:

> In your meeting it will be important to
> reiterate to Suazo the importance we attach
> to his continued cooperation in enabling
> the FDN [contras] to remain a viable ele-
> ment of pressure on the Sandinistas. With-
> out making the linkage too explicit, it
> would be useful to remind Suazo that in
> return for our help—in the form of security
> assurances as well as aid—we do expect
> cooperation in pursuit of our mutual objec-
> tives. In this regard, you could underline
> the seriousness of security commitment,
> which the Hondurans seem to regard as
> the main quid-pro-quo for cooperating with
> the FDN.[26]

When asked to explain this passage in his
deposition at the trial of Poindexter, President
Reagan said:

> A: Well, again, I think it is the same tone.
> That we don't want to press them to go
> so far that they challenge the Sandinista
> government and wind up in open hostilities
> with them. And the—it would be useful
> however to remind them that in return for
> our help in the form of security assurances
> as well as aid that we do expect coopera-
> tion. That we feel that there is an obliga-
> tion on their part, too.
>
> Q: Right. So, in other words, if some aid
> and assistance is given to them, you would
> expect some aid and assistance back from
> them—.
>
> A: Yes.
>
> Q: . . . in combating the spread of the
> Sandinistas?
>
> A: Yeah.[27]

There is little doubt from the record that in
their dealings with the Central American countries, the Administration, including the President, reminded the military and political leaders
of those countries, who were dependent on U.S.
aid and support, that support for the contras
was a tacit condition for continuation of financial and other support.

## The Resupply Organization

The President was regularly briefed by
McFarlane and Poindexter on the progress and
growth of the contra force and its operations
during the 1984–86 period.[28] At times the President almost seemed to claim responsibility for
their activities.[29] But in his answers to the
Grand Jury's interrogatories, he denied either
authorizing or approving a transfer of contra-
support functions from the CIA to the NSC:

> I did not authorize or approve of the trans-
> fer to the NSC or any of its staff any
> function or operation performed by the
> CIA with respect to the Nicaraguan Free-
> dom Fighters. I do not recall anyone ever
> asking me to approve or authorize the
> transfer of any function or operation from
> the CIA to the NSC, and I do not recall
> ever discussing such transfer.[30]

> *          *          *

> Beyond [Presidential Findings, National
> Security Decision Directives, and advocacy
> of third-country assistance], my instructions
> with regard to the support for the Freedom
> Fighters were usually of a general nature,
> and I do not now recall any authorization
> or approvals of specific actions with re-
> spect to the Freedom Fighters.

[25] Recommended Telephone Call, 4/25/85, ALU 0097413–14.
[26] Memorandum from McFarlane Re: "Meeting with Honduran President Suazo", 5/21/85, ALU 0086547–60.
[27] Reagan, *Poindexter* Trial Testimony, 2/16/90, p. 109.

[28] Poindexter, Grand Jury, 11/28/90, pp. 60–63.
[29] Reagan, Remarks and a Question-and-Answer Session With Southeast Regional Editors and Broadcasters, 5/15/87, *Public Papers of the
Presidents*, 1987, Vol. I, p. 514: "These [the contras] are people who
are fighting for democracy and freedom in their country. And here
there's no question about my being informed. I've known what's going
on there. As a matter of fact, for quite a long time now, a matter
of years, I have been publicly speaking of the necessity of the American
people to support our program of aid to those freedom fighters down
there in order to prevent there being established a Soviet beachhead
here in the Western Hemisphere, in addition to the one we already
have in Cuba. And to suggest that I am just finding out or that
things are being exposed that I didn't know about—no. Yes, I was
kept briefed on that. As a matter of fact, I was very definitely involved
in the decisions on the support to the freedom fighters. It was my
idea to begin with."
[30] Reagan, Grand Jury Interrogatories, Answer to Question 8.

With regard to Richard V. Secord and Albert Hakim, I do not recall approving or authorizing any action concerning them with regard to the Freedom Fighters or of meeting either individual during this time frame.[31]

\*     \*     \*

I knew that Lt. Col. North's responsibilities included work related to Central America and, specifically, Nicaragua. However, prior to my conversations with Attorney General Meese on November 24 and 25, 1986 concerning what has come to be known as the "diversion", I did not know that Lt. Col. North participated in planning, directing or advising NFF military or paramilitary operations or logistical support for such operations. Although I heard about allegations in the press that Lt. Col. North was engaged in such activities, I understood that these allegations were incorrect.[32]

In his testimony in *United States* v. *Poindexter*, the President said he generally recalled North as a "communicator" between the U.S. Government and the contras.[33] The President said he did not have "any inkling" that the NSC staff was guiding the contras' strategy or that North was participating in planning and directing and advising the contras' military activities, including giving logistical support to them.[34] Elaborating on his Interrogatory Answers, Reagan testified that he had "heard reports about" Secord and Hakim in connection with contra assistance[35] and he recalled that Secord had "some kind of aero business" or "delivery business" and "might have been involved with delivering some aid to the contras when it was legal to provide such aid."[36] The President also recalled being informed by Poindexter about a Costa Rican airstrip, which Mr. Reagan said he "hoped that it would be used in the delivery of when once again we could supply, keep the contras supplied, that it could be involved in the—used there, if there

was need for a refueling or anything of that kind of plane."[37] The President went on to speculate that the aircraft using the airstrip would have been "some of those that weren't officially planes of ours that had been helping in the past in deliveries to the contras." He added it seemed "logical" that Secord would have been involved in that.[38]

The President to this extent admitted to a good basic understanding of the logistics of supplying the contras' southern front from Ilopango air base in El Salvador: planes that were not "officially" U.S. government, using an airstrip in a neutral country to refuel for the long round trip from Ilopango, along the Pacific to Nicaragua near the Costa Rican border to avoid overflying Nicaragua.

McFarlane testified that he kept the President apprised of what he was doing with respect to the contras, including what was "close to the line."[39] Poindexter believed that the President would certainly have known that North was the NSC's action officer on Central America, and that the NSC was keeping close track of the situation in that region. Poindexter did not recall any conversation with the President about the breadth of these actions.[40] In a Grand Jury appearance, Poindexter recalled that he did tell President Reagan that Secord was "heading up the private operations to actually provide the logistics support to the contras."[41] Poindexter did not recall whether the President was told about the June 1985 Miami meeting in which North with Secord assumed control of the resupply operation.[42]

That the documentary record of precisely what was passed along to the President regarding the details of North's secret resupply operation is sparse is not surprising, considering the wholesale destruction of records by North. One surviving North document that reached the President was an October 30, 1985, memorandum requesting presidential approval of U.S.

[31] Ibid., Answer to Question 9.
[32] Ibid., Answer to Question 10.
[33] Reagan, *Poindexter* Trial Testimony, 2/16/90, pp.131–38.
[34] Ibid., 2/17/90, p. 170.
[35] Ibid., p. 192.
[36] Ibid., 2/16/90, p. 21.

[37] Ibid., p. 121.
[38] Ibid., p. 122.
[39] McFarlane, Select Committees Testimony, 5/13/87, p. 98.
[40] Poindexter, Select Committees Deposition, 5/2/87, pp. 221–22; Ibid., 6/17/87, pp. 315–16; Poindexter, Select Committees Testimony, 7/15/87, pp. 138–41; Ibid., 7/20/87 pp. 3, 10.
[41] Poindexter, Grand Jury, 11/28/90, p. 72.
[42] Ibid., pp. 71–73.

reconnaissance flights over Nicaragua.[43] It is initialed "approve" by Poindexter, and also bears the words "President Approved." Poindexter said this meant that he briefed the President orally on the content of the document rather than giving him the document to read.[44] Poindexter did not recall whether he briefed the President on an attached, supplementary note from North which says in part:

> You should also tell the President that we intend to air-drop [the intelligence obtained from the reconnaissance flights] to two Resistance [contra] units deployed along the Rio Escondito, along with two Honduran provided 106 mm recoilless rifles which will be used to sink one or both of the arms carriers which show up in photograph at Tab I.

Accordingly, there is some evidence indicating that the President was exposed to information about North's activities both in briefings from McFarlane and Poindexter and from documents. The President attached great importance during this period to the success of the contra effort. His personal diary is replete with references to the contra-aid struggle with Congress.[45] It showed he followed the debate on the various contra-aid proposals on Capitol Hill very closely. There were frequent references to poll results regarding the lack of public support for the contra cause. Both McFarlane and Poindexter reported regularly to Reagan on the state of the contras. The question of how to continue their financial support was discussed at several NSPG sessions.

There is no question that within the Administration, President Reagan's support for the success of the contras assured high-level guidance for North from Casey, McFarlane and Poindexter.[46] North's requests for assistance re-

ceived warm and generous responses from working groups within the national security community.[47] Ambassadors, assistant secretaries, CIA experts, and high-ranking military and intelligence officers responded to North's requests with alacrity. Only the impression, right or wrong, that North had the tacit authorization of the chief executive can explain this degree of support and cooperation in an area of manifest congressional hostility.

In spite of his insulation from North and his activities by McFarlane and Poindexter, President Reagan had to know the contras were being held together, as he directed. He knew that the funds from the Saudis had run out, but somehow other sources of funding were not only enabling the contras to survive, but to grow. When the press or Congress raised questions about the scope of the NSC and North's involvement, the President relied on McFarlane and Poindexter to respond to these allegations. The President, having issued generalized instructions to his subordinates that they stay within the law, relied upon the generalized assurances from McFarlane and Poindexter that his instructions were being followed.[48]

Proof of President Reagan's authorization or knowledge of North's illegal activities, beyond a reasonable doubt, would have required more than the non-specific testimony that McFarlane and Poindexter were willing to give and that the few surviving documents would establish. The President's own activities on behalf of the contras were not on the face of it activities forbidden by criminal law.

Procuring foreign assistance for the pursuit of objectives approved by Congress, such as the recent war with Iraq, is quite different from procuring foreign assistance for an objective rejected or prohibited by Congress. But diplomatic intercourse with the heads of foreign states is an essential presidential function. Even statutory restrictions in this field may be questionable. The constitutional remedy is impeachment. It is hardly a field for the application of criminal law. No criminal statute attempts to deal with this problem.

[43] Memorandum from North to McFarlane, 10/30/85, ALU 0060483–86.

[44] Poindexter, Grand Jury, 11/28/90, p. 86–87.

[45] The OIC was permitted to read excepts from the President's diary entries from 1984–87 deemed relevant to Iran/contra by White House counsel. The OIC reviewers were not permitted to make copies, so the references to President Reagan's Diary quoted here, except where otherwise attributed, reflect OIC attorneys' notes of the excerpts.

[46] Reagan, Grand Jury Interrogatories, Answer to Question 9. When asked whether he authorized Casey, among others, to take action with respect to the contras during the Boland cut-off period, the President said the question was too broad to be answered specifically. He conceded that Administration policy was to support the contras. "Thus,

Administration officials were generally authorized to implement that policy." (Ibid.)

[47] See North chapter.

[48] Reagan, *Poindexter* Trial Testimony, 2/16/90, pp. 53–54.

# The Iran Hostage Initiative, 1985–1986

In an effort to convince elements in Iran to use their influence to obtain the release of U.S. hostages in Lebanon, the President and his advisers in 1985 embarked upon the sale of arms to Iran, first through Israel, and subsequently directly through the CIA, under the operating direction of North, and using the Secord-Hakim "Enterprise" as a cut-out to disguise CIA involvement. In both phases, the President directed that Congress not be notified.[49]

In the first phase, beginning in mid-1985, the President was informed of and approved in advance an Israeli shipment of 504 Israeli-owned U.S.-made TOW antitank missiles to Iran in August and September and a November shipment of Israeli-owned U.S. HAWK anti-aircraft missiles.[50] The weapons were to be paid for by Iran and the Israeli stocks were to be replenished by the United States, which originally sold the weapons to Israel.

The second phase in which the United States itself transferred weapons to Iran through the CIA and the Enterprise included 1,000 TOW missiles sent to Iran in February 1986 and 240 spare parts for HAWK missile systems sent in May and August 1986. In May 1986, the United States also sent 508 TOW missiles to Israel as part of the promised replenishment. In October 1986 a second group of 500 TOW missiles from the United States was delivered through the CIA and the Enterprise to Israel. The older-model TOWs the Israelis had received in May were then shipped to Iran.

The Iranian representatives paid the Enterprise in advance for each 1986 shipment. The Enterprise reimbursed the CIA. During 1986 there was a substantial difference, aggregating roughly $16 million, after costs of delivery, between amounts collected by the Enterprise from Iran and the amounts transmitted by the Enterprise to the CIA to pay the Department of Defense for the weapons. The President's Finding authorizing the transaction specified the initia-

tive's purposes; they did not include funding the contras or profiteering by Government agents.[51]

The facts of the ill-fated Iran arms sales have been widely covered since the secret initiative began unraveling publicly in early November 1986. The question here is whether President Reagan violated any criminal law with respect to approving the arms sales to Iran, by failing to execute an appropriate Finding or a written determination authorizing NSC involvement, or by ordering that the arms sales not be reported to Congress.

In the case of the two 1985 Israeli arms transfers, President Reagan knew from the outset that he was acting in conflict with his own announced policies of not rewarding hostage takers and of not selling arms to nations sponsoring terrorism. He knew this activity was politically and legally questionable.[52] Two of his principal advisers, Secretary of Defense Casper W. Weinberger and Secretary of State Shultz, both opposed the initiative for those and other reasons. Nonetheless, the President decided to proceed, and he directed that Congress not be notified.[53]

There was no way in which President Reagan's action could be squared with the Arms Export Control Act (AECA). The AECA forbade the retransfer of U.S. arms to a third country unless the United States itself could make the transfer directly. It required certifications from the recipient country concerning further transfer. Finally, it required reports to the Speaker of the House and the Senate Foreign Relations Committee concerning retransfer agreements and notice to Congress 30 days after the end of each quarter of a transfer of more than $1 million of major defense equipment.[54]

These requirements were raised forcefully by Weinberger in November 1985 telephone conversations with McFarlane and in the December

---

[49] Ibid., 2/17/90, p. 235.

[50] The President was briefed in advance on each group of weapons sold to Iran. With respect to the November 1985 HAWK shipment, the President was also told what happened to it (see Regan, Grand Jury, 2/3/88, p. 61–64; see also Poindexter Notes, 11/25/85, 000037–38). On December 5, 1985, President Reagan signed a Finding to validate it retroactively.

[51] The January 17, 1986, Iran arms Finding listed three purposes: "(1) establishing a more moderate government in Iran; (2) obtaining from [elements in Iran] significant intelligence not otherwise obtainable, to determine the current Iranian Government's intentions with respect to its neighbors and with respect to terrorist acts, and (3) furthering the release of the American hostages held in Beirut and preventing additional terrorist acts by these groups." (Presidential Finding, 1/17/86, AKW 001921.)

[52] Reagan, Poindexter Trial Testimony, 2/16/90, p. 16–19.

[53] See the December 5, 1985, retroactive Finding referred to in footnote 50.

[54] 22 U.S.C. § 2753(a).

7, 1985, meeting of Shultz and Weinberger with the President and others. On December 7, President Reagan was defiant. Poindexter had apparently passed to him North's prediction that the American hostages would likely be killed if the arms transfers did not proceed. President Reagan said he could explain to the American people a violation of the statute, but could not explain letting the hostages be killed for fear of violating a statute.

When interviewed by Independent Counsel on July 24, 1992, President Reagan, although no longer remembering the December 1985 conversation itself, confirmed it in the sense that he believed that it was what he would have said, and that the views expressed were still held by him. President Reagan's defiance, if it had been public, would have presented an outright constitutional confrontation with Congress. The question would have been the validity of a statutory restriction upon President Reagan's view of his constitutional powers as commander-in-chief and as the officer responsible for dealing with foreign nations.

Without any criminal sanction specifically provided for AECA violations, the question was whether this secret non-compliance with the AECA could be said to be a conspiracy to defraud the United States by the President and those assisting him in carrying out the transaction. In Independent Counsel's judgment, prosecution for such non-compliance would not have been appropriate. Right or wrong, the President's determination that secrecy was necessary to protect the hostages from murder was a matter for him to decide. Certainly, it was not a frivolous concern, nor was his view of his constitutional powers and responsibilities.

The second statute relative to the Iranian arms sales was the National Security Act of 1947, as amended.[55] This Act was considered first in connection with the *1986* arms sales but also, after the November 1986 exposure, as a retroactive validation of the *1985* arms sales. These opinions will be discussed in the chronological order in which they were given.

In January 1986, the President was informed by Attorney General Meese that he could avoid the Arms Export Control Act. This opinion was based upon an October 5, 1981, opinion of Attorney General William French Smith that if the President determined that neither the Foreign Assistance Act nor the Arms Export Control Act could be used, he could approve a transfer outside the context of these statutes if he determined that the authorities of the Economy Act and the National Security Act should be utilized in order to achieve "a significant intelligence objective." Whereas Attorney General Smith advised that reporting requirements imposed by the Intelligence Oversight Act of 1980 required that the House and Senate Intelligence Committees be informed of the President's determination, Attorney General Meese took a more extreme view that the National Security Act implicitly authorized the President to withhold any prior or contemporaneous notice to Congress, even the limited notice to the leadership of the intelligence committees and the leadership of the two houses of Congress.[56]

Section 501(a) of the National Security Act of 1947, as amended, provides

> To the extent consistent with all applicable authorities and duties, including those conferred by the Constitution upon the executive and legislative branches of the Government, and to the extent consistent with due regard for the protection from unauthorized disclosure of classified information and information relating to intelligence sources and methods, the Director of Central Intelligence and the heads of all departments, agencies, and other entities of the United States involved in intelligence activities shall—
>
> (1) keep the Select Committee on Intelligence of the Senate and Permanent Committee on Intelligence of the House of Representatives . . . fully and currently informed of all intelligence activities . . . including any significant anticipated intelligence activity, except that . . . (B) if the President determines it is essential to limit prior notice to meet extraordinary circumstances affecting vital interests of the United States, such notice shall be limited to the chairman and ranking minority mem-

---

55 50 U.S.C. § 413. The Foreign Assistance Act, 22 U.S.C. § 2314, is arguably inapplicable. It concerns government-to-government transfers, not sales to individuals.

56 Meese, Select Committees Testimony, 7/28/87, pp. 6, 26; ibid., 7/29/87, pp. 45–46.

bers of the intelligence committees, the Speaker and minority leader of the House of Representatives, and the majority and minority leaders of the Senate[.]

For the purposes of this section, the transfer of defense articles exceeding $1 million value by an intelligence agency to a recipient outside that agency was defined as a "significant anticipated intelligence activity" by the Fiscal Year 1986 Intelligence Authorization Act.[57]

Section 501(b) provides

The President shall fully inform the intelligence committees in a timely fashion of intelligence operations in foreign countries . . . for which prior notice was not given under subsection (a) of this section and shall provide a statement of the reasons for not giving prior notice.

Meese and the general counsel of the CIA advised President Reagan in 1986 that he could direct that notice not be given to any member of Congress. They reasoned that subsection (b) implied that the President, under certain circumstances, could avoid any notice to Congress, even the limited notice provided in § 501(a)(1)(B). They supported this conclusion by the introductory language of subsection (a), which is a lengthy expression of deference to the President's other duties and constitutional powers.

Section 501(b) could well be read more straightforwardly as a requirement that, in timely fashion, the eight specified representatives and senators be informed of intelligence operations specified in § 501(a)(1)(B) which permitted notice limited to eight persons. Nevertheless, Meese's more extreme view that the President could forbid any notice whatsoever to any member of Congress had been expounded previously within the CIA and could not in a criminal case be treated as legally insupportable or frivolous. Under these circumstances, § 501 of the National Security Act, with its deferential concern for the President's status in national security matters, would be poor support for criminal prosecution. In itself, it provided no criminal penalty for violation and, ordinarily, a President relying upon an opinion of the attorney general interpreting its deferential language could hardly be said to be conspiring to defraud the United States.

After Meese learned in 1986 of the November 1985 shipments, he had the problem of legality analyzed by Assistant Attorney General Charles Cooper, the head of the Office of Legal Counsel in the Department of Justice. In a December 17, 1986, memorandum to Meese, Cooper reconfirmed that the AECA did not apply to the *1986* arms sales to Iran. He concluded that the National Security Act *implicitly* recognizes the President's discretion to authorize weapons transfers outside the AECA as part of an activity conducted by an "intelligence agency," such as the CIA.[58]

The Hughes-Ryan Amendment to the Foreign Assistance Act required that before the CIA might engage in such operations in a foreign country the President must "find" that the operation is "important to the national security of the United States." [59]

The Israeli arms shipments in *1985*, which the U.S. had approved, presented a problem. If the CIA was involved, there had to be a presidential Finding or the AECA would apply. Since there was no Finding, the AECA appeared to apply. In his memorandum dated more than three weeks after Meese's weekend investigation, Cooper ultimately took the position that the 1985 arms sales were legal under the President's inherent powers as implicitly recognized by the National Security Act.[60]

With respect to the August and September 1985 TOW shipments, Cooper explained that only the NSC, not the CIA, was involved. Therefore, no Finding was necessary. Assuming the NSC is an "intelligence agency" for these purposes, which Cooper found "clear," the shipments would be legal under the National Security Act.[61] This disregards Executive Order 12333. Before an agency other than the CIA

---

[57] P.L. 99–169, § 502(b).

[58] Memorandum from Cooper to Meese, 12/17/86, pp. 5–6, ALV 077747–48.

[59] 22 U.S.C. § 662.

[60] Memorandum from Cooper to Meese, 12/17/86, p. 17, ALV 007760.

[61] Ibid., p. 5, ALV 007748. Ironically, Meese maintained that the Boland Amendment, which restricted actions of "intelligence agencies," did not apply to the NSC because it was not an "intelligence agency." Meese testified that "certainly the NSC is not an intelligence agency" and in his "opinion the NSC staff would not be considered an intelligence agency within the general meaning of the term. (Meese, Select Committees Deposition, 7/8/87, p. 33.)

could undertake a covert action outside the United States, that order specified that the President make a determination that the agency was more appropriate than the CIA to discharge the covert action. National Security Decision Directive (NSDD) No. 159 provided that the presidential determination under Executive Order 12333 must be made in writing.

Because the CIA was involved in the November 1985 HAWK shipment, however, the Hughes-Ryan Amendment required a presidential Finding. Cooper elided that problem with an "oral finding" theory. McFarlane had testified that the President had orally authorized the November 1985 HAWK shipment in advance. According to Cooper, that satisfied the Hughes-Ryan requirement that the President "find" the operation "important to the national security of the United States." There remained the question of congressional notification. The National Security Act required the President to give Congress "timely" notice of "intelligence operations in foreign countries." [62] The Administration took the position that because the lives of the hostages were at risk, it was not "timely" to notify Congress until the hostages were safe.[63] President Reagan did not comply with Executive Order 12333 and NSDD 159. Whether a president is subject to his own Executive Order that had no criminal penalties was not a question to be settled by criminal prosecution.

The November 1985 HAWK shipment had been significantly aided by the CIA: first, by its effort to use intelligence resources abroad to clear the snarled Israeli transportation effort; and, second, by using its own proprietary—an airline that it owned—to carry the HAWKs from Israel to Iran. The National Security Act required a Finding for such CIA involvement. CIA General Counsel Sporkin concluded that this Finding could be signed retroactively. Accordingly, on December 5, 1985, ten days after the HAWK shipment, President Reagan signed a Finding that it was in the national interest to further the sale of weapons to appropriate persons in order to facilitate the release of American hostages, and retroactively authorizing the CIA to aid such an effort.[64] There was

no evidence that the President knew in advance that the CIA was going to participate in the HAWK transaction.

None of the above statutes, the Executive Order, or the NSDD, provided for a criminal penalty. Thus their violation rises to a level of criminality only in the event of a criminal conspiracy. Independent Counsel has taken the position, and the District Court agreed, that a charge under the conspiracy statute, 18 U.S.C. § 371, may be based upon a conspiracy, through deceitful and dishonest means, to violate a federal civil law or to prevent the Government from conducting its operations and implementing its policies honestly and faithfully. While such a charge was applicable under the facts in the *North* conspiracy count, involving unauthorized arms proceeds hidden in secret Swiss accounts to be used for other unauthorized activities, this hardly applied to the facts surrounding the President's initial decision to proceed with the arms sales to Iran. Congress was ultimately deceived, but the President's professed motive for secrecy—a desire to protect the lives of the hostages and to effect their release—had at least a surface plausibility.

## The October–November 1986 Cover-up of Iran/Contra

With the downing of one of the Enterprise contra-resupply planes by the Nicaraguans on October 5, 1986, and their capture of the surviving crew member, American Eugene Hasenfus, the unraveling of the NSC's secret contra-resupply operation began.

Despite immediate U.S. denials that either Hasenfus or the aircraft was connected to the U.S. Government or working under the direction of any American official or agency, evidence began piling up that the elaborate resupply network was being directed by North out of his NSC office.

The Hasenfus shootdown did not create much of a stir with the President. On October 7, Poindexter briefed Reagan, telling him that the Hasenfus operation was not connected with the

---

[62] 50 U.S.C. § 413(b).

[63] Meese, Select Committees Testimony, 7/28/87, pp. 197–98.

[64] President Reagan has said he does not recall signing the December 1985 Finding, but Poindexter testified that the President signed it on

December 5. Poindexter testified that it was kept in his office safe until he destroyed it on or about November 21, 1986. North testified in his trial that he and Commander Paul Thompson, the NSC's legal counsel, witnessed the destruction of the Finding.

Government.[65] The President did not even
record the Hasenfus shootdown or the press reaction to it in his personal diary. In the President's Grand Jury Interrogatory Answers (45–
47) Reagan gives this account:

> Admiral Poindexter assured me that the
> Hasenfus operation had no connection to
> the United States Government whatsoever.
> When I asked whether General John
> Singlaub might be involved in this oper-
> ation as had been reported in the press,
> I was told "no" by Admiral Poindexter.
> On the following day, October 8, 1986,
> also at an NSB [National Security Brief-
> ing], Admiral Poindexter confirmed there
> had been no U.S. Government involve-
> ment. Consequently, immediately following
> this NSB, when I departed the South Lawn
> *en route* to Raleigh, North Carolina, I an-
> swered in the negative when asked by a
> reporter whether there had been any U.S.
> involvement in this operation. (Tab 45–
> 47B).

> Though the subject was not raised in my
> November 19, 1986, press conference, I
> was given talking points in preparation for
> that conference which stated that the
> downed aircraft was not a U.S. Govern-
> ment aircraft or involved in any U.S. Gov-
> ernment operation (Tab 45–47C).

Independent Counsel could not prove that
President Reagan knew there was Government
involvement in the Hasenfus operation. He apparently had been told by Poindexter on several
occasions that there was none. The press and
some members of Congress were skeptical as
contrary evidence accumulated. But spokesmen
for the State and Defense departments and the
CIA continued the denials. Leading them was
Assistant Secretary of State Elliott Abrams, who
steadfastly denied before Congress and the public that the United States was involved in the
resupply effort.[66] As far as is known, no one
on the inside sought to protect the President's

credibility by telling him the truth or warning
him against falsely denying a U.S. connection.

## The Unraveling of the Iran Initiative

Hostage David Jacobsen was released November 2, 1986. Poindexter and North were hopeful
that a second hostage would also be released
and discussions with Iranian contacts were still
going on. When the story broke on November
3, 1986, that McFarlane had led a U.S. mission
to Tehran and that the U.S. Government had
sold weapons to Iran in exchange for hostages,
a shocked Congress and national press corps
began questioning the stark disparity between
the reported secret arms sales and the Administration's public policies calling for a boycott
of arms sales to Iran and the refusal to reward
terrorism. The angry public reaction stunned the
Administration, which spent the next three
weeks trying to stem the protest, first by
stonewalling and attempting to deny the story,
then by making highly selective admissions
aimed at stanching the flow of politically damaging information as much as possible.

The initial reaction to stonewall is reflected
in the notes of Rodney McDaniel, executive
secretary of the NSC, taken during the President's daily national security briefings for November 6 and November 7, 1986. The notes
reflect that a "no comment" posture was adopted.[67] The President's initial public statements
embodied the stonewall. On November 6, the
President answered a press question as follows:

Q: Mr. President, do we have a deal going
with Iran of some sort?

The President: No comment, but could I
suggest an appeal to all of you with regard
to this: that the speculation, the commenting and all, on a story that came out of
the Middle East, and that to us has no
foundation, that all of that is making it
more difficult for us in our effort to get
the other hostages free.[68]

65 Poindexter, Grand Jury, 3/6/91, pp. 140–41.

66 Abrams pleaded guilty October 7, 1991, to two misdemeanor
counts of withholding information from Congress about secret Government efforts to support the contras during the Boland period. He was
pardoned by President Bush on December 24, 1992.

67 McDaniel Notes, 11/6/86, ALU 0128263–64.

68 "Remarks on Signing the Immigration Reform and Control Act
of 1986," 11/6/86, *Public Papers of the Presidents,* Ronald Reagan,
1986, Vol. II, pp. 1521–22.

On the next day, the President tried again to silence the controversy, as he was questioned by the press on his meeting with Jacobsen, who was at a White House ceremony celebrating his release:

Q: Mr. President, the Iranians are saying that if you'll release some of those weapons, they'll intercede to free the rest of the hostages. Will you?

The President: Bill, I think in view of this statement, this is exactly what I tried to tell you last night. There's no way that we can answer questions having anything to do with this without endangering the people we're trying to rescue.[69]

On November 7, there was the first reference in a national security briefing to the need to discuss Iran with congressional leaders.[70] At about the same time, Poindexter directed North to develop a chronology of the Iran initiative.[71]

The Presidential diary entry for November 7, 1986, contains the following passage: "Discussion of how [to] handle press who are off on wild story originating in Beirut—I've proposed message be we can't and won't answer Q's [questions] because would endanger those we are trying to help." In his 1990 book *An American Life*, Reagan published that entry in this form:

Usual meetings. Discussion of how to handle press who are off on a wild story built on unfounded story originating in Beirut that we bought hostage Jacobsen's freedom with weapons to Iran. We've tried 'no comment.' I've proposed and our message will be: 'We can't and won't answer any questions on this subject because to do so will endanger the lives of those we are trying to help.'[72]

Over the next few days, there were a number of White House discussions about whether to reveal more about the Iran matter, with the White House staff arguing for greater disclosure

and Poindexter and Casey advising a continued "no comment."[73]

On November 10, 1986, President Reagan, Vice President Bush, Poindexter, White House Chief of Staff Donald T. Regan, Shultz, Weinberger, Casey, Meese, and Deputy National Security Adviser Alton Keel held a 90-minute meeting about both the Iran initiative and its disclosure.[74] OIC obtained copies of notes taken by Regan, Weinberger, Meese, and Keel concerning what was said at this meeting.[75] In Shultz's case, the OIC has a transcription of his notes by his aide M. Charles Hill, as well as Hill's notes of Shultz's after-the-fact "read-out" or recounting of the meeting.[76] The various notes differ in some ways, but they share one attribute that is striking: All of them reflect a purported description of the Iran initiative by Poindexter which began with the January 17, 1986, Finding; they refer to a 1985 Israeli shipment of 500 TOWs that the United States had found out about "after the fact" and agreed to replenish; they make no mention of the November 1985 HAWK transaction or the December 1985 Finding.

Neither the President nor any of the others corrected Poindexter's false account. Much of the meeting was spent debating whether to issue any sort of public statement about the Iran matter; a part of that discussion, as captured in Regan's notes, is as follows:

*Pres* We must say something but not much.

*John* [Poindexter] If we go with this [a proposed brief statement drafted by Casey] we end our Iranian contacts.

*DTR* [Regan] Must get a statement out now, we are being attacked, and we are being hurt. Losing credibility.

*Pres* Must say something because I'm being held out to dry. Have not dealt with terrorists, don't know who they are. This is long·range Iranian policy. No further speculation or answers so as not to endan-

69 "Remarks and an Informal Exchange with Reporters Prior to a Meeting with David Jacobsen," 11/7/86, *Public Papers of the Presidents*, Ronald Reagan, 1986, Vol. II, pp. 1533–34.
70 McDaniel Note, 11/7/86, ALU 0128264.
71 North, *North Trial Testimony*, 4/7/89, pp. 7032, 7036–37.
72 Reagan, *An American Life*, p. 527 (Simon & Schuster 1990).

73 Regan, Grand Jury, 2/26/88, pp. 32–34.
74 DCI (Casey) schedule, 11/10/86, ER 326–27.
75 Regan Notes, 11/10/86, ALU 024673–87; Memorandum from Weinberger to the Record, 11/10/86, ALZ 0041725–27; Meese Notes, 11/10/86, ALV 065209–12; Keel Note, 11/10/86, AKW 047247–55.
76 Hill Notes, 11/10/86, ANS 0001766–67, 0001762–64.

ger hostages. We won't pay any money, or give anything to terrorists.

*JP* [Poindexter] Say less about what we are doing, more about what we are not doing.[77]

After the meeting, work continued on a statement; according to Regan's notes, that afternoon "A lot of info [was] cut out by Ollie [North] and others at NSC due to their conversations with Iranians in Geneva over weekend." Weinberger, Meese, Casey, and the President signed off on a statement for release that evening.[78] The statement said:

> The President today met with his senior national security advisers regarding the status of the American hostages in Lebanon. The meeting was prompted by the President's concern for the safety of the remaining hostages and his fear that the spate of speculative stories which have arisen since the release of David Jacobsen may put them and others at risk.
>
> During the meeting, the President reviewed ongoing efforts to achieve the release of all the hostages, as well as our other broad policy concerns in the Middle East and Persian Gulf. As has been the case in similar meetings with the President and his senior advisors on this matter, there was unanimous support for the President. While specific decisions discussed at the meeting cannot be divulged, the President did ask that it be reemphasized that no U.S. laws have been or will be violated and that our policy of not making concessions to terrorists remains intact.
>
> At the conclusion of the meeting, the President made it clear to all that he appreciated their support and efforts to gain the safe release of all the hostages. Stressing the fact that hostage lives are at stake, the President asked his advisers to ensure that their departments refrain from making

comments or speculating about these matters.[79]

## The Initial Briefings of Congress

On November 12, 1986, the Administration held a briefing for Senate Majority Leader Robert Dole, Senate Minority Leader Robert Byrd, House Majority Leader Jim Wright, and House Minority Whip Richard Cheney. According to NSC counsel Paul Thompson's notes [80] and Meese's notes,[81] the Administration was represented at this meeting by the President, the Vice President, Shultz, Weinberger, Meese, Casey, Regan, Poindexter, Keel, Will Ball, Larry Speakes, and Thompson. The meeting began with a preliminary statement by the President, which Thompson recorded as follows:

1) principally a cov[ert] intell[igence] op[eration]

2) not a rogue op

3) no nego[tiation]s terrorists

4) enhance position in ME [Middle East]

The President's description ignored the two 1985 Israeli shipments.

Then, according to both sets of notes, Poindexter took over with a lengthy narrative. Poindexter again began with the January 17, 1986, Finding, and then described the McFarlane trip to Tehran, listed the 1986 weapons shipments to Iran (omitting the October 1986 shipment), and concluded with the statement "Mr. [President], those are all the facts." [82] The only references to the 1985 phase of the initiative are oblique; Thompson's notes show Poindexter stating that "Israelis are [probably] still shipping to Iran," [83] which Meese's notes expand into a statement that "Israelis may be continuing to ship arms to Iran (w/o [with-

---

79 Statement by Principal Deputy Press Secretary Speakes on the American Hostages in Lebanon, 11/10/86, *Public Papers of the Presidents,* Ronald Reagan, 1986, Vol. II, p. 1539.

80 Thompson Notes, 11/12/86, 11/13/86, 11/21/86, AKW 001390–463.

81 Meese Note, 11/12/86, ALV 065197–99.

82 Thompson Note, 11/12/86, AKW 001402.

83 Ibid.

77 Regan Note, 11/10/86, ALU 024673–87.

78 Ibid., ALU 024687.

out] our authorization) as they did before our contacts began.'' [84]

According to Regan's notes, later in the meeting Sen. Byrd asked when the initial contact was made, and Poindexter replied: ''in 1985 but no transfer of material—took time to assess contact & issue finding[.]'' [85]

The President and the other Administration principals in attendance, said nothing to correct the false report to the congressional leaders— that the Finding preceded all arms shipments. In his diary entry for November 12, 1986, President Reagan did not mention the meeting with congressional leaders:

> This whole irresponsible press bilge about hostages and Iran has gotten totally out of hand. The media looks like it's trying to create another Watergate. I laid down the law in the morning meetings. I want to go public personally and tell the people the truth. We're trying to arrange it for tomorrow. [86]

The President's televised speech to the nation on November 13, 1986, did not ''tell the people the truth'' about the Iran initiative.[87] Instead, it reflected the new version of the facts that the Administration had settled on for public-relations purposes. It stressed four main points:

—the weapons shipments were not ransom for the hostages,

—the quantities of weapons involved in the initiative were small,

—the weapons were ''defensive'' in nature, and

—the goals of the initiative went beyond arms for hostages and included renewing the United States' relationship with Iran, bringing an honorable end to the Iran/Iraq war, eliminating state-sponsored terrorism, and obtaining the safe return of the hostages.

The President was silent about the 1985 Israeli shipments of U.S. arms to Iran.

It was against this background that Poindexter and Casey prepared for their testimony before the congressional intelligence committees, which were embarking upon an inquiry into the Iran initiative. There is no suggestion that the President told them what to say—but if they told the truth about the 1985 shipments their testimony would be inconsistent with what congressional leaders were told in their briefing by the President and Poindexter. And it was to provide the essential facts for this crucial testimony that McFarlane, North and other officials were assembling a chronology of the Iran initiative. McFarlane, Poindexter, North and others sought to falsify an original CIA chronology—which was reasonably accurate except that it failed to mention the diversion—by distancing the Administration from the two 1985 Israeli shipments.

As facts about the arms sales were dribbling out from a variety of sources, Administration officials continued to resist divulging additional information. In a briefing of reporters before the President's November 13 televised address, Poindexter fielded a series of questions about a possible connection between the September 1985 release of American hostage Benjamin Weir and a shipment of arms to Israel:

> Q: Could you say then what prompted the release of Benjamin Weir then in September of '85? What event do you think was related to his release?
>
> SENIOR ADMINISTRATION OFFICIAL [Poindexter]: Well, I think that it was a matter of our talking to the contacts through our channel, making the case as to what our long-range objectives were, demonstrating our good faith—
>
> Q: How did you do that?
>
> Q: How was that done?
>
> SENIOR ADMINISTRATION OFFICIAL: Well, that was one of the motivations behind the small amount of stuff that we transferred to them.
>
> Q: But that was done later?
>
> Q: But where—before this January document was signed?

---

[84] Meese Note, 11/12/86, ALU 065197–99.
[85] Regan Note, 11/12/86, ALU 0139141.
[86] Reagan, *An American Life*, p. 528.
[87] Reagan, Address By the President to the Nation, 11/13/86, ALU 018811–14.

SENIOR ADMINISTRATION OFFICIAL: The problem is—and don't draw any inferences from this—but there are other countries involved, but I don't want to confirm what countries those are and—because I think that it is still important that that be protected. And going back to the question you asked me earlier, there was one shipment that was made not by us, but by a third country prior to the signing of that document.

Q: This shipment to Israel?

SENIOR ADMINISTRATION OFFICIAL: I'm not confirming that, George.

Q: Was that on our behalf?

SENIOR ADMINISTRATION OFFICIAL: It was done in our interests.

Q: Sir, what—

Q: Was that before Weir was released?

SENIOR ADMINISTRATION OFFICIAL: I honestly don't know. And if I knew, I don't think I would tell you precisely.

Q: You just said previously that you did not condone any shipments.

SENIOR ADMINISTRATION OFFICIAL: I went back and corrected—there was one exception and that was the one I just described.

Q: And that was—

SENIOR ADMINISTRATION OFFICIAL: That was it.

Q: And that was around the time of Weir's release. When you said demonstrating our good faith we have to assume—infer from what you've said that there was some kind of quid pro quo.

SENIOR ADMINISTRATION OFFICIAL: It was in the general time frame.[88]

Regan subsequently admitted to reporters that "we had condoned a shipment of arms by Israel to Iran and had replenished it."[89] The admis-

sions by Poindexter and Regan concerning U.S. approval of the 1985 Israeli TOW shipment left the November 1985 HAWK shipment, the related December 1985 Finding, and the diversion as the major remaining undisclosed facts concerning the Iran initiative. The week of November 17, 1986, saw drastic changes in the NSC Iran chronology—which omitted the diversion throughout, but which up to then contained a relatively truthful, if incomplete, account of the November 1985 HAWK shipment similar to that contain in the early versions of the CIA chronology.[90] First, Administration officials moved toward omission of the November shipment entirely and, later in the week, toward the affirmatively false statement that the United States had believed that the shipment contained oil-drilling parts.[91]

On the afternoon of November 19, the President received a personally delivered warning from Secretary Shultz that "[w]e've been deceived and lied to and you have to watch out about saying no arms for hostages."[92] Despite this cautionary warning, the President that night made yet one more effort to quell public criticism in a nationally televised press conference. During the questioning the President flatly denied the 1985 phase of the Iran initiative or any involvement by third countries. In follow-up questioning, the President was asked:

Q: Mr. President, going back over your answers tonight about the arms shipments and the numbers of them, are you telling us tonight that the only shipments with which we were involved were the one or two that followed your January 17th finding and that, whatever your aides have said on background or on the record, there are no other shipments with which the U.S. condoned?

THE PRESIDENT: That's right. I'm saying nothing but the missiles that we sold—and remember, there are too many people that are saying "gave." They bought them.

Andrea?

88 Background Briefing by Senior Administration Official, 11/13/86, AKW 028978–79.
89 Regan, Grand Jury, 2/26/88, p. 41.
90 Subject: Background and Chronology of Special Project, AKW 010038–40; Index of Logs Used By Poindexter, *Poindexter* GX 124.
91 U.S./Iranian contacts and the American Hostages, 11/20/86, AKW 000151–73.
92 Shultz, Select Committees Testimony, 7/23/87, p. 110.

Q: Mr. President, to follow up on that, we've been told by the Chief of Staff Donald Regan that we condoned, this government condoned an Israeli shipment in September of 1985, shortly before the release of hostage Benjamin Weir. That was four months before your intelligence finding on January 17th that you say gave you the legal authority not to notify Congress. Can you clear that up why we were not—why this government was not in violation of its arms embargo and of the notification to Congress for having condoned American-made weapons shipped to Iran in September 1985?

THE PRESIDENT: No, that—I've never heard Mr. Regan say that and I'll ask him about that, because . . . we waived it for a specific purpose, in fact, with four goals in mind.[93]

Immediately after the press conference, the President's aides tried to bring the President's comments into conformance with the earlier Poindexter/Regan remarks by issuing the following correction in the President's name:

There may be some misunderstanding of one of my answers tonight. There was a third country involved in our secret project with Iran. But taking this into account, all of the shipments of the token amounts of defensive arms and parts that I have authorized or condoned taken in total could be placed aboard a single cargo aircraft. This includes all shipments by the United States or any third country. Any other shipments by third countries were not authorized by the U.S. government.[94]

Secretary Shultz called the President following the press conference and warned him that he had made many wrong or misleading statements. Shultz asked for a meeting with the President the next day to discuss the matter further. The evening of November 20, 1986, Shultz and Regan met with the President in the family quarters. Shultz told the President that he was being briefed with information that

was not correct.[95] Regan recalled that Shultz told the President that Abraham Sofaer, the State Department legal adviser, was worried about what Casey was going to say in his testimony the next day. Sofaer was specifically concerned about the likelihood of a public discrepancy between Casey's testimony about the 1985 HAWK shipment and Shultz's recollection that he was briefed about the planned HAWK shipment by McFarlane during the Geneva summit meeting with Soviet leader Mikhail Gorbachev.[96]

The President's recollection of the meeting, according to his Grand Jury Interrogatory Answers, was that: "On Thursday evening, November 20, 1986, Secretary Shultz informed me of discrepancies between his recollection and what he understood would be the testimony of Director Casey the following morning on arms shipments to Iran." [97] But the most detailed account of what Shultz told the President is contained in Charles Hill's notes of Shultz's statement to Meese during Meese's "fact finding," on November 22. According to Hill's notes, Shultz told Meese:

You should know I went to [President] on Thurs. night. Asked to go see him. Went w/DR [Regan] to family qtrs. I had called after press conf. to tell him he did fine job but a lot of yr stmts. won't stand up to scrutiny & I'll come tell you what you sd [said] was wrong. How you have those ideas I don't know but it's wrong— and I described Bud [McFarlane] talk to me in Geneva [in which McFarlane briefed Shultz on the upcoming Israeli HAWK shipment]. [President] sd oh I kn[ew] about that—but that wasn't arms for hostages! I sd no one looking at the record will believe that.[98]

The next day the President directed Meese to conduct an inquiry to gather the facts about the Iran initiative. President Reagan, in response to Grand Jury Interrogatory 49, gave this account of his decision:

---

93 News Conference by the President, 11/19/86, ALU 016823.
94 Statement by the President, 11/19/86, ALU 016815.

95 Shultz, Select Committees Testimony, 7/23/87, pp. 111–14.
96 Regan, Select Committees Testimony, 7/15/87, pp. 39–42.
97 Reagan, Grand Jury Interrogatories, Answer to Question 49.
98 Hill Note, 11/22/86, ANS 0001883.

The next morning, Friday, November 21, at 11:32 a.m., according to my records, the Attorney General met with me and reported his concerns about the need for an accurate account, particularly in view of upcoming testimony to Congressional Committees. It was at this meeting that I directed Attorney General Meese to gather the facts over the weekend and report his findings to me by Monday, November 24.

By the time the President was directing Meese to conduct the inquiry, both Casey and Poindexter had begun giving their false accounts of the Iran initiative to congressional committees, the very thing Shultz had sought to head off.[99] President Reagan, in the *Poindexter* trial, testified that he did not authorize Poindexter to make any false statement to Congress.[100] The President made a similar statement regarding Casey's testimony in answer to Grand Jury Interrogatory 49.

When Meese began the weekend inquiry on November 21, the big problem was to resolve discrepancies between various accounts of the 1985 Israeli shipments and the legal problems those shipments posed, particularly the HAWK missile shipment in November. In his interview with Shultz on Saturday, November 22, Meese told Shultz:

> Certain things cd [could] be violation of a law. [President] didn't know about HAWK in Nov. If it happened & [President] didn't report to Congress, it's a violation. He [the President] sd to me if it happened I want to tell Congress not have them tell me.[101]

After Meese's aides found a copy of the North diversion memo in North's files on November 22, the 1985 Israeli arms shipments receded in importance, according to Meese.[102] In his testimony in the *North* trial, Meese conceded that upon learning of the Iran/contra diversion he feared that the merger of two controversial Administration activities—support of the contras and the sale of arms to Iran which the President

had ordered be kept secret from Congress—could lead to impeachment. Meese made the admission in cross examination by North's attorney:

> Q: And you sense immediately, when you heard that [the diversion], that could create an enormous political problem because it merged or married together two separate problems that the Administration had; One, support of the Freedom Fighters which was hotly contested, and two, the sale of arms to Iran which had been by order of the Finding kept from Congress. Correct?
>
> A: Yes. I was concerned that the two major policy issues within the Administration at the time would be merged together and this would—could complicate the ability of the President in both of the issues.
>
> Q: In fact, your assessment at the time was that unless something was done, a strong response, that the merging of those two factors could very well cause the possible toppling of the President himself. Correct?
>
> A: Yes.
>
> Q: And there was discussion, in fact, that on the days November 23 and 24th that unless the Administration, unless you and the President himself, put out to the public the facts of the use of residuals for the Freedom Fighters, unless you got it out the door first, it could possibly lead to impeachment by the Congress, correct?
>
> A: Yes. That was a concern, that political opponents might try that kind of tactic.
>
> The Court: And you discussed that with the President? He [North attorney Brendan Sullivan] is asking you.
>
> A: I believe I discussed it with the President. I certainly discussed it with others in high-ranking positions such as the Chief of Staff.[103]

Poindexter and North recognized the problems that would flow from the disclosure of the diversion, which North called the "secret

99 See Poindexter and Casey chapters.
100 Reagan, *Poindexter* Trial Testimony, 2/17/90, pp. 250–51.
101 Hill Note, 11/22/86, ANS 0001888.
102 Meese, OIC Interview, 5/11/92, pp. 55–56.
103 Meese, *North* Trial Testimony, 3/28/89, p. 5750.

within the secret.'' [104] Discovery of the diversion would have in turn exposed the entire, apparently unauthorized and illegal NSC contraresupply program that North directed from late 1984 to October 1986. Poindexter had succeeded in keeping the diversion under wraps by the simple expedient of instructing North to leave it out of the NSC's accounts of the Iran matter and making no reference to it himself in response to the Congressional and press demands for an explanation of the Iran initiative.[105] Poindexter testified that as late as November 19, 1986, when the President made his second public appearance to answer questions about the Iran initiative, he was still determined to keep knowledge of the diversion away from the President [106]—despite McFarlane's reminder to Poindexter on that same day that ''you have a problem about the use of the Iranian money.'' [107]

In addition, Poindexter testified that he neither sought nor received the President's authorization to destroy the December 1985 Iran Finding.[108] In his Grand Jury testimony, Poindexter stated he recalls no discussion with President Reagan of the destruction of any Iran or contra-related document during October or November 1986.[109] President Reagan testified at his deposition that he did not authorize Poindexter to destroy any document related to Iran/contra.[110] Regarding the destruction of documents by North or others at the NSC, the President's Grand Jury Interrogatory Answer states:

> At no time did I authorize or approve of the destruction or alteration of documents, relating to Iranian arms transactions or relating to the NFF [contras], by LtCol North or any other officer or employee of the United States or by anyone else. I did not learn of any such destruction or alteration prior to November 26, 1986. I do not possess any independent knowledge of these activities.[111]

After ascertaining from Poindexter that he was aware of the diversion and had not told the President about it, Meese informed the President along with Regan about North's account of the diversion and Poindexter's acknowledgement of it on November 24. Both Meese and Regan testified that the President appeared ''shocked'' and ''surprised.'' [112]

Later on November 24, when Meese briefed the other top national security officials at a senior advisers' meeting about the results of his inquiry, he did not mention the diversion. Instead, the meeting developed into a dispute between Poindexter and Shultz as to the continuation of the initiative and a response by Poindexter and Meese to Regan's question about President Reagan's knowledge of the 1985 HAWK shipment. Meese reported that there was a legal problem with the November 1985 HAWK shipment, but he stated that the President ''did not know.'' [113] This was at odds with Shultz's account to Meese just two days before that the President did recall having contemporaneous knowledge of the HAWK shipment. Additionally, Poindexter asserted that McFarlane conducted the 1985 transactions all alone, without documentation.[114] No one spoke up to correct these misstatements, although most of those at the meeting knew they were wrong.

The morning of the next day, November 25, Meese and the President briefed Cabinet members about the diversion. Then the President and Meese, accompanied by Shultz, Casey and Regan, briefed congressional leaders at a White House meeting. The discussion focused upon the diversion, the current status of the Iran initiative, and future inquiries and investigations into the Iran matter. The subject of the 1985 Israeli shipments did not come up.[115]

At noon, the President and Meese held a press conference. In a brief initial statement, the President said that Meese's weekend review of the Iran initiative had turned up information that ''I was not fully informed on the nature of one of the activities undertaken,'' which

[104] North, *North* Trial Testimony, 4/13/89, p. 7669.
[105] Poindexter, Select Committees Deposition, 7/2/87, pp. 12–13; Poindexter, Select Committees Testimony, 7/20/87, p. 127.
[106] Ibid., pp. 188–89.
[107] McFarlane, *North* Trial Testimony, 3/14/89, p. 4277.
[108] Poindexter, Select Committees Testimony, 7/15/87, pp. 50, 53.
[109] Poindexter, Grand Jury, 11/14/90, pp. 88–91.
[110] Reagan, *Poindexter* Trial Testimony, 2/16/90, p. 160; Ibid., 2/17/90, p. 267.
[111] Reagan, Grand Jury Interrogatories, Answer to Question 50.

[112] Meese, Grand Jury, 2/17/88, pp. 51–56; Regan, Grand Jury, 2/3/88, pp. 43–47.
[113] Regan Note, 11/24/86, ALU 0139379.
[114] Weinberger Meeting Note, 11/24/86, ALZ 0040669LL.
[115] Richardson Note, 11/25/86, Cong. Ex. EM–53.

raised "serious questions of propriety." [116] The President announced the resignation of Poindexter, the firing of North, the appointment of a special review board to determine the role of the NSC in the matter, and a continuation of the Justice Department review. The President turned the podium over to Meese to announce the diversion and then left the briefing room, declining to answer questions.[117]

Meese laid out a somewhat garbled account of the diversion, which, partly as a result of North's description of it, seemed to put the Israelis, not the Secord-Hakim "Enterprise," at the center of the profiteering and secret Swiss accounts. Then Meese faced a barrage of questions, including questions about the 1985 Israeli shipments, to which he gave erroneous and misleading answers.[118]

That evening, President Reagan telephoned North. In his Grand Jury Interrogatory Answer, the President described the call as follows:

> On November 25, 1986, I telephoned LtCol North. Our records reflect that my phone call lasted 2 minutes, from 6:43 p.m. to 6:45 p.m., and was placed to the Sheraton Hotel in Tyson's Corner, Virginia.
>
> I told LtCol North generally that I regretted the circumstances surrounding his departure from the NSC staff and that I had no personal animus against him. I may have referred to LtCol North as a national hero (referring to his military service). I do not recall discussing the substance of any of the events that had given rise to his departure. I do not recall specifically LtCol North's replies.
>
> No one suggested that I make this call. I do not recall anyone being present with me when I spoke to LtCol North and, to my knowledge, the two of us were the only parties to the conversation. I did it solely out of personal compassion for LtCol North.[119]

Robert Earl, North's assistant, said that North told him that the President had said it was important that the President not know.[120] North testified that Earl was mistaken. North said he told Earl that the President had said, "I just didn't know." [121]

## The President's Culpability for November 1986 Crimes

The question of whether the President, in the discharge of his constitutional office, is criminally liable for false statements and obstruction of congressional inquiries regarding his activities is not a ready field for criminal prosecution. The President is quite different from any subordinate in his relationship with Congress. But the fundamental reason for lack of prosecutorial effort was the absence of proof beyond a reasonable doubt that the President knew that the statements being made to Congress were false, or that acts of obstruction were being committed by Poindexter, North and others.

President Reagan has testified that he did not and would not authorize any false statement to Congress by Poindexter in connection with the Iran initiative.[122] Similarly, he denied knowledge of Casey's incomplete and inaccurate testimony on November 21, 1986. Reagan's answer to Grand Jury Interrogatory 49 acknowledges that the President was aware that Casey was scheduled to testify and that Shultz was concerned with his testimony the next morning. But the President went on to state:

> I did not know of, authorize, or approve any statements made to Congress by Director Casey concerning any Iranian arms transaction or concerning aid to the NFF [contras]. It is not my practice to review the Congressional testimony of my senior officials. Director Casey did write me a letter, dated November 23, 1986, and attached with it a copy of his written remarks before the House and Senate Intelligence Committees on November 21,

---

116 "Remarks Announcing the Review of the National Security Council's Role in the Iran Arms and Contra Aid Controversy," 11/25/86, *Public Papers of the Presidents*, 1986, Vol. II, p. 1587.

117 Ibid.

118 Transcript of Meese's News Conference, 11/25/86.

119 Reagan, Grand Jury Interrogatories, Answer to Question 51.

120 Earl, Grand Jury, 5/1/87, pp. 117–19. ("Colonel North turned and confided, 'And you know what'—again I don't have the exact wording so I'm just going to relay the thrust of what he said—that the President had told him that it was important that he not know; that he was told that it was important that he not know.")

121 North, Select Committees Deposition, 7/1/87, pp. 17–18.

122 Reagan, *Poindexter* Trial Testimony, 2/17/90, p. 152.

1986. In his letter he described his testimony in general terms.[123]

The state of the President's knowledge of the 1985 Israeli shipments as of November 1986 is a difficult matter to ascertain. The President's early statements regarding that shipment wandered from an outright denial of knowledge to an account which ultimately resembled McFarlane's testimony that the President had approved that Israeli action in advance and agreed to replenishment of Israeli weapons stocks.[124] At his deposition in *Poindexter*, President Reagan stated that he could not recall whether he remembered the November 1985 HAWK shipment at the time he met with congressional leaders on November 12, 1986, or even whether he had heard about it before the Lebanese newspaper article revealed secret U.S. arms sales to Iran on November 3, 1986.[125]

On the other hand, his diary contained a number of entries regarding the early days of the initiative, starting July 17, 1985, when, while in the hospital, he noted "strange sounds coming from some Iranians—Bud M. [McFarlane] will be here tomorrow to talk about it—could be a breakthrough on 7 kidnap victims—evidently Iranian economy disintegrating fast under strains of war." The next day, the President's diary records his meeting with McFarlane: "Bud came by—seems 2 members of the Iranian govt. want to establish talks with us—I'm sending Bud to meet with them in a neutral country." On August 6, he simply noted "Rumors of 5 to 7 hostages to be released no confirmation." On August 23, although cryptically written, the President's diary notation suggests his approval for the Israeli TOW shipment: "Received 'secret phone' call from Bud McFarlane—seems a man high up in the Iranian govt. believes he can deliver all or part of the 7 kidnap victims—I had a few decisions to make about a few points—but they were easy to make—now we must wait." On September 15, President Reagan noted in his diary: "Release of Rev. Weir; told by mystery man in Beirut others will follow."

The President's entries in November 1985 do not refer specifically to HAWKs, but clearly he was following the course of the initiative. The pertinent entries are as follows:

> 11/22/85 brief NSC on hostages in Beirut—we have an undercover thing going by way of an Iranian which could get them sprung momentarily

> 11/23/85 still sweating out our undercover effort to get hostages out of Beirut

> 12/5/85 NSC Briefing—probably Buds last—subject our undercover effort to free our 5 hostages—complex undertaking with only a few in on it-won't even write in this diary what we're up to

> 12/7/85 meeting with Regan, Weinberger, McFarlane, Poindexter, Shultz & Mahan [sic, CIA Deputy Director John McMahon] of CIA-complex plan which could return our 5 hostages & help some officials in Iran who want better relationship with us—Israel would sell weapons to Iran, hostages released as soon as delivered in installments by air—weapons go to moderate leaders in army who are essential if to be change[d] to more stable govt—we then sell Israel replacements—none of this is a gift. [126]

In his autobiography, Reagan rendered this same diary entry as follows:

> Saturday, Dec. 7—Pearl Harbor Day: I . . . had a meeting with Don R, Cap W, Bud M, John P, George S and McMahon of CIA. This has to do with the complex plan which could return our five hostages and help some officials in Iran who want to turn that country from its present course and onto a better relationship with us. It calls for Israel selling some weapons to Iran. As they are delivered in installments by air, our hostages will be released. The weapons will go to the moderate leaders in the army who are essential if there is to be a change to a more stable government. We then sell Israel replacements for the delivered weapons. None of this is a gift. The Iranians pay cash for the weapons—so does Israel.

123 Reagan, Grand Jury Interrogatories, Answer to Question 49.
124 Tower Commission Report at III–7.
125 Reagan, *Poindexter* Trial Testimony, 2/16/90, pp. 37–38.
126 OIC Review of Reagan Diary, 1987.

George Shultz, Cap and Don are opposed. Congress has imposed a law on us that we can't sell Iran weapons or sell any other country weapons for resale to Iran. George also thinks this violates our policy of not paying off terrorists. I claim the weapons are for those who want to change the government of Iran and no ransom is being paid for the hostages. No direct sale would be made by us to Iran but we would be replacing the weapons sold by Israel.

We're at a stalemate. Bud is flying to London where the Israelis and Iranian agents are. Britain has no embargo on selling to Iran. . . . The plan is set for Wednesday.[127]

The President's subsequent diary entries reflect his disappointment with the London meeting, but his decision to go ahead with direct U.S. sales under the January 17, 1986, Finding:

12/9/85 Bud back from London but not in office yet—his meeting with Iranians did not achieve its purpose to persuade them to free our hostages first—their top man said he believed if he took that proposal to the terrorists they would kill our people

12/10/85 Iranian "go between" turns out to [sic] a devious character—our plan regarding the hostages is a "no go"

1/17/86 only thing waiting was N.S.C. wanting decisions on our effort to get our 5 hostages out of Lebanon—involves selling TOW anti-tank missiles to Iran—I gave a go ahead.[128]

In addition to having his diary entries of the previous year to help his staff refresh his recollection, the President on November 19 and November 20, 1986, received direct information from Shultz regarding Shultz's contemporaneous knowledge of the November 1985 HAWK shipment. Shultz said he told the President that McFarlane reported on the HAWK shipment during the summit meeting with Gorbachev in Geneva. According to Shultz, President Reagan responded that "oh I kn[ew] about that."[129]

The foregoing facts would suggest that the President, during the first three weeks in November 1986, knowingly participated or at least acquiesced in the efforts of Casey, Poindexter and North to minimize or hide his advance approval of and participation in the 1985 Israeli arms shipments to Iran without notice to Congress.

Yet, such a conclusion runs against President Reagan's seeming blindness to reality when it came to the rationalization of some of his Iran and hostage policies. The portrayal of President Reagan in the notes of Regan and Weinberger, and Shultz's read outs to Hill, not only the November 24, 1986, meeting but beginning at least on December 7, 1985, show a consistent reiteration of the President's position. The simple fact is that President Reagan seems not to have been ashamed of what he had done. He had convinced himself that he was not trading arms for hostages, that he was selling arms to develop a new opening with Iran, and that the recovery of the hostages was incidental to a broader purpose. He disdained the restrictions of the Arms Export Control Act. He made that clear as he brushed off Weinberger's concerns about illegality on December 7, 1985. At the November 24, 1986, meeting he was "v[ery] hot under the collar & determined he is totally right."[130]

In his deposition given to Independent Counsel in July 1992, his responses were still consistent with that position. His memory had obviously failed. He had little recollection of the meetings and the details of the transactions. When his diary notes or other documents were presented to him which expressed his 1985 and 1986 position, he was again firm in his statements that they sounded like something he would have said and that he still believed them to be true.

## The President's Responses to Formal Inquiries

This final section considers whether the President committed any crimes in his responses to

127 *An American Life*, p. 510.
128 OIC Review of Reagan Diary, 1987.

129 Hill Note, 11/22/86, ANS 0001883.
130 Hill Note, 11/24/86, ANS 0001894–909.

two principal investigations that followed the November 25, 1986, disclosure of the Iran/contra diversion. He provided statements or testimony to both the Tower Commission inquiry and the criminal investigation conducted by OIC.[131] President Reagan was not asked to testify before the hearings conducted by the congressional Iran/contra Select Committees or to provide the Committees with a deposition or statement.

## President Reagan's Statements to the Tower Commission

President Reagan signed Executive Order 12575 on December 1, 1986, which established a Special Review Board "to review activities of the National Security Council" in the wake of the Iran/contra disclosures. President Reagan named former Sen. John Tower as chairman and appointed former Sen. Edmund Muskie and retired Gen. Brent Scowcroft as members of the board which became known as the Tower Commission. The President directed the board to submit its findings and recommendations to him at the conclusion of its inquiry. The Tower Commission conducted numerous interviews and reviewed hundreds of documents in its three-month inquiry. In its letter submitting its report to President Reagan on February 26, 1987, the Commission stated that in addition to the evaluative mission described in the Executive Order, "[a]t your direction, we also focused on the Iran/Contra matter and sought to follow your injunction that 'all the facts come out.' "

The Tower Commission conducted two interviews with President Reagan and was provided excerpts from his diary. The Commission also received a letter from the President correcting one aspect of his accounts at those interviews. The Commission's Report sought to draw conclusions concerning the President's knowledge and authorization of the Iran initiative in general, and of four controversial Iran/contra events in particular: (1) the August–September 1985 Israeli TOW shipment; (2) the November 1985 Israeli HAWK shipment; (3) the diversion; and (4) NSC staff assistance to the contras during the Boland period. President Reagan's responses

to the Commission in these four areas are summarized in the Tower report as follows:

### The August/September 1985 TOW Shipment

In his meeting with the Board on January 26, 1987, the President said that sometime in August he approved the shipment of arms by Israel to Iran. He was uncertain as to the precise date. The President also said that he approved replenishment of any arms transferred by Israel to Iran. Mr. McFarlane's testimony of January 16, 1986, before the Senate Foreign Relations Committee, which the President embraced, takes the same position. This portion of Mr. McFarlane's testimony was specifically highlighted on the copy of testimony given by the President to the Board.

In his meeting with the Board on February 11, the President said that he and Mr. Regan had gone over the matter a number of times and that Mr. Regan had a firm recollection that the President had not authorized the August shipment in advance. The President said he did not recall authorizing the August shipment in advance. He noted that very possibly, the transfer was brought to him as already completed. He said that subsequently there were arms shipments he authorized that may have had to do with replenishment, and that this approval for replenishment could have taken place in September. The President stated that he had been "surprised" that the Israelis had shipped arms to Iran, and that this fact caused the President to conclude that he had not approved the transfer in advance.

In a subsequent letter to the Board received on February 20, 1987, the President wrote: "In trying to recall events that happened eighteen months ago I'm afraid that I let myself be influenced by others' recollections, not my own . . ."

". . . I have no personal notes or records to help my recollection on this matter. The only honest answer is to state that try as I might, I cannot recall anything whatsoever about wheth-

[131] Reagan was interviewed by the Tower Commission on January 26, 1987 and on February 11, 1987, and by OIC on July 24, 1992, and he provided interrogatory answers to the Grand Jury in late 1987.

er I approved an Israeli sale in advance or whether I approved replenishment of Israeli stocks around August of 1985. My answer therefore and the simple truth is, 'I don't remember—period.' ''

The Board tried to resolve the question of whether the President gave prior approval to Israel's transfer of arms to Iran. We could not do so conclusively.

We believe that an Israeli request for approval of such a transfer was discussed before the President in early August. We believe that Secretary Shultz and Secretary Weinberger expressed at times vigorous opposition to the proposal. The President agreed to replenish Israeli stocks. We are persuaded that he most likely provided this approval prior to the first shipment by Israel.

In coming to this conclusion, it is of paramount importance that the President never opposed the idea of Israel transferring arms to Iran. Indeed, four months after the August shipment, the President authorized the United States government to undertake directly the very same operation that Israel had proposed. Even if Mr. McFarlane did not have the President's explicit prior approval, he clearly had his full support.[132]

### The November 1985 HAWK Shipment

In his first meeting with the Board on January 16, 1987, the President said he did not remember how the November shipment came about. The President said he objected to the shipment, and that, as a result of that objection, the shipment was returned to Israel.

In his second meeting with the Board on February 11, 1987, the President stated that both he and Mr. Regan agreed that they cannot remember any meeting or conversation in general about a HAWK shipment. The President said he did not remember

anything about a call-back of the HAWKs.[133]

### The Diversion

The President said he had no knowledge of the diversion prior to his conversation with Attorney General Meese on November 25, [sic] 1986. No evidence has come to light to suggest otherwise. Contemporaneous Justice Department staff notes of LtCol North's interview with Attorney General Meese on November 23, 1986, show North telling the Attorney General that only he, Mr. McFarlane, and VADM Poindexter were aware of the diversion.[134]

### The NSC Staff and Support for the Contras

The President told the Board on January 26, 1987, that he did not know that the NSC staff was engaged in helping the contras. The Board is aware of no evidence to suggest that the President was aware of LtCol North's activities.[135]

False statements to the Tower Commission could be punishable under 18 U.S.C. § 1001 (penalizing material false statements to a department or agency of the United States in a matter within its jurisdiction).

Of the President's statements to the Tower Commission on the four key subjects, only the President's claimed lack of knowledge of the diversion remains totally unimpeached. Nevertheless, the fundamental barrier to concluding that any of the President's various statements to the Tower Commission was criminally false is that it was virtually impossible to prove beyond a reasonable doubt what the President remembered in January and February of 1987.[136] The Tower Commission interviews were not recorded or transcribed; only notes were taken. Although it seems obvious that President Reagan made hopelessly conflicting statements to the Commission, it would be impossible to

---

[132] Tower Commission Report at III–7–8; see also ibid. at B–19–20.

[133] Ibid., p. III–9; ibid., at B–37.

[134] Ibid., p. III–21.

[135] Ibid., III–24; ibid., at C–14.

[136] In an extensive interview of Reagan conducted in Los Angeles in July 1992, Independent Counsel satisfied himself that President Reagan's memory of the Iran initiative and much of his memory of contra support during the Boland cut-off period is now very faded.

prove beyond a reasonable doubt that any misstatement was intentional or willful.[137]

## The President's Sworn Answers to Grand Jury Interrogatories and His Deposition at the Trial of Admiral Poindexter

In his Grand Jury Interrogatory answers and at his deposition, the President again provided information regarding the four key areas of his knowledge and authorization that have been identified above. In response to written interrogatories, the President in November 1987 made these key statements:

*The August/September 1985 TOW Shipment*

Mr. McFarlane briefed me about an approach by individuals in Iran while I was in the hospital in July 1985, but I do not specifically recall any discussion of the sale of arms by Israel as being part of that initiative at that time. I do recall that later in the summer or fall of 1985 I was advised that Israel sought to ship TOWs to individuals in Iran who would influence the Hazballah to free our hostages. It was part of Israel's plan that it would abort the sale if it became apparent that the hostages would not be released. My best recollection is that, at that time, I agreed that Israel should be permitted to purchase replacement TOWs from the United States. I am aware that Robert McFarlane has testified that I was briefed on all of these matters while I was in the hospital. I do not recall, however, the precise date on which I was told of the delivery of TOW missiles by Israel to Iran, nor the precise date on which I authorized the replenishment of the TOWs by the United States to Israel. I do not recall any discussion of price whatsoever.[138]

*The November 1985 HAWK Shipment*

At the time of the shipment of HAWKs by Israel to Iran, I was in Geneva meeting

Secretary General Gorbachev and discussing with him United States-Soviet relations.

I was told at that time that there was a possibility that the hostages might be released, but I do not recall that the shipment of HAWK missiles was involved. I have no recollection today whether I authorized or approved the shipment of HAWKs by Israel to Iran in November 1985, nor do I recall undertaking at that time a commitment to replenish those HAWKs from United States inventory. While I initially told the Tower Board that I disapproved the transfer, I later advised the Board that I simply had no recollection on this issue. I am aware that Don Regan has stated that in November 1985 in Geneva we were told to expect a shipment of HAWKs by Israel to Iran and that I approved such a transfer but made no commitment on replenishment. I am also aware that Robert McFarlane has stated that he advised me of the shipment but said that the shipment was comprised of oil drilling equipment. I have no current recollection whatsoever of approving or disapproving this shipment or replenishment. I do not recall any discussion of prices at all, but I recall that any weapons involved in the initiative generally were to be paid for by the recipient country.[139]

*          *          *

I do not recall signing a Finding relating to Iranian arms transactions in November or December 1985. I am aware that an unsigned version of such a Finding exists . . . although I am told that a signed version has not been found. I have been advised that the CIA was told contemporaneously that on December 5, 1985, I signed a Finding relating to this initiative. While I do not deny having signed such a Finding, I have no current recollection of doing so.

In November and December 1985, I was briefed on an initiative involving Israel's

---

[137] Additionally, a diary kept by White House Counsel Peter Wallison indicates President Reagan's state of confusion as his staff tried to prepare him for the Tower Commission interview. See Regan chapter.

[138] Reagan, Grand Jury Interrogatories, Answer to Question 23; see also Reagan, *Poindexter* Trial Testimony, 2/16/90, pp. 16–20; ibid., 2/17/90, pp. 226–28.

[139] Reagan, Grand Jury Interrogatories, Answer to Question 24; see also Reagan, *Poindexter* Trial Testimony, 2/16/90, pp. 35–37; ibid., 2/17/90, p. 229.

attempts to secure the return of our hostages and an initiative to facilitate a dialogue between our Government and moderate leaders in Iran. I approved of such a initiative and directed my National Security Adviser Robert McFarlane to take part in such a dialogue. My review of the unsigned Finding . . . leads me to believe that I would have understood it to relate to such an initiative.[140]

### The Diversion

The first time I learned that the proceeds of any Iranian arms transactions might have been paid to any account used to provide weapons and military aid to the Nicaraguan Freedom Fighters—what has been termed the "diversion"—was on November 24, 1986, when Attorney General Edwin Meese reported to me that a memorandum had been found referring to such a use. I immediately instructed that the NSC, the leadership in Congress and the general public be told of this development.

I never authorized nor approved the "diversion," nor was I ever asked to authorize or approve it. I can recall no conversation or discussion whatsoever of any such idea prior to my conversation with the Attorney General. As noted above, I was unaware that any profits or "residual funds" were to be generated by such sales.

It was only as the investigation by the Tower Board got underway that I learned of the operational roles of North, Secord or Hakim. I do not recall authorizing or approving, nor do I believe I was ever asked to authorize or to approve, operational details, such as what accounts were to receive payments.

It was only in my discussions with Attorney General Meese on November 24, 1986, and after that I learned any details of any bank accounts into which the proceeds of arms shipments were paid, or the retention of these proceeds by anyone other than the U.S. Government. I do not recall any

discussion prior to that time concerning the proceeds of such sales, nor do I recall being asked for authority by anyone to use, control or retain these funds.[141]

### NSC Staff Assistance to the Contras

I was generally aware that some assistance was flowing from the private sources to the NFF [contras] and that some of this assistance would have included military support. This information was public knowledge as early as 1985 and was even mentioned in Congressional debate about a request for funding in August 1985. Until the plane carrying Mr. Hasenfus was shot down in October 1986, I do not recall knowing of specific individuals or groups engaged in this activity and was unaware of any connection with the U.S. Government. I believed such activity to be similar to efforts by Americans in other conflicts. Even after Mr. Hasenfus was shot down, I was told that he was not participating in a U.S. sponsored operation, and I was not informed of any particulars of that operation beyond what was in the news media. It was not until after November 25, 1986, when the full details of these operations became public, that I learned the nature and extent of the private support network and the role of certain U.S. officials in it.

\*          \*          \*

Although I did not seek or directly encourage private citizens to provide military support, I did encourage William Simon and others to provide humanitarian assistance through the Nicaraguan Freedom Fund. . . . I also knew, as had been previously reported in the press, that Mrs. Garwood had contributed money to refurbish a Medevac helicopter. I understood her contributions to be of a humanitarian nature, and, when I met with Mrs. Garwood, this subject was not discussed.[142]

---

[140] Reagan, Grand Jury Interrogatories, Answer to Question 27; see also Reagan, *Poindexter* Trial Testimony, 2/17/90, pp. 231–32.

[141] Reagan, Grand Jury Interrogatories, Answer to Questions 36–38; see also Reagan, *Poindexter* Trial Testimony, 2/16/90, pp. 29, 155–57; ibid., 2/17/90, pp. 236–37, 243–44, 276–82, 289–90.

[142] Reagan, Grand Jury Interrogatories, Answer to Questions 14–17.

Regarding his knowledge of the North-run contra-resupply operation, the President said:

> I did not authorize or approve of the transfer to the NSC or any of its staff any function or operation performed by the CIA with respect to the Nicaraguan Freedom Fighters. I do not recall anyone ever asking me to approve or authorize the transfer of any function or operation from the CIA to the NSC, and I do not recall ever discussing such transfer.[143]

*       *       *

> Beyond [Presidential Findings, NSDDs, and advocacy of third-country assistance], my instructions with regard to support for the Freedom Fighters were usually of a general nature, and I do not now recall any authorizations or approvals of specific actions with respect to the Freedom Fighters.

> With regard to Richard V. Secord and Albert Hakim, I do not recall approving or authorizing any action concerning them with regard to the Freedom Fighters or of meeting either individual during this timeframe.[144]

> I knew that LtCol North's responsibilities included work related to Central America and, specifically, Nicaragua. However, prior to my conversations with Attorney General Meese on November 24 and 25, 1986, concerning what has come to be known as the ''diversion,'' I did not know that LtCol North participated in planning, directing or advising NFF military or paramilitary operations or logistical support for such operations. Although I heard about allegations in the press that LtCol North was engaged in such activities, I understood that these allegations were incorrect. . . .[145]

This office is not aware of evidence to prove that President Reagan intentionally made material false statements or committed perjury in his answers to this office's Interrogatories, which were submitted as sworn testimony to the Grand Jury, or in his deposition in the *Poindexter* trial. The President's responses to the Interrogatories were carefully and professionally crafted, unlike his presentation to the Tower Commission. While there is a substantial amount of failure to recall and vagueness in the President's responses, both to the Interrogatories and in his later deposition in the *Poindexter* Trial, this standing alone does not warrant a criminal charge.[146] By July 1992, when Reagan agreed to a final, extensive interview with Independent Counsel, it was obvious that the former President truly lacked specific recollection of even the major Iran/contra events which took place in 1984–1987.

---

[143] Ibid., Answer to Question 8.
[144] Ibid., Answer to Question 9.

[145] Ibid., Answer to Question 10.
[146] For a full account of the President's testimony in *Poindexter*, see Poindexter chapter.

# Chapter 28
# George Bush

George Bush served as vice president through the Reagan presidency from 1981 to 1989. In January 1989, he succeeded Reagan as President. It was in his capacity as President that Bush committed what will likely become his most memorable act in connection with Iran/contra. On December 24, 1992, twelve days before former Secretary of Defense Caspar W. Weinberger was to go to trial, Bush pardoned him.[1] In issuing pardons to Weinberger and five other Iran/contra defendants, President Bush charged that Independent Counsel's prosecutions represented the "criminalization of policy differences."

The criminal investigation of Bush was regrettably incomplete. Before Bush's election as President, the investigation was primarily concerned with the operational conspiracy and the careful evaluation of the cases against former National Security Adviser John M. Poindexter and Lt. Col. Oliver L. North of the National Security Council staff, prior to their indictment in March 1988. This included a review of any exculpatory material that might have shown authorization for their conduct. In the course of this investigation, Vice President Bush was deposed on January 11, 1988.

A year later Bush was President-elect, and OIC was engaged in the intensive preparation for the trial of North, which began on January 31, 1989. After the completion of the trials of North and Poindexter and the pleas of guilty of retired Air Force Maj. Gen. Richard V.

Secord and Albert Hakim, OIC broadened its investigation to those supporting and supervising Poindexter and North. This investigation developed a large amount of new material with which it intended to question President Bush. His interrogation was left to the end because, as President, he obviously could not be questioned repeatedly. It was Independent Counsel's expectation that he would be available after the completion of the 1992 Presidential election campaign.

In light of his access to information, Bush would have been an important witness. In an early interview with the FBI in December 1986 and in the OIC deposition in January 1988, Bush acknowledged that he was regularly informed of events connected with the Iran arms sales, including the 1985 Israeli missile shipments.[2] These statements conflicted with his more extreme public assertions that he was "out of the loop" regarding the operational details of the Iran initiative and was generally unaware of the strong opposition to the arms sales by Secretary of Defense Weinberger and Secretary of State George P. Shultz. He denied knowledge of the diversion of proceeds from the arms sales to assist the contras.[3] He also denied knowledge of the secret contra-resupply operation supervised by North.[4]

In 1991 and 1992, Independent Counsel uncovered important evidence in the form of withheld documents and contemporaneous notes that raised significant questions about the earlier ac-

---

[1] President Bush also pardoned former National Security Adviser Robert C. McFarlane, former Assistant Secretary of State Elliott Abrams, former CIA Central American Task Force Chief Alan D. Fiers, Jr., former CIA Deputy Director for Operations Clair E. George, and former CIA Counter-Terrorism Chief Duane R. Clarridge. The Weinberger pardon marked the first time a President ever pardoned someone in whose trial he might have been called as a witness, because the President was knowledgeable of factual events underlying the case.

[2] Bush, FBI 302, 12/12/86; Bush, OIC Deposition, 1/11/88. But Bush's recollection was very general and he did not recall specific details of meetings in which the Iran arms sales were discussed.

[3] Bush, FBI 302, 12/12/86, p. 3; Bush, OIC Deposition, 1/11/88, p. 17. During his interview with the FBI, Bush said he would be willing to take a polygraph examination concerning his lack of prior knowledge of the diversion.

[4] Bush, OIC Deposition, 1/11/88, p. 154.

counts provided by high Administration officials. The personal diary of Vice President Bush was disclosed to Independent Counsel only in December 1992, despite early and repeated requests for such documents. This late disclosure prompted a special investigation into why the diary had not been produced previously, and the substance of the diary.

Following the pardons, Bush refused to be interviewed unless the interview was limited to his non-production of his diary and personal notes. Because such a limited deposition would not serve a basic investigative purpose and because its occurrence would give the misleading impression of cooperation where there was none, Independent Counsel declined to accept these conditions. A Grand Jury subpoena was not issued because OIC did not believe there was an appropriate likelihood of a criminal prosecution. Bush's notes themselves proved not as significant as those of Weinberger and Shultz aides Charles Hill and Nicholas Platt, and the statute of limitations had passed on most of the relevant acts and statements of Bush.

## The Bush Diary

On December 11, 1992, Chester Paul Beach, Jr., associate counsel to President Bush, informed the OIC that a diary, kept by Bush, dating back to his vice presidency, had not been produced to Independent Counsel. It consisted of Bush's nightly dictation concerning the events of the day. Although the diary contained many personal and political observations, it also contained a substantial number of references to the events surrounding the Iran/contra matter and the subsequent investigation. Accordingly, the diary was responsive to at least two document requests sent to the White House by the OIC in 1987 and 1992.

Bush began in November 1986 keeping a daily "political diary" tracking his bid for the Presidency in 1988.[5] Most of the dictation was transcribed by Betty Green, a secretary in the Vice President's Houston, Texas, office.[6] She believed she first started transcribing the dictation in February 1987.[7] Bush's Special Assistant, Don Rhodes, would receive cassette tapes from Bush at his residence and deliver them to Green in Houston.[8] On a couple of occasions, Rhodes received transcripts from Green and returned them to Bush. Neither Rhodes nor Green knew what Vice President Bush did with the transcripts once he received them.

Jack Steel, the head of Bush's Houston office, knew Green was transcribing dictation for Bush and that it was personal, but he was not aware of the substance.[9] Other than Bush, Green, Rhodes and Steel, there is no evidence that others knew of the existence of the diary prior to September 1992. Others knew that he would occasionally dictate his thoughts, but no one knew that it was part of a daily diary.[10]

## The White House Response to OIC's 1987 Document Request

On March 27, 1987, OIC's request for the production of documents was circulated throughout the White House complex, including the Office of the Vice President (OVP), by A.B. Culvahouse, counsel to President Reagan.[11] This document request represented the product of negotiations between the White House, the congressional Select Committees and the OIC to develop an omnibus document request.[12] A cover memorandum attached to the document

---

[5] The first entry in the diary reads: "This is November 4, 1986, the beginning of what I hope will be an accurate diary, with at least five and maybe 15 minutes a day on observations about my run for the presidency in 1988." (Bush Diary, 11/4/86.) Prior to November of 1986, Vice President Bush did, on occasion, dictate his thoughts in conjunction with a particular historical event, such as the hospitalization of President Reagan in July 1985.

[6] During his vice presidency, Bush had six offices in the following locations: the West Wing of the White House; the Old Executive Office Building; the Dirksen Senate Office Building; the Capitol; the Vice Presidential Residence; and Houston, Texas. The primary function of the Houston Office was to respond to public correspondence. (Presock, FBI 302, 3/17/93, p. 1.)

[7] Green, FBI 302, 2/18/93, p. 2.

[8] Rhodes, FBI 302, 2/18/93, pp. 2–4.

[9] Steel, FBI 302, 2/18/93, p. 2.

[10] OVP Chief of Staff Craig L. Fuller recalled observing Bush occasionally dictating when he obviously was not working on correspondence. (Fuller, FBI 302, 2/19/93, p. 2.) Rose Zamaria, Special Assistant to President Bush, was aware that Bush made "sporadic" dictation of his thoughts, although she does not know when he began this practice. (Zamaria, FBI 302, 2/17/93, p. 2.) Another special assistant, Susie Peake, transcribed some Bush dictation in 1989 concerning his trip to China and again in 1991 concerning the Gulf War. (Peake, FBI 302, 2/18/93, p. 2.) Zamaria and Peake were not aware of Bush dictating a diary that dated back to November 1986.

[11] Memorandum from Culvahouse to Assistants To The President, et al., 3/27/87, ARZ 003929–37. This document was generated, in part, in response to a letter from Independent Counsel to Culvahouse's predecessor, Peter J. Wallison, dated February 27, 1987. This letter forwarded the initial document request from the OIC to the Executive Branch.

[12] Letter from Friedman to Wallison, 2/27/87, ARZ 004369–70.

request stated that the request included "all personal and official records" of the staff members of the White House, NSC, and the Executive Office of the President.[13] The attached request explicitly identified relevant "notes," "diaries," and "audio tapes" among the materials required to be produced. As a result of the prior negotiations, the document request was limited to material from the period January 20, 1981 to January 2, 1987.[14]

Following the disclosure of the existence of the Bush diary, President Bush retained private counsel. In January 1993, his counsel conducted an internal investigation and reported that Bush did not recall reviewing the 1987 document request and was not aware that it called for the production of personal diaries.

There was, however, substantial evidence that a copy of the March 1987 document request was received by Vice President Bush, and that the requirements of the request, including the demand for personal materials and documents, were communicated to Bush by his counsel, C. Boyden Gray.

The memorandum circulated by Culvahouse was received by Craig L. Fuller in his capacity of chief of staff for the OVP.[15] On April 1, 1987, he delegated responsibility to Gray and John P. Schmitz, deputy counsel to the Vice President.[16] On April 8, 1987, Gray and Schmitz circulated a memorandum to the "heads" of the OVP offices.[17] They stated that the document request "covers all personal and official records of OVP staff members."

The Vice President's West Wing Office contained the largest collection of what would be considered Bush personal materials. Patty Presock, an administrative assistant to Bush, was considered the "head" of this office, with the only other staff person being Susie Peake. On April 8, 1987, Presock received a memorandum from Schmitz following up on an earlier telephone conversation and forwarding a copy of the document request.[18] The last sentence of the memorandum stated:

Boyden will talk to the Vice President about the extent to which this request applies to your office's records.

Beach, in an interview with the OIC, stated that Gray informed him on December 12, 1992 that he had this conversation with Bush in 1987.[19]

Others support Beach. Fuller said he understood that Bush reviewed the document request in 1987, although Gray was the one handling that issue.[20] Fuller did not recall whether he, himself, provided a copy of the document request to Bush or whether it was done through Gray.[21] The first Fuller learned that Bush did not recall seeing the document request was in his recent interview with Bush's private lawyers.[22]

Bush's general awareness of the problem of personal notes and diaries is documented in a January 30, 1987, Bush handwritten note, produced from a set of files known as his "chron files."[23] It includes the statement "memo from counsel—all notes, memos, documents etc."[24] This predated the March 1987 document request, but followed a narrower early document request of the Attorney General.

This Bush note was followed by a February 2, 1987, memorandum from Fuller to White House Chief of Staff Donald T. Regan concerning the production of the Reagan handwritten notes and diary. Fuller wrote "it's only a matter of time until someone calls for the 'diary.' "[25] The memorandum discussed the need to develop a plan to "satisfy" the OIC and congressional investigators. The memorandum was initialed by Bush and stamped "V.P. Has Seen."[26]

Culvahouse did not recall Bush being present at any meetings relating to the 1987 document

---

[13] Memorandum from Culvahouse to Assistants To The President, et al., 3/27/87, ARZ 003929–37.

[14] Ibid.

[15] Memorandum from Fuller to Gray, 4/1/87, ARZ 003928.

[16] Ibid.

[17] Memorandum from Gray/Schmitz to Heads of OVP Offices, 4/8/87, ARZ 003486–95.

[18] Memorandum from Schmitz to Presock, 4/8/87, ARZ 004336.

[19] Beach, FBI 302, 3/9/93, pp. 4–6. Beach's recollection of the conversation with Gray is memorialized in contemporaneous notes Beach made during the conversation on December 12, 1992. (Beach, "Notes of Interviews Re V.P. Diary Excerpts.") This conversation, and the corresponding notes, were the product of an "internal investigation" conducted by Beach following the discovery of the Bush diary.

[20] Fuller, FBI 302, 2/19/93, pp. 3–4.

[21] Ibid.

[22] Ibid.

[23] The "chron files" consist of chronologically sorted daily files of various documents and were maintained by Susie Peake. Chron file documents include correspondence, memoranda, calendars, phone logs and personal notes written or typed by Vice President Bush.

[24] Bush Note, 1/30/87, ARZ 000772.

[25] Memorandum from Fuller to Regan, 2/2/87, ARZ 000787.

[26] Collamore, FBI 302, 3/12/93, p. 2.

request.[27] Culvahouse did recall discussions with Gray concerning Bush "notes."[28] According to Culvahouse, the OVP was handling the production of Bush "notes" with the same sensitivity, and following the same procedures, as the White House was using to handle the Reagan diary.[29]

Jack Steel and Betty Green of the Houston office both recalled receiving the 1987 document request but did not feel that the documents in the Houston office, including the tapes, were relevant.[30] Don Rhodes, head of Bush's Dirksen Building office, received a copy of the 1987 request, but did not believe that the tapes would be relevant.[31]

Related to the issue of the diary was the production of the chron files. When the Iran/contra document request was circulated, Bush instructed Peake to "just give them everything."[32] Peake boxed up the entire collection of chron files and put them in Gray's office. Subsequently, the personal notes were segregated from the other documents in the chron files in anticipation of production of the chron files to the OIC.

Pursuant to negotiation between Gray and the OIC, Bush's November and December 1986 chron files, responsive to the 1987 document request (that cut off on January 2, 1987), were made available for review just prior to Vice President Bush's deposition in January 1988.[33] The relevant personal notes for this period were excerpted by Gray and were also made available at this time.

## The White House Response to OIC's 1992 Document Request

On June 30, 1992, the OIC transmitted a broader document request to the White House calling for the production of any diaries kept by George Bush during the period May 1, 1985, through December 1, 1987.[34] The primary effect of the 1992 Request was to extend the earlier request for diaries through December 1, 1987. This request received considerable attention within the White House during the summer of 1992. Various members of the White House Counsel's office wrote memoranda and held meetings discussing how the White House should respond.

There is no evidence that anyone involved in formulating the White House response knew of the existence of the Bush diaries at the time. Each has stated that the discussions focused on the chron files from the period January 3, 1987 through December 1, 1987. These discussions ended when the OIC, on September 15, 1992, delayed the response date until after the November 3, 1992 Presidential election.[35]

In a memorandum to Gray and Schmitz written on September 15, 1992, Beach told them of the extension of time to respond to the 1992 request.[36] It also stated:

> [The OIC has] indicated, as a "heads-up," that they have a "wealth of new information" since they last interviewed the President four years ago, and that they would probably ask that he respond to some additional interrogatories—*after the election.*[37]

Prior to this call from the OIC, the OIC requested full access to whatever materials existed. The White House wanted to provide only limited access to relevant extracts that had been agreed upon in 1987 with respect to the Reagan diaries and the 1986 Bush chron files.[38] The gist of White House internal discussions was a decision that Gray should actually begin the process of reviewing the 1987 chron files. According to Bush counsel Janet Rehnquist, Gray was going to conduct this review alone.

Gray apparently began such a review of the 1987 chron files in the late summer of 1992. Witnesses (including Beach, William Lytton and Rehnquist) stated that Gray had the 1987 chron

[27] Culvahouse, FBI 302, 3/19/93, p. 4–5.
[28] Ibid.
[29] Ibid.
[30] Steel, FBI 302, 2/18/93, pp. 3–4; Green, FBI 302, 2/18/93, p. 3.
[31] Rhodes, FBI 302, 2/18/93, p. 5.
[32] Peake, FBI 302, 2/18/93, p 3.
[33] Prior to the discovery of the Bush diary, many of the members of Bush's staff referred to the chron files as a "diary." (Beach, FBI 302, 3/9/93, p. 7.) In fact, prior to the disclosure of the Bush diary, the White House Counsel had acknowledged that the chron file "diary" was responsive to OIC document requests calling for production of a "diary." (Memorandum from Rehnquist to File, 7/10/92, ARZ 003193–94.)

[34] Letter from Barrett to Rehnquist, 6/30/92, ARZ 004164A–65.
[35] Memorandum from Beach to Gray, 9/15/92, ARZ 003527–28.
[36] Ibid.
[37] Ibid. (emphasis in original). The White House counsel never interpreted the September 15th call extending the document-request response date to imply that the OIC had dropped its June 1992 request. To the contrary, the White House understood that the request was "deferred" until after the election, when the White House was expecting the OIC to call about it. (Beach, FBI 302, 3/9/93, p. 12.)
[38] Memorandum from Rehnquist to file, 7/10/92, ARZ 003193–94.

files in his office beginning some time during the summer of 1992.

## Discovery of the Dictated Diary Transcript

The Bush diaries did not become known to anyone other than Bush, Rhodes, Steel and Green prior to September 1992. Sometime between September 18 and September 24, 1992, the diary transcripts were discovered by Presock while she was conducting an inventory of the Bush family safes located on the third floor of the White House residence.[39] The diary consisted of a typed transcript, which had been organized in binders. Presock knew the diary notes were important to Iran/contra investigators based on a request she had received a few months earlier for similar documents.[40]

Presock told President Bush of her discovery early on the morning of September 25. This meeting took place in Rose Zamaria's office adjacent to the Oval Office. Presock pointed out to President Bush that the diary transcript made repeated references to Iran/contra. President Bush took little interest and stated "let's call Boyden and he can sort it out."[41] Later that day, Gray came to Presock's office and reviewed the diary transcript.[42]

Knowledge of the existence of the diary went no farther than Boyden Gray until December 1, 1992. At a December 1, 1992, White House counsel meeting attended by Gray, Schmitz, Beach and Lee Liberman, there was a brief discussion referring to document production.[43] Gray did not reveal that what had been discovered was a diary. He did refer to newly discovered material as containing Iran/contra "stuff" and new 1986 Bush "stuff." At this meeting Gray asked Beach if he had heard from the OIC on its outstanding request. When Beach

said no, Gray said that the White House should probably "goose them on it," because there were some 1986 materials that had not been produced.[44]

Gray, himself, decided to delay notifying the Independent Counsel of the existence of the diaries.[45] Gray had his secretary type up diary excerpts relevant to Iran/contra for his staff to review.[46] These excerpts were reviewed on approximately Monday, December 7, 1992. The staff members concluded that the material was plainly relevant and should be produced.[47]

On December 9, 1992, the White House made its first attempt to inform the Independent Counsel of the existence of the Bush diary.[48] It was not until Friday, December 11, 1992, that Independent Counsel actually received the information.

## Production of Documents From the White House

In 1993, the OIC requested certain documents relevant to the diary production and to Iran/contra generally. Bush's new private counsel took over the production of official documents from the White House. They adopted a very narrow approach to the OIC document request, allowing production of only those materials that related to the production of the diary. They claimed that all other documents requested were protected by the attorney-client privilege.[49]

The OIC also requested relevant documents of each witness interviewed regarding document production. Every witness complied except Schmitz, who asserted that his documents were privileged work product.

Bush's counsel asserted that the failure to produce Bush's November and December 1986 diary notes was inadvertent. However, one Bush 1987 diary entry raises questions about Bush's willingness to cooperate fully with investigators. During 1987 Secretary of State George P. Shultz had turned over to investigators certain notes detailing personal meetings with President

[39] Presock, FBI 302, 1/19/93, pp. 1–3.

[40] Presock recalled a search for a Bush diary in July 1992 by the White House Counsel's office. She believed it was in response to the OIC request. Presock did not recall any diary being found at that time. (Presock, FBI 302, 1/19/93, pp. 4–5.)

[41] Ibid., p. 6.

[42] When interviewed by Beach in December 1992, Gray thought he recalled Presock saying she found the diaries in August, before the Republican Convention, and thought he might have learned of them prior to late September. (Beach, FBI 302, 3/9/93, p. 7.) However, Gray had no precise memory of the dates, and Presock had documentary evidence, along with Rose Zamaria's recollection, supporting the late-September date. (Ibid.)

[43] Liberman, FBI 302, 3/16/93, p. 7.

[44] Ibid., p. 6.

[45] Ibid., p. 11. No discussion took place, to Beach's knowledge. Clearly uncomfortable with the question, Beach carefully stated that he and his colleagues "recognized that Boyden had made a difficult decision" regarding delayed notification.

[46] Ibid., p. 4.

[47] Ibid.

[48] Ibid.

[49] Letter from Sollers to Gillen, 1/27/93.

Reagan that were relevant to Iran/contra. When Bush became aware of Shultz's note production, he responded as follows in his personal diary:

> Howard Baker in the presence of the President, told me today that George Shultz had kept 700 pages of personal notes, dictated to his staff . . . Notes on personal meetings he had with the President. I found this almost inconceivable. Not only that he kept the notes, but that he'd turned them all over to Congress . . . I would never do it. I would never surrender such documents and I wouldn't keep such detailed notes.[50]

This note, which was not among selected diary notes Bush released publicly in 1993, would have been used to question Bush about his cooperation with investigators if he had consented to the requested Independent Counsel deposition in 1993.

## Request to Interview Boyden Gray and John Schmitz

Much of the evidence relating to the failure to produce the diary focuses on Gray, Bush's counsel as Vice President and as President, and his deputy, Schmitz. On January 11, 1993, OIC wrote Gray and Schmitz requesting production of relevant documents and requesting an interview.[51] Subject to a non-waiver agreement, Gray and Schmitz produced their appointment calendars and a folder of documents.[52] Schmitz kept a personal diary that covered the relevant period (1987–1992), but he refused to produce it, asserting that any relevant excerpts were protected as work-product.

Gray and Schmitz finally refused to be interviewed by Independent Counsel. The OIC had been willing to limit the scope of the their interviews to questions directly related to the

timing of the production to the OIC of President Bush's diary tapes and transcripts for periods prior to 1988 and the production of the chron files.[53] In addition, the OIC agreed to a non-waiver of any privilege of Bush, excepting the Fifth Amendment privilege against self-incrimination.[54]

During the negotiations with Gray and Schmitz, the OIC learned that their lawyer, Richard Willard, had been consulted regarding the production of Bush documents prior to Gray's revelation of the Bush diary.[55] Lee Liberman, an associate counsel to the President, stated in an interview, that she and Beach had consulted Willard in December 1992 concerning the production of the diary.[56]

Willard was thus potentially a witness. The OIC asked to question Willard before he attended the interviews of Gray and Schmitz to determine whether a conflict existed. Willard refused to be interviewed by the OIC and his clients refused to be interviewed without his presence as counsel.[57] Willard claimed that his involvement in the White House production of the diary was solely as counsel to Gray and Schmitz,[58] and subject to work-product protection.[59]

The OIC then agreed to allow Willard to be present during the interviews of Gray and Schmitz.[60] Gray and Schmitz still refused to

---

[50] Bush Diary, 7/20/87.

[51] The document request was limited to "personal and official documents and other materials that relate in any way to your service in the Executive Branch from 1986 through the present as it relates to any aspect of the Iran/contra matter, including document requests from this Office or any other Iran/Contra investigation." (Letters from Harleston to Gray/Schmitz, 1/11/93.)

[52] The non-waiver agreement stated:
This review will not waive and will be without prejudice to any privilege against disclosure that may exist with respect to any of the documents, including the attorney-client privilege.
(Letter From Harleston to Willard, 2/10/93.)

[53] Letter from Harleston to Willard, 3/23/93.

[54] Ibid.

[55] The OIC's concern over a potential conflict with Willard serving as Gray's and Schmitz's attorney stems primarily from a Janet Rehnquist note of a conversation she had with Willard. The note reads:
Richard Willard:
—Right to be concerned
—Obstructing
—Covering up
—process has been sloppy over the years
—not atty client or work product materials
—make this kind of material in a Special way
—shakier
(Rehnquist Note, ALU 0141477.)
Rehnquist had a poor memory of this conversation; her note is not dated. She believed it related to the 1992 Request, but was essentially guessing when she tried to interpret the phrases. But Rehnquist clearly remembered that she did not learn of the Bush diaries until she read about them in the newspapers. This conversation with Willard, then, does not relate to the diaries. (Rehnquist, FBI 302, 3/17/93, pp. 12–13.)

[56] Liberman, FBI 302, 3/16/92, p.11. In fact, Liberman stated that Gray put Willard in contact with Beach and her. (Ibid.) It was from Willard that Liberman first learned that the "stuff" Gray had discovered was in fact the Bush diary. (Ibid.)

[57] Letter from Willard to Harleston, 3/29/93, 026101.

[58] Ibid.

[59] Ibid.

[60] Letter from Harleston to Willard, 4/8/93.

be interviewed,[61] claiming that the characterization of Willard as a potential witness could "unfairly cast doubt on the legitimacy of the proposed interviews."[62] Finally, they insisted upon a non-waiver provision that extended to any privilege held by Gray and Schmitz as well as President Bush.[63] Such a non-agreement would have included the Fifth Amendment privilege against self-incrimination and would essentially allow Gray and Schmitz to testify under a grant of immunity. The OIC refused to agree.[64] Gray and Schmitz refused to consent to an interview.[65]

## Interview of President Bush

The OIC informed the White House in the summer of 1992 that based on new information it had obtained since last interviewing Bush in 1988, the OIC anticipated the need to ask President Bush to respond to further questioning.[66] The White House provided no response to this statement. While President Bush made numerous public statements extolling his cooperation with the Independent Counsel's investigation,[67] that, in fact, had not been the case: Inside the White House it appears he had little intention of cooperating with Independent Counsel. In August 1992, there were discussions among White House counsel about not allowing the

OIC to interview President Bush.[68] According to Janet Rehnquist:

> This matter was discussed among Lytton, Schmitz, Gray and Rehnquist. Their position was they were going to tell the OIC to "pound sand" on the Bush interview issue. Their position was that interviews had already been done, that an election was going on and that enough was enough. There was no discussion about how the newly-revealed Caspar Weinberger material that had come to light might justify a new interview.[69]

The White House remained cognizant of Independent Counsel's interest in questioning Bush through the fall of 1992.[70] Following the disclosure of the Bush diary in December 1992, the OIC reiterated that interest.[71] In late February 1993, Bush informed Independent Counsel of his unwillingness to be deposed. Specifically, his counsel set forth six professed obstacles preventing a deposition of the kind OIC sought.[72] The most serious of his objections was his unwillingness to answer questions except regarding non-production of his diary. This position essentially denied the OIC the opportunity to question Bush on issues pertaining to his knowledge of Iran/contra.

There remained the alternative of a Grand Jury subpoena. Independent Counsel concluded that this recourse should not be used unless it was reasonably likely to lead to a criminal prosecution. It was important to avoid the appearance of Grand Jury use to obtain material for a report. It was also important to avoid any appearance of retaliation for the pardon of Weinberger. Under the circumstances, particularly because of the passage of time, it was

---

[61] Letter from Willard to Harleston, 4/16/93, 026988.

[62] Ibid.

[63] Ibid.

[64] Letter from Parsigian to Willard, 4/21/93, 027075.

[65] This was not the OIC's first encounter with non-cooperation on the part of Gray. In a May 23, 1991, FBI interview regarding Donald Gregg, Gray asserted on behalf of President Bush attorney-client privilege to many of the questions asked involving conversations between Gray and other members of the OVP staff. (Gray, FBI 302, 5/23/91.)

[66] The OIC did indicate that the questioning would probably be in the form of interrogatories. (Memorandum from Beach to Gray/Schmitz, 9/15/92, ARZ 003527–28.)

[67] For example, in a September 11, 1992, *Los Angeles Times* article, Bush was quoted as stating: "I have nothing to explain. I've given every bit of evidence I have to these thousands of investigators. And nobody has suggested that I've done anything wrong at all." ("Iran-Contra Issue Haunts GOP Ticket," *The Los Angeles Times*, 9/11/92, p. A1.)

In 1988, Bush stated publicly: "The President and I cooperated fully with the various investigations, turned over thousands of documents and directed our staffs to do the same." ("'There Never Was a Formal Meeting' on Iran Initiative"—Vice President Bush's responses to Mary McGrory's questions, *The Washington Post*, 1/14/88, p. 2.)

In 1989, Bush stated publicly: "Certainly, I would see that if any documents are in control of this administration, relevant documents, that we would live assiduously by those guidelines . . . set up to determine what documents would be made available." ("Bush Doubts Contra Files Withheld," *The Washington Times*, 4/21/89, p. 5A.)

[68] Rehnquist, FBI 302, 3/17/93, p. 9.

[69] Ibid.

[70] Memorandum from Beach to Gray/Schmitz, 11/4/92, ARZ 003525.

[71] On December 14, 1992, Deputy Independent Counsel Craig A. Gillen informed Paul Beach, Associate Counsel to the President, that it would probably be necessary for the OIC to depose President Bush. (Letter from Gillen to Sollers, 2/23/93.) On January 5, 13 and 15 and February 9, 1993, Gillen informed King & Spalding, counsel for President Bush, of the outstanding request to depose the President. (Ibid.)

[72] The six reasons for not agreeing to a deposition addressed the following: (1) who would conduct the deposition; (2) the scope of the deposition; (3) the imposition of a time limitation; (4) the use of interrogatories in lieu of a deposition; (5) the location; and (6) assurances concerning the purpose of the inquiry and Independent Counsel's intentions with regard to President Bush. (Letter from Sollers to Gillen, 2/24/93.)

decided that a Grand Jury subpoena would be inappropriate.

## Remaining Questions for President Bush

Independent Counsel's continuing investigation exposed evidence that called into question previous statements made by Vice President Bush concerning his knowledge of and involvement in the Iran/contra matter. The purpose of a second interview with Bush was to resolve inconsistencies. The second interview would have focused primarily on these areas:

1. The 1985 arms sales to Iran through the Israelis, particularly the presidential briefings leading up to them, and the briefing and meetings leading to the January 7, 1986, meeting of the President and his senior advisers regarding a continuation of the Iran arms sales.

2. Bush's meeting with Israeli official Amiram Nir in July 1986, particularly focusing on Secord's recollection that after Bush's report of this meeting, Reagan authorized the resumption of the Iran arms sales.[73]

3. The November 1986 period in which the President and his advisers tried to deal with the political uproar created by the public disclosure of the Iran arms sales. Bush would have been interrogated regarding contemporaneous notes of President Reagan's senior advisers, and his conversations with Attorney General Meese on this subject.

4. Bush's knowledge of or involvement in any quid-pro-quo arrangements with Central American or other countries in exchange for their support of the contras.

5. Bush diary entries concerning his national security adviser Donald P. Gregg and deputy Samuel J. Watson's statements denying that they informed Bush of contra-support activities.

6. The Vice President's contacts with North, particularly an August 6, 1986, meeting—the period when Gregg alleged that he learned of Felix Rodriguez's role in North's contra-resupply operation—and Gregg's August 8 and 12, 1986, meetings with representatives of agencies connected to contra resupply. Gregg denied reporting these meetings to Bush until December 1986, and Bush has stated that he did not learn of Rodriguez's role in the contra-resupply effort until then.

7. Bush's failure to produce until December 1992, the diary that Bush began creating in November 1986.

### November 1986

An area of special concern in questioning Bush would have been based on the recently obtained notes of Weinberger, Regan, and others, which provided valuable insight into the November 1986 period and the actions of the Reagan administration officials as they attempted to deal with the disclosure of the Iran initiative. The notes and Bush's diary also shed light on the extent of the Vice President's involvement in those events.[74]

The question was whether high Administration officials in November 1986 sought to create a false and inaccurate account of the Iran arms sales to protect themselves and the President from allegations of possible illegality and a confrontation with Congress regarding President Reagan's deliberate disregard of statutory restrictions on arms sales to terrorist countries.

On November 10, 1986, Bush was present at a meeting of the President with his senior advisers when Poindexter described the Iran initiative as beginning in January 1986, not 1985.

On November 12, Bush was present at a briefing of the congressional leadership on the facts of the Iran initiative when Poindexter again repeated his false and incomplete account. When Sen. Robert Byrd asked Poindexter if any weapons had been shipped in 1985,

---

[73] Secord and Wurts, *Honored and Betrayed* (John Wiley & Sons 1992), p. 282.

[74] For example, Bush on November 5, 1986, noted in his diary: On the news at this time is the question of the hostages. . . . [[D]iscussion of Bud McFarlane having been held prisoner in Iran. . . . I'm one of the few people that know fully the details, and there is a lot of flack and misinformation out there. It is not a subject we can talk about.
(Bush Diary, 11/5/86, ALU 0140191)

Poindexter replied that there had been contacts but that no materiel had been moved until 1986.[75]

Bush had been present at McFarlane's 1985 intelligence briefings in advance of the November 1985 HAWK shipment. In his interview with the FBI in December 1986, Bush recalled having knowledge of 1985 shipment.[76] In his 1988 deposition with the OIC, he recalled the Israeli TOW shipments and also appeared to allude to the November 1985 HAWK shipment, stating that:

> I do recall a third country landing rights situation. I remember that distinctly and what I remember, and this is fairly vague, but that there was an airplane that was supposed to land, pick up weapons, and fly to Israel—I mean to Iran—and once it was either airborne or landed over there, why then you were going to have this other half of this deal that I described, some facilitation of the release of hostages, not the actual release of them—or more; I thought it was supposed to be more.[77]

So when Bush heard Meese at the November 24, 1986, meeting of senior Administration officials state that the November 1985 HAWK shipment was "[n]ot legal because no finding," and add that the "President not informed,"[78] Bush was in a well-informed position to know the President had known of this shipment.

Independent Counsel was also concerned whether in the November 1986 period there was an effort to coerce Shultz into becoming more supportive of the President's Iran arms sales policy and conforming his testimony to others', for example, President Reagan's insistence that the Iran initiative was not an arms-for-hostages exchange.[79]

Earlier that month, Shultz unsuccessfully tried to persuade Bush to refrain from denying that the Iran initiative was an arms-for-hostages deal. On November 9, Shultz met privately with Bush and refuted Bush's public denial that there had

been an arms-for-hostages exchange with Iran. In his book published in 1993, Shultz recalled the meeting and said he reminded Bush that he had been present when arms-for-hostages had been discussed.[80] Shultz recounted the meeting as follows:

> I put my views to him: I didn't know much about what had actually transpired, but I knew . . . such an action would never stand up in public. Bush admonished me, asking emphatically whether I realized that there are major strategic objectives being pursued with Iran. He said that he was very careful about what he said.
>
> "You can't be *technically right*; you have to be right," I responded. I reminded him that he had been present at a meeting [January 7, 1986] where arms for Iran and hostage releases had been proposed and that he had made no objection, despite the opposition of both Cap and me. "That's where you are," I said. There was considerable tension between us when we parted.[81]

Bush noted the meeting with Shultz in his diary, stating that he was concerned about reports that Shultz might resign and that he felt "cut out" on the Iran initiative. Bush gave the following account:

> Indeed, he [Shultz] had felt cut out. And, he was dealing from less than a full deck on the Iran situation. He distrusts not only North, but he feels that I'm in jeopardy . . . myself. He thought he had heard me say something that later proved to be a lie, and his advice to me as a person interested in my future, "don't get involved in this."[82]

Bush's diary is replete with mentions of the behind-the-scenes intrigue regarding how to handle the growing political crisis over the disclosure of the Iran arms sales, with Shultz pushing for a public disclosure of the facts and Poindexter and Casey opposing this. By November 14, Bush and Regan were also pushing

---

[75] Regan Notes, 11/12/86, ALU 0139132–49.

[76] Bush, FBI 302, 12/12/86, p. 2.

[77] Bush, OIC Deposition, 1/11/88, pp. 80–81. Bush also stated that the President was informed of the 1985 shipments.

[78] Weinberger Meeting Notes, 11/24/86, ALZ 0040669MM (emphasis in original).

[79] Address by the President to the Nation, 11/13/86, ALU 018811–14. News Conference by the President, 11/19/86, ALU 016817–27.

[80] Shultz, *Turmoil and Triumph* (Chas. Scribner's Sons 1993), p. 809.

[81] Ibid. (emphasis in original).

[82] Bush Diary, 11/9/86, ALU 0140194.

for a public disclosure of the facts. Bush's diary entry on November 14 notes:

> I keep urging total disclosure, and not making statements that are not accurate. I know George Shultz feels this way. Also, being sure that our mechanical procedures inside the White House are proper. It leads me to feel, again, certainly for the future, that we should not have CIA Director as part of the cabinet; that all findings should be properly found. There's friction—a little between Don [Regan] and Poindexter now.[83]

By the next day, Bush observed in his diary that Shultz was again the topic of discussion. "[S]hultz . . . Don Regan whispered to me that we're having real problems with Shultz. That Shultz was not on board at all. I told him that I'd call him [Shultz] on Sunday."[84] On November 16, Bush called Regan regarding his comments about Shultz the previous day:

> I called him [Regan] today to see what he meant and he said that Shultz wanted to come out and say, "well, from now on, it would all be done in the State Department and no more arms of any kind to Iran." Regan's point is that this makes the President look like he was "wrong". . . . I'm not sure that we've [seen] the end of all of this.[85]

By November 18, Bush recorded that two different sources were reporting that "Howard Baker would be willing to be Secretary of State, and that he wouldn't run from that post against me [in the 1988 presidential race]. We'd been told this once before, a couple of years ago. I love Howard, but it does seem like the vultures are circling over George Shultz."[86]

Bush noted that he met with the President privately the next day. "We talked about the need to get the Shultz resignation stories in shape. In fact, there was friction between State and the White House. Shultz feeling he was closed out. The White House feeling that Shultz was cutting and running . . . separating himself

out."[87] On November 20, Bush again met privately with the Reagan:

> The President tells me that at lunch, "I really had a shocker. Don Regan has just told me that George Shultz has told him Poindexter has to go or he goes." It doesn't sound like George, this kind of ultimatum. We talked at length and I suggested to the President that the only thing he could do was call a Monday meeting which he decided to do to get the key NSC players together and to get them all to lay it on the table and to just simply say, "we're going to hammer this thing out and what are you upset about, George? What are you upset about, Poindexter?" The problem is—and I showed him certain clippings—that Poindexter, Don Regan and George are all out there with leaks and peddling their own line. Regan, for example, says, "I'm a team player.["] Everybody at State rallies around George, and it gets him all upset. And, when Regan says, or uses the word "negotiate" or allegedly makes some comment about Israel, everybody—State and NSC—gets upset with him.[88]

Bush continued his discussion of this meeting with the President in his diary notes on the following day. He noted that when the President told him that about Shultz's ultimatum, "I told the President, 'you simply cannot be held hostage. I love George Shultz. I want him to stay. It will hurt your short run. But, no President can have a Cabinet set the terms under which he will stay. It is impossible.'" In the same diary entry, Bush expressed concern about Poindexter: "On Poindexter, I'm concerned because today—on Friday—some new revelation that there were arms shipped in September of '85. The President having said that none were and I don't know what that's all about, but I walked into Don Regan's at lunch today and he said, 'well, there's a new bomb shell.'"[89]

Bush and Regan had been aware of the September 1985 TOW shipment, as was the President. Thus the "bombshell" was not the fact

83 Ibid., 11/14/86, ALU 0140198–99.
84 Ibid., 11/15/86, ALU 0140200.
85 Ibid., 11/16/86, ALU 0140201.
86 Ibid., 11/18/86, ALU 0140202.

87 Ibid., 11/19/86, ALU 0140203.
88 Ibid., 11/20/86, ALU 0140204–05.
89 Ibid., 11/21/86, ALU 0140206.

of the shipment, but that it had been made public.

Bush's diary entry for November 24 described the afternoon meeting of the President and his senior advisers. Unlike the notes of Weinberger and Regan, he did not record the substance of the meeting—including Meese's report on his weekend inquiry and the possibility that the November 1985 HAWK shipment was in violation of law.

## The Bush Diary

Had a final Bush interview occurred, the questioning regarding the non-production of Bush's diary would have focused on the decision of Bush and or Gray not to disclose the existence of the diary initially in April 1987, in response to OIC's document request, and to delay its ultimate production until December 1992. The questioning would have addressed Bush's familiarity with the 1987 OIC and congressional document requests, and his knowledge of the production of the Reagan diary in 1987. It would have sought an explanation of his previously described July 20, 1987, diary note condemning Shultz for producing Charles Hill's daily notes of Shultz's thoughts, discussions and activities.

It also would have covered Bush's diary entry of November 25, 1986, regarding a telephone call he had with North following his firing, and the substance of information he obtained from North and relayed to President Reagan regarding the fact that Israeli officials were extremely upset about the day's events.

# Chapter 29
# Donald P. Gregg

Donald P. Gregg in 1951 began a career of more than 30 years with the Central Intelligence Agency. That service included several overseas postings, including a tour in South Vietnam during the war. In 1979 Gregg was detailed by the CIA to the National Security Council staff, where his responsibilities included Asian affairs and intelligence matters. Following the election of Ronald Reagan in 1980, the new Administration requested that Gregg remain at the NSC. Until 1982, Gregg headed the NSC's Intelligence Directorate. In August 1982, he resigned from the CIA and accepted the position of national security adviser to Vice President George Bush, holding that position until the end of the Reagan Administration. In early 1989, President Bush nominated Gregg to be U.S. ambassador to the Republic of South Korea. Gregg was confirmed by the Senate for this position on September 12, 1989, and served as ambassador until 1993.

During the Vietnam War, Gregg supervised CIA officer Felix Rodriguez and they kept in contact following the war. Gregg introduced Rodriguez to Vice President Bush in January 1985, and Rodriguez met with the Vice President again in Washington, D.C., in May 1986. He also met Vice President Bush briefly in Miami on May 20, 1986. As a teenager, Rodriguez had participated in the ill-fated Bay of Pigs invasion of Cuba and remained, following that debacle, an ardent anti-communist.

In 1985 and 1986, Rodriguez worked out of the Ilopango air base in El Salvador, where he assisted the Salvadoran Air Force in anti-guerrilla counterinsurgency tactics. In late 1985 and during 1986, Rodriguez—whose alias was "Max Gomez"—became increasingly involved in the contra-resupply effort that was based at Ilopango at that time. Because of Rodriguez's close association with General Juan Bustillo, who headed the Salvadoran Air Force, Rodriguez was vital to Lt. Col. Oliver L. North's contra-resupply operation by coordinating flights based at Ilopango.

Following the shootdown of the contra-resupply aircraft carrying American Eugene Hasenfus on October 5, 1986, Rodriguez became a center of public and congressional attention. Because of Rodriguez's close friendship with Gregg and his three personal meetings with Vice President Bush, questions arose whether the contra-resupply operation was being directed by Gregg through Rodriguez. Questions also arose about when the Vice President's office became aware of Rodriguez's and North's active participation in the contra-resupply operation at Ilopango.

Both Gregg and his deputy, Col. Samuel J. Watson III, were investigated for possible false testimony regarding their denial of knowledge of Rodriguez's involvement in North's contra-resupply operation. OIC obtained Watson's immunized testimony in an effort to further its investigation. Despite unresolved conflicts between documentary evidence and the testimony of the principal witnesses, OIC determined that it could not prove beyond a reasonable doubt a criminal case against Gregg.

## Gregg, Rodriguez and North

When Gregg assumed his position as assistant to the Vice President for national security affairs in August 1982, he consciously disassociated himself from former colleagues with whom he had worked during his CIA career. The exception to that rule was Felix Rodriguez. Gregg testified: ". . . I have made it a conscious decision really not to reach back into that part of my life to bring other people forward. Felix is the only exception I have made to that."[1] Gregg lost track of Rodriguez for a period of time after Vietnam and did not see him until the early 1980s, when Rodriguez came to Washington sporadically and talked with Gregg about old times. Gregg was not certain what Rodriguez was doing at that time, and he did not inquire; however, they remained friends.[2]

Rodriguez visited Gregg in Washington in March 1983 and left him a proposal for helicopter anti-guerrilla operations in Central America.[3] Gregg forwarded Rodriguez's plan with a favorable recommendation to Deputy National Security Adviser Robert C. McFarlane.[4] McFarlane forwarded it on to North for his summary and recommendation.[5] North did not recall what action, if any, he took in response to McFarlane's directive.[6]

North first met Rodriguez on December 21, 1984.[7] Subsequently, North solicited Rodriguez to assist him and retired Air Force Maj. Gen. Richard V. Secord in the contra-resupply operation based out of Ilopango airfield in El Salvador. What role, if any, Gregg played in the introduction of Rodriguez to North and whether Gregg was aware of North's intentions to recruit Rodriguez for the resupply operation was relevant to Iran/contra investigators and was a matter of concern to the Senate Foreign Relations Committee (SFRC) conducting confirmation hearings on Gregg's ambassadorial nomination in May 1989.

One month before Gregg's confirmation hearings for the ambassadorship in May 1989, North testified at his trial that Gregg was the person who introduced him to Rodriguez.[8] In discussing his formal solicitation letter to Rodriguez, dated September 20, 1985, North testified that "I believe that once I had talked to Mr. Gregg about it [the solicitation] I talked to Mr.

McFarlane about it, about the fact that he [Rodriguez] would be able to assist in that country."[9]

During the confirmation proceedings, Gregg categorically denied North's trial assertions: "I am mentioned, by North, for the first time, on page 7,345 of the trial record, and he makes two assertions there, one, that I introduced him to Felix, and two, that he talked to me before he recruited Felix. And I regret to say that both of those are incorrect."[10] OIC obtained no evidence contradicting Gregg's denials; North did not back up his trial assertions with further evidence in the Grand Jury.

After the Rodriguez introduction became an issue at North's trial, William R. Bode, a former Department of State official, wrote an April 25, 1989, letter to Gregg based upon his review of his calendar entries. Bode's recollection was that he had referred Rodriguez to North on the occasion of their initial meeting on December 21, 1984.[11] This is corroborated by North's own notebook entry. On December 21, 1984, at 10:30 a.m. North writes "Call from Bill Bode." Underneath that entry is the name "Felix Rodriguez."[12] Rodriguez said it was Bode who made the arrangements for him to meet North.

Rodriguez also met with Gregg on that day and expressed his interest in going to El Salvador to work with the Salvadoran Air Force. Gregg recommended meetings with several other Administration officials.[13]

Gregg promptly reported to Vice President Bush after his meeting with Rodriguez. According to Gregg, he said, "My friend Felix, who was a remarkable former agency employee who was a counterinsurgency expert[,] wants to go down and help with El Salvador. And I am going to introduce him to Tony Motley, Tom Pickering, and Nestor Sanchez and see if he can sell himself to those men." Gregg stated that the Vice President said "Fine."[14]

---

[1] Gregg, Grand Jury, 10/23/87, p. 18.

[2] Gregg, Senate Foreign Relations Committee (SFRC) Testimony, 5/12/89, pp. 72–73.

[3] Ibid., pp. 54–55, 73–74; Tactical Task Force Report, 3/4/82, AKW 027860–66.

[4] Memorandum from Gregg to McFarlane, 3/17/83, AKW 027859–66 (attaching Tactical Task Force Report).

[5] Ibid.

[6] North, Grand Jury, 7/6/90, p. 17.

[7] North's schedule card in his handwriting reads: "1545 Felix Rodriguez (will be seeing Gregg at 1600)." North Schedule Card, 12/21/84, AKW 003167.

[8] North, North Trial Testimony, 4/11/89, p. 7435.

[9] Ibid.

[10] Gregg, SFRC Confirmation Hearings, 5/12/89, p. 122.

[11] Letter from Bode to Gregg, 4/25/89, ASX 0000003.

[12] North Notebook, 12/21/84, AMX 000267; North, Grand Jury, 7/6/90, p. 19.

[13] Statement by OVP Press Secretary, 12/15/86, ALU 012418 (attaching summary of Rodriguez contacts); Gregg, SFRC Testimony, 5/12/89, pp. 56–58, 75.

[14] Gregg, SFRC Testimony, 5/12/89, pp. 75–76. Motley was the assistant secretary of state for inter-American affairs; Thomas R. Pickering was U.S. ambassador in El Salvador; and Nestor Sanchez, a former CIA official, was deputy assistant secretary of defense for international security affairs.

Although Rodriguez testified that his goal was to assist in the Salvadoran anti-guerrilla program during late 1984 and early 1985, the evidence shows that he was also interested in contra-related matters.

At North's request, Rodriguez in January 1985 met Robert Owen, an associate of North, at the Key Bridge Marriott Hotel in Rosslyn, Virginia.[15] Owen wrote North a two-page letter regarding his meeting with Rodriguez, mentioning "FR's project" and "those who will be put under FR's care." The letter reports that Rodriguez wanted information on communications, command and control locations, which ideally would include "primary and secondary targets, both military and civilian." [16] Rodriguez acknowledged that the letter recounts their conversation, which was based on problems Rodriguez had observed on visits to contra camps.[17] Rodriguez testified that none of the projects he discussed with Owen were implemented because Rodriguez was mainly interested in El Salvador.[18]

Gregg arranged for Rodriguez to meet Vice President Bush on January 22, 1985. According to Gregg, the purpose of the meeting was to inform Bush that Rodriguez wanted to work in El Salvador against the guerrillas.[19] The meeting occurred in the Vice President's Old Executive Office Building office. According to Rodriguez, he met briefly with the Vice President, showing him his photo album, discussing Rodriguez's experiences in the CIA and watching a television report on the Bush family.[20]

On January 24, 1985, Rodriguez first met General Adolfo Blandon, the Salvadoran military chief of staff, and on January 30, 1985, he met with General Bustillo, commander of the Salvadoran Air Force. Both approved Rodriguez's planned assistance. Bustillo told

him he could stay at Ilopango Military Air Base outside of San Salvador and agreed to put him in contact with air force officers.[21]

As Rodriguez was completing his consultations with U.S. and Salvadoran officials, Thomas R. Pickering, the U.S. ambassador to El Salvador, learned of Rodriguez's planned mission. Pickering immediately raised a number of questions with a senior CIA field officer in Central America, who referred them to CIA headquarters. The field officer's January 31, 1985, cable says that Pickering wanted "help in finding out who Felix Rodriguez is and what is behind his apparent mission to El Salvador." CIA officers also reported that Pickering had been told that NSC staff members Nestor Sanchez and Constantine Menges were sending Rodriguez there "to 'solve the insurgency problems.'" Pickering wondered whether this had been coordinated with CIA headquarters and, if not, Pickering wanted the CIA "to learn about who is footing bill" for Rodriguez.[22]

On February 2, CIA headquarters responded to Pickering's questions about Rodriguez. Headquarters reported that Rodriguez had recently visited Langley, claiming that Salvadoran generals Blandon and Bustillo had welcomed his offer to help fight the guerrillas and stating that he had discussed this matter with Vice President Bush, Motley, North, Sanchez and Gregg. CIA headquarters also stressed, however, that "Rodriguez' visit is totally unrelated to [CIA]. . . ." [23]

The day the CIA answered his query, Pickering sent a cable to General Paul Gorman, chief of the U.S. Southern Command in Panama. Pickering summarized his knowledge of Rodriguez, his mission with the Salvadoran military and his high-level contacts in the U.S. Government. Pickering also reiterated his concern about Rodriguez's proposed mission in El Salvador and recommended that Gorman meet with Rodriguez to evaluate him and to clarify the U.S. approach in El Salvador.

On February 8, 1985, Gorman spoke with North about Rodriguez, the contras and U.S.

[15] Owen, Select Committees Testimony, 5/19/87, p. 201; Rodriguez, Select Committees Testimony, 5/28/87, pp. 119–21.

[16] Letter from Owen to North, 1/27/85, AKW 016393–94.

[17] Rodriguez, Grand Jury, 12/4/87, pp. 23–24.

[18] Ibid., pp. 24–25.

[19] Statement by Press Secretary attaching Summary of Contacts with Felix Rodriguez, 12/15/86, ALU 012418; Gregg, Grand Jury, 10/9/87, p. 52.

[20] Rodriguez, Grand Jury, 12/4/87, pp. 19–20. North's interest in Rodriguez continued. A 1/28/85 North notebook entry reflects a telephone call from Clair George, Director of Operations for the CIA: "Felix R w/ V.P. feedback from Don." (North Notebook, 1/28/85, AMX 003918.) Gregg's telephone log indicates that he had a secure telephone conversation with George on January 24, 1985. (Gregg Phone Log, 1/24/85, ALU 022016.)

[21] Rodriguez and Weisman, Shadow Warrior, pp. 222–23 (1989) (hereafter, Shadow Warrior).

[22] CIA Cable, 1/31/85, DO 166759.

[23] DIRECTOR 243316, 2/2/85, DO 166760.

assistance to Salvadoran anti-guerrilla forces.[24] In a subsequent cable to Pickering, Gorman reported that Rodriguez "has been put into play by Ollie North, and, while well acquainted, does not have higher backing." Gorman also reported that North "assures me that his intent was to focus Rodriguez on forces operating elsewhere in CentAm" and that, in response to Gorman's view that the Salvadoran Air Force was getting more than enough advice at the moment, "Ollie rogered, and said that Rodriguez can be much more useful in other places, where aid and advice is much scarcer." [25]

On February 14, 1985, Rodriguez met with Gorman in Panama City. They discussed Rodriguez's planned consulting role with the Salvadoran Air Force. Rodriguez also told Gorman of an immediate obligation to deliver equipment to contra forces, purchased with funds Rodriguez had received from contra leader Adolfo Calero. A few days later, Gorman told North that he had instructed Rodriguez to make the contras his priority.[26] Rodriguez later testified that his short-term priority during early 1985 was the delivery of security equipment to facilitate night supply drops to the contras, and that this must have been what Gorman was referring to in his conversation with North.[27]

On February 15, 1985, Gorman sent Rodriguez by military jet to El Salvador, where he met Pickering and U.S. Army Col. James J. Steele, commander of the U.S. Military Group in El Salvador. Rodriguez briefed them on his proposed helicopter counter-insurgency operations and his short-term, higher-priority mission for the contras. In his reporting cable to Gorman and back to the Department of State, Pickering effectively approved Rodriguez's plan to work with Bustillo, under the close supervision of Steele and on the conditions that Rodriguez avoid civilian casualties and not fly combat missions.[28] Pickering also asked the State Department to "brief Don Gregg in the VP's office for me."

Rodriguez immediately traveled to Washington to report on his meetings in Central America. On February 19, 1985, Rodriguez met with

Gregg in his office and told him of his successful meetings with Gorman, Pickering and Steele.[29] Rodriguez also met with North, whose notes show they discussed specific types of U.S. military assistance for El Salvador.[30]

In mid-March 1985, after first satisfying his obligation to deliver contra supplies to Honduras,[31] Rodriguez relocated to Ilopango air base. The next month, he began flying anti-guerrilla helicopter operations with the Salvadoran Air Force.

On April 20, 1985, after a helicopter operation succeeded in capturing a Salvadoran guerrilla leader and obtaining valuable intelligence information,[32] Rodriguez wrote a letter thanking Gregg for his and the Vice President's support and asking Gregg to write a note thanking Steele for the support he had given Rodriguez.[33] On April 29, Gregg sent a letter thanking Steele "for giving Felix your confidence and support, without which he feels he could not have gotten things under way." [34] On June 5, 1985, Rodriguez introduced Gregg to Steele at the Key Bridge Marriott Hotel in Rosslyn, Virginia.

## The September 10, 1986, Meeting

Congress in August 1985 authorized $27 million for humanitarian assistance to be administered through a newly created State Department office, the Nicaraguan Humanitarian Assistance Organization (NHAO).

In September 1985, Rodriguez's name began to surface in Administration circles in the context of the contra-resupply effort.[35] Similarly, Gregg appeared to be involved in discussions concerning the contras. A North notebook entry at 4:30 p.m. on September 10, 1985, seems to reflect a meeting between North, Gregg and Steele relating to problems with contra resupply:

1630—Mtg w/ Jim Steele/Don Gregg

[24] North Notebook, 2/8/85, AMX 003963.

[25] San Salvador 01792, 2/12/85, ALV 000148.

[26] North Notebook, 2/19/85, AMX 000466.

[27] Rodriguez, Grand Jury, 5/3/91, pp. 54–55.

[28] US SOUTHCOM Cable, 2/14/85, AMY 001054–55.

[29] Shadow Warrior, p. 227; OVP Summary of Contacts with Felix Rodriguez, 12/15/86, ALU 012418.

[30] North Notebook, 2/19/85, AMX 000467. Although North and Gregg spoke on February 26, 1985, there is no record of the substance of their conversation. (Gregg Phone Log, 2/26/85, ALU 22034.)

[31] Rodriguez, Grand Jury, 12/4/87, p. 31.

[32] Shadow Warrior, pp. 231–33, 242.

[33] Letter from Rodriguez to Gregg, 4/20/85, ALU 012402–05. On May 31, 1985, Rodriguez signed a similar note, which he sent along with a photograph of himself to Gregg in Washington. (Letter from Rodriguez to Gregg, 5/31/85, ALU 011618.)

[34] Letter from Gregg to Steele, 4/29/85, AKW 029991.

[35] See, for example, Abrams, Fiers, and Corr chapters.

Approached by

Mario del Amico
   claims to be close to Aplicano
   claims to be close to FDN [contras]
says radar coverage was prob.
   for flights out of Aguacate [Honduras]
wants to use
Talked to Blandon who
   said Tamarindo (near
   la Union) [in El Salvador] could be used
Says Bermudez was prepared
   to devote a special ops [operations] unit
   astride FMLN [ 36] log lines.
Introduced by Wally Greshiem\Litton
Calero/Bermudez visit to
   Ilopango to estab.
   log support./maint. for
—Del Amico convinced Blandon to
   give FDN 1K FN mags.
   Blandon never paid for mags. . . .37

North's note appears to cast doubt upon Gregg's sworn testimony that he was unaware of North's involvement with contra-resupply prior to the summer of 1986. The notes mention an arms dealer in Central America, Mario Dellamico, who apparently claimed to be close to Honduran Col. Hector Aplicano and to the contras.38 The notes reflect a discussion about the problem of Nicaraguan radar coverage of contra flights out of Aguacate, Honduras. The notes also reflect a discussion about the contras creating a special operations unit to interdict Salvadoran insurgents' supplies from Nicaragua into El Salvador. Apparently contra leaders Calero and Bermudez visited Ilopango to assess that location for logistical support for unspecified military activities. The notes apparently reflect that Dellamico convinced Salvadoran General Blandon to give the contras a thousand magazines for Belgian rifles, for which he was never paid.

In addition to North's notebook entry, his September 10, 1985, schedule card reflects a handwritten entry at 4:30 p.m. for Gregg. North explained that the addition of his handwritten note to his already typed, prepared schedule

would indicate that someone added a meeting with him at the last minute.39

After reviewing his schedule card and notebook entry of the meeting with Steele/Gregg, North testified that this notebook entry appeared to reflect a scheduled meeting with Don Gregg at 4:30 p.m. on September 10, 1985.40 North, however, did not specifically remember having this discussion with Steele or Gregg.41

Gregg disputed this North notebook entry. Gregg testified that he did not recall meeting with North and Steele about the matters presented in the notes. Steele also did not believe that he, Gregg and North had discussions about contra resupply. Steele said that following a meeting with Gregg in September 1985, he possibly met with North to discuss these matters, but Steele did not place Gregg in the meeting.42

## North Recruits Rodriguez

On September 20, 1985, North wrote a "Dear Felix" letter formally requesting Rodriguez's assistance at Ilopango to facilitate the operation of contra-resupply planes. In the letter, North asked Rodriguez not to inform CIA field personnel or Dellamico about his request, and to destroy the letter after reading it. North informed Rodriguez that he would be contacted by an individual who would identify himself as being sent by "Mr. Green." 43

Rodriguez testified that when he met with North on October 17, 1985, in Washington, North told him not to reveal Rodriguez's assistance to the resupply to anyone on the "second floor," a reference to the Office of the Vice President. Rodriguez testified that he obeyed North's instruction and did not discuss contra-resupply with Gregg until August 8, 1986. Rodriguez said he did not reveal to Gregg the North letter of solicitation until December

36 The guerrilla movement in El Salvador.
37 North Note, 9/10/85, AMX 001726–27.
38 For a more complete discussion of Dellamico's activities, see CIA Subject #1 chapter.
39 North, Grand Jury, 7/6/90, p. 73–74.
40 Ibid., p. 75.
41 Ibid., p. 82.
42 Steele, Grand Jury, 2/6/91, pp. 34–37. Steele's continued denial of Gregg's involvement in a September 10, 1985, meeting added credibility to Gregg's denials. Steele in lengthy interviews with OIC in 1990 and 1991 made incriminating statements about his own conduct. In light of Steele's candor about his own complicity in operational matters at Ilopango, his continued insistence that he did not remember a substantive meeting with North and Gregg seemed credible. On the other hand, Steele failed a polygraph question that squarely addressed Gregg's attendance at the September 1985 meeting with North. (Polygraph Report of Steele, 9/18/90.)
43 Letter from North to Rodriguez, 9/20/85, AKW 022740–43.

1986.[44] North, however, denied telling Rodriguez not to tell Gregg about the "Dear Felix" letter.[45] Rather than attempting to hide his association with Rodriguez, contemporaneously created documents indicate that North willingly shared this information with other Administration officials. North's notebook of October 1, 1985, contains an entry which states: "Don Gregg: Maximo Gomez [Rodriguez] 27–31–59." [46]

North did not remember whether this entry indicated that he obtained Rodriguez's Salvadoran phone number from Gregg, or that he possibly supplied Gregg with the number.[47] However, the entry shows that North was not reluctant to discuss Rodriguez and his alias "Gomez" with Gregg during this period. Indeed, during a RIG meeting the same day to implement the NHAO funding, North shared information regarding Rodriguez with other Administration officials from the Department of State and the CIA. The notes of Ambassador Robert Duemling, head of NHAO, reflect the following:

> (North) can use—
> Mr. Green said to call—
> Maximo Gomez [Rodriguez]
> 273159 in San Salvador
> Will airlift the stuff from Salvador.[48]

Duemling's note reflects that Gomez (Rodriguez) would be awaiting a call from a representative from Mr. Green, as North had indicated in the "Dear Felix" letter. Additionally, the Duemling note reflects the same telephone number attributed to Rodriguez in the earlier North notebook entry. North testified that he had no reason to conceal from other Government officials his knowledge of Rodriguez's alias, his telephone number, or the fact of his availability.[49]

In mid-December 1985, Rodriguez received a call from Rafael Quintero, an associate of Secord. Quintero said he was calling on behalf of "Mr. Green." Rodriguez and Quintero had known each other for some time but had a falling out because of Quintero's relationship with former CIA officer and convicted felon Edwin Wilson, and with Thomas Clines and Frank Terpil, who had been involved with Wilson.[50] As a result of Quintero's call, Rodriguez arranged for the landing of a 707 aircraft from Europe that brought weapons to Ilopango for the contras.

Following news media coverage in October 1985, Honduras prohibited direct humanitarian aid flights for the contras from the United States to Honduras. Arrangements were made permitting the supplies to be flown to Ilopango in El Salvador and ultimately delivered to the contras. A number of U.S. officials flew to Ilopango and attended a meeting on December 30, 1985, to discuss the logistics of providing the NHAO aid. Among others, North, CIA Central American Task Force Chief Alan D. Fiers, Jr., State Department official William Walker, NHAO official Cresencio Arcos and U.S. Ambassador to El Salvador Edwin G. Corr met with Bustillo at Ilopango air base. Rodriguez also was present.

After receiving a mid-December 1985 State Department cable reflecting concern over the Honduran situation, Gregg's deputy Watson bracketed for Gregg a segment of the cable addressing alternative means of moving essential supplies to the contras. At the top of the cable Watson wrote: "Don—Suggest you read carefully—could have serious effect on our supplies to Contras." [51]

Rodriguez's resupply efforts became more concentrated in January and February 1986. In January, Rodriguez met Richard B. Gadd, a Secord associate, at Ilopango. Gadd became responsible for advising Rodriguez of the arriving planes.[52] By this time, Rodriguez's use of the alias "Gomez" was being openly discussed in Washington within the Restricted Interagency Group (RIG), which focused on Central American issues. During late January and early February 1986, Rodriguez's coordination of NHAO flights and his involvement with lethal-resupply

44 Rodriguez, Grand Jury, 5/3/91, p. 66.

45 North, Grand Jury, 7/11/90, p. 22.

46 North Notebook, 10/1/85, AMX 001787.

47 North, Grand Jury, 7/11/90, pp. 15–17.

48 Duemling Note, 10/1/85, GP 0025170–78.

49 North, Grand Jury, 7/11/90, p. 31. In the Grand Jury, North did not recall whether he asked Gregg whether he could utilize Rodriguez in resupply efforts, contrary to his own trial testimony. (North, Grand Jury, 7/6/90, pp. 117–18, 122; North, Grand Jury, 7/11/90, pp. 31–32.)

50 Quintero, Grand Jury, 1/6/88, pp. 192–97; Quintero, North Trial Testimony, 3/2/89, pp. 2915–16; Rodriguez, Grand Jury, 5/3/91, pp. 119–21.

51 State 388960, 12/23/85, ALU 011860.

52 Rodriguez, FBI 302, 12/29/86.

activities became an issue of concern to the CIA and Department of State officials. There is no documentary evidence, however, that links CIA and State Department concern about Rodriguez to Gregg or to any other member of the Office of the Vice President.[53]

Only one witness, Steele, told Independent Counsel that Gregg may have known of Rodriguez's assistance to the contra-resupply effort during the January 1986 period. Steele recalled that during a visit to Washington in January 1986, he dropped by briefly to say hello to Gregg. At the end of the conversation, Gregg asked Steele " 'Is Felix taking a lot of risks flying?' or 'Is Felix still flying a lot?' " Steele responded, "Felix is not doing a lot of flying because he's spending a lot of time helping the contras."[54]

## The Watson February 1986 Memorandum

In mid-January 1986, the Vice President's deputy national security adviser Watson went to Central America to familiarize himself with the region. For a portion of his trip, he was escorted by Rodriguez.[55] Both men denied that they discussed Rodriguez's involvement in contra resupply. Nevertheless, on February 4, 1986, Watson wrote a memorandum regarding his trip to Honduras and El Salvador and the state of the contras. Watson's memorandum for Vice President Bush was channeled through Gregg. In his memorandum, Watson noted that he "visited the DFR's [contras'] main aerial re-supply base [at Aguacate, Honduras] and looked at their DC-6 (not the best for infiltration and flying in between mountains), their parachuting packing and rigging facilities and their ammunition and supply warehouses." Gregg marked the memorandum for Bush, noting at the top: "Good report from Sam."[56]

One portion of the Watson memorandum, concerning the contras, particularly drew Gregg's attention:

> What is lacking is our ability to provide outright logistical support, advice, planning, or even direction of cross-border operations. As you know, we are proscribed by Congress from any of these more active measures.

Gregg underlined the portion of the paragraph which read "to provide outright logistical support, advice, planning, or even direction of cross-border operations." In the margin of the memorandum Gregg wrote, "Felix agrees with this—It is a major shortcoming."[57] Gregg testified that he and the Vice President never had a discussion about the logistical problems that the contras faced, reiterating that he had never discussed contra-resupply with the Vice President.[58]

An additional Office of the Vice President document appears to contradict Gregg's testimony that he never discussed contra-resupply with Rodriguez or with the Vice President. On March 6, 1986, Watson attached to a memo for Bush a note and a December 21, 1985, cable from the U.S. Embassy in Managua, Nicaragua, regarding consolidation of Sandinista power. On the first page of the Embassy cable Gregg wrote:

> A sober analysis of the Sandinistas' hold on power. The means suggested to counter this hold will not be enough. The central point is that Contra actions + internal political opposition need to be coordinated. Felix says we are doing nothing to direct the Contra planning. . . .[59]

## The May 1, 1986, Rodriguez/Bush Meeting: "Resupply of the Contras"

On April 11, 1986, Rodriguez assisted in the flight of an L-100 aircraft from Ilopango to

---

[53] Gregg and Watson were not regular members of the RIG, which often specifically discussed contra-related matters. Although Watson, as an Office of the Vice President representative, had asked to attend RIG meetings, Abrams denied him access. (Gregg, Grand Jury, 10/23/87, p. 25.) Abrams nevertheless told the FBI that he believed that he told Gregg about Rodriguez's activity in the private resupply network. (Abrams, FBI 302, 6/15/88, p. 2.)

[54] Steele, FBI 302, 2/5/91, p. 2.

[55] Watson schedule, 1/86, ALU 025485–86.

[56] Memorandum from Watson to Bush, 2/4/86, ALU 25448–50.

[57] Ibid. Gregg, SFRC Testimony, 5/12/89, pp. 107–8.

[58] Ibid., p. 109. Rodriguez testified in 1991 that he did not discuss the topics reflected in Watson's memorandum with either Gregg or Watson, and that until August 8, 1986, he did not discuss any of those subject matters with Gregg. (Rodriguez, Grand Jury, 5/3/91, pp. 194, 196.)

[59] Briefing Memorandum, 3/6/86, ALU 025418–22.

drop lethal supplies to contra forces on the southern military front in Nicaragua. This was the first lethal-resupply flight to the southern front forces.

Rodriguez, however, was becoming disenchanted with his role in Salvador and on April 16, 1986, he called the Office of the Vice President to request a meeting with Vice President Bush. That call resulted in the production of a scheduling memorandum detailing the purpose of Rodriguez's meeting with Bush—which ultimately took place May 1, 1986—as a discussion regarding "resupply of the Contras." This memorandum, which Gregg revealed to investigators in December 1986, cast doubt on testimony that Rodriguez did not discuss contra-resupply with the Vice President.[60]

Rodriguez called the Office of the Vice President on April 16, 1986, and spoke with secretary Phyllis Byrne. Byrne's shorthand notes of that conversation translate as follows:

Felix:—El Salvador
503 27 1996 late night or early morning
7–9:30 a.m.
Late p.m.—235566
Dinner—stay 2–3 hours
Sleep at air base.
21st—talk to the VP for a short time.[61]

Byrne then prepared a scheduling proposal memorandum in Gregg's name for Debbie Hutton, an OVP employee. The memorandum requested a 15-minute meeting on April 22 or 23 for "Felix Rodriguez, a counterinsurgency expert visiting from El Salvador . . . [t]o brief the Vice President on the status of the war in El Salvador [sic] and resupply of the Contras." Byrne penned in the initials "DG" next to Gregg's name on the memorandum. The proposed meeting date range was altered by hand on the typed memorandum to read "April 28 to May 2."[62]

Rodriguez did not inform Byrne of the purpose of his meeting with the Vice President. When she was typing the proposed scheduling memorandum, she asked Watson what the purpose of the meeting would be. In response to Byrne's request, Watson provided her with the phrase "To brief the Vice President on the status of the war in El Salvador and resupply of the contras."[63]

Watson repeatedly denied supplying Byrne with the wording in this phrase. Byrne, however, was not familiar with the term "resupply" and she testified that she had never used it or heard it before she received the phrase from Watson for the scheduling memorandum.[64] Gregg speculated in congressional testimony that the phrase "resupply of the Contras" might actually have meant "resupply of the copters," and could have referred to needed supplies for helicopter operations for the Salvadoran Air Force.[65] However, in 1987, Col. Watson testified that as a military man, "resupply" was a technical term with a very specific meaning—the provision of food, ammunition, batteries, water and bullets to troops, by way of truck, helicopter, airplane or on foot. Watson testified that he did not believe that the term "resupply" would apply to obtaining helicopters or helicopter parts.[66]

Stephanie VanDevander, Watson's secretary at the time, remembered hearing Byrne ask Watson for language to use in the memorandum. She remembered Watson giving a response that she could not hear. However, following Watson's response to Byrne's question, Byrne typed the memorandum. Subsequently, VanDevander became aware of the conflict of Watson's and Byrne's recollection of this occasion. On the day she left the Vice President's office in February 1988, she informed Gregg that Watson had not been completely forthcoming on the matter of the scheduled proposal memorandum.[67]

In spite of the direct contradiction between Watson's testimony and that of two of the support staff in the Office of the Vice President,

[60] Gregg brought this note to the attention of the investigators and focused on it during his initial FBI interview on December 15, 1986. Although this note creates concern about the veracity of portions of Gregg's testimony, it is noteworthy that the document was produced and focused upon by Gregg early in the investigation.

[61] Note and Transcription from Byrne, 6/16/87.

[62] Schedule Proposal, 4/16/86, ALU 012415.

[63] Byrne, Grand Jury, 10/23/87, pp. 13–17.

[64] Ibid., p. 20. Rodriguez testified that he did not mention resupply of the contras in his conversation with Byrne. (Rodriguez, Grand Jury, 5/10/91, p. 10.)

[65] Gregg, SFRC Testimony, 5/12/89, p. 104. Gregg also referred to a June 1986 memorandum to the Vice President titled "Subject: Helicopters for El Salvador." The memorandum states that "Last month [May 1986] Felix Rodriguez raised with you a problem the Salvadoran Air Force was having getting spare parts for their Hughes 500 helicopters. . . ." (Memorandum from Gregg and Watson to Bush, 6/3/86, ALU 012376.)

[66] Watson, Grand Jury, 10/14/87, pp. 102–3.

[67] VanDevander, FBI 302, 11/30/90, pp. 7–9.

Independent Counsel determined in the summer of 1991 that he would not seek an indictment against Watson but rather would compel his testimony before the Grand Jury through use immunity. This was not productive. During his appearances before the Grand Jury in 1991 and 1992, Watson's testimony was heavily laced with answers of "I do not recall" and "I do not remember." [68]

Following his call to the Office of the Vice President on April 16, Rodriguez participated in a meeting on April 20, 1986, at Ilopango with North, Secord and others involved in the resupply operation. Rodriguez testified that he had misgivings about certain aspects of the re-supply operation. He was concerned that the airplanes used in the resupply operations were being purchased at a considerable profit to the individuals involved, and he did not believe North's statement that the aircraft were actually donations from a European country. Additionally, Rodriguez was concerned about the role of Secord because he associated Secord with Quintero, Clines and Edwin Wilson. The linkage of those individuals with Qadhafi and Libya greatly disturbed Rodriguez.[69] A combination of factors led Rodriguez to inform Ambassador Corr on April 24, 1986, that he was tired, and because he had been separated from his family for a long time, he planned on leaving.[70]

Watson remembered getting the briefing memorandum dated April 30—the day before the meeting with the Vice President—which repeated its planned purpose: "Briefing on the status of the war in El Salvador, and resupply of the Contras." [71]

The evening before the meeting with the Vice President, Rodriguez met Watson for drinks at a Washington restaurant. Watson and Rodriguez did not recall what was discussed.[72]

The next day, on May 1, Rodriguez went to North's office prior to his meeting with the Vice President. Rodriguez informed North that he was tired and planned on leaving El Sal-

vador. North tried to convince Rodriguez to stay.[73]

Rodriguez then met with the Vice President and, by all accounts, the topic of contra-resupply was not discussed. Rodriguez showed the Vice President photos from his helicopter project in El Salvador.[74] During most of the meeting the participants were the Vice President, Gregg, Watson, Rodriguez and Nicholas Brady, whom the Vice President asked to sit in because of his interest in Central America.[75] Toward the end of the meeting, North brought in Corr. Corr praised Rodriguez to the Vice President, saying he was doing a magnificent job and that he would like Rodriguez to stay in El Salvador. Rodriguez had not mentioned to the Vice President his plans to depart; after Corr's praise, Rodriguez chose not to bring it up.[76]

Following the meeting with Vice President Bush, Rodriguez returned to Salvador and in May 1986 met Robert Dutton, who replaced Gadd as Secord's principal supervisor of the resupply operation. During that meeting, Rodriguez told Dutton he had a very close relationship with the Vice President and a number of his people.[77] Rodriguez's boasting of his relationship with the Vice President was a continual problem.[78]

## Rodriguez's June 25, 1986, Meetings With North and Watson

In June 1986, North asked Dutton to bring Rodriguez to Washington for a meeting, because North had information that Rodriguez had been discussing contra-resupply plans over an open telephone. Rodriguez on June 25, 1986, met with North and Dutton in the Old Executive Office Building. During the meeting, there was a brief discussion about reorganization of the resupply operation at Ilopango. North then told Rodriguez that he had documented proof of Rodriguez talking over open phone lines and

[68] The futility of the Watson Grand Jury examination was illustrated by his response of "I do not recall" when asked whether he ever chose deliberately to answer "I do not recall" to a question about the "resupply of the contras" memo prepared by Byrne. (Watson, Grand Jury, 1/24/92, pp. 112–16.)

[69] Rodriguez, Grand Jury, 5/10/91, pp. 43–59.

[70] Ibid., pp. 43, 45, 87–88.

[71] Watson, Grand Jury, 1/24/92, p. 81.

[72] Ibid., p. 92; Rodriguez, Grand Jury, 5/10/91, p. 62.

[73] Ibid., pp. 69, 84–85.

[74] Ibid., p. 81.

[75] Ibid.

[76] Ibid., pp. 83–85.

[77] Dutton, Select Committees Testimony, 5/27/87, pp. 23–24, 44; Dutton, North Trial Testimony, 3/6/89, pp. 3275–78, 3311–13, 3332.

[78] Abrams, Grand Jury, 11/6/91, pp. 45–46; Fiers, FBI 302, 7/18/91, p. 2; North Notebook, 1/9/86, AMX 000876 ("Felix talking too much about VP connection").

was concerned he might compromise the entire operation.[79] Rodriguez became angry and showed North a photocopy of a letter from one of the resupply pilots describing the poor quality of the aircraft and the dangerous conditions that existed in the resupply operation at Ilopango.[80] Rodriguez asked if Dutton would leave the room and in Dutton's absence Rodriguez complained that Secord's associate Thomas Clines was selling $3.50 hand grenades for $9.00 to $9.50 to the contras.[81] Rodriguez testified that North said there had been no money exchanged, the materials were a donation from a European country, and Clines was a patriot. Finally Rodriguez stated that he had to leave to go to the Vice President's office to pick up pictures taken of Bush and Bustillo's wife at a Miami event.[82]

In the Vice President's office, Rodriguez ran into Watson, and they sat in Gregg's office and had a brief conversation about helicopter parts.[83] Shortly thereafter, North walked into the room with Dutton. Rodriguez remembers North stating that he arrived to escort Rodriguez back when he was finished. Watson's notes of a much later meeting, which were withheld until 1991, suggest that North introduced Dutton as "our man for resupply." Watson could not remember this when he testified in 1992. Rodriguez denied it.[84]

In the Grand Jury, Watson was confronted with his own notes of a December 17, 1986, meeting among Gregg, Watson, Byrne, and vice presidential lawyers C. Boyden Gray and John Schmitz.[85] The notes attribute the following remark to Watson during the meeting: "Was Dutton the guy Earl or North brought in one day—'Our man for resupply'?"[86] Watson's recollection of the Dutton meeting was not refreshed by his own note.[87]

## Gregg's August 8, 1986, Meeting With Rodriguez

The conflict between North and Rodriguez intensified throughout the summer of 1986. Rodriguez was concerned that the airplanes, which he believed had been donated to the contras, would be claimed as an asset of Secord's resupply operation once Congress approved $100 million in contra aid, expected in the fall of 1986. Because of this concern, Rodriguez arranged to have armed guards placed on the planes to ensure their return to Ilopango.[88] On July 29, 1986, Watson, appearing at a White House meeting in place of Gregg, received a whispered message from North concerning Rodriguez's interference with the resupply operation. Watson's initial notes read as follows:

> . . . Max shut down pilots resupply . . .[89]

The same day, Secord sent a message to Dutton recommending that the operation be moved out of Ilopango because of problems with Rodriguez.[90] On July 31, 1986, either North or North's assistant Robert Earl complained to Watson that Rodriguez had stolen two airplanes from Miami and had taken them to El Salvador. When Watson asked for additional information, he was told, "just tell Felix to cut 'it' out."[91] The next day, North again complained to Watson about Rodriguez, claiming Rodriguez has "screwed up S [southern] front."[92]

The conflict between Rodriguez and the North-Secord resupply operation reached a climax following Rodriguez's flight from Miami to El Salvador on a C–123 loaded with spare parts for planes at Ilopango. Quintero called Rodriguez claiming that Rodriguez had stolen the plane and demanded that it and its cargo be returned to Miami.[93] North called Gregg and told him that Rodriguez had stolen a plane. Gregg called Rodriguez and asked him about

[79] Rodriguez, Grand Jury, 5/10/91, pp. 111–12; Dutton, Select Committees Testimony, 5/27/87, pp. 49–50; Dutton, *North* Trial Testimony, 3/6/89, p. 3286.

[80] Rodriguez, Grand Jury, 5/10/91, p. 113.

[81] Ibid., p. 114.

[82] Ibid., p. 115.

[83] Ibid., p. 117.

[84] Ibid., pp. 118–20.

[85] Watson, Grand Jury, 2/7/92, p. 79.

[86] Watson Note, 12/17/86, ALU 0136580.

[87] Watson, Grand Jury, 2/7/92, p. 151.

[88] Rodriguez, Select Committees Testimony, 5/28/87, pp. 101–2.

[89] Watson Note, 7/29/86, ALU 011950–51. This note is another piece of evidence that contradicts Rodriguez's assertion that North did not want the Office of the Vice President to know about their activities.

[90] KL–43 Message from Secord to Dutton, 7/29/86, 00360–61.

[91] Memorandum from Watson, 12/17/86, ALU 025490.

[92] Watson Note, 8/1/86, ALU 011952.

[93] Rodriguez, FBI 302, 12/29/86, p. 8; Rodriguez, Grand Jury, 5/10/91, pp. 125–29.

the stolen plane. Rodriguez called Gregg back and told him that he needed to talk with him.[94] At 9:30 a.m. on August 8, 1986, Rodriguez met with Gregg and Watson at the Old Executive Office Building.

Following the Iran/contra revelations on November 25, 1986, the Office of the Vice President on December 15, 1986, produced a chronology of meetings with Rodriguez. According to the chronology, during this August 8, 1986, meeting, Rodriguez expressed "his concerns that the informal contra supply organization which then existed might not survive until the United States Government organization directed by CIA to implement delivery of funds and equipment recently authorized by Congress could be established . . ."[95] The chronology stated that this meeting was the first time Rodriguez discussed contra resupply with anyone in the Office of the Vice President. The chronology further asserted that Rodriguez mentioned he was concerned about the poor quality of the aircraft being used in the contra-resupply operation.[96]

Gregg was questioned extensively about his meeting with Rodriguez on August 8, 1986. He was asked whether he informed the Vice President of Rodriguez's complaints. During his first investigative interview on Iran/contra matters on December 15, 1986, Gregg told the FBI that he did not have direct knowledge from his conversation with Rodriguez in August 1986 that Rodriguez was involved in the resupply operation. Gregg only suspected Rodriguez had knowledge of the operation because Rodriguez had worked at Ilopango air base where the operation apparently was run.[97] Gregg provided the FBI with a chronology of contacts with Rodriguez, which did not describe Rodriguez's complaints about North during the August 8, 1986, meeting. Additionally, the chronology stated it was not until November 7, 1986, that Rodriguez met with Gregg and Watson and indicated that he personally had assisted the contra-resupply effort.[98]

Later, Gregg testified in 1987 that in late December 1986 Rodriguez told him that he had been formally solicited by North to assist and had been told not to tell Gregg about his activities.[99] Gregg described Rodriguez's August revelations as "the tip of the iceberg" and stated he was not fully aware of his involvement in contra resupply until he put the pieces together in December 1986.[100]

An analysis of Gregg and Watson's notes of the Rodriguez meeting, coupled with Rodriguez's subsequent testimony, raised concerns about Gregg's assertions. Gregg's notes read:

Felix—8 Aug '86
Using Ed Wilson group for supplies.
Felix used by Ollie [North] to get Contra
planes repaired at Ilopango
"Mr. Green" = Rafael Quintero
Felix knew him at Bay of Pigs, also
close to Tom Clines whom Felix
used to know—split over Libya.
A swap of weapons for $
was arranged to get aid for Contras
Clines & General Secord tied in.
Hand grenades bought for $3—
sold for $9.
Felix planned to quit in May.
DICK GADD purchases things
got 1st Caribou—big profit
Clines is getting $ from Saudis
or whoever: buying things at great
profit. He hired pilots for Qadhafi with
 Wilson
BOB DUTTON brought in as mgr [manager]
for project after a flap. He & Felix
got into a conflict. Tried to set up a
proper org. to sell to CIA.
CIA said no—people involved said
we'll keep what we have.

[page 2:]
Dick Gadd rip off $20,000 on
a commo gear piece.
Gadd getting rip off on two workers
$650 a day.
C–123 was seen as a donation

94 Ibid., p. 130.
95 Summary of Contacts with Felix Rodriguez, 12/15/86, ALU 012419.
96 Ibid.
97 Gregg, FBI 302, 12/15/86, p. 4.
98 Summary of Contacts with Felix Rodriguez, 12/15/86, ALU 012420. Gregg also maintained that he did not inform the Vice President

about his August 8 meeting with Rodriguez. (Gregg, FBI 302, 12/15/86, p. 4.)
99 Gregg, Grand Jury, 10/23/87, p. 68.
100 Gregg, SFRC Testimony, 5/12/89, pp. 118–19.

by Bustillo.
Was sitting in Miami with
medicine Felix got from Mayor
of W. Miami [Reboredo] IV's, spare parts
Bermudez asked Mayor to come in
to Contra base
Southern Air Transport said plane
OK to go. Called Jim Steele.
Rafael said NO

---

Quintero said ops "finished"
Bustillo angry—feels plane is a
donation—was told so by Ollie
C–123 & 2 others are held on the base
by order of Bustillo
Steele will not release planes
Feels as Felix does.

[page 3:]
Bustillo feels US credibility
at stake—now feels it has been
a $ making process. He feels
3 planes belong to Contras.
He offered the base to Contras
on his own.
If planes pulled back, Bustillo
will be angered & will close base
down.
Felix can get Bustillo to
release the planes.[101]

Rodriguez remembered telling Gregg about North being involved with the Edwin Wilson group. Rodriguez thought that the effect could be worse than Watergate, because of North's position as an NSC staff officer, his responsibility for anti-terrorism efforts, and his involvement with a group of people connected to terrorists like Libya's Mu'ammar Qadhafi through Wilson.[102] Rodriguez explained that the only reason he told Gregg about these matters in August 1986 is because North asked Gregg to use his influence with Rodriguez to release the airplane.[103]

Rodriguez was asked whether he told Gregg the contents of the September 20, 1985, "Dear Felix" letter. Rodriguez responded that Gregg

had asked him how he got involved in the operation and Rodriguez "probably mentioned the fact that Oliver North had told me that a guy by the name of Mr. Green was going to call him to help in this maintenance of the aircraft."[104] However, Rodriguez did not remember whether he specifically mentioned the letter. Rodriguez testified that he did not hold anything back from Gregg during their meeting on August 8, including his own role in the contra-resupply effort.[105]

Watson acknowledged the correlation between Gregg's notes and the "Dear Felix" letter.[106] However, Watson did not recall Rodriguez mentioning the letter in the meeting, even though his own notes of the meeting contain the word "letter."[107] Gregg was so concerned over what Rodriguez was telling him that he called and asked Earl, North's deputy, to join them in the meeting.[108]

## Gregg's August 12, 1986, Meeting Regarding Rodriguez and the Contra-Resupply Operation

Following the Rodriguez meeting, Gregg called a meeting of U.S. Government officials in his office on August 12, 1986, to discuss issues raised by Rodriguez. Gregg met with Raymond Burghardt of the NSC staff, Corr, Earl, Fiers, Steele, Walker and Watson. According to the December 15, 1986, Office of the Vice President chronology, the purpose of the meeting

---

[101] Gregg Notes, 8/8/86, AKW 029885–87.
[102] Rodriguez, Grand Jury, 5/10/91, pp. 140–41. Rodriguez was aware of Quintero's involvement in the resupply operation as early as December 1985 and that of Secord before his May 1, 1986, meeting with the Vice President.
[103] Ibid., p. 142.

[104] Ibid., p. 155.
[105] Ibid., pp. 158–59. Additionally, Rodriguez did not recall ever using the phraseology "swap of weapons for dollars." (Ibid., p. 160.) Rodriguez also said Quintero or someone in Central America had mentioned that Saudi money was being pumped into the operation. (Ibid., 5/10/91, p. 161.)
[106] Watson, Grand Jury, 4/10/92, p. 80.
[107] Ibid., p. 82; Watson Note, 8/8/86, ALU 0136944. Watson's recollection is that Rodriguez did not say anything about his own role with resupply during the August 8 meeting, notwithstanding Gregg's note. (Watson, Grand Jury, 4/10/92, p. 107.)
[108] Central to Gregg's concern was the involvement of Thomas Clines. Earl's August 8, 1986 note attributes the following to Gregg:
   Don Gregg:
   Tom Clines = snake! (would sell his mother)
(Earl Note, 8/8/86, AMT 00612.) Clines testified that he saw Gregg in the OEOB in the middle of June 1985, while Clines was walking with Secord and North. Clines and Gregg knew each other from their days at the CIA. Clines told Gregg he was "with these guys [North and Secord] working on the contra thing." (Clines, Grand Jury, 4/19/91, pp. 19–21.)

was "to pass along the concerns mentioned by Mr. Rodriguez." [109]

According to Burghardt, the topics discussed went beyond Rodriguez's concerns and included what would happen to supplies stored for the contras at Ilopango after Congress authorized $100 million in assistance, what would happen to the old aircraft, and what role Rodriguez would play in the further resupply operations.[110] Earl's notes of the meeting reflect no detailed discussion of the concerns described by Rodriguez to Gregg on August 8, 1986, involving Wilson, Quintero, Clines, Secord and the Libya connection to North. Earl's notes reflect primarily operational concerns about transition from the contra-resupply operation at Ilopango to Government-authorized, CIA-directed resupply:

> Corr
> Concerned on transition
>   Busti[ll]o concerned FDN [contras]
>   getting       screwed
>       (re A/C) [aircraft].
> Equip being taken?
> Urgent need for resupply of [the] southern
>   front.
> —123 Miami →
> Felix Rodriguez—compadres w/ Busti[ll]o.
>
>             *       *       *
>
> bottom line = sell A/C & money to FDN.
> Corr recommends this.
> Or, ON [North] to explain who owns A/C
>   to Busti[ll]o—
> Corr doesn't think this will work.
> Felix needs to be eased out w/ honor.
> Corr doesn't mind either way, but Corr thinks
> he's been instrumen-        | 3 months
> tal                         |
>                             |
>                             |
> Ilopango = [Classified   |   continuation
>   information withheld]
>   not 1st choice
> Felix claims working w/ VP blessing for CIA.
>
>             *       *       *
>
> Corr sees no legal alternative to Felix ([CIA]
> & Steele can't ~~tough~~ touch it)

> Corr can't see any way to operate
> Mario Delameco, Miami = Felix contact
>   (Cuban
>       → cut this link.
> Calero—Martin link = a problem too. [111]

After the August 12, 1986 meeting, Rodriguez told Gregg that everything was fine; the resupply flights were continuing.[112] Rodriguez continued his resupply activities until he temporarily left El Salvador for medical reasons in September 1986. Rodriguez was in Miami when the Hasenfus plane was shot down on October 5, 1986.

## Abrams and North's General Recollections of Discussions With Gregg Regarding Rodriguez and Contra Resupply

After Elliott Abrams pleaded guilty and agreed to cooperate with Independent Counsel, Abrams gave testimony relevant to whether Gregg was aware of Rodriguez's contra activities prior to August 1986.

Abrams remembered that he was concerned that Rodriguez, who went to El Salvador to be involved in counterinsurgency efforts, became a part of the contra-resupply effort. Abrams said Rodriguez talked too much about the Vice President.[113] Abrams' concern was that because Rodriguez was a part of the resupply operation and was boasting of his vice presidential connections, he would create the erroneous impression that the Office of the Vice President had some sort of linkage to the contra-resupply operation.[114] Abrams believes he spoke at least once to Gregg in person about this problem.[115] Abrams did not specifically recall when this meeting occurred, but he believed it occurred in the first half of 1986.[116]

North also had a general, but not specific, recollection of addressing the Rodriguez problem with Gregg before August 1986. North generally recalled discussing with Gregg

[109] Summary of Contacts with Felix Rodriguez, 12/15/86, ALU 012419.
[110] Burghardt, FBI 302, 2/27/87, p. 6.
[111] Earl Notes, 8/12/86 (emphasis in original).
[112] Rodriguez, Grand Jury, 5/10/91, pp. 168–71; Gregg, SFRC Deposition, 5/12/89, p. 135.
[113] Abrams, Grand Jury, 11/6/91, p. 45.
[114] Ibid., pp. 47–48.
[115] Ibid., p. 46.
[116] Ibid., p. 47.

Rodriguez's boasting about his connection with the Office of the Vice President.[117]

## The Hasenfus Shoot-Down

On October 5, 1986, prior to the enactment of a pending authorization for CIA support for the contras and a $100 million appropriation, an aircraft carrying weapons and other supplies to the contras was shot down over Nicaragua. Three crewmen were killed. An American citizen, Eugene Hasenfus, the sole survivor, was captured by the Nicaraguans.

That day Rodriguez unsuccessfully attempted to call Gregg to inform him of the missing plane. He reached Watson, who in turn notified the White House Situation Room.[118] The following day, Rodriguez called Watson again and told him that the airplane was one of North's. Watson's notes of the calls from Rodriguez read as follows:

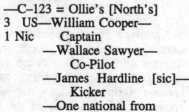

10/6 → Good poss. [possibility] lost in water
    1. Bad area
    2. Friendly in S [South]
    3. in water
       —No radio =
       —C–123 = Ollie's [North's]
       3   US—William Cooper—
       1 Nic    Captain
       —Wallace Sawyer—
          Co-Pilot
       —James Hardline [sic]—
          Kicker
       —One national from
          Nic [119]

Watson told Gregg of Rodriguez's call. Gregg's immediate assumption was that the plane was a part of the resupply operation Rodriguez had described to him and Watson in August 1986. Gregg understood North to be "acting as chairman of the board" for the operation.[120]

According to Gregg's later testimony, he did not have contact with Rodriguez from the summer of 1986 until November 7.[121] Rodriguez,

however, had a faint recollection of talking with Gregg within 72 hours after the plane was shot down.[122] Rodriguez said that when he spoke with Gregg, he did not tell him the downed plane was one of North's because "[h]e already knew." [123] Gregg also told Craig L. Fuller, Vice President Bush's chief of staff, that Rodriguez was hiding out in Miami and would not be talking to the press.[124] Gregg reasserted this on October 13, 1986, in a message that was cabled to Corr.[125]

On October 9, 1986, Hasenfus, then in Nicaraguan custody, stated he had made 10 flights to supply the contras—six out of Ilopango airfield in El Salvador—and had worked with "Max Gomez" and "Ramon Medina," whom he said were CIA employees. Hasenfus stated that Gomez and Medina oversaw the housing for the crews, transportation, refueling and flight plans.[126]

On October 10, 1986, *The San Francisco Examiner*, citing an unidentified source, reported that Gomez had received direction not from the CIA but from the White House, especially from the NSC. The story said that Gomez, also known as Felix Rodriguez, had been assigned to Ilopango air base in El Salvador by Gregg. According to the newspaper's source, "the initial deal (to place Gomez at Ilopango) was cut by Gregg after the fellow (Gomez) was introduced directly to George Bush." The article cited Gomez's close connections with the Salvadoran military and stated that he flew helicopters for the Salvadoran Air Force.[127] Gayle Fisher, spokeswoman for Bush, was quoted as saying that Gregg was not available for comment. Fisher also said, "Gregg is not involved

117 North, Grand Jury, 7/11/90, p. 20. Gregg acknowledged that North called him to complain that Rodriguez had "too high a posture." (Gregg, FBI 302, 12/15/86, p. 3; Gregg, Deposition, 5/18/87, p. 72.)
118 White House Situation Room log entry, 10/6/86, 0250 hours, AKW 042275–76.
119 Watson Notes, 10/6/86, ALU 025478.
120 Gregg, Grand Jury, 10/23/87, pp. 77–78.
121 Gregg, Select Committees Deposition, 5/18/87, p. 80.

122 Rodriguez, Grand Jury, 5/10/91, p. 175.
123 Ibid., pp. 175–77. See also Gregg Telephone Log, 10/15/86, ALU 022218 (indicating Gregg took call from Rodriguez).
124 Fuller, FBI 302, 12/14/90, p. 3.
125 Memorandum from Gregg to Corr through the White House Situation Room, Re: Vice President's Statements Regarding Hasenfus/Gomez, 10/13/86, ALU 012377 ("FYI, I have talked to Felix who I think intends to keep a low profile in Miami. It might be well if [U.S. Army Col.] Jim Steele [commander of the U.S. Military Group in El Salvador] keeps him informed of developments in El Salvador as necessary."). Four days later, the Department of State transmitted another copy of Gregg's memorandum to Corr. (State 326682, 10/17/86, ALW 030376–83.)
126 State Cable, 10/9/86, ALW 0026774.
127 "Contra Plane Linked to Bush," *The San Francisco Examiner*, 10/10/86, p. 1.

in any type of situation like that, like the weapons to the contras from El Salvador." [128]

In response to the article, Bush's office issued a statement regarding the allegations: "There is no one on the Vice President's staff who is directing or coordinating an operation in Central America. Allegations to that effect are simply not true." [129] The Vice President's statement was approved by Gregg before it was issued. [130]

On October 10, 1986, Watson typed a page of talking points for guidance for Vice President Bush on the subject of the downed plane and the Office of the Vice President's connection to Rodriguez. The document describes "Felix" as a great man, a hero, who has provided assistance to El Salvador's fight against communism. The document adds: "Don't know Max Gomez." [131] Watson had "a feeling" that the talking points never got to Vice President Bush but Watson did not know "whether I did it and gave it to Don [Gregg] or what. I just don't know." [132]

On October 11, 1986, *The Los Angeles Times* reported that Gomez had told associates he reported to Vice President Bush about his activities as head of the secret air-supply operation that lost a cargo plane in Nicaragua. Gomez allegedly stated that he met with Bush twice and had been operating in Nicaragua with the Vice President's knowledge and approval, the source said. Similarly, sources close to Bush told *The Washington Post* that the Vice President acknowledged meeting Gomez once or twice and expressing approval of his efforts to help the contras. However, those sources stated they knew nothing of any direct assistance given to Gomez by Bush or his staff. [133]

On October 11, 1986, Bush denied that he had any connection with the plane crash whatsoever. When asked about Gomez, Bush stated "I know Felix Gomez," mixing Rodriguez's true first name with his alias surname. Bush acknowledged meeting Gomez twice, once in January 1985 and again in May 1986. Bush stated that the only discussions he ever had with him related to El Salvador. [134] Bush stated that he did not speak directly or indirectly with Gomez about Nicaragua. When asked whether other branches of the Government had talked to him, Bush responded "Well, I don't know the facts on that." [135]

On October 13, 1986, Gregg sent a message to Corr through the White House Situation Room:

Subject: Vice President's Statements Regarding Hasenfus/Gomez.
1. The Vice President wanted you to know what he had said about the Hasenfus/Gomez affair on the record. A transcript of his press conference follows: (Note to Situation Room, please send copy from attached press statement.)
2. We have noted various denials of knowledgeability coming out of El Salvador regarding Gomez's activities. The Vice President and his staff will not be saying anything further on the record in hopes of keeping the story from getting more complicated.
3. FYI, I have talked to Felix, who I think intends to keep a low profile in Miami. It might be well if Jim Steele keeps him informed of developments in El Salvador as necessary. [136]

Because of the media stories linking Rodriguez/Gomez with the Vice President's office, congressional committees investigating the Hasenfus shootdown in October 1986 asked Reagan Administration officials about their knowledge of these allegations. On October 14, 1986, before the House Permanent Select Committee on Intelligence, Assistant Secretary of State Elliott Abrams, speaking for the Administration, stated that it was his understanding that Gregg knew Rodriguez and introduced him to the Salvadorans in 1984 to work with the Salvadoran Air Force. Abrams added that the Vice

128 Ibid. Fisher remembered the call from *The San Francisco Examiner*. One of the questions asked was: "Did Don Gregg know Max Gomez?" She personally asked Gregg the question and "Gregg gave her a flat 'no' answer with no explanation." (Fisher, FBI 302, 5/17/91, p. 3.)

129 Statement by the Press Secretary, 10/10/86, ALU 0134718.

130 Fitzwater, FBI 302, 11/8/90, pp. 7–8.

131 Memorandum re: Nicaragua, 10/10/86, ALU 025354.

132 Watson, Grand Jury, 10/14/87, pp. 168–70.

133 "Bush is Linked to Head of Contra Aid Network," *The Washington Post*, 10/11/86, p. A1.

134 Excerpts of Press Conference Remarks by Bush, 10/11/86, ALU 009984–86, ALU 0138407–9.

135 Ibid.

136 Memorandum from Gregg to Corr through the White House Situation Room, Re: Vice President's Statements Regarding Hasenfus/Gomez, 10/13/86, ALU 012377; *accord* State 326682, 10/13/86, ALW 030376–83 (Telegram from Gregg to Corr, transmitted 10/17/86).

President was aware of Rodriguez's involvement on behalf of the Salvadoran Air Force in their air/ground helicopter operations, but that there was no knowledge that Rodriguez was or at what point he moved off into conducting activities on behalf of the contras.[137]

Abrams' statement was consistent with the public response by the Vice President's office to the Rodriguez allegations. However, on October 16, 1986, while in transit to El Salvador to survey earthquake damage, Abrams reported to Shultz regarding the Rodriguez connection to the Office of the Vice President:

> Felix Rodrigues [sic]—Bush did know him from CIA days. FR [Rodriguez] is ex-CIA. In El Salv [Salvador] he goes around to bars saying he is buddy of Bush. A yr [year] ago Pdx [Poindexter] + Ollie [North] told VP staff stop protecting FR as a friend—we want to get rid of him from his involvmt [involvement] w [with] private ops. Nothing was done so he still is there shooting his mouth off.[138]

After landing in San Salvador, Shultz received the text of a letter from Bush, which had been delivered to the Department of State, with information to be passed to President Duarte. The message addressed the conflict between the government of El Salvador's denials of Gomez's involvement on their behalf in El Salvador and Bush's public statement on October 11 about Gomez's involvement in the counter-insurgency. Bush wanted Duarte to know that he only met Gomez twice and never discussed anything with him but counter-insurgency against the guerrillas in El Salvador. Bush extended his regrets that "this has become public."[139]

After public disclosure of the Iran/contra affair in November 1986, there was a new round of questions about Felix Rodriguez and the Office of the Vice President. On December 2, 1986, after being confronted by a television crew in the driveway of his home, Gregg stated that the only thing that he'd talked to "Max" [Gomez/Rodriguez] about was "his involvement in the insurgency in El Salvador."[140] When the questions persisted, the Office of the Vice President on December 15, 1986, released a chronology detailing contacts between Rodriguez and members of the Office of the Vice President, including Vice President Bush.[141]

## Gregg's Statements to Iran/Contra Investigators

Beginning on December 15, 1986, until January 15, 1989, Gregg testified or gave formal statements to the FBI, the Select Committees, the federal Grand Jury and the Senate Foreign Relations Committee concerning his involvement in and knowledge of events relevant to Iran/contra. Gregg's testimony was essentially consistent.

According to Gregg, he and Rodriguez maintained a close relationship since they worked together for the CIA in South Vietnam. Rodriguez came to Gregg in 1984 or 1985 with a proposal to train the Salvadoran Air Force to conduct helicopter counter-insurgency operations similar to those used by Rodriguez in Vietnam. Because this particular technique had proved effective in fighting guerrilla units in Vietnam, Gregg believed Rodriguez's proposal was a good one and assisted him in getting in touch with various U.S. officials who could approve Rodriguez's involvement in El Salvador.

In January 1985, Gregg introduced Rodriguez to Vice President Bush. Rodriguez met with

---

[137] Abrams, HPSCI Testimony, 10/14/86, pp. 23–24. Following the testimony, Gregg actually sent manufactured buttons over to the CIA which read "Who is Max Gomez?" and "I'm Max Gomez." They were a source of great humor at CIA. (Fiers, FBI 302, 7/23/91, p. 12; George, *George*, Trial Testimony, 8/13/92, pp. 3404–5.)

[138] Hill Note, 10/16/86, ANS 001661.

[139] Letter from Bush to Shultz, 10/16/86, ALW 0030249 (with handwritten note: "Passed to the Secretary in El Salvador who told Duarte himself."); STATE 324973, 10/16/86, ALW 0030246–47 (Department of State telegram, cabled to Shultz's aircraft); Note from Keith Eddins to Shultz, 10/16/86, ALV 001412 (with handwritten postscript by Charles Hill); Hill Note, 10/16/86, ANS 0001661. Elliott Abrams subsequently wrote to Under Secretary of State Michael H. Armacost that Duarte and the Salvadoran high command were "privately resentful that our own government unwittingly put them in a difficult position." (Memorandum from Abrams to Armacost, 10/21/86, ALW 0026749–51.)

[140] The CBS Evening News, 12/15/86 & 12/16/86. Gregg did not reveal his August 8, 1986, meeting with Rodriguez about contra-resupply. In March 1987, Vice President Bush defended Gregg by saying that he "forgot" about his August 8, 1986, meeting with Rodriguez when he told reporters he had never talked with Rodriguez about contra resupply. In response to a question concerning the difference of forgetting and lying, Bush said "Well, maybe it's the same. I don't know. But I don't see it as a major felony case, frankly." ("Bush Is Mystery Man of Iran Affair," *The Washington Post*, 3/23/87, p. A1.)

[141] This chronology was amended on May 14, 1987, to include an aspect of the meeting between Rodriguez and Watson that occurred on June 25, 1986.

the Vice President again on May 1, 1986, in Washington, D.C. Gregg said that contra resupply was not discussed during these meetings and that the topic of both sessions was the guerrilla anti-insurgency effort in El Salvador.

Gregg denied introducing Rodriguez to Oliver North and denied that he and North had a conversation about Rodriguez prior to North's recruitment of Rodriguez for the resupply operation at Ilopango Air Base. In fact, Gregg testified that he was unaware until August 1986 that Rodriguez was involved in any way in activities relating to the support of the contras.

Gregg testified that prior to August 1986, he and Rodriguez never discussed contra resupply. Gregg testified that he did not inform Vice President Bush about anything that Rodriguez informed him of on August 8, 1986. Gregg said he believed that ''secondhand allegations of corruption by some seedy Americans in an obscure air base in Central America'' in August 1986 were not worth elevating to the attention of the Vice President.[142]

Although Gregg said he knew that North had been involved as liaison with the resupply network, Gregg said he was unaware that North was involved in helping facilitate the supply of lethal aid to the contras prior to August 8, 1986, when Gregg met with Rodriguez.[143] Even after Rodriguez explained North's involvement in the resupply operation, Gregg testified that he did not have a sense that anything was ''ipso facto'' against the law.[144] Gregg denied that he or anyone within the Office of the Vice President directed the resupply operation in any manner, specifically by controlling Felix Rodriguez's activities regarding resupply.

## Independent Counsel's Investigation

President Bush in early 1989 nominated Gregg to be U.S. Ambassador to the Republic of South Korea. During his confirmation hearings before the Senate Foreign Relations Committee in May and June 1989, Gregg was confronted with various documents and testimony which seemed to contradict certain aspects of his prior testimony. Gregg's testimony, however, was gen-

erally consistent with his previous statements to Iran/contra investigators. In spite of concern expressed by some of the senators on the committee, Gregg was confirmed.

In the summer of 1990, OIC asked Gregg to submit to a polygraph examination regarding certain aspects of his prior testimony.[145]

On July 24, 1990, a polygraph examination was conducted by the Federal Bureau of Investigation at its Washington Metropolitan Field Office. Following a discussion with Gregg, the polygraph examination was conducted using the following relevant questions:

1. Prior to August 1986, did you know that Felix Rodriguez was assisting the Nicaraguan contras?

2. Prior to August 1986 were you aware that Felix Rodriguez was working with Oliver North to assist the Nicaraguan contras?

3. Were you ever involved in a plan to delay the release of the hostages in Iran until after the 1980 Presidential election? [146]

4. Prior to his media statement in October 1986, had you told then-Vice President Bush that persons in the U.S. Government were covertly and/or illegally involved in providing military supplies and assistance to the Nicaraguan contras?

5. Have you deliberately provided any false or misleading information in your testimony before Congress or a Federal Grand Jury?

After the examination, it was the opinion of the FBI examiner that Gregg's negative responses to each of the above questions indicated deception. Gregg was informed of the examiner's opinion. He suggested that he be reexamined, amending the questions to read as follows:

1. Have you ever given any false or misleading testimony about Felix Rodriguez to

---

142 Gregg, Grand Jury, 10/23/87, pp. 63–65.
143 Gregg, Select Committees Deposition, 5/18/87, pp. 26–27.
144 Ibid., p. 34.

145 Gregg had told the FBI in December 1986 that he would take a polygraph examination regarding Iran/contra matters. (Gregg, FBI 302, 12/15/86, p. 8.)
146 The OIC reported this question and answer to the Department of Justice in 1990. In 1992, in response to its omnibus request for information in the possession of the OIC, this aspect of Gregg's polygraph examination also was disclosed to the House Committee investigating the ''October Surprise.''

the Grand Jury or the congressional investigating committees?

2. Have you ever given any false or misleading testimony regarding Oliver North to the Grand Jury or the congressional investigating committees?

Following the completion and subsequent review, it was the opinion of the examiner that Gregg's negative responses to the two questions were indicative of deception.

Gregg was asked if he wanted to be polygraphed by another examiner or to be reexamined after a period of reflection. He stated that he did not feel either to be necessary.[147]

OIC's investigation reviewed a number of sworn statements by Gregg regarding his lack of knowledge prior to August 1986 of the involvement of North and Rodriguez with the contra-resupply effort. Gregg testified that he was unaware prior to June 1986 of *any* involvement by North with the contra resupply operation:

Q: Now through June of '86, did you know whether he [North] had any involvement with the contra resupply operation?

A: "He" being North?

Q: Colonel North.

A: No. I was out of the country for a fair part of June '86.

Q: And you didn't know at any time prior to June '86?

A: No.[148]

Similarly, Gregg testified that prior to August 8, 1986, he did not know that Rodriguez was involved in contra-resupply:

Q: And it's your testimony that prior to August 8, 1986, to be specific, you did not know that Felix Rodriguez was also involved in the Contra resupply effort?

A: That is correct.[149]

Gregg testified during his confirmation hearings that in his many meetings with Rodriguez prior to August 1986, Rodriguez never mentioned his efforts on behalf of Contra resupply:

SENATOR CRANSTON: Is it still your testimony that prior to August 8th, 1986, Rodriguez never mentioned the status of his Contra resupply efforts during his numerous face-to-face meetings with you in Washington?

MR. GREGG: Never.[150]

During his Select Committees deposition in 1987, Gregg was asked why he did not report to Vice President Bush what Rodriguez had told him in the August 8, 1986, meeting concerning the resupply operation. Gregg responded:

Well, I felt that it was a very murky business. I spend a great deal of my time trying to send things to the Vice President that I think are really Vice Presidential. I try to keep him focused, help him keep focused on arms control or Mideast peace or things of that nature. *We had never discussed the contras.* We had no responsibility for it. We had no expertise in it. . . .[151]

When confronted at his confirmation hearings in 1989 with documentary evidence that seemed to contradict that testimony, Gregg testified that he meant that he had never discussed contra-resupply with the Vice President.[152]

## Conclusion

There was no credible evidence obtained that the Vice President or any member of his staff directed or actively participated in the contra-resupply effort that existed during the Boland Amendment prohibition on military aid to the contras. To the contrary, the Office of the Vice President's staff was largely excluded from RIG meetings where contra matters were discussed and during which, particularly in the summer of 1986, North openly discussed operational details of his contra efforts. During 1985 and 1986, when Abrams, North and Fiers met to

---

[147] On August 22, 1990, Gregg's attorney provided Independent Counsel with a report of the results of a polygraph examination conducted by a private examiner retained by Gregg. That examiner, who asked a different series of questions, concluded that Gregg's answers were truthful.

[148] Gregg, Select Committees Deposition, 5/18/87, p. 11.

[149] Gregg, Grand Jury, 10/9/87, p. 48.

[150] Gregg, SFRC, 5/12/89, p. 101. See also Gregg, Grand Jury, 10/23/87, p. 64.

[151] Gregg, Select Committees Deposition, 5/18/87, pp. 30–31 (emphasis added).

[152] Gregg, Confirmation Hearings, 5/12/89, p. 109.

discuss Central American matters too sensitive for the RIG, there is no evidence that the Office of the Vice President's staff was included or even informed of their discussions.

During his trial, North alleged that Gregg was the person who introduced him to Rodriguez and that he contacted Gregg before recruiting Rodriguez to assist him in the contra-resupply effort. Gregg denied both assertions. The evidence suggests that Gregg's denials are correct. It appears that William Bode of the State Department, not Gregg, introduced Rodriguez to North. Additionally, there is no direct evidence that North sought Gregg's approval prior to writing his "Dear Felix" recruitment letter to Rodriguez in September 1985.

The question of whether Gregg was aware of Rodriguez's role in contra resupply or whether he was aware of North's involvement in resupply prior to August 1986 is more problematic. A recurring problem in the investigation of the Office of the Vice President was a conflict between contemporaneously created documents—which apparently impute knowledge of North and Rodriguez's activities to the Office of the Vice President—and subsequent testimony by Gregg, Watson, Rodriguez and others which contradicted those documents.

North's September 10, 1985, notebook entry reflecting an apparent discussion between North, Gregg and Steele about operational contra-resupply issues is not corroborated by a *specific* recollection of the meeting by either North or Steele.

North's notebook entry of October 1, 1985, and Duemling's NHAO meeting notes of the same day show that North did not try to hide Rodriguez from other Government officials, contrary to Rodriguez's claim that North asked him not to tell Gregg or the OVP of his contra-resupply activities.

Watson's note to Gregg on the top of a December 1985 State Department cable, "Don—Suggest you read carefully. Could have serious effect on our supplies to the contras," conflicts with Gregg's later assertions that the Office of the Vice President did not concern itself or have any expertise in contra-resupply issues.

Gregg's handwritten note to Vice President Bush on a February 4, 1986, Watson memorandum stating "Felix agrees with this" in reference to problems in contra logistical support, appears to reflect conversations between Gregg and Rodriguez regarding contra planning. Gregg's forwarding of that information to the Vice President reflects his understanding that the Vice President was interested in contra resupply. The same is true of Gregg's handwritten note to the Vice President on March 6, 1986, which expressed concern about contra activity.

The schedule memorandum detailing the purpose of Rodriguez's visit with the Vice President on May 1, 1986, as a discussion regarding "resupply of the contras" is another example of a contemporaneously created document that appears to be in conflict with the subsequent testimony of Gregg and Watson. Even Watson and Gregg's own notes of their August 8, 1986, meeting with Rodriguez contradict in part their subsequent explanations of that meeting. Yet, Rodriguez supported Gregg's denials of any discussion with Rodriguez about his or North's involvement in lethal contra-resupply operations prior to August 1986.

These documents—combined with the general, non-specific, recollections of Abrams, Steele and North which contradict portions of Gregg's sworn testimony—were insufficient to support a prosecution requiring proof beyond a reasonable doubt.

There was strong evidence that following the shootdown of the Hasenfus plane, Gregg and Watson were aware of North's connection to the resupply operation. Rodriguez informed them of North's involvement in August 1986, and Rodriguez called Watson on October 6, 1986, to let him know the downed plane was one of North's. They remained silent as Administration representatives publicly stated that there was no U.S. involvement in the flight.

Despite these acts of concealment, the evidence did not prove that Watson or Gregg committed a chargeable offense following the Hasenfus shootdown. No chargeable offense could be proved beyond a reasonable doubt.

# Chapter 30
# Donald T. Regan

Donald T. Regan was White House chief of staff from February 1985 to February 1987. He was forced to resign because he was unable to contain the continuing political damage being done to President Reagan by public exposure of the Iran/contra matters. In the White House, Regan controlled access to the President and oversaw his schedule. He attended President Reagan's national security briefings each morning and was present during the most significant White House meetings among Iran/contra principals.

Regan served the President throughout the Iran/contra period but he was not in a position to authorize operations. The area of inquiry, therefore, focused on actions he took in response to the November 1986 exposure of Iran/contra matters and in subsequent testimony about those matters.

Throughout November and December 1986, after the Iran and contra matters became public, Regan was in frequent contact with CIA Director William J. Casey, National Security Adviser John M. Poindexter, Attorney General Edwin Meese III and Defense Secretary Caspar W. Weinberger. He was less frequently in contact with Secretary of State George P. Shultz. There are no documented contacts between Regan and former National Security Adviser Robert C. McFarlane or U.S. Marine Lt. Col. Oliver L. North of the NSC staff during this period.

In early testimony about the November-December 1986 period, Regan recounted in colorful anecdotal terms his and President Reagan's surprise and shock at the details of Iran/contra matters as they purportedly became known to them. But Regan did not explain in any depth the steps that he and other top Administration aides took in response to the worst political crisis of the Reagan presidency.

Clearly Regan attempted to serve President Reagan's interests by protecting him from the political and legal damage of Iran/contra. The question was whether Regan, in concert with the President's other top advisers, helped choreograph a cover-up by agreeing to a false version of the arms sales to obscure legally questionable activity.

Independent Counsel did not charge Regan with a crime. Evidence of the apparent November 1986 cover-up of the President's knowledge and approval of the November 1985 HAWK missile shipment—and Regan's participation in it—was not developed by Independent Counsel until 1992, when he obtained previously withheld notes from Weinberger and Regan indicating that Meese appeared to have spearheaded an effort among top officials to falsely deny presidential awareness of the HAWK transaction. When Regan in 1992 was questioned about these events, he was forthcoming and candid in his responses. In addition, when Independent Counsel late in 1991 subpoenaed additional notes from Regan, he cooperated.

## The Regan Notes

In 1991, Independent Counsel undertook a full review to determine whether Administration officials had complied with document requests. It was determined that White House production of Regan documents had been late and incomplete. There had been conflicting evidence whether he had taken notes during his tenure as White House chief of staff. He had stated in various testimony that he did not take or keep notes of important meetings. But his aides said he took copious notes with the expectation that he would write a book about his White House experiences.[1]

Regan late in 1991 admitted that he had copies of relevant notes.[2] When subpoenaed, he granted investigators access to them. Of special interest to Independent Counsel were Regan's notes of the November 24, 1986, meeting of the President and his senior national security advisers in which Meese falsely stated that the President had no knowledge of the possibly illegal November 1985 HAWK missile shipment to Iran. These late-produced Regan notes conformed in crucial respects to Weinberger's notes of the same meeting, which also had been obtained only recently.

Because Regan said he had only copies—not originals—of his notes, Independent Counsel on May 8, 1992, subpoenaed the White House for all original notes, notebooks and other documents created by or for Regan. The White House reported that it could not locate them, either in its own files or in the files of the Reagan Presidential Library.[3]

## Regan's Response to Public Exposure of the Iran Arms Sales

Regan repeatedly testified that he advocated full public disclosure of the facts of the Iran arms sales, following the first press revelations in early November 1986. But as November and December 1986 played out, Regan and other senior officials were not so much disclosing new information as begrudgingly admitting to facts appearing in press reports and emanating from congressional investigations.

On November 6, 1986, Meese and Regan met briefly with President Reagan in the afternoon. Regan did not recall the meeting.[4] Regan's notes from that date suggest concerns about impending congressional inquiries:

Demos will start in
investigations
Hollings—textile
Kennedy—Meese
Any skeletons will come [5]

On November 7, 1986, Regan had breakfast with Poindexter. In a computer note that evening to McFarlane, Poindexter said Regan "agreed that he would keep his mouth shut." [6]

Several sets of notes of a White House meeting of President Reagan with his top national security advisers on November 10, 1986, state that Regan urged the issuance of a public statement on the arms sales because the Administration was losing credibility.

In this November 10 meeting, Poindexter laid out a version of the Iran arms sales that essentially omitted the 1985 transactions and falsely asserted that U.S. officials discovered the early Israeli shipments by stumbling across a warehouse of Israeli-owned U.S. weapons in Portugal. Regan did not dispute Poindexter's version, even though he had directly contrary information. Regan said he did not question Poindexter's omission of the 1985 shipments because other officials in the meeting also knew about them. Regan said he assumed Poindexter was addressing only those shipments that occurred after Poindexter became national security adviser in December 1985.[7]

The public statement resulting from the meeting did not disclose any facts or even confirm that arms sales had occurred; it merely asserted that no laws had been broken in U.S. efforts to win the freedom of American hostages and that the President had the support of his advisers in those efforts.[8]

Regan did not specifically recall that Shultz disagreed with Poindexter after the November 10 meeting about the President's proposed public statement and that all of the President's advisers supported the Iran policy. Regan said he did recall that "Mrs. Reagan, Poindexter, and several others were upset with George Shultz in and around this time because he was using or saying one type of thing and the rest were

---

[1] In fact, Regan did write a book, *For The Record* (Harcourt Brace Jovanovich 1988), about his experiences in the White House. In his book (p. xiii) he stated: "All my life I have kept detailed notes of my workaday actions and conversations, and I did the same while I worked for the President."

[2] Regan admitted a life-long practice of taking notes. (Regan, Grand Jury, 5/8/92, pp. 5–22.) He said Independent Counsel may not have seen the notes he took and kept in a "book file" in preparation for writing a book. But he denied any intention to withhold notes and any conversations among Administration officials about not producing documents. He said any failure of his own to produce notes was due to inadvertence or misfiling.

[3] Letter from Rademaker to Barrett, 5/12/92, AKW 0086056–57.

[4] Regan, Grand Jury, 8/12/92, p. 43.

[5] Regan Note, 11/6/86, ALU 0139111.

[6] PROFs Note from Poindexter to McFarlane, 11/7/86, AKW 021625.

[7] Regan, Grand Jury, 5/8/92, pp. 96–97.

[8] Statement by Principal Deputy Press Secretary Speakes on the American Hostages in Lebanon, 11/10/86, Public Papers of the Presidents, Ronald Reagan, 1986, p. 1539.

saying something else and he seemed to be off making remarks that indicated he was in disagreement with the President on some of these matters." [9]

On November 12, 1986, Regan met with Shultz, shortly before President Reagan and Poindexter briefed congressional leaders on the Iran arms deals. According to Regan's notes, Shultz expressed consternation over the Iran arms sales. Regan, however, urged Shultz to "stay on board":

> Shultz came in to see me re Iran. Gave his side of why he disagrees with Pres' policies. I heard him out. Denies he had a hand in drafting "Finding" of Jan. 17 '86 on Iran and overtures to them. JP [Poindexter] had told me he was in room when Bill [Casey], Ed Meese, & JP were drafting.
>
> Says this is swapping arms for hostages no matter what we say, and undercuts our efforts with allies, particularly Italians & [Italian Prime Minister] Craxi who want to sell arms.
>
> Is going to tell Pres of his feelings. Urged him to stay on board. We getting murdered in Press. I want to go public. Pres, VP & JP saying no—too risky.
>
> He says I'm right, & he'll urge telling the story.[10]

In the November 12, 1986, briefing of congressional leaders, Regan noted that Poindexter, in response to a question from Senator Byrd, stated that there was "no transfer of material" in 1985 because it "took time to assess contact &. issue finding." This was contrary to Regan's own knowledge of the 1985 shipments.[11] Regan conceded that he knew this but said he was not concerned about it at the time.[12]

Throughout November 1986, Regan was in frequent contact with Nancy Reagan, the President's wife, about mounting public furor over the Iran arms sales. On November 12, Regan noted a morning phone call with Nancy Reagan:

"Pres[ident] + 1st Lady very upset." . . . McFarlane—told her we're going to have to dump hostages to save Pres[ident]'[s] reputation, if necessary She agreed. Risking Presidency.[13]

Regan explained:

> Q: When you have down here "Risking presidency," what was that a reference to?
>
> A: That, similar to Watergate, he might be impeached; that we were risking the President's tenure in office, his presidency and his reputation. The longer this story persisted, the more the fingers were pointing at Ronald Reagan as either being inept, devious, or all of the above, and that we couldn't allow this situation to go on. We were going to have to end it somehow or other.[14]

Regan said the subject of impeachment was never openly discussed in the White House:

> . . . it was a no-no word. . . . You never used the word impeachment except to yourself because that was something no one wanted to even think about, but as chief of staff I felt I should at least look that beast in the eye to see, you know, were we going up here to another Watergate, what are we doing here?[15]

On November 13, 1986, President Reagan in a televised address admitted for the first time that the United States had been selling arms to Iran. The speech was short on details and misleading regarding the nature of the weapons shipments. Regan said the President's speech "wasn't the whole truth," and it underscored Regan's growing concern about a lack of factual information coming from the NSC staff to the President.[16]

By mid-November, Regan and Poindexter were briefing the press on the arms deals, essentially repeating the facts as given to congressional leaders on November 12 and in the President's November 13 televised address, with some additional details.

---

9 Regan, Grand Jury, 8/12/92, p. 59.
10 Regan Note, 11/12/86, ALU 0139130–31.
11 Ibid., ALU 0139132–49.
12 Regan, Grand Jury, 5/8/92, p. 105.

13 Regan Note, 11/12/86, ALU 0138701.
14 Regan, Grand Jury, 5/8/92, p. 99.
15 Ibid., pp. 110–11.
16 Ibid., p. 112.

On November 16, 1986, *The New York Times* published an interview with Regan in which he said he was part of the White House "shovel brigade that follow[s] parade down Main Street . . ." He boasted of successful damage control following other troubling incidents and suggested that the Administration would also prevail over the Iran flap.[17] Regan had begun publicly blaming McFarlane for dragging the President into the arms deals.

As controversy over the arms sales persisted, the President decided to hold a news conference on November 19, 1986, in an attempt to quell the turmoil. Instead, the President's performance only fueled the debate, particularly because he made several glaring factual misstatements about the role of other countries in the arms sales. Regan said the role of Israel was the "centerpiece" of Reagan's confusion

> because Poindexter and I think it was Al Keel, who was then his assistant—it may have been still Rod McDaniel, I'm not sure, but I have to think it was Keel— were telling the President that he shouldn't speak up about Israel, that Israel's role in this should be downplayed, we should not feature it, and he should be cautious about acknowledging the Israeli role.[18]

Regan said the President was

> stumbling all over the place and looking very inept and weak and willful during that press conference. Why? Well, he had had all the briefings but he was confused in his own mind because he knew some things that he was being told, "Don't say." Other things he was being told "Say it this way," and still other things he was being told to ignore. So the poor guy couldn't get it straight.[19]

By the time of the President's news conference on November 19, 1986, Regan had privately briefed some reporters and told them that third countries had been involved in the early arms shipments to Iran. He said in a November 14, 1986, press briefing that the United States had decided in the summer of 1985 to allow the shipment of defensive arms in response to a "request" by a third party: "And we agreed that if that third party wanted to sell weapons of that same nature as we were discussing, we would not object to that."[20] This admission by Regan caused reporters to challenge later statements made by President Reagan on November 19, when he said there were no third countries involved in the arms shipments. Consequently, the White House was forced to issue a correction of the President's statements following his press conference.

Following the press conference, Shultz called Regan to schedule a meeting with the President to discuss factual problems in the President's statements. Regan arranged a meeting for Shultz and the President for the following afternoon.

In advance of his meeting with the President, Shultz met with Regan at 10:45 a.m. on November 20, 1986, to discuss inaccuracies in the President's press conference. Afterwards, Shultz told Charles Hill, his executive assistant, that he had:

> A very hard conversation w DR [Regan]. Went through all the p[oin]ts, errors. Bill Rogers to look into it. P [President], w [with] VP told Pdx [Poindexter] of my telling him things were wrong—sh[ould] convene a meeting to go over what everybody knows & get it together. On Monday. P [President] will think it over at ranch.

> I s[ai]d that's a formula for catastrophe. Have to make decisions. Here they are. Make them. You can't wait around. The longer you wait the worse it gets. Not a matter of getting our lines straight and work as a team. Think of the future.

> Don [Regan] seemed v. subdued. Feels maybe his staff work bad. My comments break into a sense of unity over there that they know what they are doing.

> Some NSC guy I overheard there scoffing at us saying we didn't know. Pretty soon they'll say we ran it all.

---

[17] *The New York Times*, "Criticism on Iran and Other Issues Put Reagan's Aides on Defensive," 11/16/86, p. 1.

[18] Regan, Grand Jury, 2/26/88, p. 39.

[19] Ibid., 5/8/92, p. 113.

[20] Transcript of Press Briefing, 11/14/86, p. 5.

After lunch I'll call him again. What will you do. Today. Tonight. At C.D. [Camp David] this weekend

\*      \*      \*

DR [Don Regan] not taking charge & VP dug in too. Not taking strong role either.[21]

Later on November 20, Shultz met with the President and Regan in the White House residence from 5:15 p.m. to 6 p.m. Shultz complained that factual misstatements by the President would not withstand scrutiny. Shultz specifically mentioned the November 1985 HAWK shipment as a clear arms-for-hostages swap. President Reagan acknowledged that he knew about the shipment but argued that it did not represent arms for hostages.

Shultz's recounting of the White House meeting to Charles Hill indicates that Shultz made little headway in impressing on the President the seriousness of his concerns:

Hot & heavy. Argued back & forth. I didn't shake him one bit. The press is the problem. His material is diff. he says. We can straighten it all out Mon. He refuses to see we have a problem. So I never got to what should be done. Nancy was not there. I had hoped she wd help.

\*      \*      \*

I'll go to the mtg Monday, but then just make it clear I have to resign. . . .[22]

Regan played no visible role in the November 20, 1986, drafting of the congressional testimony of Casey and Poindexter for the next day, although Casey told CIA Deputy Director Robert Gates in a taped phone call during the week of November 18 that he planned to speak to Regan about the testimony.[23] Regan did have contact with both Casey and Poindexter on November 20. Regan met Casey briefly at 3 p.m. He said Casey told him of financial irregularities in the Iran arms transactions.[24] Then after attending the meeting between Shultz and Presi-

dent Reagan, Regan met with Poindexter from 6:12 to 6:45 p.m.[25]

Regan said he finally got a copy of the NSC chronology from Poindexter on November 21, 1986. David Chew, White House staff secretary, had alerted him after the November 19 press conference that he had seen North with a chronology of the arms sales, but North had refused to give Chew a copy. Regan gave the chronology to White House Counsel Peter J. Wallison to review, expressing doubts about its accuracy.

## Legal Concerns: White House Counsel Questions the 1985 Shipments

Throughout November 1986, White House Counsel Wallison, a close Regan adviser, repeatedly raised with Regan his concerns about possible legal problems of the Iran arms sales. As the facts of the shipments became clearer, Wallison's concerns intensified, peaking on November 21 when he first learned of a possibly illegal November 1985 HAWK shipment.

Wallison's diary reflects that he reported facts to Regan as he learned them, but Regan did not share with Wallison his own knowledge of the transactions. The diary shows that Meese was firmly in charge of exploring the arms sales and containing their legal ramifications. Wallison was excluded. Wallison was concerned that Meese was not the proper person to conduct the investigation and that Regan was unwilling to intervene in the matter.

Wallison wrote in his diary that on November 7, 1986, he first raised concerns with Regan about the legality of the Iran arms sales under the Arms Export Control Act (AECA). At that time Wallison had not focused on the 1985 shipments, because he had no facts about them. According to Wallison, Regan told him to review the AECA questions with Poindexter. At a meeting the same day, Poindexter told Wallison that "the AG [Attorney General] had been involved from the beginning in this matter and should be the lawyer consulted on any other issues of legality."[26]

21 Hill Note, 11/20/86, ANS 0001866 (emphasis in original).
22 Ibid., ANS 0001871.
23 PRT–250 Call from Gates to Casey, 11/18/86.
24 Regan, FBI 302, 3/6/91.

25 Poindexter Appointment Schedule, 11/20/86, AKW 044200.
26 Wallison Diary, 11/7/86, ALU 0138211.

On the morning of November 10, 1986, Wallison again raised his concerns with Regan. Wallison wrote in his diary that he was "unhappy" with a public statement issued by the White House that "all laws had been complied with. I was told that this is what the AG wanted said." [27] On November 11, 1986, Wallison discussed some of his concerns with David Doherty, CIA General Counsel, and gave Regan a memo outlining the legal questions. On November 12, 1986, Wallison told Regan that "unless the operation could be portrayed as a diplomatic move, it would have had to have been reported as a covert action in advance." [28] Regan suggested that Wallison raise the issue with Meese.

Wallison called Meese on the morning of November 12, 1986, and found out he was in Poindexter's office. Wallison asked Poindexter's aide Paul Thompson, the NSC counsel, if he could join the meeting. After checking, Thompson "returned in a minute with the statement that Poindexter and Meese were 'discussing something else.'" [29]

On November 13, 1986, Wallison told Regan he had concluded that the AECA placed an "absolute prohibition" on arms sales to Iran without prior notice to Congress. At an early afternoon meeting to prepare President Reagan's televised speech, Poindexter's deputy Alton Keel "exploded" when Wallison tried to omit a line stating that all laws had been complied with; Keel said that this is what the President, the attorney general and the national security adviser wanted. Wallison reached Meese late in the afternoon to discuss the AECA, and Meese said he would have Assistant Attorney General Charles Cooper call him. When Cooper telephoned Wallison, Cooper said he was "relying on a theory developed by the State Dept. in 1981 that there was no need to comply with the AECA at all if the export is part of an intelligence operation." [30]

At about this time, the White House made public the fact that the President in a covert-action Finding in January 1986 had authorized the arms sales, in conformance with the legal theory Cooper had expounded to Wallison. On

November 15, 1986, *The Washington Post* published an interview with Poindexter in which he stated: "[The] finding only existed in its original form in my safe." [31] *The New York Times* reported that, according to someone who had seen the order, a classified executive order (presumably the Finding) explicitly said Congress was not to be told of the Iran arms sales because of "security risks." [32] Other news reports quoted White House spokesman Larry Speakes confirming CIA involvement in the arms sales.

On November 18, 1986, Wallison convened a meeting of general counsel—including Thompson, Abraham Sofaer of the State Department, Lawrence Garrett of the Defense Department, Cooper, David Doherty of the CIA and a Joint Chiefs of Staff lawyer—to agree on common legal theories to support the arms sales in upcoming congressional testimony. According to Wallison, Cooper was surprised to learn of a September 1985 Iran arms shipment and said he would ask Meese for more facts. [33] Wallison, Garrett and Sofaer wanted an NSC chronology of events, but Thompson told them he doubted that one would be made available. [34]

The next day, in preparation for the President's November 19, 1986, press conference, Meese said it would be best for President Reagan to cite the Attorney General as the authority on legal issues, according to Wallison. [35]

On November 20, 1986, Wallison in the late afternoon met with Cooper and Thompson, who, according to Wallison, appeared shaken after having reviewed a draft of Casey's congressional testimony, which was to be given the following day. Then Wallison received a call from Sofaer, who asked Wallison whether he knew about the November 1985 HAWKs shipment; Wallison said he did not. Wallison asked Cooper and Thompson whether they had heard about this, and they said no. Wallison considered this the most serious disclosure of all. [36]

---

[27] Ibid., ALU 0138220.
[28] Ibid., ALU 0138221.
[29] Ibid., ALU 0138222.
[30] Ibid., ALU 0138223.

[31] *The Washington Post*, "Reagan Ordered Casey to Keep Iran Mission from Congress; Written Notice Conflicted with CIA Chief's Pledge," 11/15/86, p. A–1.
[32] *The New York Times*, "White House Says CIA Had Role in Iran Operation," 11/15/86, p. 1.
[33] In fact, the Israeli sale of 504 U.S. TOW missiles to Iran occurred in two shipments, one in August 1985 and a second in September 1985.
[34] Wallison Diary, 11/18/86, ALU 138227.
[35] Ibid., 11/19/86, ALU 138231.
[36] Ibid., ALU 0138235–36.

Wallison told Regan of the November 1985 HAWKs shipment on the morning of November 21, 1986, noting that it meant that the arms shipments in which the United States was involved pre-dated the January 1986 covert-action Finding, which authorized the later shipments. Regan had known of the HAWK shipment; he was present with President Reagan in Geneva when McFarlane alerted the President to expect it. Regan apparently did not share with Wallison the facts as he knew them, even though he was seeking Wallison's legal guidance.[37]

Regan could not explain why he did not inform Wallison of his own knowledge of the November 1985 HAWK shipment, but he denied attempting to hide that fact from Wallison.[38] Asked whether in the November 1986 assembling of facts about the Iran arms sales he ever volunteered to anyone his own knowledge of the HAWK shipment, Regan said he did not because he was not asked.[39]

## The Weekend Probe

Late on the morning of November 21, 1986, President Reagan, Regan, Meese and Poindexter met in the Oval Office to discuss the need to reconcile differing versions of the facts of the Iran arms sales. By this time, it was obvious that there were serious discrepancies in the details of the arms deals laid out by the principals. It was also clear that the November 1985 HAWK shipment posed serious legal problems. Regan said his memory of the Oval Office meeting was "hazy," but "[t]he gist of it was that the thing didn't hang together. Again every time you seemed to have one piece nailed down, something else popped up that negated that or changed that. It was a fluid situation." Regan said Poindexter suggested that they let the matter blow over, but Meese wanted to investigate. Regan said he got angry and said, "Let's get this thing buttoned up once and for all."[40]

Regan said the need for Meese's weekend investigation arose from factual discrepancies that became apparent in the November 20, 1986, preparation of Casey and Poindexter's

congressional testimony. But Regan also cited pricing information available in highly reliable intelligence reports about the arms sales as a factor that prompted the investigation, just as Meese stated several days later in his November 25, 1986, disclosure of the Iran/contra diversion.

Regan in later testimony reasserted that highly reliable intelligence reports helped precipitate the weekend investigation. He said the intelligence "was one of the things that was puzzling the Attorney General from it and also the State Department." Regan said the intelligence reports

> gave the Attorney General the first clue that somebody wasn't telling the straight story because we had [intelligence reports] that indicated the Iranians were paying X but we were only getting Y and there was a difference, and the Attorney General was trying to reconcile why would the Iranians be [paying] a price higher than we were showing they were getting and they couldn't do that.[41]

This would support the view that Meese was looking for evidence of a funding diversion when he initiated his weekend probe.[42] Independent Counsel could not find other supporting proof of this.

At 1:45 p.m. on November 21, 1986, Regan called Wallison into his office to tell him about Meese's pending investigation. Wallison raised concerns about a conflict of interest in Meese investigating a White House matter. Regan gave Wallison a copy of the arms sales chronology he had obtained from Poindexter and asked Wallison to review it and suggest questions for the upcoming November 24 meeting at which Meese was to present his findings. Wallison

---

[37] Regan was with the President in Geneva in November 1985 when McFarlane briefed them and Shultz on the HAWK shipment.

[38] Regan, Grand Jury, 5/8/92, p. 133.

[39] Ibid., 8/12/92, pp. 61–62.

[40] Ibid., 2/26/88, pp. 52–53.

[41] Regan, FBI 302, 7/14/87, pp. 69–70.

[42] Meese, in disclosing the Iran-contra diversion at the November 25, 1986, press conference, alluded to information in the highly reliable intelligence reports as a reason he undertook the weekend investigation. In fact, DOJ official John McGinniss spent the early morning hours of November 22, 1986, reviewing the reports, after Meese and his top aides learned that Senate Select Committee on Intelligence members had based some of their questioning of Casey on the basis of this intelligence. Further circumstantial evidence that Meese and his aides were looking for reasons to explain pricing irregularities is the fact that rumors of a diversion were already circulating at the CIA, that some CIA officials had knowledge of it, and that even State Department officials before the diversion discovery were suspicious of Southern Air Transport's role in both Iran and contra activities (according to Charles Hill's notes and a comment by Shultz to Meese about a possible mixing of the two activities in a interview on the morning of November 22, 1986).

did so in an unsigned, undated memo delivered to Regan's house on Friday, November 21, 1986.[43]

## Regan's Contacts During the November 22–23, 1986, Weekend

Regan described his contacts with Casey and other top officials over the November 22–23, 1986, weekend only in vague terms:

> There were lots of phone calls back and forth, nothing specific with the Attorney General. Casey had called me some point along the way here and I was unable to get him on Friday and I'm not sure whether I went out Friday night or did something and therefore on Saturday tried to get back to Casey and I recall missing him and then I'm not sure whether we finally did talk about. I'm inclined to say, yes we did talk over the weekend but it was strictly he wanted to tell me that his testimony up on the Hill had gone well and he thought he had discussed the subject in enough detail to satisfy the House Intelligence Committee.[44]

Regan said he received calls over the weekend from officials who were going to appear on the Sunday television talk shows, but "I was no part of the investigation nor was I questioned."[45]

On Saturday, November 22, 1986, Regan called Casey at 2:45 p.m., and at 2:51 p.m. Casey called Regan, apparently while Casey was having lunch with Poindexter and North in Poindexter's office.[46] According to Regan's "Chief of Staff Calls" phone log, Regan called Casey again on Saturday at 4:53 p.m. and at 6:45 p.m. On Sunday, November 23, 1986 at 9:52 a.m. Regan called Casey. At 12:35 p.m.

Meese called Regan.[47] The substance of these calls could not be determined.

## November 24: Regan Learns of Meese's Discovery of the Diversion

On November 24, 1986, Regan met throughout the day with the President and other senior advisers. Meese testified that he informed the President and Regan on November 24 of his weekend discovery of the diversion. But November 24 proved to be significant in another respect: At an afternoon meeting of the President and his senior advisers (including Regan), Meese informed the group that the November 1985 HAWK missile shipment to Iran was possibly illegal. He stated, falsely, that the President was not aware of the transaction.

Regan's notes of the November 24, 1986, meeting, obtained early in 1992, confirmed and illuminated notes of the same meeting taken by Caspar Weinberger. Regan asked the key question at the meeting: Did the President acquiesce in the November 1985 HAWK shipment? It was one of a list of questions prepared for him by Wallison.

Regan's notes reflect "DTR [Regan] asked about shipment of HAWK missiles to Iran in Nov."[48] Weinberger's notes are more specific: "Don Regan: Did we object to Israeli sending Hawks shipment missiles to Iran?"[49] Weinberger's notes reflect an initial response by Poindexter that "From July '85 to Dec. 7 McFarlane handled this all alone—no documentation . . ." Regan's notes do not reflect Poindexter's response. But both sets of notes indicate that Meese gave a lengthy answer to Regan's question, informing the group:

> Shultz told in Geneva by Bud [McFarlane]—delivery of weapons & maybe hostages out. Didn't approve. Pres only told maybe hostages out in short order.
>
> Plane unable to land in Iran. Smaller plane arranged only 18 missiles aboard—wrong

---

43 Memorandum from Wallison, circa 11/21/86, ALU 0138936.

44 Regan, FBI 302, 7/14/87, p. 61.

45 Regan, Select Committees Testimony, 7/30/87, p. 129.

46 The Select Committees asserted that Regan called Poindexter while Poindexter was having lunch with Casey and North on November 22, 1986. When asked about this by the Select Committees, Regan said he probably called Poindexter to get the answer to a technical question in anticipation of the Sunday talk shows. (Regan, Select Committees Testimony, 7/30/87, p. 130.) Records obtained by OIC, however, do not indicate that Regan called Poindexter at all; the call by Regan to Poindexter's office may have been recorded as his 2:45 p.m./2:51 p.m. calls with Casey.

47 Meese Phone Notes, 11/23/86, AMS 000654.

48 Regan Note, 11/24/86, ALU 0139378.

49 Weinberger Meeting Note, 11/24/86, ALZ 0040669KK.

ones. No specific ok for HAWKS [.] Returned in Feb. from Israeli stocks.

Bud told Geo. [Shultz] hostages out first, then arms in. Did not take place.

Maybe a violation of law if arms shipped w/o [without] a finding. But Pres did not know—Cap [Weinberger] denies knowing. Israelis may have done this on their own. But it was a low level contact that did this, probably using Pres' name.[50]

Independent Counsel questioned whether Regan had agreed with any of the other participants before the meeting to ask the question that prompted Meese's response. Regan denied that he had.[51]

Regan already knew the true answer to the question that he asked, from his direct participation in the November 1985 briefing in Geneva that McFarlane gave the President about the impending HAWKs shipment. Regan said he did not remember whether he told Wallison he already knew the answer.[52] Regan said virtually all of the other meeting participants knew Meese's statements regarding the state of President Reagan's knowledge to be incorrect.[53] Regan said he, the President, Vice President Bush, Shultz, Poindexter, and probably Casey knew the statements were wrong; he was uncertain about Meese's knowledge:[54]

Q: Can you explain to us why people who were witting about the Presidential knowledge and approval of the November Hawk shipment did not speak up during this meeting to correct the record on a matter that the Attorney General focused on as possibly dealing with a violation of American law?

A: I can only describe as best I can the mental attitude of one of them, to wit, myself; why didn't I speak up at that point. First of all, he said it's a possible violation. Wallison had told me a possible violation. We had not had an opinion that yes, it

is a violation for this, this, and this reason. Obviously we were waiting to be told specifically is this a violation. That's my attitude now, right or wrong. Second, I was very concerned about the diversion of funds, what is this all about? What new turn is this Iranian arms shipment going to take with diversion of funds? So that was on my mind. Before I start an outburst in this meeting and getting everybody upset, let's get the rest of the facts. Maybe we have found why we had been so puzzled as to why we couldn't get a chronology. So I was waiting for the Meese meeting with the President before speaking up on that particular subject, that is the Hawk missiles in '85. . . .

Q: Was your attitude that until we know that this was not a violation of the law, I'm not going to be the one to announce to this group that the President knew and approved it?

A: Very probable.[55]

## Regan on November 25, 1986

On November 25, 1986, Regan's day revolved around public disclosure of the Iran/contra diversion and deciding how to contain the public firestorm that was sure to follow.[56]

There are no known notes of President Reagan's 9:00 a.m. meeting with Vice President Bush, Regan and Meese, or of President Reagan's 9:38–9:55 a.m. meeting with Vice

---

[50] Regan Note, 11/24/86, ALU 0139378–79.

[51] Regan, Grand Jury, 5/8/92, p. 136.

[52] Ibid., p. 135. In the Grand Jury on 8/12/92 (p. 87–88) Regan said he may have discussed with Wallison "some of the possible answers" to the questions Wallison prepared for the November 24, 1986, meeting.

[53] Ibid., 5/8/92, pp. 141–54.

[54] Ibid., 8/12/92, pp. 94–97.

[55] Ibid., 5/8/92, pp. 154–57.

[56] Regan called Meese at 6:30 a.m. Meese received the message from his driver while he was at Casey's home, and Meese returned the call from there. Meese testified that Regan told him he had determined overnight that he wanted to talk to Poindexter at 8 a.m. and tell him he should resign. Meese said he did not tell Regan he would be meeting with Poindexter before then. Meese said that on November 24, 1986, Poindexter had expressed a desire to hear from Meese whether he would have to resign, and "so I felt an obligation, him having told me that and Don having told me what his views were, to impart that information to Admiral Poindexter before Mr. Regan talked to him." (Meese, Grand Jury, 2/17/88, pp. 80–84.)

According to Poindexter, Meese told Poindexter at their Justice Department meeting to submit his letter of resignation. Poindexter went back to the White House, left a message in Regan's office that he wanted to meet with him, went back to his own office to eat his breakfast, "and a few minutes later Don Regan came in, and I told him that I was going to resign." Poindexter said he does not recall Regan asking him whether he told the President about the diversion. Poindexter testified there was no scolding or reprimand. (Poindexter, Select Committees Testimony, 7/16/87, pp. 88–89.)

President Bush, Regan and Meese and Poindexter, at which Poindexter resigned.

According to Wallison, Regan told him and another Regan aide, Dennis Thomas, on November 24, 1986, that the diverted payments had been made in November 1985 for the HAWKs, and he asked Wallison whether that was unlawful. Wallison said if the money were U.S. money it would be illegal, but if it were Israeli money the situation was not as clear.[57]

On November 25, 1986, Wallison noted a significant change in the story from what Regan had told him the previous day. In a meeting with congressional leaders at 11 a.m., Meese described the transaction unclearly, dating the diversion as taking place in 1986. Dennis Thomas asked Wallison to pass a note to Meese to the effect that he should specify that the money was deposited in the Swiss account in the fall of 1985. Wallison handed the note to Regan for Meese, but Regan returned the note saying the events occurred in 1986. "This was not what Regan had told us yesterday, nor was the fact that the arms involved—according to the AG's account—were US rather than Israeli arms," Wallison wrote. "Thomas and I vividly recalled Regan's talking yesterday about Hawk missiles with the Star of David on them." [58] Wallison later told OIC that he did not follow up on the issue of whether the diversion had occurred in relation to the HAWKs shipment.[59]

Regan's notes of the briefing of congressional leaders on the morning of November 25, 1986, show that Meese made no mention of 1985 shipments in connection with the diversion:

> In 1986—4 arms shipments Feb, May, July, Oct 29. Israel sent arms to Iran who previously had deposited money in bank acct. Israel overcharged. Iran paid to Israel—Israel put over charge into Swiss acct (3 of them) Calero of Contras established these. Contras drew funds total value $10–$30 myn [million] from 3 shipments. Ollie North knew of this— Poindexter had suspicions did not investigate. Did not question it. Happened 3 times in 1986.[60]

President Reagan opened a press briefing to announce the Iran/contra diversion shortly after noon on November 25, 1986. After stating that he did not know certain unspecified details of the arms sales and that North had been fired and Poindexter had resigned, the President turned the floor over to Meese, who disclosed the diversion. Reagan, Regan and Weinberger watched Meese's briefing on television in a room off the Oval Office.

## Regan's Changing Testimony About His Contacts With Casey

Regan testified that he did not learn of the Iran/contra diversion until Meese told him about it on November 24, 1986. The record is murky, however, regarding when Regan learned of financial problems in the Iran arms sales. Regan testified repeatedly that Casey informed him of the problems generally. But Regan's testimony regarding the timing and specifics of his knowledge was inconsistent, placing it as early as October 1986 or as late as November 20, 1986:

> —Asked by OIC on July 14, 1987, whether he had any conversations with Casey in October 1986 about Roy Furmark,[61] Regan said no. "Casey did tell me on or about the time that the story was breaking in Lebanon that he had had a Canadian contact who was telling him that this story was getting around in the Middle East." [62] Regan said Casey did not initially mention money worries in connection with the Canadian: "It was only later that I became aware that it was the Furmark story, the name Furmark, and that fact that the Canadians were actually looking for money.[63] . . ."

> —Regan in a congressional deposition on July 15, 1987, said Casey told him about an unnamed Canadian contact on November 3 or 4, 1986: "Casey had told me without using the name Furmark that a Canadian friend of his had told him that the

57 Wallison Diary, 11/24/86, ALU 0138242.
58 Ibid., 11/25/86, ALU 0138244.
59 Wallison, FBI 302, 10/5/92, p. 12.
60 Regan Note, 11/25/86, ALU 139169.

61 Furmark, a long-time Casey acquaintance, was the New York businessman and partner of financier Adnan Khashoggi who personally communicated to Casey in October 1986 threats of exposure of the Iran arms sales by disgruntled Canadian investors.
62 Regan, FBI 302, 7/14/87, p. 92.
63 Ibid., pp. 93–94.

news of McFarlane's visit and arms shipments by us and Israel to Iran was pretty well known in certain circles, and that this thing was coming unglued."[64]

—Regan in the Grand Jury on February 3, 1988, said Casey mentioned Furmark's involvement in the arms deals to him in late October 1986.[65]

—In an interview with OIC on March 6, 1991, Regan said he met with Casey on November 20, 1986, and Casey at that time told him about financial problems and the involvement of Furmark and Khashoggi in the Iran initiative. Regan said that he probably shared what he learned from Casey with Wallison.[66]

There is evidence that Regan was Casey's choice as the person who should be informed about Iran arms sale money problems. Furmark said he met on November 24, 1986, with Casey at the CIA and told him that arms financier Adnan Khashoggi had invested $25 million in the Iran transactions, and that millions of dollars were unaccounted for. Furmark told Casey that arms dealer Manucher Ghorbanifar believed the excess money had gone to the contras. According to Furmark, an excited Casey tried to call Donald Regan but he was not in, so Casey called North.[67]

Independent Counsel obtained no documentary evidence clarifying when Casey informed Regan of financial irregularities in the Iran arms sales. Regan was initially untruthful about at least one significant meeting with Casey on the evening of November 24, 1986, but Regan later corrected the record: He initially denied having discussed with Casey the discovery of the

Iran/contra diversion on November 24 but later admitted he had.

On the evening of November 24, 1986, Regan met with Casey at CIA headquarters, at Casey's urgent insistence. Regan in his Select Committees Deposition of March 3, 1987, was asked whether he discussed the diversion with Casey at their meeting:

A: Only to the effect that there were— no, I didn't. Let me back up. I did not discuss the precise nature of what Ed Meese, the Attorney General, had told the President.

Q: Why was that?

A: Well, at this point I didn't know who knew what, or who was guilty of what, and I thought the less I talk about it, the better off the Attorney General and his investigators would be.

Q: But didn't you want to know what your friend, William Casey, knew of this?

A: I knew that Ed Meese had been talking to him.[68]

But Casey, who died in May 1987, told the House Intelligence Committee on December 11, 1986, that Regan told him on November 24, 1986, that he had

. . . some evidence of a diversion. . . . Don Regan stopped in to see me on the way home. This had been arranged over the weekend when I was supposed to see if we were able to meet; and we were not able to meet, so that was the first I had any inkling of a diversion.[69]

Meese complicated the matter for Regan in a Select Committees deposition on July 8, 1987. Meese testified that when he saw Casey privately early on November 25, 1986, Casey was already aware of the diversion:

He heard about it, I believe, from Don Regan the previous evening, I believe. . . . Well, he had heard from Don Regan that there had been a diversion and that Poindexter was planning to resign and that

---

[64] Regan, Select Committees Deposition, 7/15/87, p. 76.

[65] Regan, Grand Jury, 2/3/88, p. 38. Regan told the Senate Select Committee on Intelligence on December 16, 1986, that Casey contacted him in late October 1986 about the arms sales, but Regan said the contact centered on Casey's request for a copy of the arms-sales Finding. Regan said he told Casey he did not have a copy of the Finding but Poindexter might. "So, later I said to Poindexter, how come we don't have a copy of that Finding?" Regan testified. "And he said I'll tell you why. He said, there's only an original and it's in my safe. I never made a copy of it." (Regan, SSCI Testimony, 12/16/86, p. 31.) Regan later told OIC that Casey wanted the Finding in late October 1986 because of an impending arms shipment to Iran. (Regan, FBI 302, 7/14/87, p. 92.)

[66] Regan, FBI 302, 3/6/91, p. 7. Wallison's diary does not reflect a conversation with Regan about Furmark and Khassoghi on November 20, 1986.

[67] Furmark, FBI 302, 2/22/88, pp. 12–13.

[68] Regan, Select Committees Deposition, 3/3/87, pp. 13–14.

[69] Casey, HPSCI Testimony, 12/11/86, pp. 77–78.

Don Regan felt that Poindexter should resign immediately and probably—I don't
know whether North was discussed, too,
or not.[70]

Regan in an interview with OIC on July 14,
1987, for the first time said he discussed with
Casey on the evening of November 24, 1986,
Meese's discovery of the diversion and the fact
that it would have to be made public.[71] On
July 15, 1987, Regan in a deposition to the
Select Committees said he told Casey about
the diversion on the evening of November 24,
1986. He told the Committees that Casey's general reaction was that public disclosure would
harm prospects for contra aid and would upset
Middle Eastern friends and Israel.[72]

In congressional testimony on July 30, 1987,
Regan said his earlier misstatements stemmed
from the fact that he was questioned in a "confusing period," following his resignation.[73]

Regan told the Grand Jury on February 3,
1988, that his November 24, 1986, meeting with
Casey lasted about 25 minutes, that they discussed the diversion and the consequences of
publicly disclosing it, and that Casey reminded
Regan he had told him earlier about a Canadian
threatening to expose the arms sales.[74]

## Late November–December 1986:
## The Fallout Continues

In the aftermath of the Iran/contra disclosures,
Regan's job became increasingly complicated.
He attempted to distance the President from
the NSC staff members who had been most
directly involved in the operations.[75] He was
confronted with Nancy Reagan's growing alarm
over the political beating her husband was taking. He and other senior Presidential aides
sought to expel Shultz from the Cabinet, because of his continued public dissent. But perhaps the most difficult task Regan had to endure
was the demands by Members of Congress and
others that he be removed as White House

Chief of Staff, so that the President could start
the last two years of his Administration with
a clean slate.

In an undated memo titled "Plan of Action,"
Regan on November 24, 1986, laid out a series
of steps to be taken in response to the public
disclosure of the Iran/contra diversion. Regan's
overall strategy, in fact, was adopted by the
White House. Among other things, he proposed
that Poindexter resign and that North be reassigned, that Poindexter's deputy Alton Keel
temporarily replace Poindexter, and that the
President announce the appointment of a special
review board to examine NSC actions. The
memo states in part:

> Tough as it seems[,] blame must be put
> at NSC's door—rogue operation, going on
> without President's knowledge or sanction.
> When suspicions arose he took charge, or-
> dered investigation, had meeting of top ad-
> visors to get at facts, and find out who
> knew what. Try to make the best of a
> sensational story. Anticipate charges of
> "out of control", "President doesn't know
> what's going on," "Who's in charge",
> "State Department is right in its suspicions
> of NSC", "secret dealing with nefarious
> characters", "Should break off any con-
> tacts with: a) Iranians, b) Contras" [76]

Regan was partly successful in distancing the
President from the actions of the NSC staff,
but he could not escape criticism. On November
25, 1986, Vice President Bush privately told
the President that "I really felt that Regan
should go, Shultz should go, and that he ought
to get this all behind him in the next couple
of months." [77] The Vice President and others
would succeed in removing Regan after only
three more months of turmoil.

Throughout December 1986, Regan's notes
record meetings with members of Congress on
Iran/contra. One set of notes—written in past
tense, unlike other Regan notes—suggest continued concern about the pre-1986 arms shipments, but do not illuminate whether the President told Congress the truth about his knowledge of them:

---

[70] Meese, Select Committees Deposition, 7/8/87, p. 126.

[71] Regan, FBI 302, 7/14/87, pp. 19–23.

[72] Regan, Select Committees Deposition, 7/15/87, pp. 73–75.

[73] Ibid., 7/30/87, pp. 109–12.

[74] Regan, Grand Jury, 2/3/88, pp. 34–38.

[75] Despite Regan's efforts, the President called North after his firing.
Regan testified that when he learned of the call, he asked the President
why he did it and told him "Well, I hope you did the right thing."
(Regan, Select Committees Testimony, 7/15/87, p. 108.)

[76] Memorandum from Regan, circa 11/24/86, ALU 010205.

[77] Bush Diary, 11/25/86, ALU 0140213.

12/2/86 Pres, VP, Dole, Michel, Simpson, Lott

Pres. outlined Iran situation
Read his TV statement on Independent Counsel, and Frank Carlucci.
Some conversation on how Congress should handle investigation.
Then DTR [Regan] asked Pres point blank—what happened, Mr. Pres what did you know—when did you know it? That's the question on these fellows mind. Tell them what you know.
He did—for 10 minutes
Then they asked questions about arms shipments before Jan '86.
Also lack of support by GS [Shultz], Bud McF, & revelation of contras.
Pres reassured them on where he stood. Tried to tell him not to beat up on press. They emphasized the magnitude of the issue. Opponents and press are after Presidency.
Make sweeping changes.
Carlucci is not enough; they said.
Lott, Cheyney [sic], Simpson, all said they needed answers.
Pres told them he knew nothing of fund as far as he knows only North & Poindexter
It is now a domestic political program, not a foreign policy matter.
May be a public apology is needed.[78]

On December 1, 1986, the Senate Select Committee on Intelligence began a preliminary investigation into Iran/contra. On December 5, 1986, Regan noted two phone conversations with Casey reflecting behind-the-scenes contacts with the committee to try to defuse the problem. Casey called Regan to inform him of a conversation he had just had with SSCI staff director Robert Bernard McMahon:

Staff director—Durenberger 'Wants to demolish this molehill'
so does most of committee
Bernie McMahon—is staff director
Casey called him back—told him he'd be hearing from someone representing me shortly

Quote above is from McMahon

\*     \*     \*

Casey—secure phone—just got an "offer of surrender" from Intell Comm counsel who says Some Sens feel nothing there—"dry hole" in hearings
How to get out of it?
Suggestion
Have Pres announce some morning soon that North violated law on contras funding did not tell us. Also Pres say Poindexter had knowledge of this should have reported it to Pres. Both of them want to tell story to public. Put them on TV Let them tell story and then Pres pardon.
[at side]: DTR [Regan] to take this on
        Paul Laxalt as intermediary . . .[79]

According to Wallison's diary, Regan instructed Wallison on December 5, 1986, to invite McMahon to the White House for a talk. Wallison told McMahon that a presidential pardon was a political "non-starter," and Wallison suggested that the President might be willing to endorse immunity for North and Poindexter to testify before Congress. McMahon told Wallison that the SSCI would resist granting immunity because of possible problems it would pose to an independent counsel.[80]

On Saturday, December 6, 1986, Casey called Wallison to ask about his conversation with McMahon, and Wallison discussed immunity with Casey. Wallison then called Regan and discussed immunity with him. Wallison called Associate Attorney General Steven Trott on December 7, 1986, to discuss the immunity matter, because Meese was not available.[81]

As December wore on, Regan and other Presidential advisers tried to remedy the fact that both North and Poindexter were refusing to testify before Congress, citing their Fifth Amendment right against self-incrimination. Their silence fueled continuing speculation about the President's involvement in Iran/contra. The consensus in the White House was that Congress should be asked to grant limited or "use" immunity from prosecution to North and Poindexter so that each of these men could effectively clear the President by stating that

---

[78] Regan notes, 12/2/86, ALU 0139177–78 (emphasis added).

[79] Ibid., 12/5/86, ALU 0139195–96.
[80] Wallison Diary, 12/5/86, ALU 0138266.
[81] Ibid., 12/6/86, ALU 0138267.

they did not inform him of the narrow issue of the Iran/contra diversion.

On December 16, 1986, President Reagan called on SSCI to grant North and Poindexter use immunity because, "We must get on with the business at hand and put this issue behind us. It is my desire to have the full story about Iran come out now—the alleged transfer of funds, the Swiss bank accounts, who was involved—everything." [82] President Reagan stated that the granting of use immunity would not prevent the Independent Counsel, who had not yet been appointed, from bringing anyone to justice.

On December 16, 1986, Regan testified before SSCI. On December 17, 1986, Regan's notes from a meeting with the President reflect continuing concern over the committee's investigative findings:

> 4. Iran—
> Durenberger says only Ollie North knew.
> RR [Reagan] didn't
> Immunity asked by RR. [83]

On December 18, 1986, Regan testified before the House Intelligence Committee. At a meeting with the President that morning before testifying, Regan noted that they discussed "Dispute between testimony of DTR [Regan] and Bud [McFarlane]." [84] On December 19, Regan noted again that he and the President in their morning meeting discussed the fact that "DTR—Regan] McFarlane differ over Israeli arms shipments in Aug. 1985." [85] The dispute, as outlined in news reports of McFarlane and Regan's congressional testimony, was over McFarlane's assertion that President Reagan had approved the August 1985 shipment in advance and Regan's contention that the President learned about it only after the fact. [86]

Regan notes apparently taken on December 18, 1986, describe the broad outlines of SSCI's anticipated findings, and how they cut in favor of the President:

> Comm (Sen. Intel) wants to give us report in 10/14 days Not just a chronology but

outline a scam by arms dealers & gvt [sic] govt's involved. Hood-winked our people. W[ou]ld brief Pres or anyone else so he knows whats [illegible word]
Can take notes—no exec summary. No interpretats No questioning of Pres—No desire to add him to witness list. Keep meeting conf. [confidential]—No press back door to Oval [87]

On December 19, 1986, Durenberger and committee staff director Bernard McMahon secretly briefed the President, Regan, Keel and Wallison about SSCI's findings. This was done without the knowledge of the committee. [88]

## Regan's Testimony on the 1985 Arms Shipments

Unlike Shultz and Weinberger, Regan did not deny knowledge of the August–September 1985 arms shipments to Iran. But his testimony shifted factually in several key respects, leaving the record unclear about the President's authorization of the early shipment and the promise to replenish Israeli stocks. Regan at first asserted that the President learned about the two-part shipment after the fact and did not approve replenishment; later, Regan testified that the President learned of the shipments in mid-transaction—after the first shipment in August but before the second in September—and that he did approve replenishment. [89]

[82] Statement on the Iran Arms and Contra Aid Controversy, 12/16/86, Public Papers of the President, Ronald Reagan, 1986, p. 1631.
[83] Regan Note, 12/17/86, ALU 0139214.
[84] Ibid., 12/18/86, ALU 0139216.
[85] Ibid., 12/19/88, ALU 01389218.
[86] 1986 Facts on File, 12/26/86.
[87] Regan Note, 12/18/86, ALU 0139217.
[88] In its preliminary report issued January 29, 1987, SSCI noted: According to testimony received by the Committee, on December 19 Senator Dave Durenberger, Chairman of the Intelligence Committee, and Bernard McMahon, the Committee's staff director, met with the President, Peter Wallison, Don Regan, and Alton Keel, at the request of the White House to discuss matters relating to the sale of arms to Iran and possible diversion of funds to the Contras. The Committee was not informed of this meeting until January 20, 1987.
According to testimony received by the Committee, on December 20 Senator Dave Durenberger and Bernard McMahon met with the Vice President, Craig Fuller and a second member of his staff to discuss matters relating to the sale of arms to Iran and possible diversion of funds to the Contras. The Committee was not informed of this meeting until January 20, 1987.
(SSCI Report on Preliminary Inquiry, 1/29/87, ALU 003546.)
[89] Regan's first testimony on the subject was before the SSCI on December 16, 1986. He testified that in August 1985 President Reagan told McFarlane that he didn't want to authorize Israeli arms shipments. In September 1985, according to Regan, McFarlane told the President about the Israeli TOW missile shipment after the fact, and the President was "quite upset" about it. Regan said the President told McFarlane to let the Israelis know of "our displeasure . . . in no uncertain terms. Period." Asked whether the President approved of the replenishment

of Israeli stocks, Regan said no. (Regan, SSCI Testimony, 12/16/86, pp. 12–13.)

In an FBI interview on December 18, 1986, Regan said McFarlane in August 1985 briefed the President on the fact that Israel wanted to sell TOWs to Iran. While the President agreed with the desirability of a dialogue with Iran, he did not approve the arms sale or replenishment, according to Regan. Regan said the only arms sales to Iran specifically authorized by the President took place in 1986. (Regan, FBI 302, 12/18/86, p. 8.)

Regan told the Tower Board on January 7, 1987, that McFarlane informed the President after Labor Day in September 1985 that the Israelis had sold arms to Iran. He said the President was upset, but "at that time did not indicate that he wanted to make a big deal out of it. It was done. It had been done. There was a possibility of a hostage coming out. He decided to leave it alone, just accept the fact that it was done, leave it there. I don't recall anything else happening, except I believe that [hostage] Benjamin Weir did come out at that time, if I'm not mistaken, or shortly thereafter." Regan said there was no specific request for replenishment at that time. (Regan, Tower Commission Interview, 1/7/87, p. 9.)

In a Select Committees deposition on March 3, 1987, Regan said he could not recall the President ever telling him that he had told McFarlane he would replenish Israeli weapons stocks. (Regan, Select Committees Deposition, 3/3/87, p. 55.) In a second deposition on July 30, 1987, Regan reaffirmed his earlier statements and added Poindexter's November 10, 1986, inaccurate recounting of events as supporting evidence:

Q: Does it sound reasonable or plausible to you knowing the Israelis they would go forward and deplete—not deplete, but diminish this inventory of TOW missiles without some sort of a guarantee that they would, in fact, be replaced at a future time?

A: I can't answer that. I don't know what was in the minds of the Israelis. What I was looking for here in my notes, I have notes somewhere that the—John Poindexter, at the November 10th meeting giving the background to everybody, in there described the fact that the Israelis had gone ahead without our permission. This is Poindexter now, who is the deputy at the time the incident happened, describing it to the rest of us and saying the same thing. So there was no presidential knowledge, no presidential concept. So the Israelis apparently took a chance that if they did something that pleased us, we would replace them.

(Regan, Select Committees Deposition, 7/30/87, pp. 117–18.)

Also on July 30, 1987, Regan said the President said when he learned in September 1985 of the shipment: "As far as any replenishment is concerned, we will cross that bridge later. I am not going to do anything about that now." Regan said he knew at the time that the Israeli delivery of TOWs was tied to the release of Weir. (Ibid., pp. 30–31.)

Regan in the Grand Jury on February 3, 1988, said about the August–September 1985 shipment: "I have always claimed and I will claim today that it was after the fact that we were notified. I don't recall being told in advance that this was happening. If I recall it, it was that we were notified by McFarlane along these lines, and I'm paraphrasing, 'Guess what those damn Israelis have done. They've already shipped TOWs to Iran, and now they're asking us to replace them.'" Regan, however, directly contradicted his earlier testimony regarding President Reagan's stand on replenishment:

Q: And after you learned of that shipment, was the issue of replenishment raised at that time?

A: Yes—toward the end of August and in September.

Q: What was your understanding, if any, of how replenishment would operate?

A: Well, at that point we were faced with a fait accompli. The deed was done. And Israel is a staunch ally of ours, and the President said, "Well, I guess we'll have to replace them." So he authorized the replenishment.

(Regan, Grand Jury, 2/3/88, pp. 55–56.)

In his February 3, 1988, Grand Jury appearance, Regan indicated that the President learned of the August–September 1985 shipments in mid-transaction. Asked whether he and the President were informed in advance of the mid-September 1985 shipment, he said: "I believe we were, because that was tied in with the original shipment. That— okay, when we replenish we'll have to replenish both the 500 and 100." (Ibid., p. 57.)

Regan's shifting testimony paralleled generalized legal worries among Administration officials about the 1985 Israeli shipments. Before Regan made his early statements about the August–September 1985 arms shipments, White House Counsel Wallison had raised with him serious concerns about their legality under the Arms Export Control Act (AECA).

Regan's testimony on the November 1985 HAWK missile shipment to Iran has been consistent, acknowledging that McFarlane briefed the President in Geneva on the HAWKs shipment as it was about to take place.[90]

## Correcting the President

Starting with his testimony before SSCI in December 1986 up until his Grand Jury appearance in February 1988, Regan maintained that President Reagan had not known about the August–September 1985 TOW shipments until after the fact and had not approved the replenishment of weapons to Israel. This put him in direct conflict with McFarlane, who had testified that

---

[90] Since his earliest testimony before the SSCI on December 16, 1986, Regan repeatedly stated that McFarlane briefed the President during the November 1985 Geneva summit on a shipment of arms from Israel to Iran via a European country.

Independent Counsel questioned Regan also about the possibility that he spoke to North about the HAWK shipment, because of a series of documented phone calls between North, Poindexter and Regan in the same time frame. Regan has testified repeatedly that the only time he ever spoke to North on the phone was on November 24, 1985, but he consistently maintained that this conversation concerned the hijacking of an Egyptian airliner. Asked by the FBI on March 6, 1991, to explain a list of calls between November 25–December 1, 1985, including some from Poindexter, Regan stated that he doesn't remember receiving any calls about the HAWK shipment. (Regan, FBI 302, 3/6/91, p. 6.) On November 23, 1985, Regan received a call from an unidentified "secure voice" at 11:44 p.m., 10 minutes before Poindexter called the President. Poindexter told the Grand jury he could not remember the purpose of this late-night call. (Poindexter, Grand Jury, 3/6/91, pp. 8–9.)

In an apparent contradiction with other Administration officials who early on maintained that President Reagan didn't learn about the true cargo of the November 1985 HAWK shipment until 1986, Regan told SSCI that a meeting in the White House residence of the principals on December 7, 1985, involved "much discussion about the shipment of those HAWK missiles." (Regan, SSCI Testimony, 12/16/86, p. 20.) Regan in his Select Committees deposition of July 15, 1987, recalled there was talk at the meeting of a need for a Finding if the initiative proceeded, but he didn't recall anyone saying one was already drafted. (Regan, Select Committees Deposition, 7/15/87, pp. 15–16.)

Regan in the Grand Jury on February 3, 1988, was shown a memo by Deputy CIA Director John McMahon, written December 7, 1985, stating that a Finding had been signed to cover the November 1985 HAWK shipment. With refreshed memory, Regan testified that he "probably did" discuss the Finding with Casey: "Because I recall that, after this event had taken place—that is, the HAWK shipments— that Casey did discuss with me the fact that there was no finding, but such a finding would be needed for the record; and he would get together with McFarlane and see that one was prepared." (Regan, Grand Jury, 2/3/88, pp. 70–71.)

President Reagan explicitly approved, in advance, the shipments and replenishment.

These contradictory claims did not cause a real problem for the White House until the presidentially appointed Tower Board in late 1986 and early 1987 interviewed McFarlane, Regan and President Reagan; the President wavered between the two versions of events, ultimately informing the Board he could not recall what had actually happened.

McFarlane gave his first interview to the Tower Board on December 11, 1986, with subsequent interviews on February 19 and 21, 1987. Regan spoke to the Board on January 7, 1986. By the time President Reagan testified about the August–September 1985 arms shipments, there was a stark factual conflict regarding his actions that only he could resolve.

The Tower Board reported that President Reagan in his first interview on January 26, 1987, said he had approved the arms shipments in August 1985. In his second interview on February 11, 1987, "the president said that he and Regan had gone over the matter repeatedly and that Regan had a firm recollection that the President had not authorized the August shipment in advance."[91] The Board noted that President Reagan relied heavily in his second interview on a memorandum prepared by Wallison, which stated that the President had been "surprised" by the August–September 1985 shipments. Finally, on February 20, 1987, President Reagan in a letter to the Board stated: "I let myself be influenced by others' recollections, not my own." President Reagan said he had no personal notes or records to refresh his memory and he "cannot recall anything whatsoever" about whether he approved the shipment or replenishment in August 1985. "My answer therefore and the simple truth is, 'I don't remember—period.'"[92]

In his book *Consequences*, John Tower, the Chairman of the Tower Board, described the Board's shock and suspicion over President Reagan's changed testimony. Tower said when he asked the President clarifying questions, the President at one point "picked up a sheet of paper and . . . said to the board, 'This is what I am supposed to say,' and proceeded to read us an answer prepared by Peter Wallison, the White House counsel." Tower wrote:

> . . . we were left with a major contradiction to deal with, which bore all the earmarks of a deliberate effort to conceal White House Chief of Staff Donald Regan's involvement in the Iran-contra affair. By convincing the president that he, the president, had not authorized the arms shipment, Regan was buttressing his own contention that he had been completely unaware of the transaction despite a reputation for tightly controlling the chain of command within the White House staff. It appeared that Regan was putting his own interests ahead of those of the president, who had promised the American people a "full and complete airing of all the facts." Given the Wallison memo, this seemed to us to be the only logical explanation for the altered testimony.[93]

In his diary, Wallison described preparing President Reagan for his initial testimony to the Tower Board, in a meeting on January 22, 1987, that included Vice President Bush, Regan and Special Counsel David Abshire. Wallison said the President used a chronology of events that Wallison had prepared and had apparently gone back to his diary to flesh it out. While the President's diary was "relatively complete," according to Wallison, it contained "no confirmation that he had approved arms sales in Aug. or Sept. of 1985." Wallison said the President had virtually no independent recollection of any of the 1985 arms shipments except for diary notes. Another preparatory meeting was held January 23, 1987.[94]

Wallison was present during President Reagan's January 26, 1987, Tower Board interview. He noted in his diary that the President said he thought he had approved the August 1985 shipment in advance. "This really surprised me," Wallison wrote. "In our earlier discussions the Pres. had no recollection of having approved this sale, and now he seemed to have a pretty clear recollection that he had done so. I could not figure out how he had come to that view, which put him at odds with Regan,

91 Tower Commission Report, 2/26/87, p. B–19.
92 Ibid., p. B–19–20.

93 Tower, *Consequences* (Little, Brown & Co., 1991), pp. 283–284.
94 Wallison Diary, 1/22/87, ALU 0138553.

the rest of the cabinet, and the written record." [95]

After the Tower interview, President Reagan met with Wallison in the Oval Office and showed him that he had found a North chronology of November 19, 1986, which Wallison told him was false. According to Wallison, the chronology helped explain President Reagan's recollection about the November 1985 HAWK shipment, but the chronology stated that he had *not* approved the Israeli shipment in advance "so his statements that he had approved had not come from that source." [96]

On January 28, 1987, Wallison gave President Reagan a memorandum on what he had earlier told the Tower Board. Reagan read the memorandum and said it seemed complete. Wallison told the President he wanted to discuss with him some of his answers. On January 30, 1987, Wallison, Regan and Abshire met with the President and asked him whether he remembered approving the August 1985 shipment, or just the fact of replenishment some time in 1986. The President "seemed at first to have no recollection," according to Wallison.

> Then Regan said that he (Regan) remembered McF. [McFarlane] telling the Pres. that the Israelis had sent the weapons without our approval, and that the Pres. was surprised and displeased. Regan said the Pres. said something like "What's done is done," but was not happy. As he listened to this, the Pres. seemed to have a recollection of this event. He said to me "You know, he's right" referring to Regan. I think at that point he genuinely had a recollection of this sequence of events, and that he had not approved the sale in advance. [97]

In early February 1987, Wallison managed to set up a second interview for the President with the Tower Board. On February 9, 1987, Wallison, Regan and Abshire met with the President to prepare him for his second interview.

Wallison advised the President to tell the Board only what he seemed to recall, according

to Wallison, about the 1985 shipments: That he was "surprised" to learn after the fact of the summer 1985 transactions, and that he had no memory of the November 1985 HAWK shipments.[98] A second preparatory session was held the morning of February 11, 1987. Wallison in his diary stated that he gave the President a memo "setting out what I understood to be his revised recollection concerning whether he had initially authorized the sale of TOWs by Israel to Iran." Wallison said the President "seemed to see the issue as a dispute between Regan and McFarlane, and did not want to take sides." [99]

In his second interview with the Tower Board, President Reagan read from the Wallison memorandum. "Unfortunately, it was written in the second person, and so he flubbed a summary of it," Wallison noted. "In all, it was a weak performance, and left the unfortunate impression that he might have been influenced to this view against his best recollection." [100]

Wallison said after the interview he became "quite concerned" that the Board might believe "we had tried to sway his recollection, perhaps in order to buttress Regan's view of events." But, Wallison said,

> It was an attempt to set the historical record straight. I had twice heard him say that he had been surprised to learn of the Israeli shipment; his notes do not disclose and [sic] approval; Shultz, Weinberger and Regan do not know of any approval; the record shows that North was not able to get replenishment of the Israelis before the Jan 17, 1986 finding was signed. All this leads to the conclusion that the Pres. did not in fact approve. Only McF. says he did, but McF.'s credibility is subject to question and he could have been protecting the Pres. by adopting the idea of an oral finding.[101]

On February 13, 1987, *The Washington Post* reported that the Tower Board was now looking into a "cover-up" by the White House to keep

---

95 Ibid., 1/26/87, ALU 0138304–05.
96 Ibid., ALU 0138305.
97 Ibid., 1/30/87, ALU 0138310.

98 Ibid., 2/9/87, ALU 0138319.
99 Ibid., 2/11/87, ALU 0138321–22.
100 Ibid., ALU 01388322–323.
101 Ibid., ALU 0138323.

the Iran arms sales from becoming public.[102] On February 14, 1987, Wallison met with the Tower Board staff about their concerns over the President's changing statements about the August 1985 shipment. The same day Wallison started to get press inquiries about a change in Reagan's testimony. The story became public in the press on February 19, 1987, and Regan was directly blamed for the President's changed testimony.[103]

In the meantime, Wallison had gathered three computer messages from McFarlane to Poindexter that confused the issue further: one dated November 7, 1986, stating that the President had not authorized the August 1985 arms shipment in advance; the second on November 18, 1986, also stating that the President did not approve a weapons transfer; and one written on November 21, 1986, in which McFarlane described a meeting with Meese and noting that Meese would be "relieved" if the President had approved the 1985 Israeli shipments in advance.[104] Wallison showed the computer notes to Regan on February 19, 1987, suggesting that McFarlane changed his version of events and that Regan's recollection was the true one.[105]

Later on, Abshire and Wallison met with President Reagan and showed him the McFarlane notes. The President read the November 18, 1986, computer message and "seemed angry about it," according to Wallison. The President said his recollection was closer to McFarlane's testimony, which he had recently re-read—that he had approved the shipment in advance. President Reagan said he had no recollection of being surprised at learning of the shipment. When Wallison and Abshire pressed him, "he finally said that he really could recall nothing of any of this—that the whole period was a blank." Abshire subsequently called Tower and told him to talk to President Reagan on the phone to hear his statement; Tower asked for a letter instead.[106]

On February 20, 1987, President Reagan sent his letter to the Tower Board. Regan, upon learning that the President said he let himself be "influenced by others' recollections," became angry, according to Wallison, and blamed the wording of the letter on Nancy Reagan.[107]

## Regan's Forced Resignation

The Tower Board controversy led to Donald Regan's ultimate dismissal as White House chief of staff, after pressure on the President to remove him had been building for months. On February 20, 1987, Vice President Bush confronted Regan about resigning, citing continuing trouble among staff and in the press. Regan, according to the Vice President, agreed to leave following the issuance of the Tower Board report.

Vice President Bush wrote: "I went in to see the President after the talk with Don Regan. The President was very, very pleased. He thanked me about three times. I gave him a full report. He was concerned that Don would walk in and see us talking, so I left after about 15 minutes." According to Vice President Bush, he and the President agreed that their discussion about Regan should be considered a "non-conversation." [108]

Vice President Bush saw Regan again February 26, 1987, and Regan informed Bush he would leave the following week. Again, the Vice President informed President Reagan of the conversation.[109]

On February 27, 1987, Regan resigned. Wallison followed him shortly thereafter.

## Decision Not To Prosecute

There were three areas of Regan's conduct that invited investigation. Independent Counsel attempted to determine whether there was a con-

102 "Tower Panel Probing Whether Iran Cover-Up Was Attempted," *The Washington Post*, 2/13/87, p. A1.

103 "President Changed Statement on 1985 Iran Arms Approval," *The Washington Post*, 2/19/87, p. A1; "Conflicts in Reagan Iran Remarks Cited," *The Los Angeles Times*, 2/19/87, p. 1.

104 PROFs Notes from McFarlane to Poindexter: 11/7/86, AKW 021626–27; 11/18/86, AKW 021672–74; 11/21/86, AKW 021677.

105 Wallison Diary, 2/19/87, ALU 0138337–39.

106 Ibid., ALU 0138339.

107 Ibid., ALU 0138571–72.

108 Bush diary, 2/20/87, ARZ 002847–48.

109 Ibid., 2/26/87, ARZ 002849. Don Regan described in his book *For The Record* a more elliptical exchange with the Vice President. According to Regan, the Vice President on February 23, 1987, called him into his office and said, "Don, why don't you stick your head into the Oval Office and talk to the President about your situation?" Regan said the Vice President explained that the President had asked him what Regan's plans were. According to Regan, the President suggested that he leave that day, before the Tower Board report came out. Regan convinced the President to allow him to stay until the following week, after it was issued. (Regan, *For The Record*, Harcourt Brace Jovanovich 1988, pp. 96–99.)

spiracy to cover up President Reagan's possible violation of the Arms Export Control Act by the 1985 arms transactions; second, whether Regan, on his own or with Wallison, deprived the Tower Board of President Reagan's honest recollection regarding his authorization of the 1985 arms transactions; and third, whether Regan willfully withheld his notes from the congressional committees and the Office of Independent Counsel.

As more extensively discussed in the section dealing with Meese, there is little doubt that Meese's November 21–24, 1986 "fact-finding" effort was, in fact, a damage-control effort. Wallison was concerned that the President had violated the Arms Export Control Act, and raised these concerns with Regan. Regan admitted to Independent Counsel his own concerns over possible impeachment of the President.[110]

Although Regan was in frequent contact with Meese and Casey during this critical period, Independent Counsel obtained no usable evi-

---

[110] The Justice Department's later rationalizations that the Arms Export Control Act did not apply were at best tenuous. Whether or not the arms transactions were illegal, they presented a clear confrontation with the statute and, accordingly, they invited consideration of harsh congressional reaction and possible impeachment, as Regan admitted.

dence that he was attempting to orchestrate a story, or that he was helping Meese do it. His notes, when ultimately produced, substantially helped develop Independent Counsel's knowledge of the facts. When Regan testified before the Grand Jury, he gave every appearance of being forthright. His testimony would have been used against Weinberger and was available against Meese. Under the circumstances, it was decided that, although the delay in the production of his notes had damaged OIC's investigation, its investigative purposes would be better served by developing him as a witness rather than a target.

Regarding the President's vacillating statements to the Tower Board, there is no direct evidence of obstruction by Regan or Wallison. Based on Wallison's diary, there seems to have been genuine confusion over the issue, and the President appeared genuinely confused about his recollection.

Regarding Regan's notes, Independent Counsel believed that primary responsibility for production rested with the White House. Regan produced copies of his notes when they were subpoenaed.

# Chapter 31
# Edwin Meese III: November 1986

Attorney General Edwin Meese III became directly involved in the Reagan Administration's secret plan to sell weapons to Iran in January 1986, when he was asked for a legal opinion to support the plan.[1] When the secret arms sales became exposed in November 1986, raising questions of legality and prompting congressional and public scrutiny, Meese became the point man for the Reagan Administration's effort, in Meese's words, "to limit the damage."[2]

Meese began with an attempt to justify legally President Reagan's failure to notify Congress of the arms sales for more than a year. His efforts led to a November 21–24 fact-finding investigation focused on the President's involvement in the November 1985 HAWK missile shipment to Iran.

The Select Iran/contra Committees criticized Meese for departing from "standard investigative techniques" in his fact-finding mission because he failed to protect National Security Council documents, many of which were altered or destroyed as he conducted one-on-one interviews with senior Administration officials without taking notes.[3] The Select Committees also faulted Meese for "incorrectly" stating in his November 25, 1986, press conference, at which he disclosed the Iran/contra diversion, that President Reagan did not learn of the 1985 shipment until February 1986. The Select Committees viewed this as an isolated error. It was not.

Meese was conducting the November 21–24 investigation as "counselor" and "friend" to the President, not as the nation's chief law en-

forcement officer. Independent Counsel concluded that he was not so much searching for the truth about the November 1985 HAWK shipment, as he was building a case of deniability for his client-in-fact, President Reagan. By this time, Meese knew that the 1985 HAWK transaction, in which the National Security Council staff and the Central Intelligence Agency were directly involved without a presidential covert-action Finding authorizing their involvement, raised serious legal questions. The President was potentially exposed to charges of illegal conduct if he was knowledgeable of the shipment and had not reported it to Congress, under the requirements of the Arms Export Control Act (AECA) and in the absence of a Finding. But Meese apparently never questioned the President himself about whether he approved or knew about the November 1985 HAWK shipment. When Meese got answers in his inquiry that did not support his defense of the President, he apparently ignored them, as he did with Secretary of State George P. Shultz's revelation on November 22 that the President had told him that he had known of the HAWK shipment in advance.

In the course of the weekend inquiry, Meese and his aides discovered in the National Security Council Office of Lt. Col. Oliver L. North a politically explosive document: An undated memorandum, apparently drafted in early April 1986, that outlined a planned diversion of $12 million in proceeds from the Iran arms sales to the Nicaraguan contras. This discovery caused the Meese inquiry to veer off onto two tracks—while facts about the 1985 HAWK shipment were still being gathered, there was a second effort to determine who knew about and who approved the diversion. After receiving

---

[1] Meese, Select Committees Testimony, 7/28/87, pp. 2–9; 21–36. Meese also supported the plan. (Ibid., pp. 5–7.)

[2] Meese, *North* Trial Testimony, 3/28/89, pp. 5747–48.

[3] Select Committees Report, pp. 10–11, pp. 20–21, pp. 306–07, p. 311, pp. 317–18.

confirmation from North that an Iran/contra diversion had occurred, Meese quietly imparted the news to the President, White House Chief of Staff Donald T. Regan and Vice President Bush on November 24, sounding them out privately on their personal knowledge of it. He did not inform a senior advisers' meeting that afternoon. He informed the Cabinet on the next day.

Meese attempted to resolve the separate but continuing problem of the HAWK shipment—particularly the President's contemporaneous knowledge—at the senior advisers' meeting on Monday, November 24, attended by President Reagan, Vice President Bush, Regan, National Security Adviser John M. Poindexter, Shultz, Secretary of Defense Caspar W. Weinberger, and CIA Director William J. Casey. In response to a question about the November 1985 HAWK shipment, Poindexter falsely claimed that before December 1985, McFarlane handled the Iran arms sales "all alone" with "no documentation."[4] Meese then added that the November 1985 HAWK shipment "[m]ay be a violation of law if arms shipped w/o a finding. But President did not know."[5] At least Meese, President Reagan, Regan, Shultz, Weinberger, Bush, and Poindexter knew that Meese's version was false, but no one spoke up to correct him. After the meeting, Shultz told his aide M. Charles Hill, "They may lay all this off on Bud [McFarlane] . . . They rearranging the record."[6]

Because Congress had already announced its intention to hold hearings on the Iran arms sales, Meese's apparent attempt to signal other Cabinet members that the party line should be that the President did not have contemporaneous knowledge of the November 1985 HAWK shipment required evaluation as an effort to obstruct a congressional inquiry.

The OIC did not learn of Meese's statements at the November 24, 1986, meeting until late 1991 and 1992, when it finally obtained notes of the meeting taken by Weinberger and Regan. Six years after the pivotal events had occurred, the trail was cold. With the principals professing no memory of often critical events, the OIC

did not uncover sufficient evidence of an obstruction to justify a prosecution.

## November 1–19, 1986

On November 3, 1986, the secret U.S. arms sales to Iran were first exposed in the press, setting off inquiries that resulted in a series of false denials by the White House. On November 5, 1986, Poindexter asked Meese for some "legal advice" on the arms sales to Iran, in anticipation of questions from Congress.[7] Two days later, Meese asked Assistant Attorney General Charles Cooper, the head of the Department of Justice Office of Legal Counsel, to research the matter, with assistance from "one other trusted person."[8] Meese told Cooper that NSC counsel Paul Thompson would be his White House contact.[9] Cooper understood that he was to research the relevant statutes and to provide an analysis of whether the arms shipments were legal.[10]

On the morning of November 10, President Reagan met in the Oval Office with his senior national security advisers, including Meese, Poindexter, Vice President Bush, Shultz, Weinberger, Casey, Regan, and Poindexter's deputy, Alton Keel, to discuss issuing a public statement on the Iran arms sales. Poindexter gave a presentation on the arms sales to Iran in which he described U.S. involvement as beginning with the January 17, 1986, presidential Finding. He omitted any mention of U.S. approval of or involvement in the 1985 shipments of arms from Israeli stocks. Instead, he asserted falsely that U.S. officials first learned of the 1985 Israeli shipments to Iran when they confronted Israeli officials after discovering a warehouse of U.S.-made arms in Portugal in 1986. According to Poindexter, Israel had responded that they were trying to get Iranian Jews out of Iran.[11]

Virtually everyone at the November 10 meeting knew that Poindexter's story was false, but no one spoke up to correct it. President Reagan, Shultz, Weinberger, Regan, Vice President Bush, and Casey all knew that at least since

---

[4] Weinberger Note, 11/24/86, ALZ 0040669LL.

[5] Regan Note, 11/24/86, ALU 0139379.

[6] Hill Note, 11/24/86, ANS 00001898.

[7] Meese, Grand Jury, 12/16/87, pp. 62–66.

[8] Meese, Select Committees Testimony, 7/28/87, pp. 42–43; Cooper, Grand Jury, 7/15/92, pp. 8–11.

[9] Ibid., pp. 22–23.

[10] Ibid., pp. 13, 15–16.

[11] Hill Note, 11/10/86, ANS 0001762; Regan Note, 11/10/86, ALU 0139114; Keel Note, 11/10/86, AKW 047247.

June 1985 Israel had proposed selling U.S. arms to Iran in an attempt to free U.S. hostages, not Iranian Jews. They also knew that the Administration had learned about the Israeli efforts directly, not from stumbling on a warehouse of weapons in Portugal. President Reagan, Regan, Shultz, Vice President Bush, and Weinberger all had advance notice of the November 1985 HAWK shipment and its purpose—to free the hostages. Casey definitely knew within a few days after the shipment and may have known in advance as well. There is no direct evidence that Meese knew about the 1985 shipments prior to this meeting.[12]

After Poindexter's presentation, the group reviewed a draft press statement prepared by Casey. Poindexter opposed issuing a public statement because it would terminate ongoing negotiations with Iran. Regan urged they issue a statement, because "we are being hung out to dry" and "[o]ur credibility is at stake."[13] President Reagan favored a statement emphasizing that the United States had not dealt with terrorists but was pursuing a long-range policy toward Iran.[14] Meese wanted the statement to include the assertion that no U.S. laws or policy had been violated, even though he had not yet received any assurance from Cooper, who was still researching the matter.[15] Meese testified that as late as November 20, 1985, he was not "fully informed" on the legal issues and was relying on Cooper.[16]

Near the end of the meeting, Shultz demanded to know whether there would be further arms sales to Iran. President Reagan responded by insisting that his advisers support the policy and to not say anything else publicly. Shultz replied that he supported the President, but not the policy.[17]

The press statement released later that day did not confirm or deny any arms sales to Iran. It simply announced that the President had met with his senior national security advisers to discuss the hostages held in Lebanon, and that no laws had been broken:

> As has been the case in similar meetings with the President and his senior advisers on this matter, there was unanimous support for the President. While specific decisions discussed at the meeting cannot be divulged, the President did ask that it be reemphasized that no U.S. laws have been or will be violated and that our policy of not making concessions to terrorists remains intact.[18]

When White House Counsel Peter J. Wallison received a copy of the statement he "was unhappy to note that it said that all laws had been complied with. I was told that this is what the AG [attorney general] wanted said."[19] Wallison had previously expressed to Regan his concern that the arms sales may have violated the Arm Export Control Act (AECA). Wallison's efforts to look into the matter had been thwarted, however, by Poindexter's unwillingness to provide him with the facts.

On November 12, 1986, a story in *The New York Times* questioned the legality of the arms sales to Iran. After learning of the report, Nancy Reagan told Don Regan that she was "very upset" by the press reports and that the policy of refusing comment on the arms sales was "[r]isking presidency."[20] Regan testified that as the Iran arms sales continued to dominate the news and the President's approval ratings plummeted, he and other officials were concerned that the scandal would become another Watergate and lead to calls for President Reagan's impeachment.[21]

---

[12] Meese denied that a September 1985 TOW missile shipment was discussed at the November 10 meeting and maintained that he did not learn of the 1985 shipments until approximately November 18, when Cooper told him about the NSC chronology. Meese's own notes of the meeting, however, belie his claim: "508 [TOWs] shipped by Israel—[U.S.] told after the fact . . . Results: . . . 3 hostages ret'd: Weir, Jako [sic, Jenco] Jacobsen." The reference to Weir's release being one of the "results" of the shipments is significant because he was released in September 1985.

[13] Weinberger Memo, 11/10/86, ALZ 0041727.

[14] Regan Note, 11/10/86, ALU 0139114; Keel Note, 11/10/86, AKW 047247.

[15] Regan Note, 11/10/86, ALU 0139114.

[16] Meese, Grand Jury, 12/16/87, p. 112. Meese's prior analysis in January 1986 that the plan was legal was based on his understanding that shipments would be authorized by a Finding signed by the President. Having just been told that in September 1985, weapons were shipped *before* any Finding, Meese, at that point, had no basis for asserting that no laws had been violated. Even if Israel had shipped the weapons without U.S. approval there would have been a violation of the Arms Export Control Act because the President had failed to report such a third-country the shipment to Congress "immediately" after learning of it.

[17] Regan Note, 11/10/86, ALU 0139126; Keel Note, 11/10/86, AKW 047255; Hill Note, 11/10/86, ANS 0001764.

[18] White House Press Statement, 11/10/86.

[19] Wallison Diary, 11/14/86, ALU 0138220, p. 251.

[20] Regan Note, 11/12/86, ALU 0138701.

[21] Regan, Grand Jury, 5/8/92, pp. 98–100.

Later on November 12, President Reagan and his top advisers, including Vice President Bush, Shultz, Weinberger, Meese, and Poindexter met with Senate leaders Robert Byrd and Robert Dole, House Speaker Jim Wright and Rep. Richard Cheney to brief them on the Iran arms sales.[22] According to Regan's notes of the meeting, Poindexter once again provided the false cover story that "Israel's participation in arms selling led us to discover arms in Portugal which Israel [was] selling to get Jews out of Iran." [23] When Sen. Byrd demanded to know when the Administration's contacts with Iran began, Poindexter responded falsely that, although the Administration had begun to explore contacts with Iran in 1985, there had been "no transfer of material" before the Finding was signed in January 1986.[24]

On November 13, 1986, Cooper gave Meese the memorandum justifying the 1986 arms shipments under the National Security Act. That evening, President Reagan delivered a nationally televised address, purporting to set out the facts of U.S. involvement in the arms sales to Iran. He publicly admitted for the first time that he had authorized "the transfer of small amounts of defensive weapons and spare parts for defensive systems to Iran." He insisted, however, that "[t]hese modest deliveries, taken together, could easily fit into a single cargo plane." He denied reports of dissension within the Administration and asserted that "all appropriate Cabinet officers were fully consulted." The President also reiterated his earlier statement that no federal laws had been broken and assured the public that "the relevant committees of Congress are being, and will be, fully informed." He did not mention the 1985 arms sales to Iran.[25]

At a meeting that morning to draft the President's address, Poindexter's deputy Alton Keel proposed inserting a sentence that all laws had been complied with. Wallison, who had been researching the question for Regan but was unable to get the facts from Poindexter, stated that the legality of the shipments had not yet been confirmed. According to Wallison, "Keel exploded, telling me that this is what the President wanted, this is what the AG [attorney general] wants, and this is what the National Security Adviser wants; that the Pres. [President] had already said as much earlier in the week; that this statute was the AG's to interpret, and I should not go around expressing disagreement with the AG's conclusions." The sentence that all laws had been complied with was inserted in the President's address over Wallison's objection.[26]

Wallison remained concerned about the legality of the shipments and tried repeatedly to discuss the subject with Meese. When Wallison finally spoke with Meese on the afternoon of November 13, Meese said he would have Cooper contact him. That evening, Cooper explained his theory on the legality of the arms shipments as set forth in the memorandum he had delivered to Meese, based on the January 1986 Finding authorizing the shipments as a covert action under the National Security Act. Cooper argued that the President had inherent constitutional powers, recognized in the National Security Act, to conduct the arms sales without notifying Congress. Wallison responded that Cooper's approach would "provoke a constitutional confrontation that we have tried to avoid in the context of the War Powers Resolution." [27]

Wallison also asked Cooper how long he had been working on this project. Cooper responded, "about a day." Wallison noted in his diary that "[i]t thus appeared that the Pres. [President] was going to state in his speech that no laws had been violated but the Justice Dept., which supposedly had given him that advice had not even begun to research the question in any depth." [28] The problem was even greater than Wallison suspected: The 1985 shipments, particularly the November HAWK shipment in which the NSC and CIA acted without a Finding, had yet to be acknowledged by Administration officials.

Dissidence about the arms sales among the President's top advisers broke into the open on Sunday, November 16, when Shultz appeared on CBS–TV's "Face the Nation." Shultz stated

22 Regan Note, 11/12/86, ALU 0139132.
23 Ibid., pp. 4–5, ALU 0139135–36.
24 Ibid., p. 10, ALU 0139141.
25 Transcript of President's Address to the Nation on the Iran Arms and Contra Aid Controversy, 11/13/86, pp. 1546–48.

26 Wallison Diary, 11/14/86, ALU 0138222–23, pp. 253–54.
27 Ibid., p. 254, ALU 0138223.
28 Ibid., p. 255, ALU 0138224.

that he opposed any further arms sales to Iran but, when pressed, conceded that he could not speak for the Administration.[29]

On November 18, Wallison called a meeting of the general counsel of the agencies involved in the Iran arms sales. Present at the meeting were Wallison, Paul Thompson from the NSC, Cooper, Abraham D. Sofaer from State, H. Lawrence Garrett III from the Defense Department, David Doherty from the CIA, and an attorney from the staff of the Joint Chiefs of Staff.[30] The purpose of the meeting, according to Wallison, "was to see if . . . [they] could agree to a common set of theories to support the position that the Administration would take in testimony and briefings on the Hill." [31]

Cooper explained his theory that the 1986 shipments were legal pursuant to the President's inherent constitutional authority as recognized by the National Security Act, and that the reporting requirements of the AECA did not apply. Cooper noted that the failure to notify Congress of the 1986 arms sales, which were authorized by the January 17 Finding, was defensible because there were precedents for delayed congressional notification of covert operations.[32] Wallison questioned whether Cooper's "exception" to the AECA could "swallow up the statute," but everyone else supported Cooper's view.[33]

Paul Thompson, general counsel to the NSC staff, briefed the group on the September 1985 TOW shipment, explaining that Israel had shipped the TOWs to Iran and that the United States replenished Israel's stocks after the January 17, 1986, Finding was signed.[34] According to Sofaer, Cooper—apparently relying on a draft chronology of the arms sales prepared by the NSC staff that he had been given the day before [35]—said that the United States had no advance knowledge of the TOW shipment but learned about it after the fact and later replenished Israel's stocks.[36] Wallison understood that U.S. officials *had* known about the shipment, but had not approved it.[37] In any event, no one had a viable legal theory for justifying the failure to report the September 1985 shipment to Congress, as required by the AECA.[38] Wallison questioned whether Meese had known of the pre-Finding shipments before telling the President everything was legal, and Cooper agreed to check with Meese.[39] Curiously, the November 1985 HAWK shipment was not discussed at the meeting, even though it was listed on the draft NSC chronology Cooper had obtained the previous day.[40]

Also at the meeting, Sofaer, Garrett, Wallison, and Cooper complained to Thompson that the NSC staff was "stiffing everybody" by withholding factual information.[41] Sofaer and Wallison stated that without the facts they could not advise their clients and Meese would have to be the sole spokesperson on the legal issues.[42] Thompson nevertheless refused to provide additional facts.[43]

Sofaer met that afternoon with Shultz's executive assistant, M. Charles Hill, to debrief him about the general counsel meeting. Sofaer told Hill that Thompson and the CIA were refusing to give the other lawyers the facts. Sofaer explained the legal rationale for the 1986 arms transfers, pursuant to the January 17 Finding and noted that there were two problems with the Administration's position. First, Sofaer noted, one of the transfers occurred after an August 1986 amendment to the AECA which "absolutely prohibit[ed] shipments to Iran." [44]

29 Weinberger's diary notes for the day reflect that he spoke to Poindexter later that day "re Shultz 'distancing himself'" from the Iran arms sales. (Weinberger Note, 11/15/86, ALZ 0040539.)

30 Wallison Note, 11/18/86, p. 258, ALU 0138204.

31 Ibid.

32 Ibid., p. 259; Sofaer Note, 11/18/86, ALV 000309.

33 Wallison Note, 11/18/86, ALV 0138228, p. 259.

34 Cooper Note, 11/18/86, ALV 077953; Cooper, FBI 302, 1/6/88, pp. 2, 5.

35 Cooper, Grand Jury, 7/15/92, pp. 23–24.

36 Sofaer, OIC Interview, 9/29/92, pp. 8–9, 15; Sofaer Note, 11/18/86, ALV 000309.

37 Wallison Note, 11/18/86, ALU 0138228, p. 269.

38 Ibid. Even Cooper was concerned, at that time, that the pre-Finding shipments might violate the AECA. (Cooper, Grand Jury, 7/15/92, p. 44.) Ultimately, however, Cooper determined that the AECA did not apply to even the pre-Finding shipments.

39 Wallison Note, 11/18/86, ALU 0138228, p. 259. Cooper could not recall agreeing to check with Meese. (Cooper, Grand Jury, 7/15/92, p. 50.)

40 Ibid., pp. 24–25. The Wallison and Sofaer notes of the meeting do not reflect any discussion of the November 1985 shipment.

41 Cooper, Grand Jury, 7/15/92, p. 32; Wallison Note, 11/18/86, pp. 258–59; Sofaer Note, 11/18/86, ALV 000309–10.

42 Wallison Note, 11/18/86, ALU 0138227–28, pp. 258–59; Sofaer Note, 11/18/86, ALV 000309–10.

43 Ibid., 259.

44 Hill Note, 11/18/86, ANS 0001837 (emphasis in original). The amendment, Section 509 of the Omnibus Diplomatic Security and Antiterrorism Act of 1986, Pub. L. No. 99–399 (1986), prohibits sending weapons to any country the Secretary of State has identified as a supporter of international terrorism. Secretary Shultz declared Iran a

The second and "more serious" problem Sofaer identified was the "Sept[ember] 1985 Israeli transfer of arms to Iran" and the subsequent replenishment of those arms by the United States,[45] because there was no Finding authorizing either action. Sofaer added that "If Admin claims we did not approve Sept 85 transfer + it can be proved we did, its a Watergate style thing." [46] Sofaer had "suspicions" that people were "trying to hide the facts" and was concerned that Poindexter and Meese were "shutting . . . [him] out" because they already had their legal arguments set and didn't want him involved because he would "only permit arguments within certain parameters." [47]

Sofaer and Under Secretary of State Michael Armacost, who was to be the State Department's representative at the November 21 hearings before the Senate and House intelligence committees, met later on November 18 with Poindexter for a further briefing on the arms sales. According to Sofaer's memorandum of the meeting, Poindexter said that McFarlane had "refused expressly to sanction" in advance Israel's September 1985 TOW shipment to Iran but had indicated that the United States would continue to sell weapons to Israel even if it proceeded with the transfer.[48] Poindexter's presentation to Sofaer and Armacost once again omitted any mention of the November 1985 HAWK shipment. According to Sofaer's memorandum, he and Armacost "emphasized the need to prepare all witnesses carefully, and to answer correctly all questions, *especially those related to activities prior to January 17.*" [49]

The morning of November 19, Shultz met with Hill, Armacost, and Deputy Secretary of State John C. Whitehead to discuss the possibility of resigning. The three agreed that Shultz and the State Department had been put in an untenable position by the public revelation that the Administration had been secretly selling arms to Iran while Shultz, who had known about the arms sales, had been promoting the official U.S. policy of discouraging arms sales to Iran and refusing to make concessions to terrorists.[50] Armacost complained that the NSC staff was "not telling . . . [State] the truth." [51]

Meanwhile, President Reagan was preparing for his press conference scheduled for that evening. Shultz met with the President that afternoon to attempt to persuade him to announce publicly that all aspects of U.S. foreign policy toward Iran would be returned to the State Department. Shultz argued that the President had been misled by his other advisers regarding Iran's role in terrorism and advised him to "watch out about saying [there had been] no deals for host[a]g[es]." [52] According to Hill's notes of Shultz's report on the meeting, Shultz also told the President his understanding of the November 1985 HAWK shipment at that meeting: "Bud once told me about a plane of arms that w[oul]d go if host[a]g[es] released—not if not. P[resident] knew of this—but it didn't come off." [53]

Meese did not participate in preparing President Reagan for the November 19 press conference, but he and Wallison agreed that the President should say he relied on Meese's advice that all the shipments were legal.[54] Wallison advised the President to "cite the AG" [55] if legal questions arose.

Despite Shultz's warning, President Reagan insisted in his press conference that evening that there had been no exchange of arms for hostages. To dispel this "widespread but mistaken perception" of the policy, Reagan pledged that there would be no further arms sales to Iran and promised again that "all information will be provided to the appropriate members of Congress." In response to questions, President Reagan stated that no third countries had been involved in the arms sales. He also denied that there had been any U.S. involvement in arms sales to Iran before the January 17, 1986,

---

supporter of terrorism in 1984. (49 Fed. Reg. 2836 (1984).) The amendment was troublesome because it appears to absolutely prohibit arms shipments to Iran unless the President (1) determines the shipment is "important to the national interests of the United States" and (2) submits a report to Congress "justifying that determination" and describing the proposed shipment." Cooper ultimately decided the amendment was irrelevant to the Iran arms sales because the AECA itself did not apply to shipments made pursuant to the President's inherent authority as implicitly recognized by the National Security Act. (Memorandum for the Attorney General, 12/17/86, p. 13, ALV 077743.)

45 Ibid.

46 Hill Note, 11/18/86, ANS 0001837 (emphasis in original).

47 Sofaer, OIC Interview, 9/29/92 pp. 23–31.

48 Memorandum of Conversation from Sofaer, 11/18/86, ALV 000329.

49 Ibid., ALV 000333.

50 Hill Note, 11/19/86, ANS 0001847.

51 Ibid.

52 Hill Note, 11/19/86, ANS 0001852.

53 Ibid.

54 Wallison Note, 11/19/86, ALU 0138231, p. 262.

55 Ibid.

Finding, even though he had just that afternoon told Shultz he knew of the November 1985 HAWK shipment.

Because Donald Regan had told reporters in an earlier briefing that the United States had acquiesced in an Israeli shipment of arms to Iran, the White House was compelled to issue a correction of the President's statement.[56]

Shultz, who watched the press conference with Hill and another aide, was alarmed by President Reagan's inaccurate statements and asked the aide to review the transcript and identify the factual errors.[57] He immediately called Regan to schedule an appointment with the President the following day.

## Conflicting Stories on the November 1985 HAWK Shipment

On November 20, 1986, Meese and Cooper met for about two hours with Casey, CIA Deputy Director Robert Gates, Poindexter, Thompson, and North in Poindexter's office to prepare Casey's congressional testimony and Poindexter's congressional briefing scheduled for the next day. Meese's role in the meeting is unclear, largely because of his own conflicting testimony. In December 1987 Meese told the Grand Jury he "had been there primarily to be available in case any legal matters came up. I don't remember that any did particularly. I think we may have talked about the Arms Export Control Act."[58] In testimony before the Senate Intelligence Committee in December 1986, however, Meese indicated that discussion of the legal issues dominated, explaining that he had been present to ensure "they had properly represented the Findings in the chronology, and *if I remember correctly we discussed the nature of the Findings, the legal theories that were involved, and it was that more than any factual basis.*"[59] Poindexter testified that Meese flagged the 1985 shipments as the key legal problem: "And sometime in that conversation Ed said that on both the September shipment of TOWs and the November shipment of HAWKs, that—I don't want to put words in his mouth, but it was something along the

line that it would make a difference whether the President approved it ahead of time or afterwards, or words to that effect."[60] This would become the theme of Meese's November 21–24 investigation as he sought to shield President Reagan from any question of illegal actions.

The meeting focused on preparing Casey's testimony on the CIA's role in the November 1985 HAWK shipment.[61] According to the draft of Casey's testimony, "We in CIA did not find out that our airline had hauled HAWK missiles into Iran until mid-January [1986] when we were told by the Iranians."[62] In fact, North and Poindexter, as well as many CIA personnel, knew in advance that the November 1985 shipment contained weapons. Casey had been told by McFarlane on November 14, 1985, that the Israelis were planning a weapons shipment to Iran; he was receiving intelligence reports which made clear the cargo was weapons, and he had seen the Finding CIA General Counsel Stanley Sporkin had prepared shortly after the shipment, which sought to retroactively authorize CIA involvement in it. Nevertheless, everyone in the meeting apparently remained silent while North revised the draft testimony to include the broader assertion that "no one in the USG [U.S. Government]" knew before January 1986 that the cargo was weapons.[63]

North also changed a statement about why the HAWKs were returned to Israel—from an accurate account that the Iranians were dissatisfied with the type of missiles they were sold to a false account that the United States was upset about the arms shipment and "jawboned" the Iranians into returning the HAWKs.[64] Again, no one challenged North's change. Cooper testified that he had "no reason

---

56 Ibid., ALU 0138232, p. 263.
57 Hill Note, 11/19/86, ANS 0001862.
58 Meese, Grand Jury, 12/16/87, p. 163.
59 Meese, SSCI Testimony, 12/17/86, p. 17 (emphasis added).

60 Poindexter, Select Committees Testimony, 6/17/87, pp. 347–49.
61 Cooper, FBI 302, 11/21/90, p. 8. Thompson testified that the HAWKs were an issue during the preparation session, because it "was still a dangling paragraph to have the CIA suddenly receiving a call from somebody, a U.S. Government person or other, and then responding to it by having a CIA aircraft made available for this. It just didn't seem very characteristic of the way the CIA normally does operations, and so I think it called a lot of attention to itself. . . . I know that was certainly a concern of the Justice Department, that why would the CIA get involved in an airplane shipment and not know more about it, the basis for it." (Thompson, Grand Jury, 5/20/87, p. 157.)
62 Draft Memorandum Re: CIA Airline Involvement, 11/20/86, AMY 000732; Cooper, Select Committees Testimony, 6/25/87, pp. 239–42.
63 Cooper, Select Committees Testimony, 6/25/87, pp. 45–46; Draft Memorandum Re: CIA Airline Involvement, AMY 000732.
64 Cooper, Grand Jury, 7/15/92, pp. 70, 39–40.

whatsoever not to accept'' North's version of the return of the HAWK missiles.[65]

Cooper said that no one objected to North's changes because, ''[i]n fact, the meeting was such that with respect to all these changes . . . North seemed to be the person who had a basis for knowing what the facts were. It was my impression that Poindexter didn't know one way or the other on this. It was my impression that Casey didn't know one way or the other on these changes, and that he was, like I was, accepting of North's information because North appeared to know what he was talking about. . . .''[66]

North, on the other hand, suggested that Casey, Thompson, Poindexter and Meese did not object to his changes, because ''they had a darned good reason for not putting the straight story out, and their reasons might have been the same as mine.''[67]

While North was shaping Casey's testimony, Hill at the State Department was briefing Sofaer and Armacost on the Iran arms sales from his contemporaneous notes to prepare for Armacost's testimony the next day. Hill disclosed that while in Geneva on November 18, 1985, McFarlane had told Shultz about a planned shipment of HAWK missiles to Iran in exchange for the release of the hostages.[68] During the briefing, Sofaer received a draft of Casey's proposed testimony.[69] Because he had just learned that Shultz knew of the November 1985 HAWK shipment in advance, Sofaer was skeptical of the assertion in Casey's draft testimony that the CIA did not learn the nature of the cargo of the November 1985 HAWK shipment until January 1986.[70] Sofaer told Hill that he was going to tell Meese and Wallison about his ''concern about <u>pre-Jan 17 '86</u> activities.''[71]

At about 2:30 p.m. on November 20, Sofaer placed a secure call to Meese. Meese was still in the White House meeting preparing Casey's testimony, so Sofaer spoke to Deputy Attorney General Arnold Burns.[72] According to Sofaer, he told Burns that he did not believe Casey's proposed testimony that everyone in the CIA thought the November 1985 shipment had contained oil-drilling parts because Shultz had contemporaneous notes that McFarlane knew the shipment was HAWK missiles.[73] After exchanging messages, Sofaer spoke again to Burns shortly before 4:00 pm. Burns said that Meese had spent the afternoon with Poindexter and Casey and ''was fully aware of the facts [Sofaer] mentioned. [Burns] said the A.G. [attorney general] was profuse in his thanks for [Sofaer's] warning, and appreciated [Sofaer's] motives, but that he (the AG) knew of certain facts that explained all these matters and that laid to rest all the problems [Sofaer] might perceive.'' According to Sofaer, Burns said ''the AG did not give him any facts, and that he was simply passing on the 'mysterious' assurance that all was well.''[74]

After the Casey testimony preparation session, Thompson and Cooper met with Wallison at Wallison's request.[75] According to Wallison, they discussed the summer 1985 TOW shipment by Israel, which, they believed, the United States subsequently condoned:

Under the law this sale—a violation of the AECA—should have been reported to Congress but was not. Neither Cooper nor Thompson could think of any way to justify this lapse, and neither could I, but I suggested that we give some consideration to arguing that when the Israelis told

[65] Ibid., p. 40.

[66] Cooper, Grand Jury, 1/11/88, pp. 55–56.

[67] North, Select Committee Testimony, 7/8/87, p. 93. North's basis for including Meese among those who knew that the United States had approved the November HAWK shipment in advance is unclear.

[68] Sofaer Note, 11/20/86, ALV 000334.

[69] Sofaer Chronology, 5/19/87, ALV 000306.

[70] Ibid.; Sofaer, Select Committees Deposition, 6/18/87, pp. 31–37.

[71] Hill Note, 11/20/86, ANS 0001867 (emphasis in original). Sofaer explained: ''A/G & P[resident] in vulnerable position. A/G gave his opinion—but probably <u>not</u> aware of pre-Jan/post-Aug activities. Yet now is being asked to support such activities. So I tho[ugh]t I'd call the A/G secure. To bring these facts to his attn, because P[resident] doesn't know the facts. And A/G opinion on post-Jan 17 acts as a wash for all arms shipments. Get every channel working to send enzyme into the system to eat away at it.'' (Ibid., ANS 0001867–68.)

[72] Sofaer, Select Committees Deposition, 6/18/87, pp. 37–40.

[73] Ibid., pp. 38–39. Burns could not recall the details of what Sofaer told him, but did not question Sofaer's version. (Burns, FBI 302, 10/29/87, p. 5.)

[74] Sofaer Note, 11/20/86, ALV 000347–48. Burns said that, although he did not understand the information Sofaer had related, he relayed it immediately to Meese. (Burns, FBI 302, 10/29/87, pp. 5–6.) Burns vividly recalls walking upstairs to Meese's office and telling him in person as Meese was preparing to leave for the airport. Meese testified that Burns called him on his car phone while he was en route to Andrews Air Force Base. Meese said he ''advised Mr. Burns that this matter was being taken care of because we just had been going through putting together what was, to the best of my knowledge at that time, an accurate description of what had occurred.'' (Meese, Select Committees Deposition, 7/8/87, p. 67.)

[75] Wallison Note, 11/20/86, ALU 0138235–36, pp. 266–67; Cooper, Grand Jury, 7/15/92, pp. 60–61.

us they had done this, the availability of the channel thus opened made the ensuing events part of an intelligence activity. This was a little farfetched in terms of the real facts, it turned out . . . and so we were thrown back to arguing that under the Const. [Constitution] the Pres. [President] has the inherent power to permit third countries to sell arms without reporting to Cong. [Congress][76]

While the meeting was in progress, Sofaer, unsatisfied with Meese's assurance that all was well, called Wallison to discuss the discrepancy between Casey's proposed testimony and Hill's notes. According to Wallison, Sofaer "was worried that the Pres. [President] had not told the truth last night [at the press conference], and hoped that the Pres. had not been informed fully." Sofaer "then asked . . . whether [Wallison] knew about the sale of Hawk missiles by Israel to Iran in November."[77] When Wallison said he did not, Sofaer told him that McFarlane had informed Shultz in Geneva in November 1985 that Israel would be shipping HAWK missiles to Iran as part of an effort to free the hostages. Sofaer also told Wallison that North had worked with the CIA to arrange for the CIA proprietary airline to deliver the missiles. This, Sofaer said, made Casey's proposed testimony that the CIA did not learn that the cargo was weapons until January 1986 highly dubious and he suggested Wallison "look into it."[78]

According to Sofaer, Wallison was "in shock" after these disclosures.[79] Wallison described his reaction as follows:

Since Cooper and Thompson were sitting right there, I asked them whether they had heard this story, and they confirmed that they had. Of course, if I had not asked they undoubtedly would not have told me voluntarily [sic].

This was perhaps the most serious disclosure of all. It indicates that well before the finding in January 1986 there had been in existence a plan to seek release of all the hostages by trading them for arms to Iran. . . . If the story is true, then everything the Pres. [President] had said about the foundations of our policy was incorrect—if he was aware of these facts. Otherwise, if the Pres. was not aware, there had been a clear violation of the export laws which had not been reported to Congress. One could hardly argue that the Pres. had invoked his constitutional powers when he was not aware of what had been planned.[80]

Cooper recalls that while he knew of the November 1985 HAWK shipment, he was immediately concerned about the accuracy of Casey's proposed testimony that "no one in the USG" learned that the cargo was weapons until January 1986.[81] According to Cooper, upon hearing of Shultz's conversation with McFarlane, he "turned to Paul Thompson and in very manly terms told him that he needed to get with North and McFarlane immediately and clear this up because that obviously was inconsistent with the information that North had just told us in Poindexter's office. . . ."[82]

Cooper then went to his office, where he spoke with Sofaer directly.[83] He told Sofaer that Casey's testimony had been changed to include the broader denial that "no one in the USG" knew that the shipment contained weapons until January 1986. Sofaer told Cooper he knew that assertion was impossible because McFarlane had informed Shultz in November 1985 that the cargo would be HAWK missiles.[84] Cooper asked if Sofaer was certain, and

[76] Ibid., ALU 0138235, p. 266.

[77] Ibid., ALU 0138236, p. 267.

[78] Sofaer, Select Committees Testimony, 6/18/87 pp. 42–43. Sofaer had not yet learned that Casey's testimony had been broadened to say that "no one in the USG" knew the cargo was weapons until January 1986.

[79] Sofaer Chronology, 5/19/87, ALV 000306.

[80] Wallison Note, 11/20/86, p. 267, ALU 0138236.

[81] Cooper, Grand Jury, 7/15/92, pp. 62–63.

[82] Ibid., p. 65.

[83] Cooper, Grand Jury, 7/15/92, p. 65. Sofaer recalled that Wallison passed the phone to Cooper during their meeting and that Sofaer told Cooper what he had told Wallison. (Sofaer, Select Committees Deposition, 6/18/87, pp. 42–43.) He recalls having a second conversation with Cooper at approximately 6:00 p.m. during which they discussed the subject in more detail. (Ibid., pp. 45–49.) Cooper did not recall speaking with Sofaer directly until the second call. (Cooper, Select Committees Testimony, 6/25/87, pp. 59–61.)

[84] Sofaer, Select Committees Deposition, 6/18/87, pp. 47–49. Sofaer also told Cooper that he thought the CIA's version of its involvement in the November HAWK shipment was "untenable as a matter of logic." (Ibid., pp. 43–44.) Sofaer did not believe the CIA would have made such a substantial effort to support a shipment of oil-drilling equipment. He analogized the oil-drilling equipment story to the type of cover story used by drug dealers who never mention drugs by

Sofaer told him of Hill's contemporaneous notes, which indicated that McFarlane specifically told Shultz the cargo was HAWKs. Cooper felt that lent "a lot of credibility" to Shultz's story and that the "gravity of the inconsistency" between Shultz's recollection and the NSC version of events was greatly increased.[85]

Sofaer told Cooper that if Casey's testimony was not corrected, he would advise Armacost to tell Congress there *was* contemporaneous U.S. Government knowledge of the November 1985 HAWK shipment, taking a direct stand against Casey.[86] Sofaer also threatened to resign if Casey's testimony was not corrected. Cooper assured Sofaer that he shared Sofaer's concerns and that he would also resign if Casey gave false testimony to Congress.[87] Cooper then tried to contact Meese.

Meanwhile, Shultz went to the White House late in the afternoon on November 20 with a list of factual errors the President had made in his press conference.[88] In the presence of Regan, Shultz attempted to persuade the President that the public would never believe that the Iran arms sales were not an "arms-for-hostages" swap.[89] Shultz again raised the November 1985 HAWK shipment as an example and argued that the plan McFarlane had outlined to Shultz in Geneva was described expressly as an arms-for-hostages deal.[90] President Reagan responded that he knew about the November 1985 shipment, "but that wasn't arms for hostages."[91]

Cooper finally reached Meese at West Point at 10:30 p.m. and told him about the factual dispute over the HAWKs.[92] According to Meese, Cooper told him "there were concerns in the State Department that there was a good deal more knowledge within the Government about the fact of HAWKS being shipped in November 1985 that was known then than anything we had been led to believe earlier that afternoon."[93] Meese paid attention to Cooper's concerns; Meese agreed that nothing should be said about the HAWK shipment until the facts were clear.[94] Meese told Cooper to contact David Doherty, general counsel of the CIA, and to go to the CIA in the morning to make sure Casey's testimony was changed.[95] At Cooper's urging, Meese decided to return to Washington the next day, cancelling a planned appearance at Harvard University.[96]

After speaking to Poindexter at 11:00 p.m., Cooper called Doherty to tell him to delete the reference in Casey's testimony to U.S. knowledge of the HAWKs shipment; Doherty advised Cooper it already had been deleted.[97] Cooper

name in conversations, referring to them euphemistically as "shirts" or other objects. (Ibid.)

[85] Cooper, Grand Jury, 7/15/92, pp. 65–66.

[86] Cooper, Select Committees Testimony, 6/25/87, p. 64.

[87] Cooper, Grand Jury, 7/15/92, pp. 80–81; Cooper, Select Committees Testimony, 6/25/87, pp. 64–65.

[88] Hill Note, 11/20/86, ALW 0059427. Weinberger, in contrast, noted that he "[w]atched President's press conference" and then "[c]alled President—to congratulate him on his press conference." (Weinberger Note, 11/19/86, ALZ 0040547.)

[89] Hill Note, 11/22/86, ALW 0059429–30.

[90] Ibid.

[91] Ibid. Shultz had briefly met with the President on November 19, before the press conference, but could not recall in his testimony whether he discussed the November 1985 shipment on the 19th or on the 20th. (Shultz, Select Committees Testimony, 7/23/87, pp. 110–12.) Hill's notes of November 19 reflect that Shultz told the President his version of the 1985 HAWK shipment discussions: "Bud once told me about a plane of arms that w[oul]d go if host[a]g[es] released—not if not. P[resident] knew of this—but it didn't come off." (Hill Note, 11/19/86, ANS 0001852.) On November 22, Shultz told Hill "I told P[resident] Thursday [November 20] of what Bud told me about Nov 85. He s[ai]d he knew it. When dug into—will be shown that P[resident] pushed these people." (Hill Note, 11/22/86, ALW

0059428.) When Shultz was interviewed by Meese, he reiterated that story. (Ibid., ALW 005929–30.) Hill's notes thus suggest that Shultz discussed the 1985 HAWK shipment with the President on both November 19 and November 20.

[92] Cooper Chronology, 11/86, ALV 077959.

[93] Meese, Select Committees Testimony, 7/8/87, p. 69.

[94] Although Meese could not recall any specifics about his conversation with Burns, he generally recalled that Burns informed him about "possible inconsistencies or inaccuracies in the proposed testimony of Mr. Casey." (Meese, Select Committees Deposition, 7/8/87, p. 68.) Meese said he "assumed" these "inconsistencies or inaccuracies" had been resolved by the changes and corrections made in the preparation session that afternoon. (Meese, Select Committees Testimony, 7/28/87, p. 68.) It is difficult to believe that Meese could reasonably have thought that any of those changes would have resolved whatever "inconsistency or inaccuracy" could have prompted an urgent call from Sofaer.

In a vague and circular response, Meese explained that the information Cooper gave him "differed—it was much—a whole new area of information that was beyond what *I had assumed* Mr. Burns was telling me because it went beyond the corrections that we had made in the testimony . . . in Mr. Poindexter's office." (Meese, Select Committees Deposition, 7/8/87, p. 72. Emphasis added.) One plausible explanation for Meese's changed reaction could be that Cooper apparently did not think the changes in the testimony made in Poindexter's office had corrected the problem Sofaer had raised. It is worth noting, however, that while Burns apparently did not tell Meese about any documentation of the inaccuracies or inconsistencies Sofaer had mentioned, (Ibid., p. 70,) Cooper told him that the State Department had a contemporaneous note that George Shultz had been informed in November 1985 by McFarlane that there were HAWKs on the shipment. (Cooper, Grand Jury, 7/15/92, p. 66.) As became apparent later in Meese's investigation, deniability of the President's involvement in the November 1985 HAWK shipment could be maintained if there were inconsistencies in memory; a contemporaneous note made it much more difficult.

[95] Meese, Select Committees Deposition, 7/8/87, pp. 74–75; Cooper, Select Committees Testimony, 6/25/87, p. 66.

[96] Ibid., p. 66.

[97] Ibid., pp. 71–72.

then called Sofaer at 11:28 p.m. and told him that Meese shared their concerns about the November 1985 shipment and that Meese had canceled his Boston trip.[98] According to Sofaer's notes, Cooper had "[v]ery many questions about CH's [Charles Hill's] notes. When taken? What written? AG [attorney general] very interested." Cooper told Sofaer that Thompson had spoken to North, who adhered to his story, and that Poindexter had tried to reach McFarlane but had been unable to do so. Cooper told Sofaer that Casey's testimony had been "[a]djusted correctly to avoid [the] issue" of the November 1985 HAWK shipment. Sofaer congratulated Cooper, and they "agreed P[resident] should not be placed at risk till truth is known. Worst outcome is 'self-immolation.' Can deal w/ legal difficulties." [99]

Although the broad assertion that "no one" in the U.S. Government knew about the shipment was deleted from Casey's opening statement to the intelligence committees on November 21, Casey did not disclose that the Administration had participated in the November 1985 HAWK shipment.[100] Casey also failed to disclose the existence of the December 1985 presidential Finding to authorize retroactively CIA participation in the transfer.[101] Casey was well aware of that Finding, which identified the November shipment as an "arms for hostages" deal, because he had sent it to Poindexter for President Reagan's signature.[102]

## Developing a "Coherent Overview"

On Friday morning, November 21, 1986, Meese returned to Washington and met with Cooper, Burns, Assistant Attorney General William Bradford Reynolds, and chief of staff John Richardson.[103] According to Cooper, the group discussed the plan he and Meese had agreed to on the night before over the phone: that

Meese would meet with the President and offer to take responsibility to investigate "the President's, the Government's knowledge" of the Iran arms sales "as accurately as possible, and completely as possible in as short a period of time as possible before some error was made." [104] During the meeting, Cooper made a preliminary list of persons to interview— McFarlane, Shultz, Sporkin, North, Poindexter, Weinberger, Vice President Bush, President Reagan, Regan, and Casey.[105]

Cooper took only two notes from his morning meeting with Meese: "Any legal problems. Are there other facts that would raise crim[inal] problems." [106] Cooper testified that there was a general concern about legal problems, including possible crimes. Cooper, at least, believed at that time that North and Poindexter had known that "there were HAWKs on the plane" and that the day before, "they were saying something to me and others in the room that they knew to be untrue and were suggesting that information should go to Congress." [107]

Meese, on the other hand, denied that the legality of the November HAWK shipment was a concern in his investigation. He testified that his inquiry was premised on the "assumption that everything was legal," and he did not "believe the question of legality ever came up until the memorandum was found [on November 22] regarding the diversion." Asked when the issue of the legality of the November HAWK shipment arose, Meese responded, "I don't know that it ever did come up." [108]

---

98 Sofaer Note, 11/20/86, ALV 000350.

99 Ibid.

100 Casey, SSCI Testimony, 11/21/86, pp. 8–9, 31–32; HPSCI Testimony, 11/21/86, pp. 5–7.

101 Poindexter later testified that it was on this day that he destroyed the December 1985 Finding because it described a straight arms-for-hostages exchange and would be politically embarrassing. (Poindexter, Select Committees Testimony, 7/15/87, pp. 44, 123.)

102 Poindexter, Select Committees Deposition, 6/17/87, pp. 370–71.

103 Cooper, Grand Jury, 7/15/92, pp. 73–77; Meese Schedule, 11/21/86, ALV 080343.

104 Cooper, Grand Jury, 7/15/92 pp. 73–76.

105 Cooper Note, 11/21/86, ALV 077958; Cooper, Grand Jury, 7/15/92, pp. 77–78. Cooper was not certain whether he made his list before the meeting or during it, but it reflected his thoughts about "who should be talked to and roughly the order in which they should be talked to." (Ibid. pp. 77–78.)

106 Cooper Note, 11/21/86, ALV 077958.

107 Cooper, Grand Jury, 7/15/92 pp. 78–82. Cooper had previously testified, when not confronted with his note, that while there was concern about contemporaneous knowledge by U.S. officials of the HAWK shipment, there was no concern about possible criminal violations. (Cooper, FBI 302, 1/6/88, p. 8; Cooper, Select Committees Deposition, 6/22/87 p. 126 (not a "suggestion or hint" of criminal violation at that point).)

108 Meese, OIC Interview, 5/11/92 pp. 35–36. Cooper had taken a similar position before being confronted with his contemporaneous notes. At the 8:30 a.m. staff meeting on November 21, 1986, which Meese did not attend because his flight did not arrive from West Point until 8:30, the third item on the agenda was "Iran—> Legality—" (Meeting Agenda, 11/21/86, ALV 033705.) John Richardson, Meese's chief of staff and one of the three trusted aides Meese chose to conduct the weekend investigation, explained, "The big problem for us was what laws might have been kicked in to

While Meese was meeting with his staff, Regan was meeting with Wallison, who had been alarmed by Sofaer's revelation that McFarlane had briefed Shultz about the November 1985 HAWK shipment in advance.[109] Wallison told Regan that this shipment "raised serious legal questions because a shipment like that would either have to be reported as a shipment by the US or as a violation of the AECA by Israel, and neither was done."[110]

After conferring with his staff, Meese met with the President, Poindexter, and Regan at 11:30 a.m. at the White House.[111] Meese explained that a problem had arisen with Casey's proposed testimony because "the CIA was doing some things, the Department of Defense was doing other things, the NSC staff had certain responsibilities, and so on, and because of the highly compartmentalized nature of the whole initiative . . . people had not talked to each other, you did not have the normal documentation and reporting, and . . . therefore there was a great deal of confusion . . ."[112] Meese told the President it was "absolutely necessary" that "someone look into the matter . . . to develop a coherent overview of the facts," and offered to do it himself.[113] The President accepted Meese's offer to "look into the matter," and asked him to report his findings at a senior advisers meeting set for November 24, 1986.[114]

Meese said he did not ask President Reagan—or Poindexter or Regan—about his knowledge of the arms sales because it "didn't seem very important" at that stage of the inquiry. Cooper testified, however, that he and Meese had "resolved" in their telephone conversation the night before that Meese "was going to go in and talk to the President *about*

*the state of the President's, the Government's knowledge of the Iran matter* and advise him that somebody needed to take responsibility for . . . collecting the facts as accurately and completely as possible."[115] Cooper included President Reagan on his list of persons to interview,[116] but Meese, on a similar list, did not.[117] In Cooper's mind, what the President knew about the November HAWK shipment and when he knew it was a "primary concern" of the investigation at that point.[118] Meese, however, has testified that he never got around to asking the President what he knew about the HAWK shipment.[119]

At 12:30 p.m., following his meeting with the President, Meese returned to the Justice Department, where he met over lunch with his investigative team, all trusted political appointees—Cooper, Reynolds and Richardson.[120] Meese wrote down a list of people to be interviewed, including McFarlane, Shultz, North, Thompson, Weinberger, Vice President Bush, and a number of CIA officials who had been involved in the November 1985 shipment. On a separate list entitled "Action," Meese listed questions to ask various people. Next to Poindexter's initials, Meese wrote "Every document, telephone logs, etc.[;] Contact person— Paul Thompson?[; and] What did GPS [(Shultz)] give to or show RR [Ronald Reagan]?" Later that afternoon, Meese telephoned Poindexter and checked off each of the three questions.[121]

Poindexter later testified that following this conversation with Meese, Poindexter called Paul Thompson and asked him to pull together the Iran documents. Later that afternoon, Thompson showed Poindexter the December 1985 Finding signed by the President, which sought to retroactively authorize the CIA's involvement in the November HAWK shipment. Poindexter then

---

focus or violated by the Administration by shipping these arms in '85, before there was a Finding in '86, and that was the entire focus [of the investigation], whether the U.S. Government knew about it and authorized it." (Richardson, Grand Jury, 12/11/87, p. 43.)

[109] Wallison Note, 11/20/86, p. 268, ALU 0138237.

[110] Ibid.

[111] Meese, Select Committees Testimony, 7/28/87 pp. 75–76; Meese Schedule, 11/21/86, ALV 080343.

[112] Ibid., p. 76.

[113] Ibid., pp. 76–77. Meese maintains that he was not acting in his capacity as attorney general in conducting an investigation, but rather was operating as any other Cabinet member might in compiling a factual "overview." (Meese, OIC interview, 5/11/92, p. 36.) In the *North* trial, Meese testified that he was acting as the President's counselor and friend. (Meese, *North* Trial Testimony, 3/28/89, pp. 5746–47.)

[114] Ibid., pp. 77–78.

[115] Cooper, Select Committees Deposition, 6/22/87, p. 122 (emphasis added); Cooper, Grand Jury, 7/15/92, pp. 75–76.

[116] Cooper Note, 11/21/86, ALV 077958.

[117] Meese Note, 11/21/86, ALV 015778.

[118] Cooper, Grand Jury testimony, 7/15/92, p. 94.

[119] Meese, OIC interview, 5/11/92, p. 72.

[120] The choice of political appointees reflected Meese's concern that the President's "political opponents . . . might try to claim that there was some kind of a cover-up and that would be a position of vulnerability even though there was absolutely no cover-up going on." (Meese, *North* Trial Testimony, 3/29/89, pp. 5854–55.)

[121] Meese Note, 11/21/86, ALV 015779; Meese, Select Committees Testimony, 7/28/87, pp. 82–84.

destroyed the only known signed version of that Finding.[122]

Meanwhile, McFarlane, who apparently had learned that the State Department had contemporaneous records relating to the November 1985 shipment, called Sofaer. Sofaer confirmed that the State Department had such records but did not disclose their contents. McFarlane asked whether Sofaer had given the records to the Justice Department, and Sofaer responded that he "had passed on some alleged facts to protect P[resident]." Sofaer advised McFarlane to keep all his records, and McFarlane agreed.[123]

Cooper called Sofaer at 3:00 p.m. to confirm that the President had authorized Meese to investigate. Cooper asked Sofaer to provide him with "all info." Charles Hill, who distrusted Meese, was reluctant to relinquish his notes to Cooper, but Sofaer told him he had no choice.[124] Hill was also concerned that Sofaer's disclosure of Hill's November 18, 1985, note, revealing a planned "arms-hostages swap" before the January 17, 1986, Finding, could "be read as GPS [Shultz] fingering McF[arlane] for something that c[oul]d get him prison."[125]

At 3:30 p.m., Cooper and Meese interviewed McFarlane. According to Cooper's notes of the interview, McFarlane told Cooper and Meese that he thought "he first learned of [the November 1985 HAWK shipment] when briefed for trip to Iran in May [1986]. Iran sent back HAWKs be/[cause] couldn't reach hi-altitude bomber. N[orth]—briefed M[cFarlane]—he was action-officer on this beginning Oct or Nov." The notes indicate that McFarlane then told Meese that he learned in Geneva on November 17 or 18, 1985, "that Isr[ael] had shipped oil equipment." McFarlane claimed Israeli Defense Minister "Rabine [sic] called from N.Y. and said they have problem w/ shipmt to Iran" and McFarlane asked North "to assist." McFarlane said North reported that the shipment "hit snag in customs in [a European country]," and McFarlane subsequently called the European officials to ask for assistance. McFarlane, according to Cooper's notes, said he "remember[ed] no mention in all this of arms" and "doesn't remember chat w/ GS [George Shultz], but probably had one."[126]

At the end of the interview, Cooper left and McFarlane and Meese had a brief private conversation. Meese testified that McFarlane "said something to the effect that I have been taking a lot of this on my shoulders[127] . . . but I want you to know—it was something to the effect he wanted me to know that the President was generally in favor of pursuing the Israelis' ideas all along."[128] Meese said he responded by telling McFarlane to "not try to think how to protect the President, just tell exactly what happened." Meese added, "I think I said something like 'If the President knew earlier, it might even be helpful as a legal matter . . .'"[129]

Cooper's notes do not reflect any question or answer regarding what McFarlane told the President about the November 1985 HAWK shipment. Cooper testified that because the President's knowledge of the November 1985 shipment was a "primary concern" at that point of the investigation, it would have been "logical" to ask McFarlane whether he had told the President about the shipment.[130] Meese, who testified that "what the President knew was not an issue at that time,"[131] said he did not ask McFarlane about what he had told the President about the November 1985 shipment.[132]

Following his interview, McFarlane sent a computer note to Poindexter stating:

[i]t appears that the matter of not notifying about the Israeli transfers can be covered

122 Poindexter, Select Committees Deposition, 5/2/87, p. 108.

123 Sofaer Chronology, 5/17/87, ALV 000308. Sofaer testified that he "assumed" McFarlane had learned of the Hill note from Meese during a Meese-McFarlane interview on November 21. (Sofaer, Select Committee Deposition, 6/18/87, p. 62.) Sofaer's chronology, however, places the call from McFarlane before 3:00 p.m., while McFarlane's interview with Meese did not begin until 3:30 p.m.

124 Sofaer Chronology, 5/17/87, ALV 000308; Hill Note, 11/21/86, ANS 0001878–79. Hill, who was traveling with Shultz to Canada on the 21st, wrote in his opening observations for the day that "Casey testimony has been changed. With recognition that Nov 85 shipment illegal, CIA & NSC both trying to say they didn't manage it—& didn't know what was in it." (Hill Note, 11/21/86, ANS 0001873.) Recording a report of the congressional briefings later that day, Hill noted "Leahy focusing on Nov '85 flt [flight] & why no one knew cargo." (Hill Note, 11/21/86, ANS 0001877, emphasis in original.)

125 Hill Note, 11/21/86, ANS 0001879.

126 Cooper Note, 11/21/86, ALV 071809–10 (emphasis in original).

127 McFarlane had by that time already made public statements in which he took responsibility for the Administration's Iran policy. (Cooper, Grand Jury, 8/5/92, p. 11.)

128 Meese, Select Committee Testimony, 7/28/87, pp. 92–93.

129 Meese, OIC Interview, 5/11/92, p. 60.

130 Cooper, Grand Jury, 7/15/92, pp. 94–95.

131 Meese, OIC Interview, 5/11/92, pp. 37–38.

132 Cooper, Grand Jury, 7/15/92, p. 101. Cooper thought McFarlane was "overwrought and nervous" and did not believe his story. (Ibid., p. 106.)

if the President made a "mental finding" before the transfers took place. Well on that score we ought to be ok because he was all for letting the Israelis do anything they wanted at the very first briefing in the hospital. Ed seemed relieved at that.[133]

Meese testified, however, that he did not recall having discussed the concept of an oral or mental finding with McFarlane.[134]

Cooper called Sofaer at about 6:30 p.m. to arrange an interview with Shultz the following morning. When Sofaer called Shultz to schedule the interview, Shultz told Sofaer that he had received a message that McFarlane had asked Shultz to call him.[135] Sofaer advised Shultz against talking to McFarlane because it could "create an appearance that he is Coordinating his position with you" and "cause the A.G. [attorney general] to feel that he is not getting your views without any effects that might result from a discussion with McFarlane."[136] Shultz spoke to Hill at 8:00 p.m., apparently to tell him about the interview with Meese the next morning. Hill suggested to Shultz that "Meese wants to see [you] to get the info on Nov '85 to show—this weekend—that P[resident] was mislead [sic]. So he can tell P[resident] on Monday."[137] Hill testified that this comment reflected his suspicion that Meese had an agenda to insulate the President from responsibility for the November 1985 shipment.[138]

Meese called Weinberger at 7:00 that evening. Weinberger wrote in his diary notes: "Ed Meese [called]—President has asked him to put together paper covering whole Iran Episode."[139] Meese later testified that he determined quickly that Weinberger (whose department was responsible for producing the weapons) could not contribute much information and that there was no need to interview him fur-

ther.[140] Contrary to Meese's conclusion, Weinberger had much valuable information, none of which was discovered until 1991, when the OIC uncovered thousands of pages of Weinberger's daily notes and high-level meeting notes.[141]

At 7:30 a.m. on Saturday, November 22, before the interview with Meese, Shultz and Hill met at the State Department. Shultz told Hill: "I told P[resident] Thursday [November 20] of what Bud [McFarlane] told me about Nov 85. He s[ai]d he knew it. When dug into—will be shown that P[resident] pushed these people."[142]

The Shultz interview began at 8:05 a.m. Present were Shultz, Hill, Meese, and Cooper. Hill and Cooper took notes. According to Hill's notes of the interview, Meese remarked, "Abe's [Sofaer's] intervention fortuitous. Key revolving around Nov 85. 18 Hawks from Isr[ael] to Ir[an]. Then returned in Feb 86. I understand y[ou] had talk w[ith] Bud [McFarlane] about it." Shultz told Meese that during the summit in Geneva on November 18, 1985, McFarlane told him about deal in which HAWK missiles would go to Iran and the hostages would be released. Hill, who stepped in to provide additional detail, described it as a "complex deal" with the arms routed through an Asian country and the hostages coming out before the arms were delivered to Iran.[143] At that point, Cooper's notes record Meese as interjecting, "[I] recall vaguely that the plan described, perhaps at Jan 7 [1986] meeting, was to not provide any arms until the hostages were released."[144]

After the interjection by Meese, Shultz began again: "You sh[oul]d know I went to P[resident] Thurs. night [November 20]. Asked to go see him. Went w[ith] DR [Regan] to family qtrs. . . . And I described Bud [McFarlane] talk to me in Geneva. P[resident] s[ai]d oh I kn [knew or know] about that— but that wasn't arms for hostg! I sd [said] no one looking at the record will believe that."[145]

[133] PROFs Note from McFarlane to Poindexter, 11/21/86, AKW 019148. McFarlane relayed a similar message to North by telephone immediately after the interview. (McFarlane, Select Committees Deposition, 7/2/87, p. 11; North Note, 11/21/86, AMX 001707.)

[134] Meese, Select Committees Testimony, 7/29/87, p. 12.

[135] Sofaer Chronology, 5/17/87, ALV 000308; Hill Note, 11/21/86, ANS 0001878. It appears from Hill's notes that McFarlane called before his interview with Meese.

[136] Memorandum from Sofaer to Shultz, 11/21/86, ALV 000358; see also Hill Note, 11/21/86, ANS 0001879 (note of 5:20 pm conversation with Sofaer).

[137] Hill Note, 11/21/86, ANS 0001880.

[138] Hill, Grand Jury, 7/10/92, pp. 157–60.

[139] Weinberger Note, 11/21/86, ALZ 0040553.

[140] Meese, OIC Interview, 5/11/92, pp. 61–64.

[141] See Weinberger section of report.

[142] Hill Note, 11/22/86, ALW 0059428.

[143] Ibid., ANS 0001882; Cooper Note, 11/22/86, ALV 071839. Cooper, Grand Jury, 8/5/92, p. 65.

[144] Cooper Note, 11/22/86, ALV 071839.

[145] Hill Note, 11/22/86, ANS 0001883. Cooper, who also took notes, recorded Shultz statement as "G.S. advised that M. [McFarlane] came to G.S. + told of deal. Pres. said he knew of it—but didn't understand

Meese, who has repeatedly claimed that he never asked the President about his knowledge of the November 1985 shipment,[146] responded that the "P[resident] didn't make notes. He had trouble remembering mtgs [meetings]." Meese then asked, "[a]s to Nov [November 1985] talk with Bud, no contact y[ou] know of that Bud had w[ith] P[resident] then?" Shultz replied, "not to my knowledge. Tho[ugh] I don't know."[147]

Later in the interview, having established that (1) Shultz did not know whether McFarlane had told the President in November 1985 about the HAWK shipment, and (2) whatever the President had said to Shultz on Thursday night was suspect because the President "didn't make notes" and "had trouble remembering mtgs," Meese told Shultz that "[c]ertain things c[oul]d be violation of a law. P[resident] didn't know about HAWKs in Nov[ember 1985]. If it happened & P[resident] didn't report to Congress, it's a violation."[148]

Cooper's notes include Shultz's statement that the President knew about the November 1985 HAWK shipment, but they omit Meese's remarks regarding legality and the President's knowledge. Cooper's notes generally track Hill's, but are less detailed: "G.S. [George Shultz] advised [President Reagan] that M[cFarlane] came to GS & told of deal[.] Pres. said he knew of it—but didn't understand it as arms for hostages, but as part of larger plan."[149] Cooper resisted interpreting his and Hill's notes as meaning that the President had said he knew of the November HAWK shipment. Even though he conceded that the entire discussion to that point in the interview concerned the November HAWK shipment and that the topic of discussion after Shultz's statement that the "Pres. said he knew of it" was the HAWK shipment, Cooper maintained that the "it" the President knew of was the Iran arms sales plan generally, not the HAWK shipment specifically.[150] According to Cooper, it would

have struck him like a "lightning bolt" if he had understood Shultz to be saying that the President had said he knew about the November 1985 HAWK shipment. Cooper added, however, that he would have taken such a revelation "with some grain of salt" because the President could be forgetful.[151] Ultimately, Cooper conceded that the "logical" interpretation of his and Hill's notes was that Shultz had told Meese that the President said he knew about the HAWK shipment in advance.[152]

Hill and Shultz told Sofaer, Nicholas Platt, Armacost, and Whitehead about the interview immediately afterward.[153] Shultz first asked Sofaer to clarify his role: Was he the President's lawyer or Shultz's lawyer? Sofaer responded that he could serve both Shultz and the President and explained that he felt an obligation to come forward with "info if indicates someone broke the law." Drawing an analogy to Watergate, Sofaer told Shultz he could not simply "step away from" evidence of wrongdoing by other officials "just bec[ause] y[ou] are a nice guy."[154] Shultz replied that he had "no trouble w[ith] being completely open about any possible violation of law," but he did have reservations about "dealing w[ith] the W[ite]H[ouse] in circ[umstance]s like this." Shultz recounted how Poindexter had provided certain false information in the November 10, 1986, meeting and cautioned Sofaer to "be careful" about providing information to the White House.[155]

Sofaer assured Shultz that "[i]n terms of the law you are out of it," but "[t]he P[resident] is in the hands of people who are lying." Shultz noted that "P[resident] says that A/G [attorney general] sh[oul]d find out if people telling him things that not true. But it is that people telling him wrong characterization. . . ." Hill remarked "[t]he P[resident] just discovered the way out—he was mislead [sic]."[156]

Shultz directed Hill to review with Sofaer his notes of the Meese interview. Hill's notes of the briefing quote Sofaer as saying, "when

---

it as arms for hostages, but as part of larger plan." (Cooper Note, 11/21/86, ALV 071840.)

[146] Meese, OIC Interview, 5/11/92, p. 41.

[147] Hill Note, 11/22/86, ANS 0001883. Meese's question to Shultz is noteworthy in light of Meese's failure to ask McFarlane directly whether he had informed President Reagan of the November 1985 HAWK shipment.

[148] Ibid., ANS 0001888.

[149] Cooper Note, 11/22/86, ALV 071840.

[150] Cooper, Grand Jury, 8/5/92, pp. 105–08.

[151] Ibid., pp. 83–85.

[152] Ibid., pp. 82, 95.

[153] Sofaer's notes indicate that he had been excluded because Platt and Hill believed that Sofaer was acting as the President's lawyer rather than protecting the State Department's interests.

[154] Hill Note, 11/22/86, ANS 0001890–91.

[155] Ibid., ANS 0001891.

[156] Ibid., ANS 0001892.

I told Meese about what you told me about McF[arlane] talk w[ith] S[hultz] in Geneva Nov 85, Meese told the P[resident] who said 'I didn't know about that. I never approved it.' "[157]

While Meese and Cooper were conducting interviews, Reynolds and Richardson were reviewing documents at the NSC. On the morning of November 22, 1986, they discovered in North's office files a memorandum that indicated that profits from the arms sales to Iran had been diverted to aid the contras. Reynolds and Richardson informed Meese of their discovery over lunch at the Old Ebbitt Grill.[158] At this point, the focus of the Meese inquiry became twofold: The continuing investigation of the HAWKs, and the question of whether an Iran/contra diversion had occurred and who had known about and approved it.

After lunch, Meese and Cooper interviewed former CIA General Counsel Stanley Sporkin about the HAWK shipments.[159] This interview apparently was the first detailed account Meese and Cooper received of the existence of a retroactive Finding for the November 1985 HAWK shipment, which Sporkin had drafted. According to Cooper's notes, Sporkin disclosed that the "two guys from operations" at the CIA who had briefed him shortly after the shipment told him the operation was, in essence, an arms-for-hostages trade; Sporkin said the draft Finding reflected that fact. Sporkin's interview therefore made clear that CIA officials knew at the time of the November 1985 shipment, or at least immediately thereafter, that the shipment contained weapons, not oil-drilling equipment as had been claimed in the NSC chronology and in Casey's original draft testimony. Cooper's handwritten notes of the Sporkin interview do not reflect whether Sporkin told them the Finding had been signed. Although Sporkin told Meese that the purpose of the December 1985 draft Finding was "to ratify anything that had already been done," Meese did not ask whether the President had signed the Finding to make it effective.[160]

Following the Sporkin interview, Cooper arranged to meet with the two men from the CIA Operations Directorate who had briefed Sporkin shortly after the 1985 HAWKs shipment. Cooper spent the evening at the CIA conducting additional interviews.[161]

On Sunday, November 23, from 2:00 p.m. to 5:45 p.m., Meese, Cooper, Richardson, and Reynolds interviewed North at the Justice Department. A list of questions drafted by Cooper aide John McGinniss focused on the November 1985 HAWK shipment. McGinniss's questions for North contained a section titled "Presidential Knowledge" that included five questions covering the President's knowledge and approval of the HAWK shipment, whether any legal advice had been sought regarding the requirements of the Arms Export Control Act, and whether the President had made a decision not to report the shipment.[162] As in his interview of McFarlane, Meese apparently did not ask North about the President's knowledge of the November HAWK shipment.

It was in this interview that Meese, in addition to questioning North about the arms sales, planned to confront him with the Iran/contra diversion memo that had been found in North's office the day before.

Meese opened by cautioning North that the "[w]orst thing [that] can happen is if someone try to conceal something to protect selves, RR [Reagan], put good spin on it. Want nothing anyone can call a coverup." North nevertheless dissembled about his knowledge that the November 1985 shipment contained HAWK missiles. North claimed that Rabin told him the shipment contained "oil related equipment," and he only learned later, from retired U.S. Air Force Maj. Gen. Richard V. Secord, that the shipment contained HAWK missiles.[163] North said he informed the CIA in late November or early December 1985 that the shipment had contained "arms + not oil drilling equipment."[164]

[157] Ibid., ANS 0001893. Sofaer testified that he never spoke directly with Meese on this issue, but dealt only with Cooper. He could not recall making the statement to Hill. (Sofaer, OIC Interview, 9/29/92, pp. 49–50.) On November 25, 1986, Hill's notes indicate that Sofaer said he "got [the] impression from Meese" that the P[resident] "didn't know" about the November 1985 HAWK shipment. To which Shultz responded, "Everybody running away from it." (Hill Note, 11/25/86, ANS 0001920.)

[158] Meese, Select Committees Testimony, 7/28/87, pp. 105–6.

[159] Cooper Chronology, ALV 077961.

[160] Cooper Note, 11/22/86, ALV 071859–61.

[161] Cooper Chronology, ALV 077961.

[162] "Questions for Oliver North," ALV 014311–13.

[163] Richardson Note, 11/23/86, ALV 071893–94.

[164] Ibid., ALV 014607.

North denied knowledge of a retroactive Finding authorizing specifically "for Hawks or future Hawks," explaining there had been "one draft re: all previous acts" that had been worked on in mid-December 1985. Meese apparently did not ask, and North did not volunteer, whether a Finding covering "all previous acts" had ever been signed.[165] North seemed to suggest it had been, however, by stating "someone ought to step up and say this [the shipment] was authorized in Nov."

As in his interview with Shultz, Meese contradicted North at one point, disagreeing with North's assertion that President Reagan was not motivated by the desire to establish a strategic relationship with Iran but rather "wanted the hostages." Meese insisted that Reagan "talked about both." [166] Meese told North, "Concern protect RR [Reagan] but we need to know facts." [167]

North recognized the seriousness of the HAWKs issue, even after being confronted with the diversion memo. North confirmed for Meese that an Iran/contra diversion had taken place, and told Meese that the only other U.S. Government officials who knew of it were Poindexter and McFarlane. North said: "If this [the diversion] doesn't come out, only other [problem] is the Nov. Hawks deal." [168]

After an hour of questioning North, Meese left the interview. Cooper, Richardson and Reynolds remained and there was further discussion of "who knew 508/Hawks?" and of the contradictions between Shultz and McFarlane's memories of their conversation in Geneva in November 1985.[169] By this point, however, at least Cooper was convinced that Shultz was telling the truth and that the President knew of, and may have approved, the pre-Finding shipments.[170]

From 9:00 a.m.–10:15 a.m., on Monday, November 24, Cooper met with Sofaer and Hill at the State Department, and Hill read Cooper a chronology of Shultz-State Department knowledge of the arms sales, prepared from Hill's notes. Hill's chronology revealed not only that McFarlane had told Shultz of the November 1985 HAWK shipment in advance but also that Poindexter had called Shultz on December 5, 1985, and told him that the shipment had "misfir[ed]" when Iran rejected the arms as too old. According to Hill's chronology, Poindexter also said he had gone to the President and urged him to stop the operation, "but the President did not want to stop." [171]

Meese, meanwhile, met privately with McFarlane from 10:00 a.m. to 10:30 a.m. on Monday, November 24, 1986, to question him about the diversion. McFarlane confirmed that North had told him about the diversion. Meese did not take notes of the interview. After the interview, McFarlane prepared a three-page letter for Meese in which he set forth his views on the Iran situation and on U.S.-Soviet relations. With respect to the Iran arms sales, McFarlane wrote, "I have written an accurate description of those events that that [sic] I believe might meet with the President's approval. I will be glad to pass it along if you wish." [172] According to McFarlane, Meese never requested a copy of the "accurate description" and McFarlane never provided it.[173]

After questioning McFarlane on November 24, Meese went to the White House to meet with Regan and President Reagan. Regan and Meese have given inconsistent testimony as to whether Meese advised President Reagan of the diversion during this morning meeting or simply alerted him to the fact that the weekend investigation had turned up evidence they needed to discuss. Meese also met privately with Vice President Bush some time before the 2:00 p.m. senior advisers' meeting where Meese was to report the findings of his investigation. Meese took no notes of the discussion but he has testified that they discussed the diversion, and Vice

165 Ibid., ALV 014612. The draft of the December 1985 retroactive Finding that survives approves "[a]ll prior actions" involving trading "munitions" to Iran to "obtain the release of Americans held hostage in the Middle East." ALV 014320.

166 Richardson Note, 11/23/86, ALV 014619.

167 Ibid., ALV 014618.

168 Ibid., ALV 014625.

169 The "508" appears to be a reference to the 504 TOW missiles transferred to Iran in August and September 1985. The "Hawks" refers to the November 1985 shipment.

170 Cooper, Grand Jury, 8/5/92, p. 124.

171 Cooper Note, ALV 071943–45; Hill handwritten chronology ALW 50566 (prepared 11/8/86).

172 Letter from McFarlane to Meese, 11/24/86, ALV 049175. Although the letter is not dated, McFarlane told the OIC that after his morning interview with Meese, he prepared the letter and dropped it off at Meese's house.

173 Untranscribed OIC interview of McFarlane. McFarlane could not recall what he stated in the "accurate description" of events. He did not retain a copy of the description. (McFarlane, OIC Interview, 10/2/92.)

President Bush indicated that he hadn't known about it.[174]

## The Senior Advisers' Meeting

The senior advisers' meeting on the afternoon of November 24, 1986, included President Reagan, Vice President Bush, Shultz, Weinberger, Meese, Casey, Regan, and Poindexter. The discussion began with a review of the Iran arms sales by CIA official George Cave, who left the meeting after his presentation. In the second portion of the meeting, Meese did not announce the discovery of the diversion; he did, however, talk about the November 1985 HAWK shipment.

According to Weinberger's notes of the meeting, Donald Regan asked whether "we object[ed] to" the November 1985 HAWK shipment.[175] Poindexter falsely responded that, before December 7, 1985, McFarlane handled the Iran arms sales "all alone" with "no documentation."[176]

Meese then told the group that McFarlane had outlined the planned shipment to Shultz in Geneva in November 1985, and briefly recounted how the shipment had gone awry, resulting in the missiles being returned to Israel in February 1986. According to Weinberger's notes, Meese advised the group that the shipment was "[n]ot legal because no Finding," but "President not informed."[177] Regan's notes similarly show that Meese stated "[m]ay be a violation of law if arms shipped w/o [without] a Finding But Pres[ident] did not know—Cap [Weinberger] denies knowing. Israelis may have done this . . . probably using Pres' [President's] name."[178] Regan's notes also reflect

Meese saying that the "Pres. [President] only told may be hostages out in short order."[179]

Assuming Meese testified truthfully when he said he did not discuss the November 1985 HAWK shipment with the President,[180] there appeared to be no factual basis for his statement. Meese's assertion that the President did not know of the November HAWK shipment directly contradicted the information Shultz had provided Meese in their Saturday interview, as well as McFarlane's assertion to Meese that the President supported and approved the arms sales from the beginning in the summer of 1985, and North's similar assertion regarding the HAWKs shipment specifically.

Cooper, who did not attend the November 24 senior advisers' meeting, had concluded from the weekend investigation that the President knew of the HAWK shipment and may have even approved it.[181] According to Cooper, however, he and Meese did not discuss their respective conclusions about the President's knowledge of the HAWK shipment.[182] He said they did not discuss what Meese would say at the senior advisers' meeting in reporting on the investigation.[183] Cooper said he felt there was no point in sharing his thoughts and conclusions with Meese because they had together interviewed McFarlane, Shultz, and North, so Meese knew what Cooper knew.[184]

In addition to Shultz and Meese, virtually everyone else present at the senior advisers meeting knew or should have known that Meese's claim that the President was "not informed" was false, but no one corrected Meese. Meese concluded the meeting by asking, "anyone know anything else that hasn't been revealed."[185] Again, no one had anything to add.

174 Bush Diary, 11/24/86, ALU 0140210; Meese, Select Committees Testimony, 7/29/87, pp. 119–20.

175 Weinberger Note, 11/24/86, ALZ 0040669KK. Regan had called Wallison into his office on the afternoon of the 21st to tell him that Meese had been asked to investigate the Iran arms sales. Regan gave Wallison a copy of the NSC chronology of the arms sales, prepared by North, and asked Wallison to review it and provide Regan with a list of questions to ask at the November 24 senior advisers' meeting. Wallison's memorandum, which he delivered to Regan at home on Friday night, focused on what the President knew about the November 1985 HAWK shipment and when he knew it. (See Regan chapter.)

176 Weinberger Note, 11/24/86, ALZ 0040669LL. As mentioned earlier, Poindexter on November 21 had destroyed the signed 1985 Finding that sought to retroactively authorize the HAWKs shipment.

177 Ibid., ALZ 0040669LL–MM (emphasis in original).

178 Regan Note, 11/24/86, ALU 0139379.

179 Ibid., ALU 0139378.

180 Meese, OIC Interview, 5/11/92, p. 41.

181 Cooper, Grand Jury, 8/5/92, p. 124.

182 Ibid., p. 128.

183 Ibid., pp. 130–31.

184 Ibid., p. 128.

185 Regan Note, 11/24/86, ALU 0139383. President Reagan had told Shultz and Regan only a few days earlier that he knew about the November 1985 shipment. Regan had not only been present for that conversation but had also been present when McFarlane briefed the President about the plan on two separate occasions in November 1985. McFarlane told Weinberger in November 1985 that the President has decided to implement the transaction through the Israelis. Casey and Poindexter both knew at least that President Reagan had attempted in December 1985 to validate retroactively the CIA's support for an arms-for-hostages transaction. Vice President Bush later said he had been present for a national security briefing in 1985 at which McFarlane explained the HAWK shipment.

In addition, although Meese had informed at least Vice President Bush and Regan and President Reagan of the diversion by this time, no one apparently wanted to discuss that information in the group.

Shultz had remarked to Hill in the morning, before the senior advisers' meeting: "They may lay all this off on Bud [McFarlane]. That won't be enough." [186] Reporting to his aides after the senior advisers' meeting, Shultz said it "was the damndest meeting." Shultz, who had expected Meese to report fully on his weekend inquiry, said Meese had "s[ai]d nothing" at the meeting. Shultz was astounded that the meeting had instead addressed the possibility of continuing the ill-fated arms-sale plan. Shultz characterized President Reagan as "v[ery] hot under the collar + determined he is totally right." [187]

Shultz also reported to Hill after the meeting that Poindexter said "McF[arlane] ran it all by himself until Dec 4 '85 + no one knows what he did. I s[ai]d I know something of what he did. An Aug. 85 mtg w P[resident] + me + Bud [McFarlane]. Bud sd all deniable. I sd impossible. They rearranging the record." [188] Shultz added that the President is "now saying he didn't know anything about Bud's Nov '85 activities"—in contrast to what the President had told Shultz just four days earlier.[189] Hill hypothesized that the White House was carrying out "thru Meese" a "carefully thought out strategy" to insulate the President and "blame it on Bud [McFarlane]." [190]

At his November 25, 1986, press conference—in which he announced the diversion of profits from the Iran arms sales to the Nicaraguan contras—Meese reiterated the false story that the President did not learn of the November 1985 HAWK shipment until February 1986.[191] He did not, however, publicly state the conclusion he had shared privately first with Shultz

and later at the senior advisers' meeting—that the November 1985 HAWK shipment was illegal because there was no Finding. In fact, he now declared all the shipments "legal." [192]

In response to a question regarding the propriety of Shultz's public criticism of the arms sales, Meese stated at the press briefing: "I think every member of the administration owes it to the President to stand shoulder-to-shoulder with him and support the policies that he has—the policy decisions he has made[.]" [193]

## Was There a Cover-Up?

Although the Select Iran/contra Committees questioned Meese closely in 1987 about his November 21–24, 1986 inquiry, they did not question him about his remarks regarding the HAWK shipment at the November 24 meeting. Their focus was on the Iran/contra diversion. The Select Committees had only two contemporaneous records of the meeting—Meese's notes and Hill's notes of Shultz's recollections immediately after the meeting. Meese's notes reflect Regan's question about the HAWK shipment and Poindexter's initial response, but they omit Meese's own lengthy presentation as to illegality and President Reagan's lack of knowledge. Hill's November 24, 1986 notes, which show that Shultz and his aides were concerned that the White House was presenting an inaccurate account of the November 1985 shipment, apparently were never explored fully by the Select Committees. They did not have the Regan and Weinberger notes cited above, which the OIC only obtained in 1992, despite having sent comprehensive document requests to both the White House and the Department of Defense in early 1987.

During their public hearings, the Select Committees did focus on the fact that Shultz had told Meese in the November 22, 1986, interview that the President knew of the November 1985 HAWK shipment. They questioned Meese closely about his assertion to the contrary at

---

186 Hill Note, 11/24/86, ANS 0001898. Hill also recorded his concerns about Shultz's position, noting that the facts in Shultz's possession "point the finger at McF[arlane] + Pdx [Poindexter] and make him [Shultz] the star witness for the prosecution. So the day he testifies is his last day in office." (Ibid., ANS 0001899.)

187 Ibid., ANS 0001894–909.

188 Ibid., ANS 0001902.

189 Platt Note, 11/24/86, ALW 0039195; see also Hill Note, 11/24/86, ANS 0001904 ("P[resident] now saying he didn't know what Bud [McFarlane] was up to.").

190 Platt Note, 11/24/86, ALW 0039196.

191 Transcript of Meese Press Conference, 11/25/86, ALV 022208.

192 Ibid., ALV 022210–11.

193 The pressure on Shultz to resign was coming from all sides. Weinberger wrote in his diary notes on November 25:

Bill Casey—on secure—thinks Shultz should go to[o] . . .

*              *              *

[Called] Bill Clark in San Luis Obisbo [sic]—Bill Fr. Smith + Pete Wilson both will call President & urge that he dump Shultz[.] (Weinberger Note, 11/25/86, ALZ 0040561–64.)

his November 25, 1986, press conference. Although they had Hill's notes, the Select Committees did not question Meese about why he had contradicted Shultz during the November 22, 1986, interview itself. They did not explore this subject with Shultz, either. The State Department, however, had anticipated such questions and prepared the following responses:

Q: *On Saturday, November 22, 1986, Mr. Meese said to you that the President did not know about the 1985 HAWK shipment when it occurred.*

A: Yes. Mr. Meese said that to me at that meeting. But I had already told Mr. Meese in that same Saturday, November 22, 1986 meeting that the President had told me he knew.

Q: *Was Mr. Meese trying to get you to change your recollection?*

A: You'll have to ask Mr. Meese.[194]

Both Shultz and Hill testified in 1992 that Meese's assertion in the interview that the President did not have contemporaneous knowledge of the November 1985 HAWK shipment struck them as peculiar at the time, given that Shultz had just told Meese the President *did* know. Shultz said he had simply assumed Meese had more information.[195] Hill, however, was more skeptical. He thought Meese was trying to get Shultz to back off of his claim that the President had admitted knowing about the HAWK shipment.[196] Hill described Meese's style of questioning as "leading," and said Meese had stood over Shultz during the interview, in a "back on your heels" manner.[197]

In May 1992, the OIC questioned Meese about the newly discovered evidence of his activities in November 1986. He admitted that Shultz had told him that the President said he knew about the November 1985 HAWK shipment,[198] but he denied that he ever had any legal concerns about the HAWK shipment.[199] When confronted with the Hill, Regan, and Weinberger notes from November 1986, he de-

nied ever having said that the November 1985 HAWK shipment violated the law or that the President did not know about the shipment:

Q: Did you express a concern to Mr. Shultz that it was important that the President not know about the '85 shipments because they could potentially be a violation of law?

A: No. I'm positive I didn't say that.

\*          \*          \*

Q: [Reading from Hill's notes of Meese's November 22, 1986, interview of Shultz] "Certain things could be violation of a law. President didn't know about HAWKS in November. If it happened and President didn't report it to Congress, it's a violation."

Do you remember making such a statement to Mr. Shultz?

A: No, I don't. I don't remember that about violation of law and that sort of thing. . . . I don't know whether he misunderstood me or what I was trying to say there.

Q: Then it says "President didn't know about HAWKS in November." Apparently you're telling Mr. Shultz that the President didn't know about HAWKS.

A: *I'm sure I would not have said that. It seems strange to have me saying that. I'm not sure what that means.*

Q: Because Mr. Shultz——

A: He had told me.

Q: ——told you that the President did know.

A: Yes, so that doesn't make any sense.[200]

Meese did not flatly deny making the statements to Shultz, but he claimed to have "no recollection of that portion of the conversation at all or whether that's accurate[.]"[201]

Meese had a similar reaction to the Weinberger and Regan notes of his comments

194 ALW 0051382.
195 Shultz, OIC Interview, 6/4/92, pp. 85–86.
196 Hill, Grand Jury, 7/10/92, pp. 165–66.
197 Ibid., pp. 167–69.
198 Meese, OIC Interview, 5/11/92, pp. 67, 70.
199 Ibid., pp. 35, 41, 67–71.

200 Ibid., pp. 67–70 (emphasis added).
201 Ibid., pp. 70–71.

at the November 24, 1986, senior advisers' meeting. He again claimed not to recall any concern or statement about the legality of the November 1985 HAWK shipment or any statement that the President did not know about the shipment.[202] Ultimately, Meese said only, "I can't explain it." [203]

When confronted with his statement in the November 25, 1986, press briefing that the President did not learn about the HAWK shipment until February 1986, Meese responded, "I'm confused now." [204]

If Meese testified truthfully when he said he did *not* ask President Reagan whether he knew about the November 1985 HAWK shipment,[205] then Meese had no factual basis for contradicting Shultz on November 22, 1986, by stating that the President did not learn of the HAWK shipment until after the fact. To the contrary, even North and McFarlane had each suggested that the President *had* approved the November 1985 HAWK shipment. The most plausible explanation for Meese's conduct is that he *was* trying to get Shultz to change his recollection. In the November 24 senior advisers' meeting, it appears Meese was trying to signal the other senior advisers that the official position should be that the President didn't know. Meese's motives for misrepresenting the President's knowledge are implicit in the preface to his statement to Shultz: "certain things could be a violation of law." Meese, in effect, signaled Shultz that to disclose the President's knowledge of the November 1985 HAWK shipment would implicate the President in an illegal activity.

According to Weinberger and Regan's notes, Meese communicated a similar message at the November 24, 1986, senior advisers' meeting, asserting again that the November 1985 shipment may have been illegal, but that the President was "not informed." Meese and Poindexter's statements at the November 24 meeting placed responsibility solely on McFarlane's shoulders, by suggesting that he had acted alone and exceeded his authority in operating without the knowledge or approval of the President. By asserting that McFarlane had "handled this all alone" with "no documentation," Poindexter suggested that McFarlane would not be able to *prove* otherwise.[206]

In 1992 Grand Jury testimony, Donald Regan conceded that he knew Meese's assertion that the President did not know about the 1985 shipment was false, and that Vice President Bush as well as Secretary Shultz also knew it was false. Regan admitted frankly that, in light of Meese's statement that the shipment *may* have been illegal, he was not willing to speak up to correct the record regarding the President's knowledge until a final determination was made regarding the legality of the shipment.[207]

Three weeks later, Cooper drew out legal theories justifying all the arms shipments. With the legal rationale in place, the need to insulate the President from knowledge of the HAWK shipment was diminished although the problem of convincing Congress of the after-the-fact rationalization remained. Over time, Administration officials acknowledged certain facts of the President's knowledge, although the record remained extremely confused because some officials, most prominently Weinberger, lied to Congress about their own knowledge of the HAWKs and continued to obfuscate in subsequent testimony. The short life of the effort to insulate the President, coupled with the passage of more than five years before the Regan and Weinberger notes were uncovered, made further pursuit of a possible conspiracy futile. The passage of time also effectively killed a case against Meese for falsely claiming in 1992 not to recall that he had legal concerns about the November 1985 HAWK shipment or that he had stated at the senior advisers' meeting that President Reagan had not known of the November 1985 HAWK shipment. The sheer passage of time made Meese's claimed failure to recall the interchange at a meeting over five years in the past, dramatic and important though it was, too difficult to refute beyond a reasonable doubt.

---

202 Ibid., pp. 80–86.
203 Ibid., p. 86.
204 Ibid., pp. 92–93.
205 Ibid., p. 41.

206 Meese had already made sure that Shultz was not aware of any direct contact by McFarlane with the President in Geneva regarding the HAWK shipment.
207 See Regan chapter.

## Other Meese Problems

Independent Counsel investigated other aspects of Meese's conduct but decided against prosecution. There follows a brief summary of these investigations.

Meese's early testimony was marked by a conspicuous lack of recollection about significant events, even in the face of contemporaneously made records and other evidence. OIC concerns were heightened when Meese in the *North* trial was able to assist the defendant by clearly recalling in 1989 information he had failed to recall much earlier, at a time nearer the events in question. The evidence against Meese for his *North* trial testimony, however, never quite supported a perjury case against him.

In a series of Grand Jury appearances and FBI interviews in 1987 and 1988, Meese was questioned extensively about a number of areas, particularly the extent of his contacts with and his knowledge of North's contra-support activities, and whether Meese sought to delay federal investigations that might have exposed those activities.

### Knowledge of North's Contra-Support Activities

Meese initially testified that he had only a "general recollection" that North "was involved in working on that whole project, the support for and assistance to the freedom fighters [contras] in Nicaragua as a part of his general responsibilities in the military office of the NSC staff." [208] He said he did not recall any conversation with North about his fundraising activities or his provision of military supplies or tactical support for the contras. Meese was unapologetic about his repeated claims of memory loss. When asked directly why he could not recall whether he knew that North was providing tactical advice to the contras, Meese said:

> Well, I can't tell you in sworn testimony here—and this is why many questions I have to say I don't have any recollection. I want to be sure that I'm not testifying in any way that could be possibly subject to contradiction later on. [209]

Meese was asked repeatedly if he ever had any discussions with North about the contras and repeatedly side-stepped the question, saying he could not recall any. But he stopped short of actually denying that he did. For instance, when asked the question before the Grand Jury, Meese said:

> Well, again, I told you that maybe a dozen times in the course of a year, it could have been as many as twenty, I would pass him [North] in the hall or see him on the street. He might have said something about that in passing but I can't recall at this time. It certainly was not anything significant. I can assure you of that. [210]

Although Meese had a close relationship with CIA Director Casey and shared with Casey a desire to see the contras survive during the Boland cut-off period, Meese consistently failed to recall any conversation with Casey regarding North's activities or the CIA director's relationship with North. In his Select Committees deposition, Meese said he could not recall any discussions with Casey about North and he didn't know "how closely or remotely they happened to work together." [211] He testified four months later that he was not aware of any special relationship between North and Casey. [212] In later Grand Jury testimony, Meese admitted to a "dim recollection" that Casey asked him in May 1984 to intercede with the Marine Corps' decision to reassign North out of the NSC staff and back into the Marines. [213] "As I recall that was a time in which Mr. Casey indicated he thought very highly of Colonel North and what he was doing with regard to Central America," Meese said. Asked whether he knew what North was doing in this regard, Meese answered, "Again it's a very dim recollection, but my recollection is that he was talking about Ollie [North] knowing the situation there and doing a good job, or words to that effect." [214]

Meese's notes of May 15, 1984, indicate that he discussed with Casey North's possible transfer and took immediate action to check North's

---

[208] Meese, Grand Jury, 11/18/87, p. 91.
[209] Ibid., 11/20/87, p. 10.

[210] Ibid., pp. 38–39.
[211] Meese, Select Committees Deposition, 7/8/87, pp. 123–24.
[212] Meese, Grand Jury, 11/11/87, p. 29.
[213] Ibid., 11/18/87, p. 97.
[214] Ibid., pp. 97–98.

status with the Marines.[215] Meese's recollection of Casey's call for help was much clearer almost 18 months later when he testified under cross examination in the *North* trial:

> I had my assistant check with Admiral Poindexter or his deputy in the National Security Council staff, and received a report that the National Security Council—the head of the National Security Council staff had approved the re-assignment in deference to Colonel North's career because the transfer back to the Marine Corps would have given him the opportunity to command a battalion at Camp Lejeune.[216]

Asked whether he dropped the matter at that point, Meese responded:

> At that time, I notified Mr. Casey of the situation, indicated we didn't want to do anything to interfere with Colonel North's career, but I said that if he wanted me to go ahead and go further and talk to General Kelley, the commandant of the Marine Corps, I would be glad to do so if he felt further action was necessary.[217]

## Advice on Whether Boland Restricted the NSC Staff

Meese testified before Congress that he did not believe that the National Security Council staff was restricted by the Boland Amendment prohibition on military aid to the contras.[218] He gave similar testimony before the Grand Jury.[219] He also testified that he did not recall giving advice to President Reagan or other Administration officials, either informally or in written opinions, regarding the Boland restrictions and which agencies were subject to them. For instance, in a Grand Jury appearance in November 1987, when Meese was asked about that, the following exchange occurred:

> Q: Well, let me ask you then specifically, between the time you became Attorney General in February of 1985 and November 25th, 1986, were you ever asked to give an official Department of Justice

Opinion on the Boland Amendment, what activity was or was not prohibited, and to whom it applied?

> A: I don't believe we were, and I have no recollection that we were. It's possible, again, that there could have been requests that I wouldn't see in the normal course of business. But I don't have any recollection of that happening.[220]

The question was then extended to include any oral, informal opinion, even in general conversation:

> Q: Now you mentioned that on occasion you would see Colonel North in the hallways over at the White House and have conversations with him. To your knowledge—well, did you ever have any conversation with him about the Boland Amendment and about whether it applied to the NSC staff or what was prohibited by it?

> A: I can't ever recall having such a conversation with Colonel North.[221]

To try to nail down the point completely regarding Meese's assertion that he gave no advice to anyone regarding the Boland restrictions, the following exchange occurred:

> Q: So just to make it clear, when [Associate Counsel] Ms. Hetherton used the term "oral opinion", sometimes when we use the word "opinion" as lawyers we are talking about something fairly formal even if it is oral. Do you recall any conversations or discussions or advice or something short of advice that you had with anybody before November of 1986 on the matter of the Boland Amendment?

> A: No.

> Q: (By Associate Counsel Judith Hetherton): So we are broadening the question now beyond Colonel North to include the President, the Vice President, the Chief of Staff, Mr. Regan, Mr. Casey, Mr. McFarlane, Admiral Poindexter, Cdr. Thompson, Craig Coy, Robert Earl, anyone

215 Meese Notes, 5/15/84, 55301467.
216 Meese, *North* Trial Testimony, 3/28/89, p. 5741.
217 Ibid.
218 Meese, Select Committees Testimony, 7/29/87, p. 310.
219 Meese, Grand Jury, 11/18/87, pp. 108–9.
220 Ibid., p. 113.
221 Ibid., pp. 113–14.

else. To your knowledge, did you have any conversations with any of them about the Boland Amendment, to whom it applied, and what it restricted?

A: I don't recall ever having such a conversation.[222]

Although President Reagan both publicly and in answer to written interrogatories posed by Independent Counsel stated that he did not believe that the Boland restrictions applied to NSC staff, the OIC found no evidence that the White House ever sought from the Justice Department a written opinion on Boland.

In the *North* trial, however, Meese had a distinctly different recollection on this subject under cross examination by North's attorney:

Q: Mr. Meese, during the timeframe 1984, did you ever have a discussion with the President in which you indicated to him what your views were with regard to whether Boland applied to the National Security Council?

A: I participated in meetings of the National Security Planning Group in which this was discussed, to the best of my recollection.

The Court: The question is——

Meese: And the President was there, and there was such a discussion.

The Court: The question is: Did you give any advice, not what anybody else said but did you give any advice as to whether it applied or not?

Meese: Yes, your honor.

The Court: What was your advice? This is the question.

Mr. Keker [Associate Counsel John Keker]: Could we have the date?

The Court: We will get the date.

Meese: I have a general recollection, your honor, of giving my opinion in those meetings, in at least one meeting, and my opinion was, and my view then and now was

that the Boland Amendment did not apply to the National Security Council staff.

The Court: And when did you give that view?

Meese: That would be in National Security Planning Group meetings, and I believe during 1984 when this was under discussion.[223]

## The Nature of Meese's Investigation

Meese was called as a Government witness in the *North* trial because two of the charges were based on North's false account of the Iran arms sales diversion and other lies he told the attorney general during a November 23, 1986, interview.

Under cross examination, Meese agreed with North's counsel that his questioning of North as part of his November 21–24 weekend inquiry was "almost like coworkers in the Administration . . . trying to understand what the basic facts" were. To the defense counsel's assertion that his inquiry, with three of his most senior assistants present, was more or less a chat among colleagues, Meese responded, "That's correct." [224] Similarly, Meese agreed when defense counsel gave this description of his mission in questioning North:

. . . And your focus was not really the focus of an attorney general wearing the attorney general's hat but it was basically to try to gather information to protect the President as best you could and deal with this enormous political problem brewing in the Congress, correct?

A: Yes.[225]

Trial Judge Gerhard A. Gesell interrupted:

The Court: Are you saying then that Lieutenant Colonel North had no obligation to answer your questions?

Meese: He would have had no obligation other than as a loyal member of the Administration and a person in the White House. In other words, there was no legal compulsion in the normal sense as there

---

222 Ibid., p. 114.

223 Meese, *North* Trial Testimony, 3/29/89, pp. 5823–24.
224 Ibid., 3/28/89, p. 5758.
225 Ibid., p. 5749.

would be perhaps in a criminal investigation.

The Court: So he could have said, I would rather not answer?

Meese: He could have said that, yes.[226]

## Meese's Awareness of Third-Country Contra Funding

On the question of the Reagan Administration's efforts to solicit third-country contributions to support the contras, Meese changed his testimony between the time he was first asked about it by the FBI in December 1986 and his appearance in the *North* trial, more than two years later. In his initial FBI interview, Meese said he had no knowledge of third-country funding for the contras.[227] Following public revelations about the misplaced $10 million Brunei contribution, Meese told the House Permanent Select Committee on Intelligence (HPSCI) that he had no "personal knowledge" of U.S. Government solicitations of third countries other than Brunei, "nor was it discussed in any NSC meetings that I can recall." [228]

After Saudi Arabia's contributions were publicly disclosed in the Select Committees hearings, Meese was asked in July 1987 by congressional investigators about his knowledge of meetings of President Reagan with King Fahd of Saudi Arabia or Prince Bandar, the Saudi ambassador to the United States. "I don't have any recollection of knowing about those meetings at the time. I think that was during 1985 and 1986; . . . Maybe it was in 1984. I don't have any—I don't recall at this time that I knew about it. It is possible that I did." [229]

Confronted with the minutes of the National Security Planning Group (NSPG) meeting on June 25, 1984, at which third-country funding for the contras was debated, Meese said: "I don't recall the meeting, no, but again the minutes here are not inconsistent with anything I generally recall." [230] The minutes quote Meese as interjecting:

As another non-practicing lawyer I want to emphasize that it's important to tell the Department of Justice that we want them to find the proper and legal basis which will permit the United States to assist in obtaining third party resources for the anti-Sandinistas [contras]. You have to give lawyers guidance when asking them a question.[231]

McFarlane testified publicly at the Select Iran/contra Committee hearings that the initial Saudi donation to the contras occurred in the spring or summer of 1984, following discussions by him with Prince Bandar. Meese recalled June 1984 discussions with the Saudis, but when asked what he knew about third-country funding, he said, "I don't recall anything that I knew at that time." Asked if he remembered any approaches to foreign countries while counselor to the President, he said: "Again I have a general recollection that those activities took place but I can't specifically recall anything." [232]

Meese's wavering recollection of what and when he knew about third-country funding for the contras solidified by the time he testified in the *North* trial:

Q: Now, in the National Security Council, as a result of your participation on the Council and as as result of your position as counselor to the president, did you learn in 1984, Mr. Meese, that Saudia [sic] Arabia was giving assistance to the United States to fund the freedom fighters [contras]?

A: I recall learning that more in my position as counselor to the president.

Q: Yes, that's what I mean, as counselor to the president.

A: Yes.

Q: Would that have been in early 1984 that you first learned about that, sir?

A: I can't place it exactly, but that sounds about right.

226 Ibid.
227 Meese, FBI 302, 12/4/86, p. 5.
228 Meese, HPSCI Testimony, 12/19/86, pp. 95–96.
229 Meese, Select Committees Deposition, 7/8/87, p. 159.
230 Meese, Grand Jury, 11/18/87, pp. 79–80.
231 Minutes of the June 24, 1984 NSPG Meeting, ALU 007874.
232 Ibid., pp. 87–88.

Q: Did you learn specifically that Mr. McFarlane was dealing with an official of the Saudi Arabian government in working out arrangements so that they would provide a million dollars a month to the freedom fighters?

A: I don't believe I knew the exact amount or the detail, but I did know generally that that was going on, yes.[233]

## Posey-Corvo Investigation

Independent Counsel investigated the circumstances surrounding Meese's intrusion in two federal investigations that could have exposed North's contra-support activities. Independent Counsel found no direct evidence that Meese obstructed either of these investigations, although he openly admitted seeking a delay in one to avoid exposure of the Iran hostage-recovery efforts.

The Posey-Corvo case was being investigated by the U.S. Attorney's Office in Miami. It involved allegations of contra-related gun-running, drug trafficking and Neutrality Act violations. Among the allegations surrounding the case were an attempted assassination plot against a U.S. ambassador. Meese and others in Washington who expressed special interest in the Posey-Corvo case cited the assassination allegations as the cause for their interest.

Jeffrey Feldman, an assistant U.S. attorney in Miami, began in early 1986 investigating the Posey-Corvo matter, based in part on allegations by Jesus Garcia, who had been convicted in December 1985 for illegal possession of a machine gun. Garcia claimed that a pro-contra mercenary group led by Thomas Posey had plotted to assassinate U.S. Ambassador to Costa Rica Lewis A. Tambs to collect a bounty placed on Tambs' head by a drug kingpin, and then to blame the assassination on Nicaragua's Sandinista government to build public support for the contras. At the same time, other sources told federal investigators that North, Robert W. Owen, and John Hull, an American rancher living in Costa Rica, were involved in gun-running.

The OIC declined to take over the Posey-Corvo case but did investigate a possible obstruction of justice regarding it. It was determined that the allegations were not supported by the evidence.

In the course of his investigation, Feldman reported hearing rumors about a contra-resupply network run by North. On a trip to Costa Rica, Feldman on March 31, 1986, laid out the assassination allegations to Tambs and CIA Costa Rican Station Chief Joseph F. Fernandez.[234] North's notebooks reflect a call from Fernandez noting Feldman's visit to Costa Rica with FBI agents.[235] On April 7, 1986, North received a memo from Owen in which he identified the investigators who came to Costa Rica and quoted Feldman as stating he was not only looking at Neutrality Act violations but also the unauthorized use of Government funds.[236]

On April 4, 1986, Feldman briefed Kellner and several other members of the U.S. Attorney's Office in Miami. Assistant U.S. Attorney David Leiwant, who was present for part of the meeting, said that Kellner received a phone call from Washington during the meeting, in which an unknown official told Kellner to go slow on the investigation.[237] Neither Feldman nor anyone else in the meeting corroborated Leiwant's allegations.

Meese's most direct involvement in the Posey-Corvo matter came during a trip with Assistant Attorney General Lowell Jensen and FBI official Oliver "Buck" Revell to Miami on April 12, 1986.

Meese inquired about the Posey-Corvo case, and Kellner said he told Meese that no credible information had been found to support either the assassination or gun-running allegations.[238] Meese denied that he asked Kellner to slow down the investigation or that he instructed anyone else to do so.[239]

After a series of delays, on October 6, 1986—one day after a contra-resupply plane carrying Eugene Hasenfus was shot down in Nicaragua—a decision was made in the U.S.

---

[233] Meese, *North* Trial Testimony, 3/29/89, p. 5824.

[234] Feldman during his presentation on the gun-running allegations showed Tambs a chart that listed North, Owen and Hull; Tambs appeared shaken, according to Feldman. (Feldman, Select Committees Deposition, 4/30/87, p. 50.) Feldman did not know that he was speaking to two Government officials who were assisting North in contra-support efforts.

[235] North Note, 3/31/86, AMX 001042–43.

[236] Memorandum from Owen to North, 4/7/86.

[237] Leiwant, FBI 302, 4/6/87, pp. 1–2, 4.

[238] Kellner, FBI 302, 4/7/87, p. 2

[239] Meese, Grand Jury, 11/18/87, pp. 146–47.

Attorney's Office in Miami to send the Posey-Corvo matter to a Grand Jury.

Independent Counsel determined that the heightened interest in the case by Washington officials was understandable in light of the alleged assassination plot. In Miami, delays in presenting the case to a Grand Jury were attributable to the fact that Feldman's superiors considered it a routine gun-running case and that the matter was not sufficiently developed. There was a large volume of serious drug and weapons cases based in Miami. During the first half of 1986, no one in the U.S. Attorney's Office was aware of North's actual involvement with the contras. When Feldman stumbled onto North's contra-resupply network in early 1986, his focus was on the gun-running and assassination aspects of the case.

The evidence did not support an obstruction charge.

## Role in Delaying FBI and Customs Investigations Into Southern Air Transport Following the Hasenfus Shootdown

Meese admitted that he sought to delay the FBI and Customs Service investigations of Southern Air Transport (SAT) in the wake of the Hasenfus shootdown on October 5, 1986. He testified that he did so at Poindexter's request and possibly also spoke to North about the matter.[240] Meese said his purpose in delaying the investigations into Southern Air Transport—which was involved in both the Iran and contra operations—was to keep Iran arms sales from being publicly exposed while hostage-rescue efforts were underway. Although there was circumstantial evidence that Meese was aware of North's contra-support activities, Independent Counsel determined that the evidence did not prove that Meese delayed the investigations of SAT for a purpose other than to protect the hostage-rescue operation.

Robert Dutton of the contra-resupply operation said North told him on October 9, 1986, that he had talked to Meese about the Customs investigation of SAT and that the matter would be taken care of.[241] A North notebook entry

suggests that North at least intended to bring it to Meese's attention:

[box] Ed Meese

—SAT EXPOSURE =
IRAN/HOSTAGE EXPOSURE [242]

Meese said he had little awareness of the Hasenfus shootdown in early October 1986 and did not recall discussing it with other Administration officials.[243]

On October 13, 1986, North noted continuing concern over exposure of the SAT matter, this time apparently connecting it to exposure of Secord's Iran involvement:

[box] Ed Meese

—SAT/RVS [Richard V. Secord]—
IRAN [244]

Meese said his involvement in the SAT investigations began October 30, 1986, when Poindexter called him to request a delay in the investigation of SAT by FBI and Customs. Meese said Poindexter told him

. . . the FBI was seeking to interview people at the Southern Air Transport or to get some records from Southern Air Transport, something along that line, and that the people they were supposed to talk with at Southern Air Transport were involved in the Iran initiative project and they were needed to be away during a certain period of time therefore, I think it was about 10 days, and would it be possible to delay the FBI interviews or contacts with them for a short time. And I said I would find out if it was, and if that would not interfere with the investigation that was being conducted, I would see if that could be done.[245]

Meese added that it was possible that Poindexter said to get back to him or North if he had any questions.[246] Meese said Poindexter probably also mentioned the Cus-

240 Meese, Grand Jury, 12/16/87, pp. 103–4.
241 Dutton, Select Committees Testimony, 5/11/87, pp. 87–88.

242 North Note, 10/10/86, AMX 001582.
243 Meese, Grand Jury, 12/16/87, p. 27.
244 North Note, 10/13/86, AMX 001586.
245 Meese, Grand Jury, 12/16/87, pp. 41–42.
246 Ibid., p. 43.

toms probe as well as the FBI probe.[247] Meese said he did not discuss with Poindexter SAT's connection to the Hasenfus case, despite a prominent story in *The Washington Post* that day reporting on the connection.[248]

Meese characterized the delay in the SAT investigations as a brief one: 10 days. The FBI investigation, however, was not resumed until November 26, 1986, after the Iran/contra diversion had been exposed. After receiving Poindexter's request for a delay in the investigations, Meese turned the matter over to Assistant Attorney General Stephen Trott. Trott called FBI Director William Webster on October 30, 1986, asking that all non-urgent investigations be stopped to keep from jeopardizing the hostage operation, and Webster agreed.

Meese spoke with Baker about the Customs investigation of SAT generally, but their recollections differ.[249] Baker said that Meese at an uncertain date approached him at a White House meeting and said he wanted to talk about an overzealous Customs investigation.[250] According to Baker, Meese said national security matters were involved but Meese did not go into specifics.[251]

A memo for the record by North on November 14, 1986, describes a conversation North had with Revell of the FBI about the investigation delay. According to the memo, Revell told him that 10 days before he

> . . . received guidance from Attorney General Meese to "suspend" the investigation of Major General Secord's involvement in support of the Nicaraguan resistance and that the Attorney General had discussed the Customs' investigation of SAT with Treasury Secretary Jim Baker. On Mr. Revell's advice, North called Associate Attorney General Stephan [sic] Trott to solicit his advice on the matter.

> At 12:10 p.m. on November 14, Trott advised North by secure phone that the Secord and SAT involvement with the Iran covert action had been the subject of a discussion between Trott and the Attorney

General and a separate discourse between the Attorney General and Treasury Secretary Baker. Trott indicated that Secretary Baker had planned to advise Customs regarding sensitivity to SAT's involvement in sensitive U.S. government operations.

> Trott informed that he would discuss this matter immediately with Attorney General Meese and indicated that he (Trott) fully understood the need not to divulge SAT or Secord's roles in support of the Iran covert action. Trott indicated that he would advise us of the results.[252]

Revell confirmed that he and North in the second week of November 1986 discussed the SAT matter and Secord.[253] Revell said he told North the FBI would continue its investigation. Revell said North's memo is accurate except that he did not tell North he had received guidance from Meese.[254]

Trott said North called him and asked that Meese intervene in the Customs investigation through Baker, to slow down the investigation or narrow the Customs subpoena for SAT documents.[255] Trott said he discussed North's call with Meese, and Meese later told him he had discussed the matter with Baker.[256] Trott's notes of the phone call with North on November 14 indicate the concerns were Iran-related:

> O.N. . . . Legit covert action . . . J.P. Customs Florida S.A.T.—6 missions into Tehran—sanctions [noted in margin: "sensitive stuff"] . . . NOT down south connected . . . *SEACORD* = Customs all S.A.T. records . . .[257]

During the second week in November 1986, FBI officials asked DOJ whether the SAT investigation could be resumed. Trott asked Meese. Meese said he called Poindexter on November 14, 1986, to asked whether the FBI could resume its inquiry of SAT; Meese said Poindexter told him on November 18 that the investigation could proceed.[258] On November

247 Ibid., pp. 41–42, 46.
248 Ibid., pp. 45–46.
249 Meese, FBI 302, 12/19/86, p. 1.
250 Baker, FBI 302, 12/18/86, p. 1.
251 Ibid.
252 North memo to the Record, 11/14/86, AKW 006105.
253 Revell, FBI 302, 12/16/86, p. 3.
254 Ibid.
255 Trott, FBI 302, 12/15/86, pp. 2–3.
256 Ibid., 3/29/88, p. 5.
257 Trott Note, 11/14/86, ALV 011083 (emphasis in original).
258 Meese, Grand Jury, 12/16/87, pp. 53–56.

20, 1986, Trott advised Revell that the FBI investigation of SAT should resume.

Although these investigations threatened the exposure of the contra-resupply operation as well as the Iran arms sales, OIC obtained no convincing evidence that Meese sought the delay for reasons other than those he claimed: keeping secret the hostage-rescue operation.

# Part X
# Political Oversight and the Rule of Law

The Iran/contra prosecutions illustrate in an especially stark fashion the tension between political oversight and enforcement of existing law. Congress's decision to compel immunized testimony from a number of Iran/contra figures pursuant to 18 U.S.C. § 6002—most notably Lt. Col. Oliver L. North and Vice Adm. John M. Poindexter—was thought important both to address an immediate crisis of political confidence and to shed light on flaws in the functioning of the national security apparatus. Ultimately, however, that decision also was fatal to the prosecutions of North and Poindexter, and made a full and equitable accounting for criminal wrongdoing impossible. That outcome holds important lessons for the future.

## Background

It was apparent from the outset of the Iran/contra investigation that congressional grants of use immunity to the principals in the affair would make prosecution of those persons problematic. The Office of Independent Counsel noted that concern in its first Interim Report, issued in April 1987, explaining that the award of immunity "will have a serious and possibly destructive impact upon a subsequent prosecution" and "might preclude future prosecution of those [immunized] individuals." The Office pointed out that, under *Kastigar* v. *United States,* 406 U.S. 441, 458 (1972), a grant of use immunity results in "a sweeping proscription of any use, direct or indirect, of the compelled testimony and any information derived therefrom." The Office accordingly took extensive steps to avoid this danger. It expedited the elements of its investigation most likely to be the subject of congressional inquiry. It memorialized the statements of potential trial witnesses—in the vernacular, "canning" them—that were made prior to the time that immunized testimony became publicly available. It implemented prophylactic procedures designed to shield prosecutors and investigators from exposure to immunized disclosures. And it urged Congress to be conservative in granting immunity.

When Congress nevertheless chose to compel testimony from North and Poindexter, these prophylactic procedures continued before the Grand Jury and at the *North* and *Poindexter* trials. Grand Jury witnesses were instructed by the Government to "make sure that your answers to our questions are based solely on your own personal knowledge and recollection of the events in question. Do not relate to us anything which you learned for the first time as a result of listening to or reading or hearing about immunized testimony." The district judge gave a similar instruction to all witnesses at the *North* trial.

The district judge presiding in the *Poindexter* case took even more extensive precautions. Prior to trial he reviewed statements made by potential trial witnesses before Poindexter's immunized testimony became publicly available, finding that all of the proposed testimony of most of these witnesses had been memorialized by that date. As for those witnesses whose trial testimony would not be limited to that "canned" prior to Poindexter's congressional appearance, the district judge found that the proposed trial testimony of most of them concerned subjects that Poindexter did not address in his immunized statements.

This left the Government still to prove that five of its potential witnesses were free of taint. The district judge ordered these witnesses to appear at a pretrial hearing. Of the three of these witnesses who subsequently testified at trial, two credibly affirmed at the hearing that their anticipated trial testimony would not be affected in any way by Poindexter's immunized statements.

The third witness, North, took a different tack. He stated at the hearing that he was unable, with respect to any relevant subject, to distinguish between what he had personally done, observed or experienced and what he had heard about the events by way of Poindexter's immunized testimony. As for Poindexter's destruction of the December 1985 presidential Finding, North acknowledged that he had seen Poindexter destroy a piece of paper, but insisted that he did not know that the document was the Finding until Poindexter stated that fact before Congress.

The district court, however, rejected North's testimony at the hearing as incredible. Basing its ruling on North's demeanor, on inconsistencies in North's testimony, and on other objective indicia that North had an untainted memory of events, the court found that North "appears to have been embarked at that time upon the calculated course of attempting to assist his former colleague and co-defendant . . . by prevaricating on various issues, including most notably the issue whether he had to rely for his recollection of events on Poindexter's immunized testimony." North accordingly was permitted to testify.

## The North and Poindexter Decisions

Both convictions were set aside by divided panels on appeal. In the *North* case, the appeals court concluded that receipt of testimony from witnesses whose memories had been refreshed by exposure to North's immunized disclosures constituted improper "evidentiary use" of North's statements. The majority accordingly directed the district court to determine on remand as to each witness whether it was possible to separate out "unspoiled memory" from that influenced by North's testimony and, if not, to exclude evidence presented by such witnesses.

The court of appeals also concluded that the trial judge's instructions to witnesses were inadequate to prevent them from testifying to mat-

ters that they had first learned from North's immunized disclosures, accepting North's argument that such witnesses could not filter their answers through the district court's "prior knowledge" test. The court therefore held that the trial judge was obligated, on remand, to hold a full hearing "that will inquire into the *content* as well as the *sources* of the Grand Jury and trial witnesses' testimony. That inquiry must proceed witness-by-witness; if necessary, it will proceed line-by-line and item-by-item." The court explained that the district judge was required to "make express findings that the government has carried [its] heavy burden as to the content of all of the testimony of each witness."

Then-Chief Judge Patricia M. Wald dissented, declining to find that the district judge's "prodigious and conscientious efforts to protect North's Fifth Amendment rights were in any way so ineffectual as to require reversal on the formalistic grounds the majority advances." She noted that virtually all of the Grand Jury evidence relating to the counts on which North was convicted had been presented *prior* to North's congressional appearance. And she found it "indeed striking that North's counsel cannot point to a single instance of alleged witness testimony tainted by exposure to North's immunized testimony." In all, she observed that the procedural regime imposed by the majority "makes a subsequent trial of any congressionally immunized witness virtually impossible."[1]

On remand, the prosecution of North was dismissed when Independent Counsel concluded that satisfaction of the court of appeals' requirements would be both very difficult and enormously burdensome.

---

[1] The court reaffirmed its initial conclusions when it denied rehearing. It did, however, appear to modify its opinion in two respects. It retreated somewhat from the suggestion in its initial opinion that the Government could establish a lack of taint only by showing that a witness never had been exposed to the immunized testimony, or that all of his evidence had been "canned" prior to exposure. At the same time, however, the court added another element to the showing required on remand: whether Government witnesses were motivated to testify by the immunized disclosures. Chief Judge Wald again dissented. She concluded that the procedures used by the district court—under which the Government effectively made a showing that no illegal use of the immunized testimony was made—were adequate; she suggested that the majority's contrary conclusion "represents an unneeded and unprecedented incursion into the trial court's discretion in managing a fair trial." She also faulted the majority for failing to realize that any use of the tainted evidence may have been too attenuated to raise constitutional concerns, noting that the question "is a deep and unsettled one in current constitutional law."

A different panel of the appeals court reversed Poindexter's convictions. The majority concluded that all of the convictions had to be set aside because, in its view, the trial court's measures failed to ensure that Poindexter's immunized testimony was not used against him at trial. In reaching this conclusion, the court of appeals restated the standard set out in *North*: "that a prohibited 'use' [of immunized testimony] occurs if a witness' recollection is refreshed by exposure to the defendant's immunized testimony, or if his testimony is in any way 'shaped, altered, or affected,' by such exposure." Under this standard, the court explained, "'the Government must demonstrate affirmatively that the immunized testimony did not . . . [have] an influence on [the trial witnesses'] thinking, even one for which they cannot at this time consciously account.'"

Although the *Poindexter* case was tried prior to the decision in *North*, the court of appeals declined to remand for new findings under the *North* standard. Focusing on North's testimony at the *Poindexter* trial, the court held that the district judge's finding that North lied when he denied having an independent recollection could not be used to support the proposition that North *did* have an untainted memory. The court of appeals also went on to reason that the district judge's finding of differences between North's account and Poindexter's immunized testimony was irrelevant, opining that a "substantially exposed witness" who has not "canned" his testimony may give evidence at trial only when he "persuasively claim[s] that he can segregate the effects of his exposure."

Chief Judge Abner J. Mikva dissented in part. Although he did not take issue with the *North* standard, he complained that in North "the Court changed the standards the special prosecutor had to meet; today we refuse to let him try to meet them." The majority's failure to accord any weight to the district judge's credibility findings, Chief Judge Mikva added, "tells future defendants that all they need to evade responsibility [to testify at trial] is a well timed case of amnesia." [2]

## The Implications of North and Poindexter

The decisions in *North* and *Poindexter* have significant implications for the interplay between congressional oversight and law enforcement. While it may affect any case in which immunity is granted, the holding in *North* will have its most profound impact on prosecutions involving public immunized testimony—in particular, testimony before Congress—that is widely disseminated. In such cases, the court of appeals' ruling on refreshed recollection will require a complex psychological inquiry into the thought processes and memory of every witness. At the same time, the large number of witnesses potentially exposed to immunized testimony in cases involving newsworthy events means that the court of appeals' draconian procedural requirements will, as Judge Wald observed, "consume[] countless extra weeks or months of trial." In all, then, the *North* ruling may, again in Judge Wald's words, amount to "an absolute deterrent of any prosecution after a grant of immunity in a high-profile case."

The decision in *Poindexter* took the *North* ruling a step further. The court purported to state its procedural holding in modest terms: focusing on North's testimony at the Poindexter trial, the court said "only that where a substantially exposed witness does not persuasively claim that he can segregate the effects of his exposure, the prosecution does not meet its burden merely by pointing to other statements of the same witness that were not themselves shown to be untainted." But while it is difficult to quarrel with that statement in the abstract, the real effect of the court's holding is dramatically broader. In fact, the court held that the Government could not carry its burden by pointing either to persuasive evidence that a witness was lying when he denied having an untainted recollection of the relevant events or to other

---

[2] There are grounds to doubt the correctness of the court of appeals' decisions in *North* and *Poindexter*. There is considerable authority for the proposition that a finding that a witness lied may be used to establish "'that the truth is the opposite of his story'" (*NLRB* v. *Walton Mfg. Co.*, 369 U.S. 404, 408 (1962) (per curiam), quoting

*Dyer* v. *MacDougall*, 201 F.2d 265, 269 (2d Cir. 1952) (L. Hand. J.))—which means that the finding that North lied when he denied having an untainted memory could have been used to establish that he *did* have an untainted memory. And the Supreme Court repeatedly has applied attenuation concepts in deciding whether evidence must be excluded under the Fourth or Fifth Amendments—concepts that were rejected by the court of appeals in *North* and *Poindexter*. See, e.g., *Nix* v. *Williams*, 467 U.S. 431, 442 (1984); *United States* v. *Crews*, 445 U.S. 463, 471 (1980). The Supreme Court denied Independent Counsel's petitions for certiorari in both cases, however, and further analysis of the constitutional issues is beyond the scope of this report.

forms of circumstantial indicia that the witness had not been affected by the immunized testimony. It bears emphasis that the court of appeals decided more than that the district judge applied the wrong standard in assessing such evidence; by refusing to remand the case, the court concluded as a matter of law that such evidence *never* may be used to carry the Government's burden. It thus is manifest that, unless the court retreats from its rule, a witness whose testimony has not been "canned" and who asserts that he has been affected by exposure to immunized disclosures will not be permitted to testify at trial, no matter how improbable or internally inconsistent his claim.

These rules will have obvious practical consequences. They will make almost impossible the prosecution of any case involving public immunized statements that requires testimony by persons sympathetic to the accused, such as co-conspirators or other associates. And the dangers of abuse and manipulation are magnified by the court of appeals' view, expressed in *North,* that a witness inclined to assist the defense may become disqualified from testifying at trial by the simple expedient of soaking *himself* in the defendant's immunized statements.[3] As the outcome of the *North* and *Poindexter* prosecutions makes graphically clear, these consequences have particular importance because the cases most sharply affected by the court of appeals' new rules will, by definition, be prosecutions involving conduct that has far-flung implications for national policy—those where Congress has determined that the national interest requires an immediate public examination of the activity at issue.

## The Competing Roles of Congress and the Independent Counsel

With this as background, the competing roles of Congress and the Executive (here represented by Independent Counsel) must be borne in mind. As Independent Counsel recognized from

the outset of his investigation, it is Congress (in the case of the Iran/contra affair, its Select Committees) that is primarily responsible for the accurate public disclosure of the facts concerning transactions such as the Iran/contra matter. Ultimately, it is Congress that is empowered to legislate in a manner that not only will preclude future similar transactions in a narrow sense, but that also will facilitate the effective management of foreign policy and that will discourage disregard for existing legal strictures.

Although the Independent Counsel also has a reporting function, his first responsibility, in contrast, is the prosecution of criminal conduct. Accordingly, it is not primarily his duty to develop for the public a knowledge of what occurred.

When a conflict between the oversight and prosecutorial roles develops—as plainly occurred in the Iran/contra affair—the law is clear that it is Congress that must prevail. This is no more than a recognition of the high political importance of Congress's responsibility. It also is the appropriate place to strike the balance, as resolution of this conflict calls for the exercise of a seasoned political judgment that must take a broad view of the national interest.

In exercising this judgment, however, it is imperative that Congress be sensitive to the dangers posed by grants of immunity to the successful prosecution of criminal conduct—and that it bear in mind, as well, the importance of the even-handed application of criminal justice. In recent years Congress has granted use immunity with some frequency, in cases including many of the most notable examples of misconduct involving public officials or matters of public policy: in addition to the Iran/contra affair, the list includes the Watergate, "Koreagate," and ABSCAM scandals; congressional ethics inquiries; impeachment proceedings against federal judges; inquiries into narcotics trafficking, assassinations, and organized crime; investigations of fraud, corruption, and mismanagement on Indian reservations; and most recently, allegations of misconduct at the Department of Housing and Urban Development and of improper favors for savings and loan officials. In all, Congress has conferred use immunity on more than 300 witnesses over the last two decades.

---

[3] As the court of appeals put it, persons sympathetic to the defense "could have held evening classes in 'the Parsing and Deconstruction of *Kastigar*' for the very purpose of 'derailing' the [Independent Counsel's] prosecution, and such a curriculum would have been simply irrelevant to the question of whether or not the prosecution's case made use of North's compelled testimony."

In the past, members of Congress may have been of the view that the experience of the Watergate cases suggests that grants of use immunity do not significantly impede successful prosecution. Even at the time, that would not have been the proper lesson to draw from Watergate. Although two immunized witnesses in the Watergate matter—John Dean and Charles Colson—subsequently pleaded guilty, no immunized Watergate witness who refused to plead guilty was successfully tried and convicted. Gordon Strachan, the only immunized witness who was charged in the Watergate cover-up indictment, never went to trial because the Watergate Special Prosecutor concluded that there was a significant possibility that Strachan eventually might prevail on his claim of taint.[4] The same thing happened in the case of Felipe De Diego, who was granted immunity by state authorities in connection with the break-in at the office of Daniel Ellsberg's psychiatrist.[5] But in any event, the decisions in *North* and *Poindexter* should lay to rest any lingering sense that a congressional grant of use immunity is not a serious bar to future prosecution.

Congressional action that precludes prosecution—or, as in Iran/contra, that makes it impossible to sustain a successful prosecution—imposes costs on society that far transcend the failure to convict a few lawbreakers. There is significant inequity when (again as in Iran/contra) the more peripheral players are convicted while the central figures in the criminal enterprise escape punishment. And perhaps more fundamentally, the failure to punish governmental lawbreakers feeds the perception that public officials are not wholly accountable for their actions. It also may lead the public to believe that no real wrongdoing took place. That is a danger in the Iran/contra affair, where Oliver North hailed the ultimate dismissal of the prosecution against him as a personal vindication. While it was, of course, nothing of the sort—North was found guilty beyond a reasonable doubt of serious criminal offenses, and the court of appeals' decision setting aside his conviction cast no doubt on his factual guilt—the risk of public confusion on the point is substantial.

This background strongly suggests that Congress should compel public testimony from a Government official suspected of criminal misconduct only in the most extraordinary circumstances. Before doing so, it should determine whether there is substantial evidence that the prospective witness was involved in a criminal transaction, whether he or she ordinarily would be a logical subject for prosecutive consideration, and whether the prospective witness had a leading or substantial role in the criminal enterprise. If so, Congress also should determine whether a less culpable person could supply the evidence sought, and what the likelihood is that the witness to be immunized will supply honest, useful and necessary information. Only if no less culpable person is available—and if the need for obtaining the information is compelling—should the prospective witness be granted immunity.

---

[4] See Strachan, *Self-Incrimination, Immunity and Watergate*, 56 Tex. L. Rev. 791, 814–820 (1978).

[5] See *United States* v. *De Diego*, 511 F.2d 818, 822–825 (D.C. Cir. 1975).

# Part XI
# Concluding Observations

The underlying facts of Iran/contra are that, regardless of criminality, President Reagan, the secretary of state, the secretary of defense, and the director of central intelligence and their necessary assistants committed themselves, however reluctantly, to two programs contrary to congressional policy and contrary to national policy. They skirted the law, some of them broke the law, and almost all of them tried to cover up the President's willful activities.

What protection do the people of the United States have against such a concerted action by such powerful officers? The Constitution provides for congressional oversight and congressional control of appropriations, but if false information is given to Congress, these checks and balances are of lessened value. Further, in the give and take of the political community, congressional oversight is often overtaken and subordinated by the need to keep Government functioning, by the need to anticipate the future, and by the ever-present requirement of maintaining consensus among the elected officials who are the Government.

The disrespect for Congress by a popular and powerful President and his appointees was obscured when Congress accepted the tendered concept of a runaway conspiracy of subordinate officers and avoided the unpleasant confrontation with a powerful President and his Cabinet. In haste to display and conclude its investigation of this unwelcome issue, Congress destroyed the most effective lines of inquiry by giving immunity to Oliver L. North and John M. Poindexter so that they could exculpate and eliminate the need for the testimony of President Reagan and Vice President Bush.

Immunity is ordinarily given by a prosecutor to a witness who will incriminate someone more important than himself. Congress gave immunity to North and Poindexter, who incriminated only themselves and who largely exculpated those responsible for the initiation, supervision and support of their activities. This delayed and infinitely complicated the effort to prosecute North and Poindexter, and it largely destroyed the likelihood that their prompt conviction and appropriate sentence would induce meaningful cooperation.

These important political decisions were properly the responsibility of Congress. It was for the Committees to decide whether the welfare of the nation was served or endangered by a continuation of its investigation, a more deliberate effort to test the self-serving denials presented by Cabinet officers and to search for the full ramifications of the activities in question. Having made this decision, however, no one could gainsay the added difficulties thrust upon Independent Counsel. These difficulties could be dealt with only by the investment of large amounts of additional time and large amounts of expense.

The role of Independent Counsel is not well understood. Comparisons to United States attorneys, county district attorneys, or private law offices do not conceive the nature of Independent Counsel. Independent Counsel is not an individual put in charge of an ongoing agency as an acting U.S. attorney might be; he is a person taken from private practice and told to create a new agency, to carry out the mission assigned by the court. It is not as though he were told to step in and try a case on the calendar of an ongoing office with full support of the Government behind him, as it would be behind the United States attorney. He is told to create an office and to confront the Govern-

ment without any expectation of real cooperation, and, indeed, with the expectation of hostility, however veiled. That hostility will manifest itself in the failure to declassify information, in the suppression of documents, and in
all of the evasive techniques of highly skilled
and large, complex organizations.

The investigation into Iran/contra nevertheless
demonstrates that the rule of law upon which
our democratic system of government depends
can be applied to the highest officials even
when they are operating in the secret areas of
diplomacy and national security.

Despite extraordinary difficulties imposed by
the destruction and withholding of records, the
need to protect classified information, and the
congressional grants of immunity to some of
the principals involved, Independent Counsel
was able to bring criminal charges against nine
government officers and five private citizens involved in illegal activities growing out of the
Iran/contra affair.

More importantly, the investigation and the
prosecutions arising out of it have provided a
much more accurate picture of how two secret
Administration policies—keeping the contras
alive "body and soul" during the Boland cut-
off period and seeking the release of Americans
held hostage by selling arms to Iran—veered
off into criminality.

Evidence obtained by Independent Counsel
establishes that the Iran/contra affair was not
an aberrational scheme carried out by a "cabal
of zealots" on the National Security Council
staff, as the congressional Select Committees
concluded in their majority report.[1] Instead, it
was the product of two foreign policy directives
by President Reagan which skirted the law and
which were executed by the NSC staff with
the knowledge and support of high officials in
the CIA, State and Defense departments, and
to a lesser extent, officials in other agencies.

Independent Counsel found no evidence of
dissent among his Cabinet officers from the
President's determination to support the contras
after federal law banned the use of appropriated
funds for that purpose in the Boland Amendment in October 1984. Even the two Cabinet
officers who opposed the sale of arms to Iran
on the grounds that it was illegal and bad pol-

icy—Defense Secretary Caspar W. Weinberger
and Secretary of State George P. Shultz—either
cooperated with the decision once made, as in
the case of Weinberger, or stood aloof from
it while being kept informed of its progress,
as was the case of Shultz.

In its report section titled "Who Was Responsible," the Select Committees named CIA
Director William Casey, National Security Advisers Robert C. McFarlane and John M.
Poindexter, along with NSC staff member Oliver L. North, and private sector operatives Richard V. Secord and Albert Hakim. With the exception of Casey who died before he could
be questioned by the OIC, Independent Counsel
charged and obtained criminal convictions of
each of the men named by Congress. There
is little doubt that, operationally, these men
were central players.

But the investigation and prosecutions have
shown that these six were not out-of-control
mavericks who acted alone without the knowledge or assistance of others. The evidence establishes that the central NSC operatives kept
their superiors—including Reagan, Bush, Shultz,
Weinberger and other high officials—informed
of their efforts generally, if not in detail, and
their superiors either condoned or turned a blind
eye to them. When it was required, the NSC
principals and their private sector operatives received the assistance of high-ranking officers
in the CIA, the Defense Department, and the
Department of State.

Of the 14 persons charged criminally during
the investigation, four were convicted of felony
charges after trial by jury, seven pleaded guilty
either to felonies or misdemeanors, and one had
his case dismissed because the Administration
refused to declassify information deemed necessary to the defendant by the trial judge. Two
cases that were awaiting trial were aborted by
pardons granted by President Bush. As this report explained earlier, many persons who committed crimes were not charged. Some minor
crimes were never investigated and some that
were investigated were not solved. But Independent Counsel believes that to the extent possible, the central Iran/contra crimes were vigorously prosecuted and the significant acts of obstruction were fully charged.

---

[1] Majority Report, p. 22.

Fundamentally, the Iran/contra affair was the first known criminal assault on the post-Watergate rules governing the activities of national security officials. Reagan Administration officials rendered these rules ineffective by creating private operations, supported with privately generated funds that successfully evaded executive and legislative oversight and control. Congress was defrauded. Its appropriations restrictions having been circumvented, Congress was led to believe that the Administration was following the law. Numerous congressional inquiries were thwarted through false testimony and the destruction and concealment of government records.

The destruction and concealment of records and information, beginning at the twilight of Iran/contra and continuing throughout subsequent investigations, should be of particular concern. Oliver North's destruction of records in October and November 1986 caused an irretrievable loss of information to the executive agencies responsible for regulating clandestine activities, to Congress, and to Independent Counsel. John Poindexter's efforts to destroy NSC electronic mail nearly resulted in comparable damage. CIA Costa Rican Station Chief Joseph F. Fernandez attempted to hide phone records that would have revealed his contacts with Enterprise activities.

This sort of obstruction continued even after Independent Counsel's appointment. In the course of his work, Independent Counsel located large caches of handwritten notes and other documents maintained by high officials that were never relinquished to investigators. Major aspects of Iran/contra would never have been uncovered had all of the officials who attempted to destroy or withhold their records of the affair succeeded. Had these contemporaneous records been produced to investigators when they were initially requested, many of the troublesome conflicts between key witnesses would have been resolved, and timely legal steps taken toward those who feigned memory lapses or lied outright.

All of this conduct—the evasions of the Executive branch and the Congress, the lies, the conspiracies, the acts of obstruction—had to be addressed by the criminal justice system.

The path Independent Counsel embarked upon in late 1986 has been a long and arduous one. When he hired 10 attorneys in early 1987, Independent Counsel's conception of the operational conspiracy—with its array of Government officials and private contractors, its web of secret foreign accounts, and its world-wide breadth—was extremely hazy. Outlining an investigation of a runaway conspiracy disavowed by the President was quite different from the ultimate investigation of the President and three major agencies, each with the power to frustrate an investigation by persisting in the classification of non-secret but embarrassing information. Completing the factual mosaic required examining pieces spread worldwide in activities that occurred over a three-year period by officials from the largest agencies of government and a host of private operatives who, by necessity, design and training, worked secretly and deceptively.

# The Role of Independent Counsel

Given the enormous autonomous power of both the Legislative and Executive branches in the modern state, the rightly celebrated constitutional checks and balances are inadequate, alone, to preserve the rule of law upon which our democracy depends.

As Watergate demonstrated, the checks and balances reach their limits in the case of criminal wrongdoing by Executive branch officials. The combination of an aggressive press, simple crimes, the White House tapes, and principled defiance by Department of Justice-appointed counsel all combined to bring Watergate to its conclusion without an independent counsel statute. It was apparent then, however, as it should be now in light of Iran/contra, that the competing roles of the attorney general, as a member of the Cabinet and presidential adviser on the one hand and chief law enforcement officer on the other, create an irreconcilable conflict of interest.

As Iran/contra demonstrated, congressional oversight alone cannot make up for deficiencies that result when an attorney general abandons that law-enforcement role in cases of Executive branch wrongdoing. Well before Attorney General Meese sought an independent counsel in

December 1986, he had already become, in effect, the President's defense lawyer, to the exclusion of his responsibilities as the nation's top law enforcement officer. By that time, crucial documents had already been destroyed and false testimony given.

Congress, with all the investigatory powers it wields in the oversight process, was not able to uncover many of these documents or disprove much of that false testimony. That inability is structural, and does not result from ill will, impatience, or character flaw on the part of any legislator. With good reason, Congress's interest in investigating Executive branch wrongdoing extends no farther than remedying perceived imbalances in its relations with the Executive branch. Except in the case of impeachment, Congress's interest does not, and should not, extend to the law-enforcement goals of deterrence, retribution and punishment.

In normal circumstances, these law-enforcement goals are the province of the Justice Department, under the direction of the attorney general. As the chief law enforcement officer of the United States, the attorney general represents the people of the United States—not the President, the Cabinet or any political party. When the attorney general cannot so represent the people, the rule of law requires that another, independent institution assume that responsibility. That is the historic role of the independent counsel.

## Problems Posed by Congressional Immunity Grants

The magnitude of Iran/contra does not by itself explain why Independent Counsel took so long to complete the task assigned by the Special Division which appointed him. The word "independent" in Independent Counsel is not quite accurate as a description of his work. Time and again this Independent Counsel found himself at the mercy of political decisions of the Congress and the Executive branch. From the date of his appointment on December 19, 1986, Independent Counsel had to race to protect his investigations and prosecutions from the congressional grants of immunity to central Enterprise conspirators. At the same time, he had to wait almost one year for records from Swiss banks and financial organizations vital to his

work. Once Congress granted immunity, Independent Counsel had to insulate himself and his staff from immunized disclosures, postponing the time he could get a wider view of the activities he was investigating.

Despite extraordinary efforts to shield the OIC from exposure to immunized testimony, the North and Poindexter convictions were overturned on appeal on the immunity issue. While the appellate panels did not find the prosecution was "tainted" by improper exposure to the immunized testimony of North or Poindexter, they ruled that the safeguards utilized by the trial courts did not ensure that witnesses' testimony was not affected by the immunized testimony.

Although Independent Counsel warned the Select Committees of the possibility that granting use immunity to principals in the Iran/contra matter might make it impossible to prosecute them successfully, he has never contended that Congress should refrain from granting use immunity to compel testimony in such important matters as Iran/contra. In matters of great national concern, Independent Counsel recognizes that intense public interest and the need for prompt and effective congressional oversight of intelligence activities may well force the Congress to act swiftly and grant immunity to principals.

But, in light of the experience of Independent Counsel in the Iran/contra cases, Congress should be aware of the fact that future immunity grants, at least in such highly publicized cases, will likely rule out criminal prosecution.

Congressional action that precludes, or makes it impossible to sustain, a prosecution has more serious consequences than simply one less conviction. There is a significant inequity when more peripheral players are convicted while central figures in a criminal enterprise escape punishment. And perhaps more fundamentally, the failure to punish governmental lawbreakers feeds the perception that public officials are not wholly accountable for their actions. In Iran/contra, it was President Reagan who first asked that North and Poindexter be given immunity so that they could exculpate him from responsibility for the diversion. A few months later, the Select Committees did that—granting immunity without any proffer to ensure honest testimony.

# The Classified Information Procedures Act

After Independent Counsel brought the principal operational conspiracy cases, he was forced to dismiss the central conspiracy charges against North, Poindexter, Hakim and Secord because the Administration, which had opposed the charge in the first instance, refused to declassify the information needed to proceed in the *North* case. Later, the entire case against Joseph F. Fernandez, the CIA's station chief in Costa Rica, was dismissed when the Administration declined to declassify information necessary for the trial. In both instances, Independent Counsel concluded that the classified information in question was already publicly known, but the Administration declined to engage in meaningful consultation with Independent Counsel before making its decision.

In any prosecution of a national security official, a tension inevitably arises between the Executive branch's duty to enforce the criminal law and its obligation to safeguard the national security through protecting classified information. The Classified Information Procedures Act (CIPA) was enacted in 1980 to assist the Department of Justice and other Executive branch agencies in resolving this tension in a manner consistent with our nation's commitment to the rule of law. Under CIPA, only the attorney general has the authority to make the decision between the Government's need to enforce the law and the Government's need to withhold information for national security reasons. If the intelligence agencies decline to declassify information deemed necessary by the trial court for the fair trial of a case, only the attorney general can overrule them. Likewise, if the attorney general decides that the information should not be disclosed, he is empowered to file a CIPA § 6(e) affidavit to prohibit the disclosure. Current law does not require that the attorney general's decision to withhold classified material from disclosure at trial meet any objective or articulated standard. No court can challenge the substance of a § 6(e) affidavit; no litigant has standing to contest the attorney general's decision to file one.

The Administration has the power to make the CIPA process work when it wants to, as in the case of alleged spies or in the trial of former Panamanian dictator Manuel Noriega. Since CIPA became law in 1980, no attorney general killed a prosecution by filing a § 6(e) affidavit until Attorney General Richard Thornburgh forced the dismissal of the *Fernandez* case in November 1989. As the *Fernandez* and *North* cases show, the Administration also has the power to derail the CIPA process when, for reasons of its own, it chooses not to make it work.

The attorney general's unrestricted CIPA § 6(e) authority becomes questionable when an independent counsel, rather than the Justice Department, has jurisdiction over the prosecution. An independent counsel is appointed only when the attorney general determines, after a preliminary investigation, that high-level officials within the Executive branch may have been involved in criminal activity or that the Department of Justice may be perceived to have a conflict of interest. The problems of conflict are compounded in CIPA because the issue involves classified information controlled by an intelligence agency in a case charging one or more of the officials of that agency in criminal activity. Congress could not have intended that CIPA—a statute designed to facilitate trials involving classified information—be used by the attorney general to control prosecutions of independent counsel.

## Final Thoughts

The Iran/contra investigation will not end the kind of abuse of power that it addressed any more than the Watergate investigation did. The criminality in both affairs did not arise primarily out of ordinary venality or greed, although some of those charged were driven by both. Instead, the crimes committed in Iran/contra were motivated by the desire of persons in high office to pursue controversial policies and goals even when the pursuit of those policies and goals was inhibited or restricted by executive orders, statutes or the constitutional system of checks and balances.

The tone in Iran/contra was set by President Reagan. He directed that the contras be supported, despite a ban on contra aid imposed on him by Congress. And he was willing to trade arms to Iran for the release of Americans held hostage in the Middle East, even if doing so was contrary to the nation's stated policy and possibly in violation of the law.

The lesson of Iran/contra is that if our system of government is to function properly, the branches of government must deal with one another honestly and cooperatively. When disputes arise between the Executive and Legislative branches, as they surely will, the laws that emerge from such disputes must be obeyed.

When a President, even with good motive and intent, chooses to skirt the laws or to circumvent them, it is incumbent upon his subordinates to resist, not join in. Their oath and fealty are to the Constitution and the rule of law, not to the man temporarily occupying the Oval Office. Congress has the duty and the power under our system of checks and balances to ensure that the President and his Cabinet officers are faithful to their oaths.

# Index